MARITIME LAW

Other books in the *Essentials of Canadian Law* Series

Statutory Interpretation

The Law of Trusts

Intellectual Property Law

Income Tax Law

Immigration Law

International Trade Law

Family Law

Legal Ethics & Professional Responsibility

Copyright Law

Criminal Law 2/e

Remedies: The Law of Damages

Individual Employment Law

The Law of Equitable Remedies

Administrative Law

Ethics and Canadian Criminal Law

Public International Law

Environmental Law 2/e

Securities Law

Constitutional Law 2/e

The Law of Evidence 3/e

The Charter of Rights and Freedoms 2/e

Youth Criminal Justice Law

Computer Law 2/e

The Law of Partnerships and Corporations 2/e

The Law of Torts 2/e

Media Law 2/e

ESSENTIALS OF CANADIAN LAW

MARITIME LAW

EDGAR GOLD
ALDO CHIRCOP
HUGH KINDRED

Marine and Environmental Law Programme
Dalhousie University

IRWIN LAW

Maritime Law
© Irwin Law Inc., 2003

All rights reserved. No part of this publication may be reproduced, stored in a retrieval system, or transmitted, in any form or by any means, without the prior written permission of the publisher or, in the case of photocopying or other reprographic copying, a licence from Access Copyright (Canadian Copyright Licensing Agency), 1 Yonge Street, Suite 1900, Toronto, Ontario, M5E 1E5.

Published in 2003 by

Irwin Law
347 Bay Street
Suite 501
Toronto, Ontario
M5H 2R7
www.irwinlaw.com

ISBN: 1-55221-086-3

National Library of Canada Cataloguing in Publication

Gold, Edgar, 1934–
    Canadian maritime law / Edgar Gold, Aldo Chircop, Hugh Kindred.

(Essentials of Canadian law)
Includes bibliographical references and index.

ISBN 1-55221-086-3

1. Maritime law—Canada. I. Chircop, Aldo E. II. Kindred, Hugh M. III. Title. IV. Series.

KE1105.G64 2003   343.7109'6   C2003-906531-6
KF1105.G64 200

The publisher acknowledges the financial support of the Government of Canada through the Book Publishing Industry Development Program (BPIDP) for its publishing activities. The publisher also acknowledges the Government of Ontario through the Ontario Media Development Corporation's Ontario Book Initiative.

Printed and bound in Canada.

1 2 3 4 5   07 06 05 04 03

SUMMARY TABLE OF CONTENTS

PREFACE xxix

ACKNOWLEDGMENTS xxxi

CHAPTER 1: Canadian Maritime Law: An Introduction *1*

CHAPTER 2: The Shipping Industry: An Overview *18*

CHAPTER 3: Admiralty Jurisdiction *99*

CHAPTER 4: The Ownership and Registration of Ships *141*

CHAPTER 5: The Safety Management of Ships *193*

CHAPTER 6: Maritime Mortgages and Liens *241*

CHAPTER 7: Marine Insurance *297*

CHAPTER 8: Carriage of Goods by Charterparty *358*

CHAPTER 9: Carriage of Goods under Bills of Lading and Similar Documents *407*

CHAPTER 10: Carriage of Passengers *479*

CHAPTER 11: Maritime Collisions *495*

CHAPTER 12: Maritime Personal Injury and Death *544*

CHAPTER 13: Maritime Pilotage *561*

CHAPTER 14: Maritime Towage *574*

CHAPTER 15: Maritime Salvage and Wreck *594*

CHAPTER 16: General Average *628*

CHAPTER 17: Marine Pollution Prevention *658*

CHAPTER 18: Limitation of Liability for Maritime Claims *718*

CHAPTER 19: Admiralty Procedure *748*
by A. William Moreira

APPENDICES *807*

LISTS *827*

TABLE OF CASES *851*

INDEX *891*

DETAILED TABLE OF CONTENTS

CHAPTER 1:
CANADIAN MARITIME LAW: AN INTRODUCTION *1*

A. Why a Textbook on Canadian Maritime Law? *1*

B. International Character of Maritime Law *6*

C. Subject-Matter of Canadian Maritime Law *9*

D. Layout of This Book *10*

E. Special Note on the *Canada Shipping Act* *14*

F. Special Note on the *United Nations Convention on the Law of the Sea* *16*

Further Readingss *17*

CHAPTER 2:
THE SHIPPING INDUSTRY: AN OVERVIEW *18*

A. Introduction *18*

B. Shipping Industry *19*
   1) Background *19*
   2) Globalization of Shipping *21*
   3) Canadian Aspects *23*

C. Ships and Ship's Equipment *24*
   1) Basic Terminology *24*
   2) Ship's Machinery *26*
   3) Ship's Hull, Superstructure, and Cargo-Handling Equipment *28*

4) Ropes and Wires 29
5) Tonnage 30
   a) Deadweight Tonnage 31
   b) Cargo Tonnage 31
   c) Displacement Tonnage 31
   d) Gross Tonnage 31
   e) Net Tonnage 32
   f) Limitation Tonnage 32
6) Draught, Load Line Marks, and Freeboard 32
7) Types of Ships 35
   a) Cargo Ships 35
      i) Cargo Liner Vessels 35
      ii) Tramp Ships 36
      iii) Specialized Cargo Ships 37
         aa) Bulk Liquid Cargo Ships 37
         bb) Dry Bulk-Cargo Ships 38
         cc) Refrigerated Cargo Ships 39
         dd) Heavy and Oversized Cargo Vessels 39
   b) Passenger Ships 39
      i) Cruise Ships 39
      ii) Passenger Ferries 40
   c) Fishing Vessels 40
   d) Other Types of Vessels 40
      i) Naval and Military Vessels 40
      ii) Other Government Vessels 41
      iii) Service Vessels 41
      iv) Pleasure Craft 41

D. Navigation and Nautical Information 42
   1) Nautical Charts 42
   2) Navigational Aids 43
      a) Compass 43
      b) Depth-Sounding Devices 45
      c) Vessel Speed Indicators 45
      d) Global Positioning Systems 46
      e) Radar 47
      f) Electronic Chart Display Information Systems 48
      g) Loran C 49
      h) Radio Direction Finding 50
      i) Decca 50
   3) Communication Aids 51
      a) Communication on Board Ships 51
      b) Communications between Ships and between Ship and Shore 52
      c) Communications for Vessels in Distress 52
   4) Maritime Weather 53

5) Ship Manoeuvring and Handling 54
   a) Propulsion 54
   b) Wake Current 56
   c) Screw-Race 56
   d) Turning Circle 57
   e) Stopping Distance 57
   f) Interaction 59
   g) Bank Effect 59
6) Ship at Sea 59
   a) Watches and Logbooks 59
   b) Master 61
   c) Officers and Crew 61

E. Ancillary Shipping Services 62
   1) Classification Society Surveyor 63
   2) Steamship Inspector 64
   3) Receiver of Wreck 66
   4) Salvage Association Surveyor 67
   5) Harbour Master 67
   6) Shipping Master 67
   7) Port Warden 68

F. Offshore Energy Sector: Maritime Aspects 69
   1) Introduction 69
   2) Offshore Drilling Operations 70
      a) Exploration Wells 70
      b) Delineation Wells 70
      c) Development Wells 70
   3) Offshore Drilling Systems 71
      a) Jack-up Rigs 71
      b) Semi-submersible Rigs 71
      c) Drill Ships 71
   4) Other Offshore Facilities and Support Systems 72
      a) Anchored Structure with Legs 73
      b) Gravity-Based Structure 73
      c) Floating Production Storage and Offloading System 73
   5) Legal Status of Offshore Facilities 73

G. Shipping and International Organizations 75
   1) Intergovernmental Organizations 77
      a) International Maritime Organisation 77
         i) Maritime Safety Committee 79
         ii) Marine Environment Protection Committee 80
         iii) Legal Committee 80
         iv) Technical Cooperation Committee 81
         v) Facilitation Committee 81

        b) International Labour Organisation 81
        c) U.N. Conference on Trade and Development 82
        d) U.N. Commission on International Trade Law 84
        e) Other International Organizations with Marine-Related Interests 85
            i) International Telecommunications Union 85
            ii) World Health Organization 86
            iii) Universal Postal Union 86
            iv) World Meteorological Organization 86
            v) International Civil Aviation Organization 86
            vi) International Hydrographic Organization 86
            vii) International Tribunal for the Law of the Sea 87
            viii) International Maritime Satellite Organization 87
            ix) International Oil Pollution Compensation Fund 87
            x) U.N. Environment Programme 87
            xi) Intergovernmental Oceanographic Commission 88
            xii) Regional Port State Inspection Systems 88
            xiii) Other Regional Organizations 88
    2) Non-Governmental Organizations 88
        a) Comité Maritime International 89
        b) International Chamber of Shipping 92
        c) International Association of Ports and Harbours 92
        d) International Association of Lighthouse Authorities 92
        e) International Union of Marine Insurers 93
        f) International Organization for Standardization 93
        g) Baltic and International Maritime Council 93
        h) International Bar Association 93
        i) International Tanker Owners Pollution Federation 93
        j) International Group of Protection and Indemnity Clubs 94
        k) International Chamber of Commerce 94
        l) International Transport Workers Federation 94
        m) International Salvage Union 94
        n) International Maritime Bureau 95
        o) International Federation of Shipmasters Associations 95
        p) International Marine Pilots Association 95
        q) International Association of Independent Tanker Owners 95
        r) International Shipping Federation 95
        s) International Association of Classification Societies 95

H. Conclusion 96

Further Readings 96

CHAPTER 3:
ADMIRALTY JURISDICTION 99

A. Introduction *99*

B. Maritime Law Jurisdiction Distinguished from Other Marine Jurisdictions *100*
   1) Distinction from Maritime Zones and Resource-Related Jurisdictions of Canada *100*
   2) Distinction from Provincial Maritime Property Rights *102*

C. Admiralty Court and Maritime Law Jurisdiction: An Historical Perspective *104*
   1) Origins and Evolution of the Admiralty Court and Jurisdiction in England *104*
   2) Evolution of the Admiralty Court and Jurisdiction in Canada *107*

D. Jurisdiction *Ratione Materiae* *111*
   1) Definition of Canadian Maritime Law *111*
   2) Statutory Framework for Jurisdiction *117*
   3) Boundaries and Frontiers of Admiralty Jurisdiction *120*

E. Provincial Considerations *131*
   1) Which Provincial Courts May Exercise Maritime Law Jurisdiction *131*
   2) Extent of Concurrency by Provincial Courts *133*
   3) Provincial Law in a Maritime Law Setting *134*
      a) Step One: Identifying the Matter at Issue *136*
      b) Step Two: Reviewing Maritime Law Sources *136*
      c) Step Three: Considering the Possibility of Reform *137*
      d) Step Four: Constitutional Analysis *137*

Further Readings *139*

CHAPTER 4:
THE OWNERSHIP AND REGISTRATION OF SHIPS *141*

A. Introduction *141*

B. A Ship and its Ownership *143*
   1) What is a Ship? *143*
      a) General Definitions *143*
      b) Vessels Not Designed for Navigation *146*
      c) Vessels Designed for Navigation, But Lacking own Propulsion *147*
      d) Offshore Installations and Structures *147*
      e) Combination of Vessels *149*
      f) Small Vessels *150*
      g) Submersibles *151*
      h) Decommissioned Ships *151*
      i) Other Vessels *152*

xii MARITIME LAW

      j) Concluding Comment on Definitions   *152*
   2) How a Ship is Owned   *153*

C. **Building a New Ship**   *155*

   1) Steamship Inspection Service   *155*
   2) Construction Agreement   *157*
      a) Planning Stage   *157*
      b) Design Stage   *157*
      c) Financing Stage   *159*
         i) Federal and Provincial Financing Programs   *159*
         ii) Builder's Mortgage   *160*
      d) Contracting and Construction Stage   *161*
         i) Contract Framework   *161*
         ii) Delivery and Delay   *164*
         iii) Warranties against Defects and Bad Workmanship   *165*

D. **Purchase of a Ship**   *169*

   1) Qualifying Ship Ownership in Canada   *169*
   2) Transferring Ownership   *170*
      a) Contract of Sale   *170*
      b) Securing a Clean Title   *173*

E. **Registration of a Ship**   *176*

   1) Ship Nationality and Canada as a Flag State   *176*
   2) Canadian Register of Ships   *179*
   3) Procedure for Registration   *180*
      a) Preliminary Steps   *180*
      b) Application for Registry   *181*
      c) Builder's Certificate and First Transfer of Title   *182*
      d) Declaration of Ownership and Declaration of Transfer of Ownership   *182*
      e) Certificate of Registry   *182*
      f) Bill of Sale   *183*
      g) Ship's Carving and Marking Note   *183*
      h) Transcript of Registry   *183*
      i) Registration of a Foreign-Built Vessel in Canada   *183*
      j) Provisional Registration   *184*
      k) Registry of Alterations, Registry Anew, and Transfer of Registry   *184*

F. **Registration under Flags of Convenience**   *184*

   1) Issues   *184*
      a) Traditional Flags of Convenience and Open Registries   *184*
      b) Flags of Environmental Convenience   *188*
   2) Factors to be Considered in Choosing a Flag of Convenience   *189*

G. Licensing *191*

Further Readings *192*

CHAPTER 5:
THE SAFETY MANAGEMENT OF SHIPS *193*

A. Introduction *193*

B. Safety of Ships *194*
   1) Background *194*
   2) Safety of Life at Sea Conventions, 1914–60 *195*
   3) Outline of *SOLAS 1974* *197*
      a) Canadian *SOLAS 1974* Regulatory System *201*
   4) Fishing Vessel Safety *202*
      a) Canadian Fishing Vessel Safety Regulatory System *203*
   5) Small Vessel Safety *203*
      a) Canadian Small Vessel Safety Regulatory System *203*
   6) Ships' Loading and Cargo Safety *205*
      a) Loading Limits for Ships *205*
         i) Canadian Load Line Regulations *206*
      b) Freight Containers *207*
         i) Canadian Sea Container Regulations *208*
      c) Dangerous Goods and Cargoes *209*
         i) Canadian Dangerous Goods Regulations *210*
   7) Offshore Drilling *211*
      a) Canadian Offshore Regulatory Regime *213*

C. Safety of Ships' Crews and Passengers *215*
   1) Crews *215*
      a) Background *215*
   2) ILO Conventions *216*
      a) *Merchant Shipping (Minimum Standards) Convention, 1976 (ILO No. 147)* *217*
      b) Canadian Adoption and Implementation of ILO Conventions *218*
   3) STCW 1978 *220*
      a) Canadian Implementation of *STCW 1978* *223*
   4) Passengers *223*
      a) *SOLAS* System for Passenger Safety *224*
      b) Canadian Implementation *225*

D. Other Safety Management Regimes *226*
   1) Background *226*
   2) *ISM Code* *226*
   3) Port State Control Systems *228*

a) *Paris MOU 1982* 228
4) Classification Societies 230
5) Maritime Security 233
6) Maritime Search and Rescue 236
7) Port Facilitation 237

E. **Conclusions** 238

Further Readings 239

CHAPTER 6:
MARITIME MORTGAGES AND LIENS 241

A. **Introduction** 241

B. **Mortgages** 242
   1) Introduction 242
      a) Ship Financing: Bottomry, Respondentia, and Mortgages 242
      b) Form, Scope, and Regulation of Ship Mortgages 243
   2) Mortgages under Federal Legislation 244
      a) Registration under *Canada Shipping Act* 245
      b) Rights of Mortgagor 246
      c) Rights of Mortgagee 249
      d) Security under *Bank Act* 251
   3) Mortgages under Provincial Legislation 253
      a) Scope of Personal Property Security Acts 253
      b) Creation and Perfection of Security Interests 255
      c) Rights of Parties 256
   4) Ranking of Mortgages 257
      a) Priority under Federal Legislation 258
      b) Priority under Provincial Legislation 262

C. **Liens** 265
   1) Introduction 265
   2) Maritime Liens 267
      a) Policy Rationale 267
      b) Definition and Characteristics 275
         i) Privileged Claim 276
         ii) Attachment to Maritime Property 276
         iii) Service Done to/Injury Caused by *Res* 277
         iv) Moment when Lien Arises 277
         v) Survival Despite Transfer of Ownership 278
         vi) Enforceability by an Action *in Rem* 278
      c) Types of Maritime Liens 279
         i) Bottomry and Respondentia 279
         ii) Collision Claims 279

  iii) Salvage Claims *280*
  iv) Unpaid Master's and Crew's Wages *280*
  v) Master's Disbursements *283*
 d) Extinguishment of Maritime Liens *285*
3) Possessory Liens *288*
4) Statutory Rights *in Rem* *290*
 a) Definition and Characteristics *290*
 b) Range of Rights *in Rem* *291*
 c) Claims that are Defeated by a Transfer of Title *292*
 d) Claims that are Not Defeated by a Transfer of Title *294*
5) Ranking of Liens and Mortgages *294*

Further Readings *295*

CHAPTER 7:
MARINE INSURANCE *297*

A. Introduction *297*

1) Origins *297*
2) Lombard and Hanseatic Initiatives *298*
3) Establishment of the English Marine Insurance Market *299*
4) Lloyd's *299*
5) Insurance Companies and Hull Clubs *300*
6) Third-Party Liability Coverage *302*
7) U.K. *Marine Insurance Act, 1906* *305*
8) Canadian Provincial Statutes *306*
9) Canadian *Marine Insurance Act, 1993* *307*

B. Basic Principles and Features *308*

1) Definitions and Terminology *308*
2) Distinctive Features *309*
3) Different Types of Marine Insurance *312*
 a) Hull and Machinery Insurance *312*
 b) Loss of Hire *315*
 c) Protection and Indemnity Insurance *316*
 d) Defence Cover *316*
 e) War-Risk Insurance *317*
 f) Cargo Insurance *318*
 g) Other Market Cover *319*
 h) Reinsurance *320*
4) Brokers and Managing General Agents *320*

C. Marine Insurance Doctrines *322*

1) Disclosure and Utmost Good Faith *322*
2) Insurable Interest *324*
3) Measure of Indemnity *325*

4) Subrogation and Abandonment 327
5) Warranties 328
6) Perils of the Sea 329

D. **The Marine Insurance Policy** 330

1) Background 330
2) Time and Voyage Policies 331
3) Marine Insurance Policy Clauses 332
   a) Navigation (Tow and Assist) Clause 334
   b) Continuation Clause 335
   c) Breach of Warranty Clause 335
   d) Sale of Vessel or Termination Clause 335
   e) Notice of Assignment Clause 335
   f) Perils Clause 335
   g) Pollution Hazard 336
   h) Three-Quarters–Collision Liability 337
   i) Sister-Ship Clause 337
   j) Duty of Assured (Sue and Labour) Clause 338
   k) Unrepaired Damage Clause 338
   l) Disbursements Clause 338
   m) Free Capture and Seizure Clause 338
   n) Risks Clause 338
   o) Transit Clause 339
   p) "Seaworthiness Admitted" Clause 339
   q) Duty of the Assured Clause 339
   r) Other Cargo Clauses 340

E. **Protection and Indemnity Insurance** 340

1) Background 340
2) P&I Club Operation and Membership 341
3) Non-club Protection and Indemnity Cover 346
4) Risk Coverage 347
   a) Protection and Indemnity Cover 347
   b) Other Risks 351

Further Readings 352

Annex 354

CHAPTER 8:
CARRIAGE OF GOODS BY CHARTERPARTY 358

A. **Introduction** 358

B. **Maritime Common Law Principles of Carriage** 360

1) Seaworthiness of the Ship 361

2) Care of the Cargo *363*
3) Deviation on the Voyage *364*
4) Delay in Delivery *368*
5) Dangerous Goods *372*
6) Freight *375*

C. **Carriage by Charterparty** *378*
1) Introduction: Kinds of Charterparties *378*
2) Charters by Demise *380*

D. **Voyage Charterparties** *381*
1) Standard Provisions *381*
2) Preliminary Voyage *383*
    a) Expected Arrival *383*
    b) Safe Ports *385*
3) Loading and Discharging Operations *387*
    a) Terms of Operation *387*
    b) Laytime and Demurrage *388*
4) Voyage *392*
    a) Seaworthiness *392*
    b) Cargo Care *393*
    c) Deviation *394*
    d) Delay *397*
5) Freight *398*

E. **Time Charterparties** *399*
1) Standard Provisions *399*
2) Particular Clauses *400*

Further Readings *405*

CHAPTER 9:
CARRIAGE OF GOODS UNDER BILLS OF LADING AND SIMILAR DOCUMENTS *407*

A. **Kinds of Liner Shipping Documents** *407*
1) Introduction *407*
2) Bills of Lading *408*
3) Bills of Lading as Evidence of the Carriage Contract *410*
4) Bills of Lading as Receipts for the Goods Carried *411*
5) Bills of Lading as Negotiable Documents of Title *413*
6) Sea Waybills and Other Sea Transport Documents *414*
7) Combined Transport Documents *416*
8) Electronic Transport Documents *418*
9) Transfer of Rights in a Bill of Lading *419*

10) Bills of Lading on a Chartered Ship 425
11) Carrier Identity and Demise Clauses 427

B. **International Rules Governing Bills of Lading** 433

C. **Application of the *Hague-Visby Rules*** 436

1) To Whom the Rules Apply 436
2) When the Rules Apply 439
   a) Geographic Scope 439
   b) Contractual Formalities 440
   c) Temporal Scope 441
3) To What the Rules Apply 444
4) How the Rules Apply 445

D. **Responsibilities of Carriers** 446

1) Bills of Lading 447
2) Seaworthiness of the Ship 449
3) Care of the Cargo 452
4) Deviation on the Voyage 452
5) Delay in Delivery 455
6) Exclusion of Liability 456
   a) Errors in Navigation 456
   b) Fire 457
   c) Perils of the Sea 459
   d) Other Dangers and Restraints 460
   e) Saving Life at Sea 460
   f) Shipper's Faults and Cargo Defects 460
   g) Latent Defects 462
   h) Any Other Cause Without Fault 463
7) Limitation of Liability 463

E. **Responsibilities of Cargo Owners** 468

1) Description of the Cargo 468
2) Dangerous Goods 469

F. **Claims and Actions** 470

1) Time Limits 470
2) Jurisdiction and Arbitration Clauses 471
3) Order and Onus of Proof 474

Further Readings 477

CHAPTER 10:
CARRIAGE OF PASSENGERS 479

A. **Introduction** 479

B. Carriage of Passengers at Common Law 480

C. Carriage Under *PAL 1974/1990* 483
   1) Scope of Application in Canada 483
   2) Carrier's Responsibilities 484
   3) Extent of Carrier's Liability 486
   4) Claims and Actions 490

D. Prospective Developments 490

Further Readings 494

CHAPTER 11:
MARITIME COLLISIONS 495

A. Introduction 495

B. Collision Regulations in 1972 497
   1) *COLREGS 1972* Part A: General Principles 498
      a) Rule 1: Application 498
      b) Rule 2: Responsibility 499
      c) Rule 3: Definitions 500
   2) *COLREGS 1972* Part B: Steering and Sailing 501
      a) Rule 4: Application 501
      b) Rule 5: Look-out 501
      c) Rule 6: Safe Speed 502
      d) Rule 7: Risk of Collision 505
      e) Rule 8: Action to Avoid Collision 505
      f) Rule 9: Narrow Channels 506
      g) Rule 10: Traffic Separation Schemes 508
      h) Rule 11: Application 509
      i) Rule 12: Sailing Vessels 509
      j) Rule 13: Overtaking 509
      k) Rule 14: Head-on Situation 510
      l) Rule 15: Crossing Situation 511
      m) Rule 16: Action by Give-Way Vessel 512
      n) Rule 17: Action by Stand-on Vessel 512
      o) Rule 18: Responsibilities between Vessels 514
      p) Rule 19: Conduct of Vessels in Restricted Visibility 514
   3) *COLREGS 1972* Part C: Lights and Shapes 515
   4) *COLREGS 1972* Part D: Sound and Light Signals 517
   5) *COLREGS 1972* Part E: Exemptions 518
   6) Canadian *Collision Regulations* Part F: Specific Canadian Provisions 518
   7) *COLREGS 1972*: Annexes I–IV 518

C. Inland Waters Rules *519*

   1) In Canada *519*
   2) In the United States *520*

D. Liability for Maritime Collisions *521*

   1) Introduction *521*
   2) Negligence *521*
   3) Statutory Provisions *522*
      a) The *Collision Avoidance Rules* *523*
   4) Defences and Division of Loss *525*
   5) Finding of "Fault" *527*
   6) Collision Damages *529*
      a) *1952 Civil Jurisdiction Convention* *530*
      b) The *Lisbon Rules* *532*
   7) U.S. Law Differences *533*

E. Liability for Collisions with Fixed and Floating Objects *536*

   1) Differences between Collisions with Fixed and Floating Objects and Collisions between Ships *536*
   2) Damage Liability Claims for Collisions with Fixed and Floating Objects *537*

F. Criminal Liability and Jurisdiction in Collision Cases *540*

   1) *1952 Penal Jurisdiction Convention* *541*
   2) Canadian *Criminal Code* *542*

Further Readings *543*

CHAPTER 12:
MARITIME PERSONAL INJURY AND DEATH *544*

A. Introduction *544*

B. Applicable Law *545*

C. Personal Injuries and Fatal Accidents in a Maritime Setting *547*

D. Claims and Claimants *551*

   1) Difference between Personal Injury and Fatal Accident Claims *551*
   2) Eligible Claimants *552*

E. Liability for Maritime Accidents *554*

   1) Standard of Care *554*
   2) Considerations Specific to Recreational Boating *554*
   3) Damages *557*
   4) Apportionment of Liability *558*

Further Readings 559

CHAPTER 13:
MARITIME PILOTAGE 561

A. Introduction 561

B. Pilotage Authorities 562

C. Pilot/Master Relationship 564
   1) Legal Status of the Pilot 564
   2) Pilot/Master Relationship 564

D. Liability 569
   1) Liability of the Master 559
   2) Liability of the Shipowner 569
   3) Liability of the Pilot 570
   4) Disciplinary Proceedings against the Pilot 570

E. Pilotage and Salvage 572

Further Readings 573

CHAPTER 14:
MARITIME TOWAGE 574

A. Introduction 574

B. Types of Tugs 575

C. Authority to Contract Towage 576

D. Contract Terms 577
   1) Implied Contract Terms 577
   2) Standard Conditions 578
      a) Liability Exemption Clauses 580
      b) Indemnity Clauses 582
   3) Commencement and Termination of Towage Operation 583
   4) Performance of the Towage Contract 585

E. Towage and the *Collision Regulations* 587

F. Towage and Salvage 588
   1) Difference between Towage and Salvage 588
   2) When Towage Can Be Converted into Salvage 589

G. Towage and Carriage of Goods 591

Further Readings 593

CHAPTER 15:
MARITIME SALVAGE AND WRECK 594

A. **Maritime Salvage** 594
   1) Introduction 594
   2) International Law 595
      a) *Assistance and Salvage Convention 1910* 595
      b) *1989 Salvage Convention* 598
   3) Canadian Law and Legislation 599
   4) Subjects of Salvage 599
   5) Salvage Operations 600
      a) Stranding 601
      b) Sinking 602
      c) Rescue (Towing) 602
   6) Salvage Services 603
   7) Required Elements for a Salvage Claim 605
      a) Danger 605
      b) Voluntariness 606
      c) Success 607
   8) Obligations of Salvor and Shipowner 609
   9) Salvage Contracts and Clauses 611
      a) Standard Salvage Contracts 612
      b) Special Compensation Clauses 614
         i) *PIOPIC* Clause 614
         ii) *SCOPIC* and *SCOPIC 2000* Clauses 614
   10) Salvage Award 617
   11) Life Salvage 618

B. **Wreck** 620
   1) Introduction 620
   2) Receiver of Wreck 620
   3) Underwater Cultural Heritage 621
   4) Wreck Removal 622
      a) General Principles 622
      b) International Rules 625

Further Readings 626

CHAPTER 16:
GENERAL AVERAGE 628

A. **Introduction: *York-Antwerp Rules*** 628

B. **Four Requirements of General Average** 631

1) Extraordinary Loss 632
   a) General Average Sacrifices 632
      i) Of the Cargo 632
      ii) Of the Ship 633
      iii) Of the Freight 634
   b) General Average Expenditures 634
      i) Salvage Costs 634
      ii) Temporary Repair and Other Port of Refuge Costs 635
      iii) Environmental Costs 636
      iv) Substituted Expenses 637
2) Intentionally and Reasonably Incurred 642
3) In Time of Peril 647
4) For the Common Safety of the Voyage 650

C. General Average Adjustment 651
   1) Valuation of Loss 652
   2) Contributory Values 653

D. Reform of General Average 655

Further Readings 656

CHAPTER 17:
MARINE POLLUTION PREVENTION 658

A. Background 658
   1) Introduction 658
   2) Developments to 1980 660
   3) Developments since 1980 665
   4) Canadian Policy, Law, and Regulation 669

B. Marine Pollution: The International Operational Regime 672
   1) *OILPOL 1954* 672
   2) *Intervention* 673
   3) *LC 1972* 674
   4) *MARPOL 73/78* 674
   5) *Basel Convention 1989* 676
   6) *OPRC 1990* 676
   7) Ballast Water Guidelines 677
   8) Port State Control Systems 678
   9) Canadian Law and Enforcement 678
      a) Transport Canada and Fisheries and Oceans Canada 679
         i) *Canada Shipping Act* and *Canada Shipping Act, 2001* 679
         ii) *AWPPA* 681
         iii) *NWPA* 681
         iv) *Canada Marine Act* 682

b) Fisheries and Oceans Canada 680
   i) Oceans Act 683
   ii) Fisheries Act 683
   iii) Coastal Fisheries Protection Act 683
c) Environment Canada 683
   i) Canadian Environmental Protection Act, 1999 684
   ii) Canada Water Act 684
   iii) Canada Wildlife Act 685
   iv) Migratory Birds Convention Act, 1994 685

C. Marine Pollution: The International Liability and Compensation Regime 686

1) CLC 1969 686
   a) Pollution from Ships 687
   b) Pollution from Floating Storage Units and Floating Production, Storage, and Offloading Units 691
2) FUND 1971 692
3) LLMC 1976 695
4) Nuclear 1971 696
5) HNS 1996 697
6) Pollution from Ships' Bunkers 699
7) Pollution from Harmful Anti-fouling Systems 700
8) Canadian Law and Policy 700
   a) Oil Pollution 701
   b) Non-oil Pollution 705
   c) Canadian Marine Pollution Response Mechanism 706
9) U.S. Law Differences 707

D. Marine Pollution: Offshore Energy Operations 708

1) Background 708
2) International Law and Related Instruments 709
   a) U.N. Law of the Sea Conventions 709
   b) MARPOL 73/78 710
   c) Other Regimes 710
   d) IMO MODU Code 1998 711
3) Liability and Compensation 711
4) Canadian Law and Policy 712

E. Conclusions 715

Further Readings 716

CHAPTER 18:
LIMITATION OF LIABILITY FOR MARITIME CLAIMS 718

A. Introduction 718

B. Who is Entitled to Limit Liability? 722

  1) Persons 722
  2) Navigable Waters 724
  3) Ships 724

C. The Right to Limit Liability 725

  1) The Right to Limitation 725
  2) Claims Not Subject to Limitation 729
  3) Conduct Barring Limitation 732

D. General Limits 734

  1) Measurement of Tonnage 734
  2) Unit of Account 734
  3) Appropriate Tonnage Unit for Limitation Purposes 735
  4) Limitation Amounts 737
     a) Ships less than 300 Tons 738
     b) Ships of more than 300 but less than 2000 Tons 738
     c) Ships more than 2000 Tons 739

E. Special Limitation Cases 739

  1) Passenger Claims 739
  2) Salvors 741
  3) Dock, Canal, and Port Owners 741
  4) Other Ocean Users 743

F. Limitation Fund 744

  1) Significance of the Fund 744
  2) Constitution of the Fund 745
  3) Distribution of the Fund 746
  4) Fund Established in a Foreign Jurisdiction 746

Further Readings 746

CHAPTER 19:
ADMIRALTY PROCEDURE 748

A. Introduction 748

  1) Overview 748
  2) Historical Perspective 748
  3) Canadian Admiralty Procedural Rules 751

B. Structure of the Federal Court of Canada 752

  1) *Federal Court Act* 752
  2) Practice before the Federal Court 752
  3) Registry Practice 753

C. **Admiralty Proceedings** 754

　　1) Initiation in Federal Court 754
　　2) Claim for Relief under or by Virtue of Canadian Maritime Law 755
　　3) Interplay between Sections 43 and 22 755
　　4) Maritime Claims in Provincial Courts 758
　　5) Practical Considerations Governing Choice of Court 759

D. **Actions in Rem** 750

　　1) Nature of the *Res* 750
　　　a) Things that are Not "Ships" 760
　　　b) Property "That is the Subject of the Action" 761
　　2) Corresponding *in Personam* Liability of the Owner of the *Res* 761
　　3) Right to Proceed *in Rem* Lost in Some Cases with Change in Ownership 763
　　4) Sister-Ship Proceedings 764
　　　a) Difference from *Arrest Convention* and U.K. Legislation 765
　　　b) Sister Ships Defined 766
　　　c) Piercing the Corporate Veil 770
　　　d) Sister-Ship Arrest Not Available if "Subject Vessel" Sold 771
　　　e) Do Maritime Liens Attach to Sister Ships? 771

E. **Arrest of the *Res*** 773

　　1) Available *in Rem* Actions 773
　　2) Theory and Purpose of Arrest 773
　　3) Territorial Scope for Service of Warrant 774
　　4) Arrest of Multiple Sister Ships? 776
　　5) "Wrongful Arrest" 778
　　6) Movement of Arrested Property 779
　　7) Marshal's Expenses of Arrest 770
　　8) Arrest Contrasted with Statutory Seizures and Detentions 781
　　　a) Safety Violations 781
　　　b) Spills of Pollutants 782
　　　c) Fisheries Offences 784
　　　d) *Immigration Act* 785
　　　e) *Customs Act* 786

F. **Release of Arrested Property** 786

G. **Caveats** 788

H. **Certain Procedural Considerations Peculiar to Admiralty** 789

　　1) Collision Cases 789
　　2) Limitation of Liability Proceedings 790
　　3) Intervention in Admiralty Litigation 791

I. **Judicial Sale of the *Res*** 791

1) Timing of Sale Order 791
  2) Required Contents of Sale Order 792
  3) Customizing the Sale Order 793
  4) Flag-State Recognition of Canadian Judicial Sale 794

J. **Distribution of Sale Proceeds** 795
  1) Introduction to Admiralty Priorities 795
  2) "Normal" Priorities in Canada 795
  3) Refinements of Certain Priorities 795
    a) Marshal's Expenses of Arrest 796
    b) Costs of Bringing the Ship to Sale 797
    c) Possessory Liens Predating Maritime Liens 797
    d) Maritime Liens 798
    e) Mortgages 799
    f) Statutory Rights *in Rem* 799
  4) Marshalling of Secured Property 800
  5) Procedure in Priorities Matters 801

K. **Mareva Injuctions and Other Pre-Judgment Attachments** 802
  1) General 802
  2) *Mareva* Injunctions 802
  3) Certain Provincial Court Orders 804

L. **Maritime Arbitration in Canada** 804

Further Readings 805

APPENDIX 1: *HAGUE-VISBY RULES* 807

APPENDIX 2: *LOF 2000* 819

APPENDIX 3: FEDERAL COURT ADMIRALTY PROCEDURE FORMS 821

ACRONYMS AND ABBREVIATIONS 827

LEGISLATION 832

INTERNATIONAL TREATIES AND AGREEMENTS 838

TABLE OF CASES 851

INDEX 891

ABOUT THE AUTHORS 905

PREFACE

While Canadian maritime law generally follows the international maritime legal system, there are numerous differences in Canadian federal legislation, as well as in case law and procedure that necessitate a distinctively Canadian text in the area. Such a work has been missing. It is hoped that this book will fill the gap and be of assistance to the maritime law community in Canada and elsewhere, including teachers, students, practitioners, regulators, and anyone else who may wish to consult a text on Canadian maritime law.

The authors were responsible for researching and writing different parts of this book. The introductory chapter was co-authored by all three. Professor Edgar Gold prepared chapters 2, 5, 7, 11, 15, and 17. Professor Aldo Chircop prepared chapters 3, 4, 6 (liens section), 12, 13, 14, and 18. Professor Hugh Kindred wrote chapters 6 (mortgages section), 8, 9, 10, and 16. A. William Moreira, Esq., Q.C., authored Chapter 19.

Edgar Gold, Aldo Chircop, and Hugh Kindred
Halifax
July 2003

ACKNOWLEDGMENTS

There were many people during the life of this textbook project who assisted in the production of this book, and whom the authors wish to acknowledge. All three authors are or have been teachers of maritime law at Dalhousie Law School, which has long specialized in the area. As a result, maritime law casebooks and materials have been produced at Dalhousie for many years, often by distinguished Canadian maritime law practitioners, such as the late Professor Arthur J. Meagher, Q.C., and the late Donald A. Kerr, Esq., Q.C. In 1975 a collection of such materials was produced by Professor Edgar Gold[1] and was regularly revised with the assistance of a number of Dalhousie law students, who went on to their own distinguished legal careers. A significant part of these materials formed the basis of some of the chapters in this book and is gratefully acknowledged.

The co-authors are especially grateful to A. William Moreira, Esq., Q.C., a partner of Stewart McKelvey Stirling Scales, Halifax, who, despite his many other commitments, answered the call for help and contributed an entire chapter on Admiralty procedure.

This project received funding support from various sources, for which the authors express their appreciation: the Foundation for Legal Studies provided a research grant to Professor Chircop; the SSHRC/Research Development Fund administered by the Faculty of Graduate Studies at Dalhousie University provided research grants to Professors Chircop and Kindred; and Dalhousie Law School provided student research assistance for the project. Dalhousie Law School Dean Dawn Russell's support for the project is also gratefully acknowledged.

The research, editing, citation, and manuscript finalization would not have been possible without the competent, efficient, and patient

---

1 E. Gold, *Canadian Maritime Law: Introductory Materials*, 9th rev. ed. (Halifax: Dalhousie Law School, 1996).

work of Carolyn Shaw, Jennifer Grandy, and Jamie Lee Angus, all LL.B. students at Dalhousie Law School, who carried out their work with dedication and good humour. Carolyn Shaw was instrumental in the early compilation of a database of cases, statutes, and literature on Canadian maritime law. Jennifer Grandy was critical for the duration of the project, working tirelessly on the extensive footnoting and formatting of most chapters. Jamie Lee Angus ensured that the text was properly formatted and citations were correct. She also prepared the final manuscript. The authors are truly grateful for this outstanding assistance. Susan Rolston prepared the index for this book, Kathleen Basque and Molly Ross assisted with word processing, and Geordie Lounsbury did most of the internal printing during the project. The authors thank them all for their excellent work. The ready support of the Dalhousie Law Library is also gratefully acknowledged.

The authors also wish to thank Jeff Miller, of Irwin Law Inc., for the constant encouragement and support he provided throughout the life of the project, which often involved authors on three different continents.

In addition to our general acknowledgements, Edgar Gold is most grateful for the assistance received from the T.C. Beirne School Law Library of the University of Queensland, Brisbane, Australia, with some of the research required. Professor Gold's long association with the Gard P&I Club, Arendal, Norway, has assisted him significantly in a number of chapters for which he had responsibility, and has also permitted him to quote extensively from two Gard publications.[2] Professor Gold's association with the World Maritime University, Malmö, Sweden, as the Canadian member of the board of governors and long-time visiting professor, greatly extended his knowledge of international maritime law and practice that is reflected in some of the chapters. Professor Gold is also most grateful to the Salvage Arbitration Branch of Lloyd's of London, for permission to reproduce *Lloyd's Open Form 2000 Salvage Agreement* in the book, as well as to Dalhousie Graphics, Dalhousie University, for assistance in creating the figures in Chapter 2. Professor Gold is especially grateful for the very valuable assistance received on specific chapters from a number of individuals. Captain Thomas Kearsey, of Survival Systems Training Inc., Dartmouth, Nova Scotia, and former principal, Nova Scotia Nautical Institute, who thoroughly checked and updated the technical section of Chapter 2 and also provided the latest bibliographic information. Peter Leckie Wright, Esq., of Insurance Dispute Resolution Services of British Columbia,

---

2 E. Gold, *Gard Handbook on Marine Pollution*, 2d ed. (Arendal: Gard A.S., 1997); E. Gold, *Gard Handbook on P&I Insurance*, 5th ed. (Arendal: Gard A.S., 2002).

Vancouver, British Columbia, and one of Canada's best-known marine insurance specialists, provided extensive comments, as well as updating, on Chapter 7. James E. Gould, Esq., Q.C., of Metcalf & Co., Halifax, Nova Scotia, and immediate past-president of the Canadian Maritime Law Association, provided very helpful comments and updating on Chapter 17; this help, which involved a significant amount of work, is not only most valuable but these chapters could not have been completed without it. Chapter 17 also benefited from the information received from Canada's Ship-Source Oil Pollution Fund, Ottawa, and its administrator, K. A. MacInnis, Esq., Q.C., who has very kindly supplied the fund's annual report and other helpful information to Professor Gold for many years. Captain Alan W. Knight, of Transport Canada, Ship Safety, Dartmouth, Nova Scotia, also kindly assisted with some questions related to Chapter 5.

In addition, Aldo Chircop expresses appreciation for the most helpful comments he received on individual chapters from the following: David Henley, Esq., and William Moreira, Esq., Q.C, of Stewart McKelvey Stirling Scales, Halifax (toward Chapter 12 and Chapter 18); the Honourable Mr. Justice Arthur J. Stone, Federal Court of Canada, Ottawa (toward Chapter 3); and Mikis Manolis, Esq., Campney and Murphy, Vancouver (toward Chapter 13 and Chapter 14).

Each of the authors is also grateful to the other two for the thorough review and helpful comments they made on each other's chapters. Edgar Gold and Hugh Kindred also express their particular gratitude to Aldo Chircop for his special contribution, made so adroitly and with unwavering good humour, in co-ordinating this project to its successful conclusion.

Last, but not least, the three authors express their affection and thanks to their spouses, Judith Gold, Andrea Chircop, and Sheila Kindred, for their usual patience, empathy, and constant support for their efforts.

Edgar Gold
Aldo Chircop
Hugh Kindred

CHAPTER 1

CANADIAN MARITIME LAW: AN INTRODUCTION

A. WHY A TEXTBOOK ON CANADIAN MARITIME LAW?

The subject-matter of this textbook is maritime law as it has been developed and practised in Canada. Maritime law — or as it is also called, Admiralty law — has been practised in Canada since at least the eighteenth century. The term "Admiralty" is derived from the period in history when the admiral of the English fleet exercised significant powers over the sovereign's naval fleet, as well as over those matters that occurred at sea over which common law courts had no jurisdiction. This specialized body of law — which has its own unique character but is linked to many other areas of law — has historically been administered by Admiralty Courts. These courts are judicial institutions that possess the competence necessary to exercise Admiralty jurisdiction. Although the term "Admiralty" is still widely used,[1] especially with reference to the Admiralty Court and Admiralty jurisdiction, a more modern and broadly encompassing term for this field of law is "maritime." Modern maritime law is significantly broader in scope than the areas traditionally addressed by admiralty law; however, there is no meaningful distinction between the two terms, which will be used interchangeably, with the exception of references to the Admiralty Court.

---

1 Especially in the United States.

Why a textbook on Canadian maritime law? Is maritime law in Canada sufficiently different from the maritime law of other countries, especially that of England from which it originates, to deserve separate treatment from a general maritime law shared by many maritime nations? More than eighty years ago Edward Courtenay Mayers wrote what remains the only comprehensive treatise on Canadian maritime law.[2] Writings and commentaries on maritime law as administered in Canada date from the second half of the nineteenth century, suggesting that the intellectual interest in the subject has been an enduring one.[3] Nevertheless, there is a fairly extensive modern literature on Canadian maritime law in both English and French, whether in the form of treatises, periodical articles, or conference proceedings, many of which have become standard reference works in various sectors of Canadian maritime law.[4] What has been missing is a textbook providing a com-

2 E.C. Mayers, *Admiralty Law and Practice in Canada* (Toronto: Carswell, 1916).
3 An earlier work by A. Howell, *Admiralty Law, Canada* (Toronto: Carswell, 1893), was not strictly a textbook. It consisted of a compendium of primary materials with annotations and an essay on the jurisdiction of admiralty courts in Canada. A slightly earlier and more general work was by E.N. Lewis, *Lewis' Law of Shipping, Being a Treatise on the Law Respecting the Inland and Sea-coast Shipping of Canada and the United States* (Toronto, Carswell, 1885). Commentaries on the work of specific Vice-Admiralty Courts in the late nineteenth century include the following: J. Stewart, *Commonplace Book and Judgments of Cases in Halifax, 1841–1851*, microfiche (Silver Springs, MD: Association for Information and Image Management, 1999); W. Young, *The Admiralty Decisions of Sir William Young* (Toronto: Carswell, 1882); W. Cook, *Cases Selected from those Heard and Determined in the Vice-Admiralty Court at Quebec* (Montreal: John Lovell, 1885); and A.A. Stockton, *Reports of Cases Decided in the Vice-Admiralty Court of New Brunswick from 1879 to 1891* (St. John, NB. J.&A. McMillan, 1894).
4 A. Bräen, *Le Droit Maritime au Québec* (Montréal: Wilson & Lafleur, 1992); J.D. Buchan, *Mortgages of Ships: Maritime Security in Canada* (Toronto: Butterworths, 1986); R.M. Fernandes, *Marine Insurance Law of Canada* (Toronto: Butterworths, 1987); R.M. Fernandes, *The Annotated Canada Shipping Act* (Toronto: Butterworths, 1988); R.M. Fernandes, *Boating Law of Canada* (Toronto: Carswell, 1989); M. Ganado & H. Kindred, *Marine Cargo Delays* (London: Lloyd's, 1990); W.W. Spicer, *Canadian Maritime Law and the Offshore: A Primer* (Calgary: Canadian Institute of Resources Law, 1984); G.R. Strathy, *The Law and Practice of General Average* (Toronto: Available from Strathy Barristers and Solicitors, 1995); G.R. Strathy & G.C. Moore, *Law & Practice of Marine Insurance in Canada* (Toronto: LexisNexis Butterworths, 2003); W. Tetley, *Marine Cargo Claims*, 3d ed. (Cowansville, QB: Yvon Blais, 1988); W. Tetley, *Maritime Liens and Claims*, 2d ed. (Cowansville, QB: Yvon Blais, 1998); and W. Tetley & R.C. Wilkins, *International Conflict of Laws: Common, Civil and Maritime* (Cowansville, QB: Yvon Blais, 1994). Several conferences, convened by the Canadian Maritime Law Association and the Canadian Bar Association, have also resulted in useful overviews of developments in Canadian maritime law.

prehensive statement on the scope and content of maritime law as it has been developed and is practised in Canada.[5]

The conspicuous absence of a current textbook useful for both student and practitioner is probably reason enough to produce one, but there are other reasons why a textbook is necessary at this stage. First, over the last twenty-five years, and most notably since 1998, there have been extensive changes in Canadian maritime law. Ever since the constitutional decisions rendered in 1977,[6] the Supreme Court of Canada and the Federal Court of Canada have been occupied in defining and developing the substantive maritime law, as originally inherited from English law, and further refining the full extent of maritime law jurisdiction at the federal and provincial levels.[7] This ongoing exercise has had an impact upon interpretations of the constitutional relationship between the federal head of power "navigation and shipping" and the provincial head of power "property and civil rights." In 1986 a further important Supreme Court of Canada case[8] highlighted the dynamic nature of maritime law by stating that it is neither static nor frozen in time. This case has facilitated a very generous interpretation of the full spatial and functional scope of maritime law as it continuously changes in response to commercial and technological forces and environmental concerns. A more recent Supreme Court decision[9] severely restricts the application of provincial law in maritime settings despite the accumulated practice. In other words, Canada's federal structure and unitary court system have distinctly influenced the judicial legal development of Canadian maritime law.

---

5   By way of recent examples of the closest works in terms of scope have been E. Gold, ed., *Canadian Maritime Law: Introductory Materials*, 9th rev. ed. (Halifax: Dalhousie Law School, 1996); and earlier versions produced since 1975 as casebooks for the teaching of maritime law at Dalhousie Law School, and also used by some other law schools in Canada; and R.M. Fernandes, *Shipping and Admiralty Law* (Toronto: Carswell, 1995), which consists of primary materials and case annotations across some selected sectors of maritime law. The most recent example is W. Tetley, *International Maritime & Admiralty Law* (Cowansville, QB: Yvon Blais, 2002), which is a significant international reference work. These books, however, cannot be characterized as textbooks.
6   *Quebec North Shore Paper Co. v. Canadian Pacific Ltd.*, [1977] 2 S.C.R. 1054; and *McNamara Construction (Western) Ltd. v. R.*, [1977] 2 S.C.R. 654.
7   For a more detailed analysis of these jurisdictional issues see Chapter 3, "Admiralty Jurisdiction."
8   *ITO International Terminal Operators Ltd. v. Miida Electronics Inc. (The Buenos Aires Maru)*, [1986] 1 S.C.R. 752.
9   *Ordon Estate v. Grail* (1996), 30 O.R. (3d) 643, aff'd [1998] 3 S.C.R. 437.

Second, the cumulative impact of these and several other recent decisions has led to the most active period of statutory development of maritime law since the *Admiralty Act, 1934*[10] and the *Canada Shipping Act, 1934*.[11] In 1993 the *Marine Insurance Act*[12] and the *Carriage of Goods by Water Act*[13] were enacted. Since then a new *Canada Shipping Act, 2001*,[14] the *Canada Marine Act*,[15] the *Canada Transportation Act*,[16] and the *Marine Liability Act*[17] have appeared. In areas relevant to maritime law a new *Canadian Environmental Protection Act, 1999*,[18] and the *Oceans Act*[19] have been passed. These legislative developments are in addition to the numerous amendments to or repeals of existing legislation. Even the Federal Court rules and procedure have changed and continue to do so,[20] and the British Columbia Supreme Court has become the first provincial superior court to adopt an Admiralty rule as part of its Rules of Court.[21]

Third, the applications of maritime law to ocean uses in Canada have also expanded and continue to do so. Until relatively recently, the bulk of maritime law applications were primarily in commercial shipping and transport matters, followed by fishing vessel activities. These "traditional" areas of application are now supplemented by offshore oil and gas activities (including their support services), especially in the Atlantic region, and recreational boating in all inland and marine waters. The increasing diversity of maritime legal issues has enriched several areas of maritime law, including maritime torts, limitation of liability, registration, and safety.

Fourth, over this period there has also been a considerable development of international maritime treaties in support of new global standards or legal harmonization, mostly under the auspices of the International Maritime Organisation (IMO).[22] This is in response to a discernible trend toward global uniformity in the regulation of all

---

10 S.C. 1934, c.31.
11 S.C. 1934, c.44.
12 S.C. 1993, c.22.
13 S.C. 1993, c.21.
14 S.C. 2001, c.26.
15 S.C. 1998, c.10.
16 S.C. 1996, c.10.
17 S.C. 2001, c.6.
18 S.C. 1999, c.33.
19 S.C. 1996, c.31.
20 See Chapter 19, "Admiralty Procedure."
21 B.C. Reg. 221/90, r.55 (British Columbia Supreme Court Rules).
22 See Chapter 2, "The Shipping Industry: An Overview."

aspects of international transport that ultimately facilitate trade. The areas covered by these new conventions include the following: arrest of ships, maritime liens and mortgages, the carriage of hazardous and noxious substances at sea, the training of seafarers, maritime safety management, marine oil pollution preparedness and response, and many others both in public and private law.[23] For a variety of reasons, Canada often has difficulties in becoming a party to international treaties. Nevertheless, Canada has accepted and implemented a large number of these international instruments. Furthermore, even where such conventions have not been formally accepted by Canada, they have frequently been adopted in national legislation anyway. This practice has resulted in a growing continuum between Canadian and international maritime law, which is also increasingly recognized by case law.

Owing to some of the influences stated above, Canadian maritime law has changed fundamentally and it would be very difficult today to teach or practise in this area of law without an understanding of how it has developed and where it stands now. In other words, it would no longer be wise to rely only on international maritime law texts without reference to those areas where Canadian law and practice has either tended to diverge significantly or developed its own subtleties. Although Canadian maritime law, as developed by legislators and courts, has tended to move toward international uniformity, there are still differences based on specific interests, public policy concerns, and relations with Canada's most important trading partners. As a result, even though Canadian maritime law shares many similarities with English maritime law, with American maritime law (as a result of a close trading and geographical relationship), and other common law and civil law jurisdictions, there are some distinctly Canadian approaches. For instance, Canadian courts are more generous than their English and Commonwealth counterparts in recognizing and enforcing foreign maritime liens that do not have counterparts in Canadian law.[24] In the area of marine insurance the Canadian system is now exclusively federal;[25] but in the

---

23 Many of these conventions will be discussed at some length in other parts of this book. However, a detailed, up-to-date listing can be found in Institute of Maritime Law, *The Ratification of Maritime Conventions*, 4 vols., Updated looseleaf service (London: Lloyd's Press, 1991–2003).
24 *Marlex Petroleum Inc. v. Har Rai (The)* (1984), 4 D.L.R. (4th) 739 (F.C.A), aff'd [1987] 1 S.C.R. 57.
25 See Chapter 7, "Marine Insurance."

United States, another federal country, it is a state matter, resulting in diversity, when compared to its uniformity in Canada.[26]

B. INTERNATIONAL CHARACTER OF MARITIME LAW

Although maritime law is part of Canadian federal law, it has a more distinctly international base than any other area of Canadian law. This fact is not surprising, as maritime law has historically evolved to service international trade.[27] Although maritime law today is more than simply such a service, it is still guided by the comity among nations. As a result, the international content and responsiveness to its international mission are evident at all levels in all sectors of maritime law.

Ships carry nationality through their flags. This means that nationality entails the application of the legal system of the state of registry, for instance, the flag state.[28] Suffice to show here that a ship when navigating at sea is, in a sense, a moving legal system that, while operating, may interact with a number of other legal systems. This may involve such situations arising from a ship colliding with other ships on the high seas, or from simply entering the maritime zones and especially the ports or internal waters of a foreign state. Furthermore, a ship may change nationality several times over its lifetime, simply by changing registry.

International trade between ports may involve vessels that are registered in one state but beneficially owned in another. Such ships may be managed and/or operated by agents in yet other states, with master and crew drawn from several states. A ship's hull and machinery insurance may be covered through London underwriters but liability or protection and indemnity (P&I) insurance is covered through a U.S., U.K.,

---

26 The leading U.S. case on this subject is *Wilburn Boat Co. v. Fireman's Fund Ins. Co.*, 75 S.Ct. 368, 348 U.S. 310 (1955), whereas the Canadian equivalent is *Triglav v. Terrasses Jewellers Inc.*, [1983] 1 S.C.R. 283. For a commentary on differences between U.S. and U.K. marine insurance law, see T.J. Schoenbaum, *Key Divergencies Between English and American Law of Marine Insurance* (Maryland: Cornell Maritime Press, 1999). For a more detailed examination of U.S. maritime law, see N.J. Healy & D.J. Sharpe, *Cases and Materials on Admiralty*, 3d ed. (St. Paul, MN: West Group, 1999); and T.J. Schoenbaum, *Admiralty and Maritime Law*, 2d ed. (St. Paul, MN: West Publishing, 1994).
27 For an extensive examination of this aspect see E. Gold, *Maritime Transport — The Evolution of International Marine Policy and Shipping Law* (Toronto: Lexington Books, 1981).
28 Chapter 4, "The Ownership and Registration of Ships."

Japanese, or Scandinavian P&I club. Cargo carried on board may be owned by many persons in various states and originate from and be intended for several destinations, subject to carriage contracts that include a choice of foreign law and a different forum for dispute settlement. Multimodality that enables cargo shipping containers to be moved from door-to-door utilizing a variety of transportation modes has further enhanced the international dimension and terrestrial reach of maritime law. The international character exists also in the range of services afforded to shipping, such as marine insurance and salvage that may involve parties, interests, and issues that cut across different legal systems and jurisdictions. Resulting from this diversity of actors, nationalities, geographical locations, and legal systems potentially involved, the practice of maritime law can be as fascinating as it is complex. Conflicts of law are very frequent, such as when a ship is arrested in Canada and lien holders advance claims based on various foreign laws. A Canadian court is expected to recognize foreign law that generates a claim, and to apply Canadian law in granting remedies.

Today a large section of the earth's hydrospace consists of national maritime zones. In the last three decades a modern system of national maritime zones has emerged in the law of the sea that entitles coastal states to exercise sovereignty or specific jurisdiction over wide sections of the oceans.[29] Coastal states have the right, as well as the responsibility, to legislate and enforce laws for a wide variety of purposes, and frequently these directly affect shipping and navigation. As ships regularly navigate through the maritime zones of various coastal states, this raises a number of issues concerning what kind of regulations may apply to ships generally, without necessarily and unjustifiably constraining international navigation. Coastal states frequently assert their authority from concerns about maritime safety and marine environmental issues. This can cause difficulties,[30] as unnecessary interference with international navigation may impede international trade. The shipping industry, therefore, needs a balanced approach to resolving the often-conflicting interests of coastal states and international community needs. This balance has been delicately crafted and re-crafted through an increasing array of international organizations and agencies as the industry becomes

---

29 *United Nations Convention on the Law of the Sea*, 10 December 1982, 1833 U.N.T.S. 3 [*UNCLOS*] (entered into force 16 November 1994). Although Canada is not yet a party to this treaty, the federal government has expressed the intention to accept it. In any case, many of the *UNCLOS* provisions have been implemented in Canadian legislation.
30 See Chapter 17, "Marine Pollution Prevention."

more and more globalized.[31] In other words, this globalizing trend has led to an increasingly international approach in establishing standards for safety and marine environmental protection.

A significant portion of modern maritime law has resulted from the initiatives of intergovernmental and non-governmental organizations aimed at developing international approaches and standards, in lieu of uniquely and exclusively national standards. The IMO, as the principal specialized U.N. agency dedicated to shipping, has developed a number of widely accepted, key international conventions affecting almost all aspects of vessel operations.[32] In addition, the Comité Maritime International (CMI) has proposed and facilitated numerous private maritime law conventions on just about all aspects of maritime law.[33] These conventions have enabled state parties to negotiate maritime law, including private maritime law, through public law-making processes. This development of international maritime law has greatly simplified and facilitated various relations between states; for example, the legal regime concerning port access and simplification of documentation and other port procedures has facilitated a more efficient turnaround of ships in port. The international requirements for training and certification of ships' officers and crew, and standards for the management of ships and shipping companies, are also aimed at creating international uniformity. In other words, international maritime law is today the most important component of maritime law, as reflected throughout this book. The necessity of an international approach to maritime law has also been clearly recognized at the highest judicial level in Canada, when it was stated that the development of the common law should consider "the fabric of the broader international community of maritime matters."[34] The Supreme Court went on to state that courts must also consider the effects of "change upon Canada's treaty obligations and international relations, as well as upon the state of international maritime law."[35] Thus, Canadian maritime law today clearly operates within a larger international legal system that relies, to a great extent, upon a regime of reciprocity among maritime nations.

---

31   See Chapter 2, "The Shipping Industry: An Overview."
32   Ibid.
33   International Maritime Committee, although the French name is generally used. It is the principal international non-governmental organization representing the private sectors of the shipping industry. The Canadian Maritime Law Association (CMLA) is CMI's Canadian member. See also Chapter 2, "The Shipping Industry: An Overview."
34   Iacobucci and Major JJ. in *Ordon Estate v. Grail*, above note 9 at 233 (S.C.C.).
35   Ibid.

C. SUBJECT-MATTER OF CANADIAN MARITIME LAW

The subject-matter of maritime law consists of the institutions that govern the origins and life of a ship. This includes the rights and responsibilities of those that have an interest in such a ship, whether involved in financing, securing, owning, managing, operating, provisioning and supplying, navigating, using its services or servicing it in any way, or regulating it, as well as those who are affected or injured by its operations.

Traditionally, a core element of maritime law is the notion of maritime property. The concept of property here is not simply a passive one (i.e., as an asset) but also an active one whereby the property achieves a measure of legal personality. The notion of maritime property in a maritime law context is based on a legal fiction that creates a "personality"; thus, the ship and other maritime property such as cargo, freight, and even the proceeds of a judicial sale, may generate rights and/or obligations in contract or in tort, in statute, or at common law. The ship itself is, therefore, considered to be a legal person capable of attracting liability. In this connection the ship can be considered as a "debtor" as well as a "tortfeasor," even though in reality those that own, manage, load, discharge, or operate the ship are the authors of any ensuing liability through their actions or inactions on or concerning the ship. The conceptualization of ship, cargo, and freight as maritime property has far-reaching legal consequences. It enables a claimant to proceed against such property on the basis of an action *in rem* (i.e., an action against the maritime property or the *res* itself). This is the quintessential, traditional action in maritime law and does not really have counterparts in other areas of law. The action starts with the "arrest" of the property (another fiction) and may result in its judicial sale. The action *in rem* is distinguished from the action *in personam* (i.e., an action against a person pursuant to a contract or tort). These two actions have a special relationship in Canada.[36]

---

36 See Chapter 3, "Admiralty Jurisdiction" and Chapter 19, "Admiralty Procedure."

D. LAYOUT OF THIS BOOK

The compilation of Canadian maritime law in this book is organized in such a way that it attempts to follow the life and operation of the ship and the various interests involved at different points and for specific purposes. After this general introduction, the basic technical aspects, as well as the commercial background to the shipping industry, are outlined in Chapter 2. This chapter also provides an overview of the industry's international connections and interests that, as already indicated above, have such a profound effect on modern maritime law.

Chapter 3, "Admiralty Jurisdiction," examines the major dispute resolution institutions in this area of law in Canada: the Admiralty Court, which in Canada is the Federal Court, and the provincial courts that still possess maritime law jurisdiction. Jurisdiction in maritime law is significantly different from other areas of law, in the sense that it is defined *ratione materiae* (i.e., by reason of the subject-matter) and, generally, is not confined in any way by location of the cause of action, nationality, or nature of the maritime claim.

Chapter 4 commences with a discussion of definitions of the ship and then moves to an application of substantive maritime law in relation to a ship in Canada starting with its construction: a naval architect is engaged and design plans may be purchased or developed, financing secured, and a shipyard contracted. Even before the ship is completed it may require a so-called builder's mortgage that provides a maritime security on the ship. At this early stage and once built, a ship needs to be inspected, classified by a classification society attesting to its design and seaworthiness, insured, and registered. A decision will need to be made as to where to register the ship, as this could have very significant financial and operational consequences. Each one of these steps engages a specific set of issues in maritime law.

Chapter 5 examines the initial operational aspects of the ship. Once ready to operate, the vessel will need a master, officers, and crew, who are likely to be contracted in part from a crewing agency. These service agreements are contracts in maritime law. In addition, international standards governing certification and training have a direct bearing on the seaworthiness of a ship. In fact, a vessel that has an incompetent crew can be deemed to lack seaworthiness, which in turn, may have serious implications during port state control inspections and affect its ability to sail on schedule. Furthermore, such unseaworthiness would also affect marine insurance coverage, arising from warranties the assured owes to the insurer, as well as liability for the carriage of goods on board.

Chapter 6 examines the fact that throughout its life the ship will continue to earn and discharge obligations arising from mortgages and liens, as well as other claims. As can already be seen, a ship may accumulate liabilities even before it sails on its first voyage. There are many ways in which a ship earns different types of liens, whether directly as a result of an incident, through contract, statutory requirements, or judicial decision — such as for towage, repairs, supply of necessaries, salvage, collisions or allisions, unpaid wages of master and crew, and so on.

Chapter 7, "Marine Insurance," provides an overview of this essential service to shipping. Before the ship starts to trade it needs various types of marine risk coverage, for hull and machinery losses, third-party liability (protection and indemnity), cargo insurance, and coverage for a variety of other risks. The marine insurance regime is one of the most ancient aspects of maritime commerce and, in fact, long precedes all other forms of insurance. It is a distinctive system with its own rules and peculiarities and is, therefore, a complex area of maritime law. It has as a particular characteristic the fundamental duty of *uberrimae fidei* (i.e., utmost good faith), requiring disclosures and various warranties that place a higher standard of good faith than normally required in contract law on the parties to the insurance agreement.

Chapter 8, "Carriage of Goods by Charterparty," Chapter 9, "Carriage of Goods under Bills of Lading and Similar Documents," and Chapter 10, "Carriage of Passengers," provide an extensive overview of the legal regime of the earning aspects of the ship. Once a commercial vessel is ready to start trading it may either be operated directly by the shipowner (including through representatives such as a ship management company or agent) or be chartered out. "Chartering" means the leasing of the ship or part of the cargo-carrying capacity of the ship. Charters may be by demise, when the shipowner gives up possession and control of the ship to the charterer. In charters that do not involve demise, the shipowner retains most of the control and simply leases the use of the ship or part of the ship for specific voyages or for a specified period of time. However, in many cases a whole ship may not be required and, instead, limited space may be required to carry goods. In such a case a different kind of contract of carriage of goods by sea is required and is evidenced by a bill of lading. The bill of lading is one of the most important instruments in maritime law as it generally performs the function of a negotiable document of title, enabling the goods on board to be traded, not only when they arrive at their destination but also while they are still at sea or in transit. Finally, the growing business of transporting passengers by water, whether on cruise vessels, ferries, or other ships, has resulted in the development of a specific legal regime for the carriage of passengers at sea. In all aspects of carriage by sea, whether of passengers or goods, there has developed a complex international regime governed by widely accepted rules and commercial practices.

Chapter 11, "Maritime Collisions," and Chapter 12, "Maritime Personal Injury and Death," examine the legal aspects of accidents that may occur during the ship's voyage. While navigating at sea all ships are governed by the international collision avoidance rules that not only establish the rules of the road at sea but also set out basic elements of good seamanship. This is a standard of due care expected from seafarers, against which they are judged when something goes wrong, such as a collision with another ship, an allision with a stationary object, loss of life or personal injury, damage to ship and cargo from various causes, and environmental damage.

Chapter 13, "Maritime Pilotage," Chapter 14, "Maritime Towage," and Chapter 15, "Maritime Salvage and Wreck," examine the services a ship may require during its voyage. Such services may be routine, such as pilotage and towage. In most Canadian ports pilotage is normally compulsory, while towage usually is not. Nevertheless, the master of a ship frequently enters towage contracts on behalf of the shipowner in order to expedite the entry or exit of the vessel from port terminals and for reasons of general maritime safety. When the ship faces a situation of extraordinary danger that could potentially result in significant risk to crew and/or passengers, serious damage to ship and/or cargo, or environmental disaster, the master may require contractual salvage services in order to bring the ship, crew and passengers, and cargo to a place of safety. Significant public policy concerns underlie the legal and moral requirement to assist ships in distress. As a result a long-established, traditional regime, designed to encourage and reward salvors for appropriate actions, has evolved. In the end a severely damaged ship may also become a wreck. This would trigger another aspect of maritime law related to wrecks.

Chapter 16, "General Average," discusses another ancient aspect of maritime law. In certain situations of danger, the master of a ship may be forced to make conscious sacrifices, such as jettisoning cargo to lighten a ship, or to incur unexpected expenditures, such as in a stranding. In order to cover this type of situation maritime law has developed the ancient institution of general average — "average" being a term of art meaning "loss" — whereby those that benefit from the sacrifice or expenditure incurred on behalf of the whole maritime adventure are required to contribute to the loss of those that suffered for the safety of others. Although technically part of the law of carriage of goods by sea, general average may also be seen as a type of collective and mutual cost-insurance by all interests on board the ship.

Chapter 17, "Marine Pollution Prevention," deals with a subject of growing importance and complexity in a much more environmentally conscious world. While vessel-source pollution accounts for less than 10 per cent of all pollution entering the oceans, commercial marine transportation has been singled out as a major culprit and is, therefore, the most heavily regulated marine activity in this area. As part of its normal operations a ship will generate significant and diverse wastes that are no longer permitted to be discharged overboard. This may include garbage, sewage, bilge wastes, waste engine oil, and oily ballast water that are now covered by a series of conventional and statutory requirements on waste management. In exceptional situations, when a ship becomes a maritime casualty, resulting in oil cargo and/or bunker fuel loss, severe damage to coastlines, coastal communities, local economies, and the marine environment generally may occur. While this type of casualty is relatively rare, there is now a well-developed international and domestic regime for shipowner and cargo liability, compensation, and cleanup. However, the emphasis is on prevention, especially on well-run ships abiding by international standards and well-trained crews, to avoid or mitigate negative impacts. International standards are applied by Canada and most other maritime states through a system of port state control inspections aimed at pushing substandard shipping out of business.

Chapter 18 addresses the unique regime that permits the shipowner to limit liability for maritime claims. There are many ways in which maritime claims may arise. Of legal concern here is the tortious action or inaction that may result in loss of life and injury, and/or damage to property. Canadian maritime law has undergone significant development in this area recently, mostly as a result of both judicial and legislative action.[37] An important and distinctive element in maritime law is the shipowner's right to limit liability, subject to a strict legal regime and in accordance with a tonnage formula.

Chapter 19 closes the ship's circular voyage as it examines the procedure that is required in order to bring a maritime action in the Canadian legal and maritime court system (described in Chapter 3.)

It should be noted that, given the complexities of maritime law, this book can only provide an overview of the various areas examined and is designed to impart basic knowledge. For more advanced insights the

---

37   *Ordon Estate v. Grail*, above note 9; and *Marine Liability Act*, above note 17.

voluminous maritime law literature must be consulted. The law is stated as it applied on 30 April 2003.

E. SPECIAL NOTE ON THE *CANADA SHIPPING ACT*

While this book was being prepared the main Canadian shipping legislation, set out in the *Canada Shipping Act*, was undergoing significant reform. A new *Canada Shipping Act, 2001*,[38] is now in existence and will, in due course, supersede the current *Canada Shipping Act*.[39] However, this change has resulted in significant problems in the regulatory area. The new Act includes considerable changes, both in form and substantive content, resulting from a lengthy review and consultative process. These changes require substantial revisions of almost all of the regulations made under the old Act as well as some entirely new ones. It is estimated that the completion of this task will take at least five years and possibly much longer. The inevitable result is that both acts will be in operation but almost all the regulations will still be derived from current statute, at least until new regulations under the *Canada Shipping Act, 2001* are available. As a result of this transitional situation, references to both statutes are made in this book. Also, it is not at all certain if the forthcoming regulations under *Canada Shipping Act, 2001* will be similar to those under the current regime. In fact, it is already apparent that there will be some significant differences, with some regulations disappearing altogether. In other words, users and readers of this book must always consult the latest information on the regulatory progress from Transport Canada and from the Canadian Coast Guard, Department of Fisheries and Oceans, which now have joint jurisdiction and responsibility over the modernization of the law.

The preparation of the new regulations has been divided into two phases. According to the latest information available, in Phase 1 the regulations are expected to be completed within four years (from 2002). These are the regulations necessary for the *Canada Shipping Act, 2001* itself to be enacted. In other words, the new Act will only come fully into force when these regulations are ready. They include the subjects outlined in Table 1.1.

---

38 Above note 14.
39 R.S.C. 1985, c.S-9.

Canadian Maritime Law: An Introduction   15

Table 1.1: Phase 1

Transport Canada	Canadian Coast Guard, Deptartment of Fisheries and Oceans
Vessel Classification by Voyage Type Regulations	Aids to Navigation Protection Regulations
Small/Medium Vessel Regulations	Boating Restriction Regulations
Crewing Regulations	Competency of Operators of Pleasure Craft Regulations
Vessel Navigation and Routing Regulations	Eastern Canada Vessel Traffic Services Zone Regulations
Load Lines/ Vessel Markings Regulations	Pleasure Craft Sewage Pollution Prevention Regulations
Ship Registration and Tonnage Regulations	Private Buoy Regulations
Inspection Regulations	Response Organizations and Oil Handling Facilities Regulations
	Sable Island Regulations
Fishing Vessel Regulations	Small Vessel Regulations
International Convention Implementation Regulations	Vessel Traffic Services Zones Regulations
Record Keeping, Information Management and Reporting Regulations	St. Clair and Detroit River Navigation Safety Regulations
Regs. Respecting the Appointment of and Conduct of Adjudicators	Heritage Wreck Regulations
Cargo Regulations	Regulations to Prescribe Vessels or Categories of Vessels as Pleasure Craft
Vessel Clearance Regulations	Large Pleasure Craft Regulations
Administrative Penalties	NORDREG (Arctic Canada VTS Zones)
Fire Safety Regulations	
Ballast Water Management	
Pollution Prevention Regulations	

In Phase 2 the regulations are expected to be completed within a further two-year period after the *Canada Shipping Act, 2001* is in force. They will be compiled jointly by Transport Canada and the Canadian Coast

16   MARITIME LAW

Guard, Department of Fisheries and Oceans. Both indicate that the compilation may take even longer. (See Table 1.2 for subject-matter.)

Table 1.2: Phase 2

Life Saving Equipment Regulations
Pollution Prevention Regulations
Marine Machinery Regulations
Procedures and Practices
Hull Construction Regulations
Navigation Safety Regulations
Regulations Excluding Certain Government Ships from the Application of the *Canada Shipping Act*
Canadian Maritime Documents
Detention, Abandonment and Sale of Vessels Regulations
Regulations Respecting Human Remains and Salvage of Heritage Wreck
State of War and Armed Conflict Regulations

F. SPECIAL NOTE ON THE *UNITED NATIONS CONVENTION ON THE LAW OF THE SEA*

The important *UN Convention on the Law of the Sea* (*UNCLOS*) is mentioned in a number of chapters of this book as it is the basis for much legislation in Canada affecting the use of Canadian waters by ships. In fact Canada only became a full party to *UNCLOS* by ratifying it on November 6, 2003.

Unfortunately, this significant legal development occurred as this book was going to press and too late to alter all its internal references to *UNCLOS*. In fact Canada's belated ratification of *UNCLOS* serves to shore up the legislative foundations of the law discussed in these pages.

FURTHER READINGS

BRÄEN, A., *Le Droit Maritime au Québec* (Montréal: Wilson & Lafleur, 1992).

BUCHAN, J.D., *Mortgages of Ships: Maritime Security in Canada* (Toronto: Butterworths, 1986).

FERNANDES, R.M., *Boating Law of Canada* (Toronto: Carswell, 1989).

——, *Shipping and Admiralty Law* (Toronto: Carswell, 1995).

——, *Marine Insurance Law of Canada* (Toronto: Butterworths, 1987).

GOLD, E., *Maritime Transport* (Toronto: Lexington, 1981).

INSTITUTE OF MARITIME LAW, *The Ratification of Maritime Conventions*, 4 vols., Updated looseleaf service (London: Lloyd's Press, 1991–2003).

SPICER, W.W., *Canadian Maritime Law and the Offshore* (Calgary: Canadian Institute of Resources Law, 1984).

STRATHY, G.R., *The Law and Practice of General Average* (Toronto: Available from Strathy Barristers and Solicitors, 1995).

STRATHY, G.R., & G.C. MOORE, *Law & Practice of Marine Insurance in Canada* (Toronto: LexisNexis Butterworths, 2003).

TETLEY, W., *Maritime Liens and Claims*, 2d ed. (Cowansville, QB: Yvon Blais, 1998).

——, *Marine Cargo Claims*, 3d ed. (Cowansville, QB: Yvon Blais, 1988).

——, *International Maritime & Admiralty Law* (Cowansville, QB: Yvon Blais, 2002).

TETLEY, W., & R.C. WILKINS, *International Conflict of Laws: Common, Civil and Maritime* (Cowansville, QB: Yvon Blais, 1994).

CHAPTER 2

THE SHIPPING INDUSTRY: AN OVERVIEW

A. INTRODUCTION

The world of ships, seafarers, the shipping industry, and international shipping organizations is unique. Although this chapter is only indirectly connected to the actual practice of maritime law, it is designed to assist those who have little awareness of the shipping industry and its various sectors. Maritime law is a very specialized area of law and some fundamental knowledge of the technical and commercial sectors of the shipping industry is essential. Furthermore, as can be seen from other chapters in this book, maritime law cases generally involve a number of technical aspects that require at least a basic appreciation of the area; for example, it would be difficult to assess a collision case without understanding the relevant ships' courses as plotted on the navigational charts.

Ships have evolved from the primitive craft of pre-history to today's highly specialized vehicle of trade; at the same time, seafarers have changed from primitive foragers or hapless impressed labourers to skilled technicians and professional mariners. In other words, ships and the environment they operate in have become complex and highly specialized in operational, managerial as well as legal terms. This chapter provides an overview of the shipping world.

B. SHIPPING INDUSTRY

Shipping is an international business and, therefore, much of it is regulated by widely accepted international rules that have been transposed into national law. Canada, as a major trading nation, is very much part of this international system. It is important to understand that shipping is a global industry that is always in transition and is continuously evolving. These factors have significant effects on the regulatory process.

1) Background

Until the 1970s shipping was part of the world's organized trade and commerce and was based on well-established procedures and legal regulations. This system had evolved from nineteenth-century British practice, when Great Britain controlled more than half the world's international seaborne trade.[1] Britain and a number of other dominant maritime states continued to control international shipping long after the Second World War. Shipping was predominantly privately owned and operated, under national flags, on distinctive trade routes with established management styles. New ships were generally ordered when replacements were required or if there was growth in a specific trading area. Payment for new vessels was usually made from retained profits or by modest bank loans, based on measurable trading prospects and a good credit record.[2] Even large oil companies and other downstream users of raw materials operated their own vessels under their specific national flags. Additional tonnage was chartered as required from independent shipowners. Bulk cargo charters were generally arranged in the London market. Liner shipping conferences were dominated by the traditional maritime states and determined their own freight rates and schedules. Ships were surveyed, classified, and insured by a very small group of institutions, often also based in London but with worldwide agencies. In other words, the period prior to the 1970s was considered to be relatively stable and prosperous for the shipping sector.

---

1 For a thorough analysis of this period see E. Gold, *Maritime Transport — The Evolution of International Marine Policy and Shipping Law* (Toronto: Lexington, 1981) cc.3–4.
2 One of the leading studies describing this period is C.E. McDowell & H.M. Gibbs, *Ocean Transportation* (Toronto: McGraw-Hill, 1954).

The profound changes that occurred in the shipping industry in the early 1970s had both political and subsequent economic causes. The closure of the Suez Canal in 1973, the cutbacks in oil production in the Middle East, the Iranian revolution, and the subsequent global recession were all causes that resulted in significant changes. In a few years shipping moved from relative stability to almost chaotic development.[3] Shipbuilding orders soared for larger vessels that had to use the Cape of Good Hope route when the Suez Canal passage became unavailable. Japan and South Korea provided significant subsidies for such ship construction in their modern, efficient, low-cost shipyards.

Also within a brief period marine technology changed significantly. This resulted in the standard 28,000 DWT (Deadweight Ton) supertankers, developed in the late 1950s, growing to the 250,000 DWT very large crude carrier (VLCC)[4] as the principal means to carry crude oil. Similar economies of scale were also developed in the dry bulk trades where the traditional 10,000 DWT tramp vessel would be replaced by a new generation of 40,000–200,000 DWT bulk carriers. Changes in the general cargo sector were equally significant owing to the evolution of container ships. Each of these new vessels would replace about seven conventional general cargo ships.[5] This technological revolution in shipping involved significant capital requirements as the traditional method of paying for ship replacements from accumulated profits was inadequate. Large bank loans became a necessity and the new shipping environment became highly geared to debt; however, banks and other financial institutions were quite willing to lend, often up to 80 to 90 per cent of ship costs, shipyards gave easy credits for new orders, and governments provided tempting tax breaks to national and foreign shipowners for vessels under their flag. However, there was an inevitable downturn. Easy financing and market processes generated an uncontrolled shipping surplus, with consequent cash-flow problems and many bankruptcies. Freight rates also fell under commensurate competitive and other pressures and some of the largest end users of shipping, such as major oil and dry bulk companies, began to dispose of their own

---

3   Gold, *Maritime Transport*, above note 1, cc.6–7; A.D. Couper, *The Geography of Sea Transport* (London: Hutchinson, 1972); B.J. Abrahamsson, *International Ocean Shipping: Current Concepts and Principles* (Boulder: Westview, 1980) c.1.
4   Vessels above this tonnage, ranging up to 500,000 DWT and known as ultra large crude carriers (ULCC), would soon follow.
5   For a general discussion of these developments see Abrahamsson, above note 3, c.1.

fleets and, instead, to charter vessels from competing independent owners at lower rates. Shipping profitability declined significantly.[6]

2) Globalization of Shipping

Since the 1970s shipping has become more international but probably at the cost of some stability. In areas such as financing, ownership, shipbuilding, crewing, and transnational aspects, the shipping industry is today the most globalized of all major industries. Today there is virtually unimpeded international mobility of capital and maritime labour in the industry. There are few barriers to entry and a relatively free choice to shippers in terms of competing vessels in the bulk cargo and most of the liner trades. The traditional freedom of the seas still permits ships to sail unimpeded, bound only by the law of the vessel's flag.[7] Even within states' 12-nautical mile (22-km) territorial sea areas, vessels are permitted to practise "innocent passage" under the new law of the sea.[8] Only upon entering the internal waters or port areas of a foreign state will the flag state's authority be overridden;[9] however, as discussed below, even here there have been significant changes.

An important part of the globalization of the shipping industry has been the lessening of the traditional link between ship ownership and flag state,[10] owing to the development of the "open registries" or "flags of convenience" system.[11] This system is principally a cost-saving device that permits ships to be registered in states for a lower price. It also permits shipowners to avoid heavier national taxation and employ seafarers at lower pay rates. The growth of open registries has been enormous, to the extent that almost half the world fleet is today within this system.[12] Some 9,689 ships, amounting to 375 million DWT, are

---

6 Abrahamsson, above note 3, cc.2–4.
7 As codified by the *United Nations Convention on the Law of the Sea*, 10 December 1982, 1833 U.N.T.S. 3 at art.87 [*UNCLOS*] (entered into force 16 November 1994; not yet accepted by Canada). See also Institute of Maritime Law, *Ratification of Maritime Conventions*, 4 vols., Updated looseleaf service (London: Lloyd's Press, 1991–2003) vol.I.1.170.
8 *Ibid.*, art.17.
9 *Ibid.*, art.8.
10 See A. Behnam, "Ending Flag State Control?" Unpub. lecture delivered to International Conference on Marine Environmental Law in Germany, April 2002.
11 See also Chapter 4, "The Ownership and Registration of Ships."
12 402 million DWT from a world total of 826 million DWT, as of January 2002. See, UNCTAD, *Review of Maritime Transport 2002* (Geneva: UNCTAD, 2002) at 25.

registered in seven major open registry states alone.[13] This also means that, in today's globalized shipping industry, a vessel could be financed, mortgaged, constructed, registered, owned, managed, operated, chartered, and insured in different states. The control of the flag state might be minimal and the crew could be drawn from almost anywhere.

The thirty-five most important maritime states control almost 95 per cent of the total world fleet with their share of over 30,000 vessels.[14] The world fleet carries almost six billion tons of cargo among one thousand main ports throughout the world.[15] The world fleet can be divided into five main groups by tonnage:[16]

- tankers: 35%
- dry bulk carriers: 35%
- general cargo ships: 13%
- container ships: 9%
- others: 8%

As discussed later in this chapter, within these groups are many specialized types of vessels, including some 250 large cruise ships, one of the fastest growing sectors in the industry. An examination of the world's twenty principal flag states indicates that beneficial ownership of vessels registered under open registry systems is still based in traditional maritime states, such as Greece, Japan, the United States, Norway, Hong Kong (China), the United Kingdom, and Germany.[17] However, there is a discernible rise of shipping in states such as China (including Hong Kong), South Korea, Singapore, Taiwan, and Brazil. Nevertheless, of the total world tonnage of 826 million DWT, the nation states with developed market economies still own 208 million DWT.[18] As already indicated, however, the major oil companies — which owned the great majority of tankers prior to the 1970s — now own only a small part of the world tanker fleet; the rest is independently owned. The dry bulk trade is almost completely independently owned. In the container trade there have been significant amalgamations and mergers to the extent that the global container vessel fleet is today operated by three or four very large alliances that are still growing.

---

13 Panama, Liberia, the Bahamas, Malta, Cyprus, Bermuda, and Vanuatu: *Review of Maritime Transport 2002*, ibid. at 33.
14 *Review of Maritime Transport*, ibid. at 31–32.
15 Ibid. at 8–10.
16 Ibid. at 18.
17 Ibid. at 34–35.
18 Ibid. at 25.

The final aspect of the globalization of the modern shipping industry is the growing internationalization of the regulatory process, owing to the fact that national flag state control over shipping has been greatly reduced by economic and technological changes in recent years, as well as the rapid growth of the open registry system. As a result, intergovernmental organizations with maritime interests — often strongly supported by a large group of non-governmental maritime organizations — have become increasingly involved in the regulatory process on a global, regional, and national basis. Their involvement is discussed in greater detail in the final section of this chapter.

3) Canadian Aspects

Although bordered by three great oceans and a major inland seaway, Canada is not a maritime state in the true sense of this expression.[19] Canada has a significant international trading sector, but its national-flag fleet is tiny. In any case, the great majority of Canadian exports move south by road and rail to the United States. Overseas exports of raw materials and manufactured goods generally move on foreign-flag vessels or open registry vessels that may or may not be beneficially Canadian-owned. In many ways Canada is a continental country with a large centrally located population connected from coast to coast by lengthy railway systems. As a result, shipping is not something that appears to rank very high in Canadian government policy priorities even though it is an essential element of Canadian trade and economy.

Nevertheless, Canada did have a more significant shipping industry in earlier times when it was an important extension of British Imperial shipping and trade policy.[20] As a result, Canada had a fairly extensive merchant marine prior to the First World War, especially on the Atlantic coast.[21] The fleet was built up again as part of Canada's efforts in the Second World War but faded when the federal govern-

---

19 N. Letalik & E. Gold, "Shipping Law in Canada: From Imperial Beginnings to National Policy?" in D. VanderZwaag, ed., *Canadian Ocean Law and Policy* (Toronto: Butterworths, 1992) at 261.

20 K.H. Burley, "Canada and the Imperial Shipping Committee" (1974) 2 J. Imperial and Commonwealth History 349.

21 See R.E. Ommer, "The Decline of the Eastern Canadian Shipping Industry, 1880–1895" (1984) 5 J. Transport History 1:24–44; E.W. Sager & G.E. Panting, *Maritime Capital: The Shipping Industry Atlantic Canada 1820–1914* (Montreal: McGill–Queen's University Press, 1990); E.W. Sager, *Seafaring Labour: The Merchant Marine of Atlantic Canada 1820–1914* (Kingston, ON: McGill–Queen's University Press, 1989); J.S. Ewart, "Merchant Shipping" (1912) 37 Can. L.T. 337.

ment decided to relinquish its interest in a government owned national fleet in the 1950s. In the subsequent period the industry was almost totally de-regulated, with some protection only for the Canadian coastal and Great Lakes trades.[22]

This development resulted in Canadian maritime law owing its origins to British law and policy.[23] "Navigation and shipping" is a class of subjects contained in Canada's *Constitution Act, 1867*.[24] However, among the subjects that had fallen under the jurisdiction of the Dominion Parliament at that time, the model for the *Canada Shipping Act* remained the British merchant shipping acts until 1934. At that stage the Dominion Parliament became legally entitled to legislate in the field of shipping law[25] and quickly passed the first two Canadian shipping acts.[26] Even this new legislation was very closely related to its British antecedents and, for that matter, to legislation in other parts of the British Commonwealth.[27] Since then Canadian shipping legislation has continued to closely reflect international maritime law as developed in the major maritime states.[28]

C. SHIPS AND SHIP'S EQUIPMENT

1) Basic Terminology

The two main parts of a ship are the hull and the machinery. The hull is the actual shell of the ship, while the machinery includes not only

---

22 *Coasting Trade Act*, S.C. 1992, c.31, as am.; P.G. Cathcart, "Deregulation in the Canadian Maritime Industry" (1988) 56 Transportation Practitioners Journal 15; see also M.R. Brooks, *Commercial Requirements for a Canadian Fleet* (Halifax, NS: Canadian Marine Transportation Centre, 1984).
23 Letalik & Gold, above note 19 at 262. See also V. Black, "One if by Land, Two if by Sea: Old Directions in Maritime Law" [1985] Maritime Law 17; T.L. McDorman, *The Development of Shipping Law and Policy in Canada: An Historical Examination of the British Influence.* Unpub. LL.M. Thesis, Dalhousie University, 1982; W. Tetley, "A Definition of Canadian Maritime Law" (1996) 30 U.B.C. L.Rev. 137.
24 (U.K.), 30 & 31 Vict., c.3, repr. R.S.C. 1985, App. II, No. 5. See also Chapter 3, "Admiralty Jurisdiction."
25 With the entry into force of the *Statute of Westminster, 1931* (U.K.), 22 Geo. V., c.4.
26 *Canada Shipping Act, 1934*, S.C. 1934, c.44; and *Admiralty Act, 1934*, S.C. 1934, c.31. See also Chapter 3, "Admiralty Jurisdiction."
27 M.L. McConnell, *A Comparative Study of the Development of Shipping Law and Policy in Canada and Australia.* Unpub. doctoral diss., University of Sydney, Faculty of Law, 1988.
28 See, e.g., W. Tetley, "The State of Maritime Law: Canada, U.S., U.K. and France" [1986] Meredith Lect. 389–404.

the engines required for propulsion but also the auxiliary equipment serving the electrical installations, cargo winches and cranes, refrigeration and air-conditioning plants, cargo pumping equipment, and so on. The front portion of the ship is termed "forward," while the extreme forward end is called the "bow" or "stem"; the rear portion of the ship is termed "aft" and the extreme rear is called the "stern." When moving bow first, the vessel is considered to be moving ahead or making headway. When moving stern first, the vessel is considered as moving astern. The midpoint of the vessel, halfway between the bow and the stern, is called "amidships." The greatest width of the hull is called the "beam." A line running from the centre of the stem to the centre of the stern — called the "fore-and-aft centre line" — is generally used to measure the length of the vessel. When standing on the fore-and-aft centre line of a vessel looking forward, the direction to the right is "starboard" or the starboard side, and the direction to the left is "port"' or the port side. Some countries use right or left instead of starboard and port, respectively. Under the *Convention on the International Regulations for Preventing Collisions at Sea, 1972 (COLREGS 1972)*,[29] at night, the starboard side is indicated by a green light, and the port side by a red light.[30] (See Figure 2.1 for an illustration of the parts of a ship.)

Figure 2.1: Parts of a Ship

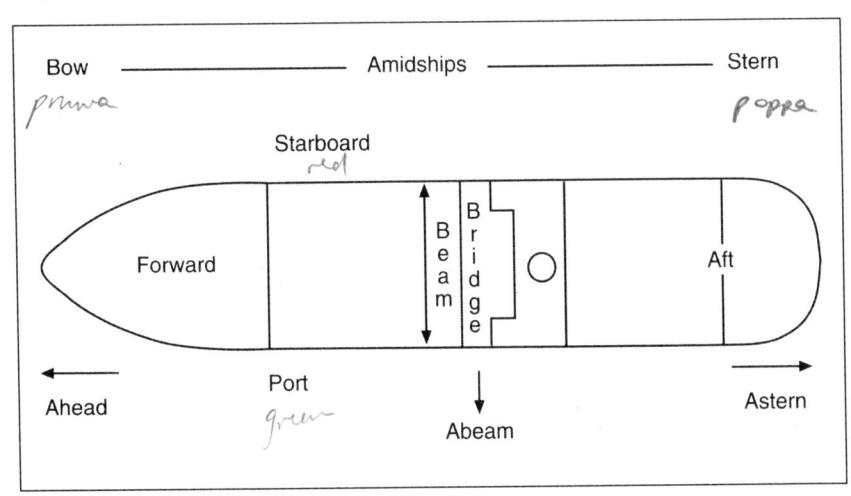

---

29 20 October 1972, 1050 U.N.T.S. 16 (entered into force 15 July 1977; Canada acceded on 15 July 1977). See also *Ratification of Maritime Conventions*, above note 7 vol.I.3.250. See also Chapter 11, "Maritime Collisions."
30 *COLREGS 1972, ibid.*, Part C, r.21.

It is frequently necessary to indicate the general direction of an object external to the ship by reference to horizontal sectors relative to a ship's fore-and-aft centre line. (See Figure 2.2) This is especially important in close-quarters situations with other vessels that could lead to a collision. Therefore, such an object may be reported as being ahead or astern, on the starboard or the port bow, on the starboard or port beam, or on the starboard or port quarter. For greater accuracy the position of the other object may be given by providing the horizontal sector direction in combination with compass points. (See also Figure 2.4.)

Figure 2.2: Horizontal Directional Sectors of a Ship

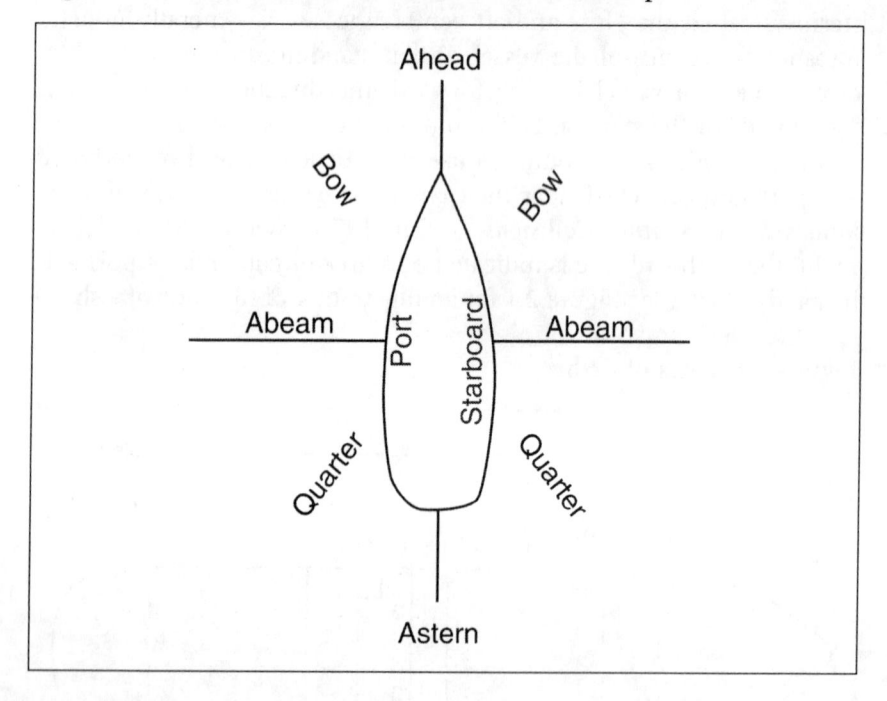

2) Ship's Machinery

A vessel's engine room, or machinery space, accommodates the ship's propulsion machinery as well as the auxiliary machinery, the generators required for lighting, cargo work, air conditioning and refrigeration, and the steering system. Up to the 1950s, this space was normally located amidships; since then there has been a tendency for most types of cargo and passenger vessels to have their engines situated further aft, thus making the widest part available for more space to accommodate cargo and passengers. Another reason for moving the engine aft is that it shortens the length of the propeller shaft and thereby greatly decreases construction costs. Engine room exhausts are usually passed through a funnel shape, often painted with the shipping line's distinguishing logo. However, many modern ships may have different exhaust arrangements. The propeller shaft, linking the propeller with the propulsion system, passes through a shaft tunnel. Vessels with twin or multiple engines could have additional propellers, or could be coupled to one propeller. In addition to the main propulsion unit, many modern vessels have a transverse propulsion unit in a tube across the hull, near the bow and/or other parts of the hull, which allows the ship to move sideways. This provides for greater manoeuvrability in confined waters, channels, ports, and harbours, when docking or undocking, and also reduces or eliminates the need for tugs.

There are many different types of propulsion systems for vessels. The traditional reciprocating steam engine is rarely used today, although vessels fitted with steam turbines may still utilize steam power. The most common propulsion machinery fitted on ships today is the multi-cylinder diesel engine operated in high or low speed. These engines range from small power plants, on board fishing and auxiliary vessels, to some of the most powerful engines installed on large passenger, container, bulk, and tank vessels. There are also other types of propulsion systems, such as diesel-electric or gas turbine, as well as the latest water jet and "azipod" propulsion systems, that dispense with the need for propellers or that combine steering and propulsion. As there are many significant marine insurance claims for machinery damage, some knowledge in this area is essential. While the use of sails in ship propulsion is now mainly confined to pleasure yachts, there are numerous passenger vessels as well as a few, mainly experimental, cargo vessels that utilize auxiliary sails as part of their propulsion system.

The rudder that directs the course of the vessel is usually located at the stern. There may be systems with twin rudders or even bow rudders for special operations. A steering engine — or engines in the case of multiple systems — drives the rudder. This is part of the vessel's auxiliary machinery. Another piece of auxiliary machinery is the ship's windlass used to lower and hoist the vessel's anchors usually located in the vessel's bow. Other auxiliary machinery include the ship's generators, which supply the vessel's electrical systems; refrigeration systems, especially on vessels carrying refrigerated cargoes; cargo pumping systems on board tank vessels; ballast pumping systems; bilge pumps; air-conditioning compressors; cargo winches or cranes; and emergency fire pumps and lifeboat machinery. In most cases, ships will be required to have backup systems for much of this machinery.

3) Ship's Hull, Superstructure, and Cargo-Handling Equipment

The vessel's hull is its main watertight compartment and consists of an outer shell constructed in accordance with the relevant specifications as required under international regulations. The shape of the hull will obviously depend on the type of vessel. Ships designed to carry solid or liquid bulk cargoes will require a hull shape that will maximize cargo capacity. Concerns about marine pollution prevention have today developed the requirement for double hulls for tank ships.[31] Vessels carrying solid bulk cargoes — such as coal, ore, and bulk chemicals — will require large, almost square, unobstructed holds with mechanically operated hatch covers for the speedy handling of cargo in order to reduce loading and discharge time in port. The actual design of the holds will depend upon the requirements of the trade for which the vessel was built. A tanker in the crude oil trade will have the hull subdivided into large cargo tanks. A tank vessel designed to carry refined products — such as gas oil, petrol, or liquid chemicals — may have a large number of smaller sub-divided tanks. Tankers may also be designed to carry other cargoes, such as vegetable oils, wine, and other food products.

A general cargo vessel, conveying a variety of goods in relatively small consignments — often known as the break-bulk trade — would have its hull divided into horizontal "tween decks" to facilitate stowage. Container ships are equipped with specially designed cellular holds to facilitate speedy loading and discharge of standardized containers;[32] such containers are slotted into the cells in the vessel's holds as well as on deck. Passenger vessels' hulls are designed in such a way that passenger space can be maximized, for instance, through the fitting of numerous horizontal decks. In all cases, international regulations will set out the requirement of watertight compartmentalization on ships. In addition, in many cases, vessels will also be fitted with double-bottom or double-skinned hulls. For tankers this will become a standard safety requirement in the near future.[33] This safety feature is designed to protect the watertight integrity of the vessel and also reduce the possibility of pollutants being spilled from vessels involved in collisions or grounding.

---

31 See also Chapter 17, "Marine Pollution Prevention."
32 See, e.g., F. Böer, *All About a Container Ship* (Herford: Koehlers, 1987).
33 The United States will implement this requirement in 2004 under its *Oil Pollution Act*, 33 U.S.C. §§2701–2761 (1990). See Chapter 17, "Marine Pollution Prevention."

The ship's superstructure is built on the upper part of the hull, generally on the top watertight horizontal deck. For most cargo vessels this will consist of a structure containing accommodation space for ship's crew as well as the navigation bridge and some type of engine exhaust system such as a funnel. There may also be some type of mast(s). There may be some other structures containing pump room auxiliary machinery, other cargo machinery, and storage spaces. Passenger vessels may have numerous decks in very large superstructures containing passenger accommodation and other hotel facilities.

The ship's cargo handling equipment will depend on the type of vessel and its trade. The traditional general cargo vessel carried its own derricks or ship's cranes with lifting capacities ranging from 0.5 to 50 tons; some ships may be fitted with jumbo derricks capable of lifting up to 200 tons. The derricks are suspended from the ship's masts and are operated by winches. However, the use of derricks is today quickly disappearing. General cargo vessels that require their own loading/unloading equipment are now generally fitted with cranes. Container ships usually depend on shore equipment for loading/unloading of containers. Some container vessels, trading to areas where no shore equipment is available, may be fitted with their own container-handling systems. Dry bulk cargo vessels also generally depend upon shore equipment for loading and discharge; however, some geared bulk vessels may have their own cargo-handling equipment in order to service ports without such equipment. Tankers always have their own cargo-pumping system fitted, although many shore terminals may have pumping and gravity systems to load/unload the cargo. There are, of course, many other specialized types of vessels that have different types of cargo-handling equipment. Some of these are described below.

4) Ropes and Wires

While containerized cargo has eliminated a considerable amount of traditional cargo-handling equipment on board ships, a significant amount of work on a ship still utilizes rope, wire rope, and chains. Accordingly, one of the predominant causes of maritime injuries is the improper use of such equipment. It is, therefore, important to have some idea of how to determine whether a rope or chain is of sufficient strength for a particular task or working load.[34] Four main types of

---

34 In accidents involving rope, wire, and chain, expert assistance will be required. In most cases the required working loads will be set by national legislation and regulation. See C.H. Brown, *Nicholl's Seamanship and Nautical Knowledge*, 22d

rope used in such maritime operations as mooring, towage, and cargo-handling are manila, sisal, coir, and synthetic fibres (i.e., polypropylene and nylon). Manila rope is made from abaca fibre, which comes from a plant belonging to the banana family. The rope is smooth, glossy, strong, flexible, very durable, easy to handle, and has a very high resistance to rotting. It was the most common natural fibre in use at sea for a long time; however, it is quite expensive and synthetic fibre ropes have now overtaken its use. Sisal fibre is taken from the long, spiny leaves of the agave plant. It has very consistent strength, very good sisal being of equal strength to medium-grade manila. Sisal rope is not generally considered suitable for marine work if manila or synthetic fibre rope is available. Coir is made from coconut fibre removed after the shell has been water-soaked for many months. This rope is very elastic, red in colour, rough to handle, floats very easily, and is extremely resistant to rotting. It is principally used in towing and docking. Polypropylene, nylon, and other synthetic ropes are now most widely used, as they are very strong, soft, and pliable; they are more modestly priced and easily obtainable than natural fibre ropes. They are also waterproof and their surfaces dry quickly; their resistance to abrasion, rot, and mildew is very good, although strong acids can damage them. Owing to its strength, steel wire rope is also frequently used in many marine operations. A modern wire rope consists of a number of strands laid around a central heart that may itself be a steel strand, steel wire rope, or a strand of vegetable or synthetic fibre. Each strand in turn is composed of a given number of individual wires again laid round a central wire or fibre core, the wire core in this case usually consists of one single wire. The strength of the wire rope depends upon the type of heart, the number of strands, and the number of wires in each strand. Chain is also used in many marine operations. It is made from steel or iron bars and is built up link by link. Each part of the chain is tested, as a defective link can only be detected by testing, and a chain is only as strong as its weakest link. The proof load of a chain is the stress applied to the chain in testing the links.

5) Tonnage

Reference has already been made to tonnage, which is an important subject in the shipping industry, as it determines in part the cost of

---

ed. (Glasgow: Brown, Son & Ferguson, 1974) c.3. See also *Canada Shipping Act*, R.S.C. 1985, c.S-9, s.338; *Canada Shipping Act, 2001*, S.C. 2001, c.26, s.120(b) that permits regulations for this area to be made.

running a ship. In general, tonnage may refer to any of three shipping aspects: the size of a vessel, the amount of cargo carried by the ship, and the ship's spatial (volumetric) capacity. The principal types of tonnage are deadweight, cargo, displacement, gross, net, and limitation.

a) Deadweight Tonnage
Deadweight tonnage (DWT) is the number of English long tons (each weighing 2,240 lb.) a vessel is capable of transporting, including cargo, passengers, crew, stores, and bunker fuel. Deadweight tonnage is used interchangeably with deadweight carrying capacity; a vessel's actual cargo-carrying capacity is less than its total deadweight tonnage.

b) Cargo Tonnage
Cargo tonnage is expressed either as a weight or volume measurement. The weight ton is usually expressed in terms of the American short ton (2,000 lb. [907 kg]), the English long ton (2,240 lb. [1016 kg]), or the metric tonne (1000 kg). A measurement ton is usually 40 cubic feet or 1.1 cubic metres.

c) Displacement Tonnage
The displacement tonnage of a vessel is the weight, in English long tons, of the ship and its contents — that is, the weight of water the ship displaces. Light displacement is the weight of the vessel without stores, bunker fuel, or cargo. Loaded displacement is the weight of the vessel plus cargo, crew, passengers, fuel, and stores. Displacement tonnage is rarely used for cargo ships because of the great difference between light and loaded displacements; it is, however, the usual method of describing the tonnage of warships.

d) Gross Tonnage
Gross tonnage (GT) applies to vessels and not to cargo. These are really measurements of space that are based on the principle that the earning capacity of a ship is mainly governed by the cubic capacity of the ship under and on the deck. The internal capacity is obtained by multiplying the length, breadth, and height of the ship in feet, with one ton being equal to 100 cubic feet. Gross tonnage, often referred to as the gross registered tonnage (GRT), is equal to the total internal capacity of the ship below the main deck plus the capacity of all enclosed spaces above deck, but with a number of exempted spaces.[35] Gross tonnage is

---

35 Light and air spaces, wheelhouse, galley, water closets, staircases, hatchways, and open shelter deck.

used as a basis for pilotage fees, dry-docking, and, sometimes, tonnage dues. Additionally, it may be used for statistical purposes, when comparing ship sizes, and as a basis for protection and indemnity insurance club entries.[36]

e) Net Tonnage

Net tonnage (NT), often referred to as net registered tonnage (NRT), expresses the space available for the accommodation of passengers and the stowage of cargo. In other words, net tonnage is the earning or revenue space on the vessel: it is equivalent to gross tonnage after subtracting certain spaces.[37] Most harbour and port dues, canal tolls, and other charges are calculated on a vessel's net registered tonnage. Accordingly naval architects and shipowners attempt to achieve a low NRT but with a maximum cubic capacity for cargo and/or passengers. In summary, the GRT is the measurement of the capacity of the vessel's closed-in spaces, and the NRT is the general estimation of the earning capacity of the ship.

f) Limitation Tonnage

Limitation tonnage (LT) is only used in calculating the limitation of liability of a vessel found liable for loss and damage arising from a marine collision or other accident.[38] There are also two other specific types of tonnage measurement, such as the Panama Canal tonnage and Suez Canal tonnage, which differ from each other as well as from other measurements. They are used to calculate fees for passage through these waterways.

6) Draught, Load Line Marks, and Freeboard

A vessel's draught refers to the actual depth of the submerged part of the hull below the waterline, measured vertically to the lowest part of the hull. Draught marks are engraved and painted, usually at the bow and stern of the vessel, indicating the number of feet or decimetres of draught at any time. Such marks are important when loading cargo on a ship in order that the ship is properly balanced, or trimmed, from

---

36   See Chapter 7, "Marine Insurance."
37   Crew accommodation, master's and officers' accommodation, navigation spaces, deck department store rooms, water ballast or freshwater tank spaces (forepeak & afterpeak tanks), pump room (on tankers), auxiliary engine spaces, and propelling machinery spaces (engine room, propeller shaft, etc.).
38   See Chapter 18, "Limitation of Liability for Maritime Claims."

bow to stern. Sufficient height of the side of a vessel above the waterline ensures the following:

- satisfactory safe handling and working of the ship,
- adequate protection for cargo hatches and ship's equipment from sea damage, and
- delivery of the cargo in good condition.

Until 1876 there were no standards with respect to how much cargo could be loaded on a ship or how deeply the hull could be submerged. Shipowners would order masters to load as much cargo as possible on their ships in order to maximize potential profits. As a result many ships were lost and that period was known as the age of the "coffin ships." Samuel Plimsoll, a British politician and shipping law reformer, advocated a basic standard for the loading of cargo and, in 1876, developed the "Plimsoll mark," (now "line") to be painted on the side of a ship to denote the maximum depth to which the ship might be loaded. (See Figure 2.3.) This height restriction of the ship's hull above the waterline would eventually be regulated by the *International Convention on Load Lines, 1966*, (LL 1966)[39] that has become widely accepted throughout the shipping world. It has been incorporated into regulations under the *Canada Shipping Act*[40] and is enforced by port wardens[41] throughout Canada.

LL 1966 requires the deck line and load line marks to be marked on the sides of vessels. The deck line is a mark amidships denoting the level of the vessel's uppermost complete watertight deck. "Freeboard" is a term used for the height between this deck or deck line and the load line. Directly below the deck line on the side of the ship is a mark called the load line disk with a line (the Plimsoll line) horizontally through its centre; the load lines are forward of this disk. There are usually six load line marks on merchant vessels, indicating different seasons and zones, and for fresh and salt water. The Plimsoll line is always on a line with the most commonly used summer load line mark. (See Figure 2.3.) A ship operating in the winter season will usually

---

39   5 April 1966, 640 U.N.T.S. 133 (entered into force 21 July 1968; entered into force in Canada 14 April 1970). See also *Ratification of Maritime Conventions*, above note 7, vol.1.3.50.
40   *Canada Shipping Act*, above note 34, s.355; *Canada Shipping Act, 2001*, above note 34, s.122.
41   Under the *Canada Shipping Act*, ibid., Part VIII, the *General Load Line Regulations*, C.R.C., c.1425, s.18 give power to port wardens to board ships, examine the load line certificate and/or determine whether the load line is submerged. The *Canada Shipping Act, 2001*, has no equivalent section and it remains to be seen if regulations drafted under this Act will continue this position and task.

34   MARITIME LAW

encounter harsher conditions than when operating in a tropical zone. As a result greater freeboard will be required in order to ensure the safety of the vessel and its cargo. On a voyage, a ship may pass through a number of zones where different load lines apply; however, the vessel is required to arrive in a zone with the proper amount of freeboard. Significant fines are imposed in Canada and elsewhere for violations of these load line regulations.[42]

Figure 2.3: The Plimsoll Line

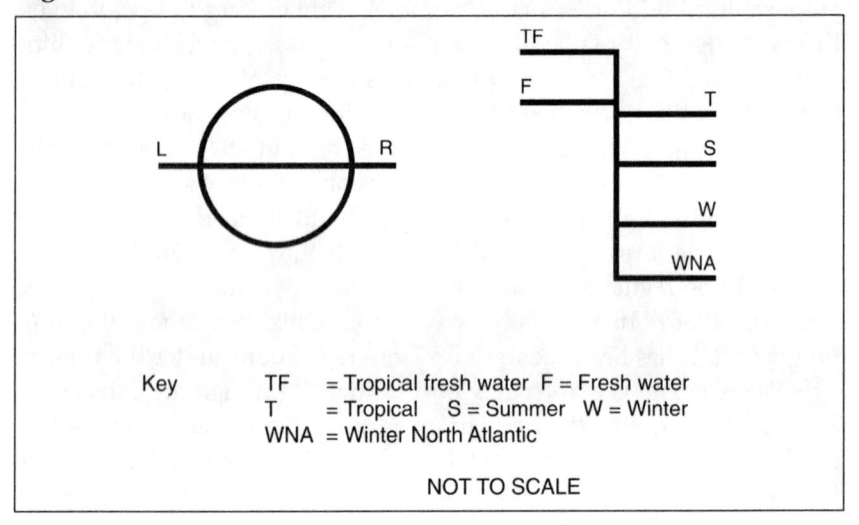

Key	TF	= Tropical fresh water	F = Fresh water
	T	= Tropical	S = Summer W = Winter
	WNA	= Winter North Atlantic	

NOT TO SCALE

The distances between the load line marks depend on the size of the ship. Classification societies measure the ship and ensure the proper positioning of these marks. The relevant society is identified by letters marked above the Plimsoll line in the load line disk. The most common abbreviations are LR (Lloyd's Registry), DNV (Det Norske Veritas — Norway), BV (Bureau Veritas — France), and ABS (American Bureau of Shipping).[43]

---

42 $1000 fine, plus $500 for each inch or fraction thereof submerged: *Canada Shipping Act*, above note 34, s.332. Contravention results in a maximum fine of $500,000 for each cm (or part of cm) the load line is submerged or eighteen months in jail: *Canada Shipping Act, 2001*, above note 34, s.110(2).

43 For a fuller explanation of classification societies, see below, G, "Shipping and International Organizations."

7) Types of Ships

There are many different types of ships in non-commercial and commercial operation.[44] In the non-commercial area, government ships include all types of military vessels, coastguard ships, fisheries patrol craft, naval auxiliary vessels, and search-and-rescue craft. Although such vessels are generally required to obey navigational rules within the limits of their abilities, they may be exempted from a number of other legal requirements. In the commercial area, ships can be broadly divided into four groups: cargo ships, passenger ships, fishing vessels, and other types of vessels.

a) Cargo Ships

There are three main divisions of cargo ships: liner vessels, tramp ships, and specialized cargo vessels. These divisions are based on the function, rather than size and speed, of the vessel.

i) *Cargo Liner Vessels*

The cargo liner vessel, or freighter as it is sometimes called, is a ship that operates on a scheduled, defined, and advertised route between specified ports of call.[45] Such vessels are classified as common carriers, offering cargo space and, sometimes, limited passenger accommodation. Cargo liners normally sail on scheduled dates regardless of whether they are fully loaded. This strict scheduling is designed so that shippers can rely on the service. Delays are, therefore, costly and the liner companies will do everything to avoid delays or unforeseen schedule changes. In order to provide this type of service — often on a weekly basis from major ports — an adequately sized fleet and a fairly large shore establishment is required. Modern liner services mostly employ containerized vessels. In many cases the major container companies provide allied or combined services so that frequent scheduling can be maintained. In recent years, there have been major amalgamations and takeovers in the container shipping business, resulting in this global trade being dominated by two or three major container business alliances.[46]

Container shipping has revolutionized global trade as it allows a door-to-door service for shippers. While container ship construction

---

44 See, e.g., A.E. Branch, *The Elements of Shipping*, 4th ed. (London: Chapman & Hall, 1977) c.4.
45 *Ibid.* at 28–29; B. Farthing, *International Shipping*, 2d ed. (London: Lloyd's Press, 1993) at 13.
46 Such as the Maersk–Sea Land Group; the P&O–Nedlloyd Group; and Hapag-Lloyd, etc. See also Farthing, *ibid.*, c.10.

costs are very high, in the longer term the expense of shipping by container is comparatively low. Advantages of shipping by container include

- significant reduction of handling costs on door-to-door transit, as containers eliminate the intermediate handling of individual articles within the container because containers are specifically designed for inter-modal transit (i.e., each container is designed so that it can be carried with equal facility by ship, rail, or truck);
- reduced risk of damage to, or theft of, the goods carried inside the container; and
- partial elimination of packaging of goods to be shipped.

In addition to the high cost of container ship construction, there are a few other disadvantages, almost all related to expenditure. These include the high initial cost of obtaining a sufficiently large number of containers to start a container service. Container services also require special port facilities to take full advantage of the system's rapid loading and discharging capabilities. These include special cranes capable of lifting the containers into and off the ship. Major container terminals are required to have the capacity to discharge and load several thousand containers per day. The disadvantages are far outweighed by the many advantages of the container system. The container trade is today firmly established and the range, size, and type of container ships that operate on the major cargo liner routes is far advanced in terms of technological sophistication from the original concept of moving trucklike boxes on board ships. The latest generation of 115,000 DWT container vessels is capable of carrying over 7,000 TEU (twenty-foot equivalent units *q.v.*) at a speed of 25 knots on around-the-world services. Such vessels will only call at major ports and containers will be shipped to such ports by smaller container feeder vessels. Although originally designed to carry all types of general cargo in packages, today containers are designed to move refrigerated cargo, hazardous and dangerous substances, bulk commodities, and liquid substances as well. In the short sea trades, vehicular commercial ferries or "Ro-Ro" (Roll-on–Roll-off) ships also provide a liner service. Such vessels permit road transport trucks and even rail carriages to be driven directly on board the vessel and then driven off at the port of destination.

ii) *Tramp Ships*

Tramp ships are cargo vessels that do not keep to a fixed route or sail to any particular schedule.[47] Their routes and ports of call are governed

---

47 Branch, above note 44 at 29–31.

solely by the availability of suitable cargoes or charters. Tramp ships are usually not specialized for specific cargoes but can carry any type of bulk or packaged cargo in large unobstructed holds. In most cases such ships are utilized in the carriage of dry bulk commodities such as grain, ore, or coal. The ships are usually chartered for a specific time or voyage.[48] Tramp shipping companies are often family-owned and are usually much smaller than their liner cargo counterparts. While the number of tramp vessels has fallen in recent years, the total volume of tramp tonnage has remained relatively stable, as many of these types of vessels are today much larger.

iii) Specialized Cargo Ships
The general purpose vessels already described above are not suitable or appropriate for a number of specialized cargoes and trades, such as oil, oil products, chemicals, certain dry bulk cargoes, liquid natural gas, liquid petroleum gas, heavy or large volume cargoes, and refrigerated cargoes. Accordingly, the shipping industry has developed specialized vessels for such trades.

aa) Bulk Liquid Cargo Ships
The global demand for oil and oil products led to the development of the tank vessel, designed to carry bulk liquid cargoes that can be loaded and discharged expeditiously.[49] A tanker's hull is sub-divided into numerous tanks, connected by a piping system to pump rooms, which load and discharge the cargo. Tankers are divided into two types: crude oil carriers and product, or parcel, tankers. As the name indicates, crude oil tankers are designed to carry crude oil from producing areas to refinery ports. Such vessels are generally large to the point where those exceeding 150,000 DWT are designated very large crude carriers (VLCCs) and those in excess of 300,000 DWT are classified as ultra large crude carriers (ULCCs). Product or parcel tankers are designed to carry refined oil products, such as gasoline, kerosene, and naphthalene. They are also often used to carry liquid bulk chemicals. They are usually smaller than crude carriers. Their hulls are also sub-divided into tanks, but there will usually be more tanks and very complex piping systems in order that many different types of oil products or chemicals may be carried. Tank vessels now comprise over 50 per cent of the world fleet. The world's tanker fleet is divided between tramp opera-

---

48 See Chapter 8, "Carriage of Goods by Charterparty."
49 G.S. Marton, *Tanker Operations*, 2d ed. (Centreville, MD: Cornell Maritime Press, 1984) c.1.

tors, operating their vessels under spot, voyage, or time charters, and those owned and operated by the major energy companies.

Another type of bulk liquid cargo vessel is the liquefied natural gas or LNG carrier, designed to carry liquefied natural gas in insulated tanks in specially designed holds at very low temperatures (-162°C [-260°F]). Although the insulated tanks may be designed in any number of ways, they are generally classified into two types: free-standing tanks or membrane tanks. LNG carriers present very little environmental risk because of the volatile nature of the cargo; on the other hand, the main hazard faced by such vessels is fire and explosion. In addition, there are also certain other hazards faced by the ship's crew when in contact with such cargo; however, the LNG industry has a very good safety record mainly owing to the high construction and operation standards of these costly ships.

Liquefied petroleum gas, which is a byproduct of the oil refining process, is today widely used in industry and transportation. This has led to the development of the liquefied petroleum gas or LPG carrier. These vessels are usually smaller than LNG carriers and are also capable of transporting liquefied gas cargoes in pressurized and/or refrigerated form in free standing insulated tanks at low temperatures. Like the LNG carrier, LPG carriers present a minimal environmental risk because of the volatile nature of their cargo. However, while petroleum gas, stored at only -50°C (-58°F), presents less danger to the crew or ship's hull than LNG carried at -162°C (-260°F), both share the chief hazard of fire, and proper insulation and storage is still essential.[50]

bb) Dry Bulk-Cargo Ships
As already indicated above, the tramp shipping industry is comprised of many bulk carriers designed to carry different dry bulk cargoes. However, in a number of trades the carriage of certain bulk cargoes has also become quite specialized. This has resulted in bulk carriers specifically designed to carry coal, bulk chemicals, and such minerals as iron ore and manganese. While the majority of such vessels depend on shore loading and discharging facilities, there are several vessels in operation that have their own loading/unloading equipment. Bulk carriers range in size from small coastal vessels to very large vessels exceeding 250,000 DWT. This industry has also produced a hybrid vessel capable of carrying both liquid and dry bulk cargoes. This is the ore/bulk/oil vessel, designed to carry different bulk commodities on different legs of a voyage.

---

50   J.R. Dudley, B.J. Scott, & E. Gold, *Towards Safer Ships and Cleaner Seas — A Handbook for Modern Tankship Operations* (Arendal, NO: Gard, 1994).

cc) Refrigerated Cargo Ships
A very specialized trade utilizes purpose-built refrigerated vessels, often called reefer vessels, designed to carry perishable products such as fruits and vegetables, chilled or frozen meat, seafood, and dairy products.[51] In general, refrigerated cargo vessels are divided into fruit carriers fitted with cool air systems to prevent fruit and vegetables from overripening, and fully refrigerated vessels capable of carrying frozen cargo at required low temperatures.

dd) Heavy and Oversize Cargo Vessels
Very heavy machinery or oversize cargo that cannot be carried on standard merchant ships, Ro-Ro, or container ships has resulted in the very specialized heavy lift shipping sector. Such ships are not only capable of lifting over 500 tons but can also carry very large pieces of equipment, including oil rigs, large boats, and railway locomotives.

It is not appropriate to provide a comprehensive listing of all types of cargo ships in this chapter. There are many other specialized cargo vessels designed to carry some specific type of cargo or for a particular trade route.

b) Passenger Ships
Passenger vessels are today not utilized for international, long-distance liner service, as they simply cannot compete with the aircraft industry. Instead, passenger vessels can be divided into two groups: cruise ships and passenger ferries.

i) Cruise Ships
Cruise ships have been an enormous growth industry in recent years.[52] There are now large passenger vessels cruising in all parts of the world, with many more vessels on order. Many of the newer vessels are huge, often exceeding 100,000 DWT, capable of carrying up to 3,000 passengers with a crew of 1,500–1,800. Instead of being floating hotels, such ships are really floating resorts. They are expensive vessels, with costs often exceeding US$250 million. Concerns have been expressed about the safety of such large vessels with close to 5,000 persons on board, and the International Maritime Organisation (IMO) is presently studying this aspect. In general, the industry has been very safety conscious stemming from a high standard of construction and emergency train-

---

51 L.G. Taylor, *Cargo Work: The Care, Handling and Carriage of Cargo*, 8th ed. (Glasgow: Brown, Son & Ferguson, 1974) c.11.
52 *Review of Maritime Transport 2002*, above note 12 at 18.

ing. In the era following the terrorist attacks in the United States on 11 September 2001, such ships also now require a high degree of security.

ii) Passenger Ferries

Ferry services can be found in many parts of the world and are, to some extent, simply an extension of the road or rail services across bodies of water. The ships involved range from small cross-river boats to very large, luxurious, high-speed vessels. In addition to carrying passengers, these vessels also often carry automobiles and transport trucks as well as rail cars. Given the large number of such vessels in operation throughout the world, this industry's safety record is reasonably good, although periodic serious accidents and disasters, such as those involving *The Herald of Free Enterprise* off Zeebrugge, Belgium,[53] and the *The Estonia* in the Baltic, illustrate the vulnerability of such vessels.

c) Fishing Vessels

There are far more fishing vessels in operation on the world's waters than commercial and pleasure craft. These range from small indigenous coastal craft to large deep-sea fish factory vessels. As there are many different fishing technologies — such as hook-and-line fishing, long lining, drift netting, purse seining, trawling, trap fishing, and bottom dragging — a great variety of craft is utilized for the various methods. As fishing operates in navigable coastal waters as well as on the high seas, it merits its own section in *COLREGS 1972*.[54] In general, most vessels are required to keep out of the way of vessels engaged in fishing, although fishing vessels are required to indicate clearly that they are fishing.

d) Other Types of Vessels

In addition to the various types of vessels already briefly listed, there are many other types of vessels covering almost every maritime service and activity. Among them are naval and military vessels, other government vessels, service vessels, and pleasure craft.

i) Naval and Military Vessels

Naval and military vessels range from giant nuclear-powered aircraft carriers and large submarines to small coastal patrol vessels. Although such ships must generally follow *COLREGS 1972* requirements,[55] they

---

53   S. Crainer, *Zeebrugge: Learning from Disaster* (London: Herald Charitable Trust, 1993).
54   Above note 29.
55   *Ibid.*, art.1; see Chapter 11, "Maritime Collisions."

are in many cases excluded from generally accepted maritime law.[56] They are often engaged in ocean exercises, frequently operate in groups, and may be engaged in sovereignty patrols, coastal embargoes, and other security related activities.

ii) Other Government Vessels
There are many types of vessels carrying out non-commercial government services in coastal and international waters, including coast guard vessels, fisheries patrol craft, customs and excise vessels, navigation aid service craft, ocean weather station vessels, hydrographic survey vessels, scientific research ships, government icebreakers, government supply and replenishment vessels, pilot vessels, government salvage and towage vessels, port and harbour service vessels, and experimental craft.

iii) Service Vessels
In addition to government service vessels, there are also many other vessels that provide services on a commercial basis, such as ocean, coastal, and harbour tugs;[57] salvage vessels;[58] offshore supply vessels; cable and pipe-laying vessels; dredgers; crew shuttle and service craft; mooring vessels; garbage and refuse craft; bunkering vessels; dry and liquid cargo barges, both self-propelled and towed; and floating cranes and other loading and discharge equipment.

iv) Pleasure Craft
There has been a phenomenal growth in the pleasure craft industry in almost all regions of the world. Such crafts operate in the internal and coastal waters of many states, as well as on the high seas, and range from small personal watercrafts to large ocean-going power-driven yachts that may be larger than small commercial ships. This growth has also led to increasing regulation.[59] Regrettably, there has been a commensurate increase in accidents involving pleasure crafts, which are often operated by persons who are insufficiently trained. These accidents can lead to significant claims.[60]

---

56   *UNCLOS*, above note 7, art.32, 95, and 236.
57   See Chapter 14, "Maritime Towage" and Chapter 13, "Maritime Pilotage."
58   See Chapter 15, "Maritime Salvage and Wreck."
59   *Canada Shipping Act, 2001*, above note 34, Part 10 deals with pleasure crafts. See also *Competency of Operators of Pleasure Craft Regulations*, S.O.R./99-53 and *Crewing Regulations*, S.O.R./97-390, s.59.
60   See Chapter 12, "Maritime Personal Injury and Death" and Chapter 18, "Limitation of Liability for Maritime Claims." See also "Summertime Sailing: Cruise Ships, Pleasure Boats, and the Law": Symposium (1998) 29 J. Mar. L. & Com. 155; *Curtis v. Jacques* (1978), 20 O.R. (2d) 552; *Horsley v. MacLaren*, [1972] S.C.R. 441.

D. NAVIGATION AND NAUTICAL INFORMATION

1) Nautical Charts

Ships are navigated safely between ports by following a selected route on a chart, which is a contour map of the seabed and its surrounding coastline. A topographic, or land surface, map provides the heights of the land contours above sea level, while a chart sets out the bathymetry. The selected route takes into account the vessel's draught in order that there will always be sufficient underwater clearance from the seabed and other undersea obstructions. The ship proceeds on compass courses along a selected route at a speed depending on the ship's operational capabilities and other external factors. Within sight of land the ship's position and progress is traditionally fixed by compass bearings related to headlands, points, and conspicuous buildings. In addition, soundings (i.e., sonic measurements comparing the actual depth of water beneath the vessel with the depths shown on the chart) provide a traditional navigational check. Charts also indicate prominent landmarks as well as lighthouses, light vessels, and buoys. Such navigational aids are illuminated with different light and colour characteristics, which assist recognition by mariners at night. When out of sight of land, a ship's position can be determined by astronomical observations and calculations, using the sun, moon, planets, and stars, with the aid of a sextant. While these traditional navigational methods are still used, modern electronic aids today not only augment the traditional methods but generally provide a more accurate and efficient system of determining the vessel's position, as outlined further below.

Most charts are based on Mercator's projection, in which the meridians (i.e., the longitude lines) are represented as being parallel to each other and perpendicular to the parallels of latitude. However, as the latitude increases, the meridians converge toward the poles. The higher the latitude (i.e., the closer to the poles) the greater is the amount of distortion resulting on the chart. Meridians, or longitude lines, run from pole to pole and are measured up to 180° east and west of the 0° (or Greenwich) meridian. Latitude parallels run horizontally around the globe and are measured up to 90° north and south of the equator. Both longitude and latitude are divided into degrees (°), minutes ('), and seconds ("). As in time measurement 60 seconds equal 1 minute and 60 minutes equal 1 degree. For example, Halifax, Nova Scotia, is located at 44°38'N (latitude) 63°35'W (longitude) and Melbourne, Australia, is located at 37°45'S (latitude) and 144°58'E (longitude).

Because 1 minute of latitude is approximately equal to 1 nautical mile, measuring latitude will not only partially determine a ship's position but also provide a basis for measuring distance. The ship's course will also be determined and set out on the nautical chart. A compass rose printed on the chart assists chart readers.

2) Navigational Aids

a) Compass

In maritime law some knowledge of compass direction is essential. A compass is an instrument that points in a fixed horizontal direction. This direction is true north in the case of a gyrocompass, and magnetic north for a magnetic compass. Compasses are divided into 360° through four quarters: north, east, south, and west, with 90° in each quarter. Older compasses were expressed in points, with the face of the compass graduated into thirty-two named points, with north, south, east, and west forming the four cardinal points (see Figure 2.4). The term "point" is also used to describe the angle of 11¼° between any two successive points of the compass; thus, two points equal an angle of 22½°, four points an angle of 45°, and eight points an angle of 90°. This method of describing an angle or direction is now used to describe a general direction, especially in terms of giving the relative direction of other ships. For example, the direction of an approaching object may be described as being two points abaft the starboard beam; since the beam is the centre line of the ship (between the bow and the stern), this would mean that the object is approaching from the right at 22½° behind the ship's centre line, or 112½° from the direction in which the vessel is pointed.

Ships have used the magnetic compass since very ancient times, although it contains two important errors — variation and deviation — which together are called magnetic compass error. Variation is the angular difference between true north and magnetic north. As previously mentioned, the magnetic compass points to magnetic rather than true north. The angle of variation differs from place to place owing to the difference between the true and magnetic poles, and the irregular pattern of the earth's magnetic field. For example, in Halifax, Nova Scotia, the difference between true and magnetic north is about 22°W, while in New York the variation is about 10°W. Deviation is the built-in compass error caused by the inherent magnetism in the steel of the vessel itself. The magnetic properties of each ship inevitably affect the magnetic compass by causing it to point in a direction determined by the combination of the earth's field (variation) and the ship's field (deviation). Deviation will vary with any change in the ship's magnetic state and will be different for various directions of the ship's head. These differences may be considerable. However, although these effects cannot be entirely eliminated, they can be sufficiently reduced by corrector magnets placed around the compass and through other means to allow the compass to be used for accurate navigation.

Figure 2.4: Ship's Compass Points

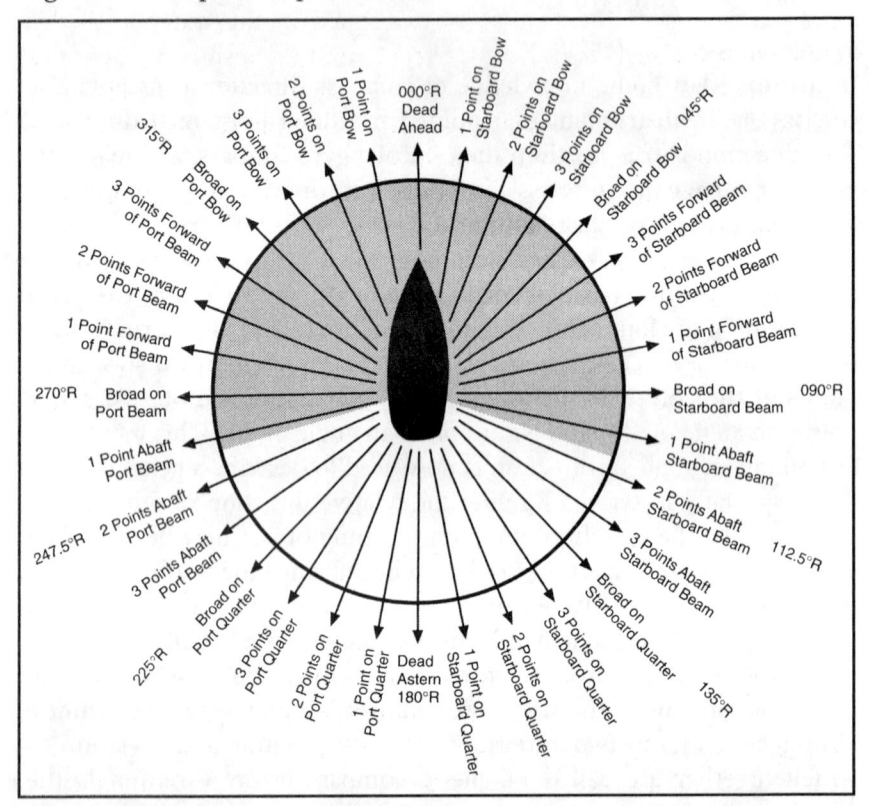

While all ships are still fitted with a magnetic compass, most ships today also have a gyrocompass that is electronically operated and more efficient and accurate than a magnetic compass. The gyrocompass is an instrument that seeks true north based on a gyroscope. As the gyrocompass points to true north, the gyrocourse of the ship and the true course are almost always identical. As a result there is no variation or deviation. The major disadvantages of the gyrocompass are that it is dependent upon electricity, and that it may take 4–8 hours to warm up and operate effectively. Today, the magnetic compass is usually only used on ships in emergencies when the gyrocompass is inoperative.

b) Depth-Sounding Devices[61]

A measurement of the depth of water is called a sounding. As already indicated, ships are interested in water depth for two reasons: first and foremost, in the interest of safety, and second, for positioning. The depth of water is usually measured in feet, metres, or fathoms (1 fathom = 6 ft. or 2 m). Traditionally soundings are taken by a lead line, a length of line marked at intervals along its length and with a lead weight at one end. The lead line is dropped in the water until the weight is on the seabed and the correct sounding is shown where the water level cuts the line. A hollow space in the bottom of the lead can be filled with grease and the nature of the sea bottom can thus be determined. As marine sounding technology has become more advanced, the lead line is now seldom used. Another older sounding method was the "patent sounder" that is also in little use today, although still fitted on older vessels. Patent-sounding machines measure the depth of water through the use of a glass tube lowered to the bottom. The inside of the tube is coated with a chemical that indicates how far the water entered the tube. The pressure at the bottom determines the entry of water, as the pressure of water on a submerged body increases with the depth to which it is submerged.

The "echo sounder," since its appearance in about 1925, has become such an important navigational aid that it is now installed in almost every ship. It is a sonar device, operating on the principle that sound travels in water at a known speed and is reflected from the seabed in the same way that a sound above sea level is reflected from hills and cliffs. The principle on which the echo sounder operates is relatively simple. Short pulses of sound are emitted from a transmitter at a rate of 5 to 600 per minute. These pulses are reflected by the seabed and received by a receiver in the ship. The depth is proportional to the measured time interval between emission and reception. This interval is measured and the depth indicated by a recorder on board the vessel. These depth recorders vary in type and sophistication and are capable of visually indicating the depth below the ship and/or provide a printed record of the depth and contours of the seabed as the ship travels over it. Modern echo sounders can also be fitted with an alarm that will sound if a water depth lower than that set by the operator is detected.

c) Vessel Speed Indicators

While a vessel's speed can be measured through taking navigational positions, mariners also need to have a constant indicator of a vessel's

---

61 Brown, above note 34 at 120–27.

speed over the ground. Traditionally the ship's "log," first invented in the sixteenth century, measured a vessel's speed.[62] The log consisted of a piece of wood attached to a line and thrown over the stern to lie like a log on the water. The first 20–30 metres of the line, known as the stray line, allowed the log to be carried beyond the wake of the vessel. At the end of the stray line a piece of material was inserted called the turnmark. Beyond this mark, the line was marked with pieces of cord, each having a certain number of knots in it. As soon as the turnmark went over the rail of the ship, a sandglass was inverted. When the sand ran out of the inverted glass, the cord nearest the rail was noted and identified by the number of knots in it. In other words, the knot as a unit of ship speed, is derived from the marks on the log line. A knot is equal to 1 nautical mile (usually 6080 ft.) per hour or, roughly, 100 feet per minute.

Since the early twentieth century, vessels were able to use "patent logs."[63] There are a variety of types. One type consists of a rotator at the end of a log line extended from the ship. The rotator revolves according to the speed of the vessel, turning the log line in a register that indicates the speed on a dial. Another type, known as the "impeller log," consists of an impeller at the end of a retractable tube located at the bottom of the ship's hull. The impeller, or rotator, contained in the tube provides a very accurate measure of the speed travelled through the water if the strength of the current is known. This information is relayed electronically to a counter. The tube must be retracted when a vessel is berthing or operating in very shallow water.

Electronic logs, sometimes called "bottom logs," determine the ship's speed by the Doppler effect of pulses in water between two small fins projecting from the bottom of the ship. Other types measure the pressure of the water exerted in a tube by the forward motion of the ship. Speeds and distance travelled are shown on dials or digital displays on the ship's navigating bridge.

d) Global Positioning Systems

The Global Positioning System (GPS) relies on satellite data and is the most advanced navigational aid available to shipping at present. These systems are also based on military technology developed during the

---

62 Brown, *ibid.* at 127–28.
63 So called because such logs were developed by patent-holding companies, such as Walker and Chernikeef, Brown, *ibid.* at 128–32.

Cold War.[64] A number of sophisticated navigational satellites in polar orbit feed constant information to GPS receivers on the earth's surface, providing extremely accurate positioning with a constant readout. The satellites transmit their positions and the vessel receiver can determine its position relative to the satellites. There are at present twenty-four satellites on six different orbital paths. It normally takes a minimum of three satellites to obtain a usable position, although input from four or more improves the accuracy. Information is injected into the satellites from ground stations to update their position information. Although not yet fitted on all ships, nor required under international conventions, GPS is quickly becoming less expensive. As a result, it is being fitted more widely. Even hand-held sets that can show an accurate position within tens of metres, as well as course, speed, and distance, are now obtainable for only a few hundred dollars.

The Differential Global Positioning System (DGPS) is today increasingly used for navigation in coastal waters. GPS works out the receiver's position from the raw data from the satellites, but such data may contain variable and random errors caused by radio waves and other factors prevalent in coastal areas. Accordingly, DGPS utilizes a ground station that receives these signals and calculates corrections for each incoming satellite signal and removes any errors. In offshore waters such accuracy is not required so the ground stations do not have great range.[65]

e) **Radar**

The word "radar" is composed of the first letters of radio detection and ranging. It is an electronic and mechanical navigational aid that not only detects the echoes of ships, buoys, or the coastline, but also measures their bearing and range, and gives a limited indication of the nature of these objects. As a result, radar serves as an anti-collision aid as well as a position finder. Radar is a particularly important aid to navigation at night, in fog, or at other times of impaired visibility. It is probably the most important development in modern navigation.[66]

---

64 *Convention on the International Maritime Satellite Organization*, 3 September 1976, 1143 U.N.T.S. 105 [INMARSAT] (entered into force 16 July 1979 and acceded to by Canada on 16 July 1979). See also *Ratification of Maritime Conventions*, above note 7, vol.I.3.260. The system is now internationally monitored, administered, and regulated by the International Maritime Satellite Organization, based in London, England. See also below G, "Shipping and International Organizations."
65 The Canadian Coast Guard provides some more detailed information on its web site: <http://www.ccg-gcc.gc.ca/dgps/maine_e.htm>.
66 See also Chapter 11, "Maritime Collisions."

Radar works on the basic principle of bouncing electronic impulses off objects through generating ultra-short high-frequency radio waves in a narrow beam. An object in the path of the beam will reflect an echo to the radar set on board the vessel. The radar receiver then calculates the range of the object and displays it on a cathode-ray radar screen. The radar antenna rotates continually so that the echoes of all objects surrounding the ship are displayed. Radar was first successfully developed and used extensively during the Second World War. After the war the development of radar exclusively for navigational purposes began. Radar systems on board vessels are today often very sophisticated. In many cases collision-avoidance systems link radar with other navigational aids and systems on board. Nevertheless, as also indicated in Chapter 11, "Maritime Collisions," radar is still a navigational aid as the systems on board have a number of limitations.[67]

f) Electronic Chart Display Information Systems

The Electronic Chart Display Information System (ECDIS) combines information from satellite positioning, radar, sonar, and paper charts in one computer-based device. ECDIS incorporates sensors that provide visible and audible warnings of potential collisions with ships or other objects, including those that may not appear on the charts. ECDIS is also capable of automatically recording the ship's previous positions, enabling a ship to retrace a known safe route and allowing investigators to trace errors after an accident. Performance standards for ECDIS were initially approved in 1995.[68] ECDIS is still being developed, although it is in full use in a number of regions, especially on shorter sea routes. It is expected that fuller, global ECDIS coverage will become available in the foreseeable future. This would eliminate the need for ships to carry an extensive collection of charts that requires constant correction, as electronic and radio signals would in future correct the electronic chart information.[69]

---

67 See, e.g., A.N. Cockcroft & J.N.F. Lameijer, *A Guide to the Collision Avoidance Rules*, 3d ed. (London: Stanford Maritime, 1982) at 53–62.
68 By the nineteenth Assembly of the International Maritime Organisation after significant preparatory work. *Performance Standards for Electronic Chart Display and Information Systems*, IMO Res. A.817(19) (1995). Transport Canada has made a decision to only implement interim ECDIS standards until global standards are available. Users of the interim system are able to obtain a reduction in Marine Service fees. See online at <http://www.ccg-gcc.gc.ca/msfdsm/archive/Oct98/Oct98FEEschedule_e.html>.
69 See <http://www.tc.gc.ca/cmac/documents/PaperChartReportEng.htm> for a Transport Canada consulting report on this subject.

ECDIS is an integrated system as it displays the electronic chart on a large computer screen. The linked GPS/DGPS information places the ship on the screen in the exact latitude and longitude. The linked radar system is able to shift the position of the ship in order that strong radar targets — such as a wharf, island, or other distinctive mark — are over the charted position of the actual radar target. The system then projects a ship shape icon, similar in scale of the chart, onto the screen. The linked gyrocompass then projects the ship shape in the actual direction that the ship is heading. In other words, the operator on the vessel is able to observe a real-time presentation of where the vessel is actually located on the chart.

Prior to the development of ECDIS, mariners had to obtain data for plotting onto a paper chart from a variety of sources (i.e., compass, radar, Loran, or other now discontinued electronic systems). The actual position, once plotted, was history immediately as the process took minutes rather than seconds. Instead ECDIS provides an accurate and present position on a continuous basis without the need for manual activities by the user. Furthermore, the ECDIS user is able to manipulate data to the extent that some charted information that may not be needed, can be deleted, or the scale of some charted information may be exaggerated for better clarity. The system is also able to sound an alarm if the ship is heading toward or is close to water depths or obstructions such as a dock, bridge pylon, or even other vessels.

The latest generation of vessels will be fitted with fully automated bridge systems that completely integrate information from a variety of data sources, such as radar, GPS/DGPS, echo sounder, compass, and log. Such an automated system is able to compute the ship's estimated (i.e., dead reckoning) position from the log and compass information and then compare it with the position provided by GPS/DGPS. If the variation is greater than a pre-set amount, an alarm will sound. This type of system is very similar to the automated, computerized, electronic information and navigation systems carried by modern aircraft. Only the flight data recorder (or, black box) system is not yet used on board ships; however, studies are under way for the fitting of such devices on board ships.

g) **Loran C**
Loran[70] C is a development of the earlier Loran A hyperbolic navigation system. The Loran system uses signals from three or more ground stations (master and two "slaves") and uses a time difference between

---

70   Loran is an acronym for *long range air navigation*.

their reception to determine the position of the receiver. Receivers then convert the time difference readings to latitude and longitude readings for display. This information can also be integrated into the ECDIS or Automated Bridge System. Loran C has a range of just under 1,000 miles (1609 km). The system was to be phased out in the early 2000s but it has been retained as a backup to GPS, in the aftermath of the terrorist incidents on 11 September 2001 in the United States, as GPS signals can be interfered with more easily than Loran C signals. In addition, many non-marine operations rely heavily on the very accurate time signals contained in the GPS and Loran signals.

h) Radio Direction Finding

Radio Direction Finding (RDF) is an electronic position-finding method used by vessels in close proximity to land.[71] It consists of a radio receiver and aerial system that determines the direction of incoming radio waves. When the angle between this direction and a known direction (e.g., true north) is found and, if the position of the transmitting station is known, it is possible to draw a line on the chart on which the ship is situated. By taking a bearing from a second station, a second position line is found. The point of intersection of the two lines can be assumed to be the position of the ship. While many ships are still fitted with RDF systems, it is less frequently used today as it has been superseded by some of the better systems outlined already. In addition, shore RDF stations are increasingly being closed in many parts of the world.

i) Decca[72]

Decca[73] is also an important marine radio locating system, particularly popular in smaller ships and fishing vessels as it determines the ship's position with a high degree of accuracy with a relatively simple onboard apparatus. The Decca system requires three or four fixed stations (called a "chain") that emit signals continuously and is based on a principle of phase difference in the reception of signals from the master and "slave" transmitters ashore. The difference in phase is depicted on special charts as hyperbolic lines, requiring some interpolation by the user in order to plot their position on the chart. Decca chains have been and are being closed down primarily because of the system's relatively short range (e.g., 300 nautical miles from the master station ashore).

---

71   Brown, above note 34 at 145–47.
72   *Ibid.* at 148–51.
73   The name is derived from the Decca Electronics Company, which developed the system.

3) Communication Aids

a) Communication on Board Ships

Communication throughout a small ship is easily accomplished by the human voice, but the larger the ship the more difficult it becomes to maintain the rapid and effective transmission of imperative orders from the navigating bridge to the various parts of the ship. As a result, numerous onboard communication devices — such as engine and docking telegraphs, telephones, public address systems, CB radio transmitters and receivers, and closed-circuit television — as well as various different electronic display devices that indicate the status of watertight doors, navigation lights, and fire and safety systems, among others, are installed in the wheelhouse that is the nerve centre of the vessel.

The telegraph is a means of transmitting orders from the bridge to the engine room.[74] The mechanical telegraph consists of wires and chains connected to handles and dials. Movement of the handle in the bridge to a particular engine order moves a pointer on a dial in the engine room to the same order. A reverse procedure is used to confirm the order from the engine room to the bridge. In each case, movement of the pointer causes a bell to ring. Electronic telegraphs are more commonly used today, operating in much the same manner as the mechanical ones. The operation of pointers is positive and instantaneous, and an alarm bell rings continuously from the time an order is given until that particular order is acknowledged. Such an arrangement has two advantages: for the bridge, the immediate operation of the alarm confirms that its order has been transmitted and, for the engine room, the fact that its bell operates continuously ensures that attention must be drawn to the telegraph, even if the duty engineer officer is elsewhere at the time. Today many recently built ships are equipped with automatic engine rooms and have what is known as bridge control. Bridge control means, as the name implies, a direct system of engine control from the bridge, which eliminates the inevitable delay that occurs with telegraphs, which depend on human response. Docking telegraphs are sometimes fitted on large ships, usually one at the stern and sometimes another at the bow. They are geared to a corresponding telegraph on the bridge in the same way as the engine-room telegraph. The orders that can be given by this system are limited to activities relating to the mooring of the ship. Today most ships have telephone and other electronic communications for this purpose.

---

74   Brown, above note 34 at 117–20.

b) Communications between Ships and between Ship and Shore

Communication between vessels, and between vessels and shore establishments, is also important — not only in emergencies but also in daily operations. Sound signalling — including use of the ship's siren, foghorn, and whistle — is an awkward method of communication restricted to emergencies when visual or radio communications are impractical. Visual signalling is accomplished by the use of panels, pyrotechnics, coloured lights, flashing lights, flags, and semaphore. Under *COLREGS 1972* requirements, some specified forms of visual and sound signals are mandatory at sea.[75] However, radio communications are now widely used and mandatory. Traditionally communication by radio telegraphy, carried out by a dedicated radio officer who kept radio watches, was required; however, the development of very efficient and effective radio telephony has eliminated the radio officer from many ships. A portion of the very high frequency (VHF) band of 30–300 MHz is reserved for maritime radio telephony communications. The primary use of the VHF communication facility is to increase the safety of the vessel by rapid direct contact with, for instance, other ships, rescue services, tugs, shore establishments, private persons, and shipping company offices. The number of applications and the use of VHF is so great that most vessels over 1,600 GT are fitted with it. In many areas, such as the Suez Canal and the St. Lawrence River, VHF is obligatory.[76]

Communications between ships, and between ship and shore, via satellite is also becoming more common today. Several commercial communications satellites are in global orbit specifically for this purpose, and the satellite system is regulated by an international agency.[77]

c) Communications for Vessels in Distress

While radio and satellite systems can all be utilized when a vessel is in distress or wishes to transmit information on other vessels in distress, a specific international system has been established under the *International Convention for the Safety of Life at Sea, 1974* (*SOLAS 1974*).[78] Under this convention the contracting governments have established a Global Maritime Distress and Safety System (GMDSS) specifically designed to

---

75 Above note 29, Rule 32ff. See also Chapter 11, "Maritime Collisions."
76 See *Canada Shipping Act*, above note 34; *VHF Radiotelephone Practices and Procedures Regulations*, S.O.R./81-364; *Ship Station (Radio) Regulations, 1999*, S.O.R./2000-260; and *Ship Station (Radio) Technical Regulations, 1999*, S.O.R./2000-265.
77 INMARSAT, above note 64.
78 1 November 1974, 1184 U.N.T.S. 2 (entered into force on 15 May 1980; entered into force in Canada on the same day). See also *Ratification of Maritime Conventions*, above note 7, vol.I.3.20. See also Chapter 5, "The Safety Management of Ships."

ensure that suitable arrangements are made for registering GMDSS identities and for making such information available to rescue co-ordination centres on a continuous basis.[79] It is expected that the GMDSS requirements will work closely with those under the *International Convention on Maritime Search and Rescue, 1979 (SAR 1979)*.[80]

4) Maritime Weather

Maritime weather is still one of the most important aspects of shipping. Despite the increasing size of ships a voyage can be affected, delayed and, in extreme cases, terminated by the effect of weather systems at sea. The waters of the ocean are never still: they are blown into waves by the wind, rise and fall with the tides, and flow with the currents, changing with the seasons of the year. However, wave action caused by wind on the surface of the sea is the most familiar and, at times, the most spectacular of all the motions of the oceans and the seas. The severity of the waves depends upon the velocity and duration of the wind and the distance over which it acts. Wind force is expressed numerically on a scale, generally, from zero to twelve, developed by Sir Francis Beaufort in 1808 for use on board ships of the Royal Navy. Since Beaufort's time many changes have taken place, but in 1941 the World Meteorological Organization[81] agreed to the use of such scale that judged the wind force from the appearance of the sea surface.

Beaufort Scale

0 calm
1 light air
2 light breeze
3 gentle breeze
4 moderate breeze
5 fresh breeze
6 strong breeze
7 near gale
8 gale
9 strong gale
10 storm

---

79 SOLAS 1974, ibid., c.IV, reg.5.1.
80 27 April 1979, 1405 U.N.T.S. 97 (entered into force 22 June 1985). See *Ratification of Maritime Conventions*, above note 7, vol.I.3.280. See also Chapter 5, "The Safety Management of Ships."
81 See below G, "Shipping and International Organizations."

54   MARITIME LAW

11 violent storm
12 hurricane

Weather can affect a ship and its cargo in at least five ways: by reducing the speed of the vessel, by damaging the cargo through ship movement, by damaging deck cargo by heavy seas on deck, by preventing proper ventilation of the cargo, and by damaging the vessel's structure and equipment through wave action. The effect of maritime weather on navigation has been recognized legally for a long time.[82] If weather or an unusual circumstance affects the voyage, and the master suspects that there may be a claim for loss, he can lodge a maritime protest before a lawyer or notary public at the first port of call after the occurrence. The object of a maritime protest is to record promptly, in an authorized form, the circumstances in which loss or damage occurred in order to attempt to exonerate master and crew from blame for any damage. Although such protests are neither compulsory nor essential in England[83] or Canada, they are a recommended precaution for the master.

5) Ship Manoeuvring and Handling[84]

Many legal claims occur as the result of errors and accidents that arise out of the manoeuvring and handling of vessels. It is, therefore, necessary to know something about this complex subject. The successful handling and manoeuvring of a ship is entirely dependent upon the handler's wide experience and knowledge of many factors, some of which are controllable while others are not. Regardless, their effects must be quickly assessed so that due allowance may be made for them.

a) Propulsion

Propulsion is the actual movement of the ship generated by the propeller (or screw). (See Figure 2.5.) The axial thrust of the propeller (i.e., the fore and aft thrust) is the force that causes a ship to move ahead or astern through the water. The amount of distance a ship moves depends primarily upon two factors: the pitch of the screw and slip. The pitch is the theoretical distance the screw would move the ship ahead in one revolution, assuming no slip, and assuming that the screw was revolving in a solid and not in water. Slip is the difference between the actual speed of the ship and the propeller (or engine)

---

82   See Chapter 8, "Carriage of Goods by Charterparty" and Chapter 9, "Carriage of Goods under Bills of Lading and Similar Documents."
83   *Santa Anna (The)* (1863), 32 L.J.M.P.M. & A. 198.
84   Brown, above note 34, c.8.

speed. This difference is owing to the yielding of the water to pressure exerted on it by the screw as it forces the ship ahead. The slip is increased by drag on the ship such as when the wind and sea are ahead of the vessel, when the submerged part of the vessel's hull is fouled by marine growth, and at lower speeds of movement.

Figure 2.5: Ship's Propeller Movement

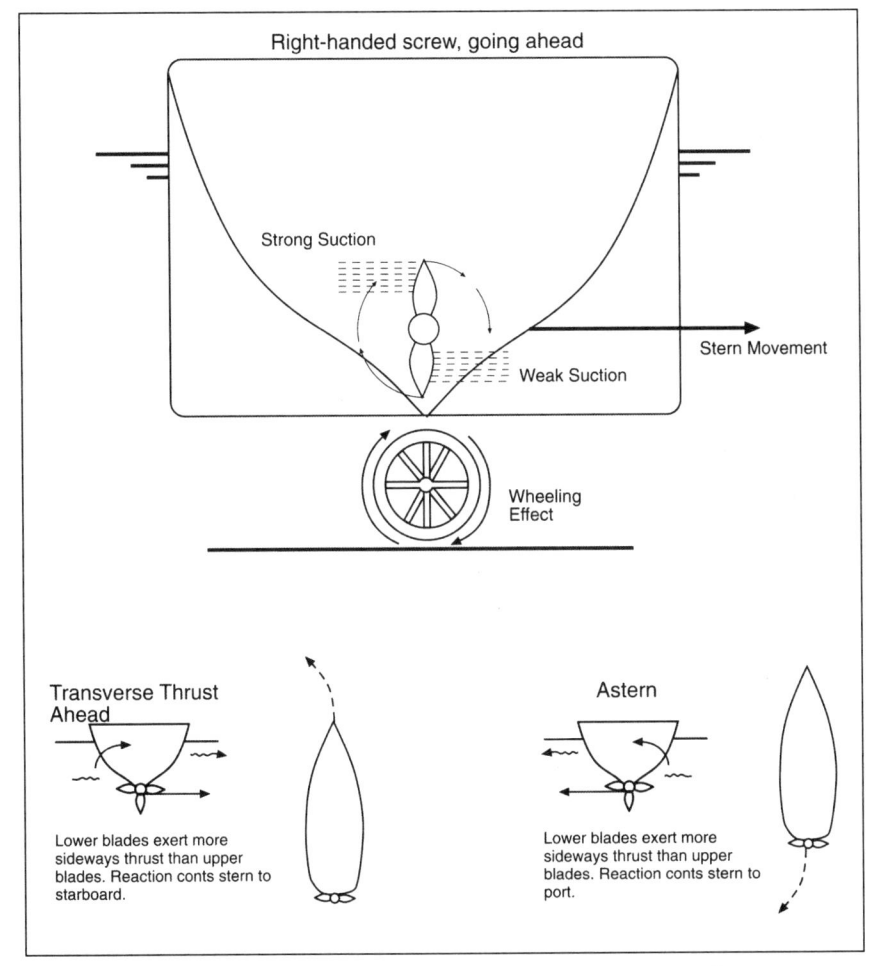

Right-handed screw, going ahead

Strong Suction

Stern Movement

Weak Suction

Wheeling Effect

Transverse Thrust Ahead

Lower blades exert more sideways thrust than upper blades. Reaction conts stern to starboard.

Astern

Lower blades exert more sideways thrust than upper blades. Reaction conts stern to port.

Ships may be fitted with between one and six propellers. By convention, engines are designed to have clockwise-turning shafts when moving ahead and viewed from astern. For this reason, right-hand propellers are nearly universal on single-screw (one propeller) ships. Twin-screw ships invariably have outward-turning screws, that is, the propeller on the right side of the ship is right-handed and that of the left side is left-handed; when going astern, both propellers naturally turn inward. A ship, however, will not move naturally in a straight line through the water because of a force coexistent with the axial (fore and aft) thrust called the transverse thrust. The transverse thrust is the sideways thrust of the propeller blades as they rotate. When going ahead on an average ship (one having a right-handed single screw), the lower blades exert more sideways thrust than do the upper blades that work near the surface. This thrust tends to pull the vessel's stern to starboard and her head to port. This effect is not very pronounced when going ahead, as the lines of a vessel are designed to feed water into the propeller when moving ahead and the upper blades are not operating in excessively broken water. However, when a right-handed propeller is moving astern, the backlash of water against the vessel's stern causes the surface water to be considerably broken. The upper blades of the propeller are therefore less effective than the lower blades, and the result is a pronounced kick of the stern to port, with the head going to starboard. This action cannot be controlled since the rudder is ineffective when going astern. Under such conditions transverse thrust may outweigh all other effects. Transverse thrust is stronger in light vessels than in loaded vessels. In a twin-screw ship, the transverse thrust of two propellers will cancel each other when going ahead. Moreover, the propellers are usually offset from the centre line, thus creating an offset effect that helps the vessel maintain a straight course.

b) Wake Current

Another factor affecting the manoeuvring and handling of a ship is the wake current. When a ship is making headway, a cavity or partial void will be created at its stern. Water will flow down the sides of the vessel and swirl in to fill this cavity. Steering will be adversely affected because the rudder will be working in what might loosely be termed a partial vacuum. Furthermore, the propeller will be working in disturbed water, speed will be lost, and vibrations will be set up. This water swirling into the cavity is called the wake current. Both cavitation and wake current increase with speed. These two factors, and their effects, will vary considerably according to the hydrodynamic lines of the vessel. For example, a beamy rectangular barge will have much larger cavitation and wake current than a sleek streamlined yacht. When a ship moves astern, the cavitation and wake current that occur at the head of the ship are minimal and do not affect the propeller or steering.

c) Screw-Race

The screw-race of the propeller will also affect steering of the vessel. As the screw worms its way through the water, it creates two spiral currents that corkscrew or curl sharply around each other after going through the propeller: these twisting currents of water are known as the screw-race. They create a transverse, or sideways, force acting on the rudder of the ship. This can be illustrated by imagining the port blades of the propeller to be coming up and the starboard blades to be going down. Water entering the propeller on the starboard side is pushed down by the downward stroke of the blades. This water crosses to port under the propeller and then curls up again; it then hits the rudder on the top half of the port side and pushes the rudder to starboard. Meanwhile, water entering the propeller on the port side is pushed up by the upward stroke of the blades. This water crosses to starboard over the propeller and the spiral effect of the propeller causes it to curl down; it then hits the rudder on the lower half of the starboard side and pushes the rudder to port. As a result, there are two transverse forces acting simultaneously on opposite sides of the rudder. However, these forces are not equal: the deeper current hitting the rudder on the lower half of the starboard side predominates (pushing the rudder to port) and causes the ship's bow to go to port and its stern to starboard. These effects are not present on twin-screw ships.

d) Turning Circle

The turning circle of a ship is also an important aspect for the ship handler to know.[85] The turning circle is roughly a circular path through which the ship moves when her course is altered through 360°. Throughout the turn, the ship's bow will be slightly inside the circle and the stem a little outside it. The pivot point of the ship is the point about which the vessel turns. This point is, for practical purposes, just forward of the bridge when it is located amidships. The turning circle is not a perfect circle as it does not link up with the original course owing to some side-slip when the circle is first begun. During the turn, the vessel suffers some deceleration; after turning 90° the vessel has lost about 25 per cent of the original speed, after a further 90° about one-third of the original speed has been lost, and thereafter the speed will remain roughly constant.

e) Stopping Distance

The stopping distance of a ship is of critical importance for mariners.[86] Both the turning circle and the stopping distance of a ship are tested when the ship is new and fully loaded. The normal stopping distance

---

85 Cockcroft & Lameijer, above note 67 at 228.
86 Ibid. at 68–72.

58 MARITIME LAW

of a ship is the distance travelled from the time a vessel moving at full speed has its engines stopped until the time the ship comes to a full stop. The "crash-stopping distance" is an emergency measure for the distance travelled by a ship from the time the vessel, moving at full speed, stopping and then reversing engines, until the time the ship reaches a full stop. (See Figure 2.6.) The ideal crash-stopping distance is considered to be the equivalent of between six and eight ship lengths. Large ships of more than 150 metres in length, which are often low powered, may have a crash stopping distances significantly in excess of this.[87] It should be noted, however, that this also depends upon the type of propulsion power, the number of engines and propellers, and the hydrodynamic shape of the hull. For example, many modern high-powered passenger and container vessels will have much shorter crash-stopping distances than more traditional cargo and tank vessels.

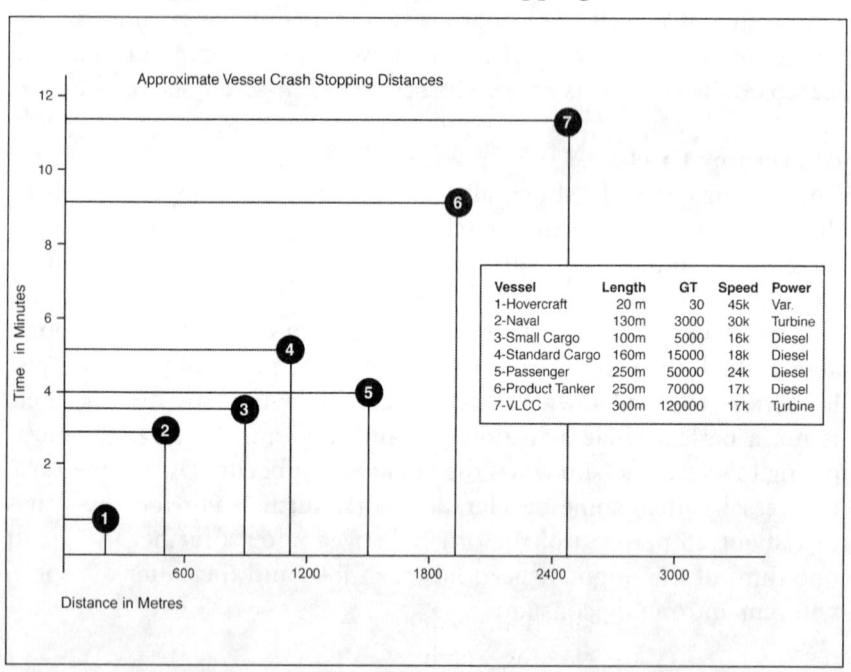

Figure 2.6: Approximate Vessel Crash-Stopping Distances

Vessel	Length	GT	Speed	Power
1-Hovercraft	20 m	30	45k	Var.
2-Naval	130m	3000	30k	Turbine
3-Small Cargo	100m	5000	16k	Diesel
4-Standard Cargo	160m	15000	18k	Diesel
5-Passenger	250m	50000	24k	Diesel
6-Product Tanker	250m	70000	17k	Diesel
7-VLCC	300m	120000	17k	Turbine

[Note that this illustration is merely a general one and not based on actual information.]

---

87 *Ibid.* at 227.

f) Interaction

Interaction is a ship movement effect that has become increasingly important in ship handling.[88] The differences in water pressure around a moving ship produce forces of attraction and repulsion between two ships moving close together in the same direction. This can cause collision.[89] These forces are usually referred to as interaction. The extent of the zone of interaction and the strength of the effect can vary according to the size and shape of the ships, their speeds, and the depth of the water. Small ships will generally experience interaction when within approximately 50 feet (15 m) of one another, and large ships when within 100 feet (30 m) of one another. While the effect of interaction does not increase greatly with higher speeds, less time is available to correct mistakes and to change the rudder angle to compensate for the effect. The strength of the interaction effect is greatly increased in shallow water.

g) Bank Effect

Bank effect or bank suction is an effect related to interaction that is caused by the action of forces produced by water pressure when a ship is moving close to a bank of a river or channel. The effect causes the stern of the ship to be attracted toward the bank and, conversely, for the bow to swing away from the bank. In an important Canadian case, serious damage — including the total loss of one vessel — was caused by the overcorrection of a ship's pilot to the effects of bank suction, resulting in a collision on the St. Lawrence River.[90]

6) Ship at Sea

a) Watches and Logbooks

The day at sea is a 24-hour day, using the 24-hour clock system, usually divided into six 4-hour periods called "watches":

00:00 to 04:00 = the middle watch
04:00 to 08:00 = the morning watch
08:00 to 12:00 = the forenoon watch
12:00 to 16:00 = the afternoon watch
16:00 to 20:00 = the evening watch
20:00 to 24:00 = the first watch

---

88   *Ibid.* at 105–07.
89   *Queen Mary (The)* (1949), 82 Ll. L.R. 303 (H.L.); see also Chapter 11, "Maritime Collisions."
90   *Nord-Deutsche Versicherungs Gesellschaft v. R.*, [1969] 1 Ex. C.R. 117, var'd [1971] S.C.R. 849; see also Chapter 11, "Maritime Collisions."

In the past, the evening watch was broken at 18:00 hours into two 2-hour periods called the first and second "dog" watches. This enabled two sets of officers of the watch, or watchkeepers, to alternate their routine day by day. However, most ships today have three sets of officers, and the dog watch practice is confined to smaller vessels with two watchkeeping officers. The officers of the watch on most ships are the chief/first officer on the morning and evening watch; second officer on the middle and afternoon watch; and third officer on the forenoon and first watch. This may, of course, vary on large passenger vessels. The duties of the officer of the watch are primarily to maintain an efficient lookout, verify the vessel's position whenever possible and necessary, ensure that the ship maintains a proper course, and record various data in the deck logbook. The deck logbook contains data such as engine movements and revolutions, weather conditions, courses steered, details of action in fog or bad visibility, the use of lights, emergency drills and measures, ballasting arrangements, and any other information related to safety. This information is virtually a diary of the ship's activities. Each page of the logbook is signed by the chief officer and countersigned by the master. A similar logbook is also kept in the engine room, covering all engine room and related activities, and is signed by the chief engineer and countersigned by the master. In many shipping companies the deck and engine logbooks are kept in rough form and then transferred into a "smooth" logbook on a daily basis. The master keeps the official logbook and all entries are signed by him and witnessed by a crew member, usually the chief officer. Under the *Canada Shipping Act*, the official logbook is a legally required document on most Canadian registered ships.[91]

The logbook contains entries related to births, deaths, and marriages on board, offences by passengers or crew, cases of sickness or injury, a list of crew members with a report on their conduct and character, details of collisions, and other matters,[92] including information from the radio logbook[93] kept by the radio officer (if one is carried). While the official logbook is the principal legal record of a vessel's

---

91 *Canada Shipping Act*, above note 34, s.261; *Canada Shipping Act, 2001*, has no equivalent provisions but it is assumed that they will be in the regulations when available. *Canada Shipping Act, 2001*, makes reference to log books in general terms only. *Canada Shipping Act*, ibid., s.266(3) prohibits false entries in a log book.
92 *Canada Shipping Act*, above note 34, s.262. There is nothing equivalent in the *Canada Shipping Act, 2001*.
93 Regulations can be made under *Canada Shipping Act*, above note 34, s.343(h). See *Ship Station (Radio) Technical Regulations, 1999*, above note 76, s.41.

activities, the deck and engine logbooks will be of prime legal interest in collision cases and other maritime accidents.

b) Master

The person in charge of a vessel, regardless whether small coaster, large tanker or huge passenger vessel, is the master. The master is entitled to be called "Captain" as a form of address, although captain is also a specific military rank. The master's duties and responsibilities are varied and expansive. The master is the shipowner's personal representative and bears the ultimate responsibility for the safe navigation of the vessel and for the efficient loading, stowage, and discharge of cargo. While the master has always had the authority to transact the ship's business in ports abroad, advances in modern communications have enabled the owner to assume more direct supervision of the ship's business abroad. On the other hand, the master, as the ship's legal representative, has assumed increasing administrative responsibilities in terms of dealing with a variety of port officials, surveyors, inspectors, customs, and immigration authorities. In some states such responsibilities are considered personal, to the extent that breaches of national laws may involve prosecution of the master often with resulting fines, detention, and even imprisonment.

c) Officers and Crew

The crew of a vessel can be conveniently divided into four departments: engine room, catering (hotel services on passenger vessels), deck, and radio (generally only on larger passenger ships). An officer, who is responsible to the master, oversees each section or department.

The deck department is the responsibility of the first mate or chief officer, who acts as the executive officer and deputy to the master. Depending on the size of the ship, the chief officer is assisted by two or more navigating officers or mates. In addition to watchkeeping, the chief officer normally supervises the handling of cargo and is responsible for the upkeep of the ship and its equipment, excluding the engine room and auxiliary power equipment. The mates also have specified tasks in addition to their watchkeeping duties, such as chart correction, cargo stowage, lifesaving and fire equipment, and docking. The deck department also includes petty officers, together with a number of deck hands including able-bodied seamen, ordinary seamen, and a middle grade known as efficient deckhands. The principal petty officer is the bosun or boatswain, who acts as the supervisor of the deckhands on a day-to-day basis. At sea the able-bodied seamen are also watchkeepers on watches similar to the navigating officers, taking their turn at steering and lookout duties. The remaining deckhands are day workers employed at sea in general duties. Many modern vessels today have multi-purpose crews, that is, seafarers who are trained and capable to work in several different positions on board the vessel.

Where applicable the radio department is staffed by radio officers. Their duties include radio watchkeeping and maintenance of the radio transmitters and receivers. The radio officer may also be responsible for the maintenance of other electronic apparatus, such as echo-sounders and radar. Today, radio officers are generally only carried on larger passenger vessels.

The engine room is supervised by the chief engineer, who is responsible to the master both for the main propulsion machinery and for auxiliaries comprising electrical plant, cargo winches, refrigeration machinery, steering gear, and air conditioning and ventilating systems. The chief engineer is also responsible for fuel, machinery maintenance, and repairs and is assisted in this task by a number of engineer and electrical officers, according to the size of the vessel. Engine room assistants, fitters, and greasers also work in the engine room. In cases of engine rooms that still require watchkeeping, engine room assistants will be on watch with the relevant engineer officers. However, most modern ships have fully or semi-automated engine rooms with computerized and/or electronically controlled operations. In such vessels, the engine department staff is principally involved in maintenance and upkeep.

On board cargo vessels the catering department is supervised by the chief steward, or catering officer, who is responsible for catering and the galley, for galley stores, and for the ship's laundry. Depending on the size of the vessel the catering department will include cooks, bakers, and assistant stewards. On passenger vessels the relevant hotel department may be a very large and important entity and may have a staff of more than a thousand persons, consisting of chefs, cooks, bakers, stewards, bar service personnel, fitness and recreation personnel, entertainers, cruise directors, cabin attendants, cleaners, laundry personnel, shop assistants, and security personnel. This service would be under the supervision of a chief purser, assisted by a large group of assistant pursers.

E. ANCILLARY SHIPPING SERVICES

During port visits the principal purpose of ships is to load and discharge cargo and passengers, carry out necessary maintenance and repairs, take on fuel and stores, and discharge and sign on crew members. The ship will also be involved in a number of administrative inspections, surveys, and visits involving classification society surveyors, steamship inspectors, receivers of wreck, salvage association surveyors, harbour masters, shipping masters, or port wardens.

1) Classification Society Surveyor

Classification societies employ surveyors in ports around the world to inspect ships to see if they are maintaining their classification.[94] The object of classification societies is to grade ships into classes, and thereby provide an authentic record of the details of the building of the ship in relation to its reliability while operating on the high seas. The main requirement of a society is to provide reliable data for underwriters insuring the hull and of the ship as a whole, as well as the cargo it carries. In addition, there is the essential requirement of the shipowner to know the quality and grade of the vessel. Thus the insurer and the shipowner are the two direct beneficiaries of the classification society. There are generally two types of classification society surveys: annual and four-yearly. The annual survey is usually conducted in dry dock, and the hull and equipment are inspected. Every four years there is a more extensive and involved survey, which can take over a month. Governments also often request classification societies to carry out statutory surveys on tonnage measurement, freeboard assignment, and safety surveys for them. The three characteristics essential to any classification society are impartiality, technical competence, and the desire to aid the shipping industry as a whole.

The first classification society was Lloyd's Register of Shipping in England; since, similar societies have developed in many other states. Lloyd's is still one of the most widely known societies with about 50 per cent of the world's ships. Some other national classification societies, which are equally efficient and also widely recognized:

- American Bureau of Shipping (ABS) — United States
- Det Norske Veritas (DNV) — Norway
- Bureau Veritas (BV) — France
- Germanischer Lloyd (GL) — Germany
- Nippon Kaiji Kyokai (NKK) — Japan
- Registro Italiano Navale (RINA) — Italy

---

94   See P. Boisson, *Safety at Sea* (Paris: Bureau Veritas, 1999) c.6; see also Chapter 5, "The Safety Management of Ships."

While classification societies may have developed to meet the requirements of marine insurance, the most important task of the societies today is to modernize their technical rules and to rationalize the survey work to meet the technical progress in shipbuilding and marine engineering. Another important function of the classification societies today is to standardize the enforcement of the provisions of the various international conventions regulating merchant shipping.[95] Compliance with these conventions quite naturally requires a high degree of uniformity in the standards of the classification societies. Coupled with the fact that, as a matter of national pride, many developing states have created their own classification societies, this highlights the need for increased co-operation among the societies to ensure uniform standards. The proliferation of classification societies has resulted in the establishment of the International Association of Classification Societies, which is attempting to ensure that the highest international standards are maintained.[96]

2) Steamship Inspector

The Steamship Inspection Service is a branch of the Department of Transport.[97] Its function is basically to administer the provisions of the *Canada Shipping Act* from offices throughout the country.[98] As a result the inspectors have very wide powers delegated directly by the minister under the current *Canada Shipping Act*. The primary duties of the service and its inspectors are as follows:

- enforcement of the *Canada Shipping Act* regulations for Canadian and foreign vessels;[99]

---

[95] Such as *SOLAS 1974*, above note 78, and *LL 1966*, above note 39. For an easily accessible, complete listing of international maritime conventions, see *Ratification of Maritime Conventions*, above note 7. See also N. Singh, *International Maritime Conventions*, 3d ed. (London: Stevens, 1983).

[96] See below G, "Shipping and International Organizations." Although numerous attempts have been made in recent years to hold classification societies liable for damages, they have generally not succeeded in court cases. See Boisson, *Safety at Sea*, above note 94 at 395–96; see also Chapter 5, "The Safety Management of Ships."

[97] See web site: <http://www.tc.gc.ca/MarineSafety/welcome.htm>.

[98] *Canada Shipping Act*, above note 34, ss.301–17; *Canada Shipping Act, 2001*, above note 34, s.11 authorizes the appointment of marine safety inspectors (ss.16(2) and 211).

[99] *Canada Shipping Act*, ibid., s.310(2); *Canada Shipping Act, 2001*, ibid., s.227.

- enforcement of *SOLAS 1974* provisions on every ship entering Canadian waters;[100]
- monitoring the condition of life-saving and fire-fighting equipment on Canadian vessels and, when appropriate, on foreign vessels;[101]
- examination and certification of masters, mates, and engineers, including *STCW* requirements;[102]
- supervision of crew engagements;[103]
- supervision of the construction of Canadian ships, including measuring vessels prior to registration in Canada;[104]
- annual and other required periodic surveys for the certification of Canadian ships;[105]
- investigations of marine accidents;[106]
- enforcement of oil pollution regulations;[107] and
- carrying out port state inspections under *Paris and Tokyo Memorandum* obligations.[108]

---

100 *Canada Shipping Act*, ibid., ss.314, 316, 328, and 331; *Canada Shipping Act, 2001*, ibid., s.227 covers both Canadian and foreign ships.
101 *Canada Shipping Act, 2001*, ibid., ss.109 and 227; *Fire Detection and Extinguishing Equipment Regulations*, C.R.C., c.1422; *Life Saving Equipment Regulations*, C.R.C., c.1436.
102 *Canada Shipping Act*, above note 34, Part II, ss.109–140 (Certificates of Officers); *Canada Shipping Act, 2001*, ibid., s.87; see also *Crewing Regulations*, above note 59, s.3. See *International Convention on Standards of Training, Certification and Watchkeeping for Seafarers*, 7 July 1978, 1361 U.N.T.S. 2 [*STCW 1978*] (entered into force 28 April 1984 and acceded to by Canada on 6 February 1988). See also *Ratification of Maritime Conventions*, above note 7, vol.I.3.90.
103 *Canada Shipping Act, 2001*, ibid., s.85.
104 *Hull Inspection Regulations*, C.R.C., c.1432; *Hull Construction Regulations*, C.R.C., c.1431.
105 *Canada Shipping Act*, above note 34 ss.323(2) and 316; *Canada Shipping Act, 2001*, above note 34, s.71.
106 *Canada Shipping Act*, ibid., s.477(1); *Canada Shipping Act, 2001*, ibid., s.149; see also *Canadian Transportation Accident Investigation and Safety Board Act*, S.C. 1989, c.3.
107 *Canada Shipping Act*, ibid., s.21; *Oil Pollution Prevention Regulations*, S.O.R./93-3; *Canada Shipping Act, 2001*, ibid., s.183.
108 *Memorandum of Understanding on Port State Control in Implementing Agreements on Maritime Safety and Protection of the Marine Environment*, 26 January 1982, 21 I.L.M. 1 [*Paris MOU 1982*] (entered into force 1 July 1982 and accepted by Canada on 3 May 1994); *Memorandum of Understanding on Port State Control in the Asia-Pacific Region, 1993*, 1 December 1993, online: <www.tokyo-mou.org> . [*Tokyo MOU 1993*] (entered into force 1 April 1994 and accepted by Canada on 15 April 1994); see also *Ratification of Maritime Conventions*, above note 7, vol.I.3.100 and 105; see also Chapter 17, "Marine Pollution Prevention." See the Transport Canada web site at: <http://www.tc.gc.ca/MarineSafety/Ships-and-operations-standards/Inspection/Port-State-Control/menu.htm>.

Under the *Canada Shipping Act, 2001*,[109] when in force, marine safety inspectors will be appointed or deployed under the *Public Service Employment Act*.[110] Under the same Act marine safety inspectors may be authorized to exercise specific functions under the Act, including *quasi*-judicial powers and the administration of examinations,[111] and to carry out inspections[112] including the following:

- inspections of hulls;
- inspections of machinery;,
- inspections of equipment;
- inspections concerning the protection of the marine environment for the purpose of Part 9 (Pollution Prevention, Department of Transport); and
- inspections of cargo.

3) Receiver of Wreck

The receiver of wreck is a senior Canadian government officer (usually from the Department of Transport) or other government-appointed person, whose powers and duties are set out in the *Canada Shipping Act*.[113] The receiver is empowered to take control of any wrecked, stranded, or distressed vessel within Canadian waters or on or near the coast but may not take charge if the master, shipowner, or cargo-owner objects.[114] The owner of the wreck may claim the wreck within one year on payment of the salvage, fees, and expenses due on the vessel. If the owner does not claim the wreck, or if the wreck consists of dangerous goods, the wreck may be sold.[115] The receiver also has the power to hear salvage claims if the amount claimed is less than $100 or where the salvage subject's value is less than $250, or if the parties agree. The receiver may seize the property within his or her district that is alleged to be liable for salvage.[116]

---

109 *Canada Shipping Act, 2001*, above note 34, s.11(1); see also Chapter 5, "The Safety Management of Ships."
110 R.S.C. 1985, c.P-33.
111 *Canada Shipping Act, 2001*, above note 34, s.16(2).
112 *Canada Shipping Act, 2001*, ibid., s.211.
113 *Canada Shipping Act*, above note 34, Part 6, ss.423 and 426; *Canada Shipping Act, 2001*, ibid., Part 7, ss.154 and 163.
114 *Canada Shipping Act*, ibid., s.427; *Canada Shipping Act, 2001*, is silent on this issue but it will probably be covered in new regulations under s.163.
115 *Canada Shipping Act*, ibid., ss.441, 443, 445, and 427; *Canada Shipping Act, 2001*, above note 34, s.160.
116 *Canada Shipping Act*, ibid., s.454; *Canada Shipping Act, 2001*, ibid., s.156.

4) Salvage Association Surveyor

Founded in 1856, the Association for the Protection of Commercial Interests as Respects Wrecked and Damaged Property, was first incorporated in England in 1867 as a non-profit organization whose basic purpose is to take the part of the insurance underwriter in every marine casualty. The association, known conveniently as the Salvage Association, covers about 85 per cent of the world's shipping fleet and has representatives in all principal ports. It does not operate salvage vessels of its own but acts in the interests of all parties concerned in cases of marine casualty when so instructed by the interested shipowner. The association negotiates salvage contracts or settlements, undertakes the survey of damaged ships and other property, and supervises their repair or disposal.[117]

5) Harbour Master

The harbour master is employed by the Canada Port Authority[118] or by local port authorities.[119] Basically, the harbour master enforces the rules and regulations of the particular harbour, for example, assigns berths, controls ship movement in port, removes wrecked ships in port, and enforces oil pollution regulations.[120]

6) Shipping Master

The shipping master operates under the Steamship Inspection Service. The shipping master's powers and duties are set out in the *Canada Shipping Act*.[121] The shipping master is basically concerned with seafarers. The primary duties are that

> Every shipping master shall:
> - Afford facilities for engaging seamen, by keeping registers of the names of seamen who apply to him for engagement, and registers

---

117 Farthing, *International Shipping*, above note 45 at 42–43. See also E. Gold, ed., *Maritime Affairs: A World Handbook*, 2d ed. (London: Longman, 1991) at 55.
118 The successor to the National Harbours Board.
119 Under the *Canada Marine Act*, S.C. 1998, c.10, s.69.
120 See, in general, *Columbia Transportation Co. v. F.P. Weaver Coal Co.*, [1950] Ex. C.R. 167; *Donnacona Paper Co. v. Desgagne*, [1959] Ex. C.R. 215; *Fraser River Harbour Commission v. Hiro Maru (The)*, [1974] 1 F.C. 490 (T.D.); and *Sociedad Transoceanica Canopus S.A. v. Canada (Nat. Harbours Board)*, [1968] 2 Ex. C.R. 330.
121 *Canada Shipping Act*, above note 34, s.142. The shipping master is not mentioned in the *Canada Shipping Act, 2001*.

of all seamen shipped or discharged by him, which registers shall be open for public inspection.
- Superintend and facilitate the engagement and discharge of seamen in the manner hereinafter provided.
- Provide means for securing the presence on board and the proper types of men who are engaged, when requested to do so, the expense of that service to be defrayed by the master, owner or agent of the ship requiring the presence of men on board.
- Facilitate the making of apprenticeships to the sea service.
- Perform such other duties relating to seamen, apprentices and merchant ships as are committed to him by this Act.[122]

Some of the shipping master's other duties are as follows:
- custody of the effects of deceased seamen in some cases,[123]
- keeping a register of deserters,[124] and
- taking charge of distressed (i.e., left behind) seamen who must be returned to their port of origin.[125]

7) Port Warden

The port warden also operates under the Steamship Inspection Service and is appointed for designated harbours or port districts. The duties and powers are set out in the current *Canada Shipping Act*.[126] The port warden is concerned with the condition and stowage of cargo, and the duties include the following:

- enforcing the international load line regulations;[127]
- determining whether a ship can carry specified cargoes, such as grain, or concentrated ores;[128]
- examining property damaged on board a ship;[129] and
- acting as an impartial arbitrator in disputes between the master of a vessel and the owner, shipper, or consignee of the cargo.[130]

---

122 *Ibid.*, s.151.
123 *Ibid.*, s.216.
124 *Ibid.*, s.252.
125 Unless taken care of by someone else: *ibid.*, s.292.
126 *Canada Shipping Act*, *ibid.*, Part VIII. As already indicated, the *Canada Shipping Act, 2001*, does not mention port wardens and it remains to be seen if regulations establishing this position under the new Act will be drafted.
127 *General Load Line Regulations*, above note 41.
128 *Canada Shipping Act*, above note 34, ss.538(2) and 540.
129 *Canada Shipping Act*, *ibid.*, s.533.
130 *Canada Shipping Act*, *ibid.*, s.549.

F. OFFSHORE ENERGY SECTOR: MARITIME ASPECTS[131]

1) Introduction

A significant amount of the world's oil and natural gas supplies is now produced in offshore areas in many parts of the world. Canada is quickly becoming an important offshore energy producer with proven resources off the east, west and Arctic coasts. While exploration for oil and natural gas began off the Canadian east coast almost half a century ago, technological advances, market conditions, and the general economy have finally reached a point that encourages the oil industry to develop these resources.[132] Furthermore, it is also likely that west coast and Arctic region resources will be developed in the foreseeable future.

While this book is principally addressing traditional shipping law, the close relationship between shipping and offshore oil and gas exploration and exploitation in a number of areas warrants a cursory examination of this increasingly important subject. It should be noted that the legal regime for offshore energy differs significantly from that established for shipping, although there are also close relationships between the two sectors in some areas.[133] Nevertheless, a number of specific Canadian acts and regulations must be consulted whenever questions related to this sector arise.[134]

---

131 There are several useful web sites on Canadian oil and gas development in the offshore: Canadian Association of Petroleum Producers <www.capp.ca>; Canada–Newfoundland Offshore Petroleum Board <www.cnopb.nfnet.com>; Canada–Nova Scotia Offshore Petroleum Board <www.cnsopb.ns.ca>; Deep Panuke Project <www.encana.com/operations_and_projects>; Hibernia <www.Hibernia.ca>; Sable Project <www.soep.com>; Terra Nova Project <www.terranovaproject.com>; and Petroleum Communications Foundation <www.Pcf.ab.ca>.

132 See, e.g., Canada–Nova Scotia Offshore Petroleum Board, *Annual Report 2000–2001* (Halifax: CNSOPB, 2001); see also Chapter 5, "The Safety Management of Ships."

133 The *Marine Liability Act*, S.C. 2001, c.6, s.38 exempts offshore energy activities from some aspects of liability and compensation in oil pollution cases; see also Chapter 17, "Marine Pollution Prevention" and Chapter 18, "Limitation of Liability for Maritime Claims." The *Canada Shipping Act, 2001*, above note 34, ss.166, 186(2), and 120(2) also set out specific requirements related to offshore energy operations; *Canada Shipping Act*, above note 34, s.655(2).

134 *Canada–Nova Scotia Offshore Petroleum Resources Accord Implementation Act*, S.C. 1988, c.28; *Canada–Newfoundland Atlantic Accord Implementation Act*, R.S.N. 1990, c.C-2; *Newfoundland Offshore Area Oil and Gas Operations Regulations*, S.O.R./88-347; *Newfoundland Offshore Petroleum Installations Regulations*, S.O.R./95-104; *Nova Scotia Offshore Petroleum Drilling Regulations*, S.O.R./92-676

The exploration for and production of oil and natural gas in offshore regions, especially in the North Atlantic, is far more challenging than producing such resources on land.[135] Offshore facilities must be designed for extreme weather conditions, deep water, and ice. At the same time, depending on their size, such facilities — or oil rigs — must be able to accommodate 25–200 workers for up to three weeks at a time in reasonable comfort. In addition to crew accommodation, such facilities would also have the following equipment on board: control and communications, anchoring or positioning, cranes, power generators, fire safety and life saving, helicopter support, storage, and waste management.

2) Offshore Drilling Operations

After receiving governmental approval, oil and gas companies normally drill three types of wells: exploration, delineation, and development. Depending on well depth and drilling conditions, such wells may take as long as three to six months to complete. The required investment is significant.

a) Exploration Wells
Exploration wells are drilled to confirm if geological formations identified from seismic surveys contain hydrocarbons.

b) Delineation Wells
If the results from exploration drilling are promising, delineation wells may be drilled into different areas of the geological formation in order to confirm the formation's dimensions as well as the characteristics of the hydrocarbon resources. This information assists in deciding if the area is economically attractive to develop further.

c) Development Wells
If the information from exploration and delineation drilling is favourable, the company will proceed to the third stage, drilling a development well. This is expected to lead to production. An outline of the

---

as am.; *Nova Scotia Offshore Petroleum Installations Regulations*, S.O.R./95-191; *Newfoundland Offshore Petroleum Drilling Regulations*, S.O.R./93-23; *Canada Oil and Gas Operations Act*, R.S.C. 1985, c. O-7; *Canada Oil and Gas Drilling Regulations*, S.O.R./79-82; *Canada Oil and Gas Production and Conservation Regulations*, S.O.R./90-791.

135 T. Robinson, *The Offshore* (St. John's: Jesperson Press, 1992); see also Canadian Association of Petroleum Producers, *Producing Oil and Gas Offshore* (Calgary: CAPP, 2001) pub.# 2001-0023.

four main types of facilities used for offshore energy exploration and production follows.

3) Offshore Drilling Systems

Offshore drilling systems are highly complex and extremely expensive. They have been developed from crude land-based systems first used over a century ago. However, the modern systems are constantly being modified and upgraded. During the drilling stage, three different types of rigs may be utilized.[136]

a) Jack-up Rigs

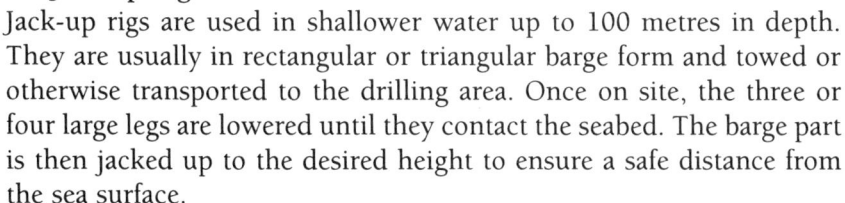

Jack-up rigs are used in shallower water up to 100 metres in depth. They are usually in rectangular or triangular barge form and towed or otherwise transported to the drilling area. Once on site, the three or four large legs are lowered until they contact the seabed. The barge part is then jacked up to the desired height to ensure a safe distance from the sea surface.

b) Semi-submersible Rigs

These are very large structures that are used in water depth of between 70 and 1000 metres using anchoring systems, or more than 1000 metres if using a dynamic positioning system. They are either towed or able to move under their own power. The working platform is supported by a series of vertical columns that sit on two or more steel pontoons that float below the sea surface during drilling operations. The platform can be raised or lowered by adjusting the amount of ballast water in the pontoons. Two methods are used to hold this type of rig in place. In water depths up to 1800 metres support vessels lay out a series of large anchors on heavy steel cables. Such anchors and cables may extend up to 1 kilometre from the rig. Special winches maintain tension on the cables. More common in deeper water is the use of dynamic positioning systems instead of anchors.

c) Drill Ships

These are the most mobile drilling units and operate in water depths of 200–1000 metres, using an anchoring system, and over 1000 metres using a dynamic positioning system. They are basically large ships fitted with a complete drilling system. They are especially useful for oper-

---

136 Robinson, *ibid.*, c.; see also Canadian Association of Petroleum Producers, *Offshore Drilling Rigs* (Calgary: CAPP, 2001) pub.# 2001-008.

ating in remote areas as they require only limited support. Drilling takes place through a large opening in the bottom of the hull, known as the "moon pool."

4) Other Offshore Facilities and Support Systems

During the drilling[137] and production phases, the offshore energy industry utilizes a significant support system consisting of rig supply and stand-by vessels, crew shuttle vessels, emergency evacuation and support craft, waste disposal craft; towage vessels, anchor and cable handling vessels, helicopter support craft, and floating storage units. Many of these are legally required under the relevant offshore legislation or licensing arrangements with the coastal state. Once an offshore well has been developed the production phase will begin.[138] While the systems for producing oil and natural gas vary widely, most support the basic functions of

- drilling and maintaining the wells used to produce oil and gas and, where required, injecting water, chemicals and, possibly, gas, back into the formation;
- processing and separating the produced mixture of oil and gas, and removing possible sand and water residues from the hydrocarbons;
- storing produced hydrocarbon liquids for later transport to markets or to a transhipment terminal;
- gathering, storing, and transporting drilling muds and other debris and effluents from the drill site; and
- gathering and processing gas and natural gas liquids and sending them through sub-sea pipelines to shore; if no processing takes place offshore, the raw gas and liquids are sent to shore through a pipeline for processing at a shore-based facility.

These functions may be combined in a single structure or carried out at separate facilities and/or separate locations. Crude oil may be stored in tanks within the production facility, or it may be transported through a pipeline to a nearby storage tanker.

While there are many different offshore production facilities, they are all made up of two separate structures:

- the "platform" that supports the upper or "topsides" facilities. The platform may float or sit on the seabed with storage silos for crude oil; and

---

137 Canadian Association of Petroleum Producers, *Drilling an Offshore Well in Atlantic Canada* (Calgary: CAPP, 2001) pub.# 2001-0022.
138 *Producing Oil and Gas Offshore*, above note 135.

- the topsides, where all the operating and support functions of the producing operations are accommodated.

In general offshore energy production, three different types of production facilities may be utilized.[139]

a) Anchored Structure with Legs
Often called a "jacket," an anchored structure with legs is usually floated by barge to the desired location. The steel or concrete legs are then lowered to the seabed in an upright position and anchored into the bottom with steel piles driven into the seafloor.

b) Gravity-Based Structure
A system using a gravity-based structure usually consists of a very large structure built of reinforced concrete, floated into position and then filled with ballast; it sits on a prepared foundation on the seafloor. Tanks in the base of the structure are used to store oil before it is shipped ashore.

c) Floating Production Storage and Offloading System
The Floating Production Storage and Offloading System (FPSO) uses a double-hulled ship-shaped vessel that contains the production, oil storage, and transhipment facilities. This vessel structure is connected to the producing wells through an internal turret that is anchored in position. The vessel structure then rotates around the turret in response to local winds, currents, and wave conditions. The turret is designed so that it can be safely disconnected from the FPSO vessel.

5) Legal Status of Offshore Facilities

Even this brief overview of offshore energy operations should illustrate their importance, complexity, and vulnerabilities. Unfortunately their status in terms of maritime law is less clear.[140] The various offshore structures move or are moved and operate in national and international navigable areas where they may be involved in marine and marine-related accidents similar to those involving normal vessels, for instance, collisions, grounding, pollution, loss of life, or personal injury. Their legal position, however, is far from clear. The first question that arises in this context is whether these facilities are "ships." As

---

139 Ibid.
140 M. Summerskill, Oil Rigs: Law and Insurance (London: Stevens, 1979).

already indicated, many of these structures float, are able to move under their own power, and, in many cases, look like ships; however, they are designed for operations that are very different from that of normal ships. Obviously, some of these structures, which are firmly fixed to the seafloor, could be classified as artificial islands rather than ships; however, many are not firmly fixed and can be moved from place to place. Legal definitions are only of limited assistance and court decisions are also of relatively little help.[141]

The *Canada Shipping Act* defines "ship" to "include every description of a vessel used in navigation and not propelled by oars."[142] However, the Federal Court of Appeal has held that a floating crane used in a port, without self-propulsion and not capable of navigation, was a "ship." The court stated that, although the crane was not capable of navigation, it was "built to do something on water requiring movement from place to place. Therefore ... the *Glenbuckie* was a ship."[143] This appears to be a very wide interpretation and would indicate that all floating offshore structures — such as jack-up rigs, semi-submersibles, drill ships, or FPSOs — would be considered to be "ships" under Canadian law. However, does this also mean that such structures are only "ships" when they are actually floating or moving but not when they are anchored or onsite engaged in offshore operations? There has been at least one Canadian court decision supporting such an illogical proposition, but that case has been neither followed nor supported.[144] In other words, until the situation is clarified either by international or national legislation or by definitive case law, it has to be assumed that offshore structures that are not permanently fixed to the seabed are "ships."[145] This also means that such structures are subject to the various provisions of maritime law discussed in this book.

---

141 W.W. Spicer, "Applications of Maritime Law to Offshore Drilling Units — The Canadian Experience" in I. Townsend-Gault, ed., *Offshore Petroleum Installations: Law and Financing. Canada and the United States* (London: International Bar Association, 1986); see also Chapter 5, "The Safety Management of Ships."
142 *Canada Shipping Act*, above note 34, s.2 defines both vessel and ship; *Canada Shipping Act, 2001*, above note 34, s.2 defines only a vessel.
143 *R. v. Saint John Shipbuilding & Drydock Co.* (1981), 126 D.L.R. (3d) 353 (F.C.A.).
144 *Dome Petroleum v. Hunt International Petroleum Co.*, [1978] 1 F.C. 11. This case is distinguished from *Shibamoto & Co. v. Western Fish Producers* (1989), 63 D.L.R. (4th) 549 (F.C.A.) and explained in the trial division hearing of the same case at (1989), 29 F.T.R. 311. It was also mentioned in *Bow Valley Husky (Bermuda) Ltd. v. Saint John Shipbuilding Ltd.* (1995), 126 D.L.R. (4th) 1.
145 See also R. Fernandes, "What is a Ship?" *Seaports and the Shipping World* (May 1983) 50; J.A. George, "When is a Watercraft a Vessel?" (1999) 35 Trial 74; W. Hohmann, "Are Offshore Drillings Rigs 'Ships' under Canadian Maritime Law?"

G. SHIPPING AND INTERNATIONAL ORGANIZATIONS

Although shipping is widely recognized as a key component of international trade, it has generally been operated and regulated by flag states on a national basis. However, this aspect has changed, quite imperceptibly, since the end of the Second World War. Today the truly international character of the shipping industry is more and more reflected by an increasingly complex and important network of international intergovernmental and non-governmental organizations that have contributed to the overall globalization of the industry.[146]

Because of its highly international character, efficient sea transportation has always required co-operation among different sectors. A ship can be owned by nationals from several different states and can fly the flag of yet another state. The vessel's construction may have been financed by institutions based in foreign states and may actually be managed or operated by or chartered to corporations in other states. Furthermore, the cargo carried on board could have been produced in any number of states and can be owned by nationals from altogether different states. Additionally, the ownership of the ship and the cargo could potentially change hands several times during the course of a single voyage. Finally, numerous underwriters from yet other states may underwrite insurance, for either the ship or its cargo, or for third-party liability. Before the goods reach their final destination, they may well have passed through the territory of any number of states. Without international co-operation, shipping would be unmanageable, if not altogether impossible. This is especially important for the legal aspects of maritime transport that demand a predictable uniform system. As a result, this uniform international approach has developed several hundred international treaties, conventions, protocols, and related instruments that form the basis of modern maritime law today.

Unfortunately, there has never been one international organization controlling and regulating sea transportation on a comprehensive, worldwide basis.[147] Despite extensive co-operation among states dating

---

[1967] Can. B. Papers 115. See also *Global Marine Drilling v. Triton Holdings Ltd.*, [1999] Scot. J. No. 238 (QL), discussed by E. Watt, "From Noah's Ark to Mobile Drilling Units" (2000) L.M.C.L.Q. 299.

146 E. Gold, "World Shipping: A Global Industry in Transition" in E.M. Borgese, A. Chircop, & M. McConnell, eds., *Ocean Yearbook 15* (Chicago: University of Chicago Press, 2001) at 267.

147 Gold, *Maritime Transport*, above note 1, cc.5–6.

back several centuries, where the saving of life at sea was concerned, it was not until 1889 that the first international maritime conference took place. This conference, held in Washington, discussed such matters as regulations for preventing collision at sea, saving of life and property from shipwreck, qualifications for officers and seamen, laws for vessels on frequented routes, and the establishment of a permanent international maritime commission. On the last point, however, the conference concluded that the establishment of such a commission was not, at that time, appropriate. Resulting from that decision, all shipping related problems that required international agreements had to be dealt with by *ad hoc* conferences. The first international organization that did useful work in the field of shipping was the League of Nations' Transit Organization, which organized the International Convention on the Regime of Maritime Ports, held in Geneva, Switzerland in 1923. The following year, the Transit Organization set up a sub-committee on Ports and Maritime Navigation, which dealt with the subjects of unifying maritime tonnage measurement rules and buoyage systems. Unfortunately, the Transit Organization ceased to exist with demise of the League following the outbreak of the Second World War. Following that war, the need for a permanent international organization was felt even more strongly. International co-operation was needed to rebuild a war-ravaged world. In other words, the critical role of international organizations in promoting co-operation among many sectors involved in shipping — whether governments, private individuals, corporations, or industry associations — was finally recognized.

The activities of international organizations cover a number of spheres of activity ranging from economic, environmental, and social to the technical aspects of merchant shipping. At first the role of such organizations was largely advisory in terms of promoting and facilitating, rather than actually regulating, the commercial and operational aspects of shipping. In more recent times, international organizations can and do play an increasingly important role in developing internationally binding treaties for shipping and in seeing that these are widely implemented. In other words, through their states members, these organizations have now adopted a law-making role that has become widely recognized and accepted in international law. At the highest level, the global United Nations Convention on the Law of the Sea (*UNCLOS*)[148] has recognized this role as the responsibility of "competent international organizations."

---

148 *UNCLOS*, above note 7.

International organizations are generally classified into two types: intergovernmental organizations (IGOs) and non-governmental organizations (NGOs). As the name indicates, IGOs are those organizations whose constituent members are state governments; however, as already suggested, international NGOs are today also of increasing importance in the globalization of the industry. Although NGOs are not directly law making in the true sense of that expression, they exert significant influence on the regulatory powers of the IGOs in the various international fora where they have consultative status. In many cases, especially at IMO meetings, the NGO input is considered essential and new conventions could neither be produced nor move forward without this expert assistance. In general, these NGOs are lobbies representing specific interests. In a complex industry, such as shipping, government regulators — whether operating nationally, regionally, or internationally — would be unrealistic to ignore this NGO advice and input. In almost all cases such co-operation leads to acceptable compromises that, in the long run, seem to work.

1) Intergovernmental Organizations

As it is necessary to have an understanding of the most important intergovernmental organizations that affect shipping, a brief outline follows.[149]

a) International Maritime Organisation
For shipping, the International Maritime Organisation (IMO) is one of the most important international organizations. The IMO is a specialized agency of the United Nations headquartered in London, Enland. Originally called the Inter-Governmental Maritime Consultative Organisation, it was established by a convention drawn up at the United Nations Maritime Conference held in Geneva, Switzerland in 1948. The convention entered into force only in March 1958, and the first meeting was held in 1959. The name was changed to International Maritime Organisation in 1982, at which time it had 122 members and 1 associate member.[150] Although it is the smallest U.N. specialized agency, it is widely considered to be one of the most effective and efficient ones. It is unique in that it is the only intergovernmental organi-

---

149 For fuller details and information on most other international organizations, see Farthing, *International Shipping*, above note 45, and Gold, *Maritime Affairs*, above note 117.
150 The IMO membership consists of 162 member states in 2003.

zation that deals solely with maritime matters. Under the terms of the *IMO Convention*[151] the organization's purposes are

- to promote and to provide the machinery for international co-operation in technical matters affecting merchant shipping, and to encourage "the highest practical standards in matters concerning maritime safety and efficiency of navigation;"[152]
- to discourage restrictive practices by shipping concerns;
- to discourage flag discrimination;
- to provide for the exchange of information among Governments on matters under consideration by IMO; and
- to give advice to other international organizations on shipping matters.

While one of the IMO's main functions is to act in a "consultative and advisory" capacity for its member states, its chief concern has been to develop international treaties and other legislation concerning maritime safety and marine pollution prevention, that is, the IMO's dual aims to achieve "safer ships and cleaner seas." By the late 1970s IMO had been able to complete a major series of conventions and, since then, has concentrated heavily on keeping legislation up to date and ensuring that it is ratified and implemented by as many states as possible. From time to time IMO develops new conventions as the need arises. This approach has been most successful. At this stage there are more than fifty IMO conventions and protocols, many of which apply to more than 90 per cent of global shipping tonnage.[153]

Like most U.N. special agencies, the IMO is operated by a secretariat, an assembly, a council, and several committees and sub-committees. The secretariat consists of the secretary general and his staff. The council, with the approval of the assembly, chooses the secretary general.[154] With his staff, the secretary general maintains the records necessary for the discharge of the functions of the organization. He also keeps member states informed about the organization's activities. Finally, the secretary general also performs other tasks assigned by the assembly, the council, or the committees. The assembly consists of all the members

---

151 *Convention on the Intergovernmental Maritime Consultative Organization*, 6 March 1948, 289 U.N.T.S. 48 [*IMO Convention*] (entered into force 17 March 1958; entered into force in Canada on the same day); see also *Ratification of Maritime Conventions*, above note 7, vol.I.1.10.
152 *IMO Convention*, ibid., art.1; see also S. Mankabady, ed., *The International Maritime Organisation* (London: Croom Helm, 1986).
153 See IMO web site at <www.imo.org>.
154 The present secretary general is William O'Neil, C.M., of Canada, whose third and final term will end in late 2003.

of *imo*. It meets in regular biennial session at which time it elects representatives to the council. Furthermore, the assembly receives and considers the reports of the council, votes on budgetary matters, and, most importantly, recommends regulations to members for adoption, that is, it might recommend that all member states pass laws or regulations regarding some aspect of marine safety.

Originally, the IMO council consisted of eighteen members who were to be the governments of the largest shipping and sea-trading states. This composition of council had led to some criticism that IMO is a mouthpiece for the large shipping and sea trading states; however, such criticism is no longer valid, if it ever was. Council membership has been progressively increased from eighteen states to twenty-four then to thirty-two, and is expected shortly to be increased to forty. This was done essentially to take into account IMO's growing states membership as well as to ensure that the views of developing states were properly represented. The council acts as the governing body of the organization between the biennial sittings of the assembly. It prepares the budget and work program for the assembly. It usually meets twice annually when it receives the reports of the committees and transmits them to the assembly. Five IMO committees perform much of the actual technical work of developing, negotiating and drafting of proposed regulations, and preliminary drafting of conventions.

i) *Maritime Safety Committee*

The Maritime Safety Committee (MSC) considers the technical work of the International Maritime Organisation related to maritime safety and is considered to be the IMO's principal technical body. The MSC's functions are to

> consider any matter within the scope of the Organisation concerned with aids to navigation, construction and equipment of vessels, manning from a safety standpoint, rules for the prevention of collisions, handling of dangerous cargoes, maritime safety procedures and requirements, hydrographic information, log-books and navigational records, marine casualty investigation, salvage and rescue, and other matters directly affecting maritime safety.[155]

The MSC is also required to provide machinery for performing any duties assigned to it by the *IMO Convention* or any duty within its scope of work that may be assigned to it by or under any international instrument and accepted by the organization. It also has the responsibility for

---

155 *IMO Convention*, above note 151, art.28.

considering and submitting recommendations and guidelines on safety for possible adoption by the assembly. The MSC operates with the assistance of nine sub-committees: Bulk Liquids and Gases, Carriage of Dangerous Goods, Solid Cargoes and Containers, Fire Protection, Radio Communications and Search and Rescue, Safety of Navigation, Ship Design and Equipment, Stability and Load Lines and Fishing Vessel Safety, Standards of Training and Watchkeeping, and Flag State Implementation.

ii) Marine Environment Protection Committee

The Marine Environment Protection Committee (MEPC) concentrates its activities on the "cleaner seas" aspect of International Maritime Organisation's "safer ships and cleaner seas" principle. The basis for this work rests on the resolutions adopted by the 1973 International Conference on Marine Pollution[156] and the Global Programme for the Protection of the Marine Environment developed under the Rio principles.[157] The MEPC is also closely involved with a number of other IMO conventions that deal with operational and liability aspects of marine pollution.[158] In addition, the MEPC serves as a useful forum for the exchange of information on pollution problems among members of IMO. In general, the work of the MEPC in providing technical expertise to its member states is expanding as the emphasis toward protecting the marine environment is increasing steadily.

iii) Legal Committee

The IMO Legal Committee[159] was established in the aftermath of the "Torrey Canyon" disaster in 1967. At that time it was seen that the existing arrangements for dealing with oil pollution disasters were in definite need of revision. The IMO council met in an extraordinary session in response to the disaster and saw the need to develop legal solutions to the problems that the "Torrey Canyon" presented.[160] The council then established the Legal Committee and asked it to draft a legal solution. In addition to its legal responsibilities, the committee also assumed responsibilities for the IMO's external relations a few years later. The Legal Committee is involved in all aspects of the IMO's development of international conventions, protocols, codes, and guide-

---

156 See Chapter 17, "Marine Pollution Prevention."
157 Ibid.
158 Ibid.
159 The present chairman of the LC is Alfred Popp, Q.C., of Canada.
160 Gold, *Maritime Transport*, above note 1 at 325–27.

lines. It meets usually twice annually. At that stage the work plan, based on requests received from member states through the Council and/or Assembly and the MSC and MEPC, is developed. The Legal Committee then starts to develop legal drafts of conventions or protocols in preparation for subsequent IMO diplomatic conferences.

iv) Technical Cooperation Committee
The Technical Cooperation Committee (TCC) was established in 1969 when the IMO became the first U.N. agency to establish this type of function on a permanent basis. This reflects the needs of the many developing countries that require significant upgrading in maritime training and technical assistance in a variety of marine-related areas. The TCC works closely with two international training institutions established under IMO auspices, the World Maritime University, established in 1983 in Malmö, Sweden, and the IMO International Maritime Law Institute, based in Malta. The IMO has generally no technical assistance funds in its own budget but derives funding from a number of states members under technical co-operation agreements.

v) Facilitation Committee
The International Maritime Organisation's Facilitation Committee is a subsidiary body of the IMO council. It was established in 1972 and deals with IMO's work in eliminating unnecessary formalities and red tape in international shipping.

b) **International Labour Organisation**
The International Labour Organisation (ILO), with headquarters in Geneva, Switzerland was created by the Peace Treaty of 1919, but became a U.N. specialized agency in 1946. It is unique as an international organization in that the representation of each member state is tripartite, that is, it includes representatives from government, labour, and employers. The principal organs of the ILO are as follows:

- the International Labour Office, which functions as the ILO's permanent secretariat;
- the governing body, which serves as the ILO's executive body; and
- the International Labour Conference, which meets annually to establish the organization's policy.

As its name would indicate, the ILO is also concerned with maritime labour.[161] In 1920, the governing body of the ILO decided at a meeting

---

161 See Chapter 5, "The Safety Management of Ships."

in Antwerp, Belgium to create a Joint Maritime Commission (JMC) to deal with maritime labour questions. The composition of the commission changes from each session as new representatives of the shipowners and seafarers are elected by the delegates to the Special Maritime Sessions of the International Labour Conference. The role of the JMC is, therefore, to prepare the preliminaries for and to advise the maritime session of the ILO. As an advisory body, the JMC presents drafts and recommendations for proposed ILO conventions and recommendations. Past work of the JMC has dealt with a broad range of subjects, including wages, hours of work and manning, company certificates, annual holidays with pay, social security, health and welfare, and safety questions, which have resulted in numerous conventions.[162] In addition to these conventions, the ILO also has passed numerous recommendations that serve as guidelines for national governments to follow.

c) **U.N. Conference on Trade and Development**

The United Nations Conference on Trade and Development (UNCTAD) is the principal organ of the U.N. General Assembly in the field of trade and development. It was established on 30 December 1964 by a General Assembly resolution as a permanent organ of the General Assembly.[163] UNCTAD has 188 member states assisted by a permanent staff of

---

162 E.g., *Convention Concerning Seafarers' Hours of Work and the Manning of Ships, 1996*, 22 October 1996, online at <www.ilo.org> (ILO No. 180, not yet in force); *Ratification of Maritime Conventions*, above note 7 vol.I.6.410; *Convention Concerning the Inspection of Seafarers' Working and Living Conditions, 1996*, 22 October 1996, online at <www.ilo.org> (ILO No. 178, entered into force 22 April 2000, but not yet accepted by Canada); *Ratification of Maritime Conventions*, above note 7, vol.I.6.390; *Convention Concerning Annual Leave with Pay for Seafarers, 1976*, 29 October 1976, 1138 U.N.T.S. 205 (ILO No. 146, entered into force 13 June 1979, but not yet accepted by Canada); *Ratification of Maritime Conventions*, above note 7, vol.I.6.320; *Convention Concerning Social Security of Seafarers*, 28 June 1946, 148 B.F.S.P. 133 (ILO No. 70, not yet in force); *Ratification of Maritime Conventions*, above note 7, vol.I.6.180; *Convention Concerning Seafarers' Pensions*, 28 June 1946, 442 U.N.T.S. 235 (ILO No. 71, entered into force on 10 October 1962 but not yet accepted by Canada); *Ratification of Maritime Conventions*, above note 7, vol.I.6.190; *Convention Concerning Liability of the Shipowner in Case of Sickness Injury or Death of Seamen*, 24 October 1936, 40 U.N.T.S. 169 (ILO No. 55, entered into force on 29 October 1939 but not yet accepted by Canada); *Ratification of Maritime Conventions*, above note 7, vol.I.6.110; *Convention Concerning Sickness Insurance for Seamen*, 24 October 1936, 40 U.N.T.S. 18 (ILO No. 56, entered into force on 9 December 1949 but not yet accepted by Canada); and *Ratification of Maritime Conventions*, above note 7 vol.I.6.120.

163 UNCTAD, *The History of UNCTAD 1964–1984* (New York: United Nations, 1985) U.N. Doc. UNCTAD/OSG/286.

450 that forms part of the U.N. Secretariat in Geneva, Switzerland. UNCTAD's principal purpose has been to accelerate the economic growth and development of developing states. Its primary connection to the maritime field relates to the shipping problems of the developing states. Normally, UNCTAD meets every four years, and since 1964, nine conferences have taken place. Between conferences UNCTAD's permanent organ, the Trade and Development Board, meets in regular annual or executive sessions to oversee the overall consistency of UNCTAD's activities with agreed priorities. At UNCTAD IX, three commissions of the board were established to perform integrated policy work in their respective areas of competence:

- the Commission on Trade in Goods and Services, and Commodities;
- the Commission on Investment, Technology and Related Financial Issues; and
- the Commission on Enterprise, Business Facilitation and Development.

The Commission on Enterprise, Business Facilitation and Development has specific responsibilities for shipping policy as it has succeeded the UNCTAD Shipping Division. This division was established very early in UNCTAD's life, originally as the Committee on Shipping and Invisibles, which was to address concerns that centred around the importance of shipping to the trade and balance of payments problems of developing states. Although at times considered to be an irritant by traditional shipping states, the Shipping Division became an effective focus for developing countries' shipping aspirations. Subjects that have been discussed by the Shipping Division include freight rates, discriminatory practices, the improvement of port facilities in developing states, and the expansion of the merchant marines of developing states, as well as the legal issues of revising the conventions in force today, which work counter to the interests of the developing states. In particular, the Shipping Division has sharply criticized the practices of private shipping conferences for maintaining high and discriminatory freight rates against the developing states. It was argued that this has presented obstacles to increasing international trade with developing states.[164] As a result, the Shipping Division created a sub-committee whose function was to work on international shipping legislation. The work of this sub-committee was then referred to the United Nations Commission on International Trade Law (UNCITRAL), which is the

---

164 M.W. Connelly, "Canadian Shipping Policies and the U.N. Conference on Trade and Development: An Analysis of UNCTAD V" (1982) 9 Maritime Policy and Management 35.

appropriate legal body to redraft and amend existing law. The most important work to result from this source is the *Convention on a Code of Conduct for Liner Conferences, 1974*.[165] Nevertheless, there has been reluctance on the part of major shipping states to ratify this convention.

In recent years UNCTAD was totally reorganized, before it almost disappeared as a result of U.N. cost cutting and other reasons. In its reorganized state the new Enterprise Commission absorbed the Shipping Division and, in general, UNCTAD's image as a "poor nations' club" has receded. Today UNCTAD has become the focal point within the U.N. system for the integrated treatment of development and inter-related issues in the areas of trade, finance, technology, investment, and sustainable development. In this new role UNCTAD's direct involvement in shipping has decreased somewhat. However, there is an IMO-UNCTAD agreement that involved UNCTAD in shipping issues and treaties that have a major commercial content; for example, the *International Convention on Maritime Liens and Mortgages, 1993*,[166] was completed under this system.

d) U.N. Commission on International Trade Law

The United Nations Commission on International Trade Law (UNCITRAL) was established as the result of a U.N. General Assembly resolution in 1966. Its mandate was to further the progressive harmonization and unification of the law of international trade by

- co-ordinating the work of organizations active in this field and encouraging co-operation among them;
- promoting wider participation in existing international conventions and wider acceptance of existing model and uniform laws;
- preparing and promoting the adoption of new international conventions, model laws, and uniform laws;
- promoting ways and means of ensuring a uniform interpretation and application of international conventions and uniform laws in the field of international trade;
- collecting and disseminating information on national legislation and modern legal developments, including case law, in the field of international law of international trade;

---

165 *Convention on a Code of Conduct for Liner Conferences,* 6 April 1974, 1334 U.N.T.S. 15 (entered into force 6 October 1983 but not accepted by Canada); *Ratification of Maritime Conventions,* above note 7, vol.I.5.210.

166 *International Convention on Maritime Liens and Mortgages, 1993,* 6 May 1993, 33 I.L.M. 353 (not yet in force); *Ratification of Maritime Conventions,* above note 7, vol.I.4.21.

- establishing and maintaining close collaboration with UNCTAD; and
- maintaining liaison with other U.N. organs and specialized agencies.

In 1971 UNCITRAL passed a resolution creating the Working Group on International Shipping Legislation. Its current work includes reexamining the existing international conventions and legislation relating to bills of lading.[167] It is the commission's task to find suitable (and acceptable) remedies in such specific problem areas. Moreover, during its existence, UNCTAD's Shipping Division has constantly focused on areas of maritime law that required revision. Once such problem areas are identified, UNCITRAL's Working Group on International Shipping Legislation would study the UNCTAD reports and either draft new legislation or revise existing legislation. The project which has taken up much of the Commission's time over the years, and still contiunes to do so, has been the law of carriage of goods by sea.

e) Other International Organizations with Marine-Related Interests

Several other intergovernmental organizations have significant involvement in the marine sector generally and in maritime law specifically. These organizations and agencies are all part of the international system that increasingly regulates, affects, governs, and supports the world shipping industry. Accordingly, anyone involved in the industry, especially in the legal or regulatory sectors, must have some basic knowledge of this organizational interface. The most important organizations and agencies are described below.

i) *International Telecommunications Union*

The International Telecommunications Union (ITU) was established in 1865 and became a U.N. specialized agency in 1947 with its headquarters in Geneva, Switzerland. Its aim is to maintain and extend international co-operation for the improvement and rational use of telecommunication. It manages the Mobile Maritime Service that handles radio communication by ships and maritime radio navigation. Conferences are convened by the ITU to create new conventions and to revise old ones. IMO representatives frequently attend these conferences to see that the maritime interests are considered. The ITU has aided considerably in the promulgation of rules and regulations that have raised the standard of telecommunications for ships, greatly increasing safety at sea.

---

167 See B in Chapter 9, "Carriage of Goods under Bills of Lading and Similar Documents."

ii) World Health Organization

The World Health Organization, also based in Geneva, Switzerland is concerned with such issues as maritime quarantine, the eradication of sea-borne epidemics, and disinfestations, which consequently affect shipping in these areas.

iii) Universal Postal Union

The Universal Postal Union was established in 1874 but is now a U.N. specialized agency. It affects shipping as it establishes the rates of carrying mail by sea. While a great deal of international and regional mail is now carried by air, there is still a significant amount of "surface" mail (i.e., carried by sea).

iv) World Meteorological Organization

The World Meteorological Organization is a U.N. specialized agency located in Geneva, Switzerland. It co-operates closely with ships at sea through monitoring marine weather forecasts and also receives weather reports from vessels. The organization works closely with national weather services in supplying regional and global information on weather.

v) International Civil Aviation Organization

As there is a considerable amount of regulatory and technical overlap between shipping and aviation, the work of the International Civil Aviation Organization also affects shipping. As a result, there is close co-operation between this aviation organization and IMO. The former is a U.N. specialized agency headquartered in Montreal, Canada since its inception in 1947.

vi) International Hydrographic Organization

The International Hydrographic Organization (IHO) is located in Monte-Carlo, Monaco and was originally established as the International Hydrographic Bureau in 1921. The name was changed with the entry into force of the *Convention on the International Hydrographic Organization* in 1970.[168] Under IHO auspices permanent associations among the hydrographic services of various maritime states have been developed. The principal purpose of the IHO is to develop uniformity in hydrographic information and documentation, including the navigational charts and other information that are essential to the safe navi-

---

168 *Convention on the International Hydrographic Organization*, 3 May 1967, 751 U.N.T.S. 41 (entered into force 22 September 1970); see Gold, *Maritime Affairs*, above note 117 at 38.

gation of ships. Recent work by the IHO includes collaboration with IMO in devising plans for a worldwide system of promulgating navigational warnings to shipping as well as new electronic technology and navigational data bases.

vii) International Tribunal for the Law of the Sea
The International Tribunal for the Law of the Sea (ITLOS) was established in 1996 in Hamburg, Germany, under the provisions of *UNCLOS*[169] as the main dispute resolution body under that convention. ITLOS can hear disputes by various means and has already decided a number of matters relating to the arrest of vessels and fisheries disputes. It can be expected that ITLOS will, in future, be increasingly involved in shipping related disputes in the public area.

viii) International Maritime Satellite Organization
The International Maritime Satellite Organization (INMARSAT) is an intergovernmental body based in London, England. As its name implies, it deals with outer-space based satellites that assist communications and navigation at sea. It sets various rules under the INMARSAT Convention.[170]

ix) International Oil Pollution Compensation Fund
The International Oil Pollution Compensation Fund, based in London, England administers the IMO's *FUND 1972 Convention*, including its 1976 and 1992 protocols.[171] The fund is specifically involved in the settlement of ship-source marine pollution claims that fall outside the normal claims settled under the *CLC 1969 Convention*.[172]

x) U.N. Environment Programme
The United Nations Environment Programme (UNEP), the U.N. agency with responsibility for the global environment, is based in Nairobi, Kenya. UNEP was established as a result of the 1972 Stockholm Conference on the Human Environment. Although UNEP deals with all aspects of environmental protection, it places special emphasis on marine pollution in thirteen areas under its Regional Seas Programme.[173]

---

169 *UNCLOS*, above note 7, Annex VI.
170 Above note 64; see also N. Jasentuilyana, "The Establishment of an International Maritime Satellite System" (1977) 2 Ann. Air & Sp. L. 249.
171 See Chapter 17, "Marine Pollution Prevention."
172 *Ibid.*
173 E. Gold, *Gard Handbook on Marine Pollution*, 2d ed. (Arendal, NO: Gard, 1997) at 38–39 and 404–19.

xi) Intergovernmental Oceanographic Commission

The Intergovernmental Oceanographic Commission is based at the Paris, France, headquarters of the United Nations Educational, Scientific, and Cultural Organization. It is mainly involved in furthering marine scientific research but, in recent years, has co-operated closely with IMO on various aspects of damage arising from ship-source marine pollution.

xii) Regional Port State Inspection Systems

Regional Port State Inspection Systems have been set up in Europe (*Paris MOU 1982*), Asia (*Tokyo MOU 1993*), South America (*Viña del Mar Agreement*), the Caribbean (*Caribbean MOU*), the Mediterranean (*Mediterranean MOU*), for the Indian Ocean (*Indian Ocean MOU*), and in other regions. These systems, set up by a regional agreement of interested states, require the inspection of ships in the ports of contracting states in order to enforce IMO, ILO, and other safety measures. Port state inspection has already made significant contributions in achieving the IMO's goal of "safer ships and cleaner seas" and, at the same time, contributes to the growing international regulatory network.[174]

xiii) Other Regional Organizations

In recent years a number of regional intergovernmental organizations have also assumed responsibilities in maritime matters, including legal development. In particular, the European Union (EU), through its Transport Directorate, has become very important in this area. Other regional organizations, such as the Association of South East Asian Nations, the Organization of American States, and the various U.N. regional economic commissions, such as the Economic Commission of West African States, the Economic Commission for Latin America and the Caribbean, and the U.N. Economic and Social Commission for Asia and the Pacific, as well as a number of others, are all becoming involved in the maritime sector. This is a growing trend.

2) Non-Governmental Organizations

There are also a large number of non-governmental organizations that have significant interests in various aspects of shipping, stemming from the fact that shipping is still principally a private sector industry with significant national, regional, and global impacts. In many cases the regulatory systems permit and encourage industry self-regulation.

---

174 *Ibid.* See also Chapter 5, "The Safety Management of Ships" and Chapter 17, "Marine Pollution Prevention."

In other areas, the most effective non-governmental organizations provide the necessary expertise required when new national, regional, and international regimes are developed. The most important of these are described below.

a) Comité Maritime International

The International Maritime Committee, more commonly known by its French title, Comité Maritime International (CMI), has its administrative office in Antwerp, Belgium, and is supported by the national maritime law associations of fifty-three states.[175] The objectives of the CMI are to

- further the unification of maritime law,
- encourage the creation of national associations for the unification of maritime law, and
- provide a forum at which the national maritime law associations can communicate and develop the law.

The representatives of the various national maritime law associations meet annually in an assembly. The assembly forms international subcommittees and working groups to prepare work for future assemblies and conferences. The work of the CMI has been of significant value to the shipping world, as the maritime law conventions established through its auspices rank among the most important ones concluded. The CMI encourages input from all sectors of the shipping industry before it drafts a convention. Draft conventions are usually the focus of CMI conferences that take place on an irregular basis but generally are held about every three to five years. Some thirty-seven international CMI conferences have been held since the institution's creation in 1897.[176] For many years, owing to special arrangements with the government of Belgium, where the CMI offices are located, the CMI prepared draft conventions that were then placed before a diplomatic conference hosted by the Belgian government. However, since the establishment of the International Maritime Organisation, the CMI has basically become an expert industry body that presents reform proposals to the IMO.

The various conventions concluded under the auspices of the CMI deal with a broad range of subjects and are outlined in greater detail, as appropriate, in many chapters of this book, and include the following:

---

175 Including the Canadian Maritime Law Association.
176 A. Lilar & C. Van den Bosch, *Le Comité Maritime International 1897–1972* (Antwerp: CMI, 1973). See also Gold, *Maritime Transport*, above note 1 at 128–31.

- Collisions between Vessels, 1910,[177]
- Assistance and Salvage at Sea, 1910,[178]
- Limitation of Liability, 1924,[179]
- Bills of Lading, 1924,[180]
- Maritime Liens and Mortgages, 1926,[181]
- Immunity of State Owned Ships, 1926/1934,[182]
- Penal Jurisdiction, 1952,[183]
- Civil Jurisdiction, 1952,[184]

---

177 *Convention for the Unification of Certain Rules Respecting Collisions Between Vessels, 1910*, 23 September 1910, U.K.T.S. 1913 No. 4 (entered into force 1 March 1913 and accepted by Canada 28 October 1914); *Ratification of Maritime Conventions*, above note 7, vol.I.3.200; see also Chapter 11, "Maritime Collisions."

178 *Convention for the Unification of Certain Rules with Respect to Assistance and Salvage at Sea, 1910*, 23 September 1910, 103 U.K.T.S. 441 (entered into force on 1 March 1913 and acceded to by Canada on 28 October 1914); *Ratification of Maritime Conventions*, above note 7, vol.I.3.210; see also Chapter 15, "Maritime Salvage and Wreck."

179 *International Convention for the Unification of Certain Rules Relating to the Limitation of Liability of Owners of Sea-Going Vessels*, 25 August 1924, 120 L.N.T.S. 123 (entered into force on 2 June 1931 but never accepted by Canada); *Ratification of Maritime Conventions*, above note 7, vol.I.2.399; see also Chapter 18, "Limitation of Liability for Maritime Claims."

180 *International Convention for the Unification of Certain Rules of Law Relating to Bills of Lading*, 25 August 1924, 120 L.N.T.S. 155 [*Hague Rules*] (entered into force 2 June 1931; not accepted, but legislatively adopted by Canada); *Ratification of Maritime Conventions*, above note 7, vol.I.5.10; see also Chapter 9, "Carriage of Goods under Bills of Lading and Similar Documents."

181 *International Convention for the Unification of Certain Rules of Law Relating to Maritime Liens and Mortgages*, 10 April 1926, 120 L.N.T.S. 187 (entered into force 2 June 1931 but never accepted by Canada); *Ratification of Maritime Conventions*, above note 7, vol.I.4.10. See also Chapter 6, "Maritime Mortgages and Liens."

182 *International Convention for the Unification of Certain Rules Concerning the Immunity of State Owned Vessels*, 10 April 1926, 176 L.N.T.S. 199 (entered into force 23 February 1936, but not accepted by Canada); *Protocol Additional to the International Convention for the Unification of Certain Rules Concerning the Immunity of State Owned Vessels of 10 April 1926*, 24 May 1934, 150 L.N.T.S. 269 (entered into force 8 January 1937 but not accepted by Canada); see also *Ratification of Maritime Conventions*, above note 7, vol.I.12.05.

183 *International Convention for the Unification of Certain Rules Relating to Penal Jurisdiction in Matters of Collision or other Incidents of Navigation*, 10 May 1952, 439 U.N.T.S. 233 (entered into force 20 November 1955 but not accepted by Canada); see also *Ratification of Maritime Conventions*, above note 7, vol.I.2.30.

184 *International Convention on Certain Rules Concerning Civil Jurisdiction in Matters of Collision*, 10 May 1952, 439 U.N.T.S. 217 (entered into force 14 September 1955 but not accepted by Canada); see also *Ratification of Maritime Conventions*, above note 7, vol.I.2.20; see also Chapter 3, "Admiralty Jurisdiction."

The Shipping Industry: An Overview 91

- Arrest of Ships, 1952,[185]
- Limitation of Liability, 1957,[186]
- Stowaways, 1957,[187]
- Carriage of Passengers, 1961,[188]
- Liability of Operators of Nuclear Ships, 1962,[189]
- Carriage of Passenger Luggage, 1967,[190]
- The 1967 Protocol to the 1910 Salvage Convention,[191]
- Maritime Liens and Mortgages, 1967,[192] and
- Vessels under Construction, 1967.[193]

185 *International Convention for the Unification of Certain Rules Relating to the Arrest of Sea-Going Ships*, 10 May 1952, 439 U.N.T.S. 193 (entered into force on 24 February 1956, but not accepted by Canada); see also *Ratification of Maritime Conventions*, above note 7, vol.I.2.10; see also Chapter 3, "Admiralty Jurisdiction"; *International Convention on Arrest of Ships, 1999*, 12 March 1999, Doc. A/CONF.188.6 has since then been concluded but is not yet in force; *Ratification of Maritime Conventions*, above note 7, vol.I.2.15.
186 *International Convention Relating to the Limitation of the Liability of Owners of Sea-Going Ships*, 10 October 1957, 1412 U.N.T.S. 73 (entered into force on 31 May 1968, but not accepted by Canada); *Ratification of Maritime Conventions*, above note 7, vol.I.2.310; see also Chapter 15, "Limitation of Liability for Maritime Claims."
187 *International Convention Relating to Stowaways*, 10 October 1957, 1957 A.M.C. No.2:1980 (not yet in force); CMI, *International Conventions on Maritime Law* (Antwerp: CMI, 1987) at 123.
188 *International Convention for the Unification of Certain Rules Relating to the Carriage of Passengers by Sea and Protocol*, 29 April 1961, 1411 U.N.T.S 81 (entered into force on 4 June 1965 but not accepted by Canada); *Ratification of Maritime Conventions*, above note 7, vol.I.5.140; see also Chapter 10, "Carriage of Passengers."
189 *International Convention on the Liability of Operators of Nuclear Ships, with Additional Protocol, 1962*, 25 May 1962, 57 A.J.I.L. 268 (not yet in force); *Ratification of Maritime Conventions*, above note 7, vol.I.7.20.
190 *International Convention for the Unification of Certain Rules Relating to the Carriage of Passengers' Luggage by Sea*, 27 May 1967, B.P.P. Misc. 7 (1968) (not yet in force); *Ratification of Maritime Conventions*, above note 7, vol.I.5.160; see also Chapter 10, "Carriage of Passengers."
191 *Protocol to Amend the Convention for the Unification of Certain Rules of Law Relating to Assistance and Salvage at Sea, 1910*, 27 May 1967, U.K.T.S. 1978 No. 22 (entered into force on 15 August 1977, but not accepted by Canada); *Ratification of Maritime Conventions*, above note 7, vol.I.3.230; see also Chapter 15, "Maritime Salvage and Wreck."
192 *International Convention for the Unification of Certain Rules Relating to Maritime Liens and Mortgages*, 27 May 1967, S.D. No.12 (1967) 3 (not yet in force); *Ratification of Maritime Conventions*, above note 7, vol.I.4.20; see also Chapter 6, "Maritime Mortgages and Liens."
193 *Convention Relating to Registration of Rights in Respect of Vessels Uunder Construction*, 27 May 1967, U.D. 1967–1968 (1):342 (not yet in force); *Ratification of Maritime Conventions*, above note 7, vol.I.4.30; see also Chapter 4, "The Ownership and Registration of Ships."

As this list of conventions indicates, the CMI has probably been the most important international non-governmental organization involved in maritime law to date. However, the CMI's role has been changing. Although the CMI will continue to prepare draft conventions on a variety of maritime law subjects, it now does this in close co-operation with a number of other NGOs and IGOs, such as IMO, EU, UNCITRAL, UNCTAD, ILO, and others. For example, during the period 2002–2003, the CMI has working groups preparing draft documentation on offshore craft and structures, maritime liability, electronic data interchange, collision and salvage, wreck removal, maritime liens and mortgages and arrest of ships, classification societies, and carriage of goods.

b) International Chamber of Shipping

The International Chamber of Shipping (ICS) has been considering matters of general shipping policy since it was founded in London, England in 1921.[194] It promotes the interests of its members (mostly national shipowners' associations) in all policy matters except for those dealing with wages, general conditions, and accommodation of seagoing personnel — dealt with by the International Shipping Federation, which is also located in London and which works in close collaboration with the ILO. The ICS membership controls more than half of the world's active trading fleets.

c) International Association of Ports and Harbours

The International Association of Ports and Harbours (IAPH) is based in Tokyo, Japan and was founded in 1955.[195] It serves as a forum for the exchange of information relevant to port and harbour organization, administration, management, development, operation, and promotion. Major concerns include encouraging the standardization and simplification of procedures governing imports, exports, and the clearance of vessels in international trade. Port development concerns revolve around dealing with large ships and with containerization.

d) International Association of Lighthouse Authorities

The International Association of Lighthouse Authorities was formed in 1957 in Paris, France, to establish a forum where the lighthouse authorities of all states would meet to discuss matters of technical information and to exchange information on recent improvements that

---

194 See Gold, *Maritime Affairs*, above note 117 at 53.
195 *Ibid.* at 52.

might be useful to other states.[196] Activities of this association include forming sub-committees to study leading lines, microwave aids to navigation, frequencies, calculation of intensity of lights, the unification of new buoyage regulations, buoy moorings, radio navigation systems, and surface colours.

e) **International Union of Marine Insurance**
The International Union of Marine Insurance was founded in 1874 and represents the interests of marine insurers and has consultative status with the IMO.[197] Its offices are located in Basel, Switzerland. This union is involved in promoting freedom of insurance in co-operation with the International Chamber of Commerce.

f) **International Organization for Standardization**
The International Organization for Standardization, in London and Geneva, creates uniform technical standards also applicable to shipping.

g) **Baltic and International Maritime Council**
The Baltic and International Maritime Council is an important international association, based in Copenhagen, Denmark, and in operation since 1905.[198] It unites shipowners and others interested in shipping to take action regarding instances of unfair charges (on imports) and claims, freight speculation, and other negative practices. It also serves as a forum for exchanging and disseminating information affecting the industry. Further work includes improving charter parties and other shipping documents. The Council has produced a number of widely used standard forms for charter parties and bills of lading.

h) **International Bar Association**
As its name implies, the International Bar Association, based in London, England unifies law practitioners from many states at the international level. The association has had a very effective maritime transport section for many years.

i) **International Tanker Owners Pollution Federation**
International Tanker Owners Pollution Federation, based in London, England,[199] was originally established to administer the Tanker Owners'

---

196 *Ibid.* 117.
197 *Ibid.* at 54–55.
198 *Ibid.* at 48–49.
199 *Ibid.* at 67.

Voluntary Agreement Concerning Liability for Oil Pollution, an important oil pollution liability agreement in effect from 1969 to 1997.[200] During this time the federation acquired a leading role in the technical aspects of oil spill response. Under new arrangements, concluded in 1996–97, the federation continues to provide very effective technical and scientific expertise in this area to its tanker-owner membership as well as to coastal states affected by marine pollution incidents.

j) **International Group of Protection and Indemnity Clubs**
The International Group of Protection and Indemnity Clubs, based in London, England, represents the interests of the major P&I clubs, based in the United Kingdom, Norway, Sweden, the United States, and Japan.[201] It has consultative status with the IMO.

k) **International Chamber of Commerce**
The International Chamber of Commerce, based in Paris, France, provides broad-based services to its worldwide global membership of national chambers of commerce. However, its Commission on Sea Transport is of considerable relevance in the maritime sector. In addition, the chamber commercial arbitration rules are widely used in maritime arbitration matters.

l) **International Transportation Workers' Federation**
The International Transportation Workers' Federation, based in London, England, has assumed an important role overseeing the rights and conditions of seafarers and ensuring the compliance with the various ILO conventions. The federation is supported by various national maritime trade unions and has been especially involved in combating abuses perceived to occur on sub-standard vessels under open registries.

m) **International Salvage Union**
The International Salvage Union, based in Rotterdam, Netherlands, represents the interests of its membership consisting of marine salvage companies based in all regions of the world. The union has consultative status at the IMO and has been principally involved in negotiating the various versions of Lloyd's Open Form salvage agreements as well as the IMO salvage conventions.[202]

---

200 See Chapter 17, "Marine Pollution Prevention."
201 See Chapter 7, "Marine Insurance."
202 See Chapter 15, "Maritime Salvage and Wreck."

n) International Maritime Bureau

The International Maritime Bureau, based in London, England with a regional office in Kuala Lumpur, Malaysia, is a specialized division of the International Chamber of Commerce, with a main objective of combating maritime fraud and criminal activities, such as piracy, theft, and hijacking, against merchant ships in various regions of the world.

o) International Shipmasters' Associations

As its name indicates, the International Shipmasters' Associations represents the various national and regional associations of shipmasters.

p) International Marine Pilots' Association

The International Marine Pilots' Association represents the various regional marine pilotage services at the international level.

q) International Association of Independent Tanker Owners

The International Association of Independent Tanker Owners, based in Oslo, Norway, represents the majority of independent tanker owners at the international level and provides a forum for the exchange of views among members. It also promotes free competition, safer tanker operations, and environmental protection.

r) International Shipping Federation

The International Shipping Federation works closely with the International Chamber of Shipping and is based in the same offices in London, England. It is mainly concerned with issues related to maritime employment and represents its shipowner members' interests in discussions on this aspect with governments and maritime unions.

s) International Association of Classification Societies

The International Association of Classification Societies was set up in 1969 by seven major classification societies,[203] but now has ten members and three associate members.[204] The association membership provides classification for more than 95 per cent of world shipping and

---

203 American Bureau of Shipping (ABS), Bureau Veritas (BV), Lloyd's Register (LR), the Japanese Register (NKK), Det Norske Veritas (DNV), and Registro Italiano (RI); see Boisson, *Safety at Sea*, above note 94 at 124ff; see also Chapter 5, "The Safety Management of Ships."

204 Additional members: China Classification Society,,Korean Register, and, Russian Maritime Register. Associate members: Croatian Register, Indian Register, and Polish Register.

more than 50 per cent of all ships. This involves in excess of half a million surveys annually, with more than six thousand surveyors based in twelve hundred offices.[205] The association aims to provide the highest possible credibility and standards of surveys for the shipping industry utilizing a stringent system of checks and balances.

H. CONCLUSION

This chapter was designed to provide a very broad outline of the shipping industry that is regulated by maritime law at the national, regional, and international levels. As indicated in the Introduction to the chapter, maritime law is based on the complex operational aspects of the shipping industry. Furthermore, an understanding of the industry's technical, operational, and commercial aspects is an essential basis to understanding its legal and regulatory aspects. As has become clear from this chapter, and as will be indicated throughout this book, maritime law is today significantly influenced by international developments in what has become a globalized industry. This is especially applicable for Canadian maritime law, as should be apparent from this chapter. Canada has generally followed international maritime law developments to the extent that many international conventions have basically become Canadian maritime law regardless of whether the actual treaty has been formally accepted.

FURTHER READING

Selected General Shipping Industry and Legal Materials

ABRAHAMSSON, B.J., *International Ocean Shipping: Current Concepts and Principles* (Boulder, CO: Westview, 1980).

BOISSON, P., *Safety at Sea* (Paris: Bureau Veritas, 1999).

BRANCH, A.E., *The Elements of Shipping* (London: Chapman & Hall, 1977).

COMITÉ MARITIME INTERNATIONAL, *International Conventions on Maritime Law* (Antwerp: CMI, 1987).

---

205 Boisson, *Safety at Sea*, above note 94 at 124.

COUPER, A.D., *The Geography of Sea Transport* (London: Hutchinson, 1972).

FARTHING, B., *International Shipping*, 2d ed. (London: Lloyd's Press, 1993).

GOLD, E., *Maritime Transport* (Toronto: Lexington, 1981).

GOLD, E., ed., *Maritime Affairs: A World Handbook*, 2d ed. (London: Longmans, 1991).

HOLMAN, H., ed., *A Handy Book for Shipowners and Masters*, 16th ed. (London: UK P&I Club, 1964).

INSTITUTE OF MARITIME LAW, *Ratification of Maritime Conventions*, 4 vols., Updated looseleaf service (London: Lloyd's Press, 1991–2003).

MANKABADY, S., ed., *The International Maritime Organisation* (London: Croom Helm, 1986).

SINGH, N., *International Maritime Conventions*, 3d ed. (London: Stevens, 1983).

UNCTAD, *Review of Maritime Transport 2002* (Geneva: UNCTAD, 2002).

VANDERZWAAG, D., ed., *Canadian Ocean Law and Policy* (Toronto: Butterworths, 1992).

Selected Technical Materials

BAPTIST, C., *Tanker Handbook for Deck Officers*, 8th ed. (Glasgow: Brown, Son & Ferguson, 2000).

BÖER, F., *All About a Container Ship* (Herford, UK: Koehlers, 1987).

BROWN, C.H., *Nicholl's Seamanship and Nautical Knowledge*, 22d ed. (Glasgow: Brown, Son & Ferguson, 1974).

CLARK, I.C., *The Management of Merchant Ship Stability, Trim and Strength* (London: Nautical Institute, 2002).

CORNISH, M. & E. IVES, *Maritime Meteorology*, 2d ed. (London: Thomas Reed, 1996).

DUDLEY, J.R., B.J. SCOTT, & E. GOLD, *Towards Safer Ships and Cleaner Seas — A Handbook for Modern Tankship Operations* (Arendal, NO: Gard A.S., 1994).

EYRES, D.J., *Ship Construction (Eyres)*, 5th ed. (London: Butterworth-Heinemann, 2001).

FOTHERGILL, M.G., *Lumber Deck Cargo Manual* (London: Nautical Institute, 2002).

HOUSE, D.J., *Cargo Work*, 6th ed. (London: Butterworth-Heinemann, 1998).

MAUDSLEY, P., *Operation of Offshore Supply and Anchor Handling Vessels* (London: Nautical Institute, 1995).

MILLER, A.G., *Basic Seamanship*, 7th ed. (Glasgow: Brown, Son & Ferguson, 1998).

MINISTRY OF DEFENCE, *Admiralty Manual of Seamanship* (London, UK: H.M. Stationery Office, 1995).

RANKIN, K.S., *Thomas' Stowage: The Properties and Stowage of Cargoes*, 4th ed. (Glasgow: Brown, Son & Ferguson, 2002).

ROBINSON, T., *The Offshore* (St. John's, NL: Jesperson Press, 1992).

SOLLY, R., *Supertankers: Anatomy and Operation* (London: Witherby, 2001).

CHAPTER 3

ADMIRALTY JURISDICTION

A. INTRODUCTION

As seen in Chapter 1, maritime law falls under Parliament's prerogative to legislate over navigation and shipping.[1] There are many reasons why the founders of Confederation decided to allocate this power to the federal legislator, and perhaps the most important is the very nature of maritime law as it relates to international activities and the need to promote uniformity not only nationally within Canada as a whole but also internationally.[2] The national argument for uniformity has not been a smooth one and has raised many fascinating issues on the nature of maritime law and the jurisdictions of the institutions that legislate or enforce it. This is the central theme of this chapter. Admiralty court and maritime law jurisdiction are two closely intertwined subjects that are best discussed in a Canadian context by cross-referencing to each other. In order to assist the reader navigate through this complex subject, it is useful to keep in mind two sets of questions that have arisen in case law and with reference to which the subject must be explained.

The first set of questions concern Canadian maritime law as a body of substantive law. The main question is this: What is Canadian maritime law? In other words, what is its scope (i.e., range of subjects) and

---

1 *Constitution Act, 1867* (U.K.), 30 & 31 Vic., c.3, s.91(10), repr. R.S.C. 1985, App. II, No. 5.
2 *Ordon Estate v. Grail* (1996), 30 O.R. (3d) 643, aff'd [1998] 3 S.C.R. 437.

content (i.e., actual substance of maritime law). There are critical subsidiary questions that need to be addressed. First, when was English maritime law "received" in Canada in order to become "Canadian" maritime law? Second, how was this body of law saved from one statute to another? Third, what is its status as a uniform body of federal law? Fourth, what is its relationship to provincial law, or can provincial law be applied in a maritime setting?

The second set of questions focus on the Federal Court as the Admiralty Court of Canada, its jurisdiction in this regard, and concurrency of that jurisdiction with provincial courts. There are four main questions here. First, what is the status and purpose of the Federal Court as a court under section 101 of the *Constitution Act, 1867*, and what is comprehended by its function for the better administration of the "laws of Canada" in a maritime context? Second, what is Admiralty jurisdiction in Canada, and what is the full extent of Federal Court Admiralty jurisdiction? Related to this question is the scope of the class of subjects comprehended by "navigation and shipping," that is, what is the area of capture of Canadian maritime law and what are its jurisdictional limits *ratione materiae*? Third, what provincial courts may exercise maritime law jurisdiction? Fourth, what is the full extent of provincial court admiralty jurisdiction? These are the questions that this chapter will attempt to answer. They are fundamental to building an understanding of what is maritime law and how admiralty jurisdiction in Canada is understood and practised.

B. MARITIME LAW JURISDICTION DISTINGUISHED FROM OTHER MARINE JURISDICTIONS

First of all, it is useful to distinguish maritime law jurisdiction from other existing or potential federal and provincial marine jurisdictions and entitlements.

1) Distinction from Maritime Zones and Resource-Related Jurisdictions of Canada

Admiralty jurisdiction should be distinguished from the exercise of other forms of marine jurisdiction permitted in the *United Nations Convention on the Law of the Sea, 1982* (*UNCLOS*).[3] Consistently with the

---

3   10 December 1982, 1833 U.N.T.S. 3 [*UNCLOS*].

UNCLOS and the *Oceans Act*,[4] Canada as a state at international law, and a coastal state in particular, exercises sovereignty, sovereign rights, or jurisdiction over various types of maritime zones, including internal waters enclosed by an extensive straight baseline system in the Arctic, Atlantic, and Pacific regions. Canada has a territorial sea of 12 nautical miles (22 km), a contiguous zone of 24 nautical miles (44.5 km), an exclusive economic zone of 200 nautical miles (370 km), and a continental shelf whose current seaward limits are undefined, but which is likely to extend well beyond 200 nautical miles (370 km) in at least the Atlantic and Arctic, if not the Pacific as well.[5] In the past Canada has claimed historic title to various inshore marine areas in the three regions, although these areas are now encompassed within Canada's straight baseline system and therefore constitute internal waters.[6] In addition, Canada exercises special environmental jurisdiction in the Arctic within 100 nautical miles (185 km) of its baselines and north of 60° latitude.[7] Through its external affairs prerogative it has been Canada, rather than the provinces, that has been able to gain law of the sea benefits and responsibilities.

At a domestic level, the *Constitution Act, 1867*, empowers the federal government to exercise exclusive legislative jurisdiction *inter alia* over navigation and shipping, and fisheries.[8] Under the *Oceans Act*, the federal government, through the Department of Fisheries and Oceans has responsibility for leading, co-ordinating, and facilitating the development of a national oceans management strategy, integrated management plans, marine protected areas, and marine environmental quality guidelines within Canada's maritime zones. The fisheries jurisdiction has been used to develop an elaborate licensing, management, and enforcement system primarily through the *Fisheries Act*[9] and related regulations. Offshore development, the laying of submarine cables, and other ocean uses have been legislated also. Aquaculture as an ocean use stands somewhat apart, as the development and management of this sector is generally a responsibility of the provinces and is coordinated with the federal government through memoranda of agreement.

---

4   *Oceans Act*, S.C. 1996, c.31.
5   Ibid., ss.4(a), 10, and 13(1)(a); Geological Survey of Canada, *Canada and Article 76 of the Law of the Sea, Defining the Limits of Canadian Resource Jurisdiction Beyond 200 Nautical Miles in the Atlantic and Artic Oceans* (Open File 3209, Ron McNab (ed.), 15 May 15 1994).
6   (1974) 12 Can. Y.B. Int'l Law 222.
7   Formerly *Arctic Waters Pollution Prevention Act*, R.S.C. 1985, c.A-12, s.2.
8   Above note 1.
9   R.S.C. 1985, c.F-14.

The exercise of these development, management, and enforcement responsibilities is not necessarily an exercise of maritime law jurisdiction. First, these jurisdictions are exercised as a result of public international law of the sea entitlements of a coastal state, that is, Canada as a state actor in international law. Second, the legislative and enforcement jurisdiction of maritime law is *ratione materiae*, and does not depend on nationality or geography, whereas the law of the sea entitlements are based on geography and specific functional jurisdictions.

However, the relevance of maritime law comes in where vessels are involved. So although the licence to explore and develop offshore resources is not a maritime law matter, claims in tort or contract against the ship (irrespective of its functions in fishing, oil and gas development, recreation, tourism, etc.) are indeed matters falling within navigation and shipping, and consequently invoke maritime law jurisdiction.

2) Distinction from Provincial Maritime Property Rights

Also to be distinguished from maritime law jurisdiction is the subject of provincial property rights or Aboriginal rights over maritime areas, which is more appropriately a constitutional matter. While Canada as a state at international law exercises sovereignty and jurisdiction over maritime areas for international law purposes, at a domestic constitutional level, individual coastal provinces may have maritime property rights. On joining Confederation the various coastal provinces, now forming part of Canada, may have brought with them maritime territory as a matter of property. The *Constitution Act, 1867*, addressed the division of powers over classes of subjects but did not alter the boundaries of provinces within which maritime areas may have been encompassed. Technically, the boundaries of a province may not be changed without its consent, and it is a matter of evidence what maritime territory is indeed part of a province today.[10]

Subsequent to Canada gaining the right to legislate extraterritorially by the *Statute of Westminster, 1931*,[11] the question of provincial entitlement to maritime areas, now covered by regimes of internal waters, territorial sea, and continental shelf at international law, was judicially considered by both the Supreme Court of Canada and provincial courts in province-specific contexts. In the 1967 *Reference Re Ownership of*

---

10   Above note 1, s.6.
11   (U.K.), 22 Geo. V., c.4.

Offshore Mineral Rights, the Supreme Court of Canada determined that the territorial sea, its seabed, and subsoil off British Columbia (Vancouver Island) belonged to Canada.[12] The Supreme Court found differently in 1984 in relation to the waters in Juan de Fuca Strait and Strait of Georgia between Vancouver Island and the B.C. mainland, when it determined that these were encompassed within the limits of British Columbia when it joined Confederation in 1871 and were, consequently, property of the province.[13] In 1983 the Newfoundland Court of Appeal found that the province did indeed have a territorial sea of 3 nautical miles (5.5 km), but that it did not have any continental shelf rights.[14] A year later the Supreme Court of Canada similarly found that Newfoundland had not acquired continental shelf rights prior to joining Confederation in 1949.[15] *R. v. Keyn*[16] featured prominently as a jumping-off point for the discussion of the territorial aspect involved. The courts accepted the view that "the realm consisted of the land within the body of the counties, that all beyond the low-water mark was high seas and that the concept of the three-mile limit was a matter of international law which could not enlarge the area of English municipal law. The latter could only be done by Act of Parliament."[17] Thus, the answer to the question, what maritime territory is part of a province, depends on the province concerned. But irrespective of the full extent of property rights, jurisdiction over navigation and shipping, and fisheries continues to remain federal by reason of section 91 of the *Constitution Act, 1867*. Therefore, provincial property rights ought to be distinguished from jurisdiction *ratione materiae*. Also under the *Oceans Act*, and to a certain extent under the Atlantic offshore accords statutes, provincial law and provincial court jurisdiction may be extended to apply to Canada's maritime zones.[18] Again, this is

---

12 [1967] S.C.R. 792.
13 *Reference Re Ownership of the Bed of the Strait of Georgia, (AG of Canada v. AG of British Columbia)* (1984), 8 D.L.R. (4th) 161 (S.C.C.).
14 *Reference Re Mineral and other Natural Resources of the Continental Shelf* (1983), 145 D.L.R. (3d) 9 (Nfld. C.A.).
15 *Reference Re the Seabed and Subsoil of the Continental Shelf Offshore Newfoundland* (1984), 5 D.L.R. (4th) 385 (S.C.C.).
16 *(The Franconia)*, [1876] 2 Ex. D. 63.
17 *Reference Re Mineral and other Natural Resources of the Continental Shelf*, above note 14 at 15.
18 *Oceans Act*, above note 4, s.9; *Canada–Newfoundland Atlantic Accord Implementation Act*, S.C. 1987, c.3, s.7; *Canada–Nova Scotia Offshore Petroleum Resources Accord Implementation Act*, S.C. 1988, c.28, s.6.

not maritime law jurisdiction. The potential extension of provincial law is intended to ensure that there is a body of law alongside federal law to govern a range of activities offshore.

C. ADMIRALTY COURT AND MARITIME LAW JURISDICTION: AN HISTORICAL PERSPECTIVE

In order to fully appreciate the nature and extent of Canadian maritime law, the status of the Federal Court as the Admiralty Court of Canada, and the system of concurrent Admiralty jurisdiction by virtue of which provincial superior courts administer maritime law in addition to the Federal Court, it is helpful to distinguish between the Admiralty court as a judicial institution and Admiralty jurisdiction as the power of a court as they evolved historically in England and were eventually transported to the colonies, including North America. At the heart of the distinction lies a historically difficult relationship between the common law courts and Admiralty courts since the creation of the latter in the late fourteenth century. It took a full five hundred years into the late nineteenth century before the conflict was resolved through the abolition of the Admiralty court as a unique judicial institution and conferring its powers, in the form of Admiralty jurisdiction, on the common law courts.

In Canada this controversy continued into the twentieth century on two grounds. The first was the relationship between the Exchequer Court and its successor, the Federal Court, both unique statutory creations for the better administration of laws of Canada, and the provincial courts as common law courts in the federal constitutional structure created in the *Constitution Act, 1867*. The second was the operation of the doctrine of reception in a maritime law context, thereby determining how much substantive maritime law was inherited from the English practice of Admiralty law, the common law, and civil law to source and nourish the statutory grant of jurisdiction to the Federal Court.

1) Origins and Evolution of the Admiralty Court and Jurisdiction in England

The commission granted to Jean de Beauchamp by Edward III in 1360 designating him as admiral of the fleets and empowering him to exercise executive and judicial jurisdiction over shipping issues — which at the time could not be effectively exercised by any other court —

would lead to the first modern Admiralty Court on common law territory. This extensive jurisdiction, which drew heavily from civilian sources and with civilians as practitioners, quickly conflicted with the jurisdictions exercised by the courts in local seaports and the common law courts so that by the period 1389–91, and again in 1400, the admiral's jurisdiction had to be limited to activities outside the realm of the Crown, that is, matters happening at sea. The common law courts and Admiralty Court would resist each other's jurisdictional encroachments. Persons instituting proceedings in the wrong court were subject to a penalty.[19] The passing of these three statutes gave the Admiralty Court jurisdiction over matters on the sea. However, this jurisdiction was statutory, as opposed to inherent, giving the common law courts the position from which they were able to limit and define the Admiralty Court's power. The interpretation of statutes was a function of the common law courts and they had the power to prohibit the Admiralty Court, when petitions or complaints were made, that actions in dispute were not within the Admiralty jurisdiction.

The Admiralty Court was not only restricted by the common law courts in the subject-matter with which it might deal, but also with regard to the location of the cause of action. The common law courts developed the practice of dealing with matters that had happened at sea by saying they had taken place on land. The location of a cause of action was not a material part in an action for contract and in that manner the common law courts dealt with contracts made outside of England. However, there were certain subjects and practices in maritime matters that the common law courts could not effectively deal with, such as maritime torts, collision, securities of ships, and pre-judgment attachment of ships. These matters maintained the framework that kept the Admiralty Court in existence. This struggle for jurisdiction between the common law courts and the Admiralty Court lasted from 1389 through the Protectorate and the Restoration to the middle of the nineteenth century, when judges in England were given both common law and admiralty jurisdiction.

The Admiralty Court gradually gained power and its jurisdiction was at a high water mark with the passing of the ordinances of 1648. The jurisdiction at that time covered practically everything of a maritime nature. The Restoration in 1660 led to a revocation of the Admiralty Court's wide jurisdiction. After the Restoration, the common law courts successfully maintained their right to prohibit suits in Admiralty

---

19 *A Remedy for him who is Wrongfully Pursued in the Court of Admiralty, 1400* (U.K.), 2 Hen. IV., c.11.

on contracts made on shore or within harbours or tidal waters, regardless of where such contracts were broken; for torts committed within the limits of a county, whether on land or sea; and for contracts made in foreign ports. Despite the fact that the patents appointing the judges in Admiralty gave them wide powers, it was held that this did not create jurisdiction. The Admiralty Court's civil jurisdiction was practically confined to contracts made and to be performed on the high seas, torts committed on the high seas, and suits for mariner's wages.

The Admiralty Court sank into relative insignificance until the necessity of having prize courts arose in the early 1800s because of the great maritime wars of this period. The judge in Admiralty at this time exercised two functions: one as a judge of the civil court, called the Instance Court, and the other as the judge of the court governing prizes, known as the Prize Court. The constant appeal to the Prize Court — more than a thousand prize cases each year between 1803 and 1811 — and the ability of Lord Stowell, then judge of Admiralty in both Instance and Prize cases, raised the Admiralty Court to an important position again. In 1833 a select committee of the House of Commons presented a report recommending the extension of the Admiralty Court's jurisdiction. This recommendation was not acted upon until 1840, when an Act of Parliament was passed to improve the practice and extend the jurisdiction of the court. It was in this year that there began a movement for the revival of the ancient English Admiralty jurisdiction. The first of the so-called Admiralty Court Acts was passed. These were followed by other Acts in 1846, 1854, 1861, and 1868. These all tended to give a broader and fuller jurisdiction to what was called by then the High Court of Admiralty. By 1873 that court had a general jurisdiction over matters of title and mortgage of ships, salvage, towage, and necessaries, building, equipping and repairing ships, claims over bills of lading and for damage to goods, questions of account between part owners, claims for life, salvage, and seamen's wages, including master's wages, and jurisdiction over any claim for damage done by any ship. The able administration of the Admiralty Court by Dr. Stephen Lushington and Sir R.J. Phillimore, combined with the development of steam shipping — leading not only to increased commerce but also to increased activity in cases of collision, salvage, and damages — helped increase the significance and importance of the Admiralty Court.

In 1873, the High Court of Admiralty was united and consolidated with the other courts of England to form the Supreme Court of Judicature. The High Court of Justice, which heard original matters, was divided into several divisions. One was known as the Probate, Divorce and Admiralty Division, to which causes of a maritime nature were assigned. The divisions of the High Court of Justice were constituted merely for the better distribution of work. All the jurisdictions vested in the High Court belonged to all the divisions alike, and all the judges of the High Court had equal power, authority, and jurisdiction — so that any judge could hear any cause or transfer it to another division. The result of this unification of the courts was to largely dispel the conflict between the Admiralty and common law courts, since both kinds of cases could be heard by the same judge in the same division of the High Court. Most importantly, the old restriction of jurisdiction to actions over subject-matter of causes arising only "upon the sea" was removed, and the question of locality and subject-matters had also disappeared to some extent. This jurisdiction continued to evolve on the basis of statute and the inherent jurisdiction of the High Court of Admiralty. In 1970 an Admiralty Court was established as part of the Queen's Bench Division of the High Court.

2) Evolution of the Admiralty Court and Jurisdiction in Canada

Admiralty law in Canada was probably first exercised in Newfoundland. In 1583 Sir Humphry Gilbert had claimed Newfoundland for England, whose western adventurers used the coast of the island as a convenient base for their fisheries. The thousands of fishermen who spent their summers in and out of the harbours were a turbulent crew. When, in 1633, the Privy Council issued regulations known as the "Western Charter" designed to cure the disorderly conduct found at the fisheries, it recognized an immemorial custom according to which the commander of the first ship to enter a harbour each season, the "admiral," was responsible for settling disputes among the ships and the inhabitants of the surrounding area. The courts presided by these fishing admirals were not Admiralty courts proper as their jurisdiction related to dealing with disorder among fisherfolk.[20] When the island was finally ceded by France to England in 1783 by the *Treaty of Paris*, the fishing "admirals" were still dispensing what passed for justice in the localities occupied by the English. However, a Vice-Admiralty Court had been established in St. John's earlier in 1765.

From 1763 until 1863, Admiralty law was administered in the present provinces of British Columbia, Newfoundland, New Brunswick, Nova Scotia, Prince Edward Island, and Quebec by Vice-Admiralty

---

20 *Cull v. Rose* (1982), 139 D.L.R. (3d) 559 (Nfld. T.D.).

judges appointed under commissions from the Admiralty in England. The commissions defined the jurisdiction of each judge. Originally the governors of the colonies were *ex officio* vice-admirals and judges of the Vice-Admiralty Courts. Later a judge of the Supreme or Superior Court of the colony would be appointed by the British Admiralty to be a judge of the Vice-Admiralty Court. Acts passed by the British Parliament in 1863 (*Vice-Admiralty Courts Act, 1863*) and 1867 (*Vice-Admiralty Courts Amendment Act, 1867*) delineated the jurisdiction of the Vice-Admiralty Courts.[21] They also provided that the Chief Justice of the Supreme Court in each British possession should be *ex officio* the judge of the Vice-Admiralty Court unless a contrary appointment was made by the Admiralty.

While Confederation did not change the scheme of Vice-Admiralty Courts it did give the jurisdiction to deal with Admiralty matters to the Dominion Parliament. The *British North America Act, 1967* (now *Constitution Act, 1867*) stated in section 91(10) that matters of "navigation and shipping" fall under the subjects within the authority of the Dominion Parliament. In 1877, by virtue of its power granted under section 101 of the *Constitution Act, 1867*, the Parliament of Canada created a Court of Maritime Jurisdiction for the province of Ontario. As this federal legislation did not conflict with the *Imperial Act of 1863*, the Dominion Parliament's actions were *intra vires*. This statute defined the jurisdiction of the Court and gave all persons the same rights and remedies as they would have had in a Vice-Admiralty Court.

In 1890 the British Parliament passed the *Colonial Courts of Admiralty Act, 1890*.[22] This act repealed all previous legislation with respect to Vice-Admiralty Courts and abolished those courts. The Act provided that the legislature of any British possession could declare any court of unlimited civil jurisdiction in that possession to be a Colonial Court of Admiralty. The jurisdiction of the court would be the same as the admiralty jurisdiction of the High Court in England, whether existing by virtue of statute or otherwise. In the following year the *Admiralty Act, 1891*,[23] was passed by the Parliament of Canada. Under this Act, the Exchequer Court, a federal court, was selected to be the court having Admiralty jurisdiction, with the Supreme Court of Canada gaining appellate jurisdiction over Admiralty matters. The Exchequer Court enjoyed the same admiralty jurisdiction and administered English mar-

---

21 (U.K.), 26 & 27 Vict., c.24; (U.K.), 30 & 31 Vict., c.45, respectively.
22 (U.K.), 53 & 54 Vict., c.27.
23 S.C. 1891, c.29.

itime law just as the High Court of England.[24] Admiralty districts were established in the provinces of British Columbia, New Brunswick, Nova Scotia, Ontario, Prince Edward Island, and Quebec, and local judges in Admiralty were appointed. The law administered at that time was by necessity English rather than Canadian, as the Dominion Parliament did not yet have the right to legislate extra-territorially. Since the realm ends at the low-water mark under common law,[25] it would have been impossible for the Parliament of Canada to pass laws relating to Admiralty matters without those laws being extra-territorial in nature, unless, of course, the acts covered actions occurring in inland waters.

In the case of Newfoundland, the Admiralty jurisdiction enjoyed by the Supreme Court as a result of the *Colonial Courts of Admiralty Act, 1890*, continued until 1949 when it was removed by the *Terms of Union*. However, this did not mean that the provincial courts in Newfoundland ceased to enjoy this jurisdiction, as the *Terms of Union*, while repealing the statutory jurisdiction, did not touch the residual Admiralty jurisdiction enjoyed by the common law courts in the province.[26]

Until 1927, it was considered by most Admiralty lawyers that any addition to the Admiralty jurisdiction of the High Court in England made after 1890 automatically applied to Canada. Judges of the Admiralty court in several districts decided cases in matters in which jurisdiction had only recently been added to the High Court on this assumption. In the case of *The Yuri Maru and The Woron*, however, the Privy Council decided that the jurisdiction of courts established under the *Colonial Courts of Admiralty Act* was that of the High Court as it existed at the date of the passing of that Act in 1890.[27]

The whole matter of the status of Admiralty courts in Canada and other dominions was considered at the Conference on the Operation of Dominion Legislation and Merchant Shipping Legislation held in 1929 in London. This conference recommended that the dominions be given power to repeal the *Colonial Courts of Admiralty Act, 1890*, and to establish Admiralty courts under their own laws.

---

24 "Although the Exchequer Court in Admiralty sits in Canada it administers the Maritime Law of England in like manner as if the cause of action were being tried and disposed of in the English Court of Admiralty" (*Robillard v. St. Roch (The)* (1921), 21 Ex. C.R. 132).
25 See *R. v. Keyn (The Franconia)*, above note 16.
26 See *Cull v. Rose*, above note 20, as distinguished by *Ontario (AG) v. Pembina Exploration Canada*, [1989] 1 S.C.R. 206 [*Pembina*]; and on the basis of *Shipman v. Phinn* (1914), 19 D.L.R. 305, aff'd (1914), 20 D.L.R. 596.
27 [1927] A.C. 906 (P.C.).

The *Statute of Westminster, 1931*, gave the Canadian Parliament the ability to legislate extra-territorially, hence the Dominion Parliament was then competent to deal with Admiralty and shipping matters.[28] The statute had this effect because it repealed the *Colonial Laws Validity Act, 1865*, so that thereafter, instead of the legislation of the Imperial Parliament overriding repugnant Dominion legislation in those areas allowed by the *Constitution Act, 1867*, legislation of the Canadian Parliament became supreme. In 1934 the *Admiralty Act, 1934*,[29] and the *Canada Shipping Act*[30] were enacted. The *Admiralty Act, 1934*, made each province, except for Alberta and Saskatchewan, an Admiralty District. The District Admiralty Court was presided over by a District Judge in Admiralty, who was generally a superior or a county court judge. The District Judge had the jurisdiction, power, and authority of a judge of the Exchequer Court with respect to the Admiralty jurisdiction of that court. Trials of maritime claims and all interlocutory applications were heard by the District Judge. Appeals from any final judgment of the District Judge were made either to the Exchequer Court or directly to the Supreme Court of Canada.

The Admiralty Court was a court of strictly limited jurisdiction. It lacked jurisdiction to hear any claims not covered by the statutory powers given the court by the *Admiralty Act, 1934*, the *Canada Shipping Act, 1934*, or any other statutory enactment. Section 18 of the *Admiralty Act, 1934*, provided that the court shall have jurisdiction over "The like places, persons, matters, and things as the Admiralty jurisdiction now possessed by the High Court of Justice in England, whether existing by virtue of any statute or otherwise."[31] In other words, the Admiralty Court in Canada had the inherent jurisdiction of the Admiralty Court in England; the statutory jurisdiction of the Admiralty Court in England; and any additional jurisdiction given to it by any statute of the Parliament of Canada. In 1971 Parliament passed the *Federal Court Act*, which established the Federal Court of Canada as successor to the Exchequer Court and Admiralty District courts, and elaborated the statutory basis of its powers, including maritime law jurisdiction.[32] The Federal Court is now the Admiralty Court for Canada, but maritime law jurisdiction continues to be exercised by the provincial courts concurrently with the Federal Court.

---

28 Above note 11.
29 S.C. 1934, c.31.
30 S.C. 1934, c.44.
31 Above note 29, s.18.
32 *Federal Court Act*, S.C. 1971, c.1.

D. JURISDICTION *RATIONE MATERIAE*

1) Definition of Canadian Maritime Law

It might seem trite at first blush to ask the question, What is Canadian maritime law? However, this deceivingly simple question has had no one simple answer; it has been in fact a subject of major controversy in the Supreme Court of Canada, and continues to provoke discussion today. The answer to the question serves not only to identify what law is applicable in a maritime context but also to define the extent of Admiralty jurisdiction *ratione materiae*. It also touches on sources of Canadian maritime law, in terms of the operation of the doctrine of reception and at what point in time, as well as the role of the common law and civil law as sources. The jurisprudence on this question has not always provided an elucidating answer. Perhaps a step back in history is an appropriate way to explain the question. Throughout the colonial period and the beginning of Confederation in 1867, the maritime law applied by the Vice-Admiralty Courts was English maritime law at the time. Developed in an English context since the fourteenth century, this law was still heavily civilian in nature, despite strong influences from the common law. In essence, maritime law had developed over the centuries into a unique body of law in England, but its civilian origins were evident all the time. Interestingly, pleading before the Admiralty Court was restricted to doctors of civil law as late as 1858, when this practice was finally abolished. The significance of the civilian heritage and common law influences would assume a special constitutional and legal significance with regards to a uniform area of law in a confederation that included both civil and common law systems.

With Confederation, the *Constitution Act, 1867*, allocated the class of subjects concerning navigation and shipping to the federal government. The *Admiralty Act, 1891*,[33] was the first maritime law statute passed by the Parliament of Canada after Confederation exercising this authority over navigation and shipping. In effect through section 4 of the 1891 Act, English maritime law at the time was received as "Canadian" maritime law with the Exchequer Court given responsibility as an Admiralty Court to administer it concurrently with provincial courts:

> Such jurisdiction, powers and authority shall be exercisable and exercised by the Exchequer Court throughout Canada, and the waters thereof, whether tidal or non-tidal, or naturally navigable or artificial-

---

33 See above note 23.

ly made so, and all persons shall, as well in such parts of Canada as have heretofore been beyond the reach of the process of any Vice-Admiralty court, as elsewhere there-in, have all rights and remedies in all matters, (including cases of contract and tort and proceedings *in rem* and *in personam*), arising out of or connected with navigation, shipping, trade or commerce, which may be had or enforced in any Colonial Court of Admiralty under *The Colonial Courts of Admiralty Act, 1890*.[34]

The English maritime law inherited was substantive law. It did not include English rules and practices of procedure in Admiralty.[35] Procedure, and more specifically its articulation into rules of court, was left to the Exchequer Court and Federal Court to develop under authority of Canadian statutes or common law. This substantive law was not developed immediately by Parliament to any significant extent, partly because Canada did not enjoy extra-territorial legislative authority. Following the *Statute of Westminster, 1931*, which finally gave Canada control over external relations, the Parliament of Canada enacted the *Admiralty Act, 1934*, which repealed the 1891 Act. There was some controversy as to whether the 1934 Act fully provided for the carrying forward of substantive maritime law on repealing the earlier Act, but the general view today is that this was indeed the case, and continued to be the case after the enactment of the *Federal Court Act* in 1971. This Act made it clear that "Canadian maritime law as it was immediately before the coming into force of this Act continues subject to such changes therein as may be made by this or any other Act."[36]

At the same time as the 1934 Act was enacted, the first *Canada Shipping Act* was also developed. The significance of this was that Canadian maritime law as inherited from English maritime law and further developed by Canadian jurisprudence, would see further development by statute. The *Federal Court Act*, section 2(1) thus defines Canadian maritime law as:

> the law that was administered by the Exchequer Court of Canada on its Admiralty side by virtue of the *Admiralty Act*, chapter A-1 of the Revised Statutes of Canada, 1970, or any other statute, or that would have been so administered if that Court had, on its Admiralty side, unlimited juris-

---

34 *Ibid.*, s.4.
35 *Oy Nokia Ab v. Martha Russ (The)*, [1973] F.C. 394; *Antares Shipping Corp. v. Capricorn (The)*, [1977] 2 S.C.R. 422 [*Antares*]; *Porto Seguro Companhia de Seguros Gerais v. Belcan S.A.*, [1997] 3 S.C.R. 1278.
36 Above note 32.

diction in relation to maritime and admiralty matters, as that law has been altered by this or any other Act of the Parliament of Canada.

Case law would highlight a number of characteristics of Canadian maritime law, such as the facts that

- its exact limits are uncertain;
- it is the same (uniform) throughout Canada irrespective of location of cause of action;
- there is overlap between maritime law and provincial law and the possibility of different outcomes depends on which body of law is applied; and
- maritime law is not part of the provincial law but is, rather, subject to the power of Parliament to repeal, abolish, and alter.[37]

Federal law is not "foreign law" to the provinces but is, rather, an integral part of the law of each province.[38]

The Supreme Court of Canada in *Buenos Aires Maru* stated that Canadian maritime law is "a body of federal law and encompassing the common law principles of tort, contract and bailment."[39] This came as a surprise, as it did not accord with historical fact. McIntyre J. also expressed the opinion that "Canadian maritime law is uniform throughout Canada." The surprise was twofold as it did not seem overtly to recognize the civilian origins of maritime law, nor the civilian maritime law of Quebec. In doing so, the decision came across in the eyes of a number of commentators that the duality of legal systems in force in the country and which are ultimately served by one Supreme Court, was not recognized. Doubtless, the intent was to ensure that Canadian maritime law, as a body of federal law, would have one authoritative federal voice and that its application would be consistent across the country, irrespective of the legal system. In fairness to the Court, it did note elsewhere in the judgment that the body of Admiralty law received from England encompassed "both specialized rules and principles of Admiralty *and* the rules and principles adopted from the common law and applied in Admiralty cases as these rules and principles have been, and continue to be, modified and expanded in Canadian jurisprudence" (emphasis added).[40]

---

37 *Associated Metals and Minerals Corp. v. Evie W (The)*, [1978] 2 F.C. 710 [*Associated Metals and Minerals*]; *Triglav v. Terrasses Jewellers Inc.*, [1983] 1 S.C.R. 283 at para 7; *ITO International Terminal Operators Ltd. v. Miida Electronics Inc. (The Buenos Aires Maru)*, [1986] 1 S.C.R. 752 at 779 [*Buenos Aires Maru*]; and *Q.N.S. Paper Co. v. Chartwell Ltd.*, [1989] 2 S.C.R. 683 at 725 [*Chartwell*].
38 *Buenos Aires Maru*, ibid. at 753.
39 *Ibid.* at 779.
40 *Ibid.* at 776.

Subsequent judgments of the same court would more explicitly recognize the important role of the civilian heritage in and continued role of civil law principles as a source of Canadian maritime law, even though they did not see it as applicable to the case at bar. *Q.N.S. Paper Co. v. Chartwell* concerned whether an agent acting on behalf of an unnamed principal is personally liable when the agent specifically indicates that it is acting as an agent.[41] Plaintiff Q.N.S sued Chartwell for stevedoring and other services in the Quebec Superior Court, and principles of the Quebec Civil Code relating to the liability of a mandatary to third persons were applied in both provincial courts. Giving judgment on behalf of the Supreme Court of Canada, La Forest J. clearly saw the suit as maritime, since it concerned a claim for stevedoring services under section 22(m) of the *Federal Court Act*.[42] As a result he proceeded to apply principles of the common law of contract and agency. However, La Forest J. recognized that there may be issues where "reference may fruitfully be made to the experience of other countries and specifically, of the genesis of Admiralty jurisdiction, to civilian experience." McLachlin J. (as she then was), in delivering judgment with Lamer J., went on to add that she would not "confine the consideration of civil law principles to situations where the English Admiralty Court had jurisdiction prior to 1934."[43] She gave three reasons. First, the maritime law inherited from England has a long international tradition, which drew also from the civil law. Second, maritime law is to a great extent international law, and there is therefore a strong commercial reason to draw on the broader backdrop of international law. Third, *Buenos Aires Maru* did not preclude the application of civil law principles in the absence of precedents in Canadian maritime law. In her view the context of commerce and shipping within which maritime and Admiralty should be interpreted "is neither a common law context, nor a civilian context; it is an international context in which both traditions may play a part."[44] As a result, the civilian tradition as a source and its role in comparative methodology in

---

41 *Chartwell*, above note 37.
42 R.S.C. 1985, c.F-7.
43 *Chartwell*, above note 37 at 697. L'Heureux-Dubé J. also noted: "This body of law encompasses not only common law principles but also civil law principles which were always part of maritime law as applied by the English High Court of Admiralty"; she went on to recall the comparative methodology used by the High Court in dealing with sources to ascertain maritime law principles. This was consistent with the international character of this law (*Chartwell*, above note 37 at 685).
44 *Ibid.* at 692.

maritime law is alive and well. Further, McLachlin J.'s thinking on the international dimension of maritime law would again be reflected in *Ordon Estate v. Grail* (discussed below).

Recalling *Associated Metals and Minerals*, the Supreme Court in *Buenos Aires Maru* also refused to accept the argument that the provincial law of Quebec may have been referentially incorporated or re-enacted as a "law of Canada."[45] The Court has stated that the Federal Court is not restricted to applying federal law only, and "where a case is 'in pith and substance' within the court's statutory jurisdiction, the Federal Court may apply provincial law incidentally necessary to resolve the issues presented by the parties."[46] However, the application of common law principles as might have been incorporated into federal maritime law does not constitute an application of provincial law. *Ordon Estate v. Grail* would in any case further severely restrict the possible application of provincial law in a maritime law setting. This inability of provincial law to apply in a supplementary manner in a maritime law setting will necessarily be expected to result in extensive federal legislative activity and Federal Court development of the common law.

International maritime law is recognized as a source for Canadian maritime law, both in statute and case law. This is not a recent phenomenon, as case law since Confederation occasionally applied rules and practices of comity among nations.[47] However, this source of law as manifested by Canadian ratification or accession has gained more explicit recognition and application in leading cases such as *Ordon Estate v. Grail* and the two most recent major federal maritime law statutes, the *Marine Liability Act* and the *Canada Shipping Act, 2001*. In *Ordon Estate v. Grail*, the Supreme Court of Canada specifically identified international law as a source and went on to refer to the *Collision Avoidance Rules, 1910*.[48] Iacobucci and Major JJ. went further to highlight the need to consider "the fabric of the broader international community of maritime nations, including the desirability of achieving uniformity between jurisdictions in maritime law matters" in developing the common law and that "the common law test must be adapted

---

45 *Buenos Aires Maru*, above note 37 at 779.
46 *Ibid.* at 781.
47 For examples with reference to the right to refuge of ships in distress see *Canada (AG) v. Natalie S. (The)*, [1932] Ex. C.R. 155; and *Cashin v. Canada*, [1935] Ex. C.R. 103. For examples with respect to collision avoidance rules, see *Nisbet Shipping v. R.*, [1951] 4 D.L.R. 225 (Ex. Ct.); *Canada v. Saint John Tug Boat Co.*, [1946] S.C.R. 466.
48 *Convention for the Unification of Certain Rules Respecting Collisions between Vessels, 1910*, 23 September 1910, U.K.T.S. 1913 No. 4.

in accordance with the nature and sources of maritime law as an international body of law whenever courts consider whether to reform Canadian maritime law."[49] Indeed, as La Forest J. pointed out earlier in *Whitbread v. Walley*, "much of maritime law is the product of international conventions" when considering the exigencies of maritime law in Canada's inland waterways.[50]

The *Canada Shipping Act, 2001*, implements numerous conventions and also provides a mechanism for the adoption of amendments to those instruments. Section 6(g) lists as an objective of the Act to "ensure that Canada can meet its international obligations under bilateral and multilateral agreements with respect to navigation and shipping." Schedule 1 of the Act lists thirty-one conventions that are the responsibility of the Minister of Transport,[51] while Schedule 2 adds two more under the responsibility of the Minister of Fisheries and Oceans.[52] Schedule 3 incorporates the entire *International Convention on Salvage, 1989*.[53] By way of further example, section 32(1) of the Act provides for referential incorporation by regulation of material produced by international bodies. An example of such a body is the International Maritime Organisation (see Chapter 2). Likewise, the *Marine Liability Act*[54] is predominantly based on international conventions or rules to which Canada is or may become a party.[55] These are a few examples and other international conventions

---

49 *Ordon Estate v. Grail*, above note 2 at para.78.
50 *Whitbread v. Walley*, [1990] 3 S.C.R. 1273 at 1294–96.
51 S.C. 2001, c.26. See, e.g., ss.2, 21, 22, 29–32, 35(1)(d), 108(2), 110(1), and 227(1), where the minister's responsibilities are stated, in addition to Sch.1.
52 See, e.g., *ibid*., ss.29, 30, 31, and 35(3)(a), where the minister's responsibilities are stated, in addition to Sch.2.
53 28 April 1989, U.K.T.S. 1996 No. 93.
54 S.C. 2001, c.6.
55 Namely the *International Convention for the Unification of Certain Rules of Law Relating to Bills of Lading*, 25 August 1924, 120 L.N.T.S. 155; *Protocol to Amend the International Convention for the Unification of Certain Rules of Law Relating to Bills of Lading, 1924*, 23 February 1968, 1412 U.N.T.S. 121 [Hague-Visby Rules]; *United Nations Convention on the Carriage of Goods by Sea*, 31 March 1978, 17 I.L.M. 608 [Hamburg Rules] (not yet in force in Canada); *Athens Convention Relating to the Carriage of Passengers and their Luggage by Sea, 1974*, 13 December 1974, 14 I.L.M. 945; *Convention on Limitation of Liability for Maritime Claims, 1976*, 19 November 1976, 1456 U.N.T.S 221 (as amended by the 1996 protocol); *International Convention on Civil Liability for Oil Pollution Damage*, 29 November 1969, 973 U.N.T.S. 3 [CLC 1969], as amended by *Protocol to Amend the International Convention on Civil Liability for Oil Pollution Damage, 1969*, 27 November 1992, U.K.T.S. 1996 No. 87 [CLC Prot 1992]; and *International Convention on the Establishment of an International Fund for Compensation for Oil Pollution Damage*, 18 December 1971, 1110 U.N.T.S. 57 [FUND 1971], as amended

are implemented in other federal maritime law statutes. In summary, the following are sources of Canadian maritime law:

- federal statutes, including the *Federal Court Act*, the *Admiralty Act, 1891*, and *Admiralty Act, 1934*, and any other maritime law statute enacted by the Parliament of Canada, such as the *Canada Shipping Act, 2001*, and *Marine Liability Act* (see Table of Legislation);
- case law: jurisprudence of English courts until 1934, the jurisprudence of Canadian courts before 1934, and since then (federal and provincial);
- principles of civil law and the common law as may be determined applicable through a comparative methodology in a maritime law setting by the Federal Court; and
- maritime law conventions to which Canada is a party.

2) Statutory Framework for Jurisdiction

The debate on the nature of Canadian maritime law has been closely intertwined with the subject of Federal Court Admiralty jurisdiction. This is not surprising as the Federal Court is a statutory creation pursuant to section 101 of the *Constitution Act, 1867*, for the better administration of laws of Canada, with a mandate that includes navigation and shipping. The meaning of "navigation and shipping" would itself raise fundamental questions concerning the frontiers, rather than boundaries, of Admiralty jurisdiction.

The starting point of discussion here is section 22(1) of the *Federal Court Act*, entitled "Navigation and Shipping":

> 1) The Trial Division has concurrent original jurisdiction as well as between subject and subject as otherwise, in all cases in which a claim for relief is made or a remedy is sought under or by virtue of Canadian maritime law or any other law of Canada relating to any matter coming within the class of subject of navigation and shipping, except to the extent that jurisdiction has been otherwise specially assigned.

The Federal Court continues to enjoy original jurisdiction, in the sense of the institution of proceedings within this court, and concurrent jurisdiction enjoyed by the Exchequer Court with provincial superior

---

by *Protocol to Amend the International Convention on the Establishment of an International Fund for Compensation for Oil Pollution Damage, 1971*, 27 November 1992, 1996 A.T.S. 3 [*FUND Prot 1992*].

courts. While the general rule supports concurrent jurisdiction, Parliament may allocate exclusive jurisdiction to one court or another. Irrespective of the court with jurisdiction, the law to be applied is Canadian maritime law[56] and any other law enacted by the Parliament of Canada in pursuit of its power under section 91(10) and section 101 of the *Constitution Act, 1867*. Subsection 22(2) continues as follows:

Maritime jurisdiction

(2) Without limiting the generality of subsection (1), it is hereby declared for greater certainty that the Trial Division has jurisdiction with respect to any one or more of the following:

(a) any claim with respect to title, possession or ownership of a ship or any part interest therein or with respect to the proceeds of sale of a ship or any part interest therein;

(b) any question arising between co-owners of a ship with respect to possession, employment or earnings of a ship;

(c) any claim in respect of a mortgage or hypothecation of, or charge on, a ship or any part interest therein or any charge in the nature of bottomry or respondentia for which a ship or part interest therein or cargo was made security;

(d) any claim for damage or for loss of life or personal injury caused by a ship either in collision or otherwise;

(e) any claim for damage sustained by, or for loss of, a ship including, without restricting the generality of the foregoing, damage to or loss of the cargo or equipment of, or any property in or on or being loaded on or off, a ship;

(f) any claim arising out of an agreement relating to the carriage of goods on a ship under a through bill of lading, or in respect of which a through bill of lading is intended to be issued, for loss or damage to goods occurring at any time or place during transit;

(g) any claim for loss of life or personal injury occurring in connection with the operation of a ship including, without restricting the generality of the foregoing, any claim for loss of life or personal injury sustained in consequence of any defect in a ship or in her apparel or equipment, or of the wrongful act, neglect or default of the owners, charterers or persons in possession or control of a ship or of the master or crew thereof or of any other per-

---

56 *Federal Court Act*, above note 32, ss.2(b) and (j); *Robert Simpson Montreal Limited v. Hamburg-America Linie Norddeutscher*, [1973] F.C. 1356 at 1361 [*Robert Simpson*].

son for whose wrongful acts, neglects or defaults the owners, charterers or persons in possession or control of the ship are responsible, being an act, neglect or default in the management of the ship, in the loading, carriage or discharge of goods on, in or from the ship or in the embarkation, carriage or disembarkation of persons on, in or from the ship;

(h) any claim for loss of or damage to goods carried in or on a ship including, without restricting the generality of the foregoing, loss of or damage to passengers' baggage or personal effects;

(i) any claim arising out of any agreement relating to the carriage of goods in or on a ship or to the use or hire of a ship whether by charter party or otherwise;

(j) any claim for salvage including, without restricting the generality of the foregoing, claims for salvage of life, cargo, equipment or other property of, from or by an aircraft to the same extent and in the same manner as if the aircraft were a ship;

(k) any claim for towage in respect of a ship or of an aircraft while the aircraft is water-borne;

(l) any claim for pilotage in respect of a ship or of an aircraft while the aircraft is water-borne;

(m) any claim in respect of goods, materials or services wherever supplied to a ship for the operation or maintenance of the ship, including, without restricting the generality of the foregoing, claims in respect of stevedoring and lighterage;

(n) any claim arising out of a contract relating to the construction, repair or equipping of a ship;

(o) any claim by a master, officer or member of the crew of a ship for wages, money, property or other remuneration or benefits arising out of his employment;

(p) any claim by a master, charterer or agent of a ship or shipowner in respect of disbursements, or by a shipper in respect of advances, made on account of a ship;

(q) any claim in respect of general average contribution;

(r) any claim arising out of or in connection with a contract of marine insurance; and

(s) any claim for dock charges, harbour dues or canal tolls including, without restricting the generality of the foregoing, charges for the use of facilities supplied in connection therewith.

Although this subsection specifies heads of maritime law jurisdiction of the Federal Court, it does so by inclusion and as a result does not provide an exhaustive list of maritime law subjects. How these heads have been treated by the courts is further discussed below. This subsection is followed by subsection 3:

Jurisdiction applicable

(3) For greater certainty, it is hereby declared that the jurisdiction conferred on the Court by this section is applicable

  (a) in relation to all ships, whether Canadian or not and wherever the residence or domicile of the owners may be;
  (b) in relation to all aircraft where the cause of action arises out of paragraphs (2)(j) to (l), whether those aircraft are Canadian or not and wherever the residence or domicile of the owners may be;
  (c) in relation to all claims, whether arising on the high seas, in Canadian waters or elsewhere and whether those waters are naturally navigable or artificially made so, including, without restricting the generality of the foregoing, in the case of salvage, claims in respect of cargo or wreck found on the shores of those waters; and
  (d) in relation to all mortgages or hypothecations of, or charges by way of security on, a ship, whether registered or not, or whether legal or equitable, and whether created under foreign law or not.

The effect of this subsection is to emphasize maritime law jurisdiction as first and foremost *ratione materiae*. Nationality of ship or aircraft, residence or domicile of the owners, location of cause of action, and nature of security on a ship do not operate as to restrict the jurisdiction of the court. However, while this subsection appears to suggest that the jurisdiction, once grounded *ratione materiae*, is limitless, the Federal Court is not always automatically the most appropriate forum to entertain a given case. Conflict of laws rules would apply when there is an actual or potentially competing forum that is a *forum conveniens*. The Federal Court's jurisdiction is further supplemented by other statutes that not only nourish the statutory grant of jurisdiction but also further define it. Reference has already been made to the two most recent statutes, the *Marine Liability Act* and the *Canada Shipping Act, 2001*. The list of maritime law statutes, or statutes with a maritime relevance, is fairly long (see Table of Legislation). Many aspects of this significant body of law are discussed in different parts of this book as appropriate.

3) Boundaries and Frontiers of Admiralty Jurisdiction

In practice in the early to mid–1970s, the jurisdiction exercised by the Federal Court over Canadian maritime law was perhaps best captured by Jackett C.J. on behalf of the Federal Court of Appeal in *Robert Simpson*, when he summarized the maritime jurisdiction of the Federal Court in four points. First, jurisdiction could be grounded on the basis of the *Admiralty Act, 1934* and other statutes administered by the Federal Court's predecessor. Second, jurisdiction could also be grounded on the basis of other law administered by the Federal Court's predecessor if it had unlimited Admiralty jurisdiction. Third, it could be grounded on the basis of a federal statute enacted under section 91(10), navigation and shipping, of the *Constitution Act, 1867*. And, fourth, it could be grounded simply on the basis of Parliament's legislative competence under section 91(10), without that competence necessarily having been exercised.[57]

In 1977 there followed two Supreme Court of Canada constitutional decisions that altered this general understanding, especially in relation to the fourth ground of jurisdiction summarized by Jackett C.J. The first of these was *Canadian Pacific Ltd. v. Quebec North Shore Paper Co.*, where the appellant Canadian Pacific, who was contracted by the plaintiff to build a marine terminal in Quebec, failed to commence work to enable timely completion.[58] The appellant was successful in contesting the jurisdiction of the Federal Court, arguing that the contract was governed by the laws of Quebec and that the action should have been brought in the Quebec Superior Court. The issue was the relationship between a claim for relief or remedy under section 23 of the Federal Court and the meaning of "administration of the laws of Canada" in section 101 of the *Constitution Act, 1867*. In delivering the Supreme Court's decision, Laskin C.J. gave "laws of Canada" an interpretation restricted to federal laws actually in force. Legislative competence *per se* or relevant existing provincial laws did not qualify as "laws of Canada" and could not confer jurisdiction on the Federal Court. It was necessary that "there be applicable and existing federal law, whether under statute or regulation or common law ... upon which the jurisdiction of the Federal Court can be exercised."[59] A somewhat similar determination was made by the Supreme Court in the second case, *McNamara Construction (Western) Ltd. v. R.*, where the Crown as plaintiff and one of the respondents alleged breach of contract in suits under section 17(4)(a) of the *Federal Court Act*. Laskin C.J. reiterated the thinking in *Quebec North Shore* and held that "judicial consideration contemplated by section 101 is not co-extensive with federal legislative

---

57 *Robert Simpson*, ibid. at 1362.
58 [1977] 2 S.C.R. 1054 [*Quebec North Shore*].
59 Ibid. at 1066.

competence."[60] Interestingly, though, both decisions recognized that Federal Court jurisdiction is not necessarily limited to legislation and that there can be federal common law.

Needless to say, these decisions caused considerable concern among maritime lawyers in the country. It was felt by some that existing federal statutes and regulations might not cover all those areas that traditionally could be brought before the Federal Court.[61] There were several areas listed under the heads of jurisdiction in section 22(2) of the *Federal Court Act*, such as marine insurance claims concerning goods originating from outside Canada, that were not nourished by federal statutes and instead drew heavily from English maritime law. The fact is that neither *Quebec North Shore* nor *McNamara* was a maritime jurisdiction case proper, and as a result the Supreme Court did not have to address the reception of English maritime law into Canada. There was also some question as to exactly what areas were included under federal common law since the Supreme Court noted that federal law included common law.

Two years later the Supreme Court had an opportunity to clarify the Federal Court's "Admiralty" jurisdiction in a subject area considered traditionally to be maritime but which under its own dictum was not nourished by a federal statute *qua* law of Canada. In *Tropwood AG v. Sivaco Wire & Nail Co.*, the facts concerned damage to cargo during shipment from Caen, France, to Montreal, Canada, and which generated an action in contract and tort by the consignee, the cargo owner, against the carrier, the shipowner.[62] The relevant provisions of the *Carriage of Goods by Water Act* (which incorporated the *Hague Rules* at the time and provided for shipments from Canadian ports)[63] and the *Canada Shipping Act* (which addressed liability of the carrier)[64] did not apply to goods shipped from abroad to Canada; the question therefore was whether the claim could be brought before the Federal Court. In delivering the Court's unanimous decision, Laskin C.J. noted that "the heads of jurisdiction specified in section 22(2) are nourished, so far as applicable law is concerned, by the ambit of Canadian maritime law or any other law of Canada relating to any matter coming within the class of navigation

---

60 [1977] 2 S.C.R. 654 [*McNamara*].
61 See for instance the following: R.W. Kerr, "Constitutional Limitations on the Admiralty Jurisdiction of the Federal Court" (1979) 5 Dal. L.J. 568; A. Braën, "Cour fédérale; compétence en amirauté" (1981) 59 Can. Bar Rev. 579; and W. Tetley, "A Definition of Canadian Maritime Law" (1996) 30 U.B.C.L. Rev. 137.
62 [1979] 2 S.C.R. 157 [*Tropwood*].
63 R.S.C. 1970, c.15.
64 R.S.C. 1985, c.S-9, s.657.

and shipping"; that Canadian maritime law included the *Admiralty Act, 1934*, and the *Admiralty Act, 1891*, which, although repealed, qualified as "any other statute" by virtue of which maritime law was administered; and that cargo damage claims were indeed within the purview of the predecessor of the Federal Court. Further, the Court found that the applicability of a foreign law in a Canadian maritime case does not necessarily reinforce the contention that there is no existing federal maritime law to deal with the cause of action. Rather, Canadian maritime law "embraces conflict rules and entitles the Federal Court to find some foreign law should be applied" to a claim before it.

A series of decisions, mostly from the Supreme Court of Canada, further explored the frontiers of maritime law. Consistently with *Tropwood*, *Antares Shipping Corp. v. The Capricorn* found that an action for the enforcement of a contract for the sale of a ship was within the jurisdiction of the Federal Court by virtue of section 22(2)(a) and to grant the relief of specific performance by virtue of section 44 of the *Federal Court Act*.[65] The Court on this issue noted the need for reliance on English maritime practice, which forms the foundation of Canadian maritime law, rather than American authorities as used by the Federal Court of Appeal and whose decision was overturned. Interestingly, plaintiff's successful action was based on section 4 of the English *Admiralty Court Act, 1840*,[66] suggesting that this long repealed statute may also qualify as "any other statute" under section 2(b) of the *Federal Court Act*. *Tropwood* principles were again re-affirmed in the context of charterparties.[67]

However, in *Quebec and Ontario Transportation Co. v. The Incan St. Laurent*, the Supreme Court unanimously upheld a decision by LeDain J.A. in the Federal Court of Appeal, finding lack of jurisdiction in the context of a dispute over joint ownership of a ship through a joint venture.[68] The joint venture, whereby a ship was to be shared equally, was part of a larger principal agreement to construct two terminals in Que-

---

65 *Tropwood*, above note 62; *Antares*, above note 35. In addition to any other relief that the court may grant or award, a mandamus, injunction, or order for specific performance may be granted or a receiver appointed by the court in all cases in which it appears to the court to be just or convenient to do so, and any such order may be made either unconditionally or upon such terms and conditions as the court deems just: *Federal Court Act*, above note 32, s.44.

66 *An Act to Improve the Practice and Extend Jurisdiction of the High Court of Admiralty of England, 1840* (U.K.), 3 & 4 Vict., c.65.

67 *Aris Steamship Co. v. Associated Metals & Minerals Corp. (The Evie W)*, [1980] 2 S.C.R. 322.

68 [1980] 2 S.C.R. 242. See also Le Dain J.A.'s reasons in [1979] 2 F.C. 834.

bec. According to the Court of Appeal the claim was not really based on Canadian maritime law, but rather was governed by Quebec civil law. *Quebec North Shore* principles appeared to draw a fine line between what was in essence a matter of property and civil rights and what was peripherally a navigation and shipping matter in the relationship between the parties. To avoid a potential contradiction in the Supreme Court's thinking, this decision should be distinguished from *Antares* on the basis that the maritime aspect of the joint venture was incidental to a preponderantly non-maritime agreement.

So when does a set of facts potentially constitute, or cease to constitute, a maritime legal issue so that provincial jurisdiction *qua* property and civil rights is engaged? In *Wire Rope Industries v. British Columbia Marine Shipbuilders* a re-socketed towing cable broke during bad weather and resulted in the loss of the tow.[69] The jurisdictional issue arose from the claim against Wire Rope, a third party, for breach of contract and negligence in the operation of re-socketing, which was not maritime *ratione loci*, but rather *ratione materiae*. If the issue were maritime, then it would be subject to Canadian maritime law, but were it otherwise B.C.'s provincial law as well as jurisdiction (*qua* property and civil rights) would be seized. The Supreme Court of Canada found the service provided by Wire Rope to be maritime in nature and therefore to fall under Canadian maritime law. Recalling *Antares* in defining the jurisdiction of the English High Court of Admiralty, which was inherited by the Exchequer Court, the Supreme Court yet again used the *Admiralty Court Act, 1840*, as a source of Canadian maritime law, section 6 of which granted jurisdiction to the High Court over "all claims and demands" *inter alia*, concerning services and necessaries supplied to a ship. This grant was carried forward through the *Admiralty Act, 1891*, the *Admiralty Act, 1934* and eventually into the *Federal Court Act* — itself a law of Canada within federal legislative competence — with section 22(2)(m) on necessaries (i.e., in this case presumably maintenance) and 22(2)(n) on repairs and equipping providing specific heads of jurisdiction over the legal issue entertained by the court. The implication was that there was federal law to be applied, and this consisted of common law principles of negligence and contract law. Interestingly at the end the Court assessed the failure of the socket as a latent defect.

Following *Wire Rope*, *Triglav v. Terrasses Jewellers Inc.*[70] pitted the classes of subjects navigation and shipping and property and civil rights directly against each other, perhaps more than ever before.

---

69 [1981] 1 S.C.R. 363 [*Wire Rope*].
70 Above note 37.

Goods were missing from a container in a warehouse in Montreal after carriage from Koper, in the former Yugoslavia. The insurance contract was between two Yugoslav companies, but a Quebec company (Terrasses, purchasers of the goods in question) had bought an interest in it. The key element in the appeal to the Supreme Court challenged the constitutionality of the *Federal Court Act* and section 22(2)(r) marine insurance head of jurisdiction in particular. Should this head of jurisdiction in the *Federal Court Act* be *ultra vires*, there could be no law of Canada under section 101 of the *Constitution Act, 1867*, to govern marine insurance. The case was particularly complex for three reasons. First, provincial jurisdiction over insurance had already been recognized in extensive case law, but none of this was in a maritime context.[71] Second, marine insurance law had long been legislated and enforced in the provinces. British Columbia, Manitoba, New Brunswick, Nova Scotia, Ontario, and Quebec[72] had such legislation modelled on the U.K. *Marine Insurance Act, 1906*,[73] whereas there was no federal marine insurance act before 1993.[74] If these could not be applied anymore, what law would govern marine insurance instead and until a formal federal enactment? Third, while there was a marine insurance contract between the insurer and consignee, the carrier was not a party. The Supreme Court found section 22(2)(r) not to be *ultra vires*. Although marine insurance was recognized as a matter falling within property and civil rights, in *Triglav v. Terrasses Jewellers Ltd.*, the Court opined that it was assigned to Parliament as part of navigation and

71 *Citizens Insurance Co. of Canada v. Parsons* (1881), 7 App. Cas. 96; *AG for Canada v. AG for Alberta*, [1916] 1 A.C. 588; *AG for Ontario v. Reciprocal Insurers*, [1924] A.C. 328; *Re The Insurance Act of Canada*, [1932] A.C. 41; *AG for Canada v. AG for Ontario*, [1937] A.C. 355; *Reference Re Special War Revenue Act, Section 16*, [1942] S.C.R. 429; *Canadian Indemnity Co. v. AG of British Columbia*, [1977] 2 S.C.R. 504.

72 British Columbia: *Insurance (Marine) Act*, R.S.B.C. 1996, c.230; Manitoba: *Marine Insurance Act*, R.S.M. 1987, c.M-40; New Brunswick: *Marine Insurance Act*, R.S.N.B. 1973, c.M-1; Nova Scotia: *Insurance Act*, R.S.N.S. 1989, c.231, ss.227–316; Ontario: *Marine Insurance Act*, R.S.O. 1990, c.M-2; Quebec: *Civil Code of Quebec*, S.Q. 1991, C.64, ss.2505–628. The Court had found it unnecessary to define the scope of provincial law, although it did recognize that the provinces also have jurisdiction over maritime law under s.92(10) of the *Constitution Act, 1867*, above note 1. None of these provinces repealed its marine insurance legislation after *Triglav v. Terrasses Jewellers Ltd.*, above note 37. In any case, the practical effect of this decision, coupled with *Ordon Estate v. Grail*, above note 2 (S.C.C.), later on is to render this legislation dead-letter law.

73 (U.K.), 6 Edw. VII., c.41.

74 This would be legislated eventually: *Marine Insurance Act*, S.C. 1993, c.22.

shipping. The Court rationalized this finding by focusing on the subject of marine insurance as a central institution of maritime law since the early origins of this legal institution. Marine insurance, with its origins in bottomry, was indeed the progenitor of all insurance law. Thus when navigation and shipping were assigned as a federal prerogative, they necessarily included the institutions of maritime law as they had developed historically! Beyond its immediate concern with marine insurance, the Court went further in *obiter dicta* to make a number of important statements on Canadian maritime law.

Despite this growing body of principles the courts had not yet articulated these into a standard test to establish more precisely the existence or otherwise of Federal Court jurisdiction over navigation and shipping. *Buenos Aires Maru* would draw on the case law to articulate such a test.[75] This was necessary because of a strong terrestrial connection in a tort setting, which theoretically could invoke jurisdiction of a province *ratione loci*. In this landmark case, carrier Mitsui subcontracted International Terminal Operators (stevedore and terminal operators) to pick up and store consignee Miida's goods on a short-term basis. The bill of lading had a Himalaya clause by virtue of which the carrier sought to extend limitation of liability to its subcontractors, and the contract between the carrier and stevedore-terminal operator expressly stated the bill of lading's limitation of liability would benefit the latter. Several cases of calculators were stolen from the warehouse. The consignee brought an action in contract and delict against the carrier and stevedore-terminal operator. The central jurisdictional issue was the negligence of the stevedore-terminal operator after goods were unloaded from a ship and temporarily stored in a warehouse. Was this navigation and shipping and therefore federal, or property and civil rights and consequently provincial? If the former, then the issue came within the ambit of the Federal Court and Canadian maritime law; if the latter, the issue could be characterized as a delict or *quasi*-delict committed in Quebec by a person domiciled in that province and therefore would engage Quebec civil law.

In addressing these questions, the Supreme Court pulled together *Quebec North Shore* and *McNamara* principles to articulate the now fundamental three-step test to determine the Federal Court's jurisdiction:

- there must be a statutory grant of jurisdiction by the federal Parliament;

---

75 Above note 37.

- there must be an existing body of federal law that is essential to the disposition of the case and that nourishes the statutory grant of jurisdiction; and
- the law must be a "law of Canada" as the phrase is used in section 101 of the *Constitution Act, 1867*.[76]

Clearly, this test did not propose new principles but, rather, re-stated judicially considered existing ones in a sequential order as criteria that have to be satisfied to ground jurisdiction. This general test would then be applied in a navigation and shipping setting. However, there still remained a question as to the scope of maritime law before it could be determined that a specific issue did indeed fall under navigation and shipping and consequently to enable the application of the three-step test. The factual scenario of this case enabled the Court to develop new flexible criteria on the ambit of maritime law. Naturally, the historical development of Canadian maritime law helped the Court trace the relaying of this body of law from one statute to another; but, other than general statutory references to the contract of carriage, there was no specific statutory mention of goods after unloading from a ship and possible claims in tort at that stage. This meant that the first category of Canadian maritime law in section 2 of the *Federal Court Act* was not helpful and therefore reliance had to be placed on the second category, that is, law that "would have been so administered if that court had on its admiralty side unlimited jurisdiction in relation to maritime and admiralty matters."[77]

The Supreme Court reviewed historical analyses by lower courts of a waxing and waning Admiralty jurisdiction to determine the full extent of jurisdiction in tort and contract, but determined that it would not "restrict the definition of maritime and Admiralty only to those claims which fit within such historical limits." History had played an important part in earlier decisions but it was time for the Court to take on an even more expansive approach to navigation and shipping. McIntyre J., in delivering the Court's judgment, stated:

> In my view the second part of the section 2 definition of Canadian maritime law was adopted for the purpose of assuring that Canadian maritime law would include an unlimited jurisdiction in relation to maritime and admiralty matters. As such, it constitutes a statutory recognition of Canadian maritime law as a body of federal law dealing with all claims in respect of maritime and admiralty matters.

---

76 *Ibid.* at 766.
77 *Ibid.* at 769.

Those matters are not to be considered as having been frozen by the *Admiralty Act, 1934*. On the contrary, the words maritime and admiralty should be interpreted within the modern context of commerce and shipping. In reality, the ambit of Canadian maritime law is limited only by the constitutional division of powers in the *Constitution Act, 1867*.[78]

Iacobucci J. would add in a later case that "such terms should rather be capable of adjusting to evolving circumstances unencumbered by rigid doctrinal categorization and historical straightjackets."[79] Still, this raises as many questions on frontiers as it answers on boundaries! Clearly the ambit of Canadian maritime law and consequent Admiralty jurisdiction have constitutional boundaries, which in themselves are significantly porous in that the class of navigation and shipping, itself one of those boundaries, is inherently flexible and subject to evolving commercial, technological, and probably also environmental forces. In this sense, using this *dictum* of the Supreme Court, that same boundary is more a frontier than a limit. The Court was conscious of this potential concern and therefore undertook further analysis to establish whether the subject-matter is "integrally connected to maritime matters as to be legitimate Canadian maritime law within federal legislative competence"[80] and thus avoid what might be in pith and substance a provincial matter. "Integral connection" was identified on the basis of three facts relating to the incidental storage of the goods as part of the contract of carriage: proximity of the terminal operation to the sea (i.e., in the port of Montreal); the connection between the terminal operator's activities in the port area and the contract of carriage in question; and the short-term nature of the storage pending final delivery to the consignee. So the connection was evidenced by a combination of the *spatial context* of the relationship between the terrestrial and maritime components of the activity, the *functional relationship* of the terrestrial service provided to the contract of carriage, and the *temporary nature* of the terrestrial service pending completion of the maritime undertaking.

As seen in the discussion on Canadian maritime law above, the Court went on to provide a basis for the application of common law principles of tort and contract, as may have been encompassed by the inherited English maritime law and further developed in Canadian jurisprudence. The Supreme Court thus satisfied the three steps it set out. The *Federal*

---

78   Ibid. at 774.
79   *Monk Corp. v. Island Fertilizers Ltd.*, [1991] 1 S.C.R. 779 at 800.
80   Ibid.

Court Act was a legitimate federal Parliament grant of jurisdiction. Canadian maritime law is a body of federal law that nourishes the statutory grant of jurisdiction. Canadian maritime law is a law of Canada as per section 101 of the *Constitution Act, 1867*. This systematic treatment of each step would set the pattern for future jurisdiction cases.

The "integral connection" analysis was applied again in *Monk Corp. v. Island Fertilizers Ltd.* Monk claimed for demurrage, delivery of excess cargo, and cost of shore-based cranes to discharge the cargo. At the heart of this case was whether the issue could be characterized as a sale of goods, thereby resulting in the application of Prince Edward Island's *Sale of Goods Act*, or a carriage of goods by sea by virtue of *Federal Court Act* section 22(2)(i) and (m). There was the possibility of a multi-contract, as distinct from a single-contract interpretation of the relationship between Monk and Island, but the better view was that there was a single contract with multiple undertakings. L'Heureux-Dubé J., dissenting, saw this as dominantly a sale of goods issue; the majority, with Iacobucci J. delivering the judgment, disagreed.[81] Several of these undertakings were distinctly maritime, such as on the one hand, Monk's purchase of marine insurance and chartering of a self-geared vessel, and on the other the discharge of the cargo by Island, including potential demurrage or dispatch. The Court noted that these are undertakings found in a contract of carriage by sea. The fact that an agreement for purchase and sale accompanied the contract of carriage does not change the nature of the contract of carriage as evidenced by a bill of lading; after all, a contract of sale normally underlies a carriage agreement. This was the general nature of the relationship between the parties. Turning to the specific claims made by Monk, these did not relate to the sale of goods itself, but rather to Island's obligation to discharge that was affected by excess product delivered. The hiring of cranes by Monk to unload the cargo was also maritime as this related to the obligation of Island to discharge the cargo from the ship. Iacobucci J. noted:

> the claims cannot properly be viewed as relating to questions encompassed by sale of goods issues such as capacity of the parties to contract, price, quality and so on... . [Therefore] Island assumed a maritime obligation that is the foundation for the claims by Monk.

---

81 Dissenting, L'Heureux-Dubé J. stated that in distinction "to the generally strict construction of Federal Court jurisdiction, this Court has, in the area of Federal Court jurisdiction over maritime law, pursued an expansive method of interpretation." *Ibid.* at 1815. The majority saw the integral connection to maritime matters stronger in this case than in *Buenos Aires Maru*, above note 37.

Parties can assume maritime obligations governed by maritime law even though they may not formally be parties to a charter-party or even a contract of carriage by sea. What is important for purposes of maritime law jurisdiction is that their claim be integrally connected with maritime matters.

The full extent of the geographical jurisdiction of the Admiralty Court in a torts setting was addressed also in *Whitbread v. Walley*, where the issue concerned tortious liability arising from a boating accident in an area located in inland waters within the province of British Columbia, as distinct from an accident at sea, and the tortfeasor's entitlement to limit liability.[82] In delivering the judgment, La Forest J. noted that "Parliament's jurisdiction over maritime law is territorially co-extensive with its jurisdiction in respect of navigable waterways" and consequently liability was a matter of maritime, not provincial law. In *obiter dicta*, La Forest J. provided a social policy reason why maritime law has to be applied uniformly over all navigable waters. It was a matter of practical necessity that the rules for safety of navigation should be the same over what is one navigational network.

In concluding this discussion of the extent of maritime law jurisdiction, it is worth pondering the extent to which Canadian maritime law jurisdiction has departed from its English origins. The breadth of this jurisdiction in Canada today is wider than it is in England, despite the common starting baseline. Maritime law jurisdiction in England today continues to be more narrowly focused, in L'Heureux-Dubé J.'s words, on claims arising in relation to ships.[83] Another example is stevedoring, which is still dealt with in the United Kingdom under the general common law jurisdiction.[84] Perhaps there are various reasons why maritime law jurisdiction has tended to be more expansive than other areas with which the Federal Court is concerned. The first is the constitutional framework of Canada, which has produced a dialectical relationship between perceptions of competing powers in the constitution over overlapping classes of subjects. Canada has not followed the English path of making maritime law and general private law jurisdiction two hats worn by the same court, except at the provincial level. That relationship between the two bodies of law has to contend with

---

82 Above note 50 at para.26.
83 *Chartwell*, above note 37 at 695.
84 *Administration of Justice Act, 1956* (U.K.), 4 & 5 Eliz. II., c.46, s.1(1)(m) and compared to *Federal Court Act*, above note 32 at s.22(2)(m); as noted by L'Heureux-Dubé J. in *Chartwell*, above note 37 at 710.

striving for uniformity in maritime law on the one hand, and lack of uniformity of provincial private law on the other.

E. PROVINCIAL CONSIDERATIONS

1) Which Provincial Courts May Exercise Maritime Law Jurisdiction?

Both before and after Confederation, provincial courts have enjoyed residual Admiralty jurisdiction concurrently with the Exchequer Court and its successor the Federal Court. The basis of provincial superior court Admiralty jurisdiction is not dependent on historical grounds as much as the jurisdiction of the Federal Court. Constitutionally, the provinces have the power to legislate for the administration of justice within their boundaries, including the establishment, maintenance, and organization of provincial civil and criminal courts.[85] This has been interpreted to empower the provincial legislatures to invest their superior courts with full jurisdiction to administer provincial, federal, and constitutional law as an expression of the unitary nature of the court system in Canada.[86]

Concurrent Admiralty jurisdiction of the superior courts in the provinces was affirmed early in *Shipman v. Phinn*, which concerned an action for damages resulting from a collision on inland waters, and where it was held that the Ontario Supreme Court had concurrent Admiralty jurisdiction with the Exchequer Court.[87] *Cull v. Rose*, which held that Newfoundland's Supreme Court had lost its Admiralty jurisdiction as a result of the *Terms of Union*, was distinguished by *Pembina* on the basis that the collision may have been outside the territorial sea or jurisdictional limits of a common law court;[88] however, the residual Admiralty jurisdiction of the provincial court continued.

There was a view until the late 1970s that, while Admiralty jurisdiction was enjoyed by provincial superior courts, this was not the case with

---

85 *Constitution Act, 1867*, above note 1, s.92(14).
86 *Pembina*, above note 26 at 217, using Hogg and Laskin as support.
87 Above note 26; see also *Tropwood*, above note 62 at 160, wherein it was stated that it was Parliament's will to establish the Federal Court to administer maritime law concurrently with provincial superior courts; *Bow Valley Husky (Bermuda) Ltd. v. Saint John Shipbuilding Ltd.* (1992), 97 Nfld. & P.E.I.R. 217 (Nfld. C.A.) [*Bow Valley*]; reaffirmed in *Ordon Estate v. Grail*, above note 2 at para.43.
88 *Cull v. Rose*, above note 20; *Pembina*, above note 26 at 21.

inferior courts. This was perhaps best illustrated in the now overruled decision of the Ontario Court of Appeal in *Hertikainen v. Kane* in considering the jurisdiction of the County Court of Ontario.[89] Contrary and more correct views in support of inferior courts' Admiralty jurisdiction were put forward by the B.C. Court of Appeal in *Balfour Guthrie (Canada) Ltd. v. Far Eastern Steamship Co.* in relation to the County Court of Vancouver,[90] and by the Quebec Court of Appeal in *General Traders v. Saguenay Shipping* with respect to the Quebec Provincial Court.[91]

Whatever doubt may have existed was removed by the Supreme Court of Canada in *Ontario (A.G.) v. Pembina Exploration Canada*, which concerned a fishing vessel that damaged its net in provincial inland waters as a result of entanglement with an unmarked gas well owned by Pembina. The constitutional questions that arose were whether the Small Claims Courts have jurisdiction pursuant to section 93 of the *Constitution Act, 1867*, and whether section 55 of the *Small Claims Courts Act* of Ontario,[92] granting that jurisdiction, conflicted with section 22 of the *Federal Court Act* and was consequently inoperative. The short question was, Could a province grant maritime law jurisdiction to a small claims court? The short answer was and is affirmative, because in the Canadian court system "judicial jurisdiction is not tied to provincial legislative jurisdiction." There is nothing in the *Federal Court Act* that confines Admiralty jurisdiction to the superior courts. Thus, the provinces — which are empowered by section 92(14) of the *Constitution Act, 1867*, to make laws for the administration of justice in the provinces — could indeed empower inferior courts with the authority to apply federal law, unless otherwise expressly stated in legislation of the federal Parliament.

Pembina is important for various reasons. It is clear that the Admiralty jurisdiction of the inferior courts is dependent on its conferment by provincial legislatures, whether expressly so or as part of a general grant of jurisdiction that would include other common law actions. The discussion focused on the jurisdiction of inferior courts over *in personam* actions. It is unclear whether this could extend to *in rem*

---

89 Held that county courts did not have admiralty jurisdiction because the province did not have the constitutional authority to confer such jurisdiction, (1975), 10 O.R. (2d) 716 (*sub nom. Heath v. Kane*), overruled by *Pembina*, ibid.
90 (1977), 82 D.L.R. (3d) 414.
91 [1983] C.A. 536.
92 R.S.O. 1980, c.476, s.55(a) provides that county courts have jurisdiction to entertain "*any action* where the amount claimed does not exceed $1,000 exclusive of interest" (emphasis added).

actions as long as they are within inferior court monetary limits: *Pembina* did not address this point directly. Ontario's *Small Claims Courts Act* grants jurisdiction over "any action." In any case, it would not be possible to proceed *in rem* at the provincial level unless provincial Rules of Court provide for such a procedure, such as those for the B.C. Supreme Court.[93] Rules of Court designate the procedure applicable, which, in an *in rem* action, starts with the arrest of the ship.

2) Extent of Concurrency by Provincial Courts

As seen earlier, Admiralty jurisdiction is shared between the Federal Court and provincial courts unless any aspect of that jurisdiction has been otherwise enjoyed. One statute, which provides some exclusivity of jurisdiction in favour of the Federal Court, is the *Canada Shipping Act*. There has now been a general re-organization of this Act, resulting in the formulation of the *Canada Shipping Act, 2001* and the *Marine Liability Act*. When the *Canada Shipping Act, 2001*, becomes fully operational there will be few areas left to the exclusive jurisdiction of the Federal Court. Prior to the *Canada Shipping Act, 2001*, the Admiralty Court was defined as the Federal Court, and where the language expressly provided, its jurisdiction over specific issues was exclusive. Thus, claims for wages of seamen in any amount, salvage and wreck, and the constitution and distribution of a limitation fund could be brought only before the Federal Court.[94] The *Canada Shipping Act, 2001*, has levelled the playing field in relation to wages, salvage, and wreck by removing the definition of Admiralty Court and thereby opening to provincial court jurisdiction those areas formerly exclusively assigned to the Federal Court. Salvage and wreck are open to "any court having jurisdiction in civil matters."[95] In the case of shares in Canadian vessels, liens of the master and crew, and claims for stevedoring services, the *Canada Shipping Act, 2001*, allows an action *in rem* in any court of competent jurisdiction whose rules provide *in rem* procedure.[96]

There are still specific issues that remain the exclusive domain of the Federal Court, most of which are found in the *Marine Liability Act*.[97] This Act defines the Admiralty Court as the Federal Court. Fol-

---

93 B.C. Reg. 221/90, r.55 (B.C. Supreme Court Rules).
94 *Canada Shipping Act*, S.C. 1998, c.6, ss.209(2), 453, and 580(1), as noted in *Ordon Estate v. Grail*, above note 2 at para.60 (S.C.C.).
95 Above note 51, s.159.
96 *Ibid.*, ss.75, 86(3), and 251(1), respectively.
97 Above note 54.

lowing *Ordon Estate v. Grail*, mere reference to the Admiralty Court in a statute should not be construed, *per se*, as an exclusive grant of jurisdiction to the Federal Court which, as a statutory creation, has no jurisdiction other than what is assigned by statute. Parliament has to "use express statutory language where it intends to assign jurisdiction to the Federal Court."[98] Therefore, the mere reference to the Admiralty Court formerly in the *Canada Shipping Act*, section 646 provisions on fatal accidents claims, in contrast to section 580(1) (i.e., constitution and distribution of a limitation fund), did not abrogate the inherent jurisdiction of the provincial superior courts over maritime fatal accident claims.[99] Indeed the Supreme Court of Canada, citing established case law, stated that "it has long been held that the provincial superior courts have jurisdiction over matters involving maritime law, including negligence actions resulting from collisions or other accidents involving vessels on inland waters."[100]

The *Marine Liability Act*, as well as the *Canada Shipping Act, 2001*, contain several references to the Admiralty Court or Federal Court. However, the only unequivocal situation where the Federal Court, *qua* Admiralty Court, is assigned exclusive jurisdiction is in section 32 of the *Marine Liability Act* with respect to the constitution and distribution of a limitation fund under Articles 11 to 13 of the *Convention on Limitation of Liability for Maritime Claims, 1976*, as amended (formerly s.580(1) in the *Canada Shipping Act*). The remaining provisions in both statutes where the Admiralty Court or Federal Court are specifically mentioned should be read as instances where a statutory court is being conferred jurisdiction without diminishing the authority of provincial courts to administer federal law within the Canadian system.[101]

3) Provincial Law in a Maritime Law Setting

In *Buenos Aires Maru* the Supreme Court of Canada considered the question as to whether when, "a case is in 'pith and substance' within the court's statutory jurisdiction, the Federal Court may apply provin-

---

98 *Ordon Estate v. Grail*, above note 2 at para.46.
99 *Ibid.* at para.57.
100 *Ibid.* at para.47.
101 Perhaps the only other section where it might be inferred that Parliament intended to confer jurisdiction on the Federal Court only is in the *Marine Liability Act*, above note 54 at s.87(2), which creates a right of appeal to the Admiralty Court from a decision of the administrator of the Ship-Source Oil Pollution Fund. The appeal in question does not appear to be a general right of appeal, but rather an appeal to this particular court.

cial law incidentally necessary to resolve the issues presented by the parties."[102] The Court did not address this matter further. In practice, and prior to *Ordon Estate v. Grail*, maritime law saw the application of provincial law in a variety of areas such as limitation periods, fatal accidents, liens and mortgages, occupiers' liability, insurance, sale of goods and bulk sales, and pollution.[103]

In two subsequent decisions, both in a torts context, the Supreme Court has taken a more definitive view on the limits of the application of provincial law. The first of these cases was *Bow Valley Husky (Bermuda) v. St. John Shipbuilding* where McLachlin J. (as she then was) rejected the application of provincial law to maritime torts, as this was seen as undercutting the uniformity of Canadian maritime law. The central issue of the potential applicability of provincial law in this context seems to depend on whether there is federal law to be applied. In *Bow Valley* the question in the eyes of the Court was "not whether there is federal maritime law on the issue, but what that law decrees."[104] Just over two decades earlier the same court in *Stein v. The Kathy K.* did indeed apply provincial tort law![105] The question was therefore raised as to whether provincial law could be applied at all in a maritime setting.

Ordon Estate v. Grail, through Iacobucci and Major JJ., provided an important test to apply in relation to the applicability or otherwise of provincial law. In this regard the question before the Court was "whether a validly enacted provincial statute of general application may be applied to deal with incidental aspects of a maritime negligence claim that is otherwise governed entirely by federal law."[106] The case

---

102 *Buenos Aires Maru*, above note 37 at 781. McIntyre J. referred to two cases to provide some support for this. *Kellog Co. v. Kellog*, [1941] S.C.R. 242 [*Kellog*], and *McNamara*, above note 60. *Kellog* seems to support this contention in the context of an employment contract and a dispute over patent rights, whereas in *McNamara* Laskin CJ. had suggested this as a possibility in a non-maritime context.
103 C.J. Giaschi, "The Constitutional Implications of *Ordon v. Grail* and the Expanding Definition of Canadian Maritime Law." Unpub. lecture delivered to Dalhousie Law School, Oct. 2000.
104 *Bow Valley*, above note 87 at para.89.
105 [1976] 2 S.C.R. 802.
106 *Ordon Estate v. Grail*, above note 2 at para.66. Further clarification of the question was advanced as follows: "This Court's recent maritime law jurisprudence makes clear that Canadian maritime law is a body of federal law, uniform across the country, within which there is no room for the application of provincial statutes. What the case law does not explicitly address, however, is whether and when it is contrary to the division of powers as set out in the *Constitution Act, 1867*, for provincial statutes of general application to apply on their own terms as provincial law within a factual context which is otherwise governed by federal maritime law" (*ibid.* at para.68).

concerned five maritime accident claims resulting in death or injury, four of which were appealed and cross-appealed to the Supreme Court. The issue underlying this question was the constitutional applicability or inapplicability of five provincial acts in Ontario in a boating accident context.[107] Case law until 1976 had indicated that in the absence of federal legislation, provincial legislation could be applied in an incidental manner,[108] but the Court noted that it had reoriented its jurisprudence since *Buenos Aires Maru*, followed by *Chartwell*, *Whitbread*, *Monk*, *Bow Valley*, and *Porto Seguro*. In reality, however, these cases did not fully rule out the potential application of provincial law in appropriate circumstances. In *Ordon Estate v. Grail*, after summarizing basic principles of Canadian maritime law, the Court felt it useful to assemble these principles and synthesize them into a four-step test, described below, for situations where a provincial statute is sought to be applied in a maritime torts context.

a) Step One: Identifying the Matter at Issue

Logically, the first step is to assess the factual scenario to see whether it should be characterized as maritime so as to fall within the exclusive federal legislative competence over navigation and shipping, or falling within provincial competence over property and civil rights or other matters exclusively assigned to the provinces. The maritime characterization has to satisfy the integral connection test based on the facts.[109]

b) Step Two: Reviewing Maritime Law Sources

Once the maritime characterization is in place, the next step is to identify applicable federal maritime law. While litigants may advance claims on the basis of principles of provincial law, the court will seek

---

107 *Family Law Act*, R.S.O. 1990, c.F-3; *An Act Respecting Compensation to the Families of Persons Killed by Accident, and in Duels*, C.S.C. 1859, c.78; *Trustee Act*, R.S.O. 1990, c.T-23; *Negligence Act*, R.S.O. 1990, c.N-1; and *Occupiers' Liability Act*, R.S.O. 1990, c.O-2.

108 *Canadian National Steamships v. Watson*, [1939] S.C.R. 11, [1939] 1 D.L.R. 273 [*Canadian National*]. B.C. law governing the responsibility of masters for the acts of their servants was applied to shipowners. In *Stein v. Kathy K. (The)*, above note 105, division of fault according to the negligence law of British Columbia was applied to an accident that occurred within the inland waters of the province. As a result of *Ordon Estate v. Grail*, *Canadian National* is no longer good law, and *Stein v. Kathy K (The)*, has lost its precedential value in relation to the applicability of the B.C. *Contributory Negligence Act*, R.S.B.C. 1960, c.74, s.2, *Ordon Estate v. Grail*, above note 2.

109 *Ordon Estate v. Grail*, above note 2 at para.73.

counterpart principles from the sources of Canadian maritime law discussed above. Litigants are urged to base their claims on Canadian maritime law. At the same time, the courts are strongly discouraged from undertaking a constitutional analysis of the applicability of provincial law before they have fully determined applicable federal law.[110]

c) Step Three: Considering the Possibility of Reform

In theory, if step two is satisfied to the extent that there is federal law applicable, there would be no need to proceed further. Should Canadian maritime law be found not to contain counterpart principles, however, courts are encouraged to undertake pre-constitutional analysis to develop the non-statutory maritime law as an exercise of the process of judicial reform established by the Supreme Court of Canada.[111] In effect, reliance on *Stein v. The Kathy K* and other previous decisions in support of the application of provincial legislation would be rendered unnecessary since, even if there is a federal statutory gap, courts are encouraged to fill that gap by finding and applying federal common law in an incremental manner before embarking on a constitutional analysis. The Supreme Court was very careful to make it clear that it is not substituting itself for the federal legislator; rather, it ensured that the role of the courts is restricted to ensuring that the common law is developed in response to social change while at the same time keeping in mind Canada's international obligations and the interests of uniformity among maritime law jurisdictions internationally.[112]

d) Step Four: Constitutional Analysis

Step four is a step of last and constitutional resort after the non-constitutional treatment in the first three steps does not result in the finding of federal law. In the assessment of provincial law, the doctrine of interjurisdictional immunity would be applied by the court, whereby in essence legislation may be read down so as not to trench on the core of a class of subject assigned to one level of government or another. Each head of federal legislative power under the *Constitution Act, 1867*, possesses "a basic, minimum, and unassailable content, which the provinces are not permitted to regulate indirectly through valid laws of general application" and, consequently, "an essential core which the

---

110 *Ibid.* at para.74.
111 More specifically, the Court referred to the following decisions to guide judicial reform: *Watkins v. Olafson*, [1989] 2 S.C.R. 750, 61 D.L.R. (4th) 577; *R. v. Salituro*, [1991] 3 S.C.R. 654; *Bow Valley*, above note 87.
112 *Ordon Estate v. Grail*, above note 2 at para.76.

provinces are not permitted to regulate indirectly."[113] The Court concluded that, accordingly, "it is constitutionally impermissible for the application of a provincial statute to have the effect of supplementing existing rules of federal maritime negligence law in such a manner that the provincial law effectively *alters* rules within the exclusive competence of Parliament or the courts to alter" (emphasis added).[114] In the context of maritime torts this is particularly important as there is an applicable and exclusively maritime standard of behaviour in the form of good seamanship.

While set out in a maritime torts context, this four-step test helps define the wider relationship between federal maritime law and provincial law.[115] The test requires maritime characterization of the facts on the basis of exclusivity, followed by a checklist of applicable federal law and, failing this, an invitation to the courts to develop non-statutory law, before considering the central question posed, that is, whether provincial law can be applied. Therefore, going back to *Buenos Aires Maru* on whether "a case is in 'pith and substance' within the court's statutory jurisdiction, the Federal Court may apply provincial law incidentally necessary to resolve the issues presented by the parties,"[116] it will be necessary to show that the provincial law concerned does not trench on a federal head of power. The provincial statutes concerned in *Ordon Estate v. Grail* were clearly problematic because they did have the potential effect of altering federal law. Hypothetically, it is still conceivable that a maritime law case might have multi-issue elements in dispute between the litigants, not all of which are necessarily maritime, in which case the dominant application of maritime law could be accompanied by a subsidiary application of provincial law. Despite the stringent test, the Court did leave the door slightly ajar for the application of provincial law and mentioned by way of example statutes setting

---

113 *Ibid.* at para. 80 and relying on *Bell Canada v. Quebec*, [1988] 1 S.C.R. 749, 51 D.L.R. (4th) 161.
114 *Ordon Estate v. Grail*, above note 2 at para.85.
115 "The constitutional analysis in the present case is necessarily specifically focussed upon the issue of maritime negligence law. Similar principles are very likely applicable in relation to the applicability of provincial statutes in other maritime law contexts, although we do not consider it appropriate at this time, in the absence of a factual backdrop plainly raising the issue, to rule on the broader applicability of the test articulated here beyond maritime negligence context": *Ordon Estate v. Grail, ibid.* at para.86.
116 Above at note 102.

rules of court and possibly taxation;[117] however, there will be exceptionally few instances in which provincial law could ever apply to the core of a maritime law case.

FURTHER READINGS

BRÄEN, A., "La juridiction en Amirauté de la Cour fédérale du Canada" (1981) 41 Rev. de Bar. 367.

——, "Cour fédérale; compétence en amirauté" (1981) 59 Can. Bar Rev. 579.

——, "La compétence maritime du Parlement canadien et ses conséquences sur l'application du Code Civil" (1986) 31 McGill L.J. 369.

——, *Le droit maritime au Québec* (Montréal: Wilson & Lafleur, 1992).

GLENN, P., "ITO — International Terminal Operators Ltd. v. Miida Electronics Inc.," Case Review (1987) 66 Can. Bar Rev. 360.

HUGHES, R.T., *2003 Annotated Federal Court Act and Rules* (Markham, ON: LexisNexis Butterworths, 2003).

KERR, R.W., "Constitutional Limitations on the Admiralty Jurisdiction of the Federal Court" (1979) 5 Dal. L.J. 568.

MAYERS, E.C., *Admiralty Law and Practice in Canada* (Toronto: Carswell, 1916).

STONE, A.J., "The Admiralty Court in Colonial Nova Scotia" (1994) Dal. L.J. 363.

——, "Canada's Admiralty Court in the Twentieth Century" (2002) 47 McGill L.J. 511.

TETLEY, W., "The Buenos Aires Maru — Has the Whole Nature of Canadian Maritime Law Been Changed?" (1988) 10 Sup. Ct. L.Rev. 399.

---

117 "At the same time, we do not wish to be understood as stating that no provincial law of general application will ever be applicable in any maritime context, whether involving maritime negligence law or not": *Ordon Estate v. Grail*, above note 2 at para.86.

———, "A Definition of Canadian Maritime Law" (1996) 30 U.B.C. L.Rev. 137.

TREMBLAY G., "L'application du droit provincial en matière maritime après l'affaire *Succession Ordon*" (1999) 59 Rev. du Bar. 679.

CHAPTER 4

THE OWNERSHIP AND REGISTRATION OF SHIPS

A. INTRODUCTION

This chapter discusses the ownership and registration of ships. It outlines the steps taken by a potential owner of a ship from the time he or she decides to build, through registration, to the time of mortgage and sale of a ship. Before embarking on a discussion of ownership and registration, it is necessary to understand what the legal notion of "ship" entails in Canadian maritime law. There are various other generic concepts, such as vessel, craft, boat, and so on, that are frequently used, and sometimes interchangeably. In Chapter 2, a variety of ships in commercial, government, and recreational service were described. However, not every shape and form of vessel qualifies as a "ship" and, because there are far-reaching legal consequences on such a designation, it is important to consider what qualifies as a "ship," for what purpose and with what consequences. Characterizing a particular structure as a "ship," or otherwise, may engage or disengage Admiralty jurisdiction. Indeed, it may give rise to a constitutional issue in terms of what head of power is being invoked when a particular structure is considered a ship or simply real property, that is, whether it is a federal (i.e., navigation and shipping) or provincial (i.e., property and civil rights) matter. The ship has a particular legal personality as maritime property and can be the subject of legal proceedings. It can cause harm to other ships or stationary objects (i.e., "damage done by ship"). The owner of a ship is entitled to limitation of liability, whether in general liability, carriage of goods, or pollution liability. Further, qualifying not simply as a "ship" but also as a particular type of ship may engage technical, safety, and environmental requirements. It is therefore useful, before proceeding with the discussion on ownership and registration, to consider how a ship is defined in Canadian maritime law and the difficulties that may be encountered.

There are different ways of acquiring ownership over a ship, such as through the construction of a new ship, or through a purchase and sale agreement, capture, inheritance, bankruptcy, or judicial sale (e.g., as a result of an action *in rem*) of an existing ship. The discussion in this chapter focuses on construction and purchase and sale agreements. Insofar as judicial sale is concerned, this subject is left for Chapter 6 and Chapter 19. The acquisition of a ship by way of capture by the Crown or by inheritance is omitted, as these have become rather unusual in modern shipping practice. Acquisition as a result of bankruptcy proceedings is more appropriately dealt with in a commercial law textbook. Canada has its own distinguishing rules on the ownership and registration of ships and the statutory requirements are set out in the current version of the *Canada Shipping Act* (Part 1: Registration, Listing, Recording and Licensing).[1] Note that important modifications are to be introduced when the *Canada Shipping Act, 2001* (Part 2: Registration, Listing and Recording)[2] is brought into force and regulations are enacted. At the time of writing, very few sections of the new Act are in force. This chapter refers to pertinent sections in both acts and regulations under the current Act.

Numerous ships in Canadian beneficial ownership are not registered in the Canadian Register of Ships. Shipping is essentially an international business and there are many states that do not maintain beneficially owned tonnage under their flag. Others compete to attract foreign tonnage. In addition to the discussion on the Canadian register, it will be necessary to consider the practice of flags of convenience and states that maintain dual registers. This discussion will be useful to understand what lures Canadian shipowners to other flags. The Canadian register is a traditional registry in many ways. There are many important legal issues, often going beyond Canadian maritime law, that need to be weighed in advising on registration under a foreign flag.

---

1   *Canada Shipping Act*, R.S.C. 1985, c.S-9.
2   *Canada Shipping Act, 2001*, S.C. 2001, c.26.

B. A SHIP AND ITS OWNERSHIP

1) What is a Ship?

a) General Definitions

In the following discussion, the generic term "vessel" will be used to capture every possible variety of ship, keeping in mind that "vessel" also has a legal definition. Not every vessel in an everyday use of the term is a "ship" in Canadian maritime law. It is unfortunate that there is no one general definition of "ship" across Canadian legislation. Federal maritime statutes and regulations use many definitions of "ship" and "vessel," mostly for two purposes: definitions for the application of general maritime statutes, such as the *Canada Shipping Act*, *Canada Shipping Act, 2001*, *Federal Court Act*, and *Marine Liability Act*, unless otherwise indicated; and modified or specialized definitions for the purposes of certain parts of the *Canada Shipping Act*, *Marine Liability Act*, and other federal statutes. In examining each definition, care must be exercised to read it against the backdrop of a statutory context or regulatory environment.

In the *Canada Shipping Act*, the following definitions of "ship" and "vessel" are currently provided:

> "ship," except in Parts II, XV and XVI, includes:
> (a) any description of vessel used in navigation and not propelled by oars, and
> (b) for the purpose of Part I and sections 574 to 581, any description of lighter, barge or like vessel used in navigation in Canada however propelled;
>
> "vessel" includes any ship or boat or any other description of vessel used or designed to be used in navigation.[3]

The major difference between the two definitions is that a "ship" includes any description of a vessel in navigational use, and excludes vessels that are propelled by oars. Therefore, neither a rowing boat nor a skiff is a ship, but each is conceivably a vessel.[4] The distinction has practical significance; for example, whereas only ships may be registered, and small vessels may be licensed, the *Collision Regulations* apply to all vessels. Also of note is the fact that the general definition of

---

3 *Canada Shipping Act*, above note 1, s.2.
4 *Edwards v. Quickenden and Forester*, [1939] P. 261.

"ship" does not apply to Part II Certification of Masters and Seamen,[5] Part XV Pollution Prevention and Response, and Part XVI Civil Liability and Compensation for Pollution.[6]

There will be a significant change when section 2 of the *Canada Shipping Act, 2001*, on definitions is brought into force. It will drop the definition of "ship" altogether and use a streamlined and more expansive definition of "vessel" for general application in the Act. The new definition of "vessel" is as follows:

> "vessel" means a boat, ship or craft designed, used or capable of being used solely or partly for navigation in, on, through or immediately above water, without regard to method or lack of propulsion, and includes such a vessel that is under construction. It does not include a floating object of a prescribed class.[7]

The new definition — by including boat and craft, partial navigational use, capability of navigation, navigation through and above water, and vessel under construction, while disregarding mode of propulsion — has fused together elements that appeared in separate definitions as well as adding new elements. The effect is a more expansive definition of "vessel," clearly a definition that intends to include, more than exclude. Exclusions apply only in relation to floating objects of a prescribed class. While the purpose is to simplify, it remains to be seen how this definition will relate to definitions in other statutes. The *Federal Court Act* defines "ship," but not "vessel." This definition has recently been consequentially amended by the *Marine Liability Act* to read as follows:

> "ship" means any vessel or craft designed, used or capable of being used solely or partly for navigation, without regard to method or lack of propulsion, and includes:
> (a) a ship in the process of construction from the time that it is capable of floating, and
> (b) a ship that has been stranded, wrecked or sunk and any part of a ship that has broken up.[8]

---

5   For the purposes of Part II there is a separate definition of "ship" that excludes pleasure craft less than twenty meters long and vessels, boats, and crafts propelled by oars or paddles. *Canada Shipping Act*, above note 1, s.109(1).
6   In Parts XV and XVI "ship" is defined to include "any description of vessel or craft designed, used or capable of being used solely or partly for navigation, without regard to method or lack of propulsion" (*ibid.*, ss.654 and 673). This definition is also used in the *Pilotage Act*, R.S.C. 1985, c.P-14, s.2.
7   *Canada Shipping Act, 2001*, above note 2, s.2.
8   *Federal Court Act*, R.S.C. 1985, c.F-7, s.2(1), as am. by *Marine Liability Act*, S.C. 2001, c.6, s.115.

The text is identical to the definition in the *Marine Liability Act* for the purposes of limitation of liability for maritime claims and liability and compensation for marine pollution.[9] This definition is important, *inter alia*, for the purposes of the heads of jurisdiction in the *Federal Court Act*, section 22(2) — which, together with section 43, is creative of various liens on the ship — and Federal Court procedure, especially the arrest and release of a ship, and the action *in rem*. The reference to any vessel or craft, both of which are considered very broad terms, encompasses anything used on or in the water, so long as there is at least partial navigational use.[10] Indeed, with reference to an earlier version of this definition, it has been held that "the definition of 'ship' in the *Federal Court Act* is not exclusive but inclusive. It thus enlarges the term."[11] Also, paragraph (b) adds another dimension to the definition that is not captured by the definitions in either the *Canada Shipping Act* or *Canada Shipping Act, 2001*. In effect, "ship" may include a vessel that is no longer in navigational use and includes part of a ship! This is not as illogical as it might sound at first: a ship in distress or a ship or part of a ship that has been lost, may still be subject to the regime of salvage and wreck.

There are other statutory definitions of "ship" but it is not necessary to consider all of these for the purposes of this chapter.[12] Rather, it is useful to examine how Canadian case law has considered a wide variety of vessels to determine whether they should be, or continue to be, considered as ships or not, or only in certain situations. The leading Canadian case defining "ship," in a non-exhaustive manner,[13] is *Canada v. Saint John Shipbuilding & Dry Dock Co.*, wherein the criteria

---

9 *Marine Liability Act*, ibid., ss.25(1) and 47.
10 *Cyber Sea Technologies Inc. v. Underwater Harvester Remotely Operated Vehicle* (2002), [2003] 1 F.C. 569 [*Cyber Sea Technologies*].
11 *Canada v. Saint John Shipbuilding and Dry Dock Co.* (1981), 43 N.R. 15 (F.C.A.) [*Canada v. Saint John Shipbuilding*]. At the time of the judgment, the Federal Court definition of "ship" included "any description of vessel, boat or craft used or capable of being used solely or partly for marine navigation without regard to method or lack of propulsion" (*Federal Court Act*, R.S.C. 1985, (2d Supp.), c.10, s.2, as am. by *Maritime Code*, S.C. 1977–78, c.41, s.4). Before the 1978 amendment, "ship" included "any description of vessel or boat used or designed for use in navigation without regard to method or lack of propulsion" (*Federal Court Act*, S.C. 1971, c.1, s.2).
12 E.g., *Transportation of Dangerous Goods Act*, 1992, S.C. 1992, c.34, s.2, the definition of "ship" specifies marine navigation. The *Marine Liability Act* contains a separate definition of "ship" for the purposes of liability for passenger carriage, above note 8, s.36(1).
13 *Cyber Sea Technologies*, above note 10.

that were applied to determine whether a crane barge was a ship were the following: it was built for use on water; it was capable of being moved from place to place, and was in fact so moved from time to time by tugs or motor boats; it was capable of carrying cargo, and had done so from time to time (e.g., loaded engine equipment and ships); and it was capable of carrying people, and had to do so to enable the crew to carry out its duties (i.e., operate the crane). The vessel was neither self-propelled, nor capable of navigation by itself, but it was "built to do something on water, requiring movement from place to place."[14] In deciding that the crane barge was a ship, the Federal Court of Appeal seems to have decided differently from similar English case law.[15]

In summary, for a vessel to qualify as a ship in Canada, the vessel must have a design that permits the performance of a maritime function and have the capability of being navigated, even if this occurs with the assistance of another vessel.

b) Vessels Not Designed for Navigation

Vessels that are not designed for navigation or that are incapable of navigation have generally not been considered to be ships. Perhaps a more appropriate description of these vessels is that they are structures constructed to perform or facilitate a particular maritime service but not navigation. A harbour dredge is one example.[16] The Burrard Yarrows, a floating drydock, was considered in *R. v. The Star Luzon*, with reference to its characteristics and function.[17] The vessel resembled a rectangular barge with high sidewalls and open ends. It was built in Japan and was towed to North Vancouver, where it was moored in a manner that allowed it to be raised and lowered while remaining centred. It had navigation lights when it was towed from Japan, but these were removed once moored. Its function was to raise ships for repair. It could be moved, but only after extensive work to remove it from its moorage. It could not be used for navigation and, when moved, was akin to cargo — possibly as machinery — at best. Even so, the owners had it registered as a ship under the *Canada Shipping Act*. However, the court found that, despite its towage from Japan, the floating drydock was not used

---

14 *Canada v. Saint John Shipbuilding*, above note 11.
15 *Merchant's Marine Insurance Ltd. v. North of England Protection and Indemnity Association* (1926), 25 Ll. L.R. 446, which concerned a crane placed on a pontoon, which could be moved from place to place. The English court held that the movement was the exception, rather than the rule. This decision was upheld on appeal, with the Court of Appeal further emphasizing function.
16 *Nithsdale (The)* (1879), 15 C.L.J. 268.
17 *R. v. Star Luzon (The)*, [1984] 1 W.W.R. 527 (B.C.S.C.).

for navigation. It was probably a vessel, at least during towage, but was not a ship for the purposes of the *Oil Pollution Prevention Regulations*. Similarly, although a different type of structure altogether, a raft of lumber (i.e., log boom) *per se* or when in tow is not a ship.[18]

c) **Vessels Designed for Navigation, But Lacking Own Propulsion**
There are vessels that are incapable of navigation on their own, but which are not necessarily disqualified from consideration as ships. It is important that such vessels must have been designed to be able to undertake some form of movement, even without their own means of propulsion. In *Falconbridge Nickel Mines Ltd. v. Chimo Shipping Ltd.*, a contract of carriage was performed in part by barges, which were used to lighter cargo from ship to shore. They were considered to be ships.[19]

A floating crane has also been treated as a ship in *Canada v. Saint John Shipbuilding*. It is significant that, while the vessel lacked its own means of propulsion and ability to navigate on its own, it could carry a crew and cargo.[20]

d) **Offshore Installations and Structures**
There is a wide diversity of vessels, including what might be more appropriately termed "installations" and "structures," used for offshore oil and gas drilling and production. Each of them has caused considerable discussion as to whether it should be considered as a ship. Drilling rigs and drillships are cases in point. Canadian statutory and subsidiary legislation does not specifically designate these as ships; for instance, the *Canada Oil and Gas Installations Regulations* define various types of installations (e.g., diving installation, drilling installation, production installation, and accommodation installation), their dependent systems (e.g., diving system and personnel accommodation), a floating platform, a mobile offshore platform, and an offshore loading system.[21] None of them is specifically defined as a ship, although each may constitute or include the utilization of vessels. A "drilling unit" is particularly relevant for this discussion, as it means "drillship, submersible, semi-submersible, barge, jack-up, or other vessel that is used in a

---

18 *Pigeon River Lumber Co. v. Mooring* (1909), 13 O.W.R. 190, aff'd 14 O.W.R. 639; *McLeod v. Minnesota Pulp & Paper Co.*, [1955] Ex. C.R. 344.
19 *R. v. Gulf of Aladdin* (1977), 34 C.C.C. (2d) 460; *Falconbridge Nickel Mines Ltd. v. Chimo Shipping Ltd.*, [1969] 2 Ex. C.R. 261, aff'd (1973) 37 D.L.R. (3d) 545 (S.C.C.).
20 *Canada v. Saint John Shipbuilding*, above note 11.
21 S.O.R./96-118, s.2(1).

drilling program and is fitted with a drilling rig, and includes other facilities related to drilling and marine activities that are installed on a vessel or platform."[22] At a minimum, however, they are all vessels and they have different designs and navigational capabilities. The jack-up rig is towed in and out of a location and, when stationary, the legs are jacked down to the seabed for stability. The semi-submersible, a floating structure, is also towed to and anchored at the drilling site. Other vessels include the tension leg platform, another floating structure anchored at the drilling site. Some vessels, such as rigs and drillships, employ dynamic positioning. Dynamic positioning technology has the effect of "virtual" anchoring of the installation to a precise location. For instance, the "JOIDES Resolution" is a drillship equipped with a computer-controlled dynamic positioning system that controls twelve thrusters and two main shafts, thereby enabling it to maintain the ship over a specific location while drilling into water depths down to 27,000 feet (8230 m).[23] The principal purpose of these installations is clearly drilling and production, not navigation, but they all require movement from one place to another and are designed to do this. In the case of dynamically positioned vessels, the drilling and the navigation are contemporaneous. Perhaps more of a challenge in treating such units as vessels is the recent technology of gravity-based structures, such as the one operating on the Hibernia oil field off the Newfoundland shore. This particular structure was designed for one movement (i.e., to the location of emplacement), and then construction of the installation was continued onsite.[24] In terms of movement, perhaps its closer next of kin is more an artificial island than an oil rig!

Offshore installations are registered like ships, are classed, can be mortgaged, require marine insurance — both for hulls and protection and indemnity — engage crews that frequently include seamen as part of the complement, are subject to regulatory inspections, and have to comply with many international maritime conventions.[25]

Dome Petroleum v. Hunt International Petroleum Co., an early decision that considered in *obiter* whether a drillship is a ship, should be considered *passé*. The case was decided on the breach of the drilling contract, which gave rise to a claim not falling under a head of juris-

---

22 Ibid.
23 "Ocean Drilling Program," online at <http://www.oceandrilling.org/ODP/ODPship.htm>.
24 "Hibernia Construction," online at: <http://www.hibernia.ca/html/about_hibernia/construction.html>.
25 W.W. Spicer, *Canadian Maritime Law and the Offshore* (Calgary: Canadian Institute of Resources Law, 1984) at 16.

diction in section 22(2) of the *Federal Court Act*. The court considered, however — most unhelpfully, and probably unnecessarily — whether a drilling system (i.e., a drilling rig mounted on a ship) constituted a ship. The court was of the view that the towing of the drillship to the drilling site was incidental to the principal activity and purpose of the ship, that is, to drill. That a vessel should be considered a ship solely on the basis of its principal function has been criticized as unhelpful.[26] Had the dispute concerned the charter of the drill ship, it could have conceivably been decided differently.

In any event, subsequent cases did not follow this line of thinking. Indeed, in *Seafarers' International Union of Canada v. Crosbie Offshore Services Ltd.*, a judicial review application, the court had no difficulty in stating that rigs are also ships. The rigs concerned were dynamically positioned vessels, had their own means of propulsion, but were towed to their drilling location. In deep water the rigs were anchored with the assistance of supply vessels.[27] Similarly at the Court of Appeal stage of *Bow Valley Husky (Bermuda) Ltd. v. Saint John Shipbuilding Ltd.*, Cam-eron J.A. considered Bow Drill III to be not only a drilling platform but also a navigable vessel, "capable of self-propulsion; even when drilling, is vulnerable to the perils of the sea; is not attached permanently to the ocean floor and, can travel world wide to drill for oil."[28] Basically, many of the activities of oil rigs are considered maritime in nature in a modern navigation and shipping context. The Supreme Court of Canada cited these views approvingly and further held that "alternatively, even if the rig is not a navigable vessel, the tort claim arising from the fire would still be a maritime matter since the main purpose of the Bow Drill III was activity in navigable waters."[29]

e) Combination of Vessels

In some instances, a combination of vessels may be considered as a single vessel or ship for certain purposes. Therefore, for the purposes of

---

26 *Dome Petroleum v. Hunt International Petroleum Co.*, [1978] 1 F.C. 11. See also *Canadian Maritime Law and the Offshore*, ibid. at 17; W.W. Spicer, "Applications of Maritime Law to Offshore Drilling Units — The Canadian Experience" in I.T. Gault, ed., *Offshore Petroleum Installations: Law and Financing, Canada and the United States* (London: International Bar Association, 1986) at 105. See also Prothonotary Hargrave's comments in *Cyber Sea Technologies*, above note 10.
27 [1982] 2 F.C. 855, (1982), 135 D.L.R. (3d) 485 (C.A.).
28 *Bow Valley Husky (Bermuda) Ltd. v. Saint John Shipbuilding Ltd.* (1995), 126 D.L.R. (4th) 1.
29 *Bow Valley Husky (Bermuda) Ltd. v. Saint John Shipbuilding Ltd.*, [1997] 3 S.C.R. 1210.

the *Collision Regulations*, a tug and a tow are considered to be one unit and are entitled to be considered as the stand-on vessel in the vicinity of other ships (see Chapter 11). The aggregate tonnage of the two may also be considered one unit for limitation of liability purposes, if the two vessels are both at fault in the collision and are commonly owned by the same person (see Chapter 14).

f) **Small Vessels**

The wide array of small pleasure craft owned by recreational users may also qualify as ships. The *Small Vessel Regulations* define a small vessel as a vessel in respect of which the regulations apply, namely, pleasure craft, vessels other than pleasure craft that do not exceed 5 tons and do not carry more than fifteen passengers, and power-driven vessels that do not exceed 15 GT and that do not carry passengers, or a fishing vessel. Flotation devices that are less than 2 metres in length and are not designed to include a motor are not affected.[30]

The courts have held that a small motor boat and an inboard motor boat are ships.[31] Similarly, a small pleasure craft operating inland is considered a ship.[32] Personal watercraft (e.g., sea-doos or jet-skis) are designed more for fast acceleration than navigation (i.e., to move from one place to another) and should therefore be distinguished from ships;[33] however, they are still vessels and their users are expected to abide by the *Small Vessel Regulations* and the standard of care for safe operation.[34] Windsurfers are vessels and require the use of life jackets under the *Small Vessel Regulations*.[35]

A remotely operated water-skiing device presented a special challenge to the B.C. Supreme Court in *R. v. Gatt*. This "craft" was designed

---

30 C.R.C., c.1487, ss.2 and 3. In an earlier version of the regulations, "vessel" included any ship or boat of any description. This was interpreted to include small dinghies, thus subjecting them to certain safety requirements (i.e., see *R. v. Vorgic*, [1983] O.J. No. 352 (H.C.J.) (QL)). The current definition clearly excludes flotation devices less than 2 meters in length.
31 *Croswell v. Daball* (1920), 47 O.L.R. 354, aff'd (1921), 49 O.L.R. 85; and *McLeod v. Ontario Minnesota Pulp & Paper Co.*, above note 18.
32 *Beaulieu v. Reliance Insurance Co. of Philadelphia* (1971), 19 D.L.R. (3d) 399, aff'd [1972] 1 O.R. 84 (C.A.).
33 *Cyber Sea Technologies*, above note 10.
34 *Field v. Poole* (1994), 51 A.C.W.S. (3d) 758 (B.C.S.C.). "Personal watercraft" is defined as "a water-driven vessel with an enclosed hull and no cockpit and a maximum length of 4 m, that is designed to be used by one or more persons while straddling, sitting, standing or kneeling" (*Small Vessel Regulations*, above note 30, s.2).
35 *PG du Québec v. Vincent*, [1984] C.S. 1037 (Qc. S.C.).

not to carry anyone but simply to tow a water-skier, with the skier operating the craft through remote control. The appellant was charged with a *Criminal Code* violation concerning the operation of a vessel while towing a person on skis without having another person on board the towing vessel. The craft was held to be a vessel within the meaning of the Code: that is, it floated, was powered at speed, was navigable, and was capable of towing a water-skier.[36]

g) Submersibles

Submersibles are likely to be considered ships. In *Cyber Sea Technologies Inc. v. Underwater Harvester Remotely Operated Vehicle*, a submersible was designed and used for logging in a flooded reservoir; it had its own propulsion but was tethered to and manoeuvred from a barge or shore cabin by means of cables and a compressed air line. Prothonotary Hargrave applied *Canada v. Saint John Shipbuilding* in concluding that it was probably a ship: the submersible was designed and built for use on water, it had its own means of propulsion and moved from place to place, it carried navigation equipment and flotation systems, and it carried inflatable balloons as cargo. The fact that it did not have a crew was not a discounting factor, for a dumb barge, which is a ship, does not have a crew. Similarly, its capability of navigation and operation under water did not diminish its characterization as a ship.[37]

h) Decommissioned Ships

It cannot be assumed that a vessel decommissioned from navigational use and converted for some other use will continue to qualify as a ship. The simple fact that the vessel was designed as a ship is not the sole applicable criterion. Therefore, a vessel that was permanently moored and used as a hotel was not considered a ship. In this case the ship was rented exclusively for use as a hotel and was the property of the province of Quebec. This constituted a local work or undertaking, thus falling within the exclusive power of the province under section 92(10) of the *Constitution Act, 1867*, and therefore the *Canada Shipping Act* was not applicable.[38] A corollary consequence of a vessel ceasing to be considered a ship could be the application of provincial or municipal tax assessment to the ship *qua* real property. In the case of a ship that was converted for use as a restaurant and secured to land, it was held that

---

36 *R. v. Gatt* (1992), 72 C.C.C. (3d) 146.
37 *Cyber Sea Technologies*, above note 10.
38 *PG du Canada v. Services d'Hôtellerie Maritimes*, [1968] C.S. 431 (Qc. S.C.).

the owners could not avoid the application of municipal tax assessment. In this case the "ship" was akin to land.[39]

A ship that is moored and awaiting dismantling continues to qualify as a ship until the ship breaking takes place. In *Hamilton Harbour Commissioners v. The AM German*, the court held that "once qualified as a 'ship' because it was designed for such use, the property never loses its classification as a ship within the meaning of the *Federal Court Act*, regardless of changes to it unless it be taken apart to the extent that the separated components would merely be individual objects which were used in the construction of the ship."[40] This view ought to be read in the context of intentional decommissioning and consequently should be distinguished from salvage and wreck, where, under the *Federal Court Act*, the definition of "ship" may still include part of a ship that has broken up.

i) Other Vessels

A vessel that operates on land and at sea, such as an amphibious vehicle, may constitute a vessel while in the water and, thereby, be subject to the *Canada Shipping Act*.[41] A hovercraft is also a ship and, therefore, could be the subject of an action *in rem*.[42] On the other hand, although a sea plane is not a ship, when on the water it is considered to be a power-driven vessel and the *Collision Regulations* apply to it.[43]

j) Concluding Comment on Definitions

There is no limit to technological ingenuity in ocean engineering. New marine structures are emerging to support novel ocean uses; for instance, aquaculture is gradually moving offshore and utilizing large submerged cages, frequently with surface structures. The at-sea extraction of energy from the ocean or wind is moving from the exploratory to a commercial phase. Exploration for deep-sea minerals will one day lead to new technologies. All of these activities can be expected to raise

---

39 *Herbstreit v. Ontario Regional Assessment Commissioner, Region 15* (1982), 38 O.R. (2d) 642 (Co. Ct.).
40 *Hamilton Harbour Commissioners v. AM German (The)*, [1973] F.C. 1254 (T.D.).
41 *R. v. General Motors Canada* (1984), 48 O.R. (2d) 204 (H.C.J.). The amphibious vehicle sank in Lake Erie with loss of life. It was held that both the *Canada Shipping Act*, above note 1, and the provincial *Occupational Health and Safety Act*, R.S.O. 1990, c.O-1, applied concurrently.
42 *Imperial Oil Ltd. v. Expo Spirit (The)*(1986), 6 F.T.R. 156, aff'd (1987), 80 N.R. 259.
43 *Ontario Central Airlines Ltd. v. Gustafson* (1957), 8 D.L.R. (2d) 584 (Ont. C.A.); *Collision Regulations*, C.R.C., c.1416.

new challenges for the extent to which Canadian maritime law is applicable. One criterion for applicability will be the extent to which new ocean technologies should be considered ships or vessels. Clearly, the capability of being used for navigation, at least at some point, will be the primary requirement to be satisfied. Navigation of a ship is to be distinguished from the simple movement of a structure as cargo. From the case law considered above, it seems that the courts are likely to assess whether a particular craft or structure is a ship, and what its responsibilities and entitlements might be, in a pragmatic, functional, and contextual manner, rather than in an abstract way. They can be expected to assess current or potential use, impact of that use on maritime matters, and the applicable regulatory scheme.

2) How a Ship is Owned

As noted in the introduction, there are various ways in which transmission of title in a ship may occur. Before moving to the construction and purchase of a ship, it is useful to explain how a ship is owned. The rules on shipowning vary significantly from one jurisdiction to another.[44] While in many cases a ship will have one or more registered owners — natural or legal, this fact *per se* might not fully indicate who actually owns the ship and where that person (or those persons) might be located. In Canada shipowning is restricted to nationals, and ship registration is indicative of ownership (i.e., legal title). Judgments in older cases debated whether registration was *prima facie* evidence, but they generally agreed that registration alone was not conclusive of ownership.[45] In comparison, many other jurisdictions have much more flexible requirements concerning nationality and, as a result, tracking down the actual ownership of a ship may require an inquiry that goes beyond the ship's registry.

Like a corporation, a ship is divided into shares and, just as the shareholder owns a part of the corporation, the share-owner owns a part of the registered ship. However, unlike a corporation — which may have a very large number of issued shares in Canada, the United Kingdom, and many other Commonwealth countries — a registered

---

44 For an explanation of shipowning requirements in many flag of convenience jurisdictions, see R. Coles & N. Ready, eds., *Ship Registration: Law and Practice* (London: Lloyd's of London Press, 2002).
45 *Lynch v. Shaw* (1859), 17 U.C.Q.B. 241; *R. v. S.G. Marshall (The)* (1870), 1 P.E.I. 316; *Haley v. Comox (The)* (1920), 20 Ex. C.R. 86; *Robillard v. St. Roch (The)* (1921), 21 Ex. C.R. 132; *Stone v. Rochepoint (The)* (1921), 21 Ex. C.R. 143.

ship is divided into only sixty-four shares.[46] In comparison, registered ships in Italy are divided into twenty-four shares, and in Cyprus and Liberia, into 100 shares.[47] In Commonwealth countries this practice dates from 1832 and seems to have evolved from the division of prize money first into eight shares and, of those shares, some would then be further divided into eighths. In any case, no more than sixty-four individuals or corporations can be registered as owners of the ship; however, each share may be jointly owned by up to five persons, legal or natural. In turn, each share or part of a share, may be corporately owned, at least in relation to commercial vessels. The owners or joint owners of the ship or shares are entered into the register.[48] Thus, there could be many share-owning interests in the ship. Moreover, there is always the possibility of another corporation owning the registered corporate owner of the ship or a share in the ship. In those jurisdictions where foreign nationality is not a bar to shipowning, it may well be that the search for the ultimate shipowner may take the researcher from one legal person to another and across different jurisdictions.

The actual owner of a ship or share should be distinguished from other persons who may have possession or control of the ship. In maritime law the rights and duties of actual owners are frequently extended to a larger range of persons who may have chartered, or have management, operation, or control of the ship. This is essential because in many cases the actual owner may not be in possession or control, yet it is necessary to ensure that the ship is managed properly and that those who manage the ship are accountable. For instance, through a bareboat charterparty (i.e., charter by demise), the actual shipowner parts with possession and control of the ship, and the charterer will hire the master and crew and manage the life of the ship. In several jurisdictions, the bareboat charterer is allowed to re-register the ship. Shipowners frequently augment their fleets through this and other types of chartering, instead of actually owning more ships. However, in all these cases where the ship is in the hands of a person other than the owner, possession and control does not translate into the full rights, privileges, and responsibilities of ownership. (See Chapter 8.) Therefore, under the *Canada Shipping Act*, while a bareboat chartered

---

46 *Canada Shipping Act*, above note 1, s.23(1); *Canada Shipping Act, 2001*, above note 2, s.53(1).
47 *Ship Registration: Law and Practice*, above note 44, at 7.
48 *Canada Shipping Act*, above note 1, s.23(2); *Canada Shipping Act, 2001*, above note 2, s.53(2).
49 *Canada Shipping Act*, ibid., s.18; *Canada Shipping Act, 2001*, ibid., s.48.

ship may be registered in Canada for the duration of the charter if its registration in a foreign country is suspended,[49] the charterer is not registered as an owner.[50] Likewise in a mortgage of a ship or a share in a ship, the mortgagee does not become owner nor does the mortgagor cease to be one;[51] however, the rights of a mortgagee and other security holders in the ship have the effect of encumbering the ship or share.

C. BUILDING A NEW SHIP

1) Steamship Inspection Service

In Canada the responsibility for the setting and implementation of standards and inspection lies with the Steamship Inspection Service. This service is run by a board and the standards applied are approved international standards, that is, standards for ships adopted under conventions of the International Maritime Organisation, and which are enacted in regulations. Where unusual design features occur, the board is responsible for deciding on standards of structural strength, safety and suitability of hulls, and machinery and equipment. Equally, the board has the power to exempt a ship from certain requirements.[52]

The actual task of surveying the machinery, hull, equipment, and electrical installations of a ship lies with steamship inspectors appointed by the Governor in Council.[53] In Canada, these persons are usually highly experienced professionals — frequently master mariners, naval architects, or marine engineers — who satisfy the qualifications and examinations set by the board, and who take an oath of office to the effect that they will not hold a financial interest in the construction or sale of steamships, nor in their equipment or machinery.[54] Ships may be inspected at any time before being put in service and thereafter. The inspectors have the power to board a ship, question or request reasonable assistance from the owner and officers, request that machinery be operated, check the certificate of registry, peruse the certification of officers, and possibly detain the ship if there is a serious breach of safety standards.[55] Ships may

---

50 *Canada Shipping Act*, ibid., s.23(4); *Canada Shipping Act, 2001*, ibid., s.53(4).
51 *Canada Shipping Act*, ibid., s.40; *Canada Shipping Act, 2001*, ibid., s.68.
52 *Canada Shipping Act*, ibid., s.305; *Canada Shipping Act, 2001*, ibid., s.108.
53 *Canada Shipping Act*, ibid., s.301; *Canada Shipping Act, 2001*, ibid., s.11(2).
54 *Canada Shipping Act*, ibid., ss.301–303.
55 *Canada Shipping Act*, ibid., ss.310–311 and 317; *Canada Shipping Act, 2001*, above note 2, s.211.

not be operated without the appropriate safety certificates.[56] Steamship inspectors are expected to do their work competently in interpreting and applying regulatory requirements under the *Canada Shipping Act*.[57] Similarly, provincial authorities responsible for establishing and monitoring standards for ship construction have a duty of care in the performance of their functions.[58]

In addition to the Steamship Inspection Service, in Canada, classification societies and surveyors may be delegated authority to conduct statutory inspections of classed ships.[59] Inspectors of such societies do not have the full powers of a steamship inspector.[60] In the past there was some delegation to classification societies for tonnage measurement and for the purposes of the *International Safety Management Code*; the expansion to broader statutory inspections, which is recent, is aimed at reducing the duplication of Steamship Service and classification society inspections, thereby increasing efficiency and reducing costs. At this time having a classification society undertake these inspections is optional and applicable to bulk cargo vessels operating on the Great Lakes; it is hoped that this process will be expanded to other vessels.[61] Agreements with a number of classification societies have already been reached. It will be interesting to see to what standard of care such organizations will be held in pursuing their work. In the *Nicholas H*, the House of Lords held that, to hold classification societies to a standard of care toward third parties — in this case cargo owners — for a carelessly performed survey of the ship, "would be unfair,

---

56 *Canada Shipping Act*, ibid., ss.316(5) and 318–319; *Canada Shipping Act, 2001*, ibid., ss.16(1), 106(2) and 107.
57 *Glovertown Shipyards Ltd. v. Hickey*, [1999] N.J. No. 169 (Nfld. S.C. (T.D.)) (QL). The steamship inspectors negligently failed to reasonably interpret and apply the tonnage guidelines. They were found contributorily negligent.
58 *Petten v. E.Y.E. Marine Consultants* (1998), 180 Nfld. & P.E.I.R. 1 (Nfld. S.C. (T.D.)) [*Petten*]. The Newfoundland Fisheries Loan Board, as it was then known, owed a duty of care to the shipyard to act thoroughly, competently, and efficiently when a construction issue arose.
59 *Canada Shipping Act*, above note 1, ss.317.1–317.3; *Canada Shipping Act, 2001*, above note 2, s.12(1). The *Classed Ships Inspection Regulations, 1988*, S.O.R./80-255, s.4, already recognized the American Bureau of Shipping and Lloyd's Register of Shipping for certain types of inspections.
60 *Canada Shipping Act*, above note 1, s.317(1); *Canada Shipping Act, 2001*, above note 2, s.211.
61 B. Streeter, unpub. address to International Conference Safer Ships — Competent Crews, convened by The Company of Master Mariners of Canada, Halifax, NS, Oct. 2001.

unjust and unreasonable ... notably because they act for the collective welfare and unlike shipowners they would not have the benefit of any limitation provision."[62] In any case, the shipowner is responsible for ensuring that the ship is seaworthy. In fact no shipowner has been successful in suing a classification society for breach of a contractual or tortious duty in surveying a damaged ship.

2) Construction Agreement

a) Planning Stage

The shipowner is first likely to consider whether to construct a new ship or simply modify a purchased used ship. In either case the prospective owner will normally consult a naval architect or issue a call for tenders from naval architecture firms, which will produce model plans for typical ships or provide a new design for the ship. The owner will have made a commercial and technological decision as to what type of ship is needed and with what capabilities in terms of, for instance, cargo- and/or passenger-carrying capacity, speed, maintenance needs, regulatory requirements (e.g., double hull), fuel consumption, and crew requirements. At this early stage the owner will also have considered a shipyard to build the ship and the eventual place of registration. The building of a ship is a major commercial decision that requires complex financial planning. The architect will be able to assist the owner by also providing a rough estimate of the cost of construction, but the shipyard will provide the precise cost.

b) Design Stage

Shipyards frequently have ready-made designs for different types of ships or are in a position to secure designs on behalf of the owner. There is always the option of a new design, so long as this conforms to approved shipbuilding standards. In such a case, the architect has a duty to exercise reasonable care and skill in designing the vessel and preparing the plans, drawings, and specifications.[63] In the case of conversion of an existing ship, there could be additional considerations concerning the extent to which the owner's specifications in the tendering process should guide the builder. A potential danger for the builder is to treat the used ship to be converted with a new ship mentality. In *Upper Lakes Shipping Ltd. v. Saint John Shipbuilding and Dry*

---

62   Marc Rich & Co. AG v. Bishop Rock Marine Co., (The Nicholas H), [1995] 2 Lloyd's L.R. 299 (H.L.) [Nicholas H] at para.75.
63   King v. Carius, [1975] F.C.J. No. 514 (T.D.).

Dock Co., a shipyard was contracted to convert a twelve-year-old bulk carrier into a self-unloader.[64] The builder was provided with drawings and specifications for the new unloading system, which included notes that they were "For General Guidance Only Not to be Used for Construction," and that "the ship side line used for this drawing was lifted from the original builder's drawing and should be checked." The builder did not take new measurements of the ship (e.g., to establish the main centre, parallel centre, and datum lines) at the outset and instead relied on the original design plans and measurements ("as built drawings") of the ship in constructing the system in pre-fabricated units. Any vessel, and especially this type of vessel, which suffers significant bulk cargo loading/unloading stresses over its lifetime, may suffer some structural distortions. The tender drawings may not be accurate and the owner, in calling for tenders, does not provide an implied or collateral warranty that the work can be done without difficulty according to the specifications and drawings provided. This principle was established by an old English case in a non-maritime context and was applied in this case.[65] The builder was not induced to rely on the "as built drawings" and therefore the owner was not under a duty of care toward him; thus, there was no negligent misrepresentation. The builder remained responsible for producing a particular result. The situation would be different if the owner actually warrants the accuracy of the drawings so that tenderers could reasonably be expected to rely on this in placing their bids.[66]

The Construction Department of the Steamship Inspection Service must approve the plans, as the ship must meet the minimum standards, such as those set out in the *Convention on the Safety of Life at Sea*.[67] It is possible for the design and construction to be exempted from certain regulatory standards in the regulations, but this requires approval from the Board of Steamship Inspectors.[68] During the construction phase, the classification surveyor will continue to oversee the building of the vessel to ensure that the standards of the society are being upheld.

---

64 [1985] F.C.J. No. 526 (T.D.), aff'd (1988), 86 N.R. 40 (F.C.A.) [*Upper Lakes Shipping*].
65 *Thorn v. Mayor & Commonality of London* (1876), 1 App. Cas 120. It was applied in *Moncton (City of) v. Aprile Contracting Ltd.* (1980), 29 N.B.R. (2d) 631 (C.A.).
66 See for instance *Cana Construction Co. v. Canada*, [1974] S.C.R. 1159, a non-maritime case, where the Crown was found liable in damages for an inaccurate estimate of the cost of subcontract work.
67 *Convention on Safety of Life at Sea*, 20 January 1914, 108 F.S.P. 283 [*SOLAS*].

Classification societies operate in relation to certain types of vessels and qualify them for the purpose of obtaining insurance coverage.

In the case of a conversion, the owner is also under a responsibility to notify the chief registrar of an alteration to a ship to the extent that it no longer corresponds to the description and particulars in the certificate of registry.[69] He or she has thirty days to notify from the completion of the alteration. In this case, the owner is responsible for arranging for a new tonnage certificate to be provided to the chief registrar.[70] If the changes are significant, the tonnage certificate provided by the tonnage measurer might indicate that the ship should be re-registered. In such a case, the existing registration will be cancelled and the owner will have to re-apply.[71]

In the case of provincial loan programs for fishing vessels, there may be a requirement of prior approval of the design, and this may be accompanied by inspections. The financing of the ship to be constructed may depend on the approval of the design by a provincial authority.

c) Financing Stage

Once the firm price is established, the potential owner will seek financing for the vessel. Financing is a critical and complex stage, and depends on the type of vessel involved. Financing for large commercial vessels tends to be international and is handled by relatively few law firms. In many cases a number of banks will be involved and complex issues concerning securities (mortgages) and insurance will arise. (These subjects are discussed in greater depth in Chapters 6 and 7.)

i) Federal and Provincial Financing Programs

Prior to 1985, the federal government operated a ship construction subsidy program. The difficulties encountered by the shipbuilding industry in Canada since then have prompted the federal government to initiate a new program of support for shipyards. In 2002 the Structured Financing Facility was launched as part of a new policy framework to support Canadian shipbuilding and the marine industrial sector with, *inter alia*, a funding commitment of $150 million over five years. Administered by Industry Canada, this new program provides tax incentives to lessees

---

68 *Canada Shipping Act*, above note 1, s.305(2.1).
69 *Canada Shipping Act*, above note 1, s.28(2); *Canada Shipping Act, 2001*, above note 2, s.58(2).
70 *Ibid*.
71 *Canada Shipping Act*, ibid., s.30(2)(c); *Canada Shipping Act, 2001*, ibid., s.60(2)(c).

and buyers of Canadian ships up to 10 per cent of the purchase price on a new ship. The support is in the form of a non-refundable loan and credit insurance for a portion of the loan or lease on a new ship.[72] Some funding also may be available through the federal government's Fishing Vessel Assistance Program for replacement of a vessel. It is important to check these sources as the terms, conditions, and existence of these programs vary from time to time — and election to election.

A potential fishing vessel owner may be able to borrow from a bank under the arrangements contained in section 427 of the *Bank Act*.[73] The procedure is available only for construction of the vessel or purchase of fishing equipment. The shipowner is borrowing money on security of future income. The owner has to give an assignment to the bank, as stipulated under section 427. This assignment may then be registered in the Canadian Register of Ships. The registration of the assignment at the register is imperative in order for the bank to have priority over subsequent recorded or registered claims against the vessel.[74]

Some provinces have small business loan legislation that may enable owners to finance small vessels. In Nova Scotia the Fisheries Loan Program provides fishermen with loans for the purpose of purchasing or building a fishing vessel, purchasing and installing engines, equipment and electronics, and undertaking technical modifications. There are various requirements, such as minimum size of vessel, possession of a fishing licence, insurance, mortgage registration (as security), and provision of a personal guarantee.[75] The province of Newfoundland and Labrador has a similar facility in the form of the Fisheries Loan Guarantee Program offered at commercial interest rates.[76] Both programs are limited to residents of the relevant province.

ii) Builder's Mortgage

In most countries, if the prospective shipowner wants to borrow money on a ship under construction, the creditor can take a chattel mortgage only on the incomplete ship and the materials used in it. In Canada, however, there is the builder's mortgage system, which makes the vessel, in the course of construction an entity for the purposes of

---

72 Online at: <http://graphics.strategis.ic.gc.ca/sc_indps/shipbuilding/graphics/sff_eng.pdf>.
73 S.C. 1991, c.46.
74 *Ibid.*, s.428(5). The assignment must also be registered under the *Bank Act*: see B(2)(d) in Chapter 6, "Security under *Bank Act*."
75 Online at: <http://www.govns.ca/nsaf/loanboards/fishlb/ vessel.htm>.
76 Online at: <http://www.gov.nf.ca/itrd/fisheries_loan.htm>.

mortgaging. The builder's mortgage is a statutory form and, under the *Canada Shipping Act*, this form must be used with very few changes.[77] The builder's mortgage will be registered at the Canadian Register of Ships.[78] There is no first or second mortgage, but there can be a series of builder's mortgages, which will rank in accordance with the time and date they are recorded in the register. The builder's mortgage is then a registered mortgage and will have priority over subsequent mortgages on the ship. The actual date of the mortgage is inconsequential as far as registered ships are concerned.[79]

As the statutory form of the builder's mortgage does not contain much information usually found in mortgage agreements — such as details regarding insurance, default, foreclosure, or varying interest — a non-registrable document, often called a Deed of Covenants, is usually prepared to supplement the actual registered mortgage. In order to give notice to title searchers, a clause will usually be put in the builder's mortgage to indicate that a Deed of Covenants was prepared. The title searcher would then go to the parties themselves to see the whole of the mortgage agreement.

d) Contracting and Construction Stage

i) Contract Framework

Having settled on the design, the shipowner will then select a shipyard to build the vessel, either by calling tenders or otherwise. There are various standard shipbuilding contracts in use, such as the Model Shipbuilding Contracts of the Shipowners Association of Japan, the Swedish Shipowners Association, and the Association of Western European Shipbuilders. There have been unsuccessful attempts at developing a uniform international approach to shipbuilding matters, such as through the *Convention Relating to Registration of Rights in Respect of Vessels under Construction, 1967*, which has not secured the support necessary to bring it into force.[80] A construction contract is desirable to the shipowner for several reasons. At common law, in the absence of such an instrument, the contract is deemed to be for a completed ship.

---

77 *Canada Shipping Act*, above note 1, s.37(2); *Canada Shipping Act, 2001*, above note 2, s.65(2).
78 *Canada Shipping Act*, ibid., s.37; *Canada Shipping Act, 2001*, ibid., s.65.
79 There was an unsuccessful attempt to promote uniformity for securities concerning ships in construction primarily through the *Convention Relating to Registration of Rights in Respect of Vessels under Construction*, 27 May 1967, B.P.P. Misc. 7 (1968) (not in force). Canada did not become a party.
80 *Ibid.*

Therefore, the title to the ship remains in the shipyard because the contract is for the sale of a future good (i.e., the ship when it is completed). It is important, however, for the owner to gain title in the ship as it is being built for four major reasons: to build up equity in the vessel, to obtain a builder's mortgage from a bank, to protect her/his interest in the vessel and its machinery in case the shipyard should go bankrupt, and to acquire an insurable interest in the vessel as it is being built and be able to safeguard the investment during construction. In Canada, a ship that is about to be built or that is under construction may be temporarily registered as a ship being built in Canada.[81] This is important for financing and other legal reasons, both from the perspective of the owner and the builder. Therefore, the owner will want the construction contract to state that the title to the ship in all stages of construction is deemed to be in the owner. This is not necessarily always the case, as the shipbuilder will also be watching out for his or her interest and may alternatively maintain title until the ship is completed. In the latter case, there is a potential risk for the owner should the shipyard become insolvent. In order to increase protection for the owner in case of the shipyard's bankruptcy, it is useful to include a clause that the prospective shipowner would acquire title to all materials and machinery as they arrive at the shipyard. This does not mean that the purchaser cannot reject the completed vessel should circumstances warrant such an action, such as a fundamental breach of contract.[82]

As the ship is being built, the shipyard will receive equipment and materials from various suppliers, who in turn will also try to protect their interests. In ship construction contracts in British Columbia, there is a practice to include a clause that passes title over purchased equipment even before it is installed in the ship.[83] However, in general, a supplier may still stipulate with the builder that title will remain with the supplier until payment is effected and, in case of default, the supplier may re-take possession. This might be possible for uninstalled equipment. But when equipment is installed into a ship, it becomes part of the ship and title to the equipment thereby passes with the title in the ship.[84] The supplier will then have only an unregistered charge

---

81 *Canada Shipping Act*, above note 1, s.19; *Canada Shipping Act, 2001*, above note 2, s.49.
82 *McDougall v. Aeromarine of Emsworth Ltd.*, [1958] 1 W.L.R. 1126 (Q.B.).
83 B.M. Caldwell, "Shipbuilding Contracts," available online at: <http://www.admiraltylaw.com/fisheries/Papers/ship_building_contracts.htm>.
84 *Hoover-Owens Rentschler Co. v. Gulf Navigation Co.* (1923), 54 O.L.R. 483: in this case, a set of engine cylinders and accessories, once installed, became part of the ship.

against the ship and, should title in the ship be passed on, the title in the equipment is consequentially transferred as well. The new owner at that point will receive clear title subject only to any registered charges[85] because claims in respect of goods, materials, and services for the operation of a ship and any claim relating to construction, repair, or equipping of a ship give rise to a statutory right *in rem*, and this type of claim is defeated by a transfer of title so that the ability to proceed *in rem* is lost.[86] Other than non-maritime law options to protect the supplier, if the equipment has considerable value (e.g., research equipment temporarily installed on an exploration vessel), one option is to secure from the owner a registered security on the ship (e.g., a mortgage).

For commercial, fishing, and some other types of vessels, the construction contract might be a lengthy and complex agreement that will address not only the construction of the hull but also the type of equipment that will be installed and its supplier(s); price; financing; performance bond requiring the owner to provide security for payment or the deposit of an agreed sum; interest payment; timelines for various stages of construction and completion; inspections, including inspections on behalf of the owner, if necessary; dock and sea trials; certificate of seaworthiness; warranties; and when the owner will take delivery. The shipbuilder will be bound to construct the vessel in a sound, proper, and workmanlike manner; using good and substantial materials and equipment; and in accordance with good shipbuilding practice.

The pricing clause will state a firm price for what is shown on the ship specifications as drawn up by the naval architect and as further agreed on during the negotiation of the contract. An omnibus clause will also be included to cover expenses arising during construction. A penalty or liquidated damages clause for late delivery may be included (discussed in detail below). There will generally be a schedule of progress payments clause, which will state how much the potential owner must pay on completion of predetermined stages of construction. It is usually in ten steps — 10 per cent on signing, 10 per cent on the laying of the keel, and so on — or possibly by stages of construction. One possible effect of payment according to stages of construction is that the contract becomes more specifically for parts of a ship

---

85　*Ibid.* The equipment supplier may seek to protect its interest in the equipment by registration under the appropriate provincial *Personal Property Security Act* prior to the installation of the items in the ship.
86　*Federal Court Act*, above note 8, ss.22(2)(m)(n) and 43(3).

leading to a completed ship;[87] thus, the shipowner is forming equity in the ship as it is being built.

ii) Delivery and Delay

The shipowner has a vital interest in the timely construction of the ship, perhaps to be available in time for the fishing season or to be able to honour commitments to charterers and cargo owners. The daily charter rate of a commercial vessel runs into many thousands of dollars, which will be to the owner's loss should the delivery of the new or converted ship be delayed. In addition to these concerns, the owner may have a crew on standby and may incur other costs while waiting for the delayed ship. At the same time, the shipyard will want the owner to take delivery of the completed ship and to clear space for the next contract. Accordingly, both sides will have an interest in agreeing on a specific delivery date, or delivery after the fulfilment of certain conditions.

Delay in delivery constitutes breach of contract. The existence or otherwise of delay has to be ascertained against the understanding concerning delivery of the ship. A contract may provide for delay to start running within a certain period from the contracted completion date (e.g., two weeks). This would give the builder some but not much flexibility. In *Petten v. E.Y.E. Marine Consultants*, the owner knew on signing the contract that construction could not start immediately because of the regulatory, planning, and financing approvals required, and accordingly there was "an implied term that the contractual delivery date would be extended to accommodate a reasonable time to construct the vessel measured from the time when all contingencies had been satisfied." The court calculated a reasonable time for construction from the date of the issuance of the permit.[88]

In so far as cause for delay is concerned, the construction time is the builder's time and it is his or her responsibility to ensure good shipbuilding practice. Thus, in *Upper Lakes Shipping*, the builder's argument that the delay resulted from the owner's failure to provide a ship that corresponded to the tender drawings was rejected since the builder failed to take into consideration that the ship being converted was a used, not a new, ship and its consequences. In addition to this failure, the shipyard had slippages in scheduling, undermanning, poor quality control, and disorganization, which all contributed to delay. On

---

87 N.J.J. Gaskell, C. Debattista, & R.J. Swatton, *Chorley and Giles' Shipping Law*, 8th ed. (London: Pitman Publishing, 1987) at 52–53.
88 Above note 58.

identifying the causes of delay, the Federal Court Trial Division concluded that they typify poor shipbuilding practice and unworkmanlike performance by any reasonable standard of probability.[89]

The construction contract may have penalty or liquidated damages clauses to govern a situation of late delivery. Liquidated damages are pre-estimated damages, normally for a specific amount multiplied by the number of days, or fractions of days, up to the date of actual delivery. If the liquidated damages have a ceiling (e.g., that in no event shall damages exceed a stipulated amount), the clause may have the effect of limiting liability, and this will be respected if it was the intention of the parties. The actual amount recoverable in damages from the builder could be significantly lower than the actual damages incurred by the owner, but courts are not likely to intervene if this is contractually agreed on by relatively equal parties.[90] For such a clause to be effective in the contract, it is important that the clause be clearly expressed, as it is likely to be read *contra proferentem*.[91]

iii) Warranties against Defects and Bad Workmanship

As with delay, the shipowner has much at stake when there are defects or bad workmanship that affect the seaworthiness of the ship. After all, the owner is responsible for the provision and maintenance of a seaworthy ship in a multitude of maritime law institutions, and his or her liability might be engaged in contract and tort law, as well as in failing to meet regulatory safety and other standards.[92] The hope is that the dock and sea trials will identify any problems that need to be rectified before delivery. Some shipowners may have their representatives present at the trials and possibly during inspections at various building stages to ensure that the ship is being built to a high standard. However, even the best built ships are likely to need some rectification of malfunctions after delivery. The warranty clause will be one of the most important in the contract and will run for a specific period, such as twelve months from the delivery date or actual delivery. Clauses vary significantly and the general intent is to ensure that the shipbuilder constructs a seaworthy ship for the intended use. He or she will war-

---

89 *Upper Lakes Shipping*, (F.T.D.), above note 64.
90 *Ibid.*, affirmed on appeal on this point.
91 *Ailsa Craig Fishing Co. v. Malvern Fishing Co.*, [1983] 1 W.L.R. 964.
92 On the shipowner's responsibility to produce a seaworthy ship, including its equipment, see *Wire Rope Industries v. British Columbia Marine Shipbuilders*, [1981] 1 S.C.R. 363, where the defect in a re-socketed towing rope was held to be a latent defect and, therefore, the owner was not negligent in rendering the tug seaworthy.

rant the design, hull, machinery, materials, equipment, and fittings against defects owing to faulty or substandard workmanship. The warranty would not apply to defects caused by misuse, improper operation, or modifications undertaken by the owner after delivery. Nor is the builder responsible for fair wear and tear, and damage resulting from the negligence of the owner or his or her servants. The captains and chief engineers of the newly delivered ship are likely to be required to keep records of and inform the owner of any malfunctions, other than minor matters that can be rectified by the crew as part of their work, which in turn will be transmitted to the builder by the owner.[93] It is important that claims are well recorded or documented since the burden to establish that the deficiencies claimed to exist, on a balance of probabilities, lies with the owner.[94]

The owner will be responsible for notifying the builder — orally or in writing and within a specified time from the date of discovery — of any defects he or she may discover. Many small matters are likely dealt with informally and, if the working relationship between the builder and owner is good, problems will be solved effectively.

The builder will retain the right to inspect the problem promptly and to verify the warranty claim, and thereafter will rectify deficiencies, undertake repairs, and replace faulty material at his or her own cost. The contract may include performance bonds, including labour and material bond, to ensure that the builder will live up to the contract. If the builder verifies an owner's claim that not all the stipulated equipment and materials were on board the ship on delivery, then the builder has to supply what is missing; but, if there is an oversupply of equipment and materials by the builder, these will go to his or her credit in any warranty claim adjustments. It is vital for the builder to honour legitimate warranty claims and therefore to respond to these communications from the owner as otherwise he or she might not be able to reject the owner's claims at a later stage.[95]

Warranty-related work would be done in the shipyard, but the parties may also agree that the work could be done at another shipyard as long as the cost does not exceed what it would have cost the original shipyard. Should the ship be sold, the warranty clause may provide for the assignment of the warranty to a new owner.

---

93 *Offshore Atlantic v. Marystown Shipyard Ltd.* (1988), 31 C.L.R. 12 (Nfld. S.C. (T.D.)), rev'd (1990), 43 C.L.R. 272 (Nfld. C.A.) [*Offshore Atlantic*].
94 *Petten*, above note 58.
95 *Offshore Atlantic*, above note 93, citing *Hughes v. Metropolitan Railway* (1877), 2 App. Cas. 439 (H.L.).

As the ship will include many different types of equipment obtained by the builder from different third-party suppliers, it is likely that the individual pieces of equipment will carry their manufacturer's warranties. The construction contract might provide for the assigning of these warranties directly to the owner; but, if it does not, this is a responsibility of builder and owner alike.[96] In the case of assigned warranties, the builder's warranty does not cover the externally warranted equipment, but the builder does remain responsible for the competent and proper installation of the equipment in accordance with the manufacturer's instructions.[97] Where the builder does not assign the third-party supplier warranties, the owner is not entitled to more than what is available under those warranties.[98]

In *Davie Shipping Ltd. v. Canada*, the builder installed a defective engine, which was supplied by a third party and damaged by fire on board a Coast Guard search-and-rescue vessel during the warranty period.[99] In its claim under the warranty, the Crown could not demonstrate with certainty what the cause of the fire was and, consequently, the builder rejected the claim. There was no evidence that the engine design or materials used were faulty or that insufficient lubrication was used. In the evidence, it appeared that a remote-control stop for the engine was negligently disconnected, there were oil leaks in the engine room, and the crew was inept in responding to the fire so that damage was not minimized. However, these failures on board the ship were not determinative or contributing factors. The most probable explanation for the fire was that dirt, remaining in the engine prior to delivery, caused the initial flashing of the bearing shells. The trial judge found that this was faulty workmanship, albeit that of the supplier rather than the builder. The builder's and supplier's argument that the source of the dirt had to be identified was not material, as it was a contractual responsibility of the supplier to flush the engine of all impurities.

Where the owner directs the supply and installation of a particular material, the builder may be held liable only for the faulty installation of that material, while the supplier has a duty to warn of any dangers posed by its product. In *Bow Valley Husky (Bermuda) Ltd. v. Saint John Shipbuilding Ltd*, the owner specifically chose the Raychem System to prevent the pipes of an oil rig, built by Saint John Shipbuilding Ltd.,

---

96 *Offshore Atlantic, ibid.*
97 Ibid.
98 Ibid.
99 (1983), 49 N.R. 305 (F.C.A.).

from freezing during the winter.[100] The system used Thermaclad wrap to keep moisture from the insulation and a heat-trace wire. The system also required the installation of a ground fault circuit breaker system to cut off the power in the event of an electrical fault to prevent arcing of the heat-trace wire, but this was not installed until after the fire. The fire that broke out on the rig caused extensive damage and put the rig out of action for several months. The owner was responsible for operating the heat-trace system without a functioning ground fault circuit breaker system. The supplier was held liable in tort for breach of its duty to warn of the inflammability of Thermaclad. The judgment against the builder was overturned by the Court — with La Forest and McLachlin JJ. dissenting on this point — holding that the duty to warn of product defects did not extend to the builder when his or her liability in the contract is limited to negligent installation, if any, of an owner-directed supply. The effect of such an agreement is to exclude all other grounds of liability for the builder, including the duty to warn. The Court held: "Where, as here, the owner specifies a particular product to be used, it is generally the owner and not the builder who, unless otherwise specified in the contract, should bear the losses that flow from the risk associated with that product's use."[101] If the builder had not used the directed supply, it would have been in breach of contract! Thus, the builder's failure to warn was not a ground for liability. The dissenting judgment on this point held that both the supplier and the builder had a duty to warn that class of persons that they ought to have known might reasonably be affected by the use of Thermaclad. That liability persists unless the owner's knowledge of the material, in full appreciation and willing assumption of the risk posed by the product, negates reasonable reliance. The dissenting judgment concluded that there was neither the degree of knowledge necessary, nor acceptance of the risk of using Thermaclad.[102]

In a worst-case scenario where the vessel is lost, it is up to the owner to prove that there is a causal connection between defective construction and the loss. In *Orr v. Ontario Boaters Brokerage Ltd.*, the plaintiff failed to establish a causal connection between the sinking and the design of the boat.[103] In *Glovertown Shipyards Ltd. v. Hickey*, the

---

100 Above note 29.
101 *Ibid.*
102 *Ibid.*
103 (1990), 24 A.C.W.S. (3d) 119 (Ont. Gen. Div.).

court similarly found against the owner.[104] The shipyard produced a seaworthy ship and, although deficiencies were found after delivery, they were addressed by the builder and suppliers. Rather, the loss was attributed to the owner in employing an unqualified master, whose negligent management and navigation led to the loss of the ship.

D. PURCHASE OF A SHIP

The other option for the shipowner is to purchase, instead of building, a new ship. Where the shipbuilder retains title in the ship under construction, on completion the owner will be purchasing the ship. As in the previous section, with a purchase the owner will need to secure financing and comply with the requirements described below.

1) Qualifying Ship Ownership in Canada

The first point to be kept in mind by a purchaser is that Canada has an important rule on qualifying ownership. By and large, Canada stresses beneficial ownership of ships or shares, and therefore only ships or shares owned or jointly owned by qualified persons may be registered in Canada.[105] The "qualified person" must be a Canadian citizen or permanent resident or, in the case of a corporation, is federally or provincially registered. An authorized representative of a Canadian ship must notify the chief registrar of changes to the owner's name within a thirty day period of the change, failing which the registration may be suspended or cancelled.[106]

If the ship is purchased by an unqualified person, any person may apply to the Federal Court for the sale of the ship to a qualified person.[107] In effect, the Federal Court is empowered to prohibit the transfer of a Canadian registered ship and, in doing so, may prohibit dealing with such a ship or its shares.[108]

---

104 [1999] N.J. No. 169 (Nfld. S.C. (T.D.)) (QL).
105 *Canada Shipping Act*, above note 1, s.23(2); *Canada Shipping Act, 2001*, above note 2, s.53(2).
106 *Canada Shipping Act*, ibid., ss.28(1) and 30(1)(d); *Canada Shipping Act, 2001*, ibid., ss.58(1) and 60(1)(d).
107 *Canada Shipping Act*, ibid., s.46; *Canada Shipping Act, 2001*, ibid., s.74.
108 *Canada Shipping Act* ibid., s.47; *Canada Shipping Act, 2001*, ibid., s.75.

2) Transferring Ownership

The sale and purchase of a ship involves ordinary contract law — in particular, sale of goods law — as well as maritime law requirements for a bill of sale. Many sales of commercial vessels use standard international forms that spell out the respective rights and duties of the seller and purchaser.[109]

a) Contract of Sale

The purchase of a ship, whether new or not, is regarded as the sale of a chattel and the transaction is governed by the relevant federal and provincial law pertaining to such matters, including laws relating to the transfer of title to goods, lending transactions and securities, and liens other than maritime liens. In order to determine whether title is effectively transferred, reference is made to the particular legislation of the jurisdiction of the sale, such as a sale of goods act, which sets out the relevant rights and obligations of the buyer and seller. It is important that all the essential procedures be fully understood and complied with in order to ensure that title will be validly transferred.

The ownership of a registered ship is transferred by a bill of sale under the *Canada Shipping Act*. The bill must be witnessed and be accompanied by a declaration of transfer by the buyer of the ship, stating that the new owners are "qualified owners" under the Act. The chief registrar must be provided with the evidence necessary to establish that the ship is entitled or required to be registered.[110] These documents along with the Appointment of Managing Owner or Manager (i.e., appointing a new manager, managing owner, or ship's husband for the vessel) have to be filed with the chief registrar before ownership of the vessel is effectively transferred. Purchase of a registered ship is simplified by the fact that the vessel's history is on record at the register.

As a sale of a chattel, the sale of a vessel is governed by the general principles of contract law. There must be an agreement between the parties for a mutual exchange of something of value. Often this will be in the form of a standard contract — particularly where a broker is involved — but, in any case, it is important that the buyer be aware that the purchase is made at his or her risk and that certain safeguards should be included in any agreement of sale. It is also important for

---

109 For a discussion of the SALEFORM standard form, see *Chorley and Giles' Shipping Law*, above note 87 at 45–49.
110 *Canada Shipping Act*, above note 1, s.45; *Canada Shipping Act, 2001*, above note 2, s.73.

conditions and warranties to be spelled out. Breach of a condition will enable the purchaser to reject the goods, whereas breach of a warranty will entitle him or her to damages only.[111] In *Fudge v. Rideau Marine (Kingston) Ltd.*, the owner/purchaser of a boat was entitled to rescind the contract with the dealer and recover the purchase price. The boat in question did not perform to the specifications and standard required, despite efforts to rectify the problem through repairs.[112]

There are differences affecting ownership between a sale and an agreement to sell, and consequent requirements to inform the registrar. As discussed in regard to construction, there are different situations as to how and when ownership is acquired, such as when the owner gradually builds equity as the ship is built; or when specific stages are completed and the ship is transferred in parts; or at the end when the ship is completed, until which time the builder retains title. In the last two options, the agreement may be an agreement to sell on completion of a stage of construction or on full completion. There is a requirement for the person in whose name a ship is recorded as being built to inform the registrar of the completion of construction and the identity of the owner, and the registrar will amend the entry in the register.[113] If this is not complied with the registrar may suspend or cancel the registration or listing.[114]

Any purchase should be subject to appropriate surveys, made at the buyer's expense, and allow the buyer to reject the vessel should it not conform to designated specifications, or require the seller to rectify the defects or make good in damages, if there has been a breach of any express or implied warranties. The surveyor is employed to make a thorough examination of the vessel as to its condition and the condition of its machinery and equipment. Apart from its usefulness in negotiating price and terms, the surveyor's report is used primarily in obtaining insurance coverage, but it can also be helpful in getting a mortgage on the vessel. If the surveyor is negligent in carrying out his or her duties, there could be liability in damages. An appropriate survey should be carried out for all aspects of the vessel (i.e., hull, machinery, and equipment).

If the vessel is sold with special equipment or ancillary items, these should be listed as agreed on by the parties and, in all cases, all terms and

---

111 *Chorley and Giles' Shipping Law*, above note 87 at 41.
112 (1991), 33 A.C.W.S. (3d) 648 (Ont. Gen. Div.).
113 *Canada Shipping Act*, above note 1, ss.28(4) and 29; *Canada Shipping Act, 2001*, above note 2, ss.58(4) and 59.
114 *Canada Shipping Act*, ibid., s.30(1); *Canada Shipping Act, 2001*, ibid., s.60(1).

conditions should be clearly spelled out in a written agreement of purchase and sale. If equipment is incorporated into the machinery of the ship, it becomes part of the ship and transfers with the title of the ship.[115]

Ships will most often be bought and sold through a broker acting for a commission, on behalf of either the purchaser or, more often, the seller, or in some instances for both parties. In any case, all the ordinary principles of agency apply, but the exact nature of the relationship between the broker, as agent, and the buyer or seller, as principal, should be clearly stipulated. Again, this will usually be in a standard form, although there is often room for negotiation as to terms, particularly in the amount of commission to be paid where a large vessel is being sold. In any event, the broker is entitled to a fee only from the party he or she actually acted for.[116] If the broker is the effective cause of the sale, the seller may not terminate a listing agreement so as to deprive the broker of the earned fee.[117]

Most jurisdictions have laws governing the lending or mortgaging aspects of a sale. These concern interest rates that may be charged and other such aspects of consumer protection in the financing of the purchase. In Canada the federal government also has enacted an *Interest Act* designed to ensure that borrowers know the cost of borrowing money to finance their purchase.[118]

There remains a shadow of uncertainty over the applicable law to a contract of sale of a ship. As seen in Chapter 3, prior to *Ordon Estate v. Grail*,[119] provincial law was applied in a maritime law context, and this included several provincial sale of goods acts. With *Ordon*, the Supreme Court of Canada adopted a stringent test to determine the applicability or otherwise of a provincial statute in a maritime setting. In a scenario since *Ordon*, at issue will be the substantive Canadian maritime law, which is federal and not provincial, governing the sale of a ship when the provisions of the *Canada Shipping Act* are deemed insufficient. While the applicability of a provincial statute in a maritime setting might be questioned, common law principles would still apply as Canadian maritime law includes common law. Presumably the 1893 English *Sale of Goods Act*[120] might still qualify as legitimate Canadian maritime law by virtue of the definition of this body of law in the

---

115 *Hoover-Owens Rentschler Co. v. Gulf Navigation Co.*, above note 84.
116 *Spellacy v. Marine Management Inc.*, [1998] N.J. No. 20 (Nfld. S.C. (T.D.)) (QL).
117 *Clift's Marine Sales (1992) Ltd. v. Moorco Inc.* (2001), 215 F.T.R. 78.
118 R.S.C. 1985, c.I-15.
119 (1996), 30 O.R. (3d) 643, aff'd [1998] 3 S.C.R. 437.
120 *Sale of Goods Act, 1893* (U.K.), 56 & 57 Vict., c.71.

Federal Court Act.[121] However, Giaschi points out: "it is not desirable that such an important area of law be regulated by a statute more than a century old."[122]

b) Securing a Clean Title
In advising on the purchase of a ship, especially a used ship, counsel should be careful in taking cautionary steps to secure a clean title. Unlike liens and securities in a non-maritime context, creditors' claims in a maritime context do not require registration. Other than a mortgage, there is no requirement to register other claims against the ship, and the non-registrable claims include powerful maritime liens that are not defeated by a transfer of title. While maritime liens are discussed at length in Chapter 6, it is worth considering some of their features to illustrate the challenge that faces a researcher of claims against the ship. A maritime lien is peculiar to the law relating to ships. It is based on the notion that a claim may be enforced against the thing itself (i.e., *in rem*), rather than against the person who owns it (i.e., *in personam*). As set out in *The Ripon City*, by Gorell Barnes J., a maritime lien results from a service done to the ship, or *res*, or from an injury caused by it.[123] The significant features of maritime liens are that they are not required to be publicly registered to be valid, and that they travel with and are enforceable against the ship even though a new owner may have no knowledge of them.[124]

Quite apart from maritime liens, which may arise under statute or at common law, liens of a non-maritime nature may arise under a number of other statutes and at common law, such as provincial statutes governing repairers' liens, warehouse keepers' claims, and claims under companies' legislation. Therefore, it is necessary to determine if there could also be a lien against the vessel pursuant to such statutes and to check at the appropriate registries to see if, in fact, such a lien exists where the owner resides and where the vessel is registered and/or situated.

Mr. Justice Arthur J. Stone, of the Federal Court of Canada, in a classic article published three decades ago entitled "Let the Boat Buyer Beware," has suggested various steps that should be taken to secure as

---

121 *Federal Court Act*, above note 8 s.2.
122 C. Giaschi, "The Constitutional Implications of *Ordon Estate v. Grail* and the Expanding Definition of Canadian Maritime Law," lecture delivered to Dalhousie Law School, Halifax, NS, Oct. 2000, online at: <http://www.admiraltylaw.com/papers/Dalspeech.htm>.
123 [1897] P. 226 at 261.
124 *Bold Buccleugh (The)* (1851), 7 Moo. P.C. 267.

clean a title as possible from the vendor and to protect the purchaser from any latent claims or claims associated with defending title.[125] That sage advice still holds today. With minor modifications, in substance the advice follows. The search should first be made for registered charges right up to the eve of the sale. Only ships registered under the *Canada Shipping Act* may have mortgages recorded; licensed vessels do not. If the vessel is registered, counsel should order an abstract of title from the registry; ascertain the identity of the registered owner(s) and title; and ascertain the existence of mortgages and any discharges.[126] If the ship has changed registry, it is useful to undertake similar searches in the previous registry or registries. If the ship is actively trading, speedy searches will be important, as the ship can continue to incur liabilities. If the ship's log book is accessible, it could be a useful indication of how well the ship is operated and it will record potentially relevant events, such as collisions the ship was involved in and matters concerning the wages of seamen.[127] The log book must remain on the vessel but may be made available for inspection.[128] Also useful in this regard are any audits according to the *International Safety Management Code* (discussed in Chapter 5) that might be available.

In the case of licensed and/or unregistered boats, a similar identification of ownership, place of ownership, owner's residence, and geographical area of operation is necessary. As will be seen below, a licensed vessel may not have mortgages registered and, consequently, much of the search will have to focus on provincially registered bills of sale, chattel mortgages, conditional sales contracts, and other kinds of personal property security interests in appropriate provincial registry offices.[129] In the case of corporate ownership, the search should include a search of corporate securities where still separated from other personal property securities.[130]

The search should also look for unregistered charges irrespective of whether the vessel is registered or licensed or not, right up to the eve of the sale. Mr. Justice Stone suggests that the making of enquiries in the geographical area of ownership and operation — whether commercial or recreational — might reveal outstanding claims against the ship,

---

125 A.J. Stone, "Let the Boat Buyer Beware" (1974) 12 Osgoode Hall L.J. 643.
126 *Ibid.* at 648.
127 See *Canada Shipping Act*, above note 1, ss.261–66.
128 *Sail Labrador Ltd. v. Challenge One (The)*, [1999] 1 S.C.R. 265. The *Canada Shipping Act*, above note 1, s.261 requires that the log book be kept on board the ship.
129 See Chapter 6, B(3) "Mortgages under Provincial Legislation."
130 See, e.g., *Corporation Securities Registration Act*, R.S.O. 1970, c.88.

such as liens for repairs, supplies, seamen's wages, damage claims, or salvage. The last three are particularly insidious, as they constitute maritime liens and are not defeated by a transfer of title. In terms of how far back in time the search should go, it is useful to keep in mind the limitation periods for these types of claims, and the fact that limitation periods vary from jurisdiction to jurisdiction. Bear in mind, however, that a court might exercise discretion as to whether it allows the continuation of proceedings as a result of a claim filed past the limitation period. The records of the Federal Court and the provincial superior court where the vessel was owned or operated ought to be checked to determine whether there are any actions *in rem* against the vessel and personal actions against the owners for unsatisfied claims. It should be remembered that the Federal Court registry in Ottawa acts as a central registry for the court in Canada but will not include information on maritime actions in other courts of competent jurisdiction.

If the title is in order and to the satisfaction of the purchaser and counsel, a bill of sale in statutory form should be executed and presented, together with other relevant documents required by the *Canada Shipping Act* for registration. In the case of a licensed vessel, one should require delivery of a duly executed deed of transfer and transfer of licence with all particulars.[131] Even before closing, however, it is necessary to ensure that all applicable taxes and other charges (e.g., statutory dues, such as port and inspection charges) are provided for and adjusted.[132] A final search for claims, including executions, is advisable. Time is of the essence, for a ship can continue to incur charges.

As a pragmatic recognition that a diligent search still might not uncover all claims against a vessel, it is useful to include in the contract a warranty by the seller (i.e., vendor's guarantee) that the vessel is being transferred free of all charges, encumbrances, and liens; that it is not subject to any action or execution at the time of the purchase; and that the seller undertakes, through an indemnification covenant, to indemnify the purchaser against all losses and costs resulting from the breach of the warranty, including costs of defending the title or claims, and that such covenant will survive the purchase.[133] Finally, marine title insurance has recently made a belated arrival in the world of shipping and is

---

131 A.J. Stone, above note 125 at 648.
132 *Ibid.* at 649. Under the *Canada Shipping Act*, above note 1, s.313 the shipowner is responsible for inspection costs. The *Canada Marine Act*, S.C. 1998, c.10, also provides for various types of fees such as, harbour dues, berthage, wharfage, duties, tolls, rates, and other charges. For instance, see the lien established in favour of a port authority and other persons in *Canada Marine Act, ibid.*, s.122.
133 A.J. Stone, *ibid.* at 649.

available in the United States for both nationally registered ships and ships registered under foreign flags. This type of insurance is also available for yachts. Marine title insurance promises to become the norm in shipping as it functions similarly to land property title insurance.

E. REGISTRATION OF A SHIP

An essential step that needs to be taken in order for a new or purchased ship to operate is registration. The shipowner will want to weigh various operational and commercial factors in deciding where to register the ship. Before proceeding with this discussion, the subject of ship nationality and Canada's responsibilities as a flag state over that ship must be addressed.

1) Ship Nationality and Canada as a Flag State

The registration of ships in Canada entails responsibilities for this country as a flag state at international law. The rights and duties of flag states are well developed and the most current statement on the international law in this regard is in Part VII, "High Seas," of the *United Nations Convention on the Law of the Sea*, many provisions of which are generally considered as customary law.[134] So although Canada is not yet a party to this important instrument, it is certainly bound by the customary law on particular matters.

Every state has the right to fix its own conditions for the granting of nationality, registration, and flying of its flag.[135] While there is a conventional law requirement that there be an existing genuine link between the ship and the state whose flag it flies, this particular requirement is not considered customary law.[136] The reality is that flags of convenience have a contrary practice, that is, they aim to encourage registration under their flag for vessels that will not have a genuine link to their flag. Flags of convenience allow foreign ownership of registered ships (more on this below). Canada, on the other hand, has adopted a genuine-link approach to registration. The nationality of the

---

134 *United Nations Convention on the Law of the Sea, 1982*, 10 December 1982, 1833 U.N.T.S. 3 Part VII [*UNCLOS*]. See also the *Convention on the High Seas, 1958*, 29 April 1958, 450 U.N.T.S. 82.
135 *UNCLOS*, ibid., art.91.
136 R.R. Churchill & A.V. Lowe, *The Law of the Sea*, 3d ed. (Manchester: Juris Publishing, Manchester University Press, 1999) at 258.

ship is a reflection of the nationality of the owner, that is, the real owner is registered as the ship or share owner. In effect, the requirement of Canadian ownership finds a parallel only with the ownership of aircraft, and the two constitute an exception to the normally unrestricted right of ownership of chattels and land in Canada.[137]

Normally, ships cannot be registered in more than one state, and a ship that sails under more than one flag for convenience purposes may be assimilated to a ship without nationality (i.e., a stateless ship).[138] A stateless ship is a ship without protection and may be visited and boarded on the high seas by the warships of any state.[139] Similarly, Canadian ships are not permitted to fly the flag of other states and, should they do so, their Canadian registration may be cancelled. There is a slightly different situation for bareboat charters, where some countries permit registration of the ship as a bareboat charter, even where that ship is also registered under another flag. Somewhat more restrictively in Canada, ships under a bareboat charter may be registered by a qualified person as long as the original registration is suspended, but the registration is only for the period of the charter and the charterer is not recorded as the owner.[140] If the charterer ceases to be in possession and control of the ship, the Chief Registrar has to be informed and, if the requirements are not met, the registration may be suspended or cancelled.[141] However, the rule remains that only one flag (i.e., that of the active registration) may be flown.

This exclusive jurisdiction of Canada is reflective of the territorial or *quasi*-territorial nature of ships. They carry the Canadian legal system on board and are, thereby, subject to Canadian sovereign legislative and enforcement control. Other flag states exercise similar exclusive sovereign control and this practice enables the maintenance of law and order at sea. As a result, Canada has the responsibility to exercise effective jurisdiction and control in administrative, technical, and social matters over its ships and to ensure that shipowners are amenable to its control.[142] This international responsibility is foundational to the maintenance of a register of ships. The power extends to

---

137 Canada, Canadian Transport Commission: Water Transport Committee, *The Ownership and Registration of Ships in Canada* (Ottawa: The Queen's Printer, 1969) at 5.
138 *UNCLOS*, above note 134, art.92.
139 *Ibid.*, art.110.
140 *Canada Shipping Act*, above note 1, ss.18 and 23(4); *Canada Shipping Act, 2001*, above note 2, ss.48 and 53(4).
141 *Canada Shipping Act*, ibid., s.28; *Canada Shipping Act, 2001*, ibid., s.58.
142 *UNCLOS*, above note 134, art.94(1).

various matters, including the maintenance of international safety and environmental standards, criminal law enforcement, and so on. Canada sets the standards and takes measures for its ships, which must be in accord with international standards, for, for instance: construction, equipment and seaworthiness; qualified master and crew, including training and work conditions, and safety and pollution prevention rules; use of signals, communications, and collision avoidance; regular inspection by qualified surveyors; and nautical publications, equipment, and instruments for safe navigation.[143] In turn, Canadian ships have a right to fly the Canadian flag and are entitled to the protection of the government of Canada, wherever they might be. This may take the form of diplomatic or consular assistance to the ship, master, and crew in situations of unlawful arrest, detention, or expropriation.

It should be pointed out that flag state jurisdiction is better described as primary, but not totally exclusive; there will be situations where the coastal state may be perfectly justified in exercising jurisdiction over foreign ships, such as where the effects of a criminal offence on board a ship passing through the territorial sea extend to the coastal state.[144] Depending on their location in another coastal state's maritime zones, Canadian ships in foreign waters are required to respect that state's laws and on many matters are also subject to its jurisdiction.[145] Similarly, a Canadian ship in a foreign port is subject to the jurisdiction of that state.

Canada exercises its international responsibilities in regard to ships through two institutions. At international maritime law, flag states are required to have a maritime administration and, in Canada, this is the Department of Transport, Marine Safety Division; various navigation and safety functions are also the responsibility of the Canadian Coast Guard, which is located in the Department of Fisheries and Oceans. Prior to 1995 the Coast Guard was part of the Department of Transport. An unfortunate division of the two as a result of a federal government re-organization has had the effect of fragmenting Canada's maritime administration.

Rules for registration of ships vary from state to state and are linked to, for instance, qualification of owners, financing arrangements, beneficial ownership, and control. The administrative aspects of these rules reflect the type of actual and effective control a state wishes to exercise over the vessels registered under its flag. In general, registra-

---

143 *Ibid.*, arts.94(3), (4), and (5).
144 *UNCLOS*, above note 134, art.27.
145 For instance, there is a duty to observe the laws and regulations of the coastal state in the exercise of innocent passage: *UNCLOS, ibid.*, art.21(4).

tion will indicate that the vessel complies with basic international rules regarding construction standards, navigational safety, manning, crew qualifications, health, and liability. Any vessel may be registered. However, under the *Canada Shipping Act*, all ships exceeding 15 GT are required to be registered. Registration in Canada provides convenient *prima facie* evidence of title and, from the standpoint of using the vessel as collateral, it enables a mortgagee to enter that mortgage on the register. Often, harbour dues and other such charges will be based on the "net registered tonnage" of the ship. Finally, in foreign waters the certificate of registry serves as the vessel's passport.

Ships involved in cabotage (or coastal trading, which is defined as trading from one port to another in Canada) must be Canadian, as this trade is reserved exclusively for Canadian ships. The *Coasting Trade Act* is a legislative attempt to protect the position of Canadian shipping with respect to this trade.[146] Where Canadian shipping is not adequate to meet the need, ships of all nations will be granted access to trade on payment of a reasonable fee to obtain a licence. This is done to ensure that shipping rates do not become unreasonably high. It is an offence for an unlicensed foreign ship to engage in coastal shipping.[147]

At present, there is no penalty imposed under the current *Canada Shipping Act* for failure to register a ship, but this will change when the new Act comes into force.[148] Currently, an unregistered ship will not be recognized in Canada and will forfeit all rights and privileges extended under the Act or those enjoyed by Canadian ships.

2) Canadian Register of Ships

The Canadian Register of Ships is maintained pursuant to the *Canada Shipping Act* and is located in the federal Department of Transport. When the *Canada Shipping Act, 2001* is fully brought into force, the register will become known as the Canadian Register of Vessels. The current Register of Ships is established and maintained by the Chief Registrar, who is located in Ottawa, and other registrars appointed by the chief registrar to service ports of registry throughout the country.[149] There are several designated ports of registry in every province and territory. Shipowners may register their ships at any port of registry.

---

146 S.C. 1992, c.31.
147 *Ibid.*, s.3(1).
148 *Canada Shipping Act*, above note 1, s.51(1); *Canada Shipping Act, 2001*, above note 2, ss.46(2) and 79(1)(a).
149 *Ibid.*, ss.13–14.

The register contains important information and documents on Canadian ships, including name, type of ship, official number, registered tonnage, name and address of owner(s), and details of mortgages secured on the ship.[150] The public at large can access information on Canadian ships. At the time of writing, the register has 46,500 ships with a total of 4.7 million GT. This is not the total number of ships in Canadian ownership, as only ships above 15 GT are required to be registered. Many boats below 15 tons would need to be licensed. Moreover, there are at least a hundred Canadian-owned ships with a total of 2.2 million GT registered under foreign flags.[151]

3) Procedure for Registration

a) Preliminary Steps

A vessel under construction that, when completed, will be a vessel registrable in Canada may be recorded, pending registration, under an assigned number and a temporary name. The vessel may be recorded as soon as it is "about to be built" by the owner, filing a Description of Ship Proposed to be Built form (Form 84-0066)[152] in the office of the registrar of ships at the port in Canada nearest to the place of the ship's construction. If a recorded vessel is sold, a bill of sale must be filed with the registrar, as ownership of the ship will be deemed to be unchanged until the recording of the bill of sale.

The first step in registering a ship is obtaining a name for the vessel. The owner submits a Notice of Name for a Ship or Change of Name of a Ship form (Form 84-0042)[153] to the registrar of the port where the vessel is intended to be registered. This form will have three alternative choices for the ship's name. The form will be forwarded to the central registry in Ottawa for approval. Approval will not be given if the names submitted are already allotted to other Canadian ships.

The owner must have the vessel measured for registration by the Government Measuring Surveyor of the Steamship Inspection Service. The surveyor will complete two documents, the Formula of Measurement and the Certificate of Survey, and send them to Ottawa for approval. The Formula of Measurement shows by what standards the ship's measurements were calculated; these standards are different for

---

150 *Canada Shipping Act*, above note 1, s.13(2).
151 Online at Transport Canada's ship registry web site: <www.tc.gc.ca/MarineSafety/Ships-and-operations-standards/registry.htm>.
152 Ship registry web site, *ibid*.
153 *Ibid*.

various classes of ships. The Certificate of Survey gives the formal particulars of the dimensions and the gross and net tonnages of the ship.

The registered tonnage of a ship is calculated in accordance with the *Ship Registration and Tonnage Regulations*.[154] The regulations do not apply to ships that do not need to be registered. For those that do need to be registered, the tonnage of the ship needs to be ascertained in accordance with the formula approved in the regulations known as *Standard for the Tonnage Measurement of Ships* (TP 13430).[155] This standard is published by the Department of Transport and is amended from time to time. The standard is based on the *International Convention on Tonnage Measurement of Ships, 1969*, which calls for specific methods of measurement of register tonnage.[156] An International Tonnage Certificate, once issued, must be maintained on board the ship.[157]

When the name of the vessel and the survey papers have been approved in Ottawa, they are forwarded to the registrar at the port where the vessel is intended to be registered. The registrar will then notify the owner that he or she is ready to proceed with the registration of the vessel. The owner will then present to the registrar the following documents:

- the Application for Registry (Form 84-0044);[158]
- the Builder's Certificate and First Transfer of Title (Form 84-0040);[159]
- the Declaration of Ownership/Declaration of Transfer of Ownership (Form 84-0002);[160] and
- the Bill of Sale (Form 84-0405),[161] if not previously filed with the registrar.

b) Application for Registry

The application is completed by the owner and is a formal request for registration. The owner also appoints a "manager," "managing owner," or "ship's husband" for the vessel, primarily for the purpose of having someone accountable for the ship. A ship's manager is a person desig-

---

154 *Ship Registration and Tonnage Regulations*, S.O.R./2000-70.
155 *Ibid.*, ss.13, 15, and 23. See ship registry web site, above note 151.
156 *International Convention on Tonnage Measurement of Ships, 1969*, 23 June 1969, 1291 U.N.T.S. 3.
157 *Ship Registration and Tonnage Regulations*, above note 154, s.12.
158 Ship registry web site, above note 151.
159 *Ibid.*
160 *Ibid.*
161 *Ibid.*

nated by a corporation to look after the business of the ship. The managing owner is a person who owns a share or shares of the ship. A ship's husband is a person designated to look after the business of the ship but who actually owns no shares.

c) **Builder's Certificate and First Transfer of Title**
This document is completed and signed by the builder of the ship. It gives the names of the shipbuilder, the shipowner, and an estimation of the dimensions and tonnage of the ship.

d) **Declaration of Ownership and Declaration of Transfer of Ownership**
As seen above, under the *Canada Shipping Act*, a Canadian ship must have "qualified" owners. In practice, there is a considerable difference between actual and beneficial ownership of registered ships. To avoid potential liabilities arising from the operation of vessels, many ships are registered under their own individual companies (one ship/one company-owner). Any liability would then be limited to that ship/company alone. In the case of flags of convenience, beneficial ownership and control of the vessel is much harder to trace. Many legal systems will not allow the veil of actual ownership to be lifted.[162] Trusts, be they express, implied, or constructive, are not entered into the Canadian register.[163] Consequently, the shipowner has complete freedom to dispose of his or her share in the ship, except, of course, when the ship is mortgaged.

e) **Certificate of Registry**
When all the above documents are completed and presented to the registrar, and when the registration fee, based on the gross tonnage of the ship, has been paid, the registrar will enter the details of the documents in the registry and will issue a Certificate of Registry, which acts as the ship's passport and remains with the vessel. The certificate will carry important information on the ship.[164] The certificate will need to be produced for inspection and constitutes evidence in a court of law.[165] The Certificate of Registry will not be delivered to the shipowner until

---

162 *Salomon v. A. Salomon & Co.*, [1897] A.C. 22.
163 *Canada Shipping Act*, above note 1, s.23(9); *Canada Shipping Act, 2001*, above note 2, s.53(9).
164 *Canada Shipping Act*, ibid., s.24; *Canada Shipping Act, 2001*, ibid., s.54.
165 *Canada Shipping Act*, ibid., s.311, re: the inspector's authority to request the certificate.

the Ship's Carving and Marking Note is returned to the registrar.[166] Also, it is important to note that the certificate carries an expiry date and will therefore need to be renewed regularly. Non-renewal may lead to suspension and eventual removal from the registry.[167] A ship may not be operated without having the certificate on board; nor can the certificate be attached by any creditor.[168]

f) Bill of Sale

Unless the bill of sale was filed for the recording of the vessel, this document must be presented to the registrar with the Application for Registry. The bill confirms that the registered owner is the actual owner of the ship and the document must be registered in order for the owner to obtain a complete title to the ship.

g) Ship's Carving and Marking Note

The vessel should be marked for identification purposes under the *Canada Shipping Act* and, until the marking is completed, the ship's Certificate of Registry is not valid. The marking includes the ship's name, register tonnage, official number, and any other information specified by the Chief Registrar. The ship has to be kept marked in the locations prescribed by law and it is an offence to deface, alter, conceal, or remove the markings.[169] On pleasure craft, the number must be fitted so that it is permanent in nature and cannot be easily removed or altered. The ship is then inspected to see that the markings are correct. If they are, then the certificate will be signed and returned to the registrar.

h) Transcript of Registry

This document will then be completed by the registrar and forwarded to the register in Ottawa, and the ship will be properly registered. It should be stressed that all documents presented to the registrar must be meticulously correct. Any errors or discrepancies can lead to delay in their processing.

i) Registration of a Foreign-Built Vessel in Canada

If a shipowner desires to register a foreign-built vessel in Canada, there are some difficulties. The Minister of Transport must consent to the

---

166 *Canada Shipping Act*, ibid., s.27(2); *Canada Shipping Act, 2001*, above note 2, s.57(2).
167 *Canada Shipping Act*, ibid., s.30; *Canada Shipping Act, 2001*, ibid., s.60.
168 *Canada Shipping Act*, ibid., s.33(4); *Canada Shipping Act, 2001*, ibid., s.63(4).
169 *Canada Shipping Act*, ibid., s.27; *Canada Shipping Act, 2001*, ibid., ss.57, 79(1)(c), and (d).

registration of a foreign-built ship.[170] Also, except for fishing vessels, duty must be paid on ships brought into Canada at the prevailing rate, unless there is a special exemption given by the minister.

j) Provisional Registration

If a shipowner purchases a ship in a foreign country and wishes to register it in Canada, he or she will have to file an Application to Obtain a Provisional Certificate of Registry for an Unregistered Ship (Form 84-0149)[171] with the Canadian Consul in the foreign country or port. This certificate expires either on arrival at a Canadian port where there is a Registrar of Shipping, or six months after the date of the document, whichever comes first.

k) Registry of Alterations, Registry Anew, and Transfer of Registry

When a ship is altered in such a way that it no longer meets its description as contained in the register, the shipowner is required to register the alteration with the registrar nearest to the port where the alterations were made. Whenever the ownership of a ship is changed, the owner(s) of the ship may register the ship anew with the registry of the port in which the ship is registered. Registry anew is not required under the *Canada Shipping Act*. If a ship is transferred to a different port, then one should obtain a Declaration of Transfer of Registry (Form 84-0048),[172] and have all the ship's owners or mortgagees send a declaration in writing to the registrar of the ship's port of registry.

F. REGISTRATION UNDER FLAGS OF CONVENIENCE

1) Issues

a) Traditional Flags of Convenience and Open Registries

So far the discussion has focused on the registration of ships in Canada. Clearly, the shipowner will have to decide whether he or she wants to register the ship in Canada or in another country. This will be primarily a business decision, although such other factors as flag loyalty and requirements of coastal trading will also influence the decision.

---

170 *Canada Shipping Act*, ibid., s.20; *Canada Shipping Act, 2001*, ibid., s.50.
171 Ship registry web site, above note 151.
172 *Ibid.*

Should a shipowner consider a foreign flag, however, there is a good likelihood that a flag of convenience, also known as open registry, will be considered.

While flags of convenience date from the sixteenth century, their modern ascendancy commenced after the Second World War when there was a tremendous need for new tonnage. Unfortunately, the lending institutions were not willing to allocate the financial resources necessary to build this new tonnage, as the fiscal policies of traditional flag states seemed to divert much of the shipowner's profits to government tax collectors, leaving little for repayment of loans. Moreover, union activity also created barriers for shipowners not using convenience flags. While the desire to escape governmental regulations might also have played a role, this was a minor factor. By 1976, over one-quarter of the world's fleet sailed under flags of convenience. Most frequently, tankers and combination bulk/oil carriers use flags of convenience, whereas cargo freighters or container ships seldom do. The principal flag of convenience states and jurisdictions today include the Bahamas, Barbados, Cambodia, the Cayman Islands, Cyprus, Gibraltar, Liberia, Malta, the Marshall Islands, Panama, Vanuatu, and several others. There is no one organization with the authority to determine what registry is a flag of convenience or not. The International Transportation Workers' Federation, an important and powerful trade union organization, has designated these and several more states.[173]

These young maritime states are by no means the only states that have adopted policies to attract shipping in similar ways, often preferring the designation of open registries. Some traditional maritime states have developed secondary registers with nuanced differences. The idea is to try to attract their owners back to their flags by providing significant incentives. The Norwegian International Ship Register and Danish International Ship Register are two examples of registers that attract beneficially owned tonnage and have entered into agreements with the national unions concerning crew wages.[174] Other secondary registers, such as the German International Register and the Spanish Register in the Canary Islands, are considered closer to the flag of convenience model.[175]

There have been various attempts through international conventions to ensure convenience states maintain some sort of watchdog agency, predominantly by extending the notion of a genuine link

---

173 *Ship Registration: Law and Practice*, above note 44 at 17.
174 Ibid.
175 Ibid.

between the ship and flag State. These efforts are intended to prevent unscrupulous owners from relying upon lax standards to allow unseaworthy ships to operate under flags of convenience. Efforts in this regard are the *Convention on the High Seas, 1958*,[176] the *United Nations Convention on the Law of the Sea, 1982*,[177] and the *United Nations Convention on Conditions for Registration of Ships, 1986*,[178] which all promote the requirement of a genuine link between a ship and a flag state, and the duties of this state to exercise effective jurisdiction and control over its ships. Flag states should have competent and adequate national maritime administrations that apply international standards. More specifically, they are expected to ensure that shipowners, managers, or operators are readily identifiable and accountable; that ships are surveyed and inspected regularly; that documentation is proper and valid; and that there is compliance with laws and regulations. However, as has been seen, this attempt at promoting a genuine link has been primarily an international conventional law effort and has certainly not succeeded in developing a customary norm in this regard.

Today flags of convenience may be defined as national flags of those states with whom shipowners register vessels in order to gain some particular benefit, more often than not a fiscal one, and without necessarily having a genuine link, whether in terms of beneficial ownership or some other close relationship — not simply a fictitious legal link — to the flag state. By registering a ship under such a flag, shipowners will avoid the fiscal obligations and the conditions and terms of employment that would have been applicable if their tonnage were entered in the register of their own states. Various characteristics of flags of convenience include allowing ownership and/or control of merchant vessels by non-citizens; maintaining easy access to the registry (i.e., allowing a ship to be registered at consulates abroad); placing few restrictions on owners to transfer their registry; keeping taxes on ship income low (i.e., a registry fee and an annual fee, based on tonnage, are normally the only charges made); and permitting the crewing of ships by non-nationals. It is not necessarily the case that a flag of convenience has lower safety standards; more often than not they apply international standards pursuant to International Maritime Organisation conventions. However, the enforcement of those standards may not be optimal, possibly because of an insufficiently developed maritime

---

176 Above note 134.
177 *Ibid.*
178 7 February 1986, 26 I.L.M. 1229 (not yet in force).

administration, irregular monitoring of registered ships, lack of experienced surveying inspectors, and a global presence ready to provide service to their ships. As a result, it does happen that flags of convenience may not have the power or the administrative capacity to impose any national or international regulations on the ships themselves.

As the *raison d'être* of flags of convenience is to decrease operating costs, it should be pointed out that the average saving resulting from operating under such a flag ranges between 14 and 20 percent.[179] A reduction of this magnitude could easily double or triple a shipowner's profit margin. Consider, for instance, the types of expenses where the shipowner has flexibility or discretion, and it will be understood why these flags are so popular and account for the bulk of the world's tonnage. A ship's main costs are mortgages, registration fees, maintenance, insurance, bunkers, disbursements, crew, and taxes. Of all these costs, a shipowner can cut expenses without affecting the safe operation of the ship only in relation to registration fees, crew's wages, and taxes. A flag of convenience will frequently have lower registration fees, allows the employment of foreign crews — so that the shipowner can shop around the world for inexpensive crew and officers — and has low or no taxes.

Critics of flags of convenience are frequently of the opinion that the qualifications of crews and the compliance of vessels with safety standards are substantially lower than with ships flying the flag of a traditional shipping state. Today requirements under the *International Convention on Standards of Training, Certification and Watchkeeping for Seafarers, 1978*, as amended,[180] and the *International Safety Management Code* are general standards irrespective of where the ship is registered, and they are applied through port state control inspection in relation to any ship. A close look at the most recent *Paris* and *Tokyo Memoranda on Port State Control*, and Canadian port state control reports shows that flags of convenience do not necessarily top the list of flag states with major deficiencies that frequently result in the detentions of ships in ports.[181]

---

179 A survey reported in R. Doganis & B.N. Metaxas, *The Impact of Flags of Convenience* (London: Polytechnic of Central London, 1976).
180 7 July 1978, 1361 U.N.T.S. 2 [*STCW 1978*].
181 *Memorandum of Understanding on Port State Control in Implementing Agreements on Maritime Safety and Protection of the Marine Environment*, 26 January 1982, 21 I.L.M. 1 [*Paris MOU 1982*]; and *Memorandum of Understanding on Port State Control in the Asia-Pacific Region, 1993*, 1 December 1993, online at: <www.tokyo-mou.org> [*Tokyo MOU 1993*].

b) Flags of Environmental Convenience

Another dimension of flags of convenience is the relatively recent phenomenon of registration of fishing vessels in states that are not parties to regional fishery agreements and organizations. This enables avoidance of fisheries quota, management, conservation, and compliance requirements. Close to Canada, this has been a problem for the Northwest Atlantic Fisheries Organization (NAFO)'s attempts over the years in managing efforts and allocations of multiple-user fisheries straddling the high seas and Canada's exclusive economic zone. Whereas member states are bound by NAFO collective decisions, non-state parties are not; as a result distant fishing fleet operators have often capitalized on this situation by registering ships under the flags of non-parties, thereby to exploit the traditional and often abused freedom to fish on the high seas.[182]

The Food and Agriculture Organisation of the United Nations (FAO) has led efforts to regulate the registration of fishing vessels for "environmental," as distinct from the usual commercial convenience. In particular, the FAO's *Agreement to Promote Compliance with International Conservation and Management Measures by Fishing Vessels on the High Seas, 1993,* is an attempt to provide restrictions on such practices and promote a genuine link between the registered fishing vessel and registering state.[183] Under the agreement, the flag state has a responsibility to take effective measures against rogue ships. Similarly, no state party will register a fishing vessel, previously registered in another contracting state, unless it is satisfied that the vessel has been removed from the registry of the previous state and is not attempting to undermine international conservation agreements.[184] Similar provisions aimed at the flag state, but backed by a tighter compliance and enforcement regime, are to be found in the *Agreement for the Implementation of the Provisions of the United Nations Convention on the Law of the Sea of 10 December 1982 Relating to the Conservation and Management of Straddling Fish Stocks*

---

182 On this problem and related compliance and enforcement concerns in the NAFO regulatory area, see D.M. Johnston, A. Chircop, & H. Williamson, *Straddling Stocks in the Northwest Atlantic: Conservation Concerns and Options*, Report to the Fisheries Council of Canada by the Marine and Environmental Law Program, Dalhousie Law School (Halifax, April 2003).

183 *Agreement to Promote Compliance with International Conservation and Management Measures by Fishing Vessels on the High Seas*, 27th Conf., UN Doc. C/93/26 (1993). Canada became a party in 1994 but at the time of writing, the *Compliance Agreement* had received eighteen acceptances, seven short of the required number to enter into force.

184 *Ibid.*, art.III.

and Highly Migratory Fish Stocks, 1995 (UNFA).[185] A flag state may authorize its fishing vessels to fish on the high seas only when it can exercise its *UNCLOS* and *UNFA* responsibilities effectively.[186] This agreement promises to address the endemic problem of flag-hopping to avoid conservation restrictions.

2) Factors to be Considered in Choosing a Flag of Convenience

Several factors should be considered in choosing one flag of convenience over another. To start, it is worth examining the tax policies of the flags that are of interest. Some states offer lengthy tax holidays, perhaps as long as twenty years. Some states allow all shares in the ship to be shares in blank, which may even prevent the registrar of companies in that state from knowing the identity of the shareholders in the shipowning company. Non-nationals may hold title to ships. Some convenience states do require that a vessel be owned by a national corporation, which is an advantage if tax avoidance is the client's primary concern. To overcome this obstacle one often follows the "double company" route. This requires, first, the incorporation in the convenience flag state of Company X, which owns the ship and, second, the incorporation of Company Y, in the same state, which owns all the shares of Company X. The client, who is not a national, holds all the shares of Company Y. As a result, Company X is qualified to own a ship as a citizen in the convenience flag state and Company Y qualifies as the beneficial owner of all of the shares of Company X.

The transfer and registration costs can be significant. It is important to factor the costs of incorporation, registration fees (per ton), continuing legal fees, costs of filing returns, maintenance of records and office, and so on. It is worth finding out how much the legal system differs from Canada's. As most Commonwealth countries based their merchant shipping acts on the U.K. *Merchant Shipping Act, 1894*,[187] for Canadian lawyers it is more convenient to choose a Commonwealth state as a flag of convenience, such as the Bahamas, or such colonial flags as Bermuda or the Cayman Islands. As Liberian and Panamanian merchant shipping law is based on the laws of the United States, American shipowners and lawyers tend to prefer those states. Knowledge about the legal system in the convenience flag state

---

185 4 December 1995, 2001 A.T.S. 8.
186 *Ibid.*, art.18(2).
187 (U.K.), 57 & 58 Vict., c.60.

becomes important in relation to the rights and obligations of mortgagees and mortgagors, and so on. A further advantage for Canadians in using a Commonwealth convenience state is that, generally, such Canadian forms as the Declaration of Ownership or the Application for Registry, are accepted there.

Research on crewing requirements may provide useful information, as crew costs range from 47 per cent of the operating costs on vessels of up to 20,000 tons to 11 per cent on vessels of 300,000 tons or more. It should be remembered that crewing costs constitute one major reason for flagging out. Also relevant is whether there is a requirement of homeport visits at regular intervals.

Finally, it is worth finding out if there are any currency controls, such as foreign exchange restrictions, in the proposed convenience flag state as well as the stability of the currency in which business will be conducted. An added consideration is the political and economic stability of the proposed state. Financiers who supply the funds for purchase or new construction should consider this point carefully. Some flags of convenience, such as Liberia and the Marshall Islands, are not necessarily administered in the country of the flag but may be run by corporations delegated to do so from overseas.

If the picture of flags of convenience is painted too brightly so far, it should be pointed out that there may be significant disadvantages in their use, since an owner who registers under such a flag will have to forgo any subsidies or inducements offered by his or her own government to its shipping industry. Also, a ship flying a convenience flag may be subject to blacklisting by unions. Moreover, there are certain factors making Canadian registration desirable, if not mandatory in some cases, such as cabotage. Although there are some quality flags of convenience, there are also those that are of poor quality. To many, poor quality flags of convenience raise serious ethical and legal questions, especially where true ownership cannot be traced; seamen are not properly protected, including when their fundamental rights are violated; crew and training certification is issued without proper quality controls; and safety standards are not enforced. While there are many reputable and conscientious shipowners, there are also those that readily exploit the weak flags. At a time when international security is at the forefront of national and international concern, the inability to trace true ownership under certain flags raises very real concerns.

Care should be exercised in selecting flags of convenience. International security and coastal environmental concerns are placing these flags under intense scrutiny. It is possible that, under international pressure, weak flags may be pushed out of business, while others may continue to thrive. For the latter, the future could be bright if they manage to promote transparency and quality, even if such traditional maritime states as the United Kingdom continue to be successful in creating new policies to induce shipowners to return to their flags. Some flags of convenience are already reacting to international concerns and are stiffening their safety regulations and enforcement procedures, aided by the underwriters and the classification societies. As their safety records improve, flags of convenience will become more respectable.

G. LICENSING

In addition to the occasional references to the licensing of boats above, more needs to be said on licensing requirements as its effects are significantly different from registration. For instance, a licence is not evidence of title and a mortgage on a licensed vessel is not registered against the licence. Also, whereas small commercial vessels are licensed by the Department of Transport's Small Vessel Licensing Program, pleasure craft are licensed by the Department of Fisheries and Oceans.

Every commercial vessel operated in Canada that does not exceed 15 GT, and every pleasure craft with 15 GT or less, and that is equipped with a motor of 7.5 kW of power or more, has to be licensed, unless it is registered under the *Canada Shipping Act*; it is registered or licensed in a foreign country and not principally maintained or operated in Canada; it is a lifeboat or other survival craft that is part of a ship's equipment; or it is an amphibious vehicle for which a provincial automobile licence for highway travel is required.[188]

Pleasure craft licences are issued without charge, but there is a charge for commercial vessels.[189] The licensing system is substantially the same as that for licensing a motor vehicle. An application form and document that establishes ownership of the vessel are submitted. Information as to the boat's length, breadth, draught, approximate register tonnage, and type of engine is required. The licence number must be noted on each side of the bow so as to be clearly visible, in block characters not less than 77 mm (3 inches) high and in a colour that contrasts with the background. As nothing should be allowed to obscure this number, the name of the boat should be placed on the stern.

As with a motor vehicle, the boat's licence and certificate of insurance should be kept with the vessel at all times. Under the *Small Vessel*

---

188 *Small Vessel Regulations*, above note 30, s.7.
189 *Ships Registry and Licensing Fees Tariff*, S.O.R./2002-172, s.2.

Regulations, a vessel is deemed to be unlicensed until it is proved otherwise.[190] Presentation of the licence is the simplest way of proving its existence. When the boat changes hands, the owner must sign the existing licence on the reverse and deliver it to the new owner. Then the previous owner must notify in writing the Department of Transport or the Department of Fisheries and Oceans at the port where the vessel is licensed of the change in ownership. The new owner must complete the transfer on the existing licence or complete the application for transfer, include the bill of sale and any other document that establishes ownership, and forward the documents to the Department of Transport or the Department of Fisheries and Oceans, as the case may be.

FURTHER READINGS

ADEMUNI-ODEKE, *Bareboat Charter (Ship) Registration* (The Hague: Kluwer Law International, 1998).

BOWTLE, G. & K. MCGUINNESS, *The Law of Ship Mortgages* (London: Lloyd'sPress, 2001).

COLES, R.M.F. & N. READY, eds., *Ship Registration: Law and Practice* (London: Lloyd's Press, 2002).

CURTIS, S., *The Law of Shipbuilding Contracts*, 2d ed. (London: Lloyd's Press, 1996).

FERNANDES, R.M., *Boating Law of Canada* (Toronto: Carswell, 1989).

GASKELL, N.J.J., *Ship Registration* (London: Sweet & Maxwell, 1993).

GASKELL, N.J.J., C. DEBATTISTA, & R.J. SWATTON, *Chorley and Giles' Shipping Law*, 8th ed. (London: Pitman Publishing, 1987).

GOLDREIN, I. & TURNER P., *Ship Sale and Purchase*, 4d ed. (London: Lloyd's of London Press, 2003).

READY, N., *Ship Registration*, 3d ed. (London: Lloyd's of London Press, 1998).

STONE, A.J., "Let the Boat Buyer Beware" (1974) 12 Osgoode Hall L.J. 643.

---

190 *Small Vessel Regulations*, above note 30, s.8(2).

CHAPTER 5

THE SAFETY MANAGEMENT OF SHIPS

A. INTRODUCTION

Like any other business, shipping depends on proper management and competent staff. In addition, as ships operate in the marine environment, with its inherent dangers and commensurate problems, crewing and management become especially critical. Accordingly, the profitable performance of a ship's voyage is closely linked to adequate maritime safety. In the modern context this link is closely monitored by international law, regional controls, national regulatory systems, and industry requirements. This legal regime is designed not only to protect ships and those who sail on them from maritime and other dangers but also to safeguard coastal states and shorelines from the dangers that ships may represent. For shipowners this regime has become at least as important as the commercial basis on which the shipping industry depends. In other words, valuable ships and equally valuable cargoes have to be managed in terms of safety as well as in terms of commercial viability. For much of its long history, maritime law appears to have been more concerned with the preservation of maritime property than with specific maritime safety. This is, in fact, reflected in the existing maritime legal regime. However, this has changed with the development of a new safety regime that forms the basis of modern ship operations. This management regime is based on considerations related to the regulation of safety at sea, the conditions of employment for seafarers, the standards of training and competence of seafarers, the management of maritime safety, the carriage of dangerous cargoes at sea, the classification of ships, regulations for ships' load lines, accident investigations, and port state control. This development has also had a significant impact on maritime law practice, which now responds as much to public maritime law aspects as it does to the more traditional private law aspects. This also means that anyone practising in the area today must have a good base of knowledge in both aspects. It is for this reason that this special chapter on safety management has been prepared.

B. SAFETY OF SHIPS

1) Background

Safety at sea includes the material state resulting from the absence of exposure to danger, as well as the regime designed to create or perpetuate such a situation.[1] This concept includes three separate aspects: the health and safety of individuals at sea, the safety of navigation, and national security in terms of national defence requirements. Maritime safety is regarded as one of the essential elements for protecting human life at sea; for protecting maritime property; and for protecting the marine environment. This is considered important enough to permit a departure from the generally overriding principle of freedom of the seas. More specifically, safety at sea includes the following:

- safety of navigation, involving the protection and saving of human life at sea, providing a defence against the perils of the sea arising from weather and sea conditions, collision, stranding, fire, and any other danger that may be encountered during the voyage by a vessel; and
- safety of trading, involving the protection of the ship against risks that may arise from such unlawful acts as piracy, terrorism, maritime fraud, restraint by states, and barratry.

In other words, safety at sea is designed to protect ships and those who sail them from maritime risks that can be defined in two broad categories: personal risks that include injuries and death resulting from accidents on board ships, and collective risks that are specifically relat-

---

1   P. Boisson, *Safety at Sea: Policies, Regulations and International Law* (Paris: Bureau Veritas, 1999) at 31. This is one of the most authoritative examinations of the subject presently available.

ed to the ship, its cargo, and its navigation.[2] Maritime risks are generally set out under seven principal casualty categories:[3]

- missing ships: ships of which no news has been received for a reasonable period of time and which are considered lost;
- fire and explosion: caused by an internal or external source;
- collision: contact with another vessel or other vessels, regardless of whether under way, moored, or anchored;[4]
- contact or allision: contact with fixed or floating objects other than ships, including docks, harbour facilities, bridges, or offshore structures;[5]
- grounding: accidental contact with the seabed or riverbed;
- loss: resulting from hull or machinery failure or damage; and
- foundering: loss or sinking of a vessel owing to heavy weather, a latent defect in the vessel, or any other consequence not already stated.

Maritime risks have been present since the sea was first used for transportation and communication.[6] Throughout maritime history, the use of the sea involved many risks that resulted in significant loss of life, injury, and loss of ships and cargo. However, the concern for safety at sea is of more recent vintage. In fact, in earlier times, the absence of safety concerns ensured that maritime commerce was mainly the preserve of adventurers. This fact was quite apparent until relatively modern times, when marine insurance documents still referred to shipping risks as "maritime adventures." As a result, the regulation of maritime safety developed only very gradually and, when it did, it was as a reactive response to serious maritime accidents and disasters.

2) Safety of Life at Sea Conventions, 1914–60

While a certain amount of maritime safety standard setting had occurred already in the nineteenth century, The Titanic disaster in 1912 was the real beginning of a truly international maritime safety regime. Just two years after the disaster, and in response to the global concern that had arisen, the first international conference on the safety of life at sea was held in London, England, at the invitation of the British govern-

---

2 Ibid. at 31.
3 As provided annually by Lloyd's Register of Shipping, at <www.lr.org/code/home.htm>.
4 See Chapter 11, "Maritime Collisions."
5 Ibid.
6 Boisson, Safety at Sea, above note 1, c.2, for a very thorough discussion of the history of safety at sea.

ment. Despite the fact that there was much opposition to the establishment of a global maritime safety regime, the conference was able to conclude the first *Convention on Safety of Life at Sea* (*SOLAS*).[7] This standard-setting process was developed significantly between the two world wars. In 1920 another international conference updated earlier rules on wireless telegraphy at sea and, at the same time, confirmed the *SOLAS* principles. Subsequent conferences finalized standard international regulations on maritime radio communications.[8] A second *SOLAS* conference in 1929 adopted a new *SOLAS* convention that included areas such as ship construction, lifesaving equipment, fire safety, wireless telegraphy equipment, navigation aids, and collision regulations.

The action was then shifted to the League of Nations, which sponsored a number of important initiatives in 1930 and 1936 that standardized maritime signalling, light vessels, lighthouses, maritime radio beacons, and the buoyage system. In the aftermath of the Second World War, a number of conferences amended existing regimes and texts and also introduced a new registered tonnage system. In 1948 the British government once again invited all states that had signed or implemented the first *SOLAS* regime, to an international conference that would revise the existing convention. The result was *SOLAS 1948*, the first fully comprehensive, international convention on safety of life at sea.[9] The fourth *SOLAS* conference in 1960 was held under the auspices of the Inter-Governmental Maritime Consultative Organisation (IMCO)[10] that had been fully established in 1958. This conference was necessitated by the fact that a number of further technical advances, which had occurred since 1948, dictated substantial revisions to *SOLAS 1948*. The result was the *SOLAS 1960* convention.[11] Each of these successive *SOLAS* conventions represents a step forward in the international development of maritime safety and, at the same time, reflects the technological progress of the world shipping industry.

---

7   20 January 1914, 108 F.S.P. 283 [*SOLAS*]. Although the first *SOLAS* convention was signed by only five states, it was extensively implemented in Britain, France, the U.S., the Scandinavian states, Canada, and Australia.
8   Washington 1927 and Madrid 1931.
9   *International Convention on Safety of Life at Sea*, 10 June 1948, 191 U.N.T.S. 3 [*SOLAS 1948*] (entered into force on 19 November 1952).
10 The predecessor of the International Maritime Organisation: see G(1)(a) in Chapter 2, "The Shipping Industry: An Overview."
11 *International Convention on Safety of Life at Sea*, 17 June 1960, 536 U.N.T.S. 27 [*SOLAS 1960*] (entered into force on 26 May 1965; entered into force in Canada on the same date); see also Institute of Maritime Law, *The Ratification of Maritime Conventions*, 4 vols., Updated looseleaf service (London: Lloyd's Press, 1991–2003) vol.I.3.10.

3) Outline of *SOLAS 1974*

In order to update *SOLAS 1960* a series of amendments were adopted by the Inter-Governmental Maritime Consultative Organization in 1966, 1967, 1969, 1971, and 1973. However, the amendment procedure in place at that time resulted in very slow acceptance. In fact none of these amendments entered into force. As a result, it was decided to hold a fifth *SOLAS* conference in 1974, which produced the *International Convention for the Safety of Life at Sea, 1974 (SOLAS 1974)* — the current treaty, which has been widely accepted.[12] It specifies the minimum standards for the construction, equipment, and operation of merchant ships. Contracting states are required to ensure that ships under their flags comply with the convention's requirements and a number of certificates attesting to this are prescribed.[13] *SOLAS 1974* has undergone some forty amendment procedures between 1981 and 2002.[14] In addition, two protocols to *SOLAS 1974* were concluded in 1978 and in 1988.[15] *SOLAS 1974* does not cover all ships; it exempts[16] warships and troop ships, cargo ships of less than 500 GT, ships not propelled by mechanical means, wooden ships of primitive build, pleasure yachts not engaged in trade, and fishing vessels. It should be noted that, unless expressly provided,[17] *SOLAS 1974* would not apply to vessels solely navigating the Great Lakes and the St. Lawrence River.[18]

SOLAS 1974, as amended, consists of 13 articles and a lengthy, comprehensive, technical annex, consisting of 12 chapters setting out 278 regulations covering the following:

- General Provisions (Regulations 1–21);

---

12   1 November 1974, 1184 U.N.T.S. 2 (entered into force on 15 May 1980); see also *Ratification of Maritime Conventions*, ibid., vol.I.3.20–41.
13   Ibid.
14   Of these forty amendments, about half have formally entered into force. Some others are, however, in force because of the IMO's tacit amendment procedure.
15   *Protocol Relating to the International Convention for the Safety of Life at Sea, 1974*, 17 February 1978, 1276 U.N.T.S. 237 [*SOLAS Prot 1978*] (entered into force on 1 May 1981; not yet accepted by Canada); *Protocol of 1988 Relating to the International Convention for the Safety of Life at Sea, 1974*, 11 November 1988, U.S. Treaty Doc. 102-2 [*SOLAS Prot 1988*] (entered into force on 3 February 2000, not yet accepted by Canada); see also *Ratification of Maritime Conventions*, above note 11, vols.I.3.30 and I.3.40.
16   *SOLAS 1974*, above note 12, c.I-3.
17   Ibid., c.V.
18   As far east as a straight line drawn from Cap des Rosiers to West Point, Anticosti Island, and on the north side of Anticosti Island, the sixty-third meridian.

- Construction — Structure, Subdivision and Stability, Machinery and Electrical Installations (Regulations 1–54);
- Construction — Fire Protection, Fire Detection and Fire Extinction (Regulations 1–63);
- Life-saving Appliances and Arrangements (Regulations 1–37);
- Radio-communications (Regulations 1–19);
- Safety of Navigation (Regulations 1–23);
- Carriage of Cargoes (Regulations 1–9);
- Carriage of Dangerous Goods (Regulations 1–16);[19]
- Nuclear Ships (Regulations 1–12);
- Management for the Safe Operation of Ships (Regulations 1–6);
- Safety Measures for High Speed Craft (Regulations 1–3);
- Special Measures to Enhance Maritime Safety (Regulations 1–4); and
- Additional Safety Measures for Bulk Carriers (Regulations 1–11).

Although *SOLAS* has as its basis the principle of flag state jurisdiction, it also provides for port state jurisdiction. States that have accepted the *SOLAS Prot 1978* are also obliged to apply the convention's requirements to ships of states that have not accepted it. This is designed to ensure that such ships are not given more favourable treatment.[20] In other words, a vessel under the flag of a state that is not party to *SOLAS* must, nevertheless, comply with its standards. Ships to which *SOLAS 1974* applies must comply with technical requirements and standards set out in the regulations contained in the annex. When a state accepts *SOLAS* these regulations are transposed into national requirements under the relevant national legislation.[21] In order to ensure compliance, ships are subjected to various periodic inspections and surveys that are carried out by qualified and authorized officers of the maritime administration of the flag state, by port state inspectors drawn from the port state's maritime administration,[22] or by qualified surveyors from organ-

---

19   See also IMO, *International Maritime Dangerous Goods Code (IMDG Code)* (London: International Maritime Organisation, 1986); IMO, *International Code on the Construction and Equipment of Ships Carrying Dangerous Chemicals in Bulk* (London: International Maritime Organisation, 1998); IMO, *International Code for the Construction and Equipment of Ships Carrying Liquefied Gases in Bulk* (London: International Maritime Organisation, 1998).
20   *SOLAS Prot 1978*, above note 15, art.II(3).
21   In Canada in the *Canada Shipping Act*, R.S.C. 1985, c.S-9, s.316; *Canada Shipping Act, 2001*, S.C. 2001, c.26, s.29; and the regulations under these Acts. These are further discussed below.
22   Under the various port state memoranda in force in a number of regions of the world. Canada is subject to the Paris and Tokyo memoranda on port state control. See below in this chapter and also, *SOLAS 1974*, above note 12, c.I-19.

izations recognized or nominated by the flag state.[23] After such inspections or surveys, the relevant maritime administration certifies the completeness and efficacy of what has taken place. The surveys and inspections required by *SOLAS* include the following:

- An initial survey is to be completed before the ship enters service.[24]
- A periodic survey is to be completed for passenger ships once every twelve months, and for cargo ships at intervals specified by the flag state's maritime administration but not exceeding five years.
- An additional survey is to be completed as the need arises (i.e., whenever any important repairs, renewals, or alterations are made).
- One intermediate survey, at least, in addition to periodic surveys, must be undergone for a tank vessel more than ten years in age during the validity of the Cargo Ship Construction Certificate and the Cargo Ship Safety Equipment Certificate.
- Unscheduled inspections are to be carried out during the validity of the Cargo Ship Construction Certificate; however, such inspections are not mandatory where the flag state has made provision for a mandatory annual survey.[25]
- Life-saving and other equipment of cargo ships are subject to an initial survey and then to subsequent surveys every two years.
- Radio, radar, and other shipboard electronic installations are subject to an initial survey and then to subsequent surveys every year.

The scope of the required surveys and inspections is set out in the regulations under Chapter 1 of the *SOLAS 1974* Annex. For example, the initial and periodic surveys must have the ability to ensure that the arrangements, materials, and scantlings of the ship's structure; boilers and other pressure vessels, their attachments, main and auxiliary machinery, including steering and associated systems; electrical installations; and other equipment are in all respects appropriate and suitable for the service for which the ship is intended. In order to ensure that an agreed international survey and inspection standard is applied, the International Maritime Organisation (IMO) has provided guidelines intended to provide a general framework on which maritime

---

23 Such as the recognized Classification Societies — generally members of the International Association of Classification Societies; see below in this chapter and G(2)(b) in Chapter 2, "The Shipping Industry: An Overview."
24 See also Chapter 4, "The Ownership and Registration of Ships."
25 Most flag states, including Canada, have regulations requiring mandatory annual surveys.

administrations can base their arrangements for carrying out such inspections.[26]

The relevant inspecting authority will issue safety certificates on the satisfactory completion of the appropriate survey. Such a certificate will indicate that the ship has met the relevant *SOLAS* requirements. The convention provides for the issue of the following certificates in Chapter 1, Regulation 12 of the *SOLAS 1974* Annex: Passenger Ship Safety Certificate,[27] Cargo Ship Safety Construction Certificate,[28] Cargo Ship Safety Equipment Certificate,[29] Cargo Ship Safety Radio Certificate,[30] Record of Equipment,[31] and Exemption Certificate.[32] These certificates are generally issued by the same authority that carries out the required surveys and inspections. Such authority assumes full responsibility for such certificates. Provision is also made for the issue of certificates by another contracting state's authority on behalf of a flag state.[33] Such certificate will have the same force and receive the same recognition as a certificate issued by a flag state. The duration and validity of these certificates is also set out under the convention and, in general, follows the survey and inspection requirements already described above.[34] Other than the Cargo Ship Safety Construction Certificate, the Cargo Ship Safety Equipment Certificate, and the Exemption Certificate, all certificates are issued for a period not exceeding twelve months. The Cargo Ship Safety Construction Certificate is issued for a period not exceeding five years. The Cargo Ship Safety Equipment Certificate is issued for a period not exceeding twenty-four months. The Exemption Certificate's validity cannot exceed the period of validity of the corresponding certificates. Certificates cease to be valid on the transfer of the ship to another flag, or if the required surveys and inspections have not been carried out within the periods prescribed under the regulations. The form of the various certificates must conform to the models set out in the *SOLAS 1974* Appendix. These certificates are important legal documents and, together with the Certificate of Registry,[35] document a ship's identity, seaworthiness, and operational capability.

---

26 See IMO Resolution A.560(14).
27 *SOLAS 1974*, above note 12, cc.II-1, II-2, III, and IV.
28 *Ibid.*, cc.I-10, II-1, and II-2.
29 *Ibid.*, cc.II-1, II-2, and III.
30 *Ibid.*, c.IV.
31 Supplementary Certificate required under the Global Maritime Distress and Safety System of 1988. See Boisson, *Safety at Sea*, above note 1 at 364–71.
32 Granted to ship as required under the relevant *SOLAS 1974* Regulations.
33 *SOLAS 1974*, above note 12, c.I-13.
34 *Ibid.*, c.I-14.
35 See E in Chapter 4, "The Ownership and Registration of Ships."

a) Canadian *SOLAS 1974* Regulatory System

Canada has accepted the *SOLAS 1974* convention, but not the 1978 and 1988 Protocols. This means that the bulk of *SOLAS 1974* is applicable under Canadian maritime law and the relevant provisions are included in the *Canada Shipping Act*,[36] as well as in the relevant regulations under the Act.[37] Among the most relevant Canadian regulations are the following:[38]

- *Marine Machinery Regulations*,[39]
- *Dangerous Goods Shipping Regulations*,[40]
- *Dangerous Bulk Materials Regulations*,[41]
- *Dangerous Chemicals and Noxious Liquid Substance Regulations*,[42]
- *Fire Detection and Extinguishing Equipment Regulations*,[43]
- *Boat and Fire Drill Regulations*,[44]
- *Navigating Appliances and Equipment Regulations*,[45]
- *Hull Construction Regulations*,[46] and
- *Hull Inspection Regulations*.[47]

These regulations are enforced by marine safety inspectors, who are empowered under the *Canada Shipping Act, 2001*,[48] to carry out inspections of ships' hulls,[49] ships' machinery, ships' equipment, and respecting the protection of the marine environment.[50]

---

36 *Canada Shipping Act*, above note 21, Part V, ss.301–421; *Canada Shipping Act, 2001*, above note 21, Part IV, ss.104–24.
37 As already indicated earlier in the book, there may be significant regulatory changes once the *Canada Shipping Act, 2001*, above note 21, is fully implemented.
38 The selection of regulations given here is for illustration purposes only; the most up-to-date official information should always be consulted. In addition, the Canadian regulatory system is presently under review as a new system will be established under the *Canada Shipping Act, 2001*, above note 21; see also R.M. Fernandes, *Shipping and Admiralty Law* (Toronto: Carswell, 1995) at 2–38ff.
39 S.O.R./90-264.
40 S.O.R./81-951 as am.
41 S.O.R./87-24 as am.
42 S.O.R./93-4.
43 C.R.C., c.1422 as am.
44 C.R.C., c.1406 as am. by S.O.R./82-1054.
45 S.O.R./84-689 as am.
46 C.R.C., c.1431.
47 C.R.C., c.1432.
48 *Canada Shipping Act, 2001*, above note 21, s.11.
49 See *R. v. Empire Sandy Inc.* (1987), 62 O.R. (2d) 641 (C.A.).
50 Under *Canada Shipping Act, 2001*, above note 21, Part 9; see also Chapter 17, "Marine Pollution Prevention."

Marine Safety Inspectors also have the power to refuse to issue the necessary *SOLAS* documentation required under the *Canada Shipping Act, 2001*,[51] in cases of non-compliance. This could, of course, result in the subject vessel being delayed or even detained. The Canadian regulatory system that incorporates *SOLAS* also includes a number of sanctions involving fines and possible imprisonment for contraventions.[52]

4) Fishing Vessel Safety

Fishing vessels are excluded under *SOLAS 1974*, owing to the significant differences in design and operation that exist between merchant ships and fishing vessels. For example, unlike merchant ships, fishing vessels frequently operate with open holds and little freeboard. Bulwark openings are often kept closed to retain the catch and therefore do not allow excess deck water to escape. Fishing vessel stability can also be directly affected by certain types of fishing operations and by the fact that they operate under different load conditions, as they take on their catch at sea. In order to address the special problems of fishing vessel safety the *Torremolinos International Convention for the Safety of Fishing Vessels, 1977* (*SFV 1977*)[53] and its protocol (*SFV Prot 1993*)[54] have been concluded. Neither the convention nor the protocol is yet in force, nor has it been accepted by Canada. One of the principal reasons why the convention has not been more widely accepted is that the great variety of fishing vessels and fishing methods makes the global implementation of a uniform system very difficult. Nevertheless, many of these international provisions have been implemented by a number of states, including Canada, which, at this stage, have not accepted the complete convention.

SFV 1977 and its 1993 protocol incorporate safety requirements for the construction and equipment of new, decked sea-going fishing vessels of 24 metres and more in length, including vessels that also process their catch. Existing vessels are only covered in respect of radio-communication requirements. The convention follows the general principles set out under the *SOLAS 1974* system. Regulations are set out in

---

51 *Canada Shipping Act, 2001*, above note 21, s.20.
52 Above note 21, ss.37–40.
53 2 April 1977, B.P.P. Misc.17 (not yet in force); see also *Ratification of Maritime Conventions*, above note 11, vol.I.3.80.
54 *Torremolinos Protocol Relating to the Torremolinos International Convention for the Safety of Fishing Vessels, 1977*, 2 April 1993, B.P.P. Misc.19 (not yet in force); see also *Ratification of Maritime Conventions*, above note 11, vol. I.3.85. This Protocol is basically designed to supersede *SFV 1977*.

ten chapters covering such areas as construction; water-tight integrity; machinery and electrical installations; unattended machinery spaces; fire protection, detection, extinction, and firefighting; protection of the crew; life-saving appliances; emergency procedures, musters, and drills; radio communications; and navigational equipment. *SFV 1977* and its 1993 protocol also provide for initial, periodic, and intermediate survey systems for fishing vessels. Such surveys and inspections by maritime authorities will result in the issue of an International Fishing Vessel Safety Certificate and, where appropriate, an International Fishing Vessel Exemption Certificate. In general, the International Fishing Vessel Safety Certificate shall not be issued with a validity of more than four years and shall not be extended for more than one year, but always subject to satisfactory intermediate and periodic inspections.

a) Canadian Fishing Vessel Safety Regulatory System

Canada has not yet accepted *SFV 1977* nor its 1993 protocol. Nevertheless, as a major fishing state Canada has developed its own fishing vessel safety regulatory systems entitled *Guide to Inspection Regulations for Small Fishing Vessels* and *Small Fishing Vessel Inspection Regulations*.[55] These regulations incorporate a number of the provisions developed under the international regime.

5) Small Vessel Safety

SOLAS 1974 does not apply to vessels under 500 GT, or other small vessels such as pleasure yachts, that are not engaged in commercial activities. However, the Maritime Safety Committee[56] of the International Maritime Organisation has recommended that states apply *SOLAS* requirements to ships that are below convention size. As there is no international regime for small vessel safety, regulation of such vessels has been left to national law.

a) Canadian Small Vessel Safety Regulatory System

Canada's extensive coastlines, rivers, and inland waters have encouraged the growth of a significant fleet of small vessels and pleasure craft. As a result, Canada has accepted the IMO recommendation that *SOLAS*-type requirements for small vessels be implemented nationally and has

---

55 Canada, Transport Canada, *Report TP 782 Guide to Inspection Regulations for Small Fishing Vessels*, online at: <www.tc.gc.ca/MarineSafety/TP/ menu.htm>; and C.R.C., c.1486 as am.

56 See G(1)(a) in Chapter 2, "The Shipping Industry: An Overview."

instituted a national regulatory system for small vessels and pleasure craft. Under the current *Canada Shipping Act*, the *Small Vessel Regulations*[57] cover the following subjects:

- pleasure craft,[58]
- engine power and load capacity,[59]
- passenger vessels under five tons,[60]
- power-driven vessels under five tons that do not carry passengers and are not pleasure craft or fishing vessels,[61]
- fire precautions,[62] and
- equipment standards.[63]

The *Canada Shipping Act, 2001*, appears to distinguish between pleasure craft and other small vessels. The *Canada Shipping Act, 2001*, specifically excludes pleasure craft from the application of the Act's safety part;[64] the new Act also sets out an extensive section covering almost all aspects of pleasure craft operations.[65] The Act defines pleasure craft to be "a vessel that is used for pleasure and does not carry passengers."[66] This seems to indicate that small vessels that are not pleasure craft will be either considered as vessels subject to standard registration under the Act,[67] or subject to new regulations not yet available. However, operators of pleasure craft are required to ensure that they meet the requirements of the regulations made under the *Canada Shipping Act, 2001*.[68] While such regulations are not yet available, the Act envisages an extensive regulatory system,[69] including offences and punishments for contraventions.[70] This appears to be in response to concerns about the increasing number of accidents involving pleasure craft in Canadian waters.

---

57 *Canada Shipping Act*, above note 21; *Small Vessel Regulations*, C.R.C., c.1487. See also Canada, Transport Canada, *Report TP 1332 Construction Standards for Small Vessels (2002)*; and *Report TP 11717E Standards for the Construction and Inspections of Small Passenger Vessels* (under review), both online at: <www.tc.gc.ca/MarineSafety/TP/menu.htm>.
58 *Canada Shipping Act*, ibid., Part II, ss.16–22.
59 *Ibid.*, Part III, ss.23–25.1.
60 *Ibid.*, Part IV, ss.26–29.
61 *Ibid.*, Part V, ss.30–35.
62 *Ibid.*, Part VI, ss.36–41.
63 *Ibid.*, Sch. III.
64 *Canada Shipping Act, 2001*, above note 21, s.105.
65 *Ibid.*, Part 10.
66 *Ibid.*, s.2.
67 *Ibid.*, s.46. See also G in Chapter 4, "The Ownership and Registration of Ships."
68 *Ibid.*, s.201.
69 *Ibid.*, s.207.
70 *Ibid.*, ss.208–209.

6) Ships' Loading and Cargo Safety

Several important factors related to safety at sea are based on how ships are loaded and the type of cargo on board. *SOLAS 1974* and the *Protocol of 1978 Relating to the International Convention for the Prevention of Pollution from Ships, 1973, (MARPOL 73/78)*[71] address the most important aspects of cargo safety related to grain and other bulk cargoes, oil and other energy products carried in bulk and cargo containers, as well as hazardous and noxious substances. However, specific regimes for freight containers and dangerous cargoes have also been developed. In addition, an important regime for loading vessels has been created.

a) Loading Limits for Ships[72]

One of the most effective ways of improving the safety of vessels consists of limiting their loaded draught (i.e., the quantity of cargo on board). While there were some regulations dating from the Middle Ages, the first rules on minimum freeboard for merchant ships date from 1875 as a consequence of Samuel Plimsoll's vigorous campaign against the "coffin ships" of that time.[73]

The modern international law on ships' load lines is largely codified in the *International Convention on Load Lines, 1966 (LL 1966)*,[74] as amended,[75] as well as its 1988 protocol, *(LL Prot 1988)*.[76] A further review of this subject is underway at the IMO at this time. LL 1966 consists of thirty-four articles and three technical annexes that are an integral part of the convention. The convention applies to all ships engaged in international voyages with the exception of warships, new ships of

---

71 *International Convention for the Prevention of Pollution from Ships, 1973*, 2 November 1973, 1340 U.N.T.S. 184 as amended by the *Protocol of 1978 Relating to the International Convention for the Prevention of Pollution from Ships, 1973*, 17 February 1978, 1340 U.N.T.S. 61 [*MARPOL 73/78*]; see Chapter 17, "Marine Pollution Prevention," for a detailed discussion of this treaty.
72 See C(6) in Chapter 2, "The Shipping Industry: An Overview," for additional information.
73 See Boisson, *Safety at Sea*, above note 1 at 201; see also C(6) in Chapter 2, "The Shipping Industry: An Overview."
74 5 April 1966, 640 U.N.T.S. 133 [*LL 1966*] (entered into force on 21 July 1968; entered into force in Canada on 14 April 1970); see also *Ratification of Maritime Conventions*, above note 11, vol.I.30.50–55.
75 *LL 1966* was amended in 1971, 1975, 1979, 1983, and 1995; however, these amendments are not yet in force.
76 *Protocol of 1988 Relating to the International Convention on Load Lines, 1966*, 11 November 1988, 2 U.S.T. 102 (entered into force on 3 February 2000; not yet accepted by Canada); see also *Ratification of Maritime Conventions*, above note 11, vol.I.3.60.

less than twenty-four metres in length, existing ships of less than 150 GT, pleasure yachts not engaged in trade, and fishing vessels. Also, the convention does not apply to ships operating solely within special areas, such as the Great Lakes of North America. Ships to which LL 1966 applies, have to be properly measured and marked[77] in accordance with Annex I of the convention. Verification is undertaken by periodic inspections and surveys carried out by the flag state's maritime administration or authorized representatives, such as classification society surveyors. Such surveys must take place

- when the vessel enters service;
- at intervals specified by the flag state's maritime administration, but not exceeding five years; and
- within three months either way of each anniversary date of the certificate.

Once the relevant survey has been completed, no changes to the ship's structure or equipment may be made without specific authorization of the flag state administration.

The national maritime administration guarantees the proper completion of such surveys through the issue of certificates as set out under the convention.[78] LL 1966 provides for the issue of an International Load Line Certificate or, where appropriate, an International Load Line Exemption Certificate. The load line certificate may not be issued with a validity exceeding five years, although an extension of up to five months may be granted. If the ship is transferred to another flag, the certificate loses its validity. Together with the ship's certificate of registration and the various *SOLAS* safety certificates, the International Load Line Certificate is an important component of the ship's official legal documentation.

i) *Canadian Load Line Regulations*
Canada is a party to LL 1966, which has been incorporated into the *Canada Shipping Act*.[79] Applicable regulations have been developed under the current *Canada Shipping Act*,[80] including *Load Line Regulations (Sea)*,[81]

---

77 Often called the "Plimsoll mark." See also C(6) in Chapter 2, "The Shipping Industry: An Overview" and E(3)(g) in Chapter 4, "The Ownership and Registration of Ships."
78 LL 1966, above note 74, Annex III.
79 *Canada Shipping Act*, above note 21, ss.352–79; *Canada Shipping Act, 2001*, above note 21, s.120(1)(h) and Sch.1.
80 *Canada Shipping Act*, ibid.; *General Load Line Regulations*, C.R.C., c.1425; no regulations under the *Canada Shipping Act, 2001*, were available at time of publication.
81 C.R.C., c.1441.

The Safety Management of Ships 207

Load Line Regulations (Inland),[82] and *Load Lines Rules for Lakes and Rivers*.[83] Although LL Prot 1988 has not formally been accepted by Canada, it has been included under the provisions of the *Canada Shipping Act, 2001*.[84] This appears to indicate that the protocol will be accepted or that its provisions may be incorporated into Canadian law without formal acceptance.

b) Freight Containers

In recent decades there has been a rapid increase in the use of freight containers for the carriage of goods by sea, the development of several generations of container ships, and the integration of transport in which the various modes are interdependent. As a result, questions of container safety have arisen, as the freight container is the common denominator in this whole, new transport system. Closely related to this is the need for standardization of freight containers to ensure progress in safety, efficiency and economy in the system. The subject of container safety has been taken up by the IMO, while standardization is within the jurisdiction of the International Organization for Standardization.[85]

As a consequence of IMO's work on container safety, the *International Convention for Safe Containers (CSC 1972)* was concluded in 1972.[86] This convention applies to the great majority of freight containers that are used internationally by all modes of transport with the exception of air. It was not intended to cover all types and sizes of containers, vans, and reusable packing boxes. Therefore, the scope of *CSC 1972* is limited to containers with corner fittings (i.e., devices that permit the handling, securing, and stacking of containers), with a bottom area of at least fourteen square metres, or seven square metres, if fitted

---

82 C.R.C., c.1440.
83 C.R.C., c.1442.
84 *Canada Shipping Act, 2001*, above note 21, Sch.1.
85 See G(2)(f) in Chapter 2, "The Shipping Industry: An Overview."
86 2 December 1972, 1064 U.N.T.S. 43 (entered into force on 6 September 1977; entered into force in Canada on 19 February 1982); *CSC 1972* amendments include *Amendments to Annex I of the International Convention for Safe Containers (CSC) of 1972*, 2 April 1981, 1263 U.N.T.S. 477; *Amendments to Annex I & II of the International Convention for Safe Containers (CSC) of 1972*, 13 June 1983, 1348 U.N.T.S. 328; and *Amendments to Annex I & II of the International Convention for Safe Containers (CSC) of 1972*, 17 May 1991, 3138 B.T.S. 6. (These amendments are all in force; a further amendment of *Amendments to the International Convention for Safe Containers (CSC) of 1972*, 4 November 1993, 42 S.I.D.A. 1, is not yet in force); see also *Ratification of Maritime Conventions*, above note 11, vol.I.3.50–60.

with top and bottom fittings. The convention sets out the approval mechanism for freight containers used in international transport. Such approval must be granted by the maritime administration of a contracting state, or an approved organization acting on behalf of such a state.[87] This covers individual and mass-produced containers.

Annex I of *CSC 1972* sets out detailed regulations for the testing, inspection, and approval of containers, and Annex II prescribes how containers should be tested through lifting, stacking, concentrated roof and floor load, transverse racking, longitudinal restraint, and end and sidewall tests. On being granted approval, the owner has to arrange that a Safety Approval Plate, in the form prescribed by *CSC 1972*, is permanently affixed to the container. Approved containers also have to be periodically inspected at intervals regulated by the relevant maritime administration. However, such intervals must not exceed five years from the date of manufacture to the date of first inspection. Subsequent inspections are required to take place at intervals not exceeding thirty months under an Approved Containers Examination Programme. The principal purpose of these inspections is to determine if the container has any defects that could cause a danger to persons. If it is determined that such danger exists, the defect has to be rectified or the approval will be withdrawn.

While the proper stowage of cargo in containers, as well as the proper handling, carriage, loading, and discharging of containers is essential to maritime safety, *CSC 1972* does not specifically address these aspects. In the convention, Annex II provides that cargo should be stowed in a container "in accordance with the recommended practices of the trade" so as to avoid undue stress. In fact, most port container handling facilities have established guidelines and rules that conform to specific practices related to the trade.[88]

i) Canadian Sea Container Regulations
Canada is a party to *CSC 1972* and has developed specific legislation for its implementation.[89] Regulations have also been developed.[90]

---

87 Such as a classification society: see below D(4), "Classification Societies" and E(1) in Chapter 2, "The Shipping Industry: An Overview."
88 See also IMCO/ILO, *Guidelines for Packing Cargo in Freight Containers* (London: IMCO, 1978).
89 *Safe Containers Convention Act*, R.S.C. 1985, c.S-1.
90 *Safe Containers Convention Regulations*, S.O.R./82-1038 as am.

c) Dangerous Goods and Cargoes

SOLAS 1974 specifically deals with the carriage of dangerous goods at sea by all ships covered under the convention.[91] The carriage of such dangerous goods is prohibited except in accordance with the convention's provisions. Most states that have accepted *SOLAS 1974*, including Canada, provide detailed instructions on the safe packing, storing, handling, and stowage of dangerous goods in order to supplement the requirements of the convention. However, despite the fact that *SOLAS 1974* provides a detailed list of the various classes of dangerous goods, it was considered necessary to provide uniform international guidelines that define the substances that would fall into each class in much greater detail. The most important and widely used of these guidelines is the *International Maritime Dangerous Goods Code (IMDG Code)* that was developed by the IMO from work that took place between 1956 and 1961.[92] The *IMDG Code* is designed to be utilized by anyone who is professionally involved with dangerous goods, including manufacturers, packers, forwarders, shippers, road and rail and sea carriers, as well as port authorities and wharf and terminal operators. The code is published by the IMO in the form of a five-volume looseleaf encyclopaedia that is frequently updated. It is divided into three parts:

- Volume I contains a general introduction, outlining the conditions of transporting dangerous goods at sea, including the designation, marking, labelling, and documenting for carriage. Annex I contains packing recommendations.
- Volumes II, III, and IV provide details on the nine categories of dangerous goods:

    Class 1: Explosive substances and articles
    Class 2: Gases, compressed, liquefied, or dissolved under pressure
    Class 3: Flammable liquids
    Class 4: Flammable solids, liable to spontaneous combustion, or that, in contact with water, emit flammable gases
    Class 5: Oxidizing substances that provoke combustion and organic peroxides that are subject to violent or explosive decomposition
    Class 6: Toxic and infectious substances
    Class 7: Radioactive materials
    Class 8: Corrosive substances

---

91 *SOLAS 1974*, above note 12, c.VII.
92 *IMDG Code*, above note 19. The code is an interpretation of *SOLAS 1974*, Part A, c.7; see Boisson, *Safety at Sea*, above note 1 at 277.

Class 9: Miscellaneous dangerous substances and articles, such as aerosols, some ammonium nitrate fertilizers, asbestos, safety matches, and substances designated as "marine pollutants"

- Volume V contains emergency procedures for ships carrying dangerous cargoes. This includes a medical first aid guide for use in accidents involving dangerous goods, the *IMO Bulk Cargo Code*, reporting procedures, the *IMO/ILO Guidelines for Packing Cargo Transport Units*, recommendations on the safe use of pesticides, and a number of other IMO recommendations.

The *IMDG Code* has been widely accepted and, while it is a recommended code rather than a legislative instrument, it has become mandatory in many states.[93] The code is almost constantly reviewed. In addition, the IMO is also engaged in efforts to harmonize the code with other transport regimes and modes.

i) Canadian Dangerous Goods Regulations

Canada has incorporated the *IMDG Code* under the *Canada Shipping Act*.[94] Applicable regulations have also been developed.[95] However, the transportation of dangerous goods in Canada is also generally controlled under the *Transportation of Dangerous Goods Act, 1992*,[96] that applies to all handling and transportation of dangerous goods by any means of transport, whether or not the goods originate from or are destined to any place in Canada. This Act is enforced through the regulations that have also been accepted by a number of provinces.[97] A number of other federal acts may also be applicable to the handling and carriage of dangerous goods.[98]

---

93 It is applied in at least 50 states, representing over 80 per cent of the global merchant fleet; see Boisson, *Safety at Sea*, above note 1 at 278.
94 *Canada Shipping Act*, above note 21, s.389; no reference to this area is made in the *Canada Shipping Act, 2001*, although regulations can be expected in future.
95 *Dangerous Goods Shipping Regulations*, S.O.R./81-951, as am. by S.O.R./94-341 as am. by S.O.R./94-554.
96 S.C. 1992, c.34; see also Fernandes, *Shipping and Admiralty Law*, above note 38 at 5-104.8, and B(5) in Chapter 8, "Dangerous Goods."
97 Fernandes, *Shipping and Admiralty Law*, ibid. at 5-126 and 5-127; see also *R. v. Nitrochem Inc.* (1992), 8 C.E.L.R. (N.S.) 283 (Ont. Prov. Div.).
98 E.g., *Atomic Energy Control Act*, R.S.C. 1985, c.A-16; *Explosives Act*, R.S.C. 1985, c.E-17; *Hazardous Products Act*, R.S.C. 1985, c.H-3; and *Nuclear Liability Act*, R.S.C. 1985, c.N-28.

7) Offshore Drilling

The exploration for and exploitation of offshore energy resources almost deserves its own separate discussion.[99] It can only be outlined here in the context of maritime safety. It is clear that the operation of highly complex installations in the marine environment, with its weather and sea-state variations, has a number of inherent risks.[100] Added to this is the potential danger from drilling for oil and natural gas, which are often found under high pressure. While safety is given very high priority by offshore operators, drilling contractors, and the major energy companies that usually sponsor such activities, accidents do occur and often involve loss of life, personal injury, and heavy pollution.[101]

Despite increasing, significant offshore activities in many parts of the world, no international convention on this activity has so far been concluded.[102] The IMO completed a *Code for the Construction and Equipment of Mobile Offshore Drilling Units (MODU Code)* in 1989 that provides basic recommendations on "design criteria, construction standards and other safety measures for mobile offshore drilling units (MODUs) so as to minimize the risk to such units, to the personnel on board, and to the environment."[103] This code covers four different types of offshore rigs representing a substantial portion of all offshore activities and operations: mobile drilling units (i.e., semi-submersibles), self-elevating units (i.e., jack-up rigs), surface units (i.e., drill ships), and column-stabilized units.[104] The code contains fourteen chapters relating to construction materials and strength subdivision, stability

---

99 See F in Chapter 2, "The Shipping Industry: An Overview."
100 See, e.g., T. Robinson, *The Offshore* (St. John's, NL: Jesperson Press, 1992); and M. Summerskill, *Oil Rigs: Law and Insurance* (London: Stevens, 1979) c.1.
101 Major offshore accidents that have occurred in recent years are "Ocean Ranger," off Canada; "Sea Gem," off the U.K. coast; and "Ixtoc I," off of Mexico; see also W.G. Carson, *The Other Price of Britain's Oil* (Oxford: Robertson, 1982).
102 Efforts have been underway through the IMO and the CMI since 1977 to create an international operational regime but have so far been unsuccessful. The most recent effort was an attempt by the Canadian Maritime Law Association during the period 1992–2000. This resulted in a draft convention that was placed before the IMO Legal Committee. However, the subject was not considered to be one that required early or urgent attention and has been removed from the IMO's task-list at this time.
103 IMO, *Code for the Construction and Equipment of Mobile Offshore Drilling Units, 1989 (IMO MODU Code)* (London: IMO, 1990) at 9.
104 E. Gold & C. Petrie, "Pollution from Offshore Activities: An Overview of the Operational, Legal and Environmental Aspects" in C.M. De La Rue, ed., *Liability for Damage to the Marine Environment* (London: Lloyd's Press, 1993) at 229.

and freeboard, machinery and electrical equipment, fire safety, life-saving equipment, radio-communication equipment, lifting devices, and helicopter facilities and operating requirements.

The IMO's *MODU Code* provides a very basic international, operational framework, but it has been left to individual states to enact and enforce their own offshore legislation. As a result, states have created a very wide variety of offshore regimes. In most cases, there will be some sort of offshore legislation and, when offshore activities are planned or take place, the coastal state and offshore operator enter into bilateral arrangements covering the specific activity. While this has created some uncertainty, especially when legal problems arise, it appears to have operated reasonably well for some time. Nevertheless, there are concerns about the lack of a comprehensive international regime when major accidents occur, increased by the fact that offshore operators and oil companies hardly ever carry out activities within the confines of the coastal areas of a single state. It is very much an international activity involving multinational corporations, operators, and crews. If there are different national rules relating to insurance, function, and operational requirements for MODUs, problems can be expected.

One of the principal problems related to the mobile offshore drilling unit is its status. Is it a ship? If the rigs are considered to be ships, then traditional maritime law will apply to offshore operations.[105] On the other hand, if a rig is not considered to be a ship but, rather, to be an artificial island or something else, a different legal regime would have to be applied.[106] Neither extreme is entirely appropriate. Most MODUs must first navigate to their operational site, that is, they move to such sites under their own power or are towed there. In other words, MODUs are a legal hybrid that must eventually have a uniform international legal regime; certain aspects of such a regime will be based on or overlap with traditional maritime law. Matters are further complicated by the fact that national laws of many coastal states do not apply beyond national boundaries except by explicit legislative enactment for the specific purpose of offshore natural resources regu-

---

105 See, e.g., Summerskill, above note 100, c.2; W. Spicer, *Canadian Maritime Law and the Offshore: A Primer,* Working Paper 6. (Calgary: Canadian Institute of Resources Law, 1984); and Chapter 4, "The Ownership and Registration of Ships," section B(1) "What is a Ship?"
106 See *Global Marine Drilling v. Triton Holdings Ltd.*, [1999] Scot. J. No. 238 (QL), discussed in E. Watt, "From Noah's Ark to Mobile Drilling Units" [2000] L.M.C.L.Q. 299.

lation.[107] Nevertheless, coastal states must provide the necessary legal regime in the absence of international law.

Offshore installations are sufficiently different from merchant ships to justify alterations in traditional maritime law. Some of the required changes may be modest (i.e., crew safety, labour standards, navigational rules when under way) and some more substantive (i.e., pollution liability, operational safety, including safety zones, platform decommissioning and removal, financing, maritime liens, and salvage). There are also substantial differences in the command structure between ships and MODUs. Once drilling operations commence, the rig is in place and cannot be moved easily. During this period the chief of drilling operations is technically in charge. Even though the MODU may have a "master" on board, this person is effectively sidelined while drilling takes place even though he or she is still "in command." This is a distinct conflict between traditional ships and MODUs and may require a new type of "rig commander." The Royal Commission enquiring into the loss of the MODU "Ocean Ranger" off Newfoundland some years ago reached this conclusion:

> The inadequacy of the practice of characterizing installations as either ships or non-ships for the purpose of how they should be operated is particularly evident. As the Royal Commission stated, a choice between two options of master marine or toolpusher is simply an inadequate response. Language and logic rebel at the concept of an entity being simultaneously what it is and what it is not. Yet legal characterization thrives on solving such problems by creating fine distinctions.[108]

a) Canadian Offshore Regulatory Regime

Canada has an important offshore oil and gas industry that is still in its infancy. Activities off the coasts of Newfoundland and Nova Scotia are well underway with potential activities in Canadian Arctic areas and off the coast of British Columbia. The existing regulatory system for offshore activities off the east coast of Canada is extremely complex, from several causes: the Canadian federal system in which the federal government has a principal responsibility for offshore activities; the multiplicity of jurisdictions over offshore activities at the federal and

---

107 See Gold & Petrie, above note 104 at 226.
108 C. Yoder, "The Canadian Regulation of Offshore Installations" in Canadian Institute of Resources Law, *Working Paper 9* (Calgary: CIRL, 1985), 91-2.

provincial levels; and a number of unresolved national and international maritime boundary problems.

The regulatory approach can be best illustrated by examining the requirements for offshore activities in the Nova Scotia region.[109] (The approach taken for activities off Newfoundland has only a few variations.) There are approximately 400,000 square kilometres of available offshore areas under Nova Scotia's jurisdiction. This area is administered by the Canada–Nova Scotia Offshore Petroleum Board (CNSOPB), which is the regulator for all offshore energy activities in the Nova Scotia offshore area.[110] In 1986 the governments of Canada and Nova Scotia set aside the issue of resource ownership and jurisdiction and through a political accord established mirror legislation providing for joint management of offshore resources: as defined under the *Canada–Nova Scotia Offshore Petroleum Resources Accord Implementation Act*,[111] and the *Canada–Nova Scotia Offshore Petroleum Resources Accord Implementation (Nova Scotia) Act*.[112] The regulatory regime for the Nova Scotia offshore area is enforced by the CNSOPB, with a mandate that covers offshore safety, environmental protection, industrial benefits and employment, licence issuance, resource management, and data collection. In addition to the CNSOPB, a number of other federal and provincial government departments and agencies are involved in the regulatory process for offshore energy activities, either as regulators or as reviewers of the process. Almost all of these have some connection with maritime safety.[113] Some of these agencies have also entered into agreements with the CNSOPB, through memoranda of understanding,

---

109 See Atlantic Canada Petroleum Institute, *Offshore Oil and Gas Approvals in Atlantic Canada* (Halifax: ACPI, 2001).
110 Its Newfoundland equivalent is the Canada-Newfoundland Offshore Petroleum Board (CNOPB).
111 S.C. 1988, c.28.
112 S.N.S. 1987, c.3.
113 Federal agencies: Canada Customs and Revenue Agency (CCRA); Canadian Environment Assessment Agency (CEAA); Canadian Transportation Agency (CTA); Citizenship and Immigration Canada (CIC); Environment Canada (EC); Fisheries and Oceans Canada (DFO); Human Resources Development Canada (HRDC); Industry Canada (IC); National Defence (DND); National Energy Board (NEB); Natural Resources Canada (NRCan); Transport Canada-Marine Safety; and Transportation Safety Board of Canada (TSB). Nova Scotia provincial agencies: Energy Resources Conservation Board (ERCB); Department of Environment and Labour; Department of Agriculture and Fisheries; Office of Aboriginal Affairs; Nova Scotia Petroleum Directorate; and Nova Scotia Utility and Review Board (NSUARB). See Atlantic Canada Petroleum Institute, above note 109, Appendix A, for a complete listing of the official mandate of these agencies.

in order to govern their relationships with respect to the regulation of offshore energy activities — especially in the safety and human resources areas. In terms of maritime law, where there is federal and provincial overlap, some jurisdictional difficulties may arise. As has already been shown, Canadian maritime law is strictly a body of federal law.[114] However, at this stage, the Supreme Court of Canada has not had an opportunity to examine a matter involving federal-provincial offshore jurisdiction that involves a maritime dispute.

C. SAFETY OF SHIPS' CREWS AND PASSENGERS

1) Crews

a) Background

The proper development and implementation of acceptable standards for the construction and equipment of vessels, as well as for their inspection, survey, and certification, are important factors in maintaining safety at sea, but they will not achieve this alone. In fact, the most crucial factor in achieving acceptable levels of maritime safety is the human element. In other words, a ship is only as good as the persons who crew it. With the continuing technological developments in shipping, the human factor has become more critical than ever. Regardless of how sophisticated modern ships might become, their safety will ultimately depend upon their crews and their professional competence and dedication. Seafaring is today a highly skilled profession involving advanced automation and instrumentation, and sophisticated electronic systems on large, specialized vessels in a world fleet of increasing size. Accordingly, the training of maritime personnel has to be given very high priority.

There is an additional factor that also centres on the human element in shipping. Seafaring has greatly changed since the end of the Second World War. Ships are much more sophisticated, highly automated, with smaller crews and much less port time. Crews have become increasingly multinational, as the former traditional maritime states that still operate the majority of the world fleet have become dependent upon maritime labour from less developed states — owing to the fact that seafarers from traditional maritime states are more reluctant to choose the sea as a career, because they have better opportunities ashore. In addition, after many years with an oversupply of maritime

---

114 See Chapter 3, "Admiralty Jurisdiction."

labour, there is now an increasing shortage, especially of seafarers with special, technical, and navigational competence. In other words, life at sea and conditions of employment on ships have become more complex and, in many cases, much more difficult. All of this has added a problematic social element to seafaring that, indirectly, also impacts on maritime safety.

It is, therefore, not that surprising that at least 80 per cent of all maritime accidents are caused by some type of human error.[115] However, the maritime community has not targeted this worrying statistic; instead the industry expends about 80 per cent of its available resources on technical solutions to maritime safety problems, leaving less than 20 per cent for issues related to the human factor.[116] It has become clear that technological improvements in the maritime sector have only a limited impact on improving safety at sea. In a number of cases it has been determined that such advances may even lead to additional risk, owing to the increased complexity of the man/machine interface. In other words, maritime safety has a critical human resource base that can only be addressed by human resource solutions.[117] The International Labour Organisation (ILO) and the International Maritime Organisation (IMO) have, to some extent, addressed this at the international level.[118]

2) ILO Conventions

The International Labour Organisation has adopted more than sixty international conventions and recommendations by its International Labour Conference during its periodic maritime sessions between 1920 and 1996.[119] These conventions and recommendations, as a body, constitute a comprehensive set of maritime standards that is often referred to as the "International Seafarers' Code" and concerns almost all aspects of the conditions of life and work of seafarers. Nevertheless,

---

115 See Boisson, *Safety at Sea*, above note 1 at 287.
116 IMO, "Role of the Human Element in Maritime Casualties." Working Paper submitted by the United States, IMO Doc. MSC 65/15/1 of 10 February 1995, cited in Boisson, *Safety at Sea*, above note 1 at 287.
117 For an extensive discussion of this whole area, see Boisson, *Safety at Sea*, above note 1, c.16.
118 See G(1) in Chapter 2, "The Shipping Industry: An Overview," for additional information on the ILO and IMO.
119 Several of these conventions have been updated and revised and, at this time, about thirty-six conventions are in effect; see *Ratification of Maritime Conventions*, above note 11, vols.I.6 and II.6.

acceptance of many of these conventions has been patchy and some are not yet in force; however, many states have accepted the recommendations and have adopted some of the standards into their own legislation as they represent minimum standards and requirements. Safety at sea has been the focus of three areas of ILO conventions: conditions of access to the seafaring profession, crew numbers, and minimum standards on board vessels. However, it is neither appropriate nor possible to provide great detail of the many ILO conventions in this book.

a) *Merchant Shipping (Minimum Standards) Convention, 1976 (ILO No. 147)*

The *Merchant Shipping (Minimum Standards) Convention, 1976*,[120] which has consolidated a number of subjects concluded in earlier separate conventions, applies to all seagoing ships carrying cargo or passengers, whether privately or publicly owned. It prescribes a set of minimum standards to be observed by shipping. Such standards cover minimum age, medical examination, certificates of competency, articles of agreement, illness and injury benefits, conditions of employment on ships, living arrangements on board vessels, prevention of accidents, and repatriation. States that have accepted this convention undertake[121] to establish legislation and regulations for vessels registered under the flag covering the following: safety standards, including standards of competency, hours of work, and manning, so as to ensure the safety of life on board vessels; appropriate social security measures; and shipboard conditions of employment and shipboard living arrangements, in so far as these are not covered by collective agreements or laid down by competent courts in a manner equally binding on the shipowners and seafarers concerned.

Any state implementing the convention must satisfy itself that the provisions of such legislation and regulations are substantially equivalent to the convention. A convention state must also exercise effective jurisdiction or control over ships that are registered in its territory in respect of the convention's requirements. Such state must also satisfy itself that measures for effective control of other shipboard conditions of employment and living arrangements, where it has no effective jurisdiction, are agreed between/among shipowners, or their organizations, and seafarers' organizations, constituted in accordance with the sub-

---

120 Also known as the *Convention Concerning Minimum Standards in Merchant Shipping*, 29 October 1976, 1259 U.N.T.S. 355 [*ILO No. 147*] (entered into force on 28 November 1981; entered into force in Canada on 25 May 1994); see also *Ratification of Maritime Conventions*, above note 11, vol.I.6.340.

121 *ILO No. 147*, ibid., art.2.

stantive provisions of a number of other, non-maritime ILO conventions covering freedom of association, protection of the right to organize, and collective bargaining.[122] Finally, the implementing state is also obliged to ensure that adequate procedures exist for the engagement and training of seafarers.

ILO No. 147 is also linked to a number of other existing maritime safety conventions — that is, SOLAS 1974, COLREGS,[123] and LL 1966 — and provides that only states that have accepted or given effect to these conventions can become parties to ILO No. 147.[124] The convention also requires that contracting states should verify, through inspections or other appropriate means, that their vessels comply with the relevant national legislation and with all other applicable ILO conventions. In order to carry out such measures for foreign ships, port state control jurisdiction is also provided under the convention.[125] This enables the port state authorities to take such measures as are necessary in order to rectify deficiencies that affect safety and health on board ships. The port state is also required to ensure that adequate procedures exist for the investigation of complaints concerning the engagement within its jurisdiction of national and foreign seafarers on foreign vessels, and to pass such complaints on to the state of registry and to the ILO director-general.[126]

b) **Canadian Adoption and Implementation of ILO Conventions**
Canada has not accepted many ILO conventions, although a considerable amount of the content of ILO conventions has been incorporated into Canadian labour and maritime legislation. In addition to the important *ILO No. 147*, Canada has accepted the following:

- Convention Fixing the Minimum Age for Admission of Children to Employment at Sea, 1920,[127]

---

122 See K.X. Li & J. Wonham, *The Role of States in Maritime Employment & Safety* (Dalian, China: Dalian Maritime University Press, 2001); see also A.D. Couper, *Voyages of Abuse — Seafarers, Human Rights and International Shipping* (London: Pluto Press, 1999).
123 *International Collision Regulations*; see Chapter 11, "Maritime Collisions."
124 *ILO No. 147*, above note 120, art.5.
125 *Ibid.*, art.4.
126 *Ibid.*, art.2(d).
127 9 July 1920, 38 U.N.T.S. 109 (entered into force on 27 September 1921; entered into force in Canada 31 March 1926); aee also *Ratification of Conventions*, above note 11, vol.I.6.10.

- *Convention Concerning Unemployment Indemnity in Case of Loss or Foundering of the Ship, 1920,*[128]
- *Convention Fixing the Minimum Age for the Admission of Young Persons to Employment as Trimmers or Stokers, 1921,*[129]
- *Convention Concerning the Compulsory Medical Examination of Children and Young Persons Employed at Sea, 1921,*[130]
- *Convention Concerning Seamen's Articles of Agreement, 1926,*[131]
- *Convention Fixing the Minimum Age for the Admission of Children to Employment at Sea (Revised), 1936,*[132]
- *Convention Concerning the Certification of Able Seamen, 1946,*[133]
- *Convention Concerning Food and Catering for Crews on Board Ship, 1946,*[134]
- *Convention Concerning the Medical Examination of Seafarers, 1946,*[135] and
- *Convention Cncerning Seafarers' National Identity Documents, 1958.*[136]

---

[128] 9 July 1920, 38 U.N.T.S. 119 (entered into force 16 March 1923; entered into force in Canada 31 March 1923); see also *Ratification of Maritime Conventions,* above note 1, vol.I.6.30.

[129] 1 November 1921, 38 U.N.T.S. 203 (entered into force 20 November 1922; entered into force in Canada 31 March 1926); see also *Ratification of Maritime Conventions,* above note 11, vol.I.6.40. As trimmers and stokers are no longer employed at sea, the convention is probably no longer applicable.

[130] 1 November 1921, 38 U.N.T.S. 217 (entered into force 20 November 1922; entered into force in Canada 31 March 1926); see also *Ratification of Maritime Conventions,* above note 11, vol.I.6.50.

[131] 24 June 1926, 38 U.N.T.S. 295 (entered into force 4 April 1928; entered into force in Canada 30 June 1938); see also *Ratification of Maritime Conventions,* above note 11, vol.I.6.60.

[132] 24 October 1936, 40 U.N.T.S. 205 (entered into force 11 April 1939; entered into force in Canada 10 September 1952); see also *Ratification of Maritime Conventions,* above note 11, vol.I.6.100. This convention has superseded the 1920 convention; however, Canada has not so far denounced the older treaty.

[133] 29 June 1946, 94 U.N.T.S. 11 (entered into force on 14 July 1951; entered into force in Canada 19 March 1952); see also *Ratification of Maritime Conventions,* above note 1, vol.I.6.200.

[134] 29 June 1946, 264 U.N.T.S. 163 (entered into force 24 March 1957; entered into force in Canada 24 March 1957); see also *Ratification of Maritime Conventions,* above note 11, vol.I.6.210.

[135] 29 June 1946, 214 U.N.T.S. 233 (entered into force 17 August 1955; entered into force in Canada 17 August 1955); see also *Ratification of Maritime Conventions,* above note 11, vol.I.6.220.

[136] 13 May 1958, 389 U.N.T.S. 277 (entered into force on 19 February 1961; entered into force in Canada 31 May 1968); see also *Ratification of Maritime Conventions,* above note 11, vol.I.6.260.

These ILO provisions are implemented in Canada in the *Canada Shipping Act*[137] and, where appropriate, in the *Canada Labour Code*, which also applies to shipping.[138] In addition, under the current *Canada Shipping Act*, a regulatory system[139] has been developed, including regulations covering the following areas: crew accommodation;[140] medical examination of seafarers; ships' food and catering; towboat crew accommodation;[141] certification of able seamen; certification of ships' cooks; and marine occupational safety and health.[142]

3) *STCW 1978*

In 1978 a diplomatic conference of the International Maritime Organisation adopted the *International Convention on Standards of Training, Certification and Watchkeeping for Seafarers (STCW 1978)*.[143] The convention lays down minimum requirements for the training, qualifications, and seagoing service for masters, navigating officers, engineer officers, radio officers, and certain categories of ratings that must be met before governments may issue certificates of competency under the convention. In addition, *STCW 1978* sets out certain principles of deck and engine watchkeeping. The convention is widely considered to be one of the most important instruments ever reached on safety at sea, as it is the first initiative taken that establishes minimum global standards for seafarers. Prior to the conclusion of *STCW 1978*, there had been no uniform international regime in this area and this aspect had been left solely to national requirements. This had become quite unsat-

---

137 See *Canada Shipping Act*, above note 21, ss.183–300; *Canada Shipping Act, 2001*, above note 21, ss.2, 21, 29(1), 30, 31, 35(1)(d), 108(2), 227(1), and Sch.1.
138 *Canada Labour Code*, R.S.C. 1985, c.L-2.
139 It should be noted that, as shipping legislation changes from *Canada Shipping Act* to *Canada Shipping Act, 2001*, both above note 21, a new regulatory system is expected to be in place in future. Accordingly, the information provided herein is for illustration only. The current valid regulations must always be consulted.
140 *Crew Accommodation Regulations*, C.R.C., c.1418.
141 *Towboat Crew Accommodation Regulations*, C.R.C., c.1498.
142 S.O.R./87-183 as am. by S.O.R./88-198; S.O.R./95-74. It should, however, be noted that Canadian seafarers injured while working on board Canadian vessels will generally be subject to provincial workers' compensation legislation. See Fernandes, *Shipping and Admiralty Law*, above note 38 at 2–65.
143 7 July 1978, 1361 U.N.T.S. 2 [*STCW 1978*] (entered into force on 28 April 1984; entered into force in Canada 6 February 1988); Amendments: 1991 (in force 1 December 1992); 1994 (in force 1 January 1996); 1995 (in force 1 February 1997); 1997 (2) (in force 1 January 1999); 1998 (in force 1 January 2003); see also *Ratification of Maritime Conventions*, above note 11, vol.1.6.90.

isfactory because of the great variation of standards that had been developed globally.

STCW 1978 contains seventeen articles covering legal issues, complemented by an extensive annex that sets out administrative and technical requirements. In addition, the IMO conference adopted twenty-three resolutions that contain more detailed provisions. Widespread acceptance of *STCW 1978* does not preclude states from adopting higher or more stringent standards. In fact, many established maritime states already developed their own training, certification, and watchkeeping standards that are in excess of *STCW 1978* requirements long ago. In other words, *STCW 1978* lays down minimum, but uniform, requirements on a global level. Under the convention, states are required to take the necessary steps to ensure that seafarers are qualified and fit for their duties in order to protect life and property at sea and to protect the marine environment.[144] *STCW 1978* is applicable to all ships, with the exception of warships, non-commercial government vessels, fishing vessels, pleasure craft, and primitive wooden ships.[145]

The basic principle of *STCW 1978* is that seafarers have to be properly trained and, consequently, duly certified.[146] Provision is made for masters, officers, and ratings who meet the standards specified in the convention's annex to be issued with certificates of competence that are recognized internationally. This annex sets out the basic requirements for such certificates as well as the syllabi to be used in examining candidates. Certain basic principles for watchkeeping standards are also included. In addition, the annex makes provisions for the continued proficiency and updating of knowledge of certified seafarers.

STCW 1978 also permits maritime administrations to depart from the regime in circumstances of "exceptional necessity" through the granting of a dispensation. Such a dispensation may permit a seafarer to serve in a capacity for which the appropriate certificate is not actually held. However, the following conditions would apply:

- the dispensation may not be issued for a period of more than six months;
- the seafarer concerned must be qualified to fill the post in a safe manner; and
- the seafarer must be in the possession of the appropriate certificate to fill the post immediately below.

---

144 *STCW 1978*, above note 143, art.I.
145 *Ibid.*, art.III. Ships engaged in certain coastal voyages are also exempted in accordance with regulations laid down by the flag state.
146 *Ibid.*, art.VI.

Such dispensations cannot be granted to masters except under extreme conditions[147] and for the shortest possible period. Dispensations for radio officers are only available under the ITU Radio Regulations.[148] In any case, all states that are parties to *STCW 1978* must submit annually a detailed list of dispensations that have been granted to vessels over 1,600 GT to the secretary general of the IMO. This is designed to ensure some degree of control in the exercise of this power, as unrestricted dispensation would clearly undermine the spirit of the convention.

Like the *SOLAS* and *LL 1966* conventions, *STCW 1978* is based on flag state jurisdiction. However, it also relies on port state control to ensure proper and efficient enforcement. Under the convention, the port state receives significant powers in respect of all ships, irrespective of flag, that are in the ports or offshore terminals within the jurisdiction of such a state. Inspections are carried out to ensure that seafarers, who are required to be certified under *STCW 1978*, hold the requisite certificate or valid dispensation. In addition, inspections must monitor that seafarers have the ability to maintain the required watchkeeping standards, if there are reasons (as specified in *STCW 1978*) to believe that such standards are not being maintained. The inspector is required to notify in writing the master or, if appropriate, the nearest diplomatic representative of the flag state, of any deficiencies found and the reasons why these may pose a danger to persons, property, or the marine environment.

STCW 1978 was substantially amended by a further IMO diplomatic conference in 1995.[149] This was necessitated by the fact that the original instrument needed updating and by some problems related to the absence of constraints in the regime. The amended instrument goes much further than the 1978 version and significantly strengthens standards. A transitional system has been created under which the IMO's Maritime Safety Committee[150] can assess the information on convention implementation supplied by contracting states. A decision can then be made whether the relevant state meets the requirements to be placed on a "white list" of states approved by the committee.

---

147 Generally *force majeure*.
148 See G(1)(e) in Chapter 2, "The Shipping Industry: An Overview."
149 During this time, a parallel IMO conference also concluded a new *International Convention on Standards of Training, Certification and Watchkeeping for Fishing Vessel Personnel*, 17 July 1995, 43 S.I.D.A. 148 [*STCW-F 1995*] that has not yet entered into force.
150 See G(1)(a) in Chapter 2, "The Shipping Industry: An Overview."

The main changes to *STCW 1978* by its subsequent amendment lie in the new structure of the convention that is now confined to legal issues. Technical requirements are rearranged in an amended *STCW* code. The amended text contains two fundamental alterations that represent a major change in the traditional mechanisms for implementing international conventions. First, the flag state's functions and responsibilities in this area are clarified; and second, the initial elements of international "control" under IMO and port state directions are set out.[151] The amended convention also takes account of technical innovations and developments, such as different working practices or the use of training simulators. Reference to the *ISM Code*[152] is also emphasized. It sets out shipping company responsibilities concerning, for instance, crewing, documentation, and data on all seafarers on board, and familiarization with tasks and ship characteristics. Finally, the 1995 amendments also simplified and accelerated the process of updating and revising the convention in future. As a result, new amendments have been able to enter into force expeditiously.

a) Canadian Implementation of *STCW 1978*

Canada is a party to *STCW 1978* and has implemented the convention's provisions through incorporation into the *Canada Shipping Act*.[153] In addition, a commensurate regulatory framework[154] has been developed in order to implement the requirements of this important convention.

4) Passengers

Although the discussion on maritime safety, as developed under the *Convention on Safety of Life at Sea* (*SOLAS*) system, includes passenger vessels generally, the subject deserves some additional specific emphasis. The safety of passengers on board ships has, for a long time, occupied a special position in international maritime regulatory activity. This is because of the variety of maritime risks to which passengers

---

151 See Boisson, *Safety at Sea*, above note 1 at 318–19
152 See below D(2), "*ISM Code*."
153 *Canada Shipping Act*, above note 21, ss.109–160; *Canada Shipping Act, 2001*, above note 21, Sch.1; no regulations under this Act have so far been developed.
154 The regulations under the *Canada Shipping Act*, above note 21, covered areas such as crewing; marine engineer examination; master and engineer dual capacity; master and mates examination; certification of lifeboat men; safe manning; home-trade, inland, and minor waters voyages; and ship's deck. This will be subject to a new regulatory framework that is being developed under the *Canada Shipping Act, 2001*, above note 21.

might be exposed, as well as the economic importance of seaborne passenger transportation. While the latter has been long overtaken by aviation, passenger shipping is still significant.[155] Furthermore, a rapid increase in cruise shipping[156] — involving some of the largest vessels ever built — has further confirmed the importance and popularity of this sector of the shipping industry.[157] Fortunately, passenger vessels have been relatively accident-free, although the potential of disaster is always present. When serious accidents do occur, they invariably involve loss of life. Tragic examples in recent years are the capsizing of the Ro-Ro ferry Herald of Free Enterprise off Zeebrugge, Belgium; the fire on board the Scandinavian Star in the North Sea; the total loss of the car ferry Estonia in the Baltic Sea; and the collision resulting in the sinking of the ferry Doña Paz in the Philippines.[158] It is, therefore, not surprising that the development of the *SOLAS* system itself arose out of The Titanic disaster in 1912.

a) *SOLAS* System for Passenger Safety[159]

As passenger safety has developed its own specialized regime within the *SOLAS 1974* framework, it is worthwhile to provide a brief description. In almost all parts of the convention, the safety of passengers is emphasized and, in many cases, involves additional requirements. Specific passenger provisions under *SOLAS 1974* include the following:[160]

Chapter I: General Provisions, Part B

Regulation 2: Passenger Ship Definition[161]

---

155 According to Lloyd's Register of Shipping, there were 2,828 passenger vessels and 2,425 passenger car ferry boats in existence in 1998. Cited in Boisson, *Safety at Sea*, above note 1 at 213.
156 It was estimated that cruise shipping attracted some 10 million passengers in 2000: cited in Boisson, *Safety at Sea*, ibid.
157 See also Chapter 2, "The Shipping Industry: An Overview."
158 The Doña Paz disaster is considered to be greatest maritime tragedy of all times as it involved the loss of 4,400 persons. In fact, it is reported that some 10,500 persons have been lost in passenger accidents in the past decade, mainly near the coasts of developing states in Asia and Africa: cited by Boisson, *Safety at Sea*, above note 1 at 213.
159 For an extensive review of this aspect, see Boisson, *Safety at Sea*, ibid., c.11.
160 *SOLAS 1974*, above note 13.
161 "A passenger ship is a ship that carries more than twelve passengers." A "passenger" is defined as "every person other than the master and members of the crew or other persons employed or engaged in any capacity on board a ship on the business of that ship and a child under one year of age" (*Canada Shipping Act, 2001*, above note 21, s.2).

Regulation 7: Surveys of Passenger Ships
Regulation 12: Passenger Ship Safety Certificate

Chapter II-1: Construction — Structure, Subdivision and Stability, Machinery and Electrical Installations

Regulations 5–12: Stability of Passenger Ships including Ro-Ro Ferries[162]
Regulation 16: Passenger Ships carrying Goods Vehicles and accompanying Personnel

Chapter II-2: Construction — Fire Protection, Fire Detection and Fire Extinction

Regulation 5: Reduction of Fire Growth Potential in Passenger Ships
Regulation 7: Fire Detection and Alarms for Passenger Ships Carrying More Than Thirty-Six Passengers
Regulation 9: Passenger Fire Control
Regulations 12–13: Notification of Passengers and Means of Escape

Chapter III: Life-Saving Appliances and Arrangements

Regulations 6–20: Requirements for Passenger and Cargo Ships
Regulations 21–30: Additional Requirements for Passenger Ships

Chapter IV: Radio Communications

Regulation 5: Distress Signal Systems

Chapter X: Safety Measures for High Speed Craft[163]

Regulations 1–3: High-Speed Craft Code.

b) Canadian Implementation

Canada is a party to *SOLAS 1974* and its amendments, and has incorporated the necessary provisions into the *Canada Shipping Act*.[164] Under this legislation a number of regulations have also been developed. Most of the *SOLAS 1974* provisions are also applicable to passenger-vessel safety. However, regulations that specifically concern passenger-vessel

---

162 These provisions were strengthened subsequent to the Herald of Free Enterprise and Estonia ferry disasters by *SOLAS 1974* amendments in 1988, 1989, 1992, and 1995.
163 Includes hovercraft, hydrofoils, jetfoils, airboats, hydrojets, and SWATH craft. Also designated as dynamically supported craft and capable of speeds of more than 30 knots and often up to 60 knots.
164 *Canada Shipping Act*, above note 21, Part V; *Canada Shipping Act, 2001*, above note 21, Part IV.

safety include hull construction,[165] hull inspection,[166] fire detection and extinguishing equipment,[167] passenger ship stability,[168] and small passenger vessels.[169]

D. OTHER SAFETY MANAGEMENT REGIMES

1) Background

The international maritime safety regimes so far outlined all have flag state jurisdiction as their basis. That factor constitutes both the strength as well as the weakness of these regimes owing to the fact that the effectiveness of the regime depends almost totally upon the commitment of the flag state to implement it. It is not surprising that some flag states are better than others. Furthermore, the open registry system[170] may also cause problems when some of these states do not follow international regime requirements sufficiently. As a result, there has been a slow, but definable, trend toward better international enforcement through port state surveys that provide an additional level of ascertaining proper implementation. As already indicated above, some development in this area has already taken place through the more recent amendments to *SOLAS 1974* and *STCW 1978*. However, these efforts have been specifically strengthened through three other international regimes: the *ISM Code*; the regional port state control regimes; and the strengthened system of ship classification. Finally, there are also three further international regimes that have an important, if indirect, impact in this area: the ship security regime; the international search and rescue system; and the port facilitation regime.

2) *ISM Code*

In 1993 an International Maritime Organisation resolution[171] concluded the *International Safety Management Code for the Safe Operation of*

---

165 Above note 46.
166 Above note 47.
167 Above note 43.
168 Canada, Transport Canada, *Report TP2237*, available online at: <www.tc.gc.ca/MarineSafety/TP/menu.htm>.
169 *Report TP11717*, above note 57.
170 See F in Chapter 4, "Registration under Flags of Convenience."
171 IMO Resolution A.741(18) of 4 November 1993.

Ships and Pollution Prevention, 1994, generally known as the *International Safety Management Code, 1994 (ISM Code)*.[172] The purpose of the *ISM Code* is to provide an international standard for the safe management and operation of ships and for marine pollution prevention. There is little doubt that this code has had far-reaching implications for almost all aspects of ship operations. For the first time an internationally agreed code sets out the management and operational requirements for vessels with a reach from "messroom to boardroom."[173] The *ISM Code* specifically states: "The cornerstone of good safety management is commitment from the top. In matters of safety and pollution prevention is the commitment, competence, attitudes and motivation of individuals at all levels that determines the end result."[174] The code sets out basic requirements for a safety management system that includes on-board, as well as shipowning company, responsibilities and authority, emergency preparedness, approved plans for shipboard operations, verification, certification and controls, and commensurate reporting systems. Under the code the shipowner is required to develop a safety management system that includes a "designated person" in its management structure, as well as an accident reporting system, a ship's maintenance record system, and periodic internal reviews and evaluations of the company's safety management system. The flag state administration, or an organization authorized by it, will audit the system and verify that it meets *SOLAS 1974*, *STCW 1978*, and related requirements. Similar inspections will also be carried out on ships. If the inspections and surveys are satisfactory, an ISM Safety Management Certificate will be issued to the ship and an ISM Document of Compliance to the shipowner.

The *ISM Code* is designed to verify and ensure compliance with the international safety regimes that have been developed. The ISM certificates will also be inspected during port state control operations and have become an important component of a vessel's legal documenta-

---

172 IMO, *International Safety Management (ISM) Code 2002* (London: IMO, 2002) [*ISM Code*] entered into effect on 1 July 1998. Amendments will be adopted, will be brought into force, and will take effect in accordance with the provisions of *SOLAS 1974*, above note 13, art.VII. The first amendment, concluded in 2000, entered into effect on 1 July 2002. The *ISM Code* can be found in *Ratification of Maritime Conventions*, above note, 11 vol.I.6.46.
173 E. Gold, *Gard Handbook on Marine Pollution*, 2d ed. (Arendal, NO: Gard, 1997) at 51. See also P. Anderson, *ISM Code: A Practical Guide to the Legal and Insurance Implications* (London: Lloyd's Press, 1998).
174 *ISM Code*, above note 172, Preamble at para.6.

tion. The *ISM Code* became mandatory on 1 July 1998.[175] Future amendments will be adopted, brought into force, and will take effect under *SOLAS 1974* provisions.[176] While it is probably too early to assess the code's success, indications are that it is generally meeting expectations.[177] As a party to *SOLAS 1974*, Canada has accepted the *ISM Code* and is expected to incorporate it into regulations to be produced under the *Canada Shipping Act, 2001*.

3) Port State Control Systems

Port state control over foreign vessels has become an important exception to flag state jurisdiction. It is a growing phenomenon as an increasing number of port and coastal states seek to ensure that substandard vessels will not cause problems in their waters. Furthermore, numerous international conventions now provide port state jurisdiction as an adjunct or alternative to flag state jurisdiction. At the highest level the *United Nations Convention on the Law of the Sea*, (*UNCLOS*) provides for limited enforcement by port states in cases where violations have taken place or where such problems are suspected.[178] However, the real impetus for a growing network of port state control systems has taken place at the regional level.

a) Paris MOU 1982

In 1982 the maritime authorities of a number of European states[179] concluded the *Memorandum of Understanding on Port State Control in implementing Agreements on Maritime Safety and Protection of the Marine Environment, 1982* (*Paris MOU 1982*).[180] Since that time several other

---

175 Under Chapter IX of *SOLAS 1974*, above note 12. It has been mandatory for tankers, bulk carriers, and passenger vessels since July 1998, and is mandatory for all other vessels, including MODUs, since July 2002.
176 *SOLAS 1974*, above note 12, art.VIII.
177 See, e.g., A. Sagen, "Operational Manuals and the ISM Code" Seaways (October 2001) at 4.
178 10 December 1982, 1833 U.N.T.S. 3, art.218 [*UNCLOS*] (entered into force on 16 November 1994, not yet ratified by Canada, although the government has expressed its commitment to ratification); see also *Ratification of Maritime Conventions*, above note 11 vol. 1.1.170.
179 Belgium, Denmark, Finland, France, Germany, Greece, Ireland, Italy, the Netherlands, Norway, Portugal, Spain, Sweden, and the U.K. (entered into force on 1 July 1982). See *Ratification of Maritime Conventions*, above note 11, vol.I.3.100.
180 26 January 1982, 21 I.L.M. 1; see *Ratification of Maritime Conventions*, above note 11, vol.I.3.100.

states, including Canada, have also become parties to this agreement.[181] The *Paris MOU 1982* sets out guidelines for an improved and harmonized system of port state control and strengthened co-operation in the exchange of information. Although specifically designed to oversee the implementation of IMO and ILO conventions, the *Paris MOU 1982* also gives effect to and, in some aspects, exceeds the port state control provisions laid down by *UNCLOS*.[182] While an MOU is basically a voluntary agreement, without the effect of a negotiated treaty, the system appears to be a viable soft law alternative that has been most effective. Under the *Paris MOU 1982*, the signing maritime authorities agree to carry out the inspections of vessels in each other's ports in order to check on safety and related matters. If a vessel lacks valid safety certificates, or if there are clear grounds that a vessel does not meet convention requirements, a more detailed inspection will follow. "Clear grounds" will also include complaints or requests from other states, or even those on board the subject vessel. Particular attention will be given to vessels carrying pollutant or hazardous cargoes, as well as vessels that have a recorded history of deficiencies. Inspecting authorities are provided with the power to demand rectification of serious problems before the problem vessel is permitted to proceed. In other cases vessels may be given permission to proceed but the authorities at the subsequent port(s) will be notified to ensure further inspection.

The system under the *Paris MOU 1982* also established an international committee to oversee the various procedures, as well as a secretariat based in The Hague, Netherlands. The MOU contains four operational annexes that contain guidelines for surveyors; deficiency forms; survey report instructions; and details of the information system on inspections. Inspection data are placed in a computer system that is not only accessible to the maritime administrations involved but also to systems under MOUs in other regions. The system established by the *Paris MOU 1982* has been most successful, averaging approximately 16,000 inspections per year.[183] It is now also closely linked to similar systems in a number of other regions of the world. This allows almost instant information to be obtained on vessels calling in many ports and permits port state inspectors to assess the condition of such vessels based on previous inspections, detentions, or deficiencies. The

---

181 Poland (1992), Canada (1994), Russia (1996), Croatia (1997), and Iceland (2000); the United States is a "co-operating observer."
182 See Gold, above note 173 at 75.
183 I.e., about one in four ships calling at MOU member states' ports (Boisson, *Safety at Sea*, above note 1 at 451).

Paris MOU 1982 initiative was considered to be important enough to be replicated in a number of other regions of the world.[184] Numerous states, including Canada, are members of more than one system.[185]

As a result of the establishment of these regional systems, an increasingly tightened international network of port state control systems is now able to target substandard vessels, detect maritime safety and labour deficiencies, and co-operate on a global level through an international data system that links the various port state control regions. The MOU port state control system and its increasing global reach complements the port state requirements set out under *SOLAS 1974, STCW 1978, MARPOL 73/78*,[186] and the *ISM Code*. It is today considered to be the most effective mechanism in the international policing of navigation and the right of self-protection of coastal states.[187] Canada participates actively in two MOU systems —Paris and Tokyo — and carries out the required inspection process under the regulatory powers of the *Canada Shipping Act*.[188]

4) Classification Societies

As the safety management of ships is also of obvious interest to shipowners and their marine insurers, not all aspects of this area are left to the relevant flag or port state maritime administrations. Classification of ships is a totally private sector service performed by a number of classification societies that play a fundamental role in preventing maritime accidents in their dual rule in the classification and certification of ships.[189] Classification societies perform services such as issuing rules for the safety of ships, including the construction of ships, and carry out regular surveys and inspections to ensure that these rules are adhered to. Their principal purpose is to protect the ship as a piece of property. Classification rules are principally applied to the structural strength of the ship's hull and the reliability of its essential machinery and equipment. Certificates to this effect, issued by the responsible

---

184 See G(1)(e)(xii) in Chapter 2, "The Shipping Industry: An Overview" and Chapter 17, "Marine Pollution Prevention."
185 Canada also participates in the *Tokyo MOU*, which applies to Asia-Pacific states.
186 See Chapter 17, "Marine Pollution Prevention."
187 Boisson, *Safety at Sea*, above note 1, c.25.
188 *Canada Shipping Act*, above note 21, ss.301–421 and relevant regulations; *Canada Shipping Act, 2001*, above note 21, s.120.
189 Boisson, *Safety at Sea*, above note 1, c.6. See also E(1) in Chapter 2, "The Shipping Industry: An Overview" and Chapter 4, "The Ownership and Registration of Ships."

classification society, are used by the shipowner to obtain marine insurance at reasonable cost.

The technical skills and experience, as well as the established international network of offices and surveyors of the classification societies, have resulted in their frequent assumption of another public service role. Some governments and their maritime administrations have delegated their powers to enforce national and international regulations on safety at sea and the protection of the marine environment. In this role, classification societies carry out the necessary inspections and surveys, order rectification as appropriate, and deliver official certificates. In other words, classification societies have an important dual function in relation to safety management of ships, as they set standards by issuing rules and guidance notes setting out technical requirements for ships, and they perform surveys and inspections to monitor that ships comply with classification society and statutory national and international rules.[190]

Classification societies were first established in the early part of the eighteenth century in order to meet the needs of marine insurers.[191] At that time underwriters had great difficulties in obtaining reliable information on which to base their premiums, or on actuarial statistics on shipwrecks, or even on ships. As a result the first maritime register of ships was set up in 1760 under the auspices of Lloyd's.[192] This register was designed to supply the basic information on ships that were to be insured as well as any related facts that affected the assessment of risks. This original initiative became the Lloyd's Register of British and Foreign Shipping in 1834, which is still in existence today. Similar registers were also established in other maritime states during this period.[193]

These original classification societies were quite successful in the latter part of the nineteenth century, as they brought measurable economic benefits to marine underwriters, for whom the high value of certain vessels represented serious risk exposure. The awareness of the actual condition of the vessels made it possible to control such risks. This method of risk management was based on rating each ship individually (i.e., classifying). Within a comparatively short period of time classification would evolve from the assignment of rating toward certi-

---

190 Boisson, *Safety at Sea*, ibid. at 119.
191 See Chapter 7, "Marine Insurance."
192 *Ibid.*
193 The "Bureau Veritas" (France, 1829); the "American Bureau of Shipping" (U.S., 1862); "Det Norske Veritas" (Norway, 1864). Other classification societies would be developed by other maritime states.

fication thereby providing the link between risk management and maritime safety. This development was accelerated by the rapid emergence of a number of technical, economic, commercial, and political factors that brought the classification societies into the modern context.

Today, classification societies are characterized by their number and diversity. They also differ significantly in size, with the smallest employing a small staff and concentrating in certain geographical areas, while the largest have a global network of surveyors. Since the 1950s the number of classification societies has grown from ten to more than fifty. Unfortunately, some do not meet the minimum standards required which has raised concern about unacceptable inconsistencies in the application of safety standards. This has affected the whole system.[194] In order to confront this concern the seven principal classification societies set up the International Association of Classification Societies (IACS) in 1969.[195] Under IACS, minimum standards for membership, a Quality Assurance System Certification program, as well as a standard-setting process have been created. IACS rules are strictly enforced and some classification societies have been suspended or have failed to gain IACS membership. At present IACS has ten members and three associate members.[196] The members are listed in order of size:[197]

- Lloyd's Register of Shipping (LR), London, England;
- Nippon Kaiji Kyokai (NKK), Tokyo, Japan;
- American Bureau of Shipping (ABS), New York, U.S.;
- Det Norske Veritas (DNV), Oslo, Norway;
- Bureau Veritas (BV), Paris, France;
- Germanischer Lloyd (GL), Hamburg, Germany;
- China Classification Society (CCS), Beijing, China;
- Russian Maritime Register of Shipping (RMR), Moscow, Russia;
- Registro Italiano Navale (RINA) Genoa, Italy; and
- Korean Register of Shipping (KR), Seoul, South Korea.

Despite its long history and generally high credibility, the classification society system appears to have lost its former privileged position within the maritime safety regime. Several high-profile maritime accidents in recent years, involving "classed" vessels that nevertheless appeared to be substandard, have contributed to this trend. Furthermore, classification societies are no longer the only standard-setting authorities;

---

194 Boisson, *Safety at Sea*, above note 1 at 123.
195 See G(2)(s) in Chapter 2, "The Shipping Industry: An Overview."
196 Croatian Register of Shipping (CRS); Indian Register of Shipping (IRS); and Polish Register of Shipping (PRS).
197 As of 2000.

they now have to share this function with some other national and international regimes. As private sector systems, classification societies have also had to face an increasing amount of legal risk owing to liability litigation.[198] Questions are also often raised as to the reliability and impartiality of a system that openly competes for business. In response, classification societies have directed their strategy toward restoring the classification system to an essential component in the prevention of accidents at sea and protecting the marine environment. This is especially critical for those flag and port states that rely totally on classification societies. It remains to be seen how this strategy will further develop in the next few years.

Canadian maritime authorities generally accept the documentation issued by classification societies, although unofficially, preference is given to certificates issued by IACS members. In any case, under the provisions of the *Canada Shipping Act,* as well as the *ISM Code,* Canada has the right to carry out onboard inspections of foreign vessels in Canadian ports if such action is warranted and even if valid classification society-issued certificates are on board. Nevertheless, Canadian maritime authorities work closely with many classification societies, which as certifying authorities, complement the official government maritime safety system.

5) Maritime Security

Piracy has existed as long as ships have sailed the seas, but unlawful acts against ships had generally been in the decline until the 1980s.[199] At that time there was renewed concern that criminal acts, and even international terrorism, might target ships and, therefore, directly affect the safety of navigation. This was graphically illustrated by the terrorist attack on the Italian passenger vessel Achille Lauro in 1985 that resulted in loss of life and injury. In response, an IMO assembly resolution called for the development of measures to prevent unlawful acts that threaten the safety of ships and the security of passengers and crews.[200] As a result, an international IMO conference in 1988 conclud-

---

198 Boisson, *Safety at Sea,* above note 1 at 132–33.
199 "Piratical" attacks on ships, involving often violent attacks on merchant vessels in coastal areas mainly for theft, have been increasing in certain Asian and African regions, to the extent that the International Chamber of Commerce has established the International Maritime Bureau (IMB), which monitors such attacks on a regular basis. See G(2)(n) in Chapter 2, "The Shipping Industry: An Overview."
200 IMO Resolution A. 584(14) of 14 November 1985, followed by the U.N. General Assembly Resolution 40/61 of 9 December 1985.

ed the *Convention for the Suppression of Unlawful Acts against the Safety of Maritime Navigation (SUA 1988)*.[201] *SUA 1988* applies to all ships, with the exception of warships and non-commercial government vessels. The convention defines the offences that would be considered as intentional and unlawful acts[202] and requires states that have accepted the convention to take such measures as are necessary to establish jurisdiction to deal with such offences, including trial and punishment and, if appropriate, extradition. States are required to fully co-operate. In other words, this type of unlawful act is to be considered to be an international offence in a similar way to aircraft hijackings some years earlier.

While *SUA 1988* was being concluded, a *Protocol for the Suppression of Unlawful Acts against the Safety of Fixed Platforms located on the Continental Shelf (SUA Prot 1988)*[203] was also developed. It established a regime similar to that under *SUA 1988* for criminal acts against fixed offshore installations. These instruments have become much more important in recent times where international terrorism appears to be on the rise and where increased criminal activities against ships are taking place. The IMO Legal Committee is currently considering an amending protocol that will expand the range of criminal offences against the safety of navigation. This problem has, obviously, become much more emphasized by the events of 11 September 2001, which illustrated the global vulnerability to terrorist action. A fully loaded passenger vessel, a large loaded tanker, a vessel loaded with liquefied natural gas, or an offshore oil platform would make excellent terrorist targets!

The *SUA* instruments are a first legal step in dealing with maritime security problems;[204] the IMO has developed a new far-reaching maritime security regime that is designed to prevent and suppress acts of terrorism and related violence against shipping. Discussion of this matter was initiated at an IMO Maritime Safety Committee[205] in May 2002 and culminated in a diplomatic conference in December 2002, which adopt-

---

201 *Convention for the Suppression of Unlawful Acts against the Safety of Maritime Navigation*, 10 March 1988, 27 I.L.M. 668 [*SUA 1988*] (entered into force on 1 March 1992; entered into force in Canada 21 July 1994); *Ratification of Maritime Conventions*, above note 11, vol.I.3.110.
202 *SUA 1988*, ibid., art.3.
203 *Protocol for the Suppression of Unlawful Acts against the Safety of Fixed Platforms located on the Continental Shelf*, 10 March 1988, 27 I.L.M. 685 (entered in to force on 1 March 1992; in force in Canada from 21 July 1994) [*SUA Prot 1988*]; *Ratification of Maritime Conventions*, above note 11, vol.I.3.120.
204 Although the international law of the sea has had anti-piracy rules for many years. See *UNCLOS*, above note 178, arts.100–107.
205 See Chapter 2, "The Shipping Industry: An Overview."

ed a number of amendments to *SOLAS 1974*[206] that will bring into force a new maritime security system. This system includes the following:

- development of an *International Ship and Port Facility Security Code* (*ISPS Code*) that will have mandatory and recommended provisions;
- requirements for Automatic Identification Systems for ships at sea;
- requirements for a Continuous Synopsis Record that will provide an onboard record of a ship's history;
- requirements for a ship security alarm system;
- requirements for port facilities that enhance security; and
- requirements for shipowners and their vessels, including the permanent marking of vessels with the required identification numbers.

Ships will in future be required to carry an International Ship Security Certificate that indicates that the ship is in compliance with the *ISPS Code*. Without such a certificate the trading capability of the ship will effectively cease, as a non-compliant vessel will be considered as a fundamental security risk.[207] However, even such a certificate will not prevent ships being subject to additional control measures from states. The principal purpose of the *ISPS Code* is to provide a standardized consistent framework for evaluating risk, enabling governments to offset changes in threat with changes in vulnerability for ships and port facilities. Three security levels, corresponding to low, medium, and high, are envisaged. Such security levels create a link between ship and port facility, as they trigger the implementation of appropriate responses and related security measures for ships and port facilities. It is expected that the new *ISPS Code* system should be in place by 1 July 2004.[208]

Several other maritime security measures are also being developed concurrently with the implementation of the regime under the International Ship Security Certificate. These include measures regarding shipping container security, the security of passenger vessels, and proper seafarer identification documentation.[209] Canada has accepted both *SUA* conventions and incorporated them into the *Canada Shipping Act* and the *Criminal Code*.[210]

---

206 Amendments to *SOLAS 1974*, above note 12, c.XI, which will have a new section on special measures to enhance maritime safety.
207 See S. Jones, "IMO's Security Deadline" Seaways (February 2003) at 13.
208 Under an implementation process set out under the *SOLAS 1974* amendment. It is expected that Canada will accept these measures promptly and incorporate them into national legislation.
209 Being developed by the ILO; see Chapter 2, "The Shipping Industry: An Overview."
210 *Canada Shipping Act, 2001*, above note 22, Sch.1, and *Criminal Code*, R.S.C. 1985, c.C-46, ss.7(2.1),(2.2), and 78, respectively.

6) Maritime Search and Rescue

In cases where maritime accidents occur, speedy maritime search and rescue efforts are essential. Several international conventions have attached importance to this aspect and have requested that coastal states make adequate arrangements to provide services to those in distress at sea. For example, under *SOLAS 1974*, a master of a ship at sea, on receiving a signal from any source that a ship or aircraft or survival craft is in distress, is bound by law to proceed at all speed to assist those in distress.[211] However, in order to ensure that a reliable, uniform, global search and rescue system is in place, an International Maritime Organisation conference in 1979 concluded the *International Convention on Maritime Search and Rescue (SAR 1979)*.[212] This instrument sets out the requirements for a uniform, international search and rescue regime. The *SAR 1979* technical annex sets out such organizational matters as establishment of rescue co-ordination centres, arrangements for the provision and co-ordination of search and rescue services, co-operation between states, preparatory measures, operating procedures, and ship reporting systems. In addition, the IMO developed guidelines in the *Merchant Ship Search and Rescue Manual (MERSAR)* and in the *Search and Rescue Manual (IMOSAR)*: *MERSAR* provides guidance for those who, during emergencies at sea, may require assistance from others or who may be able to provide such assistance themselves, and *IMOSAR* provides guidelines for a uniform international search and rescue policy, encouraging all coastal states to develop their rescue organizations along similar lines. This system is also closely linked to the Global Maritime Distress and Safety System.

Modern satellite and related technology is today also involved in search and rescue efforts. In this connection the *Convention on the International Maritime Satellite Organization (INMARSAT)* as amended, and its operating agreement, concluded in 1976,[213] are quite relevant for maritime safety. It has been shown that satellite-based communication systems are not only able to provide reliable and highly accurate information from and to vessels in distress but can also provide information on weather systems and conditions, shipping lanes, and the presence of vessels in sea areas. An even more specific and accurate space-based search

---

211 *SOLAS 1974*, above note 12, Annex, c.V, Reg. 10.
212 27 April 1979, 1405 U.N.T.S. 97 (entered into force on 22 June 1985); see also *Ratification of Maritime Conventions*, above note 11, vol.I.3.280.
213 3 September 1976, 1143 U.N.T.S. 105 (entered into force on 16 July 1979); see also *Ratification of Maritime Conventions*, above note 11, vol.I.3.260–74. Amendments are not yet in force.

and rescue system was established by the governments of the United States, Russia, Canada, and France in 1984, resulting in the *International COSPASS-SARSAT Programme Agreement (COS-SAR 1988)*.[214] This agreement augments and strengthens the *INMARSAT* and other systems that were already in place. Canada has accepted *SAR 1979*, which has been incorporated into the *Canada Shipping Act*.[215]

7) Port Facilitation

This chapter — as well as most of the book's other chapters —have demonstrated the growing complexity of the international, regional, and national regimes that shipping faces today. This has raised some concerns that, although increasing, commensurate formalities and documentary requirements may have a positive impact on the safety management of ships, they could also slow down or hinder the smooth flow of international commerce. This concern was already recognized some forty years ago, when, in 1962, the International Maritime Organisation set up a group of experts to study a draft document on this problem, prepared by the IMO secretariat.[216] This group concluded its deliberations in 1964 with the tabling of a draft convention that was eventually adopted by an IMO diplomatic conference in 1965. The *Convention on Facilitation of International Maritime Traffic (FAL 1965)*,[217] as amended, aims at facilitating maritime trade by securing uniformity in formalities, documentary requirements, and procedures on the entry of all ships engaged in international trade into national jurisdiction; and arrival in, stay in, and departure from ports. Under *FAL 1965*, unification is aimed at facilitation and expediting trade, in contrast to the requirements under the other conventions that are principally concerned with the enforcement of maritime safety, the protection of the marine environment, and maritime security.

---

214 1 July 1988, 1518 U.N.T.S. 209 (entered into force on 30 August 1988); Canada was one of the original sponsors of this agreement. See also, *Ratification of Maritime Conventions*, above note 11, vol.I.3.310.
215 *Canada Shipping Act, 2001*, above note 22, Sch.1.
216 S. Mankabady, *International Shipping Law*, vol. I (London: Euromoney Publications, 1991) at 164.
217 9 April 1965, 591 U.N.T.S. 265 [*FAL 1965*] (entered into force on 5 March 1967; entered into force in Canada 26 September 1967). Amendments of 1969, 1973, 1977, 1986, 1987, 1990, 1992, 1993, and 1996 are all in force; 2002 amendments are not yet in force. See also *Ratification of Maritime Conventions*, above note 11, vol.I.5.150.

The convention makes a strict distinction between standards and recommended practices, and sets out a list of the only documents that a port authority may require from ships on arrival or departure:[218] general declaration, cargo declaration, ship's stores declaration, crew's effects declaration, crew list, passenger list, mail document required under the Universal Postal Union treaty,[219] and maritime declaration of health. However, the port state authority would normally also request on arrival the various safety-related and marine pollution protection documents. Finally, it is also most likely that the port state may now require security-related documentation.

E. CONCLUSIONS

Devoting a whole chapter in a maritime law text to the area of maritime safety is unusual but the maritime safety management of ships has today become a critical part of ship operation. While the shipping industry has always been preoccupied with maritime safety, today's complex regulatory framework under the IMO's global principle of safer ships and cleaner seas has assumed, and continues to assume, a role of increasing importance. A significant regulatory network that has national, regional, and global dimensions today confronts ships and their operators. Failure to observe any part of the regulatory requirements, especially in terms of safety, will inevitably involve delay, increased costs, and sanctions ranging from fines to imprisonment. New initiatives, such as that introduced under the *ISM Code*, have moved the responsibility for safety management from the ship, where it traditionally resided, to the higher levels of corporate ship management. This also means that safety management responsibility and liability are now more closely linked. This is, without question, part of Canadian marine policy as expressed in some of the legislation discussed in the chapter. The safety management of ships has, therefore, become an integral part of the overall management aspect of ship operations. This provides maritime lawyers with a much broader scope of practice, as it has implications for such areas as maritime employment and labour, protection of the marine environment, safety of life and property, commercial operations, protection of investments, and commercial credibility and reputation. Accordingly, the subject not only

---

218 *FAL 1965, ibid.*, Annex, s.2.1.
219 See G(1)(e)(iii) in Chapter 2, "The Shipping Industry: An Overview."

requires full consideration in all operational, commercial, and legal decisions but deserves its own chapter in this type of book.

FURTHER READINGS

ATLANTIC CANADA PETROLEUM INSTITUTE, *Offshore Oil and Gas Approvals in Atlantic Canada* (Halifax: ACPI, 2001).

BIST, D.S., *Safety and Security at Sea* (London: Butterworth-Heineman, 2000).

BOISSON, P., *Safety at Sea: Policies, Regulations and International Law* (Paris: Bureau Veritas, 1999).

CARSON, W.G., *The Other Price of Britain's Oil — Safety and Control in the North Sea* (Oxford: Martin Robertson, 1982).

COUPER, A.D., *Voyages of Abuse — Seafarers, Human Rights and International Shipping* (London: Pluto Press, 1999).

EYRES, D.J., *Ship Construction*, 5th ed. (London: Butterworth-Heineman, 2001).

FERNANDES, R.M., *Shipping and Admiralty Law* (Toronto: Carswell, 1995).

GOLD, E., *Gard Handbook on P&I Insurance*, 5th ed. (Arendal, NO: Gard A.S., 2002).

GRAY, J., M. MONDAY, & G. STUBBLEFIELD, *Maritime Terror* (London: Paladin, 2000).

INSTITUTE OF MARINE ENGINEERS, *New Safety Culture* (London: Institute of Marine Engineers, 1998).

LI, K.X. & J. WONHAM, *The Role of States in Maritime Employment and Safety* (Dalian, China: Dalian Maritime University Press, 2001).

MERCHANT NAVY TRAINING BOARD, *Basic Safety Training: Personal Survival, Fire Prevention* (London: Merchant Navy Training Board, 1998).

ROBINSON, T., *The Offshore* (St. John's, NL: Jesperson Press, 1992).

SAGEN, A. & P. Mitchell, *Safety and Health at Sea* (London: Witherby, 2002).

SPICER, W., *Canadian Maritime Law and the Offshore — A Primer*, Working Paper 6 (Calgary: Canadian Institute of Resources Law, 1984).

SUMMERSKILL, M., *Oil Rigs: Law and Insurance* (London: Stevens, 1979).

CHAPTER 6

MARITIME MORTGAGES AND LIENS

A. INTRODUCTION

As a rule, a shipowner requires continuing financing to build, to operate, and eventually to decommission a ship. In all likelihood, the ship — especially if it is a commercial vessel — will carry mortgages and hypothecs that are necessary not only to build or to buy the ship but also to finance its operations and to upgrade it from time to time. The mortgage constitutes a consensual security interest in the ship as maritime property given by the shipowner, as mortgagor, in return for a loan. The security of the mortgage may be enhanced by the secured creditor, or mortgagee, by registering it in a public register along with the ship and its owner. Then other creditors or interested parties can discover the existence of the mortgage by a search of the register and may act toward the ship in light of it. In addition, from the moment the first keel plate is laid in the shipyard and throughout its life, the ship will have numerous responsibilities in contract, in tort, and by statute. Once operational the ship will be chartered, possibly also sub-chartered. It will need to be supplied regularly and repaired or upgraded as needed. Its owner will sell its cargo and passenger space. The ship is capable of causing unforeseeable damage through collision or otherwise. Persons on board may suffer fatal accidents or personal injuries. No one can forecast where the ship may need unexpected assistance from strangers when encountering perils of the sea. The ship will need to be berthed, be docked, use pilots, or pass through a canal and can thereby incur charges on a regular basis. All these events in the life of a ship translate into various types of charges, most notably maritime liens, possessory liens, statutory rights *in rem*, and claims of statutory authorities.

For creditors, many risks arise from the international nature of the ship's business. The ship is mobile property, moving from jurisdiction to jurisdiction, across what may be very different legal systems. The ship may incur liabilities or be used as security in different ways. The security, perhaps in the form of mortgage including hypothec, or lien, may be enforceable in different ways from one jurisdiction to another. Also, the ship is an evasive kind of property that can easily slip out of the hands of a person suffering loss or injury, or of a person having incurred expenses on its behalf or provided supplies and services to it. The ship may escape from a jurisdiction, and a creditor may have no choice but to institute proceedings against it in the first available jurisdiction. The owner of the ship is not always known, his or her financial standing may be equally unknown, and the courts of the country of registry may be inefficient or too expensive to approach. Thus, personal actions for damages may not be a satisfactory remedy for an aggrieved party.

If a creditor forecloses on a mortgage, or the owner declares bankruptcy, or the ship is unable to meet its obligations for any other reason, the ship will be subject to an action *in rem* that will lead to a judicial sale of the ship, and as a result the proceeds of the sale will be distributed among the creditors. These are the concerns of this chapter, which is divided for convenience into two parts: one on mortgages, followed by one on liens.

B. MORTGAGES

1) Introduction

a) Ship Financing: Bottomry, Respondentia, and Mortgages

A mortgage of a ship is a common way of financing its construction or purchase. In essence a mortgage provides a creditor with security for the repayment of a loan or the performance of some other obligation by the acquisition of a proprietary interest in the ship. It may in fact be used to secure any financial obligation involving the acquisition or operation of a ship. Historically, operational necessaries during a voyage were financed by bottomry or respondentia bonds. In situations of unforeseen necessity the master of the ship could grant a bottomry bond over the ship or a respondentia bond over the cargo as security for money borrowed to enable the ship to continue the voyage. The bondholder thereby gained an interest in the ship or the cargo and therefore in the success of the voyage.[1] If the ship was lost before its voyage was completed the bond was void. A prerequisite to the grant of a bottomry bond, in addition to necessity, was the inability of the master to communicate with the owner about the ship's necessitous situation. Nowadays almost instantaneous communication with ships worldwide is possible so the use of bottomry and respondentia bonds has sunk into desuetude.

The use of ship mortgages grew up through the nineteenth century at common law until it came to be regulated in the United Kingdom by merchant shipping legislation. This legislation, carried forward in Canada by the *Canada Shipping Act*, enhances the security of a ship mortgage by a statutory scheme of registration. However, a ship mortgage can never give a creditor complete security for repayment of a loan. The ship may founder or may sail to ports whose courts may not enforce the mortgage. In addition other maritime securities, such as liens, may take priority over the mortgage. Hence creditors usually look for additional security, such as a right to the proceeds of the insurance policies on the ship and an assignment of any time charterparty or a charge on the freight to be earned by the ship.

b) Form, Scope, and Regulation of Ship Mortgages

No special form has to be used to grant a ship mortgage, but there are statutory requirements for its registration. Hence, ship mortgages are usually drawn in two parts: a registerable document containing only the details required for federal registration, and a collateral loan agreement. The latter expresses the rights and obligations of the mortgagor and mortgagee that are not controlled by statute. Typically the mortgagor is bound, *inter alia*

- to pay the principal and interest on schedule,
- not to impair the validity or ranking of the mortgage,
- to maintain the vessel in a seaworthy condition and to operate it safely,
- to report any casualties to the vessel,
- not to do anything that would imperil the vessel's registration,
- not to transfer or demise charter the vessel without consent,
- to keep the ship adequately insured, and
- to permit the mortgagee, on reasonable notice, to inspect the vessel.

---

1 *St. George (The)* (1926), 25 Ll. L.R. 97 (Adm. Ct.). Technically bottomry and respondentia are maritime liens: see below at note 192.

The loan agreement also defines the circumstances in which the mortgagor will be regarded as defaulting and the mortgagee may take possession of the ship in realization of his or her security.

The subject-matter of a ship mortgage is not limited to the hull of the vessel but includes all its machinery and equipment, indeed everything on board that the vessel requires for its navigation.[2] More than one mortgagee on a ship may be granted but successive mortgages obviously involve greater risk and therefore they incur higher rates of interest. The mortgage of a ship, however, does not include a security interest in its earnings or its bunkers, unless expressly agreed,[3] nor in its insurance.[4] Both may be secured independently of the ship mortgage by appropriate agreement but will then need to be registered provincially.

A ship is a prime example of moveable personal property that falls within the constitutional jurisdiction of the provinces. Consequently a ship mortgage is subject to the regulation of provincial personal property security acts and consumer credit legislation. At the same time federal jurisdiction over shipping and navigation allows for federal control of ship mortgages under the *Canada Shipping Act*; in addition, the federal *Bank Act* grants chartered banks a special form of security when they finance one class of vessels, namely fishing boats. All these acts contain systems for the registration of security interests and, to varying extent, provisions about the powers and priorities of the secured parties. Fortunately, the constitutional principle of federal paramountcy provides a certain degree of order in the event of overlap and conflict among the legislation, so this chapter discusses ship mortgages first under federal legislation and then under provincial statutes.

2) Mortgages under Federal Legislation

The principal means of taking security in a Canadian ship is by a mortgage registered under the *Canada Shipping Act*.[5] In addition, the financ-

---

2   *Coltman v. Chamberlain* (1890), 25 Q.B.D. 328.
3   *Keith v. Burrows* (1877), 2 App. Cas. 636; *Liverpool Marine Credit Co. v. Wilson* (1872), L.R. 7 Ch. App. 507; *Pan Oak (The)*, [1992] 2 Lloyd's L.R. 36 (Adm. Ct.).
4   *Basildon (The)*, [1967] 2 Lloyd's Rep. 134 (Adm. Ct.); however, the mortgagee frequently takes an assignment of the insurance in the collateral loan agreement.
5   *Canada Shipping Act*, R.S.C. 1985, c.S-9 as am. by S.C. 1998, c.16, s.3; *Canada Shipping Act, 2001*, S.C. 2001, c.26. The Act's mortgage provisions originated from the U.K. merchant shipping legislation. International attempts to harmonize the ship mortgage regime are not reflected in the Act, as Canada, along with the United Kingdom and the United States, is not a party to the Brussels Conventions on Maritime Liens and Mortgages, 1926 and 1967 [10 April 1926,

ing of fishing vessels by a chartered bank may also be secured under the *Bank Act*.[6] (This special form of security is discussed after the general scheme of the *Canada Shipping Act*.)

a) **Registration under *Canada Shipping Act***

A ship mortgage may only be registered under the *Canada Shipping Act* if the ship appears on the Canadian Register of Ships. This register, discussed in Chapter 4, is divided into parts, including a general register of ships, a small vessel licensing system,[7] and a record of new buildings.[8] A "small vessel" is a vessel of less than 15 tons.[9] A small vessel or pleasure craft need not to be but may be entered on the register of ships. In any event, it is subject to licensing, which is an identification system only and carries none of the implications of ownership that registration does. In order for a ship to be registered, it must be owned by a "qualified person," that is, an individual or corporation bearing Canadian nationality.[10] The Act allows the registered owner of a ship[11] to grant a mortgage, which, except in the case of small vessels, may be registered against the ship.[12] The Act also permits the registration of a mortgage against a vessel that is recorded as being built in Canada.[13]

Statutory forms for ship and builders' mortgages are provided by the chief registrar.[14] They are simple documents that record only the name of the ship and its details, the name of the mortgagor and the

---

120 L.N.T.S. 187 (in force 2 June 1931); 27 May 1967, S.D. No. 12 (1967) 3, (not in force)], nor to the more recent *International Convention on Maritime Liens and Mortgages*, 1993 [6 May 1993, 33 I.L.M. 353 (not in force)].

6 S.C. 1991, c.46. See also the *Fisheries Improvement Loans Act*, R.S.C. 1985, c.F-22, by which loans to finance fishing activities may be guaranteed by the federal government provided they are secured on the fishing vessels. Some provinces offer similar fishing vessel financing on like terms.

7 The licensing system will become a small-vessel register under the *Canada Shipping Act, 2001*, above note 5, s.43(1).

8 *Canada Shipping Act*, above note 5, s.19; *Canada Shipping Act, 2001*, ibid., s.49.

9 See the *Small Vessel Regulations*, C.R.C., c.1487 as am. by S.O.R./2002-171 for the precise definition of "small vessels." See also G in Chapter 4, "Licensing."

10 *Canada Shipping Act*, above note 5, ss.2 and 16; *Canada Shipping Act, 2001*, above note 5, ss.2 and 46(1).

11 Whether of the whole of the ship or only a share of it.

12 *Canada Shipping Act*, above note 5, s.37(1); *Canada Shipping Act, 2001*, above note 5, s.65(1).

13 This subject is discussed in Chapter 4, C, "Building a New Ship." *Canada Shipping Act*, ibid., s.37(1); *Canada Shipping Act, 2001*, ibid., s.65(1). Cf. U.K. law, which has no equivalent provision: see G. Bowtle & K.P. McGuiness, *The Law of Ship Mortgages* (London: Lloyd's Press, 2001) at 54.

14 Available online at: <www.tc.gc.ca/shipregistry>.

number of shares in the ship owned, the name of the mortgagee, and the financial obligations involved. The prescribed forms allow for a mortgage to secure a principal sum and a fixed rate of interest, or a mortgage to secure an account current, that is, a continuing security for a balance that may fluctuate and an interest rate that may change. An account current mortgage is the more flexible of the two kinds of mortgage because it allows for future advances, perhaps to cover operations or repairs to the ship after the initial loan for its purchase, and it can be used to accommodate financing by a revolving line of credit.

The statutory form also expressly grants the mortgage and usually, by addition, refers to the collateral loan agreement as well. The document itself is filed with the registrar, who gives it a time and date of entry on the register as a matter of record of its standing.[15] No other charges on a ship are registerable under the *Canada Shipping Act* so there is no public record of any maritime and other liens against it. A prospective purchaser of a ship may search the register to determine its registered owner and the existence of any mortgages against it but will not discover other maritime securities and will not even be given access to check the list of licensed small vessels.

Historically, ship mortgages were regulated by the law of chattel mortgages, which was developed from real property mortgage law. This body of law has now been overtaken by the *Canada Shipping Act* and the provincial personal property security acts. One important effect is that a ship mortgage does not amount to a transfer of title to the ship to the mortgagee with an equity of redemption remaining in the mortgagor, as traditional mortgage law would hold. The *Canada Shipping Act* provides that "[a] mortgage of a vessel ... does not have the effect of a mortgagee becoming, or the mortgager ceasing to be, the owner of the vessel, except to the extent necessary to make the vessel ... available as security under the mortgage."[16] In other words, on mortgaging a ship, the shipowner remains the owner but his or her use of it becomes subject to the rights of and duties toward the mortgagee.

b) Rights of Mortgagor

As owner, the mortgagor has the right to use the ship in any way he or she wishes provided that he or she does not impair the security of the

---

15 *Canada Shipping Act*, above note 5, ss.37(2) and (3); *Canada Shipping Act, 2001*, above note 5, ss.65(2) and (3).
16 *Canada Shipping Act*, ibid., s.40; *Canada Shipping Act, 2001*, ibid., s.68. The provincial personal property security acts recognize a ship mortgage as a "security interest" in the vessel: see below B(3), "Mortgages under Provincial Legislation."

mortgagee[17] or break any restrictive covenants that may be included in the collateral loan agreement. For a commercial ship in particular, the mortgagor needs this power in order to earn profits with the ship from which to repay the mortgage loan and interest.[18] The corollary of this power is that any transaction undertaken by the mortgagor, so long as it does not impair the mortgage security, will also bind the mortgagee. Therefore, if the mortgagor charters the vessel, the mortgagee may only take possession of the ship subject to the ongoing charter.[19] But along with the mortgagor's right to use the ship and thus to earn freight or hire — unless they are also specifically assigned, goes the obligation to pay all expenses in operating the ship as well as the costs of maintenance and insurance to preserve its value as a security.[20] The mortgagor's right to use the ship also includes the right to sell it, provided there is no prohibition in the loan agreement, because the mortgagee's security is not necessarily impaired by the transfer of ownership of the vessel to another.[21]

The mortgagor's use of the ship must not "materially impair"[22] the sufficiency of the mortgagee's security. Whether it does is a question of fact in each case. A mortgagee who takes possession of the ship cannot repudiate a contract made by the mortgagor just because it is unfavourable.[23] So, for instance, a charter that will take the ship out of Canada to some jurisdiction where it will be harder for the mortgagor to enforce the security is not materially prejudicial to the mortgage;[24] nor is the fact that the ship becomes burdened by a maritime lien for payment of a reward for salvage services necessitated by a marine peril, provided the encumbrance is not allowed to remain.[25]

The mortgagee may only object if the impairment materially affects the value of the mortgaged property: for example, a charterparty that

---

17 *Collins v. Lamport* (1864), 11 L.T. 497 (Ch,). See also *Canada Shipping Act*, ibid., s.40; *Canada Shipping Act, 2001*, ibid., s.68.
18 The mortgagor is free to let the ship lie idle if he or she so wishes, and the mortgagee cannot interfere so long as the mortgage is not in default.
19 *Heather Bell (The)*, [1901] P. 143; *Myrto (The)*, [1977] 2 Lloyd's L.R. 243 (Q.B.). But the mortgagee is not bound by the commitments the mortgagor has undertaken but cannot fulfil: see *Myrto (The)*, ibid.
20 Mortgagees are free to pay the ship's debts if they choose, which they might be inclined to do to protect their security, as when the ship is arrested, and then to recover the payments from the mortgagors: see, e.g., *Orchis (The)* (1890), 15 P.D. 38.
21 See *Blanche (The)* (1887), 58 L.T. 592 (Adm. Ct.).
22 *Collins v. Lamport*, above note 17 at 499.
23 *Heather Bell (The)*, above note 19 at 151.
24 *Fanchon (The)* (1880), 5 P.D. 173.
25 *Manor (The)*, [1907] P. 339 at 362.

binds the ship for an unduly long time or to unusual and extraordinary provisions that thereby injure its sale value in the hands of the mortgagee is materially prejudicial to the mortgage security;[26] other examples include ordering the ship to carry contraband in time of war[27] or assume other risks that render it uninsurable; or chartering the ship improvidently, when it is already loaded with debts and the mortgagor is impecunious.[28] In addition to the legal prohibition against material impairment of the security in the ship, the loan agreement will typically include many clauses protecting the mortgagor's interests, the breach of which may amount to default of the mortgage.

If the mortgagor engages the ship in a way that does impair the mortgage security, the mortgagee — when he or she takes possession of the ship — may repudiate the engagement. The contract is unenforceable against the mortgagee, but the other contracting party may seek damages for breach of contract from the mortgagor.[29] On the other hand, if the mortgagee alleges erroneously that the mortgage security has been materially prejudiced and he or she consequently interferes wrongly in the contractual engagements of the ship, he or she will be liable in tort to the other contracting party.[30]

The sale of the ship will affect the mortgage when ownership is transferred to an unqualified person, essentially a foreign individual or corporation; then registration of the ship in Canada must be cancelled,[31] although it will normally be approved in the foreign state. However, the *Canada Shipping Act* expressly states that cancellation of the registration of the vessel does not affect the registration of the mortgage against it.[32] Yet, obviously, if the ship is registered in a foreign port, the unsatisfied mortgage, were it to remain on the Canadian registry, would not be readily discoverable and the mortgagee's exposure to risk from competing security interests would be increased. Instead the Act makes other provision for the protection of the mortgagee: before cancellation of the ship's registration, the registrar must give all registered mortgagees notice of the change in ownership and sufficient opportunity to arrange for the transfer of the ship to a qualified owner so that

---

26 Examples in *Heather Bell (The)*, above note 19 at 152. See also *Celtic King (The)*, [1894] P. 175.
27 *Law Guarantee & Trust Society v. Russian Bank for Foreign Trade*, [1905] 1 K.B. 815.
28 *Myrto(The)*, above note 19; *Manor (The)*, above note 25.
29 *Celtic King (The)*, above note 26 at 190.
30 *Myrto (The)*, above note 19 at 254.
31 *Canada Shipping Act*, above note 5, ss.30(2)(b) and (4); *Canada Shipping Act, 2001*, above note 5, ss.60(2)(b) and (4).
32 *Canada Shipping Act*, ibid., s.31; *Canada Shipping Act, 2001*, ibid., s.61.

it will remain on the Canadian register, or to apply to the Federal Court for a judicial sale,[33] from which the mortgagor's loan may be satisfied.

In addition to using the ship, the mortgagor has the right to redeem his or her vessel. By making due repayment of the outstanding loan and the agreed interest, the mortgagor is entitled to have the security and its registration discharged.[34] That is to say, the mortgagee must endorse the original mortgage as paid and return it to the mortgagor, who, as shipowner, must then notify the registrar to correct the register by expunging the mortgage.[35]

c) **Rights of Mortgagee**
The principal rights of the mortgagee are to take possession and to sell the ship. He or she is also free to transfer the mortgage for value if he or she so wishes. The mortgagee has no right to interfere with the mortgagor's ongoing use of the ship until either the mortgage goes into default or the security in the ship is impaired.[36] On either of these events occurring, the mortgagee is entitled to enter into possession of the ship. In practice this power is usually regulated by the terms of the original loan agreement.[37] The mortgagee may take actual possession by going, or putting a representative, on board, but that is not always feasible if the ship is on some distant voyage. Constructively taking possession will suffice if the mortgagee manifests a clear and obvious intention of assuming the right of ownership of the ship,[38] for instance, by informing the master and giving fresh sailing instructions or by appointing a new ship's agent, or by informing the mortgagor and any charterer.[39] The effect of going into possession is to put the mortgagee in the position of owner, with all its attendant benefits and responsibilities.[40] Hence the mortgagee may collect any freight payable on the ship

---

33 *Canada Shipping Act*, ibid., ss.30(3) and 45; *Canada Shipping Act, 2001*, ibid., ss.60(3) and 74. Section 75 of the *Canada Shipping Act, 2001* also gives the court discretion to prohibit any dealing with a Canadian ship for a limited time. Judicial sale is discussed in I, in Chapter 19, "Judicial Sale of the *Res*."
34 *Yolanda Barbara (The)*, [1961] 2 Lloyd's Rep. 337 (Adm. Ct.).
35 *Canada Shipping Act*, above note 5, s.28(1); *Canada Shipping Act, 2001*, above note 5, s.58(1).
36 *Blanche (The)*, above note 21. The mortgagee may have no right to seize and sell the ship even when the mortgage is in arrears if it contains a pay-as-you-earn clause and the ship has no net earnings: *Banco do Brasil S.A. v. Alexandros G. Tsavliris (The)* (1987), 12 F.T.R. 278.
37 *Banque Worms v. Maule (The)*, [1997] 1 Lloyd's L.R. 419 (P.C.).
38 *Benwell Tower (The)* (1895), 72 L.T. 664 (Adm. Ct.).
39 *Rusden v. Pope* (1868), L.R. 3 Ex. 269.
40 *Brown v. Tanner* (1868), L.R. 3 Ch. App. 597.

subsequent to taking possession of it.[41] He or she may also assume the benefits of any contract regarding the use of the ship, such as a charterparty, but he or she is also bound by its terms until its conclusion, provided it does not impair his or her security.[42] In addition, the mortgagee who operates the ship, whether for him- or herself pending sale or in performance of a subsisting charterparty, is bound to pay its costs and expenses.

Pending sale of the ship, the mortgagee's main responsibility is to exercise reasonable care of the vessel, since he or she will have to account to the mortgagor for his or her actions. Similarly the mortgagee must make good faith efforts to obtain the best possible price for the ship,[43] or he or she may become liable in damages to the mortgagor.[44] The mortgagee's right of sale is expressed in the *Canada Shipping Act*[45] as an "absolute power" subject only to limitations stated in the registered mortgage. This cannot be taken literally, however, for the mortgagee has no right to interfere with the mortgagor's rightful use of the ship. The phrase must therefore mean that the mortgagee has an unfettered right of sale once he or she has lawfully taken possession of the ship. The mortgagee may proceed with the sale in one of two ways: he or she may conduct the sale him- or herself, or he or she may arrest the ship and proceed by an action *in rem* to a court-administered sale. The processes and effects of the two methods of sale are different and have differing benefits and disadvantages. A sale by the mortgagee is generally simpler, cheaper, and quicker but can only pass to the purchaser as good a title to the ship as the mortgagee held. All mortgages, whether registered or not, are extinguished by the sale but, if the mortgagor has allowed the ship to become encumbered with maritime and other liens that run with the ship, these will be passed on to the purchaser as well. Alternatively, the mortgagee will be put to the effort and expense of providing the purchaser with an indemnity in respect of any claims that may subsequently surface.

---

41 *Ibid.* and above note 39. The mortgagor is entitled to keep the freight already earned and paid.
42 See *Fanchon (The)*, above note 24.
43 *Weir & Lewisporte Shipyards Ltd. v. Bank of Nova Scotia* (1979), 30 Nfld. & P.E.I.R. 223 (Nfld. S.C. T.D.); *Bank of Scotland v. Nel (The)*, [2001] 1 F.C. 408.
44 *Gulf & Fraser Fishermen's Credit Union v. Calm C Fish Ltd. (The Calm C)*, [1975] 1 Lloyd's L.R. 188 (B.C.C.A.).
45 *Canada Shipping Act*, above note 5, s.41(1); *Canada Shipping Act, 2001*, above note 5, s.69(1).

Where a number of parties assert an interest in the ship, the mortgagee may elect to have the ship sold by the Federal Court pursuant to its *in rem* jurisdiction.[46] The chief advantage of this route is that a court-ordered sale will cleanse the ship of all existing liens and encumbrances, as well as all mortgages, so that the purchaser acquires a clear title.[47] A second or subsequent mortgagee may have to adopt this procedure for sale since he or she is prohibited from selling the vessel him- or herself without the agreement of every prior mortgagee.[48] The disadvantage of a judicial sale is the higher cost and time it takes to complete the necessary appraisals, pay the marshall's fees, and resolve any contested claims. Whichever way the sale is conducted, after it has been completed, the registrar must be informed of the changes so that the register can be appropriately amended.[49]

Apart from enforcing the security, the mortgagor is free at any time to dispose of his or her interest in the mortgage. The *Canada Shipping Act* permits the transfer of a registered mortgage to any person, not just qualified persons, but it also requires that the registrar be informed of the transfer so that the register may also be altered.[50] A statutory form for doing so is provided on the reverse side of the registered mortgage. Similarly a mortgage may be transmitted as a result of the marriage, death, or bankruptcy of the mortgagee or possibly by court order and the registrar must be notified by the transferee of this change as well.[51] Furthermore, the mortgagee's rights are not affected by the bankruptcy of the mortgagor after registration of the mortgage.[52]

d) Security under *Bank Act*

In addition to ship mortgages under the *Canada Shipping Act*, certain vessels may also be subject to another federal statute that provides a unique form of security for the chartered banks. Since the nineteenth century, the *Bank Act*, as part of federal government economic policy to encourage development of the resources of the young Dominion of Canada, had granted, and continues to grant, Canadian banks the right to take a special security for loans to producers of primary products

---

46 *Federal Court Act*, R.S.C. 1985, c.F-7, s.22; see Chapter 19, "Admiralty Procedure."
47 *Osborn Refrigeration Sales & Service Inc.,v. Atlantean I (The)* (1982), 7 D.L.R. (4th) 395 (F.C.A.) [*The Atlantean I*].
48 *Canada Shipping Act*, above note 5, s.41(2); *Canada Shipping Act, 2001*, above note 5, s.69(2).
49 *Canada Shipping Act*, ibid., s.28(1); *Canada Shipping Act, 2001*, ibid., s.58(1).
50 *Canada Shipping Act*, ibid., s.43(1); *Canada Shipping Act, 2001*, ibid., s.71.
51 *Canada Shipping Act*, ibid., s.44; *Canada Shipping Act, 2001*, ibid., s.72.
52 *Canada Shipping Act*, ibid., s.42; *Canada Shipping Act, 2001*, ibid., s.70.

and manufacturers. This legislation affects shipping inasmuch as two of the closely prescribed classes of business borrowers are people in aquaculture and fishing, who may give their vessels as security.[53] The *Bank Act* establishes a system of registration of a bank's security with the Bank of Canada[54] but the method of registering is different from the *Canada Shipping Act*. Under that Act the statutory mortgage form itself is filed with the registrar of ships but, under the *Bank Act*, only a notice of intention to take security, signed by the debtor, is required.[55] The description of the secured property, including vessels, and the amount of the loan and interest, as well as all the other clauses of the security agreement, are private matters that do not appear on the public register. Such a notice filing system is extremely flexible. One result is that the bank's security agreement may secure loans made before, at the time of, or after the agreement is executed, as its terms may state.[56] Another consequence is that a bank can register at any time in advance of taking security as the notice is only an expression of its intentions. However, the failure to register before receiving security cannot be cured and will result in the bank's security interest being void as against creditors of the borrower and subsequent purchasers and mortgagees from the borrower in good faith.[57]

The bank may take a security interest over both the present and the after acquired property of the borrower.[58] Thus, the bank may attach its security to a vessel used for fishing or aquaculture that is currently owned or subsequently acquired. The rights that the bank acquires are said to be "the same rights and powers as if the bank had acquired a warehouse receipt or bill of lading in which that property was described."[59] This obscure language is taken to vest such rights and title as the debtor has in the bank.[60] In any case, whatever the security agreement's terms may be, the bank also has a statutory power of seizure[61]

---

53 *Bank Act*, above note 6, ss.425 and 427.
54 *Ibid.*, ss.427(4) and (5).
55 *Ibid.*, ss.427(4) and (5).
56 *Ibid.*, s.429(1).
57 *Ibid.*, s.427(4)(a). See also *Canadian Imperial Bank of Commerce v. 281787 Alberta Ltd. (Crockett's Western Wear)*, [1984] 5 W.W.R. 283 (Alta. C.A.).
58 *Bank Act, ibid.*, ss.427(2)(a) and (b).
59 *Ibid.*, s.427(2)(c).
60 *Royal Bank of Canada v. Nova Scotia (Workers/Workmen's Compensation Board)*, [1936] S.C.R. 560; *Bank of Montreal v. Hall*, [1990] 1 S.C.R. 121.
61 *Bank Act* above note 6, s.427(3). See also *National Bank of Canada v. Atomic Slipper Co.*, [1991] 1 S.C.R. 1059.

and sale.[62] Prerequisite to the exercise of the bank's right of seizure is the borrower's non-payment of the loan or failure to care for the secured property.[63] However, the property referred to by the Act would include vessels used for fishing but not necessarily those used for aquaculture.

After taking possession of the secured vessel the bank may exercise a statutory power of sale by public auction for default in repayment of the loan.[64] The right of sale for other breaches of the security agreement will depend upon its terms. In conducting the sale, the bank must act in good faith and in a timely and commercially appropriate manner.[65] This duty includes giving the defaulting owner of a fishing or aquaculture vessel notice of the impending sale. By the sale the purchaser acquires such rights and title in the vessel, including any encumbrances such as liens, as the former owner had.

It is evident from this outline of *Bank Act* security that there is overlap and conflict in the provisions of the *Canada Shipping Act* and the *Bank Act* for taking security in fishing and aquaculture vessels. In an effort to avoid confusion the *Bank Act* addresses the interrelation of the two statutes. If a fishing vessel is recorded or registered under the *Canada Shipping Act*, a bank may also register its *Bank Act* security against the vessel on the register and will thereby acquire all the rights, in addition to its *Bank Act* rights, as if it were a registered ship mortgagee. Furthermore, in a competition between a registered *Bank Act* security and any other interest, such as a mortgage that is registered against the fishing vessel, priority will be determined by the order of registration under the *Canada Shipping Act*.[66] Such alignment of the two acts is not, unfortunately, expressed to apply to aquaculture vessels.

3) Mortgages under Provincial Legislation

a) Scope of Personal Property Security Acts

A lender who does not take and register a ship mortgage under the *Canada Shipping Act* may still acquire a valid security interest in a vessel under provincial legislation. A vessel, whether a large ship or a small craft, is a species of moveable personal property that is subject to

---

62 *Bank Act*, ibid., s.428(7).
63 Ibid., s.427(3).
64 Ibid., s.428(7).
65 Ibid., s.428(10).
66 Ibid., ss.428(5) and (6), subject to prospective amendment by *Canada Shipping Act, 2001*, above note 5, s.275 to align the *Bank Act* with the *Canada Shipping Act, 2001* when that statute comes into force.

provincial jurisdiction over local property.[67] Federal statutes, such as the *Canada Shipping Act* and the *Bank Act*, do not oust this jurisdiction; they merely override it, under the constitutional doctrine of paramountcy to the extent that the federal and provincial statutes overlap and conflict. So, if a lender takes a ship mortgage but fails to register it under the *Canada Shipping Act* or obtains a security interest in a vessel by agreement with the owner by any other means, the mortgage may still be protected by provincial law.[68]

To speak of mortgages under provincial law is really a misnomer. The form of a mortgage may be used but is not necessary, and the law historically associated with mortgages is irrelevant under modern personal property security legislation. Nowadays, leaving aside the civil law province of Quebec,[69] provincial legislation recognizes, and fully regulates, a generalized security interest in personal property. These personal property security acts[70] provide a unitary system of registration for all kinds of security in personal property and a single set of rules about their appendant rights, responsibilities, and ranking. These acts are also nearly uniform throughout common law Canada.

The personal property security acts apply to every transaction that, in substance, creates a security interest in personal property to secure payment or performance of an obligation, without regard to its form. They list, as examples, a number of well-known security arrangements, including chattel mortgages.[71] The personal property in which security is taken is known under this legislation as "collateral," which is divis-

---

67 *Constitution Act, 1867* (U.K.), 30 & 31 Vict., c.3, s.92, reprinted in R.S.C. 1985, App. II, No. 5.
68 P.W. Hogg, *Constitutional Law of Canada*, 4th ed. (Scarborough, ON: Carswell, 1997) at c.16. See also *Bank of Montreal v. Hall*, above note 60. When a ship mortgage in statutory form is registered under the *Canada Shipping Act* it is undoubtedly regulated exclusively by federal maritime law. Whether security interests in ships that are not registered under the Act are subject to provincial statutes concerning personal property security has not so far been clearly determined, while in principle and commercial practice there are strong reasons to believe they are: see R.J. Wood, "The Nature and Definition of Federal Security Interest" (2000) 34 C.B.L.J. 65.
69 Which applies a distinctly different personal property security regime: see *Civil Code of Quebec*, S.Q., 1991, c.64, (C.C.Q.) Book Six, Title Three–Hypothecs and Book Nine–Publication of Rights.
70 For instance Nova Scotia: *Personal Property Security Act*, S.N.S. 1995–96, c.13 [*NSPPSA*]; Ontario: *Personal Property Security Act*, R.S.O. 1990, c.P.10 [*OPPSA*]; British Columbia: *Personal Property Security Act*, R.S.B.C. 1996, c.359 [*BCPPSA*].
71 *NSPPSA*, ibid., s.4; *OPPSA*, ibid., s.2; *BCPPSA*, ibid., s.2.

ible into several categories.[72] Ships and boats are treated as "goods" and sub-classified as equipment if put to business use, or as "consumer goods" if used for personal enjoyment. Freight and the benefit of insurance policies on vessels, when taken as security, are categorized as "intangibles."[73] Some personal property security acts make allowance for the potential for overlap with federal security acts. Thus the Nova Scotia Act excludes from its application ship mortgages registered under the *Canada Shipping Act* and security interests regulated by the *Bank Act*.[74] Others use more general language to exclude security agreements governed by any federal act.[75] Yet others, like Ontario, make no reference to security interests under federal law and therefore do not exclude duplicative registration under provincial law, with consequent complications later over priority of status. Yet even where *Bank Act* security is excluded from provincial registration, the banks can and do take a second security interest under provincial law. These opportunities for duplication impose additional complexity on the ranking of competing security interests.

b) Creation and Perfection of Security Interests

A security interest is created and protected under the personal property security acts by three steps — agreement, attachment, and perfection. There is no set form for the security agreement except that it must contain a written description of the collateral by item or kind, covering all the debtor's present and after-acquired personal property, and must be signed by the debtor.[76] The personal property security acts expressly allow creditors to grant present and future loans[77] so that, in one security agreement, they can organize a revolving line of credit or account current financing. Similarly the acts permit security to be taken in both present and future personal property of the debtor,[78] so that creditors can prospectively secure future advances against substitute or additional collateral as the debtor acquires it. The security agreement attaches to the collateral as soon as the secured party gives value and the debtor has or obtains rights in the collateral.[79] The

---

72 NSPPSA, ibid., s.2; OPPSA, ibid., s.1; BCPPSA, ibid., s.1.
73 Ibid.
74 NSPPSA, ibid., s.5.
75 E.g., Saskatchewan: *Personal Property Security Act*, 1993, S.S. 1993, c.P-6.2, s.4.
76 NSPPSA, above note 70, s.11; OPPSA, above note 70, s.9; BCPPSA, above note 70, s.10.
77 NSPPSA, ibid., s.15; OPPSA, ibid., s.13; BCPPSA, ibid., s.14.
78 NSPPSA, ibid., s.14; OPPSA, ibid., s.12; BCPPSA, ibid., s.13.
79 NSPPSA, ibid., s.13; OPPSA, ibid., s.11; BCPPSA, ibid., s.12.

secured party provides "value" by giving the loan or, sooner, by contractually promising to make an immediate or a future advance.[80] The security interest is thereby created between the parties by attachment of the collateral, and may be perfected as against third parties by registration of the agreement or possession of the collateral.[81]

The registration systems under the personal property security acts use notice filing procedures, such as the *Bank Act*, but are also increasingly electronic. Indeed, the systems in the Atlantic provinces are wholly electronic. Registration in Nova Scotia, for instance, is completed by electronic filing of a "financing statement" containing only the proper name and address of the debtor and the secured party, a description of the collateral, and the agreed duration of the security agreement.[82] Some goods, including boats, are designated as serial number goods; if the secured vessel is a consumer good, its serial number must be included in the financing statement. If it is business equipment, its serial number need not be recorded to achieve perfection but, if it is not, the security interest may be subordinated to other interests.[83]

On filing, the registry places a time and date stamp on the record,[84] which is used to establish the priority status of the secured interest. Since this is a notice filing system, the personal property security acts permit the secured party to file a financing statement at any time, so it is obviously in his or her interest to do so as early as possible, even before the security agreement is concluded. It matters not in what order the three steps of agreement, attachment, and registration are completed — although perfection cannot be achieved until all three have been accomplished.[85]

c) Rights of Parties

Under the personal property security acts, a fully perfected security interest takes priority over all unperfected ones.[86] However, the security of a perfected security interest is not perfect. The acts only regulate consensual security interests and so a cluster of liens, both maritime and statutory that arise by law, are beyond the reach of these acts. Thus, liens may still take priority over perfected security interests if the law

---

80 *NSPPSA, ibid.*, s.2; *OPPSA, ibid.*, s.1; *BCPPSA, ibid.*, s.1.
81 *NSPPSA, ibid.*, ss.25 and 26; *OPPSA, ibid.*, ss.22 and 23; *BCPPSA, ibid.*, ss.24 and 25.
82 N.S. Reg. 129/97, Part III.
83 *NSPPSA*, above note 70, s.36(4); *BCPPSA*, above note 70, s.35(4); N.S. Reg. 129/97, s.2(t); B.C.Reg. 227/2002, s.1.
84 *NSPPSA, ibid.*, s.44(4); *BCPPSA, ibid.*, s.43(2); R.R.O. 1990, Reg. 912, ss.26 and 26.1.
85 *NSPPSA, ibid.*, s.20; *OPPSA*, above note 70, s.19; *BCPPSA, ibid.*, s.19.

governing them so ordains.[87] Further, in some provinces, a judgment creditor is allowed to register a notice of judgment in the personal property security act registry and so achieve priority over any unperfected or subsequent security interest.[88]

An unperfected security interest is still valid, so a ship mortgage that is not registered either under the *Canada Shipping Act* or the local personal property security act is still enforceable against the shipowner. However, it is liable to be subordinated by any registered interest.[89] Furthermore, it is at risk of a sale of the vessel to a purchaser for value without knowledge of the security interest.[90] While the sale of the collateral is a breach of the security agreement, the acts prefer the claim of the innocent purchaser, who thereby acquires the debtor's whole interest in the vessel free of the security interest; however, the secured party's rights against the debtor are not defeated and the security interest automatically shifts onto the proceeds of the sale in the hands of the debtor.[91]

In the event of default by the debtor, the secured party may liquidate the security. The personal property security acts establish a detailed set of steps to enforcement that itemize progressively the rights of the secured party and the protections of the defaulting debtor.[92] The secured party's rights are, basically, to seize and sell the collateral "in good faith and in a commercially reasonable manner."[93] The defaulting debtor must be notified before the secured party takes possession of the vessel or moves to collect the freight, if attached under the security agreement.[94] The debtor must also be given a detailed statutory notice before any sale of the collateral[95] in order to afford him or her the opportunity to raise the money necessary to pay the outstanding debt and so redeem the vessel, or at least to pay the arrears and expenses to

---

86 NSPPSA, ibid., s.36(1)(b); OPPSA, ibid., s.20(1)(a); BCPPSA, ibid., s.35(1)(b).
87 See below C, "Liens."
88 NSPPSA, above note 70, s.21(1). In other provinces the judgment creditor must execute against the debtor's assets before priority can be asserted: see BCPPSA, above note 70, s.20(a); OPPSA, above note 70, s.20(1)(a).
89 NSPPSA, ibid., s.36(1)(b); OPPSA, ibid., s.20(1)(a); BCPPSA, ibid., s.35(1)(b).
90 NSPPSA, ibid., s.21(3); OPPSA, ibid., s.20(1)(c); BCPPSA, ibid., s.20(c).
91 NSPPSA, ibid., s.29; OPPSA, ibid., s.25; BCPPSA, ibid., s.28. But the creditor may have to take steps to perfect the security in the proceeds.
92 NSPPSA, ibid., Part V; OPPSA, ibid., Part V; BCPPSA, ibid., Part 5.
93 NSPPSA, ibid., s.66(2); OPPSA, ibid., s.63(2); BCPPSA, ibid., s.68(2).
94 NSPPSA, ibid., ss.58 and 59; OPPSA, ibid., s.61; BCPPSA, ibid., ss.57 and 58. If the debtor is insolvent, the secured party may also have to satisfy the notice requirements of the *Bankruptcy and Insolvency Act*, R.S.C. 1985, c.B-3, s.244, before seizing the secured vessel.
95 NSPPSA, ibid., s.60; OPPSA, ibid., s.63; BCPPSA, ibid., s.59.

date and so cure the default and reinstate the security agreement as an ongoing arrangement.[96] The debtor is entitled to an account of the proceeds of sale and to any surplus after the secured party and all other creditors have been paid in full.[97] If the proceeds of the sale are insufficient to repay the secured party, the debtor remains liable for the deficiency.[98] The secured party must also give a good account of the conduct of the sale and act in all respects in a commercially reasonable way.[99] If he or she does not, the debtor is entitled to damages for breach of any obligation under the personal property security acts.[100] Where the collateral is a consumer good, such as a yacht or pleasure craft, the debtor is also entitled to the benefit of consumer protection laws, which will override the acts.[101] In addition, some provinces impose limitations on the secured party's enforcement powers by compelling an election between seizure of the collateral and suit against the debtor.[102]

The rights of enforcement under the personal property security acts are available to all the secured parties. Subordinated ones do not need the consent of the prior ranking parties to proceed toward seizure and sale of the collateral on default but obviously will not be paid out of the proceeds before those with priority have been satisfied. However, a secured party with prior ranking, who considers that enforcement of the security, even though the debtor is in default, will prejudice his or her interests, may apply to the court for a stay of enforcement or other appropriate order.[103] Secured parties may also contract in the security agreement to appoint and employ a receiver or receiver-manager to administer the enforcement process and to manage the collateral for profit in the interim as appropriate.[104]

4) Ranking of Mortgages

When several security interests are taken in the same vessel but its sale value is insufficient to generate sufficient proceeds to satisfy them all,

---

96 *NSPPSA, ibid.*, s.63; *OPPSA, ibid.*, s.66; *BCPPSA, ibid.*, s.62.
97 *NSPPSA, ibid.*, s.61; *OPPSA, ibid.*, s.64; *BCPPSA, ibid.*, s.60.
98 *Ibid.*
99 *NSPPSA, ibid.*, ss.61(4) and 66(2); *OPPSA, ibid.*, ss.64 and 63(2); *BCPPSA, ibid.*, ss.60(3) and 68(2).
100 *NSPPSA, ibid.*, s.67; *BCPPSA, ibid.*, s.69.
101 *NSPPSA, ibid.*, s.71(1); *OPPSA*, above note 70, s.73; *BCPPSA, ibid.*, s.74.
102 E.g. *BCPPSA, ibid.*, s.67.
103 *NSPPSA*, above note 70, s.64; *OPPSA*, above note 70, s.67; *BCPPSA*, above note 70, s.63.
104 *NSPPSA, ibid.*, s.65; *OPPSA, ibid.*, s.60; *BCPPSA, ibid.*, s.64.

their order of priority must be determined. Prior mortgagees are always entitled to be paid in full before subordinate creditors receive anything: this is one reason why security is taken in the first place. But ordering the priority of ship mortgages can be complex because more than one statute may be involved. It is a particularly uncertain task where the interests in contest engage both federal and provincial secured transaction regimes. For this reason, the ranking of security interests taken under federal legislation, namely the *Canada Shipping Act* and the *Bank Act*, will be discussed before priorities under provincial personal property security acts are considered.

a) Priority under Federal Legislation
Ship mortgages registered under the *Canada Shipping Act* take priority according to the date of their registration,[105] regardless of when they were made. It is also irrelevant whether the first mortgagee to register had knowledge of an existing but unregistered mortgagee. The Act establishes a rule that prefers the swiftest to register; however, the Act also allows for voluntary subordination agreements between successive mortgagees, since it permits the priority of mortgages to be changed if all the mortgagees lodge their written consent with the registrar.[106] Competing ship mortgages taken on statutory forms but never registered under the *Canada Shipping Act* fall outside these priority rules but are governed by the provincial personal property security acts' rules, discussed below.

The rule that priority among registered mortgagees follows the order of their registration may, perhaps, be disturbed in the event that the prior mortgagee makes further advances after registration of a subsequent mortgage. The common law principle that allows a first mortgagee to tack on to its account all further advances[107] in priority to a second mortgagee's claim, even though the advances were made subsequent to the second mortgage, has been applied to registered ship mortgages.[108] However, an account current mortgagee may not take

---

105 *Canada Shipping Act*, above note 5, s.39(1); *Canada Shipping Act, 2001*, above note 5, s.67(1).
106 *Canada Shipping Act*, ibid., s.39(2); *Canada Shipping Act, 2001*, ibid., s.67(2).
107 Provided they were agreed with the mortgagor as part of the cumulative debt the mortgage secures.
108 *Liverpool Marine Credit Co. v. Wilson*, above note 3 at 512. This case also established that a registered mortgagee who, on the default of the mortgagor, takes possession of the ship also thereby obtains a legal right to collect the freight that has not yet been earned in priority to a subsequent mortgagee or an assignee of the freight of which the registered mortgagee was unaware.

advantage of this principle to acquire priority over a second mortgagee in respect of further advances made after the first mortgagee had notice of the second mortgage.[109] This outcome supposes that the registration of the second mortgage does not provide constructive notice to the first mortgagee. The result is commercially reasonable since the second mortgagee may be expected to search the register and so to discover the prior account current mortgage, but the first mortgagee is hardly likely to make a search every time a further advance is granted. Indeed, when a line of credit is advanced, it is the mortgagor who decides when it is drawn on, so there is no reason for the first mortgagee's registered security to be put at risk unless the mortgagee has actual knowledge of the subsequent mortgagee's security interest and is, therefore, in a position to take such defensive action as seems appropriate.

Under the *Bank Act* a secured bank is said to have "priority over all rights subsequently acquired in, on or in respect of" the secured property as well as over an unpaid vendor's claim or existing lien of which the bank was unaware.[110] Thus, unlike the *Canada Shipping Act*, the *Bank Act* ranks competing security interests of banks in vessels used for fishing and aquaculture according to the order in which their security is executed.[111] Registration of a notice of intention to take security is a necessary step to perfect a *Bank Act* security[112] but it is not determinative of its priority.

Given the statutory provision at the federal level of two distinct kinds of security in ships under two different acts, the opportunity exists for competition to arise between a ship mortgagee under the *Canada Shipping Act* and a secured bank under the *Bank Act* for priority of security in the same vessel. Neither statute addresses such a competition directly, but the *Bank Act* aligns the two acts to the extent that it permits a bank to register its *Bank Act* security under the *Canada Shipping Act*. Such registration accords the bank all the rights and priority as if it held a ship mortgage under the Act.[113] This power of a secured bank to register under the *Canada Shipping Act*, however, cannot be exercised before the vessel itself is registered, since the Act operates by registering interests against registered ships. A bank may, therefore, hold a security interest in a ves-

---

109 This is the rule in *Hopkinson v. Rolt* (1861), 5 L.T. 90 (H.L.), as applied to ship mortgages in *Benwell Tower (The)*, above note 38.
110 *Bank Act*, above note 6, s.428(1).
111 *Royal Bank of Canada v. Bank of Montreal* (1976), 67 D.L.R. (3d) 755 (Sask. C.A.).
112 Failure to register renders the bank's security void as against all the debtor's creditors: *Bank Act*, above note 6, s.427(4).
113 See the discussion above at note 66.

sel that it is unable to perfect under the *Canada Shipping Act* before the vessel and a mortgage against it are both registered under the Act.

Royal Bank of Canada v. Queen Charlotte Fisheries Ltd.[114] presented such a situation. The bank held a perfected security interest against a fishing vessel under the *Bank Act* and also registered this interest under the *Canada Shipping Act* after it learned of the registration of the vessel under that Act. But in the meantime Queen Charlotte Fisheries took a ship mortgage, which it registered before the Bank under the *Canada Shipping Act*. The court, however, preferred the bank's security interest. It held that the bank, lacking the opportunity to register under the *Canada Shipping Act* at the time it took its security, had done all it could by registering under the *Bank Act* to give notice of its security interest in the vessel. Since Queen Charlotte Fisheries knew about the bank's involvement in the financing of the fishing vessel, its mortgage was subordinated to the bank's security interest, even though it was second in order of registration under the *Canada Shipping Act*.

While the priorities among security interests under the different federal acts have been largely resolved, the competition that may arise when a federal *Bank Act* security and a provincial personal property security acts security are taken in the same vessel remains much more uncertain. It may be thought, pursuant to the constitutional doctrine of paramountcy,[115] that, since the two schemes are virtually incompatible,[116] a *Bank Act* security will always prevail.[117] Banks cannot be required to register their *Bank Act* securities under provincial personal property security acts, which, in any event, do not regulate any but provincially recognized security interests. However, in at least two provinces, the courts have, controversially, determined the priority between competing *Bank Act* and personal property security act's security interests according to their order of creation.[118] These decisions seem to be predicated on the fact that a *Bank Act* security, like a mortgage, attaches only to the extent of the debtor's rights in the property. Thus, a bank's *Bank Act* security will capture the whole of a shipowner's ownership or title to a vessel, unless it is already charged with a

---

114 (1981), 13 B.L.R. 306, aff'd (1983), 50 B.C.L.R. 128 (C.A.).
115 See Hogg, above note 68.
116 *Bank of Montreal v. Hall*, above note 60.
117 C.Walsh, *An Introduction to the New Brunswick Personal Property Security Act* (Fredericton, NB: Geographic Information, 1995) at 51.
118 *Bank of Montreal v. Pulsar Ventures Inc.*(1987), 42 D.L.R. (4th) 385 (Sask. C.A.); *Birch Hills Credit Union Ltd. v. CIBC* (1988), 52 D.L.R. (4th) 113 (Sask. C.A.); *Bank of Nova Scotia v. Harvester Credit Corp. of Canada Ltd.* (1990), 73 D.L.R. (4th) 385 (C.A.).

personal property security act's security interest, when the *Bank Act* security can only attach to the encumbered property interest that the shipowner retains. Legislative action is probably necessary to resolve the uncertainty in the law but federal/provincial agreement on the form of such legislation has yet to be reached.[119]

b) Priority under Provincial Legislation

Under the provincial personal property security acts, a perfected security interest is ranked ahead of all unperfected ones.[120] The order of priority of unperfected security interests is determined by their time of attachment.[121] Between competing perfected security interests, such as two interests in the same vessel perfected by registration, priority is fixed by the order of registration regardless of which was the first to become fully perfected.[122] It is therefore possible for a lender against security in a vessel to acquire priority over an existing lender, who also has a perfected security in the same vessel, by registering in advance of execution of the loan agreement or attachment of the debtor's collateral and before the existing lender registers.

Where a judgment creditor has exercised the right to register a notice of judgment, the secured party who has a perfected interest has priority to the extent of all advances made before he or she learns about the registration of the judgment.[123] Actual knowledge of the registration of the judgment is necessary since the act of registration is not constructive notice to the whole world.[124] Further advances, made after the secured party is aware of the registered judgment, will be subordinated to the extent of the judgment. The personal property security acts, therefore, permit the secured party to stop payment of future advances that he or she promised in the security agreement;[125] for instance, if a secured party perfects security for a revolving line of credit and a judgment creditor afterward registers notice of the judgment,

---

119 During 2003 the Uniform Law Conference of Canada and the Law Commission of Canada were engaged in a joint project to harmonize the federal *Bank Act* and provincial personal property security acts' secured transaction regimes.
120 *NSPPSA*, above note 70, s.36(1)(b); *OPPSA*, above note 70, s.20(1)(a); *BCPPSA*, above note 70, s.35(1)(b).
121 *NSPPSA, ibid.*, s.36(1)(c); *OPPSA, ibid.*, s.30(1); *BCPPSA, ibid.*, s.35(1)(c).
122 *NSPPSA, ibid.*, s.36(1)(a); *OPPSA, ibid.*, s.30(1); *BCPPSA, ibid.*, s.35(1)(a).
123 *NSPPSA, ibid.*, s.36(6); *BCPPSA, ibid.*, s.35(b).
124 *NSPPSA, ibid.*, ss. 3(1) and 48; *OPPSA*, above note 70, ss.46(5) and 69; *BCPPSA, ibid.*, ss.47 and 72.
125 *NSPPSA, ibid.*, s.15(2); *BCPPSA, ibid.*, s.14(2).

the secured party may elect to terminate the line of credit or to pay off the judgment creditor and allow the debtor to continue borrowing, as seems commercially more appropriate.

These rules of priority are subject to a special rule of super-priority of a perfected purchase money security interest;[126] for example, where a financer lends money to allow the borrower to buy a vessel and perfects a security interest in the vessel within fifteen days of the borrower acquiring possession of it, the financer is entitled to the preferred status of a purchase money security interest holder. The personal property security acts grant a perfected purchase money security interest priority over any other security interest, even a previously registered and perfected one, as well as a previously registered judgment debt.[127] This rule in favour of perfected purchase money security interest defeats the situational monopoly that the first secured party, such as a bank, may set up by taking a general security interest over the whole of the debtor's personal property, both present and future. Thus, the purchase money security interest rule preserves the opportunity for competition in the credit market, which might otherwise be smothered by the general financer, unless it were willing voluntarily to subordinate its prior security interest to the holder of the purchase money security interest. However, the purchase money security interest's super-priority is only accorded to an interest securing an advance given to enable the debtor to purchase the collateral and only when it is perfected in a timely manner.

The rights of a secured party, whether he or she holds a purchase money security interest or an ordinary security interest, may also be extended by the operation of a statutory rule concerning dealings with the collateral. If the debtor, in breach of the security agreement, sells the secured vessel or assigns the secured freight, the security interest continues in the collateral and extends to the proceeds of sale or assignment as well:[128] that is, the secured party may follow the collateral into the hands of the buyer or assignee and demand the proceeds from the debtor. Indeed, if the debtor disposes of the proceeds so as to give rise to other proceeds, the secured party may both collect those proceeds from the debtor and follow the original proceeds into the hands of their transferees, so far as they remain identifiable and trace-

---

126 *NSPPSA, ibid.*, s.2; *OPPSA*, above note 70, s.1(1); *BCPPSA, ibid.*, s.1.
127 *NSPPSA, ibid.*, ss.23 and 35; *OPPSA, ibid.*, ss.20(3) and 33; *BCPPSA, ibid.*, ss.22 and 34.
128 *NSPPSA, ibid.*, s.29(1); *OPPSA, ibid.*, s.25(1); *BCPPSA, ibid.*, s.28(1).

able.[129] Suppose, for example, a consumer debtor trades a secured yacht for a motor launch but, not liking it, soon sells it for cash and a van. The secured party — assuming that his or her security interest is perfected — is entitled to try to enforce it against the yacht, as original collateral, and the motor launch, the cash, and the van, as derivative proceeds of the debtor's wrongful dealings. However, such accumulative rights may not net the secured party more than the market value of the collateral at the date it was wrongfully disposed of,[130] or the outstanding balance of the debt due, whichever is the lesser. But in order for the secured party to enforce his or her rights in the proceeds against anyone other than the debtor, he or she will need to ensure that his or her security interest in them is perfected. The personal property security acts accept that perfection by registration of the original security interest is sufficient to continuously perfect the additional security interest in the proceeds, if they are cash or cheques, or collateral of the same kind as the original; or the financing statement is designed in advance to describe the proceeds. If the proceeds do not meet these requirements, the secured party must take affirmative steps independently to perfect his or her security interest in them within fifteen days of its attachment.[131] If the secured party does not do so, his or her security interest in the proceeds will not be continuously perfected and so his or her priority status in them — but not in the original collateral — will be lost. As a result, his or her unperfected security interest in the proceeds in the hands of the debtor will be subordinated to other perfected security interests and registered judgment debts and even to unknowing buyers of the proceeds from the debtor.[132] For instance, in the example given above concerning the wrongful disposal of a secured yacht, the lack of perfection of the secured party's interest in the proceeds for whatever technical reason would mean that he or she could not overreach the buyer of the motor launch from the debtor, or any other secured party who held a perfected security interest that attached

---

129 *NSPPSA, ibid.*, s.2(ag); *OPPSA, ibid.*, s.1; *BCPPSA, ibid.*, s.1. See also *Agricultural Credit Corp. of Saskatchewan v. Pettyjohn* (1991), 79 D.L.R. (4th) 22 (Sask. C.A.). However, security interests, even perfected purchase money security interests, in traceable proceeds in the form of money or instruments such as cheques, promissory notes, or chattel paper, may be subordinated by the special rules for the protection of their holders for value: see *NSPPSA, ibid.*, s.32; *OPPSA, ibid.*, ss.28 and 29; and *BCPPSA, ibid.*, s.31.
130 *NSPPSA, ibid.*, s.29(2); *BCPPSA, ibid.*, s.28(1).
131 *NSPPSA, ibid.*, ss.29(3) and (4); *OPPSA*, above note 70, ss.25(2)–(5); *BCPPSA, ibid.*, ss.28(2) and (3).
132 *NSPPSA, ibid.*, s.21(3); *OPPSA, ibid.*, 20(1)(c); *BCPPSA, ibid.*, s.20(c).

to the van in the possession of the debtor. However the secured party's right to follow the yacht into the hands of its buyer would not be lost provided, as the example indicated, the original security interest in it was perfected.

The provincial personal property security acts are relatively recent reformatory statutes, which, as can be seen, establish a new and comprehensive regime governing security interests in vessels that is totally different from the mortgage-like regimes of the *Canada Shipping Act* and the *Bank Act*. Since security interests in ships and boats may still be acquired in the form of mortgages, care must be taken to determine by which statutory scheme they are governed. Distinction made between federal and provincial regulation according to whether the security is a legal or an equitable mortgage, as suggested in some older texts, has been overtaken by the legislative reforms. The mode of perfection of the security in the vessel — registration under which Act? — is now likely to be indicative of the applicable law.

C. LIENS

1) Introduction

Special tools have been devised since early days to protect persons and property that have come into contact with the ship and have suffered damage or incurred expense thereby. The lien in a maritime context is one such tool. It emerged in a civilian context and was adopted and further developed in English maritime law. It was then inherited by Canada and applied to its own maritime policy context. For many Commonwealth countries, generally, the law of liens is very similar, if not identical, to that prevailing in the United Kingdom. The common law has played an important role in shaping liens and the remedies they provide. Also, in many modern states, including the United States and Canada, the legislator has intervened in the maritime domain to create certain privileges for government and many statutory bodies providing services. New liens and rights of action for maritime creditors have also been established. This diversity enriches but also complicates the law of liens, especially considering that very often the ranking of claims and distribution of limited proceeds will include claims from different jurisdictions where debts are incurred by a ship as part of its international business. Similarities aside, there are also many important differences in the law and practice of liens, including differences in the substantive rights, remedies, ranking, and limitation periods.

Even the concepts do not lend themselves to easy translation or interpretation across different languages and legal cultures.[133] Translations at times use *mortgage* in English and *hypothèque* in French (*hipoteca* in Spanish) as equivalents despite the subtle differences.[134] In one old case, an English court equated the French *hypothèque* to the maritime lien in English law.[135] Courts have also ranked maritime liens ahead of mortgages. It is no wonder that the discourse on this subject is one of the most complex in international maritime law and practice.

The international maritime community has over decades been very conscious of the need for international uniformity in securities over ships and how they should be enforced. After all, this subject is essential for the financing of all aspects of the maritime adventure, without which international seaborne trade could not prosper. Whereas historically international consistency was promoted primarily through custom and comity among nations, in more modern times attempts at promoting uniformity have been undertaken through a process of unification of rules by way of treaty law. There have been three such attempts focusing on liens: the *International Convention for the Unification of Certain Rules Relating to Maritime Liens and Mortgages, 1926*;[136] the *International Convention for the Unification of Certain Rules Relating to Maritime Liens and Mortgages, 1967*;[137] and the *International Convention on Maritime Liens and Mortgages, 1993*.[138] Of the three conventions on liens and mortgages, only the 1926 convention ever came into force. Canada is not a party to any of these conventions.[139]

The lien is security for a claim over the ship, cargo, or freight as maritime property, and which public and judicial policy protect irrespective of which legal system or jurisdiction generates it. Liens may attach to maritime property under principles of maritime law and gen-

---

133 See J.C. Gémar, *Traduire ou l'art d'interpréter — Langue, droit et société: Élements de jurilinguistique*, v. 2 (Québec: Presses de l'Université du Québec, 1995).
134 G. Capellas-Espuny, "The Problem of Terminological Equivalence in International Maritime Law," 3(3) Translation J. (1999), online at: <http://accurapid.com/journal/09legal1.htm>.
135 *Colorado (The)*, [1923] P. 102 (C.A.) [*The Colorado*].
136 Above note 5.
137 *Ibid*.
138 *Ibid*.
139 Canada has not always become party to conventions it supports, e.g., *Convention on Limitation of Liability for Maritime Claims, 1976*, 19 November 1976, 1456 U.N.T.S. 221 [LLMC 1976]; and *Athens Convention Relating to the Carriage of Passengers and their Luggage by Sea, 1974*, 13 December 1974, 14 I.L.M. 945 [PAL 1974], which are implemented through the *Marine Liability Act*, S.C. 2001, c.6; see Chapter 18, "Limitation of Liability for Maritime Claims."

eral law, such as contract, tort, or statutory law. The focus here is on liens that arise in a maritime law context, that is, marine liens, because these claims are entitled to prioritization in the distribution of the proceeds from a judicial sale. "Marine lien" is not a term of art and is used in this chapter as a generic concept that captures the main categories of liens and claims in a maritime context. Those main categories are referred to by their terms of art, namely, maritime liens, possessory liens, and statutory rights *in rem*. There are also other liens and claims that are established by statute.

2) Maritime Liens

a) Policy Rationale

The maritime lien on the ship, cargo, or freight is unique to shipping. To understand its underlying rationale, it is necessary to consider the various characteristics of maritime property, and especially the ship. Maritime property is not necessarily always in the immediate possession and control of the owner. The ship needs necessary expenditures to undertake and continue a maritime adventure. It needs to be navigated or managed professionally. It can cause injury to others. It can change its nationality with ease and can be registered under a flag with which it bears no beneficial link. Throughout its life, the ship can engage various creditors. And yet, in order for the ship to be an instrument of trade, it needs certain services. There has long been recognition of "creditors of necessity" in the maritime adventure: persons providing essential navigation services to the ship (i.e., master and crew); the person incurring necessary expenditures (i.e., disbursements) and by earning personal liabilities, in lieu of the owner, to enable the ship to undertake and continue the maritime adventure (i.e., master); persons assisting ships, cargoes, and crews in situations of distress (i.e., salvors); persons suffering injury or loss caused by the ship; and creditors who advance money to the ship against a mortgage bond tied to the fate of the ship or cargo (i.e., bottomry and respondentia, respectively). These persons have been perceived either as providing fundamental services to the ship, or as victims of a maritime tort that must be compensated by the negligent ship. Because the ship very often was viewed as the most important security for claims against it, and yet was mobile and could keep incurring liabilities to the disadvantage of creditors of necessity, these persons were deemed to deserve special protection in general maritime law. So out of necessity, and eventually tradition, there emerged a category of persons that deserved a special lien, that is, a kind of security interest in the maritime property for services to it, or damage caused by it, and enforceable against it. In this regard, Binnie J. observed in *Holt Cargo Systems Inc. v. ABC Containerline N.V.*: "[P]racticality required an *in rem* proceeding against the ship as distinguished from an *in personam* action against the shipowner."[140]

There was also recognition since early days that the owner, who undertook the major risk in the maritime adventure and who may not always have had direct and complete control over the ship, especially when voyages took long periods to complete, also deserved protection. Over time the owner came to enjoy certain privileges, such as limitation of liability, whereas the creditors of necessity were given a privileged security over the ship without the need for any pre-creation formalities. The privilege over the property was granted, but the owner retained possession and control over the ship; if the owner sold the ship, the privilege survived.

As discussed in various chapters, shipping is an international business operation during which a ship may earn liens in different jurisdictions, and this raises two issues: the first in relation to the most appropriate court to enforce the claim, and the second the extent to which an enforcing court will grant appropriate recognition and relief to all those international claims. The Supreme Court of Canada has recently had an opportunity in *Holt Cargo Systems* to consider whether the Federal Court is the most appropriate forum for an action *in rem* when the creditor instituting it is in the United States and for services provided there, the bankrupt shipowner and trustee in bankruptcy are located in Belgium, the owner's assets and numerous creditors distributed in various countries, and the only Canadian link is the arrest of the ship in Halifax, Nova Scotia. Binnie J. held that "the 'real and substantive connection' test must take into account the special lifestyle of ocean-going freighters."[141] In effect, lack of such a connection does not remove the jurisdiction of a Canadian court grounded *in rem*. It has been said that this approach may encourage forum shopping, but then again the very nature of maritime liens has to be taken into consideration. The logic and necessity of maritime liens and the need for their enforcement by the first available court makes every port a potential forum.[142]

---

140 *Holt Cargo Systems Inc. v. ABC Containerline N.V.*, [2001] 3 S.C.R. 907 [*Holt Cargo Systems*].
141 *Holt Cargo Systems*, ibid., para.93.
142 Per Lord Simon, *Atlantic Star (The)*, [1973] 2 All E.R. 175 at 198 (H.L.); cited in *Holt Cargo Systems*, ibid., para.94; and *Antares Shipping Corp. v. Capricorn (The)*, [1977] 2 S.C.R. 422 at 453.

Second, a ship may have a mortgage in Canada and incur maritime liens from one or more jurisdictions. When those securities are enforced against the ship, a court will recognize the *lex causae* or *lex loci* (i.e., the foreign law that generated the lien), then apply the *lex fori* (i.e., the law of the forum where proceedings are instituted) in granting the remedy, including the ranking of the respective claims for satisfaction. (The rules in this area are in the realm of conflict of laws, rather than maritime law, and consequently are not discussed in detail in this chapter. The reader is referred to the excellent reference works on conflict of laws at the end of this chapter.) As a matter of public and judicial policy, the maritime lien will be enforced to ensure that creditors' claims are not easily frustrated by moving the ship from one jurisdiction to another. General maritime law and the legislator protect or grant maritime liens and the courts enforce them. The Exchequer Court (Nova Scotia Admiralty District) held in *The Strandhill*:

> If a maritime lien exists it cannot be shaken off by changing the location of the *res*. A foreign judgment *in rem* creates a maritime lien and even though such a judgment could not have been obtained in the courts of this country, it will be enforced here by an action *in rem*. But a maritime lien may be created by foreign law otherwise than by a judgment *in rem*; and if it be so created I think it can be equally enforced here in the same way. If the plaintiffs have lawfully acquired the right to the *res* even under foreign law, it would be strange if they had not the liberty to enforce it here in the only court providing relief *in rem*.[143]

A majority of the Supreme Court went on to hold that in the process of enforcing the foreign lien, the Court would look to the *lex loci* (i.e., the foreign law) to determine the legitimacy of the right, then apply the *lex fori* in granting a Canadian remedy.[144] Canadian courts were echoing principles of conflict of laws adopted by U.K. courts.

It can be expected that the recognition of a foreign lien as a maritime lien in the *lex fori* can be a complex matter and the consequences are likely to be very significant. In determining the respective ranking or priority based on the nature of the security, the court will determine whose claim is discharged first from what are frequently insufficient proceeds! In *The Colorado*, the ranking between a claim for repairs (i.e.,

---

143 *Strandhill (The) v. Walter W. Hodder Co.*, [1926] Ex.C.R. 226 at 229, aff'd [1926] S.C.R. 680 [*The Strandhill*]. This case concerned the Admiralty Court's jurisdiction to entertain such claims, rather than ranking. The law applicable at the time was U.K. Admiralty law. See also *Marquis v. Astoria (The)*, [1931] Ex. C.R. 195.
144 *The Strandhill*, ibid.

necessaries) under English law and a French mortgage secured by a hypothec was considered.[145] Under English law, a mortgage ranks ahead of a claim for repairs, with the latter claim generating only a right of action *in rem*. A key question was the exact nature of the hypothec, which survived the transfer of ownership, and what its equivalent was under English law. Lord Bankes noted that the evidence did not clear the doubt altogether, but he agreed with the trial judge that "the right created by the mortgage deed was a higher right than a mere right to proceed *in rem*, and though not capable of exact description in terms applicable to well-recognized English rights, it yet had attributes that entitled it to rank on a question of priorities in the same class as a maritime lien or the right created by an English mortgage."[146] Lords Scrutton and Atkin similarly equated the hypothec to or found strong resemblance between it and the maritime lien in English law.[147] Therefore, the hypothec was ranked ahead of the repairers' claim.

Like their U.K. counterparts, Canadian courts have developed a strong tradition of enforcing foreign liens. However, judicial policy in this country has been more receptive and generous toward liens that do not have a counterpart in Canadian maritime law. This difference came out particularly clearly in related comments of the Judicial Committee of the Privy Council and the Supreme Court of Canada in a series of cases. The first case was *Todd Shipyards Corp. v. Altema Compania Maritima SA (The Ioannis Daskalelis)*, in which the Supreme Court recognized as a maritime lien a claim that would not have given rise to a maritime lien if that claim had arisen in Canada. Typically, the issue was raised in a ranking context, specifically the prioritization between a claim for necessary repairs provided to a ship in New York and a mortgage contracted in Greece.[148] In the United States, the claim for necessaries is, by statute, a maritime lien that takes precedence over the mortgage. In Canada, as in the United Kingdom, the claim for necessaries is, at the most, a statutory right *in rem* ranking below mortgages. The Canadian Court applied the *Strandhill* and *Colorado* principles, looked at the substantive rights of the creditors under the respective proper laws to establish their precise nature, and then applied the *lex fori* order of payment "for a right of that particular kind."[149] In the case

---

145 Above note 135.
146 *Ibid.* at 107.
147 *Ibid.* at 109 and 111.
148 *Todd Shipyards Corp. v. Altema Compania Maritima SA (The Ioannis Daskalelis)*, [1974] S.C.R. 1248 [*The Ioannis Daskalelis*].
149 *Ibid.* at 1254.

of the necessaries lien — which is a maritime lien in the United States — "that particular kind" meant the same species of maritime liens in Canada. This generous recognition of the foreign lien was affirmed in the interests of international comity.

The *Ioannis Daskalelis* case in turn influenced the Court of Appeal, High Court of Singapore, in *The Halcyon Isle* case, which involved a similar scenario with a claim for repairs effected in New York and a British mortgage.[150] If the claim for necessaries (i.e., repairs being considered necessaries) were to be recognized as a maritime lien, it would obviously rank ahead of the mortgage. The Court of Appeal decided in the same way as the Supreme Court of Canada. The decision was appealed to the Privy Council, which, with a narrow majority judgment, gave earlier decisions and the rule on recognition of foreign liens a far narrower interpretation than that of the Supreme Court. Per Lord Diplock, the Privy Council was similarly motivated by international comity but decided differently, based on the conception that under the English rules of conflict of laws

> maritime claims are classified as giving rise to maritime liens which are enforceable in actions *in rem* in English Courts where and only where the events on which the claim is founded would have given rise to a maritime lien in English law, if those events had occurred within the territorial jurisdiction of the English court.[151]

Further, the majority judgment proceeded to interpret the nature of the maritime lien in English law as "involving rights that are procedural or remedial only, and accordingly the question whether a particular class of claim gives rise to a maritime lien or not as being one to be determined by English law as the *lex fori*."[152] The consequence was that the claim for repairs, as a claim of necessaries, could not be recognized as a maritime lien and, therefore, the mortgage ranked ahead of necessaries. In effect, the Privy Council (1) considered whether the situation that generated the foreign maritime lien would have generated the same lien in the lex fori (i.e., English law); and (2) if the answer in (1) was in the affirmative, the foreign lien would have been enforced as a maritime lien; but, (3) if the answer in (1) was negative, the foreign lien could only be applied as an unsecured claim. According to the Privy Council, in its decision in *The Ioannis Daskalelis* the Supreme Court of

---

150 *Bankers Trust v. Todd Shipyards (The Halcyon Isle)*, [1981] A.C. 221 (P.C.) [*The Halcyon Isle*].
151 *Ibid.* at 238.
152 *Ibid.* at 238.

Canada misunderstood the judgment in *The Colorado*.[153] The two dissenting judgments of Lords Salmon and Scarman emphasized the policy and equity concerns behind foreign lien recognition and expressed an opinion founded on their view of the balance of authorities, comity, conflict of laws, and natural justice. Non-recognition of the necessaries lien in this case deprived the shipyard of its lien, which otherwise appeared to have global validity. Had the yard not thought it was getting the lien, it would not have let the ship leave; by letting the ship depart, the yard expended money and labour for the benefit of another creditor who did nothing to ameliorate the value of the *res*.[154]

The Privy Council's decision left the impression that it did not fully appreciate that Canadian maritime law and policy on this matter were different from English maritime law in two important ways. First, Canadian courts treat the maritime lien not simply as remedial, but also as substantive (i.e., both a right and a remedy). The right has a proprietary character and therefore the attachment of a lien to the *res* has the effect of detracting something from the full ownership of the *res*. Hence, the invocation of the *lex causae* (i.e., the foreign maritime law that generated the lien) is a necessary first step to determine the existence of the right in conflict of laws. Second, the recognition of foreign maritime liens in Canada is not only based on principles of conflict of laws and general comity among nations but also on a public policy in support of maritime liens where and however they are generated. These differences were explained by the B.C. Court of Appeal in *Marlex Petroleum Inc. v. The Har Rai*.[155] The case involved a claim of a supplier of oil against a ship, when the ship was under a charterparty containing a prohibition-of-lien clause. The issue was whether the supplier could institute an action *in rem* when the owner was not liable *in personam*. (This particular issue is discussed below.) The key point here is whether in this case U.S. law enabled the claimant to generate a maritime lien and, if so, whether such lien would be recognized as a maritime lien by a Canadian enforcing court. In the United States, a supplier to a charterer may presume that the charterer was duly authorized by the shipowner to incur a necessaries lien, as long as the supplier had no actual knowledge of the prohibition-of-lien clause. In this case, the supplier had no such knowledge. The Court of Appeal saw no reason to deny recognition of this lien as a maritime lien and to treat it

---

153 *Ibid*.
154 *Ibid*. at 242–50.
155 *Marlex Petroleum Inc. v. Har Rai (The)* (1984), 4 D.L.R. (4th) 739 (F.C.A.), aff'd [1987] 1 S.C.R. 57 [*The Har Rai*].

accordingly for the purposes of a Canadian remedy, even though the owner was not liable *in personam*:

> There is no question that the recognition of maritime liens is an important question of policy in maritime law on which there have been strong differences of view among the maritime nations. It is also clear that the test applied in Canada to the recognition of a foreign maritime lien differs from that which now applies in England [referring to *The Halcyon Isle*].
>
> ...
>
> The result to which the principle of presumed authority may lead under United States law is not so offensive to Canadian maritime law as to require the refusal of recognition.[156]

This line of thought was followed in *Oregon Stevedoring Co. v. The Number Four* but this time in connection with a query as to whether a claim for stevedoring charges generated in the United States — which in that country is established as a maritime lien by statute — should be recognized as a maritime lien in Canada when, in the *Federal Court Act*, it is treated as a mere statutory right *in rem*.[157] A more recent re-statement was by the Supreme Court in *Holt Cargo Systems*, where the Court was made particularly conscious of the likelihood that the claimant, a maritime lien holder, would be particularly disadvantaged if Canadian proceedings were stayed in favour of a Belgian bankruptcy forum, where the claim for stevedoring would not be recognized as a maritime lien but simply as an unsecured claim.[158]

The Federal Court's readiness to assume jurisdiction, even without a substantial connection to Canada, and its authority to provide extensive recognition to foreign maritime liens draws upon Canadian maritime law as defined in section 2 and the general grant of jurisdiction in section 22(1) in the *Federal Court Act*.[159] Therefore, the generous Canadian maritime law and policy position and underlying rationale

---

156 *Ibid.* at 744 (F.C.A.) Where the prohibition-of-lien clause is inserted in the charterparty and also posted throughout the ship, the maritime lien may still accrue in favour of a supplier, where he or she is not personally informed and does not deliver the supplies personally: (*Kirgan Holding S.A. v. Panamax Leader (The)* (2002), 225 F.T.R. 273.
157 [1984] F.C.J. No. 121 (T.D.) (QL) [*The Number Four*].
158 *Holt Cargo Systems*, above note 141, paras.41–49. Similarly, in a bankruptcy context, secured maritime creditors are protected as a matter of public policy (*ibid.*, para.53).
159 Above note 44.

for the recognition of foreign maritime liens has been re-confirmed beyond any doubt. This is not to say that recognition will know no bounds. The limit to recognition of foreign claims will be reached when recognition runs counter to or is offensive to Canadian public policy, law, or procedure.[160]

This policy position does have anomalous side effects. Identical claims for the supply of necessaries, the first generated in Canada and the second in the United States, will be treated differently. In Canada, the claim for necessaries generates only a statutory right *in rem*, whereas, in the United States, the same claim generates the more powerful maritime lien. A right *in rem* generated in Canada and sought to be enforced in the United States does not rank as a maritime lien. So whereas a Canadian court will enforce the U.S. claim for necessaries as a maritime lien, the same Canadian claim will be treated as something much less in the United States *and* in Canada.[161] The courts have been able to do this by considering the American maritime lien for necessaries as a lien captured under section 22(1), and the Canadian claim as falling under section 22(2)(m) as a mere right *in rem*. Thus, when Canadian and American suppliers of necessaries compete for the same limited fund, in Canada a combination of policy and comity will produce uneven treatment for those suppliers. This is a long-standing situation whose time has probably come for reconsideration. The Federal Court recently had an opportunity to do so in *Fraser Shipyard & Industrial Ltd. v. The Atlantis Two*. The court was invited to consider the issue of fairness toward Canadian claimants vis-à-vis the priority enjoyed by American claimants of necessaries but declined, suggesting instead that this is more an issue for legislative change.[162] The situation in this case gave rise to another concern, that an American lien — in this situation a breach of a charterparty — that ranked behind a mortgage in the United States, ranked as a maritime lien and therefore ahead of a mortgage in Canada! The situation continues to raise concern among practitioners.[163]

---

160 *The Strandhill*, above note 144; *Holt Cargo Systems*, above note 141, para.41.
161 *The Har Rai*, above note 156.
162 In *Fraser Shipyard & Industrial Centre Ltd. v. Expedient Maritime Co. (The Atlantis Two)* (1999), 170 F.T.R. 1, rev'd (1999), 170 F.T.R. 57 [*The Atlantis Two*].
163 This problem and possible solutions were recently considered by the B.C. Maritime Law Section of the Canadian Bar Association in Vancouver on 27 February 2003. The meeting adopted motions recognizing that there is a situation of inequity between Canadian and U.S. suppliers under Canadian law and that there should be legislative change adopting the *Halcyon Isle* principles to resolve the problem by applying the law of the forum to determine whether a claim has the status of a maritime lien or not. An alternative motion proposing legislative

There are two arguments in favour of change to be considered. The first is that, as the economies of Canada and the United States continue to integrate, greater uniformity in maritime law should be pursued, to the extent that it does not offend public policy. Second, the exercise of international comity by Canadian courts has important functions beyond mere courtesy but does not have to occur at the expense of uniformity. Canadian courts have held that international comity in private international law has order and fairness as objectives, and that it has been "the objective of international maritime law for centuries to create order and fairness for those engaged in maritime commerce."[164] It is hard to see where the fairness lies with such differentiation between identical claimants in what is an increasingly integrated market.[165] One way of addressing this anomaly in ranking is for the Federal Court to use its equitable jurisdiction to ensure equal ranking for claims that are alike not just in form, but also in substance (i.e., like treatment for like claims). In a modern context a functional and equitable approach, in lieu of a purely formalistic application, is preferable and consistent with the way maritime law and policy have evolved in Canada.

b) Definition and Characteristics

Maritime liens have been defined in various ways.[166] *The Frank and Troy* case provided a useful working definition of maritime liens: "A maritime lien may be defined as a privileged claim, upon maritime property, for services done to it or injury caused by it, arising from the moment when the claim attaches, travelling with the property unconditionally, and enforced by means of an action *in rem*."[167] Using this def-

---

    change to elevate the Canadian claim for necessaries to maritime lien status was not passed.

164 *Holt Cargo Systems*, above note 141, para.68, and citing a stream of case authority: *R. v. Zingre*, [1981] 2 S.C.R. 392 at 401; *R. v. Spencer*, [1985] 2 S.C.R. 278 at 283; *Morguard Investments Ltd. v. De Savoye*, [1990] 3 S.C.R. 1077; and *Tolofson v. Jensen*, [1994] 3 S.C.R. 1022 at 1058.

165 A good example of the problems that can arise in this context is *Imperial Oil Ltd. v. Petromar Inc.*, [2001] F.C.A. 391. This was a case where the Trial Division and Court of Appeal came to different conclusions as to whether the applicable law to determine a claim for necessaries was Canadian or American. The Trial Division concluded that American law governed so that a maritime lien was created. The Court of Appeal weighted the connecting factors and concluded differently, and therefore no maritime lien arose.

166 For various definitions see W. Tetley, *Maritime Liens and Claims*, 2d ed. (Cowanville, QC: Yvon Blais, 1998) at 56–60.

167 *Comeau's Sea Foods Ltd. v. Frank and Troy (The)*, [1971] F.C. 556 (T.D.) [*The Frank and Troy*].

inition, the basic elements of the maritime lien are as follows: a privileged claim, attaching to maritime property, for service done to it or injury caused by it, arising from the moment when the claim attaches, travelling with the property unconditionally, and enforced by means of an action *in rem*. These elements are discussed below.

i) Privileged Claim

A maritime lien is a privileged claim for it generally ranks in priority above all other claims against maritime property, whether they arose prior to or subsequent to the attachment of the maritime lien. The consequence is that, in general, maritime liens will rank ahead even of claims that tend to better the condition of the ship, for example, a repairer without a possessory lien or a supplier of necessaries. As a legal interest, it will also rank ahead of equitable interests.[168] There can be situations where, in the interests of equity, a court may upset the normal ranking of maritime priorities. Unlike its predecessor, the Exchequer Court, the Federal Court of Canada is a court of equity as well as court of Admiralty law.[169] It is therefore in a position to change the maritime lien's privileged ranking on the basis of equitable principles, although the changes are likely to be exceptional and/or minor, and to prevent an obvious injustice as a result of strict ranking.[170]

ii) Attachment to Maritime Property

A maritime lien attaches to the vessel, to cargo, to proceeds of their judicial sale, and to freight. The lien attaches to the whole of the *res* and not only to a part of it.[171] The term "vessel" includes the appurtenances, such as tackle, apparel, furniture, engines, and boilers,[172] as well as the wreck thereof.[173] The notion of appurtenances is not exhaustive and has evolved to include other items and situations[174] but

---

168 *Scott Steel Ltd. v. Alarissa (The)*, [1996] 2 F.C .883 (T.D.) [*The Alarissa*].
169 For a view on the Exchequer Court's lack of equitable jurisdiction, see *Montreal Dry Docks & Ship Repairing Co. v. Halifax Shipyards Ltd.* (1920), 60 S.C.R. 359 [*Montreal Dry Docks*]; and Prothonotary Hargrave's observations in *The Alarissa*, above note 168, paras.10–22.
170 E.g., see *The Atlantean I*, above note 47, and *Metaxas v. Galaxias (The)*, [1990] 2 F.C. 400 (T.D.). This practice is the same in the United Kingdom: see *Lyrma (No. 2) (The)*, [1978] 2 Lloyd's L.R. 30.
171 *Neptune (The)* (1824), 1 Hag. 227, 166 E.R. 81.
172 *Dundee (The)* (1824), 1 Hag. 109, 166 E.R. 39.
173 *Aline (The)* (1840), 1 W. Robb. 111, 166 E.R. 514.
174 See J.D. Buchan, *Mortgages of Ships: Marine Security in Canada* (Toronto: Butterworths, 1986) at 33; S.F. Friedell, ed., *Benedict on Admiralty*, 7th ed. (San Fransisco: LexisNexis, 2002) v.1 at §167 and v.2 at §32.

does not include bunkers.[175] All accretions made to the vessel, including repairs, are equally subject to the lien, except when made by a third party whose interest should be protected by the court.[176] The maritime lien does not attach to sister ships.[177]

iii) Service Done to/Injury Caused by Res
The event that gives rise to the maritime lien is an eligible service to the ship or damage caused by it. In Canadian law, the only eligible services are master's and crew's wages, master's disbursements, salvage, bottomry, and respondentia. (Each maritime lien is discussed below.) In many jurisdictions, including Canada, a ship that receives repairs does not give rise to a maritime lien but rather to an unsecured claim.[178] Thus the existence of a maritime lien depends upon whether the law that generates the claim treats it as a maritime lien. Maritime liens arise by operation of law, hence their impact on third parties. But contracting parties cannot agree to create a maritime lien that is enforceable against non-consenting parties.[179] Nor may an individual simply create a maritime lien for his or her own benefit.[180] Whether a lien results from services rendered depends not only on the agreement and actual performance of the services but also on the nature of and associated circumstances around the services.[181] It is important that the service done to the *res* be one that does in fact give rise to a maritime lien.

iv) Moment when Lien Arises
A maritime lien attaches to the *res* from the time the event occurred that gave rise to the lien but remains inchoate until called into effect by proceedings *in rem*, whereupon it relates to the period when it first attached.[182] It does not require any judicial action to be created, nor does it require a deed or registration to become active. And here is the major difficulty with the maritime lien in general maritime law: unlike

---

175 *The Atlantis Two*, above note 162.
176 *Montreal Dry Docks*, above note 169.
177 *The Atlantis Two*, above note 162.
178 *Benson Brothers Shipbuilding v. Miss Donna (The)*, [1978] 1 F.C. 379 (T.D.).
179 *Toronto Harbour Commissioners. v. Toryoung II (The)*, [1976] 1 F.C. 191 [*The Toryoung II*], concerned an attempt by the two parties to establish a salvage lien in a settlement agreement. The court held they could only bind themselves and not third parties.
180 *McBride v. American (The)*, [1924] Ex. C.R. 227 [*The American*]. In this case the master incurred liabilities that he could not claim as a disbursements lien.
181 *The Toryoung II*, above note 179.
182 *Bold Buccleugh (The)* (1851), 7 Moo. P.C. 267.

the mortgage or hypothec, it is not registered, so that it could cause difficulties to unsuspecting buyers or mortgagees. This particular characteristic is a serious consideration during a title search (as discussed in Chapter 4).[183]

v) *Survival Despite Transfer of Ownership*
Unless extinguished, a maritime lien travels with the *res* regardless of change of ownership. Therefore, a sale of the maritime property *per se* does not extinguish the lien. There is a danger here for the *bona fide* purchaser, who may think the purchase is free and clear of all encumbrances, when in reality there might still be an attachment that survives the transfer. In *British Columbia (A.G.) v. The Bermuda* the new owner discovered a maritime lien generated as a result of damage done by the ship seven months after the purchase.[184] The ship had been trading away from home port in the meantime and the log had no reference to an accident. The court held that the lien survived.

This old rule comes with a proviso. The lien holder must take action to enforce the lien with reasonable diligence and good faith.[185] In *The Bermuda*, the damage was caused on 8 October 1919, the last bill for repairs for that damage was received on 16 March 1920, and the writ was served on the new owners on 19 November 1920. The ship was purchased on 15 May 1920. The court found that the delay in the enforcement of the lien was not unreasonable.[186] A longer period than that might still be acceptable to the courts.[187]

The only situations where the undischarged maritime lien does not continue to travel with the *res* is in the case of a judicial sale or where the limitation period expires (as discussed below).

vi) *Enforceability by an Action* in Rem
As a secured claim the maritime lien can only be enforced by proceedings *in rem* in the Admiralty Court. As seen in Chapter 3, the Admiralty Court in Canada is the Federal Court, and this is the court where the action tends to be instituted.[188] However, other courts of competent jurisdiction may also entertain an action *in rem* if the rules of procedure

---

183 A.J. Stone, "Let the Boat Buyer Beware" (1974) 12 Osgoode Hall L.J. 643.
184 *British Columbia (AG) v. Bermuda (The)*, [1923] Ex. C.R. 107, [1923] 2 D.L.R. 272 [*The Bermuda*].
185 *Bold Buccleugh (The)*, in *obiter*, above note 182.
186 *The Bermuda*, above note 184.
187 *Kennedy v. Surrey (The)* (1905), 11 B.C.L.R. 499. In this case the delay in suing was twenty-three months.
188 *Federal Court Act*, above note 46, s.43.

of such courts provide for such an action (e.g., British Columbia Supreme Court Rules).[189] The holder of the lien cannot, of his or her own power, seize, retain, or sell the *res* but must institute proceedings, including arrest of the *res*, in accordance with Admiralty procedure (see Chapter 19).

The Federal Court's far-reaching remedial authority concerning maritime liens lies in the *Federal Court Act*, in particular section 2, which defines Canadian maritime law; section 22(1), which is the general grant of Admiralty jurisdiction to the Federal Court; and section 22(2), which also recognizes various maritime liens and statutory rights *in rem*. Section 43 of the *Federal Court Act* places a limitation on the exercise of the statutory right *in rem* where there is no liability *in personam*.[190] This restriction does not apply to maritime liens whose relief is sought under section 22(1), and because a maritime lien survives a transfer of ownership and continues to attach to the *res* at the cost of the new owner.[191]

c) Types of Maritime Liens

i) Bottomry and Respondentia

Although archaic and probably obsolete, bottomry and respondentia claims are still recognized in the *Federal Court Act*.[192] Bottomry is the pledging of a ship by the master as security in order to obtain a loan to enable the ship to complete a voyage when outside its home port; respondentia is the same except the cargo of a ship is pledged. The contracts for these loans are known, respectively, as bottomry and respondentia bonds. As soon as such a bond is executed, a lien attaches to the secured property. Unlike most other maritime liens, claims for bottomry and respondentia are considered transferable.[193]

ii) Collision Claims

The collisions lien is a maritime tort lien. It arises when damage is done by a ship to another ship or other property as a result of a wrongful act of navigation from want of skill or negligence.[194] No maritime lien will exist if the person in charge or possession of the ship has no authority

---

189 B.C. Reg. 221/90, r.55 (B.C. Supreme Court Rules).
190 *Westcan Stevedoring Ltd. v. Armar (The)*, [1973] F.C. 1232; *McCain Produce Co. v. Rea (The)* (1977), 80 D.L.R. (3d) 105, [1978] 1 F.C. 686 (T.D.)
191 *McCain Produce Co. v. Rea (The)*, ibid.
192 *Federal Court Act*, above note 46, s.22(2)(c).
193 *The Alarissa*, above note 168. *Federal Court Act*, ibid., s.22(2)(d).
194 *Ripon City (The)*, [1897] P. 226. See *Federal Court Act*, ibid., s.22(2)(e).

to have such control or possession.[195] Similarly, there is no maritime lien against the ship, where the owner parts with the ship under compulsion and has no authority over the master and crew.[196] Because this is a collision lien, the damage must be done by the ship, and not simply by the crew of the ship, that is, the ship must be the instrument of the damage, possibly as a result of wrongful navigation.[197] The lien arising from a collision is not transferable.[198]

iii) Salvage Claims

The lien for salvage is created by the rendering of salvage services to a maritime property, including the raising of the wreck from a sunken state.[199] The circumstances surrounding the service must be such as to qualify the service as salvage, and that the service is actually performed.[200] The lien attaches immediately on the performance of the salvage services and attaches to the salved vessel, its cargo, and its freight.[201] The foundation of the lien for salvage depends upon a beneficial service rendered to a *res*, so a maritime lien attaches regardless of who may have been in control of the vessel when the salvage services were rendered.[202] It is essential that the salvage be successful for a lien to be generated.[203]

iv) Unpaid Master's and Crew's Wages

The fourth type of maritime lien is for unpaid wages of the master and crew.[204] While technically the master is not a seaman but a "mariner,"

---

195 *Upson Walton Co. v. Brian Boru (The)* (1906), 10 Ex. C.R. 176.
196 *Sylvan Arrow (The),* [1923] P. 220. In this case the ship, under control of the U.S. government as a result of a requisition charter, became involved in a collision. The persons navigating the ship at the time were servants of the U.S. government.
197 *St. Lawrence Transportation Co. v. Amedee T. (The),* [1924] Ex. C.R. 204.
198 *Duff v. Progress (The),* [1928] Ex. C.R. 157.
199 *Federal Court Act,* above note 46, s.22(2)(j). The recovery of a sunken dredge with its contents constitutes a salvage service, which creates a maritime lien. *Simpson v. Kruger (The)* (1914), 19 Ex. C.R. 64.
200 *The Toryoung II,* above note 179.
201 *Charlotte Wylie (The)* (1846), 2 Wm. Robb. 495, 166 E.R. 842. A maritime lien for salvage arises when the service is performed: *Johnson v. Charles S. Neff (The)* (1918), 18 Ex. C.R. 159.
202 *Calypso (The)* (1828), 2 Hagg. 209, 166 E.R. 221.
203 Success is an essential element in salvage, and no lien attaches in a case of attempted salvage where the services rendered produce no result and in no way contribute to the subsequent salving of the boat. *Canadian Dredging Company v. Mike Corry (The)* (1917), 19 Ex. C.R. 61.
204 *Federal Court Act,* above note 46, s.22(2)(o), master's and crew's wages.

the lien for his or her wages is in general the same as that of any seaman.[205] Which persons qualify as "crew" is an important question, because not all persons who work on or provide a service to the ship are considered part of the crew complement. Only those persons considered as crew are entitled to a maritime lien for unpaid wages. The courts have considered a variety of situations. Two seamen who were part of the original crew complement and became responsible solely for the watchkeeping of a ship under arrest could, even in the absence of a master, officers, and other complement, constitute a crew.[206] However, where watchmen and caretakers were employed without having a relationship to the ship, they did not constitute crew.[207] Today the crew of a ship must be related to the type of ship in question and the functions that need to be performed to enable the ship to perform as intended. On a cruise ship, this could mean a wider range of persons than the normal seafarer complement, such as entertainers, shopkeepers, beauticians, or pool attendants.[208] The issue has not been fully addressed in a modern context by the Canadian courts. An old case denied a musician a lien for wages[209] but, more recently, musicians did get a lien for unpaid wages.[210] In a modern shipping and navigation context, the reality is that there are specialized ships able to function as intended only with a very diverse combination of human capabilities on board. Bearing in mind the original rationale for the lien for wages, that is, to protect the master and crew from abuse, there is no reason why the diverse complement of a cruise ship should not be similarly protected.

The lien for wages attaches to the ship and freight, provided the wages are earned on board the ship under an ordinary mariner's contract.[211] The lien attaches to the ship and independently of any personal obligation of the owner.[212] The consequence is far-reaching, as the

---

205 *Stone v. Rochepoint (The)* (1921), 21 Ex. C.R. 143.
206 *Balodis v. Prince George (The)*, [1985] 1 F.C. 890 (T.D.).
207 *Jorgensen v. Chasina (The)*, [1926] 1 W.W.R. 632; *Nicholson v. Joyland (The)*, [1931] Ex. C.R. 70.
208 W. Moreira, "Loveboat Meets Law and Order: Admiralty Issues in the Cruise Industry," a paper presented to Dalhousie Law School, October 2002, available online at: <www.cmla.org> under "Reports & Papers."
209 *McElhaney v. Flora (The)* (1898), 6 Ex. C.R. 129.
210 *Metaxas v. Galaxias (The)*, above note 170.
211 *Castlegate (The)*, [1893] A.C. 38 at 52; *Fugère v. Duchess of York (The)*, [1924] Ex. C.R. 95.
212 *Fugère v. Duchess of York (The)*, ibid., citing *The Castlegate*, ibid. as authority.

master and crew are entitled to enforce their lien against the ship, even when they are hired by a charterer rather than by the owner.[213]

It is questionable whether wages earned under a special contract give rise to a maritime lien.[214] It does not affect the right to the lien that the master and crew were engaged by a person who has no right to engage them, so long as they earn the wages on the ship.[215] Moreover, in a modern context, where crewing agencies intervene between the crew and the owner, the crew may also have a right of action in contract against the agency.

Until relatively recently, Canadian courts followed an old rule that the lien for the crew's wages is not transferable, so that the person who paid their wages did not enjoy a right of subrogation.[216] There seemed to be a public policy rationale against allowing the transfer of the remedy.[217] This rule changed in part, to the extent that the lien became transferable if approved by the court.[218] A total re-examination of this old rule occurred with *Metaxas v. The Galaxias (No. 2)*.[219] In this case, several Greek seamen were stranded as a result of the seizure and sale of their ship. Rouleau J. held: "it may now be safely said that where a seamen's benevolent organization under authority of statute pays the repatriation costs of stranded sailors in Canada, it is clearly in keeping with current policy that such a payment be given the protection of a maritime lien or its equivalent."[220] A reason behind the old rule was the protection of seamen from creditors; however, the court saw that this consideration could not really apply to a humanitarian organization transferring funds to stranded seamen directly. The court went even further to assert that in the interests of equity the seamen's right to

---

213 *Fugère v. Duchess of York (The)*, ibid. The court allowed the claims of the master and engineer against the ship.
214 *British Trade (The)*, [1924] P. 104.
215 *Edwin (The)* (1864), Br. & Lush. 281, 167 E.R. 365.
216 *Petone (The)*, [1917] P. 198, followed by *Bonham v. Sarnor (The)* (1918), 21 Ex. C.R. 183. See also *McCullough v. Samuel Marshall (The)*, [1924] Ex. C.R. 53.
217 *Rankin v. Eliza Fisher (The)* (1895), 4 Ex. C.R. 461.
218 *Ross v. Aragon (The)*, [1943] Ex. C.R. 41. See also *The Alarissa*, above note 168. See also *Finansbanken ASA v. GTS Katie (The)*, [2002] F.C.T. 74, where it was held that under Canadian law a wage claim could not be assigned or subrogated without the consent of the court, and that, in any case, there must be the agreement of the crew.
219 [1989] 1 F.C. 386 (T.D.).
220 *Ibid*. An assignment of wages and repatriation costs in favour of a mortgagee was recognized by the court in *Bank of Scotland v. Nel (The)*, [2001] 1 F.C. 408. Costs incurred by the Crown for the care of the crew were also ranked high in *Neves v. Kristina Logos (The)*, [2002] F.C.A. 502, affirming in part [2001] F.C.T. 1034.

transfer the lien ought to be recognized as otherwise other creditors would be unjustifiably enriched.

The claim for wages tends to rank high. However, where the master personally guarantees the mortgage, then his or her claim will not be preferred. The court will look at the true ownership of the ship.[221]

v) Master's Disbursements
Although very unusual, the lien for master's disbursements may still be claimed but probably in rather unique circumstances in this age of modern communications and electronic commerce. Particular circumstances and conditions generated this maritime lien. Historically, disbursements and liabilities made or incurred by a master were eligible for a maritime lien when he or she was unable to or could not easily communicate with the shipowner, possibly even while in a home port, in order to secure authority to incur expenses for the ship.[222] The only disbursements and liabilities that created this lien were those made by the master by virtue of his or her general authority, in the ordinary course of his or her employment, and for which the master could pledge the owner's credit.[223] Such expenses were incurred in a personal capacity but on account of the ship. Therefore, if the master incurred expenses on behalf of the charterer, his or her employer, rather than the owner, the lien did not arise because the master would have no authority to pledge the owner's credit.[224]

Not all expenditures incurred by the master are eligible expenses. In *McBride v. The American*, the master claimed for amounts paid for provisions and for guarantees he provided to the ship's agents to pay for wages and provisions. The agents had been paying the bills when they declined to continue advances, and the master gave the guarantee. The court held he was not in a position to claim a disbursements lien because he was in "constant and direct communication with the owners or with those acting on their behalf, and the liability incurred by him was made after the ship had been arrested by another claimant."[225] The master did not have the authority to "create a maritime lien in his own favour merely by adding his own liability to that of the owners for necessaries for the ship whether in the form of wages or otherwise."[226]

---

221 *Stone v. Rochepoint (The)*, above note 205.
222 *Symes v. City of Windsor (The)* (1895), 4 Ex. C.R. 362, aff'd 4 Ex. C.R. 400.
223 *Ripon City (The)*, above note 194.
224 *Fugère v. Duchess of York (The)*, above note 211.
225 *The American*, above note 180.
226 *Ibid.*

The expenses claimed were not necessary. The court also declined to recognize his expenditures as necessaries. This case is to be contrasted to *Reide v. The Queen of the Isles*, where the master borrowed money and made necessary expenditures for the proper working and management of the ship.[227] He had made a joint note with the owner enabling him to be paid out of the earnings of the ship and then used the note to borrow money. The court recognized his lien and the limit of liability for his claim was the value of the ship and freight. In the recent case, *Doris v. The Ferdinand*, the question arose as to whether the chief executive officer of a shipowning company could claim a lien for alleged disbursements expenses and whether the various claims put forward fell within the ambit of disbursements.[228] The expenditures were for principal and interest payments for loans for the shipowning company and monthly interest charges on the chief executive officer's personal lines of credit used for his business and family expenses. He was held not to be in the position of master and the expenditures were not disbursements for several reasons. First, the expenditures were not for necessaries (i.e., goods, materials, and services for the operation and maintenance of the ship) but for the operation of the shipowning company. Second, the CEO acted not in the capacity of a master but rather as a minority shareholder and financier of the shipowning company. Third, he was not a traditional master of a ship but the directing mind of the owners, whereas the disbursements lien was instituted for a master who could not communicate with the owner of the ship.

There seems to be inconsistency as to how disbursements are treated in different federal statutes. On the one hand the *Federal Court Act* lists the master's, charterer's, agent's, and shipper's disbursements as a class of claim that may be defeated by a transfer of title — suggesting a statutory right *in rem* rather than a maritime lien.[229] On the other hand the *Canada Shipping Act* does not provide a similar generic provision but rather provides clearer and more purposive text: the master has "the same rights, liens and remedies properly made or incurred by him on account of the ship as a master has for the recovery of his wages."[230] The latter Act leaves no doubt that the claim for disbursements is on par with the maritime lien for wages. Perhaps a discussion of the true status of this lien is more academic than practical, given the rarity of this type of claim. However, even from a purely theoretical

---

227 (1892), 3 Ex. C.R. 258.
228 *Doris v. Ferdinand (The)* (1998), 155 F.T.R. 236.
229 *Federal Court Act*, above note 46, s.22(2)(p).
230 *Canada Shipping Act*, above note 5, s.212.

perspective, the better view as to which of the two provisions should prevail is probably Professor Tetley's, who is of the opinion that the more specific language of the *Canada Shipping Act* is a clear — perhaps even clearer — indication of parliamentary intent to consider the master's disbursements as a maritime lien.[231] In contrast, the *Federal Court Act* provision has more general language and reference to a variety of persons. In any case, recalling *The Har Rai* case, there is a good argument to be had in support of the master's disbursements as a maritime lien on the basis of the *Federal Court Act*'s general grant of jurisdiction under section 22(1) and the definition of Canadian maritime law in section 2: "[T]he limitations applicable to a mere statutory right *in rem* are not in principle necessarily applicable to a maritime lien. They are two different things."[232]

d) Extinguishment of Maritime Liens

The maritime lien is an invisible charge on the *res*, but it is not indelible and may be subject to extinguishment in several ways.[233] Generally, there is extinguishment by payment and acceptance of the amount of the claim.[234] However, there is also extinguishment where the claimant elects to take securities in place of cash[235] or where a seaman, on being offered his or her wages, leaves them on deposit.[236] If other securities are contracted for repayment of necessaries, such as a mortgage or promissory note, the lien is not necessarily lost. In such situations, the lien must be expressly waived to be defeated.[237] A maritime lien is also generally extinguished by the giving of bail into court, the bail being a substitute for the ship with the effect that "the ship is wholly released from the cause of action, and cannot be arrested again for that cause of action."[238] In *N.M. Paterson & Sons Ltd. v. The Birchglen*, the Federal Court Trial Division dismissed a motion for a declaration that a maritime lien was extinguished as a result of an undertaking filed

---

231 W. Tetley, *Maritime Liens and Claims*, above note 166 at 429.
232 *The Har Rai*, above note 155 at 745.
233 *Canada Shipping Act*, above note 5, s.471; *Canada Shipping Act, 2001*, above note 5, s.145.
234 *Oxley v. Spearwater* (1867), 7 N.S.R. 144.
235 *Simlah (The)* (1851), 15 Jr. 865. See also *N.M. Patterson & Sons Ltd. v. Birchglen (The)*, [1990] 3 F.C.3 01 (T.D.) [*The Birchglen*].
236 *Rainbow (The)* (1885), 53 L.T. 91, 5 Asp. 479.
237 *Richardson International Ltd. v. Mys Chikhacheva (The)* (2001), 200 F.T.R. 76, aff'd [2002] 4 F.C. 80.
238 *Wild Ranger (The)*, [1863] Br. & Lush. 84.

by the insurers.[239] In this case, tugs were involved in a collision with the plaintiff's ship and the tugowners wished to sell the tugs. The insurer's undertaking was in the form of a letter to make good any damage award, but the plaintiff objected to the motion. The court felt it was premature to declare the tugs free of encumbrances. In rationalizing the decision, the court noted judicial reluctance to adhere to the principle that a maritime lien is completely extinguished by the posting of bail (i.e., in the case of arrest) or other security. The equating of the security posted with bail was probably not helpful, as bail is under judicial supervision, while the security is contractual.[240] The caution here is that, in the absence of express waiver of the lien by the lien holder, it cannot be assumed that the posting of security will extinguish the lien.

The lien may also be extinguished by statute where a limitation period is provided and the creditor has not enforced it during that period; for example, unless the time is extended by the court, a maritime lien for salvage, as well as for property damage arising out of a collision, is time barred after two years.[241] There is no international uniformity on limitation periods and one would need to refer to the appropriate statute. The *International Convention on Maritime Liens and Mortgages, 1993*, attempted to promote a one-year limitation period, but this instrument has not received sufficient international support to enter into force.[242] Actions in the Federal Court are subject to the limitation or prescription periods applicable in the province where the cause of action arises. When the cause of action arises elsewhere the limitation period is six years from the time the cause of action arises.[243]

Delay in enforcing the lien may be excused, such as where the ship subject to the maritime lien does not come within the court's jurisdiction, or where witnesses are not available.[244] However, in general there is a duty for the lien holder to exercise reasonable diligence and follow-up in good faith. The courts retain an equitable discretion when the claim is not proceeded with expeditiously, and unjustifiably so (i.e., laches). The expectation is not that the lien holder must do everything

---

239 *The Birchglen*, above note 235.
240 *Ibid*. A constraint for the court's competence in issuing a declaratory judgment of the type requested was the interlocutory nature of the proceeding. A court can grant a free and clear title only by judicial sale.
241 *Canada Shipping Act*, above note 5, s.471; *Canada Shipping Act, 2001*, above note 5, s.145.
242 Above note 138, art.9(1).
243 *Federal Court Act*, above note 46, s.39.
244 *Bold Buccleugh (The)*, above note 182; *The Bermuda*, above note 184.

possible but, rather, to do what could reasonably be required under ordinary circumstances, having regard to expense and difficulty.[245] Otherwise, a maritime lien may be lost by failure to exercise reasonable diligence in bringing proceedings to arrest the *res*, or by negligence or delay affecting the rights of third parties.[246] What constitutes due diligence in prosecuting a claim at the earliest opportunity, so that the interests of third parties are not duly affected, is determined on a case-by-case basis.[247] While the right to proceed *in rem* may be lost as a result of inexcusable delay, there might still be the possibility of recourse *in personam*.[248] A maritime lien is extinguished by the loss or destruction of the *res*, although it may be enforced against the fragments.[249] In fact, for the purposes of Federal Court jurisdiction, the definition of "ship" includes part of a ship and therefore an action *in rem* may be exercised against the remnants of the ship.[250] This is conceivable in the case of wreck and the salvor's lien in salving the wreck.

Maritime liens are not extinguished by a sale of the *res* other than under a court order,[251] by fruitless proceedings *in personam*, nor by the release of a claim against the owners personally, as this would not release the *res*;[252] nor are maritime liens extinguished by the owner's death or bankruptcy;[253] by an agreement to refer the claim to arbitration;[254] by a

---

245 *Europa (The)* (1863), 15 E.R. 803; *Fraser v. Jean and Joyce (The)*, [1941] Ex. C.R. 43 [*The Jean and Joyce*]. In the latter case, while the claim was for master's wages, the claimant was also in partnership as a temporary co-owner.
246 *The Jean and Joyce*, ibid.
247 *Kong Magnus (The)*, [1891] P. 223 at 233. In this old case the delay was eleven years (today, of course, there is a limitation period). The Norwegian owners of the defendant ship argued that, since the collision with the British ship (which was lost) the plaintiffs had numerous opportunities to act against the defendant ship. The ship had visited British ports on numerous occasions. There were also changes in the interest and ownership of the ship and many of the crew were no longer available as witnesses. Even so, the court allowed the action to proceed on the basis of considerations of equity and because the defendants failed to show why the merits could not be considered. See also *The Jean and Joyce*, ibid., where a maritime lien was lost through a failure to prosecute diligently.
248 *Canada Steamship Lines v. Rival (The)*, [1937] 3 D.L.R. 148 (Ex. Ct.).
249 *Neptune (The)* (1824), 1 Hagg. 227 at 238, 166 E.R. 81 at 85. In this case crew members were able to recover their wages from a fund formed as a result of what was left of the lost ship. Crew members in this case also acted as salvors.
250 *Federal Court Act*, above note 46, s.2(1), as am. by *Marine Liability Act*, above note 139, s.115.
251 *Bold Buccleugh (The)*, above note 182.
252 *Chieftain (The)*, [1863] Br. & Lush. 212, 8 L.T. 120.
253 *Goulandris (The)*, [1927] P. 182.
254 *Purissima Concepcion (The)* (1848), 7 Notes of Cases 503.

winding-up order against the owners of the ship;[255] by a salvor giving a receipt in full payment, in ignorance of the full extent of his services;[256] or by a salvor entering into a "no cure–no pay" agreement.[257]

When the vessel is sold under a court order granted in proceedings *in rem*, a maritime lien is laundered in so far as the *res* is concerned;[258] however, the lien attaches to the proceeds of the sale of the maritime property, while they remain in the hands of the court.[259]

3) Possessory Liens

At common law, a possessory lien holder has the right to retain possession of goods belonging to another until debts to the lien holder have been discharged. Possessory liens usually arise in connection with a shipbuilder's claim for work completed for the unpaid portion of the price, with a ship repairer's claim for repairs, with a shipowner's claim for freight, with a cargo owner's claim for general average contribution, with a salvor in relation to the award for the salved *res*, and with other persons who may provide a particular service to specific equipment on the ship.[260] Possessory liens are also affected by provincial statutes, which have the effect of codifying the common law on this subject. The lien holder must remain continuously in possession of the goods if the lien is to continue.[261] The "possession" serves as security for the unpaid debt, and loss of that possession is tantamount to loss of the security; however, the underlying personal cause of action subsists. Possession can also be through representation, such as the presence of a representative of the builder on board the ship while the ship is undertaking sea trials with the owner's crew on board.[262] Simple arrest of a vessel and the leaving of tools on board do not amount to possession.[263] Also, pos-

---

255 *Cella (The)* (1888), 13 P.D. 82.
256 *Silver Bullion (The)* (1854), 2 Sp. Ecc. & Ad. 70, 164 E.R. 312.
257 *Goulandris (The)*, above note 253.
258 *Ibid.*
259 *Optima (The)* (1905), 10 Asp. M.L.C. 147, 93 L.T. 638; *Acrux (The)* (1962), 1 Lloyd's Rep. 405 at 409.
260 In *Re Westlake* (1881), 16 Ch. D. 604 engineers retained a possessory lien over steam engine equipment. A supplier of materials to a ship, who has possession of the ship, is recognized as having a possessory lien (Buchan, above note 174 at 95).
261 *Rumely v. Vera M (The)*, [1923] Ex. C.R. 36. The lien is lost if the lienholder causes the arrest of the vessel and gives up possession to the marshal.
262 *The Alarissa*, above note 168, para.28.

session need not be exclusive, such as where some of the repair work is subcontracted.[264]

The possessory lien holder has no power of sale unless it has been given to him or her expressly by statute. A possessory lien cannot be enforced in the Admiralty Court, but it is recognized and protected by the court if the *res* has been arrested to enforce another claim.[265] A possessory lien holder should intervene in the existing action and request recognition and protection.[266] This can be a significant limitation because the lien holder may continue to incur expenses until the *res* is actually sold. Not all expenses will be covered by the lien itself, as for example the costs of storage.[267] The principle here is that the lien holder cannot add to the liabilities of the *res* outside the contract.

In the case of a shipbuilder, proper extras such as time, equipment, and money may be covered. The builder's lien commences from the time the first keel plate is laid but comes into play only when the builder becomes an unpaid under the contract.[268] If the building contract provides for successive payments according to stages of completion, with the owner retaining property rights, the lien will cover the residue of the price still due for a specific completed stage, even though the work on the whole ship is not yet completed. If the plans for the building of the ship continue to evolve during construction, the lien will cover any changes duly authorized by the owners.[269] If the *res* is sold during construction, the lien holder will not lose the security. Therefore, a new owner of a ship under construction would still have to contend with the possessory lien held by the builder for the outstanding debt of the previous owner.[270]

---

263 *Ibid.*, para.89.
264 *Earle's Shipbuilding Engineering Co. v. Gefion and Fourth Shipbuilding & Engineering Co.* (1922), 10 Ll. L.R. 305.
265 Tetley, *Maritime Liens and Claims*, above note 166.
266 *Tergeste (The)*, [1903] P. 26; *Montreal Dry Docks*, above note 169 at 370.
267 *Somes v. British Empire Shipping Co.*, [1843–60] All E.R. Rep. 844 (H.L.). In *Canadian Imperial Bank of Commerce v. Barkley Sound (The)*, [1999] B.C.J. No. 512 (S.C.) (QL), the repairer was allowed to claim storage costs incurred while the work was under way and up to the point of re-launching. Storage costs incurred after the work was completed were deemed to simply protect the repairer's interests and were not allowed.
268 *The Alarissa*, above note 168, para.60.
269 *The Alarissa, ibid.*, para.34. It is possible that the full value of the work completed may not be precisely known, but the lien holder will have to prove value on a motion for distribution. *Ibid.*
270 *Woods v. Russell* (1822), 5 B. & Ald. 942, 106 E.R. 1436 (K.B.).

As discussed in Chapter 19, in general, possessory liens under Canadian maritime law rank after maritime liens but before mortgages. However, it has been held in the case of a shipbuilder that the possessory lien that pre-dates maritime liens actually ranks ahead of the maritime liens and any other claims.[271] Also, where the shipbuilder acts in good faith and enhances the value of the *res*, his or her claim should be satisfied in priority to that of other creditors.[272] The relationship between a mortgagee and the holder of a possessory lien can be a difficult one. In a case where a mortgagee sells or causes a repairer or supplier of materials to lose the possessory lien before its discharge, it has been held that the mortgagee is liable to pay for the discharge of the lien.[273] Generally, there is no issue of ranking of possessory liens *inter se* because there can only be one "possession" at a time for lien purposes.[274] Liens created under provincial statutes, whether possessory or non-possessory, do not affect the priorities under Canadian maritime law and, in fact, rank behind mortgages.[275]

4) Statutory Rights *in Rem*

a) Definition and Characteristics

Whereas the maritime lien arises out of general maritime law and the inherent jurisdiction of the Admiralty Court, a statutory right *in rem* is established by statutes conferring jurisdiction on this court. Technically, the statutory right *in rem* is the conferment by statute of a particular judicial course of action to enforce a debt, rather than the creation of a lien as security on the happening of an event.[276] These enlarging statutes not only give the Admiralty Court jurisdiction over new types of claims but also increase the jurisdiction of the court over traditional claims over which it has inherent jurisdiction, such as maritime liens. Thus, statutory rights *in rem* are all matters giving rise to Admiralty jurisdiction *in rem*, except for maritime liens, possessory liens, and mortgages.

A statutory right *in rem* differs basically from a maritime lien in three respects: first, it accrues only from the day of the arrest and is

---

271 *Tergeste (The)*, above note 266.
272 *Montreal Dry Docks*, above note 169.
273 *Weir v. Bank of Nova Scotia* (1979), 30 Nfld. & P.E.I.R. 223 (Nfld. T.D.); *Greeley v. Tami Joan (The)* (1997), 135 F.T.R. 290. See also Buchan, above note 174 at 96.
274 *Greeley v. Tami Joan (The)*, ibid.
275 *Finning Ltd. v. Federal Business Development Bank* (1989), 56 D.L.R. (4th) 379. See also *Federal Business Development Bank v. Winder 4135 (The)*, [1986] 2 F.C. 154 (T.D.).
276 *Benson Brothers Shipbuilding v. Miss Donna (The)*, above note 178 at 384.

subject to claims already subsisting against the *res*;[277] second, normally, it is defeated by a transfer of title unless otherwise provided by statute; and third, the owner must be personally liable. In the institution of the action *in rem* the position of a maritime lien holder needs to be differentiated from the holder of a mere statutory right *in rem*. For the statutory right *in rem* to be exercised, for example in the case of necessaries and stevedoring charges supplied in Canada, there must be *in personam* liability of the owner; otherwise the action *in rem* will fail.[278] If those same claims generate maritime liens outside Canada, then they will be enforceable in Canada as maritime liens and not as statutory rights *in rem*, such as in the case of necessaries and stevedoring claims generated in the United States but enforced in Canada.[279]

b) Range of Rights *in Rem*

Table 6.1 lists the maritime claims over which the Federal Court has jurisdiction, including statutory rights *in rem*, under section 22(2) of the *Federal Court Act*. These claims are not exhaustive because they do not limit the generality of section 22(1) for general maritime law purposes. The majority of section 22(2) claims are statutory rights *in rem* and this discussion now focuses on these. It is important to distinguish between rights that are defeated by a transfer of title and rights that are not so defeated. Unless otherwise provided by statute, the rights *in rem* rank below mortgages, which is rather low in the overall scheme for distribution of proceeds. The courts have shown flexibility on this latter point when issues of equity arose. In *Bank of Scotland v. The Nel*, a medical clinic's claim for medical supplies to the ship was allowed because the clinic had a duty to assist seafarers with their medical needs. Although not a maritime lien, the clinic's claim was given an enhanced priority similar to such a lien.[280] In another case, the court granted an enhanced priority to a ship repairer, whose claim normally gives rise to a statutory right *in rem* similar to a maritime lien for work that enhances the value of a vessel when that work is required as a result of a port state control inspection. Not to do so would have resulted in unjust enrichment on the part of other creditors.[281]

---

277 *Cella (The)*, above note 255.
278 *Westcan Stevedoring Ltd. v. Armar (The)*, above note 190; *McCain Produce Co. v. Rea (The)*, above note 191.
279 *The Har Rai*, above note 155; and *The Number Four*, above note 157.
280 *Bank of Scotland v. Nel (The)*, above note 220.
281 *The Atlantis Two*, above note 162.

There are several maritime law statutes that either reinforce claims contemplated by the *Federal Court Act*, or that provide additional rights, including rights *in rem*, generally in favour of government or statutory authorities, and frequently with the privilege of prioritized ranking. Statutory bodies may be responsible for managing harbours, ports, docks, and canals, as well as providing other services to navigation and shipping, and the fees for their services are frequently protected. Tetley calls these "special legislative rights [that] constitute true first rights which governments have given to themselves by legislation, in pursuit of various policy objectives."[282] The author argues that these types of claims have not been given the attention they deserve and that the *International Convention on Maritime Liens and Mortgages, 1993*, is unlikely to receive enough ratifications to enter into force because it did not take into consideration these rights in state practice.[283]

c) Claims that are Defeated by a Transfer of Title

Sections 43(2) and (3) of the *Federal Court Act* identify several rights *in rem* against the ship, cargo, and freight that are defeated by a transfer of title. As identified in Table 6.1 these are as follows: (e) claims for damage sustained by or loss of a ship, including damage to or loss of cargo or equipment or any property in or on or being loaded on or off a ship;[284] (f) claims from the carriage of goods under a through bill of lading;[285] (g) claims for loss of life or personal injury as a result of operation or management of the ship (non-collision related), such as negligence or equipment defects;[286] (h) claims for damage to goods and personal baggage/effects carried on a ship;[287] (i) claims arising from agreements related to the carriage of goods, including charterparties;[288] (k) towage claims;[289] (m) necessaries claims, including stevedoring and

---

282 Tetley, *Maritime Liens and Claims*, above note 166 at 71. An example is *Holt Cargo Systems*, where the Halifax Port Corporation's claim for port dues for The Brussel was granted priority over all other claims, except wages on the basis of s.43(5) of the *Canada Ports Corporation Act*. *Holt Cargo Systems Inc.v. ABC Containerline N.V. (The Brussel)*, [1997] 3 F.C. 187.
283 Tetley, *ibid*. at 214.
284 *Marine Liability Act*, above note 139, Part 5.
285 *Ibid*.
286 *Ibid*., Part 1.
287 *Ibid*., Parts 4 and 5.
288 *Ibid*., Part 5.
289 The status of towage claims was addressed by several cases, including *Martin v. Ed McWilliams (The)* (1919), 18 Ex. C.R. 470; *Neville Canneries v. Santa Maria (The)* (1917), 16 Ex. C.R. 481; and *Stack v. Leopold (The)* (1918), 18 Ex. C.R. 325.

lighterage;[290] (n) shipbuilding, equipping, or repairing claims; (p) master's disbursements claims;[291] and (r) marine insurance claims.[292] In order not to lose the right to proceed *in rem* in these cases, the *res* must be beneficially owned by the same person both at the time of the cause of action and the commencement of the action. Should the creditor lose the right to proceed *in rem*, he or she will only be able to proceed against the debtor *in personam*.

Table 6.1 Maritime Claims in the *Federal Court Act*

Subs. 22(2) claims	Nature of Claim	Nature of Claim	Defeated by Transfer of Title Under ss.43(2) and (3)?
(a)	Title and possession	Right *in rem*	No
(b)	Disputes between co-owners concerning possession and use of ship	Right *in rem*	No
(c)	Mortgages, hypothecs, and other securities	Mortgages	No
(d)	Damage, loss of life, and personal injury caused by ship in collision or otherwise	Maritime lien	No
(e)	Damage to or loss of ship, cargo, equipment and any property during loading/unloading	Right *in rem*	Yes
(f)	Damage to goods during carriage by ship and transit	Right *in rem*	Yes
(g)	Loss of life or personal injury during the operation of a ship	Right *in rem*	Yes
(h)	Damage to cargo and passengers' luggage	Right *in rem*	Yes
(i)	Hire and charterparties	Right *in rem*	Yes
(j)	Salvage	Maritime lien	No
(k)	Towage	Right *in rem*	Yes
(l)	Pilotage	Right *in rem*	No
(m)	Necessaries	Right *in rem*	Yes
(n)	Construction, repair, and equipping of ship	Right *in rem*	Yes
(o)	Wages of seafarers	Maritime lien	No
(p)	Disbursements	Right *in rem*	Yes
(q)	General average	Right *in rem*	No
(r)	Marine insurance	Right *in rem*	Yes
(s)	Port, canal, dock, and related charges	Right *in rem*	No

---

290 *Coastal Equipment Agencies Ltd. v. Comer (The)*, [1970] 1 Ex. C.R. 13, aff'd by S.C.C., claimant for necessaries is in the same position as an unsecured creditor and needs leave of court to institute proceedings.
291 *Canada Shipping Act*, above note 5.
292 *Marine Insurance Act*, S.C. 1993, c.22.

d) Claims that are Not Defeated by a Transfer of Title

In contrast to the claims listed above, there are also several other claims that are not defeated by a transfer of title, and will therefore travel with the *res* to the new owner. As listed in Table 6.1, the claims concerned are as follows: (a) claims as to title, possession, or ownership or part-ownership of a vessel, or the proceeds of sale; (b) disputes between co-owners of a ship as to possession, employment, or earnings; (d) claims for damage, death, or personal injury caused by a ship in a collision or otherwise;[293] (l) pilotage claims;[294] (q) claims for general average contribution; and (s) dock, harbour and canal dues, and charges, including use of related facilities.[295] The effect of section 43(3) of the *Federal Court Act* on these claims is to pass on to them the important characteristic of survivability of the maritime lien but without making them maritime liens.

5) Ranking of Liens and Mortgages

Secured interests in ships, whether they are acquired by agreement like mortgages, or arise by law like maritime liens, possessory liens, and rights *in rem*, provide protection for their holders against non-payment of the secured debts by the shipowner. Hence they have no operative effect until the shipowner defaults on the obligations incurred and

---

[293] A distinction needs to be made between (1) damage, death, and personal injury as a result of a collision; and (2) damage, death, and personal injury not resulting from a collision but from some other mishap. Claims under (1) constitute maritime liens under general maritime law, *Federal Court Act*, above note 46, s.22(1); and claims under (2) are rights *in rem* (*Federal Court Act*, ibid.) Case law has adopted a flexible position on damage done by ship. The damage need not be caused directly by the ship, but may be linked to the ship indirectly or as a result of actions by the crew. E.g., the dropping or dragging of anchor that causes damage to the property of a third party is damage done by ship. By analogy, where the crew carries out maintenance on the ship and its actions (e.g., spray painting) cause damage to neighbouring property, that also constitutes damage done by ship because the crew is an integral part of the ship and maintenance of a ship is essential.

[294] *Pilotage Act*, R.S.C. 1985, c.P-14. The Act does not confer a priority, but a lien for pilotage services has been granted in several cases, in effect given priority. However, there is no agreement that this claim amounts to a maritime lien. For lien recognition see *Holt Cargo Systems*, above note 141; *The Atlantean I*, above note 47; *Ultramar Canada Inc. v. Pierson Steamships* (1982), 43 C.B.R. (N.S.) 9; *Östgöta Enskilda Bank v. Sea Star (The)* (1994), 78 F.T.R. 304, held that a maritime lien has not been established.

[295] *Canada Marine Act*, S.C. 1998, c.10; *Harbour Commissions Act*, R.S.C. 1985, c.H-1.

enforcement of the security is required. This process is usually commenced by the arrest of the ship and the institution of an action *in rem* leading to a judicial sale. Then all creditors, secured and unsecured, will attempt to prove their claims in the action and the court will have to priorize their order of recovery from the sale proceeds. This complex matter is the subject of detailed judge-made rules of procedure or statutory provision and, accordingly, is discussed in Chapter 19.

FURTHER READINGS

BOWTLE, G. & K.P. MCGUINNESS, *The Law of Ship Mortgages* (London: Lloyd's of London Press, 2001).

BUCHAN, J.D., *Mortgages of Ships: Maritime Security in Canada* (Toronto: Butterworths, 1986).

CASTEL, J.-G., *Canadian Conflict of Laws*, 5th ed. (Toronto: Butterworths, 2002).

CURTIS, S., *The Law of Shipbuilding Contracts*, 2d ed. (London: Lloyd's of London Press, 1996).

JACKSON, D., *Enforcement of Maritime Claims*, 3d ed. (London: Lloyd's Law Publications, 2000).

MARGOLIS, R.A. & C.J. GIASCHI, "Priorities and Bankruptcy in Admiralty" (paper presented at the Admiralty Law Programme of the CMLA, April 2002) online at: <www.admiraltylaw.com>.

MEESON, N., *Ship and Aircraft Mortgages* (London: Lloyd's of London Press, 1989).

STONE, A.J., "Let the Boat Buyer Beware" (1974) 12 Osgoode Hall L.J. 643.

TETLEY, W., *International Conflict of Laws: Common, Civil and Maritime* (Cowansville, QB: Yvon Blais, 1994).

——, *Maritime Liens and Claims*, 2d ed. (Cowansville, QB: Yvon Blais, 1998).

——, *International Maritime and Admiralty Law* (Cowansville, QB: Yvon Blais, 2002).

THOMAS, D.R., *Maritime Liens* (London: Stevens & Sons, 1980).

WOOD, R.J., "The Nature and Definition of Federal Security Interests" (2000) 34 C.B.L.J. 65.

ZIEGEL, J. S., "Ships at Sea, International Insolvencies and Divided Courts" (1998) 50 Can. Bar Rev. 310.

CHAPTER 7

MARINE INSURANCE

A. INTRODUCTION

Marine insurance, the earliest form of risk coverage, is a very ancient sector of maritime law. It is, therefore, helpful to know something of its history in order to understand how marine insurance operates today.[1]

1) Origins

The origins of marine insurance are "veiled in antiquity and lost in obscurity."[2] It appears that the Phoenicians already practised a form of bottomry, an advance of money on the security of a vessel that is not recoverable if the vessel is subsequently totally lost before arrival. Even earlier, a form of bottomry was used by the Babylonians and, possibly, by the ancient Hindus. Bottomry was originally a type of marine insurance, as the lender of money on bottomry made the advance before the adventure was commenced and, thereby, financed the adventurer. Bottomry is today rarely used, although in an emergency it could still

---

1 For a detailed examination of the history of marine insurance, see V. Dover, *A Handbook to Marine Insurance*, 8th ed. (London: Witherby, 1975) c.1; and C. O'May, *Marine Insurance: Law and Policy* (London: Sweet & Maxwell, 1993) c.1.
2 E. Gold, *Canadian Admiralty Law: Introductory Materials*, Rev. 9th ed. (Halifax: Dalhousie Law School, 1996) at 161. See also G.S. Staring & G.L. Waddell, "Marine Insurance" (1999) 73 Tul. L. Rev. 1619.

enable the master of a vessel to obtain advances to allow the voyage to continue. The concept of marine insurance as protection against loss by maritime perils has been traced from at least 215 BC, when the Roman government was required by the suppliers of military stores to accept "all risk of loss, arising from the attacks of enemies or from storms, to the supplies which they placed in the ships."[3] By 50 BC, references show that certain essential elements of modern marine insurance were already present, including, the requirement of an insurable interest, the assumption of the risk by someone other than the owner of the property, and the payment of a premium as a consideration for the indemnities offered.

2) Lombard and Hanseatic Initiatives

The further development of marine insurance is relatively obscure until the thirteenth century. The real origins of marine insurance, as it is practised today, can be traced to Italy at that time. It was associated with the merchants of the cities of Lombardy, and Florence, at about AD 1250. Lombard merchants wrote the oldest existing insurance policy, dated 23 October 1347, that insured the ship Santa Clara on a voyage from Genoa to Majorca. The Lombards also migrated to other countries and, by the fourteenth century, were practising marine insurance in England, Belgium, and France, as well as in Italy. Contemporaneously with the Lombards, the merchants of the Hansa towns in northern Germany were also practising marine insurance. In the thirteenth century, these towns formed the Hanseatic League, which would control world shipping until the sixteenth century. Some of the Hansa merchants migrated to England and would eventually monopolize English overseas trade, while the Lombards controlled banking in England. Both groups also engaged in marine insurance. However, the antipathy of English merchants to the Lombard and Hansa monopoly led to their expulsion from England in 1483 and 1597, respectively. The instigators of the expulsion did not desire the destruction of English trade but merely the transfer of control into English hands. The English merchants at this time had been participating in marine insurance but the alien merchants were considered to be much more successful.

---

3   Dover, *A Handbook to Marine Insurance*, above note 1 at 2.

3) Establishment of the English Marine Insurance Market

With the expulsion of the alien merchants, the British monopoly of marine insurance was assured. The first English statute relating to marine insurance was *An Act Touching Policies of Assurances Used Among Merchants*,[4] drafted in 1601 by Sir Francis Bacon but based on the insurance wording created by the Hanseatic League. The preamble of the 1601 statute illustrates not only the basic principles of marine insurance, as still practised today, but also how firmly these principles were already established in the early seventeenth century:

> And whereas it has been time out of minde an usage amongst merchantes, both of these realms and of foreign nations when they make any great adventure (specially into remote parts) to give some consideration of money to other persons (which commonly are in no small number) to have from them assurance made of the goods, merchandises, ships and things adventured or some part thereof, at such rates and in such sort as the parties assurers and parties assured can agree, which course of dealing is commonly termed a policy of assurance; by means of which policy of assurance it cometh to pass that upon the loss or perishing of any ship there followeth not the undoing of any man, but the loss lighteth rather easily upon many than heavily upon few, and rather upon them that adventure not than those that do adventure, whereby all merchantes, especially the younger sort are allured to venture more willingly and more freely.

The market for marine insurance was the forecourt of the Royal Exchange, a general commodities market, until the rise of Lloyd's Coffee House in the seventeenth century.

4) Lloyd's

The early London coffee houses were not only centres of literary interest and debate but also of commerce. They had significant political influence, to the extent that King Charles II tried unsuccessfully to suppress them. Among the many seventeenth century London coffee houses was one owned by Edward Lloyd, situated on Tower Street near the Thames; Lloyd's Coffee House attracted the patronage of those interested in and connected with the sea. Lloyd's was merely a convenient and congenial place for merchants of common interest to meet, carry out commercial transactions, and arrange marine insurance. No

---

4   *1601* (U.K.), 43 Eliz., c.12.

insurance companies existed at that time. Only individuals who became known as "underwriters" — as they wrote their names and signatures beneath the wording on insurance policies, in order to provide a personal guarantee for a commercial venture — practised marine insurance. As time passed, Lloyd's Coffee House became generally recognized as a likely place for persons wanting insurance cover to find such marine underwriters. Edward Lloyd encouraged this by providing his customers with pen, ink, paper, and shipping information obtained from the waterfront by runners. In 1696 he published a newssheet called *Lloyd's News*, which was discontinued after he found himself in difficulties for inaccurately publishing proceedings of the House of Lords. Short-lived as it was, *Lloyd's News* can be seen as the forerunner of *Lloyd's List*, London's oldest daily newspaper that first appeared in 1734, twenty-one years after Lloyd's death.

In 1769 the reputation of Lloyd's Coffee House as a meeting place for merchant insurers was threatened by gambling among the customers. As a result, the serious insurance element set up an alternate establishment called New Lloyd's; two years later, insufficient space in the new coffee house led to the formation of the First Committee of Lloyd's in 1771. The committee was elected from among seventy-nine merchants, underwriters, and brokers at the coffee house, and each member of the committee paid £100 into the Bank of England for the purpose of acquiring larger premises. For the next century, the restricting of membership and introduction of subscriptions further developed the private club characteristics of Lloyd's, and an elected committee was provided with increased authority. In 1779 a general meeting of Lloyd's adopted standard forms of insurance policies, the S policy for insurance on the ship, and the G policy for insurance of goods. By 1780 a common form known as the S.G. Form of Policy was adopted that, until recent years, remained substantially unaltered. Today Lloyd's remains the world's principal market for all types of insurance, including marine insurance.

5) Insurance Companies and Hull Clubs

The first major marine insurance companies were established at the time when the infamous South Sea Bubble burst in the early 1700s. The South Sea Company had been incorporated in 1710 with a charter that gave it a monopoly on trade within the South Seas (i.e., South America). The company, after realizing that its trading opportunities in that area were not sufficient to be very profitable, came up with a scheme to convert the entire national debt of England into a "single redeemable obligation" to the company at a low rate of interest in return for a monopoly on British foreign trade outside Europe. The government accepted the scheme with some modifications and the market value of the company's shares soared rapidly. On 30 January 1720, £100 of stock could have been bought for £129; on 24 June 1720, the price had reached £1,050. The price rose in part because of ambitious, and probably fraudulent, offers by the directors of the company to pay an annual dividend of at least 50 per cent. In June 1720 the financial frenzy of people buying stock in the South Sea Company had reached such heights that the government resorted to a statutory control over joint-stock companies.[5] This legislation, known as the *Bubble Act*, declared a company without a charter to be illegal and thereby ensured that chartered companies would become monopolies.

The *Bubble Act* also contained charters for two major marine insurance companies.[6] These companies had each offered to pay the government £300,000 in return for the grant of a charter. It was intended at first to grant the two companies a complete monopoly of marine insurance but, as a result of pressure from Lloyd's underwriters, this was eventually limited to a monopoly as far as companies were concerned. As a result, the rights of private individuals to freely practise marine insurance were not affected. While it was anticipated that private underwriters would suffer in competing with the insurance companies, this did not occur. In fact, the business of the private insurers expanded rapidly. As the companies offered cover of only a very restricted nature and consistently refused to underwrite any but the safest risks, this defeated the entire purpose of company monopoly. For example, by 1809, only about half of all the marine risks that might have been insured in England were, in fact, so insured. Moreover, the two companies between them handled less than 4 per cent of the total marine risks underwritten. Individual underwriters handled the remainder.[7] During this period brokerage commission charges were also very high. The average was about 25 per cent of the total premium paid to the underwriter.

In 1810 a Select Committee appointed by the British government to consider the state of marine insurance in Great Britain issued its

---

5   By introducing *An Act for Securing Certain Powers and Privileges Intended to be Granted by His Majesty by Two Charters for Assurance of Ships and Merchandises at Sea, for Lending Money Upon Bottomry; and for Restraining Several Extravagant and Unwarrantable Practices Therein Mentioned*, 1714 (U.K.), 6 Geo. I., c.18.
6   The Royal Exchange Assurance Company and the London Assurance Company.
7   Dover, *A Handbook to Marine Insurance*, above note 1 at 43–45.

report. The committee found that, during the period August to December, many of the principal underwriters withdrew from Lloyd's, allegedly for purposes of relaxation but probably from fear of the higher risks involved during the winter. Owing to the lack of competition, the premiums charged during these months were particularly high. The danger of an individual underwriter being unable to meet his obligations was found to be relatively great. There was evidence that, although many merchants would have preferred to insure with the companies, even at a higher premium, they were unable to do so. Even though the situation in London was considered to be unsatisfactory, the difficulties encountered by traders in other British ports were even greater, owing to the fact that both insurance companies and the Lloyd's underwriters operated from London with practices principally designed for the trade of that port. As a result, groups of shipowners at various ports banded together to form "hull clubs," which provided insurance coverage, despite the statutory prohibition, on a mutual basis, that is, with each member of the club underwriting a share of the total risk of the club members' ships. On the recommendation of the Select Committee, the monopoly of the two insurance companies was removed in 1824. Several other marine insurance companies were then founded, operating on both mutual and non-mutual principles. In practice, however, the individual Lloyd's underwriters were able to quote better rates. The Lloyd's standard hull policy did not contain many of the deductions contained in those offered by the mutual clubs that, in any case, could not offer the facilities and organization that had been built up by Lloyd's. The early system of calls adopted by the hull clubs also had the effect that good shipowners basically subsidized those with frequent claims. This resulted in the better shipowners insuring their vessels with Lloyd's. As a result, the hull clubs, left only with those risks that were unacceptable elsewhere, declined in importance.[8]

6) Third-Party Liability Coverage

The period of decline of the hull clubs coincided with the growth of shipowners' third-party liabilities that, until the nineteenth century, had not presented serious problems. In 1846 Lord Campbell's *Fatal Accidents Act* [9] was passed, providing for compensation to the dependants of persons who lost their lives "by the wrongful act, neglect or

---

8 E. Gold, *Gard Handbook on P&I Insurance*, 5th ed. (Arendal: Gard, 2002) c.1.
9 *An Act for Compensating the Families of Persons Killed by Accidents, 1846* (U.K.), 9 & 10 Vict., c.93.

default of another person." The rise in emigration from Great Britain enormously increased the potential liability of shipowners. The standard Lloyd's marine insurance policy made virtually no provision for third-party liabilities and underwriters, realizing the size of the potential risk, were apparently unwilling to cover such risks.

Shipowners agitated to have their liabilities limited, and new legislation in 1854[10] provided for the limitation for loss of life and personal-injury liability of shipowners. Even with this limitation, shipowners found themselves in a vulnerable position, as they were, to a large extent, not covered for such risks arising from collision. The amount recoverable under the marine insurance policy was limited to the insured value of the vessel. Because of this limited coverage, if a vessel was lost from a collision at sea and the assured had a liability for damage caused to the other ship, the shipowner would have to bear what could be an appreciable loss. This difficulty was exacerbated by a case in 1835 that established liability for collision damage to another ship was not a "peril of the sea" and therefore was not covered in the standard form of marine insurance policy;[11] as a result of this decision, a standard clause called the "running-down clause" was developed and attached to the policy. For an additional premium, cover was provided for three-quarters of collision liability toward another ship and its cargo. The remaining one-quarter liability was excluded, presumably to encourage shipping interests to take due precautions against collision. Even so, this clause was not immediately adopted into general use, since many underwriters feared that this protection would result in carelessness on the part of masters and owners and cause an increasing number of collisions. In fact, in 1854, Lloyd's unsuccessfully lobbied for legislation prohibiting the insurance of collision liability.

These developments created considerable concern among shipowners, who felt that they needed coverage designed to protect them from the various third-party liabilities to which they were now exposed. In 1855 this concern resulted in the founding of the first mutual protection club, the Shipowners' Mutual Protection Society.[12] In common with the other protection societies that were established in response to the *Merchant Shipping Act* of 1854, the Shipowners' Mutual Protection Society was a descendant of one of the early hull clubs. The original rules of the society provided cover only for liability in respect of death

---

10 *Merchant Shipping Act, 1854* (U.K.), 17 & 18 Vict., c.104.
11 *de Vaux v. Salvador* (1836), 111 E.R. 845.
12 Now the Britannia Steam Ship Insurance Association Limited, one of the principal U.K. P&I clubs.

and personal injury claims, for the one-quarter collision liability not covered by the hull insurers and for excess collision liability, that is, the liability for collision claims in excess of the sums insured under the hull policy.[13]

At first, these new mutual clubs were described simply as "protecting" societies. The class of risks to which the term "indemnity" would apply had yet to be developed and accepted. However, in 1870, the sinking of The Westenhope resulted in a case that would be another important landmark in the history of protection and indemnity insurance.[14] The vessel in the case was carrying a cargo bound for Cape Town, but instead of proceeding directly, the ship diverted to Port Elizabeth, where some additional cargo was loaded. However, the vessel was later lost *en route* to Cape Town. Without deviation, its owners would have avoided any liability for the cargo, by virtue of the extensive exclusion clauses in the contract of carriage. However, the court held that the deviation to Port Elizabeth prevented the shipowners from relying on their exclusion clauses and that they were, therefore, liable for the loss of the cargo. At that time cargo liability was not covered by the protecting societies, as shipowners were usually able to rely on exclusion clauses to escape responsibility for any cargo loss or damage. This case showed clearly that this form of defence was not infallible. Accordingly, in 1874, the first indemnity club was formed to provide cover for liability for loss of or damage to cargo, then known as an indemnity risk. The protecting societies amended their rules so that they also provided indemnity cover, and thereby became protection and indemnity (P&I) clubs.[15]

In 1893 the need for insurance cover for cargo liability was further reinforced by the introduction, in 1893, of the U.S. *Harter Act*,[16] which restricted the right of shipowners to rely on exclusion clauses in their bills of lading and required them to exercise due diligence to make their

---

13 S. Hazelwood, *P&I Clubs: Law and Practice*, 3d ed. (London: Lloyd's Press, 2000) at 6–8.
14 *Westenhope (The)* (1870) [unreported]. Cited in M. Mustill & J.C.B. Gilman, eds., *Arnould's Law of Marine Insurance and Average*, 16th ed. (London: Stevens, 1981) vol.1 at 186.
15 The Westenhope was entered with the North of England Protection Association, which denied indemnity to the shipowner for the cargo liability, as this risk had not been contemplated in the club's rules. As a result, the shipowners entered with the North of England Protection Association supported the creation of a cover to indemnify members against this form of risk and the term "indemnity" was adopted. See Hazelwood, *P&I Clubs*, above note 13 at 7.
16 46 U.S.C. §§190–95 (1893).

ships seaworthy. The *Hague Rules*,[17] widely adopted in 1924, extended these principles throughout the world. At about this time the various P&I clubs also began to offer defence cover, as club managers perceived the need to provide shipowners not only with insurance for legal costs but also to provide advisory and claims handling service for all P&I and many non-P&I matters. While the P&I clubs were evolving in England, similar developments were taking place in Scandinavia.[18]

7) U.K. *Marine Insurance Act, 1906*

The first English statute dealing with marine insurance was enacted in 1601. The next statute, passed in 1745,[19] prohibited the making of policies of marine insurance on subject-matters in which the insured had no interest. Before this Act, proof of insurable interest was not necessary in England as "the policy was considered to be the proof of interest." Various other acts, dealing primarily with formalities of policy and penalties of fraudulent claims, were enacted from 1748 to 1803.[20] It was not until the close of the nineteenth century that any serious attempt was made to codify the law relating to marine insurance. There had been relatively little litigation on marine insurance matters in the previous century-and-a-half; however, it became evident to the shipping community that, in order to promote the smoother working of marine insurance, something needed to be done. Primarily due to the efforts of a Birmingham County Court judge, Sir M.D. Chalmers, in collaboration with a practising underwriter, Sir Douglas Owen, the Marine Insurance Codification Bill was introduced in the House of Lords in 1894. Eventually an amended version of the Bill was passed as *An Act to Codify the Law Relating to Marine Insurance*.[21] The *Marine Insurance Act, 1906*,[22] as it is more commonly known, did not remodel existing law relating to marine insurance but merely codified previous decisions and customary practice. It did, however, alter the pre-existing law in a number of aspects. The Act approved, although it did not compel, the use of the Lloyd's S.G. Form of Policy that was printed, together with the Rules of Construction, as the First Schedule to the Statute. This is perhaps explained by the fact that the S.G. Form has

---

17 See Chapter 9, "Carriage of Goods under Bills of Lading and Similar Documents."
18 Gold, *Gard Handbook*, above note 8 at 68ff.
19 *Marine Insurance Act, 1745* (U.K.), 19 Geo. II., c.37.
20 Dover, *A Handbook to Marine Insurance*, above note 1 at 46–51.
21 *Ibid.*
22 (U.K.), 6 Edw. VII., c.41. See E.R. Hardy Ivamy, *Chalmers' Marine Insurance Act 1906*, 9th ed. (London: Butterworths, 1983) for a complete annotation of the Act.

"generations of legal interpretations hanging almost to every word, and almost certainly to every sentence."[23] Without question this Act had a profound influence on marine insurance legislation in all parts of the Commonwealth and elsewhere.

8) Canadian Provincial Statutes

British marine insurance law, as set out in the *Marine Insurance Act, 1906*, also formed the basis of all Canadian provincial and federal marine insurance legislation. This Act also had a significant influence on the development of U.S. marine insurance law.[24] In Canada, the U.K. Act was incorporated almost verbatim into the marine insurance acts in British Columbia,[25] Manitoba,[26] New Brunswick,[27] Nova Scotia,[28] and Ontario.[29] In Saskatchewan, Alberta, Newfoundland, and Prince Edward Island, marine insurance contracts have been regulated under common law principles or general insurance legislation. Quebec marine insurance law is based on the *Civil Code of Quebec*.[30] Other provinces have specifically defined marine insurance provisions in their insurance statutes,[31] while still other provinces and territories have specifically excluded marine insurance contracts from their insurance legislation.[32] However, as discussed further below, Canadian provincial and territorial marine insurance legislation is no longer applicable, as the subject has moved firmly into federal jurisdiction.[33] In other words, provincial and territo-

---

23 Dover, *A Handbook to Marine Insurance*, above note 1 at 50. While the S.G. Form has also been criticized, Sir Douglas Owen has observed that "if such a contract were to be drawn up for the first time today it would be put down as the work of a lunatic endowed with a private sense of humour" (cited by Dover, at 50).
24 N.J. Healy & D.J. Sharpe, *Cases and Materials on Admiralty*, 2d ed. (St. Paul, MN: West Publishing, 1994) at 792–93.
25 *Insurance (Marine) Act*, R.S.B.C. 1996, c.230.
26 *Marine Insurance Act*, R.S.M. 1987, c.M-40.
27 *Marine Insurance Act*, R.S.N.B. 1973, c.M-1.
28 *Insurance Act*, R.S.N.S. 1989, c.231.
29 *Marine Insurance Act*, R.S.O. 1990 c.M-2. See also R.M. Fernandes, *Marine Insurance Law in Canada* (Toronto: Butterworths, 1987), which provides a full, although now dated, annotation of the Ontario legislation, as well as an excellent outline of Canadian marine insurance law generally.
30 S.Q. 1991, c.64, arts.2505–628 C.C.Q. (1991).
31 Saskatchewan: *Saskatchewan Insurance Act*, R.S.S. 1978, c.S-26; Alberta: *Insurance Act*, R.S.A. 1980, c.I-5; Prince Edward Island: *Insurance Act*, R.S.P.E.I. 1988, c.I-4.
32 Yukon: *Insurance Act*, R.S.Y. 1986, c.91; Northwest Territories: *Insurance Act*, R.S.N.W.T. 1988, c.I-4; Newfoundland: *Insurance Act*, R.S.N. 1990, c.I-12.
33 For a detailed discussion of this aspect see Chapter 3, "Admiralty Jurisdiction," especially section E.

rial marine insurance law is no longer in effect and the cases involving such legislation are only of interest in terms of applying the provisions of Canadian federal legislation.

9) Canadian *Marine Insurance Act, 1993*

By the mid–1980s it was widely felt that marine insurance law in Canada needed not only to be unified but that it should also be subject to a federal statute. This was, to a great extent, owing to decisions by the Supreme Court of Canada holding that marine insurance was basically a federal responsibility.[34] During the discussions to develop a federal marine insurance statute, the federal government initially resisted any attempt at developing such legislation with the 1906 U.K. Act as a base. However, after further discussions between the government and the Canadian Board of Marine Underwriters, the Canadian Maritime Law Association, and other interested parties, it was decided that the 1906 U.K. Act, which had already been so widely used in most Canadian jurisdictions, should again be used as a basis for the new federal Act. In the drafting of the new Act, several minor changes to the 1906 model were made, basically involving the rearrangement and consolidation of some sections as well as the modernization of certain archaic expressions. The resulting Canadian *Marine Insurance Act*[35] entered into force in 1993. While the various provincial and territorial statutes are, in theory, still in force,[36] the new statute is now the pre-eminent expression of statutory marine insurance law in Canada; provincial and territorial marine insurance legislation has become redundant. This was further firmly confirmed when the Supreme Court in 1998 sum-

---

34 *Triglav v. Terrasses Jewellers Inc.*, [1983] 1 S.C.R. 283; *ITO International Terminal Operators Ltd. v. Miida Electronics Inc., (The Buenos Aires Maru)*, [1986] 1 S.C.R. 752. Although the law of agency is not maritime law. See *Intermunicipality Realty & Development Corp. v. Gore Mutual Insurance Co.*, [1978] 2 F.C. 691. See also W. Tetley, "Marine Insurance and the Conflict of Laws" (1994) 4 C.I.L.R. 301 at 309; M. Turcotte "Federal Court and Marine Insurance" (1983) 1 Can. J. Ins. L. 25; W. Tetley, "A Definition of Canadian Maritime Law" (1996) 30 U.B.C. L.Rev. 137. See also Chapter 3, "Admiralty Jurisdiction" for a wide-ranging discussion of these developments.

35 S.C. 1993, c.22.

36 See Tetley, "Marine Insurance and the Conflict of Laws," above note 34; A. Braën, "Questions de compétence; la compétence législative en matière d'assurance maritime; la compétence en amirauté de la cour provinciale" (1985) 16 R. Gen. 195. See also *Sunrise Co. v. Lake Winnipeg (The)* (1987), 12 F.T.R. 57; and *Monk Corp. v. Island Fertilizers Ltd.*, [1991] 1 S.C.R. 779.

marized basic principles of Canadian maritime law.[37] In addition, the Supreme Court also set out a four-step process that would test any situation where provincial or territorial legislation is to be applied.[38] It is unlikely that any Canadian provincial or territorial marine insurance legislation could survive this test.

Nevertheless, the large body of case law developed in Canada under the 1906 U.K. Act and its various Canadian provincial and territorial equivalents is still valid. As these statutes, as well as the Canadian *Marine Insurance Act, 1993*, all have different section numbers, care has to be taken when reading cases that refer specifically to marine insurance legislation. As a result, it may be necessary to consult a table of concordance setting out the equivalent section numbers of the various acts (see Annex to this chapter).

B. BASIC PRINCIPLES AND FEATURES

1) Definitions and Terminology

The parties, or "principals," to a marine insurance contract are the "insured" or "assured," and the "insurer" or "underwriter." If the insurer is a company, then the employee of that company who is authorized to bind the company on insurance risks is known as the underwriter. It is usual for a deputy underwriter to be appointed with full authority to act in the absence of the underwriter. The term "risk" in marine insurance is most frequently used to signify the whole insurance proposition, rather than in its special sense of "peril" or "hazard" that may be more specifically defined in the policy. When an application is made through a broker[39] to an insurer and the risk is accepted, it is generally "placed" in one of the major insurance "markets."[40]

The Canadian *Marine Insurance Act, 1993*, provides the following definition of marine insurance: "A contract of marine insurance is a contract whereby the insurer undertakes to indemnify the assured, in manner and to the extent thereby agreed, against marine losses, that is to say, the losses incident to a marine adventure."[41] In other words, a

---

37 *Ordon Estate v. Grail*, [1998] 3 S.C.R. 437.
38 *Ibid.*, paras.73ff. See also E in Chapter 3, "Admiralty Jurisdiction."
39 See below, B(4) "Brokers and Managing General Agents."
40 See Dover, *A Handbook to Marine Insurance*, above note 1 at c.11. For an excellent explanation of market practice, see *Edinburgh Assurance v. R.L. Burns*, 1980 A.M.C. 1261 at 1269 (D.C. Cal. 1979).
41 Above note 35, c.22, s.6(1). See also concordance in the Annex to this chapter.

contract of insurance protecting the insured against liabilities or losses arising out of a marine adventure will be deemed to be a contract of marine insurance. The Act stipulates that a "marine adventure" exists when the ship or the goods are exposed to maritime perils that are defined as follows: "'Maritime perils' means the perils consequent on, or incidental to the navigation of the sea, that is to say, perils of the seas, fire, war perils, pirates, rovers, thieves, captures, seizures, restraints and detainments of princes and people, jettisons, barratry and any other perils, either of the like kind or which may be designated by the policy."[42] Like all insurance contracts, a marine insurance contract is set out in the form of a marine insurance policy that contains the agreement between insurers and insured, and is construed by the ordinary principles of contract law. In other words, like all commercial documents, marine insurance policies are to be construed to give effect of the intention of the parties. In the first place, this intention is provided by the words in the policy, interpreted, if necessary, by additional or special circumstances. Other rules of construction may also have a bearing on the interpretation of the policy; for example, if the policy contains additional printed and written language, greater weight will, generally, be accorded to such added clauses as have been specifically inserted. While technical terms may have an ordinary meaning, evidence can be introduced to show that they have a different or special meaning in the insurance industry. Also geographical terms are considered to have been used in their commercial sense as understood by shipowners, shippers, and insurers generally. If ambiguities are found in the insurance contract, the language of the policy is construed against the individual who drafted it.[43]

2) Distinctive Features

Marine insurance is divided into two main categories: in the first the subject of insurance is the cargo, being carried in whole or in part by sea, and in the second, the subject of insurance is the ship itself. Protection and indemnity (P&I) insurance belongs to the latter category. There are some features of marine insurance that distinguish it from other types of non-life insurance: for example, P&I insurance covers the liabilities arising out of the operations of an ocean going vessel that may trade worldwide. The insurer is exposed to liabilities and losses

---

42 Ibid., s.2(1).
43 A.L. Parks, *The Law and Practice of Marine Insurance and Average*, 2d ed. (Centreville, MD: Cornell Maritime Press, 1987) c.VIII.

arising out of many different incidents and subject to a wide range of different jurisdictions and rules of law. As a result, marine insurance is closely connected to international maritime law. It follows that solid knowledge about foreign legal regimes and international rules and conventions, governing the shipowner's liability, as well as the management and operation of the ship in general, is of crucial importance for the insurer's risk and claims assessment. The role played by the insurance industry in the development of maritime law has always been most important, owing to the fact that maritime law appears to react to shipping disasters that provoke discussion about the state and adequacy of the law, and to the need for legal reform. One of the earliest examples of this process was The Titanic disaster that led directly to the development of the first safety of life at sea convention (*SOLAS 1974*).[44] Since then, there have been many similar examples, where a major maritime incident leads to new international legislation. Support from the insurance industry, especially P&I insurers, has been instrumental in the development of such new legislation, particularly in terms of liability coverage. For instance, the flooding and capsize of the Ro-Ro ferry Herald of Free Enterprise off Zeebrugge, Belgium, in March 1987, resulting in the loss of almost two hundred lives,[45] led to initiatives[46] that almost tripled the compensation payable to passengers.[47] The *International Convention on Civil Liability for Oil Pollution Damage, 1969* (*CLC 1969*)[48] resulted directly out of the grounding of the tanker Torrey Canyon near

---

44 The most recent *SOLAS* convention is the *International Convention on the Safety of Life at Sea, 1974*, 1 November 1974, 1184 U.N.T.S. 2 [*SOLAS 1974*]. See also Institute of Maritime Law, *Ratification of Maritime Conventions*, 4 vols., Updated looseleaf service (London: Lloyd's Press, 1991–2003) vol.I.3.20. For greater detail on *SOLAS 1974*, see Chapter 2, "The Shipping Industry: An Overview," and Chapter 5, "The Safety Management of Ships."

45 See S.Crainer, *Zeebrugge: Learning from Disaster* (London: Herald Charitable Trust, 1993).

46 Protocol to the Athens Convention Relating to the Carriage of Passengers and their Luggage by Sea, 1974, 29 March 1990, U.K.T.S. 1989, No. 43 [PAL Prot 1990] (not yet in force, but applied in Canadian legislation). See also *Ratification of Maritime Conventions*, above note 44, vol.I.5.201. See also Chapter 10, "Carriage of Passengers," and Chapter 12, "Maritime Personal Injury and Death."

47 Athens Convention Relating to the Carriage of Passengers and their Luggage by Sea, 1974, 13 December 1974, 14 I.L.M. 945 [PAL 1974] (entered into force on 28 April 1987; applied in Canada by legislation). See also *Ratification of Maritime Conventions*, above note 44, vol.I.5.190. See also Chapter 10, "Carriage of Passengers" and Chapter 12, "Maritime Personal Injury and Death."

48 29 November 1969, 973 U.N.T.S. 3. See also *Ratification of Maritime Conventions*, above note 44, vol.I.7.30. For more details see Chapter 17, "Marine Pollution Prevention."

the U.K. coast in March 1967.[49] In other words, without the full participation and commitment of the maritime underwriting community, most of the liability regimes developed in the last century would not have been created, nor would they function as well as they do.

Another special feature of marine insurance is that a major part of the business is underwritten through the three principal markets in London, Scandinavia, and France. There are a number of smaller markets in the United States, Germany, Italy, Japan, and Russia. The U.S. market is particularly strong in the cargo insurance area. Canada is a very minor player providing mostly branch plant services for the major markets.[50] As a result of this market concentration, a limited but widely accepted number of standard terms and conditions has been developed. The best-known examples are the *London Institute Clauses*.[51] In addition, the various P&I underwriters' rules are built on the basis of a common platform for the scope of the cover, namely the Pooling Agreement that constitutes the legal basis for the P&I clubs' claims-sharing arrangement and collective purchasing of market reinsurance. While individual club's rules may differ in layout, the material contents are, to a large extent, similar in terms of the types of liabilities and losses falling within the cover. Finally, another feature of marine insurance is that it is normally subject to specific legislation. The marine insurance industry is international in scope, with most of the major interested parties operating on a global basis. As a result of the similarity of the standard insurance product offered, competition among the various insurers mainly focuses on premium price and service to customers and members, rather than on the terms and conditions determining the scope of the various covers. With P&I insurance, there is also a certain amount of restraint on competition in terms of "premium rating," the term used by the mutual clubs when a ship is transferred from one club to another.[52]

---

49 E. Gold, *Gard Handbook on Marine Pollution*, 2d ed. (Arendal: Gard, 1998) at 31–32. See Chapter 17, "Marine Pollution Prevention." *CLC 1969* changed the traditional damage liability base from one of proven fault or negligence to one of strict liability. Besides increasing the shipowner's liability, it also introduced a system of certification making insurance compulsory.

50 Canadian marine underwriters have also established a small niche market in the area of insurance for Arctic navigational risks. See K.J. Spears, "Arctic Marine Risks: The Interaction of Marine Insurance and Arctic Shipping" (Halifax, NS: International Institute for Transportation and Ocean Policy Studies, 1986).

51 See below D(3), p. 332.

52 Gold, *Gard Handbook*, above note 8 at 136. See also Chapter 2, "The Shipping Industry: An Overview."

3) Different Types of Marine Insurance

A shipowner requires at least three different types of insurance. First, there should be protection against loss of or damage to the shipowner's property — generally the ship and its equipment. Second, there is a requirement for coverage for financial compensation in the event of loss of income if the vessel is unemployed over a longer period of time as a result of a casualty. Third, there should be coverage for third-party liabilities arising out of the operation of the ship. The latter is described as the protection and indemnity (P&I) cover. On the other hand, the owner of a cargo transported by sea will require marine insurance coverage for loss of or damage to the cargo.[53] Such cover may also be extended for other risks, such as contributions in general average[54] and salvage[55] that may arise during the carriage of the cargo. Cover may be provided under various commercial arrangements, for instance, door-to-door, port-to-port, transshipment, on-deck stowage, containerized, special handling, bulk commodities, and dangerous goods. Other risk covers are also taken out in order to protect possible gaps between the standard insurance covers available in the market or other special needs. Such insurance can either be specially designed for the individual owner, or can be a standard product available in the market, covering specific requirements for a particular trade or group of owners. An example of the latter is the special guarantee facilities established to assist tanker owners, trading to the United States, in obtaining Certificates of Financial Responsibility as required under the U.S. *Oil Pollution Act, 1990*.[56]

a) Hull and Machinery Insurance[57]

The subject of the hull and machinery insurance is the ship itself. Coverage for risks that arise will be provided by hull and machinery underwriters and/or insurance companies. Given the large variety of ships in

---

53 For an extensive examination of the maritime claims area, see W. Tetley, *Maritime Liens and Claims* (Cowansville, QB: Yvon Blais, 1998).
54 See Chapter 16, "General Average."
55 See Chapter 15, "Maritime Salvage and Wreck."
56 33 U.S.C. §§2701–2761 (1990). See also Chapter 17 "Marine Pollution Prevention."
57 The leading English texts in this area are Arnould, *Marine Insurance and Average*, above note 14; E.R. Hardy-Ivamy, *Marine Insurance*, 4th ed. (London: Butterworths, 1985); R.J. Lambeth, ed., *Templeman on Marine Insurance: Its Principles and Practice*, 6th ed. (London: Pitman, 1986); Dover, *A Handbook to Marine Insurance*, above note 1; and O'May, above note 1. The principal U.S. texts are A.L. Parks, *The Law and Practice of Marine Insurance and Average* (Centreville, MD: Cornell Maritime Press, 1987); L.J. Buglass, *Marine Insurance and General Average in the United States* (Cambridge, MD: Cornell Maritime Press, 1973);

operation globally, ranging from large tankers, container vessels, and cruise ships, to fishing boats, pleasure craft, and tugs, the hull and machinery insurance business has also become equally diverse and specialized. In other words, there are specific marine underwriting markets for each type of vessel, the trade the vessel is engaged in, and often also the type of cargo carried.[58]

The term "ship" comprises both the hull and the machinery, including equipment, spare parts, bunkers, and lubrication oil. Supplies and other engine and deck materials intended for consumption are normally excluded. A prerequisite for covering equipment and spare parts under the ship's hull and machinery policy is that the items are on board the ship. The term "on board" means that the object in question must be on board for an indefinite or prolonged period of time; for example, an object, such as a fork lift truck, that has been brought on board to be used during loading or discharging, will not be covered by the hull and machinery insurance while it is on board.

Traditionally, hull and machinery insurance covers three different types of losses: total loss of the ship, damage to the ship, and the owner's liability for damage to another ship as a result of a collision. The term "total loss" comprises three different eventualities: actual total loss of the ship, constructive total loss of the ship, and a missing or abandoned ship.[59] Actual total loss includes both actual loss of the ship and so-called "unrepairability."[60] There will, of course, be a gradual transition from an absolute loss of the ship, for example, where it has foundered in such deep water that it is impossible to reach, to cases where it is a question of economic assessment whether to undertake salvage and repair work. In this context, "repairs" mean operations that will restore the ship to its state prior to the damage.

Constructive total loss[61] entitles the owner to claim compensation for total loss of the vessel if conditions for condemnation are met. In other words, such conditions require that the costs of repairing the ship will amount to at least 80 per cent of the insured value or the value of

---

Healy & Sharpe, above note 24, c.XI; and T.J. Schoenbaum, *Admiralty and Maritime Law*, 3d ed. (St. Paul, MN: West Publishing, 2001) c.13. The most recent Canadian text is: G..R. Strathy & G.C. Moore, *Law & Practice of Marine Insurance in Canada* (Toronto: LexisNexis Butterworths, 2003).

58 See Chapter 2, "The Shipping Industry: An Overview."
59 *Phoenix Insurance v. McGhee* (1890), 18 S.C.R. 61. *Nova Scotia Marine Insurance Co. v. L.P. Churchill & Co.* (1896), 26 S.C.R. 65.
60 *Anchor Marine Insurance v. Keith* (1884), 9 S.C.R. 483. *Gallagher v. Taylor* (1881), 5 S.C.R. 368.
61 *Marine Insurance Act, 1993*, above note 35, s.57.

the ship after repairs. If the insured value is less than the value after repairs, the latter shall be used in determining whether or not the ship shall be treated as a constructive total loss.[62] However, in general, in constructive total loss cases, notice of abandonment is usually required.[63] A shipowner can also claim compensation for a total loss if the ship has been reported missing, after a certain period of time has elapsed from the date on which the ship was expected to arrive at a port.[64] Likewise the owner may claim total loss if the ship has been abandoned by the crew, without its subsequent destiny being known, when a certain period of time has elapsed from the date of the abandonment.

In this connection, the term "damage" refers to cases where the ship, as a result of an incident, has suffered damage but is not a total loss under the applicable rules.[65] As a starting point, the owner is entitled — subject to the applicable deductible — to be compensated for the costs of repairing the damage in such a manner that the ship is restored to the condition it was in prior to the occurrence of the damage.[66] However, there are some qualifications; for example, the assured must accept that damaged parts of the ship are repaired rather than replaced with new parts. Another established principle is that only the actual damage will be repaired. Thus, an owner has no automatic right to claim compensation for unrepaired damage, unless the ship has been sold in the meantime or ownership has otherwise been transferred to a third party.

Finally, hull and machinery insurance can also cover the owner's liability arising from collision or striking by the ship. While there has been a limited trend under which P&I insurance assumes the entire collision liability, most shipowners still choose to be covered for collision liability by hull and machinery underwriters. However, in the case of a collision, even if the hull and machinery insurer covers collision liability, there is still need for P&I insurance, primarily because the hull and machinery collision cover is narrower in scope than P&I cover. For example, hull and machinery insurance does not cover the

---

62 *Irvin v. Hine*, [1950] 1 K.B. 555, 83 Ll. L.R. 162; *Rodocanachi v. Elliott* (1874), L.R. 9 C.P. 518, 43 L.J.C.P. 255; *Bamburi (The) v. Compton*, [1982] Com. L.R. 31, [1982] 1 Lloyd's L.R. 312.

63 *Phoenix Insurance*, above note 59. See also *Rose v. Weekes* (1984), 7 C.C.L.I. 287 (F.C.T.D.); *Providence Washington Insurance v. Corbett* (1884), 9 S.C.R. 256.
Under the *Marine Insurance Act, 1993*, above note 35, s.59, in an actual total loss the insured does not have to give notice of abandonment.

64 *Marine Insurance Act ,1993*, above note 35, s.56.

65 *Ibid.*, ss.54–55 and 61–62.

66 *Gerow v. British American Assurance Co.* (1889), 16 S.C.R. 524.

shipowner's liability for any pollution or personal injury claims that might arise from the collision. Second, the hull and machinery insurer's liability is limited to the sum insured and set out in the contract of insurance. Such sum will, in practice, only be the assessed insurable value of the ship.

b) **Loss of Hire**
Loss of hire insurance covers the insured shipowner's loss of income as a result of the ship being off hire or otherwise suffering a loss of operational time for a period of time.[67] This is a relatively new type of cover, as the first insurance contracts for this type of risk were entered into only after the end of the Second World War.[68] Originally, this type of insurance was designed for ships on time charterparties[69] but has since evolved and may now cover the shipowner's loss of income, regardless of the nature of the ship's employment. Loss of hire insurance is, in principle, similar to the type of insurance that is arranged by shore-based businesses covering loss of use or loss of income.

Although loss of hire insurance covers the insured owner's loss of income as a result of the ship being off hire, or otherwise suffering a loss of time, not all such situations will fall within the cover. Coverage is restricted to loss of hire as a result of damage to the ship, which is recoverable under the vessel's hull and machinery policy. For example, the loss of hire insurance will compensate the owner's loss of income during the period of repair for hull damage following a collision with another ship. On the other hand, an off-hire period under a time charterparty, resulting from ordinary maintenance work, will not be compensated. A claim against the loss of hire insurer has to be calculated on the basis of the time during which the ship has been deprived of income. The loss of time is a key factor in the calculation, and certain principles have been developed depending on whether the ship is on a time or a voyage charter. In the case of time charterparties, the starting point is the period the vessel is off hire under the terms of the charter. Under a voyage charterparty, the calculation of the loss of time becomes more complicated, because the freight is not directly linked to the time taken to complete the voyage. As a general rule, the loss of time will normally be deemed to be the increase in time needed to complete the voyage the vessel was performing at the time of the casualty. This will

---

67 See, e.g., H.S. Lund, J. Heimset, & T. Eilertsen, *Handbook on Loss of Hire Insurance* (Bergen: Bergen Hull Club, 1999).
68 Gold, *Gard Handbook*, above note 8 at 79–80.
69 See Chapter 8, "Carriage of Goods by Charterparty."

include repair time and time lost during deviation to the port of refuge or the repair facility.

The owner's daily loss of income has to be calculated either on the basis of a fixed amount, if such an amount is stated in the contract of insurance. Otherwise the calculation will be based on the amount of freight or hire payable under the ship's current contract of employment, less any savings owing to the vessel being out of regular service. The insurer's overall liability for loss of time arising out of any one casualty is normally limited to a fixed daily amount multiplied by a certain number of days. Recovery under a loss of hire insurance will also be subject to a deductible period amounting to a certain number of days.

c) Protection and Indemnity Insurance

Protection and indemnity (P&I) insurance has been developed over the last 150 years in response to the need by shipowners for insurance cover for third-party liabilities that were not recoverable under the standard hull and machinery policies.[70] The original purpose of P&I insurance was to protect shipowners against liability in respect of personal injury and death, one-quarter collision liability not covered by hull and machinery insurance and/or mutual hull clubs, and excess collision liability, that is, the liability in excess of the sum insured in the hull policy. However, the standard, modern P&I policy includes coverage for a very wide range of liabilities and losses that a shipowner may incur including the following: liabilities arising from the carriage of cargo; marine pollution liability; liability for loss of life and injury to crew members, passengers, and others, such as stevedores; liability for damage to fixed or floating objects; and liability arising out of a collision with another ship. The operational aspects of P&I cover are discussed more extensively below.

d) Defence Cover

Defence cover belongs in the category of "standard additional covers." The defence cover — or Freight, Demurrage, and Defence cover, as is its official name — offers the owner insurance against legal and other costs incurred in connection with certain types of disputes arising out of the operation of the ship. An important element of this cover is the service and expertise offered by the relevant P&I club, through its in-house team of lawyers, who handle defence cases on a daily basis, and the service offered by the club's correspondents around the world (discussed below).

---

70 Hazelwood, *P&I Clubs*, above note 13; Gold, *Gard Handbook*, above note 8, Part II.

e) War-Risk Insurance

The term "marine insurance" includes both marine perils and war-risk perils; however, it is usual to distinguish between these perils when describing the covers available. In English practice, war perils are excluded from the ordinary marine cover on hull and machinery and for loss of hire, as well as from the standard P&I cover, by the so-called "war-risks" exclusion clause. There are two reasons for the distinction between standard marine and war perils: first, different insurers usually underwrite the two perils; and second, there is also a different scope of the cover as such, that is, the types of liabilities and losses that fall within the various cover.[71] War-risk insurance is a very specialized area and the number of underwriters willing to undertake such insurance is quite limited. A few such underwriters are based in the London market with even fewer in other markets. While the number of leaders offering this type of cover is small, the capacity to provide insurance is quite significant. Shipowners in several states have also formed mutual war risk associations. Most of these associations are controlled by shipowners that utilize specific national flags; reinsurance, however, is usually arranged in the London market.[72]

The shipowner's basic insurance needs will normally be covered by three different types of insurance: hull and machinery, loss of hire, and P&I insurance. Insurance against war risks is quite different, however; for example, the war-risks insurance covers hull and machinery, loss of hire, protection and indemnity, and occupational injury. Cargo insurance is usually not covered for this risk, although special cover may be obtained in some cases.[73] Coverage for war risks under most cargo policies is usually extended by the incorporation of the *Institute War Clauses*[74] in the policy at current additional premiums. In addition to the standard hull and machinery-type losses, war-risks insurance will also compensate the owner for the total loss of the ship, if he or she has been deprived of the ship by the intervention of a foreign state power. Furthermore, the loss of hire element will also include loss of time, if the ship is forced into a port by a foreign state power for the purpose of capture or temporary detention, regardless of whether there is physical damage to the ship. Finally, the war-risk cover includes coverage for liabilities and expenses that would have been covered under the ship's nor-

---

71   For a full explanation on this subject, see M.D. Miller, *Marine War Risk Insurance* (London: Lloyd's Press, 1990).
72   Gold, *Gard Handbook*, above note 8 at 81ff.
73   Hardy Ivamy, above note 22 at 219.
74   *Ibid.* at 219–24.

mal P&I insurance, if the event had not been caused by a war risk; for example, if a shipowner has been held liable for oil pollution damage caused by a war peril, such as a Second World War mine, it will be covered by the war-risk underwriter. Some market differences should be noted, as, for example, the London market does not cover requisition of the ship by a foreign state power. There are also some differences in the types of liabilities and losses that fall within the cover. The most important difference is that the standard London terms do not include P&I liabilities. This means that separate war-risk P&I insurance has to be obtained; it can normally be arranged through the owner's P&I club.

A special feature of the war-risk cover is the right of the insurer to suspend the cover under certain, critical circumstances; for example, an outbreak of war between major global powers could result in the total cancellation of such insurance. Furthermore, a war-risks underwriter has the discretion and is entitled to change the trading limits set out in the policy at any time. It should be noted that there is a distinction between "excluded areas" and "conditional areas": in an excluded area the ship will be without cover, while in a conditional area the ship will be covered against payment of an additional premium. The war-risk cover is also subject to an upper limit that will normally be the agreed insurable value of the ship. Another aspect of war risk cover relates to coverage for terrorism risks that has become especially important in the aftermath of the events of 11 September 2001 in the United States. This is now a special war-risks P&I cover that is underwritten by the relevant P&I insurer.

f) Cargo Insurance

The marine insurance of cargoes transported at sea is one of the major sectors of the global insurance market. In many cases a marine insurance policy may cover the risks related to a single valuable item, such as a ship or a large bulk shipment. However, as global trading still involves sea carriage for many individual shipments, a general cargo vessel or a container ship may have literally thousands of such items on board, all carried under specific cargo policies. Furthermore, as the ownership interest in such cargo may change a number of times during the carriage, there may be a number of assignments of policies and new policies during this period. In general, cargo will be insured under standard cargo policies that will also be claused as required, using the *Institute Cargo Clauses* system (outlined below). There will be specific policy coverage for different cargoes, as developed for the various types of cargo that can be carried, such as coal and other bulk commodities, oil and other liquid cargoes, lumber, general cargo, containers, refrigerated and perishable cargoes, dangerous goods, and heavy lifts.[75] A regular exporter may have commercial requirements that are not easily satisfied by negotiating individual risk coverage on each consignment. Instead, there may be a requirement to arrange insurance that could cover a variety of different cargoes over a longer period. Freight-forwarders, who may offer marine insurance coverage as part of their services, may require similar flexibility. As a result, in addition to the standard S.G. Form of Policy, insurers also offer an open or floating policy[76] for a fixed sum with the subject-matter only described in very general terms. As cargo is consigned, a declaration[77] is made under the policy and a certificate is issued. Floating cargo policies are most frequently governed by the London marine insurance market's *Institute Standard Conditions for Cargo Contracts* that set out the general conditions for the operation of the system.[78]

g) Other Market Cover

A number of other different covers is available in the marine insurance markets. Some are standard products, while others are specifically designed to meet individual shipowners' needs. For example, during recent years there has been an increasing demand for insurance covering contractual cargo liabilities beyond the restrictions laid down in P&I club rules that are based on the *Hague/Hague-Visby Rules* limits.[79] Special cover needs have also emerged in the cruise industry, such as the cruise ship operator's liability for passengers while on shore excursions from the ship, brought about by the extension of the operator's liability under the rules that have been implemented in most European countries.[80] While the various insurance products differ substantially in terms of the nature of the cover and the economic interests that are the subject of the insurance, most have one thing in common: they cover either gaps in the standard insurance products available in the market, or respond to individual owner's special needs.

---

75 See Chapter 2, "The Shipping Industry: An Overview;" Chapter 8, "Carriage of Goods by Charterparty;" and Chapter 9, "Carriage of Goods under Bills of Lading and Similar Documents."
76 *Marine Insurance Act ,1993*, above note 35, s.31.
77 See *General Marine Assurance Co. v. Ocean Marine Insurance Co.* (1899), 16 Qc. S.C. 170.
78 See R. Grime, *Shipping Law*, 2d ed. (London: Sweet & Maxwell, 1991) at 388; Hardy Ivamy, above note 22 at 45–46.
79 See C in Chapter 9, "Carriage of Goods under Bills of Lading and Similar Documents."
80 European Union Council Directive 90/314/EEC, "EU Directive on Package Travel, Package Holidays and Package Tours".

h) Reinsurance

Reinsurance is a system under which insurers cover their risk exposure on insurance policies they have issued or are about to issue.[81] It is not a system exclusive to marine insurance and can work in a number of different ways. For example, insurers may have reinsurance treaties under which they assign some of their risk and some of the premium received. This is a very specialized area of insurance law that cannot be discussed at any length in this book. There are a number of different types of reinsurance, such as Facultative Reinsurances, Excess of Loss Reinsurances, and Umbrella Cover. Alternatively, a specific risk can be wholly or partly reinsured. There are various ways this can operate. Insurers may only reinsure total losses and cover partial losses themselves.[82] In P&I insurance, the various P&I clubs carry a certain amount of risk exposure themselves. Larger risks are reinsured through the International Group of P&I Clubs, which also reinsure this individual club exposure. The reinsurance policy does not provide coverage for the original subject of insurance but, instead, covers the insurer's risk exposure on such a subject. In other words, the insured shipowner has no right to claim directly against the reinsurer. Almost all reinsurance policies state that it is "a reinsurance, subject to the same clauses and conditions as the original policy, and to pay as may be paid thereon."[83] This means that the reinsurer has the same payment obligation as the original insurer.[84] Even in cases where the original insurer becomes insolvent, the reinsurer is liable for the whole amount, as that would have been the obligation of the reinsured.[85]

4) Brokers and Managing General Agents

As marine insurance is a highly specialized business it requires expert knowledge. This is one of the reasons why an insurance broker is almost always engaged to negotiate with the insurers on behalf of the prospective insured. The other reason is that almost all marine insurers are unwilling to negotiate directly with a prospective client. Insurance brokers are compensated for their services by means of a deduction,

---

81 *Marine Insurance Act, 1993*, above note 35, s.14.
82 *General Accident Fire and Life Assurance Co. v. Tanter (The Zephyr)*, [1985] 2 Lloyd's L.R. 529 (C.A.).
83 N.J.J. Gaskell, C. Debattista & R.J. Swatton, *Chorley & Giles' Shipping Law*, 8th ed. (London: Pitman, 1987) at 538.
84 *Chippendale v. Holt* (1895), 1 Com. Cas. 197. See also Hardy Ivamy, above note 22 at 16ff.
85 *Re Eddystone Marine Insurance Co.*, [1892] 2 Ch. 423.

called "brokerage," from the gross premium payable to the insurer. In general the marine insurance broker is considered to be the agent of the insured, while the broker is directly liable to the insurer for the premium.[86] Brokers work closely with insurers, but they are primarily agents of the assured. This not only brings in the law of agency but may also cause complications.[87] In many cases, the insurance broker may take a leading role by devising the terms of the policy; arranging the insurance with the insurer; arranging reinsurance and, often, selling the whole package to insurers as well as insureds. This may, at times, lead to possible conflict of interest.[88] A broker acts as an agent on behalf of the broker's principal. This creates a number of legal rights and duties between such principal and third parties. The extent of a broker's power to act for his or her principal in this agency relationship is expressed in the broker's authority. For a marine insurance broker, this authority may be implied or express. In law, the implied authority is to carry out acts that are required by the main authority, that is, carrying out the business required by the marine insurance market.[89]

The marine insurance broker must carry out the instructions given by the principal and is considered to be absolutely liable if he or she fails to do this.[90] If he or she has doubts, the broker must refer to the principal for further instructions. This is today much easier than it was before the era of rapid communications when brokers often had to act without specific instructions.[91] Like any professional, the marine insurance broker is under a duty to use reasonable care in carrying out the duties that are appropriate to his or her profession. This means that the broker must arrange the insurance cover with all proper skill, ensure that all appropriate clauses are attached to the policy, and that the risk is properly described and valued. A broker who fails to carry out instructions properly or who, through negligence, fails to arrange the insurance cover required, will be liable for damages to the principal

---

86 *Marine Insurance Act, 1993*, above note 35, ss.47–49. See also A.B. Oland, "Ships Agents and Ships Brokers: The Authority Extended to them by their Principals" in *Maritime Law: Third International Conference* (Vancouver, BC, 1986) 11.1. See also P.T. Perkins, "Marine Insurance: The Legal Relationship between the Underwriter and the Broker in Canada" (1986) Meredith Lect. 361; *O'Keefe & Lynch v. Toronto Insurance and Vessel Agency*, [1926] 4 D.L.R. 477 (Ont. S.C.).
87 See *Anglo-African Merchants v. Bayley*, [1970] 1 Q.B. 311, [1969] 2 W.L.R. 686.
88 *Vesta v. Butcher*, [1989] 1 All E.R. 402.
89 Grime, above note 78 at 357.
90 *Ibid.* at 360.
91 See *Dickson & Co. v. Devitt* (1916), 21 Com. Cas. 291, 86 L.J. K.B. 315; and *The Zephyr*, above note 82.

who engaged him or her. The measure of damages will, generally, be the difference in value between the insurance that should have been arranged and that (if any) that was finally arranged.[92] It should also be noted that in Canada, where many of the principal maritime centres, such as Montreal, Halifax, and Vancouver, are located at great distances from the major marine insurance markets, such as London and New York, a system known as Managing General Agents has been developed. The agency is usually a highly credible and reputable insurance agency that is delegated responsibilities to handle significant underwriting and claims on behalf of underwriters. This system has worked extremely well in Canada[93] and has contributed greatly to the development of Canadian marine insurance practice.

C. MARINE INSURANCE DOCTRINES

There are a number of basic marine insurance doctrines[94] that must be considered, as they apply to all aspects of coverage.

1) Disclosure and Utmost Good Faith

Both parties to a marine insurance contract must observe utmost good faith, often expressed under its legal principle of *uberrimae fidei* (utmost good faith).[95] When a contract is being negotiated, the insurer must be able to make an informed decision about whether to accept the risk. It would be unworkable if the insurer were required to check and assess all the material facts involved in the proposed risk. Furthermore, there may be facts that are only known to the proposer or prospective insured. Accordingly, the proposer is under a legal duty to disclose and represent all facts that are material to the proposed risk. On the other hand, the prospective insurer must also act in good faith, as was stated almost 250 years ago: "good faith forbids either party, by concealing what he privately knows, to draw the other into a bargain from his ignorance of that fact, and from his believing to the contrary."[96] In other words, in making a full disclosure, the proposer must ensure that

---

92 See also *Vesta v. Butcher*, above note 88.
93 As well as in the U.S., where it is also widely utilized.
94 See Gold, *Gard Handbook*, above note 8 at 172ff.
95 *Marine Insurance Act, 1993*, above note 35, s.20.
96 Lord Mansfield in *Carter v. Boehm* (1766), 3 Burr. 1905.

what is proposed to the insurer is true and correct.[97] This includes every material representation made during the negotiation. If there is evidence that such a representation is untrue, the insurer has the option to avoid the contract.[98] A material representation is one that would influence the judgment of a prudent insurer in fixing the premium or in determining whether the risk shall be taken.[99] However, the proposer need not disclose circumstances that diminish the risk or factors that are known or ought to be known by the insurer.[100] Furthermore, the duty to prove the materiality of any undisclosed information lies with the insurer.[101]

Disclosure problems continue to be the subject of frequent litigation.[102] However, in recent years courts have further refined the requirements under this important insurance principle by introducing the notions of "decisive influence" and "inducement" during the contractual negotiations.[103] It was also held that although the duty of utmost good faith continued to apply after the contract was originally concluded, this was not the same as the duty owed at the pre-contractual stage. Thus, only fraud in the claims process would defeat a claim, while the only duty imposed on the assured was to act honestly.[104] Furthermore, it was held that an insurer may not avoid the contract unless it can be shown

---

97 *Strive Shipping Corp. v. Hellenic Mutual War Risk Association (The Grecia Express)*, [2002] 2 Lloyd's L.R. 88.
98 *Intermunicipality Realty & Development Corp. v. Gore Mutual Insurance Co.*, above note 34; *Degroot v. J.T. O'Bryan & Co.* (1979), 15 B.C.L.R. 271 (C.A.); *Fudge v. Charter Marine Insurance* (1992), 97 Nfld. & P.E.I.R. 91 (Nfld. S.C.); *James Yachts v. Thames and Mersey Marine Insurance*, [1977] 1 Lloyd's L.R. 206 (B.C.S.C.) [*James Yachts*]; *McFaul v. Montreal Inland Insurance Co.* (1845), 2 U.C.Q.B. 59 (C.A.); *Litsion Pride (The)*, [1985] 1 Lloyd's L.R. 437.
99 *Desrosiers v. Fishing Vessel Insurance Plan* (1994), 87 F.T.R. 101.
100 *Century Insurance Co. of Canada v. Case Existological Laboratories (The Bamcell II)*, [1983] 2 S.C.R. 47 [*The Bamcell II*].
101 *Amo Containers v. Drake Insurance* (1984), 51 Nfld. & P.E.I.R. 55 (Nfld. S.C. (T.D.)); *1013799 Ontario Ltd. v. Kent Line International* (2000), 22 C.C.L.I. (3d) 312 (Ont. S.C.)
102 See, e.g., recent U.K. cases such as *Manifest Shipping & Co. v. Uni-Polaris Insurance Co. (The Star Sea)*, [2001] 1 Lloyd's L.R. 389 (H.L.), aff'g [1997] 1 Lloyd's L.R. 360 (C.A.) [*Manifest Shipping*]; *K/S Merc-Scandia XXXXII v. Certain Lloyd's Underwriters, (The Mercadian Continent)*, [2001] 2 Lloyd's L.R. 563 [*K/S Merc-Scandia*]; and *Decorum Investments Ltd. v. Atkin (The Elena G)*, [2001] 2 Lloyd's L.R. 378.
103 *Container Transport International Inc. v. Oceanus Mutual U/W Association (Bermuda) Ltd.*, [1984] 1 Lloyd's L.R. 476; *Pan Atlantic Insurance Co. v. Pine Top Insurance Co.*, [1995] 1 A.C. 501.
104 *Manifest Shipping*, above note 102.

that a fraud was relevant to the insurer's ultimate liability under the policy to the extent that it would entitle termination of the policy.[105]

2) Insurable Interest

One of the fundamental principles of marine insurance is that the insured must have an insurable interest in the object of the insurance.[106] Such an interest is defined as where a person stands in an "equitable relation to the marine adventure or to any insurable property at risk therein, in consequence of which he may benefit by the safety or due arrival of the insurable property, or may be prejudiced by its loss, or by damage thereto, or by the detention thereof, or may incur liability in respect thereof."[107] The purpose of the marine insurance contract is to reimburse the insured for a loss resulting from an insured risk. In order to suffer a loss, the insured must have an insurable interest.[108] Otherwise, no loss can be suffered and there is nothing to reimburse. However, unlike other branches of insurance, the proposer need not have an insurable interest at the time the insurance is effected but must have such an interest when the loss occurs.[109] In general, insurable interest is tied to the passing of the risk. For example, risk is usually not passed from seller to purchaser until all cargo has been loaded on board the vessel.[110] The most obvious example of an insurable interest is the ownership of cargo on board a ship, or the vessel itself[111] — although the shipowner also has an insurable interest in freight.[112] However, it should be noted that, if a shipping company owns the vessel, it is the

---

105 *K/S Merc-Scandia*, above note 102. See also *Agapitos v. Agnew (The Aegeon)*, [2002] 2 Lloyd's L.R. 42.
106 *Marine Insurance Act, 1993*, above note 35, s.8.
107 *Ibid.*
108 *Balix Furniture and Appliances Ltd. v. Maritime Insurance Co.*, [1978] O.J. No. 1514 (QL); *Merchants Marine Insurance Co. of Canada v. Rumsey* (1884), 9 S.C.R. 577; *Phoenix Assurance v. Golden Imports* (1989), 43 C.C.L.I. 313 (B.C. Co. Ct.).
109 *Catherwood Towing v. Commercial Union Assurance* (1996), 26 B.C.L.R. (3d) 57 (C.A.).
110 *Green Forest Lumber v. General Security Insurance*, [1980] 1 S.C.R. 176; *Orchard v. Aetna Insurance Co.* (1856), 5 U.C.C.P. 445 (C.A.).
111 Including part interest, interest in an unfinished vessel and mortgage interest. *Anchor Marine Insurance v. Keith*, above note 60; *Clark v. Scottish Imperial Insurance* (1879), 4 S.C.R. 192; *Crawford v. St. Lawrence Insurance Co.* (1851), 8 U.C.Q.B. 135 (C.A.); *Merchants Marine Insurance v. Barss* (1888), 15 S.C.R. 185.
112 *Driscoll v. Millville Marine Insurance Co.* (1883), 23 N.B.R. 160 (C.A.), rev'd (1884), 11 S.C.R. 183; *Burrard Towing v. Reed Stenhouse* (1996), 19 B.C.L.R. (3d) 391 (C.A.).

corporation and not the shareholders that is the owner. As a corporation is a legal entity separate from the shareholders, even the owner of all the shares in the company does not have an insurable interest.[113]

3) Measure of Indemnity

Closely related to the doctrine of insurable interest is the principle of indemnity under which the insured is entitled to be compensated precisely to the extent of the pecuniary loss suffered. Such loss must have resulted from an insured peril. In fact, a marine insurance contract is legally a contract of indemnity. Nevertheless, not every marine insurance contract will provide a complete measure of indemnity for the insured. In many cases this measure has been agreed on when the contract of insurance was concluded. Such an indemnity may be less, or even more, than the ideal pecuniary indemnity.[114] This marine insurance peculiarity is owing to the fact that some policies may be considered as valued and some unvalued.[115] The difference between these two types of policy is that, in the valued policy, the value of the subject-matter is expressly stated and, in the absence of fraud, this value is conclusive and binding on the parties; on the other hand, an unvalued policy has no specified value stated in the policy and the payment, if a loss occurs, will be the insurable value, calculated under general insurance principles, as set out in the relevant legislation.[116] Most hull and machinery, and many cargo marine policies are valued, so that, in the absence of fraud, even those that are significantly overvalued, are acceptable.[117]

Even evidence of the vast overvaluation of a ship need not be construed as fraud. For example, The Borre was insured for £2,000 under a policy in which the vessel's value was stated to be £5,000. In effect, this was a policy for partial rather than for the full value of the ship as established by the agreed evaluation (£5,000). This is an example of insurance for part-value, or under-insurance, as the assured assumed £3,000 of the ship's total value (i.e., the difference between the agreed

---

113 *Salomon v. A. Salomon & Co.*, [1897] A.C. 22. This is not the same under U.S. law, where shareholders are permitted to have an insurable interest. See Parks, above note 43 at 524.
114 *Goole and Hull Steamship Towing Co. v. Ocean Marine Insurance Co.* (1929), 29 Ll. L.R. 242.
115 *Marine Insurance Act, 1993*, above note 35, s.30.
116 *Ibid.*, s.19.
117 *General Shipping & Forwarding Co. v. British General Ins. Co. (The Borre)* (1923), 15 Ll. L.R. 175.

value of the ship and the value covered by the insurer). In fact, the market value of the ship was only £1,500. The ship became a total loss and the insurer was obliged to pay £2,000. The insurer protested on the ground that the ship was grossly overvalued. It was held that the assured's claim should succeed, as there was no evidence of fraud.[118] To change the facts somewhat, had The Borre only been a partial loss, requiring repairs costing only £500, the underwriter would only have been required to pay £200 as the assured had assumed responsibility for three-fifths of the agreed value of the ship.

It may be easier to understand this concept, if one remembers that, in many cases, several different underwriters insure one vessel. For instance, suppose a ship is valued at $5 million. Underwriter A might take up $1 million of the risk, underwriter B $2 million, and underwriter C $500,000. If the shipowner is unwilling or unable to obtain further coverage, he will become his own insurer for the balance of $1.5 million. It is immaterial to underwriters A, B, and C whether the shipowner finds another underwriter for this portion, as each is only responsible for his or her part of the risk of the total value of the vessel. If the ship becomes a total loss, then each pays the full agreed share amount; but, if the ship is only a partial loss, for example, $1 million, then each bears only his or her proportion of the loss. For example, A would bear 20 per cent ($1 million divided by $5 million) of the loss, or, $200,000; B would bear 40 per cent or $400,000; C would bear 10 per cent or $100,000; and the shipowner would be responsible for 30 per cent or $300,000, the balance of the loss.

It should be noted that the same scheme of proportionality does not cover partial losses when the ship is overinsured. If a ship is valued at $3 million but is insured for $5 million and a partial loss occurs, resulting in $2.5-million–worth of damage, the assured does not recover five-thirds of the partial loss ($4,170,000) but only $2.5 million. This is owing to the fact that the assured is only entitled to the "reasonable cost of repairs" in the event of a partial loss.[119] However, had the ship been a total loss, the owner would have received the full $5 million.

Coverage under unvalued policies differs from that under valued policies. In the case of an unvalued policy, the principle of ideal indemnity applies up to the total value of the policy. The following example may help to demonstrate the practical and legal differences between the two types of policies. Where a ship has an actual value at the time of

---

118 *Ibid.* See also *Fudge v. Charter Marine Insurance*, above note 98.
119 *Marine Insurance Act, 1993*, above note 35, s.68.

loss of $100,000 and the ship is a total loss, under an unvalued policy covering losses up to $200,000, the owner will recover $100,000; while under a valued policy in which the agreed value of the ship is $200,000, the owner will recover the actual extent of his or her loss as determined by the policy, that is, $200,000. In other words, subject to express provisions in the policy, in the case of a total loss, the amount the assured can recover under an unvalued policy is the insurable value of the subject-matter and, in a valued policy, the sum fixed by the policy.

4) Subrogation and Abandonment

The doctrine of subrogation is the right of the insurer to step into the shoes of the insured when a loss has been paid. This ensures that the insured will not make a profit out of a loss for which an indemnity has been received.[120] However, subrogation is a right and not an obligation. Where the insurer has paid a total loss or a total loss of a part, such insurer is entitled — but not required — to take over the interest of the insured in the subject-matter. There may, of course, be occasions when it is not in the interest of the insurer to do so, for instance, when there are potential liabilities involved. Under the doctrine of subrogation the insurer is strictly confined to the rights of the insured.[121] In most cases this will involve litigation against the party that may have caused the loss in the first place. In such cases the insurer can litigate in the name of the insured who has been indemnified, in order that the insurer can recover some or all of the indemnity from those who may have been responsible for the loss in the first place.

The doctrine of subrogation is closely related to the doctrine of abandonment, a legal mechanism under which the insured gives notice to the insurer that the insured property, or what remains of it, has been abandoned. Where there is a valid abandonment the insurer is entitled to take over all proprietary rights and interests of the insured in the abandoned property. Nevertheless, a notice of abandonment by the insured does not have to be accepted by the insurer. In fact, it is almost standard practice for insurers to reject notices of abandonment. In

---

120 *Ibid.*, s.81. See also *Castellain v. Preston* (1883), 7 A.C. 333 (Q.B.).
121 *Yorkshire Insurance Co. v. Nisbet Shipping Co.*, [1961] 2 All E.R. 487; *Chubb Insurance Co. of Canada v. Cast Line Ltd.*, [2001] R.R.A. 765; *Fraser River Pile & Dredge v. Can-Dive Services*, [1999] 3 S.C.R. 108; *Manning v. Boston Insurance* (1962), 34 D.L.R. (2d) 140 (P.E.I. S.C.); *Rose v. Borisko Brothers Ltd.* (1983), 41 O.R. (2d) 606, 147 D.L.R. (3d) 191 (C.A.); *Canadian National Railway v. Canadian Industries Ltd.*, [1941] S.C.R. 591, [1941] 4 D.L.R. 561.

most cases, this position is taken as insurers wish to avoid further liabilities that may exist, such as wreck removal, oil pollution cleanup, or disposal of damaged cargo.[122]

5) Warranties[123]

In marine insurance contracts, a warranty is a promise by the insured that some particular action shall or shall not be taken, or that some condition shall be fulfilled, or where the insured affirms or denies some specific state of facts.[124] Such a warranty may be express[125] or implied,[126] and must be strictly complied with whether it is material to the risk or not. If it is not complied with, the insurer is discharged from all contractual obligations from the date of the breach;[127] examples are not operating a vessel in ice-infested waters, not carrying inflammable or explosive cargoes, or not operating in areas that are subject to armed conflict or similar disturbances.[128] As there may be many different conditions,[129] this is an area of frequent litigation.[130] In many cases the question arises of whether a condition in an insurance policy is a "true" warranty,[131] a "suspending condition," or a "promissory" warranty,[132] and what the intention of the parties to such conditions were when the

---

122 *Marwell Equipment and British Columbia Bridge & Dredging Co. v. Vancouver Tug Boat Co.* (1960), 26 D.L.R. (2d) 80 (S.C.C.); *Gallagher v. Taylor*, above note 60.
123 See *Marine Insurance Act, 1993*, above note 35, ss.32–39.
124 *Ibid.*, s.32. See also *The Bamcell II*, above note 100.
125 *Ibid.*, *Marine Insurance Act, 1993*, s.33.
126 *Conohan v. Cooperators (The)*, [2000] 2 F.C. 238 (T.D.).
127 *Shearwater Marine v. Guardian Insurance Co. of Canada* (1997), 29 B.C.L.R. (3d) 13, aff'd (1998), 60 B.C.L.R. (3d) 37; *Riverside Landmark v. Northumberland General Insurance* (1984), 8 C.C.L.I. 118 (Ont. S.C.).
128 There are many other examples: see, e.g., *Billings v. Zurich Insurance Co.* (1987), 27 C.C.L.I. 60 (Ont. Dist. Ct.).
129 In marine insurance a "warranty" is equivalent to a "condition" in general insurance law. See *Britsky Building Movers v. Dominion Insurance Corp.*, [1981] I.L.R. 1-1420 (Man. Co. Ct.). But cf. *The Bamcell II*, above note 100.
130 *Lewis v. Canada* (1995), 98 F.T.R. 278; *Norlympia Seafoods Ltd. v. Dale & Co.*, [1983] I.L.R. 1-1688 (B.C.S.C.); *Britsky Building Movers v. Dominion Insurance Corp.*, *ibid.*; *James Yachts*, above note 98; *Bank of British North America v. Western Assurance Co.* (1884), 7 O.R. 166 (H.C.); *Demitri v. General Accident Indemnity* (1996), 41 C.C.L.I. (2d) 49 (B.C.S.C.).
131 *Norlympia Seafoods v. Dale & Co.*, *ibid.*; *Insurance Co. of North America v. Thompson* (1987), 31 C.C.L.I. 285.
132 *Elkhorn Developments v. Sovereign General Insurance* (2000), 18 C.C.L.I. (3d) 203 (B.C.S.C.). *The Bamcell II*, above note 100.

policy was agreed.[133] There is also an implied warranty of seaworthiness[134] in every voyage policy, although not in a time policy. However, where the insured sends an unseaworthy vessel to sea, the insurer under a time policy is not liable for any losses that can be attributed to the unseaworthy condition. In terms of marine insurance, a ship is considered seaworthy when it is reasonably fit in all respects to encounter the ordinary perils of the seas for the venture insured.[135]

6) Perils of the Sea

The term "perils of the sea" has been defined as "those which are peculiar to the sea, which are of an extraordinary nature or arise from an irresistible force or overwhelming power, and which cannot be guarded against by the ordinary exertions of human skill and prudence."[136] In other words the term only includes fortuitous accidents or casualties of the seas but not the ordinary action of the wind and waves.[137] The perils were set out in the standard S.G. Form of Policy and had changed very little since the seventeenth century;[138] in 1980, however, the archaic language was eliminated and an updated list of maritime perils was developed: "'Maritime Perils' means the perils consequent on or incidental to navigation, including perils of the seas, fire, war perils, acts of pirates or thieves, captures, seizures, restraints, detainment of princes and peoples, jettisons, barratry, and all other perils of a like kind and, in respect of a marine policy, any peril designated by the policy."[139] In general, it is up to the insured to show that the loss was caused by a peril insured against.[140] This can be achieved by proof of the proximate cause of the loss through factual evidence;[141] it has been suggested,

---

133 *The Bamcell II*, ibid. Also, *Federal Business Development Bank v. Commonwealth Insurance Co.*, [1979] B.C.J. No. 578 (QL).
134 *Atwood v. R.* (1985), 10 C.C.L.I. 62 (F.C.T.D.).
135 *Marine Insurance Act, 1993*, above note 35, s.37. See also *Laing v. Boreal Pacific* (2000), 264 N.R. 378 (F.C.A.). See also B in Chapter 8, "Carriage of Goods by Charterparty," but note that the concept of seaworthiness is not the same for all purposes under marine insurance and carriage of goods.
136 *J. Gerber & Co. v. S.S. Sabine Howaldt*, 1971 A.M.C. 539.
137 Hardy Ivamy, above note 22 at 154.
138 Anon., "Perils of the Sea and Marine Insurance" (1984) 2 Can. J. Ins. L. 14.
139 *Marine Insurance Act, 1993*, above note 35, s.2.
140 *Stad v. Fireman's Fund Insurance Co.*, [1979] I.L.R. 1-1070 (B.C.S.C.). See also M. Turcotte, "Proving Perils of the Sea" (1984) 2 Can. J. Ins. L. 57.
141 *H.B. Nickerson & Sons v. Insurance Co. of North America (The J.E. Kenney)*, [1984] 1 F.C. 575 (C.A.).

however, that, if an insured peril was the dominant or proximate cause of the loss, the policy should be liberally interpreted.[142] Nevertheless, if a claim is made in this area, the insured also has to show that those on the ship exercised due diligence in their attempts to avert or reduce the loss;[143] negligence may not necessarily invalidate the policy.[144]

D. THE MARINE INSURANCE POLICY

1) Background

As marine insurance policies are subject to the general rules of contract law, any ambiguity in the contract is construed against the writer.[145] The terms of the policy, however, are to be interpreted in their commercial and customary sense and usage[146] and, whenever possible, the policy should be given effect.[147] However, the form of the policy used in marine insurance changed in the 1980s. This was in part a response to criticisms that the language and terms used in the old Lloyd's S.G. Form of Policy no longer adequately expressed the true intentions of the parties and could lead to difficulties in interpretation.[148] Courts had to exercise more than reasonable interpretative powers in order to determine whether or not there were risks covered under the policy. In addition, there was a demand by a number of developing states, expressed through the United Nations Conference on Trade and Development (UNCTAD),[149] that a new international approach to marine insurance was required and that such an approach need not necessarily be based on the traditions of the London market. The London market responded relatively quickly. The old Lloyd's S.G. form was eliminated in favour of a simpler document, which lists most of the

---

142 *Kaufman v. New York Underwriters Insurance Co.*, [1955] O.R. 311 (H.C.J.).
143 Unless the policy contains an "Inchmaree Clause" (see below D(3)(f) p. 335). *Morris v. Canada (Min. of Fisheries & Oceans)* (1991), 47 F.T.R. 271; *Atwood v. R.*, above note 134; *Coast Ferries v. Century Insurance Co. of Canada* (1975), 48 D.L.R. (3d) 310 (S.C.C.).
144 *The Bamcell II*, above note 100.
145 *Mowat v. Boston Marine Insurance* (1896), 26 S.C.R. 47.
146 *Providence Washington Insurance v. Gerow* (1890), 17 S.C.R. 387.
147 *British America Assurance v. William Law & Co.* (1892), 21 S.C.R. 325.
148 Such as those identified in *Shell International Petroleum Co. v. Gibbs (The Salem)* (1983), 2 A.C. 375 (H.L.).
149 See G(1)(c) in Chapter 2, "The Shipping Industry: An Overview" regarding UNCTAD.

vital information required: the policy number, the name of the assured, the vessel, the voyage or period of insurance, the subject-matter insured, the agreed value (if any), the amount insured, the premium to be paid, the clauses and endorsements to be attached, and any special conditions and warranties to be noted. In other words, the traditional S.G. Policy Form, contained as the First Schedule in the U.K. *Marine Insurance Act, 1906*,[150] has been superseded. On the other hand, the Canadian *Marine Insurance Act, 1993*, contains a schedule that sets out the requirements for the construction of the policy.[151]

2) Time and Voyage Policies

Marine insurance is written in time or in voyage policies:[152] a time policy covers a risk between specified time periods, while a voyage policy covers risks for a specified voyage or series of voyages. This is rather similar to the approach used for time and voyage charterparties.[153] Time policies are generally utilized to cover ships, while voyage policies are more frequently used to cover risks to cargo, often under the floating cover system. P&I cover is usually offered for a whole policy year, commencing on 20 February, and is considered a time policy.[154] Time policies are relatively simple. Cover commences and ceases at a contracted, specified, and predictable time.[155] However, such policies usually contain a clause that continues cover, even after the expiry time if the vessel is at sea, is in distress, or is in a port of refuge, providing that notice of this has been given to the insurer.[156] Voyage policies may, at times, cause difficulties.[157] Such policies cover risks on a specified voyage and the property will not be covered unless the specified voyage is prosecuted. The defined voyage is strictly interpreted. If the voyage is defined as from A to B, the vessel cannot proceed from A to C, or C to D, even if the alternative destinations are geographically very close. In other

---

150 As well as in Canadian provincial insurance legislation.
151 *Marine Insurance Act, 1993*, above note 35.
152 *Ibid.*, s.29.
153 See C in Chapter 8, "Carriage of Goods by Charterparty."
154 See Grime, above note 78 at 380 and 384. See also *Compania Maritima San Basilio S.A. v. Oceanus Mutual Underwriting Association (Bermuda) Ltd. (The Eurysthenes)*, [1976] 2 Lloyd's L.R. 171 (C.A.) [*The Eurysthenes*].
155 *The Eurysthenes, ibid.*
156 *Institute Time Clauses (Hulls), 1983*, cl.2, in R. Merkin, *Marine Insurance Legislation* (London: LLP, 2000) [*ITC-Hulls*]; *International Hull Clauses, 2002*, cl.12 [*IHC*] in R. Merkin, *Marine Insurance Legislation* (London: LLP, 2000).
157 See Hardy Ivamy, above note 22 at 39ff.

words, if either the port of departure or the port of destination is changed, the cover will not attach at all.[158]

In addition, voyage policies are also strictly interpreted in terms of when the cover actually commences; for example, if goods are stored in a port terminal prior to or at the end of the voyage, they will not be covered unless this has been specified in the policy. In most cases, even if the policy contains warehouse-to-warehouse or transit clauses, coverage will only be during the actual transit of the goods to and from the vessel and not during storage.[159] Deviation[160] from the specified voyage in the policy is also very strictly interpreted in a similar way to deviation in charterparties.[161] However, modern practice has mitigated the strict interpretation to some extent; in fact, marine insurance legislation now provides a number of excuses for deviation or delay:[162]

- when authorized by any special term in the policy,
- when caused by circumstances beyond the control of the master or his or her employer,
- when reasonably necessary for the safety of the vessel or property insured,
- for the purpose of saving human life or assisting a vessel in distress,
- where necessary in order to obtain urgent medical assistance for a person on board,
- when necessary to comply with an express or implied warranty in the policy, and
- in cases of a deviation involving barratry.

3) Marine Insurance Policy Clauses

The actual terms of the coverage in a marine insurance policy are contained in the clauses that are inserted.[163] These are based on standard sets of clauses that have been drawn up by the Institute of London Underwriters. This organization, composed of insurance underwriters from Lloyd's and other groups, was established in 1884. It was respon-

---

158 *Marine Insurance Act, 1993*, above note 35, s.41.
159 Grime, above note 78 at 384–86. See also *Safadi v. Western Assurance* (1933), 46 Ll. L.R. 140 (K.B.).
160 Grime, ibid.; *Marine Insurance Act, 1993*, above note 35, s.43.
161 See B(3) & D(4)(c) in Chapter 8, "Carriage of Goods by Charterparty."
162 *Marine Insurance Act, 1993*, above note 35, s.45.
163 Marginal clauses that are not considered to be representative of the contract agreed to by the parties, however, will not have this effect: see *Symington & Co. v. Union Insurance Society of Canton* (1928), 30 Ll. L.R. 280 (C.A.).

sible for the movement toward standardization of marine insurance clauses, those issued under its authority being universally known as Institute clauses. These clauses, either singularly or in sets, are now almost invariably attached to the policy in accordance with the wishes of the parties. In cases where the new format policy is used, these clauses are the policy. In the Canadian context, it should be noted that several special clauses have also been developed and adapted in various Canadian regions in order to accommodate specific requirements.[164]

During the long period of time that the London market had risen in importance as a global insurance centre, the shipping and insurance communities had already developed a number of widely accepted standard terms that could be inserted into marine insurance policies. Such terms covered almost every known eventuality, specialty, or trade. The London market had no complete set of terms and conditions, so these rules of practice and standard terms and conditions have been developed on the basis of various clauses successfully used over a long period of time. The U.K. *Marine Insurance Act, 1906*, represented to a great extent the codification of the standard clauses and rules of practice existing at the beginning of the last century. The Institute of London Underwriters subsequently combined most of these clauses and provisions in a collection entitled *London Institute Clauses*. Since 1983 most London underwriters have used these clauses for coverage of hull and machinery, cargo, and war risks.[165] The standard terms and conditions for hull and machinery are set out in the *Institute Time Clauses, Hulls* (*ITC-Hulls*).[166] On 1 November 2002, after a lengthy consultation process with the shipping and marine insurance markets, the Joint Hull Committee of the Institute of London Underwriters launched the new *International Hull Clauses, 2002* (*IHC*).[167] These new clauses will be

---

164 E.g., *Canadian Hulls (Pacific) Form; Great Lakes Form; Marine Insurance (Logs) Form; and Pacific Scow Cargo Clauses*. In a number of cases, these and other forms and clauses are applicable both in Canada as well as the United States. The Canadian insurance industry has also developed a number of specialized fishing vessel insurance forms that service the extensive Canadian fishing vessel insurance market.
165 It should be noted that a set of *American Institute Clauses* was also developed. These basically followed the English model, although with some rearrangement, modification of wording, and Americanized spelling. See Staring & Waddell, above note 2 at 1619. See also Buglass, above note 57 at 307ff.
166 A revised *ITC (Hulls)* was introduced on 1 November 1995 but did not gain wide acceptance in the market.
167 See Holman Fenwick & Willan, Newsletter, "The International Hull Clauses — A New Perspective" (London, November 2002).

phased in gradually but are expected to supersede the *ITC-Hulls* system in due course. This also means that both systems will be in use in the foreseeable future. This should not cause major difficulties, as the new system is to a great extent simply modernizing the older version. The new *IHC* system is also attempting to rectify a number of uncertainties that had arisen under the 1983 version.[168] In addition, several new clauses have been added.[169] Finally, there have been very significant amendments in respect of claims handling procedures.[170]

The standard terms and conditions for cargo are contained in the *Institute Cargo Clauses, A, B, and C*. The differences among the A, B, and C *Institute Cargo Clauses* relate to the risks that they are intended to cover.[171] War risks are covered under *Institute War and Strike Clauses, Hulls*. The standard English condition for loss of hire insurance is known as the ABS condition or Loss of Charter Hire Insurance — Including War. A very brief summary of the most important *ITC-Hulls* clauses, *IHC* clauses, and *Institute Cargo Clauses* follows.[172]

a) Navigation (Tow and Assist) Clause

The purpose of this hulls clause is to ensure that the vessel is covered at all times, whether at sea, in port, in dry dock, or on trial trips. The navigation (tow and assist) clause places restrictions on towage operations to the extent that towage is not permitted except during entry or exit from ports or when in need of assistance.[173] Under the *ITC-Hull* system, a breach of this provision was considered to be a breach of war-

---

168 Such as clarifying the "jurisdiction of the English court" under *IHC*, above note 156, cl.1.3, in response to the decision in *Al Wahab (The)*, [1983] 2 Lloyd's L.R. 365; and *IHC*, above note 156, cl.2.2.2 confirming that the costs of correcting latent defects is excluded. See *Nukila (The)*, [1997] 2 Lloyd's L.R. 146.
169 *IHC*, ibid., cl.13 Classification and ISM; cl.36 Re-commissioning Limits; cl.37 Helicopter Engagement; cl.38 Premium Payment; cl.41 Fixed and Floating Objects; cl.43 General Average Absorption; cl.44 Additional Perils.
170 *IHC*, ibid., cl.45 Leading Underwriters; cl.46 Notice of Claims; cl.48 Duties of the Assured; cl.49 Duties of Underwriters; cl.50 Provision of Security; cl.51 Payment of Claims; cl.52 Recoveries; cl.53 Dispute Resolution.
171 For a more detailed description, see *Chorley & Giles*, above note 83 at 554ff; or consult the actual Institute Cargo Clauses. See also Fernandes, above note 29 at Appendix G.
172 This is only a very brief overview, as it is not possible to provide full details here. The actual documentation should always be consulted.
173 See Chapter 14, "Maritime Towage." See also T.S. Hawkins, "Tug and Tow in British Columbia: The Course Changes for Owners and Insurers" (1997) 5 Int. Ins. L.R. 29; *Burrard Towing v. Reed Stenhouse*, above note 112; *Catherwood Towing v. Commercial Union Assurance*, above note 109.

ranty. However, the *IHC* version now simply treats such a breach as a breach of condition.[174] The *IHC* also now includes an additional clause on navigational limits that works in conjunction with this section.[175]

b) Continuation Clause

This hulls clause ensures that a vessel will continue to be covered under a policy that expires while the vessel is at sea, in distress, or in a port of refuge, at a *pro rata* premium, until arrival at the port of destination.

c) Breach of Warranty Clause

This hulls clause on breach of warranty is also known as the held covered clause, as it provides that the vessel is held covered in the event that any of the conditions in the policy are breached. However, this applies only if the insurer is notified by the insured as soon as such breach is known to the insured. Any change in the policy and any additional premium payable have to be agreed to by the parties.

d) Sale of Vessel or Termination Clause

As the management of a vessel is an extremely important factor in assessing hull risks, the sale of vessel or termination clause provides that coverage will cease if there is a change in the vessel's classification, ownership, flag of registry, charter, or management.

e) Notice of Assignment Clause

This hulls clause, notice of assignment, prohibits the assignment of the policy or funds payable under the policy unless a dated notice of assignment, signed by the insured, is endorsed on the policy and the policy is produced before any claim is paid. This ensures that the insurer is made aware of any assignment of the policy.

f) Perils Clause

The perils clause of the *ITC-Hulls* and the *IHC* is divided into two parts: the first lists the stated perils,[176] and the second contains the balance of what is known as the *Inchmaree*[177] clause that covers the listed losses but states that "such loss or damage has not resulted from want of due

---

174 *IHC*, above note 156, cls.10 and 11.
175 *Ibid.*, cl.34.
176 *Ibid.*, paras.1.1–1.8.
177 *Ibid.*, paras.2.1–2.5; *Thames and Mersey Marine Insurance Co. v. Hamilton, Fraser & Co. (The Inchmaree)* (1887), 12 A.C. 484.

diligence[178] by the assured, owners, or managers." Under the perils clause the insurance policy now covers loss or damage to the subject-matter insured caused by the following:

- perils of the seas, rivers, lakes, or other navigable waters;[179]
- fire or explosion;
- violent theft by persons from outside the vessel;
- jettison;
- piracy;
- contact with aircraft, helicopters, satellites, or similar objects, or objects falling therefrom, land conveyance, dock or harbour equipment, or installation;
- earthquake, volcanic eruption, or lightning;
- accidents in loading, discharging, or shifting cargo, fuel, or stores;
- any latent defect in the machinery or hull but only to the extent that repair costs for damage so caused exceeds the cost that would have been incurred to correct the latent defect;[180]
- bursting of boilers, breakage of shafts, or any latent defect in machinery or hull;
- negligence of master, officers, crew, or pilots;
- negligence of repairers or charterers provided such repairers are not assured this insurance; and
- barratry of master, officers, and crew.

Any of the perils named in the clause must have originated as an accident.[181] However, a latent defect becoming apparent through ordinary wear and tear is outside the scope of the policy.[182]

g) Pollution Hazard

The pollution hazard clause is a comparatively modern hulls clause that provides coverage for loss or damage to a vessel that is directly

---

178 See *Coast Ferries v. Century Insurance of Canada*, above note 143.
179 *Russell v. Canadian General Insurance Co.* (1999), 11 C.C.L.I. (3d) 284 (Ont. Ct. Gen. Div.).
180 As already indicated above, this aspect has been clarified under the new *IHC*. See above note 169.
181 *Stad v. Fireman's Fund Insurance Co.*, above note 140; *Anderson v. Dale & Co.*, [1994] B.C.J. No. 3347 (QL).
182 *Scindia S.S. Co. v. London Assurance Co.* (1936), 56 Ll. L.R. 136; *Russell v. Aetna Insurance Co.* (1975), 75 I.L.R. 1-699 at 1276, [1975] O.J. No. 911 (QL) (S.C.C.A.); *Scottish Metropolitan Assurance Co. v. Canada Steamship Lines Ltd.*, [1930] S.C.R. 262. As already indicated above, this has been clarified under *IHC*. See also *Nukila (The)*, above note 168.

caused by government authorities to prevent or mitigate a pollution hazard that did not result from a lack of due diligence by the insured.[183]

h) Three-Quarters–Collision Liability

This hulls clause was formerly known as the "Running-Down" clause and covers tort liability arising from the collision between vessels. The three-quarters–collision liability clause indicates that the insurer is only required to indemnify the insured for three-quarters of any sum or sums "paid by the assured to any other person or persons by reason of the assured becoming legally liable by way of damages."[184] The clause also confirms that the insurer's liability does not exceed three-quarters of the insured value of the vessel and, therefore, clarifies that the indemnity is based on this value alone.[185] The wording of the present clause makes it clear that the insurer is only liable to indemnify the assured for three-quarters of any sum or sums "paid by the assured to any other person or persons by reason of the assured becoming legally liable by way of damages," rather than as a consequence of a collision with another vessel what the assured is "liable to pay and shall pay by way of damages." It is not yet clear whether the change in wording will produce any significant difference in practice: for example, if the assured should become bankrupt between the award and recovery by the third party, would the insurer still be liable?[186] Nevertheless, the *IHC* system now permits underwriters to accept four-quarters–collision liability if they so wish.[187] Finally, under the new *IHC*, the underwriter's exposure to legal costs incurred by the assured in contesting liability is limited to one-quarter of the insured value of the vessel.[188]

i) Sister-Ship Clause

Under the sister-ship clause, the insured is permitted to claim damages from the different insurers of any other vessel liable for damage, where such vessel is owned by the same insured.

---

183 See also Chapter 17, "Marine Pollution Prevention."
184 It should be noted that this clause is generally applicable only to U.K. policies. The Norwegian Hull Plan covers full insurance. See Gold, *Gard Handbook*, above note 8, c.6.
185 See also Chapter 11, "Maritime Collisions."
186 In England under the *Third Parties (Rights Against Insurers) Act, 1930* (U.K.), 20 & 21 Geo. V., c.25, s.1, the answer would be in the affirmative. However, there are no similar statutory provisions in Canada. But see *Manning v. Boston Insurance Co.*, above note 121.
187 This is in line with the Norwegian and some other European systems: see *IHC*, above note 156, cl.40.
188 *IHC, ibid.*, cl.6.

j) Duty of Assured (Sue and Labour) Clause[189]

This hulls clause — the duty of assured (sue and labour) clause — provides payment for expenses incurred by the insured shipowner in taking necessary action for the purpose of averting or minimizing a loss for which the insurer would be liable, including legal expenses. Although previously considered to be a legal act, such action is considered a positive duty.[190] The expenses involved are, however, proportionate to the insured or agreed value stated in the policy and may, therefore, have little or no relationship to the actual value of the vessel.

k) Unrepaired Damage Clause

Formerly known as the valuation clause, the unrepaired damage hulls clause covered situations where a constructive total loss was claimed on the ground that the repair costs would be greater than the vessel's repaired value. In such cases the insured value was considered to be the repaired value. However, this caused some confusion because of the difficulty in estimating the repaired value. The new clause has clarified this problem.

l) Disbursements Clause

This hulls provision, formerly known as the disbursements warranty, is designed to prevent the shipowner from insuring against all risks for a comparatively low value and then making up the total loss value, or overinsuring, at a lower rate of premium through a series of policies on interests ancillary to the hull insurance. The amount of such additional insurance is limited to the percentages specified in the clause.

m) Free Capture and Seizure Clause

The free of capture and seizure (FC&S) clause was first introduced in 1898 and excludes war and similar risks that are subject to special separate risk cover.

n) Risks Clause

The archaic list of perils has now disappeared from the policy form; instead, the cargo form now lists the specific risks against which the cargo is covered. As the cargo clauses are issued in three different versions, the main differences are between the risks covered. The A clause

---

189 See *Marine Insurance Act, 1993*, above note 35, s.79.
190 H.A. Dilworth, "Preventing a Loss" in *Maritime Law: Third International Conference* (Vancouver, BC, 1986) at 9.1. See also *Integrated Container Service Inc. v. British Traders Insurance Co.*, [1984] 1 Lloyd's L.R. 154 (C.A.).

is the most wide-ranging and covers "all risks of loss or damage to the subject-matter insured," subject to a list of enumerated exceptions. Risks covered by the B and C clauses are enumerated individually. Under the B clause, the cargo is covered against loss or damage by the entry of seawater into the vessel or container; additional listed perils are general average sacrifice,[191] jettison, or washing overboard; fire and explosion; stranding, sinking, or capsizing of the carrying vessel; collision of the carrying vessel; and discharge of the cargo in a port of distress. The C clause cover is not as wide as the B cover.

o) **Transit Clause**

The modern transit cargo clause is based on the traditional warehouse-to-warehouse clause. Under this clause insurance cover is maintained despite deviation of the carrying vessel generally granted by the cargo owner. Cover is also maintained in the event of a forced discharge of the cargo, and its reshipment or transhipment.

p) **"Seaworthiness Admitted" Clause**

The "seaworthiness admitted" cargo clause stipulates that the insurance premium is payable even when the loss of the cargo was attributable to the fault of the shipowner, or the shipowner's servants, provided that the cargo owner had no knowledge of the fault. Under the clause the insurer waives any breach of the implied warranty of seaworthiness that in a voyage policy requires the vessel to be seaworthy at the commencement of each stage of the voyage.[192] However, such breach will not be waived in cases where the insured or his or her servants are aware of the unseaworthiness. The clause also waives any breach of the implied warranty that the vessel should be reasonably fit to carry the cargo.[193]

q) **Duty of the Assured Clause**

The duty of the assured cargo clause requires the insured to assist in keeping claims and damage to a minimum. In order to do this, the insured and his or her servants and agents must take such measures as may reasonably be expected for the purpose of averting or minimizing the risk. This is similar to the *ITC-Hulls* sue and labour clause. However, if additional expenses are involved in order that the insured can comply with these requirements, such costs are borne by the insurer.[194]

---

191 See Chapter 16, "General Average."
192 *Marine Insurance Act, 1993*, above note 35, s.37.
193 *Ibid.*, s.38.
194 *Netherlands Insurance Co. v. Karl Ljungberg & Co.*, [1986] 2 Lloyd's L.R. 19 (P.C.).

r) Other Cargo Clauses

There are a number of other cargo clauses that can be inserted into the policy when required.[195] Special clauses also cover commodities such as coal, oil, and jute and include increased value clauses covering price fluctuations during transit. Of increasing importance are container clauses. While the goods loaded inside containers are covered under the standard goods policies, the containers themselves are of significant value and require separate insurance coverage.[196]

E. PROTECTION AND INDEMNITY INSURANCE

1) Background[197]

Protection and indemnity (P&I) insurance originated in England in the mid–nineteenth century.[198] It provides third-party–liability coverage that evolved in part from the mutual protection system offered by the early hull clubs, and partly in response to the increases in liability faced by shipowners. Hull and machinery underwriters were, at that time, unwilling or unable to provide such additional coverage. The early mutual clubs were established in order to provide hull coverage for shipowners who could not otherwise obtain coverage from the few companies that had a monopoly in the London insurance market. However, the P&I clubs were introduced to cover risks such as the one-quarter–collision liability and potential liability for death and personal injury. This coverage was known as liability protection insurance. After 1870, when a shipowner was held liable for the loss of cargo that had been carried beyond its destination, the North of England Association offered insurance for this type of loss in a separate class within the mutual club. This was called indemnity insurance. Before 1870, cargo underwriters, having paid the cargo owners for their losses, could not exercise their right to sue the shipowners for the value of the loss under the doctrine of subrogation. In other words, protection

---

195 Such as covering Strikes and Civil Commotion.
196 See *Integrated Container Service Inc. v. British Traders Insurance Co.*, above note 190.
197 For a full discussion on P&I insurance, see Hazelwood, *P&I Clubs*, above note 13 and Gold, *Gard Handbook*, above note 8.
198 The first P&I "club," called the Shipowners' Mutual Protection Society was established in 1855 and still operates as The Britannia Steamship Insurance Association.

insurance covers liabilities arising from the ownership of the vessel, while indemnity insurance covers liabilities arising out of the operation of the vessel. During the century that followed, shipowners and ship operators had to face a steadily increasing burden of liability. However, this development has been paralleled by a corresponding growth in the scope of the cover provided by P&I clubs. P&I insurance is now an essential requirement for shipowners. In fact, in terms of law practice, it is in the protection and indemnity area that most activity takes place. While hull and machinery insurance cases may often involve major claims, it is in the protection and indemnity area that the day-to-day claims arising out of modern ship operations are to be found.

2) P&I Club Operation and Membership

Originally P&I clubs were established as unincorporated associations with their members having the dual role of insurers and insureds. This led to some problems, especially when litigation was involved. In response, P&I clubs were incorporated so that they now have a separate legal structure from their members. As a result, they are able to enter into separate contracts of insurance with such members. Most of the U.K. P&I clubs are established as companies limited by guarantee. Accordingly, a P&I club is required to have a corporate structure that includes documents, such as statutes and rules representing and regulating the contract of insurance between the club and the member. As insurers, P&I clubs issue general insurance provisions covering the basic principles related to risks covered, claims settlement procedures, and the payment of premiums. P&I clubs do not normally operate with traditional insurance contracts. Instead their insurance provisions are set out in the club's rules, with the specific terms and conditions, applicable to each member, set out in the certificate of entry. Most P&I clubs have also established subsidiaries and branch offices in other states. Such branches provide not only useful local contact with members and insurance brokers but also serve as claims representatives. In addition to such branch offices, P&I clubs also appoint correspondents in all the major ports of the world. Such correspondents assist the clubs and their members with claims that arise locally.

A member of a mutual, not-for-profit P&I club is both an insurer and an insured. The club members have reciprocal rights and obligations and are dependent on their fellow members for the success of the club. As an insurer, the member is obliged to pay sufficient premiums and, when required, sufficient additional calls to enable the club to discharge all claims. Accordingly, each member shares in the risks of the others and, as a result, has a direct interest in who is admitted to membership and how the other members conduct their business. As an insured, the member has a right to be indemnified by the club for certain liabilities and losses that the member incurs in direct connection with the operation of an entered ship.

One of the defining characteristics of a mutual club is its non-profit nature. Instead it is operated only for the benefit of its members, who are both the owners of the capital and the customers of the club or the insurers and the insureds. The income of the club, which is principally provided by the members through premiums and calls, is only required to be sufficient to meet the liabilities of the club and for the establishment of adequate reserves. There is no element of profit for external capital providers. In other words, mutual insurance means, in practice, insurance at cost. Most P&I clubs treat the insurance of risks by balancing the club's assets and liabilities on an annual basis. The members entered in each policy year pay calls to discharge the liabilities incurred in that policy year. It is contrary to the spirit of mutuality that the members entered in one year should pay liabilities incurred in another. It is, however, inevitable that this may occasionally occur, such as when clubs create reserves from assets of one year to pay claims in another, in an endeavour to equalize calls and to provide for catastrophic claims.

This mutuality of interest among the members is manifested in the way the directors or managers of the club are expected to conduct the day-to-day business of the club. The rules of the mutual clubs will usually confer on the directors or managers a large degree of discretion. Such discretion enables the directors or managers of the club to protect the mutual interests of the shipowner members as a whole in conducting the business of the club. The club's executive committee has the discretion to extend the club cover, as appropriate, on a case-by-case basis to liabilities not otherwise covered under the club's rules. This is known as the omnibus provision. Furthermore, under the standard terms of the defence cover, the club has a discretionary right to reject a claim, in whole or in part, for a variety of reasons.

A mutual risk will normally be regarded as a risk that is commonly borne by shipowners. In fact, insurance for these types of risks formed the basis for the establishment of P&I clubs. Directors and managers bear this in mind when exercising their discretion, and, therefore, generally favour accepting claims that arise from what are considered to be mutual risks. On the other hand, claims arising from risks that are particular only to the business of the member bringing such claims, or that are otherwise not normal shipowners' risks, will be rejected. It is for this reason that cover for certain specialized operations is generally excluded; for example, an additional voyage premium is usually levied to cover the oil pollution risk of trading to the United States.[199]

The discretion in the decision-making process by the club's directors is only subject to judicial review when it is alleged that such directors have exceeded their authority or failed to apply the rules of natural justice.[200] A court will normally assume that the directors have acted in good faith and the onus of proving otherwise, which is not easily discharged, is on the party bringing the allegations.[201] Entry of a ship by an owner, operator, or charterer will automatically result in club membership. If the entry is arranged by more than one such entity on a joint basis, they will be classified as joint members. The term "ship" can also include certain floating structures such as oil rigs and other structures used in offshore energy development.[202]

A shipowner is the individual or company, whether incorporated or not, who has legal title to the ship. The shipowner may be a part owner, with only title to part of a ship, or sharing such title with another co-owner. For registration purposes ships are often divided into shares,[203] and different persons can own such shares or they can be jointly owned by a number of individuals. Any type of charterer — whether bareboat, demise, time, or voyage charterer — can arrange an entry and become a member of a P&I club. However, time or voyage charterers cannot be joint members and are entered on a fixed premium basis. Such members are entitled to all the benefits of club membership, including the right to vote.

P&I clubs can accept an entry of a ship by way of reinsurance from a primary insurer of protection and indemnity risks of that ship. If this occurs, the club has the discretion in deciding whether such primary insurer, owner, operator, or charterer is accepted as a member. Furthermore, a member who owns more than one ship is entitled to enter one or more with one P&I club and the others with another club. Membership commences on the first entry and ends on termination of the last of the member's vessels. Termination or cessation of an entry of a ship can be initiated by the member or by the club or, in certain events, may

---

199 See Chapter 17, "Marine Pollution Prevention."
200 See C.V.G. Siderurgicia Del Orinoco S.A. v. London Steamship Owner's Mutual Insurance Association Ltd. (The Vainqueur Jose), [1979] 1 Lloyd's L.R. 557.
201 Hazelwood, P&I Clubs, above note 13 at 25–32. This is one of the most definitive treatises on P&I clubs presently available.
202 See F in Chapter 2, "The Shipping Industry: An Overview" and Chapter 17, "Marine Pollution Prevention."
203 E.g., Canadian and U.K. flag ships are often divided into 64 shares; Liberian flag ships are divided into 100 shares.

arise automatically. As the club is only liable for claims during the period of entry, the member will continue to be liable for premiums on a *pro rata* basis in cases where the insurance is terminated or ceases. As already indicated, the terms and conditions of the contract between the member and the club are evidenced by the certificate of entry and are subject to the P&I club's statutes and rules and, where applicable, further special conditions.

Members have no direct liability for insurance claims and other obligations; mutual members, however, are required to provide their P&I club with sufficient funds to enable it to discharge claims obligations. Any claimant must take action against the P&I club and not its members. If the club is unable to satisfy such claims, the claimant has no course of action against the members. Alternatively, where there is a surplus on the closing of a policy year, this may be repaid to members who were entered in that year.

Although P&I clubs maintain their independence, autonomy, and competitiveness, they have all agreed to co-operate with each other as members of the International Group of P&I Clubs. This group was previously known as the London Group of P&I Clubs, when it only comprised the London-based P&I clubs; it was renamed in 1979 when the three Scandinavian P&I clubs and the Japan Club became members or indirect members through reinsurance arrangements. This change and expansion was necessary in order to spread increasingly large financial risks across all the clubs, and also to take advantage of the resulting, increased purchasing power in obtaining reinsurance for larger and, potentially catastrophic, claims. The International Group of P&I Clubs[204] was incorporated in 1981 and obtained observer status at the International Maritime Organisation at the same time. The International Group also manages the pooling agreement that shares major risk exposures among its membership. The history of P&I clubs' co-operation is very much reflected in the development of the pooling agreement and the International Group Agreement. The pooling agreement has its origins in the nineteenth century. The so-called London Group of P&I Clubs, which at that time consisted of six clubs, entered into the first claims-sharing agreement in 1899. The principal purpose of the pooling agreement was the same then as it is today. It constituted the legal framework for claims sharing among the group clubs. Only later, in 1951, did it also become the vehicle for the collective purchase of market reinsurance cover.[205] Some mechanisms have always been

---

204 See G(2)(j) in Chapter 2, "The Shipping Industry: An Overview."
205 Hazelwood, *P&I Clubs*, above note 13 at 385.

necessary to ensure a certain level of discipline among the parties to the pooling agreement, and this is equally true today as it was in 1899. Some time after the first pooling agreement was created, an understanding was established between the parties restricting competition between the clubs. This restriction has subsequently been laid down in the International Group Agreement. The pooling agreement is the legal framework for claims sharing among the international group clubs. It is also the vehicle for the collective purchase of market reinsurance cover. In contrast to club rules, the pooling agreement does not contain any provision listing all types of liabilities and losses falling within the cover and is, therefore, not a named risk reinsurance. The key determinants for pool cover are whether the claim in question has arisen in respect of the insured owner's interest in the entered ship and in connection with the operation of such ship, and whether the relevant claim is not excluded by virtue of any of the exclusions contained in the appendices, under Excluded Risks and Excluded Losses.[206]

The scope of the pooling agreement is quite wide and includes the various types of liabilities an owner may incur in connection with the operation of the ship. However, the list of excluded risks and losses narrows the scope of the pool cover to what is today the standard protection and indemnity cover offered by all group clubs; for example, the list of excluded risks contains the standard war-risk and nuclear-risk exclusion clauses, while the list of excluded losses contains provisions dealing with, *inter alia*, excess *Hague-Visby* liability,[207] delivery of cargo without production of the relevant bill of lading,[208] various exclusions with regard to specialized operations, and claims covered under other insurances. In practice, the list of excluded losses contained in the agreement is of great importance because it restricts the scope of the pool cover to those categories of liabilities and losses that are considered to be of such a homogeneous nature that they are suitable for claims sharing on a mutual basis. When new categories of liabilities arise or new legislation is introduced that alter shipowners' liabilities, or certain categories of shipowners' liabilities, the member clubs to the pooling agreement must then consider whether to amend the list of excluded losses.

Currently, thirteen P&I clubs are members of the international group. This group provides liability insurance for more than 90 per cent of the world's shipowners. The current members of the international group are as follows:

---

206 International Group Pooling Agreement, 1999–2000, Appendices IV and V.
207 See C in Chapter 9, "Carriage of Goods under Bills of Lading and Similar Documents."
208 *Ibid.*

- Assuranceforeningen Gard (Norway),
- Assuranceforeningen Skuld (Norway),
- The Britannia Steamship Insurance Association Ltd. (U.K.),
- The Japan Ship Owners' Mutual Protection and Indemnity Association (Japan),
- The London Steamship Owners' Mutual Insurance Association Ltd. (U.K.),
- The North of England Protecting and Indemnity Association Ltd. (U.K.),
- The Shipowners' Mutual Protection and Indemnity Association (U.K.),
- The Standard Steamship Owners' Protection and Indemnity Association Ltd. (U.K.),
- The Steamship Mutual Underwriting Association Ltd. (U.K.),
- Sveriges Ångfartygs Assurans Forening (The Swedish Club, Sweden),
- The United Kingdom Steamship Assurance Association (The U.K. Club, U.K.),
- The West of England Shipowners' Mutual Insurance Association (U.K.), and
- The American Club (U.S.).

3) Non-club Protection and Indemnity Cover

While the international group's P&I clubs cover more than 90 per cent of world shipping, the remainder is covered outside the club system. This is especially true in the Canadian and U.S. context where a considerable amount of protection and indemnity coverage is provided through Marine Underwriting Companies and Managing General Agents based in major regional maritime centres in Canada and in the United States. There are a number of reasons why such coverage has been developed:

- the risk to be covered may not require the type of coverage provided by P&I clubs;
- risk coverage may not be available under standard P&I club cover;
- it may be more convenient to have cover that is underwritten locally;
- local coverage may be more competitive; and
- highly specialized operations may require to be underwritten locally or regionally.

The policies provided are customarily written on a flat premium basis with terms and conditions that are competitive with the major P&I clubs and would normally include a fixed limit of liability. This is, of course, a major difference from the unlimited liability provided by the P&I clubs. However, as just indicated, unlimited coverage may not be needed. Coverage is normally obtained from local or regional insurance companies and could be reinsured almost anywhere. The type of business underwritten by these local facilities would normally comprise both fleets as well as individual vessels operating in virtually any type of domestic, localized, or regional service including ferries, tugs and barges, fishing vessels, coastal and inland vessels, specialized service vessels, and tankers.

4) Risk Coverage

a) Protection and Indemnity Cover

Protection and indemnity insurance covers most of the risks in ship operations that are not covered by hull and machinery insurance. In addition to the basic principles of general insurance law, there are four factors that are of particular importance with respect to the structure of the P&I cover. First, the cover has always been developed as a direct response to shipowners' need for liability insurance; thus, only those liabilities and losses that are identified in P&I club rules are covered. In other words, P&I club cover is a named-risk insurance. Second, there must always be a link to an insured ship; liabilities and losses incurred by a shipowner without any connection to an insured ship fall outside P&I club cover. Third, the cover is unlimited save for the theoretical limit introduced on overspill claims.[209] However, the owner is always required to make use of the right to limit liability under any applicable rule of law.[210] Finally, the protection and indemnity cover is an indemnity insurance, which means that the P&I club is only obliged to indemnify the assured when the latter has discharged any liabilities to third-party claimants. Named-risk insurance means that only the categories of liabilities and losses set out in the rules of the individual club fall within the cover. These categories are set out in the P&I club's rules and are continually reviewed and amended by the clubs in response to changing market conditions. The principal types of liabilities and losses now covered are as follows:[211]

---

209 An Overspill Claim is one that exceeds the upper limit of the International Group of P&I clubs market reinsurance cover.
210 See Chapter 18, "Limitation of Liability for Maritime Claims."
211 At least thirty different risks are listed in most P&I clubs' rules. See, e.g., A.S. Gard, *Gard P&I: Statutes and Rules 2003* (Arendal: Gard A.S., 2003) Pt.II, c.1.

- liability arising from carriage of cargo;
- pollution liability;
- liability for death of or injury to crew members, passengers, and others, such as stevedores, on board ships;
- damage to fixed and floating objects and to other property;
- such part of the liability for collision damage that is not covered under the ship's hull policy;
- excess liability arising out of a collision, including that which is in excess of the limit of the hull policy; and
- wreck removal.

The expression "liabilities, losses, costs, and expenses" is generally used in P&I club rules to describe the individual category of liabilities and losses falling within the cover. In other words, the use of this expression represents in itself a restriction in the cover. First, the word "liabilities" defines "legal" liabilities; for example, P&I clubs do not cover voluntary or *ex gratia* payments made by a club member to third parties for the member's own commercial reasons, in the absence of any legal liability. Legal liabilities can arise by means of a contract entered into by the member, in tort, or under other statutory obligation. Neither jurisdiction nor the law under which liability arises is material. Under local laws liability may be based on a member's negligence (e.g., in the case of a collision), or it may be a strict or absolute liability, created by statute and imposed without any negligence on the part of the member (e.g., the damage to fixed or floating objects). Liabilities, losses, costs, and expenses that would not have arisen, but for the terms of a contract of indemnity entered into by, or on behalf of, the member are not covered unless the terms have been approved by the P&I club prior to the liability having been incurred. Similarly, the club provides no cover for liabilities resulting from the terms of a contract prohibited by the club or arising where a member has omitted to use contractual terms required. The expression "losses, costs, and expenses" covers not only losses arising out of a member's liability to a third party but also losses, costs, and expenses suffered by the member him- or herself, where the club rules permit the member to recover such losses from the club. Examples include the following:

- diversion expenses;
- expenses incurred in dealing with stowaways, illegal immigrants, and refugees;
- costs and expenses of wreck removal;[212]

---

212 See Chapter 15, "Maritime Salvage and Wreck."

- irrecoverable general average expenditure;[213]
- the cost of measures taken to avert or minimize loss; and
- disinfection and quarantine expenses.

Some of these expenses may only be recoverable if incurred with the prior approval of the club.

The liabilities, losses, costs, and expenses must be incurred either by the member directly or by servants, agents, or independent contractors for whose acts or omissions the member is held vicariously liable; for example, the member may have a direct liability to a third party for loss or damage caused by the acts or omissions of his or her employees, on the basis that an employer is vicariously liable for acts of his or her employees that are performed in the course of their employment. Where a member's servant, agent, or independent contractor incurs a direct liability to a third party in the course of his or her employment, the member may be obliged to indemnify him or her for that liability. This obligation may arise under a specific term of the contract between the member and the servant, agent, or independent contractor, or under the general law. While the P&I club does not insure servants, agents, or independent contractors themselves and will not reimburse them directly for liabilities they incur, the club will cover the member for the indemnity payment for which the member is liable. This cover is dependent on the liability that is incurred by the servants, agenst, or independent contractors, being one that would have been covered by the club if the member had incurred it directly. The member must directly incur the liability. Accordingly, the club will not cover *in rem* claims against the ship, incurred by someone other than the member, for example, a previous owner or a bareboat/demise charterer who is not entered with the club.

The P&I club does not require that a competent court or arbitration tribunal must first determine any liability incurred by a member to a third-party claimant. In the event of a claim, it is sufficient that the club, after its own investigation, is satisfied that the member is under a liability, or likely to be under a liability, to the claimant. Frequently, especially in the case of cargo and personal injury claims, there is some doubt whether the member has a liability to the claimant and there may be the possibility to settle the claim on a compromise basis. In such cases the club will cover the member's agreed compromise liability, providing it has approved the settlement. P&I cover is limited to named liabilities, losses, costs, and expenses that are incurred in direct

---

213 See Chapter 16, "General Average."

connection with the operation of an entered ship. This is also a prerequisite for a claim to be eligible for reinsurance under the pooling agreement. For this reason there must be a direct causal link between the operation of the entered ship, and the incident giving rise to the relevant liability, loss, cost, or expense. The incident must result from the operation of the ship and not from some other cause.

Any liability, loss, cost, or expense arising from other aspects of a member's business activities, apart from the operation of the entered ship, fall outside the scope of the cover. Moreover, the liability, loss, cost, or expense must relate specifically to the entered ship. The club's cover will not respond to liabilities incurred in connection with the member's general business operations that do not have a direct connection with an entered ship, such as liabilities incurred by a cruise vessel operator in respect of his or her land-based ticket and sales staff. The club's cover only comprises liabilities, losses, costs, and expenses that arise out of the member's interest in the entered ship. This will generally refer to the capacity in which the club has insured the member. If a member incurs a liability, loss, cost, or expense in a capacity other than the one in which he or she has been insured, such liability, loss, cost, or expense will not be covered.

In addition to these specific areas of cover, most P&I clubs also have an omnibus rule, which gives them wide discretion in authorizing the payment of any claims that the club feels are within the scope of the association. This rule is frequently used and constitutes one of the major advantages of this type of mutual marine insurance over that obtainable on a traditional marine insurance market. Furthermore, one of the greatest advantages of P&I insurance is that, in most cases, there is no limit on the amount of coverage for members' liabilities. An important exception is liability for oil pollution liability, which requires specific coverage that is also usually arranged by the shipowner member's P&I club.[214] P&I clubs also provide guarantees or bonds for shipowners in certain situations, such as arrest proceedings. If the circumstances that give rise to such an arrest were a risk covered by the P&I club, the necessary bond or guarantee will usually be provided. Even in cases where the risk was not covered under the P&I policy, the P&I club may still provide the bond but may require counter-security from the shipowner or charterer member.

---

214 Under the *CLC*, above note 48. See Chapter 17, "Marine Pollution Prevention." In any case, the International Group of P&I Clubs has set a limit of US$1 billion for 2002–03. See Gold, *Gard Handbook*, above note 8 at 455–57. *CLC* coverage is usually arranged by the shipowner member's P&I club.

b) Other Risks

Several other risks may be covered or coverage may be arranged by P&I clubs or by mutual associations formed especially to handle such risks, including freight, demurrage, and defence risks; war risks; and other specialized market covers. Freight, demurrage, and defence coverage consists of standard additional coverage arranged by a P&I club and covers costs and expenses related to claims and liabilities for the following:

- freight (i.e., the amount of money paid for the carriage of goods);
- demurrage (i.e., a penalty payable to the shipowner in carriage contracts for delay in loading or unloading of the cargo);[215]
- defence (i.e., legal expenses not ordinarily covered in P&I insurance); and
- offshore energy operations (a very specialized risk area covered by a few P&I clubs; in most cases, such operations will be covered by a separate set of P&I rules and liability will be limited).[216]

War-risk insurance is handled either by P&I clubs or War Risks associations and provides coverage for losses incurred in hostile territories in wartime, or from riots, sabotage, revolutions, and piracy. Finally, there is also some other specialized coverage that is designed to meet specific needs including the following:

- insurance coverage for contractual cargo liabilities beyond the restrictions laid down in P&I club rules that are based on the *Hague/Hague-Visby Rules* limits;[217]
- cruise ship operator's liability for passengers while on shore excursions from the ship; and
- oil pollution liability under international regimes.[218]

It is in the P&I area that most legal activity takes place on a day-to-day basis. P&I coverage is the shipowner's third-party insurance providing

---

215 See D(3)(b) in Chapter 8, "Laytime and Demurrage."
216 Usually US$100 million; as a result, additional liability coverage is normally arranged. See also E. Gold, "Pollution from Offshore Activities — An Overview of the Operational, Legal and Environmental Aspects" and S.-H. Svensen, "Pollution from Offshore Activities — Liability and P&I Insurance Aspects" in C.M. De La Rue, ed., *Liability for Damage to the Environment* (London: Lloyd's Press, 1993); W.J. Hope-Ross, "Insurance and Indemnity Problems in Offshore Drilling Operations" (1973) 11 Alta. L.Rev. 471. See also F in Chapter 2, "The Shipping Industry: An Overview" and B(7) in Chapter 5, "The Safety Management of Ships."
217 See C in Chapter 9, "Carriage of Goods under Bills of Lading and Similar Documents."
218 See Chapter 17, "Marine Pollution Prevention."

risk coverage for operational exposure through protection from liabilities and by indemnifying those who suffer damage from most operations.

FURTHER READINGS

BUGLASS, L.J., *Marine Insurance and General Average in the United States*, 3d ed. (Cambridge, MA: Cornell Maritime Press, 1991).

DOVER, V., *A Handbook on Marine Insurance*, 8th ed. (London: Witherby, 1975).

FERNANDES, R.M., *Marine Insurance Law in Canada* (Toronto: Butterworths, 1987).

GOLD, E., *Gard Handbook on P&I Insurance*, 5th ed. (Arendal, NO: Gard A.S., 2002).

HARDY IVAMY, E.R., *Marine Insurance*, 4th ed. (London: Butterworths, 1985).

———, *Chalmers' Marine Insurance Act of 1906*, 10th ed. (London: Butterworths, 1993).

HAZELWOOD, S., *P&I Clubs: Law and Practice*, 3d ed. (London: Stevens, 2000).

HEALY, N.J. & D.J. SHARPE, *Cases and Materials on Admiralty*, 3d ed. (St. Paul, MN: West Publishing, 1999) Part IV.

LAMBETH, R.J., ed., *Templeman on Marine Insurance: Principles and Practice*, 6th ed. (London: Pitman, 1986).

MILLER, M.D., *Marine War Risk Insurance* (London: Lloyd's Press, 1990).

MUSTILL, M. & J.C.B. Gilman, eds., *Arnould's Law of Marine Insurance and Average*, 3 vols., 16th ed. (London: Stevens, 1981 & 1997).

O'MAY, C., *Marine Insurance: Law and Policy* (London: Sweet & Maxwell, 1993).

PARKS, A.L., *The Law and Practice of Marine Insurance and Average* (Centreville, MD: Cornell Maritime Press, 1987).

STRATHY, G.R. & G.C. MOORE, *Law & Practice of Marine Insurance in Canada* (Toronto: LexisNexis Butterworths, 2003).

SUMMERSKILL, M., *Oil Rigs: Law and Insurance* (London: Stevens, 1979).

TETLEY, W., *Marine Cargo Claims*, 3d ed. (Cowansville, QB: Yvon Blais, 1988).

ANNEX
CANADIAN MARINE INSURANCE LEGISLATION CONCORDANCE

The following concordance table covers the sections in the U.K., Canadian federal, Ontario, British Columbia, Manitoba, New Brunswick, and Nova Scotia marine insurance acts. As already indicated above, Canadian provincial marine insurance legislation is no longer applicable as it has been superseded by the federal *Marine Insurance Act, 1993*.

Table 7.1 Legislation Concordance of Canadian Marine Insurance

Section	U.K.[1]	CA[2]	ON[3]	BC[4]	MN[5]	NB[6]	NS[7]
Interpretation & Application	90	2–5	1	1		1	227
Marine Insurance Defined	1	6	2	2	2	2	228
Mixed Risks	2	6	3	3	3	3	229
Contractual Requirement	3	6	4	4	4–5	4	230
Wagering & Gaming Void	4	18	5	5	6	5	231
Insurable Interest	5	8	6	6	7	6	232
Attachment of Interest	6	7	7	7	8	7	233
Contingent/ Defeasible Interest	7	9	8	8	9	8	234
Partial Interest	8	10	9	9	10	9	235
Reinsurance	9	14	10	10	11	10	236
Bottomry	10	15	11	11	12	11	237
Master's/Crew Wages	11	11	12	12	13	12	238
Advance Freight	12	12	13	13	14	13	239
Insurance Charges	13	13	14	14	15	14	240

---

1 *Marine Insurance Act, 1906*, above note 22.
2 *Marine Insurance Act, 1993*, above note 35.
3 *Marine Insurance Act*, above note 29.
4 *Insurance (Marine) Act*, above note 25.
5 *Marine Insurance Act*, above note 26.
6 *Marine Insurance Act*, above note 27.
7 *Insurance Act*, above note 28, Part IX.

Marine Insurance

Section	U.K.	CA	ON	BC	MN	NB	NS
Quantum of Interest	14	16	15	15	16	15	241
Assignment of Interest	15	17	16	16	17	16	242
Insurable Value	16	19	17	17	18	17	243
Good Faith	17	20	18	18	19	18	244
Disclosure by Insured	18	21	19	19	20	19	245
Disclosure by Insurance Agent	19	21	20	20	21	20	246
Representations	20	22	21	21	22	21	247
Conclusion of Contract	21	23	22	22	23	22	248
Contract embodied in Policy	22	25	23	23	24	23	249
Content of Policy	23	26	24	24	25	24	250
Signature of Insurer	24	27	25	25	26	25	251
Voyage & Time Policies	25	29	26	26	27	26	252
Designation of Subject-Matter	26	28	27	27	28	27	253
Type of Policy	27	30	28	28	29	28	254
Unvalued Policy	28	30	29	29	30	29	255
Floating Policy	29	31	30	30	31	30	256
Policy Form	30	–	31	31	–	31	257
Premium Arrangement	31	–	32	32	32	32	258
Double Insurance	32	86	33	33	34	33	259
Warranty	33	32	34	34	35	34	260
Warranty Breach Excuse	34	39	35	35	36	35	261
Express Warranties	35	33	36	36	37	36	262
Warranty of Neutrality	36	36	37	37	38	37	263
Warranty of Nationality	37	35	38	38	39	38	264
Warranty of Safety	38	–	39	39	40	39	265
Warranty of Seaworthiness	39	37	40	40	41	40	266
Warranty re Goods	40	38	41	41	42	41	267
Warranty of Legality	41	34	42	42	43	42	268

356   MARITIME LAW

Section	U.K.	CA	ON	BC	MN	NB	NS
Commencement of Risk	42	40	43	43	44	43	269
Alteration of Departure Port	43	41	44	44	45	44	270
Different Destination	44	41	45	45	46	45	271
Change of Voyage	45	42	46	46	47	46	272
Deviation	46	43	47	47	48	47	273
Several Discharge Ports	47	43	48	48	49	48	274
Delay in Voyage	48	44	49	49	50	49	275
Deviation/Delay Excuses	49	45	50	50	51	50	276
Policy Assignment	50	51	51	51	52	51	277
No Assignment without Interest	51	52	52	52	53	52	278
Premium Payment	52	47–48	53	53	54	53	279
Policy effected by Broker	53	49	54	54	55	54	280
Effect of Receipt	54	50	55	55	56	55	281
Included/Excluded Losses	55	53	56	56	57	56	282
Partial/Total Loss	56	54–55, 61, 62	57	57	58	57	283
Actual Total Loss	57	56	58	58	59	58	284
Missing Ship	58	56	59	59	60	59	285
Transhipment, etc.	59	46	60	60	61	60	286
Constructive Total Loss defined	60	57	61	61	62	61	287
Constructive Total Loss Effect	61	57	62	62	63	62	288
Abandonment Notice	62	58–59	63	63	64	63	289
Effect of Abandonment	63	60	64	64	65	64	290
Particular Average Loss	64	63	65	65	66	65	291
Salvage Charges Recovery	65	64	66	66	67	66	292
General Average Loss	66	65	67	67	68	67	293
Insurer's Liability	67	66	68	68	69	68	294
Total	68	67	69	69	70	69	295
Partial Loss of Ship	69	68	70	70	71	70	296
Partial Loss of Freight	70	69	71	71	72	71	297
Partial Loss of Goods	71	70	72	72	73	72	298

Section	U.K.	CA	ON	BC	MN	NB	NS
Apportionment of Valuation	72	71	73	73	74	73	299
General Average Contributions	73	72	74	74	75	74	300
Liabilities to Third Parties	74	73	75	75	76	75	301
Measure of Indemnity	75	74	76	76	77	76	302
Proportional Liability	–	75	–	–	–	–	–
Construction	–	76	–	–	–	–	–
Particular Average Warranties	76	77	77	77	78	77	303
Successive Losses	77	78	78	78	79	78	304
Sue and Labour	78	79	79	79	80	79	305
Duty to Diminish Loss	–	80	–	–	–	–	–
Subrogation	79	81	80	80	81	80	306
Contribution	80	87	81	81	82	81	307
Effect of Underinsurance	81	88	82	82	83	82	308
Return of Premium	82	82	83	83	84	83	309
Return by Agreement	83	83	84	84	85	84	310
Failure of Consideration	84	84–84	85	85	86	85	311
Mutual Insurance	85	89	86	86	87	86	312
Ratification	86	24	87	87	88	87	313
Variation of Obligations	87	90	88	88	89	88	314
Reasonable Time	88	91	89	89	90	89	315
Rules of Common Law	89	–	80	90	91	90	316

CHAPTER 8

CARRIAGE OF GOODS BY CHARTERPARTY

A. INTRODUCTION

Cargoes carried by sea are governed by two separate and strikingly different regimes according to the kinds of goods involved and the type of ships in which they are transported. For practical reasons, goods are moved across the oceans either in bulk or in packaged form. The type of cargo determines the way in which it will be handled; therefore, oil, ores, grains, timber, and other primary products are transported in bulk, while manufactured products and personal goods are moved in individual protective packages, otherwise known as break bulk goods. Such packages are typically made up into units, for ease of handling by forklift trucks and cranes, by strapping them together on pallets or stuffing them in 20- or 40-foot (6- or 12-meter) metal containers. Very large and unwieldy items, like yachts and earth moving equipment, may be shipped as single units with a minimum of wrapping.

Different kinds of cargoes not only demand different types of ships but, more importantly from a legal perspective, different modes of operation. A bulk cargo, as the name suggests, generally occupies all the carrying space of the ship, which, accordingly, will be directed by the cargo owner to proceed more or less directly to a selected destination. Therefore, ships that carry bulk goods tramp from port to port around the world, as cargoes are available and cargo owners engage them. Such tramp ships do not sail to a schedule but carry their cargoes by individual agreements with the cargo owners in contracts known as charterparties. Packaged goods may be numerous but not individually bulky and, so, they need to be combined to fill the holds of a ship. In fact, a modern container ship may carry several thousand containers of goods belonging to hundreds of different owners. Such multiple ownership of cargoes on the same ship inevitably means the vessel must sail on a pre-arranged schedule of ports and timetable. Equally, the shipowner cannot negotiate individual terms of carriage with each cargo owner but offers transportation services on a set of standard trading conditions made available in advance. Such liner service, as it is called, is recorded for each cargo in a bill of lading or similar document.

As the manner of moving goods by tramp ships or liner service determines the kind of contractual document under which they are carried, so the legal regime governing the relations between the shipowner and the cargo owner will differ. Charterparties are regulated by the maritime common law of contracts as to their validity, interpretation, and effect. In principle, therefore, the parties have freedom to contract as seems fit, overlaid only by a multitude of standard clauses and cases interpreting their technical meanings. Bills of lading, on the other hand, are now governed by one or other sets of internationally uniform rules. As the maritime common law proved to be an inadequate regimen to balance the shipowner's and cargo owner's risks in the estimation of most countries, a set of rules, known as the *Hague Rules*,[1] was agreed in 1924 to limit the freedom of contract in the liner trades. Subsequent technological improvements in ships and their equipment, as well as the development of cargo-handling methods, have necessitated extensive reform of the *Hague Rules*, but no general international agreement on one new set of rules has yet been achieved. As a result, bills of lading are largely regulated by national legislation that imposes some variant of the *Hague Rules*.

This division of applicable legal regimes is not, in practice, so simple. In particular, goods are frequently carried under bills of lading on a chartered ship. Bulk cargoes of oil are typically processed this way so that they may be sold in the market, often many times over, by negotiation of the bills of lading while the carrying ship is still at sea. Again, when a charterer loads goods of another person, that cargo owner will always need a bill of lading or similar document as evidence of the transaction. The legal implications of issuing bills of lading for the car-

---

1 *International Convention for the Unification of Certain Rules of Law Relating to Bills of Lading*, 25 August 1924, 120 L.N.T.S. 155 [*Hague Rules*].

riage of goods on a chartered ship can quickly become complex. It is not easy to determine the intended contractual relations among three parties to two different contracts, especially when the terms of the charterparty and the bill of lading are not aligned and complementary. The difficulties are compounded by the multiplicity of documents that may be involved, such as when bills of lading are issued for goods being carried on a voyage-chartered ship that has been time-chartered from the charterer by demise or the shipowner.

Such is the difference in the law regulating tramp ships carrying goods in bulk under charterparties, and liner vessels moving packaged goods covered by bills of lading, that this subject calls for separate treatment in this and the following chapter. Accordingly, the law surrounding charterparties is explained in this chapter and the regulation of bills of lading and similar documents is discussed in Chapter 9. There are, however, a set of fundamental obligations in maritime common law that are borne by the carrier and cargo owner in any transit of goods, be it processed under a charterparty, a bill of lading, or any other document. As these obligations reflect the commercial elements of every ocean transport transaction, they will be discussed first.

B. MARITIME COMMON LAW PRINCIPLES OF CARRIAGE

In the absence of contrary agreement or mandatory legislation, the parties to any contract for the carriage of goods by water will bear a number of obligations implied by Canadian maritime common law, as follows:

- obligations on the carrier:
  - to provide a seaworthy ship,
  - to care for the cargo,
  - not to deviate on the voyage, and
  - to deliver the cargo without delay;
- obligations on the cargo owner:
  - not to ship dangerous goods without appropriate warning, and
  - to pay the freight (transport charge);
- obligations shared by carrier and cargo owner:
  - general average.

Each obligation will be discussed in turn, except for general average, which is the subject of Chapter 16.

1) Seaworthiness of the Ship

The implied obligation of seaworthiness requires the shipowner to put up a ship that is in every way suitable for the contracted voyage. The courts have interpreted this obligation broadly as requiring that the hull, machinery, and all operational parts of the ship must be fit for the particular voyage intended in light of the route, sea conditions, weather, and other hazards reasonably to be expected at that time of year.[2] Seaworthiness also connotes other ship related attributes. The vessel must be properly supplied and provisioned and also properly equipped for navigation.[3] It must, of course, satisfy all mandatory laws regarding surveys, onboard documentation, and operational standards.[4] It must carry a full complement of competent crew which has been adequately trained in seamanship for its rank and in the operational and safety procedures of the ship.[5] In addition, the ship must be cargo-worthy in the sense that it is appropriate as well as prepared to receive and care for the particular kind of cargo it is contracted to carry.[6] Further, seaworthiness includes not only the suitability of the cargo holds but also the way in which the cargo is stowed. A ship is not seaworthy if bad stowage results in an overladen or unbalanced vessel that is not fit to go to sea.[7] These features of a seaworthy vessel are not static but change in the course of time as newer and better shipping and navigational equipment and technology become available. The dynamic standard is a relative one. A ship cannot be expected to be provided with all the very latest technology but is required to carry equipment of an opera-

---

2   *Lyon v. Mells* (1804), 5 East 428, 102 E.R. 1134; *Stanton v. Richardson* (1874), L.R. 9 C.P. 390; *McFadden v. Blue Star Line*, [1905] 1 K.B. 697 [*McFadden*].
3   *Toepfer G.m.b.h. v. Tossa Marine Co. (The Derby)*, [1985] 2 Lloyd's L.R. 325 (C.A.) [*Toepfer*].
4   Which now include the *ISM Code*: see D(2) in Chapter 5, "*ISM Code*." And see *Levy v. Costerton* (1816), 4 Camp. 389, 171 E.R. 124; *Cheikh Boutros Selin El-Khoury v. Ceylon Shipping Lines Ltd. (The Madeleine)*, [1967] 2 Lloyd's Rep. 224; *Toepfer*, ibid.
5   *Standard Oil Co. of New York v. Clan Line Steamers*, [1924] A.C. 100; *Hong Kong Fir Shipping Co. v. Kawasaki Kisen Kaisha Ltd.*, [1962] 2 Q.B. 26 (C.A.); *Makedonia (The)*, [1962] 1 Lloyd's Rep. 316; *N.M. Paterson & Sons Ltd. v. Robin Hood Flour Mills Ltd. (The Farrandoc)*, [1968] 1 Ex. C.R. 175.
6   *Joseph A. Likely Ltd. v. AW Duckett & Co.* (1916), 53 S.C.R. 471; *Grand Bank Fisheries Ltd. v. Lake & Lake Ltd.*, [1955] 4 D.L.R. 493, 37 M.P.R. 97; *Good Friend (The)*, [1984] 2 Lloyd's L.R. 586.
7   *Elder, Dempster & Co. v. Paterson, Zochonis & Co.*, [1924] A.C. 522 at 561; *Re Unus Shipping Co.*, [1937] 2 D.L.R. 239 (N.S.S.C.).

tional standard that is at least as good as is currently in general use in the industry.[8]

At common law the undertaking that the ship is seaworthy is absolute,[9] but the standard by which seaworthiness is measured is relative to the ordinary perils that may be expected to be encountered in the particular voyage at that time of year by the specific cargo.[10] One way of expressing the test of seaworthiness is to ask, "Would a prudent owner have required [the defect] to be made good before sending his ship to sea had he known of it?"[11] Further, although it is customarily said that the ship must be seaworthy at the beginning of the voyage, it may be more appropriate to speak of stages of the voyage where it is so divisible. For instance, the ship must be cargo-worthy when notice of readiness to load is given,[12] even though repairs to the hull or the engines are still proceeding and are only completed shortly before the ship is loaded and, in that respect, is ready to sail. Other examples of a voyage in stages include a transit partly through freshwater, such as the St. Lawrence River, and partly across the sea, or passage necessarily interrupted to call at intermediate ports for bunker fuel.[13] It has been held that "there is a different degree of seaworthiness required by law, according to the different stage or portion of the voyage which the vessel successively has to pass through, and the difficulties she has to encounter."[14] It is sufficient if the ship is seaworthy in respect of each stage before it embarks on that stage of the voyage.

The obligation of seaworthiness is neither a condition nor a warranty of the contract but an intermediate or innominate term, for breach of which the consequences depend on its seriousness.[15] If the unseaworthiness of the ship is sufficiently serious, such that it cannot be remedied in a reasonable time, it will be treated as if it were a breach of a condition that may terminate the carriage contract if the voyage

---

8   *Bradley & Sons v. Federal Steam Navigation Co.* (1927), 27 Ll. L.R. 395; *Australian Star (The)* (1940), 67 Ll. L.R. 110; *Peter Paul v. Christer Salen (The)*, 152 F. Supp 410 (S.D.N.Y. 1957).
9   *Steel v. State Line Steamship Co.* (1877), 3 App. Cas. 72 [*Steel*]; *Grand Bank Fisheries Ltd. v. Lake & Lake Ltd.*, above note 6.
10 *Steel*, ibid.; *Hedley v. Pinkney & Sons Steamship Co.*, [1894] A.C. 222.
11 *McFadden*, above note 2 at 706, quoting *Carver on Carriage By Sea*, s.18.
12 *McFadden*, ibid.; *A.E. Reed & Co. v. Page, Son & East Ltd.*, [1927] 1 K.B. 743 at 755.
13 *Vortigern (The)*, [1899] P. 140.
14 *Quebec Marine Ins. Co. v. Commercial Bank of Canada* (1870), L.R. 3 P.C. 234.
15 *Hong Kong Fir Shipping Co. v. Kawasaki Kisen Kaisha Ltd.*, above note 5; *Mihalis Angelos (The)*, [1971] 1 Q.B. 164.

has not begun.[16] Once the voyage is underway this remedy is no longer open to the charterer. Usually, cargo losses whenever they happen, provided they were caused by the unseaworthy condition of the ship before the voyage,[17] will be remedied by payment of damages in compensation. If the ship is seaworthy when it sails but becomes unseaworthy during the voyage, there is no breach of the implied obligation; liability for any cargo loss will be determined by reference to the cause of the loss and the shipowner's duty of cargo care.

2) Care of the Cargo

"[E]very shipowner who carries goods for hire in his ship ... undertakes to carry them at his own absolute risk, the act of God or of the Queen's enemies alone excepted."[18] The burden of this obligation was explained by Lord Wright in *Paterson Steamships Ltd. v. Canadian Cooperative Wheat Producers Ltd.*, when he said of a carrier of goods by sea or water: "At common law, he was called an insurer, that is he was absolutely responsible for delivering in like order and condition at the destination the goods bailed to him for carriage."[19] The shipowner's obligation to care for the cargo was never utterly absolute. Lord Wright also admitted the exceptions of loss or damage by acts "of God or the Queen's enemies." To these may be added certain failings of the cargo and the cargo owner. The shipowner is not liable for cargo loss resulting from "inherent vice," that is, by the internal deterioration of the goods over the time of the voyage.[20] Nor is the shipowner responsible for damage resulting from defective or insufficient packing of the goods by the shipper, for "no person is entitled to claim compensation from others for damage occasioned by his neglect to do something which it was his duty to do."[21] A fifth exception to the common law obligation

---

16 E.g., *Stanton v. Richardson*, above note 2.
17 *Europa (The)*, [1908] P. 84.
18 *Liver Alkali Co. v. Johnson* (1874), L.R. 9 Ex. 338 at 344.
19 [1934] A.C. 538 at 544 (P.C.) [*Paterson Steamships*]. Lord Wright implies the origin of this obligation is bailment, which harkens back to Holt C.J.'s judgment in *Coggs v. Bernard* (1703), 2 LD. Raym. 909, 92 E.R. 107, that public carriers by water bear this heavy duty out of a public policy to protect the cargo owner's property against the risk of clandestine collusion of the carrier with thieves to steal it. Holt C.J. also pointed out that this strict obligation is an exception to the usual common law rule that bailees for reward are required to exercise reasonable care.
20 *Blower v. Great Western Railway* (1872), L.R. 7 C.P. 655; *Nugent v. Smith* (1876), 1 C.P.D. 423.
21 *Barbour v. South East Railway* (1876), 34 L.T. 67 at 68.

is a "general average act," for instance, an intentional sacrifice of some cargo in order to save the ship and the rest of the cargo from a common peril during the voyage.[22]

The exceptions do not avail the shipowner, however, if he or she does not take reasonable measures to guard against their operation or their effects. Negligence on the part of the shipowner will exclude the exception for loss as a result, for instance, of an act of God.[23] Also, as exceptions to the shipowner's duty of care for the cargo, they do not afford any relief to the absolute duty at common law to provide a seaworthy ship.

3) Deviation on the Voyage

In addition to caring for the cargo, the shipowner is obliged by law to prosecute the voyage without unjustifiable deviation[24] or unreasonable delay.[25] The ship must not depart from its proper course, which is either an agreed route or, failing any agreement, the usual trade route. The carriage contract might specify a voyage from A to B with an intermediate port of call at C. Then voyaging from A to B via C would not be a deviation, but calling at D would be. In the absence of an agreement about the route, the usual trade route to follow is typically the most direct geographical route, though it is open to the shipowner to show that a different route is the customary one.[26] For instance, a ship may call at a particular intermediate port for bunkers if it is normal commercial practice to do so.[27]

A deviation off course is justified if it is made to save life or to preserve the safety of the ship and/or the cargo. At common law, deviation to save lives, for instance of persons on another ship in peril, is always justified but a deviation to save or salvage property is not.[28] Deviation to protect the voyage from grave peril, such as severe weather, ice, or

---

22 See Chapter 16, "General Average."
23 *Siordet v. Hall* (1828), 130 E.R. 902, where negligence in filling a boiler overnight allowed frost (the act of God) to freeze and burst a connecting pipe, causing damage to the cargo. See also *Wilson, Sons & Co. v. Xantho (The)* (1887), 12 App. Cas. 503; and *Paterson Steamships*, above note 19.
24 *Davis v. Garrett* (1830), 6 Bing. 716, 130 E.R. 1456.
25 Discussed below in B(4), " Delay in Delivery."
26 *Reardon Smith Line Ltd. v. Black Sea and Baltic General Insurance Co.*, [1939] A.C. 562 [*Reardon Smith Line Ltd.*]; *Achille Lauro Fu Gioacchino & Co. v. Total Societa Italiana Per Azioni*, [1968] 2 Lloyd's L.R. 247.
27 *Reardon Smith Line Ltd.*, ibid.
28 *Scaramanga v. Stamp* (1880), 5 C.P.D. 295, 42 L.T. 840.

pirates, is also acceptable.[29] Indeed the master bears the duty, on behalf of the shipowner, to care for the cargo and thus has the authority, even an obligation, to deviate as necessary; this authority includes entering an unscheduled port for repairs even though they are required because the ship was not seaworthy at the beginning of the voyage.[30] But the deviation and delay must be kept to minimum. In *Burns v. Cassels*,[31] a ship heading for Bathurst, New Brunswick, in the Gulf of St. Lawrence, began to leak near Scatterie, off Cape Breton, Nova Scotia; the captain sailed to Saint John, New Brunswick, in the Bay of Fundy, for repairs. The Court held this was not a justifiable deviation, as the ship might readily have gone to the much closer port of Sydney, Nova Scotia, for repair. In addition to geographic deviations, some other breaches of the carriage contract have sometimes been treated as *quasi*-deviations; examples are stowage of cargo on deck without authorization,[32] lengthy delay,[33] and overcarriage of the cargo.[34] The importance of characterizing these kinds of default as if they were deviations lies in the extreme legal consequences, discussed below. The reason for treating them as deviations is thought to be related to the seriousness of the breach of the carriage contract. All involve essentially a different voyage than the one contracted, with the result that insurance for the contracted voyage, at least under traditional policies, will likely not cover it. The use of this legal fiction has been more prevalent in the United States than elsewhere, though not without criticism.[35]

Deviation is regarded as so serious a breach that it goes to the root of the carriage contract. As a consequence, according to the older cases,

---

29 *Teutonia (The)* (1872), L.R. 4 P.C. 171.
30 *Kish v. Taylor*, [1912] A.C. 604.
31 (1886), 26 N.B.R. 20, aff'd 14 S.C.R. 256.
32 *Wibau Maschinenfabric Hartman S.A. v. Mackinnon & Mackenzie (The Chanda)*, [1989] 2 Lloyd's L.R. 494 (Q.B.); *Tasman Express Ltd. v. JJ Case (Australia) Pty. Ltd. (The Canterbury Express)* (1992), 111 F.L.R. 108 (N.S.W.C.A.) [*The Canterbury Express*].
33 *Citta di Messina (The)*, 169 F. 472 (D.C.N.Y. 1909); *Cunard Steamship Co. v. Buerger*, [1927] A.C. 1 (H.L.); *Jones v. Flying Clipper (The)*, 116 F. Supp. 386 (D.C.N.Y. 1953); *Atlantic Mutual Ins. Co. v. Poseidon Schiffahrt*, 313 F.2d 872 (7th Cir. 1963); *Hellenic Army Command v. MV Livorno*, 1981 A.M.C. 1288 (D.C.N.Y. 1981).
34 *Hoskyn v. Silver Line Ltd. (Silvercypress)*, 63 F. Supp. 452 (D.C.N.Y. 1943). Unauthorized transshipment has also been declared to be a deviation: see *Insurance Co. of North America v. S/S American Argosy*, 1984 A.M.C. 186 (S.D.N.Y. 1983).
35 See *Iligan International Steel Mills Inc. v. S.S. John Weyerhaeuser*, 507 F.2d 68, 1975 A.M.C. 33 (2d Cir. 1974); and *Sedco Inc. v. S.S. Strathewe*, 1986 A.M.C. 2801 (2d Cir. 1986).

the contract is displaced and all its provisions, including freight and exemption clauses, no longer benefit the shipowner.[36] Further, as a condition precedent of the contract is broken, it does not matter that the deviation was not the cause of the cargo loss.[37] For example, in *J. Thorley Ltd. v. Orchis Steamship Co. Ltd.*,[38] the cargo was damaged through negligence during its discharge, but the shipowner was not allowed to shelter behind the exception clause covering the incident, because the ship had abrogated the carriage contract by a deviation earlier in the voyage. The shipowner could only escape these dire consequences if either the cargo owner condoned the deviation and treated the contract as subsisting, suing only for the damage, if any, caused by the deviation itself, or the shipowner proved the loss would have occurred even in the absence of the deviation, through an event, such as an act of God or the Queen's enemies, or of the cargo owner, that was excusable at common law.[39] These propositions of law in the older cases left unexplained what terms of carriage arose after a deviation in the subsequent voyage to the contracted destination. In particular, if the ship were to complete the voyage, what freight would the shipowner be entitled to be paid?[40] The judgment in *J. Thorley Ltd.*[41] suggested only that the parties would be bound by such obligations as could be implied from the completion of the voyage. Subsequently, the House of Lords sought to dissolve these uncertainties in *Hain Steamship Co. v. Tate & Lyle Ltd.*[42] Lord Atkin famously reinterpreted the consequences of an unjustified deviation in ordinary contract terms, opining that

> I venture to think that the truth is that the departure from the voyage contracted to be made is a breach by the shipowner of his contract, but a breach of such a serious character that however slight the deviation the other party to the contract is entitled to treat it as going to the root of the contract, and to declare himself as no longer bound by any of its terms … . No doubt the extreme gravity attached to a devi-

---

36 *Davis v. Garrett*, above note 24; *Glynn v. Margeston & Co.*, [1893] A.C. 351; *J. Thorley Ltd. v. Orchis Steamship Co.*, [1907] 1 K.B. 660 (C.A.) [*J. Thorley Ltd.*].
37 *Davis v. Garrett*, ibid.; *J. Thorley Ltd.*, ibid.
38 Above note 36.
39 *Davis v. Garrett*, above note 24; *James Morrison & Co. v. Shaw, Savill and Albion Co.*, [1916] 2 K.B. 783 (C.A.).
40 *Hain Steamship Co. v. Tate & Lyle Ltd.*, [1936] 2 All E.R. 597 (H.L.) [*Hain Steamship*], subsequently indicated the shipowner might claim freight on a *quantum meruit* basis.
41 Above note 36.
42 Above note 40.

ation in contracts of carriage is justified by the fact that the insured cargo owner when the ship has deviated has become uninsured ... . If this view be correct then the breach by deviation does not automatically cancel the express contract, otherwise the shipowner by his own wrong can get rid of his own contract ... the event falls within the ordinary law of contract. The party who is affected by the breach has the right to say, I am not bound by the contract whether it is expressed in the charterparty, bill of lading or otherwise ... But on the other hand, as he can elect to treat the contract as ended, so he can elect to treat the contract as subsisting: and if he does this with knowledge of his rights he must in accordance with the general law of contract be held bound.[43]

Therefore, the consequences of the deviation, however slight, are decided by the election of the cargo claimant, even though a decision to waive the breach must clearly show an intention to treat the carriage contract as still binding.[44]

Unfortunately this judgment on the effects of deviation in sea carriage contracts became the source of the so-called doctrine of fundamental breach in the law of contracts generally. When the incorrectness of this doctrine was finally and fully exposed,[45] the question was then opened whether its eradication from the law of contracts affected maritime cases of deviation. If the principles of the *Hain Steamship* case were no longer sound, then whether an exclusion clause would protect a shipowner after a deviation would seem to become a matter of construction of the contract, rather than the cargo claimant's election. In *Photo Production Ltd. v. Securicor Transport*[46] Lord Wilberforce was of the view that it was preferable that the rules surrounding unjustified deviations should be considered *sui generis* on account of their historical and commercial reasons. Most subsequent courts appear to have adopted this view, although not always without doubts.[47] The issue is particularly acute over the proper legal consequences of *quasi*-deviations. In *The Antares*,[48] Lloyd L.J. favoured the view that geographical

---

43 *Hain Steamship, ibid.* at 601.
44 *Ibid.* at 602.
45 *Photo Production Ltd. v. Securicor Transport Ltd.*, [1980] A.C. 827 [*Photo Production Ltd.*]; *Beaufort Realties (1964) Inc. v. Chomedy Aluminum Co.*, [1980] 2 S.C.R. 718.
46 *Photo Production Ltd., ibid.* at 845.
47 E.g., *The Canterbury Express*, above note 32.
48 *Kenya Railways v. Antares Co. (The Antares)*, [1987] 1 Lloyd's L.R. 424 at 430 (C.A.) [*The Antares*]. See also *The Canterbury Express, ibid.*

deviation cases should now be assimilated fully with the ordinary law of contracts, and that the instant case of *quasi*-deviation through unauthorized deck carriage would not be treated otherwise.

4) Delay in Delivery

In addition to transporting the cargo to the agreed destination without deviation, the carrier is also bound to deliver it with dispatch. This duty of timely performance is different in character and effect from the other common law obligations on the carrier. Damage to the cargo as a result of unseaworthiness or lack of care occurs at a particular moment and results in the physical loss and permanent deprivation of the goods. Delay does not happen at one moment but is a continuous feature of the voyage, which culminates in a breach of duty only if delivery is ultimately made out of time. Even so, the cargo owner is only temporarily, not permanently, deprived of the goods and thus suffers primarily economic, rather than physical, losses.

Given its continuous and fluid nature, any number of incidents throughout the voyage may result in delay. Later than expected arrival of the ship at the port of loading, time wasted in loading or sailing, slow going on the voyage, and labour hindrances in discharging may all found delay if the time lost is not made up before delivery. In other words, delay can arise from the actions or inactions of the carrier at any time from the moment the carriage contract comes into effect but it will not be determined to amount to a breach until the contract ceases.

The carriage contract may set a specific date for its performance, in which case a breach will occur if the required act is not done by the stated time, regardless of the reason, unless an express exception excuses the carrier. Thus, when the date by which a ship will sail is fixed by contract, the carrier will be held strictly liable if the ship does not depart on time.[49] In commercial contracts fixed times for performance are normally treated as conditions that required precise compliance.[50] The breach of a condition allows the injured party to treat the contract as terminated. So, if the ship does not sail by the agreed date, the cargo owner may throw up the contract and recover any deposit paid;[51] if this

---

49 E.g., *Simpson v. Young* (1859), 1 F. & F. 708, 175 E.R. 917.
50 *Bowes v. Shand* (1877), 2 App. Cas. 455 (H.L.); *Bunge Corp. v. Tradax S.A.*, [1981] 2 All E.R. 513 (H.L.), where Lord Wilberforce said "broadly speaking time will be considered of the essence in 'mercantile' contracts" (at 542). But cf. *Sail Labrador Ltd. v. Challenge One (The)*, [1999] 1 S.C.R. 265 [*Sail Labrador Ltd.*].
51 *Cranston v. Marshall* (1850), 5 Ex. 395, 155 E.R. 172.

course is not desirable or is not practical because the voyage has begun, the cargo owner may seek damages in compensation.[52] In the absence of express times for arriving, loading, sailing, or delivering, the carrier bears a duty implied by common law to complete the carriage contract without unreasonable delay.[53] This is an objective standard of performance. It is also a standard of fault liability and is therefore distinctly different from the strict liability that is imposed for unseaworthiness of the ship or deviation on the voyage. The carrier will not be liable even for protracted delay if it arose from causes beyond his or her control and he or she was not negligent.[54] The carrier is expected to use "such diligence in the performance [of the contract] as a person of ordinary diligence and prudence would use in like circumstances."[55] So, for example, obstructions *en route*,[56] repairs necessitated by accidents during the voyage,[57] congestion in port,[58] or strikes of dock workers[59] are all incidents that are likely to cause delay but not to incur liability.

If a delay becomes inevitable, the carrier bears a further set of responsibilities to try to avoid or minimize its effects.[60] He or she must inform the shipper of any expected delay[61] and should reasonably anticipate and guard against its effects; for instance, a ship carrying a perishable cargo should not enter a strike bound port.[62] The carrier must also make an effort to overcome the delay[63] and resume the voyage promptly after the cause of the delay has ended.[64] Once again, the

---

52   *Behn v. Burness* (1863), 3 B. & S. 751, 122 E.R. 281 (Ex. Ct.).
53   *Hales v. London and North Western Railway Co.* (1863), 4 B. & S. 66, 122 E.R. 384 (Q.B.); *Wilhelm (The)* (1866), 14 L.T. 636 (Adm. Ct.); *Hick v. Raymond & Reid*, [1893] A.C. 22 (H.L.); *Moel Tryvan Ship Co. v. Andrew Weir & Co.*, [1910] 2 K.B. 844 (C.A.).
54   *Hick v. Raymond & Reid*, ibid. at 32–33; *Briddon v. Great Northern Railway Co.* (1858), 28 L.J. Ex. 51.
55   *Panola (The)*, 1925 A.M.C. 1173 at 1183 (2d Cir. 1925).
56   *New Orleans (City of) v. Southern Scrap Material Co.*, 491 F. Supp. 46 (E.D. La. 1980).
57   *Plow City (The)*, 23 F. Supp. 548 (D. Pa. 1937).
58   *American Steel Co. of Cuba v. Transmarine Corp.*, 1929 A.M.C. 1516 (D.C.N.Y.).
59   *Hick v. Raymond & Reid*, above note 53.
60   See M.R. Ganado & H.M. Kindred, *Marine Cargo Delays* (London: Lloyd's Press, 1990) at c.5.
61   *Gray v. Seaboard Air Line Railway Co.*, 102 S.E. 512 (S.C. 1918); *Page Communications Engineers Inc. v. Hellemic Lines Ltd.*, 356 F. Supp. 456 (D.D.C. 1973).
62   *Crelinsten Fruit Co. v. Mormacsaga (The)*, [1969] 1 Lloyd's L.R. 515 (Ex. Ct.).
63   *American Steel Co. of Cuba v. Transmarine Corp.*, above note 58; *J.M. Rodriguez & Co. v. Moore–McCormack Lines Inc.*, 1973 A.M.C. 1463 (N.Y. 1973).
64   *Bowman v. Teall*, 23 Wend. 307 (N.Y. Sup. Ct. 1840); *Reed & Rice Co. v. Wood*, 120 S.E. 874 (Va. C.A. 1924).

carrier is only required to take reasonable measures to avoid or to overcome delay, but the standard of reasonable conduct is relative to the advances that have occurred in shipping and communications. Modern equipment allows carriers to anticipate and guard against delays with more foresightedness than in the past. Current shipping aids give carriers more choices of action to overcome delays nowadays.

The carrier who commits an unreasonable delay is ordinarily liable to compensate the cargo owner in damages.[65] But when the delay is not only unreasonably committed but also unduly long, it can have more serious consequences. Plainly a carrier should not be permitted to purchase delay indefinitely by the payment of damages. Devlin J. stated the problem in *Universal Cargo Carriers Corp. v. Citati*:

> Where time is not of the essence of the contract — in other words, when delay is only a breach of warranty — how long must the delay last before the aggrieved party is entitled to throw up the contract? The theoretical answer is not in doubt. The aggrieved party is relieved from his obligations when the delay becomes so long as to go to the root of the contract and amount to a repudiation of it.[66]

Later in his judgment Devlin J. provided a practical answer to his own question by saying that, to bring a carriage contract to an end for breach of warranty, there has to be a delay so great as to frustrate its commercial purposes.[67] The application of this legal principle of commercial frustration is a question of fact in every case. Its application must also be kept distinct from another kind of frustration, namely, the dissolution of a contract upon a supervening event that renders its performance impossible.

In order to establish a claim for delay the cargo owner must prove his or her loss, the delay, and the negligent or unreasonable conduct of the carrier in respect of the delay. This is a much greater burden of proof than is required of the cargo claimant for physical loss or damage to the goods. In claims for physical loss, simply proving damage to the goods while in the custody of the carrier is sufficient because the carrier bears strict liability for the cargo unless he or she can establish a lawful excuse. But claims for delay require the cargo owner to establish the carrier's

---

65 *Behn v. Burness*, above note 52; *Hadley v. Baxendale* (1854), 9 Ex. 341, 156 E.R. 145; *Hong Kong Fir Shipping Co. v. Kawasaki Kisen Kaisha Ltd.*, above note 15; *Satef-Huttenes Albertus v. Paloma Tercera Shipping Co. (The Pegase)*, [1981] 1 Lloyd's L.R. 175 (Q.B.).
66 [1957] 2 Q.B. 401 at 426.
67 *Ibid.* at 430. See also *Carvill v. Schoffield* (1883), 9 S.C.R. 370; *Hong Kong Fir Shipping Co. v. Kawasaki Kisen Kaisha Ltd.*, above note 15.

fault liability.[68] These principles of proof have clear application when the claim of delay is independent of any other events on the voyage. However, more often than not, delay is associated with other defaults of the carrier and then complex issues of causation and proof can arise.

Sometimes the causes of loss and delay are successive, such as when a ship puts to sea but, owing to its unseaworthy condition, the voyage is interrupted for repairs and so the cargo is delayed in delivery. The delay for repairs is the proximate cause of the loss that is claimed but it is hardly the primary, material, real, or effective cause (the courts use different terms).[69] It is obvious that the significant cause in law is the ship's unseaworthy condition at the outset and so the shipowner's liability will be judged by the standards and proof of seaworthiness, however reasonable the conduct and time taken for repairs may have been.

In other situations, two distinct causes of loss may occur in such a way that the first incident places the cargo at risk of the second. For instance, if goods, while negligently delayed in the port of loading, are destroyed by fire, there are two dependent yet distinct causes of the loss incurred. The House of Lords has approached this kind of situation by holding the carrier liable following an unreasonable delay if he or she should have foreseen the event that, but for the delay, would not have operated to induce the loss. In *Monarch Steamship Co. v. Karlshamns Oljefabriker (A/B)*,[70] the ship was delayed on the voyage by its unseaworthiness and so never reached its intended destination in Sweden because, in the meantime, the Second World War broke out and the British Admiralty ordered the vessel diverted to Glasgow, Scotland. The goods were subsequently shipped to Sweden on neutral vessels, and the Swedish cargo owners sued for the expense of the transshipment. The shipowners attempted to excuse themselves under a war-risks clause in the contract, which exonerated them for compliance with the British government's order. Nevertheless they were held liable because, in the House of Lords judgment, they could have foreseen the outbreak of war and so should have anticipated that the delay might result in the ship's diversion, which gave rise to the cargo claimant's loss.[71]

---

68 See *Wilhelm (The)*, above note 53; *Tuladi (The)*, 1927 A.M.C. 894 (E.D. La. 1927); *Fruitex Corp. v. GTS Eurofreighter*, 1980 A.M.C. 2710 (S.D.N.Y. 1980); and Ganado & Kindred, above note 60 at 77.
69 See *Smith, Hogg & Co. v. Black Sea and Baltic General Insurance Co.*, [1940] A.C. 997 at 1003–05 (H.L.).
70 [1949] A.C. 196.
71 See also *Malcolm Baxter, Jr. (The)*, 277 U.S. 323 (D.N.Y. 1928). Other approaches to this kind of situation are discussed in Ganado & Kindred, above note 60 at 63–69.

5) Dangerous Goods

Turning from the carrier's fundamental obligations, it is appropriate to describe, in turn, the cargo owner's two principal duties regarding dangerous goods and freight. By maritime common law the cargo owner bears an obligation not to ship goods that have a dangerous character without giving due notice to the carrier.[72] The purpose of this rule is to ensure that the carrier knows the risks involved in accepting the goods, as well as how to handle them, and to provide him or her with the opportunity to refuse their carriage. The shipper will be strictly liable for any loss occasioned by shipping dangerous goods without notice: ignorance of their dangerous nature is no defense for the cargo owner.[73] This common law duty is backed up by legislation, in particular the *Canada Shipping Act*, which requires the shipper to give notice of the nature of the goods in writing[74] and grants the master of a Canadian ship the right to refuse to take on board any package suspected of containing dangerous goods.[75]

"Dangerous goods" are not limited to naturally explosive, flammable, toxic, or corrosive substances but include anything that might cause a danger to the ship or other cargo.[76] Seemingly innocuous goods can become a danger because of the risks of sea carriage. For example, a cargo of wheat if wetted may expand with such pressure as to burst the seams of the ship's hull. Although a cargo may not endanger the safety of the vessel, it may still be "dangerous" at common law if it causes the ship to be quarantined or detained under government order. The *Canada Shipping Act* provides an equally generic definition:[77] "[D]angerous goods ... means goods that by reason of their nature, quantity or mode of stowage are either singly or collectively liable to endanger the lives of the passengers or imperil the ship."[78] But the Act also includes every substance declared dangerous by the regulations. In fact extensive regulations, reflecting the safety of life at sea convention, *SOLAS 1974*, cover a huge array of packaged goods, bulk materials,

---

72 *Brass v. Maitland* (1856), 6 E. & B. 470, 119 E.R. 940 (Q.B.); *Shaw Savill & Albion Co. v. Electric Reduction Sales Co. (The Mahia)*, [1955] 1 Lloyd's Rep. 264 (Qc. S.C.) [*The Mahia*]; *Effort Shipping Co. v. Linden Management S.A. (The Giannis NK)*, [1998] A.C. 605 (H.L.) [*The Giannis NK*].
73 *Brass v. Maitland*, ibid.; *The Giannis NK*, ibid.
74 R.S.C. 1985, c.S-9, s.389(3).
75 Ibid. s.389(4).
76 E.g., *Brass v. Maitland*, above note 72.
77 *Mitchell, Cotts & Co. v. Steel Brothers & Co.*, [1916] 2 K.B. 610.
78 Above note 74, s.2.

chemicals, and hazardous liquids that are identified as dangerous.[79] These are extended by the *Transportation of Dangerous Goods Act, 1992*[80] which, for sea carriage, applies the *International Maritime Dangerous Goods Code* of the International Maritime Organisation and the *Canadian Environmental Protection Act, 1999*,[81] and which implements the *Basel Convention on the Movement of Hazardous Wastes*. This mass of legislation provides directions for every named product as to the manner in which it must be packaged or prepared for transportation, marked, handled, stowed, and carried.[82] This dangerous goods legislation does not supersede the common law but extends it. Even so incidents can occasionally occur that are not determined by the legislation or its regulations and the court is called to apply the principles of the common law. In *Heath Steele Mines Ltd. v. The Erwin Schröder*,[83] a bulk cargo of copper concentrate in granular form shifted when the ship encountered severe weather. The ship listed so badly that the master brought the ship to the nearest port and unloaded the cargo, claiming that it was dangerous. The court found the *Canadian Concentrates Code*[84] of that time inadequate and held, in the face of conflicting expert evidence, the master could not have been expected to have known about the risks and precautions in carrying copper concentrate. The shipper was held liable for shipping dangerous goods without notice to the carrier.

The consequences of shipping dangerous goods depend on whether appropriate notice was given to the carrier. If no notice was given, and the danger becomes active, the goods may be offloaded.[85] Indeed, under the *Canada Shipping Act*, the master may throw overboard any dangerous goods that contravene the legislation or regulations for carrying them without any civil or criminal liability for their loss.[86] If

---

79 See the *Dangerous Goods Shipping Regulations*, S.O.R./81-951; *Dangerous Bulk Materials Regulations*, S.O.R./87-24; and *Dangerous Chemicals and Noxious Liquid Substances Regulations*, S.O.R./93-4. See also B(6)(c) in Chapter 5, "Dangerous Goods and Cargoes."
80 S.C. 1992, c.34. See also the *Transportation of Dangerous Goods Regulations*, S.O.R./2001-306.
81 S.C. 1999, c.33, Part 7, Div.8.
82 Failure to comply with the regulations by either the shipper or the carrier is an offence: *Canada Shipping Act*, above note 74, ss.389(2) and (7).
83 [1969] 1 Lloyd's L.R. 370 (Ex. Ct.), aff'd [1970] Ex. C.R. 426 [*Heath Steele Mines*]; *Micada Compania Naviera S.A. v. Texim*, [1968] 2 Lloyd's L.R. 57 (Q.B.).
84 Issued under an earlier version of *Canada Shipping Act*, above note 74.
85 E.g., *Heath Steele Mines*, above note 83.
86 Above note 74, s.389(5). Alternatively they may be forfeited and disposed of under court directions: *ibid.* s.390. In addition any ship found to be carrying dangerous goods contrary to the statutory standards may be detained: *ibid.* s.389(6).

notice of the dangerous goods was given — or none was necessary because the carrier already knew of the danger[87] — and he or she agrees to carry them, the carrier accepts responsibility for their safe transportation according to the normal standards of care for goods of that type. Thus, when a carrier accepted a cargo of Nova Scotia coal, which turned out to be somewhat gassier than other coal and so caused an explosion and injuries on board, the court held that the carrier also accepted the risk of such an accident. The usual precautions for carrying coal were employed by the carrier but proved insufficient in this case.[88] But acceptance of the goods for carriage with notice of their nature will not place the risk on the carrier if he or she cannot be expected to appreciate the danger and so is unable to guard against it: *Heath Steele Mines*, described previously, is such an example.[89]

The uncertainty in determining whether the shipper supplied the carrier with a notice sufficient to allow him or her to appreciate the risks of danger involved and to realize the precautions in handling, stowing, and carrying the goods that should be taken is much alleviated by the detailed statutory regulations. These rules place requirements on both parties. In addition to giving written notice to the carrier, the shipper must also properly pack and mark and safely deliver the goods to the carrier. In its turn, the carrier must comply with all the statutory standards for handling, stowing, carrying, and discharging the dangerous goods. The carrier cannot claim he or she was not adequately informed by the shipper when there are publicly proclaimed procedures to be followed. For example, in *The Mahia*,[90] all parties knew the dangerous character of the shipment of sodium chloride. The shipper fulfilled the packing and labelling requirements for such a cargo and it was uneventfully carried from Montreal, Canada, to Melbourne, Australia. There, through blatant negligence in discharging by stevedores, explosions, fire, deaths, injuries, and damage to the ship ensued. Since the stevedores were the uninstructed agents of the ship, the shipowner was held responsible for its own losses.

---

87 By reason of the common knowledge in the shipping industry of the risks associated with those kinds of goods or by prior dealings with the shipper: see, e.g., *The Mahia*, above note 72.
88 *Athanasia Comminos (The)*, [1990] 1 Lloyd's L.R. 277. See also *Atlantic Duchess (The)*, [1957] 2 Lloyd's Rep. 55.
89 See also *Micada Compania Naviera S.A. v. Texim*, above note 83.
90 Above note 72.

6) Freight

"Freight" is defined as "the price to be paid for the actual carriage of the goods."[91] Typically the freight is set at a fixed rate per unit by weight or volume of the cargo, but the shipper and the carrier are free to agree to any terms they wish about its calculation and payment. At common law freight is payable when earned, that is, by carriage of the goods to their destination. Indeed delivery of the cargo by the carrier and payment of freight by the cargo owner are concurrent requirements.[92] The carrier is entitled to the freight when ready and willing to deliver but is prevented by default of the cargo owner; however, no freight is payable if the goods are lost or destroyed on the voyage. It does not matter whether the loss of the goods was the fault of the carrier or not; the freight has not been earned. As excepted peril may afford protection to the carrier from suit for the cargo loss, it does not confer a right to freight in the absence of express terms in the carriage contract. If part of the cargo is lost and part delivered, the carrier is entitled to pro rated freight on the portion delivered.[93]

Freight is payable in full on cargo that is delivered damaged, as opposed to lost or destroyed, because it has been earned.[94] But delivery of cargo that is so damaged as to have lost the character of the goods described in the carriage document does not earn the carrier any freight. This is a question of fact, the test being whether the goods, in their deteriorated condition, have become for business purposes something different.[95] For instance, no freight was payable on a cargo of dates that, after sinking with the ship and being raised, was found to be a pulpy and fermenting mass unfit for human consumption, even though some dates were still recognizable and retained a remedial value for other purposes.[96] Even if the goods are delivered damaged, full freight is payable. The cargo owner may not claim any deduction

---

91 *Edmonstone v. Young* (1862), 12 U.C.C.P. 437 at 442. The term "hire" is commonly used with reference to the price for the use of the ship under time charterparties.
92 *Black v. Rose* (1864), 2 Moore N.S. 277, 15 E.R. 906; *Dakin v. Oxley* (1864), 15 C.B. (N.S.) 647, 6 E.R. 938; *Aries Tanker Corp. v. Total Transport Ltd. (The Aries)*, [1977] 1 Lloyd's L.R. 334 (H.L.) [*The Aries*]; *Henricksens Rederi A/S v. T.H.Z. Rolimpex (The Brede)*, [1973] 2 Lloyd's L.R. 333 (C.A.) [*The Brede*].
93 *Dakin v. Oxley*, ibid.; *Ritchie v. Atkinson* (1808), 10 East. 294, 103 E.R. 787.
94 *Halcrow v. Lemesurier* (1884), 10 Q.L.R. 239 (Q.B.).
95 *Asfar v. Blundell*, [1896] 1 Q.B. 123 (C.A.).
96 Ibid.; see also *Montedison v. Icroma (The Caspian Sea)*, [1980] 1 Lloyd's L.R. 91 (Q.B.).

or set-off, but he or she is not denied a separate action or counterclaim for the damage.[97] This old and singular rule of English law has been reiterated by the House of Lords in *The Aries*[98] in more recent times.[99] Under U.S. maritime law, a form of set-off known as recoupment is permitted to the cargo owner.[100] If early Canadian cases seemed to permit set-offs, more recently the Federal Court of Appeal has relied on the English rule as authoritative.[101]

Given the risk to the carrier that effort and expense may be outlaid without freight ever being earned, carriage contracts regularly include terms that vary the implied obligation at common law. Several types of clauses are used. For instance, advance freight indicates the freight must be paid in advance of loading or sailing or some specified event at the beginning of the voyage.[102] If paid in advance of an accident to the ship or cargo — the more so where the contract contains a clause such as "ship and/or goods, lost or not lost"[103] — the freight cannot be recovered.[104] But if the loss of the goods occurred in circumstances that render the carrier liable, then the freight paid in advance may be recouped as part of the cargo owner's loss.[105]

Advance freight is distinct from cash in advance for disbursements. When freight is payable on delivery, the carriage contract may call for cash contributions by the cargo owner to cover certain costs of the voyage such as pilotage fees, harbour dues, and wharfage. Advances of funds for such disbursements are not payment of freight; rather, they are loans accountable against the freight when due or recoverable if the freight is not earned.[106] Advance freight or freight paid in advance must also be distinguished from prepaid freight, as the latter "means only that the carrier must look to the shipper and not the consignee for pay-

---

97 *Dakin v. Oxley*, above note 92; *The Brede*, above note 92.
98 *The Aries*, above note 92. See also *Colonial Bank v. European Grain & Shipping Ltd. (The Dominique)*, [1989] 1 Lloyd's L.R. 431 (H.L.) [*The Dominique*].
99 The rule is modified in application to claims for unpaid hire under time charters by equitable principles of set off: see the discussion below at note 223.
100 *Shipping Corp. of India v. Pan American Seafood Inc.*, 583 F. Supp. 1555 (S.D.N.Y. 1984).
101 *S.S. Steamship Co. v. Eastern Caribbean Container Line*, [1986] 2 F.C. 27.
102 See *Karin Vatis (The)*, [1988] 2 Lloyd's L.R. 330 (C.A.); *The Dominique*, above note 98.
103 See, e.g., *Compania Naviera General v. Kerametal (The Lorna I)*, [1983] 1 Lloyd's L.R. 373 (C.A.).
104 *Allison v. Bristol Marine Insurance* (1876), 1 App. Cas. 209 (H.L.) [*Allison v. Bristol*].
105 *Great Indian Peninsula Railway v. Turnbull* (1885), 53 L.T. 325 (Q.B.).
106 *Hicks v. Shield* (1857), 7 E. & B. 633, 119 E.R. 1380; *De Silvale v. Kendall* (1915), 4 M. & S. 37, 105 E.R. 749.

ment of the freight and is obliged, in the absence of other considerations, to deliver up the cargo to the consignee without regard to whether, in fact, it has been paid the freight."[107]

Sometimes freight is agreed as a lump sum for the voyage rather than specifying it as a quantitative rate per unit of cargo. Then the whole of the lump sum is earned and payable, whatever the volume of cargo is loaded, as soon as any part of it is delivered.[108] Since freight is earned at common law by delivery at the agreed destination, no freight is payable for delivery at an intermediate port. However, partial or *pro rata* freight may become payable when the parties vary the carriage contract so that the cargo owner agrees to accept delivery at the intermediate port.[109] Two other freight terms are used to describe payments due to the carrier when the cargo owner does not fulfil his or her obligations. First, when the carrier is prevented from delivering the goods for reasons beyond his or her control and is unable to obtain instructions from the cargo owner, the carrier must make alternative arrangements for landing or transshipping them or overcarrying them to another port or returning them to the port of loading. The expense of these arrangements, having been made to protect the cargo owner's interests in the goods, are then chargeable as "back freight."[110] Second, the carriage contract typically requires the shipper to load a full cargo so that the carrier may maximize the freight to be earned by the voyage. If the shipper fails to do so and leaves empty or dead cargo space, the carrier has a good claim for breach of contract. His or her compensation is the net freight that would have been earned had the dead space been used; hence it is called "dead freight."[111] Since the claim is really for damages for breach of contract, the carrier must try to mitigate the loss by making a reasonable effort to obtain other cargo to fill the dead space.

The person responsible for paying the freight is the shipper, since he or she is the cargo party to the carriage contract with the carrier, but their agreement typically includes a term making delivery conditional on payment by the consignee and any subsequent cargo interests. If the

---

107 Per Mahoney J. in *Chastine Maersk (The) v. Trans-Mar Trading Co.*, [1974] F.C.J. No. 1003 (T.D.) (QL).
108 *Robinson v. Knights* (1873), L.R. 8 C.P. 465; *Thomas v. Harrowing Steamship Co.*, [1915] A.C. 58 (H.L.).
109 *Hunter v. Prinsep* (1808), 10 East 378, 103 E.R. 818; *Hopper v. Burness* (1876), 1 C.P.D. 137; *St. Enoch Shipping Co. v. Phosphate Mining Co.* (1914), [1916] 2 K.B. 624.
110 *Cargo Ex Argos* (1873), L.R. 5 P.C. 134.
111 *McLean and Hope v. Fleming* (1871), L.R. 2 Sc. & Div. 128.

freight is not paid, the carrier may assert a common law lien over the cargo.[112] Usually the carriage contract also extends a lien for advance freight and dead freight. The common law lien is good against everyone who acquires an interest in the goods, for example, the consignee and his or her sub-purchasers.[113] A contractual lien is only effective *inter partes* (i.e., against the shipper). At common law, the carrier's lien is a possessory right, thus it has two limiting features: first, it continues only so long as the carrier remains in possession of the goods, and, second, it only permits the carrier to retain the goods, as encouragement to the cargo owner to pay the overdue freight. However, the *Canada Shipping Act* extends the rights of the carrier in a couple of significant ways. The carrier may discharge the goods and place them in the custody of a warehouse without losing the lien, provided written notice of it is given to the warehouse keeper.[114] Then, if the freight has not been paid after ninety days,[115] enough of the goods may be advertised and sold by public auction to cover the costs of the sale, the safekeeping charges of the warehouse, and the overdue freight.[116]

Following this survey of Canadian maritime common law principles of carriage, it is now practical to discuss the law about charterparties. The next section proceeds to distinguish the different kinds of charterparties, to review their typical clauses, and to explore how they have been interpreted and applied against the background of the fundamental obligations of the carrier and cargo owner at common law that have just been explained.

C. CARRIAGE BY CHARTERPARTY

1) Introduction: Kinds of Charterparties

A charterparty is a contract with a shipowner for the use of the whole carrying capacity of a ship by the charterer. The name "charterparty" is derived from the Latin *carta partita*. In times past the contract was inscribed by hand in duplicate, then divided in two by deliberately jagged or indented cut lines; the shipowner and the charterer then each

---

112 *Kirchner v. Venus* (1859), 12 Moo. P.C. 361, 14 E.R. 948.
113 *Allison v. Bristol*, above note 104.
114 Above note 74, s.597; *Canada Shipping Act, 2001*, S.C. 2001, c.26, s.248.
115 Or sooner, if the goods are perishable.
116 *Canada Shipping Act*, above note 74, s.600; *Canada Shipping Act, 2001*, above note 114, s.249. If the goods are being imported any customs and excise duties that are payable will take priority in the distribution of the sale monies: *ibid*.

received a *carta partita*, which could be quickly matched in the event of a dispute over terms by the indentations along the line of partition.[117]

In general, there are three types of charterparty: charters by demise, voyage charters, and time charters. A charter by demise is not a carriage contract at all; rather, it is a lease of a vessel without regard to the charterer's purposes for the use of it. Consequently, charters by demise, also called "bare-boat charters," need to be distinguished from true charterparties. Voyage and time charters are simply different ways of contracting for the shipowner's provision of the services of the ship. Under a voyage charterparty, the shipowner agrees to accept a cargo for a specified voyage between two named ports. By a time charterparty, the shipowner contracts to hire out the vessel for the carriage of cargo for as many voyages and ports, within agreed limits, as the charterer desires within a specified time.[118] These categories of charterparty are not rigid. The freedom of contract ensures that varieties of agreement within and between voyage and time charters are concluded. For instance an agreement for as many consecutive voyages as possible within a specified time is a consecutive voyage charterparty, although its purpose hardly differs from a time charter. Conversely, a trip time charter is a charter for the time it takes the ship to complete a specified voyage or round trip, which appears to be similar to a voyage charterparty. From a legal perspective, however, significant differences exist in the allocation of responsibility for the running costs of the ship.

Contracts of affreightment are a further category of carriage contract. Strictly speaking, every contract for the carriage of goods by sea is a contract of affreightment, but, in practice, the name has become attached to large volume contracts. The volume and availability of the cargo may not be definitely known in advance, so the parties contract for a variable number of voyages, or "liftings," within a fixed period of time. These kinds of arrangements are frequently used for the transportation of equipment and materials for major turnkey projects at a specified rate as the construction project proceeds. Contracts of affreightment thus bear many characteristics of voyage charterparties but also some of time charters.

Nowadays a practice has developed of sharing the carrying capacity of a ship by the use of "slot charters." An owner or time charterer who does not require the whole of the ship will time-charter a portion

---

117 This previously common practice in the preparation of legal documents is also the reason for naming them "indentures."
118 See *Skibs Snefonn v. Kawasaki Kisen Kaisha Ltd. (The Berge Tasta)*, [1975] 1 Lloyd's L.R. 422 at 424 (Q.B.); *Whistler International Ltd. v. Kawasaki Kisen Kaisha (The Hill Harmony)*, [2001] 1 A.C. 638 (H.L.).

of its holds. These slot charters may in turn be filled with the goods of a voyage charterer or of shippers under bills of lading. For instance, liner shipping companies may slot-charter spaces on their container ships to competitors who ship their own customers' containers of goods, as a way of consolidating cargo deliveries on the same route and reducing overall operating costs.

This text now proceeds by differentiating charters by demise, then discusses the typical clauses and legal consequences first of voyage charters and then of time charters.

2) Charters by Demise

A charter by demise is a lease of the hull and equipment of a ship. The charterer must crew it, provision it and supply it: in short, he or she accepts a bare-boat charter and agrees to run it at his or her risk and expense. In effect the charterer becomes a disponent owner under a "bare-boat" charter. Such a contract is different from other charterparties because it is not a hiring of the services of the shipowner to carry cargo: it is a hiring of the ship alone. Bare-boat charters may be used to hire out pleasure craft and are also employed in financing large ships. The true owner signs a demise charter for the vessel with the financier, who fulfils the role of registered owner. The importance of the distinction lies in the allocation of the costs and risks in running the ship. Under a demise charter the charterer is responsible for the ship. If the ship is involved in a collision, the charterer must answer to the owner for any damage incurred. If loss is incurred by a third party's cargo, the shipper's claim lies against the charterer, as disponent owner, not against the shipowner. Under voyage and time charterparties the owner remains in control of the ship and runs it at his or her own risk and cost. The charterer may only direct the employment of the ship and pays freight or hire for the shipowner's services.

Whether a particular agreement is a charter by demise or not depends on the intention of the parties not the form of document used. The main criterion for distinguishing bare-boat charters from other charterparties involves the appointment and payment of the master and crew. Are they intended to be the employees of the charterer or the owner? The answer is not always obvious on the facts. In *Baumwoll v. Furness*,[119] the owner provided insurance and maintenance of the ship and reserved the right to appoint the ship's engineer. But, because the charterer paid the master and crew, the court held that the possession

---

119 [1893] A.C. 8.

and control of the ship had passed to the charterer, so the arrangement was a charter by demise; hence the shipowner was not liable for a cargo claim on bills of lading signed by the master.

In the Canadian case of *Outtrim v. British Columbia*,[120] a motor vessel was hired to Peck, on behalf of the B.C. Crown. When his intended assistant proved unavailable, Outtrim, the owner, engaged and paid Dewar to go in his place. Subsequently the motor vessel was negligently run aground and damaged while Dewar was in control. In determining whether the amended arrangement was a charter by demise, the court noted that the important question was not whether Dewar physically controlled the vessel but whether he did so as of right or only at Peck's service and orders. In the event, the court held the hiring was by demise and so the Crown, through Peck, was liable for the negligence of Dewar, resulting in the injury to the motor vessel and the failure to redeliver it in the same condition as it had been received.

D. VOYAGE CHARTERPARTIES

1) Standard Provisions

In essence a voyage charterparty is a contract between the shipowner and the charterer for the carriage of a specific cargo between two named ports. Since it is regulated only by maritime common law, the parties are free to contract on any terms they wish. In the absence of agreed terms, the five fundamental obligations previously discussed will be implied in the contract by common law. In practice, little is left to implications of law. Charterparties are lengthy agreements full of elaborate contractual clauses encompassing many time-honoured phrases that have accumulated technical meanings through years of judicial interpretation.[121] Far from being freely negotiated contracts *de novo*, charterparties appear in a large variety of standard printed forms, customized for particular types of trade and routes. For instance, BIMCO[122] publishes a collection of forms of approved charterparty documents dealing with such trades as cement, coal, fertilizers, gas, grain, ores, stone, and wood as well as for oil and other tanker business, most of which are specifically designed for use over named customary routes.

---

120 [1948] 3 D.L.R. 273 (B.C.C.A.).
121 See the comments of Lord Diplock in *Federal Commerce & Navigation Co. v. Tradax Export S.A. (The Marratha Envoy)*, [1978] A.C. 1 at 8.
122 Baltic and International Maritime Council, a leading commercial shipping organization.

Voyage charter forms bear descriptive short form names. Some well-known ones are GENCON, ASBATANKVOY, SHELLVOY, GASVOY, and MULTIDOC. These standard forms are kept up to date by amendment as fresh decisions interpreting their clauses may demand. Such standardization has not induced simplicity. The chartering market is a highly technical business, added to which freight rates can be extremely volatile. As a result, it is run by professional agents or brokers who "fix" (i.e., agree) charters for their principals, often "subject to details." Such details may include substantial alteration of the terms of whatever printed form of charterparty has been selected.

Regardless of this complexity, every charterparty must attend to a number of standard concerns of the shipowner and the charterer. Therefore, voyage charterparties typically contain a large number of clauses covering the following range of matters:

- description of the ship,
- seaworthiness of the ship,
- preliminary voyage to the port of loading,
- cancellation of the charterparty,
- loading a full cargo,
- loading and discharging costs and time (laytime and demurrage),
- issuing bills of lading for the cargo,
- carriage of the cargo to destination,
- liberty to deviate on the voyage,
- exemption from liability for excepted perils,
- payment of freight,
- liens on the cargo for unpaid freight and other charges,
- cesser clause,
- general average (plus New Jason clause),
- strikes and lock outs in port,
- war risks,
- ice conditions,
- collisions (both-to-blame clause),
- choice of forum or choice of arbitration, and
- broker's commission.

This list of incidents concerns different aspects of the carriage transaction that may conveniently be divided into the preliminary voyage to the port of loading, the loading operation, the delivery voyage, the discharging and delivery of the cargo, and the payment of freight. The following discussion of voyage charterparties is organized along the same lines, only combining, for convenience, the operations of loading and discharging. By way of example of how these matters may be handled, reference will be made to BIMCO's most general charter designed for trades in which there is no other approved form, code-named GENCON.

2) Preliminary Voyage

The basic terms of the charterparty, which is signed by both parties, typically[123] begin by describing the shipowner; the charterer; and the shipper, if different from the charterer; the vessel, its tonnage, and carrying capacity; its present position and the date by which it may be expected to be ready to load; the loading and discharging ports; the type of cargo; and the freight rate. They continue by binding the ship to proceed to the loading port, to load the cargo, to proceed to the discharging port, and to deliver the cargo. In return the charterer agrees to provide a full and complete cargo for the ship and to pay the freight. The shipowner requires the charterer to fill the ship so that the maximum freight can be earned, but, if the charterer's own cargo is insufficient, he or she is permitted to direct the master to sign bills of lading on behalf of the shipowner for the carriage of additional goods of other shippers. In respect of the preliminary voyage, these terms raise concerns for the charterer about the expected arrival time of the ship and for the shipowner about the safety of the port of loading.

a) Expected Arrival

The stated day by which the ship may be expected ready to load is an important date for both the charterer and the shipowner: it is when the charterer must have the cargo ready in the loading port. It is also the date by which the shipowner should ensure the ship has arrived at the port of loading in a fit state to receive the cargo. Whether the naming of this day is a condition of the charterparty or only a warranty is a matter of construction of the parties' intention. The difference becomes important in the event the ship is late. If the stated date of arrival of the ship is a fixed one, it is more likely it will be characterized as a condition, the breach of which will permit the charterer to treat the charterparty as repudiated and to refuse to load.[124] The obligation is also breached if the stated date is not an honest or reasonable expectation of arrival.[125] Since

---

123 See, e.g., GENCON, cl.1, online at: <http:www.bimco.dk/BIMCO%20Documents/Gencon%2094.pdf>.
124 See, e.g., *Glaholm v. Hays* (1841), 2 Man. & G. 257, 133 E.R. 743; and *Michalis Angelos (The)*, above note 15.
125 *Sanday v. Keighley, Maxted & Co.* (1922), 10 Ll. L.R. 738 (C.A.); *Michalis Angelos (The)*, ibid.; *Geogas S.A. v. Trammo Gas Ltd. (The Baleares)*, [1993] 1 Lloyd's L.R. 215 (C.A.); *Re Empire Shipping Co. & Hall Bryan Ltd.*, [1940] 1 D.L.R. 695 (B.S.S.C.).

the charterparty ordinarily states where the ship is located at the time it is signed, an estimate can be made whether it would be reasonable for the preliminary voyage to the port of loading to be completed in time. In making this calculation, due allowance must also be made for any anticipated repairs to the ship and any preparations to receive the cargo, as well as any mandatory inspections or surveys. However, the ship may be engaged in other trade in the course of the preliminary voyage. The shipowner will want to use the earning power of the ship as fully as possible and is obviously free to employ it for other cargoes on the way to the port of loading. But if he or she accepts a cargo whose delivery necessarily means the ship will be late in arriving at the loading port, he or she can no longer be said to have a reasonable expectation of fulfilling his or her obligation. If the expected date of arrival is not a condition precedent, then the shipowner's obligation is only to exercise reasonable diligence to try to attain it and the breach of that duty is the breach of a warranty remediable by the payment of damages. However, time clauses in commercial contracts have usually been enforced by the courts as conditions.[126]

For all these reasons, as well as the vagaries of weather conditions and the risks of navigation, shipowners typically avoid guaranteeing arrival times and add exculpatory clauses to their contracts. For instance, the GENCON charter clause 1 asserts that the ship will be "expected ready to load under this Charter about" the date indicated. "On or about" is time-honoured language to indicate the expected date is not a day certain. Further, a broad disclaimer clause in GENCON clause 2 asserts: "Owners are to be responsible ... for delay in delivery of the goods only in case the ... delay has been caused ... by the personal act or default of the Owners or their manager." Such a clause probably does not cover a situation when the ship is late in arriving because the owner sent it on another voyage that made it impossible to be on time, but it will excuse a host of other causes of delay during the preliminary voyage, provided the ship has actually begun the preliminary voyage and is not engaged in some other charter voyage.[127]

In return for such liberty in arrival time, voyage charterparties frequently grant the charterer a right of cancellation.[128] That is to say, if the ship is not ready to load by a certain date the charterer has the option

---

126 *Bowes v. Shand*, above note 50; *Bunge Corp. v. Tradax S.A.*, above note 50. Cp. *Sail Labrador Ltd.*, above note 50.
127 See *Monroe Brothers Ltd. v. Ryan*, [1935] 2 K.B. 28 (C.A.); and *Louis Dreyfus & Co. v. Lauro* (1938), 60 Ll. L.R. 94 (K.B.).
128 Such as GENCON, above note 123, cl.10.

of unilaterally terminating the contract. The cancellation date is agreed as some day, say ten, after the expected date of arrival. Since cancellation is an option, the charterer may condone the late arrival of the ship and proceed to load the cargo anyway. This will likely be the preferable choice if freight rates have risen meanwhile. If they have fallen, the charterer will more likely search around for another vessel and then exercise the cancellation right. For the shipowner such waiting is wasted earning time for his or her ship, so the cancellation clause is often qualified by a provision stating the period in which it may be exercised. Until the right of cancellation is exercised, the contract is still on foot and so the ship must proceed with all reasonable haste to the loading port, even if it is already late.[129] Further, even when the charterer cancels the charterparty, he or she is not prevented from seeking damages from the shipowner for the losses consequent upon the ship's delay, if they are not precluded by the shipowner's disclaimer clause.

b) Safe Ports
In addition to arriving on time, the ship must dock in the port or in the berth within the port named in the charterparty. Sometimes[130] the charterparty leaves the choice of the port[131] or the berth, or both, open for the charterer to nominate within a specified time. Then the shipowner is bound to send the ship to the nominated place.[132] However, the shipowner will be concerned that the place of loading[133] is safe for the ship. To control this risk, charterparties regularly require the charterer to nominate a "safe port" or, where the port is specified in the contract, to qualify it by declaring that the ship shall proceed there "or so near thereto as she may safely get and be always afloat."[134] A requirement on the charterer to name a safe port or berth switches the risk of damage to the ship from the shipowner to the charterer. His or her nomination of a place is taken to warrant that it is safe for the ship. If it is not, the shipowner may refuse to send the ship there. If the ship enters a nominated port or berth that is unsafe, the shipowner may seek damages

---

129 *Moel Tryvan Ship Co, Ltd. v. Andrew Weir & Co.*, above note 53; Cp. *Democritos (The)*, [1976] 2 Lloyd's L.R. 149 (C.A.).
130 Especially as regards destination ports, since the cargo may be sold during the voyage, and the availability of berths and discharging services may not be known until the ship approaches its destination.
131 Usually within a limited range of ports.
132 *Reardon Smith Line v. Australian Wheat Board (The Houston City)*, [1956] A.C. 266 (P.C.).
133 Or discharging.
134 E.g., GENCON, above note 123, cl.1.

from the charterer for breach of contract.[135] The time at which this determination of safety has to be made is at the moment the charterer makes the nomination. The charterer is not in breach of the charterparty if, when he or she names the port or berth, it is prospectively safe for the ship, even though it becomes unsafe later.[136]

The measure of whether a port is safe was classically stated by Sellers L.J. in *Leeds Shipping Co. v. Société Francaise Bunge, (The Eastern City).*[137] A port is safe if "in the relevant period of time, the particular ship can reach it, use it and return from it without, in the absence of some abnormal occurrence, being exposed to danger which cannot be avoided by good navigation and seamanship." This is a test of risk of harm. Exposure to danger does not require actual injury to the ship. The port or berth is unsafe if, not withstanding good navigation, there is still risk of injury to the ship.[138]

Whether a port is dangerous is a question of both physical and political safety in respect of the particular ship and has to be determined as a matter of fact at the relevant time. Danger of harm may arise from such obvious physical risks as harbour obstructions, sandbars, winter ice, and congestion, but also from political risks like the outbreak of armed conflict, blockade, or quarantine. However, the risk of harm must always be more than the ship, by good navigation and seamanship, could avoid. The alternative formulation of the safe ports clause — that the ship will go to the nearest safe place — gives the shipowner greater control over the situation. It grants him or her the right, after sending the ship toward the named port and waiting a reasonable time nearby in order to determine that it cannot be reached safely,[139] so to inform the charterer and to move the ship to the nearest suitable place. The criterion is whether the ship can stay in the port or berth "safely ... always afloat." This criterion is not met if the ship cannot remain afloat because of tidal movements or changes in draught through loading of the cargo.[140]

---

135 *Kodros Shipping v. Empreso Cubana (The Evia) (No. 2),* [1983] 1 A.C. 736 (H.L.) [*The Evia*]; *Reardon Smith Line Ltd.,* above note 26; *Leeds Shipping Co. v. Société Francaise Bunge (The Eastern City),* [1958] 2 Lloyd's Rep. 127 (C.A.) [*The Eastern City*]; *Motor Oil Hellas (Corinth) Refineries v. Shipping Corp. of India (The Kanchenjunga),* [1990] 1 Lloyd's L.R. 391 (H.L.).
136 *The Evia, ibid.* In these circumstances the charterer is probably obliged to nominate an alternative safe port or berth, as least in the case of time charters.
137 Above note 135 at 131.
138 *Kristiansands Tankredere A/S v. Standard Tankers (Bahamas) Ltd. (The Polyglory),* [1977] 2 Lloyd's L.R. 353 (Q.B.).
139 *Dahl v. Nelson* (1881), 6 App. Cas. 38.
140 *Shield v. Wilkins* (1850), 5 Ex. 304, 155 E.R. 130; *Alhambra (The)* (1881), 6 P.D. 68 (C.A.); *Treglia v. Smith's Timber Co.* (1896), 1 Com. Cas. 360.

3) Loading and Discharging Operations

a) Terms of Operation

The loading and discharging of a voyage chartered ship are frequently shared operations between the shipowner and charterer or other cargo owners.[141] The actual tasks are usually carried out by a stevedoring firm on the waterfront, with assistance, maybe, of crew members under the direction of an officer of the ship, such as the supercargo. The agreement between the shipowner and the charterer is, therefore, essentially about who is to arrange and pay the considerable expense for loading or unloading. At a minimum the charterer must bring the cargo to the dock, and usually alongside the ship in reach of its tackle, when it is ready to load.[142] This is known in the trade as "gross terms." However, the charterer may agree to undertake some or all of the loading, stowing, and trimming of the cargo, including the provision of necessary dunnage or separation boards. Acronyms are frequently used to signify the charterer's choice to load and unload (i.e., FIO, standing for free in and out) or additionally to stow (i.e., FIOS) and to trim (i.e., FIOST).[143] If damage is occasioned to the ship or cargo by these operations, the charterer will be liable, even though they are all nominally, or even expressly, under the supervision of the master since he or she has the responsibility to ensure the stowage of the cargo does not affect the seaworthiness of the ship.[144]

But in the absence of agreement that the charterer is to load and stow, the primary duty of stowing the cargo falls on the shipowner. In *N.M. Paterson & Sons v. Mannix Ltd.*,[145] the charterer's employees did the major part of the work of lashing and securing a heavy mechanical shovel that subsequently broke loose and was lost during the voyage; yet the inspection and approval of the stowing of the shovel by the ship's officers, who were in a better position than the charterers to know its effects as deck cargo on the stability of the ship, negated any implication of an agreement to relieve the shipowner of his or her obligations toward the cargo at law.

---

141 *Harris v. Best, Ryley & Co.* (1892), 68 L.T. 76 (C.A.).
142 *Ibid.*; *N.M. Paterson & Sons Ltd. v. Mannix Ltd*, [1966] S.C.R. 180.
143 See, e.g., GENCON, above note 123, cl.5.
144 Unless the master actually intervenes. *Balli Trading Ltd. v. Afalona Shipping Co. (The Coral)*, [1993] 1 Lloyd's L.R. 1 (C.A.); *Canadian Transport Co. v. Court Line (The Ovington Court)*, [1940] A.C. 934 (H.L.).
145 Above note 142.

b) **Laytime and Demurrage**

A second consideration about loading and discharging is how long the operations will take. The charterer is generally not too concerned about the time taken, except to the extent he or she is paying for the operations or has a delivery date to his or her own client to meet, because he or she has to pay for the use of the vessel for the voyage in any event. The shipowner, however, is greatly concerned to ensure speedy loading and unloading, since time spent in port is time lost employing the ship on another voyage. Consequently, voyage charterparties usually contain stipulations as to the amount of time allowed for loading and unloading, commonly known as "laytime." Laytime may be specified in days (i.e., calendar days of twenty-four hours) or hours, and for loading and discharging separately or in aggregate; it may also be expressed to be calculated as running days inclusively, or running working days, or running days except Sundays and holidays, any of which may be stated to be subject to the weather permitting work.[146] Sometimes the rate is fixed by reference to the ship's hatches worked per day. Occasionally the charterparty calls for loading to take place as fast as the ship can receive the cargo, or does not specify laytime at all. In both cases the charterer bears a duty, implied by law, to complete the operation of loading or discharging in a reasonable time in light of the cargo handling methods obtaining in the port.[147]

Laytime begins to run when the ship has arrived in port and is ready to load or discharge. At common law the shipowner must give the charterer notice of the ship's readiness to load,[148] but no such notice is required at the discharging port.[149] The receiver of the cargo must watch out of the ship, since the shipowner may not know who to notify if the goods have been sold *en route*. In practice, most charterparties expressly require notice of readiness at both loading and discharging ports.[150]

If notice of readiness is given prematurely, that is, before the ship has arrived and is actually ready to receive cargo, it is ineffective and a new notice must be given when the ship is truly ready.[151] To be ready

---

146 See, e.g., GENCON, above note 123, cl.6; and *Knox Bros. Ltd. v. Healthfield (The)*, [1924] Ex. C.R. 73.
147 *Hick v. Raymond & Reid*, above note 53; *Postlethwaite v. Freeland* (1880), 5 App. Cas. 599 (H.L.).
148 *Stanton v. Austin* (1872), L.R. 7 C.P. 651.
149 *Harman v. Mant* (1815), 4 Camp. 161, 171 E.R. 52; *Pagnan & Fratelli v. Tradax Export S.A.*, [1969] 2 Lloyd's L.R. 150 (Q.B.); *Transgrain Shipping BV v. Global Transporte Oceanico S.A. (The Mexico 1)*, [1990] 1 Lloyd's L.R. 507 [*The Mexico 1*].
150 For instance, GENCON, above note 123, cl.6(c).
151 *The Mexico 1*, above note 149.

to load, the ship must be "completely ready and discharged in all her holds so as to give the [charterer] complete control of every portion of the ship available for cargo."[152] One might add that the cargo spaces must be appropriately cleaned or prepared for the particular cargo to be loaded.[153]

When a ship can be said to have arrived is a more complex matter that depends upon whether the charterparty specifies, or allows the charterer to nominate,[154] a port or the docks within the port or a specific berth. Under a berth charterparty, laytime does not begin before the ship has arrived at the specified berth.[155] Similarly, if a port is named, and by usage there is only one place within it to load, the ship must go to that place. For example, in *Midland Navigation Co. v. Dominion Elevator Co.*,[156] the ship arrived at Fort William, but owing to the queue of ships waiting to load grain from the elevators, it could not go under the only loading chute until just two hours before the time limit in the contract for receiving a full load. The Supreme Court held it insufficient for the ship simply to report in at Fort William. It had to reach the customary and usual place for loading grain in the port in enough time to allow for the loading of a full cargo, it being no excuse that the port was so congested that the ship had to wait in line. Under a dock or port charterparty — the docks or port having several berths or wharves — if a berth convenient to the charterer to load is immediately available the ship must go to it.[157] But if, through congestion, none is available, the ship must reach a position within the docks or the port where it is "at the immediate and effective disposition of the charterer."[158] Anchoring at the usual waiting place for ships will typically constitute arrival,[159] provided that that place is within the limits of the docks or the port. Some ports are so large and busy, and their

---

152 *Groves, MacLean & Co. v. Volkart Bros.* (1884), 1 T.L.R. 92, per Lopes J. at 92–93, aff'd (1885), 1 T.L.R. 454 (C.A.).
153 *Compania Nedelka v. Tradax S.A. (The Tres Flores)*, [1974] Q.B. 264.
154 The charterer's failure to make a nomination is a breach of contract that also prevents the arrival of the ship: *Zim Israel Navigation Co. v. Tradax Export S.A. (The Timna)*, [1970] 2 Lloyd's L.R. 409 (Q.B.), aff'd on other grounds, [1971] 2 Lloyd's L.R. 91 (C.A.).
155 *Stag Line Ltd. v. Board of Trade*, [1950] 2 K.B. 194; *EL Oldendorff & Co. GmbH v. Tradax Export, (The Johanna Oldendorff)*, [1974] A.C. 479 at 557 (H.L.) [*The Johanna Oldendorff*].
156 (1904), 34 S.C.R. 578.
157 *The Johanna Oldendorff*, above note 154 at 557.
158 *Ibid.* per Lord Reid at 535.
159 *Ibid.* See also *Venizelos A.N.E. of Athens v. Société Commerciale de Cereales of Zurich (The Prometheus)*, [1974] 1 Lloyd's L.R. 350 (Q.B.).

traffic and pilotage schemes organized in such a way that the usual waiting place for ships is outside the legal limits of the port. Nevertheless, a ship cannot be said to have arrived by waiting there, since it has not yet entered the port.[160]

Once the ship has arrived, laytime may begin if the ship is also ready to load and notice of its readiness has been given to the charterer. Then the burden of delay of getting into a berth falls on the charterer as part of the permitted laytime. But until the ship has arrived, even if it is waiting at the port, the time lost is borne by the shipowner, for the ship is technically still on the preliminary voyage. With a view to making the charterer always bear the burden of delay in the port, the charterparty may include a clause stating "time lost in waiting for berth to count as loading or discharging time,"[161] or causing laytime to begin for the ship "whether in berth or not" (wibon clause). For good measure, the charterparty may also state that "time actually used before commencement of laytime shall count."[162] Such a clause would cover any loading or discharging undertaken before the appointed hour of commencement of laytime or before a valid notice of readiness is given.[163] When laytime commences, it generally runs continuously. It may be suspended by express provision in the charterparty, such as the operation of a strike clause;[164] but a general exception clause for delay caused by circumstances beyond the charterer's control will only interrupt the running of laytime if it is clearly intended to apply to laytime.[165]

If the charterer exceeds the laytime, he or she is in breach of contract and will be liable to pay damages to the shipowner for detention of the ship. Against such an uncertain risk for both parties, the charterparty usually includes a liquidated damages clause for the payment of what is known as "demurrage." Demurrage is typically quoted at a certain rate per day and *pro rata* for a part day. If no limit is set to the number of days on demurrage, the shipowner is bound to keep the ship at the loading port as long as it is necessary for the charterer to load, or

---

160 *Federal Commerce and Navigation Co. v. Tradax Export S.A. (The Maratha Envoy)*, above note 121.
161 GENCON, above note 123, cl.6(c). And see *Darrah (The)*, [1976] 1 Lloyd's L.R. 285 (C.A.).
162 *Ibid.*
163 As occurred in *Pteroti Compania Naviera S.A. v. National Coal Board*, [1958] 1 Q.B. 469.
164 Discussed below at note 172.
165 *Amstelmolen (The)*, [1961] 2 Lloyd's Rep. 1 (C.A.); *Sametiet M/T Johs Stove v. Istanbul Petrol Rafinerisi A/S (The Johs Stove)*, [1984] 1 Lloyd's L.R. 38 (Q.B.).

at least until commercial frustration overtakes their contract,[166] since the charterer is paying extra for the privilege of detaining the ship. Commonly, however, a fixed number of days on demurrage is stipulated in the charterparty,[167] so that holding over longer is a breach of contract. The number of days may be set for loading and discharging altogether and, when this is combined with a right, if granted in the charterparty, to average out the laytime for loading and discharging,[168] the charterer has maximum flexibility. If, for instance, loading is unduly extended, he or she can use up all the laytime and even some of the demurrage time and take the risk that he or she can complete discharging at destination at a faster rate than estimated in allocating laytime.

Demurrage begins to run immediately once laytime has expired and runs continuously, unless there are specific exceptions expressed in the charterparty[169] or it is interrupted by an act of the shipowner for his or her own purposes, such as moving the ship to refuel it.[170] Some charterparties also include an incentive to charterers to complete loading and discharging faster than the allowed laytime by rewarding them with "dispatch money." This is a rebate of freight at a stipulated daily rate for every day of time saved in port and is often fixed at half the demurrage rate.[171]

A strike bound port of loading or discharge is a hazard that is beyond the control of both the shipowner and charterer. It is usually an expensive risk in time and money that may by chance fall on either party. If the port suffers a strike as the ship approaches the port, the waiting period is at the shipowner's expense. If the strike occurs when the ship has arrived the cost falls on the charterer as wasted laytime plus demurrage and even damages for detention if the work stoppage is a long one. In the face of this largely unpredictable risk charterparties frequently make provision to distribute the burden. For instance

---

166 *Inverkip Steamship Co. v. Bunge & Co.*, [1917] 2 K.B. 193 (C.A.); *Universal Cargo Carriers Corp. v. Citati*, above note 66. Frustration of the commercial object of the carriage contract is discussed above after note 66.
167 For instance GENCON, above note 123, cl.7, allows ten running days altogether.
168 Also called "reversible laytime."
169 Such as a strike clause, discussed below at note 172.
170 *Ropner Shipping Co. v. Cleeves Western Valleys Anthracite Collieries Ltd.*, [1927] 1 K.B. 879 (C.A.). See also *Blue Anchor Line Ltd. v. Alfred C. Toepfer International GmbH (The Union Amsterdam)*, [1982] 2 Lloyd's L.R. 432.
171 See *Fury Shipping Co. v. State Trading Corp. of India Ltd. (The Atlantic Sun)*, [1972] 1 Lloyd's L.R. 509 (Q.B.).

the CENTROCON strike clause[172] states: "If the cargo cannot be loaded by reason of ... a strike or lock-out ... the time for loading or discharging, as the case may be, shall not count during the continuance of such causes." The GENCON strike clause[173] is more radical: it opens by relieving both parties from liability for the consequences of a strike or lockout that prevents fulfilment of any obligations under the charter. Thus the shipowner will not be held responsible for delayed arrival on account of a strike nor for delay after the strike ends on account of the congestion in the port that it occasioned.[174] Similarly, if the ship has arrived and then a strike ensues, time lost waiting should not be counted against the charterer for the purposes of laytime and demurrage.

Release from their obligations by the strike, however, necessitates that the parties make other arrangements. So, for instance, the GENCON strike clause provides in regard to loading that, if a strike ensues as the ship approaches the port, the charterer may be asked to agree to reckon the laytime as if there was no strike, or the shipowner may cancel the charter. In the event of a strike at the discharging port that lasts more than forty-eight hours, the cargo owner is given the option of keeping the ship waiting and paying demurrage at half the rate, after laytime has elapsed, or of naming an alternative safe port of discharge. In practice, arrangements in the event of strikes are necessary and quite varied.

4) Voyage

Before the ship departs the loading port on the voyage, the owner has an implied obligation at common law to ensure it is seaworthy. During the voyage the shipowner impliedly undertakes to care for the cargo and to deliver it without deviation or delay. These four stringent duties at common law have been discussed earlier; in practice, they are customarily varied by express terms of the charterparty, as this section explains.

a) Seaworthiness

By maritime common law the shipowner is required to provide a ship that is in every way fit for the contracted voyage. However, this obligation is always subject to the parties' freedom to contract differently. But

---

172 SYNACOMEX, cl.30, "Amended CENTROCON Strike Clause," online at: <http://www.BIMCO.dk/BIMCO%20Documents/SYNACOMEX%2090.pdf>. But as to its effect in face of a "time lost waiting for berth to count as laytime" clause see *Ionian Navigation Co. v. Atlantic Shipping Co., (The Loucas N)*, [1971] 1 Lloyd's L.R. 215 (C.A.).

173 GENCON, above note 123, cl.15.

174 See *Salamis Shipping v. Edm. Van Meerbeek & Co. (The Onisilos)*, [1971] 2 Q.B. 500.

courts demand clear words to cut down or exclude the obligation. A general exemption clause is likely to be viewed strictly as affecting only the express obligations of the charterparty, and not its implied undertakings, unless it cannot be read otherwise.[175] In an extremely wide disclaimer clause, the GENCON charter explicitly states that the shipowner is not responsible for any loss arising "from unseaworthiness of the vessel on loading or commencement of the voyage or at any time whatsoever."[176] The deliberate exemption from liability for unseaworthiness could hardly be clearer.

b) Cargo Care

The shipowner's strict liability at common law for the care of the cargo was always subject to four exceptions, namely, acts of God, acts of the queen's enemies, inherent vice of the cargo, and defaults by the shipper, because they are incidents beyond his or her control.[177] In practice, shipowners exercise their freedom of contract to disclaim liability for a very much longer list of possible incidents of the voyage. In addition to the four common law exceptions, the list of incidents might refer to other events beyond the shipowner's control as well causes of cargo loss within his or her control, such as the following:

- perils of the sea,
- fire,
- war,
- civil unrest,
- arrest,
- quarantine,
- strikes and lock outs,
- saving life at sea,
- insufficiency of cargo packing,
- inadequacy of cargo marks,
- latent defects in the ship, and
- error in navigation of the ship.

All these incidents are discussed more particularly in the context of the enumeration of excepted perils in the *Hague-Visby Rules* governing carriage under bills of lading (in Chapter 9).[178] Yet, express exceptions in

---

175 E.g., *Nelson Line (Liverpool) Ltd. v. James Nelson & Sons Ltd.*, [1908] A.C. 16.
176 GENCON, above note 123, cl.2.
177 See *Paterson Steamships Ltd. v. Canadian Co-op. Wheat Producers Ltd.*, and the discussion of the case, above at note 19.
178 Under D(6) in Chapter 9, "Exclusion of Liability," on liability for cargo damage in the event of collision and the use of the "both to blame collision clause" in charterparties, see D in Chapter 11 "Maritime Collisions."

charterparties must be clear and unambiguous, or else, like any uncertain contract term, they will be construed narrowly *contra proferentem*. Courts are particularly concerned by clauses that may exempt shipowners from liability for the consequences of their own negligence.[179] A general disclaimer of liability is unlikely to be read as exempting negligent conduct. An express exemption from responsibility for the neglect or default of the master, crew, and other employees will be effective[180] but will also be construed literally as limited to those persons. Therefore, the shipowner may still be held liable for cargo losses resulting from their negligent acts, if he or she was negligent in appointing employees who were incompetent or untrained for their tasks.[181] But an express exemption for the shipowner's own personal negligence is permissible.

c) Deviation

Like other common law obligations, the shipowner's duty not to deviate from the proper course of the voyage may be, and frequently is, subject to contrary arrangements in the charterparty, which are known as "liberty clauses." Some liberty clauses appear to be very wide. For instance, the "deviation clause" in the GENCON charter[182] states: "The vessel has the liberty to call at any port or ports in any order, for any purpose, to sail without pilots, to tow and/or assist vessels in all situations, and also to deviate for the purpose of saving life and/or property." On the face of this clause, all limitations against deviation are set aside, and the ship can sail in any direction the shipowner desires. However, courts construe such clauses much more narrowly. The liberty "to call at any port" will be read as freedom to call at a port along the voyage in the geographical order.[183] The liberty "to call at any port or ports in any order" will allow a ship to make calls at ports out of geographical order, as long as they are all along the usual route of the voyage.[184] In reaching such interpretations, the courts seek to give commercial efficacy to the intentions of the contracting parties. The principle employed is that "the described voyage and the liberty to

---

179 See *Canada Steamship Lines v. King (The)*, [1952] A.C. 192 (P.C.); *Lamport & Holt Lines v. Coubro & Scrutton (The Raphael)*, [1982] 2 Lloyd's L.R. 42 (C.A.).
180 E.g., *Elder, Dempster & Co. v. Paterson, Zochonis & Co.*, above note 7; *Carron Park (The)* (1890), 15 P.D. 203; Cp. *Accomac (The)* (1890), 15 P.D. 208. And see GENCON, above note 123, cl.2.
181 See *Chartered Bank of India v. Netherlands India Steam Navigation Co.* (1883), 10 Q.B.D. 521 at 532.
182 GENCON, above note 123, cl.3.
183 *Leduc v. Ward* (1888), 20 Q.B.D. 475; *Glynn v. Margeston & Co.*, above note 36.
184 *Glynn v. Margeston & Co.*, ibid.

deviate, must be read together and reconciled, and that a liberty, however generally worded, could not frustrate but must be subordinate to the described voyage."[185] The courts also balance the business advantage that a shipper gets from the ship having a degree of liberty to deviate by reason of the lower freight that may, as a result, be charged.[186] Thus, a clause so broadly worded as to grant the ship liberty

> to proceed to or return to and stay at any ports or places whatsoever (although in a contrary direction to or out of or beyond the route of the said port of delivery) once or oftener in any order, backwards or forwards, for loading or discharging cargo, passengers, coals or stones, or for any purpose whatsoever[187]

will permit the ship to go to any place for any purpose provided the course of action it actually pursues does not frustrate the commercial object of the voyage.[188] Other liberty clauses are frequently added to permit the ship to deviate in foreseeable situations that are beyond the shipowner's control. Typical incidents are the onset of strikes, warfare, and ice. In the event of a strike in the port of discharge, a strike clause[189] may permit the ship to sail or remove to a substitute safe port in fulfilment of the carriage agreement. It is often difficult to forecast whether a strike will occur before or during the time a ship is due to arrive at the discharging port. It is equally problematic to foresee whether a strike in progress at the port will end quickly enough to permit timely delivery by the ship. That is the value to the shipowner of a liberty to deviate from a strikebound port, but it may also, on occasion, become a duty, as the case of *The Mormacsaga*[190] illustrates. This ship was carrying a cargo of oranges from Santos, Brazil, to Montreal, Canada, with a scheduled call at Jacksonville, Florida, which was strikebound from June. The ship docked in Jacksonville in July and, as a result of being caught in the strike until September, the cargo of oranges perished. The shipowner pleaded in defence a clause exempting liability resulting from strikes and argued that the strike seemed likely to end without delay; however, the court held that the shipowner failed to act with reasonable care for the preservation of the cargo in not directing the ship to deviate away from Jacksonville as a liberty clause in the carriage contract permitted.

---

185 *Frenkel v. MacAndrews & Co.*, [1929] A.C. 545 per Lord Sumner at 562.
186 *Connolly Shaw Ltd. v. A/S Det Nordenfjeldske D/S* (1934), 49 Ll. L.R. 183 at 189 (K.B.).
187 *Ibid.* at 185. See also GENCON, above note 123, cl.16.
188 *Ibid.*
189 See, e.g., GENCON, above note 123, cl.15, discussed above at note 173.
190 [1968] 2 Lloyd's L.R. 184 (Ex. Ct.).

A war-risks clause may also be included in the charterparty in order to provide against all kinds of hostilities as well as port blockades. The GENCON war-risks clause,[191] for example, gives the ship liberty to comply with any order of a government or belligerent party to the hostilities. It also entitles the shipowner, before loading begins and in the face of war risks at any stage of the voyage, to cancel the charter. If the risk of hostilities engulfing the ship arises after it has sailed, the charterer may name an alternative safe destination or, failing any nomination, the shipowner is given the liberty to substitute a different discharging port in fulfilment of the carriage contract.[192] But a war-risks clause may not always operate to protect a shipowner from liability in the event of war. For example, in *Monarch Steamship Co. v. Karlshamns Oljefabriker A/B*,[193] the ship was prohibited by government order from proceeding beyond Glasgow, Scotland, on account of the outbreak of war between Britain and Germany. The shipowners sought to rely on a war-risks clause, which exonerated them in the event of compliance with an order of the flag state, to excuse their non-fulfilment of the carriage contract; however, the court held that the clause did not protect the shipowners because the outbreak of war was eminently foreseeable and the effective cause of the ship incurring this risk was its delay in sailing because of its unseaworthiness.

Ice blocking a port is another foreseeable risk, especially in trade to northern ports in Canada. Against such a risk a general ice clause may be added to the charterparty. For instance, the GENCON ice clause[194] makes special arrangements to vary the charter accordingly as the ice blocks the loading or discharging port. If the loading port is blocked by ice the ship need not wait to enter and load and the charter becomes null and void. If the ship is at risk of being frozen in while loading, the master is at liberty to leave with a part cargo, and the charterer will be charged freight pro rated on the goods actually delivered. If the port of discharge is inaccessible on account of ice, the cargo receivers may name an alternative port for delivery, or, if the ship risks being iced in while discharging, the master may order it away to the nearest accessible and safe discharging port. Both results are treated as substitute performance of the voyage.

---

191 GENCON, above note 123, cl.16.
192 See *Renton (G.H.) & Co. v. Palmyra Trading Corp. of Panama*, [1957] A.C. 149; *Luigi Monta of Genoa v. Cechofracht Co.*, [1956] 2 Q.B. 552.
193 Above note 70. See discussion under section B(4), "Delay in Delivery" in this chapter.
194 GENCON, above note 123, cl.17.

d) Delay

The carrier's implied undertaking not to delay in the voyage is frequently disclaimed, or at least the remedy for it is limited, by the terms of the charterparty.[195] In any case the carrier is not liable for reasonable delays.[196] So, if a seaworthy ship suffers a casualty as a result of a peril of the seas, the time taken to repair *en route*, even though it prolongs the voyage, is not an unreasonable delay in breach of the carriage contract. However, the charterparty may be affected even when it includes an exception for delay in two recognized but not common situations. First, if the delay is tantamount to a deviation, then the consequences of a deviation will be incurred. They, it may be recalled,[197] can result in the termination of the carriage contract along with any exemption from liability for the carrier that it may contain.[198] However, courts seem less inclined nowadays to regard lengthy delays as *quasi*-deviations or to apply such a drastic rule instead of the ordinary principles of contractual remedies.[199] Second, a prolonged delay may result in the commercial frustration of the carriage contract. The doctrine of frustration applies when an unforeseen delay occurs, without any fault of either party, and the voyage is so interrupted that its eventual completion would not accomplish the objectives of the contract.[200] Such cases are, by their nature, uncommon. The outbreak of hostilities at destination is an example of an incident that may induce frustration, but often the charterparty includes a war-risks clause to regulate this eventuality.

When the carriage is frustrated, the contract automatically comes to an end and the parties are released from all further obligations. In addition any money paid by a party without receiving any consideration may be recovered.[201] However, this remedy does not apply to advance freight paid by the cargo owner.[202] The inequity between the parties of the contractual consequences that may be incurred when frustration of the voyage takes place are somewhat alleviated in many jurisdictions, including most provinces of Canada, by frustrated contracts statutes. However, no such legislation has been enacted by the

---

195 See, e.g., GENCON, *ibid.*, cls.2 and 12.
196 See the discussion of the common law obligation above at note 53.
197 See the discussion above at note 36.
198 See, e.g., *Scaramanga v. Stamp*, above note 28 at 299.
199 See *The Antares*, above note 48.
200 *Admiral Shipping Co. v. Weidner, Hopkins & Co.*, [1916] 1 K.B. 429, aff'd [1917] 1 K.B. 222.
201 *Fibrosa Spolka Akcyjna v. Fairbairn Lawson Combe Barbour Ltd.*, [1943] A.C. 32.
202 See *De Silvale v. Kendall*, above note 106; *Allison v. Bristol Marine Insurance*, above note 105, and the discussion there of advance freight.

federal Parliament, so it remains to be seen whether the courts might develop the aged common law consequences of frustration in exercise of their reformatory powers under *Ordon Estate v. Grail*.[203]

5) Freight

Typical terms used in a voyage charterparty regarding freight have already been discussed along with the obligation to pay at common law.[204] In addition, the carrier has a common law possessory lien on the cargo for non-payment of the freight and, typically, a contractual lien for non-payment of freight, dead freight, demurrage, and damages for detention.[205] The charterer will want to escape these obligations whenever he or she loads cargo of other persons who should bear the responsibility for their payment. This can be achieved, if the shipowner agrees, by inclusion of a "cesser clause" in the charterparty. By this clause, the charterer's liability is made to cease at some point during the charter, typically when the third party's goods are loaded. A cesser clause, however, will only be effective to relieve the charterer to the extent that the shipowner has an alternative remedy against the cargo and the persons interested in it.[206] Hence, for the cesser clause to be effective, it is essential for the charterer to ensure that the bill of lading issued to the shipper of the loaded cargo effectively incorporates the terms of the charterparty, including the freight and lien clauses.[207] Further, the shipowner must have a valid contract of carriage with whoever subsequently may become the holder of the bill of lading.[208] Even so, the cesser clause will not be effective to relieve the charterer of liability for the freight and other charges to the extent that the shipowner is unable to enforce the lien against the cargo for the full amount due. For example, if the freight under the bill of lading is less than in the charterparty or the lien is ineffective in the destination port, the charterer will retain responsibility to pay the shipowner.[209]

---

203 [1998] 3 S.C.R. 437, discussed in E(3) of Chapter 3, "Provincial Law in a Maritime Law Setting."
204 See above B(6), "Freight."
205 See the discussion of freight liens above at note 112ff.
206 *Overseas Transportation Co. v. Mineralimportexport (The Sinoe)*, [1971] 1 Lloyd's L.R. 514 at 516, aff'd [1972] 1 Lloyd's L.R. 201 (C.A.) [*The Sinoe*]; *Cunard Carrier (The), Eleranta and Martha*, [1977] 2 Lloyd's L.R. 261 at 263 [*The Cunard Carrier*].
207 See A(10) in Chapter 9, "Bills of Lading on a Chartered Ship."
208 See A(9) in Chapter 9, "Transfer of Rights in a Bill of Lading."
209 *Hansen v. Harold Brothers*, [1894] 1 Q.B. 612; *The Sinoe*, above note 207; *The Cunard Carrier*, above note 206; *Action S.A. v. Britannic Shipping Corp. (The Aegis Britanic)*, [1987] 1 Lloyd's L.R. 119 (C.A.).

E. TIME CHARTERPARTIES

1) Standard Provisions

Under a time, as compared to a voyage, charterparty the ship is contracted for a specified time rather than a particular voyage. Therefore, a time charter grants the charterer the use of the ship for a prolonged period to undertake any number of successive voyages. For instance, a liner shipping company, short of a vessel under repair, may charter a replacement on its scheduled service for the time being. Yet the time charter is like a voyage charter in that, in both arrangements, the shipowner continues to have control of the ship and, hence, the responsibility to manage and navigate it, while the charterer has the right to direct its employment. Therefore, most of the standard provisions of voyage charterparties find counterparts in time charterparties. The differences in their terms are mostly from the need for additional clauses in time charters to regulate the charterer's greater powers to determine the cargoes to be loaded, the ports to be visited, and the voyages to be made within the period specified in the charter. A list of standard provisions in a general time charterparty is likely to include the following matters:

- description of the ship,
- time and place of its delivery and redelivery,
- cancellation of the charterparty,
- trade limits and excluded cargoes,
- efficient state and cargo fitness of the ship,
- running costs of the ship,
- employment and indemnity by the charterer,
- hire,
- breakdown (off-hire clause),
- excepted perils,
- owner's liens,
- war risks,
- ice conditions,
- salvage,
- general average,
- choice of forum or choice of arbitration, and
- broker's commission.

In light of the replication of many of the clauses found in voyage charterparties, only a brief explanation of the major differences of time charterparties is provided here. Such an outline inevitably must overlook the great range of specialized time charters, particularly in the tanker trades, which contain distinctive clauses, in favour of reference to a widely used, general time charterparty, such as the New York Produce Exchange Time Charter (NYPE) or, as referred to here, BIMCO's BALTIME form.

2) Particular Clauses

The description of the ship, its condition, and its capacities are much greater in a time, than in a voyage, charterparty because the charterer has a much wider power and responsibility for its use. Thus, in addition to the ship's name and class, the opening clause of a time charterparty typically also records the vessel's tonnage, cargo capacity, fuel capacity, engine horse power, and speed capability at a rate of consumption of fuel. These details are necessary for the time charterer in organizing and pre-figuring the voyages on which he or she wishes to order the ship. The charterparty states that the shipowner lets and the charterer hires the ship for a specified period after delivery at the named port. The timing of the preliminary voyage to the port of delivery depends upon the shipowner making reasonable efforts at dispatch, as under a voyage charterparty. Similarly, a cancellation clause protects the charterer. Since the charterer will have the power to employ the ship as desired, the shipowner will be concerned that it is not abused or damaged, nor engaged in trade for which it is unsuitable. Hence, time charterparties include clauses that exclude unlawful traffic and named kinds of cargoes. They may also limit the ship to a certain range of ports, such as Elbe-Brest limits or North American east coast ports, in order to protect it from the risks and requirements of other ports of the world. Furthermore, as discussed for voyage charterparties, time charters also restrict the charterer's use of the ship to voyages between safe ports.[210]

In time charters, the shipowner's common law duty to provide a seaworthy ship is generally overreached by larger express obligations to deliver a vessel "in every way fitted for ordinary cargo service" and to maintain it in "a thoroughly efficient state."[211] In other words, the shipowner undertakes that the ship will be seaworthy and cargo-worthy throughout all the voyages on which it is lawfully sent. But this obligation is not interpreted to mean the ship must be maintained in a

---

210 *G.W. Grace & Co. v. General Steam Navigation Co.*, [1950] 2 K.B. 383.
211 E.g., BALTIME, cls.1 and 3, online at <http://www.bimco.dk/BIMCO%20Documents/BALTIME%201939.pdf>.

thoroughly efficient state for all purposes all of the time: it requires the shipowner to ensure that the ship is fit to discharge efficiently the immediate task in the voyage. For instance, a ship that breaks down on the voyage and has to be towed to its destination may be in breach of this obligation;[212] but, if its winches and tackle are in running order, it will be considered to be in an efficient state for its immediate task of discharging the cargo at the destination.[213]

The provisioning of the ship under a time charterparty falls much more heavily on the charterer since he or she has much greater freedom for its employment. Typically the shipowner, as part of the management of the ship, must provide the vessel and all its machinery and equipment as well as a complete and competent crew along with its provisions and stores. The charterer must arrange and pay for practically everything else required for the voyages on which the ship is sent, including all loading and discharging operations, water, fuel, port charges, pilotage fees, and other charges incidentally incurred *en route*.[214] In return for payment of these costs and hire, the charterer has full use of the ship. The master must take directions from the charterer as to the ship's voyages and must prosecute them with reasonable dispatch. The master must also accept cargo and issue bills of lading, which ordinarily[215] will bind the shipowner in contract with the cargo owners who are not parties to the time charter,[216] but in return the charterer will be expected to provide an indemnity for any liability that arises from giving such instructions.[217]

The risks of delay in a voyage under a time charterparty are the reverse of voyage charterparties. The shipowner does not care how much time the ship wastes as hire is payable all the while. Consequently, a time charter does not contain any laytime or demurrage clauses. But the charterer will be concerned that the ship works speedily in order to maximize its use and is, to a degree, protected by the shipowner's obligation to provide an efficient ship and the master's duty to undertake the voyages with dispatch.[218] The charterer may also be per-

---

212 Subject to the breakdown, off-hire, and exceptions clauses in the charterparty.
213 *Hogarth v. Miller Bros. & Co.*, [1891] A.C. 48 (H.L.).
214 See, e.g., BALTIME, above note 211, cls.3 and 4. Clause 13 also imposes liability on the charterer for any loss or damage to the ship or its owner resulting from breach of these terms.
215 Subject to any cesser clause, discussed above at note 206, or demise clause, discussed in A(11) in Chapter 9, "Carrier Identity and Demise Clauses."
216 *Paterson Steamships Ltd. v. ALCAN*, [1951] S.C.R. 852.
217 See, e.g., BALTIME, above note 211, cl.9.
218 Also the important off-hire clause discussed below in this chapter.

mitted to expedite port operations by working the ship both day and night, subject to paying for the crew's overtime.[219]

Hire, rather than freight, is the word used in time charterparties to denote the cost of the use of the vessel by the charterer. It is usually expressed at a certain rate, often per deadweight ton, calculated daily and payable monthly in advance. The precise terms are strictly enforced by the courts.[220] Shipowners invariably contract for the right to withdraw the vessel from the charterer's service in breach of payment of hire[221] and regularly exercise this right at the slightest default in timely performance, if the market rate of hire for their vessel has risen. As some protection against such harsh consequences, especially where the lateness of payment is not the fault of the charterer, the charterparty may include a provision known as an "anti-technicality clause," which requires the shipowner to give notice of intention to withdraw the ship if hire is not fully paid within a specified number of hours. Hire must not only be paid on time, it must also be paid in full. However, unlike freight due under a voyage charter against which no set-off by the charterer is allowed,[222] deductions from the payment of hire under a time charter are allowed in some circumstances. The charterer is now entitled to an equitable set-off from the hire of a reasonably assessed amount in respect of loss of use of the ship by reason of the shipowner's breach of contract.[223] The claim to set off must be for reasons associated with the obligation to pay the hire such as losses consequent on loss of use of the vessel: the charterer may not set off against hire claims for damage to the cargo.[224] If the charterer makes a wrongful or excessive deduction, the tender of hire will amount to

---

219 See, e.g., BALTIME, above note 211, cl.17.
220 Because time stipulations in commercial contracts are generally treated as conditions: see *Bunge Corp. v. Tradax S.A.*, above note 50. Examples of the court's strict enforcement are *Zim Israel Navigation Co. v. Effy Shipping Corp. (The Effy)*, [1972] 1 Lloyd's L.R. 18; *Mardorf Peach & Co. v. Attica Sea Carriers Corp. (The Laconia)*, [1977] A.C. 850 (H.L.); and *Scandinavian Trading Tanker Co. A.B. v. Flota Petrolera Ecuatoriana (The Scaptrade)*, [1983] 2 A.C. 694 (H.L.).
221 E.g., BALTIME, above note 211, cl.6.
222 See the discussion above at note 98.
223 *Federal Commerce & Navigation Ltd. v. Molena Alpha Inc. (The Nanfri)*, [1978] Q.B. 927 (C.A.), aff'd on other grounds, [1979] 1 All E.R. 307 (H.L.). See also *Santiren Shipping Ltd. v. Unimarine (The Chrysovalandou Dyo)*, [1981] 1 Lloyd's L.R. 159 (Q.B.); and *Ionna (The)*, [1985] 2 Lloyd's L.R. 164.
224 *Leon Corp. v. Atlantic Lines and Navigation Co. (The Leon)*, [1985] 2 Lloyd's L.R. 470; *Century Textiles and Industry Ltd. v. Tomoe Shipping Co. (The Aditya Vaibhav)*, [1991] 1 Lloyd's L.R. 573.

underpayment in breach of the charterparty, permitting the shipowner to withdraw the ship.[225]

In the event the ship breaks down or suffers a casualty, the charterer's obligation to pay the hire may be suspended. The "off-hire" clause, as it is often called, in the BALTIME charter[226] suspends hire whenever the ship is docked to maintain its efficiency for more than twenty-four hours. Incidents that are likely to require the ship to go into dock include repairs necessitated by negligent navigation, excusable accident or simply wear and tear, and regular servicing and surveys needed to retain its class and certification. Other incidents that are often specified as grounds for suspension of hire are deficiencies in crew's complement, fire, grounding, and general average acts. Hire is only suspended for events that fall within the specific terms of the particular off-hire clause, but a further clause usually included in time charters causes hire to cease completely if the ship is lost at sea.[227]

Whether the incident permitting suspension of hire constitutes a breach of contract by the shipowner is a coincidental feature. Conversely, not every default of the shipowner activates the off-hire clause. However, a breach of the charterparty that does allow the charterer to suspend payment of hire does not prevent him or her from suing the shipowner for damages as well. Suspension of hire is an express right in particular situations distinct from the remedies available for breach of contract. But the charterer may not be able to recover compensation for losses sustained as well as suspend payment of hire if the breach is excused by the terms of the charterparty. Time charters usually contain broad disclaimers of liability for the shipowner. The exceptions clause in the BALTIME charter, for instance, exempts the shipowner from all liability, even when the master and crew are negligent, except for damage and delay caused by the owner's personal act or omission.[228]

At the expiry of the charter the charterer must redeliver the ship to the owner in the same condition as it was received saving for fair wear

---

225 *China National Foreign Trade Transportation Corp. v. Evlogia Shipping Co. (The Mihalios Xilas)*, [1979] 2 Lloyd's L.R. 303 (H.L.).
226 BALTIME, above note 210, cl.11. An unusual form of off-hire clause was discussed by the Supreme Court of Canada in *Deep Sea Tankers Ltd. v. Tricape (The)*, [1958] S.C.R. 585.
227 See, e.g., BALTIME, above note 211, cl.16.
228 See ibid., cl.13. For interpretation of this clause see *Brabant (The)*, [1967] 1 Q.B. 588; *Apollonius (The)*, [1978] 1 Lloyd's L.R. 53 (Q.B.); *Tor Line v. Alltrans Group of Canada Ltd., (The TFL Prosperity)*, [1984] 1 Lloyd's L.R. 123 (H.L.); and the discussion of exemption clauses above at note 179ff.

and tear in the meantime.[229] The ship may also be required to contain a specified volume of fuel, for which the shipowner will repay the charterer,[230] so that the ship is capable of sailing to a refueling port or other destination more convenient to the shipowner.[231]

The precise time and even place of redelivery cannot be fixed in advance as no one can be sure how long the ship's last voyage will actually take. Hence, the charterer is expected to redeliver the ship about the expiry of the charter, paying hire up until it is in fact redelivered.[232] But the date of redelivery is not infinitely flexible. The charterer is only entitled to order the ship on a last voyage that may be objectively estimated to bring the ship to the place of redelivery reasonably close in time to the stated expiry of the charter.[233] Any other ordered voyage would be illegitimate.

The express terms of the charterparty can, of course, vary these common law principles of redelivery. If a margin of time for redelivery at the end of charter is granted by the charterparty, the ship must be redelivered within that time and any overlap will constitute a breach.[234] The BALTIME charter[235] protects the shipowner's interest in the hire by specifying that payment for the service of the ship beyond the termination date of the charter shall not be at the rate of hire but at the then market rate, if it is higher. For the convenience also of the shipowner in preparing to accept the vessel, the same BALTIME clause requires the charterer to give up to ten days' notice of when and where, within a specified range of ports, redelivery may be expected to be made.

The shipowner's remedies for late redelivery of the ship vary according to whether its last voyage was a legitimate one. If the final voyage was legitimate when ordered but, in the event the ship is delayed beyond the expiry date in the charterparty and any reasonable margin of extension without fault of the shipowner, the charterer must pay for any loss suffered by the shipowner. In other words, the charterer must pay hire until the ship is actually redelivered and, if the mar-

---

229 See, e.g., BALTIME, above note 211, cl.7.
230 Just as the charterer will have paid the shipowner for the bunkers on board when the ship was delivered.
231 See, e.g., BALTIME, above note 211, cl.5.
232 *Watson Steamship Co. v. Merryweather & Co.*, [1913] 18 Com. Cas. 294 [*Watson Steamship Co.*]; *London & Overseas Freighters Ltd. v. Timber Shipping Co. (The London Explorer)*, [1972] A.C. 1 (H.L.) [*The London Explorer*].
233 *Watson Steamship Co.*, ibid; *Democritos (The)*, above note 129.
234 *Alma Shipping Corp. of Monrovia v. Montovani (The Dione)*, [1975] 1 Lloyd's L.R. 115 (C.A.) [*The Dione*]; *The London Explorer*, above note 232.
235 BALTIME, above note 211, cl.7.

ket has risen, he or she must also pay damages equal to the difference between the charter hire and the market rate for the period after the final terminal date of the charterparty.[236] If the ship is ordered on an illegitimate final voyage, the shipowner has an option. He or she can accept the situation and demand hire to the date of redelivery plus damages for any losses since the final terminal date of the charter, just as he or she would for a legitimate voyage that overlaps the final expiry of the charter.[237] Alternatively, the shipowner can object to the order for the illegitimate voyage and demand the charterer make a different one. If the charterer refuses, the shipowner may treat the charterer's conduct as a repudiatory breach of contract, may bring the charterparty to an end immediately, and may sue for damages.[238] If the charterer redelivers the ship before the charter period expires or in a state of disrepair, he or she is in breach of contract and must pay damages for premature redelivery[239] or the repairs, repsectively.[240]

Other typical clauses in time charters bear sufficient resemblance to voyage charters that reference may be made to their discussion in the previous section. Even so, this commentary is a bare outline of the principles of the law of charterparties, which has been built up over centuries through thousands of cases interpreting hundreds of differing contractual clauses.

FURTHER READINGS

BOYD, S.C., A.S. BURROWS, & D. FOXTON, *Scrutton on Charterparties and Bills of Lading*, 20th ed. (London: Sweet & Maxwell, 1996).

COLINVAUX, R., *Carver's Carriage by Sea*, 13th ed. (London: Stevens, 1982).

COOKE, J., et al., *Voyage Charters*, 2d ed. (London: Lloyd's Press, 2001).

DAVIS, M., *Bareboat Charters* (London: Lloyd's Press, 2000).

---

236 *Hyundai Merchant Marine Co. v. Gesuri Chartering Co. (The Peoina)*, [1991] 1 Lloyd's L.R. 100 (C.A.).
237 *Ibid.*; *The Dione*, above note 234 at 118.
238 *The Dione*, above note 234; *Torvald Klaveness A/S v. Arni Maritime Corp. (The Gregor)*, [1995] 1 Lloyd's L.R. 1 (H.L.).
239 *Alaskan Trader, No. 2 (The)*, [1983] 2 Lloyd's L.R. 645 (Q.B.).
240 *Attica Sea Carriers Corp. v. Ferrostaal Poseidon Bulk Gmbh (The Puerto Buitrago)*, [1976] 1 Lloyd's L.R. 250 (C.A.). The damages payable may also include the shipowner's loss of profit while the ship is being repaired.

GORTON, L., R. IHRE, & A. SANDEVÄRN, *Shipping and Chartering Practice*, 5th ed. (London: Lloyd's Press, 1999).

SCHOFIELD, J., *Laytime and Demurrage*, 3d ed. (London: Lloyd's Press, 1996).

SUMMERSKILL, M.B., *Laytime*, 4th ed. (London: Stevens, 1989).

UNCTAD, *Charterparties*, UN Doc. TD/B/C.4/ISL/13 (1974).

VENTRIS, F.M., *Tanker Voyage Charterparties* (London: Kluwer Law, 1986).

WILFORD, M., T. Coghlin, & J.D. Kimball, *Time Charters*, 5th ed. (London: Lloyd's Press, 2003).

WILLIAMS, H. *Chartering Documents*, 4th ed. (London: Lloyd's Press, 1999).

CHAPTER 9

CARRIAGE OF GOODS UNDER BILLS OF LADING AND SIMILAR DOCUMENTS

A. KINDS OF LINER SHIPPING DOCUMENTS

1) Introduction

As explained in the last chapter, the delivery of goods by sea is processed and regulated in distinctly different ways determined by the nature of the cargo. While tramp ships carry goods, such as raw materials, in bulk under charterparties, liner vessels transport packaged and unitized goods, typically merchandise and processed products, under bills of lading and similar documents. During the nineteenth and well into the twentieth century, the use of bills of lading to process the carriage of goods in liner services was practically ubiquitous. Informal documents, such as mate's receipts, and delivery orders designating individual shares in a cargo, were also used but uncommonly. Later in the twentieth century, however, the advantageous advances in cargo handling techniques, achieved by the introduction of containers, and in the processing of transactions made possible by the application of computers have transformed the carriage of goods by liner ships. As a result of these changes, a variety of new transport documents has been developed and put increasingly into use in place of bills of lading. These documents include sea waybills, which are simpler instruments than bills of lading, and combined transport documents, which are used for through carriage by sea and multimodal movements. In addition these paper-based processes are now in progress of being transformed into electronic documents.

While the variety of shipping documents used in liner services has increased in recent years, the law governing all of them has remained substantially the same since 1924. Unlike charterparties, which have been left to the freedom of the contracting parties, liner services have been the subject of government regulation for over a century. To avoid the confusion that multiple national regimes would create, an internationally uniform set of rules, known as the *Hague Rules*, was agreed in 1924.[1] These rules have been amended more than once and alternative sets of rules have been agreed but not widely applied. Undoubtedly a new internationally uniform regime that meets the needs of carriers and cargo owners operating modern containerized traffic by streamlined and computerized processes is required. The ongoing efforts to establish such a regime by governmental agreement internationally is proving very difficult. Meanwhile Canada applies[2] an amended version of the *Hague Rules*, known as the *Hague-Visby Rules*.[3] Accordingly, this chapter addresses first the legal character and functions of the various liner shipping documents, then the Canadian application of the international *Hague-Visby Rules*.

2) Bills of Lading

A bill of lading is a document used in international sales to process the delivery of goods by sea. It is widely employed in liner shipping and on chartered ships in some trades. Issued by the carrier to the shipper, alias consignor, of the goods, it traditionally has three functions:[4]

- as evidence of the contract of carriage,
- as a receipt by the carrier for the goods to be carried, and
- as a document of title to the goods.

---

1   By the *International Convention for the Unification of Certain Rules of Law Relating to Bills of Lading*, 25 August 1924, 120 L.N.T.S. 155 [*Hague Rules*].
2   By the *Marine Liability Act*, S.C. 2001, c.6, Part 5 & Sch. 3.
3   *Protocol to Amend the International Convention for the Unification of Certain Rules of Law Relating to Bills of Lading, 1924*, 23 February 1968, 1412 U.N.T.S. 121, U.K.T.S. 1977 No.83. See Appendix 1, *Hague-Visby Rules*, as enacted by the Canadian *Marine Liability Act*, ibid.
4   See *Canadian General Electric v. Armateurs du St. Laurent Inc. (The Maurice Desgagnés)*, [1977] 1 F.C. 215 [*Canadian General Electric*]; and the definition of a bill of lading in the *Hamburg Rules*, art.1(7) enacted in the *Marine Liability Act*, above note 2, Sch.4.

Early bills of lading were merely receipts for goods received by a carrier. Progressively conditions of carriage were included in them, especially as standard form contracts became prevalent. Their status as documents of title was eventually accepted by the common law in 1782 when the commercial practice of negotiating the shipper's right to the goods by endorsing the bill of lading in favour of the consignee or purchaser was recognized in the case of *Lickbarrow v. Mason*.[5]

Its status as a negotiable document of title is what distinguishes the ordinary ocean bill of lading from all other documents used to process carriage transactions, in particular road and rail bills of lading, non-negotiable bills of lading — sometimes called "straight bills" in the United States — sea waybills, dock receipts, and delivery orders. The cases do not so much define a bill of lading as describe its three functions and list its typical contents. The usual indications on the document are its title of negotiable bill of lading and its directions to deliver the goods to the named consignee "or to order."[6] Transport documents that do not bear this time-honoured phrase are not likely to be documents of title but, rather, non-negotiable documents representing only receipt of the goods and the terms of their carriage.

The form of a bill of lading now follows a fairly standardized two-page format in which all the details of the particular cargo and its carriage are entered on the front, and the shipping company's standard trading terms appear in fine print on the back. At the foot of the first page, just above the signature line, there is generally a statement that incorporates the clauses on the back of the form as part of the operative conditions of carriage. Some shortform or blank-backed bills of lading omit the printed clauses and instead incorporate the carrier's standard terms by reference to them at their business premises. The fine-print clauses of a typical bill of lading are numerous and extensive. They set out the carrier's standard trading conditions as they vary his or her implied common law undertakings while reflecting the mandatory obligations of the *Hague-Visby Rules*. The clauses usually deal with the following range of matters:

- application of the *Hague* or *Hague-Visby Rules* (paramount clause),
- non-responsibility for cargo before loading and after discharge,
- non-responsibility for deck cargo and live animals,
- containerized cargo,

---

5   [1794] 5 T. R. 367, 101 E.R. 206.
6   *Henderson & Co. v. Comptoir d'Escompte de Paris* (1873), L.R. 5 P.C. 253; *Canadian General Electric*, above note 4; see also *Hamburg Rules*, above note 4, art.1(7).

- liberty to deviate on the voyage,
- transshipment of the cargo,
- forwarding cargo to destination,
- discharge and delivery,
- freight,
- lien and right of sale over cargo for unpaid freight and other charges,
- limitation of carrier's liability,
- exemption of employees and sub-contractors from liability (Himalaya clause),
- waiver of cargo owner's claims,
- general average (plus New Jason clause),
- war risks,
- ice conditions,
- collisions (both-to-blame clause),
- carrier identity (demise clause),
- choice of governing law, and
- choice of forum for disputes.

Bills of lading are typically issued in sets of three or even five copies. One or more is given to the shipper for transmittal to the consignee, one is kept by the shipping company for its records, and one is carried on board attached to the manifest of the ship. The last is required for customs purposes for entry of the ship at the port of discharge, as well as to match the original bill that must be presented by the consignee or endorsee in exchange for delivery of the goods.[7] The practice of issuing sets of bills of lading reflects the vagaries and inefficiencies of communications in times past; the principle remains that once one copy has been validly presented to the carrier, the rest stand void.[8]

3) Bills of Lading as Evidence of the Carriage Contract

Although regularly treated as a contract of carriage, a bill of lading is, in strict law, only evidence of the terms of that contract.[9] The shipper ordinarily makes the contract at the time of engaging transport with

---

7   Stettin (The) (1889), 14 P.D. 142; Barclays Bank Ltd. v. Commissioners of Customs and Excise, [1963] 1 Lloyd's Rep. 81 at 88–89 [Barclays Bank Ltd.]; Sze Hai Tong Bank Ltd. v. Rambler Cycle Co., [1959] A.C. 576 (P.C.) [Sze Hai Tong Bank].
8   Glyn Mills Currie & Co. v. East and West India Dock Co. (1882), 7 App. Cas. 591.
9   Ardennes (The), [1951] 1 K.B. 55, [1950] 2 All E.R. 517; Fleet Express Lines Ltd. v. Continental Can Co., [1969] 2 O.R. 97 (H.C.J.); Grace Plastics Ltd. v. Bernd Wesch II (The), [1971] F.C. 273; Saint John Shipbuilding and Dry Dock Co. v. Kingsland Maritime Corp. (1981), 126 D.L.R. (3d) 332 (F.C.A.) [Saint John Shipbuilding].

the ship's agent. This agreement will be reached well in advance of receipt of the goods by the carrier. The bill of lading, issued at least after receipt and ordinarily after shipment of the goods and signed on behalf of the shipowner only, does not conclude the carriage contract. However, the common law respects the commercial practicalities of the situation and ordinarily treats the terms and conditions of the bill of lading issued by the shipowner as the best evidence of the contract, unless there are grounds to disturb the assumption.[10] This approach reflects customary usage: shippers are assumed to know a carrier's terms of trade when engaging in repeat transactions and, even if it is a new shipper, it will be presumed to accept the shipowner's terms if they are not out of the ordinary for that trade.[11] However, the shipper may always try to prove the introduction of a novel and unusually burdensome condition without adequate notice,[12] or to establish an agreement, even orally, to a specific condition, different from the printed terms on the back of the bill of lading.[13]

4) Bills of Lading as Receipts for the Goods Carried

In addition to being evidence of the contract of carriage, the bill of lading is the carrier's acknowledgment of receipt of the goods described. Issued by the master of the carrying ship on behalf of the carrier, it is usually signed on his or her behalf by the ship's agents at the port of loading. Traditionally a "shipped" bill of lading is issued as or after the vessel leaves the port, signifying the goods are laden or shipped on board. More recently, especially in the container trades, "received-for-shipment" bills of lading are being issued when the goods are accepted on behalf of the ship at the loading terminal.[14] In either case, at common law, once the ship or its agent receives the cargo, the carrier becomes at least a bailee for reward with associated duties of custody and care of the goods.[15] In the hands of the shipper, the bill of lading is

---

10 *Ardennes (The)*, ibid.
11 *Anticosti Shipping Co. v. St-Amand*, [1959] S.C.R. 372; *Captain v. Far Eastern Steamship Co.* (1978), 97 D.L.R. (3d) 250 (B.C.S.C.).
12 *Anglo Oriental Rugs Ltd. v. March Shipping Ltd.*, [1993] O.J. No. 1075 (QL).
13 *Ardennes (The)*, above note 9; *Saint John Shipbuilding*, above note 9.
14 A "received" bill of lading may be turned into a "shipped" bill of lading if subsequently so marked by the ship's agent.
15 Maritime common law may impose heavier duties on carriers than other bailees, subject to the terms of the carriage contract, including any disclaimer clauses: see B(1), "Seaworthiness of the Ship" and B(2), "Care of the Cargo" in Chapter 8.

a receipt evidencing these obligations. The face of the bill of lading records a number of details about the shipment, including the following:

- shipper's name and address,
- consignee's name and address,
- name and address of the party to notify at destination if different from consignee,
- description of the goods,
- marks and numbers of the goods,
- quantity or weight of the goods,
- number of packages,
- name of the vessel and voyage number,
- port of loading,
- port of discharge,
- place where freight is payable,
- name of shipping line,
- master's signature,
- place and date of issue, and
- number of original bills of lading.

Usually the shipper, or the forwarding agent, supplies these details and even prepares a blank form bill of lading of the shipping company. On signature and dating on behalf of the carrier, the bill becomes a receipt as to kind, quantity, and condition of the cargo described. Usually the bill of lading includes a statement that the goods are "received in apparent good order and condition," in which case the document is termed a "clean" bill.[16] But the carrier is always at liberty to note on the bill of lading the actual deteriorated condition of the goods or their packages noticed on loading,[17] in which case the bill is said to be "claused." In any event, the carrier's receipt only represents the apparent condition of the goods, because their actual condition inside packages or containers is not visible.[18]

Frequently the carrier will seek to disclaim liability for these representations as to kind, quantity, and condition by the use of printed clauses such as "weight and quantity unknown" or "shipper's load and count" placed just above the master's signature. The cases are divided

---

16 *Canada and Dominion Sugar Co. v. Canadian National (West Indies) Steamships*, [1947] A.C. 46 at 53 (P.C.) [*Canada and Dominion Sugar*].
17 See, e.g., *Hellenic Lines v. Louis Dreyfus Corp.*, 249 F. Supp. 526 at 528 (S.D.N.Y. 1966).
18 *Marbig Rexel Pty. Ltd. v. ABC Container Line N.V.*, [1992] 2 Lloyd's L.R. 636 (N.S.W.S.C.) [*Marbig Rexel*].

as to the effectiveness of such clauses;[19] but perhaps the better view is that, unless the bill of lading is specifically claused because the carrier could not reasonably ascertain the quantity or weight,[20] the cargo owner may rely on the written representations. However, the assertion on a bill of lading that a container, which was stuffed and sealed by the shipper, is "said to contain" certain goods is generally acceptable since the carrier has no means, short of opening the load, to discover the kind, quantity, or condition of the contents.[21]

5) Bills of Lading as Negotiable Documents of Title

The third and truly exceptional function of the bill of lading is as a negotiable document of title to the goods while they remain in the carrier's custody. Since *Lickbarrow v. Mason*,[22] the common law has accepted the commercial practice of trading the bill of lading as if it were the goods while they are in carriage. The transaction is completed simply by endorsing the bill with the name of the transferee under signature of the transferor, the last holder of the bill, and delivering possession of it.[23] Strictly speaking, the value represented by the bill of lading is not negotiated, as a negotiable instrument, such as a cheque may be, but is simply transferred. A bill of lading may be transferred by this simple process as often as desired, the last named transferee or holder being entitled to receive the goods from the carrier. As a document of title, however, the bill of lading must be surrendered to the carrier, who is bound by common law only to deliver the goods on presentation of the properly endorsed document by the last named holder.[24]

Delivery of the goods by the carrier in the absence of the bill of lading is a breach of the carriage contract, exposing the carrier to liability

---

19 Cp. *Patagonier v. Spear & Thorpe* (1933), 47 Ll. L.R. 59; *Canada and Dominion Sugar*, above note 16; *AG of Ceylon v. Seindia Steam Navigation Co.*, [1962] A.C. 60 (P.C.); *Coutinho Caro & Co. v. Ermua (The)*, [1982] 1 F.C. 252; and *Noble Resource Ltd. v. Cavalier Shipping Corp., (The Atlas)*, [1996] 1 Lloyd's L.R. 642 (Q.B.).
20 See *Hague-Visby Rules*, above note 3, art.III(3); and discussion in D(1), "Bills of Lading" below.
21 E.g. *Esmeralda (The)*, [1988] 1 Lloyd's L.R. 206 (N.S.W.S.C.); and *Marbig Rexel*, above note 18.
22 Above note 5. See also *Sewell v. Burdick* (1884), 10 App. Cas. 74.
23 A "bearer" bill may be transferred by delivery alone; it is one in which no consignee is named or the named consignee endorses by signature in blank.
24 See *S.A. Sucre Export v. Northern River Shipping Ltd. (The Sormovskiy 3068)*, [1994] 2 Lloyd's L.R. 266 (Q.B.) [*The Sormovskiy 3068*]; *East West Corp. v. DKBS 1912*, [2003] 1 Lloyd's Rep. 239 at 257 (C.A.); and the cases above in note 7.

to the bill of lading holder if he or she does not happen to be the recipient of the delivery.[25] However, the necessity of presenting the bill of lading becomes an impediment to the efficient flow of trade where the goods arrive before the documents and both the carrier and consignee, being the rightful recipient, want to proceed with discharge and delivery. The speed and tight sailing schedules of modern container lines, for instance, make this a not infrequent event. Therefore, a practice has grown up of carriers making delivery in the absence of a bill of lading against a letter of indemnity from the receiver, usually with the backing of a bank.[26] This practice increases the costs and risks of both parties and is not a defence to a subsequent claim by the holder of the bill of lading.[27] For these reasons non-negotiable transport documents have been introduced in place of bills of lading where appropriate.

6) Sea Waybills and Other Sea Transport Documents

The negotiable bill of lading is a convenient document for merchants and bankers who want to buy or to borrow money against goods in transit, but such transactions are now much less common than they used to be. Containers of merchandise, for instance, are typically transported directly to the ultimate recipient. As a result, shipping companies have developed simpler documents that may look much like bills of lading but are made out to a named consignee only. Not being "to order," they are not documents of title and cannot be endorsed so as to transfer any interest in the goods they describe. Many titles have been assigned to these transport documents by the companies that designed and sought to introduce them, but the shipping industry seems now to have settled on the generic name of "sea waybill." Even so, no legal incidents hang on this name: its significance lies in its indication that this class of documents has different functions from those of bills of lading. Not being documents of title, sea waybills act only as receipts for the goods and evidence of the carriage contract. As such, they do not have to be presented to the carrier in return for the cargo, for they are only documentary evidence in the hands of the consignee of his or her rights to the goods. To receive delivery, the would-be recipient sim-

---

25 *Sze Hai Tong Bank*, above note 7; *Barclays Bank Ltd.*, above note 7; *Kuwait Petroleum Corp. v. I & D Oil Carriers Ltd. (The Houda)*, [1994] 2 Lloyd's L.R. 541 (C.A.).
26 *The Sormovskiy 3068*, above note 24.
27 See the cases above in note 25.

ply has to provide identification to the carrier demonstrating that he or she is the consignee named in the sea waybill.[28]

A variety of other documents are used in the course of transporting goods by sea. Their legal effect, as with all carriage documents, depends upon the substantive intent of their issuance and their customary standing in the trade.[29] A cargo of goods may pass through many hands in the course of sea transport, including the loading dock or terminal, a port warehouse, and a stevedoring firm as well as one or more carrying vessels. Receipts for the goods will be issued by each recipient to the transferor as a record of the transfer and custody of the cargo. Thus dock receipts and mate's receipts (i.e., acknowledgments by the ship's officer or agent) may be tendered as evidence of the receipt or loading of the goods when there is a dispute as to their number, quality, or apparent condition.[30] In addition a mate's receipt is evidence of the right to receive, in exchange, the bill of lading when it is issued.[31]

When bills of lading are written to cover cargoes carried in bulk, such as oil or grain, but deliverable to several different recipients, additional documents are necessary to effect separation of their interests. Then delivery orders recording the volume or quantity of the share of the whole cargo may be issued to the consignees.[32] In such cases, care must be taken to determine whether such a delivery order was issued by the carrier, or by the shipper or exporting merchant. Only a ship's delivery order can be used against the carrier; a merchant's delivery order will suffice, however, if it has been attorned to (i.e., signed or otherwise acknowledged) by the carrier.[33] Even then, the delivery order is not a substitute for the bill of lading and is not a negotiable document of title:[34] it is simply additional documentary evidence, like a receipt, of the named party's expected share of the cargo.

---

28 No special form of identification is necessary but sometimes presentation is requested of the *pro forma* invoice, which is a price quotation sent by the shipper/exporter in advance of the goods to the consignee/importer to enable him or her to obtain an import licence or to arrange financing.
29 I.e., mate's receipts are typically only receipts but have become documents of title by established custom in some trades: see *Kum v. Wah Tat Bank Ltd.*, [1971] 1 Lloyd's L.R. 439 (P.C.).
30 *Canada and Dominion Sugar Co.*, above note 16.
31 *Nippon Yusen Kaisha v. Ramjiban Serowgee*, [1938] A.C. 429.
32 *Julia (The)*, [1949] A.C. 293 at 322 (H.L.); *Cremer v. General Carriers S.A. (The Dona Mari)*, [1973] 2 Lloyd's L.R. 366 [*The Dona Mari*].
33 *Colin & Shields v. W. Weddel & Co.*, [1952] 1 All E.R. 1021, aff'd [1952] 2 All E.R. 337 (C.A.); *The Dona Mari*, ibid.
34 *Margarine Union Gmbh v. Cambay Prince S.S. Co. (The Wear Breeze)*, [1967] 2 Lloyd's Rep. 315 [*The Wear Breeze*].

7) Combined Transport Documents

Under modern systems of transport, goods are frequently carried by more than one ship and even by more than one mode. In the container trades, for instance, door-to-door service from the shipper to the consignee is common. Such multimodal service typically involves surface transport of the container by road or rail or both to the port of loading, mainline sea carriage to a hub port, transshipment onto a feeder line to the port of discharge, and oncarriage overland to the destination. In these circumstances the number and variety of transport documents that may be issued are increased enormously.

Concerning the sea carriage portion of such a multimodal movement, three generic classes of documents are of distinct legal significance. First, where goods are carried by sea on more than one ship, one "through" bill of lading may be issued by the first and contracting carrier to cover all segments of the transit, or separate documents may be written by each carrier.[35] Where a through bill is issued, care must be taken to determine from the fine printed terms whether the contracting carrier accepts responsibility for the goods for the whole transit, including the time they are actually being moved by the oncarrier, or if the contracting carrier limits its responsibilities to the time it has possession and custody of the goods, providing only the services of a forwarding agent for the shipper in arranging their oncarriage with the actual carrier.[36] In the latter case, the purported through bill of lading may effect delivery as desired but in law amounts to a segmented movement under two separate contracts with two different carriers. Second, a multimodal movement of goods is commonly processed nowadays under a single multimodal or combined transport document.[37] The typical document assigns responsibility for the goods to the contracting carrier for their safe carriage and delivery through all modes of transport.[38] The contracting party is then known usually as the multimodal transport operator (MTO). It may be a shipping line, working ashore as it were, or the first actual carrier, such as a railway company, or an international freight forwarder, or other transport logistics company. The first MTOs were unimodal carriers who expanded

---

35 *Louis Dreyfus & Co. v. Paterson Steamships Ltd.*, 1930 A.M.C. 1555 (2d Cir. 1930); *Pioneer Land*, 1957 A.M.C. 50 at 56 (S.D.N.Y. 1956).
36 Ibid.
37 See R. DeWit, *Multimodal Transport* (London: Lloyd's Press, 1990); H. Kindred & M. Brooks, *Multimodal Transport Rules* (London: Kluwer Law, 1997).
38 Even so, different regimes of liability may still apply to the goods in different modes: see Kindred & Brooks, *ibid*.

their businesses by offering multimodal service. Now there are numerous MTOs that have organized multimodal service companies, although they do not operate any transport equipment; they are, in fact, non-vessel/vehicle–owning multimodal transport operators (NVOMTOs). This distinction in the class of MTOs may be important in a business sense in terms of the financial viability and transport efficacy of the contractor but has no legal consequences.

Care must still be taken to ensure the multimodal transport document does indeed cast the contractor as an MTO, that is, as fully responsible for the whole movement to final delivery. For instance, freight forwarders are traditionally agents for the shipper in arranging delivery of the goods by carriers they select.[39] As agents, they owe a duty of care in arranging carriage but they contract on behalf of their principal, the shipper,[40] who thereby acquires privity of contract separately with the carrier on each segment of carriage. More recently freight forwarders have perceived the business opportunity of offering multimodal services, that is, constituting themselves as NVOMTOs. Indeed, out of concern to provide competitive operations, they frequently offer forwarding, consolidating, and transporting services in any combination the customer desires.

The third generic class of transport document is the freight forwarder's house bill. This standardized document may include clauses evincing an intention to act either as principal with full responsibility as an MTO, or alternatively as agent with the limited duties of a forwarder, as appropriate.[41] Such a document creates legal complexity in trying to determine the intent of the contracting parties[42] as to the extent of responsibility that has been accepted.[43] Indeed it is necessary to determine the level of responsibility in respect of the particular incident out

---

39 *Jones v. European General Express Co.* (1920), 90 L.J.K.B. 159 at 160. For an example of the sea and land carriers having separate responsibilities under one combined transport document, see *Lutfy Ltd. v. Canadian Pacific Railway Co.*, [1973] F.C. 1115.

40 *C.A. Pisani & Co. v. Brown, Jenkinson & Co.* (1939), 64 Ll. L.R. 340 (K.B.); *Marston Excelsior Ltd. v. Arbuckle, Smith & Co.*, [1971] 2 Lloyd's L.R. 306 (C.A.).

41 See, e.g., the standard trading conditions of the Canadian International Freight Forwarders Association, which provide suitable clauses for both roles to be included in the same contract.

42 The intention of the parties is crucial to deciding the nature of their contractual relationship: *W.T. Lamb and Sons v. Goring Brick Co.*, [1932] 1 K.B. 710.

43 *Troy v. Eastern Company of Warehouses (The)* (1921), 8 Ll. L.R. 17 (C.A.); *Salsi v. Jetspeed Air Services Ltd.*, [1977] 2 Lloyd's L.R. 57 (Q.B.); *Tetroc Ltd. v. Cross-Con International Ltd.*, [1981] 1 Lloyd's L.R. 192; *Carrington Shipways Pty. Ltd. v. Patrick Operations Pty. Ltd. (The Cape Comorin)* (1991), 24 N.S.W.L.R. 745 (C.A.).

of which a claim has arisen, since the freight forwarder may have different roles in different phases of the carriage transaction.[44]

Whenever a default in service under a multimodal transport document occurs, the cargo owner needs only look to the MTO for satisfaction, however and wherever in the transport chain it happened. Receipts and even bills of lading will be issued by the actual carriers but these are of no concern to the cargo owner. They are, however, of great importance to the MTO, which, in the role of the shipper on the underlying carriage contracts, will want to rely on them in order to seek indemnity for compensation paid to the cargo owner from the actual carrier in default. Whether multimodal transport documents are negotiable documents of title has not been settled by the courts, and legal opinions vary.[45] The market has accepted their transferability, however; in particular the banks have agreed to their use in financing export sales by documentary letters of credit.[46]

8) Electronic Transport Documents

Paper processes traditionally used in transport are increasingly being replaced by electronic transactions. The efficiencies of cargo handling achievable with containers and container ships demand equally streamlined processing systems. Major transatlantic container lines became computerized and interconnected among all their offices and port agencies in the early 1970s. Now transactions are executed electronically with customers and with customs. Part of the pressure to substitute sea waybills for bills of lading was a desire by shipping companies to standardize the format and streamline the contents of shipping documents,[47] so that transport data need only be entered by hand once into a computer yet can be replicated in print[48] or electronically whenever

---

44 *Maheno (The)*, [1977] 1 Lloyd's L.R. 81 (N.Z.S.C.).
45 The cases and views are canvassed by C. Debattista, *Sale of Goods Carried by Sea* (London: Butterworths, 1990) at 211–28. This issue has been resolved in the United Kingdom by reform legislation: see C. Debattista, *Sale of Goods Carried by Sea*, 2d ed. (London: Butterworths, 1998) at 40–43.
46 See the International Chamber of Commerce, Uniform Customs and Practice for Documentary Credits (UCP500) ICC Publication No. 500/2.
47 The Canadian General Standards Board has adopted a Canadian Trade Document Alignment System based on the United Nations Layout Key for Trade Documents, which standardizes the size, format, and information of all documents customarily used in international trade.
48 The printed version generally takes on the form of a blank back document that refers to the carrier's standard trading forms, which are accessible at its business premises.

and wherever required. In this respect, sea waybills and their electronic equivalents have become a great success in the shipping industry. Bills of lading, on the other hand, are not yet being replicated electronically in the industry. Several trial schemes have been undertaken,[49] and a set of rules to govern the electronic transaction, including the transfer of rights to the goods, has been designed and promulgated[50] but none has found general commercial acceptability. The main obstacle surrounds the unique negotiability function of the bill of lading. While the technology is available to replicate this function electronically and securely, the various parties to a sale and transport of goods, especially the banks who traditionally finance the transaction on the basis of a shipped bill of lading, are not assured of its business efficacy.

In any event, the maritime laws surrounding execution of electronic transport transactions are the same as those for processing paper documents. These laws inhibit electronic transactions, or at least claims arising therefrom, in many ways because they assume the use of paper as the medium of communication. Fortunately, general legislation, such as the *Personal Information and Electronic Documents Act*,[51] and specific amendments to existing statutes are slowly permitting electronic alternatives to writing, signatures, paper records, documentary proof, and suchlike obstacles in order to facilitate electronic commence generally.

9) Transfer of Rights in a Bill of Lading

While negotiation of a bill of lading, by endorsement and delivery,[52] entitles the new holder to rights in the goods, no rights are transferred in the contract of carriage evidenced by the bill of lading. Recognition at common law of the transferability of the bill of lading as a negotiable document of title[53] does not extend to its contractual functions.[54] Indeed, the common law does not, in general, admit assignment of

---

49 E.g., the Bills of Lading in Europe or BOLERO project.
50 See Comité Maritime International, Rules for Electronic Bills of Lading, 1990, online at: <http://www.comitemaritime.org/cmidocs/rulesebla.html>; and H. Kindred, "Trading Internationally by Electronic Bills of Lading" (1992) 7 B.F.L.R. 265.
51 S.C. 2000, c.5, Part 2. See also the *Canada Evidence Act*, R.S.C. 1985, c.C-5, ss.31.1–31.8.
52 Discussed above at note 23.
53 In *Lickbarrow v. Mason*, above note 5.
54 *Thompson v. Dominy* (1845), 14 M. & W. 403, 153 E.R. 532. Assignments of contracts were first made possible in equity and subsequently by statute.

contractual rights. Hence the endorsee of a bill of lading may be in the position of being able to demonstrate entitlement to the goods in the hands of the carrier but unable to pursue the carrier in contract for their misdelivery. Conversely, the carrier may be bound to deliver the goods on presentation of the properly endorsed bill of lading but unable to assert a contractual claim against its holder, for example, for any outstanding freight or demurrage. This unsatisfactory state of affairs is substantially alleviated by the *Bills of Lading Act*.[55] Copied from the U.K. legislation of 1855,[56] section 2 provides:

> Every consignee ... and every endorsee of a bill of lading to whom the property in the goods therein mentioned passes upon or by reason of such consignment or endorsement, has and is vested with all such rights of action and is subject to all such liabilities in respect of such goods as if the contract contained in the bill of lading had been made with himself.

As a result of this provision, in most situations on the negotiation of the bill of lading, the new holder — either consignee or subsequent endorsee — is deemed to have assumed the rights and responsibilities of the contract "contained in" the bill of lading. Thus, privity of contract arises statutorily between the carrier and the cargo owner, holder of the bill of lading. There is some difficulty with the clause "contained in" the bill of lading since, strictly speaking, that document is only evidence of the terms of the carriage contract,[57] but the courts have rejected too technical an interpretation of the statute as defeating its curative purposes.[58]

Two other interpretive considerations present much more substantial limitations on the application of the Act. First, it only applies to bills of lading. Although a bill of lading is not defined in the Act, its ubiquitous usage at the time the statute was initially enacted leaves no doubt as to the kind of document intended, to the exclusion of the more recently introduced sea waybills and similar transport documents. Second, the statutory transfer of contractual rights and duties only occurs when the bill of lading is dealt with in such a way that "the

---

55 R.S.C. 1985, c.B-5.
56 *An Act to Amend the Law Relating to Bills of Lading, 1855* (U.K.), 18 & 19 Vict., c.111. The English Act has since been repealed and usefully replaced by a much more broadly facilitative statute, the *Carriage of Goods by Sea Act, 1992* (U.K.), 1992, c.50, but no such legislative reform has yet occurred in Canada.
57 Discussed above at note 9.
58 See *Leduc v. Ward* (1888), 20 Q.B.D. 475 (C.A.); and *Hain Steamship Co. v. Tate and Lyle Ltd.* (1936), 55 Ll. L.R. 159 (H.L.).

property in the goods therein mentioned passes upon or by reason of ... consignment or endorsement."[59] This clause not only excludes all carriage transactions processed under sea waybills and other non-negotiable transport documents but also some covered by genuine bills of lading. The passing of property in the goods is old common law language for the transfer of title or ownership, which is regulated by the law of contracts of sale of goods.[60] This law impacts the maritime law of contracts of carriage by limiting the range of situations in which the *Bills of Lading Act* will take effect, even though a bill of lading is transferred. In particular, the rights and duties under the carriage contract will not be transferred with the bill of lading when

- it is not properly endorsed or negotiated;
- it does not pass property in the goods because title to them has already been transferred;[61]
- it does not pass property in the goods because they are being carried in bulk and title to the portions, which have multiple owners, cannot be transferred according to sales law until they are ascertained by discharge and delivery;[62]
- it is delivered for a purpose other than entitling the holder to a title interest in the goods; or
- although contractually intended, it was never issued.

Bills of lading are most commonly endorsed so as to sell or to mortgage the title to the goods, but they may also be transferred for other reasons outside the *Bills of Lading Act*. For instance, they may be delivered to an agent in order to sell the goods on behalf of their owner or to a bank as a pledge of the goods. In *Insurance Co. of North America v. Colonial Steamships Ltd.*,[63] the bill of lading was transferred to the cargo insurers as proof of the goods claimed to have been lost. Since no property or title interest passed to the insurers they could not claim any benefit from the *Bills of Lading Act* and so had no contractual rights against the carrier.

Where section 2 of the *Bills of Lading Act* takes effect, section 3 goes on to preserve certain pre-existing rights of the original parties. It states:

---

59 *Sewell v. Burdick*, above note 22; *Aramis (The)*, [1989] 1 Lloyd's L.R. 213.
60 See G.H.L. Fridman, *Sale of Goods in Canada*, 4th ed. (Scarborough: Carswell, 1995) c.4; and M.G. Bridge, *Sale of Goods* (Toronto: Butterworths, 1988) c.4.
61 *Delfini (The)*, [1990] 1 Lloyd's L.R. 252.
62 This is a situation in which delivery orders are typically issued to the transferees but, not being bills of lading, they are also outside the Act's application.
63 [1942] S.C.R. 357.

Nothing in this Act prejudices or affects
(a) any right of stoppage in transitu;
(b) any right of an unpaid vendor under the Civil Code of the Province of Quebec;
(c) any right to claim freight against the original shipper or owner; or
(d) any liability of the consignee or endorsee by reason or in consequence of his being such consignee or endorsee, or of his receipt of the goods by reason or in consequence of such consignment or endorsement[64]

Thus, for instance, the shipper cannot escape liability for an outstanding obligation for prepaid freight owing to the carrier, as in fact, "the statute creates a new liability, but it does not exonerate the person who has entered into an express contract."[65] The House of Lords has confirmed this interpretation of the Act, noting the difference in wording in section 2 regarding rights and liabilities. The new holder of the bill of lading is transferred the rights of the shipper but is made subject to the same liabilities as the shipper. Thus the shipper remains liable to the carrier, for example, for shipping dangerous goods without warning.[66]

If the *Bills of Lading Act* does not apply to the carriage contract in question, then recourse must be had to other less certain arguments at common law. In *Brandt v. Liverpool, Brazil and River Plate Steam Navigation Co.*,[67] the court was very ready to imply a contract at common law between the receivers — to whom the bill of lading had been endorsed as pledgees — and the carrier as a result of their conduct on discharge of the cargo. From the presentation of the bill of lading by the holder together with the freight, and the acceptance of the shipowner by delivery of the goods, a contract was inferred according to the terms of the bill of lading. Implying such a contract gives business efficacy to the carriage transaction but also creates legal difficulties, not least as to the terms and conditions of this contract. Is it to be assumed they are the same as those evidenced by the bill of lading or other transport document issued to the shipper?[68] In *Brandt's* case the cargo claimant was allowed to sue for delayed delivery on a contract

---

64 *Bills of Lading Act*, above note 55, s.3.
65 Per Pollock C.B. in *Fox v. Nott* (1861), 6 H. & N. 630 at 636, 158 E.R. 260 at 263.
66 *Effort Shipping Co. v. Linden Management S.A., (The Giannis NK)*, [1998] A.C. 605 (H.L.).
67 [1924] 1 K.B. 575 (C.A.) [*Brandt's*].
68 See *Captain Gregos (No. 2) (The)*, [1990] 2 Lloyd's L.R. 395 (C.A.); *Quadro Shipping NV v. Bizley & Co. (The Protea Trader)* (1992), 113 F.L.R. 280 (N.S.W.C.A.).

that impliedly contained the bill of lading's terms. More recent cases, however, have demanded proof of some obligations owed between cargo owner and carrier from which a contract can be implied.[69] As a result, the implied contract approach is not as reliable a solution as it once seemed to be.

A second common law solution involves the doctrine of agency. The consignee can establish a contract with the carrier if it can be shown that the shipper made the original agreement both for itself and on behalf of the consignee. Carriers who issue sea waybills frequently employ this approach by including in the printed clauses on the front of the document language that clearly indicates the shipper accepts the conditions of carriage for itself and on behalf of the consignee, and warrants it has authority to do so.[70] The absence of cases interpreting such clauses suggests their use is effective, but there must be some doubt in those instances when the shipper accepts the carriage contract before a consignee has even been identified.[71]

The operation of the *Bills of Lading Act* also affects the original shipper's right to sue on the carriage contract. Prior to the Act, since the consignee could not sue on the contract, even though he or she had become the owner of the goods, the shipper frequently did so and the fruits of the action were regarded by the court as held in trust by the shipper for the consignee. This rule, found in *Dunlop v. Lambert*,[72] was allowed as an exception to the common law principle that compensation can only be recovered to the extent of the damage to the property of the claimant, whenever it could be shown that the contracting shipper and carrier anticipated a transfer of ownership of the goods to the consignee. With the enactment of the *Bills of Lading Act*, consignees became able to sue for themselves in most cases and the rule in *Dunlop v. Lambert* lost much of its importance. However, in *The Albazero*,[73] the consignee, as cargo owner, could not take advantage of the Act and, therefore, when the shipper brought suit against the carrier, the issue was raised whether the rule in *Dunlop v. Lambert* had been disturbed by the legislation. The House of Lords held that the rule still persists but curtailed its operation

---

69 *Aramis (The)*, above note 59; *Captain Gregos (No. 2) (The)*, ibid.; *Mitsui & Co. v. Novorossiysk Shipping Co. (The Gudermes)*, [1993] 1 Lloyd's L.R. 311.
70 See the voluntary Sea Waybills Rules 1990 promulgated by the Comité Maritime International, online at <http://www.comitemaritime.org/cmidocs/rulessaway.html>.
71 The principle of agent for an undisclosed principal does not normally extend to a non-existent principal!
72 (1839), 6 Cl. & F. 600, 7 E.R. 824 (H.L.).
73 [1977] A.C. 774.

by stating that, in view of its rationale, it cannot apply where the *Bills of Lading Act* gives consignees their own right of action.[74]

If the cargo owner — whether as consignee, endorsee on a bill of lading, or holder of some other transport document — is unable to sue[75] on the carriage contract, he or she may still bring an action in tort. Sea carriage is, in essence, a species of bailment for reward and so the common law imposes on carriers a duty of care for the goods in their charge, which is owed to the cargo owners, whether they are in privity of contract or not. This is the basis on which actual carriers, to whom goods are transshipped by the contracting carrier, are responsible to their owners. The transaction is said to be a "bailment on terms" where the carrier and the cargo owner are within privity of a contract that governs their responsibilities.[76] When there is no privity of contract, the duty of care arises from the principles of negligence established in *Donoghue v. Stevenson*.[77] In such cases the carrier will be held to a standard of reasonable care in all the circumstances. However, the duty of care for property in tort is traditionally only owed to the person who is the owner, or has at least the immediate right to possession of the property, at the time it is damaged.[78] Hence a consignee or other receiver of goods who becomes owner of the cargo while it is in transit, but only after it has suffered damage, will have no right to sue for the loss.[79] As a result, the right of action in tort may depend upon the chance timing whether the consignee took up the carriage documents or otherwise became owner of the cargo before or after a marine incident that was probably unknown to him or her at the time. An attempt in the English courts to extend a right of action to the person who bears the risk of loss or damage[80] — and thereby to permit a consignee who was not the cargo owner when the goods were injured but had assumed the risk of their loss on loading[81] — was repulsed by the House of Lords, who have maintained the traditional rule.[82]

The rule is bound up with the principle of tort law that a claim in negligence may be brought for personal injury and property damage

---

74 Absent a special agreement with the carrier in favour of the shipper or charterer.
75 Or be sued.
76 See *Pioneer Container (The)*, [1994] 2 A.C. 324 (P.C.).
77 [1932] A.C. 562.
78 *The Wear Breeze*, above note 34.
79 *Ibid*.
80 Cf. *Irene's Success (The)*, [1981] 2 Lloyd's L.R. 635; and *Elafi (The)*, [1981] 2 Lloyd's L.R. 679.
81 As is customary under FOB contract terms.
82 *Leigh and Sillivan Ltd. v. Aliakmon Shipping Ltd. (The Aliakmon)*, [1986] 1 A.C. 785.

but not for pure economic loss. Although at one time relaxed somewhat in English law,[83] this principle has been affirmed once more by the House of Lords.[84] However, in Canada and elsewhere,[85] the courts have departed from strict application of the principle. According to the Supreme Court of Canada in *Jervis Crown*,[86] tortious liability in Canada depends upon a case-by-case analysis of the proximity of the parties involved and the foreseeability of the damage suffered. Pursuant to this authority, the Federal Court in *The Lara S.*[87] held the shipowner liable in tort for negligent stowage of the goods, even though the plaintiff had no proprietary or possessory interest in them at that time.

10) Bills of Lading on a Chartered Ship

While the usual carrying trades of chartered ships and liner vessels are quite distinct,[88] sometimes bills of lading are issued to cover cargo on a ship under charter. This may happen, for instance, when a vessel is time-chartered into a liner service. It also occurs on a voyage chartered vessel when it is carrying a bulk cargo, such as oil, to several consignees or when, not having a full load, it accepts additional cargo from other shippers. The practice frequently raises two legal problems. One involves the identity of the carrier — shipowner or charterer — under the bill of lading (discussed in the next subsection). The other problem concerns the terms of the carriage contract evidenced by the bill of lading. As discussed previously,[89] a charterparty, other than a charter by demise, is a contract of carriage signed by both shipowner and charterer. Therefore, a bill of lading issued by the ship to the charterer as shipper does not evidence, and cannot unilaterally alter, the terms of the contract already agreed in the charterparty.[90] However, if the bill of lading is negotiated,

---

83   *Anns v. Merton London Borough Council*, [1978] A.C. 728.
84   *Murphy v. Brentwood District Council*, [1991] 1 A.C. 398.
85   In Australia, see *Caltex Oil (Australia) Pty. Ltd. v. Dredge Willemstad (The)* (1976), 136 C.L.R. 529.
86   *Canadian National Railway Co. v. Norsk Pacific Steamship Co. (Jervis Crown)*, [1992] 1 S.C.R. 1021 [*Jervis Crown*]. See also *Bow Valley Husky (Bermuda) Ltd. v. Saint John Shipbuilding Ltd.*, [1997] 3 S.C.R. 210, 153 D.L.R. (4th) 385 (S.C.C.).
87   *Canastrand Industries Ltd. v. Lara S. (The)*, [1993] 2 F.C. 553, aff'd (1994), 176 N.R. 30 (F.C.A.).
88   See discussion in A in Chapter 8, "Introduction."
89   See Chapter 8, "Carriage of Goods by Charterparty."
90   *Rodocanachi, Sons & Co. v. Milburn Bros.* (1886), 18 Q.B.D. 67; *Great Lakes Paper Co. Ltd. v. Paterson Steamships Ltd.*, [1951] 3 D.L.R. 518 (Ex. Ct.); *President of India v. Metcalfe Shipping Co. (The Dunelmia)*, [1970] 1 Q.B. 289 [*The Dunelmia*]. The charterparty's terms may be subsequently altered by a bill of lading or any

the endorsee is not privy to the charterparty and is bound to rely, in the ordinary way, on the printed conditions in the bill of lading as the best evidence of the terms of the carriage contract.[91] Similarly, if the charterer arranges for the ship to load cargoes of other shippers and bills of lading are issued directly to them, these documents, and not the charterparty, will regulate the terms on which their goods are carried.

The result of both kinds of situations is the potential for inconsistency between the terms of carriage found in the charterparty and the bills of lading. The confusion may occur because the charterer issues its own bill of lading to the shipper or because the shipowner's printed bill of lading is used but it is not consistent with the charterparty, which, although likely based on a published standard form, tends to be individually negotiated. In order to attempt to avoid such confusion of contractual clauses it is customary for bills of lading to incorporate the terms of the charterparty by reference.[92] This practice may raise two further problems of interpretation: the first concerns the scope of the charterparty terms that are intended to be incorporated, and the second involves their construction in the face of inconsistency with other conditions in the bill of lading. The latter problems are a matter of contract construction from case to case. Regarding the scope of incorporated terms, the courts have provided some guidance as to the effect of several commonly used phrases of incorporation. First, the reference in the bill of lading may not identify any particular charterparty.[93] This, in the view of the courts, is not a problem because they will assume the reference is to whatever charterparty covers the goods in carriage.[94] Second, the general language of the incorporation clause itself may create uncertainty as to what terms are effectively incorporated. Third, the incorporated terms may not make immediate sense in the context of the bill of lading. On the last two classes of problems, the courts have expressed views that are ably organized in *Scrutton on Charterparties and Bills of Lading*.[95]

---

    other form of agreement that evinces the parties' mutual intent to do so: see *Oyler v. Merriam* (1922–24), 56 N.S.R. 64; and *The Dunelmia, ibid.*

91 *Leduc v. Ward*, above note 58.

92 Bills of lading that are well designed to operate on chartered ships contain very few of the standard clauses but instead incorporate all the terms of the relevant charterparty: see, e.g., BIMCO's "Congenbill," online at: <http://www.bimco.dk/BIMCO%20Documents/CONGENBILL%201994.pdf>.

93 Frequently the clause refers to "the charterparty dated _____" with the date left blank.

94 E.g., *San Nicholas (The)*, [1976] 1 Lloyd's L.R. 8 (C.A.).

95 S.C. Boyd, A.S. Burrows, & D. Foxton, *Scrutton on Charterparties and Bills of Lading*, 20th ed. (London: Sweet & Maxwell, 1996) at 77–80.

Given the principle of interpretation of contracts that a clause that is capable of bearing more than one meaning shall be construed *contra proferentem*, incorporation clauses have been strictly construed. A clause incorporating "freight and all other conditions as per charter" only covers the obligations of the consignee/receiver. In particular, it does not incorporate any disclaimers of liability of the shipowner: that would require a more general phrase such as "all conditions and exceptions." An even more general expression such as "all the terms, provisions, and exceptions" are "very wide words of incorporation, and are sufficient to bring into the bill of lading almost everything which is in the charterparty"[96] to the extent that they are sensible in the context of the bill of lading. Arbitration clauses in charterparties are something of an exception since they do not relate to the shipment, carriage, or delivery of goods or payment of freight; therefore they need to be specifically incorporated in the bill of lading, or the charterparty clause itself must evince an intention of governing disputes under the bill of lading.[97]

Notwithstanding these helpful guidelines about the effects of incorporation clauses, inconsistencies between the terms of the charterparty and of the bill of lading frequently occur. Then, it may be asked, does the holder of the bill of lading, not being the charterer, have the right to rely on its terms against the shipowner? If so, and supposing they are more onerous than the charterparty, does the shipowner have a right to indemnity from the charterer? The answers intimately involve issues about who contracted on whose behalf with whom and, hence, are concerned with the identity of the carrier.

11) Carrier Identity and Demise Clauses

The traditional process in issuing bills of lading involves the signature of the master of the carrying ship for and on behalf of the shipowner. In actual practice, the master rarely signs them in person; a signature is added by the ship's agent, a terminal operator, the charterer of the ship, or some such person acting for the master. When bills of lading are issued under the signature of a charterer for goods being carried on a chartered ship, the question may arise as to the identity of the carrier. Does the cargo owner contract for carriage with the shipowner, the charterer, or possibly both? The basic approach of the courts to this interpretive problem is to assume, in the absence of contrary evidence, that the charterer signed the bill of lading in the ordinary way on behalf

---

96 *Ibid.* at 79.
97 *Ibid.* at 79–80.

of the master and therefore the shipowner is the carrier. This approach was well established by 1951 when Rand J. wrote in the Supreme Court decision in *Paterson Steamships Ltd. v. ALCAN*:

> Under ... a [time] charter, and in the absence of an undertaking on the part of the charterer, the owner remains the carrier for the shipper, and in issuing bills of lading the captain acts as his agent. In this case, the bill of lading was signed for the captain by the agents appointed by the charterers certainly for themselves and probably for the vessel also ... .
>
> It is, I think, too late in the day to call in question the relation of the time charterer or his or the ship's agent towards cargo ... . The captain is bound to sign the bills of lading as presented, assuming them not to be in conflict with the terms of the charter party. The practical necessities involved in that situation were long ago appreciated by the courts and the authority of the charterer to sign for the captain confirmed.
>
> For the purpose of committing cargo to carriage, the captain, the charterer and the ships agents are all agents of the owner, acting in the name of the captain.[98]

This approach to identifying the carrier leaves open the possibility that it may be the charterer, if there is appropriate evidence of such intent. Such a determination depends upon "the construction of the bill of lading, together with so many of the terms of the ... charterparty as are incorporated in it, in the light of the surrounding circumstances; and the intention sought is not subjective but what the defendant [charterer] must be fairly understood to have intended."[99] Thus in *Namchow Chemical* the New South Wales Court of Appeal decided that bills of lading printed up by the charterer and bearing its name were, in all the circumstances, intended to be issued on its own account, notwithstanding they had been signed by an employee of the charterer over the printed words "For Master."[100] Again, in *Comorant Bulk Carriers Inc. v. Canficorp Ltd.*,[101] the Federal Court of Appeal decided that in circumstances that included a booking note and a bill of lading — which

---

98 [1951] S.C.R. 852 at 854 [*Paterson Steamships Ltd.*]. See also *Aris Steamship Co. v. Associated Metals & Minerals Corp., (The Evie W)* [1980] 2 S.C.R. 322; *Berkshire (The)*, [1974] 1 Lloyd's L.R. 185 (Q.B.); *Rewia (The)*, [1991] 2 Lloyd's L.R. 325 (C.A.).
99 *Namchow Chemical v. Botany Bay Shipping Co. (Aust.) Pty. Ltd.*, [1982] 2 N.S.W.L.R. 523 at 528 (C.A.).
100 *Ibid.*
101 (1984), 54 N.R. 66.

described the charterer as "Carrier" but nowhere named the shipowner — the charterer was contractually bound. The practical difficulty for the cargo claimant lies in identifying whom to sue correctly in advance since the risk of mistake is to be non-suited. The best course of action would be to join both the shipowner and charterer as defendants but that often cannot be done in one and the same jurisdiction.

Charterers do not like to be held responsible for the carriage of the goods because they generally have no control over how the cargo is treated once it is loaded. The chartered ship is still crewed, managed, and navigated by the owner. Hence, quite often the bill of lading or other transport document includes an identity of carrier clause or, its variant, a demise clause. The intent of these clauses is to establish with clarity that the shipowner is the carrier and that the charterer has no responsibilities for the safety of the goods, at least after loading. A typical demise clause might read as follows:

> If the ship is not owned by or chartered by demise to the company or line by whom the Bill of Lading is issued ... the Bill of Lading shall take effect as a contract with the Owner or demise charterer as the case may be as principal made through the agency of the said company or line who act as agents only and shall be under no personal liability whatsoever in respect thereof.[102]

An identity of carrier clause is usually more direct in stating that the carrier is the shipowner and the charterer is only the agent of the shipper.[103] Traditionally these types of clauses have been accepted and enforced by the courts and still are in England.[104] However, some Canadian decisions question their effect or deny their enforceability. The earlier cases, such as *Delano Corp. of America*,[105] seem to have been based on a misreading of the Supreme Court of Canada's opinion in *Paterson Steamships Ltd.*, quoted earlier,[106] to the effect that the charterer can never be the carrier but always signs the bills of lading as agent for the shipowner. But Rand J. qualified his remarks in two important

---

102 See, e.g., *Berkshire (The)*, above note 98.
103 See, e.g., *Iristo*, 1941 A.M.C. 1744 (S.D.N.Y.); *Ines (The)*, [1995] 2 Lloyd's L.R. 144 (Q.B.); and *Hector (The)*, [1998] 2 Lloyd's L.R. 287 (Q.B.).
104 *Delano Corp. of America v. Saguenay Terminals Ltd.*, [1965] 2 Ex. C.R. 313 [*Delano Corp. of America*]; *Grace Kennedy Co. v. Canada Jamaica Line*, [1967] 1 Lloyd's Rep. 336; *Berkshire (The)*, above note 98; *Jalamohan (The)*, [1988] 1 Lloyd's L.R. 443 (Q.B.); *Ines (The)*, ibid.; *Starsin (The)*, [2001] 1 Lloyd's L.R. 437 (C.A.). But see *Hector (The)*, ibid.
105 Ibid.
106 Above at note 98.

respects — by admitting that the charterer might have given an undertaking of carriage and by noting the charterer signed the transport documents for itself as well as for the ship. More recent cases show the courts have accepted that indeed the charterer may commit itself as carrier,[107] so that there is no reason to read a demise clause or an identity of carrier clause blindly as confirming the shipowner's status as exclusive carrier when the situation or the parties' intentions imply otherwise. *The Mica*[108] was one of the first Canadian cases in which the charterer was denied the protection of a demise clause[109] and held liable as a contracting carrier. In *Carling O'Keefe Breweries of Canada v. CN Marine*,[110] the court held the charterer liable as carrier despite a demise clause on account of the way it behaved, including its dealings with the shipper, the provision of its own bill of lading, its signature thereon in its own behalf, and its operations in loading and stowing the cargo. Yet more recent cases have upheld identity of carrier clauses even where the bills of lading were issued by the charterers on their own forms but there were no other circumstances implying they were carriers.[111]

An alternative approach to the problems surrounding the carrier's identity reflects the fact that sea carriage is a multifaceted task that may engage both the shipowner and the charterer. Most cases only involve argument as to whether a single defendant before the court is or is not the carrier. As a matter of principle, when the charterer and the shipowner both participate in the carriage, they may be held jointly responsible as carriers. This approach was foreshadowed in the *Paterson Steamships Ltd.* case, as noted previously,[112] when Rand J. observed that the bill of lading was signed by the charterers both for themselves and for the shipowner. Since the action was only against the shipowner, the Court had no occasion to decide whether the charterer might also have been responsible.

---

107 See *Venezuela (The)*, [1980] 1 Lloyd's L.R. 393 (Q.B.); *The Ines*, above note 103; *Starsin (The)*, above note 104; and *Hector (The)*, above note 103.
108 *Canadian Klockner Ltd. v. D/SA/S Flint*, [1973] 2 Lloyd's L.R. 478 (F.C.T.D.) [*The Mica*].
109 On the grounds that the clause relieved the charterer from liability for breach of a duty under the *Hague Rules*, above note 1, art.III(2) and was therefore null and void under art.III(8). As to the *Hague Rules*, see below at C(4), "How the Rules Apply."
110 (1987), 7 F.T.R. 178 (T.D.), varied (1989), 104 N.R. 166 (F.C.A.). See also *Comorant Bulk Carriers Inc. v. Canficorp Ltd.*, above note 101; and *Canastrand Industries Ltd. v. Lara S. (The)*, above note 87.
111 *Union Carbide Corp. v. Fednav Ltd. (The Hudson Bay)* (1997), 131 F.T.R. 241, 1998 A.M.C. 429 and *Jian Sheng Co. v. Great Tempo*, [1998] 3 F.C. 418 (C.A.).
112 Above note 98.

Subsequent cases occasionally have held shipowner and charterer jointly liable as carriers. In *Comorant Bulk Carriers Inc. v. Canficop Ltd.*,[113] the charterer was held liable on the particular facts; however, the shipowner's possible responsibility was also acknowledged. In *Canastrand Industries Ltd. v. The Lara S.*,[114] the charterer and shipowner were held jointly and severally liable because the carriage transaction amounted to a joint venture. Indeed, the charterer is frequently responsible for portside activities such as loading, stowing, and discharging, as well as for giving directions for the voyage, while the shipowner bears the duties of movement and care of the cargo at sea. In such circumstances, it remains for the courts to determine whether the charterer and the shipowner are truly jointly responsible as carriers for the whole carriage, or possibly severally liable for the separate parts of it that they each undertake.

The issuance of bills of lading on a chartered ship can also raise problems surrounding the authority of the master, or another person representing him or her, to sign them. The shipowner will be concerned that the terms of carriage evidenced by the bills of lading being issued to third-party shippers are consistent with the charterparty contract. For this reason the terms of the charterparty are often incorporated in bills of lading and, in addition, the charterparty itself frequently includes a clause to the effect that "the master is to sign bills of lading ... as presented without prejudice to this charterparty."[115] Yet it may happen that the shipowner is faced with two sets of conditions of carriage, one with the shipper or endorsee evidenced by the bill of lading on more onerous terms or at a lower freight rate than the other with the charterer. If this should occur, to what extent is the shipowner bound? The solution depends upon the scope of authority the shipowner has extended to the master, his or her employee and agent. Ordinarily the master has no implied authority to vary the charterparty in signing a bill of lading and so the shipowner may wish to refuse to recognize those terms in it that are different. This occurred in the early case of *Grant v. Norway*,[116] when the shipowner proved that the quantity of goods said to have been shipped according to the signed bill of lading was not in fact put on board and thereby established a good

---

113 Above note 101.
114 Above note 87.
115 Cf. GENCON Charter, cl.9, online at <http:www.bimco.dk/BIMCO%20Documents/Gencon%2094.pdf>.
116 (1851), 10 C.B. 665, 138 E.R. 263. And see *Brown & Root Ltd. v. Chimo Shipping Ltd.*, [1967] S.C.R. 642.

defence to a claim for their loss. But this "rule in *Grant v. Norway*" has been much criticized and confined because the shipper and, more particularly, subsequent holders of the bill of lading are bound to rely on the faith of its representations as to the goods described and the terms of their delivery. Indeed, the *Hague-Visby Rules* create an irrebuttable presumption as to the quantity or weight and apparent condition of the goods described in the bill of lading when it comes into the hands of an endorsee in good faith.[117]

When the shipowner is excused liability by reason of proof that the master negligently or fraudulently signed the bill of lading for goods that were not shipped, the master or other signatory may yet be held liable to the cargo owner. Where the *Bills of Lading Act* applies,[118] representations in the bill of lading about the goods shipped are deemed conclusive evidence against the actual signatory in favour of a consignee or endorsee in good faith and for value, without actual knowledge of the inaccuracy.[119] (In any case, the master owes a duty of care to the cargo owner while the goods are in his or her charge during his or her employ.[120]) But the master, or signatory, may escape personal liability if it can be shown that the error was not his or her fault.[121] When the shipowner is exposed to greater liability toward the cargo owner than expected because the master signed bills of lading "as presented by the charterer" that were not consistent with the charterparty, the shipowner will want recompense from the charterer. Perhaps the charterer is in breach of its duty in presenting the master with bills of lading whose terms differ from the charterparty. In any event, even though the master may sign them, the terms of the charterparty are not altered,[122] and consequently the charterer ought to indemnify the shipowner for the loss occasioned by the variations in the bills of lading.[123] To be sure of this right of indemnification, an express clause about it is commonly included by shipowners in their charterparties.

---

117 See the discussion of the *Hague-Visby Rules*, art.III(4), below at note 209.
118 Above note 55. Carriage under the sea waybills, for instance, is outside the application of the Act.
119 *Bills of Lading Act*, ibid., s.4.
120 *Cominco Ltd. v. Bilton* (1970), 15 D.L.R. (3d) 60 (S.C.C.).
121 *Bills of Lading Act*, above note 55, s.4.
122 Unless there is evidence to show that the shipowner and charterer mutually intended to amend their contract.
123 See *Krüger & Co. v. Moel Tryvan Shipping Co.*, [1907] A.C. 272.

B. INTERNATIONAL RULES GOVERNING BILLS OF LADING

In the nineteenth century the carriage of goods by sea was regulated only by the common law. This law made common carriers of cargo virtually insurers of the goods in their charge. They could avoid liability for loss or damage to the goods only if they proved the loss was due to an "act of God" or the "Queen's enemies."[124] However the principle of freedom of contract, supported by *laissez faire* economic attitudes of the time, permitted shipowners to write conditions into their bills of lading and standard trading terms that relieved themselves of the severity of the common law. Indeed, in time they exercised their contractual power over shippers to exempt them very generously from cargo liability. As a result a number of states, led by the enactment in the United States of the *Harter Act* in 1893,[125] began to pass legislation to regulate the carriage of goods by sea. So began a struggle, which continues into the twenty-first century, to establish a fair and acceptable allocation of risks and responsibilities between carriers and cargo owners of goods transported under bills of lading. It soon became clear that a proliferation of national legislation imposing differing rules on merchant ships, which, by the nature of their business, call in many different countries, would cause legal confusion and inhibit trade. A movement therefore arose to establish an internationally uniform set of rules, initiated in the International Maritime Committee of the International Law Association — which subsequently was established independently as the Comité Maritime International (CMI) — and was taken up by leading maritime states in the early part of the twentieth century. It resulted in the conclusion at Brussels, Belgium, on 25 August 1924 of the *International Convention for the Unification of Certain Rules of Law Relating to Bills of Lading*,[126] better known as the *Hague Rules* after the place where they were first provisionally adopted. Although never a party to this convention, Canada implemented its rules as national law by enactment in the *Carriage of Goods by Water Act, 1936*.[127]

---

124 *Paterson Steamships Ltd. v. Canadian Co-operative Wheat Producers Ltd.*, [1934] A.C. 538 (P.C.).
125 46 U.S.C. §§190–96 (1893). The *Harter Act* was followed by New Zealand: *Shipping and Seamen Act, 1903*; Australia: *Sea-Carriage of Goods Act, 1904*; and Canada: *Water-Carriage of Goods Act, 1910*, S.C. 1910, c.61.
126 25 August 1924, 120 L.N.T.S. 155.
127 R.S.C. 1985, c.C-27.

The *Hague Rules* became widely adopted nationally around the world and thus largely fulfilled the need for a uniform international regime governing carriage by sea. However, in the course of the twentieth century great changes occurred in vessel design, cargo-handling techniques, and communication technology as well as in trade development and economic trends. As a result the *Hague Rules* came to be regarded by some, especially cargo owners, as outmoded and increasingly unfair. Pressure to review and revise the *Hague Rules* became irresistible but the ability to establish a new set of internationally uniform rules that is acceptable worldwide has so far proved illusory. As a result, the *Visby Protocol*[128] to the *Hague Rules*, done in 1968, together with the *SDR Protocol* of 1979,[129] compete unequally with the *Hamburg Rules* found in the *United Nations Convention on the Carriage of Goods by Sea of 1978*.[130] About two dozen states, few of whom are significant maritime trading nations, apply the *Hamburg Rules*. The rest of the world operates under the *Hague Rules* or the *Hague-Visby Rules* or some variant of them. Canada legislated both the *Hague-Visby Rules* and the *Hamburg Rules* onto the statute book with the enactment of the *Carriage of Goods by Water Act* in 1993,[131] which has now been replaced by the *Marine Liability Act*, Part 5.[132] For the time being the *Hague-Visby Rules*, including the *SDR Protocol*, have the force of law in Canada. They may be replaced by the *Hamburg Rules* at any time by order in council[133] pursuant to a recommendation of the Minister of Transport, who, in any event, must report to Parliament on the question before 2005 and every five years thereafter.[134]

Other developments have also contributed to the disruption of the once relatively uniform international regime for the sea carriage of goods. The advent of containerized traffic precipitated the shift to multimodal means of transporting goods. This commercial development led to a legal initiative to conclude the *United Nations Convention on International Multimodal Transport of Goods* in 1980.[135] Since the marine

---

128 *Protocol to Amend the International Convention for the Unification of Certain Rules of Law Relating to Bills of Lading, 1924*, above note 3.
129 *Protocol Amending the International Convention for the Unification of Certain Rules of Law Relating to Bills of Lading, 1924*, 21 December 1979, 1412 U.N.T.S. 121, U.K.T.S. 1984 No. 28.
130 31 March, 1978, 17 I.L.M. 608 [*Hamburg Rules*].
131 S.C. 1993, c.21, which repealed the old Act of 1936.
132 Above note 2, s.130.
133 *Ibid.* ss.43(4) and 131(2).
134 *Ibid.* s.44.
135 U.N. Doc. TD/MT/CONF/17 (1980). The delivery of goods by sea may also become affected by the *Convention on the Liability of Operators of Transport Terminals in International Trade, 1991*, 19 April 1991, 30 I.L.M. 1503 (not in force).

mode is such a significant part of the multimodal movement of goods, this convention will potentially have a great impact on the carriage of goods by sea. However, the transport rules it establishes, modelled after the *Hamburg Rules* for sea carriage, will not come into force as long as the convention languishes, awaiting ratification by a sufficient number of states to bring it into operation. Yet the convention provided the impetus for the United Nations Conference on Trade and Development (UNCTAD), by which it was originally sponsored, and the International Chamber of Commerce (ICC) to develop from its contents the *UNCTAD/ICC Rules for Multimodal Transport Documents, 1992*.[136] These rules are not mandatory, but are available for voluntary incorporation in transport documents, and have attained widespread recognition by being adopted in the standard form documents of FIATA,[137] the international association of international freight forwarders, and BIMCO,[138] a leading commercial shipping organization. At the same time, an increasing number of countries from Scandinavia to China have been revising their sea carriage laws and adopting national variants of the *Hague-Visby Rules* and the *Hamburg Rules*. The United States, having enforced the unamended *Hague Rules* since 1936[139] for lack of national agreement on how to amend the law, has finally produced a draft for a reformed act.[140] This bill, were it to be enacted as a new *Carriage of Goods by Sea Act*, would add another national variant to the Hague-Visby and Hamburg mix of rules, including a much more extensive jurisdictional reach for U.S. courts and partially multimodal operation in some situations.

As a result of all these developments, the uniformity of sea carriage laws sought at the beginning of the twentieth century through agreement on the *Hague Rules*, for the benefit of enhanced facilitation and efficiency of world trade, was rapidly dissolving at the end of the century. Alarmed by this prospect, as well as the loud objections internationally to some aspects of the U.S. proposals to reform its national law, the United Nations Commission on International Trade Law (UNCITRAL), which had sponsored the *Hamburg Rules*, began once more a search for an internationally acceptable, single uniform set of transport rules for the twenty-first century. With vigorous input into the interna-

---

136 ICC Publication No. 481.
137 The International Federation of Freight Forwarders Associations. The acronym is formed from the French title of the organization.
138 The Baltic and International Maritime Council.
139 *Carriage of Goods by Sea Act*, 46 App. U.S.C.A. §§1300–15 (1936).
140 The work was carried forward by the U.S. Maritime Law Association as COGSA '99 and was introduced to Congress via the Senate but has not progressed.

tional discussions by the CMI, UNCITRAL had developed, by the end of 2002, a *Draft Instrument on Transport Law*,[141] which would establish a new liability regime for the carriage of goods.

From the Canadian viewpoint, the law applicable to the sea carriage of goods is found in the *Hague-Visby Rules* as enacted in the *Marine Liability Act*[142] and, beyond them, in the common law.[143] While the *Hamburg Rules* appear on the statute book, scant attention will be paid to them in this text as they are not in force in Canada and are unlikely to be brought into operation, if ever, while the international community continues to debate UNCITRAL's draft instrument for a new transport regime. The rest of this chapter therefore addresses the Canadian application of the *Hague-Visby Rules*, first as to the technical issues surrounding their scope of operation, then successively as to the obligations of carriers and of cargo owners, and finally as to the processing of claims and actions for breach.

C. APPLICATION OF THE *HAGUE-VISBY RULES*

The *Hague-Visby Rules*, in force in Canada by virtue of the *Marine Liability Act*,[144] establish a regime for the distribution of risks and responsibilities in the carriage of goods by sea between carriers and cargo owners, as well as their servants and agents. These rules do not apply to every aspect of sea carriage,[145] so it is important at the outset to take precise note of their scope. There are four pertinent aspects to the operation of the rules, which are captured by the questions to whom, when, to what, and how do they apply?[146]

1) To Whom the Rules Apply

The *Hague-Visby Rules* apply to all participants in the movement of goods by sea, including carriers, cargo owners, their employees such as the master and crew, and their independent contractors, for example,

---

141 See UNCITRAL's web site at <http://www.uncitral.org/english/commiss/geninfo.htm> for the *Draft Instrument* and subsequent work on it.
142 Above note 2, s.130 and Sch.3.
143 As to the sources of Canadian maritime law, including maritime common law, see Chapter 3, "Admiralty Jurisdiction."
144 Above note 2, s.130 and Sch.3 (see Appendix 1 in this book).
145 Maritime common law fills out the sea carriage regime.
146 *Hague-Visby Rules*, above note 3, art.I(a) (see Appendix 1 in this book).

stevedores and longshore workers. "Carriers" are not so much defined by the *Hague-Visby Rules* as stated to "include the owner or the charterer who enters into a contract of carriage." Thus the rules leave the identity of the carrier in each case to the common law rules of construction of contracts.[147] Moreover, the inclusion of shipowner or charterer does not exclude other possible contracting carriers, such as freight forwarders or MTOs, nor actual carriers, when the responsibility of moving the cargo is divided. The rules do not draw these distinctions sharply so it depends on the instant situation how they should be interpreted. For instance, presumably both contracting and actual carriers have duties of care for the cargo under article III(2), but only the contracting carrier has the responsibility of issuing a bill of lading to the shipper under article III(3). "Cargo owners" are undefined in the *Hague-Visby Rules*, which only refer to the rights and obligations of the shipper. Nevertheless, the rules anticipate that the bill of lading may be "transferred to a third party,"[148] that is, to a consignee or other endorsee; so, it is reasonable to refer to the "cargo owner" as the party who has rights under the rules against the carrier at a particular moment of carriage.

Employees and contractors are treated differently at common law. An employer is vicariously responsible for the acts of employees but not for the actions of independent contractors.[149] At the same time, employees remain personally liable in tort for the wrongs they commit in the course of their employment.[150] The *Hague-Visby Rules* recognize these principles of liability with extensions; article IV bis states:

> 2. If ... an action is brought against a servant or agent of the carrier (such servant or agent not being an independent contractor), such servant or agent shall be entitled to avail himself of the defences and limits of liability which the carrier is entitled to invoke under these Rules.

Nevertheless the protection from liability granted by this provision does not avail an employee if it is proved that the wrongful act or omission was "done with intent to cause damage or recklessly and with knowledge that damage would probably result."[151]

---

147 See above in A(11), "Carrier Identity and Demise Clauses."
148 *Hague-Visby Rules*, above note 3, art.III(4). See above in A(9), "Transfer of Rights in a Bill of Lading."
149 *St. John (City of) v. Donald*, [1926] S.C.R. 371 at 383; *671122 Ontario Ltd. v. Sagaz Industries Canada Inc.*, [2001] 2 S.C.R. 983.
150 See *Cominco Ltd. v. Bilton*, above note 120.
151 *Hague-Visby Rules*, above note 3, art.IV, bis(4).

438   MARITIME LAW

Masters and crew members and other individual employees of the carrier are not often sued,[152] probably on account of their limited personal resources, but stevedores, terminal operators, and other suppliers of shore-based cargo handling services to shipowners frequently are. As independent contractors, they do not create liability by their acts for the carrier, but neither can they benefit from the statutory extension by the rules of the carrier's defences and limitations of liability.[153] As a result it has become customary for stevedores to demand in their contract of services with the carrier protection from liability in handling the goods, and for the carrier to include in the bill of lading with the shipper a so-called "Himalaya Clause."[154] Its provisions purport to limit, or even exclude, the stevedores' responsibility for the goods put in their charge, whether their duties arise under the *Hague-Visby Rules* or at common law. Since this exculpatory clause appears in the contract[155] made between shipper and carrier, it troubled the courts for a considerable time how its protections could be relied on by stevedores who have no direct privity of contract with the cargo owner; however, by cutting through the technical analysis of contract law to the commercial realities of the transaction, the courts have now recognized the efficacy and enforceability of the Himalaya clause.[156]

---

152 But see *Cominco Ltd. v. Bilton*, above note 120; and *Adler v. Dickson*, [1954] 2 Lloyd's Rep. 267 (Q.B.).
153 There remains a kernal of doubt about this distinction in the *Hague-Visby Rules*, as civilian jurisdictions do not recognize the category of independent contractor and would, it seems, treat all who act for the carrier as either a servant or an agent.
154 After the name of the ship in *Adler v. Dickson, ibid*. As an alternative to a Himalaya clause, carriers may include a circular indemnity clause by which the cargo claimant is required to indemnify the carrier for compensating the stevedores to the extent they had to satisfy the claim of the cargo owner! Such a clause has also been upheld: *Nippon Yusen Kaisha v. International Import and Export Ltd. (The Elbe Maru)*, [1978] 1 Lloyd's L.R. 206; and *Broken Hill Pty. Co. v. Hapag-Lloyd Aktiengesellschaft*, [1980] 2 N.S.W.L.R. 572.
155 Evidenced by the bill of lading.
156 Cf. *Midland Silicones Ltd. v. Scruttons Ltd.*, [1962] A.C. 446 (H.L.); *Canadian General Electric v. Pickford & Black Ltd., (The Lake Bosomtwe)*, [1971] S.C.R. 41; *New Zealand Shipping Co. v. A.M. Satterthwaite & Co. (The Eurymedon)*, [1974] 1 Lloyd's L.R. 544 (H.L.); *Port Jackson Stevedoring Pty. Ltd.v. Salmon and Spraggon (Australia) Pty. Ltd. (The New York Star)*, [1980] 2 Lloyd's L.R. 317 (P.C.), esp. Lord Wilberforce's remarks at 371; *ITO International Terminal Operators Ltd. v. Miida Electronics Inc. (The Buenos Aires Maru)*, [1986] 1 S.C.R. 752. Even so, a Himalaya clause in the bill of lading may not benefit stevedores who do not have a contract with the carrier that binds the carrier to demand such a clause of the shippers: *Saint John Shipbuilding*, above note 9. And see W. Tetley, *Marine Cargo Claims*, 3d ed. (Cowansville, QB: Yvon Blais, 1988) at 757–66.

In establishing the enforceability of the Himalaya clause, the courts have been less careful about their scope. In their most general form, these clauses appear to exclude the stevedores or terminal operators from all liability. One may wonder why a disclaimer clause imposed on the shipper by the carrier's bill of lading should be interpreted to afford any greater excuse from liability than the minimum responsibility of the carrier. Some courts have noted that the Himalaya clause cannot afford protection to stevedores when their activities are outside the scope of the carriage contract.[157] Surely the efficacy of the carriage transaction that has allowed the stevedores to rely, as third-party beneficiaries, on the Himalaya clause should also curtail its effects to correspond with the liability imposed by law on the carrier and his or her employees, at least during the period of application of the *Hague-Visby Rules*.[158]

2) When the Rules Apply

The scope of application of the *Hague-Visby Rules* is not necessarily coextensive with the contract of carriage. The carrier may undertake greater responsibilities than the rules require but cannot contract for less.[159] When the carriage exceeds the demands of the rules, it will be regulated by maritime common law. Consequently it is important to know when the application of the rules begins and ends. In fact their operation depends upon a range of geographic, contractual, and temporal circumstances.

a) Geographic Scope

As Canada is not a party to the Brussels Convention, the *Hague-Visby Rules* operate in Canadian law only to the extent they are given effect by legislation, namely, the *Marine Liability Act*.[160] Section 43 of the Act makes the rules operate on contracts of carriage for the international

---

157 *Port Jackson Stevedoring Pty. Ltd. v. Salmon and Spraggon (Australia) Pty. Ltd. (The New York Star)*, [1979] 1 Lloyd's L.R. 298 (H.C.A.), aff'd [1980] 2 Lloyd's L.R. 317; *Burke Motors Ltd. v. Mersey Docks and Harbours Co.*, [1986] 1 Lloyd's L.R. 155 at 162.
158 Cf. *Starsin (The)*, above note 104.
159 Because the *Hague-Visby Rules*, above note 3, art.111(8) prohibit disclaimers or waivers of liability: see below C(4), "How the Rules Apply."
160 Above note 2, s.130.

delivery of goods, according to article X of the rules, and also in the Canadian coasting trade, unless the parties agree otherwise. Article X seeks to give wide application to the rules through the use of three independent criteria. The rules apply to a carriage between two different states whenever

- a bill of lading is issued in a contracting state,
- the carriage is from a port in a contracting state, or
- the contract evidenced by the bill of lading incorporates the rules.

The Canadian legislation extends these criteria still further by defining a "contracting state" as any state that gives the rules the force of law nationally even though, like Canada, it is not a party to the Brussels Convention. The first two of these criteria give statutory force to the *Hague-Visby Rules* on carriage both to and from Canada,[161] provided the claim is brought in Canada.[162] The third criterion, in effect, gives the force of law to the rules even when they are only contractually incorporated by the parties. Ordinarily, in such instances the rules would have no greater impact than other terms of the carriage contract and so it might be possible for the carrier to disclaim the responsibilities they set down.[163] But the attachment of the mandatory power of the Act even to contractual invocations of the rules means their minimum statutory standards cannot be overridden.[164]

b) Contractual Formalities

Even when the operation of the *Hague-Visby Rules* is mandated, they do not apply to every carriage transaction. This is the result of defining a "contract of carriage" under the rules in a limited way by reference to transport documents. The rules apply only to "contracts of carriage covered by a bill of lading or any similar document of title."[165] The range of "similar documents of title" is not clear but may well include a combined transport document as far as it applies to the sea leg of the movement, and to a delivery order when issued or attorned to by the carrier.[166] Transport documents that are not documents of title, such as

---

161 Unlike the unreformed *Hague Rules*, which only apply to outward carriage.
162 If the claim is brought abroad, the law of that forum or the choice of law of the parties may be applied.
163 See *Atlantic Consolidated Foods Ltd. v. Doroty (The)*, [1979] 1 F.C. 283, aff'd [1981] 1 F.C. 783 (C.A.).
164 *Morviken (The)*, [1983] 1 Lloyd's L.R. 1 (H.L.).
165 *Hague-Visby Rules*, above note 3, art.I(b).
166 See *The Dona Mari*, above note 32.

sea waybills,[167] are outside the operation of the rules.[168] Even so, it is common for carriers to incorporate the rules in their sea waybills because of the advantageous limitations of liability they grant. Such incorporation certainly gives contractual effect to the rules.

The courts have accepted that a contract of carriage is "covered" by a bill of lading even if one is not actually issued, provided that it was the parties' intention to use one. In the leading Canadian case, a bill of lading was prepared but never issued.[169] Another case also applied the rules to a claim for loss on loading, before the shipped bill of lading could be issued by the carrier.[170]

When a bill of lading is issued on a chartered ship, the application of the rules will depend upon who is holder of the bill. Article V of the rules expressly states that they are not applicable to charterparties.[171] Since the charterparty is the contract of carriage between the shipowner and the charterer, it follows that any bill of lading issued to the charterer will not be regulated by the rules either.[172] However, once the bill of lading comes into the hands of a different holder, such as an endorsee from the charterer, and thus assumes independent contractual effect between the holder and the carrier, the rules will attach to it.[173]

c) **Temporal Scope**

Statutory application of the *Hague-Visby Rules* is further constrained by a limited definition of "carriage of goods" as "the period from the time when the goods are loaded on to the time they are discharged from the ship."[174] Thus the period of responsibility under the rules may be shorter than the time the carrier actually has charge of the goods under the

---

167 See the discussion above in A(6), "Sea Waybills and Other Sea Transport Documents."
168 For a contrary argument, see W. Tetley, *Marine Cargo Claims*, above note 156 at 944.
169 *Anticosti Shipping Co. v. St-Amand*, above note 11, following *Pyrene Co. v. Scindia Navigation Co.*, [1954] 2 Q.B. 402.
170 *A.R. Kitson Trucking Ltd. v. Rivtow Straits Ltd.* (1975), 55 D.L.R. (3d) 462 (B.C.S.C.). See also *Falconbridge Nickel Mines Ltd. v. Chimo Shipping Ltd.*, [1974] S.C.R. 933.
171 The rules may, however, apply if the charterparty itself contractually incorporates them, but the practice presents interpretational difficulties: see *Adamastos Shipping Co. v. Anglo-Saxon Petroleum Co.*, [1959] A.C. 133.
172 The bill of lading in the hands of the charterer is a receipt for the goods and a document of title.
173 *Hague-Visby Rules*, above note 3, art.I(b).
174 *Hague-Visby Rules*, ibid., art.I(e).

carriage contract. Even when the rules operate at loading before the bill of lading is issued,[175] they do not extend to receipt of the goods before loading.[176] Thus in a contract for port-to-port carriage, evidenced, for instance, by a received for shipment bill of lading, the rules will only apply during the period the goods are loaded. The courts have defined this time as beginning when the ship's tackle or other loading equipment first hooks on to the cargo for the purpose of loading it aboard, and ending when the lifting gear is disconnected after discharge,[177] all of which is commonly described as the period from tackle to tackle. Any other interpretation would defeat the carrier's substantive obligations toward the cargo under the rules.[178] However, the cargo owner, especially if it is a charterer, may participate in the acts of loading or unloading. In such circumstances the same English authorities concluded that the parties may, by their contract, allocate the responsibilities at loading and discharge but cannot alter the standard of performance of those responsibilities as set by the rules.

Before loading and after discharge, the carrier and cargo owner are, by article VII of the rules, free to contract as they see fit. While the *Canada Shipping Act*[179] imposes on carriers a duty of care and diligence in the custody and conveyance of goods from the moment they are received, this obligation is expressly subject to Part 5 of the *Marine Liability Act*, which imposes the *Hague-Visby Rules*. Therefore, the freedom of contract granted by article VII seems to override the *Canada Shipping Act* when the particular carriage is covered by a bill of lading subject to the rules.

At common law the carrier's responsibility as bailee to care for the cargo continues until delivery. This event likely occurs later than discharge, since the cargo owner does not usually receive the goods over the ship's rail. Yet carriers' bill of lading terms frequently call on the cargo owner to take delivery on discharge and disclaim all responsibility for the goods from that moment. The courts have held no objection

---

175 See above note 169.
176 Unless expressly made to do so by the contract.
177 See *Pyrene Co. v. Scindia Navigation Co.*, above note 169; and *Falconbridge Nickel Mines Ltd. v. Chimo Shipping Ltd.*, above note 170.
178 Expressed in *Hague-Visby Rules*, above note 3, art.III(2) and discussed below in D(3), "Care of the Cargo."
179 *Canada Shipping Act*, R.S.C. 1985, c.S-9, s.586; *Canada Shipping Act, 2001*, S.C. 2001, c.26, s.250. See also *Canada Shipping Act, ibid.*, ss.585, 596–604. Regarding the common law position, see *East West Corp. v. DKBS 1912*, above note 24 at 257.

to enforcing such terms, beyond the period of application of the *Hague-Visby Rules*, where, on a true construction, they define the contractual extent of the carriage.[180]

Sometimes cargoes are transshipped between two carriers, perhaps with a storage period ashore, in the course of conveyance to their destination port. When this occurs out of necessity, such as when the contracting carrier's ship breaks down or suffers an accident, the owner is still responsible for the delivery of the goods.[181] When, as in the container trades, it is anticipated that the goods may be transferred from a main line ship at a hub port onto a feeder vessel for local delivery, the scope of the contracting carrier's liability under the *Hague-Visby Rules* will depend upon how the contract of carriage is arranged.

If the bill of lading is worded so as to provide through carriage to destination, the contracting carrier must be taken to be responsible under the rules even for that part of the movement that is subcontracted.[182] Where a liberty clause is included in the bill of lading, it makes a difference whether its wording simply permits transshipment without disturbing the contracting carrier's responsibilities for through carriage, or whether it should be construed, with other clauses, as terminating the contract of carriage with the initial carrier at the point of intermediate discharge and so ending responsibility under the rules.[183] The difficulty in making this determination is clouded by a Canadian case in which there was clear agreement that the goods would be transshipped between two vessels belonging to the contracting carrier but the cargo was damaged in the port of transshipment. The court held that the loss occurred outside the scope of application of the rules, yet found the carrier liable for breach of the carriage contract.[184]

---

180 Cp. *Prins Willem III (The)*, [1972] 2 D.L.R. 124, [1973] 2 Lloyd's L.R. 124 (Que. C.A.); with *R. v. Montreal Shipping Co.*, [1956] Ex. C.R. 280.

181 The carrier is bound to commit reasonable efforts and expense to overcome the obstacle to the voyage and, if it be removed, he or she has a right to transship the goods in order to earn the freight: see *Ferruzzi France SA v. Oceania Maritime Inc. (The Palmea)*, [1988] 2 Lloyd's L.R. 261; and *Hill v. Wilson* (1879), 4 C.P.D. 329 at 333.

182 Indeed without a clause granting liberty to transship the carrier probably should not.

183 See *Marcellino Gonzalez v. James Nourse Ltd.*, [1936] 1 K.B. 565; *Mayhew Foods Ltd. v. Overseas Containers Ltd.*, [1984] 1 Lloyd's L.R. 317; and *Anders Maersk (The)*, [1986] 1 Lloyd's L.R. 483 (H.K. H.C. Adm.).

184 *Captain v. Far Eastern Steamship Co.*, above note 11.

3) To What the Rules Apply

The *Hague-Visby Rules* apply to goods "of every kind whatsoever, except live animals and cargo which by the contract of carriage is stated as being carried on deck and is so carried."[185] The decision to exclude live animals and deck cargo reflects their greater risks of damage at sea than under deck cargo. The allocation of risks established by the rules did not seem appropriate to these special cargoes. The result, however, is to expose live animals and deck cargo to the rules of common law, that is, unlimited liability on the carrier unless the responsibility is contractually disclaimed.[186] The frequent disclaimer of liability for live animals is of less concern because such cargo obviously presents special difficulties and risks, and generally requires onboard care by animal keepers who are likely to be the employees of the shipper, rather than the carrier. The exclusion of deck cargo is less appropriate, especially in modern container ships where containers are stowed above or below deck according to the order and convenience of stowing them, without regard to their contents. The risks faced by above-deck containers is somewhat greater than below-deck ones, but nothing like as severe as the perils encountered in former times by sailing ships carrying cargo such as lumber exposed on deck because it was too long for the holds.

Exclusion from the operation of the rules depends upon two criteria: carriage on deck and contractual statement of this fact. The cargo owner is entitled to assume the goods are being carried under deck, and therefore protected, and the rules apply to them unless informed and agreed otherwise.[187] Indeed older cases have held that the carriage of cargo on deck without the shipper's consent is so grave a breach as to be tantamount to deviation. The result is to displace the principle of limited liability under the rules and to expose the carrier to unlimited liability, regardless of any contractual disclaimer clauses.[188] Yet a general "liberty" clause in the bill of lading, which states cargo may be car-

---

185 *Hague-Visby Rules*, above note 3, art.I(c). The definition appears to include every imaginable product and by-product, such as wood chips: *Tahsis Co. v. Vancouver Tug Boat Co.* (1965), 54 W.W.R. 395 (B.C.S.C.).

186 As in *H.B. Contracting Ltd. v. Northland Shipping (1962) Co.* (1971), 24 D.L.R. (3d) 209 (B.C.C.A.).

187 A clean bill of lading implies this situation because it bears no clause on its face stating the goods are stowed on deck.

188 *Svenska Traktor v. Maritime Agencies Ltd.*, [1953] 2 Q.B. 295 [*Svenska Traktor*]; *St. Simeon Navigation Inc. v. A. Couturier & Fils Ltdee.*, [1974] S.C.R. 1176 [*St. Simeon Navigation*]. And see B(3) in Chapter 8, "Deviation on the Voyage."

ried on deck, is insufficient: the rules require a definite statement that they are being so carried.[189]

These rulings present problems for container ships, since carriers cannot foretell which containers will be stowed above deck, nor wish to make any such distinction. However, they may urge a custom of the trade in their favour. An argument can be made that a liberty clause is sufficient where ondeck carriage is the usual or customary carrying place for the cargo, such as containers.[190] More frequently the bills of lading include a clause that extends the rules to containers stowed on the deck, thus establishing a uniform regime for all containers on board. This simple solution meets the cargo owner's expectations and provides the carrier with the assurance of limited liability.[191]

One further curious exclusion of the rules is found in article VI. This provision exempts the carriage of "particular goods" provided they are not carried under a bill of lading but are, instead, shipped against a non-negotiable receipt that is so marked and expresses the terms of agreement of carriage. When these simple conditions are met, article VI permits the carrier and cargo owner to set almost any conditions of carriage they like and to circumvent the minimum standards of responsibility of the rules. The destruction of the impact of the rules, however, has not occurred. While "particular goods" are not defined, the article indicates that its provisions do not apply to "ordinary commercial shipments made in the ordinary course of trade" but only to other cargoes, which, by their character, require special terms. The exclusion of ordinary trade transactions severely limits the resort to article VI, which, accordingly, appears to have been included in order to allow for experimentation with unusual cargoes and the development of new cargo-handling techniques. In any event, resort to article VI does not seem to occur in practice nor to have been the subject of comment by the courts.

4) How the Rules Apply

The responsibilities established by the *Hague-Visby Rules* are mandatory. The rules are intended to be an internationally uniform set of min-

---

189 *Svenska Traktor*, ibid.; *Grace Plastics Ltd. v. Bernd Wesch II (The)*, above note 9; *St. Simeon Navigation*, ibid. See also *Sheerwood v. Lake Eyre (The)*, [1970] Ex. C.R. 672; *Colonial Yacht Harbour Ltd. v. Octavia (The)*, [1980] 1 F.C. 331.
190 See *Guadano v. Hamburg Chicago Line*, [1973] F.C. 726.
191 Which is insurable, unlike the fundamental breaches of contract found in the cases above in note 188.

imum standards of responsibility for the carriage of goods. Their mandatory character is imposed by article III(8), which provides that any contractual clause that would have the effect of lessening the liability of the carrier is null and void.[192] That they are minimum standards is confirmed by article V, which permits carriers to contractually surrender their rights under the rules or to increase their responsibilities, provided the alterations are expressed in the bill of lading. These provisions do not prohibit the use of disclaimer clauses; indeed they are permissible and enforceable for matters beyond the reach of the rules.[193] However, general liberty clauses will be read down so as not to contravene the rules,[194] and specific clauses that appear legitimate on their face will not be allowed to operate if their substantive effect would be to lessen the carrier's liability.[195]

While much of the international uniformity of the regime that the rules were intended to provide has now been lost,[196] their operation still has to mesh with other carriage laws, both nationally and internationally. The courts have taken note of the international origins of the rules[197] and are ready to avert to foreign precedents where the law is similar.[198] The rules themselves also state in article VIII[199] that they do not affect the operation of the shipowner's additional right by statute, pursuant to international convention, to limit liability according to the tonnage of the ship.[200]

D. RESPONSIBILITIES OF CARRIERS

The *Hague-Visby Rules* allocate responsibility between the carrier and the cargo owner for the safe carriage of the goods. They regulate near-

---

192 E.g., *Bruck Mills Ltd. v. Black Sea Steamship Co.*, [1973] F.C. 387.
193 Such as before loading or after discharge.
194 *Nabob Foods Ltd. v. Cape Corso (The)*, [1954] 2 Lloyd's L.R. 40 (Ex. Ct.).
195 See above note 192.
196 See above B, "International Rules Governing Bills of Lading."
197 *Stag Line Ltd. v. Foscolo, Mango & Co.*, [1932] A.C. 328 (H.L.); *Maxine Footwear Co. v. Canadian Government Merchant Marine Ltd.*, [1959] A.C. 589 (P.C.); *Dominion Glass Co. v. Anglo Indian (The)*, [1944] S.C.R. 409 at 420.
198 *Falconbridge Nickel Mines Ltd. v. Chimo Shipping Ltd.*, above note 170.
199 See also *Hague-Visby Rules*, above note 3. art.IX.
200 The right is granted by the *Convention on Limitation of Liability for Maritime Claims, 1976*, 19 November 1976, 1456 U.N.T.S. 221, as amended and applied in Canada by virtue of the *Marine Liability Act*, above note 2, Part 3, especially ss.26 and 42; see Chapter 18, "Limitation of Liability for Maritime Claims."

ly every aspect of ocean transport. Consequently, they overlap all of the fundamental obligations implied by maritime common law in the carriage contract, as discussed in Chapter 8.[201] Since the *Hague-Visby Rules* have the force of statute, where they differ from common law principles, their application has overriding effect. But the common law and the rules are not coextensive. Further, the rules were originally drafted in light of experience of the operation of the common law. So the obligations of the carriage parties under the *Hague-Visby Rules* have to be understood in the context of the maritime common law in which they are embedded.[202] Accordingly the rules are discussed here with reference to the common law principles explained previously. This and the next section of this chapter divide consideration of the obligations imposed by the rules first by considering their effects on carriers and then on cargo owners.

1) Bills of Lading

As discussed previously,[203] the bill of lading issued by the carrier plays a crucial multifunctional role at common law in the transport of goods by sea. In addition, the *Hague-Visby Rules*, although they do not define a bill of lading, impose a number of further requirements on its contents and operation. After the shipper delivers the goods to the carrier for carriage, he or she is entitled to demand a bill of lading. This will only be a received for shipment bill if the goods are not then loaded but, once they are, the shipper may ask for a shipped bill or the carrier may note the facts of shipment on the existing received bill, if one was issued.[204]

The contents of the bill of lading must also include a number of details that will make it a serviceable receipt. A received bill must show the identifying marks on the cargo as well as the number of packages or the quantity or the weight of the goods. It must also express the apparent order and condition of the goods. The carrier must fill in these details as supplied in writing by the shipper unless he or she has reason to believe they are inaccurate, or he or she has no means of

---

201 In B in Chapter 8, "Maritime Common Law Principles of Carriage."
202 Not forgetting the international rules were prepared also in light of maritime legal practice in civil law jurisdictions and were intended to provide a single uniform international regime.
203 See above A(2), "Bills of Lading."
204 *Hague-Visby Rules*, above note 3, arts. III(3) and (7).

checking them.[205] A shipped bill has to contain all the details of a received bill plus the name of the carrying ship and the date of shipment.[206] In practice several other details are also added, including the names of the carrier, the shipper, and the consignee or notify party, the ports of loading and discharge, and any other particulars of importance to the execution of that transaction. Once issued under the signature of the master, the bill of lading is *prima facie* evidence in the hands of the shipper of receipt by the carrier of the goods as described.[207] When the bill is transferred to another party, such as a consignee or an endorsee[208] who takes it in good faith, its contents become irrebuttable.[209] The rules prohibit proof to the contrary out of protection for the transferee of the bill of lading, who is bound to rely on its statements about the goods, given their absence at sea and unavailability for inspection.

There appears to be no penalty for supplying a bill of lading that does not comply with the rules, or indeed for failure to issue one at all. It is the shipper's right and responsibility to demand a bill of lading and check that it is in compliance, otherwise the document as issued will govern their relations.[210] The shipper's principal concern is to be issued with a clean bill that will satisfy a bank or endorsee. The carrier's interest is contrary: it is to clause a bill, or to refuse to accept the shipper's description of the load and count, where there is doubt about it so as to avoid being held responsible for delivering goods that vary from those represented. Such contention provides opportunity for collusion between the carrier and the shipper. On occasion a carrier will issue a clean bill of lading on provision by the shipper of a letter of indemnity for any liability the carrier may incur. Where there is genuine dispute between the carrier and the shipper about the description of the

---

205 *Hague-Visby Rules*, ibid., art.III(3).
206 *Hague-Visby Rules*, ibid., art.III(7).
207 *Hague-Visby Rules*, ibid., art.III(4).
208 As to the means of transfer, see the discussion above in A(5), "Bills of Lading as Negotiable Documents of Title."
209 *Hague-Visby Rules*, above note 3, art.III(4). A consignee may not be able to take advantage of this rule where the bill is directly made out to his or her order since there would be no transfer of it. But an argument based on estoppel at common law was always available under the unamended *Hague Rules*, which never went further than admitting the bill of lading as *prima facie* evidence: see *Silver v. Ocean Steamship Co.*, [1930] 1 K.B. 416; *Canada and Dominion Sugar Co.*, above note 16; and *Westcoast Food Brokers v. Hoyanger (The)* (1979), 31 N.R. 82 (F.C.A.).
210 See *AG of Ceylon v. Seindia Steam Navigation Co.*, above note 19.

cargo, this practice is not unlawful[211] but still to be discouraged, since it tends to mislead subsequent transferees. Where there is no disagreement about the cargo but the carrier connives with the shipper, the bill of lading is a fraud on the transferees, and the letter of indemnity is unenforceable against the shipper.[212]

2) Seaworthiness of the Ship

The carrier has a duty at common law and under the *Hague-Visby Rules* both to carry and to care for the goods. These fundamental obligations are captured in the rules by article II: "under every contract of carriage of goods by water the carrier, in relation to the loading, handling, stowage, carriage, custody, care and discharge of such goods, shall be subject to the responsibilities and liabilities and entitled to the rights and immunities hereinafter set forth." The first step toward fulfilling these requirements of the rules is the provision of a suitable carrying ship. Article III(I) specifies:

> The carrier shall be bound, before and at the beginning of the voyage, to exercise due diligence to
> (a) make the ship seaworthy;
> (b) properly man, equip and supply the ship;
> (c) make the holds, refrigerating and cool chambers, and all other parts of the ship in which goods are carried, fit and safe for their reception, carriage and preservation.

The implied undertaking at common law to put up a seaworthy ship is an absolute obligation[213] but, as can be seen in article III(I), under the *Hague-Visby Rules* the carrier's duty is limited to exercising due diligence to provide one. In return for this reduction in responsibility, the duty can no longer be disclaimed.[214] Further, if a claim of loss as a result of unseaworthiness of the ship should arise, the carrier, not the cargo claimant, bears the burden of proving due diligence to render the ship seaworthy in order to escape liability.[215]

---

211 *Brown, Jenkinson & Co. v. Percy Dalton Ltd.*, [1957] 2 Lloyd's L.R. 1 (C.A.).
212 *Ibid.*; and *Silver v. Ocean Steamship Co.*, above note 209.
213 Discussed above in B(1) in Chapter 8, "Seaworthiness of the Ship."
214 Because of *Hague-Visby Rules*, above note 3, art.III(8).
215 *Hague-Visby Rules*, *ibid.*, art.IV(1). See also below F(3), "Order and Onus of Proof." Alternatively, the carrier may prove the failure to exercise due diligence did not cause the loss: *Kuo International Oil Ltd. v. Daisy Shipping Co. (The Yamatogawa)*, [1990] 2 Lloyd's L.R. 39.

Article III(1) describes many of the attributes of a seaworthy ship but not all. (The multiple characteristics of seaworthiness are discussed in Chapter 8.[216]) In short, they include the condition of the ship's hull, the machinery and navigational equipment, the complement and qualification of the crew, the ship's operational procedures, and the suitability of the cargo spaces for the particular cargo, as well as bad stowage that endangers the safety of the ship. The carrier's obligation is limited to exercising due diligence to ready the ship in all these respects. The standard of "due diligence" is akin to the common law's duty of care. Bearing in mind this expression was agreed internationally for use in both common law and civil law countries, an exact measure is not to be expected. It is usually equated to reasonable diligence in light of the known or reasonably anticipated circumstances of the contemplated voyage.[217] The duty is not delegable. The carrier is not only vicariously responsible for the acts and defaults of employees, such as crew, but also of independent contractors who may be engaged in place of or in addition to employees. It is not sufficient for a carrier to exercise good judgment in selecting and contracting with a competent and respected firm: the individuals hired must also exercise due diligence in their tasks.[218] However, the carrier will satisfy the standard of due diligence even if the contracted workers fail to discern a flaw in the ship that subsequently leads to cargo damage if they can be shown, by the carrier, to have been acting carefully and competently nonetheless.[219]

Further, the carrier's duty toward the ship only applies from the time it is under his or her control. The carrier cannot be held responsible for defects in the ship's design and building that are not detectable by due diligence unless he or she was involved in its construction. The carrier's responsibility is to make sure by careful and skilful inspection of the ship when he or she receives it that it is in a fit condition.[220] His

---

216 Above in B(1), "Seaworthiness of the Ship."
217 *Grain Growers Export Co. v. Canada Steamship Lines Ltd.* (1918), 43 O.L.R. 330; *Hamildoc (The)*, 1950 A.M.C. 1973 (Que. C.A.); *Union of India v. NV Reederj Amsterdam (The Amstelslot)*, [1963] 2 Lloyd's Rep. 223 (H.L.); *British Columbia Sugar Refining Co. v. Thor I (The)*, [1965] 2 Ex. C.R. 469 [*The Thor I*]; *Hellenic Dolphin (The)*, [1978] 2 Lloyd's L.R. 336.
218 *Riverstone Meat Co v. Lancashire Shipping Co. (The Muncaster Castle)*, [1961] A.C. 807 [*The Muncaster Castle*]; at the time, the House of Lords decision occasioned much surprise and resistance among shipowners as it was seen to be close to reintroducing an absolute standard of liability.
219 *Union of India v. N.V. Reederij Amsterdam*, above note 217.
220 *W. Angliss v. Peninsular & Orient Steam Navigation Co.*, [1927] 2 K.B. 456; *The Muncaster Castle*, above note 218; *The Thor I*, above note 217.

or her duty is to "make the ship seaworthy" by repairing it, as necessary, and preparing it for the intended voyage. A surveyor's certificate as to the seaworthiness of a ship at the time of its acquisition is probably sufficient but is not adequate to establish the carrier's due diligence toward the vessel once it is in his or her operation.[221]

According to article III(1) of the rules, the carrier is bound to exercise due diligence "before and at the beginning of the voyage." In other words, the obligation is to prepare the ship for the contracted voyage. It ends when the ship departs upon the voyage. During the voyage the carrier will have duties of care for the cargo,[222] which may be affected by the maintenance of the condition of the ship, but otherwise there is no continuing duty regarding seaworthiness.[223] When the obligation can be said to have begun has proven more contentious: it has been held to start at least from the beginning of loading and to continue through to the moment the ship sails. Thus, when fire, attributed to a lack of due diligence, destroyed a loaded cargo before the ship sailed, the vessel was found unseaworthy from the time the fire started.[224] But, where cargo is to be picked up during the voyage at an intermediate port, it is unclear whether the carrier is bound to exercise due diligence to ready the ship in every respect for all the cargoes to be lifted along the way prior to departing from the originating port, especially when the necessary action is simple to perform and is commonly postponed until the ship is underway. Article III(1) is regarded as an overriding obligation. The carrier may not rely on any exculpatory exceptions found in article IV(2)[225] until it has demonstrated that due diligence was exercised to make the ship seaworthy.[226] The carrier must make this proof, after the cargo claimant has established a *prima facie* case of loss owing to unseaworthiness of the vessel.[227]

---

221 *Ibid.* and *The Muncaster Castle, ibid.* at first instance; *Waddle v. Wallsend Shipping Co.*, [1952] 2 Lloyd's Rep. 105; *Charles Goodfellow Lumber Sales Ltd. v. Verreault*, [1971] S.C.R. 522 at 541.
222 See below D(3), "Care of the Cargo."
223 *Leesh River Tea Co. v. British India Steam Navigation Co. (The Chyebassa)*, [1966] 2 Lloyd's Rep. 193, [1967] 2 Q.B. 250 (C.A.).
224 *Maxine Footwear Co. v. Canadian Government Merchant Marine Ltd.*, above note 197. And see *Makedonia (The)*, [1962] 1 Lloyd's Rep. 316.
225 Discussed below in D(6), "Exclusion of Liability."
226 *Maxine Footwear Co. v. Canadian Government Merchant Marine Ltd.*, above note 197.
227 *Hague-Visby Rules*, above note 3, art.IV(1). See further below in F(3), "Order and Onus of Proof."

3) Care of the Cargo

The carrier has a duty of care for the cargo, which is spelled out in the *Hague-Visby Rules* in more detail than at common law.[228] Article III(2) provides: "Subject to the provisions of Article IV, the carrier shall properly and carefully load, handle, stow, carry, keep, care for and discharge the goods carried." In other words, the carrier's duty of care extends to every aspect of handling of the cargo. The standard of care requires the carrier to act "properly and carefully." These words have been read by the courts as signifying distinct yet cumulative duties. "Carefully" means exercising the degree of skill and care that a reasonably competent person in the trade ought to display in the particular circumstances involved in the task required.[229] "Properly" means acting in accordance with a system that, in light of the standards of practice in the shipping industry and the knowledge the carrier has or ought to have about the nature of the cargo, is both appropriate and adequately maintained.[230] In sum, the carrier must look after the cargo according to a sound system operated with reasonable care. While article III(2) refers to every aspect of handling the cargo, including loading and discharging, it is often the case that the shipper or consignee takes some part in those operations. Where bills of lading are issued for goods laden on a chartered ship, it is common for the parties to contract on the basis of FIOST (free in and out, stowed, and trimmed)[231] or some variant of those terms. English courts have accepted this practice as permissible under the *Hague-Visby Rules*, interpreting them to mean the carrier must act properly and carefully toward the cargo throughout the contract to which he or she has agreed. In other words the parties are free to set the scope of their responsibilities on which the rules then mandatorily fasten the standard of duties.[232]

---

228 As to which, see discussion in B(2) in Chapter 8, "Care of the Cargo."

229 See *Bache v. Silver Line Ltd. (The Silver Sandal)*, 110 F.2d 60 (2d Cir. 1940); *Falconbridge Nickel Mines Ltd. v. Chimo Shipping Ltd.*, above note 170; *Federal Commerce and Navigation Co. v. Eisenerz-G.m.b.H. (The Oak Hill)*, [1974] S.C.R. 1225.

230 *G.H. Renton & Co. v. Palmyra Trading Corp. of Panama*, [1957] A.C. 149 (H.L.); *Albacora S.R.L. v. Westcott & Laurance Line Ltd.*, [1966] 2 Lloyd's Rep. 53 (H.L.); *Atlantic Consolidated Foods Ltd. v. Doroty (The)*, above note 163.

231 See the discussion of FIOST and its variants in D(3)(a) of Chapter 8, "Terms of Operation."

232 *Pyrene Co. v. Scindia Navigation Co.*, above note 169; *G.H. Renton & Co. Ltd. v. Palmyra Trading Corp. of Panama*, above note 230. American courts seem to treat the loading and discharging operations as non-delegable, so the carrier remains responsible for them even when he or she contracts out of their performance: see *Associated Metals & Minerals Corp. v. M/V Arktis Sky*, 978 F.2d 47 (2d Cir. 1992).

The corollary of this approach to interpreting the rules is that the carrier is not bound to agree to load or discharge cargo or even to accept particular goods, but, if he or she does so, he or she cannot escape the responsibilities imposed by article III(2).[233] Nor can the carrier delegate them. The carrier is liable for the negligent performance of these obligations whether committed by him- or herself or by his or her employees or subcontractors.[234] Similarly the carrier will be liable for breach of the duty of care toward one cargo owner when another cargo owner negligently causes the damage while loading or stowing his or her own goods, as agreed with the carrier.

The carrier's duties in article III(2) are expressed in its opening words to be subject to the exceptions from liability contained in article IV. This formulation is significantly different from article III(1) on seaworthiness, which is not expressly subjected to article IV.[235] The difference in wording might suggest that the carrier may escape the duty of care for the cargo whenever he or she can prove one of the exceptions in article IV, but the courts have interpreted article III(2) more narrowly. They have worked from the common law principles that the carrier is strictly responsible for the care of the cargo and cannot take advantage of exceptions from liability if his or her conduct is negligent.[236] Similarly they have held that the exceptions in article IV, or at least those that do not explicitly speak to negligence,[237] are of no avail to the carrier when he or she is in breach of article III(2).[238] This approach also implies, although the point seems unsettled, that the burden of proof of negligence and breach of article III(2) falls on the claimant, cargo owner.[239]

---

233 *Bruck Mills Ltd. v. Black Sea Steamship Co.*, above note 192.
234 *International Packers London Ltd. v. Ocean Steam Ship Co.*, [1955] 2 Lloyd's Rep. 218.
235 The distinction was part of the basis for the holding in *Maxine Footwear Co. v. Canadian Government Merchant Marine Ltd.*, discussed above at note 197, that the *Hague-Visby Rules*, above note 3, art.III(1) is an overriding obligation.
236 See the discussion of the carrier's common law duty of care in B(2) in Chapter 8, "Care of the Cargo."
237 E.g., *Hague-Visby Rules*, above note 3, art.IV(2)(a) and (b), discussed below in D(6), "Exclusion of Liability."
238 *Gamlen Chemical Co. v. Shipping Corp. of India*, [1978] 2 N.S.W.L.R. 12; *Atlantic Consolidated Foods Ltd. v. Doroty (The)*, above note 163; *Guadano v. Hamburg Chicago Line*, above note 190.
239 See below in F(3), "Order and Onus of Proof."

4) Deviation on the Voyage

The *Hague-Visby Rules* article IV(4) permit "any reasonable deviation" in the voyage but they do not define what deviation is. Once again the courts seek to interpret the rules in light of the common law duty not to deviate.[240] That principle demands that the ship does not stray during the voyage from its agreed or customary course to destination. No difficulty is encountered under the *Hague-Visby Rules* when the parties agree a particular route different from the customary one between the loading and discharging ports: the rules simply apply to the scope of the contract defined by the parties.[241] But problems can arise when liberty clauses[242] are included or incorporated in the bill of lading. In construing such a clause together with the described voyage, the courts will seek to give business efficacy to the parties' contract[243] and also to judge whether the way the liberty is exercised is reasonable under the rules.[244] In effect a general liberty clause in a bill of lading adds almost nothing, since the carrier has a right to make reasonable deviations but cannot contractually lessen or relieve his or her liability under the rules. The test whether a deviation is reasonable, and therefore justifiable, was formulated by Lord Atkin in *Stag Line Ltd. v. Foscolo, Mango & Co.* as the following question: "[W]hat departure from the contract voyage might a prudent person controlling the voyage at the time make and maintain, having in mind all the relevant circumstances existing at the time, including the terms of the contract and the interests of all parties concerned?"[245] Article IV(4) itself provides two examples of reasonable grounds to deviate — saving life and rescuing property — although it is generally agreed that, in respect of saving property, the carrier may not deviate simply to earn a salvage award. Other obvious examples are deviating into a port of refuge or overcarrying the cargo because the destination port is strikebound. Article IV(4) says nothing about the consequences of an unjustifiable deviation but the courts have applied the remedies at common law.[246] That is to say, deviation is so serious a breach that the cargo owner may elect to treat the carriage

---

240 Discussed in B(3) in Chapter 8, "Deviation on the Voyage."
241 Pursuant to *G.H. Renton & Co. v. Palmyra Trading Corp. of Panama*, above note 230.
242 Discussed in connection with voyage charterparties above in D(4)(c) in Chapter 8, "Deviation."
243 *Ibid.*
244 *Stag Line Ltd. v. Foscolo, Mango & Co.*, above note 197.
245 *Ibid.* at 343.
246 See above note 240.

contract as no longer binding.[247] If that occurs, then the *Hague-Visby Rules* implied in the contract are also set aside and, with them, the right of the carrier to limit his or her liability.[248]

5) Delay in Delivery

Delayed delivery of the goods is not expressly regulated by the *Hague-Visby Rules* even though it may constitute a breach of the carriage contract at common law.[249] As pointed out previously,[250] the character of a breach by delay is different from other kinds of breach of contract. While delay may, in hindsight, have been triggered by a particular incident, there can be no determination of any breach until the end of the voyage. Further, the cargo owner is only temporarily, not permanently, deprived of the goods and consequently suffers purely economic, and rarely any physical,[251] losses. From a commercial point of view, however, especially under modern systems of just-in-time supply, delays in delivery can be just as financially injurious as deliveries of damaged goods. Quite often delay arises in connection with some other obligation of the carrier under the *Hague-Visby Rules*. For instance, a deviation on the voyage frequently causes delay as well. Similarly a ship that goes to sea in an unseaworthy condition is also likely to suffer delay on the voyage. In instances when delay is combined with another breach of contract, the carrier's liability will generally be determined by the rules governing that other default. Then the delay will likely only affect the outcome of the cargo owner's claim, if at all, in assessing the damages payable by the carrier.

When delay is the sole or primary cause of the cargo owner's loss, such as when the ship is late in departing or goes slow in the voyage, the carrier's liability will be determined by the standard of care of the cargo imposed by article III(2) of the *Hague-Visby Rules*. No particular difficulty has been encountered in subsuming issues of delay under the rules[252]

---

247 *Ibid.* at note 42ff.
248 Confirmed in *Stag Line Ltd. v. Foscolo, Mango & Co.*, above note 197, even though *Hague-Visby Rules*, above note 3, art.IV(5) appear to permit the carrier to limit liability "in any event": see below D(7), "Limitation of Liability."
249 See B(4) in Chapter 8, "Delay in Delivery."
250 *Ibid.*
251 A perishable cargo may suffer physical deterioration simply through delay.
252 See *Anglo Saxon Petroleum Co. v. Adamastos Shipping Co.*, [1957] 2 Q.B. 233 at 253 (C.A.), aff'd, on this point, [1959] A.C. 133; *G.H. Renton & Co. Ltd. v. Palmyra Trading Corp. of Panama*, above note 230; and *St. Lawrence Construction Ltd. v. Federal Commerce and Navigation Co.*, [1985] 1 F.C. 767 (C.A.).

and the carrier's duty to "properly and carefully" handle and carry the cargo clearly implies an obligation to deliver it with reasonable dispatch. The cargo owner's problem is not likely to be establishing the breach of the carriage contract by an unreasonable delay so much as difficulty in demonstrating that the full extent of damages that he or she claims ought reasonably to have been foreseen by the carrier as liable to result if the ship delays.[253] While temporary loss of the use of the goods or diminution in their market value is usually reasonably foreseeable, the carrier is less likely to be expected to anticipate all the cargo owner's loss of business profits and other consequential losses.[254]

6) Exclusion of Liability

While the carrier is not free to disclaim any of the responsibilities implied by the *Hague-Visby Rules*,[255] article IV(2) provides a total of seventeen exceptions to liability. This list of exemptions reflects the catalogue of "excepted perils" that carriers customarily included in the standard trading terms of their bills of lading in order to negate the heavy obligations of the common law before the *Hague Rules* were concluded. The exceptions found in article IV(2) are an important part of the international bargain expressed in the *Hague-Visby Rules* that the carrier is bound to observe a minimum standard of responsibilities toward the cargo but, in return, may limit his or her liability for default. The exceptions define those minimum responsibilities by refining the obligations regarding seaworthiness, cargo care, deviation, and delay found in articles III(1)–(2) and IV(1). Unfortunately the number and complexity of the exceptions have occasioned a great deal of disagreement and litigation about the carrier's responsibilities. The exceptions are of three kinds: some protect the carrier from liability when the cause of loss was an act of the cargo owner; some exempt the carrier from liability when the causative incident was unforeseen and beyond his or her control; and others simply excuse the carrier for malfeasance.

a) Errors in Navigation
Article IV(2)(a) continues to raise controversy because it permits the carrier to escape liability for the negligence of employees. It expressly

---

253 This is a modernized version of the famous test for the measure of damages in *Hadley v. Baxendale* (1854), 9 Ex. 341, 156 E.R. 145, itself a case of delay in delivery: see *Pegase (The)*, [1981] 1 Lloyd's L.R. 175 (Q.B.).
254 See M. Ganado & H. Kindred, *Marine Cargo Delays* (London: Lloyd's Press, 1990) c.8.
255 By reason of *Hague-Visby Rules*, above note 3, art.III(8) discussed above in C(4), "How the Rules Apply."

negates responsibility for loss arising from an "act, neglect or default of the master, mariner, pilot, or the servant of the carrier in the navigation or in the management of the ship." Historically this exception was justified on the basis that shipowners lacked the means to communicate with their ships on long and distant voyages. Masters had to act on their own judgment, which, it was asserted, should not be attributed to the shipowner. Modern communications systems have largely defeated this rationale, but shipowners still claim the benefit of the exception. But the courts interpret the exception narrowly. It has no application to the carrier's duty to exercise due diligence to make the ship seaworthy under article III(1);[256] nor is it a defence to a claim for lack of cargo care under article III(2) if the negligence was committed by the carrier.

Article IV(2)(a) protects the carrier from liability for the negligent acts of the master, crew, and other employees only, and, the courts have determined, only in respect of an error in navigation or management of the ship as a ship. A distinction must be drawn between a lack of care for the cargo and a lack of care toward the ship, though the cargo may indirectly be affected.[257] For example, the failure to use the ship's refrigeration system effectively during the voyage clearly affects only the cargo, so the carrier cannot rely on the exception.[258] But where a ship suffers an accident and the master take steps to staunch the entry of water, albeit negligently, and the cargo is also damaged, the carrier may claim the benefit of the exception because the master's acts primarily affect the safety and preservation of the vessel though they incidentally have consequences for the cargo as well.[259]

b) Fire
Article IV(2)(b) exempts the carrier from liability for damage to cargo resulting from fire, "unless caused by the actual fault or privity of the carrier." Thus the carrier cannot escape liability for fire damage if the fire was caused by the carrier's lack of due diligence to make the ship

---

256 Because the *Hague-Visby Rules*, above note 3, art.III(1) are an overriding obligation of the carrier, as discussed above in D(2), "Seaworthiness of the Ship."
257 See the dissent of Greer L.J. in *Gosse Millerd Ltd. v. Canadian Government Merchant Marine, Ltd.*, [1928] 1 K.B. 717 (C.A.), approved on appeal by the House of Lords, [1929] A.C. 223 and adopted in Canada: *Kalamazoo Paper Company v. Canadian Pacific Railway Co.*, [1950] S.C.R. 356; *Leval & Co. v. Colonial Steamships Ltd.*, [1961] S.C.R. 221; *Thor I (The)*, above note 217; and *Washington (The)*, [1976] 2 Lloyd's L.R. 453 (F.C.).
258 *Foreman and Ellams Ltd. v. Federal Steam Navigation Co.*, [1928] 2 K.B. 424.
259 *Leval & Co. v. Colonial Steamships Ltd.*, above note 257.

seaworthy, as required by article III(1).[260] Nor may the carrier rely on the fire exception if the fire resulted from any other personal negligence. When the carrier is a corporation it will be regarded at fault if the senior officer responsible for the management of the company's ships is negligent. The test is whether the official is the directing mind of the corporation,[261] at least in respect of its shipping activities.[262] This officer is now likely to be the authorized representative required to be designated under the *Canada Shipping Act, 2001*, as responsible for all matters relating to the ship.[263] The carrier, however, may claim the benefit of the exception for damage to the cargo by a fire caused by the negligence of any lesser employees.

The exception covers damage by actual fire, which means there must be ignition or flame involved. Heat alone is not enough, but damage by heat is included if flame is present.[264] So also included is cargo damage resulting from reasonable efforts to extinguish the fire; for example, if water is used to douse the fire, damage by the water is included with the fire damage.[265] However, the carrier has a continuing duty of care toward the fire-damaged goods and any other cargoes on board. He or she must act reasonably in making efforts to extinguish the fire and in protecting the various cargoes from collateral damage by his or her fire-fighting activities and materials.[266] The ship must also be crewed by seafarers whom the carrier has made diligent efforts to train properly in fire-fighting techniques, otherwise the exception will be of no avail.[267] To claim the benefit of the exception the carrier must prove that the fire caused the cargo owner's loss. Who has to prove that the carrier was without personal fault, however, is less clear. Canadian courts seem divided over the issue,[268] but a plain reading would suggest the cargo claimant has to

---

260 *Maxine Footwear Co. v. Canadian Government Merchant Marine Ltd.*, above note 197.
261 *Lennard's Carrying Co. v. Asiatic Petroleum Co.*, [1915] A.C. 705 (H.L.); *Leval & Co. v. Colonial Steamships Ltd.*, above note 257.
262 *Lady Gwendolen (The)*, [1965] 1 Lloyd's Rep. 335 (C.A.).
263 Above note 179, s.14, pursuant to the *International Safety Management Code* (*ISM Code*): see D(2) in Chapter 5, "*ISM Code*." Canada has no fire statute affecting this issue, unlike the United Kingdom and the United States, for which, see W. Tetley, *Marine Cargo Claims*, above note 156 at 422–28.
264 *Tempus Shipping Co. v. Louis Dreyfus*, [1930] 1 K.B. 699; *David McNair & Co. v. Santa Malta (The)*, [1967] 2 Lloyd's Rep. 391 (Ex. Ct.).
265 *Diamond (The)*, [1906] P. 282.
266 *Liberty Shipping Lim. Procs.*, 1973 A.M.C. 2241 (W.D. Wash.).
267 *Ibid.*
268 Cf. *Drew Brown Ltd. v. Orient Trader (The)*, [1972] 1 Lloyd's Rep. 35, aff'd [1974] S.C.R. 1286; *Maxine Footwear Co. v. Canadian Government Merchant Marine Ltd.*,

prove the carrier's actual fault or privity. This interpretation is contextually supported by the exception in article IV(2)(q),[269] which is also lost if the carrier was personally at fault. In that article proof of the carrier's actual fault is expressly stated to be on the carrier.

c) Perils of the Sea

Acts of God and perils of sea that overtake the ship are, by article IV(2)(c)–(d) of the *Hague-Visby Rules*, grounds for exempting the carrier from liability for the cargo loss they cause provided he or she first proves due diligence to make the ship seaworthy.[270] The difference between acts of God and perils of the sea is largely a matter of degree. An act of God is some incident from natural causes, although not necessarily of the sea, that could not have been prevented by any amount of foresight and care reasonably to be expected of the carrier.[271] For instance, an extraordinarily high or freak wave that swamps the ship may be an act of God.[272] A peril of the sea is a danger from water, wind, and weather of such a degree that the risk of damage to the cargo arising from it could not have been foreseen or guarded against as one of the probable incidents of the voyage.[273] However, the degree of severity of the weather, according to Canadian courts, need not be great. The peril does not have to be extraordinary or irresistible, but it must be of such violence that the damage caused cannot be attributed to negligence in protecting the cargo.[274] In other words, the peril must be an unforeseeable danger "of the sea" on the particular route of the voyage at that particular time of year.[275]

---

above note 197; and *Norman v. Canadian National Railway* (1980), 27 Nfld. & P.E.I.R. 451 (Nfld. S.C.) at 514, although these decisions may be infected by foreign precedents that involved fire statutes unknown to Canadian law: see above note 263.
269 See below D(6)(h), "Any Other Cause Without Fault."
270 *Charles Goodfellow Lumber Sales Ltd. v. Verreault*, above note 221.
271 *Nugent v. Smith* (1876), 1 C.P.D. 423; *Turgel Fur Co. Ltd. v. Northumberland Ferries Ltd.* (1966), 59 D.L.R. (2d) 1 (N.S.S.C.).
272 *Turgel Fur Co. v. Northumberland Ferries Ltd.*, ibid.
273 *Charles Goodfellow Lumber Sales Ltd. v. Verreault*, above note 221; *Falconbridge Nickel Mines Ltd. v. Chimo Shipping Ltd.*, above note 170; *Canadian National Steamships v. Bayliss*, [1937] S.C.R. 261 at 263; *N.M. Paterson & Sons Ltd. v. Mannix Ltd.*, [1966] S.C.R. 180 at 188.
274 *Keystone Transports Ltd. v. Dominion Steel & Coal Co.*, [1942] S.C.R. 495. U.K. and U.S. courts permit only extraordinary weather conditions to constitute a peril of the sea: see, e.g., *W. Angliss Co. v. P. & O. Steam Navigation Co.* (1927), 28 Ll. L.R. 202; and *Giulia (The)*, 218 F. 744 (2d Cir. 1914).
275 See *Bruck Mills Ltd. v. Black Sea Steamship Co.*, above note 192; *Washington (The)*, above note 257; and *G.E. Crippen v. Vancouver Tug Boat Co.*, [1971] 2 Lloyd's Rep. 207 (Ex. Ct.).

The carrier must also prove that such a peril was the cause of the cargo owner's loss.[276]

d) Other Dangers and Restraints

Article IV(2) of the *Hague-Visby Rules* lists a variety of other perils or dangers that a ship may run into but for the consequences of which the carrier will be excused liability: acts of war; acts of public enemies; arrest or restraint by princes, rulers, or people, or seizure under legal process; quarantine restrictions; riots and civil commotions; and strikes, lockouts, or restraints of labour.[277] These archaic phrases reflect the time-honoured exceptions found in bills of lading prior to the *Hague Rules*, but their scope and intent is still clear. All of these exemptions from liability are granted because the incidents are beyond the control of the carrier; however, the carrier has a continuing duty of care for the cargo and, so, should avoid placing the ship and cargo in the face of anticipated danger where reasonably possible.[278] For instance, the carrier should not direct the ship into a strike-bound port, especially if the cargo is perishable, but should carry the goods to an alternative safe port of discharge.[279]

e) Saving Life at Sea

Consistent with the carrier's right to make reasonable deviations,[280] article IV(2)(l) exempts him or her from liability for attempting to save life or property at sea.

f) Shipper's Faults and Cargo Defects

The carrier will not be held liable for injury to the cargo that arises from some cause within the sphere of responsibility of the cargo owner. Article IV(2) of the *Hague-Visby Rules* exempts the carrier for loss due to the acts or omissions of the shipper or owner and his or her agents, or as a result of inherent vice or defect, insufficient packing, or inadequate marking of the goods.[281] Inherent vice is an intrinsic characteris-

---

276 *Falconbridge Nickel Mines Ltd. v. Chimo Shipping Ltd.*, above note 170.
277 *Hague-Visby Rules*, above note 3, arts.IV(2)(e), (f), (g), (h), (k), and (j), respectively.
278 *Morrisey v. S.S.A. & J. Faith*, 252 F. Supp. 54 (N.D. Ohio 1965); *Sedco Inc. v. SS Strathewe*, 800 F.2d 27 (2d Cir. 1986). And see *Svenska Traktor*, above note 188. But the negligence of the carrier's employees may be excepted: see above 6(a), "Errors in Navigation."
279 *Crelinsten Fruit Co. v. Mormacsaga (The)*, [1968] 2 Lloyd's Rep. 184 (Ex. Ct.). See also *United States v. Lykes Bros. Steamship Co*, 511 F.2d 218 (5th Cir. 1975).
280 Discussed above in D(4), "Deviation on the Voyage."
281 *Hague-Visby Rules*, above note 3, arts.IV(2)(i), (m), (n), and (o), respectively.

tic of the cargo, which, by natural processes, results in change to the goods in the course of a voyage. A common form of inherent vice is wastage in bulk or weight, which is also known as *freinte de route*, such as occurs to cargoes of flour or wine during transportation. A hidden defect, by comparison, is something abnormal but hidden in the goods. Since the carrier has a duty of care for all cargo, the inherent vice or defect must be something that he or she could not be expected to guard against; for instance, if perishable goods require chilled or cooled chambers, the carrier would be in breach of his or her duty of care if the ship failed to provide such conditions.[282] Similarly, the carrier must stow and carry the goods in an appropriate way in light of his or her knowledge, or the knowledge the carrier ought reasonably to be imputed to have, of the inherent characteristics of the goods.[283] However, the carrier is not responsible for the inevitable ripening and maturity of a cargo, such as apples, which may take place in the course of a voyage.[284] It is the shipper's duty to load a cargo fit for the voyage, for the carrier only warrants by a clean bill of lading that its apparent order and condition is good.[285]

The packing of goods is not sufficient if it cannot withstand the risks of handling and the ship's movements reasonably to be expected in the course of carriage by sea. The customary packing for sea carriage in the trade is usually sufficient. So, when no wrapping is normally undertaken, such as with automobiles, the carrier cannot assert insufficiency of packing as an excuse from liability.[286] But it is always a question of fact in the particular circumstances whether the shipper's packing was insufficient or whether the carrier's stowage was inappropriate.[287] Carriers regularly raise the plea of insufficiency of packing when goods stuffed in a container by the shipper are damaged because the condition of the cargo is not apparent.[288] But in other situations

---

282 *Albacora S.R.L. v. Westcott & Laurance Line Ltd.*, above note 230 at 59.
283 *G.E. Crippen v. Vancouver Tug Boat Co. Ltd.*, above note 275; *David McNair & Co. v. Santa Malta (The)*, above note 264; *William B. Branson Ltd. v. Jadranska Slobodna Plovidba (The Split)*, [1973] 2 Lloyd's Rep. 535 (F.C.).
284 *Westcoast Food Brokers Ltd. v. Hoyanger (The)* (1980), above note 209; *Eastwest Produce Co. v. Nordnes (The)*, [1956] Ex. C.R. 328.
285 See the discussion above in D(1), "Bills of Lading." Where the carrier has knowledge that the cargo is unfit for the voyage, the bill of lading ought to be appropriately claused.
286 *Nissan Automobile Co (Canada) v. Continental Shipper (The)*, [1976] 2 Lloyd's Rep. 234 (F.C.A.) .
287 See *G.E. Crippen v. Vancouver Tug Boat Co. Ltd.*, above note 275.
288 E.g., *Guadano v. Hamburg Chicago Line*, above note 190.

where the inadequacy of the packing is evident at loading, the carrier should clause the bill of lading. Otherwise the carrier may be prevented from relying on the exception against the consignee of the goods as a result of being estopped from denying the accuracy of the bill of lading against a subsequent holder, by reason of article III(IV).[289]

Marks on the goods are not inadequate simply because they are inaccurate. For the carrier to benefit from this exception, he or she must prove the marks were so insufficient that the goods became unidentifiable to the carriage contract with the cargo owner[290] and so were misdelivered or mixed with other goods. If the carrier cannot establish the inadequacy of the cargo's marks against the consignee, he or she may be able to claim indemnity from the shipper for breach of the guarantee of their accuracy imposed by article III(5). In addition, by article IV(5)(h), the carrier is completely absolved of liability, even against an innocent consignee who relied on the bill of lading, if the nature of the goods is knowingly misstated by the shipper. Such misdescription may be deliberately made by a shipper to incur a lower freight rate or a lesser customs duty; but, if the carrier is a party to the misstatement, he or she cannot invoke the protection of the rules.

Any other defaults of the shipper or a subsequent cargo owner that are not related to the specific exceptions for inherent vice, insufficient packing, or inadequate marking of the goods will excuse the carrier from liability for loss under the general words of article IV(2)(i). But the carrier must prove that the cargo owner's act or omission caused the loss incurred. If there is more than one contributing cause, the carrier must demonstrate what loss or damage falls within the exception from liability claimed, or the carrier will be liable for the whole loss.[291]

g) Latent Defects

The carrier is also exempt from liability for loss and damage resulting from "latent defects not discoverable by due diligence" (article IV(2)(p)). Since the exemption refers to defects in the ship, not the cargo,[292] it seems to overlap with the carrier's duty to exercise due diligence to make the ship seaworthy under article III(1).[293] The carrier will not be liable for cargo losses caused by the unseaworthiness of the ship pro-

---

[289] Discussed above at note 207. And see *Silver v. Ocean Steamship Co.*, above note 209.
[290] *Sandeman & Sons v. Tyzack & Branfoot Steamship Co.*, [1913] A.C. 680.
[291] *Ibid.*; *Gosse Millerd, Ltd. v. Canadian Government Merchant Marine Ltd.*, above note 257; *Tolmidis (The)*, [1983] 1 Lloyd's L.R. 530 (C.A.).
[292] See inherent vice or defect, above at note 281ff.
[293] Discussed above in D(2), "Seaworthiness of the Ship."

vided he or she proves that he or she exercised due diligence to render the vessel seaworthy, even though a hidden defect was overlooked if it could not be discovered by reasonable diligence.[294] But the rule and the exception are not coextensive. The carrier is only bound to make the ship seaworthy before the voyage. The exception may avail the carrier for defects not discoverable by due diligence during the voyage, such as in the event of ship inspections or surveys. The exception also confirms that the carrier is not responsible for latent defects in the ship before he or she acquired it, provided they were not discoverable by a diligent inspection of the vessel on delivery.[295]

h) Any Other Cause Without Fault

Article IV(2)(q) of the *Hague-Visby Rules* concludes the lengthy list of carrier's exemptions from liability with a general excuse for loss from any other cause provided it arose without the fault or privity of the carrier or the fault or neglect of his or her agents and employees. The significance of this exception lies in the burden of proof that is expressly placed on the carrier to demonstrate the absence of default both personally and by employees and agents. The most common occasion when the carrier claims the benefit of this exception is loss by theft of the cargo.[296] But if suspicion of the pilferage falls on stevedores contracted to work the ship by the carrier, or their associates, the carrier cannot escape liability unless he or she proves that the loss occurred without any fault on the part of his or her agents and employees.[297]

7) Limitation of Liability

Article IV(5)(a) of the *Hague-Visby Rules* grants the carrier a limit to his or her liability for injury to the cargo in broad language:

> Unless the nature and value of such goods have been declared by the shipper before shipment and inserted in the bill of lading, neither the carrier nor the ship shall in any event be or become liable for any loss or damage to or in connection with the goods in an amount exceeding 666.67 units of account per package or unit or 2 units of account

---

294 E.g., *Hellenic Dolphin (The)*, above note 217.
295 See above at note 220.
296 *Leesh River Tea Co. v. British India Steam Navigation Co. (The Chyebassa)*, above note 223.
297 *Heyn v. Ocean Steamship Co.* (1927), 27 Ll. L.R. 158. See also *G.E. Crippen v. Vancouver Tug Boat Co.*, above note 275, for an example regarding stowage without negligence.

per kilogramme of gross weight of the goods lost or damaged, whichever is the higher.

The unit of account referred to is the Special Drawing Right (SDR) as defined by the International Monetary Fund. The value of 1 SDR is calculated daily from the market values of a basket of major currencies and is used to fix the comparative values of other national currencies. (In 2003 the Canadian equivalent of 1 SDR fluctuated around Can$2.) Use of the SDR as the unit of account alleviates the previous problem of divergence in national exchange rates and, therefore, in the maximum amount of compensation actually recovered by the cargo owner. Although SDRs induce a much greater degree of stability and uniformity in the monetary limits of liability, they cannot protect against world inflation and the consequent devaluation of currencies as a whole.

The carrier's limit of liability is set at 666.67 SDR per package or unit, or 2 SDR per kilo, whichever is the higher. Greater compensation may become payable by prior agreement to a higher maximum amount,[298] or, as the opening words of article IV(5)(a) declare, when the actual value of the goods, as declared by the shipper, is included in the bill of lading. In practice, bills of lading rarely include the value of the goods because, it seems, carriers are apt to charge increased freight by value at such a rate that shippers find it more economical to buy insurance instead. In addition to the limit of liability per item of cargo, the total amount recoverable is also fixed. By article IV(5)(b), the aggregate compensation payable is calculated by reference to the value the goods would have had if they had arrived whole and on time at the port of discharge. Their value is fixed according to the commodity exchange price, or market price or, if none, the normal value of like goods. This approach comports with the common law method of valuation by assessing the arrived sound market value of the goods.

The aggregate limit of liability only operates when the actual loss of the cargo owner exceeds the arrived sound market value of the goods. The carrier must prove his or her actual loss according to the ordinary common law rules for the measurement of contract damages expressed in *Hadley v. Baxendale*;[299] these include a duty on the cargo claimant to mitigate the loss.[300] For instance, where goods are delivered

---

298 *Hague-Visby Rules*, above note 3, art.IV(5)(g).
299 Above note 253. See also *Koufos v. C. Czarnikow Ltd., (The Heron II)*, [1969] 1 A.C. 350 (H.L.); *Pegase (The)*, above note 253; and *B.D.C. Ltd. v. Hofstrand Farms Ltd.* (1986), 26 D.L.R. (4th) 1 (S.C.C.).
300 *Blenheim (The)* (1885), 10 P.D. 167; *British Westinghouse Electric Co. v. Underground Electric Railways Co.*, [1912] A.C. 673 (H.L.); *Sunnyside Greenhouses Ltd.*

damaged, the cargo owner must attempt to salvage their remaining value by use or sale and his or her damages will be calculated by subtracting the arrived damaged market value of the goods from their arrived sound market value. Allowance must also be made for any natural shrinkage, evaporation, or deterioration of the cargo normally to be expected during the voyage.[301] But the cargo owner is entitled to a fair margin of profit lost by damage or loss of the goods,[302] as well as further consequential losses that the carrier may reasonably have foreseen as liable to result from his or her breach of the carriage contract.[303]

The limits of liability apply whether the action against the carrier is founded in tort or contract. They also benefit the carrier's employees — but not subcontractors — who may be sued by the cargo owner. Further, the aggregate compensation recoverable for all the claims made against the carrier, and the crew and other employees arising out of the same incident is, in effect, limited to the arrived sound market value of the goods as declared in article IV(5)(b).[304] Application of the rule of limitation of liability by package, unit, or weight is straightforward when the goods are itemized and fully wrapped. The limit of liability for partially packaged and unwrapped goods is calculated by item or unit. Canadian courts have interpreted "unit" to mean shipping unit,[305] as opposed to freight unit.[306] Thus, liability for bulky items that cannot be packed or do not require packaging will be limited by the unit, unless limitation by weight would produce a higher ceiling of compensation. Trucks,[307] tractors, generators,[308] and roll-on/roll-off cargo generally are examples of units of goods.[309]

Commonly small packages of goods are consolidated for convenience in a crate, on a pallet, or in a metal container. Then the question arises whether such consolidation reduces the assembled number of

---

v. *Golden West Seeds Ltd.* (1972), 27 D.L.R. (3d) 434 (Alta. C.A.), aff'd [1973] 3 W.W.R. 288 (S.C.C.); *Asamera Oil Corp. v. Sea Oil & General Corp.*, [1979] 1 S.C.R. 633.

301 Also known as *freinte de route*.
302 *Crelinsten Fruit Co. v. Mormacsaga (The)*, above note 279.
303 See *Pegase (The)*, above note 253.
304 *Hague-Visby Rules*, above note 3, art.IV *bis*(1)–(3).
305 See *Falconbridge Nickel Mines Ltd. v. Chimo Shipping Ltd.*, above note 170.
306 Which is the U.S. interpretation as a result of the addition of "customary freight" to "unit" in the version of the *Hague Rules* enacted in the U.S. *Carriage of Goods by Sea Act*, above note 139, §1304(5).
307 E.g., *Anticosti Shipping Co. v. St-Amand*, above note 11.
308 E.g., *Falconbridge Nickel Mines Ltd. v. Chimo Shipping Ltd.*, above note 170.
309 *Coutinho, Caro & Co. v. Ermua (The)*, [1979] 2 F.C. 528 (T.D.) is an instructive example of calculating liability by units.

packages to a single unit. Carriage in containers formerly caused the most difficulty in applying the limited liability rule because the carrier cannot ascertain the number of packages in a container stuffed and sealed by the shipper, who, additionally, may not have packed the goods to the degree necessary to withstand a sea voyage without the container. Article IV(5)(c) now affirms the prevalent court practice of looking to the intention of the parties principally as expressed in the bill of lading.[310] When the number of packages or units is enumerated in the bill of lading that will be deemed the number for the purposes of limiting liability, and any clause in the carriage contract THAT is intended to define "package" differently will be void for contradiction of article III(8). If the shipper does not declare the number of packages in a container and ensure it is recorded on the bill of lading, then the container itself will be treated as the package or unit. Thus, for example, traditional bulk goods that are unitized in containers will carry liability limited by the container or their weight, whichever is greater.

While article IV(5)(a) clearly addresses liability for loss and damage to goods, there is some uncertainty how it applies to liability for delay. The express references to physical loss and damage might be read as excluding economic losses, for instance, by delay.[311] That could mean the carrier would be exposed to unlimited liability for economic loss or that he or she could, by contract, disclaim all such liability. Either way, this interpretation contradicts the spirit and intention of the *Hague-Visby Rules* that the carrier shall bear mandatory minimum responsibility for the safe carriage and delivery of the goods in return for a maximum amount of liability in the event of default. Moreover, as noted above, courts permit claims in appropriate cases for loss of business profits when goods are lost or damaged to be limited by reference to article IV(5)(a); so, it would seem distinctly odd if they were not also to do so in the event of loss of business profits by delay. After all, there is no difference in kind in the economic loss suffered by the cargo owner whether the goods are delivered damaged or delayed.

It may be better to interpret article IV(5)(a) as intended to cover all kinds of cargo losses, thereby affirming the objective of the *Hague-Visby Rules* to provide an undivided regulatory regime for the carriage as a whole. Support for this view can be found in article IV(5)(a) as it states that, "in any event," the carrier shall not become liable "for loss or damage to or in connection with the goods" in excess of the limits

---

310 *Consumers Distributing Co. v. Dart Containerline Co.* (1980), 31 N.R. 181 (F.C.A.).
311 Cp. W. Tetley, *Marine Cargo Claims*, above note 156 at 342–43; and Ganado & Kindred, *Marine Cargo Delays*, above note 254 at 149–51.

specified. Economic loss by reason of delay in delivery is loss "in connection with" the goods. Of some remaining concern is the calculation of the limit of liability if no packages or units of goods are lost or damaged. In fact, the package-unit-weight method of article IV(5)(a) is still appropriate. In principle, if all the goods are delayed, the maximum liability should be the same as if they had all been lost or destroyed, for in both situations all of them are affected.[312]

Limitation of liability for loss following a deviation of the ship has also raised interpretive problems. The consequences of an unjustified deviation are peculiarly drastic: the cargo owner may elect to treat the carriage contract as terminated.[313] In that event none of the terms of the contract, including those implied by the *Hague-Visby Rules*, continue to oblige the cargo owner or benefit the carrier. Thus the carrier's right to limit liability under article IV(5)(a) will be of no effect. Objection has been made to this interpretative result on the grounds that it defeats the integrity and balance of rights and duties between ship and cargo owners so carefully crafted in the rules. It also seems to contradict the wording and the spirit of article IV(5)(a), which asserts the carrier's liability is limited "in any event." However, the House of Lords has confirmed that the statutory rights of the carrier are lost to the carrier who breaches the carriage contract by an unjustifiable deviation.[314]

The right of the carrier to limit liability may also be overreached in other exceptional circumstances. By article IV(5)(e) the carrier will lose the benefit of limitation if the cargo claimant proves his or her "damage resulted from an act or omission of the carrier done with intent to cause damage, or recklessly and with knowledge that damage would probably result." Apart from a deliberate sacrifice of cargo as a general average act,[315] it would be most unusual for a carrier to commit such wanton or reckless disregard for the cargo and therefore to expose him or her to unlimited liability. In any event, in addition to the limited liability provisions of the *Hague-Visby Rules*, the carrier may also take any benefit to be gained from the right of general limitation of liability calculated by the tonnage of the ship.[316] This parallel right is expressly preserved by the *Marine Liability Act* in enacting the *Hague-Visby Rules*.[317]

---

312 See Ganado & Kindred, *ibid.*
313 See discussion above in D(4), "Deviation on the Voyage."
314 *Stag Line Ltd. v. Foscolo, Mango & Co.*, above note 197.
315 Which may be regulated by a lawful provision outside of the Rules: *Hague-Visby Rules*, above note 3, art.V. And see Chapter 16, "General Average."
316 See Chapter 18, "Limitation of Liability for Maritime Claims."
317 Above note 2, s.42.

E. RESPONSIBILITIES OF CARGO OWNERS

The *Hague-Visby Rules* are chiefly concerned with striking a balance between the carrier's minimum responsibilities and maximum liabilities. Rather less attention is paid to the cargo owner's responsibilities, which are, in any case, of lesser extent. At common law the shipper is bound to deliver the cargo to the carrier in proper order and not to ship dangerous goods without due notice. Also, either the shipper or the consignee, according to the tenor of the carriage contract, is obliged to pay the freight.[318] The *Hague-Visby Rules* only address the first of these two obligations and do so in separate provisions regarding the description and the danger of the goods, as divided in the discussion below.

1) Description of the Cargo

When the shipper delivers the goods to the carrier for carriage he or she typically provides a description of their contents, their marks, their number, and their quantity or weight. On delivery, the shipper is entitled to demand a received bill of lading in which the carrier must enter the marks and the number or quantity or weight of the goods as provided by the shipper,[319] as well as their apparent order and condition.[320] In return for the issuance of a bill of lading article III(5) of the *Hague-Visby Rules* imposes on the shipper a personal guarantee of the accuracy of the particulars it contains that were supplied by him or her. This rule provides important protection for the carrier when the bill of lading is transferred to the consignee or subsequent holders. All holders subsequent to the shipper, who act in good faith, are entitled to rely on the accuracy of the bill of lading.[321] In any action by such a cargo owner for misdelivery, the carrier is estopped from attempting to prove the inaccuracy of its particulars. However, the carrier may take up the guarantee of the shipper and bring an action for indemnity to the extent of his or her liability to the cargo owner as a result of the shipper's inaccuracies. But the shipper is only liable for the consequences of inaccurate particulars in the bill of lading that were supplied by him or her. As article IV(3) of the rules makes abundantly clear, the ship-

---

318 See discussion of these obligations above in Chapter 8 in B(5), "Dangerous Goods" and B(6), "Freight."
319 Unless the carrier has reason to believe they are inaccurate or cannot be checked.
320 See *Hague-Visby Rules*, above note 3, art.III(3) discussed above at note 205ff.
321 See *Hague-Visby Rules*, above note 3, art III(4) discussed above at note 207ff.

per is not responsible for any losses of the carrier that arise without fault or neglect by the shipper or his or her employees.

2) Dangerous Goods

Both the cargo owner and the carrier share elaborate duties by common law and statute in the movement of dangerous goods (discussed in Chapter 8, under "Maritime Common Law Principles of Carriage — Dangerous Goods"). The shipper has the primary responsibility, for the shipper may not deliver dangerous goods for carriage without giving the carrier appropriate notice of their hazardous character and, if necessary, instructions on how to handle them. If the carrier accepts dangerous goods for carriage, the carrier also accepts responsibility for properly and carefully carrying them in light of their hazardous characteristics. In addition to those general principles of the common law, the *Canada Shipping Act*[322] and other federal statutes impose detailed requirements on all aspects of the packing, handling, and moving of an enormous range of potentially dangerous cargoes. The *Hague-Visby Rules* add very little to this large body of regulations. First, the *Marine Liability Act*, in adopting the rules into Canadian law, subjects their operation to the dangerous goods provisions of the *Canada Shipping Act*.[323] Second, the *Hague-Visby Rules* merely, but importantly, protect the carrier from liability for breach of the carriage contract in exercising the right, recognized at common law, to get rid of dangerous goods if necessary. Article IV(6) of the rules provides for two typical situations.

If dangerous goods are loaded without the consent of the carrier, they may be landed, destroyed, or rendered harmless by the carrier without him or her becoming liable for the cargo owner's loss. Moreover, the shipper of the dangerous goods will become liable for all the damage that results from their shipment, whether to the carrying ship or other cargo or persons on board. If dangerous goods are shipped with the consent of the carrier, then the carrier and not the shipper accepts responsibility for any injury that may occur during carriage, just as the carrier does for ordinary cargo. But, because of their dangerous character, article IV(6) grants the carrier the power to dispose of the goods if their danger should materialize without liability for their loss or destruction to the cargo owner.[324]

---

322 Above note 179, ss.389 and 390, discussed above in Chapter 8 in B(5), "Dangerous Goods."
323 Above note 2, s.42.
324 Except in general average, as to which see Chapter 16, "General Average."

The protective rights of the carrier under article IV(6) are free standing provisions and are not subject to other rules. In other words, the shipper cannot plead exemption from liability under article IV(3) that he or she is not responsible for losses sustained without his or her fault. The House of Lords has confirmed that the shipper is strictly liable for shipping dangerous goods even when he or she does not know of their danger, and article IV(3) provides no defence against this liability.[325]

F. CLAIMS AND ACTIONS

1) Time Limits

If the cargo is lost, damaged, or delayed the cargo claimant will be subject to time limits at two stages of proceeding with a claim. Early notice of claim and timely commencement of action are both required of the cargo owner. Notice of the claim and the nature of the loss incurred must be given to the carrier in writing. Article III(6) of the *Hague-Visby Rules* demands that the claimant give notice at the time the goods are delivered, unless the damage is not apparent, in which case three days of grace are allowed.[326] If timely notice is not given, the carrier is entitled to assume *prima facie* that the delivery of the cargo was in order. Article III(6) is a practical provision that serves to inform the carrier about an impending claim and the need to preserve available evidence to answer it. The carrier and the cargo claimant are also bound to afford each other reasonable facilities to collect evidence relevant to the claim. The brevity of the time limits, however, can cause difficulties for claimants, especially where the goods are being carried in a sealed container, which after discharge from the ship, is not received and opened by the cargo owner until some time later at some inland destination.

The consequences for the cargo claimant of a failure to give appropriate notice are, however, not severe. The cargo owner's claim is not barred but he or she may face an increase in the burden of proof of loss in any subsequent proceedings, which he or she bears in any event.[327] In the event of a dispute, the court may be more reluctant to accept the cargo owner's claim for alleged loss if notice of it was not given to the carrier.

---

325 *The Giannis NK*, above note 66.
326 No notice is required if the goods are subjected to a joint survey or inspection on receipt.
327 See, e.g., *Southern Cross*, 1940 A.M.C. 59 (S.D.N.Y. 1939); and *C. Itoh & Co. (America) Inc. v. Hellenic Lines Ltd.*, 1979 A.M.C. 1923 (S.D.N.Y.).

Suits[328] for disputed claims must be begun by the cargo owner within a year of delivery of the goods or when they should have been delivered, otherwise they will be time barred.[329] This limitation of actions speeds up the settlement of claims and prevents carriers from contractually imposing shorter time limits.[330] In practice, even one year is often too short a time to settle claims so the parties commonly agree, as article III(6) permits, to an extension of time. When the contracting carrier was not personally responsible for the claimant's loss, he or she will want to seek indemnity from the performing carrier at fault. But suit against the actual carrier would also be subject to the same time bar, which would be particularly limiting if the cargo claimant does not bring his or her action until the last minute. Article III(6) *bis* therefore grants the contracting carrier an extended period of not less than three months after the time limit of one year on the cargo claimant's action in which to institute proceedings for indemnity from the defaulting carrier, as local law may permit.

Proceedings against the carrier for a cause of action arising outside the application of the *Hague-Visby Rules* are not subject to their time bar of one year. For instance, a suit for loss or damage to the cargo after discharge yet still in the custody of the carrier is not affected by the one-year limitation period.[331]

2) Jurisdiction and Arbitration Clauses

Choice of law and choice of forum clauses, or an arbitration clause are often included in bills of lading. None of them is regulated by the *Hague-Visby Rules*, which means the carrier has considerable latitude to make arrangements for resolving disputes in his or her standard trading terms at his or her convenience. Canadian courts usually respect and enforce jurisdiction clauses. They will take jurisdiction under a choice of forum clause naming Canada, even though the carriage transaction and all the parties to it are foreign.[332] Further, if a cargo owner brings suit in Canada contrary to a jurisdiction clause the courts have

---

328 Which include arbitrations: *Merak (The)*, [1965] P. 223 (C.A.).
329 *Hague-Visby Rules*, above note 3, art.III(6).
330 *Transworld Oil (USA) Inc. v. Minos Compania Naveria SA (The Leni)*, [1992] 2 Lloyd's L.R. 48.
331 *Schweizerische Metallwerke Selve & Co. v. Atlantic Container Line Ltd.* (1986), 63 N.R. 104 (F.C.A.).
332 *United Nations v. Atlantic Seaways Corp.*, [1979] 2 F.C. 541.

a discretion to grant a stay of the action,[333] which, in the past, they have ordinarily exercised in favour of a stay. A recent Supreme Court of Canada decision has confirmed that there must be a strong cause for not ordering a stay of proceedings, which the cargo claimant has the burden of establishing.[334] The court will take into account all the circumstances of the case including where the evidence is located, where the trial would be convenient, whether foreign law applies, to what countries the parties are connected, whether the carrier is simply seeking procedural advantage, and whether the cargo claimant's interests would be prejudiced by a foreign trial.[335] However, a forum selection clause should be rejected if the foreign court would apply law that would lessen the carrier's alleged liability, contrary to article III(8) of the *Hague-Visby Rules*.[336] Nor should a Canadian court honour a choice of law clause that selects the law of a jurisdiction in which the carrier would benefit from lower liability than mandated by the *Hague-Visby Rules* as applied in Canada.

The judicial discretion to exercise stays of action is now subject to new rights of proceedings of cargo owners introduced by the *Marine Liability Act* in 2001.[337] Regardless of the terms of a foreign forum selection clause, the cargo claimant may bring his or her suit in a Canadian court provided that

- the port of loading or discharge was in Canada,
- the defendant carrier has a business office or agency in Canada, or
- the carriage contract was concluded in Canada.

Hence, when a cargo owner receives delayed or damaged goods that are landed in Canada, he or she may sue the carrier locally, even if their contract names a foreign jurisdiction for the resolution of their disputes.[338] However, a cargo owner who is not a member of one of the classes of claimants designated by the Act but arrests the ship in Canada, will, it seems, have to accept the court's discretionary decision whether his or her action should be stayed according to existing principles.

---

333 See the *Federal Court Act*, R.S.C. 1985, c.F-7, s.50(1); and *N.B. Electric Power Commission v. Maritime Electric Co.* (1985), 60 N.R. 203 (F.C.A.).
334 *Z.I. Pompey Industrie v. ECU-Line N.V.*, [2003] S.C.C. 27, which approved and applied the U.K. approach propounded by Brandon J. in *Eleftheria (The)*, [1969] 1 Lloyd's Rep. 237, and prior Canadian court practice in doing so too.
335 *Ibid*.
336 *Agro Co. of Canada Ltd. v. Regal Scout (The)* (1983), 148 D.L.R. (3d) 412; *Hollandia (The)*, [1983] 1 A.C. 565.
337 Above note 2, s.46.
338 But by *Marine Liability Act*, above note 2, s.46(2) after the claim arises, the cargo claimant may agree to the choice of any forum with the carrier.

Arbitration is essentially adjudication according to a body of law in a particular place by a private tribunal, all of which are selected by agreement of the parties. One reason why maritime commercial arbitration is favoured in shipping circles is that the widely dispersed shipping community can call on some highly expert and technically very knowledgeable arbitrators who operate internationally from well-established arbitral centres that have well-regarded arbitral procedures.[339] Arbitration clauses are like jurisdiction clauses in expressing the parties' choice of forum and governing law and, thus, they are subject to the same kind of body of judicial principles as well as the provisions of the *Marine Liability Act*. In addition, when a cargo owner tries to bring a court action contrary to an agreement for arbitration, the judicial discretion to stay the action in favour of arbitration is further constrained by the *New York Convention*.[340] This international agreement — which is given legal effect federally in Canada by the *United Nations Foreign Arbitral Awards Convention Act*[341] — requires the court to stay local court proceedings in breach of a foreign arbitration selection clause in a contract when requested by one of the parties.[342]

An added complication of arbitration clauses is that they are often included in the terms of a bill of lading by incorporation from a charterparty. Issues can then arise as to whether the incorporation clause sufficiently clearly includes the arbitration clause of the charterparty and how to construe the bill of lading if its terms are not wholly consistent with the charterparty.[343]

When an arbitral award is made but not honoured, the cargo owner will want to enforce it against the carrier or his or her property wherever it can be located. But since arbitration is a private adjudication, it cannot be assumed that the local court will allow it to be executed against the carrier's property without careful judicial scrutiny, if at all. This

---

339 Pre-eminently in London, England and New York, U.S.A. In Canada, international arbitration centres have been established in Vancouver, Ottawa, and Quebec City and maritime arbitrations in particular are undertaken by members of the Association of Maritime Arbitrators of Canada and the Vancouver Maritime Arbitrators' Association.
340 *Convention on the Recognition and Enforcement of Foreign Arbitral Awards*, 10 June 1958, 330 U.N.T.S. 3.
341 R.S.C. 1985, c.16 (2nd Supp.) See also the *Commercial Arbitration Act*, R.S.C. 1985, c.17 (2d Supp.), which adopts the *United Nations Commission on International Trade Law Model Law on International Commercial Arbitration* [UNCITRAL Model Law].
342 Above note 340, art.2. And see *UNCITRAL Model Law*, ibid., arts.7 and 8.
343 These issues are discussed above in A(10), "Bills of Lading on a Chartered Ship."

impediment to the international operation of the arbitral process has been largely overcome by the *New York Convention*.[344] It requires a court that is invited to recognize a foreign arbitral award to enforce it with a minimum of judicial review.[345] The convention is now widely adopted among maritime trading states, including Canada,[346] so maritime arbitral awards for and against Canadians are highly likely to be enforced.

3) Order and Onus of Proof

The provisions of the *Hague-Visby Rules* establishing the responsibilities of carriers are unfortunately complex. A series of general obligations in articles III and IV(1) are subject to a lengthy list of exceptions in article IV(2) and elsewhere. Such complexity raises difficult questions about the order and burden of proof of a cargo claim. Reference to proof burdens have been made throughout the chapter as appropriate but, at the risk of over-simplifying still contentious issues, it may be useful to summarize the shifting onus in one place. Ordinarily a plaintiff who sues in either contract or tort has to establish both the defendant's default and that it caused the loss proven. Since a sea carriage contract has grown up from ideas of bailment, the cargo claimant does not carry so heavy a burden of proof; he or she simply has to show that the goods were lost or damaged while in the custody of the carrier in order to establish a *prima facie* case. This is usually accomplished by producing a clean bill of lading describing the goods agreed to be carried and providing evidence of the extent of their loss or damage at destination. It then falls to the carrier — not the claimant as in general contract law — to establish the cause of the loss and some reason why he or she is not responsible for that cause, typically by claiming the benefit of an exemption clause in the carriage contract. Onto this platform the *Hague-Visby Rules* impliedly impose a number of special rules about proof: first, and fundamentally, they seem to assert a different order of proof according to whether the claim is for breach of article III(1) regarding seaworthiness of the ship or article III(2) about care of the cargo; second, and subsidiarily, they add special rules of proof regarding deviation, delay, and a number of the exceptions from liability in article IV(2).

Concerning unseaworthiness, once the cargo owner has made out a *prima facie* case of loss, the carrier must come forward with evidence

---

344 Above note 340.
345 *Ibid.*, arts.III–VI. And see *UNCITRAL Model Law, ibid.*, arts.34–36.
346 *Ibid.*

of his or her due diligence to make the ship seaworthy before he or she may claim the benefit of an exculpatory cause in article IV(2). The burden of proving diligence falls on the carrier, and not, as one might assume, on the cargo claimant, because article III(1) is an overriding obligation,[347] and article IV(1) expressly imposes it. The cargo claimant may then respond by attempting to contradict the carrier's evidence of diligence, or to dispute the application of the exception, or perhaps to show the loss was really caused by the carrier's negligence in caring for the cargo under article III(2). When the case is argued as a breach of cargo care under article III(2), the order of proof is somewhat different. Since it is expressed to be subject to article IV it seems that, as soon as the cargo owner has established a *prima facie* case of loss, the carrier may assert an exception from article IV(2). Then the cargo claimant has to dispute the operation of the exception or prove the carrier's negligence toward the cargo.[348] Even so, the carrier will not be allowed to benefit from most of the exceptions in article IV(2) if he or she was negligent,[349] so he or she has to rebut the cargo claimant's evidence or show that the negligence was not the cause of the loss.

When the cargo claim is about repudiation of the carriage contract by breach of a condition precedent on account of the ship's deviation on the voyage, the rules of proof are distorted by the feature that proof of the cause of the loss traditionally is not relevant.[350] The carrier may only escape liability for whatever befalls the cargo if he or she can prove not merely that their injury might have occurred but that it must have befallen them whether the ship deviated or not.[351]

Should a claim of delay be brought in conjunction with an assertion of unseaworthiness or deviation, the carrier's liability will be determined together according to the rules for the primary reason for the cargo owner's loss.[352] If the claim is for delayed delivery alone, it will be subsumed under the carrier's duty of cargo care in article III(2) and, so,

---

347 See *Maxine Footwear Co. v. Canadian Government Merchant Marine Ltd.*, above note 197 and the discussion there. Cf. *Hellenic Dolphin (The)*, above note 217.
348 *Albacora S.R.L. v. Westcott & Laurance Line Ltd.*, above note 230 and the discussion at note 235.
349 *Gamlen Chemical Co. v. Shipping Corp. of India*, above note 238; *Atlantic Consolidated Foods Ltd. v. Doroty (The)*, above note 163.
350 *J. Thorley Ltd. v. Orchis Steamship Co.*, [1907] 1 K.B. 660 (C.A.). But Tetley, above note 156 at 750–51 suggests today all jurisdictions require a causal connection.
351 *Davis v. Garrett* (1830), 6 Bing. 716, 130 E.R. 1456; *James Morrison & Co. v. Shaw, Savill and Albion Co. Ltd.*, [1916] 2 K.B. 783 (C.A.).
352 See above D(5), "Delay in Delivery."

the cargo claimant will have to prove the negligence of the carrier that caused the unreasonable delay.

Whenever the carrier alleges the protection of an exception in article IV(2), he or she must prove it was the cause of the cargo owner's loss.[353] But the operation of some exceptions is also affected by the presence of negligence. Thus, in article IV(2)(a), negligence of the carrier's employees in the navigation or management of the ship can be an excuse from liability for lack of cargo care, if the carrier proves their neglectful acts caused the cargo loss.[354] When fire is the asserted ground of exception pursuant to article IV(2)(b), the carrier must be personally faultless, but which party has to prove the matter has not been settled by the courts. Probably the cargo claimant has to prove the carrier's fault or privity[355] and thus the burden of proof is switched back to the cargo owner, even though much of the evidence of the carrier's conduct is likely within his or her control. By contrast, the carrier's right to assert any other cause of loss in article IV(2)(q) is expressly dependent upon his or her proof of the absence of fault by him- or herself or by his or her employees and agents.

In most disputed claims both parties will bring forth such evidence as they have and the case will be determined on the balance of probabilities in the ordinary way. But when the cause of loss cannot be proved or the evidence is utterly conflicting, the party that bears the burden of proof will fail. In these situations, careful attention to the order of proof — as it arguably switches between the cargo claimant and the carrier — is essential.

As the contents of this chapter show, the *Hague-Visby Rules* are unhelpfully constrained by their aged origins in the *Hague Rules*. Fit as they may have been to the shipping industry of the early twentieth century, the rules are inadequate for seaborne trade at the beginning of the twenty-first century and are out of line with the regulatory regimes of other modes of transport. Most observers take the view that the carriage by sea of packaged and other break bulk goods and merchandise needs a new and uniform set of rules, but international agreement on their terms has so far proved elusive.[356] The *Hamburg Rules*, concluded

---

353 *Antigoni (The)*, [1991] 1 Lloyd's Rep. 209 (C.A.). When there are two concurrent causes of the loss the carrier's proof of the excepted cause is not enough: *Smith, Hogg & Co. v. Black Sea and Baltic General Insurance Co.*, [1940] A.C. 997 (H.L.); and *Torenia (The)*, [1983] 2 Lloyd's Rep. 210.
354 See above D(6)(a), "Errors in Navigation."
355 See above D(6)(b), "Fire."
356 See the discussion of such attempts above in B, "International Rules Governing Bills of Lading."

in 1978 and promoted by developing countries, have not turned out to be acceptable to the major maritime states. The new initiative within UNCITRAL, promoted by the CMI, has advanced to the stage of a United Nations *Draft Instrument on Transport Law*, but there is little confidence that an international agreement will be achieved any time soon. Meanwhile, the *Hague-Visby Rules*, with such judicial adaptation as their statutory status in Canada permits, will have to suffice.

FURTHER READINGS

BAUGHEN, S., *Shipping Law*, 2d ed. (London: Cavendish Publishing, 2001) cc.1–6.

BOYD, S.C, A.S. BURROWS, & D. FOXTON, *Scrutton on Charterparties and Bills of Lading*, 20th ed. (London: Sweet & Maxwell, 1996).

CASHMORE, C., *Parties to a Contract of Carriage* (London: Lloyd's Press, 1990).

DEBATTISTA, C., *The Sale of Goods Carried by Sea*, 2d ed. (London: Butterworths, 1998).

DEWIT, R., *Multimodal Transport* (London: Lloyd's Press, 1995).

GANADO, M. & H. KINDRED, *Marine Cargo Delays* (London: Lloyd's Press, 1990).

GASKELL, N., R. ASARIOTIS, & Y. BAATZ, *Bills of Lading: Law and Contracts* (London: Lloyd's Press, 2000).

KINDRED, H., et al., *The Future of Canadian Carriage of Goods by Water Law* (Halifax, NS: Dalhousie Ocean Studies Program, 1982).

KINDRED, H. & M. BROOKS, *Multimodal Transport Rules* (London: Kluwer Law, 1997).

MANKABADY, S., ed., *The Hamburg Rules on the Carriage of Goods by Sea* (Sythoff: Leiden & Boston 1978).

STURLEY, M.F., *Benedict on Admiralty*, 7th ed. (Newark, NJ: Matthew Bender, looseleaf) vol.2A.

———, *The Legislative History of the Carriage of Goods by Sea Act and the Trávaux Préparatoires of the Hague Rules* (Littleton, CO: F.B. Rothman, 1990).

TETLEY, W., *Marine Cargo Claims*, 3d ed. (Cowansville, QC: Yvon Blais, 1988).

TREITEL, SIR G.H., & F.M.B. REYNOLDS, *Carver on Bills of Lading* (London: Sweet & Maxwell, 2002).

CHAPTER 10

CARRIAGE OF PASSENGERS

A. INTRODUCTION

The movement of people by water has become a huge sector of business in recent years and continues to grow. Canada has shared in this expansion. In addition to the constant flow of traditional ferry traffic, people now engage in a great variety of water sports and leisure activities at sea. Ferries traverse the coasts, lakes, and rivers of Canada: some are within a province or territory, others are between provinces, and several make international connections with the United States. Leisure activities include such pursuits as harbour sightseeing tours, sport fishing trips, adventure holidays on wilderness rivers, sea kayaking and scuba diving excursions, and sail training aboard "tall" ships. Boating is another immensely popular and widespread pastime, ranging from rowboats and jet skis through sailing yachts of various sizes to ocean-going pleasure craft navigated by professional sailors. Most populous of all is the resurgent cruise industry. Cruise ships carrying about 3,000 passengers each and resembling floating holiday resorts already call at Canadian ports. Even bigger vessels are under construction and dozens of orders for luxurious new ships have been placed to meet the surging interest in cruising. The ultimate cruise ship, perhaps, is the grandiosely named The World, which provides floating "permanent residencies" for its apartment owners and lessees.

Until 2001 there was no specific legislative regime in Canada to regulate the carriage of passengers in any of its many forms: only Canadian maritime common law governed. Then the *Marine Liability Act*[1] was passed and, in it, the *Athens Convention Relating to the Carriage of Passengers and their Luggage by Sea, 1974 (PAL 1974)* was implemented.[2] Although *PAL 1974* was concluded in 1974, it was not immediately adopted by Canada because it was thought not to have achieved an equitable balance between carrier and passenger interests regarding the basis of responsibility, and the nature and limitation of liability.[3] After some of these deficiencies were sufficiently amended by a protocol in 1990,[4] *PAL 1974/1990* was included in the Canadian shipping law reforms of the 1990s. Even so, Canada is not a party to the convention but simply enforces its contents as national law.[5] While the *PAL 1974/1990* regime governs passengers, which constitute by far the largest but not the whole class of persons transported by sea, the maritime common law remains in force. Accordingly this chapter contains, first, a brief outline of the common law respecting the carriage of passengers, then an explanation of the regime of *PAL 1974/1990* as it is applied in Canada.

B. CARRIAGE OF PASSENGERS AT COMMON LAW

A shipowner owes a duty implied by common law to exercise reasonable and proper care of passengers.[6] Liability for breach of this duty is incurred by a negligent act or omission of the shipowner, or his or her employees, unlike the strict responsibility imposed on a carrier of goods.[7] However, the shipowner is vicariously responsible for the neg-

---

1   S.C. 2001, c.6.
2   *Ibid.*, Part 4 and Sch.2; *Athens Convention Relating to the Carriage of Passengers and their Luggage by Sea, 1974*, 13 December 1974, 14 I.L.M. 945.
3   Canada, Canadian Transport Commission, *Liability for the Carriage of Passengers by Water in Canada*, (Ottawa: 1980) at 93.
4   A new protocol of further amendments was concluded in the IMO, on 1 November 2002. It will enter into force twelve months after acceptance by ten states, when the whole will be renamed the *Athens Convention Relating to the Carriage of Passengers and their Luggage by Sea, 2002*, 1 November 2002, IMO, LEG/CON 13.NF.2 (2003) [*PAL 2002*].
5   *Marine Liability Act*, above note 1, ss.35, 37, 38, 40, and Sch.2.
6   *MacDonald v. Saint John* (1885), 25 N.B.R. 318 (C.A.), aff'd (1886), 14 S.C.R. 1; *Smitton v. Orient Steam Navigation Co.* (1907), 23 T.L.R. 359 (K.B.).
7   See below note 17.

ligent acts of employees committed in the course of their employment,[8] and they remain personally liable for their faults.[9] "Passengers" are people carried on a ship, usually by agreement, for a fee. Family and friends of a fee-paying passenger, when allowed onto the ship as visitors, are probably also to be classed as passengers. But crew members and other employees of the shipowner, as well as charterers and their families and guests, are not passengers.[10] Individuals who are rescued at sea or become stowaways are not passengers either. Passengers are distinguished as having contracted for carriage against payment of passage money. (The carrier's responsibility for the safety of the crew and other non-passengers on board, as well as liability in the event of their injury is regulated by a different body of law discussed in Chapter 5 under "The Safety of Ships' Crew and Passengers," and in Chapter 12.)

The carrier's duty of care for passengers extends to the reasonable provision of food and accommodation during the voyage,[11] and requires the master and crew to exercise skill in navigating and managing the ship so as to protect the passengers from harm.[12] The duty includes giving due warning of dangers and taking appropriate safety measures:[13]

---

8   *Brown v. Marine Atlantic* (1998), 163 Nfld. & P.E.I.R. 164 (Nfld. S.C.).
9   *Anderson v. Harrison* (1977), 4 B.C.L.R. 320 (S.C.).
10 See *Canada Shipping Act*, R.S.C. 1985, c.S-9, s.2; *Canada Shipping Act, 2001*, S.C. 2001, c.26, s.2; and *R. v. Empire Sandy Inc.* (1987), 62 O.R. (2d) 641 (C.A.). Cruise ships employ a huge range of personnel besides crew members, such as cooks, waiters, bar staff, stewards, porters, laundry workers, cabin attendants, stores people, entertainers, casino staff, physicians, nurses, and their various supervisors and managers. They often also carry hairdressers, masseuses, manicurists, fitness trainers, photographers, art sellers, and gift shop and souvenir sellers, who may be employees of the cruise operator or of an independent concessionnaire. None of these people are passengers. Canadian law takes the broad view that all direct employees of the cruise ship, at least, are members of the crew: see *Metaxas v. Galaxias (No. 2) (The)*, [1989] 1 F.C. 386 (T.D.).
11 *Young v. Fewson* (1837), 8 c. & P. 55, 173 E.R. 396; *Andrews v. Little* (1887), 3 T.L.R. 544 (C.A.). The carrier must also provide reasonable facilities for the passenger's luggage: *Upperton v. Union-Castle Mail Steamship Co.* (1902), 19 T.L.R. 123, aff'd (1903), 19 T.L.R. 687 (C.A.).
12 *Canada Shipping Act*, above note 10, ss.562.1, 338, and 335; *Canada Shipping Act, 2001*, above note 10, s.109. Numerous regulations made under the *Canada Shipping Act* affect the standards of safety and management of the ship and quality of seamanship of the crew, all of which nourish the carrier's duty of care toward passengers: see *Canada v. Saskatchewan Wheat Pool*, [1983] 1 S.C.R. 205. See also, *Rast v. Killoran*, [1995] B.C.J. No.1354 (S.C.) (QL).
13 See *McAdam v. Ross* (1890), 22 N.S.R. 264; *Dominion Fish Co. v. Isbester* (1910), 43 S.C.R. 637; and *Efford v. Bondy*, [1996] B.C.J. No.171 (S.C.) (QL). If through want of navigational skill the ship collides with another vessel causing injury to

indeed, "the risk reasonably to be perceived defines the duty to be obeyed."[14] The carrier's responsibility also extends beyond actual carriage to the provision of reasonably safe embarking and landing places.[15]

Passengers' luggage is regulated differently, according to the degree of control the owner exercises over it.[16] Items kept within a passenger's personal custody are treated the same as the passenger. But personal luggage taken on board under the carrier's custody is carried like other goods. That is to say, the carrier owes an absolute duty to deliver them as they were received subject only to acts of God or of the Queen's enemies, or defective packing by their owner.[17] These duties are subject to contrary agreement by the parties. Carriers may, and frequently do, disclaim their common law duties or limit the extent of their liability, typically by the terms of carriage printed on the tickets issued to passengers. Such clauses are enforceable if passengers are given appropriate notice of them.[18] Furthermore, the passenger's ticket may limit the scope of the contract of carriage so that other services beyond transportation or cruising, such as hairdressing on board or excursions ashore, will be subject to separate agreements with independent operators. In addition, carriers may take advantage of any statute that also happens to affect their common law duties of care toward passengers

---

its passengers, the carrier is liable to those passengers as well as the ones injured on his or her own ship: *Mills v. Armstrong (The Bernina)* (1888), 13 App. Cas. 1 (H.L.).

14 Quoted by Barry J. in *Cole v. Canadian Pacific Ltd.* (1978), 22 N.B.R. (2d) 328 at 334 (Q.B.).

15 *MacDonald v. Saint John*, above note 6; *Brown v. Marine Atlantic*, above note 8; *Anderson v. Harrison*, above note 9; *R. v. Canada Steamship Lines*, [1927] S.C.R. 68.

16 *Smitton v. Orient Steam Navigation Co.*, above note 6.

17 *Ibid.*, and *Jenkyns v. Southampton, etc., Steam Packet Co.* (1919), 35 T.L.R. 264 (K.B.); *Turgel Fur Co. v. Northumberland Ferries Ltd.* (1966), 59 D.L.R. (2d) 1 (N.S.S.C.) See also the discussion at note 71 in Chapter 8, "Carriage of Goods by Charterparty."

18 *Turgel Fur Co.*, *ibid.*; *Cole v. CP Ltd.*, above note 14; *Adler v. Dickson (The Himalaya)*, [1954] 2 Lloyd's Rep. 267 (C.A.); *Craven v. Strand Holidays (Canada) Ltd.* (1982), 40 O.R. (2d) 186 (C.A.); *Interfoto Library Ltd. v. Stiletto Visual Programmes Ltd.*, [1989] 1 Q.B. 433 (C.A.); *Dillon v. Baltic Shipping Co. (The Mikhail Lermontov)*, [1990] 1 Lloyd's L.R. 579 (N.S.W.S.C.); *Trigg v. MI Movers International Transport Services Ltd.* (1991), 4 O.R. (3d) 562 (C.A.); *Trepanier v. Kloster Cruise Ltd.* (1995), 23 O.R. (3d) 398 (Gen. Div.). On this point U.S. law is sharply different. By 46 USC §183 clauses that attempt to limit or exclude the carrier's liability for negligence are ineffective as against public policy. Since most cruise ships that visit Canada are likely to call at U.S. ports also, this rule may have a significant effect on injured passengers' claims.

and their luggage. In particular they may assert a statutory limit to their liability measured by the tonnage of the ship involved[19] (discussed in Chapter 18). They may also demand an apportionment of liability if the claiming passengers negligently contributed to their own injuries[20] (discussed in Chapter 12).

C. CARRIAGE UNDER *PAL 1974/1990*

1) Scope of Application in Canada

PAL 1974/1990 addresses the responsibilities of carriers of passengers and their luggage by sea. It establishes minimum mandatory obligations and sets maximum limits of liability for a breach. (As the laws respecting passengers and regarding luggage are somewhat different, they are discussed separately.) The *Marine Liability Act*[21] implements the convention in Canadian law in an extended way. *PAL 1974/1990* applies to international carriage by sea going ships but, in Canadian law, is made to operate on all kinds of ships in both salt and fresh waters, and regardless whether the voyage is a wholly national or an international trip.[22] Even where the voyage is international, but is not to or from Canada, the convention's rules will still apply if the ship is registered (flagged), or if the carriage contract was made in a state party.[23] The rules of the convention apply to the contracting carrier and any other performing carriers. Thus, tour operators and cruise companies may be subjected to *PAL 1974/1990* whether they are shipowners or not. The contracting carrier remains responsible for the whole carriage, including the acts of performing carriers and their employees.[24] A performing carrier is only responsible for the operations it performs and is not bound by any special obligations, beyond the convention's require-

---

19 See the *Marine Liability Act*, above note 1, Part 3.
20 *Ibid.*, Parts 1 and 2. Passengers are also bound to comply with the directions of the master and crew members given pursuant to the safety provisions of the *Canada Shipping Act, 2001*, above note 10, s.115. Failure to do so may be viewed as contributory negligence to any injury sustained.
21 *Ibid.*, ss.35, 37, and 38. Since the legislation is new there were no reported cases interpreting its application at least up to May 2003.
22 *Ibid.*, ss.36, 37(2), and Sch.2, art.1(3) and (9). *PAL 1974* is also applied in U.K. law but not in the United States, where common law principles still govern, subject to statutory provisions, see, eg., above note 18.
23 *Marine Liability Act, ibid.*, Sch.2, art.2.
24 *Ibid.*, Sch.2, arts.1(1) and 4.

ments, which the carrier may have agreed to, unless it also accepts them.[25] The convention expressly applies to commercial carriage undertaken by public authorities,[26] such as government ferry services.

The carrier's obligations are owed to passengers and their luggage. A passenger includes anyone on a ship under a contract of carriage by water, or who is on board with the carrier's consent because he or she is accompanying vehicles or live animals that are being carried under contract for the carriage of goods.[27] The definition excludes non–fare-paying persons, such as the carrier's employees, including the master, the crew, and all others who are engaged to supply services to passengers on board.[28] It also excludes others who have no contract of carriage, such as charterers and their guests, as well as individuals who are transported privately and not on commercial or public vessels.[29] "Luggage" means anything carried for a passenger, including vehicles, provided it is not transported under a separate contract for the carriage of goods.[30] In some circumstances, the convention makes special provision for "cabin luggage," that is, items of luggage that passengers retain in their custody, whether on their persons, in their cabins, or in their vehicles.[31]

The provisions of the convention are mandatory law. All attempts by the carrier to disclaim responsibility or to lower the limits of liability are null and void. Nor can passengers waive their rights prior to the casualty on which their claims are based.[32]

2) Carrier's Responsibilities

The basis of the carrier's responsibility is demonstrable fault.[33] By Article 3, the carrier is liable for damage caused by an incident in the carriage that results in the death or personal injury of a passenger or the loss or damage of luggage, if the incident was owing to the fault or neg-

---

25 Ibid., Sch.2, art.4(3).
26 Ibid., Sch.2, art.21.
27 Ibid., s.36(2), Sch.2, art.1(4).
28 Ibid., s.37(2)(b). The definition appears to exclude onboard service providers whether employed by the carrier or by an independent concessionnaire.
29 Ibid.
30 Ibid., Sch.2, art.1(5). But luggage does not include live animals, such as, presumably, passengers' pets.
31 Ibid., Sch.2, art.1(6).
32 Ibid., Sch.2, art.18.
33 Actions against the carrier's employees are subject to the same rules of responsibility as suits against the carrier: ibid., Sch.2, art.11.

lect of the carrier or employees in the course of their employment.[34] The burden of proving that the incident that caused the loss or injury occurred in the course of the carriage, as well as the extent of loss, lies on the claimant passenger.[35] This burden is subject to the following important exceptions. If a claim for death or personal injury to a passenger or for loss or damage to cabin luggage arises as a result of shipwreck, collision, stranding, explosion, fire, or a defect in the ship, the fault or neglect of the carrier and employees is presumed.[36] Thus the carrier, in these situations, must disprove his or her own and his or her employee's negligence in order to escape responsibility. The fact that the incident was caused by third parties — such as an explosion or fire set by terrorists or pirates, or a collision created by the manoeuvres of another ship — is not of itself sufficient to exonerate the carrier. The carrier would still seem to have to demonstrate that all reasonable measures were taken to prevent, avoid, or forestall the consequences of foreseeable incidents. In the case of loss or damage to luggage, other than cabin luggage, the carrier is always presumed at fault, unless he or she proves the contrary.[37]

In the event of death and personal injury caused by incidents other than the enumerated ones, the passenger claimant has to prove the carrier's own or vicarious fault affirmatively.[38] Thus accidents to passengers claimed to have been caused by the misuse or careless use of the ship's equipment by the crew, or the failure to give appropriate warning by the master in the event of potentially dangerous manoeuvres, would have to be proved by the claimants. Similarly, the fault of employees on the ship, not being crew members, who cause the ill health or physical injury of a passenger by the way they provide a service for which they are employed — such as hair dressing, swimming instruction, or aerobic exercise on a cruise ship — must also be established by the claimant.

The distinction in the allocation of the burden of proof of fault is, in a manner of speaking, between defects or events involving the ship as a whole and all those aboard, and other incidents in the management of the ship in which only some passengers face the risk of harm. The

---

34 The *2002 Protocol to the Athens Convention*, above note 4, would alter the basis of the carrier's responsibility under the *Marine Liability Act*, ibid., Sch.2, art.3 to strict liability in shipping related incidents.
35 *Marine Liability Act*, above note 1, Sch.2, art.3(2).
36 Ibid., Sch.2, art.3(3).
37 Ibid.
38 Ibid.

line dividing shipping incidents from other faults may not be entirely clear, however. If the claimant passenger neglected safety procedures and warnings, or behaved foolishly, the carrier will be relieved of liability to the extent that he or she can prove the contributory negligence of the passenger.[39] In any event, whoever has the burden of proof of fault, the passenger always has to prove the extent of his or her injuries. The standards of responsibility expressed in PAL 1974/1990 are the only grounds on which claims for the death or injury of passengers, or the loss or damage of luggage, may be brought since the convention expressly prohibits any other actions.[40] However, other kinds of claims, for instance pecuniary loss to passengers, such as might arise if the ship deviates on the voyage or is delayed in arriving at its destination on schedule, appear to be outside the convention and are, therefore, permissible if suitable grounds exist at common law.

3) Extent of Carrier's Liability

Limiting the carrier's liability for death or personal injury is a contentious matter,[41] yet it is a common practice in international conventions for the transportation of passengers in all modes. Even so, contention continues about the maximum amount of liability that is appropriate. Canada did not adopt PAL 1974 in its original form in part because it was thought the limits of liability set in 1974 were too low. While they were increased by the 1990 protocol and are now part of Canadian law, the protocol concluded in 2002, when it comes into force,[42] will raise the limits of liability considerably higher still.[43]

---

39 Ibid., Sch.2, art.6. See also *Marine Liability Act*, ibid., Part 2, discussed in Chapter 12, "Maritime Personal Injury and Death."
40 Ibid., Sch.2, art.14.
41 This is one reason why the United States is not a party to PAL 1974. However, U.S. law does allow overall limitation by ship's tonnage and U.S. courts may recognize the limits of liability of PAL 1974 if they are properly incorporated or statutorily applicable to the passenger's contract and the voyage does not touch any U.S. port: *Mills v. Renaissance Cruises Inc.*, 1993 A.M.C. 131 (N.D. Cal. 1992).
42 Above note 4.
43 An expedited method of amending the limits of liability was added by the *Protocol to the Athens Convention Relating to the Carriage of Passengers and their Luggage by Sea*, 29 March 1990, U.K.T.S. 1989 No.43. These provisions, plus a power by order in council to adopt into Canadian law any changes made pursuant to them, have been enacted by the *Marine Liability Act*, above note 1, s.40 and Sch.2, Part 2.

Table 10.1 *PAL 1974/1990*

Type of Claim	Limit of Liability in SDR[44]	Can$ approx.
Personal Injury	175,000	350,000
Cabin Luggage	1,800	3,600
Vehicle	10,000	20,000
– deductible	300	600
Other Luggage	2,700	5,400
– deductible	135	270 *

In mid–2003 the limits of liability of the carrier for the death or injury of a passenger was 175,000 SDR. (See Table 10.1.) This limit may be set higher by national legislation[45] but has not been in Canada. As passenger vessels, such as cruise ships, become more popular and larger, the implications of this limit grow ever greater. In the event of a catastrophic casualty, a vessel carrying 1,000 passengers faces a risk of 175 million SDR, or approximately Can$350 million. The newest cruise ships, which may accommodate 3,000 voyagers, could incur liability in excess of 500 million SDR, or Can$1 billion. To these huge sums there must be added the carrier's liability for the costs of repatriation of passengers who are unhurt, as well as for the death or injury of any of the crew and staff, who, on a large cruise ship, could number 1,000 or more persons. The limits of liability for loss or damage to luggage are modest by comparison and are divided into three classes. The carrier's maximum liability for cabin luggage per passenger is 1,800 SDR; for an accompanying vehicle and any luggage in it, it is 10,000 SDR; and for all other baggage of the passenger it is 2,700 SDR.[46] (See Table 10.1.) Compensable loss of luggage includes not only physical damage or destruction but also pecuniary loss resulting from the carrier's failure or unreasonable delay in redelivering the passenger's lug-

---

44   *Marine Liability Act*, ibid., Sch.2, arts.7(1) and 9. The unit of account known as SDR, or special drawing right as defined by the International Monetary Fund, reflects the daily average value of a basket of leading national currencies as they fluctuate on the international money markets: 1 SDR was worth approximately Can$2 at time of writing.
45   *Ibid.*, Sch.2, art.7(2).
46   *Ibid.*, Sch.2, art.8. The carrier is allowed to agree with the passenger to charge a deductible of up to 300 SDR for a vehicle and up to 135 SDR for all other luggage: *ibid.*, Sch.2, art.8(4).
47   *Ibid.*, Sch.2, art.1(7). Delay caused by strikes, however, is excusable. There is no equivalent right to compensation for delay in delivering the passenger to destination because, under *PAL 1974/1990*, the carrier is only liable for the death or injury of a passenger: see above note 34.

gage.[47] However, loss of valuables, such as money, negotiable securities, gold, silverware, jewellery, ornaments, and works of art is not compensable unless the items were deposited with the carrier for safekeeping.[48] These limits are the maximum amounts in aggregate that a passenger may recover for personal injury or loss of luggage, even if separate claims are successfully pursued against the contracting carrier, the performing carrier, and their employees.[49] However, the passenger and the carrier may agree in writing to higher limits of liability,[50] but such an agreement will not affect the performing carrier unless he or she also expressly accepts it in writing.[51]

The only other way that the claimant passenger can recover full compensation in excess of the fixed limits of liability is to prove that the carrier's personal wrongdoing[52] was so culpable that he or she is disentitled to limit liability. But overreaching the statutory limits is difficult: the carrier must be shown to have acted, or failed to act, with intent to cause injury or damage, or recklessly and with knowledge that injury or damage would probably result.[53] In addition to these rules in PAL 1974/1990 about the limits of liability, the carrier may also be entitled to apply the overall limits of liability measured by the tonnage of the ship. Part 3 of the *Marine Liability Act* enacts the international *Convention on Limitation of Liability for Maritime Claims, 1976* (LLMC 1976),[54] which applies to all claims for loss of life or personal injury, and for loss or damage to property.[55] For the time being at least, the provisions of LLMC 1976 largely match PAL 1974/1990. The limit of liability for personal injuries is 175,000 SDR,[56] or Can$350,000 per

---

48 *Marine Liability Act*, ibid., Sch.2, art.5.
49 Ibid., Sch.2, art.12.
50 Ibid., Sch.2, art.10.
51 Ibid., Sch.2, art.4(3).
52 Intentionally injurious or reckless acts by crew members do not defeat the carrier's right to limit liability, but they would destroy their own protection from full liability if personally sued: see *R.G. Mayer (T/A Granville Coaches) v. P & O Ferries Ltd. (The Lion)*, [1990] 2 Lloyd's L.R. 144 (Q.B.); and *Marine Liability Act*, ibid., Sch.2, art.13(2).
53 *Marine Liability Act*, ibid., Sch.2, art.13(1).
54 19 November 1976, 1456 U.N.T.S. 221; ibid., Part 3 and Sch.1, discussed in Chapter 18, "Limitation of Liability for Maritime Claims."
55 *Marine Liability Act*, ibid., Sch.1, art.2(1).
56 Ibid., Sch.1, art.7. For a ship that is not required to hold a Canadian marine certificate under the *Canada Shipping Act*, above note 10, Part 4 (Safety) authorizing its maximum number of passengers, the limit of liability is the greater of 2m SDR or 175,000 SDR times the number of passengers actually on board: above note 1, Part 3, s.29(1).

person, and this ceiling on compensation may only be pierced by the personal wanton act or omission of the carrier.[57]

There are, however, two small but potentially significant differences in the application of the two regimes. While the carrier's maximum liability under *PAL 1974/1990* is calculated by multiplying 175,000 SDR by the number of passengers on board,[58] the ceiling on liability under *LLMC 1976* is 175,000 SDR times the number of passengers the ship is authorized to carry;[59] hence, when a less than full load of passengers is carried, the carrier's aggregate limit of liability will be greater under *LLMC 1976* than under *PAL 1974/1990*. Indeed the carrier could be liable to pay in excess of 175,000 SDR per injured passenger. In addition, under *PAL 1974/1990*, the liability limit applies throughout the carriage;[60] but, under *LLMC 1976*, it operates on each "distinct occasion" that a casualty occurs during the voyage.[61] Thus, passengers who suffer multiple injuries as the result of two or more incidents during carriage are entitled, under *LLMC 1976*, to benefit from compensation that is limited separately for each accident, not cumulatively as it would be under *PAL 1974/1990*. Once again, then, liability under *LLMC 1976* could exceed that payable under *PAL 1974/1990*. Absent any cases on these new provisions in Canadian law, it is uncertain how these two regimes limiting liability will be applied on the, probably infrequent, occasions when their operation conflicts.

Given the huge aggregate liability that a large ferry or cruise ship disaster may incur, it is not surprising that concern has arisen over the ability of a carrier to pay the required compensation, limited or not. In 2002 the International Maritime Organisation considered how to require financial security of carriers. The resulting 2002 protocol adds a new Article 4 to the convention that will, when in force,[62] require carriers to purchase sufficient insurance coverage and will grant claimants a direct right of action against the liability insurers. Meanwhile, Canada has enacted enabling power to make regulations in respect of compulsory insurance or other proof of financial security by carriers.[63]

---

57 *Marine Liability Act*, ibid., Sch.1, art.4.
58 Ibid., Sch.2, arts.7 and 11.
59 Ibid., Sch.1, art.7.
60 Ibid., Sch.2, art.7.
61 Ibid., Sch.1, art.7.
62 Above note 4.
63 *Marine Liability Act*, above note 1, s.39.

4) Claims and Actions

When luggage is lost or damaged, the passenger is expected to give written notice of a claim to the carrier. If the damage is apparent, the notice should be given for cabin luggage at the time of disembarking, and for other luggage at the time it is redelivered. If the damage is not apparent, the claimant has fifteen days in which to provide the notice. If the claimant fails to give timely notice he or she is deemed to have received his or her luggage undamaged.[64] However, such a failure on the part of the claimant does not defeat his or her right of action: it simply imposes the burden of proof on him or her to rebut the presumption and prove that the luggage was, in fact, damaged or lost. Any legal suit the claimant brings, whether for personal injury or luggage loss, must be commenced within two years, measured from the date of disembarkation, or it will be time-barred.[65] The claimant may also select his or her preferred forum from a choice of five locations: the principal place of the carrier's business; the departure port; the destination port; in the state where the claimant has a permanent residence; or where the contract was concluded, if the carrier has a place of business there.[66] The claimant has the right to make this choice of forum regardless whether the contract of carriage names some other place, but after the injury or loss has been incurred, the carrier and the passenger are free to agree on any curial jurisdiction or arbitration.[67]

D. PROSPECTIVE DEVELOPMENTS

The upsurge of interest in cruising and the growth in the size of passenger vessels are both putting pressure on the liability regime of *PAL 1974/1990*. The catastrophic ferry accidents to The Herald of Free Enterprise in 1987, when 188 people died, and The Estonia in 1994, when 852 people were killed, have already affected the increase in the limit of liability per passenger to 175,000 SDR by the protocol of 1990. The new protocol of 2002, when it comes into force,[68] will raise the ceiling sharply in two tiers. (See Table 10.2.) The new limit of liability will be 250,000 SDR but, for injury resulting from shipping incidents — now

---

64 *Ibid.*, Sch.2, art.15.
65 *Ibid.*, Sch.2, art.16.
66 *Ibid.*, Sch.2, art.17(1).
67 *Ibid.*, Sch.2, art.17(2).
68 Above note 4.

to be described as acts of war, hostilities, civil war, insurrection, natural phenomena of an exceptional inevitable and irresistible character, or acts or omissions done with intent to cause the incident by a third party[69] — the carrier will be presumed to be liable for up to 400,000 SDR, unless he or she proves the loss occurred without his or her fault or neglect. Such high limits of liability will create tensions within both the shipowning industry and the insurance community.

Table 10.2 PAL 2002

Type of Claim	Limit of Liability in SDR[70]	Can$ approx.
Personal Injury from		
– shipping incidents	400,000	800,000
– other incidents	250,000	500,000
Cabin Luggage	2,250	4,500
Vehicle	12,700	25,400
– deductible by agreement	330	660
Other Luggage	3,375	6,750
– deductible by agreement	149	298

Owners of passenger vessels will be concerned about the consequences of the new increases in liability under *PAL 2002* for their right to limit their liability by the tonnage of their vessels under *LLMC 1976*. Under *PAL 2002*, shipowners will become liable up to 250,000 SDR, or possibly 400,000 SDR, times the number of passengers on board, while, under *LLMC 1976*, they are entitled to limit their liability to 175,000 SDR times the number of passengers authorized to be carried. Hence, a fully loaded ferry or cruise ship will risk liability up to 143 per cent, or even 228 per cent, greater than the limit set by *LLMC 1976*. Unless the limit of *LLMC 1976* is also moved upward to complement the changes wrought by *PAL 2002*, shipowners will undoubtedly seek ways to take advantage of the lower limit of liability under *LLMC 1976* in this apparent conflict of regimes. One argument might focus on the shipowner's right to constitute a fund in court equal to the limit of liability applicable to the ship under *LLMC 1976*.[71] When such a fund is constituted, any passenger who makes a claim against it would become barred from exercising any right against any other assets of the shipowner, such as the ship itself. In this way, perhaps, shipowners

---

69 Cf. the existing description of shipping incidents, above note 36.
70 *Marine Liability Act*, above note 1, Sch.2, arts.7(1) and 9.
71 *Ibid.*, Sch.1, art.11.

may try to control their liability toward passenger claimants according to the lower established practices of *LLMC 1976*.

Insurers are already voicing concerns about the insurability of large passenger ships, even before the new provisions for compulsory insurance coverage under the *PAL 2002* come into force. P&I club managers, in particular, point out that the aggregate liability being risked by a large ferry or cruise ship operator under the current regime (175,000 SDR per passenger) far outstrips the limit of liability of ships of like tonnage for all other sorts of claims under *LLMC 1976*. In short, the mutuality of risks, which lies at the heart of P&I club indemnity, is shattered by the much greater potential liability of passenger ship operators. Non-passenger shipowners are not disposed to pay passenger claims against ferry and cruise ship owners, who are fellow members of the P&I club, that are disproportionately greater than the risks of their own shipping activities. Should owners of large passenger ships, as a consequence, become excluded from the existing P&I clubs, they would face extraordinarily high expenses to constitute a new mutual club among themselves, or they might find their ships uninsurable, unless they can develop a way to extract a levy from their customers.[72] Either way, the impact on costs or services to cruise passengers, in particular, could be substantial.

The threat of terrorist activity against shipping is another unlooked for development that has to be faced. Large passenger vessels are obviously an easy target of terrorism. A tragic precedent was set in 1985 when The *Achille Lauro*, carrying 400 passengers on a cruise in the Mediterranean, was hijacked by armed terrorists, who killed an elderly and disabled American and pushed him overboard. The incident led to the conclusion of the *Convention for the Suppression of Unlawful Acts against the Safety of Maritime Navigation, 1988*,[73] which established international criminal offences against ships and imposes national responsibilities for their prosecution.

More recently, the International Maritime Organisation (IMO) has responded to the renewed worldwide threats of terrorism with several new initiatives to enhance the security of ships. Most relevant to the

---

72 Akin to the oil pollution funds, constituted by both shipowners and cargo owners, as discussed in C in Chapter 17, "Marine Pollution: The International Liability and Compensation Regime."

73 10 March 1988, 27 I.L.M. 668 [*SUA 1988*]. This convention has come into force for seventy-three states representing 75 per cent by tonnage of all merchant shipping and is implemented by Canada in the *Criminal Code*, R.S.C. 1985, c.C-46, ss.7(2.1)–(2.2) and 78.1.

carriage of passengers is the possible creation of additional offences concerning terrorism against ships[74] and the conclusion in December 2002 of the *International Ship and Port Facility Security Code*[75] as a further amendment of the *International Convention for the Safety of Life at Sea (SOLAS 1974)*.[76] These measures will require, for example, security plans and security officers for ships, personal background checks and physical screening of passengers, and restrictions on access by visitors to cruise ships in port, not unlike the controls already familiar to air travellers. Canada has expressed the determination to enforce these new security measures by announced increases in the surveillance of ships and passengers by greater numbers of immigration officers, marine screening officers and security inspectors, and RCMP officers. Many of these measures are already in place by reason of the *Marine Transportation Security Act*[77] and its cruise ship security regulations.[78] The Act also grants the Minister of Transport enabling powers to prescribe further security regulations mandated by the IMO.

Apart from the threat of politically motivated terrorist acts, passenger ships are always at risk from ordinary criminal activity. These incidents may be individualized attacks against particular persons or their property, or major criminal strikes against the ship as a whole and all those on board. For instance, in 1990 more than 150 lives were lost when criminals deliberately set fire to the cruise ship Scandinavian Star in the Baltic Sea. Responsibility for such criminal activity is imposed in Canada by the public law controls of the *Criminal Code* and Part 4 of the *Canada Shipping Act, 2001*.[79] It is not the target of the private law civil liability provisions of *PAL 1974/1990*. However, should mass crimes against passengers occur, whether of a terrorist character or not, ship operators are likely to face very large claims for compensation. If the criminal activity were foreseeable and preventable by reasonable means, especially if the means form part of legislated security standards for ships, courts may in future hold shipowners and operators liable for their neglect of security precautions, just as they are responsible under *PAL 1974/1990* for any other fault in protecting against more traditional maritime risks, when transporting passengers.

---

74 Under discussion in 2003 in the Legal Committee of the International Maritime Organisation.
75 Discussed in D(5) of Chapter 5, "Maritime Security."
76 Discussed in B(3) in Chapter 5, "Outline of *SOLAS 1974*."
77 S.C. 1994, c.40 as am. by S.C. 2001, c.29, ss.56–59.
78 SOR/97-270.
79 Discussed in Chapter 5, "The Safety Management of Ships."

FURTHER READINGS

HILL, C., *Maritime Law*, 5th ed. (London: Lloyd's Press, 1998) c.12.

SCHOENBAUM, T.J., *Admiralty and Maritime Law*, 3d ed. (St. Paul, MN: West, 2001) 181–90.

CHAPTER 11

MARITIME COLLISIONS

A. INTRODUCTION

Reported shipping incidents have decreased by over 50 per cent in the last ten years.[1] Yet despite the advances in marine technology, sophisticated electronic, satellite, and other navigational aids, as well as new training methods for those operating vessels, maritime accidents generally — and marine collisions specifically — continue to feature prominently in annual maritime casualty statistics. Although collisions rarely represent a major sector of such statistics,[2] when they do occur they always involve significant losses. This is not surprising. When two large steel structures come into contact, even at low speeds, severe damage to the vessels involved and other consequential losses are generally the result. They often include death and personal injury, marine pollution, fire, explosion, cargo loss, and damage. As a result, over its long history, maritime law has developed a very complex and highly specialized sector related specifically to marine collision.[3] A collision is

---

1 Canada, Transportation Safety Board, *Annual Report to Parliament 2000–2001* (Ottawa: Transport Canada) c.6 [TSB Report].
2 In 2000, 90 per cent of all marine accidents in Canada involved ships and included grounding, striking, collision, fire, and sinking. Less than 4 per cent (14 out of 458 in 2001) involved collisions. TSB Report, above note 1.
3 E. Gold, "Foreword" in N.J. Healy & J.C. Sweeney, *The Law of Marine Collision* (Centreville, MD: Cornell Maritime Press, 1998) at xix.

495

defined as "the violent encounter of a moving body with another."[4] Marine collisions do not necessarily involve contact between two moving vessels. There may also be contact between a moving vessel and a stationary object, such as an anchored or berthed vessel, or an object that is not afloat at all, such as a bridge, wharf, crane, offshore structure, or even equipment protruding from another vessel.[5]

The origins of maritime collision law are obscure and probably predate Roman law, which mentions a number of cases. However, at that time there were no specific navigational rules, other than maritime custom, and the jurisprudence was more concerned with fault and liability for loss and damage. This approach continued into the Middle Ages and beyond as maritime law became generally more established. However, maritime law was still mainly preoccupied with fault and damage liability, and the first statutory rules or regulations concerning navigation would not appear until 1840, when the Trinity House Navigational Rules were established.[6] This was followed by the first U.K. statute that embodied navigational rules in 1846, which was itself followed by further statutory rules in 1851, 1854, and 1858.[7] A complete new set of regulations, applicable also to all British colonies, including Canada, was promulgated by the British Board of Trade in 1863;[8] by 1868 some thirty-three maritime states had indicated to the U.K. that they would be bound by such rules even in international waters.

The first diplomatic conference on navigational rules, which was convened by the U.S. president in Washington in 1889, resulted in the first comprehensive set of international navigational regulations that became effective in 1897.[9] Subsequent international conferences in Brussels, Belgium, in 1910 and in London, England, in 1948 and 1960 made a series of further changes to what had by that time become the international collision regulations. During colonial times and beyond, Canada had fully accepted these rules. This means that for well over a century a widely accepted set of international navigational rules for the

---

4   Oxford English Dictionary, 1991, s.v. "collision."
5   Strictly speaking a collision between a moving vessel and a stationary object is termed an "allision." However, as this term is rarely used, the word "collision" is employed throughout this chapter in describing contacts between vessels as well as between vessels and other objects.
6   See D.R. Owen, "The Origins and Development of Marine Collision Law" (1977) 51 Tul. L.Rev. 759 for an exhaustive examination of the history of maritime collision law.
7   *Ibid.* at 784.
8   *Merchant Shipping Act Amendment Act, 1862* (U.K.), 25 & 26 Vict., c.63, Table C.
9   Healy & Sweeney, above note 3 at 7.

conduct of vessels at sea has been in existence.[10] These rules are not designed for the finding of liability, fault, or damages for insurance purposes. (The breach of the rules, nevertheless, leads in most cases to such a finding as is discussed later in this chapter.[11])

B. COLLISION REGULATIONS IN 1972

The navigational rules currently in use throughout the world are the result of a major revision undertaken by the International Maritime Organisation in 1972 that resulted in the *Convention on the International Regulations for Preventing Collisions at Sea, 1972 (COLREGS 1972)*.[12] These regulations have been accepted by almost all states and are applicable "to all vessels upon the high seas and in all waters connected therewith."[13] Under these regulations, states are permitted to make specific rules for harbours, rivers, lakes, roadsteads, and inland waterways connected to the high seas. However, such rules should comply as closely as possible with the main rules.[14] Canada accepted *COLREGS 1972* in 1975, enacting regulations accordingly under the *Canada Shipping Act*;[15] these regulations implement *COLREGS 1972* and apply to all Canadian vessels anywhere in the world and to any vessel within the territorial and internal waters of Canada, but include certain modifications that accommodate inland waters navigation as well as seasonal requirements.

COLREGS 1972 are divided into five parts and have four attached annexes. Part A (rules 1–3) deals with general principles; Part B (rules 4–19) contains the steering and sailing rules of special relevance in collision matters; Part C (rules 20–31) governs the lights and shapes that ships must show for identification purposes; Part D (rules 32–37) sets

---

10 For a detailed examination of the history of the collision regulations, see one of the leading texts on the area: S. Gault, ed., *Marsden on Collisions at Sea*, 12th ed. (London: Sweet & Maxwell, 1998) [*Marsden*].
11 See also Chapter 18, "Limitation of Liability for Maritime Claims."
12 20 October 1972, 1050 U.N.T.S. 16 (entered into force 15 July 1977, am. 1981, 1987, 1989, and 1993). See also Institute of Maritime Law, *The Ratification of Maritime Conventions*, 4 vols., Updated looseleaf service. (London: Lloyd's Press, 1991–2003) vol.1.3.250.
13 *COLREGS 1972*, ibid., r.1(a).
14 *Ibid.*, r.1(b).
15 *Canada Shipping Act*, R.S.C. 1985, c.S-9, s.562(11); *Canada Shipping Act, 2001*, S.C. 2001, c.26, Sch.1; *Collision Regulations*, C.R.C., c.1416, s.3. The Regulations entered into force in Canada on 15 July 1977. See R.M. Fernandes, *Shipping and Admiralty Law* (Toronto: Carswell, 1995) at 3-5.

out the required sound and light signals; and Part E (rule 38) contains information on exempted vessels. Annex I deals with the positioning and technical details of lights and shapes; Annex II deals with additional signals for fishing vessels fishing in close proximity; Annex III provides technical details of sound signal appliances; and Annex IV lists the various distress signals. While it is not appropriate to provide great detail on the actual content of the *COLREGS 1972* in this book,[16] some illustrations of operational action or inaction that lead to collision may be helpful. It should be noted that, while Canada has incorporated *COLREGS 1972* into the existing Canadian *Collision Regulations*, some individual rules have been modified for Canadian waters.[17] There are also additional Canadian provisions not found in the international convention.

1) *COLREGS 1972* Part A: General Principles (Rules 1–3)

a) Rule 1: Application

Rule 1 of *COLREGS 1972* states that the regulations apply to "all vessels upon the high seas and in all waters connected therewith navigable by seagoing vessels." "High seas" is defined in the *United Nations Convention on the Law of the Sea, 1982 (UNCLOS)*,[18] and "all waters connected therewith navigable by seagoing vessels"[19] would include all other waters, such as rivers, straits, canals, lakes, bays, gulfs, territorial seas, and exclusive economic zones that are not considered to be part of the high seas, but are connected to the high seas and are navigable by seagoing vessels.[20] The only exception relates to waters that have been covered by special national regulations. Rule 1 sets out the right of states to make local and inland waters rules, the right of states to make specific rules for warships, vessels sailing in convoy, or fishing vessels fishing as a fleet, and the authority given to the International

---

16 For details on the regulations see, e.g., A.N. Cockcroft & J.N.F. Lameijer, *A Guide to the Collision Avoidance Rules*, 3d ed. (London: Stanford Maritime, 1982).
17 Canadian *Collision Regulations*, above note 15, as am. by S.O.R./83-202; S.O.R./90-702. See Fernandes, *Shipping and Admiralty Law*, above note 15 at 3–6.
18 10 December 1982, 1833 U.N.T.S. 3 (entered into force on 16 November 1994), at art.86. See also *Ratification of Maritime Conventions*, above note 12 vol.I.1.170. Canada has not yet ratified this convention. However, the Canadian government has stated on a number of occasions that it will ratify the convention in due course. Rule 1(f) and (g) as am. by S.O.R./83-202, s.3; S.O.R./90-702, ss.4 and 5 contain Canadian modifications relating to lights and sound-signalling equipment.
19 For a definition of "seagoing vessel" see *Salt Union (The) v. Wood*, [1893] 1 Q.B. 370.
20 See, e.g., *Faethon (The)*, [1987] 1 Lloyd's L.R. 538; and *Rankin v. De Coster*, [1975] 2 Lloyd's L.R. 84.

Maritime Organisation[21] to establish vessel traffic separation schemes. However, any rules that are made by states are required to comply as closely as possible to the relevant rule under COLREGS 1972.[22]

b) Rule 2: Responsibility

COLREGS 1972 rule 2 specifically disallows any exoneration of mariners from negligence for any action taken or not taken under the regulations. As a result, liability is always present when negligence occurs. Such liability depends upon the action or inaction measured against what is required by the standard of care of the ordinary seaman. This standard is difficult to define, as it is dependent upon the particular circumstances and facts of each case.[23] For example, following the COLREGS 1972 but in defiance of good seamanship in special circumstances will not result in exoneration. In other words, while the COLREGS 1972 will create claims, they cannot be used as a defence for a negligent act. There is, obviously, a large number of court decisions on this but, in summary, the law states:[24]

- A vessel underway would be expected to keep clear of an anchored vessel as a matter of good seamanship; however, a vessel underway but stopped cannot rely on other vessels keeping clear, unless that vessel is "not under command" within the meaning of the regulations and is displaying the appropriate signals.[25]
- When a vessel anchors, it must do so without endangering other vessels that may be navigating in close proximity or anchored close by; sufficient cable must be put out and a second anchor used if necessary.[26]
- In extremely restricted visibility, a vessel without operational radar may not be justified in being underway at all and may have to anchor to await repairs or clearing conditions.[27]

---

21 See Chapter 2, "The Shipping Industry: An Overview."
22 Healy & Sweeney, above note 3 at 73–74; *Marsden*, above note 10 at 117–22. Fernandes, above note 15 at 3-5 and 3-6.
23 See, e.g., *Navios Enterprise (The) v. Puritan (The)*, [1998] 2 Lloyd's L.R. 16 at 24 [*The Navios Enterprise*].
24 See some of the major treatises on collision law, i.e., Healy & Sweeney, above note 3; *Marsden*, above note 10; and H.M.C. Holdert & F.J. Buzek, *Collision Cases — Judgements and Diagrams* (London: Lloyd's Press, 1984). See also Fernandes, above note 15 at 3-7.
25 Cockcroft & Lameijer, above note 16 at 22.
26 *Northampton (The)* (1853), 1 Ecc. & Adm. 152 at 160; *Persian (The)*, 181 F. 439 (2d Cir. 1910); Healy & Sweeney, above note 3 at 76; *Marsden*, above note 10 at 125–30.
27 Cockcroft & Lameijer, above note 16 at 22.

- When two vessels are approaching one another near a difficult bend in a tidal river, the vessel having the tide against it is under a duty to wait and let the other vessel pass.[28]
- The effects of shallow water must always be taken into account; this will affect the draught and trim, may cause vessels to "squat" and also cause changing interaction between passing vessels.[29]
- If conditions or special circumstances arise that are either not covered by the COLREGS 1972 or where a departure from the rules is necessary, vessels must exercise extreme caution in taking whatever action is necessary to avoid collision.[30]
- Even though mariners must proceed on the general assumption that other vessels will observe the rules, there may be circumstances where a departure from the rules is not only necessary but required; however, under such circumstances, any departure from the rules imposes a heavy burden of proof:
  – that the circumstances were exceptional or the departure was necessary in order to avoid an immediate danger; and,
  – that the actions undertaken to avoid the danger were reasonable under the prevailing circumstances.[31]

c) **Rule 3: Definitions**

Rule 3 of the COLREGS 1972 contains the most important definitions in the regulations, such as for vessel; power-driven vessel; sailing vessel; fishing vessel; seaplane; vessel not under command; vessel restricted in the ability to manoeuvre; vessel constrained by draught, underway, length and breadth; vessels in sight of one another; and restricted visibility. Each of these expressions has a practical application as well as a legal interpretation.[32]

---

28 *Talabot (The)* (1890), 15 P.D. 194; *Toluca (The)*, [1981] 2 Lloyd's L.R. 548, aff'd [1984] 1 Lloyd's L.R. 131 (C.A.).
29 Healy & Sweeney, above note 3 at 76; Cockcroft & Lameijer, above note 16 at 23.
30 Healy & Sweeney, ibid. at 77.
31 Marsden, above note 10 at 139–40; *Kitano Maru (S.S.) v. S.S. Otranto*, [1931] A.C. 194; *Agra (The) and Elizabeth Jenkins* (1867), L.R. 1 P.C. 501; *Concordia (The)* (1866), L.R. 1 A. & E. 93; *Mauch Chunk (The)*, 154 F. 182 (2d Cir. 1907); *Zim Israel Nav. Co. v. American Press (The)*, 222 F. Supp. 947, 1964 A.M.C. 1008 (D.C.N.Y. 1963), aff'd 336 F.2d 150, 1964 A.M.C. 2537 (2d Cir. 1964); *Imo (The) v. General Transatlantic Co.*, [1920] 2 W.W.R. 428, 51 D.L.R. 403 (P.C.); *Crown Steamship Co. v. Lady of Gaspe (The)* (1914), 17 Ex. C.R. 191; *Lionel (The) v. Manchester Merchant (The)*, [1970] S.C.R. 538.
32 See Fernandes, above note 15 at 3–12.

2) *COLREGS 1972* Part B: Steering and Sailing (Rules 4–19)

Mariners are expected to have very specific knowledge of the regulations. However, any breach of these regulations will always provide *prima facie* evidence of negligence that has to be answered. This is especially so in cases where a breach of the steering and sailing rules appears to have occurred. The part of the regulations covering the steering and sailing rules is divided into three sections: rules 4–10, rules 11–18, and rule 19.

a) Rule 4: Application

Rule 4 of the *COLREGS 1972* simply states that Section I covers the "Conduct of Vessels in any Condition of Visibility." This section, consisting of rules 4–10, is of a general nature, applying to navigation in all conditions of visibility. The regulations cover speed, proper use of radar, avoidance of a succession of small alterations, and the necessity to check the effectiveness of avoiding action.

b) Rule 5: Look-out

Many collisions occur because of the lack of a proper look-out.[33] Even the lack of warning of an impending collision does not relieve the other vessel from having a proper look-out.[34] This has become especially problematic with modern vessels operated by smaller crews. Nevertheless, maritime law does not make allowances for this and has interpreted a proper look-out to include the following:

- visual look-out,
- aural look-out, and
- the intelligent interpretation of data received from such electronic navigational aids as radar or shore-based radar stations.

---

33 *Marsden*, above note 10 at 152–54; Healy & Sweeney, above note 3 at 92–104; *Kwok v. British Columbia Ferry Corp.* (1987), 20 B.C.L.R. (2d) 318; see also *Conrad v. Snair* (1994), 135 N.S.R. (2d) 19; *Brown v. Harvey* (1992), 37 A.C.W.S. 5 (B.C.S.C.); *Stein v. Kathy K (The)*, [1976] 2 S.C.R. 802; *Kenney v. Cape York (The)* (1989), 25 F.T.R. 139; *Robertson v. Maple Prince (The)*, [1955] Ex. C.R. 221; *Canada Steamship Lines v. Waldemar Peter (The)*, [1957] Ex. C.R. 254; *El Progreso v. Ralph Misener (The)* (1986), 6 F.T.R. 46; *Sociedad Transoceanica Canopus S.A. v. Canada (Nat. Harbours Board)*, [1968] 2 Ex. C.R. 330; *Bentley v. MacDonald* (1977), 27 N.S.R. (2d) 152 (T.D.); *Bischler v. Stoparyk* (1979), 9 Alta. L.R. (2d) 1 (T.D.); and *Chester Sailing Society v. Flinn* (1981), 44 N.S.R. (2d) 105. See also Fernandes, above note 15 at 3-14ff for additional cases.

34 *Egmont Towing & Sorting Ltd. v. Telendos (The)* (1982), 43 N.R. 147.

In general, where neither vessel involved in a collision kept a proper radar look-out, both vessels have been held equally at fault.[35] It has also been made quite clear that simply monitoring or observing a radar screen, without proper plotting, is not a proper look-out.[36] In fact, there has been a number of so-called "radar-assisted collisions" that have occurred from reliance on radar information to the exclusion of other information.[37] The number of persons required to constitute a proper look-out will depend upon a number of factors, such as the size of the vessel, the degree of visibility, and the density of traffic. In most cases one person may be sufficient, providing such person is reasonably trained or experienced.[38] It is also important to ensure that the look-out is posted in a place on the vessel where there is an unobstructed view. In many instances it may be best to post a look-out on the bow or the wing of the navigating bridge.

c) **Rule 6: Safe Speed**
Many collisions occur because of vessels operating at speeds that are subsequently found to be unsafe under the prevailing circumstances.[39] There is no simple rule that is always applicable to determine what is

---

35 See, e.g., *Bovenkerk (The)*, [1973] 1 Lloyd's L.R. 63 (Q.B. (Adm. Div.)); *Skyron and Hel (The)*, [1994] 2 Lloyd's L.R. 254; *Da Ye (The)*, [1993] 1 Lloyd's L.R. 30; *The Navios Enterprise*, above note 23; and *Marie Skou (The) v. Nippon Yusen Kaisha Ltd.*, [1971] S.C.R. 233.

36 See *Dagmar Salen (The) v. Puget Sound Navigation Co.*, [1951] S.C.R. 608; *Maloja II (The)*, [1993] 1 Lloyd's L.R. 48 at 55; *Glucometer II (The) and St. Michael (The)*, [1989] 1 Lloyd's L.R. 54; and *Afran Transport Co. v. Bergechief (The)*, 274 F.2d 469 (2d Cir. 1960). The automatic radar plotting aid (ARPA) is now frequently fitted on board newer vessels. Under U.S. regulations, vessels over 10,000 GT constructed after 1 September 1984 must be fitted with ARPA if they carry oil or hazardous materials in bulk or in residue in U.S. navigable waters or if they transfer such substances in any port or place within U.S. jurisdiction. The Canadian regulations on the subject are found in *Navigating Appliances and Equipment Regulations*, S.O.R./84-869, s.20 as am. by S.O.R./87-353, s.3 & S.O.R./2001-83, s.12.

37 See *Marie Skou (The) v. Nippon Yusen Kaisha Ltd.*, above note 35; *Anna Salen (The)*, [1954] 1 Lloyd's Rep. 475; and Healy & Sweeney, above note 3 at 116; see also Chapter 2, "The Shipping Industry: An Overview," for more information on radar.

38 See also *Recommendation on Basic Principles & Operational Guidance Relating to Navigational Watchkeeping*, IMO Res. A.285 (VIII); see also D(6) in Chapter 2, "The Shipping Industry: An Overview."

39 *Sanwa (The) and Chayangstar (The)*, [1998] 1 Lloyd's L.R. 283; see also Marsden, above note 10 at 164–71; Healy & Sweeney, above note 3 at 104–24; *Perrigoue v. British Columbia Ferry Authority*, [1966] Ex. C.R. 744; *Kingcome Navigation v. Perdia*, [1966] Ex. C.R. 656; *Conrad v. Snair*, above note 33. See also Fernandes, above note 15 at 3-19ff.

the safe speed. However, rule 6 of the *COLREGS 1972* provides a number of operational examples of circumstances to be taken into account in determining safe speed. In other words, the word "safe" has to be interpreted in a relative sense: vessels must proceed at a speed that is considered safe for each particular circumstance: that is, clear visibility on the open ocean, clear visibility in restricted waters or in dense traffic, in restricted visibility, or with restricted draught. In other words, adhering to safe speed is considered to be good seamanship.[40]

An earlier version of the collision regulations required that vessels proceed at a moderate speed in accordance with prevailing conditions. It was subsequently considered that "safe" speed was a better requirement, as a vessel that, in restricted visibility, had reduced speed from 22 to 11 knots had moderated its speed but was still proceeding at a speed that was not safe. While it is sometimes asserted that being able to stop a vessel in half the range of visibility may be a safe speed,[41] the so-called "half-range of visibility" rule is not always appropriate and, therefore, does not constitute a reliable rule of law.[42] Unsafe speed does not always mean excessive speed. There may be circumstances when an increase in speed may be a safe manoeuvre; for example, a modern, highly manoeuvrable vessel in good visibility in a close-quarters situation may be able to increase speed in order to clear the area and thereby avoid risk of collision.

Rule 6 also takes account of the widespread use of radar and provides a number of additional factors to be taken into account by vessels with operational radar. However, while radar and other modern electronic navigational aids offer significant assistance to mariners, they have to be used with caution. Radar is considered to be among "all available means in the prevailing circumstances" by which a look-out is to be kept.[43] However, mariners must also be aware of the limitations and constraints imposed by the use of radar as set out in rule 6.[44] In addition, the following limitations have to be taken into account when using radar:

---

40   *Nordic Ferry (The)*, [1991] 2 Lloyd's L.R. 591.
41   *Glorious (The)* (1933), 44 Ll. L.R. 321.
42   Healy & Sweeney, above note 3 at 117–18.
43   *Pulkovo (The) and Oden (The)*, [1989] 1 Lloyd's L.R. 280.
44   See a full discussion on this in Healy & Sweeney, above note 3 at 113–17, as well as the technical discussion in Cockcroft & Lameijer, above note 16 at 47–52. Also, R.O. Gerrity, "Radar Information Applied to Rules of Avoiding Collision" (1962) 5 Can. Bar. J. 290. See also D(2)(e) in Chapter 2, "The Shipping Industry: An Overview."

- Radar is a mechanical/electronic system and, therefore, liable to failure and faulty operation.
- Blind sectors and shadow sectors may be caused by parts of the ship's structure (such as funnel and masts) that interfere with or obscure the radar beam. False echoes may be displayed on the screen by returning signals bouncing off structures such as the funnel or a ship close by.
- Abnormal weather conditions can give rise to "false" echoes and cluttering of the screen; for example, echoes may be returned by rain.
- Reduction in performance may be caused by improper setting of the controls.
- There is a great variety in the reflecting properties of different targets, as well as in the range at which they may be detected; even at short range small targets, such as pleasure and fishing craft, may not be detected unless they are fitted with a proper radar reflector.
- Skill, experience, and time are required for the proper interpretation of the information depicted on the radar screen. A single observation of the screen indicates only the range and bearing of a target. Such information as aspect (way of heading), true course, relative course, may be deduced from a series of observations, but alterations in any of these may not be discernible until a further time interval has elapsed. False echoes may appear on the screen from a variety of causes, and experience is necessary so that these may be recognized.
- An echo on a radar screen provides no direct indication of the type or size or other characteristics of the vessel detected. Nor does it provide more than a very approximate idea of the size of the target.

Canadian collision regulations have modified rule 6 to include a prohibition of operating vessels at a speed that would adversely affect certain other activities such as towing, dredging, and passing grounded vessels and wrecks.[45] The Canadian regulations also include provisions requiring notice that must be given of precautions to be taken in special circumstances, such as abnormal water levels or ice conditions.[46]

---

45 Rule 6(c) and (d) as am. by S.O.R./83-202, ss.3 (8) and (9); S.O.R./90-702, s.7; Fernandes, above note 15 at 3-20.
46 Ibid. See also *Bischler v. Stoparyk*, above note 33; *Clackamas (The Ship) v. Schooner Cape d'Or*, [1926] S.C.R. 331; *Lubrolake (The) v. Sarniadoc (The)*, [1959] Ex. C.R. 131; and *Perrigoue v. British Columbia Ferry Authority*, above note 39.

d) Rule 7: Risk of Collision

Many collisions occur because the vessels involved failed to appreciate or determine that a risk of collision had developed.[47] In other words, careful observation matures into inference and prediction on what may occur. Rule 7 of the *COLREGS 1972* requires vessels to be constantly aware of the risk of collision and to determine, if in the presence of other vessels, whether such a risk exists. This determination must be made through "all available means," for instance, look-out, electronic plotting, or bearings. While the language here is similar to that of rule 6, the purpose is different. In determining if risk of collision exists with a vessel that has been visually sighted, the taking of frequent compass bearings may be especially important. If such bearings do not appreciably change risk of collision exists.[48] In clear weather the use of radar and associated equipment is more likely to be considered necessary for determining risk of collision with an approaching or crossing vessel than for the purpose of keeping a general look-out.[49] Other available means of determining risk of collision must also be utilized if appropriate; for example, in restricted waters the use of VHF (very high frequency) radio-telephony may be helpful in contacting other vessels in order to determine action that is being taken. However, this must also be undertaken with great care in order to avoid confusion.[50]

e) Rule 8: Action to Avoid Collision

Rule 8 of the *COLREGS 1972* applies to all vessels, including the "give-way" vessel.[51] In many cases collisions occur because of inadequate or

---

47 Marsden, above note 10 at 171–75; Fernandes, above note 15 at 3-22.1ff; Healy & Sweeney, above note 3 at 125–34; *Canadian Pacific Railway v. Bermuda (The)* (1910), 13 Ex. C.R. 389; *Kwok v. British Columbia Ferry Corp.*, above note 33; *Egmont Towing & Sorting Ltd. v. Telendos (The)*, above note 34.
48 *British Aviator (The)*, [1965] 1 Lloyd's Rep. 271; *Koscierzyna (The) and Hanjin Singapore (The)*, [1996] 2 Lloyd's L.R. 124, 130 (C.A.).
49 *Roseline (The)*, [1981] 2 Lloyd's L.R. 410, 415; *Gannet (The)*, [1967] 1 Lloyd's Rep. 97; *Linde (The)*, [1969] 2 Lloyd's L.R. 556.
50 *Mineral Dampier (The) v. Hanjin Madras (The)*, [2001] Lloyd's L.R. 419; *Bovenkerk (The)*, above note 35; *Tenes (The)*, [1989] 2 Lloyd's L.R. 367; *Sanwa (The) and Chayangstar Star (The)*, above note 39; *Aleksandr Marinesko v. Quint Star (The)*, [1998] 1 Lloyd's L.R. 265 at 278; *Rederiet Odfjell A/S v. Vesuvio (The)*, [1930] Ex. C.R. 207; *Dagmar Salen (The) v. Puget Sound Navigation Co.*, [1950] Ex. C.R. 283, rev'd in part [1951] S.C.R. 608; *Canadian Pacific Railway v. Vancouver Tug Boat Co.*, [1957] Ex. C.R. 95; *Polish Ocean Lines v. Maple Branch (The)* (1982), 15 A.C.W.S. (2d) 61.
51 *Kwok v. British Columbia Ferry Corp.*, above note 33.

incorrect action taken to avoid collision.[52] Rule 8 requires avoidance action to be taken early, to be positive, and to be with the observance of good seamanship.[53] In many cases a substantial course alteration alone may be sufficient.[54] In all situations passing at a safe distance from other vessels is the ultimate aim.[55] However, rule 8 also requires vessels to reduce or reverse speed or stop altogether, if necessary, to avoid collision or to permit more time to assess a potentially dangerous situation.[56] Rule 8 is not applicable where there is no immediate danger to the stand-on vessel (i.e., the vessel that is expected to maintain its course and speed).

f) Rule 9: Narrow Channels

In deciding whether a given stretch of water is a narrow channel, courts usually take into account the evidence of local seamen and experts. In general, a narrow channel is defined on a case-by-case basis as a question of fact;[57] there is no set minimum length to define a narrow channel.[58] The term "fairway" is usually considered to be a deep-water channel within the narrow channel.[59] Owing to the variance in the draughts of ships, a vessel with a shallow draught must keep farther to the starboard side of the channel than vessels of deeper draught.[60] However, vessels are not expected to put themselves in danger, or to make

---

52 Marsden, above note 10 at 175–80; Healy & Sweeney, above note 3 at 134–43.
53 See, e.g., *Golden Mistral (The)*, [1986] 1 Lloyd's L.R. 407; and *Oliver J. Olson & Co. v. S.S. Marine Leopard*, 356 F.2d 728, 1966 A.M.C. 1064 (9th Cir. 1966).
54 See *Billings Victory (The)* (1949), 82 Ll. L.R. 877 (Adm. Div.); and *British Aviator (The)*, above note 48.
55 See *Ouro Fino (The)*, [1986] 2 Lloyd's L.R. 466, aff'd [1988] 2 Lloyd's L.R. 325 (C.A.).
56 Fernandes, above note 15 at 3-24. *Faethon (The)*, above note 20 at 545; *Heminger v. Porter (The)* (1898), 6 Ex. C.R. 208; *Richelieu (The) v. Cie de Navigation Saguenay & Lac St. Jean*, [1945] S.C.R. 659; *Imperial Oil Ltd. v. Willowbranch (The)*, [1964] S.C.R. 402; *Sea Prince Fishing v. Kalamalka (The)* (1967), 61 D.L.R. (2d) 700 (Ex. Ct.).
57 Fernandes, above note 15 at 3-26. *Canadian Pacific Railway v. Camosun (The)*, [1925] Ex. C.R. 39; *Imperial Oil v. Willowbranch (The)*, ibid.
58 *Tucker v. Tecumseh (The)* (1905), 10 Ex. C.R. 149.
59 I.e., that portion of the channel that is usually depicted by pecked lines on nautical charts. See *Koningin Juliana (The)*, [1974] 2 Lloyd's L.R. 353 at 362 (C.A.); see also Marsden, above note 10 at 180–184; and *New Ontario Steamship Co. v. Montreal Transportation Co.* (1907), 11 Ex. C.R. 113, rev'd (1908) 40 S.C.R. 160.
60 *Koskeemo (The) v. Pacific Rover (The)*, [1974] 1 F.C. 256; *Mersey No. 30 (The)*, [1952] 2 Lloyd's Rep. 183; *Osprey (The)*, [1967] 1 Lloyd's Rep. 76; *British Patrol (The)*, [1967] 2 Lloyd's Rep. 16, aff'd [1968] 1 Lloyd's L.R. 117 (C.A.); *Maritime Harmony (The)*, [1982] 2 Lloyd's L.R. 400; *Union Steamship Co. v. New York and Virginia Steamship Co. (The Pennsylvania)*, 65 U.S. 307 at 314 (1860).

frequent alterations of course in order to keep near to the outer limit of every part of the channel.[61] Vessels are also required to make use of radar and other navigational instruments to ensure that they are keeping as near to the outer limit as is safe and practicable.[62] Small craft and fishing and sailing vessels are required to keep clear of vessels that can only navigate within the channel or fairway. The implication of rule 9 of the COLREGS 1972 is that fishing is only permitted in a channel when fishing vessels are able to get an early indication of the approach of other vessels, which would allow them to clear the passage in sufficient time.

Rule 9(d) attempts to reduce the number of dangerous crossings in narrow channels or fairways, often caused by relatively small vessels that could usually avoid the danger by waiting until the passage is clear, or by better anticipating the prevailing traffic situation. Another problem might arise from the increasing size of vessels: such vessels can only proceed through channels in favourable high-tide conditions but at increased speeds because of time limitations. In such cases there is often insufficient room for overtaking, unless the vessel being overtaken is willing to move out of the way to allow the overtaking vessel safe passage. This only applies to vessels in sight of one another and the necessary communication is usually achieved through whistle signals, VHF radio, and radio telephone. Finally, rule 9 also stipulates the necessary sound signals to be used in cases where a vessel approaches a bend or a section of the channel where other vessels may be obscured.

Rule 9 has received a number of modifications under the Canadian *Collision Regulations*, including the requirement that vessels in the waters of the Great Lakes basin signal their intention to cross other ships in a narrow channel. There are also some different signals to be used by ships in the Great Lakes basin. For example, for vessels navigating in Canadian narrow waters, the vessel travelling with the current has to decide on which side to pass the other vessel and is required to communicate this to the oncoming vessel moving upstream. Also certain vessels (e.g., barges, inconspicuous vessels, or those partly submerged) must not impede the progress of others travelling through the channel.[63]

---

61 *Marsden*, above note 10 at 185.
62 *British Tenacity (The)*, [1963] 2 Lloyd's Rep. 1.
63 Rule 9(h)–(k) as am. by S.O.R./83-202, ss.3(10) and (11). Fernandes, above note 15 at 3-27. *Maggie (The) v. Honovera (The)* (1916), 54 S.C.R. 51; *Sunrise Co. v. Lake Winnipeg (The)* (1987), 12 F.T.R. 57; *Egmont Towing & Sorting Ltd. v. Telendos (The)*, above note 34; *Calvin Austin (The) v. Lovitt* (1905), 35 S.C.R. 616; *Standard Oil Co. v. Ikala (The)*, [1929] Ex. C.R. 230; *Kingdoc (The) v. Canada Steamship Lines*, [1931] S.C.R. 288; *New England Fish Co. of Oregon v. Britameri-*

g) Rule 10: Traffic Separation Schemes[64]

Traffic Separation Schemes (TSS),[65] Vessel Traffic Reporting Systems (VTRS),[66] and Vessel Traffic Management Systems (VTMS) are specifically designed to separate vessels in order to avoid collisions.[67] Many collisions still occur within or close to such systems, however, because vessels either do not obey the *COLREGS 1972* that still apply fully within such systems,[68] or simply navigate improperly within such systems on the basis of fixed assumptions in the face of changing data.[69] Rule 10 sets out the general operational criteria when using TSS areas. The general rationale is that by separating traffic into two lanes the risk of collision is reduced. However, the rule also recognizes the various dangers that are created by such a separation; for example, crossing TSS areas can often lead to collisions unless crossing takes place as close to right angles to the TSS as possible.[70] In addition, rule 10 refers to a number of other aspects that may lead to collision or risk of collision.[71]

In Canada, the regulations are modified and require that TSS are published in either a Notice to Mariners or Notice of Shipping (rule 10(m)). Furthermore, fishing vessels — while fishing — in a routing system, or vessels involved in certain activities in Canadian waters, are exempt from TSS rules, the use of a TSS, as well as the requirement to cross such systems at right angles (rule 10(o)(p)). Vessels of less than

---

can, [1959] Ex. C.R. 256; *Kingcome Navigation v. Perdia*, above note 39; *Sea Prince Fishing v. Kalamalka (The)*, above note 56; *Queen Charlotte Fisheries v. Tyee Shell (The)*, [1966] Ex. C.R. 724; *Prins Frederik Willem (The) v. Gayport Shipping*, [1960] Ex. C.R. 274; *Lionel (The) v. Manchester Merchant (The)*, above note 31.

64 For a detailed analysis of this area, see E. Gold, "Vessel Traffic Regulation: The Interface of Maritime Safety and Operational Freedom" (1983) 14 J. Marit. L. & Com. 1. See also Fernandes, above note 15 at 3-32.

65 Defined as "a routing measure aimed at the separation of opposing streams of traffic by appropriate means and by the establishment of traffic lanes": per Sheen, J. in *Achilleus (The)*, [1985] 2 Lloyd's L.R. 338 at 342).

66 Canada established one of the most advanced VTR systems in 1989 under the *Canada Shipping Act*. See *Canada Shipping Act*, above note 15, s.562; *Canada Shipping Act, 2001*, above note 15, part V; see *Eastern Canada Vessel Traffic Services Zone Regulations*, S.O.R./89-99 as am. by S.O.R./96-215.

67 Marsden, above note 10 at 190–201; Healy & Sweeney, above note 3 at 153–65.

68 See, e.g., *Genimar (The)*, [1972] 2 Lloyd's L.R. 17.

69 See, e.g., *Estrella (The)*, [1977] 1 Lloyd's L.R. 525; *Eglantine, Credo and Inez (The)*, [1990] 2 Lloyd's L.R. 390 (C.A.).

70 *Century Dawn v. Asian Energy (The)*, [1994] 1 Lloyd's L.R. 138 at 150, aff'd [1996] 1 Lloyd's L.R. 125 (C.A.).

71 See *Marsden*, above note 10 at 195–201; Cockcroft & Lameijer, above note 16 at 82–95.

twenty metres in length are to use TSS where available. Transatlantic voyages are to avoid the Grand Banks of Newfoundland and Labrador north of 43°N where possible (rule (10(q)).[72]

h) **Rule 11: Application**
This rule simply states that Section II of *COLREGS 1972*, consisting of rules 12–18, applies only to vessels in sight of one another.

i) **Rule 12: Sailing Vessels**
Rule 12 of *COLREGS 1972* is one of the oldest navigational directions in existence and pre-dates the age of power-driven ships: it sets out the navigational rules for sailing vessels. While sailing vessels are today rarely used in commercial shipping, collisions may still occur, especially among sailing vessels engaged in racing. As a result, rule 12 follows the basic principles of the *International Yacht Racing Rules*. These rules govern encounters between yachts racing each other. In encounters between such yachts and third vessels, the *COLREGS 1972* apply.[73]

j) **Rule 13: Overtaking**
Overtaking is also a surprisingly frequent cause of collision.[74] Rule 13 of *COLREGS 1972* clearly states that any vessel is considered to be overtaking when coming up with another vessel from a direction more than 22.5° abaft its beam[75] and must keep out of the way of the vessel being overtaken. If doubt exists, the faster vessel should assume that it is overtaking.[76] There is some question as to whether the overtaking rule applies before risk of collision can be determined.[77] This arises out

---

72 Rule 10(m)–(q) as am. by S.O.R./83-202, ss.3(12)–(15); S.O.R./90-702, s.9; S.O.R./91-275, s.1. See Fernandes, above note 15 at 3-33. See also *Irish Shipping Ltd. v. R.*, [1977] 1 F.C. 485.
73 Marsden, above note 10 at 203; *Blanc v. Emilien Burke (The)* (1919), 19 Ex. C.R. 24, 46 D.L.R. 59; *Chester Sailing Society v. Flinn*, above note 33.
74 Marsden, above note 10 at 203–06; Healy & Sweeney, above note 3 at 168–82. *Chester Sailing Society v. Flinn*, above note 33; *Egmont Towing & Sorting Ltd. v. Telendos (The)*, above note 34; *MacDonald v. Atlantic Salvage*, [1925] Ex. C.R. 209; *Kwok v. British Columbia Ferry Corp.*, above note 33; *Sincennes-McNaughton v. Steel Chemist (The)*, [1928] Ex. C.R. 182; *Merlo, Merlo & Ray v. Harry R. Jones (The)*, [1925] Ex. C.R. 183; *Bentley v. MacDonald*, above note 33; *R. v. Petite*, [1933] Ex. C.R. 186.
75 See Figure 2.4 in Chapter 2.
76 *Manchester Regiment (The)* (1938), 60 Ll. L.R. 279; *Jones v. Texaco Panama Inc. (The Texaco Ohio)*, 428 F.Supp. 1333, 1977 A.M.C. 1249 (D.C. La. 1977).
77 See *Nowy Sacz (The)*, [1976] 2 Lloyd's L.R. 682, rev'd [1977] 2 Lloyd's L.R. 91 (C.A.); and *Auriga (The)*, [1977] 1 Lloyd's L.R. 384.

of the difficulty that often exists when determining whether a crossing or overtaking situation exists.[78] In taking avoiding action the overtaking vessel must ensure that such action does not take it so near the vessel overtaken that hydrodynamic interaction may occur.[79] This type of close proximity between vessels can lead to serious collisions.[80] The Canadian *Collision Regulations* redefine when one vessel is deemed to be overtaking another during navigation in the Great Lakes basin.[81]

k) Rule 14: Head-on Situation

A situation of two vessels colliding head-on has the potential of the most serious damage. It still occurs frequently, even when relatively minor avoiding action could have prevented the collision.[82] The expression in rule 14 of *COLREGS 1972* of "vessels meeting end-on or nearly end-on" has been interpreted to mean opposing courses that are within of about 6° of one another. It also means that this situation arises when one vessel sees the other ahead or nearly ahead, or when by night one vessel could see the other vessel's masthead navigation lights in line or nearly in line and/or both of the other vessel's side navigation lights.[83] The rule indicates that it is the direction of the ship's head and not the vessel's course that must be used to determine whether a head-on situation exists and, if it does exist, each vessel must alter course to starboard.[84] Furthermore, if a vessel is in any doubt whether a head-on situation exists, it shall be assumed that it does exist. In general, in a collision situation, rules 13, 14, and 15 must be considered together in order for a court to decide whether the collision occurred while the ships were overtaking, crossing, or in a head-on situation.[85]

---

78 See also rule 15. This problem is thoroughly discussed in P.K. Mukherjee, "Overtaking or Crossing: Judicial Interpretation and the Mariner's Dilemma" (1992) 23 J. Mar. L. & Com. 247; and by S. Harley, "Overtaking or Crossing" (Safety at Sea International, June 1977).
79 See D(5)(f) in Chapter 2, "The Shipping Industry: An Overview" for an explanation of interaction.
80 *Queen Mary (The)* (1949), 82 Ll. L.R. 303; *Jan Laurenz (The)*, [1972] 1 Lloyd's L.R. 404, aff'd [1973] 1 Lloyd's L.R. 329 (C.A.); *Iran Torab (The)*, [1988] 2 Lloyd's L.R. 38.
81 Rule 13(e) as am. by S.O.R./83-202, ss.3(16), (17), and (18) (overtaking). See Fernandes, above note 15 at 3-37.
82 *Marsden*, above note 10 at 206–08; Healy & Sweeney, above note 3 at 182–87.
83 Healy & Sweeney, above note 3 at 184.
84 See, e.g., *Kaituna (The)* (1933), 46 Ll. L.R. 200; *Gulf Stream (The)*, 43 F. 895 (D.C.N.Y. 1890); *British Engineer (The)* (1945), 78 Ll. L.R. 31; and *Koskeemo (The) v. Pacific Rover (The)*, above note 60.
85 Fernandes, above note 15 at 3-39.

l) **Rule 15: Crossing Situation**

Vessels crossing at sea are also often involved in collision situations,[86] despite the very clear requirement in rule 15 of *COLREGS 1972* that the vessel that has the other on its starboard or right side, must keep clear of the other ship. This should be achieved by any of the following actions:

- altering course to starboard so as to pass astern of the other vessel,
- reducing the speed sufficiently to allow the other vessel to cross ahead, or
- making a full-turn alteration to port.

In some cases doubt may arise as to whether there is a crossing or overtaking situation;[87] if such doubt occurs, this rule does not apply.[88] However, rule 15 does apply in situations where the overtaking (rule 13) and head-on (rule 14) regulations do not apply. In other words, rule 15 applies in cases where, if each vessel keeps its course and speed, the two vessels would arrive at a crossing point at the same time or at nearly the same time. The relative speeds of the vessels or their distance from one another are not relevant.[89] The principal purpose of rule 15 is to place a duty on the give-way vessel to keep clear of the stand-on vessel; however, in order to do this, the give-way vessel must be able to determine what the stand-on vessel is doing.[90] In any case, in keeping clear the give-way vessel is required to avoid crossing ahead of the other vessel.[91] Under the Canadian *Collision Regulations*, a modified rule 15 requires crossing vessels to keep clear of another power-driven vessel except in an area north of Ile Rouge on the St. Lawrence River.[92]

---

86   Marsden, above note 10 at 208–13; Healy & Sweeney, above note 3 at 188–98.
87   See *Auriga (The)*, above note 77; see also Mukherjee, and Harley, above note 78; *Albano (The) v. Allan Lines Steamship Co.* (1906), 37 S.C.R. 284, [1907] A.C. 193.
88   In those cases see rules 13(c) and 14(c); see also *Da Ye (The)*, above note 35.
89   *Maloja II (The)*, above note 36; *E.R. Wallonia (The)*, [1987] 2 Lloyd's L.R. 485.
90   *Lorentzen v. Alcoa Rambler (The)*, [1949] A.C. 236; *Savina (The)*, [1974] 2 Lloyd's L.R. 317 (Q.B. Adm. Crt.), rev'd [1975] 2 Lloyd's L.R. 141 (C.A.), aff'd [1976] 2 Lloyd's L.R. 123 (H.L.); *Sestriere (The)*, [1976] 1 Lloyd's L.R. 125; *Avance (The)*, [1979] 1 Lloyd's L.R. 143.
91   *Dona Myrto (The)*, [1959] 1 Lloyd's Rep. 203; *Angelic Spirit (The) and Y Mariner (The)*, [1994] 2 Lloyd's L.R. 595; *Koskeemo (The) v. Pacific Rover (The)*, above note 60; *Bentley v. MacDonald*, above note 33; *R. v. Levis Ferry*, [1962] S.C.R. 629; *Bischler v. Stoparyk*, above note 33; *R. v. Harlem (The)* (1919), 59 S.C.R. 653; *Cavalier (The) v. Liverpool Shipping Co.*, [1931] Ex. C.R. 205.
92   Rule 15(b) as am. by S.O.R./83-202, ss.3(20) and (21); S.O.R./90-702, s.10. Fernandes, above note 15 at 3-40.

m) Rule 16: Action by Give-Way Vessel

Rule 16 of COLREGS 1972 simply states that a vessel that is required to keep out of the way of another vessel it must take early and substantial action in order to do so when possible. Such action can be taken by alterations in either course or speed or both.[93]

n) Rule 17: Action by Stand-on Vessel

Rule 17 of COLREGS 1972 is one of the most difficult regulations and is often termed the "agony-of-collision" rule by mariners.[94] It is best illustrated by what has been termed the "four stages of a collision situation":[95]

Stage 1: At long range and before risk of collision exists, both vessels are free to take any avoidance action.

Stage 2: When risk of collision first begins to apply, the give-way vessel is required to take early and substantial action to achieve a safe passing distance; the other vessel must keep its course and speed.[96]

Stage 3: When it becomes apparent that the give-way vessel is not taking appropriate action under the rules, the stand-on vessel is required to give the sound signal under rule 34(d)[97] and is permitted to take action to avoid collision by her action alone,[98] but must not alter course to port to avoid another vessel on its port side; the give-way vessel is not relieved of its obligation to keep out of the way.

---

93 *Billings Victory (The)*, above note 54 at 881; *Royalgate (The)*, [1967] 1 Lloyd's Rep. 352; see also *Maloja II (The)*, above note 36 at 48–49; *Chester Sailing Society v. Flinn*, above note 33; *El Progresso v. Ralph Misener (The)*, above note 33; *Polish Ocean Lines v. Maple Branch (The)*, above note 50; *Marie Skou (The) v. Nippon Yusen Kaisha Ltd.*, above note 35. Fernandes, *Shipping and Admiralty Law*, above note 15 at 3-42.

94 The revisions found in the COLREGS 1972, above note 12, have reduced the difficulties contained in this rule to some extent. See *Marsden*, above note 10 at 213–18; and Healy & Sweeney, above note 3 at 190–98, for an extensive discussion of rule 17.

95 Cockcroft & Lameijer, above note 16 at 124–25.

96 *Roanoke (The)*, [1908] P. 231 at 239; *Echo (The)*, [1917] P. 132; *Dona Myrto (The)*, above note 91; *Egmont Towing & Sorting Ltd. v. Telendos (The)*, above note 34.

97 At least five short blasts in rapid succession. This may be supplemented by a similar light signal.

98 *Iran Torab (The)*, above note 80; *Lok Vivek (The) and Common Venture (The)*, [1995] 2 Lloyd's L.R. 230; *Angelic Spirit (The) and Y Mariner (The)*, above note 91; *Koscierzyna (The) and Hanjin Singapore (The)*, above note 48.

Stage 4: When collision cannot be avoided by the give-way vessel alone, the stand-on vessel is required to take such action as will best avoid collision.[99]

The moment when the time for the last decision arises is often considered to be the "agony of collision." However, courts have recognized the difficulties involved in judging when this moment arises; for example, it has been held that, if a master has done his or her best to choose the right moment to take action, but it is later shown that the action was taken too early or too late, he or she will not be held responsible.[100] In other words, the actions of prudent seamanship will not be judged by subsequent "mathematical calculations."[101] Nevertheless, the stand-on vessel must take action when it is apparent that such action is required in order to avoid a collision.[102] It is also considered to be good seamanship to at least attempt to communicate with the give-way vessel.

It should also be noted that under rule 17(b) as well as under rule 2(b),[103] a vessel has the right and obligation to depart from the required regulations, if such a departure is necessary in order to avoid immediate danger.[104] The actual point at which such a departure becomes necessary will depend upon the judgment of a competent master based on all existing facts.[105] In addition, if a collision becomes inevitable or unavoidable, a master is unlikely to be held negligent merely for attempting to manoeuvre the vessel in order to reduce the expected damage, whether successful or not.[106]

---

99 *Albano (The) v. Allan Line Steamship Co.*, above note 87; *Kitano Maru (S.S.) v. S.S. Otranto*, above note 31; *Jaladhir (The)*, [1961] 2 Lloyd's Rep. 13; *Nordic Ferry (The)*, above note 40; *Aracelio Iglesias (The)*, [1968] 1 Lloyd's L.R. 131; *Da Ye (The)*, above note 35.
100 The cases in this area are reviewed in *Queen Mary (The)*, above note 80 at 325; see also *F.J. Wolf (The)*, [1946] P. 91 at 95; *E.R. Wallonia (The)*, above note 89.
101 Lord Strathclyde in *Compagnie des Forges d'Homecourt v. Gibsons & Co.*, [1920] S.C. 247 at 260; see also *Aracelio Iglesias (The)*, above note 99.
102 *Tojo Maru (The)*, [1968] 1 Lloyd's L.R. 365 at 368; *Jaladhir (The)*, above note 99 at 16; *Ek (The)*, [1966] 1 Lloyd's Rep. 440 at 447; *Petroship B (The)*, [1986] 2 Lloyd's L.R. 251.
103 Rule 2: Responsibility.
104 See *Saragossa (The)* (1892), 7 Asp. M.C. 289 at 291; *Heranger (S.S.) v. S.S. Diamond*, [1939] A.C. 94 at 102.
105 Marsden, above note 10 at 216.
106 *State of Himachal Pradesh (The)*, [1985] 2 Lloyd's L.R. 573, aff'd [1987] 2 Lloyd's L.R. 97 (C.A.); *Da Ye (The)*, above note 35; *Watts v. John Irwin (The)* (1909), 12 Ex. C.R. 374; *Cleeve (The) v. Prince Rupert (The)* (1917), 20 Ex. C.R. 441.

o) Rule 18: Responsibilities Between Vessels

Many collisions still occur because of a lack of understanding among vessels of their responsibilities toward one another, especially when hampered vessels are involved. Rule 18 of *COLREGS 1972* sets up a system of privileges that apply, with the exception of the requirements of the rules for narrow channels, traffic separation schemes, and overtaking.[107] In other words, these privileges apply in substitution of the steering and sailing rules that are normally applicable for sailing vessels, head-on, and crossing rules. In other words, rule 18 is designed to protect hampered or more vulnerable vessels that, owing to their operational limitation (i.e., not under command, constrained by draught, fishing, or sailing),[108] are less likely to avoid a collision than normal power-driven vessels. As a result, under the hierarchy of vulnerability set up under rule 18, vessels that are less vulnerable or hampered must yield to more vulnerable vessels, as long as the latter satisfy the conditions laid down in rule 3. In general, it has to be noted that rules 9, 10, and 13 take precedence over rule 18.[109]

p) Rule 19: Conduct of Vessels in Restricted Visibility

Section III of Part B of the *COLREGS 1972* covers the Conduct of Vessels in Restricted Visibility; it consists only of rule 19, which applies only to vessels "not in sight of one another." Such collisions are generally caused by excessive speed and/or improper look-out in restricted visibility. This has always been and continues to be the single most serious cause of collision.[110] Rule 19 applies not only when navigating in restricted visibility but also "near" such conditions.[111] Furthermore, the application of rule 19 is not restricted to cases where a risk of collision

---

107 Marsden, above note 10 at 218–24; Healy & Sweeney, above note 3 at 199.
108 See above, definitions in rule 3.
109 Fernandes, above note 15 at 3-44; *Tilley v. Georgian Bay Airways*, [1950] O.W.N. 852; *Ontario Central Airlines v. Gustafson* (1957), 8 D.L.R. (2d) 584 (Ont. C.A.); *Hirtle v. Shanalian (The)*, [1939] Ex. C.R. 50, [1939] 4 D.L.R. 278.
110 Marsden, above note 10 at 224–32; Healy & Sweeney, above note 3 at 200–05. *Lubrolake (The) v. Sarniadoc (The)*, above note 46; *Imperial Oil v. Willowbranch (The)*, above note 56; *Elders Grain Company v. M/V Ralph Misener* (1997), 125 F.T.R. 209; *Eastern Steamship Co. v. Canada Atlantic Transit Co.*, [1929] Ex. C.R. 103; *Red Barge Line Ltd. v. Poplarboy (The)*, [1932] Ex. C.R. 209; *Benmaple (The) v. Lafayette (The)*, [1941] S.C.R. 66; *Rover Shipping Co. v. Kaipaki (The)*, [1948] Ex. C.R. 507; *Fanad Head (The) v. Adams*, [1949] S.C.R. 407; *Marie Skou (The) v. Nippon Yusen Kaisha Ltd.*, above note 35; *Ontario Central Airlines v. Gustafson*, above note 109; *Canada Steamship Lines v. Maria Paolina G. (The)*, [1954] Ex. C.R. 211.
111 Healy & Sweeney, above note 3 at 202; see also *St. Paul (The)*, [1909] P. 43.

exists but applies in all cases of restricted visibility.[112] Sighting another vessel by radar is not considered to be "in sight of" under the rules.[113] However, if a vessel detects another vessel by radar alone, it can be determined whether a close-quarters situation could arise; if so, the first vessel is required to take avoiding action "in ample time."[114] Although the rule does not set out the form such avoiding action should take,[115] it suggests actions that should be avoided, such as alterations to port and alterations toward the other vessel.[116]

Unless a determination has been made that risk of collision does not exist,[117] if a vessel detects another vessel ahead, speed has to be reduced to an operational minimum and to "navigate with extreme caution."[118] While the term "safe speed" is already clearly defined in rule 6, in restricted visibility, there may be further factors that have to be taken into account; excessive speed in restricted visibility, regardless of circumstances,[119] is never acceptable.[120]

3) *COLREGS 1972* Part C: Lights and Shapes (Rules 20–31)

Part C of *COLREGS 1972* sets out rules 20–31, under which ships must carry certain lights and shapes that identify their operational capacity by day and night.[121] Such lights[122] must be carried from sunset to sunrise in all weathers and at all other times in restricted visibility.[123] A vessel will be held at fault if such lights are not shown, even if the lights

---

112 *Da Ye (The)*, above note 35; *Skyron and Hel (The)*, above note 35.
113 *Gunnar Knudsen (The)*, [1961] 2 Lloyd's Rep. 433.
114 *Pulkovo (The) and Oden (The)*, above note 43 at 287.
115 Although such action would probably have to comply with rule 8.
116 *Roseline (The)*, above note 49 at 417; *Sanshin Victory (The)*, [1980] 2 Lloyd's L.R. 359; *Maloja II (The)*, above note 36.
117 *Marsden*, above note 10 at 229.
118 Rule 19(c). In previous versions the requirement under these circumstances was to stop engines altogether. Accordingly, caution should be exercised when using cases that were decided on this issue under pre-1972 collision regulations.
119 See *Campania (The)*, [1901] P. 289; and *Lady Gwendolen (The)*, [1964] 2 Lloyd's Rep. 99, aff'd [1965] 1 Lloyd's L.R. 335 (C.A.).
120 See, e.g., *Glorious (The)*, above note 41; and *Eglantine, Credo and Inez (The)*, above note 69.
121 See *Marsden*, above note 10 at 233–54 for a full discussion on Part C. See also Healy & Sweeney, above note 3 at 208ff, for a series of excellent illustrations of the various lights.
122 Rules 21–31 and Annexes I and II.
123 *Roseline (The)*, above note 49.

in question had been accidentally extinguished.[124] Under this section of the *COLREGS 1972*, a ship is also not permitted to show misleading or confusing lights.[125] Shapes are equivalent to the lights but are displayed in daytime and in good visibility. The rules in this section of *COLREGS 1972* set out the definitions and requirements of the various lights and shapes that have to be carried. This includes specifications, including visibility requirements for masthead, stern and side navigation lights; towing lights; all-round lights; and flashing lights. In addition, the specifications and requirements are set out for lights that have to be displayed by towing vessels, vessels towed, sailing vessels, vessels under oars, fishing vessels, vessels not under command or restricted in their ability to manoeuvre, vessels constrained by their draught, pilot vessels, vessels at anchor, vessel aground, and seaplanes.[126] This part of the rules has been modified in the Canadian *Collision Regulations* that have developed a series of additional and/or different requirements. These include changes in definitions and specific lighting requirements for different types of vessels.[127]

---

124 *C.M. Palmer (The) and Larnax (The)* (1873), 2 Asp. M.C. 94; *Saxonia and Eclipse (The)* (1862), Lush. 410 at 422; *Kingsland (The)* (1945), 78 Ll. L.R. 259; *Chester O. Swain (The)*, 76 F.2d 890, 1935 A.M.C. 613 (2d Cir. 1935).
125 *Hassell (The)*, [1919] P. 355; *Truculent (HMS)*, [1951] 2 Lloyd's Rep. 308; *Sanshin Victory (The)*, above note 116; *Ouro Fino (The)*, above note 55; *Djerada (The)*, [1976] 1 Lloyd's L.R. 50.
126 See Cockcroft & Lameijer, above note 16, for a very helpful series of illustrations of the various lights and shapes at 176ff. See also *Sea Prince Fishing v. Kalamalka (The)*, above note 56; *Clark v. Kona Winds Yacht Charters Ltd.* (1990), 34 F.T.R. 211; and *Lubrolake (The) v. Sarniadoc (The)*, above note 46.
127 Rule 21(g) and (h) as am. by S.O.R./83-202, ss.3(22) and (23); and S.O.R./88-10, s.1, & S.O.R./90-702, s.11 (high-speed vessels); rule 23(d) and (e) as am. by S.O.R./83-202, ss.3(26) and (27) (power-driven vessels); rule 24(j)–(p) as am. by S.O.R./83-202, ss.3(28)–(32), & S.O.R./85-397, s.1(1) (towing and pushing); rule 25(f) as am. by S.O.R./83-202, ss.3(33), (34), and (35) (sailing vessels); rule 26(f) as am. by S.O.R./83-202, ss.3(36) and (37) (fishing vessels); rule 28(b) as am. by S.O.R./83-202, ss.3(41), (42), and (43) (vessels constrained by their draught); rule 30(g) and (h) as am. by S.O.R./83-202, ss.3(45) and (46), & S.O.R./91-275, s.2 (vessels aground); see Fernandes, *Shipping and Admiralty Law*, above note 15 at 3-53ff. See also *Canada Steamship Lines v. John B. Ketchum II*, [1925] S.C.R. 81; *Ontario Gravel Freighting Co. v. Matthews Steamship Co.*, [1927] S.C.R. 92; *Sea Prince Fishing v. Kalamalka (The)*, above note 56; *Lionel (The) v. Manchester Merchant (The)*, above note 31; *El Progreso v. Ralph Misener (The)*, above note 33; *Harbour Navigation Co. v. Dinteldyk (The)*, [1925] Ex. C.R. 10; *Kajat v. Arctic Taglu (The)* (1997), 135 F.T.R. 161, rev'd (2000), 252 N.S.R. 152; *B.W.B. Navigation Co. v. Kiltuish (The)* (1922), 21 Ex. C.R. 398; *Maplehurst (The) v. George Hall Coal Co.*, [1923] S.C.R. 507; *Freiya (The) v. RS (The)* (1922), 21 Ex. C.R. 232; *Curtis v. Jacques* (1978), 20 O.R. (2d) 552, 88 D.L.R. (3d) 112 (H.C.J.).

4) *COLREGS 1972* Part D: Sound and Light Signals (Rules 32–37)

Part D of the *COLREGS 1972* requires ships to be equipped with certain equipment with which they can give the sound and light signals required under rules 32–37, and the types of sound and light signals required when manoeuvring. Equipment to be carried includes whistles, bells, gongs, or such other equipment that has similar characteristics.[128] Rule 34 sets out the requirements for the mandatory[129] manoeuvring and warning signals to be given by power-driven vessels in sight of one another. Failure to give such signals, or improper or inadequate signals, may be considered negligence as it can lead to collision.[130] Rule 35 provides the mandatory sound signals required to be given by all types of vessels in restricted visibility. Failure to give such signals will be considered negligent.[131] Under rule 36 vessels are permitted to make light and sound signals in order to attract attention provided that such signals cannot be mistaken for manoeuvring or warning signals required under the rules. A vessel can be considered as negligent if such warning signals are not given when it would have assisted the situation.[132] Rule 37 sets out the requirement that vessels in distress and needing assistance are to use the distress signals described in Annex IV of *COLREGS 1972*. The use of these signals is mandatory and a failure to observe this will be considered negligent.[133] Nevertheless, a lighting or sound signal infraction must generally be connected to the cause of a collision before a vessel can be held liable.[134] It should be noted that Canadian collision regulations have made modifications under which certain vessels less than 12 metres in length must comply with some international regulations applicable to vessels more than 12 metres in length.[135] There are

---

128 The technical specifications of such equipment are set out in Annex III of the Regulations.
129 Regardless of whether the sound signal can be heard. See also *Lucile Bloomfield (The)*, [1966] 2 Lloyd's Rep. 239 at 246, aff'd [1967] 1 Lloyd's Rep. 341 (C.A.).
130 See *Marsden*, above note 10 at 256; see also *Martin Fierro (The)*, [1974] 2 Lloyd's L.R. 203, aff'd [1975] 2 Lloyd's L.R. 130 (C.A.); *Kylix (The) and Rustringen (The)*, [1979] 1 Lloyd's L.R. 133; *Faethon (The)*, above note 20; *E.R. Wallonia (The)*, above note 89; *Statue of Liberty (The)*, [1970] 2 Lloyd's L.R. 151, aff'd [1971] 2 Lloyd's L.R. 277 (H.L.); *Maritime Harmony (The)*, above note 60; and *Aleksandr Marinesko v. Quint Star (The)*, above note 50.
131 *Nordic Ferry (The)*, above note 40 at 598; *Maloja II (The)*, above note 36.
132 *Sabine (The)*, [1974] 1 Lloyd's L.R. 465; *Stein v. Kathy K (The)*, above note 33.
133 *Unitia (The)*, [1953] 1 Lloyd's Rep. 481.
134 Rule 35. See Fernandes, above note 15 at 3-75.
135 Rule 33(c) as am. by S.O.R./83-202, ss.3(47), (48), and (49) (sound signalling equipment); rule 35(k) as am. by S.O.R./83-202, ss.3(53)–(58) (sound signal requirements in restricted visibility).

also additional manoeuvring and warning signals required under the Canadian regulations.[136]

5) *COLREGS 1972* Part E: Exemptions (Rule 38)

Part E, which consists only of rule 38, sets out the transitional provisions for the application of *COLREGS 1972*. The rule contains some temporary and some permanent exemptions applicable to older vessels that may otherwise be unable to comply with the regulations.

6) Canadian *Collision Regulations* Part F: Specific Canadian Provisions (Rules 39–46)

Part F contains specific Canadian provisions. These include special signals for dangerous goods (rule 39), radar reflectors and transponders (rule 41), additional requirements for energy exploration or exploitation vessels (rule 42), safety zones around energy exploration or exploitation vessels (rule 43), ocean data acquisition systems (rule 44), blue flashing light requirement (rule 45), and alternate system of navigation lights (rule 46).[137]

7) *COLREGS 1972*: Annexes I–IV

Some of the *COLREGS 1972* annexes have already been referred to. Annex I sets out the Positioning and Technical Details of Lights and Shapes, which includes definitions; vertical and horizontal positioning and spacing of lights; details of location of direction-indicating lights for fishing vessels, dredgers, and vessels engaged in underwater operations; screens for sidelights; shapes; colour specifications of lights; intensity of electric and non-electric lights; horizontal and vertical sectors; manoeuvring light; and the required approvals for such equipment. Annex II prescribes Additional Signals for Fishing Vessels Fishing in Close Proximity, including a general statement, signals for trawlers, and signals for purse seine fishing vessels. Annex III sets out the Technical Details of Sound Signal Appliances, which includes whistles, bell or gong, and the required approvals for such appliances. Finally, Annex

---

136 Rule 34(k) as am. by S.O.R./83-202, ss.3(50), (51), and (52), & S.O.R./85-397, s.1(2) (manoeuvring and warning signals). See also *Richelieu (The) v. Cie de Navigation Saguenay & Lac St. Jean*, above note 56.
137 Fernandes, above note 15 at 3-79ff.

Maritime Collisions 519

IV sets out the various approved distress signals that a vessel may exhibit, either individually or together, in order to indicate distress and need of assistance. Most provisions of the annexes have certain Canadian modifications whether in the form of additional definitions, special signals, or authority granting provisions.

C. INLAND WATERS RULES

COLREGS 1972 apply "to all vessels upon the high seas and in all waters connected therewith navigable by seagoing vessels."[138] The rules also permit special rules for inland waterways connected with the high seas and navigable by seagoing vessels to be made by appropriate authorities.[139] In other words, this is chiefly of concern to seagoing vessels entering pilotage waters and not to harbour, river, and lake craft. In many states the COLREGS 1972 are, in fact, made applicable to inland waters. However, that is not always the case. While efforts are made to ensure that inland rules conform as closely as possible to the COLREGS, in several regions there are significant differences. Of particular importance for Canada are the rules applicable to almost all North American inland waters. Seagoing vessels will have to switch from COLREGS 1972 to the inland rules when they pass the inland waters demarcation line. There may be instances where risk of collision develops with one vessel still within COLREGS 1972 jurisdiction and the other within inland waters. In such a situation each vessel must navigate in accordance with the rules that will be in effect when they are at their closest point.

1) In Canada

Canada has a significant inland waters system. The regulations covering these waters[140] conform very closely to the Canadian *Collision Regulations*[141] under the COLREGS 1972. However, there are differences

---

138 COLREGS 1972, above note 12, r.1(a).
139 Ibid., r.1(b).
140 See *Burlington Canal Regulations*, S.O.R./89-222 as am. by S.O.R./95-372; *Eastern Canada Vessel Traffic Services Zone Regulations*, above note 66; *Home-trade Inland & Minor Waters Voyages Regulations*, C.R.C., c.1430, as am. by S.O.R./79-91, s.1; *St. Clair & Detroit River Navigation Safety Regulations*, S.O.R./84-335; and *Small Vessel Regulations*, C.R.C., c.1487 as amended.
141 Above note 15.

relating to lights and shapes, manoeuvring and sound signals, ship-to-ship and ship-to-shore communications, radio requirements, and certain special equipment. There are also additional Canadian rules for fishing vessels off the Canadian west coast, for deep draft vessels, and for small vessels.[142] Otherwise the Canadian *Collision Regulations* apply to all Canadian waters and fishing zones other than the Great Lakes, their connecting and tributary waters, and the Ottawa and St. Lawrence rivers and their tributaries as far east as the lower exit of the St. Lambert Lock in the St. Lawrence Seaway near Montreal.

2) In the United States

As Canada shares a significant area of inland waters and other waterways with the United States, the U.S. inland navigational rules are of specific interest. Until 1981 there were three sets of statutory navigational rules in force for the different inland waters of the United States. These were the *Inland Rules*, the *Great Lakes Rules*, and the *Western Rivers Rules*. These rules were in use in those areas where the *COLREGS 1972* were not applicable. For seagoing vessels this four-rule system had the potential to cause problems. Accordingly the U.S. Coast Guard, together with the maritime industry, had advocated for many years that the Inland Rules should be revised and simplified. Finally, in 1980 the U.S. Congress enacted a new statute that gave effect to the current *Inland Rules*.[143] These rules have been in effect since 1983 and have been amended on several occasions. Although these rules recognize the special navigational conditions existing on the western rivers and the Great Lakes, in general, they apply on all U.S. inland waters that are not covered by the *COLREGS 1972*. The Inland Rules now comply much more closely with the *COLREGS 1972*, even in terms of their numbering and layout, and have only one additional annex.[144] As a result, there are now very few differences between the U.S. and Canadian inland waters rules. This is an important improvement, especially for navigation in inland waters that are shared and used by both countries.

---

142 *Small Vessel Regulations*, above note 140.
143 N.J. Healy & D.J. Sharpe, *Cases and Materials on Admiralty*, 3d ed. (St. Paul, MN: West Publishing, 1999) at 591.
144 Annex V covers pilot rules, mainly concerning lights for law enforcement vessels and barges: *ibid.* at 593.

D. LIABILITY FOR MARITIME COLLISIONS

1) Introduction

A maritime collision usually amounts to a tort. Liability for damages resulting from a collision between ships, or between a ship and another object, such as a wharf, depends upon the following:

- a failure under the general principles of negligence to exercise due nautical skill and prudence in the navigation or management of a ship; or
- a violation of the rules of navigation as established by custom or statute, which contributes to the cause of the collision.

Where damage is done to persons or to property of any kind on land or on water, owing to the negligent navigation or management of a vessel, a cause of action arises against those who, by their own negligence or by the negligence of their servants or agents, caused such damage to be done. Such liability may arise under common law, statute, and, in very serious cases, criminal law.[145]

2) Negligence

The essential elements of actionable negligence were already stated in 1823 to be

> a want of that attention and vigilance which is due to the security of other vessels that are navigating on the same seas, and which, if so far neglected as to become, however unintentionally, the cause of damage of any extent to such other vessels, the maritime law considers as a dereliction of bounden duty, entitling the sufferer to reparation in damages.[146]

It has been suggested that there is no distinction between common law and maritime law as to what constitutes negligence causing damage,[147] but the test of negligence under maritime law is not determined by the actions of the ordinary "man" but rather by the actions of the ordinary "seaman." Dr. Lushington has stated: "We are not to expect extraordi-

---

145 See *Criminal Code*, R.S.C. 1985, c.C-46 for provisions related to the operation of ships, dangerous operation of a vehicle (s.249(1)(b)); unseaworthy vessel operation (s.251); and operating a vehicle while impaired (s.253).
146 By Lord Stowell in *Dundee (The)* (1824), 1 Hag. Adm. 109 at 120.
147 *Cayzer v. Carron Co.* (1884), 9 A.C. 873 at 880.

nary skill or extraordinary diligence, but that degree of skill and that degree of diligence which is generally to be found in persons who discharge their duty."[148] Accordingly, maritime law requires a professional seafarer to exhibit ordinary presence of mind and ordinary skill. At a moment of great difficulty or danger, however, a seafarer may do, or omit to do, something that may contribute to the collision, without thereby showing a deficiency in ordinary skill, care, or nerve; for example a wrong decision, taken in the "agony of collision," is not negligence and, unless the emergency was caused by the vessel's fault initially, the ship will not incur liability.[149] These general principles will apply to both shipowners as well as those who operate vessels. Any subsequent contributory negligence and apportionment of liability are applied to ship operations under federal legislation.[150] Negligence defences — such as inevitable accident, *novus actus interveniens* (a new act intervening),[151] and the agony of the moment — are all recognized in maritime proceedings. In addition, Canadian legislation also permits shipowners and vessel operators to limit their liability.[152]

3) Statutory Provisions[153]

Collision rules established by custom have nearly all been superseded by statutory rules such as the *COLREGS 1972*. However, compliance with an existing customary rule will not excuse the nonobservance of

---

148 *Thomas Powell and Cuba (The)* (1866), 14 L.T. 603 at 603.
149 *Sisters (The)* (1876), 1 P.D. 117; *Kenney v. Cape York (The)*, above note 33; *Koskeemo (The) v. Pacific Rover (The)*, above note 60; *Billings Victory (The)*, above note 54; *Maplehurst (The) v. George Hall Coal Co.*, above note 127; *Sunrise Co. v. Lake Winnipeg (The)*, above note 63; *Rhone (The) v. Peter A.B. Widener (The)*, [1993] 1 S.C.R. 497; *Marie Skou (The) v. Nippon Yusen Kaisha Ltd.*, above note 35; *Cuba (The) v. McMillan* (1896), 26 S.C.R. 651.
150 *Canada Shipping Act*, above note 15, Part IX. This subject is now covered by the *Marine Liability Act*, S.C. 2001, c.6. Provincial negligence legislation is no longer applicable subsequent to *Bow Valley Husky (Bermuda) Ltd. v. Saint John Shipbuilding Ltd.*, [1997] 3 S.C.R. 1210; and *Ordon Estate v. Grail*, [1998] 3 S.C.R. 437. See also Chapter 3, "Admiralty Jurisdiction."
151 The doctrine that a negligent party is not liable for damage done to another if the chain of causation between the negligent act and the subsequent damage is broken by the intervening act of a third party.
152 *Marine Liability Act*, above note 150. See Fernandes, above note 15 at 3-1; see also Chapter 18, "Limitation of Liability for Maritime Claims."
153 *Marine Liability Act*, ibid., s.17;, *Canada Shipping Act*, above note 15, Part IX; *Canada Shipping Act, 2001*, above note 15, ss.219–20; see also *Stein v. Kathy K (The)*, above note 33.

a statutory rule.[154] The collision regulations were first given statutory force in Britain in 1846; however, the effect of a violation of one of the rules has changed since then. From 1873 to 1911, any infringement of the rules, which might possibly have contributed to a collision, rendered a vessel blameworthy, unless it could be shown that the departure from the rules was necessary. This doctrine was called "statutory presumption of fault." It was an extremely harsh rule, however, as it was quite possible that a minor regulatory infringement need not necessarily be the cause of the collision.

a) The *Collision Avoidance Rules*

The international response to the widespread concern created by the statutory presumption of fault rule was the *Convention for the Unification of Certain Rules Respecting Collisions between Vessels, 1910* (*Collision Avoidance Rules*), which has been accepted by many states.[155] Under this convention, when two or more vessels are at fault, the liability of each vessel is in proportion to its degree of fault. In order to establish such proportion the causation and blameworthiness have to be established. When it is shown that the faults cannot be established accurately, or if they are equal, liability is apportioned equally.[156] Under the *Collision Avoidance Rules*, a vessel involved in a collision is not liable for damage to cargo or other property belonging to third parties, except in proportion to its degree of fault. On the other hand, vessels at fault have joint and several liability for damages resulting from death or personal injury, without prejudice to the right of a vessel that has paid more than its proper proportion to recover contribution from the other vessel or vessels at fault.[157] However, under Canadian law, parties at fault are jointly and severally liable to those who suffered a loss but only liable in proportion to each other.[158] As the 1910 convention only has relevance to the establishment of the degree of fault of the vessels involved, it does not restrict the right of any innocent vessel or party to take legal action against either of the two negligent vessels jointly or

---

154 *Hjortholm (The)* (1935), 52 Ll. L.R. 223 at 228; *Pearl (The)* (1948), 82 Ll. L.R. 15 at 21.
155 23 September 1910, 4 B.T.S. 6677 (entered into force on 1 March 1913; entered into effect in Canada on 25 October 1914). See also *Ratification of Maritime Conventions*, above note 12 vol.I.3.200. It should be noted that this convention has not been accepted by the United States.
156 *Collision Avoidance Rules*, ibid. at art.4. This principle is also codified in the *Marine Liability Act*, above note 150, s.17(1).
157 *Collision Avoidance Rules*, ibid., art.4.
158 *Marine Liability Act*, above note 150, s.17(3).

severally for its entire loss. However, no liability attaches to any vessel whose fault did not contribute to the loss.

Under the *Collision Avoidance Rules*, "freight" includes passage or hire funds.[159] "Damages" include salvage or other expenses directly related to the collision.[160] On the other hand, the defendant to the action is free to use any defences available in addition to the right to limit liability.[161] In most cases involving damage to cargo, if the fault that caused the collision is an "error in navigation," the shipowner/carrier will have access to the "error in navigation" exception available under the *Hague Rules* or the *Visby Protocol*,[162] or under legislation giving effect to such rules, or under another contract of affreightment. However, it should be noted that, in cases involving states that have accepted the *Hamburg Rules* that do not provide the errors in navigation exoneration, this exclusion would not be applicable.[163] With the acceptance of the *Collision Avoidance Rules*, there was, once again, a requirement to prove that nonobservance of a regulation was the cause, or part of the cause, of a collision or of the damage resulting from the collision. In other words, the law was restored to what it had been prior to 1873. This system imposes a duty on the tribunal hearing the case to examine all phases of the accident. Canadian legislation, implementing the 1910 convention provisions, provides that where damage arises from a breach of the *COLREGS 1972*, such damage will be considered to have been caused by the wilful default of those in charge of the vessel.[164]

---

159 *Ibid.*, s.15(1).
160 *Ibid.*, s.15(2).
161 *Ibid.*, Part 3 (limitation of liability). See also Chapter 18, "Limitation of Liability for Maritime Claims."
162 *International Convention for the Unification of Certain Rules of Law Relating to Bills of Lading*, 25 August 1924, 120 L.N.T.S. 155 [*Hague Rules*] (in force since 2 June 1931; applied in Canada by statute); *Protocol to Amend the International Convention for the Unification of Certain Rules of Law Relating to Bills of Lading, 1924*, 23 February 1968, 1412 U.N.T.S. 121 [*Visby Protocol*] (in force since 23 June 1977; applied in Canada by statute). See also *Ratification of Maritime Conventions*, above note 12 vols.1.5.10 and 1.5.20. See D(6)(a) in Chapter 9, "Carriage of Goods under Bills of Lading and Similar Documents" for detailed information on this area. See also *Marine Liability Act*, above note 150, ss.43 and 45. See Appendix 1, *Hague-Visby Rules*.
163 *United Nations Convention on the Carriage of Goods by Sea*, 31 March 1978, 17 I.L.M. 608 [*Hamburg Rules*] (in force since 1 November 1992; not accepted by Canada). See also *Ratification of Maritime Conventions*, above note 12 vol.I.5.220.

4) Defences and Division of Loss

Like all types of marine casualties, liability for marine collision is based on a finding of fault that has caused or contributed to the damage incurred. This rule has been consistently applied from earliest times.[165] There are two exceptions. First, on very rare occasions, a collision may occur as a result of an "inevitable accident,"[166] such as a sudden unpredicted storm of such intensity as to cause a properly anchored vessel to drag its anchor and collide with another vessel. The defences of inevitable accident and contributory negligence can be used in maritime as well as in common law.[167] The defence of inevitable accident is available if it can be shown that the proximate cause of the accident was some external event beyond the ship's control that could not be avoided by ordinary care and skill or by common foresight. Second, there is the even rarer case of "inscrutable fault," where a court[168] concludes that the collision could not have occurred unless someone erred but that the error cannot be allocated to either party or both parties. An example would be a collision in fair weather, resulting in the loss of both vessels and all those on watch on both vessels. In such no-fault cases — and it has to be emphasized that they are extremely rare — the loss "lies where it falls"; that is, each side bears its own damages, and neither has a claim against the other.[169] Both of these doctrines can generally be regarded to cover situations where there is a failure to find proof of fault. If it can be shown that the plaintiff's subsequent intervening act was the proximate cause of the accident then the principle of *novus actus interveniens*[170] can be applied.[171]

---

164 *Canada Shipping Act*, above note 15, s.564(3); *Canada Shipping Act, 2001*, above note 15, s.38 creates an offence to breach regulations created under the Act. See also Fernandes, above note 15 at 3-1.
165 For a searching review of this history, see Owen, above note 6.
166 In French law termed as "unavoidable accident."
167 *Sea Lion (The)* (1921), 20 Ex. C.R. 137; *Bell Telephone Co. of Canada v. Mar-Tirenno (The)*, [1974] 1 F.C. 294.
168 This is usually a defence brought in U.S. courts. See Healy & Sweeney, above note 3 at 42–43.
169 *Ibid.* Some relevant cases are thoroughly reviewed by S. Chameides, "Inscrutable Fault in Collision Litigation" (1978) 9 J. Mar. L. & Com. 363; however, see the decision of Posner Cir. J. in *Rodi Yachts Inc. v. National Marine*, 984 F.2d 880, 1993 A.M.C. 913, 922 (7th Cir. 1993).
170 Above note 151.
171 *Letnik v. Metropolitan Toronto (Municipality of)*, [1988] 2 F.C. 399.

There is no difference between maritime law and common law as to what amounts to contributory negligence.[172] However, in maritime law, the rule as to the division of the loss has differed at times. At common law, contributory negligence was a complete bar to recovery, and the loss lay where it fell. However, there was a difference in maritime law between 1873 and 1911. During this period, when both vessels in a collision were to blame, the loss was divided equally between the two ships regardless of the proportion of fault.[173] This rule was changed by the *Collision Avoidance Rules*,[174] accepted in England in 1911,[175] and in Canada in 1914.[176] The principle established by this convention provided that liability should be apportioned according to the degree of each vessel's fault.[177] In any case the bar to contributory negligence claims in Canada was firmly removed by the Supreme Court in 1997 and confirmed by legislation.[178] Canada's *Marine Liability Act* also provides limitation periods within which an action must be brought. A possible plaintiff has two years, from the time the cause of action arose, to bring an action.[179] This period can be extended at the discretion of the court.[180] There must be at least two vessels involved for the limitation period to apply.[181]

Shipowners and operators will be liable for damage to other vessels or fixed and floating objects, such as wharves, docks, piers, cranes, buoys, and other personal property as well as for personal injury and death; the vessel involved, however, may have a counterclaim against harbour or dock authorities for providing unsafe conditions.[182] In addition, the federal government also has the responsibility to keep navigable waterways safely buoyed, marked, and lit; the government will be

---

172 *Bow Valley Husky (Bermuda) Ltd. v. Saint John Shipbuilding Ltd.*, above note 150.
173 *Ward v. Yosemite (The)* (1894), 4 Ex. C.R. 241.
174 Above note 155.
175 By the *Maritime Conventions Act, 1911* (U.K.), 1-2 Geo. V., c.57. Collision cases decided in Britain between 1873 and 1911 should therefore be treated with caution.
176 *Maritime Conventions Act, 1914*, S.C. 1914, c.13. Collision cases decided in Canada between 1873 and 1914 should be treated with caution.
177 *Marine Liability Act*, above note 150, s.17. See also *Princess Adelaide (The)* v. *Fred Olsen & Co.*, [1931] S.C.R. 254.
178 *Bow Valley Husky (Bermuda) Ltd. v. Saint John Shipbuilding Ltd.*, above note 150, consolidated in the *Marine Liability Act, ibid.*, s.17.
179 *Marine Liability Act, ibid.*, s.23.
180 *Hartikainen v. Kane (No. 2)* (1976), 15 O.R. (2d) 262 (H.C.J.).
181 *Hovey v. Swan* (1978), 19 O.R. (2d) 725, 86 D.L.R. (3d) 478 (H.C.J.).
182 See Fernandes, above note 15 at 4-54ff, for a listing of some of the relevant Canadian legislation in this area.

liable for negligence in this area,[183] even though such liability may also be limited.[184]

5) Finding of Fault

Fault involves both a causative act and blameworthiness for a navigational error. In the common law system this is considered to be a maritime tort. This implies negligence or "a failure to exercise that degree of skill and care which are ordinarily to be found in a competent seaman" under the prevailing circumstances.[185] It is considered to be the duty of a master to act with reasonable skill and care toward other users of the sea. The proper question to be posed is as follows: could the collision have been prevented by the exercise of ordinary care, caution, and skill? The standard of care is the same for all vessels, regardless of type, trade, or size. This has been defined legally: "the standard of skill and care to be applied by the Court is that of the ordinary mariner and not the extraordinary one, and seamen under criticism should be judged by reference to the situation as it reasonably appeared to them at the time, and not by hindsight."[186]

In almost all collision cases, a breach of one or more of the *COLREGS 1972* rules is a key factor in the finding of fault or negligence. This is directly linked to the damage assessment and subsequent apportionment of blame and damages in any civil litigation that will, almost inevitably, arise. In other words, unless it can be proven clearly that the breach of the *COLREGS 1972* was in no way connected to the collision, which would be quite rare, fault and negligence will be found.[187] However, the court will have discretion in how technically the *COLREGS 1972* will be applied in each case.[188] Furthermore, in most jurisdictions there may also be criminal charges arising out of a collision, especially if personal injury, loss of life, pollution, or other damage to public property is involved; in such a situation the owner of the vessel, the master, and any other person responsible for the conduct of

---

183 *Ibid.* at 4-54, 55. See also *R. v. Nord-Deutsche Versicherungs Gesellschaft*, [1971] S.C.R. 849.
184 *Canada Shipping Act, 2001*, above note 15, ss.268.1 and 295–98; see *Crown Liability Act*, R.S.C. 1985, c.C-50.
185 Viscount Maugham in *Llanover (The)* (1945), 78 Ll. L.R. 461 at 468.
186 Brandon J. in *Boleslaw Chrobry (The)*, [1974] 2 Lloyd's L.R. 308 at 316.
187 *Coniston (The) v. Walrod* (1918), 19 Ex. C.R. 238, 49 D.L.R. 200; *Forward v. Birgitte (The)* (1904), 9 Ex. C.R. 339; *Dominion Shipping Co. v. D'Entremont*, [1948] 4 D.L.R. 719; *Lubrolake (The) v. Sarniadoc (The)*, above note 46.
188 *Brazeau v. Deroy* (1995), 53 A.C.W.S. (3d) 239 (Que. C.A.).

the vessel will be charged with a criminal offence. A defence to such charges will require evidence that the person so charged took all reasonable precautions to avoid committing the offence.[189]

Fault is not precluded by the existence of restricted visibility, severe weather conditions, and other marine perils. The standard of care against which fault is measured is based on three broad principles:

- general concepts of prudent seamanship and reasonable care,[190]
- statutory and regulatory rules governing the movement and management of vessels and other marine structures, and
- recognized customs and usages.[191]

Accordingly, if negligence is present, liability for collision can be imposed even in the absence of a statutory breach. Nevertheless, the most frequent source of liability for collision is the violation of a statute or regulation. These can range from a local harbour bylaw to highest-level international treaty law, such as the *COLREGS 1972*. In most collision cases, the burden of proof rests on the party asserting a cause of action against the other party in order to establish its existence. Normally, the owner or operator of each vessel alleges fault on the part of the other; where both vessels have suffered damage and the owner of one vessel institutes an action against the other, the latter will generally file a counterclaim. In such cases, each party has the burden of proving a cause of action against the other. In cases where two moving vessels collide but there is no indication of any statutory fault, the burden of proof has to be met by any evidence that is available alone.[192]

There may be some areas, involving damage arising from maritime collisions, where strict liability may be applied and fault is not a real consideration. This is especially so in cases involving ship-generated marine pollution from oil and hazardous and noxious substances. These are considered to be complete offences against the public welfare. As a result, such offences normally merit their own compensation

---

189 See, e.g., C. Hill, *Maritime Law*, 4th ed. (London: Lloyd's Press, 1995) at 259.
190 *Robert J. Paisley (The) v. James Richardson & Sons Ltd.*, [1929] S.C.R. 359, rev'd [1930] 2 D.L.R. 257 (P.C.). *A/S Ornen v. Duteous (The)* (1986), 4 F.T.R. 122, [1987] 1 F.C. 270; *Pembina Resources v. ULS International Inc.* (1989), [1990] 1 F.C. 666.
191 See C & D in Chapter 7, "Marine Insurance." See also T.J. Schoenbaum, *Admiralty and Maritime Law*, 2d ed. (St. Paul, MN: West Publishing, 1994) at 715.
192 See Healy & Sweeney, above note 3 at 44; *Dagmar Salen (The) v. Puget Sound Navigation Co.* (S.C.C.), above note 36.

and liability regimes,[193] and shipowners arrange special insurance coverage accordingly.[194]

6) Collision Damages

Collision damages in most maritime states are based on the objective that the injured party should, to the extent possible, be put in the same financial position that the party was in before the collision occurred.[195] This means in practice that, when a vessel is lost as a result of the fault of another vessel, the owners of the lost vessel are entitled to recover its market value, if there is one. In the case of warships or other public service vessels, where there is no market value, their value must be established in some other way, for example, by a formula based on reconstruction cost less depreciation.[196] When the damage is partial, the owner is entitled to damages based on the difference between the vessel's value immediately before and after the collision, which is calculated by adding the following:

- the cost of repairs;
- the expenses incidental to such repairs (i.e., the cost of dry docking, pilotage, and towage in and out of the repair location, survey fees); and
- the cost of maintaining the vessel and profits lost during repairs.

The theory is that the sound market value of the vessel has been reduced by the sum of these items as a result of the collision.[197]

In recent years injured parties have also been able to make claims in order to recover economic losses arising out of maritime acci-

---

193 See Chapter 17, "Marine Pollution Prevention" for a full discussion of the various legal regimes applicable.
194 See E. Gold, *Gard Handbook on P&I Insurance*, 5th ed. (Arendal, NO: Gard, 2002) Part VI.
195 Subject to the right of limitation of liability. See Chapter 18, "Limitation of Liability for Maritime Claims," and C(3) in Chapter 7, "Marine Insurance." See also Fernandes, above note 15 at 3-143.
196 See *Standard Oil Co. v. Southern Pacific Railroad Co. (The Proteus and The Cushing)*, 268 U.S. 146, 45 S.Ct. 465, 1925 A.M.C. 779 (1925).
197 *Pembina Resources v. ULS International*, above note 190; *Engine & Leasing Co. v. Atlantic Towing Ltd.* (1993), 157 N.R. 292 (F.C.A.), aff'd (1993), 164 N.R. 398 (F.C.A.).
198 *Deep Sea Tankers Ltd. v. Tricape (The)*, [1958] S.C.R. 585, 16 D.L.R. (2d) 600; *Canaport Ltd. v. Beaurivage (The)* (1986), 1 F.T.R. 161; *Sunrise Co. v. Lake Winnipeg (The)* (1987), 12 F.T.R. 57, var'd (1988), 28 F.T.R. 78, aff'd [1991] 1 S.C.R. 3.

dents.[198] The general principles followed in such claims are that such losses may be claimed in cases where:[199]

- the defendant owed a duty of care to the particular plaintiff,
- the duty was breached,
- the economic loss flowed directly from the breach, and
- the economic loss was reasonably foreseeable.

Under certain circumstances, such claims may also be made by third parties on economic loss for damage to property belonging to others.[200] Damages for personal injuries are also generally recoverable under the *restitutio in integrum* (restoration to the original position) principle.[201] This will involve recovery for pecuniary losses occurring to the date of trial, costs of future care, damages for loss of future earning capacity as well as non-pecuniary losses such as damages for pain and suffering, loss of enjoyment of life, loss of expectation of life, mental anguish, and emotional trauma.[202] Dependents of the deceased or injured individual may also be able to make claims for pecuniary and non-pecuniary losses suffered.[203]

a) 1952 Civil Jurisdiction Convention

In many cases problems arise when vessels under different flags and claimants of different nationalities are involved. This may lead to conflicts of law difficulties, especially in terms of jurisdiction, damage awards, and the enforcement of such awards. This has led to an attempt by the Comité Maritime International (CMI)[204] to resolve these difficulties through an international treaty. The *International Convention on Certain Rules Concerning Civil Jurisdiction in Matters of Collision, 1952 (1952 Civil Jurisdiction Convention)*[205] applies not only to collisions but

---

199 *Interocean Shipping Co. v. Atlantic Splendour (The)*, [1984] 1 F.C. 931.
200 *Canadian National Railway v. Norsk Pacific Steamship Co.* (1989), 26 F.T.R. 81, aff'd [1990] 3 F.C. 114 (C.A.), aff'd [1992] 1 S.C.R. 1021. See M.R. McGuigan, "The Jervis Crown Case: A Jurisprudential Analysis" (1993) 25 Ottawa L.Rev. 61. See also *Bow Valley Husky (Bermuda) Ltd. v. Saint John Shipbuilding Ltd.*, above note 150.
201 See also Chapter 12, "Maritime Personal Injury and Death."
202 Fernandes, above note 15 at 3-143. See also Chapter 10, "Carriage of Passengers."
203 *Marine Liability Act*, above note 150, ss.6–13. See also *Andrews v. Grand & Toy Alberta Ltd.*, [1978] 2 S.C.R. 229; *Arnold v. Teno*, [1978] 2 S.C.R. 287; *Thornton v. Prince George (Board of Education)*, [1978] 2 S.C.R. 267; *Lindal v. Lindal*, [1981] 2 S.C.R. 629.
204 See G(2)(a) in Chapter 2, "The Shipping Industry: An Overview."
205 10 May 1952, 439 U.N.T.S. 217 (entered into force 14 September 1955; fairly widely accepted, but not by Canada nor the United States). See also *Ratification of Maritime Conventions*, above note 12 vol.I.2.20.

also to damages caused by inappropriate operations, the failure to operate properly, or non-compliance with regulations, even in cases when there has not been an actual collision. While this treaty has not been ratified by Canada, some of its principles have been incorporated into Canadian practice.[206] The convention does not affect domestic legislation covering warships or other public service vessels; claims arising from contracts of carriage or other carriage are also not affected. However, it applies to all interested parties when all the vessels involved belong to contracting states. Nevertheless, a contracting state may apply it to interested parties of a non-contracting state on principles of reciprocity.[207] However, when all parties involved belong to the state where the claim is being heard, national law and not the convention applies. Under these basic principles, litigation for damages caused by a collision between seagoing vessels or between a seagoing vessel and an inland navigational craft can be commenced

- in the defendant's habitual residence or place of business;
- where the defendant's vessel or a sister ship[208] has been properly arrested or a security has been deposited in lieu of such arrest; and
- in the case of a collision within port or inland waters areas, within the jurisdiction of such areas.

The claimant in the case has the right of choice among these jurisdictions. However, such claimant may not bring a similar action in another jurisdiction without discontinuing the initial action. Nevertheless, these provisions do not prejudice the right of the parties involved to bring a collision claim before another forum by agreement or to arbitrate the claim. Counterclaims arising out of the same collision may be brought before the forum that has the initial jurisdiction in the case.

The *1952 Civil Jurisdiction Convention* attempts to present a compromise between common and civil law concepts of jurisdiction. It follows the civil law principle of connecting factors but, at the same time, adds to the list of such factors the common law principle of the *in rem* procedure of ship arrest or the depositing of security to avoid arrest. While the convention has been in force since 1955 and has been accepted by a large number of major maritime states, a significant

---

206 See Chapter 19, "Admiralty Procedure" for a full outline of the Canadian aspects of this area.
207 See Healy & Sweeney, above note 3 at 18–20 for an excellent discussion of this area.
208 See *Holt Cargo Systems Inc. v. ABC Containerline N.V. (The Brussel)* (2000), 185 F.T.R. 145. See also (C)(4) in Chapter 6, "Maritime Mortgages and Liens."

532   MARITIME LAW

group of states has not accepted it.[209] Various reasons for this have been put forward,[210] among them the following:

- the absence of rules for the avoidance of duplications of actions;
- the exclusion of all government vessels, including those used purely for commercial purposes;
- the absence of choice of law provisions; and
- the absence of provisions concerning recognition and enforcement of judgments.

In response, the CMI[211] produced a new draft convention in 1977.[212] This draft was subsequently submitted to the International Maritime Organisation for further consideration; however, owing to the pressure of other matters the IMO Legal Committee has not yet taken up the subject for further consideration.[213]

b) The *Lisbon Rules*

In an effort to unify the widely varying methods of assessing damages in collision cases, the Comité Maritime International adopted the *CMI Lisbon Rules on Compensation for Damages in Collision Cases* (*The Lisbon Rules*) in 1987.[214] These rules are neither statutory in form nor intent but are designed as a set of principles recommended for voluntary adoption by shipowners, insurers, and, where appropriate or necessary, by courts. They could also be adopted by states as model laws. The *Lisbon Rules* are a practical set of guidelines designed to deal with problems that may arise out of a collisions, including the following:

- damages for the total or partial loss of a vessel,
- the method of calculating damages for loss of use of a vessel during the time required for repairs,
- the allowance of interest on damages,
- currency exchange problems arising when repair and other expenses are incurred in more than one state, and

---

209 Including Canada, the United States, Japan, Russia, the Scandinavian states, Brazil, and the Netherlands.
210 Provided and cited by Healy & Sweeney, above note 3 at 19–20.
211 See G(2)(a) in Chapter 2, "The Shipping Industry: An Overview."
212 *International Convention for the Unification of certain Rules Concerning Civil Jurisdiction, Choice of Law, and Recognition and Enforcement of Judgments in Matters of Collision*, 16 June 1977, International Maritime Committee Documentation, vol.1 (London Draft) 22, 1977 CMI Doc. 104.
213 Details of the draft can be found in Healy & Sweeney, above note 3 at 20–22.
214 The *Lisbon Rules* are reproduced in Healy & Sweeney, *ibid.* at 573–77.

- salvage and general average in relation to cargo losses resulting from collisions.[215]

Although the *Lisbon Rules* do not have the force of law, they are designed to be used in negotiations as guidance on what can and cannot be recovered; they therefore contribute to the more efficient and practical handling of maritime claims. Nevertheless, utilization of the rules has been very slow and there is, as yet, no evidence that they have been widely used in Canada.

7) U.S. Law Differences

The *COLREGS 1972* have been accepted widely by almost all maritime states. There are no essential differences in law among states in the treatment of sole-fault collisions, but international uniformity has not yet been achieved in respect of both-to-blame collisions. While the *Collision Avoidance Rules*[216] have been accepted by many states, an important exception is the United States. The United States is Canada's major trading partner and significant inland waters are shared between the two states; as a result, there is substantial maritime sector activity between Canada and the United States at all levels. It is, therefore, necessary to briefly outline the differences that exist in U.S. law. Prior to 1975 U.S. law followed the pre–1910 international provisions that divided damages equally to both vessels involved in a collision regardless of the degree of fault involved. However, it took another sixty-five years for U.S. law to overturn this often unjust rule. In 1975 in a landmark case, the U.S. Supreme Court overruled the "divided-damages rule" and adopted the same proportional fault rule as that set out under the *Collision Avoidance Rules*.[217] As a result, while the United States has never accepted the convention, all U.S. cases on this aspect handed down prior to 1975 are no longer applicable. This means that the international law provisions, as developed under the *Collision Avoidance Rules*, and the U.S. law are now substantially the same.

However, in terms of apportionment of damages between vessels in both-to-blame collision cases, with respect to cargo damage, substantial differences between U.S. and international law remain. For exam-

---

215 Healy & Sweeney, *ibid.* at 338, 344, and 355. See also J. Warot, "A Comment on the Lisbon Rules on Compensation for Damages in Collision Cases" (1987) 18 J. Mar. L. & Com. 583.
216 Above note 155.
217 *United States v. Reliable Transfer Co.*, 421 U.S. 397, 95 S.Ct. 1708, 44 L. Ed. 2d 251, 1975 A.M.C. 541 (1975).

ple, under the *Collision Avoidance Rules*, if the non-carrying vessel is found to be 40 per cent to blame, the cargo interests could recover a maximum of 40 per cent of their damages from the carrier. But since 1924, if the fault is considered an error in navigation, such as a breach of the *COLREGS 1972*, the carrier is usually not liable at all. This is because of the errors in navigation exception in the *Hague Rules*, the *Hague-Visby Rules*, or other contract of affreightment giving effect to such rules.[218] In that case, the cargo interests will be limited to the 40 per cent recoverable from the non-carrier.[219] In the rarer situation, where the fault has arisen from a failure to use due diligence before and after the commencement of the voyage, in terms of the seaworthiness of the vessel's navigational equipment or problems related to the crew, the remaining 60 per cent of cargo damages will be recoverable from the carrier on the basis of a breach of the contract of carriage. However, this is again quite different under U.S. law. The 1975 U.S. Supreme Court decision that incorporated the international proportional fault rule into U.S. maritime law has not affected the "innocent cargo" rule. Under this rule, the cargo interests in a both-to-blame collision case may recover 100 per cent of their damages from the non-carrying vessel. In such a case, the non-carrier who pays or is obliged to pay the full cargo claims has the right to add such payments to its list of damages for apportionment between the two vessels.[220] This leads to a strange anomaly: in such a both-to-blame collision case the carrier indirectly bears a percentage of the loss of the cargo that is carried, proportionate to the carrier's degree of fault; on the other hand, if the carrier had been solely at fault, and the loss of the cargo was caused by an excepted peril, the carrier would have totally escaped liability.

In order to avoid indirect liability for cargo damage in both-to-blame collision cases, carriers have devised the "both-to-blame collision clause" that is included in most modern contracts of affreightment. The effect of this clause is that, in cases where cargo damage occurs as a result of a both-to-blame collision, the cargo owners promise to indemnify the owner of the cargo-carrying vessel to the extent of that portion of the carrier's liability to the other vessel. This clause is considered valid internationally when included in charterparties and other interna-

---

218 See D(6)(a) in Chapter 9, "Carriage of Goods under Bills of Lading and Similar Documents."
219 Under the *Hamburg Rules*, above note 163, exoneration in respect of errors in navigation does not exist.
220 For an excellent analysis of this area, see Healy & Sweeney, above note 3 at 312ff.

tionally accepted contracts of affreightment. Nevertheless, the clause has been declared invalid and unenforceable in the United States, as it was considered to create immunity from the consequences of negligence.[221] Although considered invalid, the clause is still frequently inserted into contracts of affreightment with a U.S. connection. It has also been suggested that the law, as defined by the U.S. Supreme Court, may apply only to regulated bills of lading and that including the clause in unregulated voyage charter parties is valid.[222]

There is one further difference between U.S. law and internationally accepted law. Under the *Pennsylvania Rule*,[223] when a collision occurs and it is shown that a vessel is at fault for breaching a statute or regulation, U.S. law shifts the burden of proof of causation from the plaintiff to the defendant. In other words, under the rule the vessel considered to have breached the rule has to show that the breach could not have been one of the causes of the collision.[224] The extraordinarily heavy burden imposed by this rule has, despite much criticism, survived the 1975 U.S. Supreme Court decision that brought the United States into line with the provisions of the 1910 *Collision Avoidance Rules* convention.[225] Leading U.S. maritime law scholars have long urged that the rule be abolished, as it seems to be basically irrelevant today.[226] U.S. courts have also recognized the harshness of an equal division of damages in the face of vastly disparate blame. This has, at times, been achieved through the application of the major-minor fault doctrine that would find a grossly negligent party solely at fault;[227] however, it has been suggested that this rule, in addition to being inherently unreliable, simply replaces harshness with unfairness.[228] Under the major-minor fault rule, the vessel considered to be primarily negligent receives 100 per cent of the blame, while the vessel with minor negligence receives none.

---

221 U.S. Supreme Court in *United States v. Atlantic Mutual Ins. Co.*, 343 U.S. 236, 72 S.Ct. 666, 96 L.Ed. 907, 1952 A.M.C. 659 (1952).
222 Schoenbaum, above note 191 at 752.
223 Named after a U.S. Supreme Court decision involving a vessel with that name. *Union Steamship Co. v. New York and Virginia Steamship Co. (The Pennsylvania)*, above note 60.
224 Healy & Sweeney, above note 3 at 46.
225 See W. Peck, "The Pennsylvania Rule since Reliable Transfer" (1984) 15 J. Mar. L. & Com. 95.
226 Healy & Sweeney, above note 3 at 45–53.
227 See, e.g., *Alexandre v. Macahan, (City of New York)*, 147 U.S. 72, 85, 13 S.Ct. 211 (1893).
228 Healy & Sharpe, above note 143 at 611.

E. LIABILITY FOR COLLISIONS WITH FIXED AND FLOATING OBJECTS

1) Differences between Collisions with Fixed and Floating Objects and Collisions between Ships

One of the principal legal differences between collisions with fixed and floating objects and collisions between vessels is that the latter are covered under international conventions while the former are not. The law in this area is, therefore, somewhat more uncertain than that regulating collisions between vessels. Claims arising out of damage from ships to such fixed and floating objects as wharves, piers, cranes, shore installations and equipment, offshore structures, pipelines, or storage facilities are generally covered under national statutes and similar legislation. In Canada, the subject is under the *Federal Court Act*.[229] In almost all cases, there will be presumption of fault on the part of the moving vessel that collides with a fixed or floating stationary structure.[230] For example, under English statutory law the owner of a ship that damages the harbour, pier, quays, or other works is responsible for such damage done by the ship or by those in charge of the ship.[231] This statutory liability is larger than the common law liability of the shipowner, as it exists whether the actual wrongdoer is the shipowner's servant or not.[232] Furthermore, English law also seems to indicate that contributory negligence by the harbour authority in the collision will not be acceptable as a defence.[233] While Canada follows these English legal principles,[234] this subject is now under Canada's *Marine Liability*

---

229 S.C. 1971, c.1, s.22(2)(d). See also *Anglo-Canadian Timber Products Ltd. v. Gulf of Georgia Towing Co.*, [1966] Ex. C.R. 855.

230 See, e.g., *Boston (City of) v. Texaco Texas (The)*, 773 F.2d 1396, 1986 A.M.C. 676 (1st Cir. 1985). See also the discussion on this point in *Steves v. Kinnie*, [1917] 1 W.W.R. 1250, 33 D.L.R. 776.

231 *Harbours, Docks and Piers Clauses Act*, 1847 (U.K.), 10 & 11 Vict., c.27, s.74.

232 *Great Western Railway Co. v. Mostyn (The)*, [1928] A.C. 57 (H.L.). See also Marsden, above note 10 at 307.

233 *Workington Harbour and Dock Board v. Tower Field*, [1951] A.C. 112 (H.L.). However, this case was decided before the *Law Reform (Contributory Negligence) Act, 1945* (U.K.), 8 & 9 Geo. VI., c.28, came into operation. This statute may have eased this strict rule somewhat. But see the Australian High Court's decision in *Octavian (The)*, [1974] 1 Lloyd's L.R. 344.

234 *Philip T. Dodge (The) v. Dominion Bridge Co.*, [1935] 4 D.L.R. 65, [1936] 1 W.W.R. 94; *Canadian Salt Co. v. Irving Cedar (The)* (2000), 193 F.T.R. 20; *Sociedad Transoceanica Canopus S.A. v. Canada (Nat. Harbours Board)*, above note 33; *Braber Equipment Ltd. v. Fraser Surrey Docks Ltd.* (1998), 42 B.L.R. (2d) 314

Act, which provides limited liability for port and harbour owners/operators in cases where there was no intent to cause damage or loss.[235] The situation is also somewhat uncertain in the United States, where some courts have held that the owners of the stationary floating or fixed object that has been damaged must first provide evidence that all pertinent statutes and regulations have been complied with before the presumption of the vessel's fault can be applied.[236] Other cases have held that the owner of the moving vessel must first establish such noncompliance by the port authority as a defence.[237] It is generally considered that cases requiring the port authority to first establish its compliance with the relevant regulations are correctly decided.[238] However, in most cases this question is not really of major practical relevance. Plaintiffs will usually indicate their compliance with the relevant law and will offer evidence in support of the allegations that led to the damage without awaiting the moving vessel's attempts to prove otherwise.

2) Damage Liability Claims for Collisions with Fixed and Floating Objects

The shipowner's liability for a collision with a fixed and floating object is similar to that in a ship-to-ship collision, that is, generally in tort, but it may also arise under contract, statute, or other regulation including the criminal law. In other words, the shipowner, both personally and through such owner's servants and agents, has a duty of care to exercise the degree of skill necessary that should have prevented a collision with a fixed and floating object. Under the laws of some states a presumption of fault on the part of the ship arises in cases where a moving vessel collides with a fixed and floating object. In such circumstances the shipowner may be placed in the position of having to prove the absence of fault on the part of the entered vessel's crew; for example, if the collision occurred because of a mechanical failure of ship's equipment, it has to be shown that improper maintenance, repair, or operation did not cause such failure.[239] It may also have to be proven that the colli-

---

(S.C.), aff'd on other grounds (1999), 130 B.C.A.C. 307. See also *Canada Shipping Act*, above note 15, Parts IX and X.
235 *Marine Liability Act*, above note 150, s.30.
236 See *Rogers v. Saeger*, 247 F.2d 758, 1958 A.M.C. 71 (10th Cir. 1957); and *Willis v. Tugs Tramp and Mars*, 216 F. Supp. 901, 1965 A.M.C. 411 (E.D. Va. 1962).
237 *Georgia Ports Authority v. Atlantic Towing Co.*, 1985 A.M.C. 332 (S.D. Ga. 1983).
238 Healy & Sweeney, above note 3 at 45.
239 See *Merchant Prince (The)* (1892), P. 179; *Henderson v. H.E. Jenkins & Sons*, [1970] A.C. 282.

sion was not caused by negligent navigation of the vessel; for example, if it can be shown that, despite the exercise of ordinary care and caution and maritime skill, the collision could not be avoided owing to the dangerous actions of another vessel, or to very adverse weather conditions,[240] liability may be avoided.

Nevertheless, in most cases of collision with a fixed and floating object, the burden of proof is re-allocated from claimant to defendant. There will be a presumption of liability on the part of the ship, and the claimant does not need to prove any specific act or omission on the part of the colliding vessel. This is rather similar to the U.S. *Pennsylvania Rule*.[241] In a collision with a fixed and floating object, the claimant must, however, show that the collision could not have occurred without the vessel's negligence; for example, if the collision occurred at night it has to be shown that the object was properly illuminated.[242] Even if the object, such as an offshore oil unit, was properly illuminated, it also must be shown that its position was properly entered on the relevant charts.

Damage claims for collisions with a fixed and floating object may also arise in contract, especially in damage claims to facilities or equipment in a port area. It is often a requirement for vessels to abide by the standard terms and "conditions of use" for the port facilities. In other cases the master may actually be requested to enter into a formal written agreement with the port or harbour authorities and, in such cases, may have to bind the shipowner under such contract. While the master has the express or implied authority to bind the shipowner, this type of contract may often have onerous terms that cannot be avoided. Furthermore, the port or harbour authority's standard terms and conditions may bind the shipowner, even though no formal contract for the use of the facilities exists. The actual or regular use of the facilities may constitute agreement to be bound by such terms and conditions.[243] On the other hand, if there is an express or implied contractual arrangement between the shipowner and the port authority, then the contract, rather than fault or negligence principles, will govern the claim. In many cases existing contracts will impose liability without fault on the vessel for any damage to a fixed and floating object, even in cases where

---

240 *Boucau (The)*, [1909] P. 163.
241 See above note 223.
242 *Merchant Prince (The)*, above note 239; and *Manorbier Castle (The)* (1922), 16 Asp. M.L.C. 151.
243 On notification of contractual terms under English law, see *Circle Freight International v. Mideast Gulf Exports*, [1988] 2 Lloyd's L.R. 427.

the port authority is solely to blame.[244] In a number of states, vessels involved in a collision with a fixed and floating object may be held strictly liable, irrespective of fault, under statute or regulation.[245] In cases where statutory strict liability applies for damage to a fixed and floating object, there may still be defences available, such as where the master and crew have abandoned the vessel prior to collision,[246] or where the collision occurred solely owing to the fault of a pilot in a compulsory pilotage area.[247]

As in other collision cases, damage claims for collisions with a fixed and floating object are also subject to the law that governs any dispute arising out of the occurrence. This will depend upon factors such as location of the collision, the agreement of the parties, the vessel's flag, and the forum where the case is heard. In cases where the vessel involved in the damage to a fixed and floating object is forced to dock for repairs, survey, or other purposes in the same jurisdiction where the damage occurred, the claimant may arrest the vessel there. This will result not only in security for the release of the vessel being demanded, but also automatically vest the local court with legal jurisdiction. Claims against the vessel colliding with a fixed and floating object may include the following:

- the reasonable cost of both temporary and permanent repairs of the fixed and floating object and its equipment, or where it is beyond economically feasible repair, its value or replacement cost;
- compensation for the loss of use of the fixed and floating object;
- liabilities of the fixed and floating object interests to third parties under statute, contract, or tort; and
- reasonable expenses incurred as a result of the collision, including costs for salvage, agents, and surveyors.

Liability[248] for contact with a fixed and floating object may also cover such objects as

- harbours, quays, docks, locks, piers, jetties, bridges, cranes, buoys, and houseboats;

---

244 See *Polyduke (The)*, [1978] 1 Lloyd's L.R. 211.
245 For example, under English law, under the *Harbours, Docks and Piers Clauses Act, 1847*, above note 231.
246 *Great Western Railway Co. v. Mostyn (The)*, above note 232.
247 *Ibid.* See also *Workington Harbour and Dock Board v. Tower Field*, above note 233; and *Pilotage Act, 1983* (U.K.), 1983 c.21, s.35.
248 Subject to Limitation of Liability. See Chapter 18, "Limitation of Liability for Maritime Claims."

- power and telephone cables and pipelines;
- oil-rigs and similar offshore installations that are considered as fixed to the seabed but that may be classified as ships if under tow or proceeding under their own power; and
- fishing nets and equipment or timber being towed.

It is regrettable that there is no clearly acceptable international regime in this area at this stage. This may well be owing to the fact that the industry has not demanded it because there have been relatively few problems. Nevertheless, it has made the law in the area less predictable, as it will always depend upon the national system.

F. CRIMINAL LIABILITY AND JURISDICTION IN COLLISION CASES

While the vast majority of legal work in marine collisions is devoted to the civil law aspects, a criminal, penal, or other administrative element may also arise. In fact, any collision is likely to involve an investigation by flag or port state authorities and, if there is loss of life, serious personal injury, or other significant damage, such an investigation may not only be formal but also compulsory.[249] This is also an obligation that has been accepted in international law.[250] In many cases such investigations, preliminary enquiries, and formal hearings are principally concerned with ascertaining what safety provisions have been breached and how such occurrences may be prevented in future. In other words, the civil law aspects of fault and negligence are not considered, even though operational fault and negligence may well be determined in such investigations.[251]

In many jurisdictions the findings of such investigations are either not available to a civil law tribunal or may not be considered. Canadian legislation does not appear to insist on investigation but leaves it to the minister's discretion.[252] Nevertheless, the Canadian Transportation Safety Board, with specific jurisdiction for the mandatory reporting of maritime accidents, has been established. This board, which in addition to maritime matters, has also responsibilities for other modes of

---

249 See Fernandes, above note 15 at 3-118ff, and also at 3-137ff.
250 *UNCLOS* art.94(7).
251 *Marsden*, above note 10 at c.21.
252 *Canada Shipping Act*, above note 15, s.477; *Canada Shipping Act, 2001*, above note 15, ss.210–20.

transport, such as aviation, railways, and pipelines, and makes recommendations designed to prevent future accidents to the federal Department of Transportation.[253] The findings of such investigations may be utilized to take action against those considered to have been negligent. For example, masters and navigating officers may have to face further formal hearings that may result in their certificates of competency or licences being cancelled or suspended. In serious cases, especially if it is determined that criminal negligence has taken place, criminal charges may be instituted against those in charge of the ship(s) involved.[254] This raises a significant jurisdictional difficulty. In a collision involving ships under different flags, with crew members of different nationalities, shipowners and cargo based in different states, as well as one or more coastal states that may have been damaged — who has jurisdiction to investigate the collision? And who can take the necessary disciplinary action that may be appropriate? While these types of questions have not yet been completely answered, a serious international attempt has been made to do so.

1) *1952 Penal Jurisdiction Convention*

The first international response to the jurisdictional difficulties discussed above is the *International Convention for the Unification of Certain Rules Relating to Penal Jurisdiction in Matters of Collision or Other Incidents of Navigation, 1952 (1952 Penal Jurisdiction Convention).*[255] This convention was developed by the Comité Maritime International[256] in response to the notorious *Lotus* case. This case arose out of a collision between a French and a Turkish vessel with loss of life on the latter. A Turkish court subsequently convicted the officers in charge of both vessels of manslaughter and jailed them.[257] The *1952 Penal Jurisdiction Convention* provides that, when a collision or other navigational incident or accident occurs outside national waters, penal or disciplinary action against the master or other responsible persons of the vessels involved may only be instituted before the judicial or

---

253 *Canadian Transportation Accident Investigation and Safety Board Act*, S.C. 1989, c.3, ss.3(2) and (3), 4, 7 and 14 (*Transportation Safety Board Regulations*, S.O.R./92-446).
254 Marsden, above note 10 at c.20.
255 10 May 1952, 439 U.N.T.S. 233 (entered into force 20 November 1955; neither Canada nor the United States has accepted this convention). See also *Ratification of Maritime Conventions*, above note 12 vol.I.2.30.
256 See G(2)(a) in Chapter 2, "The Shipping Industry: An Overview."
257 *Lotus (The), (France v. Turkey)* (1927), P.C.I.J. (Ser. A.) No. 10.

administrative tribunals of the flag state. Furthermore, no arrest or detention of the vessel may be ordered, even as a measure of investigation, by any tribunal other than that of the flag state. However, the convention allows any state to permit its own authorities to take any action in respect of certificates of competency or licences issued by that state, or to prosecute its own nationals for offences committed on board vessels of other states. The principal provisions of the *1952 Penal Jurisdiction Convention* were subsequently incorporated into the *Convention on the High Seas, 1958*.[258] This convention confirmed that no penal proceedings may be commenced against the navigating officers of a vessel except before the authorities of the vessel's flag state or the state of which the officers are nationals. These principles were further codified in the *United Nations Convention on the Law of the Sea (UNCLOS)*, the latest international instrument, in virtually identical language.[259]

2) Canadian *Criminal Code*

Although the *1952 Penal Jurisdiction Convention* has been widely accepted, it has not been ratified by Canada at this stage. Canada is also not a party to the *Convention on the High Seas, 1958* nor to *UNCLOS*. However, the Canadian government has expressed its commitment to accept this instrument; when this occurs, Canada will be in line with the general principles set out in the *1952 Penal Jurisdiction Convention*. In any case, the basic principles of this convention have been generally accepted in Canada. Canada has also incorporated a number of criminal offences, arising out of maritime collisions, into the Canadian *Criminal Code*.[260] Offences included are as follows: dangerous operation of a vessel,[261] failure to stop after an accident,[262] operating a vessel while impaired,[263] and joy riding.[264]

---

258 29 April 1958, 450 U.N.T.S. 82, art.11(1) (entered into force 30 September 1962; not accepted by Canada). See also *Ratification of Maritime Conventions*, above note 12 vol.I.1.100.
259 *UNCLOS*, above note 250, art.97(1).
260 For application of Canadian criminal law in collision cases, see *R. v. Wade* (1975), 23 C.C.C. (2d) 572 (N.S. Co. Ct.); *R. v. Cole* (1976), 31 C.C.C. (2d) 427; *R. v. Ernst* (1979), 50 C.C.C. (2d) 320 (N.S.C.A.); *R. v. Stogdale* (1993), 46 M.V.R. (2d) 279, rev'd (1995), 20 M.V.R. (3d) 168; *R. v. Walters* (1977), 5 B.C.L.R. 280; and *Eastaway v. Lavalee* (1912), 5 D.L.R. 229. See also Fernandes, above note 15 at 3-137ff.
261 *Criminal Code*, above note 145, s.249(1b).
262 *Ibid.*, s.252.
263 *Ibid.*, s.253.
264 *Ibid.*, ss.255–59 and 235.

FURTHER READINGS

BOISSON, P., *Safety at Sea* (Paris: Bureau Veritas, 1999) c.19.

CAHILL, R.A., *Collisions and their Causes*, 3d ed. (London: Nautical Institute, 2002).

COCKCROFT, A.N. & J.N.F. LAMEIJER, *A Guide to the Collision Avoidance Rules*, 12th ed. (London: Stanford Maritime, 1982).

FERNANDES, R.M., *Shipping and Admiralty Law* (Scarborough, ON: Carswell, 1995) c.3.

GASKELL, N.J.J., C. Debattista, & R.J. Swatton, *Chorley and Giles' Shipping Law*, 8th ed. (London: Pitman, 1987) c.21.

GAULT, S., *Marsden on Collisions at Sea*, 12th ed. (London: Sweet & Maxwell, 1998).

GOLD, E., *Gard Handbook on P&I Insurance*, 5th ed. (Arendal, NO: Gard A.S., 2002) c.9.

HEALY, N.J. & D.J. SHARPE, *Cases and Materials on Admiralty*, 3d ed. (St. Paul, MN: West Publishing, 1999) c.VII.

HEALY, N.J., & J.C. SWEENEY, *The Law of Marine Collision* (Centreville, MD: Cornell Maritime Press, 1998).

HOLDERT, H.M.C. & F.J. BUZEK, *Collisions Cases: Judgements and Diagrams* (London: Lloyd's Press, 1984).

OWEN, D., "The Origin and Development of Marine Collision Law" (1975) 51 Tul. L. Rev. 759.

SCHOENBAUM, T.J., *Admiralty and Maritime Law*, 3d ed. (St. Paul, MN: West Publishing, 2001) c.12.

CHAPTER 12

MARITIME PERSONAL INJURY AND DEATH

A. INTRODUCTION

Maritime torts may arise in a wide variety of situations. They include collisions between ships; between ships and such stationary objects as cables, jetties, and bridges; groundings; marine pollution; property damage; injuries on board ships; faulty equipment; or unprofessional services leading to loss or cargo damage. The resulting loss may include loss of life or personal injury, property damage, loss of earnings, loss of amenities, and damage to the marine environment. Maritime torts can arise in almost any institution of maritime law and can generate liabilities alongside breaches of contract and other statutory liabilities. There is no limit to the type of actions or inactions and consequent losses that give rise to liability in tort. Various aspects of maritime tort law are addressed in the chapters on collisions, carriage of goods, general average, towage, salvage, and marine pollution. For the most part those chapters address damage to property and the marine environment. The focus of this chapter is on personal injury and death as a result of an accident in a Canadian maritime law context, other than to paying passengers (whose rights are discussed in Chapter 10.)

B. APPLICABLE LAW

As seen earlier in Chapter 3, the applicable law in a maritime tort setting is federal maritime law, both statutory and common law. *Ordon Estate v. Grail* is a seminal decision that has had the effect of severely limiting the application of provincial law in a maritime setting.[1] Prior to *Ordon*, *Stein v. The Kathy K* allowed the application of provincial law in relation to accidents taking place within the inland waters of a province.[2] For a long time, the *Canada Shipping Act* contained antiquated provisions on maritime torts, in particular in regard to the persons who could claim as a result of personal injuries and fatalities, and the nature of claimable damages. There were also inconsistent limitation periods. The courts responded to these deficiencies in different ways. Occasionally they applied provincial family and negligence law. The effect was considerable as, in this manner, the range of dependants included siblings, and the damages that could be claimed included loss of care, guidance, and companionship — neither of which was allowed in Canadian maritime law.[3] In other instances courts displayed reluctance in applying provincial law to maritime torts at all.[4] *Ordon* removed this uncertainty by establishing the four-step test to determine the applicability of a provincial statute in a maritime law setting (discussed earlier), and by developing maritime tort law in this area to extend the notion of damages. At the same time, *Ordon* provided a catalyst for Parliament to legislate the judicial development in that case and to address deficiencies that the Supreme Court of Canada could not redress through judicial intervention, such as the range of eligible claimants.

---

1 [1998] 3 S.C.R. 437 [*Ordon*]. The Supreme Court had earlier affirmed the uniform application of Canadian maritime law irrespective of the type of navigable waters, *Whitbread v. Walley*, [1990] 3 S.C.R. 1273.
2 [1976] 2 S.C.R. 802. The substantive law of the province concerning the division of fault was found applicable.
3 *Palleschi v. Romita*, [1988] O.J. No. 822 (Dist. Ct.) (QL). In *Harrison v. Nelson* (1991), 28 A.C.W.S. (3d) 6 (F.T.D.), an action in the Federal Court parallel to an action in the Ontario Court General Division was stayed, as Ontarian actions were more comprehensive, commenced earlier, and were considered to be more advanced.
4 *Shulman (Guardian ad litem of) v. McCallum*, [1991] 6 W.W.R. 470 (B.C.S.C.), aff'd (1993), 105 D.L.R. (4th) 327 (B.C.C.A.) In this case, the court refused to apply the *Family Compensation Act*, R.S.B.C. 1979, c.120, in relation to a boating accident and held that the matter was properly governed by Canadian maritime law. *Liznick v. Hamelin*, [1994] O.J. No. 624 at para.25 (Ont. Gen. Div.) (QL) held that "derivative claims authorized by the *Family Law Act* cannot have application in actions arising in a maritime context."

The new *Marine Liability Act*, which entered into force on 8 August 2001, consolidates various liability regimes, namely liability for personal injuries and fatalities, general limitation of liability, liability for carriage of passengers by water, liability for carriage of goods by water, and liability and compensation for marine pollution.[5] These diverse subject areas were previously treated separately in the *Canada Shipping Act*[6] and *Carriage of Goods by Water Act*.[7] As part of the process of reforming the *Canada Shipping Act*, it was thought that marine liabilities could more efficiently be consolidated into one dedicated statute, for instance, the *Marine Liability Act*; thus, the new *Canada Shipping Act, 2001*,[8] could focus on the actual operation of the ship.

There are other instances where maritime torts can be committed and fatalities, injuries, and property damage or loss are sustained in situations other than collision. Even in these instances, the applicable law is federal and not provincial. The plaintiff in *Bow Valley Husky (Bermuda) Ltd. v. Saint John Shipbuilding Ltd.*, which concerned damage sustained by fire on board an oil rig, argued unsuccessfully that uniformity is necessary only in matters of navigation and shipping, such as the *Collision Avoidance Rules*.[9] For reasons of policy uniformity, Canadian maritime tort law is not restricted to the application of good seamanship and the *Collision Avoidance Rules* but, rather, extends to any cause of action in tort, *ratione materiae* or *ratione loci*. This was re-affirmed in *Ordon*, which extended this thinking beyond provincial contributory negligence statutes to provincial statutes of general application in a maritime negligence claim.[10] An issue that remained unsettled until *Ordon* was whether provincial family, negligence, and trustee statutes could be applied in relation to claims arising out of personal injuries or fatalities occurring in inland waters, especially in light of the fact that Canadian maritime law lacked the breadth and depth of provincial law on the range of damages and eligible dependants in negligence claims. *Ordon* re-affirmed the applicability of Canadian maritime law and further developed its content to enable its modern application to negligence claims.

One question that *Ordon* left unanswered was whether provincial occupiers' liability statutes were also constitutionally inapplicable to the

---

5   S.C 2001, c.6.
6   R.S.C. 1985, c.S-9.
7   S.C. 1993, c.21 [repealed].
8   S.C. 2001, c.26, not yet in force.
9   *Bow Valley Husky (Bermuda) Ltd. v. Saint John Shipbuilding Ltd.*, [1997] 3 S.C.R. 1210 at 1259–60.
10 *Ordon*, above note 1 at para.93.

extent that some of these purported to cover negligence in a maritime context. The definitions of "premises" in the occupiers' liability statutes of Alberta, British Columbia, Manitoba, Nova Scotia, and Ontario include ships and vessels. In Manitoba, Nova Scotia, and Ontario, the same statute includes "water" in the definition of "premises."[11] The effect of these statutes is to replace the common law duty of care of an occupier of premises, then extend the legislated duty to the navigation and shipping domain. The Supreme Court acknowledged that the question concerning the applicability of Ontario's *Occupiers' Liability Act* is valid but did not address it, since that action was not before it.[12] However, a broad reading of the *Ordon* four-part test to determine whether a provincial statute is applicable in a maritime negligence claim (discussed in Chapter 3, section E) suggests that provincial occupiers' liability statutes are unlikely to survive the second or third step of the test, especially since the Supreme Court has significantly developed maritime tort law and is likely to continue to do so.

C. PERSONAL INJURIES AND FATAL ACCIDENTS IN A MARITIME SETTING

A variety of persons may suffer personal injury or a fatal accident in a maritime setting. The particular significance of the existence of a contractual arrangement lies in the potential modification of the liabilities for fatalities and personal injuries that a tortfeasor would normally be subject to in the absence of any agreement. The rights of a ship or person found liable or that settle a claim are subject to any existing contract between the claimant and tortfeasor. This could include agreement on liability issues.

First, there are persons who are employed to work on board the ship, such as the crew. A ship has a master and crew complement. In

---

11 AB: *Occupiers' Liability Act*, R.S.A. 1980, c.O-4, s.1; BC: *Occupiers' Liability Act*, R.S.B.C. 1996, c.337, s.1; MB: *Occupiers' Liability Act*, R.S.M. 1987, c.O-8, s.1; Manitoba also excludes the application of the *Occupiers' Liability Act* to a contract of carriage, ibid., s.9(2)(c); NS: *Occupiers' Liability Act*, S.N.S. 1996, c.27, s.2; ON: *Occupiers' Liability Act*, R.S.O. 1990, c.O-2, s.21. For commentaries on these provincial statutes, see A.M. Linden, *Canadian Tort Law*, 7th ed. (Markham, ON: Butterworths, 2001) at 651–72.
12 *Ordon*, above note 1 at para.141. The Ontario Court of Appeal's decision on the Lac Seul case was not appealed to the Supreme Court: *Ordon Estate v. Grail* (1996), 30 O.R. (3d) 643.
13 *Marine Liability Act*, above note 5, s.22.

the case of offshore installations and structures, this category of persons includes drill and other support crew for onsite operations; technically these persons are not seamen. In the case of recreational vessels such as cruise liners, the crew may be even more diverse and may include housekeepers, entertainers, and other staff.[14] The contractual relationship is between the employer — who may be the shipowner or operator in the case of an offshore installation, the charterer, or the ship manager — and each member of the crew on an individual basis. The shipowner or operator has a duty to operate a seaworthy ship[15] and to take reasonable measures for the safety of employees.[16] The employees engage the vicarious liability of the employer. Frequently, intervening agencies provide crews and other personnel, acting as intermediaries between the shipowner and the employees. In these cases it is possible that the contract of employment may not be entered into directly with the shipowner. The crew works in a technologically demanding, and physically and mentally stressful environment, frequently far from land. The occupational health considerations are much more significant than in a terrestrial working environment as the nearest medical support may indeed be very distant and, consequently, access to health professionals may be constrained. Because of operational, commercial, and practical considerations, the level of medical expertise on board will tend to be limited and, consequently, maritime or aerial evacuation of injured persons is frequently necessary, although not always possible. International standards for a safe working environment exist under such instruments as *International Convention on Standards of Training, Certification and Watchkeeping for Seafarers*[17] and *Convention Concerning Minimum Standards in Merchant Shipping, (ILO No. 147)*[18] — to which Canada is a party. The two conventions have been implemented under the *Canada Shipping Act* and regulations (see Chapter 5, section C). At the same time, seamen and other professionals in the marine environment are expected to work competently as well as to exercise due diligence.

---

14 *Metaxas v. Galaxias (No.2) (The)*, [1989] 1 F.C. 386 at 390 (T.D.)
15 *Pare v. Rail & Water Terminal (Que)*, [1978] 1 F.C. 23 at para.3. Even though the ship was under charter, the shipowner was not freed of liability to third parties for ensuring reasonable seaworthiness in order to avoid danger to those that use it.
16 Per Lord Watson: "at common law, a master who employs a servant in work of a dangerous character is bound to take all reasonable precautions for the workman's safety" in *Smith v. Baker*, [1891] A.C. 325 at 353.
17 7 July 1978, 1361 U.N.T.S. 2 [*STCW 1978*] (entered into force 28 April 1984).
18 29 October 1976, 1259 U.N.T.S. 335 [*ILO No.147*] (entered into force 28 November 1981).

Second, there are injuries or fatal accidents arising out of collisions involving any ship or craft. As discussed in the previous chapter, there is a duty on those operating a ship to navigate it safely.[19]

Third, there are persons who provide temporary services to ships, such as harbour pilots. They owe a duty of due diligence and professional service to the ship. Such persons may enjoy contractual or statutory protection from liability, or even benefit from limitation of liability.[20] Likewise, the ship operator owes a duty of care to such persons. There is no presumption of negligence against the ship or ship operator.[21]

Fourth, there are paying passengers on board certain ships, such as cruise liners, ferries, recreational vessels (e.g., tour boats), and other craft. Their relationship with the ship and ship operator is governed by a contract between carrier and passenger. The carrier is required to operate a seaworthy ship and navigate it safely.[22] Passengers are not expected to have any particular maritime expertise but are expected to be diligent, follow safety instructions, and other rules in the contract of carriage.[23] The regime governing the liability of the carrier and performing carrier for damage suffered as a result of the death of or personal injury to a passenger is to be found in the *Athens Convention Relating to the Carriage of Passengers and their Luggage by Sea, 1974*, which is implemented in the *Marine Liability Act*.[24] (More about this subject can be read in Chapter 10.)

---

19 *Stein v. Kathy K (The)*, above note 2; *Bentley v. MacDonald* (1977), 27 N.S.R. (2d) 152; *Kwok v. British Columbia Ferry Corp.* (1987), 20 B.C.L.R. (2d) 318, aff'd (1989), 37 B.C.L.R. (2d) 236; *Liznick v. Hamelin*, above note 4.

20 The liability limit of a harbour pilot is $1,000. *Pilotage Act*, R.S.C. 1985, c.P-14, s.40.

21 In *Ferguson v. Arctic Transportation* (1988), 147 F.T.R. 96, a pilot employed by the Panama Canal Authority providing service to a ship transiting the Panama Canal was injured when an insurance wire used to secure the barge to other vessels snagged under water, snapped, and knocked him unconscious. The plaintiff failed to show a causal link between his injury and negligence by the ship operator.

22 *Rast v. Killoran*, [1995] B.C.J. No. 1354 (S.C.) (QL). The operator lost control of the throttle handle in a hired boat that collided with a submerged object, and a passenger was injured. The operator was negligent in losing control of the boat and by tightening the throttle screw.

23 Insufficient safety instructions by an operator may constitute negligence: *Efford v. Bondy*, [1996] B.C.J. No. 171 (B.C.S.C.) (QL). Also, the *Small Vessel Regulations*, C.R.C., c.1487, s.26, require persons in charge of vessels of not more than 5 tons to brief passengers concerning safety and emergency procedures and to demonstrate use of life jackets, in both official languages if necessary.

24 13 December 1974, 14 I.L.M. 945; *Marine Liability Act*, above note 5, s.35.

Fifth, there may be visitors on board ships, and their situation is different in the absence of a contractual employment or passage relationship. A duty of care is expected of them and the host ship.[25] In the case of guest boaters on recreational vessels, such as sailing boats, the boat owner or operator is required to abide by good seamanship and applicable regulations, such as the *Collision Regulations, Small Vessel Regulations, Boating Restrictions Regulations*, and the *Competency of Operators of Pleasure Craft Regulations*.[26]

Sixth, there are situations involving boat rental that are akin to charters. The boat owner is required to maintain boats in a seaworthy state and to ensure that renters are competent in their operation and are not impaired. The same applies to a boat owner who loans the boat. The renter is expected to exercise good seamanship in navigating the boat. Both owner and renter have duties under the regulations listed in the preceding paragraph.[27]

Seventh, there are incidents of recreational towing, situations such as water skiing, para-kiting and towage of other flotation devices, which may be remunerated or gratuitous. A duty of care is owed by the driver to the person being towed, or on the tow; at the same time, the latter has a duty to exercise due diligence.[28]

---

25 *Clark v. Kona Winds Yacht Charters Ltd.* (1990), 34 F.T.R. 211 (T.D.), aff'd (1995), 184 N.R. 355 (C.A.). Even though the action was brought by the plaintiff against the ship she was on, its owner, and barge owner (i.e., the other vessel involved in the collision), the action was allowed against the ship. The ship was the cause of the accident and not the unlit barge, which itself was in violation of the *Collision Regulations*, C.R.C., c.1416. In *Curtis v. Jacques* (1978), 20 O.R. (2d) 552, a gratuitous passenger was injured severely when the boat she was on collided with another at night. Neither boat carried the required lights. The action was allowed against the two negligent operators but not the boat owners.

26 *Collision Regulations*, ibid.; *Small Vessel Regulations*, above note 23; *Boating Restrictions Regulations*, C.R.C., c.1407 as am; *Competency of Operators of Pleasure Craft Regulations*, S.O.R./99-53.

27 *Field v. Poole* (1994), 51 A.C.W.S. (3d) 758 (B.C.S.C.).

28 In *Martin v. Derrach* (1997), 148 Nfld. & P.E.I.R. 127 (P.E.I.S.C.), the plaintiff water skier was negligent when she deliberately steered and collided into a stationary boat. The driver did not breach the duty of care, and the skier had control over the direction of her movement. In *Chamberland v. Fleming* (1984), 29 C.C.L.T. 213, 12 D.L.R. (4th) 688 (Alta. Q.B.), a motor boat wave upset a canoe; the person in the canoe had little experience with canoes, could not swim, and was not wearing a life jacket. While the deceased was contributorily negligent, liability was apportioned between the operator and the owner. A duty of self-care on the deceased was not imposed, as this would have had the effect of sanctioning the negligent behaviour of the persons causing the injury.

Eighth, there are persons who are injured through the negligent vessel navigation of others but who are not on a ship, such as recreational water users or swimmers. There is a duty of due diligence on both the boater and the recreational user. Naturally, the boater is held to the good seamanship standard applicable to recreational boaters.[29]

Finally, there are unusual situations where the negligence of a person on land may cause injury to someone at sea.[30]

D. CLAIMS AND CLAIMANTS

1) Difference between Personal Injury and Fatal Accident Claims

So far personal injuries and fatalities have been referred to together. (The procedural aspects of the actions they give rise to are discussed in Chapter 19.) At this point there are some differences between the two that ought to be highlighted. These are in effect two different types of personal actions and have different historical origins with distinct legal impact. A personal injuries claim was originally developed in the common law, and it entitled the injured person to claim damages against the tortfeasor. This claim was further provided in the *Canada Shipping Act* and today is to be found in the *Marine Liability Act*. A fatal accident claim is not a common law creation but originated by statute. An old common law maxim held that *actio personalis moritur cum persona* (personal action for damages "dies" with the deceased). This harsh rule left the surviving dependants without a cause of action against the tortfeasor. The situation was adjusted to some extent through statutory intervention with the U.K. *Fatal Accidents Act* in 1846, which introduced the claim for dependants in the context of a fatality as a result of a person's wrongful act or omission.[31] As in the claim for personal injury, the fatal accident claim was introduced into the *Canada Shipping*

---

29 *Cox v. Brown* (1996), 4 C.P.C. (4th) 110 (B.C.C.A.), concerned a person injured by a boat while swimming in a lake. See also *Carra v. Lake* (1995), 53 A.C.W.S. (3d) 986 (Que. C.A.).

30 In *Leischner v. West Kootenay Power & Light Co.* (1986), 24 D.L.R. (4th) 641 (B.C.C.A.), a passenger on a sailboat was electrocuted when the mast touched a low-hanging power line above a boat-launching ramp; the power company and the city shared 80 per cent of the fault, with the boat owner being responsible for the remainder.

31 *An Act for Compensating the Families of Persons Killed by Accidents, 1846* (U.K.), 9 & 10 Vict., c.93.

Act but was also judicially developed by *Ordon* (as discussed below) before consolidation in the *Marine Liability Act*. The fatal accident claim is therefore a statutory right of action. Parliament has legislated the problem and thus occupied the field. As a result there continues to be no claim for maritime wrongful death under non-statutory Canadian maritime law. This has been reasserted recently in *Nicholson v. Canada*.[32] The victim was the master of a self-propelled barge, who died after the barge struck a rock in a river and capsized. His dependants were left without a claim after the limitation period in the *Canada Shipping Act* expired before they filed their claim. In the absence of a statutory right of action, counsel for the dependants argued that they were entitled to a claim for maritime wrongful death under non-statutory principles, which were not time-barred or were not subject to statutory limitation periods. Relying on *Ordon*, the Federal Court (Trial Division) rejected this argument.[33]

2) Eligible Claimants

The injured party continues to enjoy all rights of action for the injury suffered. In the case of fatal accidents, a claim by the executor of the estate of the deceased used to be barred. Through judicial reform, *Ordon* changed this anachronistic situation by removing the bar in non-statutory maritime law, thereby allowing the executor or administrator of the estate to advance a claim for negligence in the name of the deceased with the same rights as a survivor. This is a survival action. The change in the common law also affects the relevant principles and procedures governing claims advanced by executors and administrators of estates. The only restriction is a claim for damages for the death or loss of life expectancy, which the court did not permit.[34] The survival action is, in effect, a new cause of action in Canadian maritime law and, consequently, should be distinguished from a dependant's claim.[35] Under the *Marine Liability Act*, the action in a fatal accident claim is to be commenced by the executor or administrator; but, if no action is commenced within six months after the death, any or all of the dependants may bring the action forward.[36]

---

32 [2000] 3 F.C. 225.
33 *Ibid.* at para.42–49.
34 *Ordon*, above note 1 at paras.114–17; applied in *Nicholson v. Canada*, above note 32 at para.65.
35 *Nicholson v. Canada*, *ibid.* at para.65.
36 *Marine Liability Act*, above note 5, s.10(2).

At common law, even though an injured person could sue for damages for his or her own injuries, dependants were allowed to recover in limited circumstances. Prior to the *Marine Liability Act*, *Ordon* had found that siblings were not included in the definition of dependants in a fatal accident claim, even though they were so included in negligence claims at common law. The reason for this finding was that fatal accident claims were considered to be creatures of statute and, therefore, only persons recognized as dependants by statute for the purposes of such claims were eligible to claim. The definition of dependants in fatal accidents in the *Canada Shipping Act* included wife, husband, parents, and children but did not include siblings.[37] Maritime common law contained the old common law bar to actions founded on the death of a third party. The Supreme Court refrained from reforming non-statutory maritime law to expand the definition in a fatal accident context to include siblings, holding that this would, in effect, be a legislative change, that is, contrary to Parliamentary intent, and not a judicial change.[38] On the other hand, the class of eligible claimants in personal injury claims is not a creature of statute but derived from the common law. Although the Supreme Court could have expanded the definition to include siblings in personal injury claims by reforming the maritime common law, it declined to do so. The Court felt it would not be appropriate for judicial reform in the case of personal injury claims without a similar reform in fatality claims.[39]

The *Marine Liability Act* has modernized and expanded the definition of "dependant" for maritime tort claims. Dependants of injured or deceased persons are entitled to claim for their loss from the tortfeasor.[40] The relationship of dependant in the case of death must occur at the time of death and, in the case of personal injury, at the time the cause of action arose. Dependant includes three categories of persons, namely, children and grandchildren,[41] spouses and cohabitants,[42] and parents and siblings.[43]

---

37   Above note 6, s.645.
38   *Ordon*, above note 1 at para.106.
39   *Ibid.* at para.107.
40   *Marine Liability Act*, above note 5, ss.6(1) and (2).
41   "[A] son, daughter, stepson, stepdaughter, grandson, granddaughter, adopted son or daughter, or an individual for whom the injured or deceased person stood in the place of a parent": *Marine Liability Act*, above note 5, s.4(a).
42   "[A] spouse, or an individual who was cohabiting with the injured or deceased person in a conjugal relationship having so cohabited for a period of at least one year": *Marine Liability Act, ibid.*, s.4(b).
43   "[A] brother, sister, father, mother, grandfather, grandmother, stepfather, stepmother, adoptive father or mother, or an individual who stood in the place of a parent": *Marine Liability Act, ibid.*, s.4(c).

E. LIABILITY FOR MARITIME ACCIDENTS

1) Standard of Care

The duty of care and related defences in a maritime context (discussed in Chapter 11, section D, in relation to liability for collisions) generally apply to maritime accidents, irrespective of location. In *Whitbread v. Walley*, La Forest J. stated that marine and inland navigable waters were subject to one uniform maritime law concerning collisions and other accidents in the course of navigation, and that this applied to commercial as well as pleasure craft.[44] The effect of this dictum is that the *Collision Avoidance Rules* and the standard of good seamanship apply to all ships. It will be recalled from the earlier discussion that liability for a maritime tort is engaged when there is a failure under the general principles of negligence to exercise due nautical skill and prudence in the navigation or management of a ship; or a violation of the rules of navigation as established by custom or statute, which contributes to the cause of the collision. The actions under scrutiny are those of the ordinary, not the extraordinary, seaman. Causation between the offending act and injury or loss must be established to found liability. There must be negligence and not simply error of judgment.[45] The consequence of culpable behaviour is to give rise to a right of action by those suffering the loss against those that caused the loss. Therefore, collision with a stationary object creates a presumption of fault against the moving ship and, unless inevitable accident is demonstrated, there will be liability toward persons that suffer injury as a result.[46]

2) Considerations Specific to Recreational Boating

Over the last three decades, there has been a steady increase in recreational boating accidents in marine and inland waters across Canada. More than 200 boating fatalities and some 6,000 non-fatal accidents occur every year.[47] The latter frequently involve personal injuries, property losses, and loss of income. The regrettable aspect of such statistics is that most incidents are preventable. The lack of due care in

---

44 *Whitbread v. Walley*, above note 1 at paras.26–30.
45 *Horsley v. MacLaren*, [1972] S.C.R. 441, (1971), 22 D.L.R. (3d) 545.
46 *Steves v. Kinnie*, [1917] 1 W.W.R. 1250, 33 D.L.R. 776.
47 See Canadian Coast Guard, "Boating Related Incidents in Canada," online at: <http://www.ccg-gcc.gc.ca/obs-bsn/sbg-gsn/incidents_e.htm>.

recreational boating accidents frequently involves lack of good seamanship by those responsible for operating pleasure craft and their employees. However, it is also often the case that the lack of ordinary diligence by ordinary persons, not seamen, is responsible for or contributes to an accident. This raises two additional dimensions to the standard of care discussed in Chapter 11. The first concerns the application of good seamanship in a recreational boating setting. High regulatory safety standards are increasingly applicable to a growing range of recreational craft. The *Small Vessel Regulations*[48] recently have been overhauled, together with the *Collision Regulations*,[49] *Boating Restrictions Regulations*,[50] *Competency of Operators of Pleasure Craft Regulations*,[51] and other regulations under the *Canada Shipping Act*.[52] There are now new thresholds for the standard of care expected from recreational boaters. All persons have a statutory duty to operate small vessels with due care and attention and reasonable consideration for other persons.[53] This aspect of maritime tort law operates alongside the more established standards concerning collisions, property damage, and accidents to passengers and crew.

Proof of competency requirements for persons operating pleasure craft are being phased in over a ten-year period. "Proof of competency" means a pleasure craft operator card, a boating safety course completion card, a rental boat safety checklist, proof of the successful completion of a boating safety course, or a certificate or other document pertaining to safety knowledge required by the regulations.[54] Boat owners, masters, operators, charterers, hirers, or persons in charge of pleas-

---

48 These regulations apply to pleasure craft, vessels of less than 5 GT that do not carry more than twelve passengers, and power-driven vessels of less than 15 tons that are neither passenger-carrying craft nor fishing vessels, above note 23. Included in the coverage of the regulations are any power boat, personal water craft, any paddling sport (e.g., kayaking), sailing, sailboarding, and recreational towing (e.g., water skiing).
49 Above note 25.
50 Above note 26.
51 *Ibid.*
52 Other relevant regulations include the *Life Saving Equipment Regulations*, C.R.C., c.1436 as am.; and *Charts and Nautical Publications Regulations*, S.O.R./95-149 as am. by S.O.R./95-536.
53 *Small Vessel Regulations*, above note 23, s.43.
54 Phase-in periods: for operators born after 1 April 1983, the requirement date is 15 September 1999; for operators of craft less than 4 metres including personal water craft, the requirement date is 15 September 2002; for all other operators, the requirement date is 15 September 2009, *Competency of Operators of Pleasure Craft Regulations*, above note 26, s.5.

ure craft have a duty not to allow a person to operate a pleasure craft unless that person is of the required age and is competent to operate such craft under the regulations.[55] There are safety of navigation restrictions on speed, distances, and trajectories from the shore for various crafts. In many areas restrictions on navigation in respect of waters within a province may be put in place by a designated provincial authority.[56] In addition to operator competency, there are seaworthiness requirements of a technical nature in terms of the design, construction, and good working order of personal protection; and boat safety, distress, and navigational equipment.[57]

The second additional dimension to the standard of care is the continued applicability of the duty of due diligence to persons who are not seamen but are in a maritime context when they suffer injury or die in an accident. In *Efford v. Bondy*, a passenger on board a rigid hull inflatable whale-watching boat was injured when the boat crossed the wake of a larger vessel. The defendant operator had a duty to warn of the danger of sitting at the bow and to provide appropriate instructions to passengers, but the plaintiff was contributorily negligent in choosing to sit in a place where there was a higher risk of injury.[58]

Finally, in addition to civil liability, operation of an unseaworthy vessel, dangerous operation of a vessel, operating a vessel in an impaired state, and failing to stop at an accident scene may incur criminal liability.[59] In those provinces where the governments concerned entered into an agreement with the federal Minister of Fisheries and Oceans about reporting procedures for pleasure craft accidents, the person responsible for the care and control of the craft is required to complete a Boating Accident Report Form and forward it to the Office of Boating Safety in the Canadian Coast Guard within fourteen days of

---

55 *Competency of Operators of Pleasure Craft Regulations*, ibid., s.2 (2.1). In the case of non-residents, unless they hold a Canadian competency certificate, a similar certificate of competency issued by the country of residence is required (s.4(2)). The *Boating Restrictions Regulations*, above note 26 s.2, set various minimum age/horsepower restrictions. A strict liability offence, subject to a defence of due diligence, is established for owners, masters, operators, charterers, hirers, or persons in charge of vessels operated in violation of these regulations. There is vicarious liability for actions of an employee, unless due diligence is exercised (s.16).
56 A designated provincial authority may request the minister to issue navigational restrictions for specified areas. *Boating Restrictions Regulations*, above note 26, s.8.1. There are restrictions in most provinces.
57 *Small Vessel Regulations*, above note 23, s.4ff.
58 *Efford v. Bondy*, above note 23.
59 *Criminal Code*, R.S.C. 1985, c.46, s.252.

the accident. Where there is serious injury to a person, a fatality, or extensive property damage, the accident has to be reported to the local police authority.[60]

3) Damages

As in general tort claims, pecuniary and non-pecuniary damages may be sought by the claimants.[61] (Sufficient to comment here on particular issues that have arisen in a maritime context.)[62] The uncertainty concerning eligible damages in Canadian maritime law existing before *Ordon* has been clarified by this decision and subsequently also by the *Marine Liability Act*. Previously, statutory maritime law was silent as to the nature of the compensable loss, and damages in the case of fatalities were restricted to pecuniary loss only.[63] Modern conceptions of damages in terms of lost guidance, care, and companionship were not recoverable in Canadian maritime law because the loss itself was non-pecuniary, despite instances of decisions to the contrary.[64] As seen earlier in the discussion of the applicable law, the effect was to encourage some courts to apply provincial law and others to apply anachronistic maritime law. In the "interests of fairness and justice" and the "dynamic and evolving fabric of our society," *Ordon* extended the definition of damages in non-statutory maritime law in line with contemporary trends in the conception of loss for both personal injuries and fatalities. The loss for which a dependant can claim damages now includes loss of guidance, care, and companionship of a dependant as long as "the

---

60 *Small Vessel Regulations*, above note 23, s.49. The Office for Boating Safety was established in the Canadian Coast Guard in 1995 to focus on recreational boating matters.
61 *Carra v. Lake*, above note 29. An accountant who was on an air mattress on a lake was injured as a result of a collision with a motor boat towing a skier. She suffered a 26 per cent loss of physical ability and, at trial, she was awarded damages for loss of salary, disbursements, and non-pecuniary damages. She appealed claiming pecuniary damages and succeeded in part. While the Court of Appeal determined that the longevity of her career as an accountant was threatened, it did not agree that this amounted to a 26 per cent loss but pecuniary damages were allowed in part.
62 In addition to the discussion in Chapter 11, for a more detailed treatment of this subject the reader is referred to Linden's classical *Canadian Tort Law*, above note 11.
63 *Canada Shipping Act*, above note 6, s.647(2).
64 *Mason v. Peters* (1982), 139 D.L.R. (3d) 104 (C.A.). This was a motor vehicle case where an award for loss, guidance, etc., was given within the purview of pecuniary damages. See also *Ordon*, above note 1 at para.98.

claimant is able to establish, among other elements of the claim, that the injury suffered was sufficiently serious that it is capable of producing a loss of guidance, care and companionship."[65]

The *Marine Liability Act* now articulates the damages recoverable by a dependant of the injured or deceased person to include "an amount to compensate for the loss of guidance, care and companionship that the dependant could reasonably have expected to receive from the injured or deceased person if the injury or death had not occurred."[66] Such damages are determined and awarded to dependants by a court in proportion to their loss.[67] Any amounts payable under an insurance contract on the death of the deceased are not taken into account in assessing damages.[68] Similarly, pension payments under workers' compensation legislation are not included in the assessment.[69] The tortfeasor may pay an amount of money into court to cover his or her liability toward persons entitled to damages.[70] The distribution of this money among claimants is then undertaken by the court in accordance with the shares determined by it.[71]

4) Apportionment of Liability

Maritime collisions frequently involve the negligence of more than one ship or person. These are situations of contributory negligence. Liability is proportionate to the degree of fault or neglect and, where this cannot be established, liability is apportioned equally. The tortfeasors are jointly and severally liable to those that suffer the loss and, as between themselves, they are liable to make a contribution to or indemnify each other to their respective degree of fault.[72] The latter rule in the *Marine Liability Act* had been anticipated earlier by *Bow Val-*

---

65 *Ordon*, above note 1 at paras.101–2.
66 *Marine Liability Act*, above note 5, s.6(3)(a). Damages also include "any amount to which a public authority may be subrogated in respect of payments consequent on the injury or death that are made to or for the benefit of the injured or deceased person or the dependant" (*ibid.*, s.6(3)(b)).
67 *Ibid.*, s.7.
68 *Ibid.*, s.6(4).
69 *Giovanni Amendola (The) v. Vae (Le)*, [1960] Ex. C.R. 492. The case concerned pension payments under the B.C. *Workmen's Compensation Act, Amended Act, 1954*, S.B.C. 1954, c.54, s.9.
70 *Marine Liability Act*, above note 5, s.8.
71 *Ibid.*, s.7. The court has discretion to postpone distribution of shares to minors and persons with a legal disability and to make any order for their protection: *Marine Liability Act*, s.9.
72 *Marine Liability Act, ibid.*, ss.17(1) and (2).

ley Husky (Bermuda) Ltd. v. Saint John Shipbuilding Ltd., which reviewed the law on maritime contributory negligence and lifted the bar to recovery. The rules on apportionment apply even where the person who suffered the loss had an opportunity to avoid it but failed to do so.[73] What remains to be discussed now is how liability is apportioned in cases of personal injury or fatality. In *Field v. Poole*, three personal water craft were rented, and two of them were involved in a collision, with two operators being injured. Liability was split in three ways between the water-craft owner and the two injured persons. The owner was 25 per cent liable for falling short of the standard of care required in renting the craft. The court held the owner had a duty to ensure that the persons renting had a basic knowledge of the craft, its operation and capacity, and the rules of the sea, and that they were not impaired by alcohol. The plaintiff, one of the two injured operators, was liable for 35 per cent for failing to exercise reasonable care in operating the craft. The second injured person was liable for 49 per cent for not steering away and slowing down to maintain a safe distance from the other craft navigated by the plaintiff and which was involved in the collision.[74] In *Efford v. Bondy*, the operator of a whale-watching boat was liable for 75 per cent of the damage, whereas the defendant was responsible for 25 per cent. The defendant was sitting at the bow of the boat when the wake of a larger vessel was crossed causing the smaller boat to come down hard. The operator had advised passengers that the roughest ride was in the bow, and that persons with back problems or who were pregnant should not sit there; passengers were not instructed on the location of the handholds nor how to brace themselves. The plaintiff was contributorily negligent in choosing to sit in the bow, when she knew or ought to have known that there was a higher risk of injury by doing so.[75]

FURTHER READINGS

CANADA, *Eliminating Outmoded Common Law Defences In Maritime Torts: A Discussion Paper* (Ottawa: Justice Canada, Admiralty and Maritime Law Section, 1994).

FERNANDES, R.M., *Boating Law of Canada* (Toronto: Carswell, 1989).

---

73 Above note 9; *Marine Liability Act*, ibid., s.21.
74 Above note 27; *Marine Liability Act*, ibid.
75 Above note 23

LINDEN, A.M., *Canadian Tort Law*, 7th ed. (Markham, ON: Butterworths, 2001).

MACGUIGAN, M.R., "The Jervis Crown Case: A Jurisprudential Analysis" (1993) 25 Ottawa L. Rev. 61.

POPP, A.H.E., "Limitation of Liability in Maritime Law — An Assessment of its Viability from a Canadian Perspective" (1993) 24 J. Mar. Law & Comm. 335.

SPICER, W. & W.H. LAURENCE, "Not Fade Away: The Re-Emergence of Common Law Defences in Canadian Maritime Law" (1992) 71 Can. Bar Rev. 700.

CHAPTER 13

MARITIME PILOTAGE

A. INTRODUCTION

When a ship comes from the high seas, is engaged in coastal trade, approaches a port and enters harbour, or moves port-to-port or even berth-to-berth, local knowledge of the area is essential to avoid accidents. Harbour authorities have the power to make local rules for maritime traffic within their jurisdiction and these local rules take precedence over the international rules for preventing collisions (discussed in Chapter 11).[1] Naturally, masters and officers of commercial and large recreational vessels cannot be expected to know the navigation rules of every harbour at which they may call on their voyage. Their ships must, therefore, engage the services of local pilots to guide them when entering or leaving a port, or navigating therein or through other confined waters such as inland waterways. Under modern conditions it would be unsafe to leave engaging a pilot to the discretion of a ship's master, so in many districts pilotage has been made compulsory. There are certain ports and harbours where pilotage is not compulsory and, in those ports where pilotage is compulsory, certain vessels are

---

1 *Convention on the International Regulations for Preventing Collisions at Sea, 1972*, 20 October 1972, 1050 U.N.T.S. 16, r.1 [*COLREGS 1972*] (entered into force 15 July 1977, am. 1981, 1987, 1989, and 1993); see also the Canadian equivalent *Collision Regulations*, C.R.C., c.1416, s.3.

exempted, such as warships, small crafts, and ferries.[2] The decision to employ a pilot or not may be a question of due care in the circumstances. In a case where pilotage is not compulsory a ship's master can be held negligent if his or her failure to use the service contributed to the accident.[3] Where pilotage is compulsory, any movement of the ship within the pilotage area necessitates the utilization of a pilot.[4]

Pilotage in Canada is presently governed by the *Pilotage Act*.[5] Before 1911, pilotage was regulated by Part VI of the *Canada Shipping Act*. The *Pilotage Act* was enacted because the pilotage legislation in the *Canada Shipping Act* was considered to be "seriously out-of-date, unnecessarily complicated, obscure and ambiguous and, in some respects, incomprehensible to those who must implement it."[6] Thus the *Pilotage Act* modernized pilotage law and empowered pilotage authorities to enact regulations for their region. It should be noted that pilotage is not regulated internationally. The principal organization representing most national pilotage groups is the International Marine Pilots' Association, located in London, England (see Chapter 2 secion G(2)(p)); the Canadian section of the international association is the Canadian Marine Pilots' Association.

B. PILOTAGE AUTHORITIES

In Canada pilotage services are offered through pilotage authorities, which are Crown corporations with public employees, but are not agents of the Crown. The four pilotage authorities in Canada — the Atlantic is based in Halifax; the Laurentian in Montreal; the Great Lakes in Cornwall, Ontario; and the Pacific in Vancouver — are set up to "establish, operate, maintain and administer in the interests of safety an efficient pilotage service" in their respective regions.[7] The operational geographical region for each authority is set out in the schedule to the *Pilotage Act*. Each of these authorities has adopted regulations

---

2   The listing of ships to make them subject to compulsory pilotage or waiver of pilotage is provided in a pilotage authority's regulations. See for instance *Atlantic Pilotage Authority Regulations*, C.R.C., c.1264, ss.4–5.
3   *Alletta (The)*, [1965] 2 Lloyd's Rep. 479.
4   *R. v. Fernandez* (1980), 29 Nfld. & P.E.I.R. 361 (Nfld. S.C.(T.D.)).
5   R.S.C. 1985, c.P-14.
6   *Report of the Royal Commission on Pilotage* (Ottawa: Queen's Printer, 1968) Part 1 at 458.
7   *Pilotage Act*, above note 5, s.18 and Sch.

for its own region.[8] The powers include the establishment of compulsory pilotage areas and pilotage requirements for certain classes of ships.[9] These powers should be read against a harbour authority's power to designate traffic control zones in order to promote "safe and efficient navigation or environmental protection in the waters of the port, with respect to ships or classes of ships."[10] The definition of "ship" for pilotage purposes includes "any description of vessel or boat used or designed for use in navigation, without regard to method or lack of propulsion."[11] Thus even a tow is subject to pilotage.

Pilotage authorities are empowered to regulate the pilotage profession in their regions. They establish certain qualifications for the training and licensing of pilots or the granting of pilotage certificates, as well as disciplinary procedures. Barring regulatory exceptions, no person can act as a pilot within a compulsory pilotage area unless he or she is licensed or is a crew member in possession of a pilotage certificate for the area.[12] Pilotage certificates are granted to mariners who show such degree of skill and local knowledge of the waters as would be considered equivalent to that required of a licensed pilot.[13] Each pilotage authority maintains a register of pilots.[14] Authorities either hire their own pilots or contract their services.[15] It is possible for pilots to form their own association which, in turn, contracts the pilotage services to an authority. Neither Canada nor an authority is liable for any damage or loss occasioned by the fault, neglect, want of skill, or wilful and wrongful act of a licensed pilot or the holder of a pilotage certificate.[16] Pilotage authorities levy charges for their services. In com-

---

8 *General Pilotage Regulations*, S.O.R./2000-132; *Atlantic Pilotage Authority Regulations*, above note 2; *Atlantic Pilotage Authority Non-Compulsory Area Regulations*, S.O.R./86-1004; *Atlantic Pilotage Tariff Regulations*, S.O.R./95-586; *Atlantic Pilotage Tariff Regulations – Newfoundland and Labrador Non-Compulsory Areas*, S.O.R./81-710; *Atlantic Pilotage Authority Pension Regulations*, C.R.C., c.1355; *Great Lakes Pilotage Regulations*, C.R.C., 1266; *Great Lakes Pilotage Tariff Regulations*, S.O.R./84-253; *Laurentian Pilotage Authority Regulations*, C.R.C., c.1268; *Laurentian Pilotage Authority District No.3 Regulations*, S.O.R./87-58; *Laurentian Pilotage Tariff Regulations*, S.O.R./2001-84; *Pacific Pilotage Regulations*, C.R.C., c.1270; *Pacific Pilotage Tariff Regulations*, S.O.R./85-583.
9 *Pilotage Act*, above note 5, s.20.
10 *Canada Marine Act*, S.C. 1998, c.10, s.56(1).
11 *Pilotage Act*, above note 5, s.2.
12 *Ibid.*, s.25(1).
13 *Ibid.*, s.22(1).
14 *Ibid.*, s.32.
15 *Ibid.*, s.15.
16 *Ibid.*, s.39.

pulsory pilotage areas the non-use of pilotage services does not discharge the master and owner from paying the charges, unless compulsory pilotage has been waived. In situations where a ship under pilotage leads another ship without a pilot, the latter is still liable for the charges. In a situation where a tug has a waiver or possesses a certificate, the tow is liable for the charges. So in effect, unless there is a waiver of compulsory pilotage, pilotage fees are levied in compulsory pilotage districts, whether a pilot is actually used or not. The master, owner, and agent are then jointly and severally liable to the authority for the charges and a ship may not get customs clearance unless those charges are paid.[17] Further, proceeding without the use of a required pilot is an offence subject to a fine on summary conviction.[18]

C. PILOT/MASTER RELATIONSHIP

1) Legal Status of the Pilot

A pilot is defined in the *Pilotage Act* as "any person not belonging to a ship who has the conduct thereof."[19] This does not mean that the pilot becomes the sole authority on the ship. As the Royal Commission on Pilotage pointed out in 1968, the conduct of a ship must not be confused with command of a ship. The latter points to power and authority, whereas the former is simply a service. Compulsory and voluntary pilotage are similar to the many other services the master contracts and/or supervises on behalf of the ship; consequently, the pilot, although not a member of the crew, is subject to the master's authority. Thus the pilot, who exercises a delegated function, can never supersede the master's authority.[20]

2) Pilot/Master Relationship

In the vast majority of cases, the relationship between the pilot and master will be straightforward and uneventful. However, that relationship can be a very difficult one. Consider the near-collision (i.e., allision) of the tanker The Diamond Star with a pier of Laviolette Bridge in Quebec in 1994, which was investigated by the Transportation Safety

---

17 Ibid., ss.42–45.
18 Ibid., s.47.
19 Ibid., s.2.
20 *Report of the Royal Commission on Pilotage*, above note 6, Part 1 at 26–27.

Board.[21] The master was on the bridge with the pilot when he noticed a pier of the bridge dead ahead of the vessel. He ordered hard-a-port helm, but the pilot immediately ordered hard-a-starboard helm. The master repeated his order and the vessel turned to port and missed the pier and bridge. As soon as the bridge was passed the master noticed a smell of alcohol on the pilot; it turned out that the pilot had a severe alcohol addiction problem.[22] The master ordered the pilot to anchor the vessel, relieved him from duty, and waited for a substitute pilot. The master used his authority to override the pilot's instructions.

While the vast majority of pilotage services in Canada are performed without incident, The Diamond Star accident is not an isolated event. A recent report of the Transportation Safety Board showed that between 1981–1992 there were 273 accidents in Canadian pilotage waters. In 200 of these occurrences the ship was under the conduct of a pilot. The contributing factors were as follows: human, as distinct from, for instance, environmental or technological, and specifically misunderstanding (seventeen accidents); inattention (pilot: twenty-eight accidents, officer-on-watch: nineteen accidents); lack of communication (twenty accidents); and misjudgment (pilot: seventy accidents, master: twenty-one accidents).[23] The first point to be made is that a licensed pilot who has the conduct of a ship is responsible to its master for the safe navigation of the vessel.[24] The master remains ultimately responsible for the safety of the ship. Thus the master may take back control of the ship and relieve the pilot from onboard duty altogether, if he or she has reason to believe that the pilot's actions are endangering the safety of the ship.[25] Even though this duty is cast as a discretionary one in the *Pilotage Act*, in reality the situation might compel the master to re-take control. The master must then provide a written report to the relevant pilotage authority explaining the action and providing reasons. It is important that the master has reasonable grounds.

---

21 Canada, *Marine Occurrence Report: Near Collision of the Tanker "Diamond Star" with a Pier of the La Violette Bridge, Quebec, 9 April 1994* (Hull, ON: Transportation Safety Board, 1994) Report No. M94L0011.
22 Pilots on duty may not consume alcohol or any drug that may impair their ability to conduct of the ship. *Pilotage Act*, above note 5, s.25(4).
23 Canada, *A Safety Study of the Operational Relationship between Ship Masters/Watchkeeping Officers and Marine Pilots* (Hull, ON: Transportation Safety Board, 1995) Report No. SM9501 [*Safety Study*].
24 *Pilotage Act*, above note 5, s.25(2). See also *Guy Mannering (The)* (1882), 4 Asp. M.L.C. 553 at 554.
25 *Pilotage Act*, ibid., s.26 (1). See also *Tower Field v. Workington Harbour and Dock Board* (1950), 84 Ll. L.R. 233; and *Ape (The)* (1914), 12 Asp. M.L.C. 487.

This raises an interesting question as to what is the precise role of the pilot. The pilot is more than an advisor and is entrusted with the navigation of the ship.[26] His or her instructions must generally be followed, since he or she may be the only person on board who has knowledge of the dangers of the locality in which the vessel is navigating. The pilot is entitled to receive assistance from the master, officers, and crew, and these persons have a duty to provide that assistance.[27] However, such duty to assist may not extend to matters of a purely local significance, which are, and ought to be, within the particular knowledge of the pilot.[28] The master is reasonably expected to rely on the advice of the pilot, and not second-guess his or her local knowledge.[29]

The safety of the ship cannot be ensured by the pilot or master acting alone, even though the master is ultimately responsible for safety. It is essential that there be an effective relationship between the pilot and the master and crew in the form of good bridge resource management. The importance of good bridge resource management, effective communication, and teamwork were underscored in *Puerto Rico Ports Authority v. M/V Manhattan Prince*, a U.S. case. As a result of serious communication problems between the pilot, the ship's officers, and a tug, this case found both the pilot and the crew liable for the ensuing collision.[30] In another case, an English one this time, the court found that, if the pilot and the master had worked as a team, the pilot would have been able to determine correctly the heading and course of the ship, thereby avoiding the collision.[31] Teamwork is therefore essential. Whereas the pilot has local knowledge, the master and crew know their ship and its particular behavioural characteristics. As a matter of good practice, this information should be exchanged, and assumptions of knowledge on either side be minimized.[32] Relevant information includes weather conditions, docking instructions, and berthing arrangements,

---

26 "[I]f anyone is merely used as an advisor and is not entrusted with the navigation of the ship, he is not the pilot of that ship. Therefore the general provisions concerning pilots do not apply to him under such circumstances" (*Report of the Royal Commission on Pilotage*, above note 6 at 23–24).
27 *Alexander Shukoff v. Gothland* (1920), 5 Ll. L.R. 237 (H.L.).
28 *Hans Hoth (The)*, [1952] 2 Lloyd's Rep. 341.
29 *Ibid.*
30 *Puerto Rico Ports Authority v. M/V Manhattan Prince*, 1990 A.M.C. 1475 at 1480-485 (C.A. 1st Cir.).
31 *Antares II (The) and Victory*, [1996] 2 Lloyd's L.R. 482 at 498 (Q.B. (Adm. Ct.)).
32 Canada, *Recommended Code of Nautical Procedures and Practices*, 3d ed. (Ottawa: Department of Transport, 1985) Report No. TP1018E at 10.

use of tugs, and location of life-saving equipment.[33] If the master is not on the bridge, the pilot should also be aware of who the most senior officer on the bridge is and any watch changes. When the pilot is on board the tow during towage, the tug has a duty to follow the instructions provided by the pilot from on board the tow.[34]

A passage plan that identifies course alteration points where position accuracy is critical should be adopted so as to avoid surprises. Information must continue to be exchanged during the passage for the pilot will need to rely on the accurate position of the ship and information flowing from a proper look-out maintained by the officer-of-the-watch. Inadequate monitoring of the ship's course has often been a problem, especially when there is total reliance on the pilot's abilities without any cross-checking against the passage plan. Interestingly, officers-of-the-watch on foreign ships are more likely to monitor the passage than their counterparts on Canadian ships.[35] Monitoring is a safety backup.

There have been several occurrences where inadequate knowledge of the English language on foreign ships in Canadian waters was a contributing factor in an accident. This is an international problem, as shipowners continue to seek cheaper crews with uneven training standards. The problem for the pilot here is that his or her instructions may not always readily be understood.[36] It is the crew's duty to see that the pilot understands communications in foreign languages on board a ship.[37]

If the master has doubts about the pilot's actions, he or she should question the pilot's intentions. If the master is not at the bridge at the time, and if the officer-of-the-watch has any doubt as to the pilot's actions or intentions, he or she should seek clarification from the pilot; if doubt persists, the master must be notified immediately. Indeed, it is recommended that the officer-of-the-watch take whatever action is necessary until the master arrives.[38] In one case a master of a ship alerted the pilot on board of a potential problem, but the pilot did nothing to correct it. The master's failure to continue to press the matter with the pilot was not considered the proximate cause of the loss.[39] The mas-

---

33 On issues of teamwork see International Chamber of Shipping, *Bridge Procedures Guide*, 3d ed. (London: ICS, 1998).
34 *Christina (The)* (1848), 3 Wm. Rob. 27, 166 E.R. 873.
35 *Safety Study*, above note 23 at 20.
36 *Ibid.* at 17–18.
37 *Ape (The)*, above note 25.
38 *Recommended Code of Nautical Procedures and Practices*, above note 32 at 25.
39 *Kagu Maru (The) v. Malta (The)* (1920), 2 Ll. L.R. 120 (H.L.).

ter must use care in the exercise of his right to interfere or to take over the conduct of the ship as he could contribute to an accident. In the grounding of The Lake Anina, a chemical tanker, the master retained conduct of the vessel in a compulsory pilotage area, even though the pilot was on board. The master believed that his knowledge of the ship made him better suited than the pilot to undertake the intended turn; while the master was counting on the pilot's advice, the two of them had different intentions as to helm and engine actions to effect the manoeuvre.[40] The Transportation Safety Board has noted that, in "compulsory pilotage areas of the St. Lawrence and Saguenay rivers, there have been several serious occurrences where masters took the conduct of their vessels while a licensed pilot was on the bridge.... In all these occurrences, there was ineffective communication as to the master's intention of taking over the conduct of the vessel."[41] The master should fully signify his or her intention to take conduct of the ship. Even where the master does not take control, he or she must not interfere unjustifiably with the pilot's instructions. The master's suggestion of alternative options, as distinct from the issuing of contradictory commands, is not interference.[42] Where the pilot is on board the tow in a towage situation, the tug master is still required to follow the pilot's instructions unless there is "wilful misconduct or gross mismanagement" on the part of the latter.[43] Both the master and pilot are responsible for the observance of the collision avoidance regulations.[44] The crew has a duty to point out to the pilot a breach of regulations.[45]

---

40 *Safety Study*, above note 23 at 15.
41 *Ibid.* at 19.
42 For a definition of "interference" see *Lochlibo (The)* (1850), 166 E.R. 978 at 985, per Lushington. "The master is not merely entitled but bound to point out to the compulsory pilot that he may be mistaken in an opinion he has formed ('The Tactician'). He is also entitled, in order to avoid immediate peril, to take the navigation out of the hands of the pilot, but if he does so he must be prepared to show justification ('The Princess Juliana')": *Tower Field v. Workington Harbour and Dock Board*, above note 25 at 259. Further on this point, see R. Douglas, et al., *Douglas and Geen on the Law of Harbours, Coasts and Pilotage*, 5th ed. (London: LLP, 1997) at 304–06.
43 *Christina (The)*, above note 34; *Smith v. St. Lawrence Tow-Boat Co.* (1873), 2 Asp. 41, 28 L.T. 885.
44 *Douglas and Geen*, above note 42 at 307–09.
45 *Ape (The)*, above note 25.

D. LIABILITY

1) Liability of the Master

Like the owner, the master navigating in a compulsory pilotage area is answerable for any loss or damage caused by the vessel or by any fault in the navigation of the vessel.[46] However, in employing the pilot, the master is acting as the agent of the owner and is thus not personally liable for any loss or damage caused by the negligent act of the pilot, provided that he or she takes care that the pilot's orders are promptly obeyed by the ship's crew. Thus the master's liability is not absolute and he or she is held responsible, whether at maritime, civil, or criminal law only for his or her own actions and omissions. The Royal Commission on Pilotage noted that "at civil law he is merely a servant of the owner and he does not incur personally any civil responsibility for any damage caused by a pilot's error in which he did not participate or which he could not have prevented."[47]

2) Liability of the Shipowner

Since the master acts as agent of the owner, the pilot becomes a servant of the owner; thus his or her conduct of the ship engages the responsibility of the shipowner.[48] Where pilotage is voluntary, the pilot is considered to be the servant of the shipowner, and the shipowner is liable for a pilot's negligent acts carried out in the course of his or her employment. In reality, this is the case irrespective of whether pilotage is voluntary or compulsory.[49] In *The Dumurra*, a ship was under the conduct of a pilot in a compulsory pilotage area when damage was caused to submarine cables.[50] The *Pilotage Act* does not exempt the shipowner or master of any ship from liability for any damage or loss occasioned by his or her ship to any person or property when the ship was under pilotage and the pilot was negligent.[51] The effect of the Act

---

46 *Pilotage Act*, above note 5, s.41.
47 *Report of the Royal Commission on Pilotage*, above note 6 at 27.
48 *Beechgrove (The)*, [1916] A.C. 364; *Thom v. Hutchison Ltd.* (1925), 21 Ll. L.R. 169.
49 The combined effect of ss.40 and 41 of the *Pilotage Act*, above note 5, would appear to place the shipowner in the same position whether pilotage is compulsory or not.
50 *Dumurra (The) v. Maritime Telegraph & Telephone Co.*, [1977] 2 F.C. 679, 15 N.R. 382 (C.A.).
51 *Pilotage Act*, above note 5, s.41. This was originally introduced as s.31, S.C., 1970–71–72, c.52.

was to remove the defence of compulsory pilotage; thus the shipowner's liability *in personam* and *in rem* liability was still engaged despite the exclusive fault of the pilot.

3) Liability of the Pilot

An act of negligence by the pilot can expose him or her to an action for damages by the ship of which he or she has conduct and by third parties.[52] To those suffering a loss, however, an action against the pilot may be of little value since a pilot is able to limit to $1,000 his or her liability for any damage or loss occasioned by his or her fault, neglect, or want of skill.[53] This limit of liability also applies to an association of pilots.

4) Disciplinary Proceedings against the Pilot

The *Pilotage Act* and *General Pilotage Regulations* stipulate standards for the pilot, forbidding him or her to be in conduct of a ship or be on duty on board in a compulsory pilotage area when:

- he or she is aware of any physical or mental disabilities that prevent him or her from meeting the pilotage qualifications;
- his or her ability is impaired by alcohol, a drug, or from any other cause; or
- his or her licence or pilotage certificate is suspended.[54]

The holder of a licence or certificate must undergo an annual medical examination.[55] While on duty the pilot must not consume alcohol or any drug that may impair his or her ability to have the conduct of the ship.[56] The pilot who is in breach of these statutory duties may be found guilty of an offence and liable on summary conviction to a fine not exceeding $5,000.[57]

Under the *Pilotage Act*, the pilotage authorities are empowered to regulate the pilotage profession. There is the possibility of suspension or cancellation of a pilot's licence or pilotage certificate for acts or omissions of a culpable nature. In *Belisle v. Minister of Transport*, the Exchequer Court quashed an order of suspension against a pilot and held that an error of judgment in a moment of difficulty or danger might not be

---

52 *Saltaro (The)*, [1958] 2 Lloyd's Rep. 232; *Hans Hoth (The)*, above note 28.
53 *Pilotage Act*, above note 5, s.40.
54 *Ibid.*, s.25(3).
55 *General Pilotage Regulations*, above note 8, s.3.
56 *Pilotage Act*, above note 5, s.25(4).
57 *General Pilotage Regulations*, above note 8, s.48.

enough to justify a suspension.[58] Consequently, not all acts or omissions are necessarily so culpable as to justify a suspension. The chair of a pilotage authority has discretionary power to suspend temporarily a licence or pilotage certificate for up to fifteen days, where the pilot reports for duty or is in conduct of a ship when he or she should not be, consumes alcohol or a drug while on duty, was negligent on duty (e.g., giving negligent instructions), or does not meet qualifications.[59] The suspension may be oral, but if so it has to be confirmed in writing with reasons within 48 hours.[60] The chair must report the suspension to the authority. The pilotage authority may confirm or revoke the suspension and suspend the licence or pilotage certificate for a period of up to a year or until such time as the "pilot" can meet the prescribed requirements, or even cancel the licence or pilotage certificate altogether.[61]

Disciplinary measures against pilots involve administrative law matters that are mostly outside the realm of maritime law.[62] However, it is pertinent to note that pilotage authorities, like all other statutory creatures, are subject to a duty of procedural fairness toward pilots in disciplinary proceedings. The procedures are, in part, prescribed through the procedures in the *Pilotage Act*, the *Pilotage Regulations*, the authorities' own procedures, and, where there are omissions, by the common law. The disciplinary proceedings are *quasi*-judicial in nature and consequently involve significant procedural safeguards. The pilot has a right to counsel assistance during disciplinary proceedings.[63] When an authority is considering suspension of a licence or pilotage certificate, it must provide the pilot with an opportunity to be heard.[64] The right to be heard applies right from the investigative stage and may necessitate the examination of witnesses.[65] While this may not be the case in the investigation procedures of other administrative bodies, in pilotage it is necessary because the pilot may be disciplined as a result of the investigation. The pilot must receive an appropriate notice or statement of

---

58 *Belisle v. Minister of Transport*, [1967] Ex. C.R. 141.
59 *Pilotage Act*, above note 5, s.27(1).
60 *Ibid.*, s.27(2).
61 *Ibid.*, s.27(3).
62 For an excellent general text on Canadian administrative law, see David J. Mullan, *Administrative Law* (Toronto: Irwin Law, 2001).
63 *Pouliot v. Canada (Minister of Transport)*, [1965] Que. P.R. 51 (S.C.) [*Pouliot*].
64 *Champoux v. Great Lakes Pilotage Authority*, [1976] 2 F.C. 399, 11 N.R. 441, 67 D.L.R. (3d) 358 (C.A.).
65 A writ of *certiorari* was granted to a pilot who was not present at the inquiry considering his action and who was not given the opportunity to examine witnesses. *Pouliot*, above note 63.

the charge entailing suspension, or extension of a suspension, that must include details of the allegation, including reasons.[66] The notice must indicate whether the proceeding concerns conduct or competence of the pilot, a list of pertinent documentation, the source of the information on which the charge is based and when it was obtained, and the action that the authority proposed to take.[67] The authority should also provide the pilot with a five-day period within which the pilot may decide, in writing, whether to request a hearing. If the pilot decides to have a hearing, the authority will then issue notice of the hearing through a prescribed form.[68] The authority has the power to determine the procedure of the hearing to enable the pilot to present a full defence.[69] For the hearing the pilot may produce his or her own witnesses and documentation and must notify the authority that he or she is doing so. The burden of proof that the conduct was not negligent lies with the pilot, rather than with the authority.[70] The authority must give reasons for its decision.[71] The pilotage authority's decision to cancel or suspend a licence or pilotage certificate may be reviewed by the Minister of Transport. The minister has the discretionary power to direct the authority to rescind the suspension or cancellation, or reduce the suspension and on such conditions as the minister may determine.[72]

E. PILOTAGE AND SALVAGE

A pilot is not entitled to leave a ship when an emergency arises. As it is his or her duty to stay with the vessel, his or her services in so doing may entitle him or her to salvage remuneration. A pilot may be entitled to a salvage reward, if there are circumstances of such danger at the commencement of services, or if circumstances of such danger super-

---

66 *Darnel v. Pacific Pilotage Authority*, [1974] 2 F.C. 580 (C.A.); *Crabbe v. Canada (Minister of Transport)*, [1972] F.C. 863 (C.A.); *General Pilotage Regulations*, above note 8, ss.17 and 18.
67 *General Pilotage Regulations*, ibid., s.18.
68 Ibid., s.19.
69 Ibid., s.25.
70 *Barker v. Pacific Pilotage Authority* (1982), 42 N.R. 598 (F.C.A.).
71 *General Pilotage Regulations*, above note 8, s.27.
72 *Pilotage Act*, above note 5, s.29.

vene after services commence that he or she could not reasonably be expected to perform them for a pilot's fee.[73]

FURTHER READINGS

CANADA, *Report of the Royal Commission on Pilotage* (Ottawa: Queen's Printer, 1968).

CANADA, *A Safety Study of the Operational Relationship between Ship Masters/Watchkeeping Officers and Marine Pilots* (Hull, QC: Transportation Safety Board, 1995) Report No. SM9501.

DOUGLAS, R., P. LANE, & M. PETO, *Douglas & Geen on the Law of Harbours, Coasts and Pilotage*, 5th ed. (London: Lloyd's Press, 1997).

GOLD, E., "Legal Problems of Compulsory Pilotage" in E. Gold, ed., *New Directions in Maritime Law* (Halifax: Dalhousie University, 1978).

PARKS, A.A. & E.V. CATTELL, *The Law of Tow, Tug and Pilotage*, 3d ed. (London: Sweet & Maxwell, 1994).

---

73 *Jonge Andries (The)*, [1857] Swab. 226. "To entitle a pilot to salvage reward the ship he assists must be in such distress as to be in danger of being lost, and such as to call upon him to run such unusual danger, or incur such unusual responsibility, or exercise such unusual skill, or perform such an unusual kind of service, as to make it unfair and unjust that he should be paid otherwise than upon the terms of salvage reward": *Akerblom v. Price* (1881), 4 Asp. M.L.C. 441, (1880), 7 Q.B.D. 127. See also *Sandefjord (The)*, [1953] 2 Lloyd's Rep. 557.

CHAPTER 14

MARITIME TOWAGE

A. INTRODUCTION

Very often ships of all sizes, including those possessing their own means of propulsion, require the assistance of another vessel to be navigated safely. Such assistance may be required to enable a ship to make or leave a berth, dock, or canal, or to perform any manoeuvre in confined areas. Some ships do not have propulsion and therefore need towage services to move them from one place to another; thus a dumb barge — an open barge with no propulsion — can only be moved in tow, and several types of offshore installations likewise require towage to and from offshore areas, frequently assisted by a flotilla of tugs. Towage is still vital in the era of very large ships, particularly bulk carriers and tankers, and, indeed, the berthing of such ships has made the role of tugs even more important. Towage is therefore an important service for safe navigation of different ships in a variety of conditions and areas. Dr. Lushington defined the towage service as "the employment of one vessel to expedite the voyage of another, when nothing more is required than the accelerating [of] her progress."[1] In practice, towage may include a variety of services, including "holding, pushing,

---

[1] *Princess Alice (The)* (1849), 3 W. Rob. 138, 139, and 140. The transportation of a ship on land is not towage: *Toronto Window Mfg. Co. v. Audrey S (The)*, [1965] 1 Ex. C.R. 83.

pulling, moving, escorting, or guiding of or standing by the hirer's vessel."[2] This service is usually provided as a result of a contract of towage and thus the fundamental responsibilities of both the ship performing the tow (the tug) and the ship being towed (the tow) are governed by the terms, conditions, and exemptions of the towage contract.

B. TYPES OF TUGS

In general, it is not necessary for the ship that provides towage to be a purpose-built vessel. Towage can be provided by any vessel, so long as it is not violating any contractual or insurance policy conditions. In most cases, however, towage is a specialized service offered by a dedicated ship with a trained crew (the tug and its crew). The tug is a vessel that provides propulsion to another vessel for a specific purpose or for a combination of uses in marine transportation. Unlike almost all other ship types, which are powered solely for their own propulsion, the efficiency of a tug as such is dependent upon the amount of power that can be transmitted by the tug to the tow through a tow rope. Problems experienced with sailing clippers were responsible for the genesis of tugboats. As English sailing vessel owners sought to compete with the faster American clippers, they realized that the passages being made by their vessels really were from warehouse to warehouse, rather than from land to land. Efforts were therefore made to reduce the time lost at either end of the voyage. Therefore, in the early days of their development, tugs were used only in sheltered waters and estuaries. Today modern tugs are capable of meeting the requirements of the shipping and other marine industries in inshore, offshore, and deep-sea areas.

There are basically three types of tugs: ocean-going and salvage, coastal, and harbour and river.[3] A tug may be designed to encompass one or more of these classifications and thereby greatly increase its earning capacity. The basic requirements of all types of tugs are stability under all conditions, manoeuvrability, and adequate towing power. Ocean-going and salvage tugs are capable of spending long periods at sea, as they may have to tow vessels several thousands of kilometres. Their main charac-

---

2 "Towing" is defined in art.1(b)(i) of U.K. Standard Conditions for Towage and Other Service, repr. in N.J.J. Gaskell, C. Debattista, & R.J. Swatton. eds., *Chorley & Giles' Shipping Law*, 8th ed. (London: Pitman, 1987) App.10.

3 E. Gold, *Gard Handbook on P&I Insurance*, 5th ed. (Arendal, NO: Gard, 2002) at 214–15.

teristics are high power, speed, and great cruising range. Towing conditions are very different in ocean service from those encountered by tugs in calm or relatively calm water. A short tow rope may be essential in crowded waters but, at sea in bad weather, a long tow rope is necessary to absorb the shock created by the varying speeds of the tug and the vessel being towed. Ocean-going tugs usually carry a considerable amount of salvage gear and fire-fighting equipment. They may even have an infirmary and cabins for rescued crews. A comprehensive range of navigational equipment is normally provided as well as powerful lighting equipment. Coastal tugs tend to be smaller versions of the ocean-going tugs, with less power, size, and cruising range. They are used primarily for towing barges of bulk cargoes. The normal duties of these vessels are assisting large vessels when they are docking or undocking or handling ships in rivers. When involved in the latter duty, the tug may not actually tow the ship but merely help to steer it in the correct channel. A general harbour tug will, normally, be about thirty-nine metres in length, simply to allow access to confined areas and to facilitate manoeuvring in tight spots and narrow channels, but river tow boats — or, more accurately, pushboats — on the Ohio and Mississippi rivers in the United States, are often extremely large and powerful vessels.

C. AUTHORITY TO CONTRACT TOWAGE

The master of a ship has authority to engage towage services that are reasonably necessary for the due performance of the voyage and is in fact under a duty to engage the assistance of a tug, if his or her vessel without such assistance is a source of danger to the property of others.[4] The master has authority to enter into a contract for towage if the terms are reasonable and benefit the owners.[5] The implied authority of the master of a ship to contract on behalf of the shipowner is limited to such contracts as relate to the usual employment of the ship. In normal circumstances, it is doubtful whether the master has an implied authority to contract to tow another vessel. Such a contract would not relate to the usual employment of the ship and would not be necessary for its safety or for the completion of the voyage. However, there are conflicting cases on this point.[6] An important consideration for the

---

4   *Gertor (The)* (1894), 7 Asp. 472.
5   *Crusader (The)*, [1907] P. 15 at 20.
6   *Thetis (The)*, [1869] L.R. 2 A&E 365, where the master was held to have an implied authority to tow vessels in distress; and *Scaramanga v. Stamp* (1880), 5

master and shipowner is whether the hull policy on the ship permits the provision of towage to other ships, except when they are in distress. Performance of towage in contradiction to the policy may invalidate the insurance cover.[7]

D. CONTRACT TERMS

1) Implied Contract Terms

There are several terms implied by law into a towage contract set out in *Halsbury's Laws of England* and approved by the Supreme Court of Canada.[8] First, at the outset of the service, the crew, tackle, and equipment are equal to the work to be accomplished in the circumstances reasonably to be expected, that is, there is seaworthiness.[9] Second, competent skill and diligence will be used in the performance of the contract.[10] Third, both the tug and the tow will perform their contractual duty, using proper skill and diligence, and neither vessel will by neglect or misconduct create unnecessary risk to the other, nor increase any risk incidental to the service undertaken.[11] The tow owner also has a responsibility to provide a seaworthy tow. Davison and Snelson state that "the duty even extends to informing the tug of any circumstances known by the tow to be adverse to the proposed endeavour, and a failure to make such disclosure may result in the contract being declared invalid or to an entitlement on the part of the tugowner to damages for any extra expense or delay incurred as a result."[12] However, this responsibility may be modified as a result of a subsequent agreement.

C.P.D. 295, where it was held that the master does not have an implied authority to tow a vessel in distress for purpose of saving property only.

7   Institute Time Policy (Hulls), cl.1.1, in R. Merkin, *Marine Insurance Legislation* (London: LLP, 2000) 228–37.
8   *Halsbury's Laws of England*, 3d ed., vol. 35 (London: Butterworth, 1961) at 589, approved in *Wire Rope Industries v. British Columbia Marine Shipbuilders*, [1981] 1 S.C.R. 363 at 392 [*Wire Rope*].
9   *Marechal Suchet (The)*, [1911] P. 1.
10 *Pointe Anne Quarries Ltd. v. MF Whalen (The)*, [1923] 1 D.L.R. 45.
11 *Bland v. Ross (The Julia)* (1861), 15 E.R. 284 (P.C.); *Julia (The)* (1861), Lush. 224, quoted in *McCormick v. Sincennes-McNaughton Lines* (1918), 18 Ex. C.R. 357.
12 R. Davison & A. Snelson, *The Law of Towage* (London: LLP, 1990) at 28. Failure of the tow owner to inform the tug of an outbreak of disease on board the tow, which results in the quarantining of the tug and tow, was held to justify a higher reward to the tug: *Kaine v. Sorensen* (1892), 1 Qc. S.C. 184.

Where the tugowner assumes the responsibility to render the tow ready to proceed safely, he or she may in effect be assuming liability for any faulty repairs and consequent loss.[13] Once a towage contract is entered into each party engages to perform his or her duty in completing it and that proper skill and diligence will be used on both tug and tow.[14] The performance of the towage contract requires the degree of caution and skill that prudent seamen normally employ in this type of operation.[15]

2) Standard Conditions

It is very often the case that standard conditions are adopted in order to modify the application of implied terms. The effect can be very significant. Take for instance the implied duty that the tug and equipment be equal to the task articulated by Dr. Lushington: the British Columbia Tugboat Owners Association Standard Towing Conditions provide that the tugboat owner has a duty of due diligence and not an absolute duty to make and keep the tug seaworthy. The Supreme Court of Canada accepted that the inclusion in the towage contract of the due diligence standard replaced any implied warranty, and thereby protected the tugowner from liability for damage, where the tugowner showed that due diligence to make the tugboat seaworthy was exercised.[16]

United Kingdom tugowners have developed a set of standard towage conditions that are meant to absolve the tugowner from all blame in almost all circumstances.[17] Because of their inclusiveness, the courts have not always looked at these kindly, often applying the *contra proferentem* principle of interpretation. Similarly, the Eastern Canadian Tug Owners' Association and the Shipping Federation of Canada agreed to the Eastern Canada Towing Conditions, which are included in any contract of towage in the region.[18] There are the British Columbia Tugboat Owners Association Standard Towing Conditions, but these do not appear to be as widely used on the west coast as the eastern association's clauses are in the Atlantic region. Again, these condi-

---

13 *Engine & Leasing Co. v. Atlantic Towing Ltd.* (1992), 51 F.T.R. 1, var'd (1993), 157 N.R. 292 (F.C.A.), aff'd (1993), 164 N.R. 398 (F.C.A.).
14 *Canada Steamship Lines v. Montreal Trust Co.*, [1940] Ex. C.R. 220; the non-availability of the tug due to its being frozen in ice is not a defence for non-performance: *Dorland v. Bonter* (1849), 5 U.C.Q.B. 583.
15 *Champlain (The) v. Canada Steamship Lines Ltd.*, [1939] Ex. C.R. 89.
16 *Wire Rope*, above note 8.
17 U.K. Standard Conditions for Towage, above note 2.
18 See Eastern Canada Towing Conditions [unpubl.] available from the Eastern Canadian Tug Owners' Association.

tions are slanted heavily in favour of the tugowner. In 1985 a different approach was taken by the Baltic and International Maritime Council, the International Salvage Union, and the European Tugowners Association, resulting in extensive standard contracts known as Towcon and Towhire. The latter contracts attempt to balance the rights and responsibilities of the tug and tow with the hope that courts will more likely apply these than the generally one-sided alternatives.[19]

There is a duty of seaworthiness at both common law and in contract and the burden of proof rests with the tug.[20] The tugowner must exercise due care and supply a tug and equipment equal to the task at hand and in the conditions expected (e.g., geographical, climatic, seasonal), otherwise he or she might not be able to rely on the standard conditions protecting him or her from liability.[21] But there is no implied warranty that the tug shall be able to accomplish the work in all circumstances and hazards. Also, the tugowner may benefit from the defence of latent defect where equipment is defective without his or her fault.[22] Impossibility of performance of the contract may discharge the tug from its obligations. If the contract is for the hire of a "named" tug or a tug selected by the tow, there is no implied obligation as to the fitness of the tug to perform the services required.[23] This effect of the distinction between a contract for a specific tug and a contract for towage services may be obviated in any case by the express terms of the contract.[24] All obligations usually implied in the contract of towage may be excluded or modified by express terms in the contract applicable to the particular circumstances.[25] Tugowners have endeavoured, by the terms of the contract, to mitigate and even escape from all liability when engaged in a towing operation. Typical clauses inserted in towage contracts are liability exemption (exculpatory) clauses in favour of the tug, indemnity clauses intended to indemnify the tugowner against lia-

---

19 Davison & Snelson, above note 12 at 45.
20 *Wire Rope*, above note 8 at 392.
21 *McKenzie Barge & Derrick Co. v. Rivtow Marine* (1968), 70 D.L.R. (2d) 409, aff'd (1969), 7 D.L.R. (3d) 96.
22 Latent defect was a defence successfully employed in relation to a defective resocketing of a tow rope in *Wire Rope*, above note 8. However, where a bent bolt, which was the cause of the equipment failure was used for several months, the defence of latent defect could not be available, as a proper gear inspection should have revealed it: see *Scottish Metropolitan Assurance Co. v. Canada Steamship Lines*, [1930] S.C.R. 262.
23 *Robertson v. Amazon Tug and Lighterage Co.* (1881), 7 Q.B.D. 598; *Champlain (The) v. Canada Steamship Lines*, above note 15 at 95.
24 *Fraser & White Ltd. v. Vernan*, [1951] 2 Lloyd's Rep. 175 at 178.
25 *West Cock (The)*, [1911] P. 23 at 31.

bility for damages to third parties arising out of the towage, and indemnity clauses to indemnify the tugowner against liability as a result of the tug's negligence. These clauses may be useful only up to a point. If there is any ambiguity or inconsistency in or among contractual terms, they are construed *contra proferentem* or disregarded altogether.[26]

For better protection from liability, tugowners are advised to consider a provision in the standard agreement that requires the tow to insure. This is a practice that has emerged in the United States where liability exemption clauses are not allowed.[27] Giaschi suggests that, in this manner, "the tugowner effectively obtains the benefit of any insurance proceeds received by the tow for the loss" and, in the event that the tow does not obtain sufficient insurance, "it will be liable to the tugowner for breach of contract to insure and will not be entitled to recover its uninsured losses."[28]

a) Liability Exemption Clauses

Liability exemption clauses attempt to exempt the tug from liability to the tow for loss or damage suffered by the tow. The tugowner's ability to enjoy exemptions is restricted where he or she fails to provide a seaworthy tug and where the towage service is not being performed.[29] Also, the tugowner may be precluded from relying on contracted exemptions if an incident or loss is caused by his or her own fundamental breach of the contract.[30] The contracted exemption must be clear and will be interpreted narrowly. In *Canadian Salt Co. v. The Irving Cedar,* the following Towcon clause was at issue: "[T]he tugowner shall not in any circumstances be liable for any loss or damage suffered by the hirer or caused to or sustained by the tow in consequence of loss or damage howsoever caused to or sustained by the tug or any proper-

---

26 *Forfarshire (The),* [1908] P. 339. "If tugowners desire to put upon the tow liability for damages to the tug by negligence of the tug, they must do so in clear unambiguous language": Hill J. in *Emily Charlotte v. Newona* (1920), 4 Ll. L.R. 156 at 158.
27 *Bisso v. Inland Waterways Corp.,* 349 U.S. 85, 1955 A.M.C. 899.
28 C. Giaschi, "Standard Towing Conditions and Agreements to Insure," paper presented to the Canadian Maritime Law Association, January 1992, online at <http://www.admiraltylaw.com/papers/TUG.htm>. An agreement to insure a clause was upheld on appeal in *St. Lawrence Cement Inc. v. Wakeham & Sons Ltd.* (1995), 26 O.R. (3d) 321. The agreement to insure was a contractual commitment not to be interpreted against the rules of interpretation for an exculpatory clause.
29 *Cap Palos (The),* [1921] P. 458.
30 *Swan, Hunter, & Wigham Richardson Ltd. v. France Fenwich Tyne & Wear Co. (The Albion),* [1953] 2 Lloyd's Rep. 82 [*The Albion*].

ty on board the tug." The tug was attempting to break ice near a wharf and assist a vessel to dock at the plaintiff's wharf, but instead the tug veered off the ice and damaged the wharf. The tugowner invoked this clause to cover the liability for damage to the wharf. However, the court accepted the plaintiff's argument instead, that this clause exempted the tug from liability only where the tug suffers damage and such damage causes damage to the tow in turn.[31]

Excessive protection through exemption clauses can be confusing and counterproductive. This can happen in standard clauses that are used in a variety of contractual situations. In *Meeker Log and Timber v. Sea IMP VIII (The)*, the towage contract between the tugowner and tow owner contained a far-reaching exemption clause that purported to cover a variety of services including towage, charter, carriage, moorage, and storage.[32] There were ambiguities and inconsistencies in the clause and this situation led Lowry J. to state that a "clause relied upon to obtain an exemption from liability that is not clear and unambiguous is no exemption at all ... . There is no telling what was agreed."[33] The tugowner could not rely on the exemption clause. In another case where the tugowner similarly could not rely on the exemption clauses because of inconsistencies, the B.C. Court of Appeal allowed reliance on conflicting limitation provisions. The courts are not as exacting in construing these provisions.[34] Exemption clauses may not apply to undertakings by the tugowner to the tow that are deemed separate from the towage contract. Therefore, in *Engine & Leasing Co. v. Atlantic Towing*, a case where the tugowner undertook to repair a barge with a list for the tow owner, then to tow the barge, the Federal Court Trial Division held that these constituted two separate undertakings. The barge capsized and sank and on a balance of probabilities, the loss was owing to faulty repairs. The tugowner could not benefit from the exculpatory clauses in the towage contract and was found liable in tort and contract. The Court of Appeal, which varied the judgment only as to quantum of damages, further held that whether there were two separate contracts was immaterial, since the exculpatory clauses could not apply before the commencement of the voyage.[35] From a tugowner's perspective, it is useful for exemption clauses to be accompanied by a time bar so as to define the actual period within which the tow owner

---

31 (2000), 193 F.T.R. 20, paras.20–22.
32 (1994), 1 B.C.L.R. (3d) 320 (S.C.).
33 *Ibid.* at 14.
34 *Primex Forest Products v. Harken Towing Co.*, [1997] B.C.J. No. 1644 (S.C.) (QL).
35 *Engine & Leasing Co. v. Atlantic Towing*, above note 13.

may bring forward a claim, failing which "the claim and all rights whatsoever and howsoever shall be absolutely barred and extinguished."[36] Again, the wording of the bar must be clear.

b) Indemnity Clauses

At common law, in the event of a collision causing damage to an innocent third ship, the situation is as follows. Where the collision is with the tug, by the tug's fault alone, the tug alone is liable. Where the collision is with the tow, the tow being alone to blame, the tow alone is liable. When a collision takes place between the tug and the innocent third vessel by the fault of the tow, the tow owners are liable in every case, and the tugowners may also be liable. When a collision takes place between the tow and a third vessel by the fault of the tug only, the tugowner is clearly liable, and the tow owner may be liable if the tow owner had control of the navigation of the tug either directly from the tow or by those in charge of the tug being his or her servants or agents.[37]

Tugowners generally try to avoid their liability through extensive indemnity clauses in the towage contract. The contract usually stipulates that if the tug should, while towing, become liable to pay damages to third parties, the tow will indemnify the tug in respect of such payments, losses, and liabilities. The tug is the servant of the tow and the hirer is thus vicariously liable. This can be significant for the tugowner, since third parties are obviously outside the towage contract and are therefore likely to proceed against the tugowner directly. There may also be strict liability involved, such as for wreck removal and marine pollution.

The indemnity clause will come into operation only during the towage service. Therefore, if the towage is interrupted, although lawfully, the clause cannot be relied on by the tug during the interval.[38] Also, if the accident occurred because of the lack of seaworthiness of the tug, unless lack of seaworthiness is expressly excepted, the indemnity clause will not operate because seaworthiness is an implied condition that is broken prior to the start of the towage contract.[39] If none of these difficulties arise, the indemnity clause applies and will result in

---

36 See International Ocean Towage Agreement [towcon], cl.24, online at <http://www.bimco.dk/BIMCO%20Documents/TOWCON.pdf>; this clause was an issue that was upheld in *Canadian Salt Co. v. Irving Cedar (The)*, above note 31.
37 *Devonshire (S.S.) v. Barge Leslie*, [1912] A.C. 634.
38 *Cap Palos (The)*, above note 29.
39 *West Cock (The)*, above note 25.

the tow paying the whole of the damages although no blame may attach to it.[40] In a situation where the tow is under charter and the negligence is that of the charterer, contribution and indemnity do not apply to the owners of the tow, as they are not party to the towage agreement.[41]

Towage contracts in British Columbia frequently contain indemnity provisions relating to environmental claims and risks associated with the transport of dangerous and hazardous goods. The towage customer must make representations with respect to marine pollutants and/or dangerous goods to the effect that the relevant regulations have been complied with, for example, the filing of a dangerous goods declaration in accordance with the *International Maritime Dangerous Goods Code* (*IMDG Code*) and other regulations concerning the transport of dangerous goods regulations. The tugowner is concerned about his or her regulatory responsibilities concerning the carriage of dangerous goods on unmanned barges, such as the documentation and personal protection requirements. These requirements apply to the tug and not to the tow.[42] The tug master about to take charge of an unmanned barge carrying dangerous goods is required to ensure that the cargo, as far as it is accessible, is properly secured and segregated.[43] However, the person in charge of the barge — assuming this has not been chartered by the tugowner — retains the duty to ensure that dangerous goods are safeguarded and handled carefully during loading and unloading from the barge.[44]

3) Commencement and Termination of Towage Operation

The exemptions from liability under the towage contract are useful only if the towage contract is in force. Until that time, the common law applies to the rights and duties of both the tug and tow. In some cases, it has been doubtful at what exact moment the towage commences. The situation at common law is unclear. *The Clan Colquhoun* has been cited as standing for the proposition that, at common law, the towage service does not commence until the tow ropes have been passed.[45]

---

40 *President Van Buren (The)* (1924), 16 Asp. M.C. 444. However see *Canada Steamship Lines v. Paisley (The)*, [1930] Ex. C.R. 105, where a provision in the contract that towage is at "owner's risk" does not absolve the tug's responsibility toward third parties in case of negligent navigation.
41 *Gravel & Lake Services v. Bay Ocean Management Inc.* (2001), 204 F.T.R. 225.
42 *Dangerous Goods Shipping Regulations*, S.O.R./81-95, s.4(2); *Dangerous Bulk Materials Regulations*, S.O.R./87-24, s.4(2).
43 *Dangerous Goods Shipping Regulations*, ibid., s.13(3).
44 *Ibid.*, s.13(1).
45 *Clan Colquhoun (The)*, [1936] P. 153 at 164.

However, the case was actually decided on the wording of the particular towage contract used.

In any case, tugowners have inserted clauses into towage contracts under which the towage service begins at an earlier stage than the passage of the tow ropes. A common clause is found in condition No. 1 of the U.K. Standard Towing Conditions. The commencement of the towage contract is at the point in time when the tug is in a position to receive orders directly from the tow.[46] Therefore, in a situation where a tow issues instructions to the tug and the tug suffers damage when it is not actually towing, and even before a line is passed, the tow is liable for the tug's damage as the contract of towage is deemed to be under way. The test applicable is as follows:

- those on board the tug can reasonably expect the ship to give the tug an order to pick up ropes or lines,
- the tug is ready to respond to such orders if given,
- the tug should be close enough to the ship for the orders to be passed direct, and
- the tug should be within hailing distance.[47]

If, although located within hailing distance of each other, neither tug nor tow is ready to receive or give orders on yielding of lines, then the tug is not yet "in a position" to receive lines, and the contract has therefore not commenced.[48] Further, the towage contract may require that the tow be ready for sea, perhaps evidenced through the provision of a marine safety certificate, and failing which, if delay results, the tug could be entitled to demurrage.[49]

Another common clause is No. 5 of the Eastern Canada Towing Conditions, which describes the operative period as "while such tug or tugs is or are in attendance upon or fast to or engaged in any manoeuvre for the purpose of making fast to or disengaging from or proceeding clear from the vessel or craft requiring the tug or tugs."[50] In examining very similar language, English courts have held that the hir-

---

46 "The expression 'whilst towing' shall cover the period commencing when the tug or tender is in a position to receive orders direct from the hirer's vessel to commence holding, pushing, pulling, moving, escorting, guiding or standing by the vessel or to pick up ropes, wires or lines, or when the towing line has been passed to or by the tug or tender, whichever is sooner": U.K. Standard Conditions for Towage, above note 2, art.1(b)(iv).
47 *Apollon (The)*, [1971] 1 Lloyd's L.R. 476 at 480.
48 *Uranienborg (The)*, [1936] P. 21.
49 *Eastern Canada Towing v. Steel & Engine Products* (1977), 24 N.S.R. (2d) 452 (C.A.).
50 Above note 18.

ing commences when the tug is actually towing but that it includes the period when the tug, which is in the vicinity of the tow, is manoeuvring to make fast.[51]

There can be situations that raise a question as to whether a contract of towage is in existence, let alone when the towage commences. In *Joint Stock Society Oceangeotechnology v. The 1201*, the tugowner entered into a verbal agreement to tow with a named tug and took the initial step by dispatching the tug from the Mediterranean to Halifax, Nova Scotia.[52] The tug was dispatched immediately and the tow owner was kept continuously informed of its progress. After 12.5 days, the tow owner cancelled the agreement and the tugowner instituted an action *in rem* for the cancellation fee and the tug's day rate in a standard form plus interest. The Federal Court Trial Division allowed the action *in rem* to proceed, as the tugowner had commenced to fulfil the terms of the contract, despite the fact that no towing had taken place.

The towage ends when the lines are finally cast off or as determined in the contract. In the U.K. Standard Towing Conditions, the relevant time is when the final orders to cease the service are given by the tow and carried out, or when the order to cast off ropes is given and carried out, or the tow line has been finally slipped, whichever is the later. An additional condition is that the tug or tender is safely clear.[53] An unintended separation as a result of an accidental parting of the tow line has been held not to terminate towage.[54] A tug's response to a distress call and leaving with the consent of the tow does not modify, terminate, revoke, or frustrate the contract; the tow is thus liable to pay the contracted hourly rate not only until the time of the distress call but until the tug eventually returns to port, as per the towage agreement.[55]

4) Performance of the Towage Contract

Safety requires that one mind should direct the manoeuvres of both the tug and the tow. It is a term of the ordinary towage contract that, as regards the conduct and navigation of the two ships, the tug and those on board it shall obey the orders of those on board the tow. This rela-

---

51 *Ramsden (The)*, [1943] P. 46.
52 [1994] 2 F.C. 265, 72 F.T.R. 211.
53 U.K. Standard Conditions for Towage, above note 2, art.1(iv).
54 *Walumba (The) v. Australian Coastal Shipping Comission*, [1964] 2 Lloyd's Rep. 387 (Vic. S.C.).
55 *Remorqueurs du Québec v. Keystone Navigation* (1990), 45 F.T.R. 64. Responding to a distress call is a statutory duty. *Canada Shipping Act*, R.S.C. 1985, c.S-9, s.384(1); *Canada Shipping Act, 2001*, S.C. 2001, c.26, s.131(1).

tionship between the two ships is expressed by the saying, "the tug is the servant of the tow."[56] There is a presumption that the tug is under the control of the tow, and that the tow has a duty not to cause damage to the tug.[57] Therefore, drifting of the tow as a result of the tow's negligence that causes damage to the tug engages the liability of the tow to the tug.[58] In some older cases this identity of the tug with the tow led to the tow being held liable for the fault of those on board the tug, where such fault was the cause of a collision between the tow and a third ship, without consideration of where the responsibility actually lay. However, these cases should be considered as overruled, and the owner of a tow will not be held liable for the acts of its tug, unless those in charge of the tug were in fact acting under the control of the owner of the tow. This is particularly relevant in situations where a dumb barge or an unmanned tow are involved: "It must, therefore, I think, now be taken as conclusively established that the question of the identity of the tow with the tug that tows her is one of fact, not law, to be determined upon the particular facts and circumstances of each case."[59] In a situation where there is a flotilla of tugs performing a towage operation, the courts are likely to identify the *de facto* master of the flotilla as the "mind" of the operation.[60]

If in consequence of the tug's obedience to the orders of the tow, the tow sustains damage, it cannot recover from the tug for its loss. But if the tow's directions are disobeyed without good cause by the tug and damage ensues to the tow, the tug will be liable for any resulting damage and may forfeit its towage reward.[61] A tug should not obey the tow's directions when they are given owing to wilful misconduct or gross mismanagement of those in charge of the tow.[62] The tug master should exercise his or her discretion as to the manoeuvres to be employed especially in situations where he or she is more competent to make this

---

56 Per Sir R. Phillimore in *Mary (The)* (1880), 5 P.D. 14 at 16. Also per Hannes J.: "it appears to me that the authorities clearly establish that the tow had, under the ordinary contract of towage, control over the tug. The tug and tow are engaged in a common undertaking of which the general management and control belongs to the tow .... It is essential to the safety of vessels being towed that there should not be a divided command, and convenience has established that the undivided authority shall belong to the tow" in *Niobe (The)* (1888), 13 P.D. 55.
57 *Hamilton Marine & Engineering v. CSL Group* (1995), 99 F.T.R. 285.
58 *Gravel & Lake Services v. Bay Ocean Management Inc.*, above note 41.
59 Per Lord Atkinson in *Devonshire (S.S.) v. Barge Leslie*, above note 37 at 656.
60 *Rhone (The) v. Peter A. B. Widener (The)*, [1993] 1 S.C.R. 497 [*The Rhone*].
61 *Spaight v. Tedcastle*, [1881] Asp. 406.
62 *Christina (The)* (1848), 3 Wm. Rob. 27, 166 E.R. 873.

decision than the tow.[63] A difficult situation may arise in situations where there is only one pilot in a towage situation and this person is located on the tow; the tug is required to follow the pilot's instructions from the tow.[64] The tow is not bound on all occasions to give detailed directions to the tug.[65] Where no directions are given by the tow, it is the duty of the tug to direct the course.[66] It is the duty of the tug to instruct the tow on the response to changing weather conditions.[67] It is always the duty of the tug, although it be controlled by the tow, to look out for both itself and the tow.[68]

E. TOWAGE AND THE *COLLISION REGULATIONS*

For the purposes of the collision avoidance regulations, the courts usually treat the tug and tow as one ship.[69] Vessels towing one or more vessels are not absolved from obeying the regulations.[70] However, under these regulations a tug and tow are considered as "a vessel restricted in its ability to manoeuvre."[71] The tug and tow are required to carry prescribed signs and lights and, if the failure to do so causes an accident, the liability toward other ships will be engaged.[72] The tug and tow constitute a "stand-on vessel" under the regulations, and other ships have to stay out of its way.[73] While it is the duty of a tug with a ship in tow to comply with the *Collision Regulations*, it is also the duty of a third ship to make allowance for the encumbered and comparatively disabled

---

63 *Isca (The)* (1886), 12 P.D. 34.
64 *Christina (The)*, above note 62.
65 *Ibid.*; *Panther (The)*, [1957] 1 All E.R. 641.
66 *Smith v. St. Lawrence Tow-Boat Co.* (1873), 2 Asp. 41.
67 *Russell v. Gloria (The)*, [1927] Ex. C.R. 162 at 166.
68 *Jane Bacon (The)* (1878), 27 W.R. 35; *Hamilton Marine & Engineering v. CSL Group*, above note 57.
69 *Canadian Dredging Co. v. Northern Navigation Co*, [1923] Ex. C.R. 189, [1924] 4 D.L.R. 1195.
70 *Lord Bangor* (1896), 8 Asp. 211.
71 *Collision Regulations*, C.R.C., c.1416, Sch.I, r.3(g)(vi). See also Chapter 11, "Maritime Collisions".
72 *Ibid.*, Sch.I, r.24; *B.W.B. Navigation Co. v. Kiltuish (The)* (1922), 21 Ex. C.R. 398; *Maplehurst (The) v. George Hall Coal Co.*, [1923] S.C.R. 507; *Keystone Transports Ltd. v. Ottawa Transportation Co.*, [1927] Ex. C.R. 123; *Lions Gate Lumber Co. v. Francis Salman (The)*, [1958] Ex. C.R. 259.
73 *Collision Regulations, ibid.*, Sch.I, r.18.

state of a tug, and to take additional care in approaching it.[74] The tug master has to anticipate the constraints of safe towage in spatially confined areas; thus, he or she is responsible for ensuring that the tow has vertical clearance for safe passage under a bridge.[75] In certain circumstances, Canadian courts will also consider the tug and tow as one unit for liability purposes. They apply the aggregate tonnage of the commonly owned wrongdoing mass in order to determine the limit of liability.[76]

F. TOWAGE AND SALVAGE

1) Difference between Towage and Salvage

Towage should be distinguished from salvage. The three essential elements of salvage — danger, voluntariness, and success — need not be present in a towage situation, or at least not in the same manner and extent. As Dr. Lushington opined, mere towage is "confined to vessels that have received no injury or damage, and that mere towage reward is payable in those cases only where the vessel receiving the service is in the same condition she would ordinarily be in without having encountered any damage or accident."[77] Towage as an operation is not without risks, but the tow is not necessarily in distress and there is no extraordinary danger that the tug is exposed to, as would be for the salvor. Another vital difference between towage and salvage is the pay. The difference in amount between the two is financially very significant. Whereas towage is paid on a rate basis, salvage is subject to an arbitration process that determines a reward which frequently represents a certain percentage of the value of the salved *res*. Consider this in the context of the fully laden modern oil tanker, Amoco Cadiz, which grounded off the coast of France, causing a catastrophic oil spill in 1978. The difference between a towage contract and a salvage agreement may have been a crucial factor in so far as the master of the vessel in difficulty was concerned. The master had a ship over which he had no control, when he tried to negotiate towage to Lyme Bay, Dorset, on a mileage tariff basis, rather than accept salvage under a *Lloyd's Standard Form of Salvage Agreement* (see Chapter 15 and Appendix 2). Valu-

---

74 *Ingomar (The)* (1920), 5 Ll. L.R. 182.
75 *Fraser River Pile & Dredge v. Empire Tug Boats* (1995), 92 F.T.R. 26.
76 *The Rhone*, above note 60. And see Chapter 18, "Limitation of Liability for Maritime Claims."
77 *Reward (The)* (1841), 1 W. Rob. 177.

able time was wasted by the master in attempting to communicate with the head office in Chicago to secure concurrence for salvage, when in reality this decision was his.[78] As in towage, the master has the authority to contract salvage. There is no maritime lien on the tow for payment of the price fixed by the towage contract but only a statutory lien. There is a maritime lien for salvage.

2) When Towage Can Be Converted into Salvage

In certain situations, towage can be transformed into a salvage service. Ordinarily, a tug has to perform its contractual service. A temporary accident necessitating an interruption of the towage and even endangering the tow will make no difference. The tug remains bound to the towage contract if, with reasonable skill and promptitude and without itself incurring any excessive risk, it can resume the towage and overcome the temporary danger.[79] If the tug, during the performance of the towage contract, rescues the tow from some unforeseen and extraordinary peril, the tug is entitled to additional remuneration in the nature of salvage. The supervening circumstances must be such as to render the provision of the required services outside the normal expectation of the contract of towage.[80] The law implies an obligation of the tug under a towage contract to render assistance to its tow in cases of unusual difficulty or danger, and a corresponding obligation on the tow to pay extra remuneration for these services, and to pay such remuneration on a salvage basis, if the tug's services save the tow from danger or contribute to its ultimate safety.[81] In this case, the towage contract is supplemented by the right of the tug to salvage, but the salvage must be effective.[82] It is also possible for an accident to render the towage contract impossible to perform. If the tug is not to blame for the accident, the towage contract terminates and the tug is under no contractual obligation to complete it.[83] In such cases the tug is not free to abandon a tow in danger. It is its duty to endeavour to save the tow, as long as the safety of the tug is not endangered; for such services the tug is entitled to be paid on a salvage basis.[84] In these situations, however, it is not

---

78 *Re Oil Spill by Amoco Cadiz*, 954 F.2d 1279 (7th Cir. 1982).
79 *Annapolis (The)* (1861), Lush. 355, 167 E.R. 151; *Liverpool (The)*, [1893] P. 154.
80 *Minnehaha (The)* (1861), Lush. 335; *Homewood (The)* (1928), 31 Ll. L.R. 336; *Slaney (The)*, [1951] 2 Lloyd's Rep. 538.
81 *Leon Blum (The)*, [1915] P. 90 at 101.
82 *Shipman v. Morrell* (1920), 19 O.W.N. 132 (C.A.).
83 *Marechal Suchet (The)*, above note 9.
84 *Russell v. Gloria (The)*, above note 67.

that towage and salvage exist side-by-side but, rather, that salvage supplants towage.[85] In general, the courts will only find this conversion to salvage when the following conditions are satisfied: there was real and unforeseen danger to the tow; a real increased risk to the tug; and exertions on the part of the tug that go appreciably beyond its contractual towage duties. It is important that it is not the inefficiency of the tug that causes the situation of danger, as in this case there would be an issue of lack of seaworthiness. The burden is on the tug to show that the change from towage became necessary because of special circumstances in the nature of *force majeure* or inevitable accident.[86] If the temporary danger to the tow is caused, or contributed to, by the tug's negligence, or if the towage contract becomes incapable of performance through the fault of the tug, the tug is not relieved of its contractual obligations, nor on grounds of public policy is it entitled to salvage.[87]

The presence of a pre-existing contractual duty can negate a salvage claim. Towage cannot be converted into salvage where there is a pre-existing arrangement for towage services. For example, in the Australian case of *The Texaco Southampton* the plaintiffs, master pilot, and crew of a tug provided towage services to a drifting and powerless stricken tanker but were not allowed to claim salvage. The tug and crew belonged to a company that was the sole supplier of towage services to Texaco, the tanker owner. The towage rates were part of a standing agreement, but the agreement did not address salvage. They knew in advance that they would tow a disabled tanker and had little if any experience in the towage of tankers in this condition; but at the same time the work was within the realm of the work normally expected in towage. The fact that a pre-arrangement was in place did not put the tug in the position of a passing ship that unexpectedly faces another ship in distress and voluntarily offers its services. The Court of Appeal thus accepted Texaco's submissions:

> (a) the tug-owner was bound by its contract to provide towing services and the plaintiffs were bound to it by their contracts of employ-

---

85 "Hence it follows that salvage services (which are voluntary and speculative) and towage services (which are contractual and rewarded in any event) cannot co-exist during the same space of time between the same parties, *Leon Blum (The)* [above note 81], although they may alternate during successive periods of time, *Aldora (The),* [1975] 1 Lloyd's L.R. 617 at 623" (per Justice Glass, *Texaco Southampton (The),* [1983] 1 Lloyd's L.R. 94 (N.S.W.C.A.)).
86 *Westbourne (The)* (1889), 14 P.D. 132.
87 *Duc d'Aumale (The),* [1904] P. 60; *Hendry Corporation v. Aircraft Rescue Vessels,* 1953 A.M.C. 2115, 113 F. Supp. 198.

ment, and none of the services rendered either by the tug-owner or the plaintiffs lay outside the scope of their respective contracts having regard to the nature of those contracts and the nature of the danger to the ship.[88]

Had the tug crew, which was bound by an employment contract, provided services in the absence of a towage contract between the tug and the salved ship, they would have been in a position to claim salvage because they would have owed no prior duty to the salved vessel.[89]

G. TOWAGE AND CARRIAGE OF GOODS

Technically there should be a clear difference between towage, as a contract for a tug to provide motive power to another ship, and the contract of affreightment, which is a contract for the carriage of goods by sea. However, there can be situations that could blur the distinction, such as when the tow carries a cargo or the tow itself is the cargo, such as a log boom. The distinction is particularly important for insurance coverage. A pertinent example is *Burrard Towing v. Reed Stenhouse*, where the tugowners demise chartered a barge to carry a cargo of scrap iron.[90] The cargo was lost and the owners claimed. The tugowners' insurer resisted the assured's claim. The tugowners' coverage seemed to contain a conflict between the towers' legal liability endorsement, which ostensibly covered property on board the tow, and an exclusion clause that excluded liability for cargo on board the insured ships. The key question was whether the towage insurance covered the cargo on the tow. The B.C. Court of Appeal decided for the insurer. In her judgment, Southin J. held that, in reading the insurance coverage as a whole, the tugowners were covered for liabilities arising from a contract of towage and not for liabilities they incurred under a contract of affreightment. The contract of towage was read specifically with reference to the motive power provided by the tug to a tow, and that a "contract to move goods from one place to another by means of a tug and barge, both supplied by the tugowner, is a contract ... for the carriage of goods." She went on to say that "the fact that a vessel called a tug has a tow does not mean that the undertaking upon which the tug is engaged is a con-

---

88 *Texaco Southampton (The)*, above note 85.
89 *Sarpen (The)*, [1916] P. 306.
90 *Burrard Towing v. Reed Stenhouse Ltd.* (1996), 19 B.C.L.R. (3d) 391 (C.A.) [*Burrard*].

tract of towage."[91] In the same judgment, Southin J. also raised a question, which remained unanswered: whether a contract to tow a log boom constitutes towage rather than carriage of goods.[92] Earlier cases had already determined that a log boom is not a ship.[93]

A converse situation arose in *Catherwood Towing v. Commercial Union Assurance Co.*, where a dumb barge ran aground with damage resulting to both barge and cargo thereon.[94] The insurer admitted liability for the barge but resisted indemnity for the cargo. The B.C. Court of Appeal ruled against the insurer this time. "Cargo" meant cargo carried on board the insured tug and coverage of this was excluded. However, the tower's liability coverage included damage to "tow or the freight thereof or to the property on board." The reference to "freight thereof" in this case was deemed to refer to the goods transported on the tow. The consequence was that the tugowner was covered for damage to cargo on the tow as a result of the fault of the tug.[95]

Policy considerations apart, there is a significant factual difference between *Catherwood* and *Burrard* that serves to distinguish towage and affreightment. In *Burrard*, the tugowner supplied both tug and tow and committed to lift and deliver the shipper's cargo. In *Catherwood*, the tugowner did not own or charter the tow but simply provided towage to a loaded barge. Another difficulty may arise when the tugowner demise charters the tow and, as a result, there is a possibility that the tugowner becomes "owner" of the tow for insurance purposes and thereby benefits from coverage of property carried on board the tow.[96] To avoid these difficulties, the insurance contract should specify the actual operation that is covered and include "owned or chartered vessels." In another interesting situation, the tugowner entered into a contract for work and services, including towage. The tugowner chartered two barges for the carriage of oil as cargo with the consent of the cargo owner. The cargo owner undertook to bear the expenses of altering the barges for the cargo to be carried and proceeded with the alterations; however, the cargo owner could not obtain cargo insurance and, consequently, the barges could not be utilized to transport the intended

---

91 Ibid. See also *A.I.M. Steel v. Gulf of Georgia Towing Co.* (1964), 48 D.L.R. (2d) 549.
92 *Burrard*, ibid. at para.21.
93 *Paterson Timber Co. v. British Columbia (The)* (1913), 16 Ex. C.R. 305; *McLeod v. Minnesota Pulp & Paper Co.*, [1955] Ex. C.R. 344.
94 *Catherwood Towing v. Commercial Union Assurance* (1996), 26 B.C.L.R. (3d) 57 (C.A.) [*Catherwood*].
95 Ibid. at 62.
96 See the reasons given by McEachern C.J. in *Burrard*, above note 90 at para.25ff.

cargo. While there is normally an implied warranty of seaworthiness in a charterparty, the contract itself and surrounding circumstances rebutted this. The parties did not intend that the responsibility to make the barges seaworthy was the tugowner's (i.e., the charterer's).[97]

A scenario where carriage, rather than towage, dominated the contract was in *British Columbia Mills, Tug & Barge Co. v. Kelley*, where a tug was time-chartered to tow log rafts. On account of severe weather the tug master did not venture out of port; while hoping for better weather, however, he kept the tug in a continuous state of readiness. The inclement weather persisted and the charter time ran out. There was no warranty that the towage would be carried within a specific time. It was held that the charterer was still liable for the hire.[98]

FURTHER READINGS

BISHOP, W.A., "The Relationship Between the Tug and Tow in the United Kingdom" (1995) Tul. L.Rev. 507.

DAVISON, R. & A. SNELSON, *The Law of Towage* (London: LLP, 1990).

GASTON, M.J. & C.E.J. DOWSWELL, *Tugs Today: Modern Vessels and Towing Techniques* (Somerset: Patrick Stephens, 1996).

GIASCHI, C., "Standard Towing Conditions and Agreements to Insure," paper presented to the Canadian Maritime Law Association, January 1992, online at <http://www.admiraltylaw.com/papers/TUG.htm>.

GOLDSTEIN, J.K., "Towage (The Future of Maritime Law in the Federal Courts: A Faculty Colloquium)" (2000) 31 J. Mar. L. & Com. 335.

HOOPER, C.D. & J.M.D. VAN HEMMEN, "Burdens of Proof Between Tugs and Tows" (1995) 70 Tul. L.Rev. 531.

KOVATS, L.J., *The Law of Tugs and Towage* (London: Rose, 1980).

LUGENBUHL, C.E. & D.B. SHARPE, "The Law of Towage at the Millennium: What Changes Are Needed?" (1999) 73 Tul. L.Rev. 1811.

PARKS, A.A. & E.V. CATTELL, *The Law of Tow, Tug and Pilotage*, 3d ed. (London: Sweet & Maxwell, 1994).

---

97 *Russell v. McColl Brothers* (1931), 40 O.W.N. 355.
98 [1923] 1 W.W.R. 597, 1 D.L.R. 1015.

CHAPTER 15

MARITIME SALVAGE AND WRECK

A. MARITIME SALVAGE

1) Introduction

Maritime salvage is concerned with the saving of life and property from the dangers of the sea. The law of maritime salvage is of very ancient origin and is generally based on the principles of equity. Under such principles a volunteer who successfully saves maritime property in danger at sea gains a right of reward from the owner. In other words, in order for a claim for such a reward to succeed, the three required elements of a maritime salvage act must all be present: voluntariness, danger, and success. This is also often expressed in the principle "no-cure–no-pay" that has been enshrined in most salvage contracts for many years. It means that no payment or reward can be claimed in the absence of any success, that is, if despite the salvor's efforts nothing has been rescued or saved. This principle has been accepted almost universally and has been confirmed by two international maritime conventions that have codified almost all traditional salvage principles established in the subject's lengthy history.[1] In practice, most commercial salvage services are today performed under some sort of salvage contract. The best known of these is the *Lloyd's Open Form of Salvage Agreement*,[2] which is widely recog-

---

1 The 1910 and 1989 salvage conventions, discussed below.
2 See Appendix 2, *Lloyd's Standard Form of Salvage Agreement*.

nized internationally; in addition to stating the "no-cure–no-pay" principle, this agreement provides for a system of arbitration for the settlement of salvage claims (discussed below).

It should be noted that in the maritime context the word "salvage" has two accepted meanings: first, the act of saving, or assisting in saving, or rescuing[3] maritime property, such as a vessel, cargo, freight, or other recognized subject of salvage, without any prior legal or contractual obligation, from a danger at sea;[4] and, second, the actual reward, remuneration, or compensation payable to the successful salvor by the beneficiary of such service. There are also three different types of salvage:

- civil salvage (i.e., the rescue of maritime property from perils of the sea in times of peace);
- life salvage (i.e., the saving or attempting to save lives on board vessels in peril on the sea); and
- military salvage (i.e., the rescue of maritime property from the enemy in wartime).[5]

In practical terms there is also what is sometimes considered to be another form of salvage related to protection of the marine environment. ("Environmental salvage" or "liability salvage"[6] is discussed more specifically below.)

2) International Law

a) *Assistance and Salvage Convention 1910*

The long-established principles of maritime salvage were codified internationally in the *Convention for the Unification of Certain Rules with Respect to Assistance and Salvage at Sea, 1910* (*Assistance and Salvage Convention 1910*).[7] The convention was accepted by a large num-

---

3 "Rescue at sea" has been advocated as a more appropriate modern definition: see E. Vincenzini, *International Salvage Law* (London: Lloyd's Press, 1992) at 3.
4 As defined in one of the leading texts on salvage law: G. Brice, *Maritime Law of Salvage*, 3d ed. (London: Sweet & Maxwell, 1999) at 1.
5 In this book, only civil and life salvage are considered.
6 See C. De La Rue & C.B. Anderson, *Shipping and the Environment* (London: Lloyd's Press, 1998) at 571. See also Chapter 17, "Marine Pollution Prevention."
7 23 September 1910, 103 U.K.F.S. 441 (entered into force 1 March 1913; in force in Canada on 28 October 1914). See also Institute of Maritime Law, *The Ratification of Maritime Conventions*, 4 vols., Updated loosefleaf service (London: Lloyd's Press, 1991–2003) vol.I.3.210. For a full discussion of this convention, see Vincenzini, above note 3.

ber of states and has worked reasonably well.[8] It reflected the principle that remuneration should be fixed by a court or arbitral tribunal in accordance with the practical circumstances of each case on the following considerations:

- the measure of success obtained;
- the efforts and skills of the salvors;
- the danger from which the salved vessel, crew, passengers, cargo, or other property was rescued;
- the time expended and expenses incurred by the salvor,
- the losses incurred by the salvor;
- the risks of liability and other risks to which the salvor was exposed;
- the value of the salvor's property and equipment made available and exposed to such risk; and
- the value of the property salved.[9]

The *Assistance and Salvage Convention 1910* also provided that any salvage agreement could be annulled or modified by a court, if it was considered that any conditions agreed on were inequitable.[10] It was also confirmed that a master was bound, as far as it would not involve the salving vessel in endangering vessel, crew, and passengers, to render assistance to any person in danger at sea.[11] In other words, the convention fully confirmed the basic property and life salvage principles that had existed since ancient times. A protocol to the 1910 convention was completed in 1967 and widened the principles of salvage by including salvage services by and to warships and other public vessels operated solely for non-commercial purposes.[12]

---

8 Now superseded by the *International Convention on Salvage, 1989*, 28 April 1989, U.K.T.S. 1996 No.93 [*1989 Salvage Convention*] (entered into force 14 July 1996; in force in Canada on the same day). As of 1 April 2003 the convention had been accepted by 43 states comprising 33 per cent of global shipping tonnage. See also *Ratification of Maritime Conventions*, above note 7 vol.I.3.320.
9 *Assistance and Salvage Convention 1910*, above note 7, art.8.
10 *Ibid.*, art.7.
11 *Ibid.*, art.11.
12 *Protocol to Amend the Convention for the Unification of Certain Rules of Law Relating to Assistance and Salvage at Sea*, 27 May 1967, U.K.T.S. 1978 No.22 (entered into force on 15 August 1977; not accepted by Canada). See also *Ratification of Maritime Conventions*, above note 7 vol.I.3.230. This convention was never widely accepted and has been superseded by the *1989 Salvage Convention*, above note 8, which exempts salvage operations involving state-owned vessels, but permits the application of the convention if so decided by a signatory state (art.4).

b) *1989 Salvage Convention*

During the late 1960s and 1970s world shipping generally, and the tanker industry specifically, was facing a number of new global and regional concerns regarding the protection of the marine environment. Larger tankers and a number of serious maritime accidents that had caused major oil spills and environmental damage had resulted in a more environmentally conscious global community focusing sharply on the shipping industry and its operations.[13] It quickly became apparent that the ancient law of salvage was no longer considered to be adequate in accommodating some of the new environmental concerns. Traditional salvage law, as embodied in the *Assistance and Salvage Convention 1910*, concerned itself solely with the saving of maritime property. The potential of significant environmental damage arising out of a maritime casualty had not been a consideration at that time.[14] However, it had then become apparent that environmental damage, which might include coastal oil pollution, the destruction of fisheries, and possible human health problems, could in serious cases far outweigh the potential value of salved property. In fact, it was considered that the prevention of pollution might be more important than the saving of maritime property. This was of particular concern to professional salvors, who felt that they were facing a new series of environmental liabilities while carrying out their traditional duties. This was especially apparent in cases where salvage services were required for badly damaged vessels carrying pollutants. In such cases the potential environmental damage might far exceed any salved value of vessel or cargo. In some cases, the salvage service might not succeed; yet there could still be significant environmental damage for which the salvor might even be held liable. Salvors stated that they could not undertake serious cases unless the legal regime was changed substantially.[15]

In order to respond to these widespread concerns, the International Maritime Organisation (IMO)[16] requested the Comité Maritime International (CMI)[17] to undertake an intensive study of the law of salvage in 1980. After further extensive negotiations, the IMO completed the *1989 Salvage Convention*.[18] The discussions that led to this treaty

---

13 E. Gold, *Gard Handbook on Marine Pollution*, 2d ed. (Arendal, NO: Gard, 1997) c.1.
14 E. Gold, "Marine Salvage Law, Supertankers and Oil Pollution: New Pressures on Ancient Law" (1981) 11 R.D.U.S. 127. See also De La Rue, above note 6 at 571.
15 E. Gold, "Marine Salvage: Towards a New Regime" (1989) 20 J. Mar. L. & Com. 487.
16 See Chapter 2, "The Shipping Industry: An Overview" at section G(1)(a) for details on the IMO.
17 *Ibid.* at section G(2)(a) for details on the CMI.
18 Above note 8.

were difficult and controversial, and the convention took a further seven years to enter into force.[19] The perceived problem was that the protection of the marine environment, which may have to take priority during salvage operations, would significantly alter the basic salvage principles that had worked so well for such a long period. In other words, the convention authorizes a departure from the traditional no-cure–no-pay principle. However, as seen below, the shipping industry had already developed a new *Lloyd's Open Form of Salvage Agreement* in 1980 (*Lloyd's Open Form '80*) that incorporated these environmental matters into the salvage service. The *1989 Salvage Convention* not only codified some of these new *Lloyd's Open Form* innovations but also went even further. The following principal changes in salvage law were incorporated:

- The scope of international salvage has been extended to include damage to the environment not only by oil but also by circumstances arising from fire, explosion, and chemical contamination.[20]
- The ingredients to be taken into account by a court or an arbitral tribunal in assessing a salvage service include efforts undertaken to prevent damage to the environment.[21]

While the reward for property salvage shall not exceed the salved value of the property saved, "special compensation" is payable to a salvor who has carried out salvage operations on a vessel or cargo that threatened damage to the environment, but has failed to earn a reward for salvage at least equivalent to his or her expenses. This special compensation, often called the safety net, is equivalent to the salvor's expenses but does not cover a profit for the work carried out. If the salvor has prevented or minimized damage to the environment, this special compensation can be enhanced by an additional increment but only up to double the expenses.[22] A salvor who has been negligent in minimizing or preventing damage to the environment may be penalized by being deprived of the whole or part of the special compensation.[23] Provisions related to jurisdiction, maritime liens, security, apportionment, limitation of time, and liability relating to the practice and procedure in settling salvage claims are updated.[24]

---

19   See Vincenzini, above note 3 at Parts 2 and 3.
20   *1989 Salvage Convention*, above note 8, art.1(d).
21   *Ibid.*, art.13(b).
22   *Ibid.*, art.14.
23   *Ibid.*, art.14(5).
24   *Ibid.*, c.IV.

3) Canadian Law and Legislation

Canada has accepted not only all of the basic principles of marine salvage law that have been established over a long period of time through common law, legal cases, and other usage but also those principles that have been codified by the 1910 and 1989 salvage treaties described above. Although the *1989 Salvage Convention* did not enter into force until 1996, it was approved and declared to have the force of law in Canada in 1989. Furthermore, it was declared that, if there was any inconsistency between the convention and the *Canada Shipping Act*, the convention would prevail.[25] Canada has ratified the *1989 Salvage Convention* and it is now part of Canadian maritime law through incorporation into the *Canada Shipping Act*.[26] In other words, with minor differences identified in this chapter, the long-established principles of international salvage, including those codified in the relevant international conventions, are part of Canadian maritime law.

4) Subjects of Salvage

At common law the only property subject to salvage was maritime property, that is, the vessel, its equipment and cargo, including flotsam,[27] jetsam,[28] and lagan,[29] the wrecked remains of any of these, and

---

25 R.M. Fernandes, *Shipping and Admiralty Law* (Toronto: Carswell, 1995) at 4-25. *Canada Shipping Act*, R.S.C. 1985, s.S-9, s.449(1) and Sch.V. See also J.J. Kavanaugh, "Implications of a New Salvage Regime for the International Salvage Union"; D.A. Kerr, "The 1989 Salvage Convention: Expediency or Equity?: The Professional Salvor's View"; R. White-Harvey & D. VanderZwaag, "Protection of the Marine Environment and the International Convention on Salvage, 1989: Much Ado about Salving?"; and J.B. Wooder, "The New Salvage Convention: An Owner's Perspective" in *New Directions in Maritime Law, 1989* (Halifax: Continuing Legal Education Society of Nova Scotia, 1989).

26 *Canada Shipping Act*, above note 25, s.449.1, as amended by S.C. 1993, c.36, s.1. See also *Canada Shipping Act, 2001*, S.C. 2001, c.26, s.142ff and Sch.3, Part 1. It should be noted that *Canada Shipping Act, 2001* is not yet in effect pending the adoption of a number of regulatory provisions. While this may take some time, the new Act will be referred to whenever appropriate throughout this chapter. Canada also has entered an exception to the *1989 Salvage Convention* related to underwater cultural heritage. See *Canada Shipping Act, 2001*, s.186.

27 Cargo or other parts of the ship that have floated off when a ship has sunk or is otherwise in distress. Defined in *Cargo Ex Schiller (The)* (1877), L.R. 2 P.D. 145 at 148.

28 Cargo or other parts of the ship that have been cast overboard or jettisoned in order to lighten a ship in distress or otherwise prevent additional danger to the ship: *Cargo Ex Schiller (The)*, ibid.

29 An archaic term denoting cargo or parts of the ship that have been jettisoned but have been marked so that the items can be recovered later: *Cargo Ex Schiller (The)*, ibid.

freight. The saving of other property, such as a navigational buoy adrift from its moorings does not give rise to a salvage award.[30] In general, this common law rule has been codified in the 1910 and 1989 conventions, and some allowances for technological changes in the maritime industry have been made.[31] The *1989 Salvage Convention* defines "vessel" and maritime "property" as follows: "Vessel means any ship or craft, or any structure capable of navigation. Property means any property not permanently and intentionally attached to the shoreline and includes freight at risk."[32] In other words, these definitions include ships and other craft, as well as ships' equipment, stores, apparel, cargo, bunkers, and freight at risk. Freight at risk would not include "hire" payments but would cover pre-paid and advance freight and, possibly, chartered freight.[33] It should be noted that the *1989 Salvage Convention* also makes an important exclusion for offshore drilling units and platforms as follows: "This convention shall not apply to fixed or floating platforms or to mobile offshore drilling units when such platforms or units are on location engaged in the exploration, exploitation or production of sea-bed mineral resources."[34] Accordingly, this exclusion only applies if such structures are on location and engaged in sea-bed mineral resource exploration, exploitation, or production. This means that, if such a structure is otherwise engaged, such as being moved, awaiting instructions, undergoing repairs, or being delivered, it could become a proper subject of salvage.[35]

5) Salvage Operations

Since earliest times, salvage has been an arduous and often frustrating task. With the passage of time, it would be expected that salvage operations would become easier, owing to improvements in equipment and

---

30 *Gas Float Whitton No. 2 (The)*, [1896] P. 42, aff'd [1897] A.C. 337. It should be noted that U.S. law may not interpret this rule as strictly: see *Colby v. Todd Packing Co.*, 77 F. Supp. 956 (1948).
31 E.g., hovercraft and aircraft are considered to be proper subjects of salvage (*Canada Shipping Act*, above note 25, s.449(1); *Canada Shipping Act, 2001*, above note 26, s.146). See also Brice, above note 4, c.3. It should be noted that the *Convention for the Unification of Certain Rules Relative to the Assistance and Salvaging of Aircraft or by Aircraft at Sea*, 29 September 1938, 8 Hudson 135, has never entered into force. See also *Ratification of Maritime Conventions*, above note 7 vol.I.3.220.
32 *1989 Salvage Convention*, above note 8, arts.1(b) and (c).
33 See Brice, above note 4, 219–25. See also *Pantanassa (The)*, [1970] P. 187 at 192.
34 *1989 Salvage Convention*, above note 8, art.3.
35 See also E in Chapter 2, "The Shipping Industry: An Overview."

the development of specialized techniques. However, with improvements in salvage equipment and techniques, there has been a commensurate increase in the size and complexity of vessels plying the seas.[36] This has led to larger and more difficult salvage operations. Furthermore, as discussed below, the increasing concern over the protection of the marine environment has confronted salvage operations with a number of new and complex problems. These are some of the reasons why professional salvage companies carry out many salvage operations today. Some are smaller, locally based operators, while others are large multinational concerns, with ships continuously on station at strategic points around the world. These companies have the expertise and the equipment to undertake each class of salvage operation. Salvage operations are generally classified into three categories: stranding, sinking, and rescue (towing). Each class of operation requires different techniques and, quite often, different equipment.[37] Salvage operations differ from the great variety of salvage services that may be performed.

a) Stranding

If a ship is merely stranded on a mud or sand bank or on a beach, and is relatively undamaged, refloating does not usually present a great problem, especially in tidal waters where it may only be necessary to wait for the next high tide to refloat the vessel. If the tidal range is such that, at low water, the ship is high and dry, refloating may still not necessarily be difficult. Land machinery may be used, for instance, to dig a channel through which the ship can be moved to deeper water, or to remove obstacles. If the vessel is holed, any water inside will run out as the tide falls. Minor leaks can be stopped with wooden plugs or wedges, and steel or wooden patches can be fitted over larger holes. If the grounding has taken place at, or near, high tide or in almost tideless waters, then the only way of refloating is by reducing the weight of the vessel in some way. If the vessel is already light (i.e., unloaded), further reduction may sometimes be achieved by pumping out ballast water or fuel oil. However, this may raise different problems, especially in harbour or coastal areas. If the ship is loaded, it is likely that only shifting or discharging of cargo may lighten the vessel sufficiently for refloating. To prevent a stranded ship from going farther aground, or being turned sideways by onshore winds at subsequent high tides, anchors can be carried out seaward into deeper water and the anchor

---

36 *Ibid.*
37 The leading practical manual on salvage operations is D. Hancox, *Reed's Commercial Salvage Practice*, 2 vol. (Sunderland: Reed Publications, 1987).

cables kept taut to prevent the vessel from shifting position. Another way to keep the ship immobile is to run wire ropes from the stranded vessel either to other vessels or to onshore apparatus.[38]

b) Sinking

If a ship has sunk in water deep enough to be completely submerged at all times, then salvage operations are, at best, difficult and, at worst, impossible. In fact, except where the wrecked ship is a navigational hazard, only the recovery of valuable cargo is normally attempted.[39] A sunken ship is invariably full or almost full of water, often holed, and frequently otherwise badly damaged. The ship may be in any position between upright and completely upside down, depending upon whether the vessel foundered through collision, fire, explosion, mine, torpedo, or by capsizing from deck damage or cargo shifting in rough weather. In cases where salvage is to be attempted, a complete survey of the wreck by divers must first be made to establish the precise angle at which the vessel is lying, the extent of the damage, and the size of the hole(s). It can then be determined whether the ship can be raised by pumping out the water, by using compressed air, by mechanical lifting, or by other means. In almost all cases, where the sinking has taken place in coastal or near-coastal waters, and where the sunken vessel has oil on board, whether as fuel or as cargo, there will be a requirement that the pollutant be removed.

c) Rescue (Towing)

Rescue salvage is, generally, operationally less complicated than the salvage of stranded or sunken vessels. Rescue salvage usually involves taking in tow, or otherwise retrieving, a vessel that has had a breakdown owing to mechanical failure or other occurrence, such as heavy weather, collision, or striking a submerged object. This type of salvage is most frequently undertaken by professional salvors, who have the necessary equipment and expertise to undertake it. However, it is also not uncommon for non-professionals to undertake rescue towage. For

---

38 In cases of grounding, as well as any other serious maritime accident that involves salvage, expert assistance will be required: see Hancox, *ibid.* See also *Century 21 Real Estate v. Wenstob* (1996), 119 F.T.R. 201; *Gleniffer (The)* (1892), 3 Ex. C.R. 57; and *Davie v. Young Hustler No.1 (The)* (1962), 32 D.L.R. (2d) 470.

39 In rare instances, such as in the case of the scuttled First World War fleet at Scapa Flow in the Orkney Islands, England, the scrap value made even difficult, expensive, and protracted salvage operations profitable. See also the discussion below in B, "Wreck."

example, a ship may be requested by another vessel that has broken down, to tow it to the nearest port or until a rescue tug arrives. Nevertheless, it is important to distinguish between towage[40] and salvage. This distinction is not always clear and in many cases a towage operation may become a salvage operation if the vessel becomes endangered and the subsequent operations move beyond what is contractually required.[41] Alternatively, if the danger is brought about by the towing vessel salvage will not be allowed.[42] It should be noted that the *1989 Salvage Convention* provides: "No payment is due under the provisions of this Convention unless the services rendered exceed what can be reasonably considered as due performance of a contract entered into before the danger arose."[43] Unfortunately, rescue salvage has become complicated by the attitude of many coastal states, especially when a vessel with pollutants on board is involved. Although offering shelter to a damaged vessel or vessel in distress has been an ancient maritime tradition, many states now often refuse access to their waters or ports for damaged ships. As a result, salvors are often forced to operate outside coastal waters with commensurate dangers and difficulties. This problem has been placed before the International Maritime Organisation on a number of occasions but has not yet been resolved.[44]

6) Salvage Services

In addition to the more traditional salvage operations, a number of different classes of salvage services would attract a salvage award. Most of

---

40 See F in Chapter 14, "Maritime Towage."
41 See Fernandes, above note 25 at 4-36. See also *Re Zambesi (The)* (1891), 3 Ex. C.R. 67, 2 B.C.R. 91; *Smith v. Smith*, [1979] 4 W.W.R. 665 (B.C.S.C.); *Dunphy's Ltd. v. Nancy Caines (The)*, [1950] 2 D.L.R. 64 (Ex. Ct.); *Bonabelle (The) v. Hazel (The)*, [1953] Ex. C.R. 192; *Burrard Towing v. T.G. McBride & Co.*, [1968] 1 Ex. C.R. 9; *Humphreys v. Florence No.2 (The)*, [1948] Ex. C.R. 426; *Larsen v. Gas Boat (The)*, [1923] Ex. C.R. 704, [1923] 2 D.L.R. 281; and *Dunsmuir v. Harold (The)* (1894), 4 Ex. C.R. 222.
42 See Brice, above note 4, c.7.
43 *1989 Salvage Convention*, above note 8, art.17. See also Brice, above note 4 at 96ff.
44 A. Chircop, "Ships in Distress, Environmental Threats to Coastal States, and Places of Refuge: New Directions for an *Ancien Regime*? (2002) 33 Ocean Devel. & Int'l L. 207. This difficulty has been in the forefront of public interest due to recent disasters involving tankers, i.e., The Erika off the coast of France, and The Prestige off the coast of Spain and is at present under intensive study by the International Maritime Organisation.

these are drawn from the large body of case law developed over many years.[45] A more up-to-date listing includes the following:[46]

- proceeding to a casualty, locating the casualty, and standing by at request;
- carrying out inspections and surveys — including diving surveys — of a casualty and assessing its predicament;
- giving advice or formulating and executing a salvage plan, including making the necessary calculations and bringing necessary craft, supplies, equipment, and personnel to the scene (i.e., hiring in as necessary);
- pumping and making necessary repairs to a damaged ship;
- refloating (e.g., by towing, use of ground tackle, lightening, or jettisoning cargo, ballasting or de-ballasting, scouring away sand);
- towing, escorting, or guiding a casualty to safety;
- beaching or holding in position a damaged ship;
- raising a sunken ship or cargo;
- fire fighting;
- arranging port entry for a badly damaged ship;
- complying with governmental requirements to allow salvage operations to proceed (e.g., requirements as to anti-pollution measures);
- saving life or prevention of damage to the environment;
- preventing a grounding or a collision or entanglement with a buoy;
- preventing piratical looting; and
- preventing or minimizing third-party claims (possibly).

This list is not exhaustive and the principles are equally applicable under U.S. law.[47] In each case the question is simply whether or not the party claiming a salvage award has satisfied the requirements of performing a salvage service within the elements outlined above. Additional examples are as follows:

- supplying a vessel with a navigator as the vessel's navigators were incapacitated due to illness,[48]

---

45 One of the classic texts on salvage law lists thirty-seven classes of salvage services; however, some of these are quite archaic: see D.W. Steel, F.D. Rose, & R. Shaw, *Kennedy and Rose on the Law of Salvage*, 6th ed. (London: Sweet & Maxwell, 2002) [Kennedy].
46 Brice, above note 4 at 104.
47 See N.J. Healy & D.J. Sharpe, *Cases and Materials on Admiralty Law*, 3d ed. (St. Paul, MN: West Publishing, 1999) c.9; and T. J. Schoenbaum, *Admiralty and Maritime Law*, 3d ed. (St. Paul, MN: West Publishing, 2001) c.16. See also De La Rue, above note 6 at 605.
48 *Skiplander (The)* (1877), 3 Asp. M.L.C. 556 at 557.

- passing on the necessary information that would lead to a salvage service,[49]
- placing a crew member on board a distressed vessel to assist it into port,[50] and
- providing labourers to shift cargo on a stranded vessel in order to lighten ship.[51]

7) Required Elements for a Salvage Claim

In addition to determining if a salvage claim is brought properly,[52] the court or arbitral tribunal will always determine if the three required elements — danger, voluntariness, and success — were present during the salvage operation when a salvage claim is made.[53]

a) Danger

In determining the presence of danger the task is to decide if, when the assistance was provided, the vessel was in a perilous situation that exposed it to loss or destruction. However, such danger need not be imminent or even actual. A reasonable apprehension of peril will be sufficient.[54] While the onus of proving that danger existed rests on those claiming a salvage award,[55] such proof is not required, nor is it usually disputed in cases where a commercial salvage contract, such as Lloyd's Standard Form of Salvage Agreement,[56] is signed. Even though the

---

49 *Aglaia (The)* (1888), L.R. 13 P.D. 160 at 161.
50 *Charles (The)* (1872), 1 Asp. M.L.C. 296 at 297–98.
51 *Antilope (The)* (1873), 1 Asp. M.L.C. 513 at 515.
52 *Canada Shipping Act*, above note 25, s.471(1) sets out a time limitation for bringing a salvage case/claim; see also *Canada Shipping Act, 2001*, above note 26, s.145.
53 *Kelloway v. Engineering Consultants*, [1972] F.C. 932; *Shanalian (The) v. Dr. Brinkley II (The)*, [1940] S.C.R. 578 [*The Shanalian*]; *Ocean Towing & Salvage Co. v. Penny Hope (The)*, [1980] F.C.J. No.1103 (T.D.) (QL) [*Ocean Towing & Salvage Co.*]. See also Fernandes, above note 25 at 4-35 and 4-27; *Gurney v. MacKay* (1875), 37 U.C.Q.B. 324; *Sherman v. Good Hope II (The)*, [1950] Ex. C.R. 430. See also Brice, above note 4 at 46.
54 Per Dr. Lushington in *Charlotte (The)* (1848), 3 Wm. Rob. 68 at 71, 166 E.R. 888 at 889; see also *Fort Myers Shell and Dredging Co. v. Barge NBC 512*, 404 F.2d 137, 1969 A.M.C. 186 (5th Cir. 1968); *Reynolds Leasing Co. v. Tug Patrice McAllister*, 572 F. Supp. 1131, 1984 A.M.C. 1903 (D.C.N.Y. 1983); and *Iron Mac Towing v. North Arm Highlander (The)* (1979), 28 N.R. 348 (F.C.A.) [*Iron Mac Towing*].
55 *Gulf of Georgia Towing Co. v. Sun Diamond (The)* (1977), 17 N.R. 356 (F.C.A.) [*Gulf of Georgia Towing Co.*].
56 See Appendix 2, *Lloyd's Standard Form of Salvage Agreement*.

danger must be real, the ignorance of those to whom the salvage service is rendered may, in fact, be an element of real danger; for example, a vessel may be in danger if its master is ignorant of local navigational dangers,[57] or possibly even where the master is frightened and incompetent. In other words, "danger" is a question of fact to be considered on a case-by-case basis.[58]

b) Voluntariness

The issue of the voluntariness in a salvage service requires a determination of whether the salvor had a legal duty to assist; for example, a contract or other legal or official obligation between salvor and the ship or property salved will generally preclude voluntariness. Salvage by Canadian Coast Guard was, in the past, not considered eligible for an award, owing to statutory duty.[59] Neither the crew nor the pilot of a ship, nor the owner, master, or crew of a tug towing the vessel under contract of towage,[60] nor the ship's agent is, under ordinary circumstances, entitled to salvage. Crew members and passengers are generally not entitled to salvage as they are considered to be acting in the interests of self-preservation.[61] However, there are some exceptions to this rule.[62] Ship's crew members can, in very exceptional cases, claim salvage if their contract of service to the vessel has ended. Such a termination can occur either by discharge by the master, the proper abandonment of the ship under the master's orders, or a hostile capture of the vessel. In one well-known case,[63] the principle of such abandonment, which had been set out almost a century earlier,[64] was restated to be that abandonment must

---

57 *Eugenie (The)* (1844), 3 Not. of Cas. 430.
58 *Pendragon Castle (The)*, 5 F.2d 56 (1924); see Fernandes, above note 25 at 4-37; see also *Canadian Pacific Navigation Co. v. CF Sargent (The)* (1893), 3 B.C.R. 5; *The Shanalian*, above note 53; *Gulf of Georgia Towing Co.*, above note 55; *Alexander v. Gambier Isle (The)*, [1948] Ex. C.R. 414; and *Johnson v. Charles S. Neff (The)* (1918), 18 Ex. C.R. 159; but see also *Trask v. Maddox* (1863), 15 E.R. 893.
59 See Fernandes, above note 25 at 4-28; but see *Walther Herwig (The) v. Fishery Products Ltd.*, [1978] 1 F.C. 111, 76 D.L.R. (3d) 757; *Manchester Liners v. Scotia Trader (The)*, [1971] F.C. 14; and P.M. Troop, "The Role of Government in the Provision of Salvage Services: A Canadian Perspective" [1985] Mar. L. 237.
60 See *Texaco Southampton (The)*, [1983] 1 Lloyd's L.R. 94 (N.S.W.C.A.); see also F in Chapter 14, "Maritime Towage" for a discussion on the circumstances where a towage contract can become a salvage service. See also *Troilus (The)*, [1951] 1 Lloyd's Rep. 467.
61 However compare *Lomonosoff (The)*, [1921] P. 97.
62 See Brice, above note 4 at 59ff, for a detailed examination of the case law in this area.
63 *San Demetrio (The)* (1941), 69 Ll. L.R. 5 at 12.
64 Per Dr. Lushington in *Florence (The)* (1852), 16 Jur. 572.

- take place at sea and not upon a coast,
- be without hope of returning (*sine spe revertendi*),
- be *bona fide* for the purpose of saving life, and
- be by order of the master in consequence of danger by reason of damage to the ship and the state of the elements.

On the other hand, the actual motivation of the salvor is irrelevant. Professional salvors, operating purely for economic gain, or salvors acting under the control or direction of a third party, such as a government agency, would still be considered "volunteers" within the meaning of this salvage principle.[65] Those that were considered to have a "statutory duty" to provide assistance at sea, such as naval and coastguard vessels, were not considered to be volunteers under traditional salvage law principles and, unless the services performed were over and above required duties, they would not be considered a salvage service.[66] However, Canadian legislation now permits Crown vessels to undertake salvage services with the same rights and remedies, as if such services had been performed by any other salvor, providing that the government vessel is a tug or specifically equipped to undertake salvage services.[67] However, the government must approve any claim for such services.[68]

c) Success

No right to a salvage reward will arise if there has been no success.[69] This means that, even in cases where the ship is lost, if something, such as cargo, equipment, or freight has been saved, a salvage service will have been successfully concluded. This is the basis of the no-cure–no-pay principle of pure salvage that differs from certain aspects of contract salvage (discussed below). The salvage service provided must assist the property in being saved, but is not required to be the final act that saves the property.[70] The salvage award is paid out of the "salved value" of the

---

65 *General Accident Indemnity Co. v. Panache IV (The)*, [1998] 2 F.C. 455, (1997) 139 F.T.R. 167.
66 Fernandes, above note 25 at 4-28. See also Brice, above note 4 at 69ff.
67 *Canada Shipping Act, 2001*, above note 26, s.143. U.K. legislation is similar: see Brice, above note 4 at 70. See also *Walther Herwig (The) v. Fishery Products Ltd.*, above note 59.
68 *Canada Shipping Act* 2001, ibid., s.143.
69 *Manchester Liners v. Scotia Trader (The)*, above note 59; *Canadian Dredging Co. v. Mike Corry (The)* (1917), 19 Ex. C.R. 61, 47 D.L.R. 495 [*The Mike Corry*]; *Gulf & Lake Navigation Co. v. Woodford (The)*, [1955] 5 S.C.R. 829.
70 Fernandes, above note 25 at 4-28.

property saved.[71] If nothing is saved there can be no reward, as expressed in a well-known case: "The first distinctive feature is that the person rendering salvage services is not entitled to any remuneration unless he saves the property in whole or in part. This is what is meant by 'success' in cases about salvage."[72] Although this rule is relatively simple, it can also be quite harsh. It may be that a salvor could expend a significant amount of effort, involving equipment and personnel, for considerable time periods. Yet the salvor will receive nothing if the ship or other maritime property that is being saved is lost. In some cases the salvor may actually succeed in bringing the damaged vessel to a place of safety only to find out that it is so badly damaged that it has no salved value. Problems may also arise in cases where more than one salvor has been involved in a "successful" salvage effort. If there had been no pre-existing agreement among the various salvors, the question then arises as to who was most instrumental in ensuring the successful effort. For example, it may well be that the first salvor on the scene may not have had the capability to ensure success until additional salvors became involved. The House of Lords has laid down a general rule in this area:

> Success is necessary for a salvage reward. Contributions to that success, or as it is sometime expressed, meritorious contributions to that success give a title to a salvage reward. Services however meritorious, which do not contribute to the ultimate success do not give a title to salvage reward. Services which rescue a vessel from one danger but end up by leaving her in a position of as great or nearly as great danger, though of another kind, are held not to contribute to the ultimate success and do not entitle to salvage reward.[73]

There is a distinct, exceptional class of cases in which the courts have awarded salvage for services to property in danger, despite that such services have not contributed to the ultimate success. This class is called services rendered "at request" or "engaged" or "employed" services. If a master of a ship in distress requests the performance of a salvage-type service that is rendered, but the ship for which the service is requested is eventually saved through some other cause, or the salving vessel is discharged by the master of the vessel in danger, after having begun the service then the court may allow a salvage reward.[74] A fur-

---

71 *The Mike Corry*, above note 69.
72 *Tojo Maru (The)*, [1972] A.C. 242 at 293.
73 *San Onofre (The)*, [1925] A.C. 246 at 262.
74 *Undaunted (The)* (1860), Lush. 90; see Brice, above note 4 at 117–18 and *Kennedy*, above note 45 at 279–85.

ther, much more critical exception to the no-cure–no-pay rule relates, of course, to salvage involving vessels carrying pollutants (discussed in more detail below).

8) Obligations of Salvor and Shipowner

Anyone who undertakes a salvage service is expected to carry out such service with reasonable skill and care — depending of course upon the circumstances of the case and the expected skill of the salvor. The *Lloyd's Open Form* contract requires that the salvor should use his or her "best endeavours" to carry out the service.[75] A higher level of skill would be expected from a professional salvor than from an amateur. In any case, a salvor is liable for ordinary negligence that occurs while carrying out the service. This was not always clear, as the *Assistance and Salvage Convention 1910* was silent on this subject; it has, however, been firmly established in case law as well as in the *1989 Salvage Convention*.[76] In 1971 the House of Lords examined the position in a landmark case in which, during salvage operations on a tanker that had been holed in a collision, a diver negligently fired a bolt into a part of the hull that had not been gas-freed. This resulted in an explosion and serious damage to the vessel. The court held that, while a salvage award had been earned, the damage caused by the salvor's negligence would have to be set off against such an award.[77]

The *1989 Salvage Convention* sets out a specific duty of care of the salvor, including due care to prevent or minimize damage to the marine environment.[78] In other words, if, during salvage operations, negligence occurs, a salvage award may still be payable, but such award will be reduced, or set off against any damage that may be assessed.[79] If the salvor is found to be guilty of gross negligence or wilful misconduct, or if there is evidence of looting or deliberate spoilage of the salved property, any award is forfeited.[80] However, in the absence of such misconduct, where salvage is attempted but is unsuccessful, the salvor is not

---

75 *Lloyd's Open Form 2000*, art.A. See Appendix 2, *Lloyd's Standard Form of Salvage Agreement*.
76 *1989 Salvage Convention*, above note 8, art.8.
77 *Tojo Maru (The)*, above note 72. See also De La Rue, above note 6 at 601.
78 *1989 Salvage Convention*, above note 8, arts.8.1(a) and (b).
79 See *Tojo Maru (The)*, above note 72; *Empacadora del Norte S.A. v. M.V. Finnco Victoria*, 1983 A.M.C. 1235 (S.D. Tex.); *Danner v. United States (The Royal Oak)*, 99 F. Supp. 880 (D.C.N.Y. 1951); see also D.R. Thomas, "Salvatorial Negligence and its Consequence" (1977) 2 L.M.C. L.Q. 167.
80 See Brice, above note 4, c.7 for an extensive discussion of this area.

responsible for losses sustained by the shipowner or other third parties.[81] Nevertheless, there may be a problem if, during an unsuccessful salvage operation, environmental damage occurs. If it is shown that the salvor could have prevented the environmental damage in some way, he or she could be held negligent.[82] Such negligence may not even have been foreseeable during a complex operation. The *1989 Salvage Convention* did not provide a solution. Whereas the convention provided "special compensation" for preventing pollution if the salvage operation is unsuccessful, in cases where there was no such prevention the salvor would be fully liable. This was considered to be an almost intolerable burden by the salvage industry, which felt that in high-risk salvage cases, involving large laden tankers, salvors would simply have insufficient liability insurance coverage. As seen below, this problem has not been totally resolved, but it has been somewhat eased.

On the other hand, during salvage operations, the shipowner also has some important obligations and responsibilities in order to assist the salvor.[83] This was codified in the *1989 Salvage Convention* where it is stated as follows:

> The owner and master of the vessel or the owner of other in danger shall owe a duty to the salvor:
> (a) to cooperate fully with him during the course of the salvage operations;
> (b) in so doing, to exercise due care to prevent or minimize damage to the environment; and
> (c) when the vessel or other property has been brought to a place of safety, to accept redelivery when reasonably requested by the salvor to do so.[84]

The principle behind this obligation has also been incorporated into the *Lloyd's Open Form* contract that states:

> Each of the owners of the property shall cooperate fully with the contractors. In particular:
> (i) the contractors may make reasonable use of the vessel's machinery, gear and equipment free of expense providing that the con-

---

81   *Re Oil Spill by Amoco Cadiz*, 1984 A.M.C. 2123 (7th Cir. 1983).
82   *North Star Marine Salvage v. Muren*, [1973] F.C. 50, 36 D.L.R. (3d) 136 [*North Star Marine Salvage*].
83   See Brice, above note 4 at 534.
84   *1989 Salvage Convention*, above note 8, art.8.2. See also *China Pacific S.A. v. Food Corporation of India (The Winson)*, [1981] 3 W.L.R. 860 (H.L.). See also *Lloyd's Open Form 2000*, Appendix 2, cl.H.

tractor shall not unnecessarily damage, abandon or sacrifice any property on board;

(ii) the contractors shall be entitled to all such information as they may reasonably require relating to the vessel or the remainder of the property provided such information is relevant to the performance of the services and is capable of being provided without undue difficulty or delay;

(iii) the owners of the property shall cooperate fully with the contractors in obtaining entry to a place of safety.[85]

It should be noted that the salvor's rights, arising out of the salvage service performed, are protected by a maritime lien that attaches to the property and that is not lost, even if the salved property is transferred to an innocent third party. Such lien is designed to ensure that any obligation the property owner may have, whether arising under contract or otherwise, can be enforced.[86] The right to a maritime lien has also been included in the *1989 Salvage Convention*.[87]

9) Salvage Contracts and Clauses

Almost all commercial salvage operations, as well as many non-commercial salvage services, are today subject to a formal contract. Such formal agreements originated in the nineteenth century.[88] A salvage agreement is a commercial contract that fixes the amount to be paid to the salvor for salvage services or provides for its assessment by arbitration.[89] However, in most cases such an agreement still leaves the right to any payment contingent on the preservation of at least some part of the maritime property at risk.[90] The master of the vessel in difficulty has the legal authority to conclude a contract for salvage services on behalf of the vessel's owner.[91] At the same time this authority is extend-

---

85　*Lloyd's Open Form 2000*, Appendix 2, cl.F.
86　*Goulandris (The)*, [1927] P. 182, (1927) 27 Ll. L.R. 120; *Alma (The)* (1862), 5 N.S.R. 789; *Pearce v. Leatherby* (1905), 6 O.W.R. 606; *Johnson v. Charles S. Neff (The)*, above note 58; *Iron Mac Towing*, above note 54. See also Fernandes, above note 25 at 4-36; Brice, above note 4 at 544; and Chapter 6, C "Liens."
87　Above note 8, art.20.
88　See Brice, above note 4, c.5.
89　*International Wrecking & Transportation Co. v. Lobb* (1886), 11 O.R. 408 (C.A.); *Connolly v. Dracona (The)* (1896), 5 Ex. C.R. 146, aff'd 5 Ex. C.R. 207; *Africa (The)* (1880), 1 Spinks E.&A. 299, 164 E.R. 173.
90　*North Star Marine Salvage*, above note 82.
91　Codified in the *1989 Salvage Convention*, above note 8, art.6(2). See also Brice, above note 4 at 326.

ed on behalf of the owners of cargo on board the vessel.[92] This authority is binding unless the following can be shown:[93]

- the circumstances of the case did not make the agreement reasonably necessary,
- the terms of the agreement illustrated that it could not be for the owner's benefit, and
- the owner of the vessel to be salved was personally present and gave the master no authority.

A salvage contract is generally strictly enforced unless the following can be shown:

- fraud was involved,[94]
- misrepresentation or non-disclosure of a material fact induced the salvors to conclude the agreement,[95]
- the terms of the agreement are inequitable,[96] and
- the agreement has been cancelled by express or implied consent of the parties.

This enforcement aspect is, of course, related to the fixing of the salvage award, which is guided by the principles of equity, even though it may be subject to contract.

a) Standard Salvage Contracts

One of the first standard salvage contracts, and the best-known, was the Lloyd's agreement that in its standardized version became known as *Lloyd's Standard Form of Salvage Agreement — No-Cure–No-Pay*, generally called the *Lloyd's Open Form of Salvor Agreement*.[97] Originally the *Lloyd's Open Form* incorporated the basic salvage law principles, as sub-

---

92 *1989 Salvage Convention*, ibid., art.6(2). But see *Industrie Chimiche Italia Centrale and Cerealfin S.A. v. Alexander G. Tsalviris & Sons Maritime Co. (The Choko Star)*, [1989] 2 Lloyd's L.R. 42, aff'd [1990] 1 Lloyd's L.R. 516 (C.A.).
93 *The Shanalian*, above note 53.
94 *Crus V (The)* (1862), Lush 583, 167 E.R. 266; *Generous (The)* (1868), L.R. 2 A. & E. 57; *Westminster (The)* (1841), 1 W. Rob. 229, 166 E.R. 558. See also Brice, above note 4 at 365.
95 *Esso Petroleum Co. v. Mardon*, [1976] Q.B. 801; *Unique Mariner (The)*, [1978] 1 Lloyd's L.R. 438. See also Brice, ibid. at 366. See also *1989 Salvage Convention*, above note 8, art.7(a).
96 *Connolly v. Dracona (The)*, above note 89; *North Star Marine Salvage*, above note 82; *Medina (The)* (1877), L.R. 2 P.D. 5. See also Brice, ibid. at 364–5. See also *1989 Salvage Convention*, ibid., art.7(b).
97 See A.F. Bessemer-Clark, "The Role of Lloyd's Open Form" (1980) 3 L.M.C.L.Q. 297.

sequently codified by the *Assistance and Salvage Convention 1910*, into a standard form of agreement that was widely known in the industry. This *Lloyd's Open Form* agreement incorporates:

- the obligations of each party regarding the performance of the salvage services,
- the requirement for the provision of security for the salvor's claim,
- the requirement for arbitration in the event of a dispute,[98] and
- the payment of salvage remuneration and other required sums.[99]

The *Lloyd's Open Form* is periodically revised or updated, and the latest version is *Lloyd's Open Form 2000*, which is a very condensed single-sheet double-sided document. (See Appendix 2.)

The environmental pressures in the late 1960s and 1970s also dictated that some modifications to traditional salvage law needed to be made. Although this resulted principally in the *1989 Salvage Convention*, there was also a significant change to the traditional *Lloyd's Open Form*, as reflected in the *Lloyd's Open Form '80* . This followed consultations among the various interested parties, such as shipowners, salvors, insurers, oil companies, and other shippers. The principal change was in respect to laden or partially laden oil tankers. In order to encourage salvors to use their best endeavours to prevent the escape of oil from the vessel during a salvage service the basic no-cure–no-pay principle was changed. If such environmental salvage efforts were unsuccessful or only partially successful, the salvor would nevertheless receive his or her reasonable expenses from the owner of the vessel and an increment not exceeding 15 per cent of such expenses, but only if and to the extent that such expenses, together with the increment, were greater than any amount otherwise recoverable in connection with the service rendered itself. The new provisions defined "expenses" as including, in addition to actual out-of-pocket costs, also a fair rate for all tugs, vessels, personnel, and other equipment used in the service. Subsequent negotiations within the industry resulted in further changes to the *Lloyd's Open Form*. As a result, by 1990, *Lloyd's Open Form 1990* had doubled the increment payable to 30 per cent with the provision, based on the *1989 Salvage Convention*, that the special compensation could be further increased but with a ceiling of double the expenses. In other words, the *Lloyd's Open Form* virtually

---

98 Under Lloyd's Standard Salvage and Arbitration Clauses and in accordance with Lloyd's Procedural Rules, administered by Lloyd's Salvage Arbitration Branch, Lloyd's, One Lime Street, London, UK, EC3M 7HA.
99 See Brice, above note 4, c.5 for a full discussion of this area.

incorporated the controversial "liability salvage"[100] ideas in response to greater global environmental concerns. However, the salvage industry was still concerned about the increasing risks faced in complex salvage operations involving vessels carrying pollutants. Furthermore, the special compensation principles set out in the new *Lloyd's Open Form*, as well as in the *1989 Salvage Convention*, had still been insufficiently tested in practice.

b) Special Compensation Clauses

i) PIOPIC *Clause*

In 1972 the International Salvage Union, which represents the world's major salvage companies, concluded an agreement with the International Group of P&I Clubs,[101] designed to lessen the marine pollution risk exposure for salvors and, at the same time, to encourage salvors to undertake difficult salvage operations involving tankers. This agreement resulted in the *P&I Oil Pollution Indemnity Clause* (*PIOPIC*), under which the P&I clubs undertook to cover certain salvors' liability exposure to pollution risks in particular conditions. This clause, when added to specific salvage and towage contracts, committed the owner and the owner's P&I club[102] to assume responsibility for all claims for oil pollution damage, including preventive measures, arising out of the salvage or towage services under the contract, up to US$15 million, less the aggregate amount of all liabilities, costs, and expenses, incurred by the owners arising out of the casualty, or US$10 million, whichever is the greater. This clause is no longer in operation, as it has been superseded by the *SCOPIC* clause, and is simply included here to illustrate the development of salvage law in recent years.

ii) SCOPIC *and* SCOPIC 2000 *Clauses*

The special compensation developed in the *1989 Salvage Convention* and the various versions of the *Lloyd's Open Form* agreement contained a number of difficulties. First, the assessment of special compensation, even in standard cases, takes a great deal of time, involving lawyers and often accountants on all sides. This also becomes very costly and leaves the salvor with considerable uncertainty as to his or her ultimate enti-

---

100 Brice, above note 3 at 409.
101 See G(2)(j) in Chapter 2, "The Shipping Industry: An Overview" and F(2) in Chapter 7, "Marine Insurance." See also E. Gold, *Gard Handbook on P&I Insurance*, 5th ed. (Arendal, NO: Gard A.S., 2002).
102 Gold, *ibid*.

tlement.[103] This problem was further exacerbated in a 1997 case that tested the special compensation clause at the House of Lords;[104] the case arose out of a serious collision in the Malacca Strait in 1992 between the tanker Nagasaki Spirit and the container vessel Ocean Blessing. A dispute arose between the salvors and the protection and indemnity underwriters over the meaning of a "fair rate" for equipment and "out-of-pocket expenses" under the special compensation provision of the *Lloyd's Open Form* agreement. The court held that neither a fair rate nor out-of-pocket expenses should contain any element of profit. This decision had severe implications for the shipping industry generally and the salvors specifically. It basically meant that there would be very little inducement for salvors to act under the *Lloyd's Open Form's* special compensation provision, especially in high-risk cases. As a result of the *Nagasaki Spirit* case, discussions commenced in 1997 to find some solutions for these concerns. After lengthy negotiations, a compromise considered to be reasonably satisfactory to all parties was achieved. This is reflected in the *Special Compensation P&I Club Clause (SCOPIC)*[105] that displaces the no-cure–no-pay principle in *Lloyd's Open Form of Salvage Agreement*.[106] The following are the main features of the *SCOPIC* clause:

- The salvor is provided with a unilateral option at any time to invoke the *SCOPIC* clause regardless of circumstances. The assessment of *SCOPIC* remuneration commences when the salvor gives notice.
- The shipowner — in practice the shipowner's protection and indemnity insurer — will provide security for the required *SCOPIC* remuneration.
- The remuneration will be based on time and material used, plus a standard 25–per-cent uplift,[107] regardless of the outcome of the operation. The *SCOPIC* clause includes rates for tugs, personnel, and equipment.

---

103 In two major cases, the time taken was four and six years respectively; the costs in each case expended by the parties exceeded £1 million: see A. Bishop, "SCOPIC Clause" Gard P&I Summer Seminar, Arendal, Norway, June 1999, online at <www.gard.no>; and J. Nixon, "Funding Salvage" *Seaways* (Aug. 2001) at 8.
104 *Semco Salvage & Marine Ltd. v. Lancer Navigation (The Nagasaki Spirit)*, [1997] 1 Lloyd's L.R. 323 (H.L.).
105 LSSA Clauses, above note 98, Appendix C.
106 If the *SCOPIC* clause is not included in the salvage contract, art.14 of *Lloyd's Open Form '90* or *Lloyd's Open Form '95* agreement on special compensation will continue to be applicable; however, see amendments incorporated into the *SCOPIC 2000* clause discussed below.
107 This is the profit denied in *The Nagasaki Spirit* case, above note 104.

- The remuneration is only payable to the extent that it exceeds the remuneration assessed on the basis of the no-cure–no-pay principle. The salvor will face a reduction of 25 per cent on the *Lloyd's Open Form* award, if such award is greater than the *SCOPIC* remuneration.
- Both the salvor and the shipowner can terminate the contract.
- The shipowner and the relevant P&I club will obtain better access to information about the salvage operation through a "Special Casualty Representative," who will be appointed by the involved P&I club once the *SCOPIC* clause has been invoked.

The *SCOPIC* clause has been designed as a very specialized accounting arrangement and has been approved by all members of the International Group of P&I Clubs. It was intended to be used on a trial basis for an initial two-year period to be incorporated into *Lloyd's Open Form* agreements with salvors who are members of the International Salvage Union.[108] However, the clause was amended again even before the expiry of the trial period. This amendment has resulted in the *SCOPIC 2000* Clause[109] that can apply to any *Lloyd's Open Form* agreement that incorporates the provisions of Article 14 of the *1989 Salvage Convention*.[110] It can, therefore, be used in conjunction with *Lloyd's Open Form 1990*, *Lloyd's Open Form 1995*, or *Lloyd's Open Form 2000*. The additional principal amendments incorporated into the *SCOPIC 2000* clause are as follows:

- Sub-clause 1 now makes clear that if a salvage operation is undertaken on the basis of a *Lloyd's Open Form* agreement incorporating the *SCOPIC 2000* clause, the traditional *Lloyd's Open Form* Article 14 safety net will not apply, even if the provisions of the *SCOPIC* clause have not been invoked.
- Sub-clause 4 is amended so that the salvor's right of withdrawal from the *SCOPIC* provisions for failure to provide *SCOPIC* security within two working days does not apply if *SCOPIC* security is provided before notice of such withdrawal is given.
- Sub-clause 6 makes it clear that *SCOPIC* remuneration is only payable in excess of any potential *Lloyd's Open Form* Article 13[111] award, even if no Article 13 award is actually sought or paid. In addition, currency adjustments are clarified in the event that the currency applying to the main salvage agreement differs from that of the *SCOPIC* clause.

---

108 International Salvage Union is the organization representing the salvage industry. See also G(2)(m) in Chapter 2, "The Shipping Industry: An Overview." See also Gold, above note 101 at 192ff.
109 Attached to Lloyd's Procedural Rules, above note 98.
110 On special compensation.
111 On criteria for fixing the award.

- The sub-clause 9 termination provisions have been amended to clarify that the salvor has the right to terminate his or her services under both the *SCOPIC* clause and the main salvage agreement in certain specified circumstances.
- Appendix A (the *SCOPIC* tariff) has been amended to
  - define the periods for which *SCOPIC* remuneration applies to personnel engaged in a salvage operation;
  - clarify how *SCOPIC* rates apply to tugs and other craft during mobilization to and demobilization from the casualty and when taking on any necessary additional personnel or equipment;
  - explain that the use of portable salvage equipment normally on board the tug shall be remunerated in the same manner as all other portable salvage equipment;
  - clarify how tugs or portable salvage equipment lost or damaged during the operation will be treated for the purposes of *SCOPIC* remuneration; and
  - clarify how the cap on the hiring of portable salvage equipment operates, and introduce a 50–per-cent standby rate for downtime on tugs and equipment and on portable salvage equipment reasonably mobilized but not utilized during the salvage operation.

10) Salvage Award

Once the salvor's right to a reward has been established the relevant court or, if a *Lloyd's Open Form* agreement is involved, salvage arbitration tribunal, has to decide what the amount of such a reward should be. The calculation of such reward is a complex, technical undertaking based on the various ingredients that make up a salvage service. Such ingredients will include the following:[112]

- with reference to the salved property:
  - the degree of danger to human life;
  - the degree of danger to the salved property; and
  - the value of the property salved.[113]

---

112 *Iron Mac Towing*, above note 54; *Ocean Towing & Salvage Co.*, above note 53; *Humphreys v. Florence No.2 (The)*, above note 41; *Falconer Fishing Fleet Ltd. v. Island Prince (The)*, [1948] Ex. C.R. 378; *Keta (The) v. Irene M. (The)*, [1959] Ex. C.R. 372, [1959] R.L. 280; *Fishery Products Ltd. v. Claudette V (The)* (1960), 44 M.P.R. 391; *Dunphy's Ltd. v. Nancy Caines (The)*, above note 41.
113 *International Wrecking & Transportation Co. v. Lobb*, above note 89; *Gleniffer (The)*, above note 38; *Hiscock v. Tommie L. Vincent (The)* (1964), 49 M.P.R. 302 (Ex. Ct.).

- with reference to the salvor:
  - the degree of danger to human life;[114]
  - the salvor's classification (professional or otherwise), skill, and conduct;[115]
  - the time occupied, and work done in the performance of the salvage service;
  - the responsibilities incurred in the performance of the salvage service, such as risk to insurers and liability to passengers or shippers through deviation or delay;
  - the loss or expense incurred in the performance of the salvage service, such as detention, loss of profitable trade, repair of damage caused to the ship, boats, or gear, fuel consumed;[116]
  - the threat to vulnerable coastal areas from pollutants;
  - in the case of professional salvors, the investment in equipment and trained personnel available for salvage services;
  - the assistance received by the salvor from other salvors,[117] other parties, and government authorities; and
  - any contribution to the salvage effort by the interests of the salved property.

11) Life Salvage

The rules governing life salvage are closely related to the general marine salvage principles outlined above.[118] The general rule is that anyone who voluntarily saves or tries to save the life of a person on board a ship in danger is entitled to claim a financial reward for such

---

114 See *Kennedy*, above note 45 at 461.
115 *Ontario v. Mar-Dive Corp.* (1997), 141 D.L.R. (4th) 577 (Ont. Ct. Gen. Div.); *Manchester Liners v. Scotia Trader (The)*, above note 59; *Magdalen Islands Steamship Co. v. Diana (The)* (1907), 11 Ex. C.R. 40; *Herring Un Ltd. v. Nina M. Conrad (The)* (1954), 32 M.P.R. 225 (Nfld. S.C.); *Cox v. Lenneard (The Trade Up)*, [1998] F.C.J. No.291 (T.D.) (QL).
116 *Jacobsen v. Archer (The)* (1894), 3 B.C.R. 374; *Vermont Steamship Co. v. Abby Palmer (The)* (1904), 9 Ex. C.R. 1.
117 *Herring Un. Ltd. v. Nina M. Conrad (The)*, above note 115.
118 *Assistance and Salvage Convention 1910*, above note 7, art.9; *1989 Salvage Convention*, above note 8, art.16; see also *United Nations Convention on the Law of the Sea*, 10 December 1982, 1833 U.N.T.S. 3, art.98 [*UNCLOS*] (entered into force on 16 November 1994; not yet accepted by Canada). See also *Ratification of Maritime Conventions*, above note 7 vol.I.1.170. See also Brice, above note 4 at 186ff.

efforts. However, such right is enforceable only against the property that has been salved and not against the person or persons saved.[119] Accordingly, the no-cure–no-pay principle still applies: if no property is salved, no life salvage is payable. There may be some exceptions in states that may provide modest discretionary rewards under statute.[120] On the other hand, if the vessel or other property has been rescued, the life salvage award will actually be enhanced.

Life salvage claims are assessed against the owner of the vessel or cargo saved. That is applicable even in cases where the life salvors themselves neither saved nor intended to save the property.[121] Furthermore, life salvage claims have priority over all other salvage claims.[122] In cases where there is no contract between salvor and the owner of the salved ship, the claim will have to be determined under either the law of the vessel's flag or the law of the state where the services were performed. However, most states have a statutory requirement that obliges masters of vessels to render assistance to any person in danger of being lost at sea, providing that such assistance can be made without danger to the vessel or the persons on such vessel.[123] This has also been codified in the *1989 Salvage Convention*.[124] Regardless of case law and statutory principles, it has always been a custom of the sea to attempt to save life. Such attempts often involve significant risks and, in many cases, expose ships and their owners to considerable commercial costs and inconvenience.[125]

---

119 *Emblem (The)*, 8. Cas. 611 (D. Me. 1840). See also M. McInnes, "Life Rescue in Maritime Law" (1994) 25 J. Mar. L. & Com. 451. See also *Canada Shipping Act*, above note 25, s.450(1).
120 In Canada under *Canada Shipping Act*, ibid., s.450(3). There is no equivalent section in *Canada Shipping Act, 2001*, above note 26. It is assumed that, when new regulations under this Act become available, this aspect will be covered. See also *Merchant Shipping Act, 1995* (U.K.), 1995, c.21, Sch.11, Pt.II, s.5(1).
121 *Coromandel (The)* (1857), Swab. 205 at 207, 166 E.R. 1097 at 1098.
122 For a comprehensive discussion of this area, see S.F. Friedell, "Compensation and Reward for Saving Life at Sea" (1979) 77 Mich. L.Rev. 1218; see also Brice, above note 4 at 187ff; and *Kennedy*, above note 45 at 99ff.
123 *Canada Shipping Act*, above note 25, s.451(1); *Canada Shipping Act, 2001*, above note 26, ss.130–32.
124 Above note 8, art.10.
125 Especially in the modern context when rescuing adventurers, refugees, boat people, and illegal immigrants. See also McInnes, above note 119.

B. WRECK

1) Introduction

In the maritime context the word "wreck" has several meanings. It usually refers to the remains of a ship that has suffered a major maritime disaster. However, it can also describe a sunken vessel, a vessel's cargo, or other artefacts of maritime historical and archaeological significance. Flotsam, jetsam, lagan,[126] and other derelict maritime property found on or near the shore will also be classified as "wreck" and are so defined in the *Canada Shipping Act*;[127] such derelict maritime property has been defined as "abandoned at sea by master and crew without hope of recovery."[128] It should be noted that under the *Canada Shipping Act*, wreck also includes aircraft that crash into the sea.[129] There may also be a relationship between wrecked property and property that has been deliberately and, often, illegally dumped at sea. In such cases a legal conflict may arise as to what legal regime would be applicable. While the rules relating to wreck may also apply to dumped items, the *London (Dumping) Convention* may also be applicable;[130] this convention is principally concerned with the protection of the marine environment,[131] while the wreck provisions are more concerned with the saving and preserving of maritime property.

2) Receiver of Wreck

It is likely that even derelict maritime property may be owned by someone — the ownership may be in doubt or unknown, however — or

---

126 See above notes 27, 28, and 29.
127 *Canada Shipping Act*, above note 25, s.2. See also *Canada Shipping Act, 2001*, above note 26, s.153.
128 Per Sir William Scott in *Aquila (The)* (1798), 1 C. Rob. 36 at 40, 165 E.R. 87 at 88; however, the rules may be somewhat different for buried and abandoned marine treasure and valuables. See S.R. Yormak, "Canadian Treasure: Law and Lore (Second Newport Symposium: Sunken Treasure; Law, Technology, and Ethics)" (1999) 30 J. Mar. L. & Com. 229.
129 *Canada Shipping Act*, above note 25, s.449(1); *Canada Shipping Act, 2001*, above note 26, s.153. See also, *Canada Shipping Act, 2001*, ibid., s.146 on aircraft salvage. These *Canada Shipping Act* provisions were applicable in the recent Swissair Flight SR111 disaster off the coast of Nova Scotia.
130 *Convention on the Prevention of Marine Pollution by Dumping of Wastes and Other Matter*, 29 December 1972, 1046 U.N.T.S. 120 [*LC 1972*] as am. (entered into force on 30 August 1975; in force in Canada on 14 December 1975). See also *Ratification of Maritime Conventions*, above note 7 vol.I.7.150.

there may competing ownership interests. In order that this status should not lead to immediate disputes, states have legislated in this area for many years. In the Commonwealth, maritime legislation generally appoints a Receiver of Wreck.[132] This official's main function is to take charge of any wreck, preserve and protect it, and deal with any salvage or other property claims that may arise.[133] The Receiver of Wreck is given full statutory powers to carry out this task. Anyone who finds a wreck or wreckage is, therefore, obliged to inform and hand over such property to the receiver.[134] The Receiver of Wreck will attempt to find the owner and/or others with interests in the property, and/or establish possible salvage rights. This may not always be easy. Even in cases where a ship has been abandoned by master and crew, the owner may still have an interest. If the owner has been paid under a hull insurance policy, the underwriters may have an interest.[135] In other cases, the owner may have really abandoned the wrecked vessel without any further interest. That may, however, involve the eventual requirement of wreck removal (discussed below).

3) Underwater Cultural Heritage

As underwater and salvage technology have improved, many historic wrecks have become accessible. This may involve access to archaeologically and historically valuable artefacts, other sunken valuables, underwater "memorial sites,"[136] and other areas of "underwater cultural heritage."[137] In order to avoid any problems that may be expected to arise out of unrestricted and indiscriminate access, such as treasure hunting, several international rules and guidelines have been developed, or are being developed. The *United Nations Convention on the*

---

131 See B(3) in Chapter 17, "Marine Pollution Prevention."
132 See *Canada Shipping Act*, above note 25, s.423; and *Canada Shipping Act, 2001*, above note 26, s.154. See also *Wreck Districts and Receivers of Wreck Order*, S.I./83-117 as am. The Receiver of Wreck is usually a senior officer of the Canadian Coast Guard and will have this responsibility under either Act.
133 It is however at the discretion of the Receiver whether to take action. See *Canada Shipping Act*, above note 25, s.428; and *Canada Shipping Act, 2001*, above note 26, s.160.
134 *Canada Shipping Act*, ibid., s.436; *Canada Shipping Act, 2001*, ibid., s.155.
135 See C(4) in Chapter 7, "Marine Insurance."
136 Generally involving vessels that have sunk with heavy loss of life such as The Titanic and more recently, The Estonia.
137 For a very thorough examination of underwater cultural heritage, see A. Strati, *The Protection of the Underwater Cultural Heritage* (Amsterdam: Martinus Nijhoff, 1995).

Law of the Sea (UNCLOS)[138] contains provisions directed at the preservation and handling of underwater cultural heritage artefacts.[139] The *1989 Salvage Convention* also gives the rights to any state to reserve the right not to apply the convention's provisions to underwater cultural heritage property and artefacts.[140]

In 1994 the International Law Association proposed a draft convention on the subject.[141] In 1996 the United Nations Educational, Scientific and Cultural Organization (UNESCO) completed a draft *Convention on the Protection of the Underwater Cultural Heritage*, which was adopted in 2001;[142] however, it appears that this convention may well be inconsistent with the rights of salvors under the *1989 Salvage Convention*. As a result, the Comité Maritime International (CMI)[143] has commenced work on a draft protocol to the *1989 Salvage Convention*. This protocol was specifically designed to protect underwater cultural heritage sites and artefacts without unreasonably restricting the rights of salvors.[144] This work is being further developed and will probably be on the agenda of the International Maritime Organisation (IMO) in the near future.[145]

4) Wreck Removal

a) General Principles

Wreck removal must be distinguished from the finding and taking possession of derelict vessels afloat or aground on or near the coast. Wrecks

---

138 Above note 118.
139 *UNCLOS*, above note 118, arts.149 and 303.
140 Above note 8, art.30(1)(d). When accepting this convention, Canada made a declaration to the effect that the right to opt out under this article would be applied if required.
141 See Brice, above note 4 at 257.
142 *Convention on the Protection of the Underwater Cultural Heritage*, 2 November 2001, 41 I.L.M. 40.
143 See G(2)(a) in Chapter 2 for more information on the Comité Maritime International.
144 See "UNESCO Draft Convention on Underwater Cultural Heritage" in CMI, *Yearbook 2000 — Singapore I — Documents for the Conference* (Brussels: CMI, 2001) at 412. This draft was discussed at the CMI's XXXVIth International Conference in Singapore in early 2001. As a result, a CMI International Working Group developed the protocol further, and handed the results of this work over to the IMO in 2002.
145 The UNESCO convention is being strongly opposed by the international salvage industry as well as a number of states, as it is considered not to distinguish sufficiently between heritage objects and traditional salvage.

may be a danger to shipping, or may interfere with coastal amenities, or even present dangers from pollutants or dangerous cargoes. Most coastal states consider the safety of navigation on waters within their jurisdiction as their responsibility. In addition to the general legal responsibility to chart and light their coastal areas, and enforce international collision, pollution, and other regulations, states also have the ultimate responsibility to mark, raise, remove, or destroy wrecked vessels or vessels' equipment, in order to prevent further casualties to other vessels. This has caused problems in many regions of the world owing to wrecks that have been abandoned and not removed. As a result, coastal states have significantly tightened wreck removal requirements, and an international convention on this issue is under consideration by the IMO. It is, therefore, quite clear that a vessel wrecked and sunk in coastal waters, harbours, ports, bays, rivers, and estuaries will generally have to be raised or otherwise removed.[146] The removal of ship and/or cargo may be carried out under private contract directly by, or under the direction of, the coastal authority, generally under a statutory power.[147] Where the wreck has any residual value it is usual for the coastal authority to have first call on any proceeds in order to compensate for any removal costs involved. Such costs may be significant. Most states have statutory provisions under which the finder is required to deliver such derelict vessels to the appropriate authority, with a right to subsequent compensation for the finder's efforts. On the other hand, wreck generally means a ship, part of a ship, or a vessel's cargo that has grounded or sunk after having "met such danger or damage as to render her no longer capable of navigation and effectively a total loss."[148]

At present, the basic rules regarding removal of wreck in place in Canada and most other coastal states are quite specific. When a marine casualty occurs, the owner(s) of the vessel(s) involved must make an immediate report to the coastal authorities so that rescue operations may be initiated to safeguard lives and property, and to prevent possible marine pollution.[149] When the vessel casualty actually becomes a wreck, the owner is responsible for marking the wreck.[150] If such marking is carried out by the coastal authorities the costs will be borne by the owner.[151] In most cases the coastal state authorities will require the

---

146 Wreck removal is also normally covered under ships' P&I insurance policies. See Gold, above note 101, c.11.
147 *Navigable Waters Protection Act*, R.S.C. 1985, c.N-22, s.16.
148 *Olympic (The)*, [1913] P. 92.
149 *Transportation Safety Board Regulations*, S.O.R./92-446, s.3.
150 *Navigable Waters Protection Act*, above note 147, s.15.
151 *Ibid.*, ss.18(1)(a) and 18(2).

owner to remove or raise the wreck or ensure that there is no obstruction to navigation.[152] Of particular concern are wrecked vessels that may contain pollutants, such as oil cargoes or bunkers.[153] Where the local authority carries out this work, the owner will be responsible for the costs involved.[154]

In some jurisdictions, shipowners have been permitted to abandon the wreck to the coastal state and then disclaim further responsibility for the wreck;[155] however, this loophole is rarely available today and cannot be relied on. In cases where the owner(s) of the wreck is/are slow in responding, or do not respond to demands to take removal action, the coastal authorities generally have the statutory power to arrange removal themselves. While such intention must be publicized, the authorities are not obliged to notify the flag state if a foreign vessel is involved.[156] Unless the wreck has to be destroyed, any refloated vessel or parts or cargo may be sold by public auction or privately under a court or executive order. The proceeds may be used to cover the expenses incurred by the local authority, which is considered to be acting on behalf of the owner. Any surplus will be held in trust for the owner for a reasonable time. At the expiry of this period, the funds may be appropriated by the coastal state. In cases where the proceeds of any sale are insufficient, or if there are no proceeds, the coastal authority will be entitled to claim the removal costs from the owner.[157] Damage to third parties occurring during the removal operations, and all risks involved, will usually be the responsibility of the shipowner.[158]

---

152 *Ibid.*, ss.15(3) and 16.
153 A notable Canadian case involved The Irving Whale, a fully loaded oil barge that had sunk and was subsequently raised at great expense over 20 years later, when there was concern that the oil on board may cause damage to the marine environment and fisheries. This case was complicated by the fact that marine pollution law was in a stage of development during the period that elapsed between the sinking and raising of the vessel.
154 *Navigable Waters Protection Act*, above note 147, ss.18(1)(b) and 18(2); *Canada (AG) v. Brister*, [1943] 3 D.L.R. 50; *R. v. Sauvageau*, [1950] S.C.R. 664; *Anderson v. R.* (1919), 59 S.C.R. 379.
155 This was possible in the United States until 1986 when the U.S. *Wreck Removal Act*, 33 U.S.C. §§409, 411, 412, 414, 415 was amended. See Schoenbaum, above note 47 at 733–34; and J. Scowcroft, "Wreck Removal: An Overview and Recent Developments" (1985) 16 J. Mar. L. & Com. 311. The U.K. law on this also appears to have been clarified: see C. Hill, *Maritime Law*, 4th ed. (London: Lloyd's Press, 1995) at 540–43. There is no such loophole under Canadian law: *Navigable Waters Protection Act*, above note 147, s.16.
156 *Navigable Waters Protection Act, ibid.*, s.19(2).
157 *Ibid.*, s.17.
158 Canadian statutory law seems to be silent on this aspect.

b) International Rules

At this stage there is no international convention that specifically addresses wreck removal. Nevertheless, the subject has been introduced at and is under study by the International Maritime Organisation. As a result, the IMO Legal Committee is presently discussing a draft convention on wreck removal[159] that is to be recommended to an IMO diplomatic conference in late 2003 or early 2004. The latest draft is a scaled down version of an earlier draft without the complex and controversial provisions on financial liability and reporting requirements. A recent IMO report indicates that there appears to be some consensus on matters such as definition of wreck, reporting and location of wrecks, rights and obligations to remove hazardous wrecks, financial liability for locating, marking and removing wrecks, and contributions from cargo interests.[160] The draft convention is designed to create an international regime, under IMO auspices, that would govern wreck removal for wrecks outside territorial seas globally. However, a number of difficulties still has to be overcome, among them the following:

- ensuring that the convention complements relevant provisions of UNCLOS[161] and the *International Convention Relating to Intervention on the High Seas in Cases of Oil Pollution Casualties, 1969, (Intervention)*;[162] and
- ensuring that the reporting and locating of wrecks is consistent with the provisions of the *SOLAS 1974*,[163] *MARPOL 73/78*,[164] and *OPRC 1990*[165] conventions.

---

159 IMO Doc. LEG 80/INF.2 of 10 September 1999.
160 IMO Doc. LEG 81/6 of 25 February 2000.
161 Above note 118, arts.56(2), 78(2), 194(4), and 225.
162 29 November 1969, 970 U.N.T.S. 211, art.V (entered into force 6 May 1975; not yet accepted by Canada). See also *Ratification of Maritime Conventions*, above note 7 vol. II.7.70; see also Chapter 17, "Marine Pollution Prevention."
163 *International Convention for the Safety of Life at Sea, 1974*, 1184 U.N.T.S. 2 [*SOLAS 1974*] (entered into force on 25 May 1980; in force in Canada on same day). See also *Ratification of Maritime Conventions*, above note 7 vol.I.3.20. See also B in Chapter 5, "The Safety Management of Ships."
164 *International Convention for the Prevention of Pollution from Ships, 1973*, 2 November 1973, 1340 U.N.T.S. 184 as am. by *Protocol of 1978 Relating to the International Convention for the Prevention of Pollution from Ships of 1973*, 17 February 1978, 1340 U.N.T.S. 61 [*MARPOL 73/78*] (entered into force on 2 October 1983; in force in Canada on 16 February 1993). See also *Ratification of Maritime Conventions*, above note 7 vol.I.7.160 and I.7.170. See also Chapter 17, "Marine Pollution Prevention."
165 *International Convention on Oil Pollution Preparedness, Response and Co-operation, 1990*, 30 November 1990, 30 I.L.M. 733 [*OPRC 1990*] (entered into force on 13

In addition a satisfactory regime under which shipowners are required to provide a comprehensive report to coastal states about any vessels that have been wrecked will have to be developed. Finally, mechanisms designed to ensure that shipowners would be required to demonstrate financial security for wrecks that threaten navigation and/or coastlines of states will also have to be developed.

FURTHER READINGS

BESSEMER-CLARK, A.F., "The Role of Lloyd's Open Form" (1980) 3 L.M.C.L.Q. 297.

BRICE, G., *Maritime Law of Salvage*, 3d ed. (London: Sweet & Maxwell, 1997).

CHIRCOP, A., "Ships in Distress, Environmental Threats to Coastal States and Places of Refuge: New Directions for an *Ancien Regime*" (2002) 33 Ocean Devel. & Int'l L. 207.

DE LA RUE, C. & C.B. ANDERSON, *Shipping and the Environment* (London: Lloyd's Press, 1998) c.14.

FERNANDES, R.M., *Shipping and Admiralty Law* (Toronto: Carswell, 1995) c.4.

GOLD, E., "Marine Salvage Law: Towards a New Regime" (1989) 20 J. Mar. L. & Com. 487.

———, "Marine Salvage Law, Supertankers and Oil Pollution: New Pressures on Ancient Law" (1981) 11 R.D.U.S. 127.

HANCOX, D., *Reed's Commercial Salvage Practice* (Sunderland: Reed's Publications, 1987).

HEALY, N.J. & D.J. Sharpe, *Cases and Materials on Admiralty Law*, 3d ed. (St. Paul, MN: West Publishing, 1999) c.9.

MCINNES, M., "Life Rescue in Maritime Law" (1994) 25 J. Mar. L. & Com. 451.

SCHOENBAUM, T.J., *Admiralty and Maritime Law*, 3d ed. (St. Paul, MN: West Publishing, 2001) c.6.

May 1995; in force in Canada on the same day). See also *Ratification of Maritime Conventions*, above note 7 vol.I.7.230. See also Chapter 17, "Marine Pollution Prevention."

SCOWCROFT, J., "Wreck Removal: An Overview and Recent Developments" (1985) 16 J. Mar. L. & Com. 311.

STEEL, D.W., F.D. ROSE, & R. SHAW, *Kennedy and Rose on the Law of Salvage*, 6th ed. (London: Sweet & Maxwell, 2002).

STRATI, A., *The Protection of Underwater Cultural Heritage* (Amsterdam: Nijhoff, 1995).

VINCENZINI, E., *International Salvage Law* (London: Lloyd's Press, 1992).

YORMAK, S.R., "Canadian Treasure: Law and Lore" (1999) 30 J. Mar. L. & Com. 229.

CHAPTER 16

GENERAL AVERAGE

A. INTRODUCTION: *YORK-ANTWERP RULES*

General average is a maritime principle about sharing loss among the parties interested in the voyage on which the loss was incurred. It is an ancient regime, adopted by the common law and recognized in the federal *Marine Insurance Act*[1] and the *Marine Liability Act*,[2] but not statutorily regulated. Typically nowadays general average is governed by the *York-Antwerp Rules* through their incorporation into the contract of carriage, whether evidenced by a charterparty or by a bill of lading. The concept of general average is generally said to have originated in the Rhodian law several centuries BC because that source is explicitly referred to in the Digest of Roman Law of the Emperor Justinian in the sixth century AD. Subsequently general average was recorded in a number of European laws and codifications, and eventually entered English common law as well.[3] Its antiquity is the cause of initial difficulty over the maritime usage of the word "average." The English expression

---

[1] S.C. 1993, c.22.
[2] S.C. 2001, c.6, Part 5.
[3] On the history of general average, see N.G. Hudson, *The York-Antwerp Rules*, 2d ed. (London: Lloyd's Press, 1996) at 1–4; J. Wilson & J. Cooke, *Lowndes and Rudolph: The Law of General Average and the York-Antwerp Rules*, 12th ed. (London: Sweet & Maxwell, 1997) at 1–11 [*Lowndes and Rudolph*]; and K. Selmer, *The Survival of General Average* (Oslo University Press, 1958) at 19–57.

apparently was derived from the French word *avarie*, which signifies damage or loss. Thus "general average" is, simply, a common loss. It is distinguished from "particular average," which is the ordinary case of individual loss.

The purpose of the legal principle of general average is to compensate a party for loss deliberately incurred to save the voyage. Compensation is made by levying a proportionate contribution on all the parties to the voyage. A commonly referred to statement of the principle of general average at common law[4] is to be found in the old English case of *Birkley v. Presgrave*: "All loss which arises in consequence of extraordinary sacrifices made or expenses incurred for the preservation of the ship and cargo comes within general average, and must be borne proportionately by all who are interested."[5] This principle has been carried into the *Marine Insurance Act*[6] in section 65:

> A general average loss is a loss caused by or directly consequential on a general average act ... . A general average act is an extraordinary sacrifice or expenditure ... that is voluntarily and reasonably incurred in time of peril for the purpose of preserving the property from peril in an adventure. Subject to the conditions imposed by maritime law, a person who incurs a general average loss is entitled to receive from the other interested persons a rateable contribution ... in respect of the loss.

However, the *Marine Insurance Act* does not attempt to regulate the application of general average and the *Marine Liability Act*,[7] by adopting the *Hague-Visby Rules* and the *Hamburg Rules* alternatively as part of Canadian law;[8] it merely acknowledges the inclusion of provisions regarding general average in contracts of carriage.[9] Consequently the operation of general average is governed by common law and, most frequently, the *York-Antwerp Rules*. The latest version of the *York-Antwerp*

---

4   See *Grover v. Bullock* (1849), 5 U.C.Q.B. 297 at 300; *Gurney v. MacKay* (1875), 37 U.C.Q.B. 324 at 339–40; *Dancey v. Burns* (1880), 31 U.C.C.P. 313 at 315; *Montreal Trust Co. v. Canadian Surety Co.* (1937), 35 C.S. 278 at 280; *Federal Commerce and Navigation Co. v. Eisenerz-G.m.b.H. (The Oak Hill)*, [1974] S.C.R. 1225 [*The Oak Hill*].
5   (1801), 1 East. 220 at 228, 102 E.R. 86 at 89. The classic formulation of the definition of general average by American courts was provided by the U.S. Supreme Court in *Star of Hope (The)*, 76 U.S. 203 at 228 (1869).
6   Above note 1.
7   Above note 2.
8   *Ibid.*, ss.43, 45, and 131(2).
9   *Ibid.*, Sch.3, art.IV, para.2 and Sch.4, art.24.

Rules was adopted by the Comité Maritime International in 1994.[10] The rules have a substantial history of their own going back through seven revisions to 1864.[11] The important point about this history is that the rules have been achieved by international agreement among the maritime commercial community. Thus, they do not have the force of law but rely for their application on voluntary acceptance and incorporation into individual contracts of carriage and insurance. In this, they have been extraordinarily successful.[12]

A less fortunate aspect of the voluntary character of the *York-Antwerp Rules* is that the printed standard forms of contracts in the shipping industry are not always up to date and may refer to earlier versions of the rules, which are not repealed, as prior legislation may be, by the revised set of 1994. Consequently, it is quite possible for current contracts to call for the adjustment of general average according to the 1974 rules or their amended version in 1990. The explanation of general average that follows is based on the *York-Antwerp Rules 1994* but also includes discussion of their differences from the 1974 rules.

The actual operation of the rules is also constrained by the opening Rule of Interpretation. The *York-Antwerp Rules* consist of seven lettered rules, A–G, containing general principles, and twenty-two numbered rules, I–XXII, dealing with particular situations. The Rule of Interpretation states: "In the adjustment of general average the following Rules shall apply to the exclusion of any Law and Practice inconsistent therewith. Except as provided by the Rule Paramount and the numbered Rules, general average shall be adjusted according to the lettered Rules." At first sight the first paragraph of this rule appears contradictory. It suggests that these voluntary rules can overreach national law. Their intention, certainly, is to provide international unification in the application of general average. To that end, the Rule of Interpretation ordains their application wherever local law permits such arrangements, as much of the private law of contracts does. An example is the clause in the *Hague-Visby Rules* that permits the inclusion "of any lawful provi-

---

10 See proceedings of the 35th Conference of the CMI at Sydney, Australia, October 1994. See York-Antwerp Rules 1994 in "Documents of the Conference" in *International Maritime Committee Yearbook 1992–1994*, Part II (Belgium: CMI, 1994) at 146. See also G(2)(a) in Chapter 2.
11 See Hudson, above note 3 at 7–13; *Lowndes and Rudolph*, above note 3 at 41–61; and L.J. Buglass, *Marine Insurance and General Average in the United States*, 2d ed. (Centerville, MD: Cornell Maritime Press, 1981) 180–85.
12 "It may safely be said that general average is the field of maritime law where the international unification effort has succeeded to the greatest degree": Selmer, above note 3 at 58.

sion regarding general average."[13] However, rules incorporated by contract can never overreach mandatory law.[14] Therefore, the *York-Antwerp Rules* cannot derogate from the binding standards of the *Hague-Visby Rules* on carriage by sea, in particular the duties of the shipowner regarding the seaworthiness of the ship and the care of the cargo.[15] The legal status of the *York-Antwerp Rules* having been established by the first paragraph of the Rule of Interpretation, the second directs the order of priority in applying them. Specifically the numbered rules take precedence over the lettered ones. Therefore, a claim in general average will only be adjusted by the general principles in the lettered rules if it is not a particular instance dealt with by a numbered rule. So, for example, a shipowner may recover under rule X certain expenses made to complete the voyage, even though they were not incurred in the face of peril, as required to qualify them as a general average expenditure under rule A. This approach to the interpretation of the *York-Antwerp Rules* seems to be widely understood and respected in the shipping industry, even in the face of the outstanding difference of opinion between the Federal Courts in the United States.[16] In other respects the interpretation of the rules in U.S. courts is generally consistent with their application in the United Kingdom and Canada.[17]

B. FOUR REQUIREMENTS OF GENERAL AVERAGE

Claims in general average must satisfy four distinguishing requirements. These requirements were foreshadowed in the common law case of *Birkley v. Presgrave* and are spelled out by the definition of general average in the *Marine Insurance Act* (both quoted previously). They are also expressed in rule A of the *York-Antwerp Rules*, which states:

---

13 Above note 9, Sch.3, art.V.
14 See *Atlantic Consolidated Foods Ltd. v. Doroty (The)*, [1979] 1 F.C. 283, aff'd [1981] 1 F.C. 783.
15 See above note 2, at Sch.3 arts.III, IV and the discussion of them in Chapter 9, "Carriage of Goods under Bills of Lading and Similar Documents." See also *The Oak Hill*, above note 4 at 1235–36.
16 Cf. *Orient Mid-East Lines v. Shipment of Rice on Board S.S. Orient Transporter*, 496 F.2d 1032 (5th Cir. 1974); and *Eagle Terminal Tankers v. Insurance Co. of U.S.S.R. (The Eagle Courier)*, 637 F.2d 890 (2d Cir. 1981) [*The Eagle Courier*], which supports the view expressed in the text.
17 Except concerning the need for the New Jason Clause as discussed below at note 79.

"There is a general average act, when, and only when, any extraordinary sacrifice or expenditure is intentionally and reasonably made or incurred for the common safety for the purpose of preserving from peril the property involved in a common maritime adventure." That is to say, the loss must result from an extraordinary sacrifice or expenditure, which was intentionally and reasonably made, in a time of peril, for the common safety of the voyage. Each of these important requirements will now be taken up individually. If a claim satisfies all these requirements, the loss, as both the Act and the rules ordain,[18] will be made up by rateable contributions from all the parties to the voyage. The issues of valuation and average adjustment that are raised in assessing compensatory contributions will be discussed subsequently. General average adjustment is an extraordinarily technical matter. Most instances are settled with the assistance of professional average adjusters: "There is little modern case law on general average. Most claims do not go into litigation."[19]

1) Extraordinary Loss

"A general average act is [either] an extraordinary sacrifice or expenditure."[20] The loss must be extraordinary in the sense that it is not a usual incident of the voyage. The word "sacrifice" inherently conveys this idea in a way that "expenditure," if unqualified, does not. Property that is sacrificed may consist of the ship, the cargo, or the freight or any combination of them. Sacrifice of each type of property will be treated separately, then expenditures, which are much the more common and complex claims in general average today, are discussed.

a) General Average Sacrifices

i) Of the Cargo
Perhaps the classic example of a general average sacrifice is the jettison of cargo. It does not matter whether the cargo was stowed on or under the deck provided it was being carried "in accordance with the recognised custom of the trade."[21] This requirement is a question of fact in

---

18 *Marine Insurance Act*, above note 1 at s.65(3); and *York-Antwerp Rules*, above note 10, r.A, para.2, respectively.
19 *Northland Navigation Co. v. Patterson Boiler Works*, [1983] 2 F.C. 59 at 64.
20 *Marine Insurance Act*, above note 1 at s.65(2).
21 *York-Antwerp Rules*, above note 10, r.I; see also to the same effect *Cameron v. Domville* (1878), 17 N.B.R. 647. The older decision at common law in *Gibb v. McDonell* (1850), 7 U.C.Q.B. 356, that cargo stowed under deck does not have

each case. Other examples of sacrifices of cargo are damage, including water damage incidental to jettison of other cargo,[22] and loss in extinguishing a fire on board ship.[23] Cargo necessarily used for fuel or damaged in the consequence of handling, discharging, storing, reloading, and stowing at a port of refuge is also admissible as general average.[24]

ii) Of the Ship
Sacrifice of the ship may be of the whole vessel, such as when it is intentionally stranded, or of parts of it or of some of its machinery, equipment, or stores. Nowadays it does not matter whether the ship might have been driven ashore if it had not been voluntarily stranded,[25] provided it was deliberately sacrificed to protect the common interests in the voyage. Therefore, the involuntary stranding of a disabled ship is not a general average act, nor is the voluntary stranding of a disabled ship, if the intention in doing so was to save the lives of those on board rather than protect the ship and cargo.[26] Damage caused to the ship or its machinery in attempting to refloat it after involuntary stranding may be admissible in general average,[27] but damage sustained by cutting away wrecked parts of the ship may not be claimed in general average.[28] Loss incurred by scuttling or beaching a burning ship or through efforts to extinguish the fire on board is recoverable in general average.[29]

The case of *Northland Navigation Co. v. Patterson Boiler Works*[30] well illustrates the kinds of sacrifices for the common benefit of the voyage that are admissible in general average. A tug was engaged to tow a barge laden with a cargo of steel buoys. When the tug encountered difficulties in the face of heavy seas, the barge was cast adrift and it ran aground. Attempts to refloat the barge proved useless, so it was abandoned. However, the cargo was subsequently saved from the barge. In these circumstances the owner of the barge claimed a general average contribution from the cargo owner. First, the court was prepared to treat the casting adrift of the barge as an extraordinary sacrifice for the

---

to contribute in general average for the jettison of cargo lawfully stowed on deck, appears to have been overtaken by modern practice and the rules.
22 *York-Antwerp Rules*, above note 10, r.II.
23 *Ibid.*, r.III.
24 *Ibid.*, r.IX and XII, respectively.
25 *Ibid.*, r.V; cp. *Dancey v. Burns*, above note 4; *Gibb v. McDonell*, above note 21.
26 *Dancey v. Burns, ibid.*
27 *York-Antwerp Rules*, above note 10, r.VII.
28 *Ibid.*, r.IV.
29 *Ibid.*, r.III.
30 Above note 19.

common safety of the tug, the barge, and the cargo. Then the expenses incurred in the futile efforts to rescue the barge and its cargo were admitted in general average. However, the contributors in general average to the expenses were held to be only the barge and the cargo, and not the tug, because there was by that time "no common tripartite peril."[31] Moreover after the barge was abandoned and the intended voyage was terminated, the further expenditures incurred to recover the steel buoys still on board the barge were particular charges for the cargo owner alone.

iii) Of the Freight

At common law, freight is earned on delivery of the cargo at destination.[32] Freight not earned as a result of ship or cargo being sacrificed is a general average loss to the shipowner. Rule XV expressly recognizes such loss. The amount to be made good is the net loss of freight. As rule XV points out, the shipowner must deduct from the gross freight lost the costs that would have been incurred to earn that freight. Where the contract of carriage calls for prepayment of freight on shipment or states that freight is due, "ship and cargo lost or not lost," the carrier is entitled to full freight, even if not earned;[33] therefore, no general average loss is incurred.[34]

b) General Average Expenditures

Expenses made on behalf of the common interests in the voyage are, in many cases, admissible in general average. The cost of salvaging ship and cargo or expenditure incidental to repairing the ship in a port of refuge are common examples. Expenses made in anticipation of greater general average expenditure — known as "substituted expenses" — and costs incurred to protect the environment may also be recovered in general average.

i) Salvage Costs

The expense of rescuing a ship from disaster so it may complete its intended voyage is a clear example of general average expenditure. At

---

31 *Ibid.* at 66.
32 *Kirchner v. Venus* (1859), 12 Moo. P.C.C. 361 at 390, 14 E.R. 948 at 959; *Gurney v. MacKay*, above note 4 at 343; *Halcrow v. Lemesurier* (1884), 10 Q.L.R. 239, 21 R.L.O.S. 28 (Q.B.); see also *C.P. Ships v. Les Industries Lyon Corduroys*, [1983] 1 F.C. 736.
33 See B(6) in Chapter 8, "Carriage of Goods by Charterparty."
34 In such cases the freight risk falls on the cargo owner and so is treated in general average as part of the cargo value. See Hudson, above note 3 at 214.

common law it was long ago held that the cost of hauling free an accidentally stranded ship may be claimed in general average.[35] The *York-Antwerp Rules* indicate also that the cost of lightening a ship that has gone ashore, by removal of its fuel, stores or cargo, as well as any damage done in the process is admissible in general average.[36] More generally, rule VI admits expenses "in the nature of salvage, whether under contract or otherwise,"[37] as general average expenditures provided they are made for the common voyage. The rule was introduced in 1974 to deal with a difference in practice between the United Kingdom, and the United States and Europe over the inclusion of salvage payments in general average. Since the case of *The Raisby*,[38] English practice was to exclude the cost of salvage services rendered by volunteers, as opposed to those incurred contractually. The effect of rule VI has been to bring English practice into line with existing U.S. practice, which has long held that amounts paid for salvage, however obtained, are admissible in general average.[39]

ii) *Temporary Repair and Other Port of Refuge Costs*
A ship that is forced to seek a port of refuge in the course of its voyage may also claim some of the expenses it incurs there in general average. The cost of necessary permanent repairs to the ship are not admissible in general average because they are an incidental part of the shipowner's responsibility to prosecute the voyage, unless the damage was sustained by a general average sacrifice. However, temporary repairs are a general average expenditure under rule X(a), when made for the safe completion of the voyage or to enable the ship to reach a port where proper repairs can be effected,[40] because, in principle, they do not add value to the ship. But the extent of inclusion in general average of temporary repairs of accidental, as opposed to sacrificial, damage may be limited by reference to the savings in expenses that otherwise would have had to be incurred.[41] Other expenses associated with going into a

---

35 *Grover v. Bullock*, above note 4.
36 *York-Antwerp Rules*, above note 10, r.VIII.
37 As to the requirements for salvage claims, see Chapter 15, "Maritime Salvage and Wreck."
38 (1885), 10 P.D. 114.
39 See *Amerada Hess Corp. v. Mobil Apex (The)*, 1979 A.M.C. 2406 (2d Cir. 1979).
40 *York-Antwerp Rules*, above note 10, r.XIV and X(a).
41 See *ibid.*, r.XIV; *Marida Ltd. v. Oswal Steel (The Bijela)*, [1994] 2 Lloyd's L.R. 1 (H.L.); see the comment on this case by N. Gaskell, "Temporary Repairs in General Average — A Solution" [1994] L.M.C.L.Q. 342; and the discussion below in B(1)(b)(iv).

port of refuge and making repairs are admissible in general average when incurred for the common interests of the voyage. The *York–Antwerp Rules* allow charges for entering or leaving the port and the cost of handling, moving, and storing any of the cargo, fuel, or stores.[42] They also include the extra wages and maintenance costs of the ship's crew,[43] fuel, and stores consumed, and port charges[44] incurred consequent on the prolongation of the voyage or the detention of the ship in port as a result of an accident or a sacrifice *en route*.[45] Moreover, these kinds of allowable expense in port need not always have been incurred in seeking refuge from a peril at sea. This is an area in which the numbered rules override the principles of the lettered rules and introduce an element of what some commentators refer to as "artificial general average," discussed later.

iii) Environmental Costs

The first environmental cost in the *York-Antwerp Rules* is found in rule VI regarding salvage. The 1974 rule on salvage was amended in 1990 to reflect the *International Convention on Salvage, 1989*, which introduced into salvage operations a duty of care to prevent or minimize damage to the environment.[46] In return for this new obligation, salvors acquired the right to receive compensation for their skill and efforts in minimizing environmental damage. Such efforts are now taken into account in fixing the size of the award for the salvage operation.[47] When the salvage operation is unsuccessful, however, the salvor, on the ancient principle of no-cure–no-pay, ordinarily receives nothing.[48] In these circumstances, the *1989 Salvage Convention* provides for "special compensation" for the salvor's efforts to protect the environment to cover the expenses involved, plus a proportionate increase, to a maximum of 100 per cent, according to the degree of success of the measures undertaken.[49] The 1990 amendments to the *York-Antwerp Rules* on

---

42 *York-Antwerp Rules*, above note 10, r.X.
43 Contrary to the old English common law rule that crew's wages are, like necessary repairs, a cost to the shipowner of completing the contracted voyage and earning the freight: see *Atwood v. Sellar & Co.* (1880), 5 Q.B.D. 286.
44 Added in the 1994 version of the rules.
45 *York-Antwerp Rules*, above note 10, r.XI.
46 28 April 1989, U.K.T.S. 1996 No. 93, art.8(1); *Canada Shipping Act*, R.S.C. 1985, c.S-9, s.449.1, Sch.V; *Canada Shipping Act, 2001*, S.C. 2001 c.26, s.142(1) and Sch.3.
47 *International Convention on Salvage*, ibid., art.13.
48 Ibid., art.14. (See also Chapter 15.)
49 For a full discussion of the convention, see Chapter 15, "Maritime Salvage and Wreck."

general average[50] adopted the distinction drawn in the *1989 Salvage Convention*. Salvage awards, including remuneration for prevention of damage to the environment, are admissible as general average expenditures provided the successful salvage operation was undertaken for the common interests in the voyage. However, when the salvage operation is unsuccessful and no common benefit is received, the salvor's special compensation is not admissible in general average.

The other set of circumstances in which, by way of exception to rule C, expenditures on environmental protection are admitted in general average is found in the new rule XI(d). It specifies that "the costs of measures undertaken" to protect the environment will be allowed in general average when they are incurred in three kinds of situation:

- for the common safety in such circumstances that, had a stranger to the voyage performed them, a salvage reward would have been earned;
- as a condition for the ship to enter, remain or depart from a port of refuge for the common safety of the voyage; and
- in connection with the discharging, storing or reloading of the cargo whenever those operations are themselves admitted in general average.

These are very limited exceptions to rule C. They only extend to the costs of preventive measures and therefore do not cover liabilities for pollution damage, compensation paid to third parties, clean up expenses, fines, and other legal penalties, or any other incidents concerning damage to the environment.

iv) Substituted Expenses
In addition to costs that qualify in general average, other non-qualifying expenses are regularly admitted when they are incurred in place of general average expenditure. These "substituted expenses" are regulated by rule F of the *York-Antwerp Rules*, which states: "Any additional expenses incurred in place of another expense which would have been allowed in general average shall be deemed to be general average and so allowed without regard to the saving, if any, to other interests, but only up to the amount of the general average expense avoided." Some examples of substituted expenses that would fall within this rule are towage of the ship from a port of refuge to its destination, transshipment and forwarding of the cargo from a port of refuge to destination, drydocking of the ship in the port of refuge with cargo on board, and additional repair costs in order to save time. The additional expense

---

50 Maintained without change in the 1994 rules.

may only be substituted for general average expenditures that are thereby avoided. They may not be accounted against ordinary ship's costs of the voyage. Therefore, towing the disabled ship to destination or forwarding the cargo there separately are ordinarily the price the shipowner must pay for earning the freight;[51] but when such measures replace the need to make general average expenditures, their cost may fairly be set off against the expenses that would otherwise have been made. Even so, as rule F states, these substituted expenses are allowed only up to the amount of general average expenditure thereby saved. Further, only expenses and not losses may be substituted. Rule F also states that no account will be taken of any saving that might be occasioned to other interests, such as a reduction in the shipowner's cost of repairs.

Chaffey v. Schooley[52] was an early common law case in which the argument was made for substituting the expense of towing a disabled ship from a port of refuge to destination. As the law then stood, the court felt constrained to reject the argument. As the tug was not required to tow the ship and cargo to safety but simply to complete the voyage, the shipowner was not entitled to substitute the cost of the tug for the charges that would have been incurred if, staying in the port to repair, the cargo had been unloaded and reloaded. However, the court thought it reasonable that such substituted charges should be allowed, as rule F now would permit.

The cost of drydocking a vessel for repairs in a port of refuge is another example of an expense that ordinarily falls on the shipowner in completing the voyage. Usually drydocking is only undertaken once the cargo has been removed from the ship; but, if the cargo is not unloaded and additional expense in stabilizing the ship in the drydock is incurred, these costs may be substituted for the general average expenditures for handling the cargo that is saved.

While the cost of repairs in the port of refuge is for the ship's account as an incident of the voyage,[53] additional expenses that save time and thereby reduce delay in the port may be substituted for the general average expenditures that would otherwise have to be incurred by the prolongation of the voyage. The decision of the Supreme Court of Canada in *Western Canada Steamship Co. v. Canadian Commercial Corp.*[54] illustrated this principle in the early days of air transport. When

---

51 *York-Antwerp Rules*, above note 10, r.VI(a), paras.2 and (b).
52 (1876), 40 U.C.Q.B. 165 (C.A.).
53 The cost of temporary repairs would be a substituted expense under r.F except that it is specifically regulated by r.XIV, discussed above at note 41.
54 [1960] S.C.R. 632.

The Lake Chilco's tail shaft broke at sea, an aircraft was specially chartered to carry an 8-ton–replacement shaft from Wales to Singapore, the port of refuge. The shipowner claimed the extra expense of chartering the airplane over the cost of sending the replacement shaft by sea under rule F. The Court granted the claim in substitution for the expenses that would have been involved if the ship had been required to remain at Singapore while a shaft was being sent by sea. Whether this particular decision in 1960 is still good law may be questioned. Probably nowadays air transport by scheduled, if not chartered, flights will be regarded as the ordinary means of transporting spare and replacement parts for a ship. As a result, the cost will likely be treated as an ordinary incident of repairs for the ship's account.

When a decision is made in a port of refuge to take the cargo out of the ship and forward it to its destination by other means of transport, an additional complexity must be faced. Once the cargo has been transshipped, the commonality of interest in the voyage is ended and therefore the shipowner is no longer entitled to any expenses in general average that are subsequently incurred, such as allowances for the wages and maintenance of the crew in the port of refuge while the ship is being repaired. To avoid this consequence, shipowners, before releasing the cargo, usually demand of the cargo owners a general average bond that includes a non-separation agreement: Such an agreement calls for general average to be adjusted by ignoring the effects of separation and forwarding of the cargo, and by treating the parties as nearly as possible in the same positions they would have occupied had the voyage been continued to completion.[55] The use of non-separation agreements became so common that their essence has now been captured in the 1994 *York-Antwerp Rules* by the addition of new paragraphs three and four to rule G. However, the application of these parts of rule G may raise a problem where the cargo owners, or one of them, demands delivery of the cargo at the port of refuge. There is clear authority in Canada for a cargo owner, who has paid the freight for the whole voyage, to request off-loading at any intermediate port where the ship docks and facilities are available. In *Ellerman Lines v. Gibbs, Nathaniel (Canada)*,[56] the cargo in question was being carried aboard The City of Colombo from India to Toronto, Canada. When the ship docked in Montreal, general average was declared and an offer was made to forward the cargo to Toronto by other means provided a non-separation agreement was accepted. The cargo owner refused and

---

55 Or until the commercial object of the voyage was frustrated.
56 [1986] 2 F.C. 463 (C.A.).

instead demanded delivery of the cargo at Montreal. The court affirmed the cargo owner's right to immediate delivery with the legal consequences that the common voyage was brought to an end and no further expenditures were admissible in general average.

This decision was rendered under the 1974 *York-Antwerp Rules*, which were incorporated in the contract of carriage. Now that the 1994 version of rule G includes a non-separation agreement, a question may arise whether the cargo owner should be able to maintain, or should be treated as having given up, the right to demand delivery on full payment of freight at an intermediate port where general average has been declared when the 1994 rules are agreed in the contract of carriage as the basis of adjustment. The answer may be that cargo owners, who implicitly agree to non-separation clauses in a carriage contract that invokes the 1994 rules, contractually accept that they may demand delivery at an intermediate port at their own expense but are still bound to contribute in general average for subsequent expenditures.[57] A contrary interpretation might be that, when cargo owners exercise their common law right to take delivery, the contract of carriage is terminated, together with the non-separation clauses of the 1994 rules incorporated in it.

Finally, in addition to characterizing a loss as extraordinary in this technical sense, it must also be shown to have been caused by a general average act. Whether the act in question was a sacrifice or an expenditure, it must also meet the test of causation expressed in rule C: "Only such losses, damages or expenses which are the direct consequence of the general average act shall be allowed in general average." This rule imposes the necessary principle that the claimed sacrifice or expenditure must have been caused by the general average act. In so doing, it also raises the problems well known to law of defining a sufficient causal connection or, conversely put, of determining when the chain of cause and effect is broken. Rule C refers to "direct consequences" thereby impliedly excluding indirect consequences of the general average act. This phraseology reflects the use of language about causation prior to the case of *The Wagon Mound*.[58] Since that case scorned this usage, the common law has spoken of reasonably foreseeable consequences of an act, although not necessarily with any greater clarity of meaning. In this uncertainty, rule C provides some help by stating in paragraph 3 a number of possible consequences that specifi-

---

57 There is a hint of this approach in the final remarks of Stone J. in *ibid.* at 482.
58 *Overseas Tankship Ltd. v. Morts Dock & Engineering Co.*, [1961] A.C. 388 [*The Wagon Mound*].

cally will not be treated as sufficiently direct. As reworded in 1994, it reads: "Demurrage, loss of market, and any loss or damage sustained or expense incurred by reason of delay, whether on the voyage or subsequently, and any indirect loss whatsoever, shall not be admitted as general average." This statement still leaves to be determined what events might constitute "indirect loss" in modern legal usage. Surprisingly perhaps, little guidance can be found in recent cases on general average. The clearest attempt at providing directions was made by Lord Denning in *Australian Coastal Shipping Commission v. Green*[59] in 1971:

> "Direct consequences" denote those consequences which flow in an unbroken sequence from the act: whereas "indirect consequences" are those in which the sequence is broken by an intervening or extraneous cause. I realise that this is not very helpful: because the metaphor "breaking the chain" of causation means one thing to one man and another thing to another but still we have to do the best we can with it.[60]

However, Lord Denning proceeded to add a helpful interpretation in modern legal phraseology when he gave his opinion:

> If the master, when he does the "general average act," ought reasonably to have foreseen that a subsequent accident of the kind might occur — or even that there was a distinct possibility of it — then the subsequent accident does not break the chain of causation. The loss or damage is the direct consequence of the original general average act.[61]

Lord Denning's views subsequently found favour in the Supreme Court of Canada in *The Oak Hill*.[62] In this case, the ship carried a cargo that included two different qualities of pig iron that had to be kept separate. As a result of stranding in the St. Lawrence River, The Oak Hill had to be repaired at Lévis, Quebec. In the course of unloading the cargo in order to make the repairs, the pig iron became irreparably mixed and effectively destroyed. The shipowner argued the loss should be admitted as general average, pursuant to rule XII, which states in part: "Damage to ... cargo ... caused in the act of discharging shall be made good as general average when and only when the cost of those measures ... is admitted in general average." The Supreme Court accepted that the unloading of the pig iron was a general average act and therefore that the cost of doing so was a general average expenditure. Nevertheless,

---

59 [1971] 1 Q.B. 456 (C.A.).
60 *Ibid.* at 461.
61 *Ibid.* at 462.
62 *The Oak Hill*, above note 4.

the Court held that the cargo damage caused in the unloading operation could not be treated as general average because it was not a direct consequence of the general average act, as required by rule C, on account of the negligence of the master in the conduct of the unloading. Having quoted from Lord Denning's judgment in *Australian Coastal Shipping Commission v. Green*,[63] Ritchie J., writing for the Court, stated:

> It appears to me that even if Lord Denning's views be accepted, it does not mean that a master is to be relieved of responsibility for his own negligence by contending that it was "reasonably foreseeable". In my view, if it be shown that loss or damage to cargo has been caused through the negligence of the master in carrying out the general average procedure, it can no longer be said that it was a direct consequence of the general average act. The chain of causation is broken by the intervention of a new cause and, in my view, it cannot have been the intention of the committee which adopted the York/Antwerp Rules that a master should be able to claim a general average loss because he was able to foresee the possibility that he would be negligent.[64]

This statement establishes two points with respect to the application of rule C: first, "the direct consequence of the general average act" minimally means, in modern parlance, a "reasonably foreseeable" result; second, as a matter of policy, negligence of the master, acting on behalf of the shipowner, may be an intervening act that breaks the chain of causation, even if it is foreseeable.[65]

2) Intentionally and Reasonably Incurred

To qualify as general average an extraordinary sacrifice or expenditure must be intentionally and reasonably made.[66] If the loss is involuntary, such as a casualty of heavy seas, it is particular average, to which the

---

63 Above note 61.
64 *The Oak Hill*, above note 4 at 1242.
65 This assistance in clarifying the application of r.C may be at the expense of creating other uncertainties. First, the court's approach seems to require a determination about the fault of the master, contrary to the principle of r.D, discussed subsequently. Second, laudable as the judicial policy may be to hold the ship responsible for negligent care of the cargo, when the carriage is covered by a bill of lading subject to the *Hague-Visby Rules*, the shipowner may be exempt from liability for the errors of the master. See the discussion of the *Hague-Visby Rules*, art.IV(2) in D(6) of Chapter 9, "Carriage of Goods under Bills of Lading and Similar Documents."
66 *Marine Insurance Act*, above note 6; *York-Antwerp Rules* 1994 r.A, quoted above at B, "Four Requirements of General Average."

ordinary rules of legal liability apply. Only when the loss is voluntarily incurred may it amount to general average. Rule III of the *York-Antwerp Rules* illustrates this point: "Damage done to a ship and cargo ... by water ... in extinguishing a fire on board ... shall be made good in general average" because the loss sustained is the result of an intentional act of protection from peril. But the damage done by the fire itself, having arisen by accident, is not admissible in general average. In addition to the requirement of intention, the act claimed in general average must also have been reasonably made. As rule A states, there is a general average act "when, and only when, any extraordinary sacrifice or expenditure is intentionally and reasonably made." In addition, immediately before rule A, a Rule Paramount directs: "In no case shall there be any allowance for sacrifice or expenditure unless reasonably made or incurred." On first reading, this reasonable principle seems innocuous and, indeed, even redundant in light of rule A. However, the Rule Paramount was introduced in the 1994 rules in response to the case of *The Alpha*[67] in which a numbered rule, that was not expressly qualified by a requirement of reasonableness, was, as the Rule of Interpretation requires, given precedence over rule A.

The actual effect of introducing a test of reasonableness of every general average act is uncertain. The decision in *The Alpha* would certainly be reversed by the Rule Paramount. That case was an instance under rule VII of damage caused to the engines while trying to refloat the ship, which was stranded in a perilous position. The facts precisely satisfied the conditions of rule VII for admitting the injury to the ship's engines in general average except for the additional element that the negligence of the master contributed substantially to the damage sustained. That fact was treated as irrelevant by the court but now, under the Rule Paramount, the unreasonableness of the master's conduct in attempting to refloat the ship would inhibit any allowance in general average for the resulting damage. This example is clear enough, yet the same result might be achieved in Canadian law, even in the absence of the Rule Paramount, in light of the approach taken in *The Oak Hill*.[68] In that case the Supreme Court refused to admit damage sustained by cargo in discharging as general average under rule XII, because it was shown to have been caused through the negligence of the master and was therefore held not to be the direct consequence of the general average act, as required by rule C. Thus, the Court applied

---

67 *Corfu Navigation Co. v. Mobil Shipping Co. (The Alpha)*, [1991] 2 Lloyd's L.R. 515 (Q.B.) [*The Alpha*].
68 Above note 4. This case was distinguished in *The Alpha*, ibid.

a test of reasonableness of the act causing the sacrifice or expenditure comparable to the Rule Paramount.

The *Marine Insurance Act*, section 65(2)[69] also requires that the general average act be "voluntarily and reasonably incurred." From this mandatory legislative definition it may be argued, though in no case does it seem to have been, that all instances of general average sacrifice and expenditure described in the numbered as well as the lettered *York-Antwerp Rules* are, on incorporation in the carriage contract, subject to this requirement of reasonableness. The Rule Paramount may also have been foreshadowed in the practices of average adjusters. There is evidence suggesting that the reasonableness of an act or expense is taken into account and therefore the Rule Paramount does not make much difference to the practice of adjustment.[70]

While the sacrifice or expenditure may have been made intentionally and reasonably and, so, qualify as a general average act, if the loss was caused by the fault of one of the parties to the voyage, that party loses all rights in general average; for example, a shipowner will not receive contributions in general average for expenses reasonably made to save the ship and cargo when they are necessitated by the unseaworthy condition of the vessel,[71] or, where the carriage contract is subject to the *Hague-Visby Rules*, the failure of the owner to exercise due diligence to make the vessel seaworthy,[72] as "the law is ... clear that a carrier is not entitled to recover from a shipper a contribution in general average where the general average situation was brought about by his own actionable fault."[73] Indeed, this legal principle continues to apply beyond the circumstances that gave rise to the general average act also to deny recovery for sacrifices and expenditures made as a consequence of the general average situation but in breach of the shipowner's continuing duty of care for the cargo during the emergency. As Ritchie J. emphasized in *The Oak Hill*:

> It would ... be wrong to assume that ... the *York/Antwerp Rules* are to be treated as a code governing the rights of the parties concerned to

---

69 Above note 6.
70 See Hudson, above note 3 at 75–76, 132–33, and 209–11.
71 *Chaffey v. Schooley*, above note 52; *Montreal Trust Co. v. Canadian Surety Co.*, above note 4; *Western Canada Steamship Co. v. Canadian Commercial Corp.*, above note 54.
72 *Canadian Transport Co. v. Hunt, Leuchers, Hepburn (The City Alberni)*, [1947] 2 D.L.R. 647 (Ex. Ct.).
73 *St. Lawrence Construction v. Federal Commerce and Navigation Co.*, [1985] 1 F.C. 767 at 788 (C.A.).

the exclusion of other rights and obligations created by the Contract of Carriage. In my opinion the effect of [the instant] Charter Party is simply to include the Rules as a part of the contract and although in carrying out the general average act the master is acting in the interest of all concerned, he is representing the owner and in so doing, his overriding duty of care for the cargo is still paramount and loss or damage sustained by the cargo through breach of this duty is not "a general average loss" to which the Rules apply.[74]

However, where there are more than two parties to the voyage in which a general average act is committed as a result of the fault of one of them, the act retains its general average character and the obligation to contribute continues between the other parties.[75]

General average situations sometimes occur as a result of fault or negligence of the shipowner or employees that is excusable in law. Under English and Canadian law the shipowner is fully entitled to participate in the general average settlement. Laskin J. in *The Orient Trader*[76] quoted approvingly from the leading English case of *Louis Dreyfus & Co. v. Tempus Shipping Co.*[77] to the effect that when the act causing the peril is not actionable, the actor is not precluded from obtaining general average contributions. The law is different in the United States. The U.S. Supreme Court held in *The Irrawaddy*[78] that exoneration from liability for fault did not entitle the shipowner to claim in general average. As a result, a practice grew up among shipowners trading to and from the United States of including a contractual clause that expressly restores their rights in general average in the event of excusable fault. It was named the Jason Clause after the case[79] in which the U.S. Supreme Court pronounced it valid. An amended version, known as the New Jason Clause, is in use today. It typically reads:

> In the event of accident, danger, damage or disaster before or after the commencement of the voyage, resulting from any cause whatsoever, whether due to negligence or not, for which, or for the consequences of which, the carrier is not responsible, by statute, contract or other-

---

74 Above note 4 at 1235–36.
75 *Nickimen Co. v. Executive Venture (The)*, [1973] F.C. 1108 at para.3, quoting *Lowndes and Rudolph*, above note 3.
76 *Drew Brown Ltd. v. Orient Trader (The)*, [1974] S.C.R. 1286 at 1333 [*The Orient Trader*]; see also *Oak Hill (The)*, above note 4 at 1246.
77 [1931] A.C. 726. See also *Goulandris Bros Ltd. v. B. Goldman & Sons Ltd.*, [1958] 1 Q.B. 74.
78 171 U.S. 187 (1898).
79 *Jason (The)*, 225 U.S. 32 (1908).

wise, the goods, shippers, consignees or owners of the goods shall contribute with the carrier in general average to the payment of any sacrifices, losses, or expenses of a general average nature that may be made or incurred and shall pay the salvage and special charges incurred in respect of the goods.

The interaction of fault and excuse becomes peculiarly difficult where the ship's wrongdoing amounts to an unreasonable deviation. The case of *The Orient Trader*[80] before the Supreme Court of Canada illustrates the difficulties. A cargo of tin slabs was being carried on *The Orient Trader* to Hamilton, Ontario. While the ship was in port at Toronto, the owners announced it would deviate to Ashtabula, Ohio but before departure an unrelated fire destroyed the vessel and seriously damaged the cargo. The cargo owners claimed against the shipowners, who counterclaimed, as it turned out, successfully in general average. The first important point to note is that the case was decided under U.S. law as the proper law of the contract of carriage. U.S. law contains a *Fire Statute*,[81] which exempts a shipowner from liability for loss or damage to cargo by fire, unless the fire was caused by the owner's default or neglect. Most of the judgments of the Supreme Court of Canada were directed to the issue whether this statutory protection outlived the ship's unreasonable deviation. The minority of two held that the unreasonable deviation was a fundamental breach, which terminated the carriage contract and with it the choice of U.S. law clause, and thus the right to rely on the U.S. *Fire Statute*; their judgment quoted *Lowndes and Rudolph* to the effect that "deviation, unless waived or justifiable, destroys all right to contribution either under the *York-Antwerp Rules* or at common law because the interests were not voluntarily parties to the new adventure constituted by the deviation."[82] The majority of three determined that, under U.S. law, the unreasonable deviation would not deprive the shipowner of the protection of the *Fire Statute* provided there was no causal connection between the deviation and the subsequent fire, as indeed there was not. Hence the cargo owner's claim was unsuccessful.

The shipowner's counterclaim for a general average contribution toward the expenses in fighting the fire still had to be determined, however, and that depended on the continued enforceability of the New Jason Clause included in the contract of carriage. Only Justice

---

80 Above note 76.
81 46 U.S.C. §182.
82 *The Orient Trader*, above note 76 at 1311.

Laskin, who was among the majority, discussed this issue. He recognized that, apart from the New Jason Clause, the unreasonable deviation would have entitled the cargo owner to avoid the carriage contract and, with it, any obligation to contribute in general average. But he went on to show that the New Jason Clause, which expressly provided for general average contributions toward loss for which the carrier was not responsible "by statute, contract or otherwise," survived as a valid arrangement between the parties to the voyage regardless of the deviation. He found comfort for this view in the House of Lords decision in *Hain Steamship Co. v. Tate & Lyle Ltd.*[83] that an unjustified deviation entitles cargo interests to elect either to treat the carriage contract as terminated or to condone the deviation and let the contract continue. The common practice of signing a general average bond is likely also to be regarded as constituting a separate agreement that survives an unjustifiable deviation.

The *York-Antwerp Rules* respect the common law rule regarding fault in a way that allows the process of general average to continue unhindered. Rule D states: "Rights to contribution in general average shall not be affected, though the event which gave rise to the sacrifice or expenditure may have been due to the fault of one of the parties to the adventure, but this shall not prejudice any remedies or defences which may be open against or to that party in respect of such fault." Canadian courts[84] accept the common view that the effect of rule D is, first, to provide for the adjustment of general average without reference to any fault that may have led to the general average act and, second, to preserve the remedies available at law against any party in fault. This expedient rule divides the complex issues of adjusting general average and determining legal liability into a two-step process, which conveniently respects the great difference in laws and professional experience that each stage engages.

3) In Time of Peril

A general average act is a sacrifice or expenditure made for the safety of the voyage in the face of peril. The act must be made "for the purpose of preserving from peril" the property involved in the voyage,[85]

---

83 [1936] 2 All E.R. 597.
84 *The Oak Hill*, above note 4 at 1238; *St. Lawrence Construction v. Federal Commerce and Navigation Co.*, above note 73 at 788.
85 *York-Antwerp Rules* 1994, r.A, above after note 17. See also the *Marine Insurance Act*, above note 1, s.65(2).

and the peril must be a danger common to both ship and cargo.[86] It is traditional at common law that "[i]mminent peril must be impending" over the voyage,[87] but this standard has become somewhat relaxed so that it is sufficient if the peril is real and substantial, even though it may not be immediate.[88] In other words, the peril may be pending rather than impending; even so there can be "no general average if the expenditure [or sacrifice] is made to avert a peril contemplated by the voyage, and thus within the scope of the shipowner's duty."[89]

The *York-Antwerp Rules* take a less stringent approach to the requirement of peril. While rule A demands the general average act be made in a time of peril, two of the numbered rules, which have overriding effect,[90] admit expenditures on certain measures in general average though incurred in the absence of any immediate danger. Rule X(b) and the dependent rule XI(b) allow as general average the expenses of handling and discharging cargo, fuel, and stores in a port of refuge as well as the wages and maintenance costs of the crew during the period of the ship's detention in specified circumstances.[91] As long as these expenses are incurred for the common safety of the ship and cargo in a time of peril, they are entirely within the general principles of general average. Thus a ship that is holed by a collision at sea and limps into a port of refuge still in danger of sinking may claim the cost of moving cargo and other detention expenses made in the course of securing its safety. Similarly, a ship that calls at an intermediate port where it suffers a collision or a fire may claim similar expenses in the course of coping with the common peril. But once the ship has achieved safety in the port of refuge, there is no longer any peril facing ship and cargo, which requires expenditure in common. The costs of necessary repairs to the ship and, along with them, any expenses for caring for the cargo and maintaining the crew during the period of detention, would ordinarily be an incident of the voyage for the shipowner's account. However rules X(b) and XI(b) allow these kinds of expenses during

---

86 *Gurney v. MacKay*, above note 4 at 341; *Western Assurance Co. v. Ontario Coal Co. of Toronto* (1892), 21 S.C.R. 383.
87 *Kidd v. Thomson* (1899), 26 O.A.R. 220 at 222.
88 *Vlassopoulos v. British and Foreign Marine Insurance Co. (The Makis)*, [1929] 1 K.B. 187; *Navigazione Generale Italiana v. Spencer Kellogg & Sons*, 92 F.2d 41 (1937) at 43; *The Eagle Courier*, above note 16 at 896.
89 *Kidd v. Thomson*, above note 87 at 222.
90 Per the rule of interpretation discussed above at note 13.
91 See the discussion below at B(1)(b)(ii), and the judgment of the Federal Court of Appeal in *Ellerman Lines v. Gibb, Nathaniel (Canada)*, above note 56.

detention of the ship in the port of refuge for repairs as general average "if the repairs were necessary for the safe prosecution of the voyage." Since no reference is made to the presence of any common peril, expenses admitted in these circumstances have been called "artificial general average."[92] An alternative view of them is that, even though the ship be made safe in the port of refuge, it would not be fit to proceed further on the voyage unrepaired; if it were to do so, it would immediately face peril at sea.

In other words, under rules X(b) and XI(b), common peril is still a prerequisite to general average expenditure but it need not be imminent or impending; it is sufficient if apprehended or anticipated. This approach to the application of the "safe prosecution clause" in these rules received the approval of the Federal Court of Appeal in *Ellerman Lines v. Gibbs, Nathaniel (Canada)*.[93] There the court held that a general average situation existed when the ship was detained in the intermediate port of Montreal for repair of engine damage discovered while in the port and required "for the safe prosecution of the voyage."[94]

In any event the scope for admission in general average of expenses in these circumstances under rules X(b) and XI(b) is restricted by a proviso that excludes them "where the damage to the ship is discovered at a port ... without accident ... connected with such damage having taken place during the voyage."[95] Thus expenses may not be claimed in general average during repairs "necessary for the safe prosecution of the voyage" when they are necessitated by some incident, even a general average act, that occurs after the ship has reached the port once the common peril of the incident has been abated. For example, if a fire breaks out on a ship while docked in an intermediate port, damage done to the ship and cargo in extinguishing the fire may be made good in general average under rule III, but expenses subsequently incurred during the detention in port as a consequence of having to repair the ship to proceed on the voyage are beyond rule III and are also excluded from rules X(b) and XI(b) by the proviso to them.

---

92 See W. Tetley, *Marine Cargo Claims*, 3d ed. (Cowansville, QB: Yvon Blais, 1988) at 729.
93 Above note 56, quoting extensively from the American case *The Eagle Courier*, above note 16.
94 *Ellerman Lines v. Gibbs, Nathaniel (Canada)*, above note 56 at 477.
95 *York-Antwerp Rules*, above note 10, r.X(b), para.1 & r.XI(b), para.2.

4) For the Common Safety of the Voyage

Loss is general average only when the act causing it is committed for the common, or general, safety of the voyage.[96] The duty to contribute in general average is predicated upon this fundamental idea that loss sustained by one or more parties to the voyage was incurred for the safety and preservation of the property of all. Success in saving and preserving the property common to the voyage is not required.[97] Loss is admissible in general average when it results from "any sacrifice or expenditure intentionally and reasonably incurred for the benefit of all."[98]

It follows from these propositions that loss resulting from sacrifice or expenditure will not be admitted in general average if it was incurred after the common voyage has been terminated. In *Ellerman Lines v. Gibbs, Nathaniel (Canada)*,[99] since the cargo owners took delivery of the cargo in Montreal, short of the contracted destination of Toronto, the court held that the connection between the ship and the cargo was permanently severed, and that any subsequent expenses were incurred for the safety of the ship alone. Similarly when a ship, loaded with coal, became stranded and was abandoned, the cargo owners were not liable to contribute in general average for the expenses incurred in subsequently trying to raise the ship and cargo because they did not face a common peril. The cargo owners were only bound to pay the much lesser cost of salvaging the cargo.[100]

The parties common to the voyage may include several ships and cargoes. One or more tugs towing one or more barges loaded with one or more cargoes is an example. Rule B, added to the *York-Antwerp Rules* in 1994 to cope with divergent practice internationally, acknowledges the unity of such a flotilla. The rules apply to the flotilla as a whole whenever measures are taken to preserve it from a common peril; but, if a vessel achieves safety simply by disconnection, it is no longer regarded as being imperilled on a common voyage with the rest of the interests — unless the disconnection itself was a general average act. This approach is concordant with the common law decided in Canada prior to 1994.[101]

---

96 *Marine Insurance Act*, above note 1, s.65(2); and the *York-Antwerp Rules* 1994, r.A, above B, "Four Requirements of General Average."
97 But contributions will be affected because they are based on the value of the property saved. See below under C(2), "Contributory Values."
98 *The Oak Hill*, above note 4 at 1234.
99 Above note 56.
100 *Western Assurance Co. v. Ontario Coal Co.*, above note 86.
101 See *Northland Navigation Co. v. Patterson Boiler Works*, above note 19; and the practice of average adjusters in British Columbia known as "Common User Apportionment" discussed by Hudson, above note 3 at 44.

C. GENERAL AVERAGE ADJUSTMENT

When general average is declared by the shipowner, a professional average adjuster is appointed whose task is to draw up a statement of adjustment. Since the process may take a considerable time, even several years, and commerce needs to continue meanwhile, it is customary for security to be taken for payment of the general average contributions that will eventually be levied. This is done with a general average bond signed by the interested parties and backed by a guarantee of the cargo insurers or a bank or by a cash deposit.[102] A claimant in general average has, under the *York-Antwerp Rules*, twelve months from the end of the common voyage to give notice of loss to the average adjuster and bears the burden of proof that the sacrifice or expenditure is properly allowable in general average.[103] What the claimant ultimately receives will not be full compensation for the loss but contributions from the other parties to the voyage in proportion to the value of their interests. In the adjustment of the general average loss, the claimant must also bear a proportionate share.

Contributions in general average depend upon an appropriate valuation of the losses sustained and the property saved. This is a highly technical matter for which average adjusters rely on a body of professional practice in addition to the guidance of a number of the *York-Antwerp Rules*. As a general proposition, rule G states: "General average shall be adjusted as regards both loss and contribution upon the basis of values at the time and place when and where the adventure ends." Thus, if the general average claim is for expenses incurred in an intermediate port during repairs and the ship completes its intended voyage, valuation of the contributing interests will be made at the port of destination; but if the voyage is abandoned at some mid-point, perhaps because the ship is wrecked or the cargo is separated or lost, contributing property will be valued at that place. As a legal consequence of this rule, and in the absence of any contractual provision, the law of the

---

102 The handling of cash deposits is regulated by *York-Antwerp Rules*, above note 10, r.XXII.
103 *Ibid.*, r.E. The 12-month time limit was added to the rules in 1994; see also *Kidd v. Thomson*, above note 87 at 222. In *Nickimen Co. v. Executive Venture (The)*, above note 75, the Federal Court provided assistance in establishing the necessary proof by issuing an order for inspection of evidence pending legal proceedings. The cargo owner was authorized to inspect the ship's engine while it was dismantled prior to repair, in order to obtain full information as to the cause of its breakdown, in expectation of litigation contesting the claim for general average contribution on the ground that the shipowner was at fault in providing an unseaworthy vessel.

place where the common voyage ends, and values are assessed, will ordinarily govern the process of general average adjustment.[104]

1) Valuation of Loss

General average expenditures obviously require no separate valuation but are admissible in the amounts paid.[105] General average sacrifices have to be individually valued. When cargo is sacrificed, the amount to be made good in general average, according to rule XVI, is its net sound value calculated from its commercial invoice, if available. When the cargo is merely damaged and sold, the proceeds of sale are subtracted from the net sound value.[106] However, sacrifice of cargo that is misdescribed by the shipper will not be admitted in general average, and damage or loss of cargo that is undervalued on shipment will be made good only up to its declared value.[107]

In cases of sacrifice of a part of the ship or its equipment that is subsequently repaired or replaced, rule XVII sets the amount recoverable in general average as "the actual reasonable cost" incurred.[108] This amount will be reduced by one-third when old materials or parts are replaced by new if the ship is more than fifteen years old.[109] When the sacrifice is not made good, the reasonable depreciation in the value of the ship is calculated and admitted, so long as it does not exceed the estimated cost of repairs. If the ship is an actual or constructive total loss, the value of its sacrifice is calculated by estimating its sound value and deducting the estimated repair costs for any damage outside general average and its sale value, if any, as a casualty. When lost freight is admissible in general average,[110] only the net loss, after deduction of the charges that would have been incurred to earn the freight, is allowed. The shipowner may also claim in general average a commission of two per cent for time and trouble in arranging the payment of disbursements for general average purposes.[111]

---

104 See also *Fletcher v. Alexander* (1868), L.R. 3 C.P. 375; and *Atwood v. Sellar & Co.*, above note 43 at 289 for a comparable rule at common law.
105 And the cost of insurance against the failure of the contributing interests is also admissible in general average: see *York-Antwerp Rules*, above note 10, r.XX, para.3.
106 Unless there is agreement as to the cargo's depreciation.
107 *York-Antwerp Rules*, above note 10, r.XIX.
108 Compare the measure of indemnity payable for damage to a ship by insurers under the *Marine Insurance Act*, above note 1, s.68.
109 *York-Antwerp Rules*, above note 10, r.XIII.
110 Above note 32.
111 *York-Antwerp Rules*, above note 10, r.XX.

2) Contributory Values

Contribution in general average is made by all parties in proportion to their interests in the voyage. Like valuation for loss, values for the contributory interests are calculated when and where the common voyage ends.[112] Therefore, the contributory values are based not on the values of the property involved at the beginning of the voyage but the values of the property saved from peril by the general average act. If, notwithstanding a general average sacrifice, the ship and cargo are totally lost, no benefit is received from the act and so no contributions are due.[113] As rule XVII of the *York-Antwerp Rules* recites, contribution in general average is made on the actual net value of the property at the termination of the voyage, to which is added the value of any property sacrificed. If the amount to be made good in general average for sacrificed property were not to be added, the owner would receive an unfair advantage in calculating the proportionate contributions. For instance, if the value of a cargo that was totally sacrificed were to be ignored, the owner would contribute nothing, and the other parties would have to make good the whole loss. Such a result would not amount to parity of contribution to the general average.

Rule XVII also provides more specific directions for assessing contributory values of the cargo, the ship, and the freight. The value of saved cargo is calculated, as for cargo loss, from its commercial invoice. To this amount is added insurance and freight, if at the cargo owner's risk; but from it is deducted any particular charges, such as discharging costs perhaps,[114] incurred after and not in relation to the general average act. However, if the goods are sold short of the destination, their sale price will be utilized instead. The ship is assessed for its market value without regard to any demise or time charter commitments. If damage that gave rise to the general average act has been repaired, then the cost of repairs must be deducted from its market value to determine its actual net value at the termination of the voyage. Net freight earned contributes separately in general average when at the risk of the shipowner and is valued at the rate due from the cargo owners. When the cargo is discharged at an intermediate port and forwarded by other means to its destination in circumstances that a non-separation agreement or the principles of rule G as amended in 1994 apply,[115] the moment and place

---

112 See r.G above after note 105 and *ibid.*, r.XVII.
113 *Fletcher v. Alexander*, above note 104 at 382.
114 *Ultramar Canada v. Mutual Marine Office* (1994), 82 F.T.R. 1.
115 Discussed above at note 57.

for fixing the contributory values of the ship and cargo need clarification. Rule XVII provides that the ship shall contribute on its value at the time of discharging the cargo in the intermediate port, but the cargo shall be assessed on its value on delivery at the original destination port.

When valuation is complete, the resulting adjustment is still subject to the common law rule that a general average contribution may not exceed the contributory value of the property on which it is levied. As a result the excess general average loss will fall where it lies, which generally is on the shipowner. In *Ultramar Canada v. Mutual Marine Office*,[116] large general average expenses were incurred in salvaging a barge and its oil cargo and in pollution clean-up. At issue was the distribution of the excess expenditure between the barge owner, the hull insurer, the cargo insurer, and the P&I club that provided the pollution insurance. The court applied the "well established principle [that] properties saved are only liable in general average up to their contributory values."[117] As a result, after the various insurers had paid the indemnities for which they were liable, the barge owner had to bear the excess cost.

Outstanding contributions are subject to interest. Rule XXI sets a rate of 7 per cent assessable until three months after the general average statement was issued.[118] Canadian courts may also award interest beyond this date up to judgment.[119] The shipowner may assert a possessory lien at common law over the cargo for unpaid contributions. The lien extends to contributions to both the shipowner and other cargo owners.[120] Usually the lien is not exercised because the cargo is released against the security of a general average bond. Since general average adjustment frequently takes years, there is a risk that claims for unpaid contributions may become time barred. At common law a contributor's liability accrues as soon as the general average sacrifice or expenditure is made although the amount due may not be determined until a long time afterward. However, the general average bond may vary this timetable by agreement that the obligation to contribute will not arise until the adjuster has completed a general average statement.[121]

---

116 Above note 114.
117 *Ibid.* at 11.
118 Under the 1974 rules, interest is payable only up to the date of the general average statement.
119 See *The Orient Trader*, above note 76; and *Ultramar Canada Inc. v. Mutual Marine Office*, above note 114.
120 *Crooks & Co. v. Allan* (1879), 5 Q.B.D. 38; *Strang, Steel & Co. v. A. Scott & Co.* (1889), 14 A.C. 601. In Canada the cargo owner may also have a maritime lien against the ship for unpaid contribution: see W. Tetley, *Maritime Liens and Claims*, 2d ed. (Cowansville, QB: Yvon Blais, 1998) at 451–52.
121 *Castle Insurance Co. v. Hong Kong Islands Shipping Co.*, [1984] 1 A.C. 226 (P.C.).

D. REFORM OF GENERAL AVERAGE

General average is an ancient and unique institution of maritime law. Yet its utility, notwithstanding its persistence, has oftentimes been called in question. General average adjustment has become so notoriously complicated, time consuming, and expensive that many commentators[122] have called for its simplification, if not outright abolition. If its scope could be cut back, the slack, it is argued, could be taken up by insurance. In practice, the scope of general average acts has steadily widened with each revision of the *York-Antwerp Rules* as more kinds of expenditures are admitted as general average. The introduction in 1890 of the principles of rules X(b) and XI(b), permitting expenditures in the absence of peril but for the safe prosecution of the voyage, opened the way to so-called "artificial" general average. Then in 1950 they were given prominence by the addition of the Rule of Interpretation that the numbered rules take precedence over the lettered rules. The amendments of 1990 moved the *York-Antwerp Rules* away from protecting only the common adventure. In response to the *International Convention on Salvage, 1989*, general average was again substantially expanded by the inclusion of salvage awards for the protection of the marine environment in some circumstances. In 1994 the latest version of the rules extended general average to expenditures made in four further, although restricted, situations to protect the marine environment.

The appeal of general average is the obvious justice and equity of its core principle that what is sacrificed for the common good of all parties to a voyage in a time of peril should be compensated by common contribution. The question is whether general average, in its modern and highly developed form, is worth the time and expense. The adjustment process regularly takes years and involves multiple costs for all parties. It is so complex that a whole profession of average adjusters is required to handle the task. It is understandable that shipowners should want to recoup their sacrifices and expenditures, but merchants find the delay of a general average claim irritating: they expect their goods, on arrival at destination with freight paid, to be available without further demands. Commercial practice and world

---

122 See, e.g., L.J. Buglass, *Marine Insurance and General Average in the United States*, 3d ed. (Centerville, MD: Cornell Maritime Press, 1991) at 328; Gilmore & Black, *The Law of Admiralty*, 2d ed. (Mineola, NY: Foundation Press, 1975) at 270; *Lowndes and Rudolph*, above note 3 at 883; Selmer, above note 3, esp. c.IX; W. Tetley, above note 120 at 441–43; and *General Average*, UN Doc. UNCTAD, TD/B/C4/ISL/58 (1991) c.VI.

trade are much changed from the days when insurance did not exist, and shipowners and cargo owners invested their fortunes in a common marine adventure. General average was eminently equitable in those circumstances of great risk. But for many years now the sense of partnership between shipowner and merchant in a hazardous adventure has been replaced by a routine marine service by a carrier for a cargo owner, like any other mode of transport.

Several possible reform proposals have been put forward[123] but none, so far, has found general favour. Reaction from the maritime community has been mixed, partly over the principles of general average and partly because of vested interests, as well as plain inertia. The source of any reformatory solution must lie in insurance, since general average today, at bottom, is simply a system of reallocating risks among insurers. Hence, there is plainly no hope of shipping industry acceptance of the abolition of general average unless shipowners and cargo owners would be put in as good a position financially under the altered insurance system, as they currently enjoy under general average. That would require a realignment of insurance arrangements and their terms and conditions involving all three types of insurers: hull, protection and indemnity, and cargo. Serious discussions about reform did take place in the International Union of Marine Insurers and in the London market for hull insurance prior to agreement on the *York-Antwerp Rules* in 1994.[124] These discussions, however, seemed to have become centred on concerns about the potential expansion of general average to cover expenditures to protect the marine environment. The insurers were generally relieved at the restrictive compromise achieved in the 1994 rules over expenditures on the environment, but the recurrent quest for simplification and even wholesale reform of general average continues.

FURTHER READINGS

BUGLASS, L.J., *Marine Insurance and General Average in the United States*, 3d ed. (Centreville, MD: Cornell Maritime Press, 1991).

HUDSON, N.G., *The York-Antwerp Rules*, 2d ed. (London: Lloyd's Press, 1996).

---

123 See *General Average*, ibid., c.VII; and *The Place of General Average in Marine Insurance Today*, UN Doc. UNCTAD/SDD/LEG 1 (1994).
124 See *General Average — Reform of the System*, UN Doc. UNCTAD/SDD/LEG/3 (1995) at 15.

MUSTALL, SIR MICHAEL & J.P. GILMAN, *Arnould's Law of Marine Insurance and Average*, 16th ed., 3 vols. (London: Stevens, 1981 & 1997).

ROSE, F.D., *General Average Law and Practice* (London: Lloyd's Press, 1997).

SELMER, K., *The Survival of General Average* (Oslo: Oslo University Press, 1958).

STRATHY, G.R., *The Law and Practice of General Average* (Toronto: Strathy Barristers and Solicitors, 1995).

STRATHY, G.R. & G.C. Moore, *Law & Practice of Marine Insurance in Canada* (Toronto: LexisNexis Butterworths, 2003).

UNITED NATIONS CONFERENCE ON TRADE AND DEVELOPMENT, *General Average*, UN Doc. TD/B/C.4/ISL/58 (1991).

——, *The Place of General Average in Marine Insurance Today*, UN Doc. UNCTAD/SDD/LEG/1 (1994).

——, *General Average — Reform of the System*, UN Doc. UNCTAD/SDD/LEG/3 (1995).

WILSON, D.J. & J.H.S. Cooke, *Lowndes & Rudolph: The Law of General Average and the York-Antwerp Rules*, 12th ed. (London: Sweet & Maxwell, 1997).

CHAPTER 17

MARINE POLLUTION PREVENTION

A. BACKGROUND

1) Introduction

The protection of the marine environment from marine pollution has today become a very complex technical and legal area. To understand the operational and legal issues some knowledge of the background of this area is not only useful but, probably, essential. Accordingly, this chapter outlines:

- how a new international operational system to prevent ship-source marine pollution was developed,
- how this operational system has been complemented by specialized compensation and liability systems, and
- how the operational and liability aspects of offshore energy development have been developed in order to protect the marine environment.

As marine pollution resulting from vessel operations and offshore energy development has national, regional, and international implications, the approach to problems in the area has been principally international. Nevertheless, Canada has played an important role in these developments, as reflected in Canadian policy, law, and regulation. This chapter addresses the prevention of marine pollution that is generated from vessel operations as well as from offshore energy operations, including operational discharges that are accidental (i.e., caused by mechanical failure, human error, or any other unforeseen circumstance) and discharges that are deliberate (i.e., caused by actual operational requirement, deliberate action, or negligent failure). Pollution of the marine environment is defined as follows:

> the introduction by man, directly or indirectly, of substances or energy into the marine environment, including estuaries, which results or is likely to result in such deleterious harm to living resources and marine life, hazards to human health, hindrance to marine activities, including fishing and other legitimate uses of the sea, impairment of quality for use of sea water and reduction of amenities.[1]

This definition is sufficiently broad to cover all types of pollutants. There has been a major effort to prevent pollution from hydrocarbons and related polluting substances carried by ships as this was, for a long period, of prime concern. Nevertheless, this concern has broadened in recent years and now includes a significant variety of substances other than oil that are considered harmful to the marine environment. Canadian law defines "pollution" even more broadly:

> a substance that, if added to any waters, would degrade or alter or form part of a process of degradation or alteration of the quality of the waters to an extent that is detrimental to their use by humans or by an animal or a plant that is useful to humans; and any water that contains a substance in such a quantity or concentration, or that has been so treated, processed or changed, by heat or other means, from a natural state, that it would, if added to any waters, degrade or alter or form part of a process of degradation or alteration of the quality of the waters to an extent that is detrimental to their use by humans or by an animal or a plant that is useful to humans.[2]

The negative effects of marine pollution on the marine environment are well documented and it is neither necessary nor appropriate to provide more than a very brief outline in this book. Hydrocarbon and chemical pollutants have negative biological impacts on the marine

---

1 *United Nations Convention on the Law of the Sea*, 10 December 1982, 1833 U.N.T.S. 3, art.1(4) [*UNCLOS*] (entered into force on 16 November 1994; not yet ratified by Canada, although the Canadian government has expressed the intention to ratify it). See also Institute of Maritime Law, *Ratification of Maritime Conventions*, 4 vols., Updated looseleaf service (London: Lloyd's Press, 1991–2003) vol.1.7.10.
2 *Canada Shipping Act, 2001*, S.C. 2001, c.26, s.165. It should be noted that this Act will only enter into force when the necessary regulatory revisions are completed, which may take some time. Throughout this chapter, references to this Act will be made whenever appropriate. (See also the explanatory note on the *Canada Shipping Act* at E in Chapter 1.)

environment from a number of effects that include lethal toxicity, sublethal effects, physical smothering, and tainting of seafoods. Such marine pollution can damage shorelines, open waters and the seabed, wetlands and estuaries, corals and mangroves, fisheries, and coastal amenities. Such damage would, obviously, also include commensurate financial, commercial, and other related losses.[3] Better knowledge of the effects of marine pollution has resulted in an increasing awareness of the environmental dangers, which has raised global environmental consciousness that, in turn, has been transposed into political action, resulting in legislative enactment. This chapter, therefore, illustrates that in the last half-century marine pollution has become a major preoccupation of the international community.

2) Developments to 1980

While there had been some concerns about ship-source marine pollution between the two world wars,[4] nothing much happened in the global, regional, or national regulatory areas until the 1950s. At that time, a rising world economy, resulting in a sharply increasing demand for hydrocarbon fuels, contributed to renewed concerns over marine pollution problems. In 1954 the first in a series of international marine pollution conventions was completed in London: the *International Convention for the Prevention of Pollution of the Sea by Oil, 1954* (*OILPOL 1954*)[5] (discussed below). Following the formation in 1958 of the Inter-Governmental Maritime Consultative Organization (IMCO), as the specialized agency of the United Nations in maritime matters,[6] the ship-source marine pollution area devolved to this agency; further *OILPOL 1954* amendments were completed in 1962, 1969, and 1971.[7] In

---

3   Discussed below in C, "Marine Pollution: The International Liability and Compensation Regime."
4   For a fuller background on the history, as well as greater detail on this whole area, see E. Gold, *Gard Handbook on Marine Pollution*, 2d ed. (Arendal, NO: Gard, 1997) at 30ff; and D.W. Abecassis & R.L. Jarashow, *Oil Pollution from Ships*, 2d ed. (London, Stevens, 1985).
5   12 May 1954, 327 U.N.T.S. 3 (entered into force 26 July 1958; accession by Canada, 26 July 1958); see also *Ratification of Maritime Conventions*, above note 1.
6   See G(1)(a) in Chapter 2, "The Shipping Industry: An Overview." IMCO is now the International Maritime Organisation.
7   *Amendments to the International Convention for the Prevention of Pollution of the Sea by Oil, 1954*, 11 April 1962, 600 U.N.T.S. 332; *Amendments to the International Convention for the Prevention of Pollution of the Sea by Oil, of 1954*, 21 October 1969, 1140 U.N.T.S. 340; *Amendments to the International Convention for the Prevention of Pollution of the Sea by Oil, of 1954, Concerning Tank Arrange-*

1958 and 1960, the first and second United Nations conferences on the law of the sea took place. These global conferences also considered the question of marine pollution, although peripherally, by including in two of the treaties provisions that states should draw up regulations to prevent pollution of the sea by oil from ships and pipelines, from exploitation of the seabed,[8] and from radioactive pollution.[9] However, the real impetus for modern marine environmental regulation occurred only just over thirty-five years ago. As has often been suggested before, almost all developments, initiatives, and improvements in maritime safety have had some type of maritime accident or disaster as a catalyst. This is equally true for marine pollution regulation. In 1967, when the tanker Torrey Canyon grounded off the British coast, causing the largest single oil spill in maritime history up to that time, a new era in environmental controls commenced.[10] The problem at that time was that this accident caught the maritime industry and its legal and underwriting sectors completely unprepared. There were no compensation schemes for pollution damage that was not even specifically covered under the standard protection and indemnity liability insurance policies[11] then in operation. The problem of dealing with the consequences of the disaster very quickly ended up at the IMCO and resulted in that organization receiving new and wider powers.[12] The expertise of the Comité Maritime International (CMI)[13] was brought in and, within two years, two new conventions related to marine pollution were concluded. First in 1969 an IMCO conference completed the *International Convention on Civil Liability for Oil Pollution Damage, 1969 (CLC 1969)*.[14] This treaty

---

ments and Size, 15 October 1971, 11 I.L.M. 267. See also *Ratification of Maritime Conventions*, above note 1, vol.I.7.10–13.

8 *Convention on the High Seas*, 29 April 1958, 450 U.N.T.S. 82, art.24 (entered into force 30 September 1962; never accepted by Canada, although many of the convention's principles were incorporated into Canadian law); see also *Ratification of Maritime Conventions*, above note 1 vol.I.1.100.

9 *Convention on the High Seas*, ibid., art.25.

10 L.S. Reycraft, "The Torrey Canyon" [1967] C.B.A. Papers 85; and E. Gold, *Maritime Transport: The Evolution of International Marine Policy and Shipping Law* (Toronto: Lexington Books, 1981) at 286–89.

11 See E in Chapter 7, "Marine Insurance."

12 Gold, above note 10, at 339ff; and N.J. Healy, "The CMI and IMCO Draft Conventions on Civil Liability for Oil Pollution" (1969) 1 J. Mar. L. & Com. 93.

13 See G(2)(a) in Chapter 2, "The Shipping Industry: An Overview."

14 29 November 1969, 973 U.N.T.S. 3 (entered into force 19 June 1975; in force in Canada since 24 April 1989); see also *Ratification of Maritime Conventions*, above note 1 vol.I.7.30. See N.J. Healy, "The International Convention on Civil Liability for Oil Polllution" (1969) 1 J. Mar. L. & Com. 317; Gold, above note 4 at 223.

made significant changes to the traditional maritime liability regime. As discussed below, *CLC 1969* changed the liability base from one of proven fault and negligence to strict liability. Also in 1969 the IMCO conference completed the *International Convention Relating to Intervention on the High Seas in Cases of Oil Pollution Casualties, 1969* (*Intervention*).[15] This convention permits coastal states to take early action in waters outside their jurisdiction against vessels that pose or may pose a threat to the marine environment from oil pollution.

During the discussions leading up to these treaties, it became clear to the shipping industry, and particularly its tanker sector, that these new conventions would take a number of years to enter into force. It was feared that public pressure could lead to unilateral legislative action by affected coastal states, unless an alternative interim voluntary compensation regime could be implemented quickly. This realization resulted in the creation of the *Tanker Owners' Voluntary Agreement Concerning Liability for Oil Pollution* (*TOVALOP*),[16] an agreement by shipowners and their protection and indemnity (P&I) underwriters, designed to encourage the cleanup of oil spills, regardless of fault, with the assurance that costs would be recovered from the relevant P&I club. Cleanup costs by governments were also covered under this scheme. This interim agreement played an important role in this area until it was terminated, almost three decades later, in 1997. However, during the 1970s, with environmental concerns sharply increasing, coastal states brought forward concerns that the *CLC 1969* compensation limits would not suffice, should a serious marine pollution incident occur. Therefore, a further international conference at IMCO decided that a supplementary convention to the *CLC 1969* was needed. This required the involvement of the international oil industry and resulted in the *International Convention on the Establishment of an International Fund for*

---

15   29 November 1969, 970 U.N.T.S. 211 (entered into force 6 May 1975; not so far accepted by Canada); see also *Ratification of Maritime Conventions*, above note 1 vol.I.7.70. See also T. McDorman & E. Gold, "The International Convention Relating to Intervention on the High Seas in Cases of Oil Pollution" in S. Mankabady, ed., *The International Maritime Organisation* (London: Croom Helm, 1984) at 280; N.J. Gaskell, C. Debattista, & R.J. Swatton, *Chorley & Giles Shipping Law*, 8th ed. (London: Pitman, 1987) at 477; and Abecassis, above note 4 at 115ff.

16   *Tanker Owners' Voluntary Agreement Concerning Liability for Oil Pollution*, 7 January 1969, published by International Tanker Owners Pollution Federation Ltd.; online at <http://www.imli.org/docs./A97B.DOC> under International Maritime Law Treaties and Legislative Instruments [*TOVALOP*] (entered into force 6 October 1969); see also *Ratification of Maritime Conventions*, above note 1 vol.I.7.60; see Gold, above note 4 at 234; and Abecassis, above note 4 at 304ff.

Maritime Pollution Prevention 663

Compensation for Oil Pollution Damage, 1971 (FUND 1971)[17] (discussed further below). *FUND 1971* significantly extended the available compensation limits, especially for serious pollution incidents. However, once again, the industry, realizing that the *FUND 1971* convention would take a number of years to enter into force, decided to develop a supplementary, interim agreement modelled on the *FUND 1971* provisions. This time the international oil industry introduced a new scheme entitled *Contract Regarding an Interim Supplement to Tanker Liability for Oil Pollution (CRISTAL)*[18] in 1971 that significantly raised the interim compensation available through *TOVALOP*. Like *TOVALOP*, the *CRISTAL* agreement was in operation until 1997.[19]

At this stage, international environmental concerns expanded very quickly, and a number of regional agreements to protect the environment from dumping into oceans were developed in Europe.[20] These were followed by the first global conference on the environment that examined all aspects of environmental deterioration at the highest level.[21] Next, another global treaty was adopted, the *Convention on the Prevention of Marine Pollution by Dumping of Wastes and Other Matters, 1972 as amended (LC 1972)*[22] (also discussed below). In late 1973, IMCO adopted the second major operational marine pollution prevention treaty, the *International Convention for the Prevention of Pollution from Ships (MARPOL 73/78)*,[23] designed to supersede *OILPOL 1954* that was out of date

---

17 18 December 1971, 1110 U.N.T.S. 57 (entered into force 16 October 1978; in force in Canada since 24 April 1989); see also *Ratification of Maritime Conventions*, above note 1 vol.1.7.90. See Gold, above note 4 at 230; and Abecassis, above note 4, c.11.

18 *Contract Regarding an Interim Supplement to Tanker Liability for Oil Pollution*, 14 January 1971, online at <http://www.imli.org/docs/A98.DOC> under International Maritime Law Treaties and Legislative Instruments [*CRISTAL*] (entered into force 1 April 1971); see *Ratifications of Maritime Conventions*, above note 1 vol.1.7.120; see also Gold above note 4 at 234; and G. Gauci, *Oil Pollution at Sea* (Chichester: Wiley, 1997) at 25–27.

19 See Gold, *ibid.* at 33–35 and 82–83.

20 Gold, *ibid.* at 36–37.

21 U.N. Conference on the Human Environment, Stockholm 1972. See UN, *Report of the United Nations Conference on the Human Environment* (New York: UN, 1973), U.N. Doc. E.73.II.A.14 (1973).

22 29 December 1972, 1046 U.N.T.S. 120 (entered into force 30 August 1975; in force in Canada since 14 December 1975); see also *Ratification of Maritime Conventions*, above note 1 vol.1.7.150. *LC 1972* is also known as the *London Convention* and was formerly known as the *London Dumping Convention*.

23 2 November 1973, 1340 U.N.T.S. 184, as am. by *Protocol of 1978 Relating to the International Convention for the Prevention of Pollution from Ships of 1973*, 17 February 1978, 1341 U.N.T.S. 3 [*MARPOL 73/78*] (entered into force on 2 October

and had, in any case, been considered to be inadequate for a variety of reasons. MARPOL is one of the most important operational conventions in existence, as it basically sets out a total preventive regime for ship-source marine pollution from all sources.[24] Also, in 1973, the United Nations commenced a lengthy debate on all aspects of ocean uses: the Third United Nations Conference on the Law of the Sea. This massive oceanic law reform movement continued until 1982, when the *United Nations Convention on the Law of the Sea, 1982 (UNCLOS)*,[25] was adopted. The conference had also focused especially on marine pollution and the resulting convention laid down a new regime for the protection of the marine environment at the highest global level. At the same time, the International Maritime Organisation (IMO[26]) was provided with its global mandate for safer ships and cleaner seas.

Marine pollution was, unfortunately, kept very much in the public eye owing to a series of major tanker disasters in the 1970s.[27] These resulted in a significant MARPOL amendment in 1978 that was especially designed to speed up the adoption of the convention itself.[28] However, a further major tanker disaster, involving the grounding of the very large crude carrier Amoco Cadiz, off the French coast, brought the subject back to the IMO. As a result, the IMO concluded the *International Convention on Standards of Training, Certification and Watchkeeping for Seafarers, as amended (STCW 1978)*,[29] which for the first time addressed the human aspect of protecting the marine environment. However, concerns for the marine environment continued unabated following a series of further major ship-source pollution cases arising from maritime accidents.[30] By 1982 there was global consensus that the liability and compensation schemes, developed in 1969/1971, were in need of revision. In particular, it was felt that the upper limits of these schemes were no longer adequate to meet the liabilities that might arise from a catastrophic oil spill. As a result, the IMO undertook the revision of the

---

1983; in force in Canada since 16 February 1993); see also *Ratification of Maritime Conventions*, above note 1 vol.I.7.170.

24 For fuller details on MARPOL 73/78 see Gold, above note 4, c.3.
25 Above note 1.
26 IMCO changed its name and acronym in May 1982.
27 See Gold, above note 4 at 40–41.
28 MARPOL would thereafter be designated as MARPOL 73/78.
29 7 July 1978, 1361 U.N.T.S. 2 (entered into force 28 February 1984; in force in Canada since 6 February 1988); see also *Ratification of Maritime Conventions*, above note 1 vol.I.3.90. See Chapter 5, "The Safety Management of Ships" for a full discussion of this convention.
30 See Gold, above note 4 at 41.

CLC 1969 and *FUND 1971* conventions, and new protocols for these treaties were concluded in 1984. Both protocols substantially raised the limitation ceilings for *CLC 1969* and *FUND 1971*, although not as high as demanded by some states. In addition, the geographical limits of the parent conventions were also extended to 200 miles (370 km) from the coast, and future amendment procedures for the conventions were simplified. Also in 1984, an attempt was made to conclude a liability and compensation convention relating to damage to the marine environment from hazardous and noxious substances carried at sea. Unfortunately, the complexity of this area, involving potential liability of manufacturers, shippers, carriers, and their respective insurers, made resolution of this issue impossible at that time. It would take a further twelve years before a satisfactory convention could be concluded.[31]

3) Developments since 1980

The following decades witnessed a number of further developments in marine pollution regulation, which had become one of the IMO's major preoccupations under its guiding principle of safer ships and cleaner seas. *UNCLOS* finally entered into force in late 1994.[32] This gave further impetus for wider acceptance of IMO conventions. *MARPOL 73/78* was being strengthened continually and underwent some eighteen substantive amendments during this period.[33] In 1989, the *Basel Convention on the Control of Transboundary Movements of Hazardous Wastes and their Disposal (Basel Convention)*[34] was concluded. This treaty, which entered into force in 1992, was designed to deal with the export of such wastes, especially from developed to developing regions of the world. As discussed below, this convention also has some implications for shipping. During this period there were also more tanker accidents involving serious pollution that further strengthened the resolve of governments in Australia, Canada, Spain, the Malacca Straits states, Italy, the United Kingdom, and, especially, the United States.[35]

In March 1989, the U.S.-flagged very large crude carrier Exxon Valdez grounded in Prince William Sound, Alaska, spilling approximately 40,000 tons of crude oil that caused serious pollution in an

---

31   To be discussed below in C(5), "*HNS 1996.*"
32   *UNCLOS*, above note 1.
33   Gold, above note 4 at 43.
34   22 March 1989, Can. T.S. 1992 No.92 (entered into force 2 May 1992; in force in Canada since 26 November 1992); see also *Ratification of Maritime Conventions*, above note 1 vol.I.7.220.
35   Gold, above note 4 at 44–46.

environmentally vulnerable area. However, the aftermath from this accident was much more wide reaching, as it would result in the departure of the United States from the traditional international pollution regime that had evolved, to take its own unilateral route in the area. This action was expressed in the form of the U.S. *Oil Pollution Act, 1990*,[36] a piece of complex legislation completely at odds with the international regime that had previously been supported by the United States.[37] While this unilateral U.S. action was — and often still is — criticized internationally, it would eventually find a certain amount of support from states that reacted strongly to marine pollution accidents involving shipping.

There was also considerable further activity at the IMO in this area. The *International Convention on Salvage (Salvage 1989)*,[38] concluded in 1989, superseded the 1910 convention by permitting salvage awards for pollution prevention, and also provided for awards to salvors who successfully prevent pollution, even in cases where the vessel cannot be saved.[39] As a direct result of The Exxon Valdez grounding and at the urging of the United States, the IMO also concluded a new *International Convention on Oil Pollution Preparedness, Response and Co-operation (OPRC 1990)* in 1990.[40] This treaty sets out a regime that provides for better co-operation among states in responding to serious marine accidents. The Regional Seas Programme of the United Nations Environment Programme (UNEP) was also expanded and would eventually encompass some thirteen regional seas, most of which would have oil spill contingency regimes as part of their jurisdiction.[41] Another regional program that was being further developed was based on the original *Memorandum of Understanding on Port State Control in Implementing Agreements on Maritime Safety and Protection of the Marine Environment (Paris MOU*

---

36   33 U.S.C. §2701; see also Gold, above note 4, c.5.
37   Gold, *ibid.*; see also E. Gold, "Marine Pollution Liability after *Exxon Valdez*: The U.S. 'All-or-Nothing' Lottery!" (1991) 22 J. Mar. L. & Com. 423; C. De La Rue & C.B. Anderson, *Shipping and the Environment* (London: Lloyd's Press, 1998) c.4; and T.J. Schoenbaum, *Admiralty and Maritime Law*, 3d ed. (St. Paul, MN: West Publishing, 2001) c.16.
38   28 April 1989, U.K.T.S. 1996 No.93 (entered into force on 14 July 1996; in force in Canada since 14 July 1996); see also *Ratification of Maritime Conventions*, above note 1 vol.I.3.320. See Chapter 15, "Maritime Salvage and Wreck."
39   *Salvage 1989, ibid.*
40   30 November 1990, 30 I.L.M. 733 (entered into force 13 May 1995; in force in Canada on 13 May 1995); see also *Ratification of Maritime Conventions*, above note 1 vol.I.7.230
41   Gold, above note 4 at 46 and Appendix IV.

1982),[42] which had been designed to assist in the implementation of marine safety and marine pollution agreements among a number of European states and Canada, in 1982.[43] Similar initiatives were eventually developed for Latin America, the Caribbean, the Asia-Pacific region, west and central Africa, the Mediterranean, the Indian Ocean, and the Black Sea[44] However, as already indicated, the aftermath of The Exxon Valdez spill resulted in the United States taking a different direction in this area. As a result, the United States was not able to accept the 1984 *CLC 1969* and *FUND 1971* protocols, which could have entered into force only with U.S. participation. Nevertheless, as these protocols were of such importance, because of their substantially raised compensation limits, the IMO convened a further international conference in 1992 that concluded the 1992 *CLC* and *FUND* protocols (discussed later in this chapter). These were basically the same as the 1984 version but did not fully depend upon U.S. participation. As there was further concern that these protocols would take some time to enter into force, *TOVALOP* and *CRISTAL* limits were raised commensurately almost immediately and the agreements were extended for a final three-year period. There was also an important development at the highest global level during this period. This was the United Nations Conference on Environment and Development (UNCED), the Earth Summit, that took place in Rio de Janeiro, Brazil, in 1992. While UNCED addressed almost all aspects of environment and development, ocean pollution received special attention.[45] The regional port state inspection regimes and UNEP regional seas systems were also further developed during this period. In late 1996, the International Tribunal for the Law of the Sea was established in Hamburg, Germany,[46] with marine pollution within its jurisdiction.

MARPOL 73/78 was also further strengthened with wide acceptance of its annexes. A new Annex VI on the prevention of air pollution by

---

42 26 January 1982, 21 I.L.M. 1 (entered into force 1 July 1982; accession by Canada on 3 May 1994); see also *Ratification of Maritime Conventions*, above note 1 vol.I.3.100. See also Chapter 5, "The Safety Management of Ships."
43 See discussion of regional agreements and MOUs in D(3) of Chapter 5, "The Safety Management of Ships."
44 *Ibid.*
45 See *Protection of the Oceans, All Kinds of Seas, including Enclosed and Semi-Enclosed Seas, and Coastal Areas and the Protection, Rational Use and Development of their Living Resources*, UNCED OR, 4th Sess., U.N. Doc. E/CN.17/1996/3; UN, *Agenda 21: A Programme of Action for Sustainable Development. Rio Declaration on Environment and Development*, GA Conf. 151/26, vol.1 (New York: UN, 1993) c.17, U.N. Doc. E.93.I.11 [Rio Declaration].
46 See G(1)(e)(vii) in Chapter 2, "The Shipping Industry: An Overview."

ships was concluded in 1997. In late 1993, a resolution at the IMO resulted in the *International Safety Management Code for the Safe Operation of Ships and Pollution Prevention (ISM Code)*.[47] This code has far-reaching implications for all aspects of ship operation, including pollution prevention.[48] The objectives of the *ISM Code* are "to ensure safety at sea, prevention of human injury or loss of life, and avoidance of damage to the environment, in particular to the marine environment and to property."[49] This is to be achieved by imposing an obligation upon the shipowner to implement a quality assurance system as well as the duty to analyze the cause and effect of non-conformity by the vessel. This requirement has an important link to P&I insurance. Unlike flag states, P&I clubs do not have the powers of enforcement for pollution and safety regulations; but, the fact that insurance cover is conditional upon the compliance with such regulations reinforces proper compliance with national and international regulations.[50] In 1995 the IMO also concluded a very substantial revision of the *STCW 1978* convention, containing some of the most far-reaching and important regulations ever faced by the shipping industry regarding seafarers' work standards. In terms of marine pollution liability and compensation, all existing regimes have so far concentrated exclusively on oil pollution. However, in 1996, the IMO was finally able to conclude its work commenced in the 1980s on liability and compensation for substances other than oil, when it concluded the *International Convention on Liability and Compensation for Damage in Connection with the Carriage of Hazardous and Noxious Substances by Sea, 1996 (HNS 1996)* (discussed below).[51] Not yet in force, this convention has important

---

47 IMO Res. A. 741(18) (4 November 1993) [*ISM Code*] (in force 1 July 1998); see *Ratification of Maritime Conventions*, above note 1 vol.I.3.46. See also Chapter 5, "The Safety Management of Ships."
48 Gold, above note 4 at 50–51 and 319–22. See also P. Anderson, *ISM Code: A Practical Guide to the Legal and Insurance Implications* (London: Lloyd's Press, 1998).
49 *ISM Code*, above note 47 art.1.2.1.
50 See Chapter 7, "Marine Insurance." See also E. Gold, *Gard Handbook on P&I Insurance*, 5th ed. (Arendal, NO: Gard A.S., 2002) at 412; and Anderson, above note 48.
51 2 May 1996, 35 I.L.M. 1406 (not yet in force); see *Ratification of Maritime Conventions*, above note 1 vol.I.7.120. A protocol to HNS 1996 and OPRC was subsequently concluded to permit states to co-operate in dealing with pollution incidents involving these substances. See *Protocol on Preparedness, Response and Co-operation to Pollution Incidents by Hazardous and Noxious Substances, 2000* (OPRC-HNS Prot 2000) 15 March 2000 (not yet in force); see *Ratification of Maritime Conventions*, above note 1 vol.I.7.232.

implications for shipping. Finally, there is also significant work in progress at the IMO in a number of areas related to protection of the marine environment, including pollution from organisms contained in ballast water, pollution from bunker oils, the adverse effect of anti-fouling paints, and wreck removal.[52]

Even this very cursory overview[53] of the background of the international regime for the prevention and control of ship-source marine pollution should indicate clearly that, in less than a half-century, marine pollution has become of major importance for all sectors of the shipping industry. There exists today a complex and formidable array of global, regional, and national[54] regulatory regimes that involve increased costs for all levels of the industry. This is in response to greatly increased international and national awareness of the dangers — real and perceived — of environmental deterioration. This raised global environmental consciousness, in turn, has been transposed into political action, resulting in legislative enactments. It does not really matter that shipping now contributes less than 10 per cent of all pollutants entering the seas. As long as serious shipping accidents and deliberate or careless and negligent pollution continues, states and the international community will react.

4) Canadian Policy, Law, and Regulation

Throughout this period, Canada has taken an aggressive position at the international, regional, and national levels on protecting the environment generally and the marine environment specifically. In fact, in the 1970s Canada was probably at the very forefront of the developments that were outlined above.[55] The catalyst for this Canadian policy position was The Torrey Canyon disaster off the U.K. and French coasts in 1967 that led to a number of important new international initiatives.

---

52 See Chapter 15, "Maritime Salvage and Wreck."
53 For greater detail, see Gold, above note 4, or one of the principal treatises, such as De La Rue, above note 37.
54 For information on national legislation to combat marine pollution, see Gold, above note 4, c.6.
55 See, e.g., E. Gold, "Pollution of the Sea and International Law: A Canadian Perspective" (1971) 3 J. Mar. L. & Com. 13; D. VanderZwaag, "Canada and Marine Environmental Protection" in D. McRae and G. Munro, eds., *Canadian Oceans Policy: National Strategies and the New Law of the Sea* (Vancouver: UBC Press, 1989); and R.M. M'Gonigle & M.W. Zacher "Canadian Foreign Policy and the Control of Marine Pollution" in R.M. M'Gonigle & M.W. Zacher, eds., *Canadian Foreign Policy and the Law of the Sea* (Vancouver: UBC Press, 1977).

Canada was not totally satisfied with the depth and strength of international response[56] and, in response, revised the *Canada Shipping Act*[57] by enacting tough new anti-marine pollution provisions. However, Canada found itself virtually alone in its concern at that time, and the new provisions were considerably watered down after effective pressure from the shipping industry and major shipping states.[58] Further concern for Canada in this area appeared with the successful Arctic transit of the U.S. tanker Manhattan in 1969 that eventually resulted in the passage of the Canadian *Arctic Waters Pollution Prevention Act* (*AWPPA*) in 1970.[59] This Act established a pollution prevention area off all Canadian coastlines above 60° N.[60] During this period Canada was also actively engaged in the Third United Nations Conference on the Law of the Sea and its predecessor, the U.N. Seabed Committee. In particular, Canada took a leading role in the negotiations on protection of the marine environment that would eventually become an important part of *UNCLOS* in 1982.[61] These provisions formed an important base for the development of international environmental law.[62]

In early 1970 Canada experienced its first serious oil pollution disaster with the grounding of the Liberian-flag tanker Arrow in Chedabucto Bay, Nova Scotia. The accident caused widespread, serious pollution of vulnerable fishing areas. A subsequent Royal Commission made a number of specific recommendations[63] that resulted in the establishment of new coastal vessel traffic zones, the Maritime Pollu-

---

56 L. Legault, "Freedom of the Seas: A Licence to Pollute?" (1971) 21 U.T.L.J. 211.
57 See *Canada Shipping Act*, R.S.C. 1985, c.S-9, Pt.XV.
58 See, e.g., N. Letalik & E. Gold, "Shipping Law in Canada: From Imperial Beginnings to National Policy" in D. VanderZwaag, ed., *Canadian Ocean Law and Policy* (Toronto: Butterworths, 1992) at 283ff; P.D. Lowry, "Marine Pollution: The Canada Shipping Act Amended" (1973) 8 U.B.C.L.Rev. 197; and F. Rigaldies, "Le Canada et la pollution de la mer par les navires" (1977) 23 McGill L.J. 334.
59 Not proclaimed until 1972. R.S.C. 1985, c.A-12; see also VanderZwaag, above note 55 at 106; and A.E. Utton, "The Arctic Waters Pollution Prevention Act and the Right of Self-Protection" (1972) 7 U.B.C.L.Rev. 221.
60 See below B(9)(a)(ii), "*AWPPA*."
61 *UNCLOS*, above note 1.
62 Letalik & Gold, above note 58. See also A.J. Sutton, "International Maritime Law" in R. St. J. Macdonald et al., eds., *Canadian Perspectives on International Law and Organization* (University of Toronto Press, 1974) at 449; Canada, *Canada and the Law of the Sea: Resource Information* (Ottawa: Department of External Affairs, 1978); and Canada, Interdepartmental Committee on the Prevention of Pollution from Shipping, *Control Of Pollution From Shipping In Waters Under Canadian Jurisdiction* (Ottawa: Coast Guard, Transport Canada, 1981).
63 Canada, Royal Commission of Inquiry, *Steam Tanker Arrow — Final Report* (Ottawa: Transport Canada, 1971).

tion Claims Fund (MPCF),[64] and a new part of the *Canada Shipping Act* that gave the federal government broad powers to pass regulations relating to marine safety and pollution prevention.[65] Two major series of new regulations were also subsequently developed.[66] By 1988–89 Canada had also further revised and upgraded the *Canada Shipping Act* to bring civil liability and compensation for oil pollution damage provisions into effect.[67] A new Ship-Source Oil Pollution Fund, (SOPF) also succeeded the earlier model.[68] The global marine environment was also, once again, the focus at Rio de Janeiro, Brazil, in 1992.[69] Canada was a vigorous participant in this effort.[70] By the end of the 1990s Canada had, therefore, developed a very complex but effective regulatory system covering ship-source marine, as well as offshore energy pollution in all Canadian waters under legislation within the jurisdiction of the principal responsible federal government ministries and departments (Transport Canada,[71] Fisheries and Oceans Canada,[72] Environment Canada,[73] and Natural Resources Canada[74]). (The actual effect of this legislative regime is discussed below.)

---

64 This would become the Ship-Source Oil Pollution Fund (SOPF) in due course. See below.
65 *Canada Shipping Act*, above note 57, ss.656–57; see also *Canada Shipping Act, 2001*, above note 2 s.182; and VanderZwaag, above note 55 at 106.
66 The *Oil Pollution Prevention Regulations*, S.O.R./93-3 as am. by S.O.R./95-352 & S.O.R./98-123; and the *Pollutant Substances Regulations*, C.R.C., c.1458 as am. by S.O.R./83-347.
67 R.S.C. 1985 (3d Supp.), c.6.
68 S.O.R./90-82; *ibid.*, s.84. The *Ship-Source Oil Pollution Fund Regulations*, S.O.R./90-82, were repealed in 2002 and replaced by *Marine Liability Regulations*, S.O.R./2002-307, Part 1.
69 See Rio Declaration, above note 45.
70 L.K. Kriwoken et al., eds., *Oceans Law and Policy in the Post–UNCED Era: Australian and Canadian Perspectives* (London: Kluwer Law International, 1996).
71 *Canada Shipping Act*, above note 57; *Canada Shipping Act, 2001*, above note 2; AWPPA, above note 59; *Marine Liability Act*, S.C. 2001, c.6; *Navigable Waters Protection Act*, R.S.C. 1985, c.N-22 [NWPA]; *Canada Marine Act*, S.C. 1998, c.10.
72 Including the Canadian Coast Guard. *Canada Shipping Act, 2001*, above note 2. Shared jurisdiction with Transport Canada; *Fisheries Act*, R.S.C. 1985, c.F-14 as am.; *Oceans Act*, S.C. 1996, c.31; *Coastal Fisheries Protection Act*, R.S.C. 1985, c.C-33 [CFPA] as am.
73 *Canada Water Act*, R.S.C. 1985, c.C-11 as am.; *Canada Wildlife Act*, R.S.C. 1985, c.W-9 as am; *Migratory Birds Convention Act, 1994*, S.C. 1994, c.22; *Canadian Environmental Protection Act, 1999*, S.C. 1999, c.33 [CEPA 1999].
74 *Canada Oil and Gas Operations Act*, R.S.C. 1985, c.O-7. This jurisdiction is shared with Indian and Northern Affairs Canada, as well as the relevant provinces under applicable accord legislation. See below in D, "Marine Pollution: Offshore Energy Operations."

While Canada has not so far ratified *UNCLOS*, many of that treaty's provisions have been incorporated into Canadian law.[75] Although Canada's record in accepting international treaties is not always totally satisfactory, with a few exceptions, Canada has accepted and implemented the most important IMO conventions in this area.[76] In addition, Canada has also developed greater co-operation with the United States on transboundary marine pollution.[77]

B. MARINE POLLUTION: THE INTERNATIONAL OPERATIONAL REGIME

The operational regime for the prevention of ship-generated marine pollution consists of a large number of very technical international instruments. Their legal implications may be understood from the following brief overview of the most relevant conventions and agreements, including such information as may be applicable to Canadian practice. (A fuller discussion of Canadian law and enforcement in this area concludes this section.)

1) OILPOL 1954

The *OILPOL 1954*[78] convention has now been superseded by the *MARPOL 73/78* convention and is, therefore, no longer fully operational. However, as many states still adhere to this convention, it must still be considered as valid.[79] *OILPOL 1954* was the first international treaty designed exclusively to deal with ship-generated oil pollution and was widely accepted. It prohibits the intentional operational discharge of

---

75 *UNCLOS*, above note 1. See, e.g., D.L. Torrens, "Protection of the Marine Environment in International Law: Toward an Effective Regime of the Law of the Sea" (1994) 19 Queen's L.J. 613.
76 S. Hawkes & R.M. M'Gonigle, "A Black (and Rising?) Tide: Controlling Maritime Oil Pollution in Canada" (1992) 30 Osgoode Hall L.J. 165.
77 See L.A. Willis, "The Crown Zellerbach Case on Marine Pollution: National and International Dimensions" (1998) 26 Can. Y.B. Int'l Law 235; J. Woodward "International Pollution Control: The United States and Canada — the International Joint Commission" (1988) 9 N.Y.L. Sch.J. Int'l & Comp. L. 325.
78 Above note 5. As am. in 1962, 1969, and 1971 (entry into force on 26 July 1958; accepted by Canada). See *Oil Pollution Prevention Regulations*, above note 66.
79 Several states, including Canada, have accepted *MARPOL 73/78* but have not as yet denounced *OILPOL 1954*.

oil, oily mixtures, and residues from vessels in specified ocean areas. Ballast discharges have to be confined to permitted areas, and all loading and discharging operations must be recorded in an oil record book that can be inspected by government authorities.

2) Intervention

The 1969 *Intervention* convention[80] provides coastal states with limited rights to take preventive measures outside their coastal jurisdiction against vessels that are considered to present a grave and imminent danger to coastlines and other coastal interests from oil pollution as a result of a maritime casualty. The convention, which entered into force in 1975, is a significant departure from traditional international legal principles that did not permit any interference in the legitimate operations of vessels on the high seas. In other words, states other than the flag state of the vessel, are permitted to take preventive and mitigating action against such vessels on the high seas, provided that there is a realistic concern that oil pollution might result in major harmful consequences. In 1973, a protocol covering substances other than oil was concluded.[81] It should, however, be noted that this convention does not apply when there is no actual or threat of oil pollution. In other words, it would not apply to wreck removal in such cases. This is one of the reasons why an international regime relating to wreck removal is being developed.[82] The *Intervention* convention has not yet been accepted by Canada; however, the *Canada Shipping Act* has given effect to much of what it contains and Canada has actually used these powers on a number of occasions.[83] It should be noted that, under the *Intervention* con-

---

80 Above note 15 (including the protocol of 1973 and amendment of 1991).
81 *Protocol Relating to Intervention on the High Seas in Cases of Marine Pollution by Substances Other Than Oil, 1973*, 2 November 1973, 1313 U.N.T.S. 3 (entered into force 30 March 1983; not yet accepted by Canada); see *Ratification of Maritime Conventions*, above note 1 vol.I.7.80.
82 See Chapter 15, "Maritime Salvage and Wreck."
83 In the *Kurdistan* case off Nova Scotia and the *Nestucca* accident off British Columbia: see *Canada Shipping Act*, above note 57, s.655, which provides application to Canadian waters and waters in the exclusive economic zone of Canada, and also applies to Canadian ships even if outside Canadian waters; s.662, on powers of pollution prevention officers; and s.664, on offences. Under the *Canada Shipping Act, 2001*, above note 2, s.189, the minister is empowered to give directions to a ship discharging a pollutant if in or about to enter Canadian waters. See also *Canada Shipping Act, 2001*, above note 2, ss.174–80 on powers of pollution prevention officers in this area. In limited circumstances the jurisdiction of the *Canada Shipping Act* can be extended outside Canadian waters.

vention, only parties to the convention are authorized to take measures on the high seas when a marine casualty has occurred and danger exists to a marine coastline.[84]

3) LC 1972

The *LC 1972* convention[85] deals with dumping, that is, the deliberate disposal of wastes and other matter other than operational discharges from vessels and aircraft. The convention has been accepted by Canada and has been implemented through legislation.[86] It establishes categories of substances and materials that are restricted or prohibited to be discharged into the sea; for example, there is a complete prohibition of certain substances that are blacklisted, and permits are required for the dumping of greylisted substances; other substances require at least national approval before they may be dumped. A wide range of pollutants is covered and a number of enforcement measures are also included. *LC 1972* has, in recent years, assumed increasing importance as the sea is often, but mistakenly, considered as an effective waste disposal area, owing to diminishing waste disposal space ashore.

4) MARPOL 73/78

The *MARPOL 73/78* convention is the most important international operational marine pollution treaty in effect today, as it addresses almost all operational problems related to pollution from ships.[87] The convention entered into force in 1983 and has been widely accepted. A

---

84 However, under the *Canada Shipping Act*, there is no requirement for a marine casualty in order to act.
85 *LC 1972*, above note 22, am. in 1978, 1980, 1989, 1993, and 1996 (entered into force in Canada on 14 December 1975). The *1996 Protocol to the Convention on the Prevention of Marine Pollution by Dumping of Wastes and Other Matters, 1972*, 7 November 1996, 36 I.L.M. 7 (not yet in force, but accepted by Canada on 15 May 2000); see *Ratification of Maritime Conventions*, above note 1 vols.I.7.150 and 152; see also *Chorley & Giles*, above note 15 at 479; and J.H. Bates, *United Kingdom Marine Pollution Law* (London: Lloyd's Press, 1985) c.7.
86 *CEPA 1999*, above note 73. See also E.L. Hughes, "Ocean Dumping and its Regulation in Canada" (1988) 26 Can. Y.B. Int'l L. 155; and *Nanoose Conversion Campaign v. Canada (Minister of Environment)* (2000), 257 N.R. 287.
87 For full details on this convention, see Gold, above note 4, c.3; and De La Rue, above note 37 at 761ff. See also International Maritime Organisation, *MARPOL 73/78*, cons. ed. (London: IMO, 1992), IMO Publ. No.IMO-520E; IMO, *MARPOL 73/78* (London: IMO, 1994), IMO Publ. No.IMO-544E (1992 am.); and *Ratification of Maritime Conventions*, above note 1 vols.I.7.160 and 170.

protocol completed in 1978, generally known as the Tanker Safety and Pollution Protocol also entered into effect at the same time. Although it purports to be a simple amending instrument, it stands on its own and is, therefore, basically a separate convention. It is for this reason that the overall convention is always designated as *MARPOL 73/78*. The six annexes to the convention set out the actual preventive regulations:

Annex I   Regulations for the Prevention of Pollution by Oil,
Annex II Regulations for the Control of Pollution by Noxious Liquid Substances in Bulk,[88]
Annex III Regulations for the Prevention of Pollution by Harmful Substances carried by Sea in Packaged Form (entered into effect in 1992),[89]
Annex IV Regulations for the Prevention of Pollution by Sewage from Ships (entered into effect on 27 September 2003),[90]
Annex V   Regulations for the Prevention of Pollution by Garbage from Ships (entered into force in 1988),[91] and
Annex VI Regulations for the Prevention of Air Pollution from Ships (not yet in force).[92]

---

88 The *MARPOL* Annexes I/II had been accepted by 125 states, comprising 97 per cent of global shipping, as of 1 April 2003 (entered into force and accepted in Canada on 16 February 1993). See *Pollutant Substances Regulations*, above note 66; *Pollutant Discharge Reporting Regulations*, S.O.R./92-351 as am. However, Canada made a reservation related to its rights to legislate a special regime for Canadian Arctic waters.

89 Annex III had been accepted by 107 states, comprising 83 per cent of global shipping, as of 1 April 2003, but not yet accepted by Canada, although the regulations have been implemented. See *Dangerous Chemicals and Noxious Liquid Substances Regulations*, S.O.R./93-4; and *Dangerous Goods Shipping Regulations*, S.O.R./81-951.

90 Annex IV had been accepted by 91 states, comprising 51 per cent of global shipping, as of 1 April 2003, but not yet accepted by Canada, although the regulations have been implemented. See *Great Lakes Sewage Pollution Prevention Regulations*, C.R.C. 1978, c.1429; *Non-Pleasure Craft Sewage Prevention Regulations*, S.O.R./91-659 as am. by S.O.R./93-251, s.17; and *Pleasure Craft Sewage Prevention Regulations*, S.O.R./91-661 as am.

91 Annex V had been accepted by 107 states, comprising 89 per cent of global shipping, as of 1 April 2003, but not yet accepted by Canada, although the regulations have been implemented. See *Garbage Pollution Prevention Regulations*, C.R.C., c.1424 as am. by S.O.R./2000-37. See *R. v. Aqua Clean Ships* (1994), 12 C.E.L.R. (N.S.) 241 (B.C. Prov. Ct.).

92 Adopted in 1997 by the International Conference of Parties to *MARPOL 73/78*. Annex VI had been accepted by 6 states, comprising 26 per cent of global shipping, as of 1 April 2003.

It should be noted that the *MARPOL* Annexes III, IV, V, and VI have not yet been accepted by Canada; however, the complete convention is listed as a part of the *Canada Shipping Act, 2001*.[93] Also, Canada has implemented a number of regulations that cover requirements under these annexes.

5) Basel Convention 1989

The *Basel Convention 1989*[94] has indirect implications for shipping. This convention, which is administered by the Basel Convention Secretariat of the United Nations Environment Programme (UNEP),[95] addresses the growing regional and global trade in hazardous wastes. These substances are often transported from highly regulated states and regions to less regulated regions. There have been a number of cases where vessels that have loaded some of these substances as legitimate cargo have been unable to discharge them. The convention basically prohibits the international movement of such substances and directs states that are parties to the treaty to dispose of such materials within their own territories.[96] The convention was amended in 1995,[97] and a protocol to the convention was concluded in 1999.[98] Canada is a party to this treaty.

6) OPRC 1990

The *OPRC 1990* convention[99] resulted from the aftermath of The Exxon Valdez accident that revealed certain weaknesses in international response and preparedness when a major oil spill occurs. The convention, which entered into force in 1995,[100] sets out the requirements for

---

93 *Canada Shipping Act*, above note 57, s.658; *Canada Shipping Act, 2001*, above note 2, s.29(1).
94 Above note 34.
95 See Chapter 2, "The Shipping Industry: An Overview."
96 A.E. Chircop, "The Marine Transportation of Hazardous and Dangerous Goods in the Law of the Sea — An Emerging Regime" (1988) 11 Dal. L.J. 612; see also M. White, *Marine Pollution Laws of the Australasian Region* (Sydney: Foundation Press, 1994) at 111ff; and Gold, above note 4 at 43–44.
97 *Amendments to the Basel Convention on the Control of Transboundary Movements of Hazardous Wastes and their Disposal, 1989*, 22 September 1995, B.P.P. Misc. 18 (1996); not yet in force. See *Ratifications of Maritime Conventions*, above note 1 vol.I.7.222.
98 Liability and compensation are discussed below in C, "Marine Pollution: The International Liability and Compensation Regime."
99 Above note 40.
100 *OPRC 1990* had been accepted by 65 states, comprising 58 per cent of global shipping, as of 1 April 2003; see also Gold, above note 4 at 45–46; and De La Rue, above note 34 at 826–33.

onboard and land-based pollution emergency plans that vessels, offshore drilling units, and shore establishments must have. The convention also sets out requirements relating to mutual assistance and international cooperation in matters such as the exchange of information on the capabilities of states to respond to oil pollution incidents, the preparation of oil pollution emergency plans, the exchange of reports on incidents of significance that may affect the marine environment of states, as well as research and development on combatting oil pollution. Canada is a party to this agreement and has developed contingency plans for this purpose.[101] In 2000 an IMO conference also adopted the *HNS–OPRC Protocol 2000*, which not only augments the *OPRC 1990* but also the *HNS* convention. This protocol is not yet in force.[102]

7) Ballast Water Guidelines

For a number of years there has been concern about the danger of transferring potentially damaging organisms among regions of the world in the ballast water loaded and discharged by vessels. A number of IMO expert committees has studied and issued circulars on the subject from time to time. However, in late 1997, the IMO Assembly approved a resolution that set out the *Guidelines for the Control and Management of Ship's Ballast Water to Minimize the Transfer of Harmful Aquatic Organisms and Pathogens*.[103] Although only issued in voluntary form at this stage, these and similar guidelines are strictly enforced by a number of states in various regions of the world.[104] Canada has included ballast water as a "pollutant" under the *Canada Shipping Act*.[105] The IMO is currently developing a set of Ballast Water Management Regulations; it was originally planned that these would become a new *MARPOL* annex, but it now appears that they will form the basis of a new IMO convention to be concluded some time in 2004.

---

101 *Canada Shipping Act*, above note 57, s.660.9; *Canada Shipping Act, 2001*, above note 2, Sch.1.
102 See above note 51.
103 IMO Res. A. 868(20) (in IMO Publication IMO-661E).
104 Especially in Australia and the United States. See, e.g., J.M. Loy, "Ballast Water Management in the Unites States — A Coast Guard Perspective" in BIMCO Review 2000 (Copenhagen: BIMCO, 2000) at 100.
105 *Canada Shipping Act*, above note 57, s.657(1); and *Canada Shipping Act, 2001*, above note 2, ss.185 and 190. Ballast water control and management regulations have also been specifically created under the *Canada Shipping Act*, as am. S.C. 1998, c.6, s.18, in force since 31 October 1998.

8) Port State Control Systems[106]

In 1982 the maritime authorities of fourteen European states concluded the *Paris MOU 1982*[107] that sets out guidelines for an improved and harmonized system of port state control and strengthened co-operation in the exchange of critical information on ship safety and marine pollution prevention. In addition, this system also now targets substandard vessels that are not meeting the requirements of the *ISM Code*[108] and provides details of detained and banned vessels on its web site and in its detailed annual reports.[109] The success of the original *Paris MOU 1982* has also led to a number of other regions implementing similar agreements.[110] While data are already being transferred between some of the existing systems, it is expected that there will eventually be a full flow of data among all regions. As a result, the port state control system has already, and will in the future, significantly augment the traditional flag-state inspection system. There is no question that this system significantly strengthens the right of coastal states to ensure that substandard shipping is targeted for violations of the international regime for safer ships and cleaner seas. Canada has been a strong participant in this development and has acceded to both the original *Paris MOU 1982* as well as the *Tokyo MOU 1993*.[111] Transport Canada's Marine Safety Branch undertakes the Canadian quota of inspections required under the memoranda of understanding in all Canadian ports.[112]

9) Canadian Law and Enforcement

Canada has accepted the principal international treaties relating to operational activities in the shipping industry that may involve marine pollution. Although the federal government is not provided with express

---

106 Gold, above note 4 at 74–78. See discussion in D(3) of Chapter 5, "The Safety Management of Ships."
107 Above note 42.
108 Above note 47. See Chapter 2, "The Shipping Industry: An Overview" and D(2) in Chapter 5, "The Safety Management of Ships." See also Anderson, above note 48.
109 The MOU web site at time of publication was <http://www.parismou.org>.
110 MOUs have been concluded in Asia (*Tokyo MOU 1993*); Latin America (*Viña del Mar Agreement 1992*); the Caribbean region (1996); the Mediterranean region (1997); the Indian Ocean region (1998); the West and Central African region (1999); and the Black Sea region (2000). Additional MOUs are being negotiated for the East African region and the Persian/Arabian Gulf region.
111 See above notes 42 and 43.
112 See Transport Canada web site: <www.tc.gc.ca/marine safety>.

authority in the Canadian constitution to regulate or control marine pollution, the federal government may make the necessary regulations under its peace, order, and good government constitutional powers, as the subject has been judged by the Supreme Court of Canada to be a national concern.[113] Canada has set up a complex regulatory enforcement system under the jurisdiction of various ministries and departments as discussed below.

a) Transport Canada and Fisheries and Oceans Canada

Transport Canada has traditionally been the principal enforcement agency for regulations relating to ship safety and marine pollution prevention, and has jurisdiction under five federal acts: *Canada Shipping Act*,[114] *Canada Shipping Act, 2001*,[115] *Arctic Waters Pollution Prevention Act*,[116] *Navigable Waters Protection Act*,[117] and *Canada Marine Act*.[118]

i) Canada Shipping Act and Canada Shipping Act, 2001

Transport Canada has functioned for a long period under the *Canada Shipping Act*[119] and its predecessors. This Act is applicable to pollution incidents, offences, regulations relating to marine pollution, pollution prevention and response, pollution prevention personnel, pollution response organizations, standards, and measures to reduce/minimize pollution. This legislation gives effect to some of the international operational conventions, described above, to which Canada is a party, including *MARPOL 73/78*[120] and *OPRC 1990*. However, the new *Canada Shipping Act, 2001*[121] provides shared responsibility between Transport Canada[122] and Fisheries and Oceans Canada.[123] Transport Canada

---

113 *R. v. Crown Zellerbach Canada Ltd.*, [1988] 1 S.C.R. 401. See also Willis above note 77; and Chapter 3, "Admiralty Jurisdiction" for a discussion of the increased powers of the federal government in maritime matters.
114 Above note 57.
115 Above note 2.
116 Above note 59.
117 Above note 71.
118 *Ibid.*
119 Above note 57, Part XV. This part was amended by S.C. 1993, c.36, s.36, and S.C. 1996, c.31, s.101. As noted in E of Chapter 1, "Canadian Maritime Law: An Introduction," the regulations made under *Canada Shipping Act* will continue to be applicable until regulations under *Canada Shipping Act, 2001* are available.
120 Above note 23.
121 Above note 2.
122 *Canada Shipping Act, 2001*, *ibid.*, Part 8.
123 *Canada Shipping Act, 2001*, *ibid.*, Part 9.

will continue to have responsibility for the areas already outlined above under *Canada Shipping Act*.[124] Shared jurisdiction includes responsibilities for discharge of oil, amount of pollutants that can be carried by ships, the creation of response organizations, appointment of pollution prevention officers, appropriate response measures, and offences. Both agencies have jurisdiction, for instance, to detain vessels and to give directions, although, under the *Canada Shipping Act*, default jurisdiction is given to Transport Canada.[125] However, amendments to the 1985 Act already provided Fisheries and Oceans Canada with certain jurisdiction in such areas as[126] *OPRC* provisions, pollution prevention provisions, standards for oil handling facilities, and measures to remedy/minimize or prevent pollution. Under both *Canada Shipping Act*s, regulations cover, and are expected to cover, a number of areas including the following:

- Garbage Pollution Prevention Regulations,
- Non-Pleasure Craft Sewage Pollution Prevention Regulations,
- Oil Pollution Prevention Regulations,
- Pleasure Craft Sewage Pollution Prevention Regulations,
- Pollutant Substances Regulations, and
- Response Organization and Oil Handling Facilities Regulations.

This shared jurisdiction can be complex and confusing; care has to be taken with the relevant regulatory provisions until a standard system under the *Canada Shipping Act, 2001* eventually becomes available.

Transport Canada is also authorized to grant permits for the discharge of pollutants under the *Canadian Environmental Protection Act, 1999 (CEPA 1999)*.[127] In the event of a spill, Transport Canada has wide powers requiring full disclosure of information.[128] Pollution offences include discharge of polluting substances, contravention of oil pollution plan requirements, and refusal or failure to proceed as directed to a place to unload a pollutant.[129] The Canadian Coast Guard, now part of Fisheries and Oceans Canada, enforces regulations related to information on oil cargoes on board vessels, as well as required information

---

124 Many of the DFO regulatory duties will be carried out by the Coast Guard, now under DFO jurisdiction.
125 *Canada Shipping Act*, above note 57, s.2.
126 *Ibid.*, ss.660.1–660.11 and 678.
127 Above note 73, s.127; *Canada Shipping Act*, above note 57, s.656(2); *Canada Shipping Act, 2001*, above note 2, s.187.
128 *Canada Shipping Act, ibid.*, s.663; *Canada Shipping Act, 2001, ibid.*, s.189.
129 *Canada Shipping Act, ibid.*, ss.662 and 664–65; *Canada Shipping Act, 2001, ibid.*, ss.191–93.

on such vessels' insurers and pollution liability insurers.[130] In addition, Fisheries and Oceans Canada also administers enforcement provisions for shore-side oil-handling facilities, in order to ensure the existence and adequacy of oil pollution prevention plans, and to prevent any discharge of pollutants during loading and unloading operations.[131]

ii) AWPPA

Transport Canada also has responsibilities under the jurisdiction of the *Arctic Waters Pollution Protection Act (AWPPA)*.[132] This legislation basically establishes a marine pollution protection regime similar to that contained in the *Canada Shipping Act*, but specifically for an area enclosed by the sixtieth parallel of north latitude, the one hundred and forty-first meridian of west longitude, and a line measured seaward from the nearest Canadian coastline to a distance of 100 miles (185 km). The *AWPPA* also

- prohibits all waste disposals into Arctic waters,
- imposes special vessel equipment and crewing requirements,
- establishes a number of special vessel traffic zones within which specified types of vessels are restricted,[133]
- permits the removal or destruction of any vessel or cargo or bunkers of vessel when serious pollution discharge occurs,[134]
- provides for additional offences committed by persons and ships,[135] and
- permits seizure and forfeiture of ship and equipment in cases of pollution offences.[136]

Similar to their powers under the *Canada Shipping Act*, pollution prevention officers are also empowered by the *AWPPA* to inspect vessels and otherwise enforce the legislative provisions.[137]

iii) NWPA

The *Navigable Waters Protection Act (NWPA)*[138] provides Transport Canada with the necessary jurisdiction to protect Canadian coastal

---

130 *Canada Shipping Act*, ibid., ss.385, 422(2), 423–75, Part VII, ss.562.15–562.2, 660.1–660.11, and 678; *Canada Shipping Act, 2001*, ibid., ss.167(1) and (2).
131 *Canada Shipping Act*, ibid., ss.2 and 660.2(4); *Canada Shipping Act, 2001*, ibid., s.191. See also *R. v. Sun Diamond (The)*, [1984] 1 F.C. 3 (T.D.).
132 Above note 59.
133 *AWPPA*, ibid., s.12; *Shipping Safety Control Zones Order*, C.R.C., c.356.
134 *AWPPA*, ibid., s.13.
135 *AWPPA*, ibid., s.19.
136 *AWPPA*, ibid., s.23.
137 *AWPPA*, ibid., ss.15–23.
138 Above note 71.

waters from unauthorized dumping, works, or construction, as well as the removal of abandoned vessels. In other words, the principal task of this legislation is to keep Canadian waterways navigable. This has certain marine pollution implications especially in the case of unauthorized activities or abandoned vessels. The Act is complementary to the *Canada Shipping Act* and other anti-pollution legislation, and includes sanctions and fines for offences under the Act. It also places an obligation requiring notification if any illegal action under the NWPA has occurred.[139] The NWPA is also linked to the new *Canada National Marine Conservation Areas Act*,[140] which is under the jurisdiction of the Minister of Canadian Heritage. This legislation envisages the setting up of national marine conservation areas that are to be specifically protected against polluting and other deleterious activities.[141] The Act includes provisions on enforcement as well as sanctions for breaches.[142]

iv) *Canada Marine Act*[143]

The *Canada Marine Act* is closely related to the NWPA as it specifically deals with the setting up, jurisdiction, and responsibilities of port authorities in Canada. Under the Act, which is under Transport Canada jurisdiction, port authorities are given responsibility for ensuring order and safety, including pollution prevention, in port areas.[144] This also includes the necessary regulations, enforcement provisions, and sanctions for breaches.[145]

b) **Fisheries and Oceans Canada**

In addition to its shared jurisdiction with Transport Canada, Fisheries and Oceans Canada also has enforcement responsibility over marine pollution under other legislation within its jurisdiction, including the *Oceans Act*,[146] *Fisheries Act*,[147] and *Coastal Fisheries Protection Act* (*CFPA*).[148]

---

139 NWPA, ibid., s.6. See also *Margrande Co. Naviera SA v. Leacliffe Hall (The)*, [1970] Ex. C.R. 870.
140 S.C. 2002, c.18.
141 *Ibid.*, ss.12–14.
142 *Ibid.*, ss.18–28.
143 Above note 71.
144 *Canada Marine Act*, ibid., s.61.
145 *Ibid.*, ss.62 and 74, 109–16, and Part 3.
146 Above note 72.
147 *Oceans Act*, ibid.
148 *Ibid.*

i) Oceans Act

The *Oceans Act* is the principal legislative instrument setting out Canada's maritime jurisdiction. It not only establishes Canada's maritime zones[149] but also sets out the national maritime strategy, as well as the powers, duties, and functions of Fisheries and Oceans Canada. These powers and duties include the promulgation of regulations that are designed to protect Canada's maritime zones and marine protected areas from illegal activities, including pollution.[150] The *Oceans Act* links most other existing Canadian marine legislation and, thereby, provides what is envisaged as an all-encompassing legislative umbrella in the maritime area.

ii) Fisheries Act

Given the importance of the fisheries for the Canadian economy, it is not surprising that the *Fisheries Act* contains strict provisions designed to ensure that the marine environment, on which the fishery depends, is protected. Accordingly, the Act's section on Fish Habitat and Pollution Prevention contains specific provisions against marine pollution. The definition of "pollution" is almost identical to that contained in the *Canada Shipping Act, 2001*.[151] Furthermore, the enforcement provisions under the act are at least as strict as those contained in the *Canada Shipping Act*, and include severe penalties.[152]

iii) Coastal Fisheries Protection Act

The principal purpose of the *Coastal Fisheries Protection Act* is to implement an international agreement on fisheries and to protect Canadian coastal fisheries from illegal fishing activities. It also provides a regulatory framework that is designed to protect the coastal fishery from other illegal activities that would include operations that endanger the marine environment.[153]

c) **Environment Canada**

The federal ministry that is responsible for Canada's general environmental regulatory regime and that works in conjunction with its

---

149 These maritime zones include the territorial sea, exclusive economic zone, and continental shelf areas as authorized by *UNCLOS*, above note 1, although this treaty has not yet been accepted by Canada.
150 *Oceans Act*, above note 72, ss.37–39.
151 Above note 2, s.165.
152 *Fisheries Act*, above note 72, ss.35, 36, and 40.
153 *CFPA 1999*, above note 72, ss.5.3 and 6.2.

provincial/territorial counterparts is Environment Canada. It also has certain direct and indirect responsibilities for marine pollution through legislation under its jurisdiction, including *Canadian Environmental Protection Act, 1999*,[154] *Canada Water Act*,[155] *Canada Wildlife Act*,[156] and *Migratory Birds Convention Act, 1994*.[157]

i) *Canadian Environmental Protection Act, 1999*

The *Canadian Environmental Protection Act, 1999* (*CEPA 1999*) is an extensive Act that excercises very broad jurisdiction on almost all aspects of pollution prevention, and the protection of environmental and human health in order to contribute to sustainable development.[158] However, several sections in the Act specifically address water pollution, including disposal at sea,[159] international water pollution,[160] as well as the control of the movement of hazardous waste, hazardous recyclable material, and prescribed non-hazardous waste for final disposal.[161] *CEPA 1999* also contains specific enforcement provisions, including use of the *Criminal Code* and high fines.[162]

ii) *Canada Water Act*

The purpose of the *Canada Water Act* is best expressed through its preamble, which states:

> pollution of the water resources of Canada is a significant and rapidly increasing threat to the health, well-being and prosperity of the people of Canada and to the quality of the Canadian environment at large and as a result it has become a matter of urgent national concern that measures be taken to provide for water quality management.

The *Canada Water Act* is especially applicable to water quality management areas and includes enforcement provisions and fines.[163]

---

154 Above note 73.
155 *CEPA 1999*, ibid.
156 *Ibid.*
157 *Ibid.*
158 The Act responds in many ways to ideas proposed by the U.N. Rio Conference, above note 45.
159 *CEPA 1999*, above note 73, Div. 3.
160 *Ibid.*, Div. 7
161 *Ibid.*, Div. 8. This division of *CEPA 1999* deals with Canada's responsibilities under the *Basel Convention*, above note 34.
162 *CEPA 1999*, ibid., ss.220–21, 272–74, 287–90, and 295.
163 *Canada Water Act*, above note 73, ss.30–31 and 36.

iii) Canada Wildlife Act
The abundance of Canadian wildlife, especially in coastal and estuary areas, can be negatively affected by marine pollution. As a result, the *Canada Wildlife Act* contains regulatory and enforcement provisions that also include marine protected areas.[164]

iv) Migratory Birds Convention Act, 1994
The *Migratory Birds Convention Act, 1994*, implements Canada's obligation under a bilateral Canada–U.S. treaty designed to protect migrating birds that cross North American land and water areas. In particular the Act protects water areas where migrating birds congregate and prohibits any act, including pollution, in such inland waters and other marine areas. The Act contains enforcement provisions as well as sanctions.[165]

Even this rapid overview of the Canadian marine pollution regulatory system should provide an adequate illustration that marine pollution offences, even for minor spills, are vigorously prosecuted in Canada under one or more regulatory instruments. In general, if there is evidence of a spill, strict liability is applied;[166] even a defence of acting reasonably is not available,[167] and, prior to 1978, not even a defence of due diligence was acceptable. Since then it appears that, in cases of public welfare offences involving *prima facie* strict liability, the defence of due diligence may be accepted, if such a defence can be proven and if the wording of the regulatory provisions that have been breached permits such an interpretation.[168] Even though both ship and person in control are subject to prosecution,[169] if a spill is caused through the negligence of shore personnel, the ship should not be convicted, particularly if due diligence on the part of the ship can be established.[170]

---

164 *Canada Wildlife Act*, above note 73, ss.11, 13, 16, and 19.
165 *Migratory Birds Convention Act, 1994*, above note 73, ss.12–16 and 19.
166 *R v. Dilkara (The)*, [1974] 1 W.W.R. 258 (B.C.C.A.); *R. v. Caird* (1993), 16 Cr. L.Q. 112 (B.C. Co. Ct.); *R. v. Esso Resources Canada*, [1983] N.W.T.R. 59.
167 *R. v. MV Allunga*, [1977] 3 W.W.R. 673 (B.C.C.A.); *R. v. Star Luzon (The)*, [1984] 1 W.W.R. 527 (T.D.); see also *R. v. J.D. Irving Ltd.*, [1999] 2 F.C. 346.
168 *R. v. Sault Ste Marie*, [1978] 2 S.C.R. 1299. See also *R. v. M.T. Barbro* (1992), 121 N.B.R. (2d) 379, 304 A.P.R. 379 (Prov. Ct.); cf. *R. v. Aran (The)* (1973), 7 C.C.C. (2d) 562 (B.C.S.C.); *R. v. Wholesale Travel Group Inc.*, [1991] 3 S.C.R. 154; *Gulf Hathi (The) v. R.* (1981), 27 B.C.L.R. 92, 58 C.C.C. (2d) 481, 121 D.L.R. (3d) 359 (C.A.); *R. v. Glenshiel Towing Co.* (2001), 154 B.C.A.C. 310; and *R. v. M/V Humber Arm (The)* (2000), N.S. Prov. Ct. Case #878518, 19 January 2000 [unreported].
169 *R. v. Westfalia (The)*, [1975] 2 W.W.R. 134, 54 D.L.R. (3d) 412 (B.C.C.A.).
170 *R. v. MV Point Vibert (The)*, [2000] N.S.J. No. 147 (Prov. Ct.) (QL); but cf. *Newfoundland Processing v. South Angela (The)*, [1997] 1 F.C. 154 (T.D.).

C. MARINE POLLUTION: THE INTERNATIONAL LIABILITY AND COMPENSATION REGIME

The traditional liability system for maritime accidents was never considered suitable for marine pollution claims that involved strict liability and could involve claims for catastrophic damage.[171] Nevertheless, until 1969, there was no specific liability regime for ship-generated pollution damage. There were only some general national laws, such as port regulations and rules related to nuisance, with commensurate moderate fines, that could be applied if required.[172] However, there were no international agreements that specifically addressed liability and compensation for pollution damage. Liability for such damage was, generally, considered to be strictly based on the traditional principle of fault. As a result, the offending vessel's financial liability was usually limited to the ship's liability tonnage as set out under the *International Convention Relating to the Limitation of the Liability of Owners of Seagoing Ships, 1957*.[173] However, the limitation amounts available were considered to be insufficient by many states generally, and for oil pollution claims specifically. This led to a series of new liability regimes.[174]

1) CLC 1969

The *International Convention on Civil Liability for Oil Pollution Damage, 1969 (CLC 1969)*,[175] provides a uniform set of international rules and procedures for determining liability and, as a consequence, also provides compensation to those who have suffered damage caused by the escape or discharge of oil from ships. The convention was revised by protocols in 1976, 1984, and 1992. Under the 1976 protocol,[176] the liability limits

---

171 See Chapter 18, "Limitation of Liability for Maritime Claims." But see *Canada Shipping Act*, above note 57, s.678.1; *Canada Shipping Act, 2001*, above note 2, s.181; and the *Marine Liability Act*, above note 71, Part 6, providing details on liability for marine pollution. See also Gauci, above note 18 for a full analysis of the current civil liability and compensation system for marine pollution damage; also De La Rue, above note 37.
172 *Esso v. Southport Corporation*, [1956] A.C. 218.
173 10 October 1957, 1412 U.N.T.S. 73 (entered into force on 31 May 1968; never accepted by Canada); see also *Ratification of Maritime Conventions*, above note 1 vol.I.2.310. See also Chapter 18, "Limitation of Liability for Maritime Claims."
174 P.D. Lowry, "The Ship Owner and Oil Pollution Liability" (1972) 18 McGill L.J. 577.
175 Above note 14; see Gauci, above note 18; De La Rue, above note 37, c.2.
176 *Protocol to the International Convention on Civil Liability for Oil Pollution Damage, 1969*, 19 November 1976, 1225 U.N.T.S. 356 [*CLC Prot 1976*] (entered into

were changed from the original gold standard of monetary calculation to the special drawing rights (SDR) of the International Monetary Fund. The 1984 protocol attempted to raise the liability limits and extend jurisdiction to the exclusive economic zone beyond states' territorial seas, but this attempt failed and the 1984 protocol did not enter into force. Nevertheless, a further, similar attempt, in 1992, was successful;[177] this protocol not only raised compensation limits substantially but also based the limitation tonnage on the vessel's gross tonnage.

a) Pollution from Ships

Only oil carried in bulk as cargo is covered under the convention and vessels in ballast are not covered under the original *CLC 1969*. However, under the *CLC Prot 1992*, "convention vessels" in ballast are covered as long as there are residues of the previous oil cargo on board. Bunker oil is covered only if it is carried as cargo, or if it escapes from a "convention vessel."[178] Liability for damage from pollution is strict and is placed on the shipowner.[179] In other words, proof of negligence is not required. The only exceptions available are where the shipowner proves that the damage

- resulted from an act of war, hostilities, civil war, or insurrection;
- resulted from a natural phenomenon of an exceptional, inevitable, or irresistible character;
- was wholly caused by an act or omission done with intent to cause damage by a third party; or
- was wholly caused by the negligence or other wrongful act of any government or other authority responsible for the maintenance of lights or other navigational aids in exercise of that function.

Actual pollution damage is defined in *CLC 1969* as follows:

> Loss or damage caused outside the ship by contamination resulting from the escape or discharge of oil from a ship, wherever such escape

---

force on 8 April 1981 and in Canada on 24 April 1989); see *Ratification of Maritime Conventions*, above note 1 vol.I.7.40.

177 *Protocol to Amend the International Convention on Civil Liability for Oil Pollution Damage, 1969*, 27 November 1992, U.K.T.S. 1996 No. 87 [*CLC Prot 1992*] (entered into force on 30 May 1996, and in Canada on 29 September 1999); see *Ratification of Maritime Conventions*, above note 1 vol.I.7.51.

178 *CLC 1969*, above note 14, art.I(1).

179 This confirms the Canadian jurisprudence (referred to above in B(9), "Canadian Law and Enforcement"); see *R. v. Sault Ste Marie*, above note 168; *R. v. City of Guildford* (1975), 27 C.C.C. (2d) 212 (Ont. Co. Ct.); *R. v. Himmerland* (1973), 2 C.E.L.R. 17; *Reference Re s.92 Motor Vehicle Act*, [1982] 2 S.C.R. 486; *R. v. Dilkara (The)*, above note 166; and *Gulf Hathi (The) v. R.*, above note 168.

or discharge may occur, [and includes] the costs of preventive measures and further loss or damage caused by preventive measures.

In general, all quantifiable damage claims are accepted. This includes contamination of property, fishing boats and gear, recreational boats, beaches, piers, and other coastal property.[180] Also included is economic loss suffered by those who depend directly upon earnings from coastal and sea-related activities. Furthermore, claims for salvage and oil recovery operations, including preventive measures, are also covered. However, difficulties arise with the proper assessment and quantification of damage to the marine environment, as the marine environment as a whole does not have a discernible, or easily quantifiable, market value.[181] As a result, claims in this area can only be accepted if a claimant, with a legal right to claim under national law, has suffered an assessable economic loss.

The convention only applies to damage caused in the territory and waters of states that have accepted the treaty. The flag state or the vessel owner's state need not be parties to the convention. Under the *CLC Prot 1992*, pollution damage is extended to a contracting state's exclusive economic zone that is established in accordance with international law or, if a state has not established such a zone, to an area beyond and adjacent to the territorial sea of that state, but not more than 200 nautical miles (370 km) from the baselines from where the territorial sea is measured.[182] The *CLC Prot 1992* defines oil as any "persistent" oil such as crude, fuel, heavy, diesel, lubricating, or whale oil.[183] Non-persistent oils and oil products, such as gasoline, kerosene, and distillates, are not covered; nor are liquid chemicals and other hazardous and noxious substances. In cases where oil escapes from two or more ships, the owners of such vessels are jointly and severally liable, subject to the

---

180 *Outhouse v. Thorshavn (The)*, [1935] Ex. C.R. 120, 4 D.L.R. 628.
181 De La Rue, above note 37 Part III; see also E. Gold, "Compensation for Ship-Source Marine Pollution: A Hypothetical Case Study" in M. J. Valencia, et al., eds., *Shipping, Energy, and Environment: Southeast Asian Perspectives for the Eighties* (Halifax: Dalhousie Ocean Studies Program, 1982) at 261.
182 *CLC Prot 1992*, above note 177, art.3.
183 "Persistent oil" has been defined as "oil that, at the time of shipment, consists predominantly of non-residual fractions and of which more than 50 per cent by volume distils at a temperature of 340°C when tested by the STM method D86/78 or any subsequent revision." See Gold, above note 4 at 225, for a more detailed description of persistent oils. Whale oil has been removed under the *CLC Prot 1992*, ibid.

defences stated above, for all pollution damage that is not reasonably separable.[184] Nevertheless, a malicious act or omission, or negligence on the part of the party suffering pollution damage, may wholly or partly exonerate the shipowner from liability.[185] On the other hand, the shipowner's liability covers damage resulting from the escape or discharge of oil, as well as the costs of preventive measures taken to prevent or minimize pollution damage.[186] Unless the pollution incident occurred owing to the shipowner's actual fault or privity,[187] the shipowner's liability is limited as follows:

- Under the *CLC 1969*: 2,000 Poincaré francs/ton, or 210 million Poincaré francs, whichever is the lesser amount.[188]
- Under the *CLC Prot 1976*: 133 SDR/ton, or 14 million SDR, whichever is the lesser amount.[189]
- Under the *CLC Prot 1992*:
  - Vessel up to 5,000 GT: 3 million SDR.[190]
  - Vessel more than 5,000 GT: 420 SDR/ton up to a ceiling of 59.7 million SDR.[191]

"Fault or privity" are commonly defined as knowledge and consent in relation to any fault, defect, or misconduct. However, the *CLC Prot 1992* introduces a tighter test that must be satisfied if the shipowner is to be deprived of the right to limit. It will have to be proved "that the pollution damage resulted from his personal act or omission, committed with intent to cause such damage, or recklessly and with knowledge that such damage would probably result."[192] Under the *CLC 1969* liability is channelled only to the registered owners of the polluting vessel. This protects other service providers, such as ship managers, officers, crew members, and pilots, from being held liable. This also means that only the party to whom liability will be channelled is required to take out the necessary compulsory insurance cover.

The *CLC 1969* also provides that the shipowner, whose liability in this area is normally covered under the protection and indemnity pol-

---

184 *CLC 1969*, above note 14, art.IV.
185 *Ibid.*, art.III(3).
186 *Ibid.*, arts.I(6) and III(1).
187 See Chapter 18, "Limitation of Liability for Maritime Claims" on the general regime of limitation of liability under the 1957 and 1967 Limitation Conventions.
188 *CLC 1969*, above note 14, art.V.
189 *CLC Prot 1976*, above note 176, art.2.
190 Expressed as units of account.
191 *CLC Prot 1992*, above note 177, art.6.
192 *Ibid.*, art.6(2).

icy,[193] is required to constitute a fund for the total sum representing the liability exposure. Under the *CLC Prot 1992*, this involves a relatively simple calculation. The vessel's gross tonnage is multiplied by the relevant unit of account (i.e., SDR) for the ship's tonnage up to a permitted limitation ceiling. This fund is then deposited, in the form of either actual funds or an acceptable guarantee, with the court or other appropriate authority in the contracting state or states where the claim for damage is being brought. The establishment of the fund is the basis on which limitation of liability is permitted by the *CLC 1992*. Unless limitation is subsequently denied, this fund will be the sole source for meeting damage claims arising out of the incident. Furthermore, no proof is required on the right to limit liability. Accordingly, if the vessel alleged to have caused the pollution damage is arrested, it must be released once the fund is constituted. The funds payable are distributed rateably to claimants, in proportion to their respective proven or quantified claims. For these purposes, the vessel owner's claim for the recovery of expenses involved in preventive measures ranks equally with other claims against the constituted fund.[194] A claimant must commence action against the shipowner within three years of the date on which the damage occurred. However, no action may be commenced after a period of six years, from the date when the incident that caused the damage occurred, has elapsed.[195]

In order to be covered under the *CLC 1992*, the vessel registered in a *CLC* state and carrying more than 2,000 tons of oil in bulk as cargo must carry commensurate insurance or other financial security up to the limits required for such vessels, as well as certificates confirming the existence of such liability coverage. *CLC* certificates are today demanded by most states as evidence of adequate coverage.[196] The certificate, a copy of which must be kept on board, contains certain specific details of the insurance coverage and must be obtained by the shipowner from the maritime authorities of the state of registry. The certificate is in a prescribed form and will normally name the liability insurer (usually the vessel's protection and indemnity insurer) or other party providing financial security for the shipowner's financial liability for pollution damage. As a result, any claim under the *CLC 1992* for pollution damage may be made directly against the insurer named in the certificate.

---

193 See Chapter 7, "Marine Insurance."
194 See De La Rue, above note 37 at 108–12; *Chorley & Giles*, above note 15 at 483ff.
195 *CLC 1969*, above note 14, art.VIII.
196 *Ibid.*, art.VII.

This also means that such insurer would have access to any defences or limitation of liability that the shipowner would have been able to invoke. In addition, the insurer may also join the shipowner as a third party to such claims.

b) Pollution from Floating Storage Units and Floating Production, Storage, and Offloading Units

Floating storage units and floating production, storage, and offloading units have been developed fairly rapidly in the last decade, as a new and economic way of storing and exploiting energy resources, especially offshore. Such units that can be moved easily from one location to another, provide an efficient and economic alternative to fixed platforms, pipelines, and onshore storage facilities. However, the legal question that arises is whether such units constitute a "ship" within the meaning of the *CLC*; the test appears to be whether *CLC 1969*[197] or the *CLC Prot 1992*[198] applies. Furthermore, even then, the answer is not entirely clear.[199] *CLC 1969* applies only if the unit is "actually carrying oil in bulk as cargo." However, the records of the IMO conference that developed the convention do not contain any indication that storage of oil afloat was considered, and it appears that "carrying oil as cargo" means that it was understood to be conveyed from one place to another. In other words, although spills from a vessel involved in carrying oil in bulk from one point to another will be covered, even if such a vessel is stationary, at anchor, or otherwise idle, spills from a vessel used to store oil are not covered under *CLC 1969*.

Under the *CLC Prot 1992*, although there appears to be more flexibility in including oil spills from floating storage units and floating production, storage, and offloading units, this is not entirely clear, as this issue was also not considered at the 1984 IMO conference that developed this protocol. Under the *CLC Prot 1992*, coverage for spills is available even where the vessel is not "actually carrying oil in bulk as cargo" but is "constructed and adapted" to do so.[200] It follows that, if this is so, the actual use to which the vessel is being put at the time of the incident should, in principle, not affect the issue. Nevertheless, it is less clear what types of vessels or structures would come within such a definition, particularly given the fact that floating storage units and

---

197 Above note 14.
198 Above note 177.
199 See De La Rue, above note 37 at 81.
200 *Ibid.* at 81.

floating production, storage, and offloading units have become very diverse. The general conclusion appears to be that each incident would be examined on a case-by-case basis. It has been suggested that these floating units did not normally fall within the scope of *CLC Prot 1992*[201] and *FUND Prot 1992*,[202] but that there was a possibility that some units might fall within such scope in particular circumstances.[203] The position taken by the International Group of P&I Clubs[204] is as follows:

- Craft constructed or adapted for production operations should not normally be considered ships within the meaning of *CLC Prot 1992*.
- Craft should not fall outside the scope of the definition on the mere ground that it is constructed or adapted for storage; and the floating storage unit should be capable of being considered to be a ship.

CLC Prot 1992 should not apply to incidents involving oil held in storage; but, where the craft is a ship, the convention should apply to movements of oil leading to discharge at another location.[205]

2) FUND 1971

The *International Convention on the Establishment of an International Fund for Compensation for Oil Pollution Damage, 1971* (*FUND 1971*) entered into force in 1978.[206] The main purpose of the *FUND 1971* convention is to provide supplementary compensation for claimants who are unable to obtain full compensation under the *CLC* and, until recently, to indemnify shipowners for a portion of their *CLC* liability. Under the convention, an intergovernmental organization to administer the *FUND 1971*, the International Oil Pollution Compensation Fund (IOPCF) was also established.[207] States that accept the *FUND 1971* con-

---

201 Above note 177.
202 *Protocol to Amend the International Convention on the Establishment of an International Fund for Compensation for Oil Pollution Damage, 1971*, 27 November 1992, 1996 A.T.S. 3 [*FUND Prot 1992*] (entered into force on 30 May 1996, and in Canada on 29 May 1999); see *Ratification of Maritime Conventions*, above note 1 vol.I.7.111.
203 *Ibid.* at 83.
204 See G(2)(j) in Chapter 2, "The Shipping Industry: An Overview" and Chapter 7, "Marine Insurance."
205 "Applicability of the 1992 Conventions to Offshore Craft" (note by the International Group of P&I Clubs to the IOPC Fund, IOPC Fund Doc. 92FUND/WGR.2/2/2 of 9 April 1999).
206 Above note 17. See also *Marine Liability Regulations*, above note 68, Part 1. See Gold, above note 4 at 80; De La Rue, above note 37 at 69–73 and 127–28; *Chorley & Giles*, above note 15 at 486–88.
207 See G(1)(e)(ix) in Chapter 2, "The Shipping Industry: An Overview."

vention are automatically members of the IOPCF. The *FUND 1971* is financed by a levy applicable to parties, such as oil companies, that receive persistent oil in *FUND 1971* member states via sea transport.[208] Three *FUND* protocols, completed in 1976, 1984,[209] and 1992,[210] are quite similar in scope to the *CLC* protocols that were concluded at the same time. The 1976 protocol[211] changed the monetary standard from the Poincaré gold franc to the unit of account or special drawing rights (SDR) of the International Monetary Fund; the 1984 protocol attempted, but failed, to raise the convention's limits and scope of applicability; but the 1992 Protocol succeeded in achieving what had been attempted in 1984.[212] Under the original *FUND*, agreement shipowners were permitted to recover increased *CLC* limits from the *FUND*; however, in reality, the *FUND* only provided shipowners with about 25 per cent of their total *CLC* liability. This indemnification was paid by the *FUND* in addition to payments under the general claims provisions. However, the *FUND Prot 1992* abolished this relief provision. As a result, such relief is only available in cases where the *FUND Prot 1992* is not applicable. The *FUND* convention provides compensation to any claimant who has suffered oil pollution damage in cases where full compensation is not available under the *CLC*, for the following reasons:

- No liability arises under the *CLC*, as the shipowner is protected by one or more of the CLC exemptions.
- The shipowner is financially unable to meet the *CLC* obligations, and the available insurance coverage is insufficient.
- The damage exceeds the shipowner's *CLC* liability.

Most claims will fall within the last category. The *FUND* convention provides the following compensation limits:

---

208 Canadian contributions to *FUND* are made by the Ship-Source Oil Pollution Fund, Ottawa: see below in C(8), "Canadian Law and Policy."
209 *Protocol of 1984 to Amend the International Convention on the Establishment of an International Fund for Compensation for Oil Pollution Damage, 1971*, 25 May 1984, 23 I.L.M. 195 [*FUND Prot 1984*] (not yet in force and not likely to be as it has been superseded by *FUND Prot 1992*); see also *Ratification of Maritime Conventions*, above note 1 vol.I.7.50.
210 Above note 202. This protocol effectively supersedes the original *FUND* provisions. See De La Rue, above note 37 at 128ff.
211 *Protocol of 1976 to the International Convention on the Establishment of an International Fund for Oil Pollution, 1971*, 19 November 1976, 16 I.L.M. 621 [*FUND Prot 1976*] (entered into force on 22 November 1994 and in Canada on 22 May 1995); see also *Ratification of Maritime Conventions*, above note 1 vol.I.7.100.
212 Gold, above note 4 at 80–81; De La Rue, above note 37, c.3.

- Under *FUND 1971* (until 1979): up to a maximum amount of 450 million Poincaré francs.[213]
- Under *FUND 1971* (1979–87): up to a maximum amount of 675 million Poincaré francs.
- Under *FUND 1971* (1987–94): up to a maximum amount of 900 million Poincaré francs.[214]
- Under *FUND Prot 199*: up to a maximum of 135 million SDRs.[215]

The IOPCF will pay compensation claims that are justified and meet the *FUND* criteria. In order to do this the claimant must follow a set procedure by producing documentation to support the claim.[216] In settling claims the IOPCF works and co-operates closely with the shipowner's P&I club. In many cases, the investigation, evaluation, and quantification of the damage is generally a joint IOPCF and P&I club exercise pursuant to a memorandum of understanding completed in 1980 between the two entities. Accordingly, claims need only be presented once. In general, the claims procedure under the *FUND* is quite similar to that under the *CLC*. However, in practice, *FUND* claims may, at times, be treated with more flexibility than *CLC* claims that may require court or arbitral resolution.

FUND claims are usually handled in accordance with the precedents set by prior *FUND* claims. When new issues arise, the IOPCF convenes a meeting of its members in order to determine the proper course of action. The IOPCF has accumulated significant expertise in handling claims, which can also provide guidance for many *CLC* claims. This is especially important for claims involving general damage to the marine environment. For example, the IOPCF has so far vigorously and successfully resisted claims that attempted to assert value for the marine environment on the basis of abstract or theoretical models. In other words, *FUND* claims must be real and quantifiable. It should be noted that the IOPCF system is at present under review. This is one of the consequences of The Erika disaster that caused serious

---

213 *FUND*, above note 17, art.4(4)(b).
214 *Ibid.*, art.4(6).
215 *FUND Prot 1992*, above note 202, art.4(a). In cases where at least three IOPC Fund members have received at least 600 million tons of contributing oil in the previous year, this limit may be increased to 200 million SDRs. This ceiling has not so far been activated.
216 This procedure is set out in the *IOPC FUND Claims Manual*. See Gold, above note 4 App.IX; and M. Jacobsson, "The International Regime of Compensation for Oil Pollution Damage and the Policy of the International Oil Pollution Compensation Funds as to the Admissibility of Claims" (2002) 1 W.M.U.J. Mar. Aff. 59.

pollution to the French coastline in December 1999.[217] As the pollution damage from that spill was expected to significantly exceed the standard *FUND* limits, the increase mechanism that has been built into the system, as a tacit amendment procedure, was triggered. In addition, the IOPCF set up a working group to make recommendations on further action. Furthermore, a number of member states also requested that the IOPCF review the international compensation regime as soon as possible.[218] After its second meeting the International Oil Pollution Compensation Fund Working Group submitted a report, which contained a recommendation that the IOPCF should set up a third tier of compensation that would be voluntary and would only be applicable to those countries that accepted such a protocol.[219] Although this recommendation was controversial, it was sent to the IMO with a recommendation that the subject be placed before a diplomatic conference.[220] It is, therefore, quite likely that some substantial changes to the *FUND* system will be put in place sooner rather than later.

3) *LLMC 1976*

The legal aspects of shipowner's limitation of liability are addressed, in some detail, in Chapter 18. This subject also has some relevance in the area of marine pollution claims. Under the *Convention on Limitation of Liability for Maritime Claims, 1976 (LLMC 1976)*,[221] claims for oil pollution damage within the meaning of the *CLC* and *FUND* conventions are specifically excluded.[222] This means, however, that claims for pollution damage falling outside these conventions must be brought under *LLMC 1976*. Furthermore, until the *HNS 1996*[223] convention enters into

---

217 See E. Gold, "Ship-Source Marine Pollution: Testing the Viability of the International Liability and Compensation System" in *BIMCO Review 2001* (Copenhagen: BIMCO, 2001) at 130. At present, the regime is undergoing additional scrutiny in the aftermath of The Prestige disaster off Spain in November 2002.
218 See Ship-Source Oil Pollution Fund, *Ship-Source Oil Pollution Fund: Administrator's Annual Report 2001–2002* (Ottawa: SOPF, 2002) at 73 [*SOPF Report*].
219 "Report on the Second Meeting of the Third International Working Group," IOPCF Doc: 92FUND/WGR.3/6. 30 March 2001.
220 *SOPF Report*, above note 218 at 75.
221 19 November 1976, 1456 U.N.T.S. 221 (entered into force 1 December 1986, but not accepted by Canada); see *Ratification of Maritime Conventions*, above note 1 vol.I.2.330. See also Chapter 18, "Limitation of Liability for Maritime Claims." As of 1 April 2003, *LLMC 1976* had been accepted by 40 states, comprising 44 per cent of world tonnage.
222 *LLMC 1976*, ibid., art.3.
223 Above note 51. See below in C(5), "*HNS 1996*."

force, claims for pollution damage from substances other than oil will also have to be made under *LLMC 1976*. Although the 1957 limitation convention[224] has been superseded by *LLMC 1976*, it is still fairly widely accepted.[225] Nevertheless, *LLMC 1976* is today the principal treaty in this area.[226] A protocol concluded in 1996, which raised the limitation amounts and provides for speedier amendment, is not yet in force.[227]

4) Nuclear 1971

Although the carriage of nuclear material at sea is on the increase, it still only comprises a very small percentage of goods moved by maritime transport. However, the damage potential is sufficiently serious for it to merit its own regime. The *Convention Relating to Civil Liability in the Field of Maritime Carriage of Nuclear Material, 1971* (*Nuclear 1971*) has been in effect since 1975.[228] This convention is basically designed to complement the Paris and Vienna conventions on nuclear damage liability,[229] which provide that, in the case of damage caused by a nuclear incident occurring during the maritime carriage of nuclear materials, the operator of a related nuclear installation is liable for such damage. Accordingly, the *Nuclear 1971* convention confirms the regime of strict liability for damage arising out of the carriage of nuclear materials at sea in specific terms. This is an area requiring special insurance coverage.

---

224 See Chapter 18, "Limitation of Liability for Maritime Claims."
225 This would include states that have accepted *LLMC 1976* but have failed to denounce the 1957 treaty.
226 Canada has not acceded to *LLMC 1976*, but its principles have been fully accepted and incorporated into the *Marine Liability Act*, above note 71, Part 3. See also Chapter 18, "Limitation of Liability for Maritime Claims."
227 *Protocol of 1996 to Amend the Convention on Limitation of Liability for Maritime Claims, 1976*, 3 May 1996, 35 I.L.M. 1406; see *Ratification of Maritime Conventions*, above note 1 vol.I.2.340. This protocol is enacted by Canada under the *Canada Shipping Act, 2001*, above note 2.
228 17 December 1971, 974 U.N.T.S. 255 (entry into force on 15 July 1975; not accepted by Canada, although probably covered under *Canada Shipping Act* and *Marine Liability Act* provisions); as of 1 April 2003, *Nuclear 1971* had only been accepted by 16 states, comprising 20 per cent of world tonnage.
229 *Convention on Third Party Liability in the Field of Nuclear Energy*, 29 July 1960, 956 U.N.T.S. 251; and *Additional Protocol to the Convention on Third Party Liability in the Field of Nuclear Energy*, 1960, 28 January 1964, 956 U.N.T.S. 335; *Convention Supplementary to the Convention on Third Party Liability in the Field of Nuclear Energy of 1960*, 31 January 1963, 1041 U.N.T.S. 358.

5) HNS 1996

Substances other than oil can cause pollution damage that is at least as, or more, serious than that caused by oil. MARPOL 73/78 now covers substances other than oil in operational terms, but liability for damage is not covered by the international regimes in place at present. In any case, there are substantial practical differences between the carriage of oil and that of hazardous and noxious substances. The carriage of oil in bulk involves a relatively small number of specialized vessels. On the other hand, most ships can carry hazardous and noxious cargoes. Because such cargoes can be carried so widely, there are still difficulties for many states on how to properly identify hazardous and noxious materials as well as what quantities of such cargo need to be carried before a contribution to the fund is triggered. After many years of preparation, and the failure of a first attempt to conclude a convention in 1984,[230] the *International Convention on Civil Liability and Compensation for Damage in Connection with the Carriage of Hazardous and Noxious Substances by Sea, 1996* (HNS 1996) was concluded.[231] The convention is not yet in force and it is likely that some years will pass before this occurs, as the entry-into-force provisions are quite complex. Nevertheless, this chapter provides an overview, as it is an extremely important instrument and is likely to be accepted by Canada before it officially enters into force.[232] The convention can only enter into force eighteen months after it has been accepted by at least twelve states, including four states each with not less than 4 million GT of shipping, and after the secretary general of the IMO has received information indicating that states that had previously received over 20,000 tonnes of HNS 1996 materials, have received during the preceding calendar year a total quantity of at least 40 million tonnes of cargo.[233] The convention defines hazardous and noxious substances as follows:

- oils carried in bulk as listed in *MARPOL* Appendix I, Annex I;
- noxious liquid substances carried in bulk as listed in *MARPOL* Appendix II, Annex II, as well as substances categorized under regulation 3(4) of *MARPOL* Annex II;

---

230 See Gold, above note 4 at 82 and 242; De La Rue, above note 37 Part II.
231 Above note 51. For full details on the *HNS* compensation regime, see De La Rue, *ibid.*
232 Canada has already imposed obligations on shipowners for spills of noxious chemicals and permits government agencies to recover costs for spill prevention and cleanup. See *Marine Liability Act*, above note 71.
233 As of 1 April 2003, *HNS 1996* had been accepted by only 3 states, comprising less than 2 per cent of world shipping.

- dangerous liquid substances carried in bulk as listed in Chapter 17 of the *International Code for the Construction and Equipment of Ships Carrying Dangerous Chemicals in Bulk, 1994 (INC Code)*;[234]
- dangerous, hazardous, and harmful substances, materials, and articles in packaged form covered under the *International Maritime Dangerous Goods Code, 1994 (IMDG Code)*;[235]
- liquefied gases as listed in Chapter 19 of the *International Code for the Construction of Ships Carrying Liquefied Gases in Bulk, 1993 (IGC Code)*;[236]
- Liquid substances carried in bulk with a flashpoint not exceeding 60°C;
- solid bulk materials possessing chemical hazards covered under the *Code of Safe Practice for Solid Bulk Cargoes*, Appendix B;[237] and
- residues from any of the materials or substances listed above.[238]

It should, however, be noted that numerous substances, such as coal and ore, are not included in this listing, despite the fact that they may be hazardous in terms of damage potential. It seems that in referring to "loss of life or personal injury on board," HNS 1996 appears to be more concerned with substances that cause damage to other materials and to the environment, owing to their inherent nature, as opposed to causing damage to the vessel from physical causes, such as shifting cargo and spontaneous combustion.

The convention, in general, follows some of the two-tier principles established under the *CLC* and *FUND* regimes for oil pollution. The first-level of coverage is as follows:

- Vessels up to 2,000 GT: 10 million SDR
- Vessels 2,001–50,000 GT: 1,500 SDR/GT in addition
- Vessels more than 50,000 GT: 360 SDR/GT in addition up to 100 million SDR.[239]

At the second level the convention establishes the International Hazardous and Noxious Substances Fund (*HNS 1996* Fund), to be administered by an assembly and a secretariat, similar to the IOPCF system. The *HNS 1996* Fund will become available when the first level is either

---

234 IMO Publication Res. A.212(VII) (IMO: London).
235 Including 1994 and 1996 amendments and supplements: IMO Res. A.120(V), IMO Publication. (IMO: London 1994) Sales No.IMO-200E.
236 IMO Publication Res. A.328(IX).
237 IMO Publication Res. A.434(XI).
238 *HNS 1996*, above note 51, art.1(5).
239 *Ibid.*, art.9(1).

unavailable or insufficient to meet damage claims and would boost compensation to a maximum of 250 million SDR.[240]

HNS 1996 provides the shipowner with the standard defences, similar to those available for oil pollution claims. The convention is not applicable to pollution damage as defined under the *CLC/FUND* regimes, nor for damage caused by radioactive material of class 7 of either the *IMDG Code* or the *Code of Safe Practice for Bulk Cargoes*, Appendix B. The territorial scope of application of the convention is also similar to the 1992 *CLC/FUND* regimes. Again, like *CLC* requirements, vessels will be required to carry a compulsory HNS 1996 Certificate, indicating that liability insurance or other financial security is in place in accordance with the convention's requirements. The HNS 1996 convention is unique in the fact that, for the first time, a liability convention combines the interests of carrier, manufacturer, shipper, and relevant state. It remains to be seen how it will operate in actual practice once it enters into force.[241]

6) Pollution from Ship's Bunkers

The *CLC/FUND* regimes cover pollution damage from ship's bunkers only for bunker spills from laden tankers or tankers carrying oil residues from a previous cargo on a ballast voyage. This has been of concern to many coastal states as the potential of pollution from bunker oil has risen sharply with the increasing amounts of bunkers carried by larger vessels. As a result, the subject was placed on the IMO agenda and, after a number of years of discussion and negotiation, a new *International Convention on Civil Liability for Bunker Oil Pollution Damage, 2001 (BUNKER 2001)* was completed by an IMO diplomatic conference in March 2001.[242] The new convention is a freestanding instrument covering pollution damage only and is modelled on the *CLC 1969*. Accordingly, a key requirement will be the need for the registered owner of a vessel to maintain compulsory insurance cover.[243] Another important requirement is the provision for direct action that would permit a claim for compensation for pollution damage to be

---

240 See De La Rue, above note 37, c.7.
241 J. MacDonald, "Implementation of the 1996 Hazardous and Noxious Substances Convention: A Few Short Steps to Canadian Law" (1998) 7 Dal. L.J. 241; A. Saheb-Ettaba, "La protection juridique de l'environnement marin dans le cadre du transport maritime de substances nocives et potentiellement dangereuses" (1998) 32 Themis 493.
242 27 March 2001, IMO Doc. LEG/CONF.12/19.
243 *BUNKER 2001, ibid.*, art.7. See also, De La Rue, above note 37, c.6.

brought directly against a liability insurer.[244] Under the new convention only ships of more than 1,000 GT are covered. In addition the scope of application covers only pollution damage in the territory, territorial sea, or exclusive economic zone of states that have accepted the convention. Preventive measures are also covered. Liability for pollution from bunkers is channelled to the shipowner, including the registered owner, bareboat charterer, operator, or manager of the polluting vessel.[245] However, any applicable national or international limitation of liability regimes, such as *LLMC 1976*, is available.[246] The IMO bunkers conference also adopted a number of resolutions connected to the new convention, covering Limitation of Liability, Promotion of Technical Co-operation, and Protection of Persons Taking Measures to Prevent or Minimize the Effects of Oil Pollution. The new convention will enter into force a year after the date on which eighteen states, including five states each with ships whose combined gross tonnage is not less than 1 million GT, have accepted it. This is likely to take some time. Nevertheless, once in force, the new convention will close the last significant gap in the international regime, designed to compensate victims of pollution damage from ships.

7) Pollution from Harmful Anti-fouling Systems

Pollution from harmful anti-fouling systems is a problem that has only been causing concern in recent years. In order to prevent the fouling of ships' underwater surfaces that causes corrosion and impedes vessel speed, the industry has developed various types of surface coatings that prevent fouling by such marine organisms as barnacles and algae.[247] Unfortunately, scientific studies have shown that the main chemical content of such paints, tributylin, is not only harmful to marine life but may also enter the food chain. In response to the concern over these perceived dangers, the IMO convened an international diplomatic conference in October 2001 that concluded the *International Convention for the Control of Harmful Anti-Fouling Systems on Ships, 2001*.[248] It had been hoped that the new convention would receive early acceptance

---

244 *BUNKER 2001*, ibid., art.7.10.
245 Ibid., art.1.
246 Ibid., art.6; see Resolution on Limitation of Liability made by the conference; and Gold, above note 50 at 435.
247 Such anti-fouling coatings are also heavily used by pleasure boats.
248 5 October 2001; not yet in force; see *Ratification of Maritime Conventions*, above note 1 vol.I.7.240.

with a five-year phase-in period. However, there now appears to be significant opposition both from shipowners as well as scientists.[249] For the shipping industry the main concern is the significant increase in costs, as the alternatives to tributylin-based paints may not only cost three times as much but may also be less effective. Scientists believe that the treaty may be difficult to enforce and that much of the illegal tributylin would end up in less affluent countries that care less about the problem. Nevertheless, it is likely that the convention will eventually enter into force as there is significant pressure from environmental organizations.

8) Canadian Law and Policy

a) Oil Pollution

As a country with one of the longest and most vulnerable coastlines in the world, Canada has not only been aware that the protection of the environment required a strong regulatory system but also that compensation and liability, when pollution damage did occur, would have to have an adequate regime.[250] Canada has generally been a strong supporter of almost all international initiatives designed to protect the marine environment. However, because of Canada's rather unwieldy legislative procedures, the acceptance of international conventions generally seems to take an inordinate amount of time. Nevertheless, Canada eventually accepts most conventions that are of importance, with one or two notable exceptions. In some cases, where there are political, constitutional, or administrative barriers to acceding to a particular treaty, Canada often implements the treaty into its domestic legislation without formally accepting it. In other cases, where Canada considers certain liability limits too low, the spirit of the treaty will be accepted into domestic legislation, but greater limitation amounts will be inserted.[251] In other words, with some exceptions, that have been noted, the international legal regime, as set out in the various IMO conventions related to marine pollution prevention and compensation and liability, is basically Canadian law. In considering liability and compensation for marine pollution damage, it may be appropriate to ask, How much

---

249 See S. Neuman, "Treaty in Trouble" *Far Eastern Economic Review* (13 March 2003) 38.
250 A.H.E. Popp, "State Responsibility and the Environment (with specific Reference to Liability and Compensation for Oil Pollution caused by Ships)" (1989) Can. Council Int'l L. Proc. 142.
251 See Chapter 18, "Limitation of Liability for Maritime Claims."

marine pollution occurs in Canadian waters? While Canada has so far been spared from a catastrophic marine pollution disaster, there are a surprising number of maritime accidents that involve marine pollution each year. These range in pollutant spills from a few litres to hundreds of tonnes, involving small and large vessels, as well as mystery spills that cannot be traced to anyone. Fortunately, Canada has established the Ship-Source Oil Pollution Fund (SOPF), which provides a detailed report on spills in Canadian waters annually.[252] The SOPF is the successor of the original Maritime Pollution Claims Fund created under amendments to the *Canada Shipping Act* in 1971.[253] The principal purpose of the latter fund at that time was to provide funds for claims in excess of shipowners' liability limits and also to provide an accessible fund that could be utilized by the Canadian government in cleanup operations. This regime was in operation from 1971 to 1989 and was funded by a levy imposed on oil companies, power generating authorities, pulp and paper manufacturers, chemical plants, and other heavy industries that utilized oil.[254]

When Canada decided to accept the international oil pollution compensation and liability regimes, already outlined above, the Maritime Pollution Claims Fund became the SOPF under the *Canada Shipping Act*.[255] The funds collected under the former fund were also transferred to the SOPF and further levies are authorized under the implementing legislation. No levies have been collected since 1976; however, for the fiscal year 2002 the Minister of Transport has the statutory power to impose a levy that is indexed annually.[256] The SOPF is based in Ottawa and is headed by an administrator who is supported by administrative, technical, and claims staff. The SOPF is effectively Canada's oil pollution compensation and liability conduit to the international compensation system, such as *CLC 1969* and *FUND 1971* and their successors, as described above. In this position the SOPF attends

---

252 The 2001–02 *SOPF Report*, above note 218, lists claims for 98 spills, including some dating from 1998.
253 *Ibid.* at i.
254 This $0.15 levy was put in place during the period 1972–79 when almost $35 million was collected. With interest this amount had increased to almost $150 million by 1989 when the MPCF was transferred to the SOPF. As of April 2002, the fund balance held by the SOPF was over $316 million. *SOPF Report, ibid.* at vii and 2.
255 However, the SOPF is now under the jurisdiction of the *Marine Liability Act*, above note 71.
256 The 2002 levy could be $0.41 per tonne of "contributing oil" imported into or shipped from a place in Canada in bulk as cargo on a ship. *SOPF Report*, above note 218 at 2.

the meetings of IOPCF and provides the Canadian financial contribution to the *FUND* system. This significantly simplified the legal process of claims for compensation and liability for marine pollution, and is very different from the rather convoluted international legal regime for the enforcement of pollution prevention provisions, as outlined above. The process has been even further eased by the one-stop link between the SOPF and the new *Marine Liability Act*.[257] Previously, a number of acts had jurisdiction for marine pollution damage and made the claims process more complex. There are, however, some specific differences between the *Marine Liability Act*, the *CLC Prot 1992*, and the *FUND Prot 1992* regimes. This is especially important in coverage for compensation for environmental damage. The *Marine Liability Act* provides:[258] "Where oil pollution damage from a ship results in impairment to the environment, the owner of the ship is liable for the cost of reasonable measures of reinstatement actually undertaken or to be undertaken." Under the *CLC Prot 1992* and *FUND Prot 1992* conventions, the definitions for "pollution damage" provide as follows:[259] "compensation for impairment of the environment, other than loss of profit from such impairment, shall be limited to costs of reasonable measures of reinstatement actually undertaken or to be undertaken."

The SOPF is basically a funding mechanism of first and last resort for marine pollution claims under the *Marine Liability Act*.[260] This Act makes the shipowner strictly liable for ship-source oil pollution damage, as well as for the costs and expenses incurred by Fisheries and Oceans Canada and others for cleanup and preventive measures. In other words, under the *Marine Liability Act* a claimant can take action against the shipowner. However, the SOPF is legally empowered to be a party to any litigation in Canadian courts against the shipowner, the liability insurer, or the IOPCF,[261] and also has the power and authority to participate in any settlement, including making payments from the fund.[262] The SOPF can also be a fund of first resort for any claimants, including the Crown. Claimants are able to file their pollution damage claim with the SOPF, which has a duty to investigate, assess, accept or reject such claims.[263] If a claim is accepted the SOPF can make an offer of compensation and, if accepted and paid, is subrogated to the rights

---

257 Above note 71.
258 *Marine Liability Act*, above note 71, s.51(2).
259 *CLC 1992*, above note 177, art.2(6)(a); *FUND 1992*, above note 202, art.2(1)(a).
260 *Marine Liability Act*, above note 71, ss.84–85.
261 *Ibid.*, s.72.
262 *Ibid.*, s.84.
263 *Ibid.*, s.85.

of the claimant and must then take all reasonable measures in order to recover what has been paid out. If a claim is rejected the claimant can appeal the SOPF decision to the Federal Court of Canada.[264]

The Ship-Source Oil Pollution Fund is required to pay claims for oil pollution damage or anticipated damage anywhere in Canada, or in Canadian waters, including the exclusive economic zone of Canada, caused by the discharge of oil from a ship. However, claims from all classes and types of ships are covered. This is broader coverage than that of the *FUND* under the IOPCF that applies only to seagoing tankers and persistent oil. Furthermore, the SOPF also provides a third layer of additional compensation in the event that coverage under *CLC Prot 1992* and *FUND Prot 1992* is either insufficient or unavailable.[265] The classes of claims for which the SOPF may be liable include the following:

- claims for oil pollution damage;
- claims for costs and expenses of oil spill cleanup, including the cost of preventive measures; and
- claims for oil pollution damage and cleanup costs where the identity of the ship that caused the discharge cannot be established (i.e., mystery spills).

A widely defined class of persons in the Canadian fishing industry may also claim for loss of income arising from a ship-source oil spill.[266] However, the present statutory claims regime, as set out in the *Marine Liability Act*,[267] is based on the polluter-pays principle that requires that

- all costs and expenses must be reasonable,
- all cleanup measures taken must be reasonable, and
- all costs and expenses must have actually been incurred.

In other words, at this stage, pollution claims must be based on actual, quantifiable damage and abstract measurements or valuations for "environmental damage" that cannot be quantified are not acceptable.

Environment Canada has set up an Environmental Damages Fund which consists of monies levied from fines imposed on polluters by the courts and representing compensation for environmental damage. The funds are made available to local groups in the same community where the pollution occurred to undertake environmental restoration work, assessment, and education. This is inconsistent with the policy devel-

---

264 See *SOPF Report*, above note 218 at 3.
265 Subject to the SOPF maximum liability of Cdn$136 million for 2002–03 that is indexed annually.
266 *Marine Liability Act*, above note 71, s.88.
267 *Ibid.*, Part 6.

oped by the IOPCF in administering *FUND Prot 1992*, which permits claims for quantifiable elements of damage that would include the reasonable costs of reinstatement of the damaged environment, as well as any loss of profit, income, or revenue resulting from damage to the marine environment by persons who depend directly on earnings from coastal or marine-related activities, for instance, those engaged in the fishing, tourist, or coastal amenities industries.[268]

b) Non-oil Pollution

The Canadian liability and compensation system for oil pollution is now well established and is generally based on a credible international regime. However, marine pollution from substances other than oil is still inadequately covered. There is, at this time, no widely accepted international regime covering liability and compensation for pollution from substances other than oil in place. The *HNS 1996* compensation, although completed in 1996, has so far attracted very few acceptances.[269] International regimes covering pollution from bunker oil[270] and from harmful anti-fouling systems[271] are very new and expected to take some time to enter into effect. On the other hand, Canada's extensive and complex marine pollution prevention law and enforcement system covers all types of marine pollution. This is reinforced by the *Marine Liability Act*, under which those responsible for ship-generated marine pollution will be held liable. The question that may arise is, If pollution from substances other than oil occurs in Canadian waters, will adequate compensation be available? The answer is that there will be adequate coverage for normal operational pollution, but probably less so for pollution arising from larger and catastrophic accidents. This is owing to the fact that, at this stage, only oil pollution is subject to the larger international compensation funds already discussed. Non-oil pollution damage compensation would, therefore, have to fall under the traditional limitation of liability regime as outlined under the *Marine Liability Act*.[272]

It has already been shown that Canada has not formally accepted the latest international limitation of liability regime, as set out in *LLMC 1976*,[273] but has incorporated the convention into the *Marine Liability*

---

268 *SOPF Report*, above note 218 at 33.
269 See above note 233.
270 See above in C(6), "Pollution from Ship's Bunkers."
271 See above in C(7), "Pollution from Harmful Anti-fouling Systems."
272 Above note 71 Part 3.
273 Above note 221.

Act with very few differences.[274] This means that pollution damage caused by substances other than oil are subject to the compensation limits set out in the *Marine Liability Act*.[275]

c) Canadian Marine Pollution Response Mechanism

The adequate response to pollutant spills has operational, as well as liability and compensation aspects, in Canada and elsewhere. Canada is party to the *International Convention on Oil Pollution Preparedness, Response and Co-operation, 1990* (OPRC 1990) regime,[276] which is given effect in the *Canada Shipping Act, 2001*.[277] As indicated in the treaty's name, states are obliged to be prepared as well as be capable to respond to oil spills. This has resulted in Transport Canada and Fisheries and Oceans Canada setting up a licensed network of private response organizations in designated geographical regions. Such response organizations are envisaged to be the first line of defence to take action in the event of oil spills.[278] Under the *Canada Shipping Act, 2001*, such response organizations may also set a schedule of fees[279] to be charged to shipowners and oil-handling facilities that enter into an arrangement with the organization as required under the Act.[280] The designated response organization is required to give notice of the intended fee schedule and the Minister of Transport Canada may review the level of fees, if there are objections.[281] The fees collected by these designated response organizations cover only the establishment and equipping of the organization, as required under the Act.[282] In case a spill actually occurs the normal liability and compensation regime will enter into effect and the costs and expenses of actually combating the spill will be recovered through the Ship-Source Oil Pollution Fund. It should be added that, although shipowners and oil-handling facilities are obliged to enter into an arrangement with one or more response organization under the *Canada Shipping Act, 2001*, they are not required to use such

---

274 *Marine Liability Act*, above note 71, Part 3. See Chapter 18, "Limitation of Liability for Maritime Claims." See also above note 226.
275 *Marine Liability Act*, ibid., ss.28–29.
276 Above note 40.
277 Above note 2, Sch.1.
278 *Ibid.*, ss.169 and 171.
279 *Ibid.*, s.170.
280 *Ibid.*, ss.167–68.
281 Such a review was undertaken in 1996. See E. Gold, J. Gratwick, & P. Yee, *Canadian Oil Spill Response Capability: An Investigation of the Proposed Fee Regime*, Final Report (Ottawa: Fisheries and Oceans Canada, 1996).
282 *Canada Shipping Act, 2001*, above note 2, s.171.

organizations and may use other private sector agencies to assist in combating spills. Nevertheless, in case of serious spills it is likely that the on-scene commander for Transport Canada or Fisheries and Oceans Canada would take over and direct operations.[283]

Once again, the weakness in the system is that it is, at this stage, designed to respond only to oil spills. That means that responses to pollution from substances other than oil are inadequately covered in Canada and elsewhere. A recent attempt at the international level has produced the *Protocol on Preparedness, Response and Co-operation to Pollution Incidents by Hazardous and Noxious Substances, 2000 (OPRC–HNS Protocol 2000)*,[284] which will, however, take some time before it can enter into force. In the meantime, spills in Canada involving pollutants other than oil will be covered by such response mechanisms as are available under existing legislation. The *Canada Shipping Act, 2001*, as well as other Canadian legislation provides an adequate enforcement regime for all types of pollution. Nevertheless, the question remains whether the response mechanism, as set out under the *Canada Shipping Act, 2001*,[285] is sufficient if a major spill from substances other than oil would occur in Canadian waters.

9) U.S. Law Differences

Problems may, however, arise in cases of transborder marine pollution involving the United States. This is owing to the fact that the United States has not accepted many IMO conventions, especially those related to compensation and liability. As indicated, the United States has legislated, and continues to legislate, unilaterally in this area. In most cases this is because U.S. policy appears to consider the internationally negotiated limitation and compensation limits to be too low. In cases where a vessel causes marine pollution in Canadian waters and damage occurs in U.S. waters or territory, problems may occur.[286] Given the close proximity of U.S. and Canadian waters, it is therefore advisable to have some understanding of some of the basic legal differences that

---

283 *Ibid.*, s.180.
284 Above note 51.
285 Above note 2, s.180
286 See A.H.E. Popp, "Legal Aspects of International Oil Spills in the Canada/US Context" (1992) 18 Can.–U.S.L.J. 309; P.G. Bernard & A.P. Mayer, "A Tale of Two Sovereigns: Canada, the United States, and Trans-Border Pollution Issues" (2000) 13 U.S.F. Mar. L.J. 125; see also "Discussion after the speeches of R.L. Jarashow and A.H.E. Popp" (1992) 18 Can.–U.S.L.J. 327; see also De La Rue, above note 37, cc.4, 21, and 23.

presently exist. First and foremost, under U.S. legislation, there is a distinct difference in the way compensation for environmental damage is handled from the *Marine Liability Act* and *CLC Prot 1992/FUND Prot 1992*. The U.S. *Oil Pollution Act, 1990*,[287] provides for payments of natural resource damage claims from the U.S. Oil Spill Liability Trust Fund. Only designated trustees are entitled to submit natural resource damages, although such "trustees are authorized to consider a plan to restore and rehabilitate or acquire the equivalent of the damaged natural resource."[288] While any properly quantified, reasonable cost for restoration or reinstatement of the marine environment that can be compensated under the *CLC Prot 1992/FUND Prot 1992* regime may be equivalent to the basic U.S. legal requirement, U.S. law goes much further and also includes compensation for the diminution in value of damaged natural resources pending restoration, plus the reasonable costs of assessing those damages. This U.S. approach takes damage claims into theoretically based assessments of environmental damage; it has moved significantly beyond the international (and *Marine Liability Act*) regime. It has obvious implications for significantly raised compensation costs. This is a matter that continues to be monitored by the Ship-Source Oil Pollution Fund and is also the subject of ongoing discussions between the responsible U.S. authorities and those representing the international regime.[289]

D. MARINE POLLUTION: OFFSHORE ENERGY OPERATIONS

1) Background

Much of this chapter discusses marine pollution generated by ships, as commensurate with the contribution of ship-source pollution to the overall pollution of the marine environment. As a result, international, regional, and national legislation has concentrated on this area. However, steadily increasing offshore operations, especially those related to the exploration and exploitation of offshore energy resources in many offshore regions of the world, have also contributed to the danger of

---

287 Above note 36. See also De La Rue, *ibid.*, c.4.
288 *SOPF Report*, above note 218 at 32.
289 *Ibid.* at 33.

marine pollution from such operations.[290] Offshore oil and gas operations are technologically sophisticated, very costly, and — as they involve the marine environment as well as sub-sea oil and gas reserves — frequently dangerous.[291] In many cases, oil and gas reserves are found under high-pressure conditions that could cause an accidental blowout resulting in fire, explosion, and uncontrolled pollution.[292] The industry's safety record is relatively good; but, when major accidents do occur, they are likely to result in loss of life, personal injury, the loss of expensive equipment, and in some cases serious marine pollution.[293]

2) International Law and Related Instruments

It may perhaps be surprising that, apart from some basic customary international law principles,[294] there is so far no international treaty or similar instrument that specifically addresses offshore operations. As a result, only very limited legal provisions related to offshore operations, including compensation and liability aspects, may be found in a number of international instruments.

a) U.N. Law of the Sea Conventions

The *1958 Continental Shelf Convention*[295] precludes offshore operations that unjustifiably interfere with navigation, fishing, conservation efforts, and scientific research.[296] Under this convention, states are also required

---

290 Several other offshore operations, such as mining, salt extraction, water production, and tidal power development may also have environmental implications: see M. McConnell, "The Other Uses of the Sea and the Seabed" in E. Gold, ed., *Maritime Affairs: A World Handbook* (Harlow: Longman, 1991) c.7.
291 See E in Chapter 2, "The Shipping Industry: An Overview." See also T. Robinson, *The Offshore: An Introduction to the Technology, Terminology and Operations of Offshore Oil Exploration* (St. John's: Jesperson Press, 1992).
292 See E. Gold & C. Petrie, "Pollution from Offshore Activities: An Overview of the Operational, Legal and Environmental Aspects" in C.M. De La Rue, ed., *Liability for Damage to the Marine Environment* (London: Lloyd's Press, 1993) at 218.
293 The largest oil spill from a drilling accident was The Ixtoc 1 blowout in 1979 off the coast of Mexico, which caused widespread coastal pollution. See Gold, above note 292 at 218. See also B.S. Middleditch, ed., *Environmental Effects of Offshore Production* (London: Plenum Press, 1981) at 3.
294 E.g., those elucidated in the *Trail Smelter* case that stands for the principle that states must refrain from acts that infringe negatively on the rights of neighbouring states. See *United States v. Canada*, 35 A.J.I.L. 684 (1941).
295 *Convention on the Continental Shelf*, 29 April 1958, 499 U.N.T.S. 311 (entered into force 10 June 1964; entered into force in Canada 8 March 1970); see also *Ratification of Maritime Conventions*, above note 1 vol.I.1.130.
296 *Ibid.*, art.5(1).

to establish 500-metre safety zones around offshore drilling units.[297] The 1958 *High Seas Convention*[298] requires states to draw up regulations for the prevention of marine pollution from pipelines or resulting from oil exploration and exploitation.[299] *UNCLOS*[300] has adopted many of the relevant principles related to offshore operations from the 1958 Geneva Conventions. However, *UNCLOS* specifically refers to measures for preventing pollution accidents, dealing with emergencies, ensuring safety, and regulating the design, construction, equipment, operation, and crewing of offshore installations.[301] The convention also requires states to co-operate to develop global and regional rules to prevent pollution from offshore installations.[302]

b) MARPOL 73/78

MARPOL 73/78 specifically excludes jurisdiction over marine pollution caused by blowout, structural failure of an oil installation, collision with such an installation, or malfunctioning of a pipeline. The convention defines discharge to exclude "release of harmful substances directly arising from the exploration, exploitation and associated offshore processing of seabed mineral resources."[303] Nevertheless, *MARPOL 73/78* also requires fixed and floating oil rigs, when engaged in the exploration and exploitation of seabed resources, to apply the rules applicable to ships of 400 GT and over.[304] The application of such rules prohibits the discharge of oil and oil mixtures into the sea. Nevertheless, such rules do not cover the many other operational aspects of offshore work that can, and often do, lead to environmental problems.[305]

c) Other Regimes

There have been a number of attempts to develop international rules for pollution damage compensation and liability that have been either very limited or unsuccessful and that are, at least at this time, not relevant for Canada. These include the *Offshore Pollution Liability Agree-*

---

297 *Ibid.*, arts.5(2) and (3).
298 *Convention on the High Seas*, above note 8.
299 *Ibid.*, art.24.
300 Above note 1.
301 *UNCLOS*, above note 1, art.194(3)(c).
302 *Ibid.*, art.208(5).
303 *MARPOL 73/78*, above note 23, art.2(3).
304 Other than oil tankers. *MARPOL 73/78*, *ibid.*, Annex I, Reg. 21.
305 See also Chapter 5, "The Safety Management of Ships" and Chapter 2, "The Shipping Industry: An Overview."

ment, 1974, (OPOL 1974)[306] and the *Convention on Civil Liability for Oil Pollution Damage Resulting from Exploration for and Exploitation of Seabed Mineral Resources, 1977, (CLEE 1977).*[307] The Comité Maritime International (CMI)[308] made an attempt to create a viable international regime for offshore operations in 1977. This effort resulted in a Draft Convention on Offshore Mobile Craft. The draft was then submitted to the International Maritime Organisation for further action. However, the subject was not considered further at the international level for a number of years. A number of serious accidents arising from offshore operations resulted in renewed interest in the subject in the late 1980s and early 1990s. As a result, the IMO requested the CMI to review or revise the 1977 draft convention and the CMI continued further work as requested. The subject is also still on the agenda of the IMO, although it is not considered to have a high priority.

d) IMO MODU Code 1998

A fairly widely accepted international functional instrument that governs the design criteria, construction standards, and other safety measures for offshore installations is the IMO's *Code for the Construction and Equipment of Mobile Offshore Drilling Units, 1998 (MODU Code 1998)*. This code covers the four main types of offshore rigs: mobile drilling units (semi-submersibles); self-elevating units (jack-up rigs); surface units (drill ships); and column-stabilized units.[309] The code is a voluntary framework for offshore operations that sets out basic, minimum standards and requirements. It is widely used in Canadian offshore energy operations.

3) Liability and Compensation

There is, at this stage, no effective international instrument that covers liability and compensation for damage arising out of offshore operations. As a result, this aspect is left to the bilateral arrangements between the coastal state, where offshore operations are to take place, and the oil company that plans to undertake such work. Accordingly,

---

306 4 September 1974, online at <www.opol.org.uk>. *OPOL 1974* is limited to a number of European states only. See Gold & Petrie, above note 292 at 247.
307 17 December 1976, 16 I.L.M. 1451 (not in force); see also *Ratification of Maritime Conventions,* above note 1 vol.1.7.390.
308 See G(2)(a) in Chapter 2, "The Shipping Industry: An Overview."
309 For technical details, see Robinson, above note 291, c.1; and F in Chapter 2, "The Shipping Industry: An Overview."

most coastal states that permit offshore operations will have developed national legislation and operational regulations that cover all aspects of offshore exploration and exploitation.[310] In many cases offshore operators will be faced with the prospect of significant liabilities in case of accidents. Such liabilities will usually be covered under a protection and indemnity insurance policy.[311] In fact, coastal states such as Canada, which have a highly regulated offshore area, will require adequate financial protection against accidents as part of the agreement under which the offshore contractor is permitted to work. Furthermore, the offshore operator will also have to provide financial guarantees that any offshore installations will be removed once operations are completed. Abandoned offshore installations may also cause navigational and environmental hazards.

4) Canadian Law and Policy

The regulatory system designed to protect the marine environment from pollution damage originating from offshore energy operations is, at this time, almost entirely left to national law and regulation. As Canada is rapidly becoming a major source of offshore energy on the Atlantic coast and in the foreseeable future the Pacific and Arctic coasts, an effective regulatory system has been developed. This covers both federal and provincial responsibilities from the constitutional accords that have been developed between the government of Canada and the provinces of Nova Scotia and Newfoundland and Labrador; at this stage, they are reflected in a number of legislative provisions[312] that cover the management and operations of offshore energy resources as well as revenue sharing and the necessary federal-provincial regulatory requirements. Under this arrangement, the Nova Scotia and the Newfoundland and Labrador offshore areas are managed, in terms of regulatory requirements, safety, environmental protection, and licensing, by joint federal-provincial boards that have been created under the accord legislation. These are the Canada–Nova Scotia Offshore Petro-

---

310 See Gold & Petrie, above note 292.
311 See S.-H. Svensen, "Pollution from Offshore Activities: Liability and P&I Insurance Aspects" in De La Rue, above note 292, c.18.
312 *Canada–Newfoundland Atlantic Accord Implementation Act*, S.C. 1987, c.3; *Canada–Newfoundland Atlantic Accord Implementation Act*, R.S.N. 1990, c.C-2; *Canada–Nova Scotia Offshore Petroleum Resources Accord Implementation Act*, S.C. 1988, c.28; *Canada–Nova Scotia Offshore Petroleum Resources Accord Implementation (Nova Scotia) Act*, S.N.S. 1987, c.3.

leum Board,[313] and the Canada–Newfoundland Offshore Petroleum Board.[314] These boards have been delegated powers under the accord legislation by the federal government and the relevant provinces specifically to regulate offshore energy development. The delegated powers include regulating activities such as the following:

- rights management,
- exploratory permits,
- exploration licences,
- exploratory drilling,
- diving and geophysical programs,
- offshore labour health and safety,
- industrial benefits and employment,
- strategic environmental assessments and reviews,[315] and
- all aspects of environmental protection.

These powers are reflected in the numerous regulations that have been developed for the Newfoundland and Labrador,[316] and for the Nova Scotia[317] offshore energy areas.

---

313 See the CNSOPB's Annual Reports and/or its web site: <www.cnsopb.ns.ca>.
314 See web site: <www.infosource.gc.ca/info1/CNP-e.html>.
315 See, e.g., Canada, Commissioner's Report, *Results of a Public Review on the Effects of Potential Oil and Gas Exploration Offshore Cape Breton* (Halifax: CNSOPB, 2002).
316 *Canada–Newfoundland Oil and Gas Spills and Debris Liability Regulations*, S.O.R./88-262; *Newfoundland Offshore Area Oil and Gas Operations Regulations*, S.O.R./88-347; *Newfoundland Offshore Area Petroleum Diving Regulations*, S.O.R./88-601; *Newfoundland Offshore Area Petroleum Geophysical Operations Regulations*, S.O.R./95-334; *Newfoundland Offshore Area Petroleum Production and Conservation Regulations*, S.O.R./95-103; *Newfoundland Offshore Area Registration Regulations*, S.O.R./88-263; *Newfoundland Offshore Certificate of Fitness Regulations*, S.O.R./95-100; *Newfoundland Offshore Petroleum Drilling Regulations*, S.O.R./93-23; *Newfoundland Offshore Petroleum Installations Regulations*, S.O.R./95-104; *Newfoundland Offshore Petroleum Resource Revenue Fund Regulations*, S.O.R./95-257.
317 *Canada–Nova Scotia Oil and Gas Spills and Debris Liability Regulations*, S.O.R./95-123; *Nova Scotia Offshore Area Petroleum Diving Regulations*, S.O.R./95-189; *Nova Scotia Offshore Area Petroleum Geophysical Operations Regulations*, S.O.R./95-144; *Nova Scotia Offshore Area Petroleum Production and Conservation Regulations*, S.O.R./95-190; *Nova Scotia Offshore Certificate of Fitness Regulations*, S.O.R./95-187; *Nova Scotia Offshore Petroleum Drilling Regulations*, S.O.R./92-676 as am.; *Nova Scotia Offshore Petroleum Installations Regulations*, S.O.R./95-191; *Nova Scotia Offshore Revenue Account Regulations*, S.O.R./93-441; *Nova Scotia Offshore Revenue Fiscal Equalization Offset Payments Regulations*, S.O.R./96-249; *Nova Scotia Resources (Ventures) Limited Drilling Assistance Regulations*, S.O.R./94-168; *Nova Scotia Share of Offshore Revenue Interim Period Payment Regulations*, S.O.R./84-848; *Nova Scotia Share of Offshore Sales Tax Payment Regulations*, S.O.R./85-912; *Offshore Area Exclusion Order*, S.O.R./84-592.

A similar regulatory system for Canadian offshore development generally has also been put in place.[318] In addition, there are separate environmental regulations that are specifically aimed at offshore development and operations.[319] While some of these regulations are not directly concerned with the protection of the environment, as the Canadian offshore energy system's environmental, safety, economic, and licensing sectors are so closely interrelated, it is usually necessary to treat the regulatory system as a whole. At this time, the only offshore energy development in Canada has taken place off the Newfoundland and Labrador, and the Nova Scotia coasts; federal legislation, however, envisages such development elsewhere. The *Canada Oil and Gas Operations Act*[320] applies in respect of the exploration and drilling for and the production, processing and transportation[321] of oil and gas in the Northwest Territories, Nunavut, and Sable Island, as well as in submarine areas not within a province in the internal waters, the territorial sea, or the continental shelf of Canada. While submarine areas that are located within a province are subject to federal-provincial arrangements, the purpose of the *Canada Oil and Gas Operations Act*[322] is to promote the following, in respect of the exploration for and exploitation of oil and gas:

- safety, particularly by encouraging persons exploring for and exploiting oil and gas to maintain a prudent regime for achieving safety;
- the protection of the environment;
- the conservation of oil and gas resources; and
- joint production arrangements.

---

318 *Canada Oil and Gas Certificate of Fitness Regulations*, S.O.R./96-114; *Canada Oil and Gas Diving Regulations*, S.O.R./88-600; *Canada Oil and Gas Drilling Regulations*, S.O.R./79-82; *Canada Oil and Gas Geophysical Operations Regulations*, S.O.R./96-117; *Canada Oil and Gas Installations Regulations*, S.O.R./96-118; *Canada Oil and Gas Operations Regulations*, S.O.R./83-149; *Canada Oil and Gas Production and Conservation Regulations*, S.O.R./90-791; *Oil and Gas Spills and Debris Liability Regulations*, S.O.R./87-331.
319 Under various regulations cited, as well as the *Canadian Environmental Assessment Act*, S.C. 1992, c.37.
320 Above note 74, s.3.
321 It should be noted that, under the *Canada Shipping Act*, s.655(2), and the *Canada Shipping Act, 2001*, ss.166(2) and 186(2), the pollution prevention and response requirements do not apply to vessels involved in the exploration or exploitation of oil as defined in the *Canada Oil and Gas Operations Act*, *ibid*.
322 *Ibid*.

E. CONCLUSIONS

The protection of the marine environment has today become a major global preoccupation. As a result, the enforcement, liability, and compensation of pollution prevention has also become an important and complex sector of maritime law. As is clear from this chapter, an impressive array of international, regional, and national laws and regulations is available to handle ship-source marine pollution, as well as pollution from offshore energy operations. Offences are prosecuted with high fines and even imprisonment, and there appears to be zero tolerance, even for pollution caused by accidents. These regimes have certain positive impacts on the protection of the marine environment; however, there is no question that pollution from ships and offshore operations contributes only a minor part of pollutants entering the seas. For example, one of the most recent studies undertaken by the U.S. National Academies Research Council indicates that the consumers of oil, and not the ships that transport it, are responsible for most petroleum that enters U.S. waters;[323] the report states that nearly 85 per cent of the 29 million gallons (110 million L) of oil that enter U.S. ocean waters annually is the result of human activities from land-based runoff, polluted rivers, aircraft, pleasure boats, and jet skis. Less than 8 per cent comes from tanker or pipeline spills, and oil extraction and exploration account for three per cent of the oil that enters the sea. In other words, the heavy media and legal concentration on marine pollution prevention from ships and oil rigs does not reflect the actual source of pollutants.

Nevertheless, ships and oil rigs have the potential to cause significant environmental damage, especially when vessels are improperly operated and/or managed. Furthermore, regular shipping accidents, involving significant pollution, ensure that the problem is there and that it requires continuing assessment at the national and international levels. For example, the recent tanker accidents involving the tanker Erika, off the French coast in December 1999, and the tanker Prestige, off the Spanish coast in November 2002, have resulted in renewed efforts by the International Maritime Organisation to tighten up international standards further. A recent submission by the European Union to the IMO proposed changes to *MARPOL 73/78* would phase out single-hull tankers earlier than originally anticipated, ban the carriage of heavy oil

---

323 Cited in "Update," Marine Log, June 2002 at 10.

in single-hull tankers, or require a Condition Assessment Scheme for all tankers that are more than fifteen years old.[324] It is, however, hoped that more sophisticated ship and rig technology, raised global safety standards, increased port state controls, and other advances will reduce ship- and rig-generated marine pollution to its lowest-ever levels. Given Canada's lengthy and vulnerable coastlines, important fisheries, and marine industries, it is certain that Canadian law and regulation will also continue to be updated in order to ensure that this occurs.

FURTHER READINGS

ABECASSIS, D.W. & R.L. JARASHOW, *Oil Pollution from Ships*, 2d ed. (London: Stevens, 1997).

BATES, J.H., *United Kingdom Marine Pollution Law* (London: Lloyd's Press, 1985).

CHIRCOP, A.E., "The Marine Transportation of Hazardous and Dangerous Goods in the Law of the Sea — An Emerging Regime" (1988) 11 Dal. L.J. 612.

DE LA RUE, C., ed., *Liability for Damage to the Environment* (London: Lloyd's Press, 1993).

DE LA RUE, C. & C.B. ANDERSON, *Shipping and the Environment* (London: Lloyd's Press, 1998).

DUDLEY, J.R., B.J. SCOTT, & E. GOLD, *Towards Safer Ships and Cleaner Seas — A Handbook for Modern Tankship Operations* (Arendal, NO: Gard A.S., 1994).

FERNANDES, R.M., *Shipping and Admiralty Law* (Toronto: Carswell, 1995) c.7.

GAUCI, G., *Pollution at Sea* (Chichester, UK: Wiley, 1997).

GOLD, E., *Gard Handbook on Marine Pollution*, 2d ed. (Arendal, NO: Gard A.S., 1997).

---

324 EU Proposal of 10 April 2003; this submission was discussed by the IMO's Marine Environmental Protection Committee in July 2003: see IMO web site: <www.imo.org>.

—, *Gard Handbook on P&I Insurance*, 5th ed. (Arendal, NO: Gard A.S., 2002) Part VI.

—, "Ship-Source Marine Pollution: Testing the Viability of the International Liability and Compensation Systems" *BIMCO Review 2001* (Copenhagen: BIMCO, 2001).

GOLD, E., J. GRATWICK, & P. YEE, *Canadian Oil Spill Response Capability: An Investigation of the Proposed Fee Regime. Final Report* (Ottawa: Fisheries and Oceans Canada, 1996).

JACOBSSON, M., "The International Regime of Compensation for Oil Pollution Damage and the Policy of the International Oil Pollution Compensation Funds as to the Admissibility of Claims" (2002) 1 W.M.U.J. Mar. Aff. 59.

KRIWOKEN, L.K., et al, eds., *Ocean Law and Policy in the Post–UNCED Era: Australian and Canadian Perspectives* (London: Kluwer International, 1996).

MACDONALD, J., "Implementation of the 1996 Hazardous and Noxious Substances Convention: A Few Short Steps to Canadian Law" (1998) 17 Dal. L.J. 241.

MIDDLEDITCH, B.S., *Environmental Effects of Offshore Production* (London: Plenum, 1981).

SCHOENBAUM, T.J, *Admiralty and Maritime Law*, 3d ed. (St. Paul, MN: West Publishing, 2001) c.16.

SUMMERSKILL, M., *Oil Rigs: Law and Insurance* (London: Stevens, 1979).

VANDERZWAAG, D., ed., *Canadian Ocean Law and Policy* (Toronto: Butterworths, 1992).

WHITE, M., *Marine Pollution Laws of the Australasian Region* (Sydney: Foundation Press, 1994).

CHAPTER 18

LIMITATION OF LIABILITY FOR MARITIME CLAIMS

A. INTRODUCTION

An important rule in maritime law that sets shipping apart from all other branches of industry and commerce is that the shipowner and certain other persons can limit their liability for loss or damage for their negligence. Broadly stated, the rule is that the owner of a negligent ship need not necessarily compensate fully those who have suffered as a result of a ship colliding with and damaging another vessel or causing loss of life or personal injury to passengers or other personnel. Usually the shipowner can limit liability according to the size of the ship. Although of very old origin, the rule was probably first codified at the time of Louis XIV in the seventeenth century. The great Dutch publicist and legal scholar, Hugo Grotius promoted it as a matter of public policy and it quickly gained acceptance at a time of growth in international trade. Essentially it was a public policy decision and was probably one of the first examples of state support for the shipping industry. The rationale behind it was that the shipowner undertook great risks in the maritime adventure and was not necessarily in control over what happened to the ship and cargo at the hands of the master and crew. The early rule allowed the shipowner to limit liability to the value of the ship and freight in cases of cargo theft. Eventually with the *Merchant Shipping Act, 1894*, the application of the rule was extended to include collision liability and a tonnage formula was used.[1] It was in the interests of trade to encourage shipowning, to protect shipowners from ruin, and ultimately to promote a climate of ascertainable risk that would encourage insurability.[2] A cost associated with such a benefit was the very real possibility that those who suffered loss as a result of the negligence of the shipowner or his or her servants might not get full compensation, possibly resulting in injustice. But, Lord Denning noted in *The Bramley Moore*, "there is not much justice in this rule; but limitation of liability is not a matter of justice. It is a rule of public policy which has its origins in history and its justification in convenience."[3] As a result, the rule continues to be controversial.

The old rule was that the shipowner could limit liability as long as he or she was not in actual fault or privity in causing the loss. If limitation was granted the burden of absorbing a marine loss often fell unfairly on those suffering the loss. In collision cases, it was virtually axiomatic that, until the case of *The Lady Gwendolen*, if the cause of a collision arose out of navigational error on the part of the master or crew, limitation of liability would be granted. *The Lady Gwendolen* applied an objective standard of the ordinarily reasonable shipowner and a paramount

---

1 *Merchant Shipping Act, 1894* (U.K.), 57 & 58 Vict., c.60. Shipping in Canada was governed by this Act until the 1931 *Statute of Westminster* enabled the enactment of the *Canada Shipping Act*.
2 Clyne J. explained this: "[b]efore the first limitation Act was passed in England in 1734 it was possible for a shipowner to sustain ruinous losses because of the acts of the master in some remote part of the world where the shipowner was unable to exert any actual control and, as a matter of policy to encourage and maintain shipping, it was deemed advisable to limit the liability of the owner to the value of the ship and her freight where there was theft of cargo by the master and crew. By successive statutes the right to limitation was extended to other cases until it has reached its present form" in *Vancouver v. Rhodes*, [1955] 1 D.L.R. 139 at 140. Similarly, Ritchie J. said: "[t]he limitation of liability provisions ... are expressly designed for the purpose of encouraging shipping and affording protection to shipowners against bearing the full impact of heavy and perhaps crippling pecuniary damage sustained by reason of the negligent navigation of their ships on the part of their servants or agents" in *British Columbia Telephone Co. v. Marpole Towing*, [1971] S.C.R 321 at 338.
3 *Bramley Moore (The)*, [1963] 2 Lloyd's Rep. 429 at 437. The tragic case of *Princess Victoria (The)*, [1953] 2 Lloyd's Rep. 619, illustrates this point. In this case the master refused to sail an unseaworthy ship, but the shipowner told the master that he would be fired unless he sailed. The ship sailed and sank in bad weather, and 133 people lost their lives. Regardless, the shipowner was still able to limit his liability.

concern for safety of life at sea as a test to assess the conduct of the shipowner in the management and control of a ship or fleet.[4] Since this case, many English cases, such as *The England*, followed the trend against the limitation of liability.[5] Similarly, many Canadian cases, such as *The Farrandoc*[6] and *The Kathy K*,[7] demonstrated the change in the courts' attitudes in favour of finding fault and privity on the part of shipowners by applying the old provisions of the *Canada Shipping Act*. In *The Kathy K*, the Court found fault because the shipowner acquiesced in the tug and tow being left in inexperienced hands, thus exposing other traffic to foreseeable potential danger. Other courts probed into the shipowner's management of the ship, found negligence, and therefore denied limitation. Actual fault or privity entailed the shipowner's actual involvement or knowledge, as distinct from vicarious liability for the acts of agents or servants. In several cases where the owner was the negligent master, the courts at times denied the "owner" the right to limit as "master" by applying an objective standard.[8] The Supreme Court re-examined the right to limitation in *The Rhone*,[9] where it granted limitation, but a radical change in favour of the right to limitation would occur only with legislative intervention.

The rationale for letting shipowners limit their liability was no longer as valid as it had been in the past. In the early days of shipping, a shipowner often did not hear of his or her ship's whereabouts for months at a time; hence, the shipowner had little or no control over his or her vessel. Then, it would have placed a heavy burden on shipowners to make them liable for the acts of their ships on the other side of the world. Today, however, communication has advanced to the point where a shipowner can be in almost constant contact with his or her ship. As well, underwriters are now far more willing to underwrite risks than they were in the past. To remedy some of the hardships that fell on claimants, it was felt that a new convention on liability limitation was necessary to find a new balance between the need to encourage shipowning on the one hand, and appropriate compensation for those who suffer loss on the other. In 1976 a conference held in London, England, produced the *Convention on Limitation of Liability for*

---

4   *Lady Gwendolen (The)*, [1965] 1 Lloyd's Rep. 335.
5   *Rederij v. England (The)*, [1973] 1 Lloyd's L.R. 373 [*The England*].
6   *Robin Hood Flour Mills v. N.M. Patterson & Sons Ltd.*, [1967] 1 Ex. C.R. 431 [*The Farrandoc*].
7   *Stein v. Kathy K (The)*, [1972] F.C. 585, aff'd [1976] 2 S.C.R. 802 [*The Kathy K*].
8   *Chernoff v. Chilcott* (1988), 27 B.C.L.R. (2d) 283; *Conrad v. Snair* (1995), 131 D.L.R. (4th) 129 (N.S.C.A.).
9   *Rhone (The) v. Peter A.B. Widener (The)*, [1993] 1 S.C.R. 497 [*The Rhone*].

Maritime Claims, 1976 (LLMC 1976).[10] In this convention a new balance was struck among an unbreakable right to limit liability, the ability for the shipowner to obtain insurance cover, and a higher amount of compensation that could be recovered, the limits of which could be revised from time to time. From an industry perspective, the outcome is an acceptable one, even though higher liability limits were put in place. From the perspective of those suffering loss there is less satisfaction, as the bar to limitation has been raised to a much higher level than ever before, there is a wider range of persons that can claim limitation, and the burden of proof has been shifted onto the victim. Hence the controversy continues!

At the international level, the concept of limitation of liability was approved and adopted in the *International Convention for the Unification of Certain Rules Relating to the Limitation of Liability of Owners of Sea-Going Vessels, 1924*;[11] the *International Convention Relating to the Limitation of Liability of Owners of Sea-Going Ships, 1957 (1957 Convention)*[12] as amended by the protocol of 1979,[13] and more recently the *LLMC 1976* as amended by the protocol of 1996.[14] Canada signed the *LLMC 1976* and protocol of 1996 on 9 September 1997 but has not ratified or acceded to either. Similarly, Canada was not a party to the first two conventions, although it had given effect to their provisions through the *Canada Shipping Act*; still, Parliament has implemented the provisions of the *LLMC 1976* and protocol of 1996 with some modifi-

---

10   19 November 1976, 1456 U.N.T.S. 221 (entered into force 1 December 1986); see Institute of Maritime Law, *Ratification of Maritime Conventions*, 4 vols., Updated looseleaf service (London: Lloyd's Press, 1991–2003). At 30 June 2002, this convention had 37 state parties representing 42.62 per cent of global tonnage: see <http://www.imo.org/Conventions>.
11   25 August 1924, 120 L.N.T.S. 123 (entered into force on 2 June 1931).
12   10 October 1957, 1412 U.N.T.S. 73 [*1957 Convention*] (entered into force 19 June 1975).
13   *Protocol Amending the International Convention Relating to the Limitation of the Liability of Owners of Sea-Going Ships*, 21 December 1979, 1412 U.N.T.S. 73 (entered into force 6 October 1984). This protocol raised limitation amounts and substituted the unit of account for the SDR.
14   *Protocol of 1996 to Amend the Convention on Limitation of Liability for Maritime Claims, 1976*, 3 May 1996, 35 I.L.M. 1406 (not yet in force). The protocol will come into force ninety days after acceptance by ten states. The protocol substantially increases the amount of compensation available and introduces a tacit acceptance procedure for further increases in liability limits. The latter will enable future increases in the limits to account for inflation. At 30 June 2002, the protocol had received 7 ratifications representing 9.40 per cent of global tonnage: see <http://www.imo.org/Conventions>.

cations through the *Marine Liability Act*.[15] For the purposes of the application of the *LLMC 1976*, Canada is deemed to be a state party.[16] The *LLMC 1976* applies whenever a person seeks to limit liability before a Canadian court or a court of a state party, or seeks the release of a ship, property, or security within the jurisdiction of such court.[17] The ship need not be a Canadian registered ship.

B. WHO IS ENTITLED TO LIMIT LIABILITY?

In the past the question as to who is ultimately responsible — especially where the shipowner is a company and the ship is chartered or managed by someone other than the actual owner — caused much difficulty. This difficulty has been addressed to the extent possible by expanding the range of persons that could be the target of a claim. Today in Canada the persons who can limit their liability in addition to any benefits from incorporation include the shipowner; charterer; manager; operator; salvor; master; crew; insurer; owners of docks, canals, and ports; and other persons for whose actions the shipowner and salvor are responsible. In this chapter these persons are referred to as "limitation claimants," as distinct from claimants against the limitation fund, that is, those suffering loss.

1) Persons

There is a wider class of persons entitled to limit their liability now than in the *1957 Convention*. The *LLMC 1976* allows the shipowner, salvor, insurer, and "any person for whose act, neglect or default the shipowner or salvor is responsible" to limit liability.[18] "Shipowner" includes the actual owner, charterer, manager, and operator. The *Marine Liability Act* expands the class of persons eligible by including "any person who has an interest in or possession of a ship from and including its launch-

---

15 S.C. 2001, c.6, Part 3 and Sch.1. Before the *Marine Liability Act*, the *LLMC 1976* and protocol of 1996 were implemented through the *Canada Shipping Act*, R.S.C. 1985, c.S-9, Sch.VI (as enacted by S.C. 1998, c.6, s.26).
16 *Marine Liability Act*, above note 15, s.27.
17 *LLMC 1976*, above note 10, art.15.
18 *Ibid.*, arts. 1 and 6. In the *1957 Convention* only the shipowner and the manager and operator of the ship, the master, the crew, and other servants were entitled to limit their liability. Similarly, the term "any person" in the *LLMC 1976* is broader than its 1957 counterpart, "master, crew, and servants of the shipowner."

ing."[19] Shipowner thereby includes not just the owner proper but also persons who may have management or control of the ship and any other person who has an interest. An action against the ship engages the liability of the shipowner. The reference to persons in possession of a ship is not in the *LLMC 1976* and constitutes a Canadian modification to enable a wider definition of shipowner. The meaning of "in possession" is potentially subject to controversy. An example contemplated during the debate on the amendments of the *Canada Shipping Act* to bring it into line with the *LLMC 1976* was the case of ship repairers who would be in possession of the ship.[20] Presumably, a creditor who forecloses on a mortgage may be said to be in possession of the ship. The question arose before the Federal Court in relation to towage in *Bayside Towing v. Canadian Pacific Railway Co.*[21] Could the tug owner be said to be in possession of the tow during towage? The Federal Court rejected this possibility on the basis of the flotilla principle and by reference to the public policy rationale for limiting liability. Likewise the reference to a person having "an interest" in the ship is a Canadian modification. It remains to be seen what persons and how close or remote their interest needs to be, and in which circumstances, before it becomes eligible. Presumably, a holder of a share in a ship has such an interest through a proprietary interest as part-owner. A mortgagee has an obvious interest and under certain conditions may enter into possession of the ship (see Chapter 6). But what about the holder of a maritime lien in Canada where, unlike the United Kingdom, the lien is not merely a procedural tool but is also deemed to carry a proprietary interest?[22] The inclusion of "salvors" into the class is a direct result of the House of Lords' decision in *The Tojo Maru*, where the salvor was held liable for the negligence of its chief diver.[23] Now "salvor," a term that includes any person rendering services in direct connection with the salvage operation, is protected by the limitation provisions. Salvage operations include a wide range of activities (see

---

19 *Marine Liability Act* above note 15, s.25(1)(b).
20 *Proceedings of the Standing Senate Committee on Transport and Communications*, 1st Sess., 36th Parl. (2 December 1997) (D.M. Collenette).
21 [2001] 2 F.C. 258 (T.D.) [*Bayside Towing*].
22 For the position in Canada, see *Todd Shipyards Corp. v. Altema Compania Maritima SA (The Ioannis Daskalelis)* (1972), 32 D.L.R. (3d) 571, [1974] S.C.R. 1248; and *Marlex Petroleum Inc. v. Har Rai (The)* (1984), 4 D.L.R. (4th) 739 (F.C.A.), upheld by S.C.C. For the position in the United Kingdom, see *Bankers Trust v. Todd Shipyards (The Halcyon Isle)*, [1981] A.C. 221 (P.C.).
23 *Tojo Maru (The)*, [1971] 1 Lloyd's L.R. 341 (H.L.).

Chapter 15).[24] "Any person" includes the master and crew and any other person in the employment of the owner, salvor, charterer, manager, or operator.[25] Understandably, the master and crew now find their positions much more vulnerable than before. In addition, "any person" may include a wide range of persons on contract service to the shipowner such as agents, stevedores, divers, and repairers.

In so far as the insurer is concerned, this "person" (i.e., limitation claimant) can benefit from limitation only in relation to those claims that are subject to limitation. Thus, if a claim is not subject to limitation of liability, there is no benefit to the insurer. This might be particularly worrying in those jurisdictions where direct action statutes are in place.[26]

2) Navigable Waters

The *LLMC 1976* anticipates that state parties may regulate the liability of ships on inland waterways. Canada has addressed this possibility in two ways: first, it extended the definition of shipowner in the *LLMC 1976*, which restricts ships to seagoing ships, by deleting the reference to "seagoing," and second, carriage is understood with reference to "water" rather than "sea." The effect is to extend the application of the convention to all navigable waters.[27]

3) Ships

For the purpose of limitation, "ship" means "any vessel or craft designed, used or capable of being used solely or partly for navigation, without regard to method or lack of propulsion." The definition includes ships under construction from the moment they are capable of floating and ships that are stranded, wrecked, or sunk, including parts of a ship.[28] Air-cushion vehicles and floating platforms constructed for natural resource utilization are not allowed to limit their liability. Further, according to the *LLMC 1976*, ships constructed for, or adapted to, and engaged in drilling are not governed by the conven-

---

24 *LLMC 1976*, above note 10, arts.1(3) and 2(1)(d)–(f).
25 *Ibid.*, art.1(4). The *1957 Convention* exempted the master, crew, and other servants of the owner from liability, even if they were in actual fault or privity to the occurrence that gave rise to the claim, above note 12, art.6(3).
26 E.g., Florida, Fla. Stat. c.624.155(1)(b)(1) (2002).
27 *Marine Liability Act*, above note 15, ss.25(1)(b)–(c).
28 *Ibid.*, s.25(1). See also Chapter 2(C).

tion, where they are subject to a higher liability limit than the general limits discussed below.[29] In the case of offshore development in Atlantic Canada, the civil liability for damage from offshore oil and gas operations arises under the common law, statute law, and contract.[30] In the Nova Scotia offshore, there is strict liability up to $30 million but, where negligence or fault is shown, liability is unlimited.[31]

C. THE RIGHT TO LIMIT LIABILITY

1) The Right to Limitation

The right to limitation arises upon certain facts and entitlements being established.[32] Given that Admiralty jurisdiction in Canada is exercised by both the Federal Court and provincial courts, the right to limitation of liability may be asserted in the filing of a defence, by way of action or counterclaim for declaratory relief in any court of competent jurisdiction.[33] However, a limitation fund may be constituted only in the Federal Court.[34] The claiming of the right of limitation does not *per se* constitute admission of liability.[35]

The *LLMC 1976* identifies classes of claims that will entitle limitation of liability. Article 2(1) sets out the following maritime claims

---

29 *LLMC 1976*, above note 10, art.15(4).
30 The financial responsibility requirements are set out in *Canada–Newfoundland Atlantic Accord Implementation Act*, R.S.C. 1987, c.3; and *Canada–Nova Scotia Offshore Petroleum Resources Accord Implementation Act*, S.C. 1988, c.28. Both federal statutes have mirror provincial statutes. For a commentary on offshore financial responsibility issues in Atlantic Canada, see B.B. de Jonge, "Financial Responsibility Requirements for Oil and Gas Activities Offshore Nova Scotia and Newfoundland" (2001) 24 Dal. L.J. 109–26.
31 *Canada–Nova Scotia Offshore Petroleum Resources Accord Implementation Act*, ibid., s.167; *Canada–Nova Scotia Oil and Gas Spills and Debris Liability Regulations*, S.O.R./95-123.
32 As Mr. Justice Clarke, of the Queen's Bench Division, Admiralty Court, found in *Capitan San Luis (The)*: "The 1976 Convention ... ha[s] conferred upon the shipowner a right to limit his liability which can only be defeated if certain facts are proved ... . [T]he right to limit under the 1976 Convention is a legal right, exercisable in circumstances which can readily be established and which can only be defeated if the claimant discharges what Mr. Justice Sheen rightly described as a 'heavy burden'" in [1993] 2 Lloyd's L.R. 573 at 579 (Q.B.D. Adm. Ct.).
33 *Marine Liability Act*, above note 15, s.32.
34 *Ibid.*, s.32(1). The limitation institutes an action in the Federal Court against the claimants. *Federal Court Rules*, S.O.R./98-106, s.496.
35 *LLMC 1976*, above note 10, art.1(7).

whatever the basis of liability might be. Liability might thereby arise in contract, tort, or statutory requirements.

> (a) claims in respect of loss of life or personal injury or loss of or damage to property (including damage to harbour works, basins and waterways and aids to navigation), occurring on board or in direct connexion with the operation of the ship or with salvage operations, and consequential loss resulting therefrom;

This class of death, personal injury, and property claims relates to events that may be on board a ship or in connection with its operation. Liabilities arising from maritime torts such as collisions, allisions, and maritime accidents give rise to the right to limitation. A potential difficulty here is the reference to "consequential loss," specifically, what and how much damage downstream from the original cause could be covered by "consequential," so that the tortfeasor's duty of care is engaged? (This is also relevant to the discussion below.)

The real innovation in the *LLMC 1976* is the inclusion of loss from delay in Article 2(1)(b):

> (b) claims in respect of loss resulting from delay in the carriage by sea of cargo, passengers or their luggage;

The carrier's liability limits are set by international standard rules applicable in Canada, such as the liability ceiling in the *Hague-Visby Rules* which is limited by unit or package in carriage contracts evidenced by a bill of lading.[36] Similarly, although not law in Canada, a liability limit is available for carriers in the *Hamburg Rules*.[37] Neither convention modifies the rights and obligations of carriers under the *LLMC 1976*. One could thereby incur liabilities under the *LLMC 1976* and one of the two carriage conventions at the same time. The carriage of passengers and their luggage involves a convergence of regimes between the *LLMC 1976* and the *Athens Convention Relating to the Carriage of Pas-*

---

36 *International Convention for the Unification of Certain Rules of Law Relating to Bills of Lading*, 25 August 1924, 120 L.N.T.S. 155 [*Hague Rules*]; and 1968 Visby Protocol: *Protocol to Amend the International Convention for the Unification of Certain Rules of Law Relating to Bills of Lading, 1924*, 23 February 1968, 1412 U.N.T.S. 121 [*Hague-Visby Rules*]; and *Protocol Amending the International Convention for the Unification of Certain Rules of Law Relating to Bills of Lading, 1924*, 21 December 1979, 1412 U.N.T.S. 121, as implemented in the *Marine Liability Act*, above note 15, Sch.3, art.IV(5). See D(7) in Chapter 9, "Carriage of Goods under Bills of Lading and Similar Documents."
37 *United Nations Convention on the Carriage of Goods by Sea*, 31 March 1978, 17 I.L.M. 608, as implemented in the *Marine Liability Act*, above note 15, Sch.4, art.6.

sengers and their Luggage by Sea, 1974 (*PAL 1974*), as amended by the protocols of 1976, 1990, and 2002.[38] Canada is not a party to *PAL 1974* or any of its protocols, but has implemented, through the *Marine Liability Act*, the convention and 1990 protocol. At the time of writing, it is unclear whether Canada will implement the 2002 protocol as well. The carrier is entitled to limit liability under this convention but, as in the *Hague-Visby* and *Hamburg Rules*, *PAL 1974* does not modify the carrier's rights or duties under the *LLMC 1976*.[39]

> (c) claims in respect of other loss resulting from infringement of rights other than contractual rights, occurring in direct connexion with the operation of the ship or salvage operations;

The claims in this class, in *LLMC 1976*, Article 2(1)(c), are also comprehended by Article 2(1)(a), but this time the loss is loss other than death, personal injury, or property, which is incurred from non-contractual rights, presumably where a duty of care is violated. One example of recoverable loss of this type is in *Kenney v. The Cape York*, which involved a collision between trawlers, where loss of fishing revenue was allowed in damages.[40] Loss of profit has also been allowed.[41]

In recalling the reference to "consequential" loss under Article 2(1)(a), but this time in the context of the generic claims under this class, it is interesting to consider the difficult and controversial notion of relational economic loss. In *Jervis Crown* a collision between a barge being towed and a bridge resulted in closure of the bridge.[42] Under contract, a third party used the bridge for rail transportation, and its clo-

---

38 13 December 1974, 14 I.L.M. 945 [*PAL 1974*]. *Protocol to the Athens Convention Relating to the Carriage of Passengers and their Luggage by Sea, 1974*, 29 March 1990, U.K.T.S. 1989 No. 43. *PAL 1974* was also amended earlier by the Protocol of 1976: *Protocol to the Athens Convention Relating to the Carriage of Passengers and their Luggage by Sea, 1974*, 19 November 1976, 16 I.L.M. 625. *PAL 1974* was further amended in 2002: *Protocol of 2002 to the Athens Convention Relating to the Carriage of Passengers and their Luggage by Sea, 1974*, 1 November 2002, LEG/CON 13.NE2 (2003), which introduced new compulsory marine insurance and raised the liability limits to much higher levels. See Chapter 10, "Carriage of Passengers."

39 *Marine Liability Act*, above note 15, Sch.2, art.19; *PAL 1974*, ibid., arts.7–8 do not limit the application of any other limitation of liability convention, i.e., *LLMC 1976*. *PAL 1974* liability limit for death or personal injury of 175,000 units of account per carriage is consistent with the limit for passenger claims under the *LLMC 1976*.

40 (1989), 25 F.T.R. 139.

41 *Shelburne Marine v. MacKinnon & Olding* (1997), 163 N.S.R. (2d) 257 (S.C.).

42 *Canadian National Railway v. Norsk Pacific Steamship Co.* (*Jervis Crown*), [1992] 1 S.C.R. 1021 [*Jervis Crown*].

sure caused loss to the third party as a result of the need to reroute its trains. A split Supreme Court of Canada allowed the claim for relational economic loss; however, more recently, the same Court decided differently on the same principle in *Bow Valley Husky (Bermuda) Ltd. v. Saint John Shipbuilding* and did not allow a claim for relational economic loss.[43] The Court did not see that the shipbuilder in this case had a duty to warn third parties and stressed the public policy considerations against this type of loss, including indeterminate liability.

For our purposes here, there is no fear that the potential liability would be indeterminate for there is a virtually unbreakable right to limit liability. The *LLMC 1976*, as implemented by the *Marine Liability Act*, establishes a general rule. The issue in this regard is not so much the danger of indeterminate liability but, rather, that a wider range of persons suffering loss might be entitled to claim against the limitation fund. Whether the courts will rethink relational economic loss as eligible loss in light of the *LLMC 1976* remains to be seen. There could be a concern that an excessive number of claimants against the limitation fund might dilute compensation. Rather than indeterminate liability, the concern could be insufficient compensation, which in itself might run counter to the public policy concern behind raising the limitation amounts.

> (d) claims in respect of the raising, removal, destruction or the rendering harmless of a ship which is sunk, wrecked, stranded or abandoned, including anything that is or has been on board such ship.

The claims under this class, in *LLMC 1976*, Article 2(1)(d), are likely to be brought forward by public authorities. Under the *Navigable Waters Protection Act*, the Minister of Fisheries and Oceans has the power to remove obstructions to navigable waters caused by wreck, sinking, lying ashore, and grounding of ships, and any expenses incurred are recoverable.[44] Similarly under the *Canada Marine Act*, a port enforcement officer has the power to remove a ship or goods that impede, interfere

---

43 *Bow Valley Husky (Bermuda) Ltd. v. Saint John Shipbuilding Ltd.*, [1997] 3 S.C.R. 1210. For pertinent remarks on relational economic loss, see A.M. Linden, *Canadian Tort Law*, 7th ed. (Markham, ON: Butterworths, 2001) at 440–43.
44 R.S.C. 1985, N-22, ss.16 and 18. In the Act, this responsibility appears to be that of the Minister of Transport, but the Minister of Fisheries and Oceans took over when the Canadian Coast Guard, together with its responsibility for the administration of the Act, was moved to the latter ministry in 1995; Bill C-55, *Public Safety Act, 2002*, 1st Sess., 37th Parl., 2001–2002, s.94, substitutes the Minister of Fisheries and Oceans for the Minister of Transport in the *Navigable Waters Protection Act*.

with, or render difficult or unsafe the use of a port area to a place that the officer considers suitable, and the costs are recoverable.[45] In contrast to Canada where these claims are subject to limitation, the United Kingdom has retained unlimited liability for wreck removal under statutory authority.[46]

> (e) claims in respect of the removal, destruction or the rendering harmless of the cargo of the ship;

This class of claims, in *LLMC 1976*, Article 2(1)(e), is similar to the previous except that it relates to cargo and must not be subject to remuneration by the person liable on the basis of a contract, as per *LLMC 1976*, Article 2(2). In Canada port authorities have similar powers over cargo as over ships in maintaining port safety and navigability.[47]

> (f) claims of a person other than the person liable in respect of measures taken in order to avert or minimize loss for which the person liable may limit his liability in accordance with this convention, and further loss caused by such measures.

This class of claims, in *LLMC 1976*, Article 2(1)(f), covers the possibility of claims advanced by third parties for costs incurred to avoid or minimize loss. This is conceivable in a situation where the shipowner engages a contractor to assist in avoiding the loss but fails to remunerate the contractor after services are rendered. The contractor can thus claim from the limitation fund. Similarly, the expenses of a public authority to remove obstacles in ports and navigable waterways discussed under Article 2(1)(d) may fall under this class as well.

2) Claims Not Subject to Limitation

The *LLMC 1976* excepts certain claims from the application of the convention, namely remuneration for salvage, contribution in general average, marine pollution damage, nuclear damage, and certain claims by servants of the shipowner or salvor. Salvage claims, other than claims resulting from the salvor's negligence, and special compensation claims under the *International Convention on Salvage, 1989*, are excluded.[48] Remuneration for such claims is based on contractual stipula-

---

45 S.C. 1998, c.10, s.123. Costs so incurred give rise to a maritime lien that ranks above all other claims, except seamen's wages: *ibid.*, s.122.
46 P. Griggs & R. Williams, *Limitation of Liability for Maritime Claims*, 3d ed. (London: LLP, 1998) at 18.
47 *Canada Marine Act*, above note 45, s.123.

tions, and industry and arbitration practices. The same presumably applies to remuneration under the *SCOPIC* clause.[49]

Claims for contribution in general average are likewise excluded, since such claims are addressed by a specialized regime.[50] General average has historically developed a different liability basis. All those interests that benefit from the intentional sacrifice or expenditure have to contribute proportionately to those that suffer the loss. In a sense, the contribution is a contingent expense of the carriage for ship and cargo owner alike; however, a claim in damages — as distinct from the contribution — against the negligent shipowner for causing the loss leading to a general average contribution is not necessarily excluded from this class of claims (e.g., where the carrier provides an unseaworthy ship).

The shipowner's limit of liability in relation to claims for oil pollution damage is excepted from the *LLMC 1976* but is covered by a separate strict liability regime involving the *International Convention on Civil Liability for Oil Pollution Damage, 1969 (CLC 1969)*, as amended over time and most recently by the 1992 protocol, and to which Canada is a party.[51] It remains to be seen whether this exclusion will eventually be extended to the *International Convention on Liability and*

---

48 *LLMC 1976* above note 10, art.3(a); 28 April 1989, U.K.T.S. 1996 No. 93.
49 See International Salvage Union web site at <http://www.marine-salvage.com/media_d.htm>. See also A(9)(b)(ii) in Chapter 15, "Maritime Salvage and Wreck."
50 The rules of contribution in general average are set out in the *York–Antwerp Rules* (discussed in Chapter 16, "General Average"). See also N.G. Hudson, *The York-Antwerp Rules*, 2d ed. (London: LLP, 1996).
51 *LLMC 1976*, above note 10, art.3(b); *CLC 1969*, 29 November 1969, 973 U.N.T.S. 3 (entered into force 19 June 1975; entered into force in Canada 24 April 1989, but denounced by Canada 29 May 1995), as am. by *Protocol to the International Convention on Civil Liability for Oil Pollution Damage, 1969*, 19 November 1976, 1225 U.N.T.S. 356; *Protocol of 1984 to Amend the International Convention on Civil Liability for Oil Pollution Damage, 1969*, 25 May 1984, 23 I.L.M. 177; *Protocol to Amend the International Convention on Civil Liability for Oil Pollution Damage, 1969*, 27 November 1992, U.K.T.S. 1996 No. 87. The convention is now applied through the *Marine Liability Act*, above note 15, Part 6, Civil Liability and Compensation for Pollution. The *CLC 1969* is accompanied by a second tier of compensation through the *International Convention on the Establishment of an International Fund for Compensation for Oil Pollution Damage*, 18 December 1971, 1110 U.N.T.S. 57 [*FUND 1971*] (entered into force 16 October 1978; ceased to be in force 24 May 2002) as am. by protocols of 1976, 1984, and 1992: *Protocol to the International Convention on the Establishment of an International Fund for Compensation for Oil Pollution Damage of December 18 1971*, 19 November 1976, 16 I.L.M. 621; *Protocol of 1984 to Amend the International Convention on the Establishment of an International Fund for Compensation for Oil Pol-*

Compensation for Damage in Connection with the Carriage of Hazardous and Noxious Substances by Sea, 1996 (HNS 1996)[52] and to the *International Convention on Civil Liability for Bunker Oil Pollution Damage, 2001*.[53] HNS 1996 adopts a strict liability regime based on the CLC 1969 and FUND 1971 convention system to compensate victims of accidents involving substances such as chemicals. (These conventions are discussed in Chapter 17, "Marine Pollution Prevention.") Also excluded are claims for liability for nuclear damage and claims against a shipowner of a nuclear ship for nuclear damage. These claims are covered by separate regimes.[54]

Normally the shipowner's or salvor's servants and their heirs, dependants, and others entitled to bring forward claims may do so under the LLMC 1976. However, in those jurisdictions where shipowners or salvors are not entitled to limit their liability or the limit of liability they are entitled to is greater than that established under the general limits in the LLMC 1976, then the convention will not apply.[55] The reason is that in this situation the domestic limit of liability is higher than that established in the convention, and shipowners and salvors are not allowed to seek the lower limit. In Canada the LLMC 1976 is law and, unless domestic liability limits that are higher than those in the convention are introduced in the future, the convention's liability limits will continue to apply.

---

lution Damage, 1971, 25 May 1984, 23 I.L.M. 195; and *Protocol to Amend the International Convention on the Establishment of an International Fund for Compensation for Oil Pollution Damage, 1971*, 27 November 1992, 1996 A.T.S. 3. The CLC 1969 and FUND 1971 convention system is discussed in detail in Chapter 17, "Marine Pollution Prevention."

52   2 May 1996, 35 I.L.M. 1406.
53   *International Convention on Civil Liability for Bunker Oil Pollution Damage, 2001*, 27 March 2001, IMO LEG/CONF.12/19 [BUNKER 2001]. See also C(6) in Chapter 17, "Marine Pollution Prevention."
54   LLMC 1976, above note 10, arts.3(c)–(d): applicable international conventions re (c) are *Convention on Third Party Liability in the Field of Nuclear Energy*, 29 July 1960, 956 U.N.T.S. 251; *Convention Supplementary to the Convention on Third Party Liability in the Field of Nuclear Energy, 1960*, 31 January 1963, 1041 U.N.T.S. 358; *Convention Relating to Civil Liability in the Field of Maritime Carriage of Nuclear Material*, 17 December 1971, 974 U.N.T.S. 255 [NUCLEAR 1971] (entered into force 15 July 1975; Canada is not a party); and re (d) *International Convention on the Liability of Operators of Nuclear Ships*, 25 May 1962, 57 A.J.I.L. 268 (not yet in force; to date, Canada is not a party to any of these instruments). Canada has occasionally implemented treaties it is not a party to, but the *Nuclear Liability Act*, R.S.C. 1985, c.N-28 does not enact any of these treaties.
55   LLMC 1976, ibid., art.3(e).

3) Conduct Barring Limitation

Under the *1957 Convention* and a previous era of the *Canada Shipping Act*, a shipowner claiming limitation of liability could do so, provided the loss did not occur with his or her actual fault or privity. In Canada this was interpreted so restrictively that limitation of liability was rarely granted. Moreover, the shipowner had the burden of proof of showing that he or she was not in actual fault or privity. Fault barred limitation. This situation has been completely reversed by the *LLMC 1976* in that the shipowner's entitlement to limit liability is removed only "if it is proved that the loss resulted from his personal act or omission, committed with the intent to cause such loss, or recklessly and with knowledge that such loss would probably result."[56] As a result, limitation of liability under the *Marine Liability Act* and the *LLMC 1976* is much easier to achieve than under the *1957 Convention*.

There are three key elements required to bar limitation. First, unlike under the old regime, the burden of proof has now shifted to the person challenging the limitation claimant's right to limitation. Second, it must be shown that the loss resulted from the personal behaviour of the limitation claimant. Even though the limitation claimant is still vicariously responsible for the acts of his or her servants, the negligent acts of servants alone are not enough. There must be a personal act or failing, that is, authorship, on the part of the limitation claimant. Unfortunately, there is no indication as to what acts committed by directors of a shipowning corporation constitute reckless acts. In the case of corporations the question as to what is "personal" could be moot. One possible interpretation is for a court to apply the doctrine of corporate identification. The court would enquire as to who is the directing mind of the corporation on matters of corporate policy by using the test in *The Rhone*.[57] A consequence of the "personal" nature of the conduct barring limitation is that it is perfectly possible in the same occurrence for the master to lose the right to limitation, while the shipowner retains it. Third, the act or omission must be either intended or reckless, and with knowledge of the probable consequences. Intentionality suggests a *mens rea*. Recklessness suggests gross negligence. In either case, there is the condition that there be knowledge, not mere speculation, that the loss would probably result. There must be much more than mere negligence. In one of the first cases in Cana-

---

56 *LLMC 1976*, ibid., art.4. In relation to docks, canals, and ports the relevant provision is the *Marine Liability Act*, above note 15, s.30(4).
57 Above note 9 at para.42.

da where a challenge to the right to limitation was advanced under the *LLMC 1976* on the basis of knowledge of the damage, recklessness, and statutory presumption, the challenge failed.[58] The defendants alleged that the actions of the plaintiffs, crew, and owners of the tug were "wilful defaults," language that is not used in the *LLMC 1976* but does appear in the *Canada Shipping Act* in connection with breaches to the collision regulations.[59] Prothonotary Hargrave, using principles of statutory interpretation, deferred to parliamentary intent in not equating wilful default to the *LLMC 1976* test for conduct barring limitation. On this point he opined:

> [I]t may be difficult for CPR [the defendants] to convince a judge that a breach of the collision regulations and the application of s.564(3) of the *Canada Shipping Act*, leading to a deemed positive act of wilfulness, which can also mean an act done in a reckless manner, intending the result, bars limitation under Article 4 [of the *LLMC 1976*].[60]

If intention or recklessness is proved, then the shipowner's right to limit liability would be lost. Where the right to limit liability is lost, it is conceivable that an underwriter might avoid liability under a marine insurance policy. The assured is subject to an implied warranty that the marine adventure insured is lawful and, to the extent that the assured has control, will be carried out in a lawful manner (i.e., warranty of legality).[61] Also, an insurer is not liable for any loss attributable to the wilful misconduct of the insured.[62] If the underwriter refuses indemnity, it is probable that the claimant might not have much option but to try to recover from the shipowner and master. At the same time, this scenario could be encouraging for the shipowner to simply abandon the arrested vessel and hide behind a convenient corporate veil, except where the veil is lifted by a court.

---

58 *Bayside Towing*, above note 21.
59 "Where any injury to a person or damage to property arises from the non-observance by any vessel or raft of any of the Collision Regulations, the injury or damage shall be deemed to have been occasioned by the wilful default of the person in charge of that raft or of the deck of that vessel at the time, unless it is shown to the satisfaction of a court that the circumstances of the case made a departure from the regulation necessary": *Canada Shipping Act*, R.S.C. 1985, c.S-9, s.564(3).
60 *Bayside Towing*, above note 21.
61 *Marine Insurance Act*, S.C. 1993, c.22, s.34. See R.M. Fernandes, ed., *Marine Insurance Law of Canada* (Toronto: Butterworths, 1987) at 62–63.
62 *Marine Insurance Act, ibid.*, s.53(2). Burden of proof rests with the insurer: see Fernandes, *ibid.* at 90ff.

D. GENERAL LIMITS

There are three general tonnage levels to determine liability limits under the *Marine Liability Act*. The Act applies the *LLMC 1976* limits as amended by the protocol of 1996, with some important modifications. It is important to note that the protocol of 1996 increased the limits of liability, simplified the scales, and left it to state parties to regulate ships less than 300 tons. Passenger claims, salvors, and dock, canal, and port owners deviate from the general limits scale. For loss of life, personal injury, and property claims, there are two separate funds. In the case of ships above 300 tons, the loss of life/personal injury does not constitute the full extent of liability in respect of all claims. In the event of mixed claims — loss of life or personal injury together with property claims arising out of the same incident — where the loss of life or personal injury fund is not sufficient to meet all claims, the right to proceed rateably with the other claims against the property loss fund is maintained. The liability limits apply to the aggregate of all claims that arise from any one distinct occasion.[63]

1) Measurement of Tonnage

Under the *LLMC 1976*, tonnage figures represent gross tonnage, a figure that is much higher than limitation tonnage used in the *1957 Convention*, which was based on a per-GT flat rate of a ship's tonnage. The tonnage of a ship is now measured according to Annex I of the *International Convention on Tonnage Measurement of Ships*.[64]

2) Unit of Account

The unit of account for those states who are members of the International Monetary Fund is no longer the gold (Poincaré) franc but the Special Drawing Rights (SDRs) of the fund.[65] The monetary liability is determined on the basis of the units of account established or calculat-

---

63 *LLMC 1976*, above note 10, art.9.
64 23 June 1969, 1291 U.N.T.S. 3 (entered into force 18 July 1982). Canada implemented the convention through the *Ship Registration and Tonnage Regulations*, S.O.R./2000-70.
65 *LLMC 1976*, above note 10, art.8. A different non–SDR formula for those not members of IMF allows conversion into gold and national currency; the underlying requirement is to approximate the real value to the SDR formula. See (D)(7) in Chapter 9.

ed at the relevant liability level and converted into SDRs. Previously under the *1957 Convention* the limitation amount was calculated in Poincaré francs, which in turn were converted into the local currency.

3) Appropriate Tonnage Unit for Limitation Purposes

The question as to what unit should be used for limitation purposes in the case of a flotilla, as distinct from a ship, has been treated somewhat differently in the United Kingdom and Canada. This question has arisen in connection with towage, where the situation may involve a tug and tow, or several tugs and a tow. In the case of a loss caused by the negligence of the tug, should the unit for limitation be the tonnage of the tug alone, or the combined tonnage of the tug or tugs and tow as one operation? This has far-reaching significance for the amount of liability subject to limitation. A tug is likely to have low tonnage. A tug towing a larger and more expensive ship, such as a liner or an oil rig, will lead to a higher liability ceiling. The *Marine Liability Act* (and previously, the *Canada Shipping Act, 1985*) and the *LLMC 1976* are silent on this question. In the United Kingdom, the law on this point has evolved. Originally English case law held that in a situation of common ownership the errors of navigation of the tug were also errors of the tow so that the shipowner's liability was engaged as owner of tug and tow, and the aggregate tonnage constituted the limitation unit.[66] This eventually evolved to the point where the ship actually at fault is considered as the sole unit for limitation. The question was considered by Lord Denning in *The Bramley Moore*, a case that involved the towing of a barge owned by two separate owners.[67] Counsel argued that the wrongdoer should be liable for the potentiality of the damage, and the greater the potential the higher the measure of liability should be. His Lordship disagreed, stating: "The principle underlying limitation of liability is that the wrongdoer should be liable according to the value of his ship and no more," even though the tug is a small ship and may tow a liner that does great damage.[68] In *obiter dicta*, he also dismissed the relevance of ownership and focused on causative negligence instead. For Lord Denning, combined tonnage for the determination of limitation of liability is appropriate where there is combined negligence, that is, the negligence causative of the damage occurs on both the tug and tow. The

---

66 *The Rhone*, above note 9, referring to a string of old English cases between 1922–50.
67 *Bramley Moore (The)*, above note 3.
68 *Ibid.* at 437.

issue arose again in front of Mr. Justice Kerr in *The Joseph Rawlinson*, this time involving common ownership of tug and tow, but the negligence was on the tug alone. Justice Kerr reluctantly followed the decision in *The Bramley Moore*.[69] In effect the innocent tonnage is exempted. However, if it happens that both the tug and tow are at fault, then the limits that both are entitled to will be available for the claimant.[70]

The position in Canada evolved out of old English case law. In *The Pacific Express v. The Salvage Princess*, where there was common ownership of tug and tow, but sole negligence of the tug, the aggregate tonnage was used as the limitation unit.[71] In *The Maple Prince*, where the tug and tow were separately owned, the tonnage of the negligent tug alone was used for limitation.[72] A distinction was drawn between commonly and separately owned tug and tow. The issue came up again with a twist in *Monarch Towing & Trading Co. v. British Columbia Cement Co.*,[73] where the limitation claimant owned the tug but was the charterer of the scow that was lost. Since, for the purposes of limitation, "owner" included charterer in the *Canada Shipping Act* at the time — and in the *LLMC 1976* as implemented by the *Marine Liability Act* today — the limitation claimant was deemed to be owner of both tug and tow. Even though the scow was unmanned, limitation of liability was assessed on the aggregate tonnage. The reasoning was that, even though the actual negligence was that of the tug, the tow was not innocent by virtue of being a servant, like the tug, of the same owner. Again the Supreme Court of Canada in *The Kathy K* addressed the question where the tug and tow had common ownership, and it decided that the aggregate tonnage of the wrongdoing mass should be the unit for limitation.[74]

The main difference between the United Kingdom and Canada seems to be the relevance or otherwise of ownership. The Supreme Court had an opportunity to consider this difference in *The Rhone* but declined to do so. In this case a flotilla of four tugs towed a barge. The tugs Ohio and South Carolina were owned by the limitation claimant. Of the entire flotilla, only The Ohio was negligent and the Court therefore limited the tonnage to The Ohio alone. Writing for the majority, Justice Iacobucci held: "Apart from the vessel responsible for the over-

---

69 *London Dredging Co. v. Greater London Council (The Joseph Rawlinson)*, [1972] 2 Lloyd's L.R. 436 [*The Joseph Rawlinson*].
70 *Smjeli (The)*, [1982] 2 Lloyd's L.R. 74.
71 [1949] Ex. C.R. 230.
72 *Robertson v. Maple Prince (The)*, [1955] Ex. C.R. 225 [*The Maple Prince*].
73 [1957] S.C.R. 816.
74 *The Kathy K*, above note 7.

all navigation of a flotilla, only those vessels of the same shipowner which physically caused or contributed to the resulting damage form the unit for which liability is limited." The South Carolina could not possibly be held liable: "it would be stretching the principles of causation beyond their proper limits to hold that a vessel not physically causing the impugned damage nor responsible for the navigation of the vessel which in fact physically caused the damage to be part of the 'wrongdoing mass.'"[75] Ownership matters only when the commonly owned vessels are all actively involved in the wrongdoing causing the damage.

The issue arose again recently in *Bayside Towing*, which was discussed earlier under the definition of shipowner.[76] A loaded scow (a dumb barge) towed by a tug collided with a bridge causing $5-million–worth of damage. The tonnage of the tug alone had a limitation fund of $500,000. The tug and scow were owned separately. Counsel for defendant argued that, although the real ownership was separate, the tug could also be said to be the "shipowner" for the tow since the tug owners were "in possession" of the scow during towage. As a result, counsel argued, the aggregate tonnage should be used to determine liability. Gibson J. rejected this argument and applied *The Rhone* principles in calculating liability on the basis of the wrongful mass, that is, the tug alone this time. In summary, the Canadian flotilla principle, whereby aggregate tonnage is used to constitute a limitation fund, applies only when there is a combination of common ownership and causative negligence.

4) Limitation Amounts

The limit of liability is calculated on the basis of a general formula that is based on a number of factors. First, it distinguishes between, on the one hand, loss of life and personal injury and, on the other, any other claim; this general formula does not apply to passenger claims, which are considered under a separate formula. Second, it identifies different levels of tonnage ranges. Third, for ships whose tonnage is 2001 tons or more, the limit is determined on the combination of a base rate plus a unit of account per ton. Collectively, these three factors constitute the formula as illustrated in Table 18.1.

---

75 *The Rhone*, above note 9 at 501.
76 Above note 21.

Table 18.1 Limits of Liability by Tonnage

Tonnage	Loss of Life and Personal Injury	All Other Claims
Less than 300	C$ 1,000,000	C$ 500,000
300–2000	SDR 2,000,000 (C$ 4,000,000)*	SDR 1,000,000 (C$ 2,000,000)*
2001–30,000	SDR 2,000,000 (C$ 4,000,000)* + SDR 800 per ton (C$ 1,600* per ton)	SDR 1,000,000 (C$ 2,000,000)* + SDR 400 per ton (C$ 800 per ton)*
30,001–70,000	SDR 2,000,000 (C$ 4,000,000)* + SDR 600 per ton (C$ 1,200 per ton)*	SDR 1,000,000 (C$ 2,000,000)* + SDR 300 per ton (C$ 600 per ton)*
More than 70,000	SDR 2,000,000 (C$ 4,000,000)* + SDR 400 per ton (C$ 800 per ton)*	SDR 1,000,000 (C$ 2,000,000)* + SDR 200 per ton (C$ 400 per ton)*

*(C$ = Approximate Value)

a) Ships less than 300 Tons

Under the *1957 Convention*, the minimum tonnage used as a base for calculating liability was 500 tons. This was raised to 2000 tons in the *LLMC 1976* while leaving the limitation system of ships less than 300 tons to the discretion of state parties.[77] As a result, the *LLMC 1976* places far greater liability on owners of small vessels than did the *1957 Convention*. The first scale consists of ships with a gross tonnage of less than 300 tons. Since the *Marine Liability Act* extends the *LLMC 1976* to all navigable waters, it can be seen that this tonnage will capture a wide variety of small ships and craft. The limit for such ships on any distinct occasion is $1 million with respect to loss of life or personal injury and $500,000 in respect of any other claims.[78] This limit does not apply to passenger claims, which are subject to the limits discussed below.

b) Ships of more than 300 but less than 2000 Tons

Ships with tonnage over 300 but less than 2000 tons have different limits for, on the one hand, claims for loss of life or personal injury, and on the other for any other claims. Claims for loss of life or personal

---

77 *LLMC 1976*, above note 10, art.15(2)(b).
78 *Marine Liability Act*, above note 15, s.28(1).

injury for any distinct occasion have a ceiling of 2 million units of account. All other claims have a limit of 1 million units of account.[79] Where the claims for loss of life or personal injury exceed the sum available, any unpaid claims will rank rateably with the other claims.[80]

c) **Ships more than 2000 Tons**

Again, a distinction is maintained between claims for loss of life or personal injury, and any other claims. In loss of life or personal injury claims the liability limit is a combination of 2 million units of account and the following sliding scale according to tonnage levels:

- 2001–30,000 tons: by 800 units of account/ton
- 30,001–70,000 tons: by 600 units of account/ton, and
- more than 70,000 tons: by 400 units of account/ton.

With respect to any other claim the liability limit is a combination of 1 million units of account and the following sliding scale according to tonnage levels:

- 2001–30,000 tons: by 400 units of account/ton
- 30,001–70,000 tons: by 300 units of account/ton, and
- more than 70,000 tons: by 200 units of account/ton.[81]

As in the case of ships between 300–2000 tons, where the claims for loss of life or personal injury exceed the sum available, any unpaid claims will rank rateably with the other claims.[82]

E. SPECIAL LIMITATION CASES

1) Passenger Claims

The subject of passenger claims is addressed comprehensively in Chapter 10, "Carriage of Passengers." A discussion of *LLMC 1976* would not be complete, however, without reference to the provisions in this convention concerning passenger claims and a consideration of the significance of the overlap between the *LLMC 1976* and *PAL 1974*. Passenger carriers comprise a new class of ships for liability purposes under the *LLMC 1976* and their liability under this convention needs to be related to *PAL 1974*,

---

79 *LLMC 1976*, above note 10, art.6(1) as am. by protocol of 1996, above note 14.
80 *Ibid.*, art.6(2).
81 *Ibid.*, art.6(1).
82 *Ibid.*, art.6(2).

since Canada has implemented both instruments in the *Marine Liability Act*. Under both instruments passengers are persons carried under a carriage contract or who accompany a vehicle or live animals under a carriage contract with the carrier's consent.[83] A carrier cannot contract out of liability to passengers for death and personal injury claims.[84] A significant difference between the formula for calculating liability for passengers and the formula for other claimants against the limitation fund is that liability for passenger claims is not based on tonnage but, rather, on a fixed number of units of account. There are different scenarios contemplated in the *LLMC 1976*. The maximum liability on any distinct occasion for claims for death or personal injury on ships that do not require a certificate under Part V of the *Canada Shipping Act* is the greater sum of 2,000,000 units of account and 175,000 units of account multiplied by the number of passengers on board the ship.[85]

In the case of claims by persons carried without a contract of carriage, the maximum liability on any distinct occasion for loss of life or personal injury is the *greater of*

- 2,000,000 units of account, and
- one of two options:
  (1) 175,000 units multiplied by the number of passengers the ship is authorized to carry under a Part V *Canada Shipping Act* certificate, or
  (2) 175,000 units multiplied by the number of persons on board the ship if no certificate is carried.[86]

The difference between (1) and (2) can be very significant as the ultimate amount of liability will depend upon either the number of persons that the ship is licensed to carry, or the actual number of passengers on board the ship.

Although the limits for death or personal injury in *PAL 1974* are comparable, the limits are applicable *per carriage* rather than on any distinct occasion as provided for in the *LLMC 1976*.[87] There could be a

---

83 *Marine Liability Act*, above note 15, s.29(4); *LLMC 1976*, above note 10, art.7; *PAL 1974*, above note 38, art.1(4).
84 *PAL 1974*, ibid., art.18.
85 *Marine Liability Act*, above note 15, s.29(1).
86 Ibid., s.29(2). This particular provision does not apply to "(a) the master of a ship, a member of a ship's crew or any other person employed or engaged in any capacity on board a ship on the business of a ship; or (b) a person carried on board a ship other than a ship operated for a commercial or public purpose." Ibid., s.29(3).
87 *PAL 1974*, above note 38, art.7.

potential inconsistency in the event that the same passenger is injured twice on the same carriage, especially since the provisions of *PAL 1974* do not override the *LLMC 1976* provisions. In effect, both limitation of liability regimes could apply side by side, if the claims are numerous and so large that one fund is insufficient to satisfy all of them.

As discussed in Chapter 10, "Carriage of Passengers," the 2002 protocol of *PAL 1974* has significantly raised the liability limits, as well as introducing compulsory insurance.[88] At this time, and with fast growing cruise ship tourism on the Atlantic and Pacific coasts, it is unclear whether Canada will opt to implement the higher limits. While the new limits are certainly a considerable improvement on the 1990 protocol limits to *PAL 1974*, it remains to be seen to what extent the new limits will be sufficient to compensate for death and personal injury claims that may involve very large cruise ships.[89]

2) Salvors

Salvors' limitation of liability is treated differently and is dependent upon whether the service is performed from the salvor's own ship. If the claim is against the shipowner of a ship rendering salvage services from that ship, or the salvor operating from such ship, then the limitations are the same as for those mentioned above. But, where the claim is made against the salvor who is not operating from a ship, or who is operating on the ship that is the object of salvage, then the limit of liability is based on 1,500 GT.[90]

3) Dock, Canal, and Port Owners

Dock, canal, and port owners have a duty of care toward those who use their facilities.[91] They are entitled to limit their liability, including lia-

---

88 For an explanation of the changes introduced by the 2002 Protocol, see "Liability Limits for Ship Passengers Raised with New Athens Convention, Compulsory Insurance Introduced" (IMO Newsroom, Press Briefing 2002), online at <http://www.imo.org/home.asp?topic_id=161>.

89 The Royal Caribbean's Voyager of the Seas is 142,000 GT in size, has a crew of 1,800 and has capacity for 3,100 passengers: see "Larger Ships, New Safety Challenges" (IMO Newsroom, Hot Topics), online at <http://www.imo.org/home.asp?topic_id=161>.

90 *LLMC 1976*, above note 10, art.6(4).

91 *Webb v. Port Bruce Harbour Co.* (1861), 19 U.C.Q.B. 623; *Grit (The)*, [1924] P. 246; *R. v. Hochelaga Shipping and Towing Co.*, [1940] S.C.R. 153; *Panagiotis TH. Coumantaros (The) v. Canada (Nat. Harbours Board)*, [1942] S.C.R. 450.

bility for the actions and omissions of persons for whom they are responsible. As in the case of ships, the rule concerning conduct barring limitation applies; that is, limitation of liability does not apply if it is proven that the loss resulted from the personal act of the owner or person for whom the owner is responsible, and "committed with intent to cause the loss or recklessly and with knowledge that the loss would probably result."[92] There is a very wide definition of "dock," which includes "wet docks and basins, tidal-docks and basins, locks, cuts, entrances, dry docks, graving docks, gridirons, slips, quays, wharfs, piers, stages, landing places, jetties and synchrolifts," whereas "owner of a dock, canal or port" is defined as including the person having the control or management of such a facility, and also includes the ship repairer that may be using the facility.[93]

A number of points need to be made in relation to this definition. The purpose behind the *Marine Liability Act*'s extension of limitation — and beyond the coverage of the *LLMC 1976* — to such service providers is a policy aimed at encouraging the provision of important services to shipping. This was applied in *Beeco Invest KS v. Canada*, where a lock wall in a Crown-owned canal collapsed and in so doing trapped a ship. The Crown, as owner of such a facility, enjoyed limitation of liability. Also interesting in this case is the extent to which the court was willing to consider the type of loss covered by limitation. There was no physical damage to the ship, but economic loss resulted. It was held that "the loss or damage to a vessel is not limited to those cases where the vessel itself or her cargo are physically damaged." Owners of docks, canals, and harbours provide services to ships, and therefore their potential liabilities include the interruption or suspension of such services and not simply physical damage that may be inflicted upon ships.[94] However, the same policy rationale was not applied in *Nord-Deutsche Versicherungs-Gesellshaft v. R.* with respect to the Crown's liability resulting from a collision between two ships, which was attributed, in part, to misplaced navigation lights on the shore of a river. The Crown was responsible for the maintenance of the navigation lights, but it did so not in the capacity of an owner of a canal or port. The Exchequer Court and the Supreme Court of Canada were of the view that because the right to limit liability is extraordinary — that is, it reduces the full liability normally applicable under the ordinary rules of the common and civil law — it must be given a strict

---

92 *Marine Liability Act*, above note 15, s.30(4).
93 *Ibid.*, s.30(5).
94 [1989] 2 F.C. 110 (C.A.).

application.[95] It is clear that the entitlement to limit liability will be strictly applied to the actual owner or person who has control or management. In so far as the ship repairer is concerned, this person is clearly entitled to limit liability while providing services to a ship in a dock, canal, or port. But is he or she entitled to limit liability only while the ship is in the dock, canal, or port, whereas the damage becomes apparent after departure from the facility? This question was considered by an English case. What is important is for the act or omission that caused the damage to have occurred while the ship was in the dock, even though it became apparent after the ship left.[96]

The maximum liability of a dock, canal, or port owner for a claim arising for a loss to a ship, cargo, or other property on any distinct occasion is the greater of two ceilings. The first is $2 million. The second is calculated on the basis of the tonnage of the largest ship that was within the area of the facility controlled or managed at the time of the loss or up to five years before that time. The tonnage of the ship is multiplied by $1,000 to arrive at the liability limit.[97] It is interesting to note that the *Marine Liability Act* has not extended the right to limitation in the case of death or personal injury, suggesting that in the case of such claims liability might be unlimited.

4) Other Ocean Users

In addition to the traditional shipping and navigation actors discussed above, there is an increasing diversity of users of Canada's marine areas but for whom limitation of liability under the *LLMC 1976* and *Marine Liability Act* does not apply. The growing list of users includes owners or operators of submarine telecommunication cables, submarine gas pipelines, aquaculture cages, and wind energy farms. In so far as the utilization of a ship in association with one of these activities is concerned, the *LLMC 1976* would naturally apply in respect to damage done by that ship. However, the significance of these new marine activities is that the ocean use involves more than the utilization of a ship. Where property damage, death, or personal injury results not from the operation of a ship, or is suffered not on a ship, there could be the possibility of unlimited liability for the owner or operator of a cable, pipeline, cage, or wind farm. There have been cases where loss was suffered by their owners or operators, but there have not been cases where

---

95 [1969] 1 Ex. C.R. 117, var'd [1971] S.C.R. 849.
96 *Mason v. Uxbridge Boat Centre and Wright*, [1980] 2 Lloyd's L.R. 592 (Q.B.).
97 *Marine Liability Act*, above note 15, s.30.

the owners or operators were authors of the loss.[98] The potential liability of these uses in a marine environmental context is not within the domain of traditional maritime law and the trade policy rationale behind limitation, and consequently, if limitation of liability were to be extended to these ocean users, it would have to be done by statute.

F. LIMITATION FUND

1) Significance of the Fund

There are two significant general implications on the establishment of a limitation fund. The first is the transfer of the potential claims arising out of a distinct occasion against the ship or other property to the fund. The effect of this is to bar any claimant against the fund from proceeding against any other assets belonging to the person claiming limitation. The second is that, on the establishment of the fund, the person claiming limitation has the right to secure the release of the ship or any property attached or security given. The overall effect is to enable those that are able to bring a claim to do so against the limitation fund.[99] However, in situations where a claimant is not able to bring a claim against the limitation fund before the court administering it, and the fund is not actually available and freely transferable in respect of such claim, the claimant could still be in a position to proceed against other assets.[100] This rule is not triggered when the fund is unable to meet fully all claims within the limit of liability, for in this situation the various claims would be pro-rated. After all, the purpose of the fund is to limit the liability of the person claiming limitation. Limitation funds bar actions against assets in foreign jurisdictions, provided that the fund is not subject to currency regulations restricting transfers out of the country.[101] Canada does not have such restrictions; however, it is conceivable that a claimant in Canada might not have his or her claim satisfied from a limitation fund in a foreign court as a result of currency controls within that jurisdiction.

---

98 E.g., see *Pembina Resources Ltd. v. ULS International Inc.* (1989), 28 F.T.R. 180, concerned the fracturing of a submarine pipeline by a ship that dragged anchor; and *Peterborough (The) v. Bell Telephone Co. of Canada*, [1952] Ex. C.R. 462, concerned the fouling of a submarine cable by a ship's anchor.
99 *LLMC 1976*, above note 10, arts.13(1)–(2).
100 *Ibid.*, art.13(3).
101 P. Griggs & R. Williams above note 46 at 59.

It is possible for a limitation claimant not to establish a fund.[102] This might arise as a defence in a maritime suit before a provincial court. The risk the limitation claimant runs is that his or her non-maritime assets may remain attached pending resolution of the suit. A payment may be made into court or a bond or guarantee filed in accordance with the rules of court of the jurisdiction concerned to cover claims, but this *per se* does not bar claims against personal assets, if the security given is deemed insufficient. In those jurisdictions where the rules of court allow for the arrest of maritime property, bail could be secured.[103]

2) Constitution of the Fund

Under the *LLMC 1976*, as implemented by the *Marine Liability Act*, a person entitled to claim limitation of liability may do so by establishing a limitation fund within a court of competent jurisdiction. In Canada, while the right to limit liability may be raised in any court of competent jurisdiction, the Federal Court retains exclusive jurisdiction over the constitution and distribution of a limitation fund.[104] So the claimant that is party to proceedings, or is an interested person (e.g., insurer) on the same subject-matter before a provincial court, has to apply to the Federal Court to constitute a limitation fund.[105] The Federal Court will determine the amount needed to cover claims and interest calculated from the date of the occurrence and will take steps for the constitution of the fund. The fund amount consists of monies deposited by, or the provision of, a financial guarantee to the satisfaction of the court from the limitation claimant or his or her insurer.[106] Once the fund is established, the Federal Court may enjoin any person from instituting or continuing proceedings on the same subject-matter in any other court.

---

102 *LLMC 1976*, above note 10, art.10; see also *Marine Liability Act*, above note 15, s.32(2).
103 B.C. Reg. 221/90, r.55.25 (British Columbia Supreme Court Rules).
104 *Marine Liability Act*, above note 15, s.32.
105 *Ibid.*, s.33(1). For some reason, in s.33, the powers of the Federal Court exclude consideration of potential applications by dock, canal, and port owners to limit their liability. Presumably the claims to limitation of these persons can still be advanced in any court of competent jurisdiction as per s.32(2), but no limitation fund is necessarily established.
106 *Ibid.*, s.33; *LLMC 1976*, above note 10, art.11.

3) Distribution of the Fund

The Federal Court will distribute the fund proportionately according to the respective liabilities among the various claims before it and emanating from foreign courts. The proportions are not affected by any lien or right. The Federal Court may also postpone distribution in relation to any person or part of the fund as it may deem appropriate. If the limitation claimant or his or her insurer has settled a claim against the fund before distribution, there is a right of subrogation to the rights of the claimant against the fund.[107] Likewise, any payments made by a public authority to injured persons or dependants of injured persons or victims of fatal accidents may give rise to a right of subrogation against the fund.[108] Also adjusted are claims subject to counterclaims by the limitation claimant, which are set off against each other and the distribution will apply to the balance, if any.[109]

4) Fund Established in a Foreign Jurisdiction

The *LLMC 1976* is a legal regime based on reciprocity among state parties, and this has implications for actions before Canadian courts. A court in Canada is bound to respect the constitution of a limitation fund in a foreign jurisdiction that is a state party to the *LLMC 1976*. Consequently, the Canadian court would be expected to release the ship or other property when such a fund is properly established. Inversely, a fund constituted in a state that is not a party is not necessarily taken into consideration in the decision to release a ship.[110]

FURTHER READINGS

ALDOUS, G., "Claims by Personal Injury and Fatal Accident Claimants on Property Funds in Limitation Proceedings" [2001] L.M.C.L.Q. 150.

BERLINGIERI, F., "Basis of Liability and Exclusions of Liability" [2002] L.M.C.L.Q. 336.

---

107 *Marine Liability Act*, above note 15, s.33(2); *LLMC 1976*, above note 10, art.12.
108 *Marine Liability Act*, above note 15, s.6(3)(b).
109 *LLMC 1976*, above note 10, art.5.
110 *Marine Liability Act*, above note 15, s.34(2).

DE JONGE, B.B., "Financial Responsibility Requirements for Oil and Gas Activities Offshore Nova Scotia and Newfoundland" (2001) 24 Dal. L.J. 109–26.

GIASCHI, C.J., "The Marine Liability Act: Parts 2, 3 and 4 — Apportionment of Liability, Limitation of Liability and Carriage of Passengers," paper presented to the Maritime Conference, 2002, online at <http://admiraltylaw.com/papers/MLA.htm>.

GRIGGS, P. & R. WILLIAMS, *Limitation of Liability for Maritime Claims*, 3d ed. (London: Lloyd's Press, 1998).

HUYBRECHTS, M., "Limitation of Liability and of Actions" [2002] L.M.C. L.Q. 370.

MACGUIGAN, M.R., "The *Jervis Crown* Case: A Jurisprudential Analysis" (1993) 25 Ottawa L.Rev. 61.

POPP, A.H.E., "Limitation of Liability in Maritime Law — An Assessment of its Viability from a Canadian Perspective" (1993) 24 J. Mar. L. & Com. 335.

CHAPTER 19

ADMIRALTY PROCEDURE

A. INTRODUCTION

1) Overview

Admiralty practice, in its broadest sense, is the practice of law in which substantive maritime law is applied. In Canada in particular, this body of law has undergone, and continues to undergo, significant growth in content and in scope of activities to which it applies. Principally, again in a Canadian context, Admiralty practice involves litigation before the Federal Court of Canada, in both *in rem* and *in personam* proceedings. Such proceedings are the substantial focus of this chapter. There are, however, other aspects of modern Admiralty practice, including *in personam* proceedings in provincial courts — and in British Columbia, *in rem* proceedings — as well as application of regulatory and penal law, chiefly federal statutes, in such areas as shipping, fisheries, pollution prevention, and offshore oil and gas exploration.

2) Historical Perspective

The origins of the English Admiralty court are lost in antiquity; scholarly writings[1] on the subject vary somewhat among themselves in the

---

1   See E.S. Roscoe, *Admiralty Jurisdiction and Practice of the High Court of Justice*, 5th ed. (London: Sweet & Maxwell, 1931); W. Senior, "The First Admiralty

detail. There is, however, general agreement that, by the middle years of the fourteenth century, there existed an officer of state called the admiral, who exercised both executive and judicial functions. As England's pre-eminence as a sea power grew, English law found it necessary to deal with spoils and prize claims against foreign powers, as well as with piracy and other offences committed at sea. However, because of its tradition of confining its jurisdiction to the English counties from which juries could be summoned, the common law was considered ill-equipped to deal with these aspects. As a result the patent of Admiral Sir John de Beauchamp, appointed in 1360, gave him or his deputy power of "taking cognizance of maritime causes and of doing justice and imprisoning offenders." As a result, the Admiral's courts, from the time of their inception, took on themselves the resolution of commercial, tort, and criminal cases that the common law courts had always considered to be in their exclusive jurisdiction. This meant that the early Admiralty courts were restrained in their operation both by prerogative writs issued by the common law courts and also by statute. Two statutes in particular in the late fourteenth century provided that "the Admirals and their deputies shall not meddle from henceforth of anything done within the realm, but only of a thing done upon the sea,"[2] and that "of all manner of contracts, pleas and quarrels, and all other things rising within the bodies of counties, as well by land as by water, and also wreck of the sea, the Admiral's court shall have no manner of cognizance, power or jurisdiction."[3] The substantive law thus administered for the centuries that followed is summarized by Williams & Bruce:

> The Admiralty court was left in possession of its jurisdiction over torts committed on the high seas, for that had never been disputed, and in suits of salvage also its authority prevailed, for that was regarded as a branch of the royal prerogative, with the exercise of which the court was properly entrusted. In suits of possession the Admiralty acquired jurisdiction, because it afforded a summary process unknown to the common law, by which the possession of the very thing in dis-

---

Judges" (1919) 35 L.Q.R. 73; R.G. Marsden, ed., *Select Pleas in the Court of Admiralty* (London: Seldon Society, 1894) vol.1, Introduction; R.G. Williams & G. Bruce, *Jurisdiction and Practice of the High Court of Admiralty* (London: Maxwell & Son, 1869); and E.C. Benedict, *Benedict on Admiralty*, 7th ed. (San Francisco: LexisNexis, 2002) vol.I.
2   *What Things the Admiral and his Deputy Shall Meddle*, 1389 (U.K.), 13 Rich. II., c.5.
3   *In What Places the Admiral's Jurisdiction Doth Lie*, 1391 (U.K.), 15 Rich. II., c.3.

pute was at once dealt with. Again, in cases of hypothecation the Admiralty was suffered to exercise jurisdiction, because the contract of hypothecation was not recognized by the common law, and it was only in Admiralty that the thing hypothecated could be proceeded directly against. Over seamen's wages the court, though only after a long struggle, obtained jurisdiction, apparently on the grounds that as the crew could sue together in the Admiralty court, the remedy was more convenient than at law, and that the seamen were entitled to the advantage the Admiralty afforded them of having the ship itself arrested as security for their wages.[4]

Additional subject-matter jurisdiction was eventually assigned to the Admiralty Court by statute — which generally did not commence until Queen Victoria's reign[5] — but it appears from the above discussion that "inherent" Admiralty jurisdiction was based in function: the extraterritorial *situs* of the cause of action and the ability of the court to seize property against which it was invited to exercise that jurisdiction. In a modern context, this latter aspect of historical Admiralty practice lives on as the *in rem* action.

There has been much debate among scholars as to the theoretical base of *in rem* proceedings. Some espouse the "personification theory" — that the ship itself is an instrument of wrongdoing and, although inanimate, is itself a defendant in proceedings before the court;[6] others hold to the "procedural theory" — that the arrest of the ship was a device that compelled, or at least provided incentive, for the shipowner to appear before the court to answer claims against him or her, at peril of being permanently deprived of his or her property.[7] Somewhat surprisingly, a contest between these two theories recently reached and required decision of the House of Lords,[8] the issue being whether judgment in an *in personam* action operated as *res judicata* and so prevented a separate *in rem* action arising out of the same facts. This decision contains a thorough review of the various times and circumstances in which each theory was ascendent in Admiralty proceedings.

---

4   Above note 1 at 9–10.
5   *Admiralty Court Act, 1840* (U.K.), 3 & 4 Vict., c.65; *Admiralty Court Act, 1861* (U.K.), 24 Vict., c.10; *Colonial Courts of Admiralty Act, 1890* (U.K.), 53 & 54 Vict., c.27 (Imp.). In a Canadian context, these were largely adopted by the *Admiralty Act, 1934*, S.C. 1934 c.31, and remained in force until repealed in 1971 on the coming into force of the *Federal Court Act*, S.C. 1971, c.1.
6   See, e.g., *Burns (The)*, [1907] P. 137.
7   See, e.g., *Terraete (The)*, [1922] P. 259 (C.A.).
8   *Indian Grace (No. 2) (The)*, [1998] 2 Lloyds L.R. 1 (H.L.).

In modern Canadian practice, certain elements of both the procedural and personification theories persist, and it may be argued that Canada has adopted a hybrid of the two schools of thought. As discussed later, Canadian law requires that there be a ship or other property that is "the subject of the action," without which there can be no *in rem* proceeding at all. Furthermore, some substantive elements of modern maritime law, such as limitation of liability based on the size of the ship, are reminiscent of the notion that the amount recovered cannot exceed the value of the wrongdoing ship. However, Canada is a "sister-ship" arrest jurisdiction, in which, in some cases, a ship other than that which is "the subject of the action" may be arrested in its stead, if the two ships are commonly owned. It is suggested that, as a device to compel the shipowner, as opposed to the ship, to honour its obligations, this is a modern manifestation of the procedural theory.

3) Canadian Admiralty Procedural Rules

The principal procedural rules in Canadian maritime practice are the *Federal Court Rules, 1998*[9] that came into force on 25 April 1998. The former rules of the Federal Court of Canada were, in some cases, substantially re-enacted, although renumbered, and in some cases changed significantly or even eliminated. When researching procedural jurisprudence in the Federal Court, it is essential to identify which sets of rules are being considered and, if the former rules, carefully check whether the present *Federal Court Rules* are the same or different. The B.C. Supreme Court, alone among provincial superior courts, permits *in rem* proceedings and exercises *in rem* jurisdiction. For its procedure the B.C. Supreme Court has adopted rules[10] substantially similar in content to the Admiralty rules of the Federal Court, but they appear not to have underlying statute law[11] corresponding to sections 22 and 43 of the *Federal Court Act*.[12] However, the *British Columbia Supreme Court Rule* 55(1)(2) provides that an *in rem* action may be brought in the B.C. Supreme Court "if the suit may be brought *in rem* in the Federal Court of Canada."[13] In practice, Federal Court practice and jurisprudence is relied on, and generally followed, in proceedings before the B.C. Supreme Court. The Federal Court's subject-matter jurisdiction in

---

9 *Federal Court Rules*, S.O.R./98-106.
10 B.C. Reg. 221/90, r.55 (*British Columbia Supreme Court Rules*).
11 See *Supreme Court Act*, R.S.B.C. 1996, c.443.
12 *Federal Court Act*, R.S.C. 1985, c.F-7, ss.22 and 43.
13 *British Columbia Supreme Court Rules*, above note 10, r.55.1.2.

Admiralty and maritime matters is concurrent with that of the provincial superior courts. *In personam* actions under substantive maritime law can equally be asserted in the Federal Court or in the provincial superior courts. In the latter courts, their own procedural rules apply in maritime matters the same as they do in all civil and commercial litigation.

B. STRUCTURE OF THE FEDERAL COURT OF CANADA

1) *Federal Court Act*[14]

The Federal Court of Canada is a creation of statute, the *Federal Court Act*, with neither independent existence nor inherent jurisdiction. The Federal Court is comprised of two divisions: the Trial Division and the Court of Appeal. Judges are separately assigned to one or other division, although all have jurisdiction to sit *ad hoc* in the other division from that to which they are appointed. All judges of the court are required to reside in the National Capital Region, but the court sits, quite literally, anywhere in Canada in which its attention is required and in which the most basic accommodation for judicial hearings can be found. Travel and mobility are among the hallmarks of the Federal Court of Canada. The Federal Court is bilingual, conducting any and all of its business in either official language. It is also bijural, in the sense that its judges include persons trained and who have practised in either the civil law or the common law. Constitutionally, however, the court may administer only federal law, which tends to be statute-based and when not so based — at least in maritime law, said to incorporate principles of contract, tort, and bailment[15] — is comprised more of common law principles. In the specific context of maritime litigation this seems incongruous, when one considers that Admiralty law finds its ancient roots in civilian legal systems in Europe.

2) Practice before the Federal Court

Any member of any Canadian law society is entitled to appear as counsel in the Federal Court, in any physical place in the country in which

---

14 Above note 12.
15 *ITO International Terminal Operators Ltd. v. Miida Electronics Inc. (The Buenos Aires Maru)*, [1986] 1 S.C.R. 752. See full discussion of Federal Court in D(2) in Chapter 3, "Admiralty Jurisdiction."

the court sits. It is rare in Admiralty proceedings for self-represented parties to appear in the court, although they have every right to do so. Because of the subject-matter with which the court typically deals (i.e., immigration, intellectual property, and federal administrative law, in addition to maritime law), the bar that regularly practices before the court tends to have restricted practices concentrated in fairly specialized substantive areas. In addition to judges of the Trial Division and the Court of Appeal, the court has prothonotaries, who unlike judges are not required to reside in Ottawa and who are, subject to their own travel obligations, available on a full-time basis in Vancouver, Toronto, and Montreal. The prothonotaries have jurisdiction to hear most motions and to preside at trials to which the "simplified proceedings" (that is, small claims) *Federal Court Rules* apply. In addition, prothonotaries, like judges on some occasions, preside over the various alternative dispute resolution (ADR) processes that the court provides and to which specific *Federal Court Rules* apply.[16] The court has regularly scheduled motions sittings in fifteen cities throughout Canada. Trials and hearings of applications are arranged as and where needed, depending primarily on the availability of judges. There are no jury trials in the Federal Court of Canada.[17]

3) Registry Practice

There are eighteen registry offices of the Federal Court, in the principal cities of every province and the three territories. Especially in Admiralty proceedings, it is essential to be aware of the services provided by the registry offices and the jurisdiction of registry officials. Registry officers, for example, issue warrants for the arrest of ships, releases of ships from arrest, and — subject to discretion to refer such matters to a judge — resolve disputes between parties as to the form of bail. For the convenience of parties and their counsel, documents may be filed by hard copy or fax in any registry office regardless of which registry in which the proceeding was commenced. This both enables relatively immediate filing from any place in Canada, and gives practitioners in western (later) time zones of the country a few hours' advantage in meeting filing deadlines, since documents can be filed by fax in the Vancouver registry before that office closes for business on the last filing date, and still be timely. A central paper file is kept at Ottawa for every proceeding in the Court.

---

16 Above note 9, rr.50 and 51.
17 *Federal Court Act*, above note 12, s.49.

C. ADMIRALTY PROCEEDINGS

1) Initiation in Federal Court

Proceedings in the Trial Division of the Federal Court take the form of actions[18] or applications.[19] Applications are generally paper-based proceedings, in which presentation to the court of *viva voce* evidence, requiring the court to make findings of disputed facts, are thought not to be required. Other than in the context of very specific problems (e.g., arbitration, fisheries, or immigration matters), applications are seldom used in Canadian maritime cases. Usually, therefore, Admiralty proceedings take the form of actions. Actions are commenced in the Trial Division by filing a statement of claim (Form 171A: see Appendix 3)[20] in any registry of the court and paying the prescribed fee.[21] The text of Form 171A is mandatory and must be followed. The portion of the document titled "Claim" is a manuscript pleading in which facts giving rise to plaintiff's claim are alleged and plaintiff's claim for relief is set out. The pleading must allege facts that, if true, disclose not only a valid cause of action but also one that is within the subject-matter jurisdiction of the Federal Court of Canada.[22] In Admiralty proceedings, this will generally be a claim for relief under or by virtue of Canadian maritime law, which could — but is not required to — be one or more of the specific kinds of claims listed in the *Federal Court Act*.[23]

The Federal Court has, and administers, its own small claims procedures, which the court refers to as "simplified actions."[24] These procedures are mandatory in all actions, including Admiralty actions and including particularly *in rem* proceedings, in which the amount claimed is $50,000 or less. The procedures vary somewhat from other actions: for example, a list of documents is served instead of an affidavit of documents;[25] discovery is by written questions and answers;[26] and, at trial, evidence in chief is tendered by way of affidavit.[27] Trials of simplified actions are generally assigned to be heard before prothono-

---

18 *Federal Court Rules*, above note 9, rr.169–299.
19 *Ibid.*, rr.300–34.
20 *Ibid.*, r.63 and Form 171A.
21 *Ibid.*, Tariff A, s.1(1)(a).
22 For further discussion, see Chapter 3, "Admiralty Jurisdiction."
23 *Federal Court Act*, above note 12, s.22(2).
24 *Federal Court Rules*, above note 9, rr.292–99.
25 *Ibid.*, r.295.
26 *Ibid.*, r.296.
27 *Ibid.*, r.299.

taries. Motions practice in simplified actions is very restricted.[28] When a motion, other than one that *Federal Court Rule* 298 permits, is appropriate (e.g., a motion for judgment in default of defence), the practice is to move concurrently for an order under rule 298(3)(a) that the action shall cease to be a simplified action, and then, for the substantive order that is sought.[29]

2) Claim for Relief under or by Virtue of Canadian Maritime Law

"Canadian maritime law" is defined in the *Federal Court Act* as follows:

> Canadian maritime law means the law that was administered by the Exchequer Court of Canada on its Admiralty side by virtue of the Admiralty Act, chapter A-1 of the Revised Statutes of Canada, 1970, or any other statute, or that would have been so administered if that Court had had, on its Admiralty side, unlimited jurisdiction in relation to maritime and Admiralty matters, as that law has been altered by this Act or any other Act of Parliament.[30]

The Trial Division has original jurisdiction, concurrent with the provincial superior courts, in cases in which a claim for relief is made under or by virtue of Canadian maritime law.[31] It is not required that claims under Canadian maritime law be asserted in actions in which one or more of the parties is a ship, or other property, even though strictly speaking the joinder of such inanimate parties is what gives an action its Admiralty character. Pure *in personam* actions engaging substantive Canadian maritime law are unquestionably within the court's subject-matter jurisdiction and are very commonly commenced.

3) Interplay between Sections 43 and 22

Section 43 of the *Federal Court Act* is a series of provisions that permits and governs *in rem* actions in the Federal Court. The section provides:

> 43. (1) Subject to subsection (4), the jurisdiction conferred on the Court by section 22 may in all cases be exercised *in personam*.

---

28 *Ibid.*, r.298.
29 *Ibid.*, r.298 and 298(3)(a).
30 Above note 12, s.2. See full discussion of nature and scope of Canadian maritime law in Chapter 3, D(1), "Definition of Canadian Maritime Law."
31 *Federal Court Act*, ibid., s.22(1).

(2) Subject to subsection (3), the jurisdiction conferred on the Court by section 22 may be exercised *in rem* against the ship, aircraft or other property that is the subject of the action, or against any proceeds of sale thereof that have been paid into court.

(3) Notwithstanding subsection (2), the jurisdiction conferred on the Court by section 22 shall not be exercised *in rem* with respect to a claim mentioned in paragraph 22(2)(*e*), (*f*), (*g*), (*h*), (*i*), (*k*), (*m*), (*n*), (*p*) or (*r*) unless, at the time of the commencement of the action, the ship, aircraft or other property that is the subject of the action is beneficially owned by the person who was the beneficial owner at the time when the cause of action arose.

(4) No action *in personam* may be commenced in Canada for a collision between ships unless
   (*a*) the defendant is a person who has a residence or place of business in Canada;
   (*b*) the cause of action arose in Canadian waters; or
   (*c*) the parties have agreed that the Court is to have jurisdiction.

(5) Subsection (4) does not apply to a counter-claim or an action for a collision, in respect of which another action has already been commenced in the Court.

(6) Where an action for a collision between ships has been commenced outside Canada, an action shall not be commenced in Canada by the same person against the same defendant on the same facts unless the action in the other jurisdiction has been discontinued.

(7) No action *in rem* may be commenced in Canada against
   (*a*) any warship, coast-guard ship or police vessel;
   (*b*) any ship owned or operated by Canada or a province, or any cargo laden thereon, where the ship is engaged on government service; or
   (*c*) any ship owned or operated by a sovereign power other than Canada, or any cargo laden thereon, with respect to any claim where, at the time the claim arises or the action is commenced, the ship is being used exclusively for non-commercial governmental purposes.

(8) The jurisdiction conferred on the Court by section 22 may be exercised *in rem* against any ship that, at the time the action is brought, is beneficially owned by the person who is the owner of the ship that is the subject of the action.

(9) In an action for a collision in which a ship, aircraft or other property of a defendant has been arrested, or security given to answer judgment against the defendant, and in which the defendant has

instituted a cross-action or counter-claim in which a ship, aircraft or other property of the plaintiff is liable to arrest but cannot be arrested, the Court may stay the proceedings in the principal action until security has been given to answer judgment in the cross-action or counter-claim.[32]

It will be seen from section 43(2) that, as long as the claim for relief engages, substantively, Canadian maritime law — including, but not necessarily, one of the kinds of claims enumerated in section 22(2)[33] — and the claim is capable if being asserted against a "ship, aircraft or other property that is the subject of the action," then the court's jurisdiction may be exercised *in rem* against that ship, aircraft, or other property. The *in rem* proceeding is the hallmark and the defining attribute of true Admiralty litigation. (Specific concerns with and jurisprudence concerning the innumerable contentious issues that arise out of section 43 are the subject of detailed discussion later in this chapter.)

There are a relatively few, but important, formal requirements for documents in *in rem* proceedings, which must be followed in every case. The style of cause must be headed "Admiralty Action *in Rem*."[34] The defendant property must be described as "the owners and all others interested in [*defendant ship or other property*]."[35] It occasionally happens in practice that plaintiffs somewhat expand this mandatory language, at least in the case of ships, to sue some variant of the words, "the owners, charterers, managers, operators and all others interested in the Ship." It is also sometimes the practice to then add "and the Ship [*name*]" or as the case may be. The use of such expansive descriptions of the *in rem* defendant is seldom if ever challenged, and there is no jurisprudence indicating the court's opinion whether the use of this language is proper or otherwise — or whether failure to follow the apparently mandatory expression "the owners and all others interested in" may nullify an attempt at commencement of *in rem* proceedings. It is highly probable, all else being equal, that, if a challenge on this basis ever had to be resolved, the court would treat the use of expansive language as a matter of form only, capable of being cured by appropriate amendment, and so not fatal to the action. It should also be noted in this context that sometimes the defendant property does not have a name: for example, a ship under construction or generic cargo on

---

32 *Ibid.*, s.43.
33 *Ibid.*, s.22(2).
34 *Federal Court Rules*, above note 9, r.477(2) and Form 477. See Appendix 3.
35 *Ibid.*, r.477(4) and Form 477.

board or discharged from a ship. In such cases, the practice is to use language that concisely but clearly identifies the defendant property, such that it can be differentiated without confusion and with reasonable certainty from other property against which plaintiff does not assert an *in rem* claim.

If plaintiff asserts also a claim *in personam* against some legal entity — whether or not the owner of the defendant property — the practice requires that the entity be separately named as a defendant and be separately served. The statement of claim must, in these cases, allege facts to support both an *in personam* action and the *in rem* action, and the prayer for relief generally separately specifies what remedy is sought as against each of the multiple defendants. Note that in cases in which *in rem* and *in personam* claims are combined, it is some practitioners' practice — although it is neither universal nor required by the *Federal Court Rules* — to alter the rule 477(2) heading on the style of cause to read "Admiralty Action *in rem* Against the Ship [*name*] and *in personam* against [*in personam defendant(s)*]."[36]

A defence in an *in rem* action must identify the legal entity that files defence on behalf of the defendant property and must also state the nature of that entity's interest in the defendant property.[37]

4) Maritime Claims in Provincial Courts

The Federal Court's original jurisdiction in maritime cases is concurrent — that is, the provincial superior courts concurrently exercise that same subject-matter jurisdiction. However, of all the provincial superior courts, only that of British Columbia has provision in its rules for *in rem* proceedings. In the superior courts of other provinces, actions claiming relief under or by virtue of Canadian maritime law may be brought *in personam*, but *in rem* proceedings are not available. Generally, if the plaintiff relies on some peculiar substantive advantage for which provision is made in provincial law — typically legislation — the plaintiff will avoid, if possible, commencing its litigation in the Federal Court of Canada. The Federal Court is a statutory court, constitutionally limited to "administration of the laws of Canada."[38] Plaintiffs, however, should be very cautious, even in provincial court, relying upon specific provincial legislation. If the subject-matter of the litiga-

---

36 Above note 9, r.477(2).
37 *Federal Court Rules*, ibid., r.480.
38 *Constitution Act, 1867*, (U.K.), 30 & 31 Vict., c.3, repr. in R.S.C. 1985, App. II, No. 5, s.101.

tion is "shipping and navigation," legislative jurisdiction in respect of which is assigned exclusively to the federal Parliament by section 91 of the *Constitution Act, 1867*,[39] provincial legislation may be incapable of applying to that subject-matter and so to the litigation in question.[40]

It should be noted that where provincial statutes are appropriately worded, claims under Canadian maritime law may equally be brought in the province's Small Claims Court. In many provinces, these courts exercise the same subject-matter jurisdiction as the superior courts, subject to monetary limits. In such cases, there is no impediment to maritime claims being asserted *in personam* in the Small Claims Courts.

5) Practical Considerations Governing Choice of Court

In addition to constitutional technicalities and niceties of jurisdiction, there are some very practical factors that influence a plaintiff's choice of court, and that should be taken into account by a plaintiff contemplating commencement of maritime litigation. These factors include whether *in rem* process is desired. If an *in rem* action is contemplated — and unless plaintiff is in a position to sue in British Columbia — then there will be little alternative but to commence proceedings in Federal Court. Material to this issue is whether the debtor is solvent, is personally amenable to the jurisdiction of the provincial court, and has assets within that court's jurisdiction against which judgment, if obtained, can be executed. If the answer to any of these questions is negative, and if the ship or other property is in Canada and available for service and arrest at the time of commencement of the action, then *in rem* proceedings in Federal Court will be in order.

A second factor is whether national enforcement process will be required. While there is legislation providing for mutual recognition and enforcement of provincial courts' judgments, the Federal Court's judgments may be executed anywhere in Canada without any further proceedings being necessary.

A third factor is whether extraprovincial compulsion of testimony may be required. Subpoenas of the Federal Court have effect anywhere in Canada.

A fourth factor is whether discovery of multiple witnesses or expert witnesses — or, alternatively, the avoidance of such discovery — will be desired. In the Federal Court, discovery is permitted only of parties

---

39 *Ibid.*, s.91.
40 *Bow Valley Husky (Bermuda) Ltd. v. Saint John Shipbuilding Ltd.*, [1997] 3 S.C.R. 1210; *Ordon Estate v. Grail*, [1998] 3 S.C.R. 437.

themselves unless the court otherwise orders, and discovery of expert witnesses is not permitted. Many provinces' rules of procedure permit unlimited fact discovery, and/or expert witness discovery. If plaintiff desires to have, or to avoid, unlimited discovery, this may be a factor influencing its choice of court in which to commence action.

There are relative merits of each court's case management system. It is held by many practitioners — whether fairly or not is debatable — that the Federal Court's somewhat inflexible filing deadlines and highly structured special management protocols create a "user-unfriendly" case management regime. The counterpart case management systems in some of the provincial courts are perceived to be more forgiving, and/or better suited to the delays inherent in transnational litigation. Conversely, some plaintiffs, desiring relative certainty of predictable progress toward trial, elect to sue in Federal Court for these very reasons.

D. ACTIONS *IN REM*

1) Nature of the *Res*

The nature of property that can be made the subject of an action *in rem*, and therefore arrested in connection with such an action, is apparently not limited by the *Federal Court Act*, which permits such action against "the ship, aircraft *or other property* that is the subject of the action,"[41] nor by the *Federal Court Rules*, which refer to "a ship or cargo *or other property*."[42]

a) Things that are Not "Ships"

In *Imperial Oil Limited v. The Expo Spirit*,[43] the property arrested was a hovercraft. The defendant had moved to set aside the arrest on grounds, *inter alia*, that that property was not a "ship." The court dismissed the motion, deciding in reference to this ground that various statutory definitions of "ship," including that referred to in the *Federal Court Act*, "encompass a craft used in navigation even if there is some airspace left between it and the water."[44] While the court certainly did not so expressly decide, this case might be taken to imply that a conveyance that is not within the statutory definition of "ship" is not

---

41 Above note 12, s.43(2).
42 Above note 9, r.479.
43 *Imperial Oil Ltd. v. Expo Spirit (The)* (1986), 6 F.T.R. 156.
44 *Federal Court Act*, above note 12, s.2.

capable of being arrested. Things that are not ships but are frequently sued *in rem* and arrested include cargo — whether on a ship, on the quay awaiting loading, or following discharge — freight, containers, and bunkers.

b) Property "That is the Subject of the Action"

The *Federal Court Act* limits the availability of an *in rem* process to the ship, aircraft or other property "that is the subject of the action."[45] It appears the court interprets these words to require that the arrested property must be the subject-matter of, or must have given rise to, the dispute between the parties.[46] The language used by the Federal Court of Appeal is that "it must be possible to say that it is the use of this ship or the carriage of this cargo that justifies the action *in rem* brought against the property arrested."[47]

2) Corresponding *in Personam* Liability of the Owner of the *Res*

It is well established that, to arrest property in an action *in rem*, there must exist corresponding liability *in personam* of the owners of that property to the plaintiff in the action.[48] This principle creates practical difficulties in several situations: for example, if the plaintiff's claim is for a debt due from the time charterer, as opposed to owner, of the ship, or if the plaintiff is an unpaid supplier or subcontractor of some third party, which in turn is owed money by the shipowner. Many creative ways are attempted to justify *in rem* actions in these kinds of situations. When challenged, they are frequently unsuccessful.

When an action *in rem* is brought to enforce a maritime lien for "necessaries" arising under U.S. law, personal liability of the shipowner for the underlying debt will not be required: *Marlex Petroleum Inc. v.*

---

45 *Ibid.*, s.43(2).
46 *Paramount Enterprises International Inc. v. An Xin Jiang (Le)* (1997), 146 F.T.R. 161, rev'd in part (1997), 147 F.T.R. 162, aff'd [2001] 2 F.C. 551, 265 N.R. 354 (C.A.).
47 *Ibid.* at 553 (C.A.).
48 *Mount Royal Walsh Inc. v. Jensen Star (The)* (1989), 99 N.R. 42 (F.C.A.), per Marceau J.A., para.30 [*The Jensen Star*]; *Frisol Bunckering BV v. MV Alexandria (The)* (1991), 47 F.T.R. 3, per Joyal J., para.29; *Feoso Oil Ltd. v. Sarla (The)* (1995), 184 N.R. 307 (F.C.A.), per Stone J.A., paras.12 and 22; *Translink France Outre Mer SA v. Pegasus Lines Ltd. SA* (1996), 207 N.R. 293 (F.C.A.) per Hugessen J.A., para.1.

The Har Rai.⁴⁹ No Canadian authority was found that considered whether lack of the owner's *in personam* liability would defeat an action *in rem* to enforce a maritime lien recognized under substantive Canadian law: for example, wages due to crew members who were employed and paid by some entity other than the shipowner. It is possible that, because a claim such as this is not among the clauses of section 22(2) that are enumerated in section 43(3) of the *Federal Court Act*, the court would consider that, as a matter of statutory interpretation, the requirement for owner's *in personam* liability does not apply. It must be said, however, that the many authorities quoted above, which require the owner's personal liability, do not appear to so decide as a matter of interpretation of section 43(3) of the *Federal Court Act*.⁵⁰

There was a time when it was thought, and some judges in *obiter dicta* speculated, that personal liability of a demise charterer of a ship — as distinct from the shipowner — would additionally support an action *in rem* against the ship and, correspondingly, a right of arrest.⁵¹ This is the case, by statute, in the United Kingdom, under the *Administration of Justice Act, 1956*,⁵² and its replacement, the *Supreme Court Act 1981*,⁵³ both of which, in turn, gave effect in the United Kingdom to the *International Convention Relating to the Arrest of Sea-Going Ships* (*Arrest Convention*). Article 3(4) of the convention provides, in part, that "when in the case of a charter by demise of a ship the charterer and not the registered owner is liable in respect of a maritime claim relating to that ship, the claimant may arrest such ship."⁵⁴ Canada has not acceded to the *Arrest Convention* nor wholly incorporated its provisions into Canadian domestic law. That Canadian law does not permit the arrest of a ship when the demise charterer, but not the owner, is liable

---

49 [1982] 2 F.C. 617 (T.D.), rev'd [1984] 2 F.C. 345 (F.C.A.), aff'd [1987] 1 S.C.R. 57 [*The Har Rai*].
50 Above note 12, s.43(3).
51 See, e.g., *Thorne Riddell Inc. v. Nicole N. Enterprises Ltd.*, [1985] 2 F.C. 31, per Addy J. at 37; *Imperial Oil Ltd. v. Expo Spirit (The)*, above note 43, per Dubé J. at 160.
52 *Administration of Justice Act, 1956* (U.K.), 4 & 5 Eliz. II, c.46.
53 *Supreme Court Act, 1981* (U.K.), 29 & 30 Eliz. II, c.54.
54 10 May 1952, 439 U.N.T.S. 193 [*Arrest Convention*]. It should be noted here that a new arrest convention, significantly altering the public international law relating to arrest of ships, was signed at Geneva, Switzerland, on 12 March 1999: *International Convention on Arrest of Ships, 1999*, 12 March 1999, Doc. A/CONF.188.6. Among many other changes, this convention would permit arrest of multiple sister-ships in respect of the same claim and would require plaintiff arresting a ship to post "counter-security" in respect of damages suffered by defendants arising from the arrest. At time of writing, this convention was not in force internationally and, as for the predecessor *Arrest Convention*, has not been ratified by Canada.

in personam for the underlying claim was settled by the Federal Court of Appeal in *The Jensen Star*.[55]

Suppliers of "necessaries" to vessels take the benefit of a rebuttable presumption that the shipowner authorized the person in possession of the vessel to order the "necessaries" for the benefit of the vessel, and on the credit of the vessel and his or her owners.[56] The presumption, however, is capable of being rebutted: for example, by the master having endorsed fuel delivery receipts with the words "for charterers' account."[57]

3) Right to Proceed *in Rem* Lost in Some Cases with Change in Ownership

If the claim is a kind described in the clauses of section 22(2) of the *Federal Court Act* that are enumerated in section 43(3) thereof, the right to proceed by way of action *in rem* is available only if "at the time of the commencement of the action the ship, aircraft or other property that is the subject of the action is beneficially owned by the person who was the beneficial owner at the time when the cause of action arose."[58] Such were the facts of *The Jensen Star*.[59] The plaintiff had performed repairs on some seventeen occasions between August 1982 and June 1984. The original owner transferred title to and registered ownership of the ship on 24 November 1983. The action *in rem* was commenced on 9 August 1984. The court held that the right to proceed *in rem* in respect of the six jobs that preceded the date of sale was lost when the ship was transferred to its new owners. As regards the eleven jobs that occurred after the sale, however, the court held, on the facts of that case, that the former owner was "tacitly authorized" by the new owner to order the work as agent for the latter and so engage the necessary *in personam* liability of the new owner in respect of the after-sale accounts.

Examination of the subject-matter of the claim is therefore necessary to ascertain whether it falls within one of the clauses of section 22(2), which are enumerated in section 43(3), that is, damage sustained by a ship;[60] carriage of goods;[61] loss of life or personal injury;[62]

---

55 Above note 48, per Marceau J.A., para.14.
56 See, e.g., *Sabb Inc. v. Shipping Ltd.*, [1976] 2 F.C. 175 (T.D.), per Dubé J. at 195; *The Jensen Star*, above note 48, per Marceau J.A., para.22.
57 *Frisol Bunkering BV v. MV Alexandria (The)*, above note 48.
58 Above note 12, s.43(3).
59 Above note 48.
60 *Federal Court Act*, above note 12, s.22(2)(e).
61 *Ibid.*, ss.22(2)(f) and 22(2)(h).
62 *Ibid.*, s.22(2)(g).

towage;[63] supplies of goods, materials, or services to a ship (so-called "necessaries" claims);[64] ship building or repairing contracts;[65] claims for master's, charterer's, or agent's disbursements;[66] or marine insurance matters.[67] If it is such a claim, then an action *in rem* and accordingly a right to apply for arrest of the property are available only if beneficial ownership of the property sought to be arrested has not changed between the "time when the cause of action arose" and the time of commencement of the action.

In the absence of statute, "true" maritime liens were enforceable by action *in rem* notwithstanding intervening change of ownership of the *res*.[68] While no authority on the point could be found, from an examination of the clauses of section 22(2) of the *Federal Court Act* that are not enumerated in section 43(3), it appears that the intent of Parliament was to preserve the right to proceed *in rem* in respect to all classes of claim traditionally thought to give rise to "true" maritime liens, as well as to certain additional classes of claim in respect to which it was considered appropriate to permit creditors to so proceed, notwithstanding transfers of beneficial ownership. It is submitted that the effect of section 43(3) in this context should be limited to modifying traditional Admiralty law only as regards the class of claim in respect to which a right to proceed *in rem* will survive a change in beneficial ownership of the *res* and, specifically, should not otherwise alter or interfere with the general law concerning the nature of, or the priority attaching to, "true" maritime liens.

4) Sister-Ship Proceedings

Canadian experience with the process of sister-ship proceedings is evolving and continues to evolve. The cases have not been without difficulty and the decisions not without controversy. A review follows of Canadian authorities to date and of U.K. authorities that may be of assistance in the interpretation of similar statutory language, with a view to identifying existing principles governing sister-ship actions in Canada, and to suggesting ways in which those principles that have yet to be established might be addressed.

---

63 *Ibid.*, s.22(2)(k).
64 *Ibid.*, s.22(2)(m).
65 *Ibid.*, s.22(2)(n).
66 *Ibid.*, s.22(2)(p).
67 *Ibid.*, s.22(2)(p).
68 *Heinrich Bjorn (The)* (1886), 11 A.C. 270 (H.L.), per Lord Watson at 276–77. See discussion in C(2) in Chapter 6, "Maritime Mortgages and Liens."

a) Difference from *Arrest Convention* and U.K. Legislation

The Canadian legislation is found in the *Federal Court Act*, section 43(8).[69] This statutory language is to be contrasted with corresponding provisions in the United Kingdom:

> In case of any such claim as is mentioned in section 20(2)(e) to (r), where
> (a) a claim arises in connection with a ship; and
> (b) the person who would be liable on the claim in an action *in personam* (the "relevant person") was, when the cause of action arose, the owner or charterer of, or in possession or in control of, the ship,
>
> an action *in rem* may (whether or not the claim gives rise to a maritime lien on that ship) be brought in the High Court against —
> (i) that ship, if at the time when the action is brought the relevant person is either the beneficial owner of that ship as respects all the shares in it or the charterer of it under a charter by demise; or
> (ii) any other ship of which, at the time when the action is brought, the relevant person is the beneficial owner as respects all shares in it.[70]

The corresponding provisions in the *Arrest Convention* state:

> (1) Subject to the provisions of paragraph (4) of this Article and Article 10, a claimant may arrest either the particular ship in respect of which the maritime claim arose, or any other ship which is owned by the person who was, at the time when the maritime claim arose, the owner of the particular ship ... .
>
> (2) Ships shall be deemed to be in the same ownership when all the shares therein are owned by the same person or persons.
>
> ...
>
> (4) When in the case of a charter by demise of a ship the charterer and not the registered owner is liable in respect of a maritime claim relating to that ship, the claimant may arrest such ship or any other ship in the ownership of the charterer by demise, subject to the provisions

---

69 See *Federal Court Act*, above note 12, s.43(8) as enacted by *Federal Court Act*, S.C. 1990, c.8, s.12, repr. above at note 32, which came into force on 1 February 1992.
70 *Supreme Court Act, 1981*, above note 53, s.21(4).

of this Convention, but no other ship in the ownership of the registered owner shall be liable to arrest in respect of any such claim.[71]

Two points are submitted as noteworthy at the outset: the U.K. statute incorporates certain features of the convention (e.g., personal liability of demise charterers giving rise to a right of arrest) but deviates from the convention by introducing the concept of "beneficial ownership." The Canadian *Federal Court Act* incorporates only the concept of sister-ship arrest from the convention and adopts the United Kingdom's incorporation of the concept of "beneficial ownership."

b) Sister Ships Defined

To summarize the decisions discussed immediately below, it is submitted that the weight of Canadian authority to date is to the effect that sister-ship proceedings are available only if both the ship that is the subject of the claim and the ship sought to be arrested have identical registered ownership. Although it appears that certain exceptions may exist (e.g., where the registered owner is a trustee), it is submitted that these exceptions will be narrowly defined and relatively seldom available.

Subsection 43(8) uses, as apparently distinct concepts, the word "owner" and the phrase "beneficially owned." Subsection 43(3) similarly uses the phrase "beneficially owned."[72] Prior to enactment of section 43(8), the Federal Court of Appeal had occasion, in *The Jensen Star*,[73] to consider the meaning of that phrase. It will be recalled that, in *The Jensen Star*, the vessel was sold, then chartered by demise to the vendor, between the commencement and the conclusion of the series of repairs in respect to which plaintiff sued *in rem* for payment; one of the issues before the court was whether the demise charterer's *in personam* liability could support an action *in rem* against the ship. On the subject of the meaning of the phrase "beneficial owner," Marceau J.A. said:

> Whatever may be the meaning of the qualifying term "beneficial," the word owner can only normally be used in reference to title in the *res* itself, a title characterized essentially by the right to dispose of the *res*. The French corresponding word "propriétaire" is equally clear in that regard .... In my view, the expression "beneficial owner" was chosen to serve as an instruction, in a system of registration of ownership rights, to look beyond the register in searching for the relevant person. But such search cannot go so far as to encompass a demise char-

---

71 *Arrest Convention*, above note 54, art.3.
72 *Federal Court Act*, above note 12, ss.43(8) and 43(3).
73 Above note 48.

terer who has no equitable or proprietary interest which could burden the title of the registered owner. As I see it, the expression "beneficial owner" serves to include someone who stands behind the registered owner in situations where the latter functions merely as an intermediary, like a trustee, a legal representative or an agent. The French corresponding expression "véritable propriétaire" leaves no doubt to that effect.[74]

In *Ssangyong Australia Pty. Ltd. v. The Looiersgracht*,[75] the plaintiff arrested the defendant ship and demanded security for alleged cargo damage suffered on board, as well as on board five additional sister ships. According to Lloyd's Register of Shipping, the six ships were owned by separate Belgian legal entities, which were said to be the equivalent of limited partnerships. One firm, described as Spliethoff's, was manager of all six vessels and was also a member of each of the six "limited partnerships." Aside from Spliethoff's, however, each of the six shipowning "limited partnerships" had different members. The plaintiff's position was that these facts disclosed "a common ownership based on management of a fleet by Spliethoff's, on ownership by Spliethoff's and also perhaps by the way in which each vessel is owned by a limited partnership."[76] Prothonotary Hargrave held that the degree of common ownership necessary to support sister-ship arrest under section 43(8) was not present and, accordingly, security was ordered in an amount representing only alleged damage to cargo on board the single ship that had been arrested. While acknowledging that the use of the concept "beneficial ownership" in both the U.K. and Canadian legislation "may be much broader than the [*Arrest Convention*] concept of legal ownership," the fact that each of the limited partnerships before the court was differently constituted prevented the application of section 43(8).[77] He concluded:

> Under our legislation it is insufficient to merely show some beneficial interest. Our legislation requires that the sister ship be "beneficially owned by the person who is *the* owner of the ship that is the subject of the action."
>
> To come within Canadian sister ship provisions there must be common complete ownership of both vessels by the same owner or owners, for that is the plain and ordinary meaning of our legislation.

---

74 *The Jensen Star*, above note 48, para.14.
75 (1994), 85 F.T.R. 265 [*The Looiersgracht*].
76 Ibid., para.13.
77 Ibid., para.17.

It is not enough to be *an* owner, but rather it must be *the* owner, that is similar complete ownership of both vessels. [Emphasis in original.][78]

It is submitted, on the basis of *The Looiersgracht* reasoning, that, in any case in which shares of two or more ships are owned by more than one person, all of each ship's shares must be owned by all of the same owners. It remains to be argued, should such a case ever reach the court, whether the proportional shareholdings of each ship would also need to be identical.

In *Hollandsche Aannaming Maatschappij v. The Ryan Leet*,[79] The Ryan Leet was arrested. The ship that was "the subject of the action" was The Terra Nova Sea. The Ryan Leet was owned by Secunda Marine Services Limited. The Terra Nova Sea was owned by Kenworthy Limited, which in turn was a wholly owned subsidiary of Secunda Marine Services Limited. Secunda Marine Services Limited moved to set aside the arrest warrant. Rothstein J. examined section 43(8) and determined that because the different concepts "owner" and "beneficially owned" were used, they must have been intended to have different meanings.[80] He went on to decide that "[t]he definition of owner, as applied to registered ships ... means the registered owner only" and "[i]n the case of registered ships, when no qualification is stated, 'owner' means the registered owner only"; he declined to impute to Parliament any intention to "pierce the corporate veil."[81] In the result Rothstein J. set aside the arrest warrant, on the basis that Kenworthy Limited, the owner of the ship that was the subject of the action, was not the beneficial owner of the arrested ship, The Ryan Leet.[82] By way of comment, it is noted that, to permit a sister-ship arrest on the facts of *The Ryan Leet*, the court would have had to conclude that the subsidiary company was the "beneficial owner" of the property of its parent company. Conceptually, these facts could be distinguished from those in which the reverse could be asserted (i.e., that when the ship that "is the subject of the action" is owned by the parent company, the ship owned by the subsidiary would be argued to be the "beneficial" property of the parent). However, given Rothstein J.'s clearly stated interpretation that section 43(8) *per se* discloses no legislative intent to "pierce the corporate veil," it is submitted that the result could well be the same in the postulated reversed factual circumstance. A more usual set of facts would

---

78 Ibid., paras.40 and 41.
79 (1997), 135 F.T.R. 67 [*The Ryan Leet*].
80 Ibid., para.7.
81 Ibid., paras.11 and 14.
82 Ibid., para.17.

be two "single-ship companies," each of which is the registered owner of a ship, and each of which is a wholly owned subsidiary, directly or indirectly, of a common parent. If, on the authority of *The Ryan Leet*, the subsidiary cannot be the "beneficial owner" of the property of the parent, would it not even further strain the statutory language to argue that the subsidiary can be the "beneficial owner" of the property of its parent's other subsidiary?[83]

Finally, subsection 43(8) was considered in the course of the court's priorities decision in *Holt Cargo Systems Inc. v. ABC Containerline N.V. (The Brussel)*.[84] Two Belgian companies, ABC Containerline N.V. and Antwerp Bulkcarriers N.V. went into bankruptcy shortly following the arrest at Halifax of the ship Brussel. The ship was judicially sold by the Federal Court and creditors of the ship were directed to file claims against the proceeds of sale in the usual way. Many claimants, relying on section 43(8), asserted a right to recover from the fund not only their accounts in relation to The Brussel but also in relation to other ships owned or managed by the bankrupt companies. On the point of which such claims could be considered for payment out of the fund in court, MacKay J. said "only those vessels owned beneficially by Bulkcarriers when the action herein commenced by the arrest of the *Brussel*, i.e., the *Antwerpen*, the *Deloris*, and the *Helen, can* be characterized as sister ships of the *Brussel* pursuant to section 43(8) of the *Federal Court Act*."[85] It is not known what evidence was or was not before the court with respect to the corporate relationship, if any, between Bulkcarriers and ABC, and no argument is said to have been made on any basis that ABC was the "beneficial owner" of ships, including The Brussel, of which Bulkcarriers was the registered owner. It is clear, however, that MacKay J. was satisfied that section 43(8) applied, in the circumstances before him, only to those ships of which Bulkcarriers was the common *registered* owner.

---

83 Those were essentially the facts of *Evpo Agnic (The)*, [1988] 2 Lloyds L.R. 411 (C.A.), the leading U.K. authority. Each of a fleet of ships was registered to a single-ship company, and all companies were said to be ultimately owned by a single businessman. Lord Donaldson, M.R., set aside the arrest warrant, saying: "The truth of the matter, as I see it, is that s.21 does not go, and is not intended to go, nearly far enough to give the plaintiffs a right of arresting a ship which is not 'the particular ship' or a sister ship, but the ship of a sister company of the owners of 'the particular ship'" (at 415). Despite differences in structure and language of the U.K. and Canadian statutes, it is submitted that they are, on this point, sufficiently similar conceptually so that *The Evpo Agnic* is likely to be very persuasive authority in Canada.
84 (2000), 185 F.T.R. 145 [*Holt Cargo Systems Inc.*].
85 *Ibid.*, para.23.

c) Piercing the Corporate Veil

The decisions discussed above acknowledge that the court has power to pierce the corporate veil and to treat ships owned by subsidiary companies as "beneficially owned" by parent companies, if the registration in the name of the subsidiary company is a sham or otherwise used for a fraudulent or deceitful purpose. In the earlier reported cases in which the court was invited to find a sham, however, the court declined to do so. See, for example, *The Glastnos*,[86] which seems to stand for the proposition that the use of single-ship companies *per se* creates no suspicion or presumption of improper motive, and *The Looiersgracht*,[87] in which Prothonotary Hargrave was satisfied that the use of one-ship "companies" is not a sham when used to reflect the fact that ships were owned by different groups in partnership. More recent Canadian jurisprudence, however, has not been as forgiving. In *Bank of Scotland v. The Nel*,[88] Prothonotary Hargrave said in part:

> In [*The*] *Ryan Leet* the term "owner," in the context of section 43(8) of the *Federal Court Act*, was held to refer only to the registered owner. In the result the right of sister ship arrest can only be invoked where the ship sought to be arrested is beneficially owned by the registered owner of the ship that gave rise to the obligation that is the cause of the action. Here I would note that the effect of this is that an owner may defeat the whole idea of sister ship arrest by placing each ship in a separate company, even though each separate company is owned by the same parent company. This I think is contrary to the intention of Parliament, that sister ship legislation is not to be so easily defeated.
>
> ...
>
> This leads to a distinction between the situation in [*The*] *Ryan Leet* and the situation here. In [*The*] *Ryan Leet* the registered owners involved were genuine operating companies, with one company owning the other. In the present case Mr. McEwen suggests and I acknowledge that he is correct, that the registered owners of the Leond Maritime fleet are sham companies and that the operating company for all ships is Leond Maritime Inc.[89]

Prothonotary Hargrave gives no indication in this decision what evidence was before him, other than the "suggestion" of claimants' coun-

---

86 [1991] 1 Lloyds L.R. 482 (Q.B.).
87 *The Looiersgracht*, above note 75.
88 [2001] 1 F.C. 408, 189 F.T.R. 230 [*The Nel*].
89 *Ibid.*, paras.113 and 116, respectively.

sel, that the shipowning companies were "shams." It is not indicated on whom lies the burden of proof of a sham, nor what facts are relevant to be considered in reaching this conclusion. The proposition in *The Nel* may be stated to be that single-ship companies are *per se* shams. It is further troubling that the discussion and finding, however supported, that the shipowning companies were shams were *obiter dicta*. The issue in the case was whether a maritime lien for necessaries, arising under U.S. law, could be enforced with maritime lien priority against a sister ship of the ship to which the supply had been made. Prothonotary Hargrave[90] held that it could not. In view of this legal conclusion, it was unnecessary for him to consider whether the ships in question were, or were not, sister ships for purposes of the *Federal Court Act*.[91]

d) Sister-Ship Arrest Not Available if "Subject Vessel" Sold

In *Noranda Sales Corp. v. Ship British Tay*,[92] the plaintiff brought an action *in rem* against two ships, The Canada Marquis and The British Tay, which were in collision with one another. Noranda's cargo, carried on board The Canada Marquis, was delayed and Noranda claimed against both vessels for alleged financial losses. Between the date of collision and the date of commencement of the action, The Canada Marquis had been sold. Noranda applied to amend its statement of claim by substituting five ships owned by the same company as had owned The Canada Marquis as defendants in place of The Canada Marquis. Denault J. denied leave to so amend, on grounds that once the right to proceed *in rem* against The Canada Marquis was lost through transfer of beneficial ownership,[93] so the right to bring action *in rem* against its sister ships was lost.[94]

e) Do Maritime Liens Attach to Sister Ships?

In *Fraser Shipyard & Industrial Centre Ltd. v. Expedient Maritime Co. (The Atlantis Two)*,[95] maritime liens in favour of U.S. suppliers of necessaries were asserted, among many other claims, against the ship Atlantis Two. Prothonotary Hargrave held that an American maritime lien is a privilege against a given ship but is not a substantive right against any other ship.[96] He concluded on this point:

---

90 Following earlier authority on this point; see below in D(4)(e).
91 Above note 12, s.43(8).
92 (1994), 77 F.T.R. 8.
93 As under the *Federal Court Act*, above note 12, s.43(3).
94 *Noranda Sales Corp. v. Ship British Tay*, above note 92, para.7.
95 (1999), 170 F.T.R. 1 [*The Atlantis Two*].
96 *Ibid.*, para.90

In this framework the substantive American maritime lien does not fit into the sister ship provision, section 43(8) of the *Federal Court Act*, which merely refers to the jurisdiction conferred on the Court by section 22 of the Act, an *in personam* jurisdiction, as being enforceable against a sister ship, not a right or privilege against one ship being enforced against another ship. If American maritime lien holders wished to use the sister ship procedure here in Canada they would need sister ship legislation in the United States to enable them to bring into Canada a full blown maritime lien against the sister ship.

Of course, a lien holder, assuming he or she also had an *in personam* right against a shipowner and assuming that shipowner was the owner of not only the wrongdoing or debtor ship but also the sister ship or ships at the relevant time, might bring that *in personam* right into Canada and enforce it, procedurally, against one or more of the sister ships. However the priority of such a claim would then only be that of a statutory right *in rem*.[97]

Prothonotary Hargrave's analysis of the non-attachment of U.S. necessaries suppliers' maritime liens to sister ships was followed by MacKay J. in *Holt Cargo Systems Inc. v. ABC Containerline N.V. (The Brussel)*.[98] In the course of that decision, MacKay J. said:

> The issue is whether the sister ship provision of the *Federal Court Act* should be construed to allow for an interpretation that would give maritime lien holders with a claim against one ship the same priority as a maritime lien in relation to a sister ship arrested in Canada, regardless of whether the claims originated in Canada or abroad. In the absence of legislation, I cannot conclude that the special priority accorded to maritime liens is portable to sister ships.
>
> ...
>
> In my opinion the holders of maritime liens against sister ships of the "Brussel" may enforce their claims against the "Brussel" under subsection 43(8) of this Court's *Federal Court Act*, but they do not have the same status as holders of traditional maritime liens against that vessel. They have a statutory right *in rem* with priority similar to that of any creditor who has an ordinary *in rem* claim against a sister ship of the "Brussel."[99]

---

97 Ibid., paras.92 and 93.
98 *Holt Cargo Systems Inc*, above note 84.
99 Ibid., paras.21 and 22.

These two cases dealt particularly with maritime liens arising under U.S. statute, and it may be arguable that the result will be different in cases involving "true" maritime liens as recognized in Canadian law. It must, however, be noted that the reasoning of both Prothonotary Hargrave in *The Atlantis Two* and MacKay J. in *The Brussel* appears to be applicable to any maritime lien, however it arises.

E. ARREST OF THE *RES*

1) Available *in Rem* Actions

Arrest of property is available "in an action *in rem*."[100] Note that a warrant will be issued only following commencement of the action. The warrant is issued by the registry officer[101] on presentation for filing of an affidavit to lead warrant that complies with Federal Court rule 481(2).[102] The warrant, the affidavit to lead warrant, and the statement of claim must all be served on the property to be arrested.[103] Following service of documents on the ship, or on property on board a ship the practice is for the sheriff to notify local authorities who must support or permit the departure of the ship (i.e., customs, pilots, harbour master, or similar authority) that the ship has been arrested. Those authorities, in practice, will not then attend the ship or clear it for departure unless and until informed by the sheriff that the ship has been released.

There are some ships (e.g., small pleasure craft and some fishing vessels) that require neither customs clearance nor a pilot to depart port. In such cases, for all practical purposes, only the sanction of contempt proceedings prevents surreptitious departure by the vessel following arrest.

2) Theory and Purpose of Arrest

Arrest procedures are available only in an action *in rem* and only after the filing of the statement of claim in that action.[104] Even though the *Federal Court Rules* do not expressly so state, it is generally accepted that a warrant for arrest can be issued only against property that has

---

100 *Federal Court Rules*, above note 9, r.481.
101 *Ibid.*, r.481(1).
102 *Ibid.*, r.481(2).
103 *Ibid.*, r.482(1).
104 *Ibid.*, r.481(1).

been identified as a defendant, or one of the defendants, in the style of cause in the *in rem* action. It is well established that arrest is a procedural device only, the use of which neither grants nor creates any substantive rights that did not otherwise exist.[105] Arrest of a ship includes arrest of all its equipment and machinery, including engines, removed and sent for repair at the time of arrest, as well as electronics that had been removed and stored for safekeeping.[106]

3) Territorial Scope for Service of Warrant

The Federal Court is a court "in and for Canada" and its process "runs throughout Canada and any other place to which legislation enacted by Parliament has been made applicable."[107] It is submitted to be clear that the court's process may be enforced, and its warrants may be served, anywhere in Canada's land areas or internal waters. As a matter of practice, most ship arrests occur, and warrants are served, in Canadian seaports, both tidal and non-tidal, without question or challenge as to territorial jurisdiction or as to validity of arrest.

Proceeding from the practical to the somewhat theoretical, under section 7 of the *Oceans Act*,[108] Canada's territorial sea — extending seaward 12 nautical miles (22 km) from baselines — "forms part of Canada." If, logistically, a circumstance presented itself — logistics including the practicality of transporting a sheriff's officer to the ship to effect service and reasonable assurance that the ship will remain safely in the place where the service occurred — there is submitted to be no reason in principle why a ship cannot be arrested anywhere in Canada's territorial sea.

Under the *Oceans Act*, Canada's exclusive economic zone extends from 12–200 nautical miles (22–370 km) seaward of baselines. Canada claims, in its exclusive economic zone, "sovereign rights" in respect of, among other things, exploitation of resources and "jurisdiction" in respect of protection of the marine environment. Assuming logistic difficulties could be overcome, it is submitted that a right of arrest in the exclusive economic zone could be argued to exist for *in rem* claims aris-

---

105 *Coastal Equipment Agencies Limited v. Comer (The)*, [1970] 1 Ex. C.R. 13, per Noël J., at 31 [*Coastal Equipment Agencies Limited*]; *Benson Brothers Shipbuilding Co. v. Miss Donna (The)*, [1978] 1 F.C. 379, per Addy J., para.22 [*Benson Brothers Shipbuilding Co.*].
106 *Pacific Tractor Rentals (V.I.) Ltd. v. Palaquin (The)* (1996), 115 F.T.R. 224.
107 *Federal Court Act*, above note 12, s.55(1).
108 S.C. 1996, c.31.

ing out of activities in respect of which Canada exercises sovereign rights or jurisdiction in the exclusive economic zone, particularly activities that are carried out there under Canadian licence. Such activities would clearly include fishing and offshore hydrocarbon exploration or development. Further, to the extent that Canada's laws relating to protection of the marine environment include provision for private compensation to be paid by polluters, one wonders whether a right of arrest of a ship, or other maritime property, would exist beyond Canada's territorial sea but within Canada's exclusive economic zone in an appropriate fact situation. A more probable — theoretically and logistically — situation would be a private claim arising in respect of an offshore drilling or production unit on location within Canada's exclusive economic zone. Such units are unlikely, for operational reasons, to be surreptitiously removed and their presence in the exclusive economic zone is necessarily under Canadian licence and to conduct an activity in respect of which Canada is sovereign in that part of the ocean. On these principles, the argument could further be made that the court's process extends to, and its warrants could be served in, that portion of the continental shelf that extends beyond Canada's exclusive economic zone.[109] Note, finally, on these points that certain sections of the *Coastal Fisheries Protection Act*[110] purport to apply for certain purposes throughout the Northwest Atlantic Fisheries Organization regulatory area — generally speaking, eastward to mid-Atlantic. Can the argument be made under section 51(1) of the *Federal Court Act*[111] that, because any Canadian legislation applies in that place, the court's process necessarily extends there for all purposes?

Beyond the territorial reach of the court's process — wherever that may end — it is well established that the court cannot and will not authorize service *ex juris* of *in rem* process.[112] This is entirely consistent with the theory of *in rem* proceedings in Admiralty: the court acquires jurisdiction over the *res* because it is arrested within the court's territorial jurisdiction, regardless of the domicile or accessibility for service of the person or entity liable *in personam* in respect of the claim.

---

109 *Ibid.*, s.20.
110 R.S.C. 1985, c.C-33.
111 Above note 12.
112 *Mesis (The) v. Louis Wolfe & Sons (Vancouver) Ltd.*, [1977] 1 F.C. 429 (C.A.); *Gilling v. Canada*, [2001] F.C.T. 1271.

4) Arrest of Multiple Sister Ships?

Article 3(3) of the *Arrest Convention* provides in part:

> A ship shall not be arrested, nor shall bail or other security be given more than once in any one or more of the jurisdictions of the Contracting States in respect of the same maritime claim by the same claimant; and ... any subsequent arrest of the ship or of any ship in the same ownership by the same claimant for the same maritime claim shall be set aside.[113]

This provision, like many others in the *Arrest Convention*, has not been incorporated into the *Federal Court Act*, leaving open for argument the proposition that Parliament intended Canadian law to differ from the provisions of the *Arrest Convention* in this respect. Although it is not yet definitively settled in Canada whether multiple sister ships may be arrested in respect of the same claim, it is submitted that the weight of U.K. authority, and such Canadian authority as presently exists, is to the effect that they may not.

In *The Banco*,[114] the plaintiffs arrested seven commonly owned vessels including The Banco. The defendants moved to set aside the arrest of the remaining six vessels. At the time, the governing U.K. legislation was the *Administration of Justice Act, 1956*, which permitted *in rem* proceedings to be brought against

(a) that ship [i.e., the subject ship of the claim], if at the time when the action is brought is beneficially owned as respects all the shares therein by that person; or
(b) any other ship which, at the time the action is brought, is beneficially owned as aforesaid.[115]

Lane J. at first instance interpreted this statutory language to mean that "ship" is singular, and one ship only, either the offending ship or any one sister ship, could be arrested in respect to any one maritime claim. Lane J. was upheld by a unanimous Court of Appeal in the following terms:

> The important word in that subsection is the word "or." It is used to express an alternative as in the phrase, "one or the other." It means that the Admiralty jurisdiction *in rem* may be invoked either against the offending ship or against any other ship in the same ownership,

---

113 *Arrest Convention*, above note 54, art.3(3).
114 *Monte Ulia v. Banco (The)*, [1970] 2 Lloyds L.R. 230 (Adm. Ct.), aff'd [1971] 1 Lloyd's L.R. 49 (C.A.) [*The Banco*].
115 *Administration of Justice Act, 1956*, above note 52, s.3(4).

but not against both. This is the natural meaning of the word "or" in this context ... I would add that the word "ship" in the phrase "any other ship," means "ship" and not "ships" (*per* Lord Denning, MR).[116]

As I have said, I think that the meaning put forward by the defendants is right. It is the unambiguous meaning of section 3(4). The word "or" expresses an alterative. "Any other ship" does not include the plural....

Article 3(3) of the [*Arrest Convention*] prohibits, for all relevant purposes, the arrest of more than one vessel by a plaintiff in respect of a maritime claim. If the plaintiffs' construction of s. 3(4) of the [*Administration of Justice Act*] were correct, Parliament would in that respect not have given effect to, but would have directly contradicted, the international obligation which Her Majesty's Government accepted by ratifying the [*Arrest Convention*]. (*per* Megaw J.A.)[117]

Looking at [section 3(4) of the *Administration of Justice Act*] as a whole the first impression made on my mind is that it provides alternatives — the offending ship or one other, so displacing the rule that the singular includes the plural. In support of this construction I add (1) that if the wider construction had been intended it could have been more simply expressed by omitting (a) and (b) after "against" and simply saying "any ship or ships beneficially owned at the same time the action is brought by the owner of the ship in connection with which the claim arose"; (2) alternatively, if the wider construction had been intended "and" would be a more appropriate conjunction than "or"; (3) if it had been intended to give rights extending beyond those provided by the [*Arrest Convention*], one would have expected very clear language to be used to emphasize the difference. (*per* Cairns J.A.)[118]

It is noted that, although section 43(8) of the *Federal Court Act* uses the word "ship" in the singular, it refers to "any ship" not "any other ship," and the word "or" does not appear in that section. For these reasons of structure, and also because Canada did not ratify the *Arrest Convention*, it is submitted to be available to argue that *The Banco* is not persuasive authority in Canada.

In *Elecnor S.A. v. The Soren Toubro*, Prothonotary Hargrave held sister-ship arrest in Canada to be permitted but not mandatory. While the

---

116 *The Banco*, above note 114 at 53.
117 *Ibid.* at 56.
118 *Ibid.* at 59.

availability of multiple arrest was not directly before him in that case, he had occasion to comment in the course of his decision:

> Mr. Justice Brandon[119] touches on the history of *in rem* proceedings before and after the 1956 enactment in Britain of the Brussels Convention of 1952 (see p. 539 et seq.). At 543 Mr. Justice Brandon comments on the English policy of allowing a plaintiff discretion to elect among sisterships:
>
>> It is no doubt desirable that a plaintiff, who has an option to proceed against any one of a number of ships owned by a defendant, should not be compelled to elect irrevocably between them when he issues his writ, but should instead be able to defer such final election until he knows that a suitable ship is about to come, or has come, within the jurisdiction.
>
> The reference to a "suitable ship" is important for *just as a plaintiff ought not to be able to arrest a whole fleet, to the detriment of the defendant who would then be forced to put up security far beyond the value of either the wrongdoing vessel or the most valuable vessel in a fleet*, a plaintiff ought not to be forced to arrest the first sistership coming into the jurisdiction, if that sistership is of minimal value compared to the wrongdoing ship. [Emphasis added.][120]

Regardless whether multiple arrest of commonly owned ships is or is not ultimately decided to be available in Canada, it is arguable that the procedural device of sister-ship arrest should not be employed to entitle plaintiff to any security greater than the value of the wrongdoing vessel. If plaintiff's right to security for its claim is a substantive and not a procedural right, then, it is submitted, to permit otherwise would offend the basic principle that *in rem* process and arrest are purely procedural and create no substantive advantage that does not otherwise exist.

5) "Wrongful Arrest"

In *Armada Lines Ltd. v. Chaleur Fertilizers Ltd.*,[121] a series of misfortunes and misunderstandings resulted in the plaintiff shipowner believing the defendant shipper had repudiated a contract that called for loading

---

119 *Berny (The)*, [1977] 2 Lloyds L.R. 533 (Q.B.).
120 *Elecnor S.A. v. Soren Toubro (The)* (1996), 114 F.T.R. 134, para.24.
121 (1995), 170 N.R. 372 (F.C.A.), rev'd [1997] 2 S.C.R. 617 [*Armada Lines Ltd.*].

at certain dates. As a result, the shipowner redirected the ship elsewhere to take on replacement cargo and sued the shipper, as well as the cargo *in rem*, for alleged commercial losses and arrested the cargo. Security was posted for the release of the cargo. On the defendants' motion some eight months later, the arrest and the security were set aside. The defendants counterclaimed against the plaintiff for damages arising out of the arrest of the cargo. Regarding the counterclaim, the trial judge is said to have decided that the arrest caused no damage to cargo owners, and that their alleged cost of $36,651 for "maintaining security" was referable to their delay in moving to set aside the arrest. In the Federal Court of Appeal, Heald J.A. considered authorities governing the grant of *Mareva* injunctions, noted that plaintiff's undertaking to respond in damages is required in such cases, and determined that those authorities "demonstrate that the plaintiff who seeks the arrest must carry the risk and burden of an illegal arrest and the consequences flowing therefrom."[122] Heald J.A. concluded that damages are payable where the arrest is without a proper legal foundation. On further appeal to the Supreme Court of Canada, the counterclaim was dismissed, the Court holding[123] that damages may be awarded for wrongful arrest only if plaintiff's conduct amounts to malice or gross negligence. It should be noted that the Supreme Court awarded to the defendants the interest component of their cost to maintain security (approximately $3,800) on the basis that this interest was properly included in recoverable party and party costs of the motion to set aside the arrest.

6) Movement of Arrested Property

Federal Court rule 484 provides: "No property arrested shall be moved without leave of the court or the consent of all parties and caveators."[124] This rule means what it literally says: to move a ship, cargo, or other property on board ship while under arrest without court authorization or all parties' consent is prohibited and is punishable as contempt of court. If, however, all parties consent, such consent is in practice documented very informally — sometimes as little as an exchange of correspondence between counsel expressing their consent, all of which is copied to the local registry office of the court.

---

122 *Ibid.*, para.33 (F.C.A.).
123 *Ibid.*, per Iacobucci J., para.24 (S.C.C.).
124 *Federal Court Rules*, above note 9, r.484.

7) Marshal's Expenses of Arrest

Expenses incurred for the purpose of maintaining and preserving the value of a ship while under arrest — sometimes called *custodia legis* expenses — are reimbursed to the party by which they were paid with the highest priority. Such reimbursement, however, is not automatic and care must be taken to pre-authorize all such expenses. In Canadian Admiralty practice, arrest does not vest the sheriff, or the plaintiff, with possession of the arrested property. By Federal Court rule 483(1), unless and until the court otherwise orders, possession of the arrested property remains in the person who was in possession immediately before the arrest.[125]

In the case of a solvent shipowner intent on securing the release of the ship and returning it to operations — and in a financial position to do so — paying or recovering maintenance expenses during arrest is seldom a concern for plaintiff or for other creditors. In the case, however, of shipowner insolvency, someone must usually take the initiative to preserve the value of the *res*, pending its sale. Because the circumstances in which these costs may be required and the kinds of expenses that may be appropriate are nearly infinitely varied, only general principles in respect of *custodia legis* expenses can be mentioned here.

Obtaining a court order to have the sheriff declared in possession, without more, does not solve the problem of paying for maintenance. In Canada at least, the sheriff has no access to public resources with which to pay such costs in anticipation of their ultimate recovery. All expenses must be funded privately — generally by some party interested in the ship, such as the mortgagee, or in the litigation; the plaintiff or some other creditor; or sometimes a collaboration of creditors. In order to be recoverable with priority as if they were marshal's expenses, all such expenses must be authorized by court order prior to being incurred.[126] The authorization is embodied in an interlocutory order — one or a series — obtained on motion brought on notice to all interests that are on file with the court (e.g., parties to another action involving the same ship would normally be served). As a rule, the court must be satisfied that the proposed expenses are reasonable in amount, and are reasonably necessary to preserve the value of the *res* pending sale for the benefit of all parties in interest. Orders are generally specifically drafted to suit the circumstances of the case. In cases in which there may be a prolonged period of arrest pending sale, provision is frequent-

---

125 *Ibid.*, r.483(1).
126 *The Atlantis Two*, above note 95, paras.45–47.

ly made for filing of periodic reports by the party making the payments, or for expiry and periodic renewal of the authorizing order.

Discharge of cargo from arrested ships is a special circumstance deserving comment. Usually, cargo is the innocent victim of the arrest of the ship. In cases in which the arrest of the ship may be prolonged, or the ultimate sale of the ship likely, it is in the cargo owner's interest to expedite carriage of the cargo to its destination by some other means. Generally — although not always[127] — it is in the plaintiff's and other creditors' interest to have the cargo removed from the ship, both to avoid responsibility for the cargo and also to facilitate marketing and sale of the ship. The U.K. practice is that cargo must bear the cost of its own discharge;[128] in U.S. practice, discharging cargo is a *custodia legis* expense.[129] There is Hong Kong authority to the effect that each case should be decided according to its own equities.[130] The point was expressly left open in a Canadian case where this aspect was argued,[131] and it was held on the facts to be premature for decision.

8) Arrest Contrasted with Statutory Seizures and Detentions

Ships may be prevented from departing Canadian ports under various statutory powers. While theoretically and substantively quite different from arrest in private *in rem* proceedings described above, these powers present very real commercial and operational problems for shipowners and must, when they arise, be dealt with by Admiralty practitioners on an urgent basis. Certain of the more common[132] statutory detention and seizure powers and how release of the ship from them is obtained, are briefly discussed below.

a) Safety Violations

Under the *Canada Shipping Act*,[133] a steamship inspector is required to detain a ship if "he considers the ship unsafe, or if a passenger ship,

---

127 *Bank of Scotland v. Nel (The)* (1997), 149 F.T.R. 271.
128 *Myrto (No. 2) (The)*, [1984] 2 Lloyd's L.R. 341.
129 *Poznam (The)*, 1927 A.M.C. 723; *Associated Metals & Minerals Corp. v. Alexander's Unity (The)*, 41 F.3d 1007 (5th Cir. 1995).
130 *Mingren Development (The)*, [1979] H.K.L.R. 159.
131 *Royal Bank of Scotland v. Kimisis III (The)*, [1999] F.C.J. No. 300 (QL).
132 Note that the statutes discussed here are not exhaustive. Statutory detention powers also exist under the *Marine Transportation Security Act*, S.C. 1994, c.40, s.16; *Canada Marine Act*, S.C. 1998, c.10, s.115; and *Canadian Transportation Accident Investigation and Safety Board Act*, S.C. 1989, c.3, s.19(14).
133 R.S.C. 1985, c.S-9, s.310(1).

unfit to carry passengers, or the machinery or equipment is defective in any way so as to expose persons on board to serious danger." Further, the steamship inspector has discretion to detain any ship "in respect of which any provisions of [the *Canada Shipping Act*] have not been complied with."[134] When a ship is ordered detained under section 310,[135] one cannot post security for its release. Release is available only when work has been completed to correct the safety deficiency. Owners and operators may and often do negotiate with authorities concerning the scope of work that will be required to correct the deficiency; typically, those negotiations are conducted by technical or operational people, as opposed to lawyers.

Under the *Canada Shipping Act, 2001*,[136] somewhat expanded powers of detention are provided. In summary, detention is, again, discretionary in the case of contravention of a "relevant provision" of the Act or regulations[137] and is mandatory in the case of the inspector believing that the ship is unsafe, is unfit to carry passengers or crew, or has defective machinery and equipment.[138] In addition, if enforcement proceedings are commenced in Canada against a foreign vessel, a detention order is mandatory in respect of that vessel. A detention order under *Canada Shipping Act, 2001*, will be required to specify what work is necessary to correct the safety deficiency and, if enforcement proceedings have been commenced, what amount and form of security must be provided to the Minister of Transport in order to have the detention rescinded.[139] Because these sections are not yet in force, it is not known whether Transport Canada will be willing to accept relatively informal security, such as P&I club letters of undertaking, to permit rescission of detention orders for ships against or in respect of which enforcement proceedings have been commenced.

b) Spills of Pollutants

Part XV of the *Canada Shipping Act*, entitled "Pollution Prevention," applies in respect of the discharge from ships of "pollutants," which are defined in regulations made under that part to include a large number of substances. As a general statement, discharge of pollutants in Canadian waters or in Canada's exclusive economic zone is an offence under

---

134 *Ibid.*, s.310(2).
135 *Ibid.*, s.310.
136 S.C. 2001, c.26, Part 11, not yet proclaimed in force.
137 *Ibid.*, s.222(1).
138 *Ibid.*, s.222(2).
139 *Ibid.*, s.222(6).

Part XV.[140] Section 672(1) provides that when a pollution prevention officer believes on reasonable grounds that an offence under Part XV has been committed, he or she may make a detention order in respect of the ship.[141] Under section 672(7), the detention order is released on the provision of financial security to the federal government.[142] While the current *Canada Shipping Act* remains in force, this part is administered by Transport Canada, which has developed a practice of accepting letters of undertaking as security for release of section 672(1) detentions, subject to the amount of security, and the creditworthiness of the entity by which the security is given, being satisfactory to Transport Canada.

Substantially similar detention powers are provided for in section 177(1) of the *Canada Shipping Act, 2001*, contained in that statute's Part 8, "Pollution Prevention and Response — Department of Fisheries and Oceans."[143] Section 177(4) provides that the notice of detention must specify "the measures to ensure compliance with this Part" and must also "if an indictment has been preferred in respect of the offence" indicate the amount and form of security that must be provided to the minister.[144] At the time of publication, this section had not been proclaimed in force and so it was not known whether section 177(4) will be interpreted to mean that security to obtain rescission of a detention notice may be provided only in cases — and in fact after — "an indictment has been preferred." As this would arguably be an absurd result, given that it would exclude security for release being possible in less serious offences for which proceedings by indictment are not taken, it is submitted to be more probable that the general power in section 177(4)(a) to require measures to be taken to support rescission of a detention notice will be interpreted to include statutory power to accept security for release in less serious matters.[145]

Furthermore, it should be noted that *Canada Shipping Act, 2001*, Part 8, when in force, will be administered by Fisheries and Oceans Canada, presumably, by the Canadian Coast Guard, which is an agency within that department and not, as is the case at present with Part XV of the *Canada Shipping Act*, by Transport Canada. It is not yet known whether Fisheries and Oceans Canada will continue Transport Cana-

---

140 *Canada Shipping Act*, above note 133. On marine pollution, see Chapter 17.
141 *Ibid.*, s.672(1).
142 *Ibid.*, s.672(7).
143 *Canada Shipping Act, 2001*, above note 136, s.177(1).
144 *Ibid.*, s.177(4).
145 *Ibid.*, ss.177(4) and 177(4)(a).

da's policy of accepting letters of undertaking as security for release of ships in pollution offence matters.

c) Fisheries Offences

The *Fisheries Act* provides that a fisheries officer may seize, among other things, any fishing vessel that the officer believes on reasonable grounds was used in the commission of an offence under the Act.[146] Under section 71(2) "a court" may order the return of the seized thing to the person from whom it was seized, "if security is given in a form and amount that is satisfactory to the Minister."[147] Note that, unlike the case of pollution offences, in which purely private security arrangements may be made between the ship and Fisheries and Oceans Canada, seizures under the *Fisheries Act* require judicial order to be released. This generally means that a seized fishing vessel cannot be released until after the commencement of a prosecution. Note also that the court may order release only on provision of security "in form and amount ... satisfactory to the Minister." Courts generally — and, it is submitted, correctly — hold that they have no authority to direct or impose on Fisheries and Oceans Canada release or security terms with which the department disagrees. For practical purposes, ships can be released from *Fisheries Act* seizures only on the department's agreement as to form and amount of security. It should be noted also that, in the event of conviction of an offence under the *Fisheries Act*,[148] the sentencing court has, under section 72(1), discretion to order forfeiture of, among other things, any ship seized under section 51. Courts frequently exercise this power in respect of fishing gear but relatively seldom in respect of ships themselves. One case in which forfeiture of a vessel was ordered — and in the final result partial forfeiture was upheld by the Supreme Court of Canada — involved the ship Kristina Logos.[149]

Separately, under the *Coastal Fisheries Protection Act*, a statute that generally prohibits unauthorized entry by foreign fishing vessels into Canadian fisheries waters, fishery officers are empowered to seize any

---

146 R.S.C. 1985, c.F-14, s.51.
147 *Ibid.*, s.71(2).
148 *Ibid.*
149 *R. v. Tavares*, (27 July 1994), Newfoundland (Prov. Ct.) [unreported], aff'd (1995), 131 Nfld. & P.E.I.R. 271 (Nfld. T.D.), rev'd (1996), 144 Nfld. & P.E.I.R. 154 (Nfld. C.A.); *R. v. Ulybel Enterprise Ltd.* (1997), 150 Nfld. & P.E.I.R. 308, rev'd in part (1999), 178 Nfld. & P.E.I.R. 321 (Nfld. C.A.), rev'd [2001] 2 S.C.R. 867. For related proceedings in Federal Court of Canada see *Neves v. Kristina Logos (The)* (1996), 124 F.T.R. 167, aff'd (1998), 225 N.R. 32 (F.C.A.); and *Neves v. Kristina Logos (Le)* (1999), 173 F.T.R. 31.

vessel "by means of or in relation to which the officer believes on reasonable grounds [an] offence has been committed."[150] Section 13 then provides:

> Where a fishing vessel or goods have been seized pursuant to section 9 and proceedings in respect of an offence under this Act have been instituted, the court or judge may, with the consent of the protection officer who made the seizure, order redelivery thereof to the person from whom the fishing vessel or goods were seized on security by bond, with two sureties, in an amount and form satisfactory to the Minister, being given to Her Majesty.[151]

Here again, a court order is required, following commencement of proceedings, to release the ship from seizure. Note that section 13 only contemplates security in the form of a bond signed by two sureties. Fisheries and Oceans Canada takes the position — again, probably correctly — that it has discretion whether to approve the identities of any proposed sureties. The department has been known to accept cash security for release of *Coastal Fisheries Protection Act* seizures — presumably on the basis that this is the best form of security; it is arguable, however, that section 13 does not give the court discretion or jurisdiction to order *Coastal Fisheries Protection Act* release for any form of security, even cash, other than the prescribed bond with two sureties.

d) *Immigration Act*

The *Immigration Act*, Part V, "Obligations of Transportation Companies,"[152] contains complex and multi-faceted provisions imposing various potential financial obligations on transportation companies, including payment of administrative fees to Citizenship and Immigration Canada and bearing the cost to remove from Canada certain persons not permitted to enter or to remain in Canada. These provisions apply equally to multiple transportation modes, not just shipping, and so their complexity tends to be compounded by generic wording when applied to marine transportation. Note also, especially in a marine transportation context, that "transportation company" is defined to include "any agent" of the person providing the transportation service. This is the source of much consternation and severe potential liabilities on the part of the port agency community — and in some circumstances even maritime law practitioners — in Canada.

---

150 Above note 110, s.9.
151 *Ibid.*, s.13.
152 R.S.C. 1985, c.I-2, Part V.

In very general terms, Citizenship and Immigration Canada, under section 92(1)–(3) may require transportation companies to deposit a "sum of money" with the federal government, for the purpose of ensuring that liabilities under the Act will be paid.[153] Failing payment, the department may detain, seize, and hold "any vehicle" — defined to include a ship — of the transportation company. The vehicle, or ship, may be released on receipt of security covering the deposit amount plus detention costs or, if lower, the value of the vehicle.[154] Citizenship and Immigration Canada will only accept cash payments as security for release from detention under Part V of the *Immigration Act*. The Act does not appear to contemplate — and, in any event, the department does not accept — any other form of security.

e) **Customs Act**

Section 110 of the *Customs Act*[155] empowers customs officers to "seize as forfeit" any "conveyance" — again defined to include a ship — that the officers believe on reasonable grounds "was made use of" in respect of a contravention of the Act. Under section 118, an officer may return the conveyance on receipt of money in an amount directed by the minister, not exceeding the value of the conveyance, or such other security as the minister authorizes.[156] It is possible to seek judicial resolution of a dispute as to the "value of the conveyance." For an interesting analysis of valuation for customs seizures purposes of a fishing vessel gainfully, if illegally, employed in the off season, see *Joys v. Minister of National Revenue*.[157]

F. RELEASE OF ARRESTED PROPERTY

A ship may be released from arrest if appropriate alternative security is provided. The security or bail to be provided to the court may take one of four forms: guarantee of a bank;[158] surety company bond in Form 486A[159] (see Appendix 3); bail bond in Form 486A;[160] or cash paid into court.[161] Note that disputes as to amount of bail must be resolved on

---

153 *Ibid.*, ss.92(1), (2), and (3).
154 *Ibid.*, ss.92(4)–(5).
155 R.S.C. 1985, c.1 (2d Supp.), s.110.
156 *Ibid.*, s.118.
157 (1995), 189 N.R. 175 (F.C.A.).
158 *Federal Court Rules*, above note 9, r.486(1)(a).
159 *Ibid.*, r.486(1)(b).
160 *Ibid.*, r.486(1)(c).
161 *Ibid.*, r.487(1).

motion to the court;[162] disputes as to form of bail or the sufficiency of surety may be resolved by the registry officer or referred by the registry officer to the court.[163] In addition to posting bail, the release of property from arrest can be obtained by order of the court or consent of the plaintiff. By order of the court,[164] it would be unusual for the court to order a release of arrest in the absence of bail or other security; however, if on motion the court should determine that the arrest was unauthorized or invalid for some reason, the court would presumably order release without security. Presumably the court would suspend the actual issuance of a release pending expiry of any applicable appeal period. For practical purposes, when arrest validity is disputed, the practice is to post bail or other security to obtain a release, then apply to the court for an order that the security be returned. By consent of the plaintiff,[165] generally, consent to release will be granted as one of the terms of a negotiated agreement for release from arrest: either by settlement and payment of the *in rem* claim, or an assurance of payment satisfactory to plaintiff, or delivery to plaintiff of a so-called letter of undertaking — typically issued by the P&I club with which the defendant ship is entered — to the effect that the issuer guarantees payment of any judgment or settlement in the litigation in which the ship was arrested. Note that "club letters" are purely private arrangements between the parties and are not filed with the court.

It is said in the jurisprudence that bail "takes the place of the ship" and should not exceed the fair market value of the ship.[166] There is sometimes concern whether claims against the security, cash, or instrument, formally provided as bail, are subject to normal Admiralty priorities; that is, whether, for example, a necessaries supplier taking security in its *in rem* action would be subject to having that security exhausted by, for example, unpaid crew or a mortgagee, of whose claim the plaintiff necessaries supplier was unaware at the time that bail was taken. As a matter of interpretation of the former (prior to 1998) Federal Court rule 1004,[167] it was said that "bail may only be taken to answer the judgment that may be given in the proceedings in which the bail was taken."[168] The corresponding 1998 rule 485 is worded differ-

---

162 *Ibid.*, r.485.
163 *Ibid.*, r.486(4).
164 *Ibid.*, r.488(1).
165 *Ibid.*, r.487(1)(c).
166 See *Scindia Steam Navigation Co. v. Canada*, [1985] F.C.J. No. 1130 (T.D.) (QL).
167 *Federal Court Rules*, C.R.C., c.663, r.1004 (1978).
168 *Transocean Gateway Corp. v. Weser Isle (The)*, [1974] 2 F.C. 90 (C.A.) [*The Weser Isle*].

ently, providing that only the court may fix the amount of bail.[169] However, it is equally clear from *The Weser Isle*[170] that bail will be paid and applied according to the terms of the instrument by which it is provided. Plaintiffs accordingly should take care to ensure that bail instruments, when taken, are appropriately worded to avoid or minimize the possibility that competing claimants may claim against the security and potentially frustrate plaintiff's ultimate recovery from it.

It is generally faster and less expensive and therefore preferable to arrange release, and bail if necessary, by agreement between the parties to the litigation. This usually requires agreement as to both form and amount of security. As to amount, the plaintiff is entitled to security representing its "best arguable case" as to quantum, limited by the value of the arrested property,[171] plus an allowance (typically 25%–33%) to cover pre-judgment interest and costs. As to form of security, the wording of a bail bond is prescribed.[172] If the defendant desires to provide a bank guarantee, the plaintiff must negotiate the form of the guarantee not only with the defendant but also, in many cases, with the defendant's bank.

G. CAVEATS

Caveats are a peculiar process of limited, but in some circumstances significant, utility. They take the form of caveat releases, caveat warrants, and caveat payments. (See Appendix 3.) A caveat warrant[173] is a notice filed with the court for the purpose of preventing the arrest of property. Before the court will issue an arrest warrant, a nationwide search for caveat warrants must be performed. If a caveat warrant is on file, the warrant will not be issued; but the entity by which the caveat warrant was signed must provide bail in, or pay into court, the amount of money set out in the caveat warrant. A caveat release[174] prevents the release of a ship in respect of which an arrest warrant has been issued and served. Before a release will be issued for an arrested ship, a nationwide search for caveat releases is similarly performed. Typically, if a

---

169 *Federal Court Rules*, above note 9, r.485.
170 *The Weser Isle*, above note 168.
171 *Brotchie v. Karey T (The)* (1994), 83 F.T.R. 262; *Amican Navigation Inc. v. Densan Shipping Co.* (1997), 137 F.T.R. 132; *NHM International Inc. v. F.C. Yachts Ltd.* (2003), 227 F.T.R. 42.
172 *Federal Court Rules*, above note 9, r.486 and Form 486A.
173 *Ibid.*, r.493(1) and Form 493A.
174 *Ibid.*, r.493(2) and Form 493B.

caveat release is on file, the shipowner must either settle the claim in respect of which the caveat release was filed or make a private arrangement with the caveator for security for that claim, in order to obtain the caveator's withdrawal of the caveat release. On filing with the court of withdrawals of all caveat releases that are on file, the court will proceed to issue a release in the usual way. A caveat payment[175] prevents payment of money out of court. This form of caveat is seldom used. It is presumed that, when a caveat payment is on file and making a payment of money out of court — which itself requires a court order[176] — is desired, the caveator would be given notice of the motion for the order for payment and would be required to show cause to justify the continued retention of the money in court.

A few practical points concerning caveat releases should be made. Bail is not available to obtain the release of a caveat. Further, filing of a caveat release in an action commenced by another plaintiff gives the caveator no procedural rights to progress that other action, aside from the right to be served with interlocutory processes as a party in interest. If security, as opposed to settlement and payment, is taken in exchange for withdrawal of a caveat release, that security must by its own terms provide for resolution of the dispute between the caveator and the shipowner. While there is no jurisprudence to this effect, practitioners generally accept that filing a caveat release is not commencement of an action for purposes of preservation of a right to proceed *in rem* in a case to which the *Federal Court Act*, section 43(2) applies.[177] Thus, if the plaintiff commences an *in rem* action, the caveator files a caveat release, and beneficial ownership of the defendant property subsequently changes, the plaintiff has the right to continue its *in rem* proceeding but the caveator will have lost its right to commence one.

H. CERTAIN PROCEDURAL CONSIDERATIONS PECULIAR TO ADMIRALTY

1) Collision Cases

Under Federal Court rule 498,[178] in cases arising out of collisions between ships, the statement of claim and statement of defence contain

---

175 *Ibid.*, r.493(3) and Form 493C.
176 *Ibid.*, r.150.
177 Above note 12, s.43(2).
178 *Federal Court Rules*, above note 9, r.498.

only sufficient particulars to identify the parties. The plaintiff and defendant, within ten days following filing of their respective pleadings, each files with the court in sealed envelopes a document detailing "preliminary acts," which must contain all of the detail listed in Federal Court rule 498(2).[179] The preliminary acts are unsealed and given to the parties after the pleadings are closed and all parties' preliminary acts have been filed. The purpose of this practice is to compel each party to disclose, in pleadings, its own complete version of the event, without being able to tailor a response to the allegations made in a previously filed pleading.

2) Limitation of Liability Proceedings

The substantive right of the shipowner to limit its liability in Admiralty is discussed in Chapter 18. Assertion of that right gives rise to some unique procedures. Statutory limitation of liability may be pleaded by way of defence, or may be asserted by the shipowner in a separate limitation of liability proceeding. When a shipowner, or some other party entitled to limit its liability, commences such a proceeding, it must do so as an action the defendants in which are all of the potential claimants known to the plaintiff.[180]

The procedural constitution of a limitation fund is contemplated by Articles 11–13 of the *Convention on Limitation of Liability for Maritime Claims*.[181] This convention, as adopted in the Canadian *Marine Liability Act*,[182] provides that the Admiralty Court has exclusive jurisdiction in respect of constitution and distribution of the limitation fund.[183] An assertive limitation proceeding by the person against whom claims are made or apprehended[184] requires that security in the amount to which liability is limited be deposited into the fund[185] and, once constituted, prevents the arrest of the ship, or requires the release of the

---

179 *Ibid.*, r.498(2).
180 *Ibid.*, r.496(1).
181 19 November 1976, 1456 U.N.T.S. 221, arts.11 and 13, as am. by Protocol of 1996 to amend the *Convention on Limitation of Liability for Maritime Claims, 1976*, 3 May 1996 35 I.L.M. 1406.
182 *Marine Liability Act*, S.C. 2001, c.6, Part 3.
183 Note that, under *Marine Liability Act*, *ibid.*, s.31(2), limitation may be pleaded by way of defence to an action in any court.
184 *Marine Liability Act*, *ibid.*, s.33(1).
185 *Convention on Limitation of Liability for Maritime Claims, 1976*, above note 181, art.11(2).
186 *Ibid.*, art.13.

ship[186] and requires all persons with claims against the ship to participate in the limitation proceedings.[187] Distribution of the fund among claimants who filed with the court generally follows the usual scheme of Admiralty priorities.[188] Note that distribution of the fund may be postponed, pending the outcome of litigation or arbitration in another jurisdiction of specific or potential claims.[189]

3) Intervention in Admiralty Litigation

The Federal Court's intervention rule[190] is of general application and is not specific to Admiralty proceedings; this rule, however, is widely used in such proceedings for a variety of purposes. In cases of shipowner insolvency, it is not unusual for mortgagees to be added as interveners, both to "defend" the substance of plaintiff's *in rem* claim and, more generally, to support the mortgagee's ability to exercise a measure of control over the process of realization of its security. When a ship is arrested, the warrant does not arrest or affect in any way property of third parties that is on board the ship.[191] Again, in maritime insolvencies or other circumstances in which a lengthy period of arrest is anticipated, third-party owners of property on board ship will wish to move the court for an order permitting removal of that property from the ship. Federal Court rule 358[192] and the following discussion can be interpreted to provide that any person may make a motion to the court — not just a party to the action in which the motion is made. The practice, however, appears to be that third parties wishing to move the court concurrently move for an order adding themselves as interveners, for the purpose of allowing them to bring the substantive motion before the court.

I. JUDICIAL SALE OF THE *RES*

1) Timing of Sale Order

It is typical in *in rem* proceedings to include in plaintiff's prayer for relief language to the following effect: "In default of payment [of the

---

187 *Marine Liability Act*, above note 182, s.33(1)(b).
188 See discussion below in J, "Distribution of Sale Proceeds."
189 *Marine Liability Act*, above note 182, s.33(2).
190 *Federal Court Rules*, above note 9, r.109.
191 *Pacific Tractor Rentals (V.I.) Ltd. v. Palaquin (The)*, above note 106.
192 *Federal Court Rules*, above note 9, r.358.

claimed judgment], an order for appraisement and sale of the defendant [property]." Again typically, at conclusion of litigation, if the plaintiff succeeds, the order for judgment will set out amounts payable to the plaintiff and grant the plaintiff liberty to apply further to the court for an order for appraisement and sale in the event of default in payment of the judgment. In cases in which judgment is entered in default of defence,[193] it is normal for the plaintiff to move concurrently, usually on a single motion, for both an order for judgment and an order for appraisement and sale of the defendant property.

Federal Court rule 490(1) permits sale of the property before judgment, at the court's discretion.[194] A motion for pre-judgment sale will normally be based on one or both of the propositions that the property is declining in value while under arrest[195] — either by its depreciable nature, or because of the cost of maintaining it while under arrest[196] — or the market for the arrested property can be expected to fall in the time that would be taken to proceed to judgment. For practical purposes, orders for pre-judgment sale are most likely to be granted in cases in which the shipowner is insolvent or has otherwise ceased operations, leading to the reasonable conclusion that the eventual sale of the ship is inevitable.[197]

2) Required Contents of Sale Order

Sales of ships, or other arrested property, are governed by Federal Court rule 490.[198] Note that on a literal reading of this rule, none of the contents of a sale order is mandatory. However, for practical purposes, all judicial sale orders must have, at minimum, the following:

- Provision for independent appraisal of the property, which generally will not be disclosed until conclusion of bidding on the sale or the opening of tenders, so as not to influence the potential price to be obtained. In those rare instances in which it is appropriate to invite the court to give its sanction to a private pre-arranged contract of sale,[199] appraisal will need to be supplied to the court on the motion

---

193 *Ibid.*, r.210.
194 *Ibid.*, r.490(1).
195 *Bank of Scotland v. Nel (The)*, above note 127.
196 *Neves v. Kristina Logos (The)*, above note 149.
197 *Canada v. Horizons Unbound* (1997), 123 F.T.R. 127.
198 *Federal Court Rules*, above note 9, r.490.
199 See, e.g., *The Nel*, above note 88.

for the sale order, so that it can be demonstrated that a fair price is being obtained.
- A process for identifying the buyer and settling upon the price to be paid. The most commonly employed methods are auction or sealed tender.[200]
- Provision that, on completion of the sale, the purchaser acquires title to the property "free and clear of all liens and encumbrances." This is the language typically employed in a sale order, notwithstanding that is goes somewhat beyond what is substantively provided for in Federal Court rule 490(3).[201]
- Provision for advertising to notify creditors of a deadline by which claims against the property must be filed with the court. Generally in those cases — which is most cases — in which the sale process itself is such that the sale is advertised to attract potential purchasers, a single advertisement, published on multiple occasions, is used for both purposes.
- Provision for payment of the sale proceeds and execution and delivery of a bill of sale by the sheriff. These are generally simple logistic issues.

Judicial sales invariably carry only assurances of good title, if it is customary in the sale order, and in the advertisement of the sale, to provide that the sale terms are "as is, where is, with all existing faults, without any allowance for deficiencies or errors of description whatsoever and without any legal or contractual representations or warranties." It is customary for the sale order to provide that if the highest bid is less than the appraised value, the court must either approve the sale or make provision for a second attempt at sale.

3) Customizing the Sale Order

Certain variations on some of the themes outlined above are common. Sale methods can and do vary. Most common are sealed tenders or auction. Occasionally, in respect of high-value ships for which a worldwide market may exist, the sale order may provide for the appointment of specialist brokers to market the ship and attempt to negotiate a sale contract — called, in this context, a sale by private treaty — to be recommended to the court for approval. Placement of advertising is generally tailor-made to suit the circumstances of the case. Usually,

---

200 Both are discussed below in I(3), "Customizing the Sale Order."
201 *Federal Court Rules*, above note 9, r.490(3).

insertion of the advertisement in each publication on at least two occasions will be required. Publications in which the advertisement will be inserted should be selected with a view to both bringing the sale to the attention of prospective buyers and bringing filing deadlines to the attention of the ship's creditors. Advertising is expensive, especially in specialized shipping publications that circulate worldwide, and balance must be sought between reasonable efforts to market the ship and controlling the cost of the sale process. Generally, the sale order will provide that prospective purchasers may inspect the ship or its onboard certificates and papers, and will either require the person in possession of the ship to provide access to the ship for these purposes, or empower the sheriff to take potential purchasers on board to do so. Also, generally, a deposit will be required to be paid and will be forfeited in the event of the successful bidder's default in completing the sale. In cases where the sale process has been by tender or auction, the order may also provide that, in the event of the high bidder's default, the ship may then be offered for sale to the next-highest bidder, in the hope of avoiding cost and delay of repeating the sale process.

The order may provide for payment of the sale proceeds by the sheriff into court to the credit of the action, or into some third party's account, usually a law firm's trust account, in either case always to abide further order of the court. Payment into trust accounts can be advantageous if, as is commonly the case with oceangoing ships, the sale price is in U.S. dollars, or if sale proceeds may remain on deposit for some considerable time awaiting a distribution order and it is desired to invest them in relatively higher-yield securities. Note that the court will only accept payments into court in Canadian currency. Further, when orders for payment are made, cheques are much more promptly obtained when drawn on solicitors' trust accounts. Payments out of court, even when authorized by order, can take significant time and, if it is desired to avoid delays in distribution when authorized, having sale proceeds elsewhere than in court can assist.

4) Flag-State Recognition of Canadian Judicial Sale

The sale order will authorize the sheriff to execute a bill of sale in respect of the defendant property to be exchanged for payment in full of the purchase price. Occasionally difficulties arise[202] in the acceptance of the bill of sale as evidence of title, or even of transfer of title in the juris-

---

202 See, e.g., *Canada v. Galaxias (The)*, [1989] 1 F.C. 375 (T.D.).

diction in which the ship is registered, or in which the purchaser desires to newly register the vessel following the sale. It is suggested that these problems, should they arise, are beyond the power of the Federal Court of Canada to correct. It is submitted that prospective purchasers should perform their own due diligence and satisfy themselves that flag-state authorities will recognize and accept the Canadian sheriff's bill of sale before committing themselves to proceed with the purchase.

J. DISTRIBUTION OF SALE PROCEEDS

1) Introduction to Admiralty Priorities

When a ship is judicially sold in the Federal Court of Canada, part of the sale process is advertisement of a notice to creditors of the ship to the effect that they are required to file proof of their claim with the court. This must be verified by an affidavit on or before a date specified in the notice. Failing to complete this requirement will result in claims against the ship being barred. It should be noted that failure to file within the limited time and failure to recover the amount of the claim in whole or in part from the sale fund, in and of themselves, have no effect on the *in personam* liability of the shipowner or anyone else for the claim. Creditors are always at liberty to proceed with *in personam* claims separate from the *in rem* process described in this section. On expiry of the deadline for filing *in rem* claims, which generally is a date following conclusion of the judicial sale, the court is in a position to distribute sale proceeds among the various claimants who filed. It is almost invariably the case that the aggregate amount of claims exceeds the amount of the fund generated by sale of the ship; therefore, a complex system of priorities must be applied to determine the order in which claims are paid from the fund. Claims, subject to proof in each case, are paid in full according to their respective priorities until the sale fund is exhausted.

2) "Normal" Priorities in Canada

Neither statute in Canada, nor treaty that Canada has ratified, sets out the ranking of priorities in Admiralty. Priorities have evolved through court judgments, originally in England and since imported to and refined in Canada. There is substantial and well-accepted Canadian authority that ranking of priorities is in the discretion of the court, and that the court's mandate is to rank claims on an equitable basis such that a just result is achieved.[203] However, it is equally clear that to overturn or to deviate from the "normal" scheme of Admiralty priorities, the court must be satisfied that there exist both "special circumstances and [a] plainly unjust result."[204] Absent special circumstances justifying equitable deviation, the "normal" ranking of Admiralty priorities in Canada is as follows:[205]

- marshal's expenses of arrest;
- costs of selling the ship, including sheriff's disbursements;
- possessory liens arising earlier in time than maritime liens;
- maritime liens, including for practical purposes special statutory liens;
- possessory liens arising later in time than maritime liens;
- mortgages, in the order of their registration; and
- statutory rights *in rem*.

3) Refinements of Certain Priorities

The simple list above generally holds true in all proceedings, but some refinements and even exceptions should be noted in respect of each category, as described below.

a) Marshal's Expenses of Arrest

In practice, the marshal seldom is put in possession of a ship under arrest and, at least in Canada, the marshal never advances public funds to maintain a ship while under arrest. Cost of maintenance of the ship while under arrest is generally borne by the shipowner in the usual course, if the shipowner is solvent. Otherwise the costs will be borne by some creditor or collective of creditors who have an interest in preserving the value of the ship while under arrest. In theory this maximizes the price for which the vessel will sell at judicial sale and so maximizes the amount of the sale fund available for creditors. When creditors desire to advance moneys for the purpose of maintaining a ship under arrest, the general practice is that they apply to the court, on notice to all known interested parties, for an order authorizing payment of specific expenses. This order usually contains a provision stating the maximum amount liable and the time frame involved. The

---

203 *Metaxas v. Galaxias (No. 2) (The)*, [1989] 1 F.C. 386 [*The Galaxias No. 2*]; *The Atlantis Two*, above note 95; *The Nel*, above note 88.
204 *The Nel*, ibid., para.63.
205 *The Galaxias No. 2*, above note 203; *The Nel*, above note 88; *The Atlantis Two*, above note 95.

order would also usually provide for the reimbursement of expenses so made "with priority equivalent to that of an Admiralty marshal for expenses of arrest," or language to similar effect.[206]

Creditors who advance custodial or maintenance expenses without seeking and obtaining prior court authorization are at risk of not recovering those outlays.[207] There are court decisions in which expenses after the arrest have been ordered to be reimbursed with priority equivalent to marshal's expenses, despite the absence of specific prior authorization, on the basis that the expenses were incurred for the benefit of all parties and in the interest of the court in facilitating the sale.[208] This authority is an example of the court exercising its equitable discretion in a priorities context and on the specific facts of the case then before it. It should not be taken as creating a rule that all generally beneficial expenses will be reimbursable in the absence of prior authorization by court order.

b) Costs of Bringing the Ship to Sale

These expenses generally include the party and party costs of the party — frequently, although not necessarily, the plaintiff in the *in rem* action — that has moved the court for an order for sale. They also, and invariably, include the disbursements incurred by, or reimbursed by the moving party to, the sheriff for arranging and conducting the sale. These include advertising costs, appraisal fees, the sheriff's fee itself, and any commissions or like expenses that may be payable on the sale.

c) Possessory Liens Predating Maritime Liens

A possessory lien gives a superior priority, but it is lost when physical possession ends. The possessory lien secures fees and charges for services performed during the period of possession (e.g., repair costs), but it does not secure costs of simply possessing the thing (e.g., berthage or moorage).[209] For practical purposes, a creditor asserting a possessory lien commences action *in rem* claiming, in addition to its claim on the merits, priority as holder of a possessory lien. If and when security is posted for the release of the ship, that security would specify that it is taken, and the ship is released, without prejudice to the plaintiff's

---

206 *The Atlantis Two*, above note 95, paras.21–23; *Holt Cargo Systems Inc.*, above note 84, para.9.
207 *The Atlantis Two*, above note 95, paras.45–47.
208 *Holt Cargo Systems Inc. v. ABC Containerline N.V.*, above note 84.
209 *The Galaxias No. 2*, above note 203 at 420. See discussion in C(3) in Chapter 6, "Maritime Mortgages and Liens."

claim to a possessory lien. The authorities indicate that a possessory lien ranks higher than a later-accruing maritime lien; however, an accrued maritime lien ranks higher than a later-arising possessory lien. Timing of accrual of liens is therefore critical in some circumstances. Any maritime lien, and any valid possessory lien, ranks higher than any mortgage, regardless of relative dates of accrual or registration.

d) Maritime Liens

In Canadian maritime law, maritime liens secure crew wages — including, in a modern context, benefits and, if applicable, repatriation costs[210] — salvage claims, and collision damage claims. Pilots' claims for their fees for services actually rendered are generally accorded maritime lien status in Canada.[211] In addition, Canada recognizes maritime liens arising under foreign law, even if Canadian law would not give rise to a maritime lien in respect of that claim or transaction. Most important of these foreign maritime liens, and the source of much litigation in Canada, is the maritime lien arising under U.S. law for necessaries supplied to a ship in the United States.[212] Under Canadian authority, the maritime lien for crew wages is paid in priority to other maritime liens.[213] Certain Canadian special statutory rights[214] are payable in priority to all claims except those of seamen for their wages. Accordingly, it appears that following pre-existing possessory liens, if any, the ranked scheme of distribution will be seafarers' claims for wages, special statutory claims, and other maritime liens. No Canadian authority directly on point could be found; it is generally accepted, however, that, if there are insufficient funds remaining to satisfy all

---

210 *Metaxas v. Galaxias (No. 4) (The)* (1988), 24 F.T.R. 243; *The Atlantis Two*, above note 95, paras.30–32. See discussions in C(2)(b)–(d) in Chapter 6, "Maritime Mortgages and Liens."

211 *Osborn Refrigeration Sales & Service Inc. v. Atlantean I (The)*, [1979] 2 F.C. 661 (T.D.) at 675–76, aff'd (1982), 52 N.R. 10 (F.C.A.); *Ultramar Canada v. Pierson Steamships* (1982), 43 C.B.R. (N.S.) 9 (F.C.T.D.) at 12.

212 *Todd Shipyards Corporation v. Altema Compania Maritima S.A. (The Ioannis Daskelelis)*, [1974] S.C.R. 1218; *The Har Rai*, above note 49. Note that this is contrary to the position under U.K. law: see *Bankers Trust v. Todd Shipyard (The Halcyon Isle)*, [1981] A.C. 221. See also discussion in C(2)(a) in Chapter 6, "Maritime Mortgages and Liens."

213 *Llido v. Lowell Thomas Explorer (The)*, [1980] 1 F.C. 339 at 344; *The Galaxias No. 2*, above note 203 at 424; *The Atlantis Two*, above note 95, para.28; *Holt Cargo Systems Inc.*, above note 84, para.10.

214 For an example of berthage owing to harbour authorities, see *Canada Marine Act*, above note 132, s.122. See also C(4) in Chapter 6, "Statutory Rights *in Rem*."

"other maritime liens" in full, those liens share the remaining funds among themselves *pari passu*. On the subject of the maritime lien for seamen's wages, it should be noted that creditors sometimes desire to pay off and repatriate the crew, both for humanitarian reasons and also for reasons of limiting the accrual of superior claims against the ship. Such creditors typically seek and obtain prior court order authorizing the payment and providing that, on making the payments, the creditor becomes assigned and subrogated to the maritime lien held by the crew in respect of their wages, or language to similar effect. There is contradictory authority in Canada as to whether such prior authorization by order is required: compare *Scott Steel v. The Alarissa*[215] with *Metaxas v. The Galaxias (No. 4)*.[216]

e) Mortgages

Mortgages rank following all maritime liens in the order in which they were registered under the *Canada Shipping Act*. If not registered, competing mortgagees' rights follow an order of ranking that depends upon the statutes governing them (as explained in B(4) in Chapter 6). It is a rare case in which the fund generated by judicial sale is even sufficient to pay out the first mortgage. In any case in which a mortgagee has participated or intends to participate in a judicial sale, reference should be made to *The Nel*.[217] Although perhaps attributable to the specific conduct of the mortgagee in that case and arguably confined to its facts, the decision can certainly be taken as authority that there are onerous duties, owed apparently to other creditors as well as to the court, placed on marine mortgagees.

f) Statutory Rights *in Rem*

Any claim that may be asserted in or by way of an *in rem* proceeding, but is not a maritime lien, a possessory lien, a special statutory right, or a mortgage, by default is treated as a statutory right *in rem*, and by definition falls to the bottom of the Admiralty Court's list of priorities. There is no Canadian jurisprudence on this point, but the practice appears to be that, in the rare case in which there are moneys left available for distribution after payment of all mortgages, the remaining *in rem* creditors would share those moneys *pari passu*.

---

215 [1996] 2 F.C. 883, para.82, aff'd on an unrelated point (1997), 125 F.T.R. 284.
    See also *Finansbanken ASA v. GTS Katie (The)* (2002), 216 F.T.R. 176.
216 Above note 210, paras.5 and 6.
217 Above note 88. See also discussion in B(2)(b) in Chapter 6, "Maritime Mortgages and Liens."

4) Marshalling of Secured Property

Marshalling was defined in *The Nel* as "a concept involving a creditor with only one fund upon which it is able to claim and a second creditor with security against two or more funds, the latter being, in some instances, required to organize recovery so as not to prejudice the former."[218] In other words, the proposition is that a creditor who has available multiple securities for its debt may be required to exhaust those in which another creditor has a security interest, before calling on those in which there is competition. In this way the payment of secured creditors is maximized. In an earlier decision in the same litigation,[219] Prothonotary Hargrave expanded on the doctrine of marshalling in Canadian maritime law. He decided as follows:

- Creditors whose status is only as holders of statutory rights *in rem*, as opposed to maritime liens, are not entitled to be treated as secured creditors, despite the arrest of the ship.[220]
- Authorities in British Columbia[221] and Ontario,[222] which hold that marshalling does not apply in favour of unsecured creditors, respectively, fail to consider earlier authorities concerning marshalling and "seem to offend against a number of equitable maxims and doctrines."[223]
- The historic development of marshalling, and the equitable principles that the doctrine embodies, do not require that marshalling not be available to ordinary contractual creditors; "the opposite is true."[224]
- On the authority of a recent decision of the Ontario Court of Appeal,[225] marshalling may be invoked against a mortgagee or doubly secured creditor, by any creditor in an inferior position. The superior creditor may be required to satisfy his or her claim from property to which the inferior creditor has no claim; if fairness demands, equity may allow the inferior creditor to stand in a supe-

---

218 *Ibid.*, para.122.
219 *Bank of Scotland v. Nel (The)*, [1998] 4 F.C. 388.
220 *Ibid.*, paras.14–15, citing *Coastal Equipment Agencies Limited* and *Benson Brothers Shipbuilding Co.*, both above note 105.
221 *Williamson v. Loonstra* (1973), 34 D.L.R. (3d) 275.
222 *Re Bread Man Inc.* (1979), 89 D.L.R. (3d) 599.
223 *Bank of Scotland v. Nel (The)*, above note 219, para.17–18.
224 *Ibid.*, para.19.
225 *Re Allison* (1998), 38 O.R. (3d) 337 (C.A.).

rior position in relation to property against which the inferior creditor otherwise has no recourse.

In Canadian Admiralty jurisprudence to date, marshalling has not *per se* been applied to upset or to justify deviation from the normal scheme of Admiralty priorities. In Admiralty, the court has in any event equitable jurisdiction to adjust priorities where doing otherwise would lead to an unjust result. It is submitted that, if equity demands some alteration of priorities so as to do justice between the parties, it is preferable to do so directly as the court has power to do.

5) Procedure in Priorities Matters

Priorities proceedings and decisions are not just a matter of categorizing the various claims that have been filed and then applying priorities' principles to the claims so categorized. Priorities litigation frequently involves serious disputes of law and fact, which the court generally must determine without the benefit of a full trial. Priorities issues are determined on motions;[226] thus, it is a paper proceeding, in which *viva voce* evidence is not heard by the court. Federal Court rule 492(d) permits the court at any time following a sale order to direct the procedure to be followed in determining the rights of the parties. Such orders are frequently sought and made, especially in cases in which there are multiple competing claimants and/or dispute as to the amount, or the priority status of some or all of the claims. Provisions typically made in a rule 492(d) order include the following:[227]

- a time limit for filing by any claimant of additional fact evidence by way of supplementary affidavit — the claim itself typically having been required to be verified by affidavit at the time that it was filed;
- time within which parties may cross-examine deponents to fact affidavits;
- time within which parties must file affidavits containing expert evidence, but note that, if foreign law is relied upon to attach maritime lien status to a particular claim, foreign law must be proved by way of expert affidavit; and
- time within which motion records including written representations must be filed.

---

226 *Federal Court Rules*, above note 9, r.491.
227 *Ibid.*, r.492(d).

K. *MAREVA* INJUNCTIONS AND OTHER PRE-JUDGMENT ATTACHMENTS

1) General

Arrest of maritime property in *in rem* actions in the Federal Court of Canada is a summary, inexpensive, and very effective process. When arrest of property is available, it is almost invariably used to obtain security for a claim, to the exclusion of other effective but more cumbersome procedures. Previously recourse to such other procedures was fairly common. This was because of the belief that either the claim was not within the Federal Court's subject-matter jurisdiction, or because the ship or property that is the subject of the action was not in the jurisdiction and available for arrest, but some other asset of the debtor shipowner was so available. In recent practice such considerations have become less compelling, because of the general expansion of the court's subject-matter jurisdiction in maritime cases,[228] and the 1992 procedural amendments permitting sister-ship arrest. There are, however, still instances in which maritime practitioners may desire the interlocutory seizure of assets other than through arrest. The available procedures to do so are briefly discussed below.

2) *Mareva* Injunctions

The *Mareva* injunction — now called a freezing injunction in England — is an interlocutory order preventing the removal of defendant's assets, usually assets specifically identified in the order, from the court's jurisdiction pending either trial of the action or the provision by defendant of security for plaintiff's claim. Originally developed by the English Court of Appeal, principally by Lord Denning,[229] as an interlocutory remedy against a defendant improperly removing property from the jurisdiction pending trial of an action, the *Mareva* injunction, at least in Canada, is theoretically available to preserve assets for plaintiff's benefit in a variety of situations. In a Canadian context, the English

---

228 *ITO International Terminal Operators Ltd. v. Miida Electronics Inc. (The Buenos Aires Maru)*, above note 15; *Monk Corp. v. Island Fertilizers Ltd.*, [1991] 1 S.C.R. 779. See generally Chapter 3, "Admiralty Jurisdiction."
229 *Nippon Yusen Kaishu v. Karageorgis*, [1975] 3 All E.R. 282 (C.A.); *Mareva Corp. Naviera SA v. International Bulkcarriers SA*, [1980] 1 All E.R. 213 (C.A.); *Rasu Maritime SA v. Perusahaan*, [1977] 3 All E.R. 324 (C.A.); *Third Chandris v. Unimarine*, [1979] 2 All E.R. 972 (C.A.).

authorities were reviewed in detail by the Ontario Court of Appeal in *Chitel v. Rothbart*.[230] MacKinnon C.J.O. held that the remedy was to be available in principle where the plaintiff[231]

- having made full disclosure including particulars of its claim against defendant and fairly stating points made against it by defendant, demonstrated a "strong *prima facie* case" on the merits;
- identifies specific assets of defendant in the jurisdiction against which the injunction can be directed;
- persuades the court that defendant is removing or there is a real risk that defendant is about to remove assets from the jurisdiction to avoid the possibility of judgment; and
- gives an undertaking to respond in damages.

The Supreme Court of Canada considered and affirmed the availability of *Mareva* injunctions in Canada in *Aetna Financial Services Ltd. v. Feigelman*.[232] Subsequent Canadian authority is conflicting as to the degree of impropriety on defendant's part, risk of which must be proved before the injunction will issue. In Nova Scotia,[233] it is said that the applicant for the injunction must "clearly [show] that the defendant has committed a fraud or is about to dispose of his assets in a way that is intended to render the plaintiff's eventual judgment fruitless." In Ontario,[234] in contrast, the court was not satisfied that "the element of fraudulent or improper purpose or design ... [is] a necessary ingredient to be established (like a strong *prima facie* case) as a condition precedent to the order." The principal disadvantages of a *Mareva* injunction relative to arrest of a ship in an *in rem* proceeding are the delay inherent in appearing before a judge, as opposed to presenting papers at the registry office, and the requirement that plaintiff give in interlocutory injunction motions an undertaking to respond in damages. Arrest of a ship involves no such requirement.

In Canadian maritime cases, *Mareva* injunctions are generally sought when arrest of property is not available — typically where there is doubt whether the Federal Court has subject-matter jurisdiction, or where the assets, removal of which is sought to be enjoined, are not the subject of the action. Further, the injunction is often used where the asset desired

---

230 (1982), 29 O.R. (2d) 513.
231 *Ibid.* at 532.
232 [1985] 1 S.C.R. 2.
233 *Magliaro v. Scotia Wholesale Ltd.* (1987), 81 N.S.R. (2d) 201 (C.A.).
234 *Kuehne & Nagel International Ltd. v. Redirack Ltd.* (1991), 47 C.L.R. 241 (Gen. Div.).

to be frozen is money on deposit with a bank in Canada, arrest of which is considered to present conceptual and logistic difficulties.

3) Certain Provincial Court Orders

In most cases, the rules of procedure of the provincial superior courts make provision for pre-judgment attachment orders in some limited circumstances. For example, in Nova Scotia, such orders are governed by Civil Procedure rule 49[235] and are available in situations very similar to those in which a *Mareva* Injunction could be sought. Note that an attachment order is issued as of right once the necessary facts are proved by affidavit and the supporting bond filed. While *Mareva* injunctions are more flexible in their terms and generally do not require the plaintiff to post a bond, they are discretionary orders. There are occasions on which the need for the order is so acute that the incremental cost of obtaining a bond justifies avoidance of judicial discretion and directs the applicant to seek an attachment order. The Supreme Court in *Aetna Financial Services v. Feigelman*[236] held that attachment orders and *Mareva* injunctions are capable of co-existing, and either is available in Canada in appropriate circumstances. It should be noted that there is no provision in the *Federal Court Rules* for attachment orders. This remedy is available, if at all, only in the provincial superior courts.

L. MARITIME ARBITRATION IN CANADA

Canada is no exception to the rule that there is a high propensity for maritime disputes to be resolved by arbitration as opposed to litigation. No Canadian city can claim to be the international shipping arbitral centre that, for example, London, England, or New York, U.S.A., is; but many contracts between domestic parties and some contracts in which the Canadian party has sufficient bargaining strength do provide for Canadian arbitration of disputes. Further, in many instances, parties may agree to submit a dispute to arbitration in Canada or to amend an existing agreement, so as to provide for a Canadian venue for arbitration after the dispute between them has arisen. Canada has adopted the UNCITRAL model *Commercial Arbitration Code* of 21 June 1985. Under

---

235 Nova Scotia, *Civil Procedure Rules*, r.49.
236 Above note 232.

federal legislation,[237] the *Commercial Arbitration Code* applies to arbitration agreements to which the federal government is privy and to "maritime and Admiralty matters." Further, under the *Commercial Arbitration Code*,[238] the arbitration agreement is required to be in writing. Canadian practice generally respects the parties' right to stipulate by agreement the procedures that will be followed in the arbitration. Where the parties fail to so stipulate or fail to agree, the procedures in the *Commercial Arbitration Code* apply by default.

There are two recognized maritime arbitration institutes in Canada — the Association of Maritime Arbitrators of Canada (AMAC) and the Vancouver Maritime Arbitrators' Association. By way of example, AMAC's rules of procedure[239] apply where the arbitration agreement stipulates AMAC arbitration, or where the arbitrator or a majority of multiple arbitrators are AMAC members. In Canada, arbitral awards, whether given in Canadian or foreign proceedings, may be registered and enforced as judgments of the Federal Court of Canada.[240] Registration proceedings are commenced by notice of application.[241] Grounds on which registration of an arbitral award may be refused by the court are limited to those listed in Article 36 of the *Commercial Arbitration Code*.[242] Notice of the registration must be served on the person against whom the award is desired to be enforced, and execution in Canada may not be commenced until proof of such service has been filed with the court.[243]

FURTHER READINGS

BENEDICT, E.C., *Benedict on Admiralty*, 7th ed. (San Francisco: LexisNexis, 2002) vol.I.

---

237 *Commercial Arbitration Act*, R.S.C. 1985, c.17 (2d Supp). Most provinces have also either incorporated the UNCITRAL *Commercial Arbitration Code* by reference in provincial law, or enacted arbitration statutes that substantially follow the language of the *Commercial Arbitration Code*. Certain controls on the situs of arbitration have recently been added in respect of cargo claims: see *Marine Liability Act*, above note 182, s.46; and discussion in F(2) in Chapter 9, "Jurisdiction and Arbitration Clauses."
238 *Ibid.*, Sch., c.II, art.7(2).
239 AMAC Rules of Procedure, online at <www.amac.ca/rules.htm>.
240 *Commercial Arbitration Act*, above note 237, Sch., c.VIII, art.35; *Federal Court Rules*, above note 9, r.324–34.
241 *Federal Court Rules*, above note 9, r.324(1).
242 *Commercial Arbitration Act*, above note 237, Sch., c.VIII, art.36.
243 *Federal Court Rules*, above note 9, r.334.

BERLINGIERI, F., *Berlingieri on the Arrest of Ships*, 3d ed. (London: Lloyd's Press, 2000).

HUGHES, R.T., *2003 Annotated Federal Court Act and Rules* (Markham, ON: LexisNexis Butterworths, 2003).

JACKSON, D., *Enforcement of Maritime Claims*, 3d ed. (London: Lloyd's Press, 2000).

MEESON, N., *Admiralty Jurisdiction and Practice* (London: Lloyd's Press, 2000).

TETLEY, W., *Maritime Liens and Claims*, 2d ed. (Cowansville, QB: Yvon Blais, 1998).

———, *International Maritime & Admiralty Law* (Cowansville, QB: Yvon Blais, 2002).

APPENDIX 1

HAGUE-VISBY RULES

Marine Liability Act, S.C. 2001 c.6, PART 5[1]

LIABILITY FOR CARRIAGE OF GOODS BY WATER

Interpretation
Definitions

41. The definitions in this section apply in this Part.

"Hague-Visby Rules"
« règles de La Haye-Visby »
"Hague-Visby Rules" means the rules set out in Schedule 3 and embodied in the International Convention for the Unification of Certain Rules of Law relating to Bills of Lading, concluded at Brussels on August 25, 1924, in the Protocol concluded at Brussels on February 23, 1968, and in the additional Protocol concluded at Brussels on December 21, 1979.

"Hamburg Rules"
« règles de Hambourg »
"Hamburg Rules" means the rules set out in Schedule 4 and embodied in the United Nations Convention on the Carriage of Goods by Sea, 1978, concluded at Hamburg on March 31, 1978.

Other statutory limitations of liability

42. Nothing in this Part affects the operation of any other Part of this Act, or sections 389, 390, 585 and 586 of the *Canada Shipping Act*, or a provision of any other Act or regulation that limits the liability of owners of ships.

Hague-Visby Rules
Effect

43. (1) The Hague-Visby Rules have the force of law in Canada in respect of contracts for the carriage of goods by water between different states as described in Article X of those Rules.

---

[1] Available online at <http://www.tc.gc.ca/acts-regulations/GENERAL/M/mla/act/mla.html#Hague-Visby%20Rules>.

Extended application

(2) The Hague-Visby Rules also apply in respect of contracts for the carriage of goods by water from one place in Canada to another place in Canada, either directly or by way of a place outside Canada, unless there is no bill of lading and the contract stipulates that those Rules do not apply.

Meaning of "Contracting State"

(3) For the purposes of this section, the expression "Contracting State" in Article X of the Hague-Visby Rules includes Canada and any state that, without being a Contracting State, gives the force of law to the rules embodied in the International Convention for the Unification of Certain Rules of Law relating to Bills of Lading, concluded at Brussels on August 25, 1924 and in the Protocol concluded at Brussels on February 23, 1968, regardless of whether that state gives the force of law to the additional Protocol concluded at Brussels on December 21, 1979.

Replacement by Hamburg Rules

(4) The Hague-Visby Rules do not apply in respect of contracts entered into after the coming into force of section 45.

Hamburg Rules
Report to Parliament

44. The Minister shall, before January 1, 2005 and every five years afterwards, consider whether the Hague-Visby Rules should be replaced by the Hamburg Rules and cause a report setting out the results of that consideration to be laid before each House of Parliament.

Effect

45. (1) The Hamburg Rules have the force of law in Canada in respect of contracts for the carriage of goods by water between different states as described in Article 2 of those Rules.

Extended application

(2) The Hamburg Rules also apply in respect of contracts for the carriage of goods by water from one place in Canada to another place in Canada, either directly or by way of a place outside Canada, unless the contract stipulates that those Rules do not apply.

Meaning of "Contracting State"

(3) For the purposes of this section, the expression "Contracting State" in Article 2 of the Hamburg Rules includes Canada and any state that gives the force of law to those Rules without being a Contracting State to the United Nations Convention on the Carriage of Goods by Sea, 1978.

References to "sea"

(4) For the purposes of this section, the word "sea" in the Hamburg Rules shall be read as "water".

Signatures

(5) For the purposes of this section, paragraph 3 of article 14 of the Hamburg Rules applies in respect of the documents referred to in article 18 of those Rules.

Institution of Proceedings in Canada
Claims not subject to Hamburg Rules

46. (1) If a contract for the carriage of goods by water to which the Hamburg Rules do not apply provides for the adjudication or arbitration of claims arising under the contract in a place other than Canada, a claimant may institute judicial or arbitral proceedings in a court or arbitral tribunal in Canada that would be competent to determine the claim if the contract had referred the claim to Canada, where

(a) the actual port of loading or discharge, or the intended port of loading or discharge under the contract, is in Canada;

(b) the person against whom the claim is made resides or has a place of business, branch or agency in Canada; or

(c) the contract was made in Canada.

Agreement to designate

(2) Notwithstanding subsection (1), the parties to a contract referred to in that subsection may, after a claim arises under the contract, designate by agreement the place where the claimant may institute judicial or arbitral proceedings.

Marine Liability Act, S.C. 2001 c.6, Schedule 3 (s.41)[2]

HAGUE-VISBY RULES

ARTICLE I
Definitions

In these Rules the following expressions have the meanings hereby assigned to them respectively, that is to say,

(a) "carrier" includes the owner or the charterer who enters into a contract of carriage with a shipper;

(b) "contract of carriage" applies only to contracts of carriage covered by a bill of lading or any similar document of title, in so far as such document relates to the carriage of goods by water, including any bill of lading or any similar document as aforesaid issued under or pursuant to a charter-party from the moment at which such bill of lading or similar document of title regulates the relations between a carrier and a holder of the same;

(c) "goods" includes goods, wares, merchandise and articles of every kind whatsoever, except live animals and cargo which by the contract of carriage is stated as being carried on deck and is so carried;

(d) "ship" means any vessel used for the carriage of goods by water;

(e) "carriage of goods" covers the period from the time when the goods are loaded on to the time they are discharged from the ship.

ARTICLE II
Risks

Subject to the provisions of Article VI, under every contract of carriage of goods by water the carrier, in relation to the loading, handling, stowage, carriage, custody, care and discharge of such goods, shall be subject to the responsibilities and liabilities and entitled to the rights and immunities hereinafter set forth.

ARTICLE III
Responsibilities and Liabilities

1. The carrier shall be bound, before and at the beginning of the voyage, to exercise due diligence to
    (a) make the ship seaworthy;
    (b) properly man, equip and supply the ship;

---

2 Available online at: <http://www.tc.gc.ca/acts-regulations/GENERAL/M/mla/act/mla.html#SCHEDULE%203>.

(c) make the holds, refrigerating and cool chambers, and all other parts of the ship in which goods are carried, fit and safe for their reception, carriage and preservation.
2. Subject to the provisions of Article IV, the carrier shall properly and carefully load, handle, stow, carry, keep, care for and discharge the goods carried.
3. After receiving the goods into his charge, the carrier, or the master or agent of the carrier, shall, on demand of the shipper, issue to the shipper a bill of lading showing among other things
   (a) the leading marks necessary for identification of the goods as the same are furnished in writing by the shipper before the loading of such goods starts, provided such marks are stamped or otherwise shown clearly upon the goods if uncovered, or on the cases or coverings in which such goods are contained, in such a manner as should ordinarily remain legible until the end of the voyage;
   (b) either the number of packages or pieces, or the quantity, or weight, as the case may be, as furnished in writing by the shipper;
   (c) the apparent order and condition of the goods:
   Provided that no carrier, master or agent of the carrier shall be bound to state or show in the bill of lading any marks, number, quantity, or weight which he has reasonable ground for suspecting not accurately to represent the goods actually received or which he has had no reasonable means of checking.
4. Such a bill of lading shall be *prima facie* evidence of the receipt by the carrier of the goods as therein described in accordance with paragraphs 3(a), (b) and (c). However, proof to the contrary shall not be admissible when the bill of lading has been transferred to a third party acting in good faith.
5. The shipper shall be deemed to have guaranteed to the carrier the accuracy at the time of shipment of the marks, number, quantity and weight, as furnished by him, and the shipper shall indemnify the carrier against all loss, damages and expenses arising or resulting from inaccuracies in such particulars. The right of the carrier to such indemnity shall in no way limit his responsibility and liability under the contract of carriage to any person other than the shipper.
6. Unless notice of loss or damage and the general nature of such loss or damage be given in writing to the carrier or his agent at the port of discharge before or at the time of the removal of the goods into the custody of the person entitled to delivery thereof under the contract of carriage, or, if the loss or damage be not apparent, within

three days, such removal shall be *prima facie* evidence of the delivery by the carrier of the goods as described in the bill of lading.

The notice in writing need not be given if the state of the goods has at the time of their receipt been the subject of joint survey or inspection.

Subject to paragraph 6 *bis* the carrier and the ship shall in any event be discharged from all liability whatsoever in respect of the goods, unless suit is brought within one year of their delivery or of the date when they should have been delivered. This period may, however, be extended if the parties so agree after the cause of action has arisen.

In the case of any actual or apprehended loss or damage the carrier and the receiver shall give all reasonable facilities to each other for inspecting and tallying the goods.

6. *bis* An action for indemnity against a third person may be brought even after the expiration of the year provided for in the preceding paragraph if brought within the time allowed by the law of the Court seized of the case. However, the time allowed shall be not less than three months, commencing from the day when the person bringing such action for indemnity has settled the claim or has been served with process in the action against himself.
7. After the goods are loaded the bill of lading to be issued by the carrier, master or agent of the carrier, to the shipper shall, if the shipper so demands, be a "shipped" bill of lading, provided that if the shipper shall have previously taken up any document of title to such goods, he shall surrender the same as against the issue of the "shipped" bill of lading, but at the option of the carrier such document of title may be noted at the port of shipment by the carrier, master, or agent with the name or names of the ship or ships upon which the goods have been shipped and the date or dates of shipment, and when so noted the same shall for the purpose of this Article be deemed to constitute a "shipped" bill of lading.
8. Any clause, covenant or agreement in a contract of carriage relieving the carrier or the ship from liability for loss or damage to or in connection with goods arising from negligence, fault or failure in the duties and obligations provided in this Article or lessening such liability otherwise than as provided in these Rules, shall be null and void and of no effect.

A benefit of insurance or similar clause shall be deemed to be a clause relieving the carrier from liability.

ARTICLE IV
Rights and Immunities

1. Neither the carrier nor the ship shall be liable for loss or damage arising or resulting from unseaworthiness unless caused by want of due diligence on the part of the carrier to make the ship seaworthy, and to secure that the ship is properly manned, equipped and supplied, and to make the holds, refrigerating and cool chambers and all other parts of the ship in which goods are carried fit and safe for their reception, carriage and preservation in accordance with the provisions of paragraph 1 of Article III.
Whenever loss or damage has resulted from unseaworthiness, the burden of proving the exercise of due diligence shall be on the carrier or other person claiming exemption under this article.
2. Neither the carrier nor the ship shall be responsible for loss or damage arising or resulting from
    (a) act, neglect, or default of the master, mariner, pilot or the servants of the carrier in the navigation or in the management of the ship;
    (b) fire, unless caused by the actual fault or privity of the carrier;
    (c) perils, dangers and accidents of the sea or other navigable waters;
    (d) act of God;
    (e) act of war;
    (f) act of public enemies;
    (g) arrest or restraint of princes, rulers or people, or seizure under legal process;
    (h) quarantine restrictions;
    (i) act or omission of the shipper or owner of the goods, his agent or representative;
    (j) strikes or lock-outs or stoppage or restraint of labour from whatever cause, whether partial or general;
    (k) riots and civil commotions;
    (l) saving or attempting to save life or property at sea;
    (m) wastage in bulk or weight or any other loss or damage arising from inherent defect, quality or vice of the goods;
    (n) insufficiency of packing;
    (o) insufficiency or inadequacy of marks;
    (p) latent defects not discoverable by due diligence;
    (q) any other cause arising without the actual fault and privity of the carrier, or without the fault or neglect of the agents or servants of the carrier, but the burden of proof shall be on the per-

son claiming the benefit of this exception to show that neither the actual fault or privity of the carrier nor the fault or neglect of the agents or servants of the carrier contributed to the loss or damage.

3. The shipper shall not be responsible for loss or damage sustained by the carrier or the ship arising or resulting from any cause without the act, fault or neglect of the shipper, his agents or his servants.

4. Any deviation in saving or attempting to save life or property at sea or any reasonable deviation shall not be deemed to be an infringement or breach of these Rules or of the contract of carriage, and the carrier shall not be liable for any loss or damage resulting therefrom.

5. (*a*) Unless the nature and value of such goods have been declared by the shipper before shipment and inserted in the bill of lading, neither the carrier nor the ship shall in any event be or become liable for any loss or damage to or in connection with the goods in an amount exceeding 666.67 units of account per package or unit or 2 units of account per kilogramme of gross weight of the goods lost or damaged, whichever is the higher.

(*b*) The total amount recoverable shall be calculated by reference to the value of such goods at the place and time at which the goods are discharged from the ship in accordance with the contract or should have been so discharged.

The value of the goods shall be fixed according to the commodity exchange price, or, if there be no such price, according to the current market price, or, if there be no commodity exchange price or current market price, by reference to the normal value of goods of the same kind and quality.

(*c*) Where a container, pallet or similar article of transport is used to consolidate goods, the number of packages or units enumerated in the bill of lading as packed in such article of transport shall be deemed the number of packages or units for the purpose of this paragraph as far as these packages or units are concerned. Except as aforesaid such article of transport shall be considered the package or unit.

(*d*) The unit of account mentioned in this Article is the Special Drawing Right as defined by the International Monetary Fund. The amounts mentioned in subparagraph (a) of this paragraph shall be converted into national currency on the basis of the value of that currency on the date to be determined by the law of the Court seized of the case. The value of the national currency, in terms of the Special Drawing Right, of a State which is a member of the International Monetary Fund, shall be calculated in accordance with the method of valuation applied by the International Monetary Fund in effect at the date in question for its operations and transactions. The value of the national currency, in terms of the Special Drawing Right, of a State which is not a member of the International Monetary Fund, shall be calculated in a manner determined by that State.

Nevertheless, a State which is not a member of the International Monetary Fund and whose law does not permit the application of the provisions of the preceding sentences may, at the time of ratification of the Protocol of 1979 or accession thereto or at any time thereafter, declare that the limits of liability provided for in this Convention to be applied in its territory shall be fixed as follows:

(i) in respect of the amount of 666.67 units of account mentioned in subparagraph (a) of paragraph 5 of this Article, 10,000 monetary units;

(ii) in respect of the amount of 2 units of account mentioned in subparagraph (a) of paragraph 5 of this Article, 30 monetary units.

The monetary unit referred to in the preceding sentence corresponds to 65.5 milligrammes of gold of millesimal fineness 900. The conversion of the amounts specified in that sentence into the national currency shall be made according to the law of the State concerned. The calculation and the conversion mentioned in the preceding sentences shall be made in such a manner as to express in the national currency of that State as far as possible the same real value for the amounts in subparagraph (a) of paragraph 5 of this Article as is expressed there in units of account.

States shall communicate to the depositary the manner of calculation or the result of the conversion as the case may be, when depositing an instrument of ratification of the Protocol of 1979 or of accession thereto and whenever there is a change in either.

(e) Neither the carrier nor the ship shall be entitled to the benefit of the limitation of liability provided for in this paragraph if it is proved that the damage resulted from an act or omission of the carrier done with intent to cause damage, or recklessly and with knowledge that damage would probably result.

(f) The declaration mentioned in subparagraph (a) of this paragraph, if embodied in the bill of lading, shall be *prima facie* evidence, but shall not be binding or conclusive on the carrier.

(g) By agreement between the carrier, master or agent of the carrier and the shipper other maximum amounts than those mentioned in subparagraph (a) of this paragraph may be fixed, provided that no maximum amount so fixed shall be less than the appropriate maximum mentioned in that subparagraph.

(h) Neither the carrier nor the ship shall be responsible in any event for loss or damage to, or in connection with, goods if the nature or value thereof has been knowingly mis-stated by the shipper in the bill of lading.

6. Goods of an inflammable, explosive or dangerous nature to the shipment whereof the carrier, master or agent of the carrier has not consented, with knowledge of their nature and character, may at any time before discharge be landed at any place or destroyed or rendered innocuous by the carrier without compensation, and the shipper of such goods shall be liable for all damages and expenses directly or indirectly arising out of or resulting from such shipment.

If any such goods shipped with such knowledge and consent shall become a danger to the ship or cargo, they may in like manner be landed at any place or destroyed or rendered innocuous by the carrier without liability on the part of the carrier except to general average, if any.

ARTICLE IV BIS
Application of Defences and Limits of Liability

1. The defences and limits of liability provided for in these Rules shall apply in any action against the carrier in respect of loss or damage to goods covered by a contract of carriage whether the action be founded in contract or in tort.
2. If such an action is brought against a servant or agent of the carrier (such servant or agent not being an independent contractor), such servant or agent shall be entitled to avail himself of the defences and limits of liability which the carrier is entitled to invoke under these Rules.
3. The aggregate of the amounts recoverable from the carrier, and such servants and agents, shall in no case exceed the limit provided for in these Rules.
4. Nevertheless, a servant or agent of the carrier shall not be entitled to avail himself of the provisions of this Article, if it is proved that the damage resulted from an act or omission of the servant or agent done with intent to cause damage or recklessly and with knowledge that damage would probably result.

ARTICLE V
Surrender of Rights and Immunities, and Increase of Responsibilities and Liabilities

A carrier shall be at liberty to surrender in whole or in part all or any of his rights and immunities or to increase any of his responsibilities and liabilities under the Rules contained in any of these Articles, provided such surrender or increase shall be embodied in the bill of lading issued to the shipper.

The provisions of these Rules shall not be applicable to charter-parties, but if bills of lading are issued in the case of a ship under a charter-party they shall comply with the terms of these Rules. Nothing in these Rules shall be held to prevent the insertion in a bill of lading of any lawful provision regarding general average.

ARTICLE VI
Special Conditions

Notwithstanding the provisions of the preceding Articles, a carrier, master or agent of the carrier and a shipper shall in regard to any particular goods be at liberty to enter into any agreement in any terms as to the responsibility and liability of the carrier for such goods, and as to the rights and immunities of the carrier in respect of such goods, or his obligation as to seaworthiness, so far as this stipulation is not contrary to public policy, or the care or diligence of his servants or agents in regard to the loading, handling, stowage, carriage, custody, care and discharge of the goods carried by water, provided that in this case no bill of lading has been or shall be issued and that the terms agreed shall be embodied in a receipt which shall be a non-negotiable document and shall be marked as such.

Any agreement so entered into shall have full legal effect.

Provided that this Article shall not apply to ordinary commercial shipments made in the ordinary course of trade, but only to other shipments where the character or condition of the property to be carried or the circumstances, terms and conditions under which the carriage is to be performed are such as reasonably to justify a special agreement.

ARTICLE VII
Limitations on the Application of the Rules

Nothing herein contained shall prevent a carrier or a shipper from entering into any agreement, stipulation, condition, reservation or exemption as to the responsibility and liability of the carrier or the ship for the loss or damage to, or in connection with the custody and care and handling of goods prior to the loading on and subsequent to the discharge from the ship on which the goods are carried by water.

ARTICLE VIII
Limitation of Liability

The provisions of these Rules shall not affect the rights and obligations of the carrier under any statute for the time being in force relating to the limitation of the liability of owners of vessels.

ARTICLE IX
Liability for Nuclear Damage

These Rules shall not affect the provisions of any international Convention or national law governing liability for nuclear damage.

ARTICLE X
Application

The provisions of these Rules shall apply to every bill of lading relating to the carriage of goods between ports in two different States if:
    (*a*) the bill of lading is issued in a Contracting State, or
    (*b*) the carriage is from a port in a Contracting State, or
    (*c*) the contract contained in or evidenced by the bill of lading provides that these Rules or legislation of any State giving effect to them are to govern the contract, whatever may be the nationality of the ship, the carrier, the shipper, the consignee, or any other interested person.

APPENDIX 2

LLOYD'S STANDARD FORM OF SALVAGE AGREEMENT

LOF 2000

LLOYD'S

LLOYD'S STANDARD FORM OF
SALVAGE AGREEMENT

(APPROVED AND PUBLISHED BY THE COUNCIL OF LLOYD'S)

NO CURE - NO PAY

1. Name of the salvage Contractors: (referred to in this agreement as "the Contractors")	2. Property to be salved. The vessel: her cargo freight bunkers stores and any other property thereon but excluding the personal effects or baggage of passengers master or crew (referred to in this agreement as "the property")
3. Agreed place of safety:	4. Agreed currency of any arbitral award and security (if other than United States dollars)
5. Date of this agreement:	6. Place of agreement:
7. Is the Scopic Clause incorporated into this agreement? State alternative : Yes/No	
8. Person signing for and on behalf of the Contractors Signature:	9. Captain or other person signing for and on behalf of the property Signature:

A. **Contractors' basic obligation:** The Contractors identified in Box 1 hereby agree to use their best endeavours to salve the property specified in Box 2 and to take the property to the place stated in Box 3 or to such other place as may hereafter be agreed. If no place is inserted in Box 3 and in the absence of any subsequent agreement as to the place where the property is to be taken the Contractors shall take the property to a place of safety.

B. **Environmental protection:** While performing the salvage services the Contractors shall also use their best endeavours to prevent or minimise damage to the environment.

C. **Scopic Clause:** Unless the word "No" in Box 7 has been deleted this agreement shall be deemed to have been made on the basis that the Scopic Clause is not incorporated and forms no part of this agreement. If the word "No" is deleted in Box 7 this shall not of itself be construed as a notice invoking the Scopic Clause within the meaning of sub-clause 2 thereof.

D. **Effect of other remedies:** Subject to the provisions of the International Convention on Salvage 1989 as incorporated into English law ("the Convention") relating to special compensation and to the Scopic Clause if incorporated the Contractors' services shall be rendered and accepted as salvage services upon the principle of "no cure - no pay" and any salvage remuneration to which the Contractors become entitled shall not be diminished by reason of the exception to the principle of "no cure - no pay" in the form of special compensation or remuneration payable to the Contractors under a Scopic Clause.

E. **Prior services:** Any salvage services rendered by the Contractors to the property before and up to the date of this agreement shall be deemed to be covered by this agreement.

F. **Duties of property owners:** Each of the owners of the property shall cooperate fully with the Contractors. In particular:

   (i) the Contractors may make reasonable use of the vessel's machinery gear and equipment free of expense provided that the Contractors shall not unnecessarily damage abandon or sacrifice any property on board;

   (ii) the Contractors shall be entitled to all such information as they may reasonably require relating to the vessel or the remainder of the property provided such information is relevant to the performance of the services and is capable of being provided without undue difficulty or delay;

   (iii) the owners of the property shall co-operate fully with the Contractors in obtaining entry to the place of safety stated in Box 3 or agreed or determined in accordance with Clause A.

G. **Rights of termination:** When there is no longer any reasonable prospect of a useful result leading to a salvage reward in accordance with Convention Articles 12 and/or 13 either the owners of the vessel or the Contractors shall be entitled to terminate the services hereunder by giving reasonable prior written notice to the other.

H. **Deemed performance:** The Contractors' services shall be deemed to have been performed when the property is in a safe condition in the place of safety stated in Box 3 or agreed or determined in accordance with Clause A. For the purpose of this provision the property shall be regarded as being in safe condition notwithstanding that the property (or part thereof) is damaged or in need of maintenance if (i) the Contractors are not obliged to remain in attendance to satisfy the requirements of any port or harbour authority, governmental agency or similar authority and (ii) the continuation of skilled salvage services from the Contractors or other salvors is no longer necessary to avoid the property becoming lost or significantly further damaged or delayed.

I. **Arbitration and the LSSA Clauses:** The Contractors' remuneration and/or special compensation shall be determined by arbitration in London in the manner prescribed by Lloyd's Standard Salvage and Arbitration Clauses ("the LSSA Clauses") and Lloyd's Procedural Rules. The provisions of the LSSA Clauses and Lloyd's Procedural Rules are deemed to be incorporated in this agreement and form an integral part hereof. Any other difference arising out of this agreement or the operations hereunder shall be referred to arbitration in the same way.

J. **Governing law:** This agreement and any arbitration hereunder shall be governed by English law.

K. **Scope of authority:** The Master or other person signing this agreement on behalf of the property identified in Box 2 enters into this agreement as agent for the respective owners thereof and binds each (but not the one for the other or himself personally) to the due performance thereof.

L. **Inducements prohibited:** No person signing this agreement or any party on whose behalf it is signed shall at any time or in any manner whatsoever offer provide make give or promise to provide or demand or take any form of inducement for entering into this agreement.

IMPORTANT NOTICES :

1. **Salvage security.** As soon as possible the owners of the vessel should notify the owners of other property on board that this agreement has been made. If the Contractors are successful the owners of such property should note that it will become necessary to provide the Contractors with salvage security promptly in accordance with Clause 4 of the LSSA Clauses referred to in Clause I. The provision of General Average security does not relieve the salved interests of their separate obligation to provide salvage security to the Contractors.

2. **Incorporated provisions.** Copies of the Scopic Clause; the LSSA Clauses and Lloyd's Procedural Rules may be obtained from (i) the Contractors or (ii) the Salvage Arbitration Branch at Lloyd's, One Lime Street, London EC3M 7HA.

Tel.No. + 44(0)20 7327 5408

Fax No. +44(0)20 7327 6827

E-mail: lloyds-salvage@lloyds.com.

www.lloyds.com

LLOYD'S

APPENDIX 3

FEDERAL COURT ADMIRALTY PROCEDURE FORMS

FORM 171A (Federal Court Rule 171)[3]

STATEMENT OF CLAIM
(General Heading — Use Form 66)
(Court seal)

STATEMENT OF CLAIM TO THE DEFENDANT

A LEGAL PROCEEDING HAS BEEN COMMENCED AGAINST YOU by the Plaintiff. The claim made against you is set out in the following pages.

IF YOU WISH TO DEFEND THIS PROCEEDING, you or a solicitor acting for you are required to prepare a statement of defence in Form 171B prescribed by the Federal Court Rules, 1998, serve it on the plaintiff's solicitor or, where the plaintiff does not have a solicitor, serve it on the plaintiff, and file it, with proof of service, at a local office of this Court, WITHIN 30 DAYS after this statement of claim is served on you, if you are served within Canada.

If you are served in the United States of America, the period for serving and filing your statement of defence is forty days. If you are served outside Canada and the United States of America, the period for serving and filing your statement of defence is sixty days.

Copies of the *Federal Court Rules*, 1998, information concerning the local offices of the Court and other necessary information may be obtained on request to the Administrator of this Court at Ottawa (telephone 613-992-4238) or at any local office.

IF YOU FAIL TO DEFEND THIS PROCEEDING, judgment may be given against you in your absence and without further notice to you.

(Date)_____
Issued by: _____
(Registry Officer)
Address of local office: _____
TO: (Name and address of each defendant)
(Separate page)

---

3 Available online at: <http://www.fct-cf.gc.ca/business/act/ forms/forms_e.shtml>.

CLAIM

1. The plaintiff claims: (State here the precise relief claimed.)
(In consecutively numbered paragraphs, set out each allegation of material fact relied on to substantiate the claim.)

The plaintiff proposes that this action be tried at (place).
(Date)

_____
(Signature of solicitor or plaintiff)
(Name, address, telephone and fax number of solicitor or plaintiff)

FORM 477 (Rule 477)

STYLE OF CAUSE — ACTION *IN REM*

(Court File No.)

FEDERAL COURT — TRIAL DIVISION

ADMIRALTY ACTION *IN REM*

BETWEEN:
(Name)
Plaintiff
– and –
The owners and all others interested in
The Ship (name)
(or)
The owners and all others interested in
The Ship (name) and freight
(or)
The owners and all others interested in
The Ship (name) and her cargo and freight
(or if the action is against cargo only)
The cargo ex The Ship (name)
(or if the action is against the proceeds realized by the sale of the ship or cargo)
The proceeds of the sale of The Ship (name)
(or)
The proceeds of the sale of the cargo of The Ship (name),
(or as the case may be)
Defendants

FORM 486A (Rule 486)

BAIL BOND

(General Heading — Use Form 477)

BAIL BOND

I, (full name and occupation of deponent), of the (City, Town, etc.) of (name) in the (County, Regional Municipality, etc.) of (name), SWEAR (or AFFIRM) THAT:

1. I submit myself to the jurisdiction of this Court and consent that if (insert name of party for whom bail is to be given, and state whether plaintiff or defendant, or as the case may be) do(es) not pay what may be adjudged against them (or as the case may be) in this action, with costs, or do(es) not pay any sum due to be paid under any agreement by which the action is settled before judgment and which is filed in this Court, execution may issue against me, my executors or administrators, or my personal property or movables, for the amount unpaid or an amount of $(amount), whichever is the lesser.

(Add where bond given by an individual:)

2. I have a net worth of more than the sum of $(state amount in which bail is to be given) after payment of all my debts, as shown by the financial statement attached as Appendix A hereto.

Sworn (or Affirmed) before me at the (City, Town, etc) of (name) in the (County, Regional Municipality, etc.) of (name) on (date).

_____
Commissioner for Taking Affidavits
(or as the case may be)

_____
(Signature of Surety)

FORM 493A (Rule 493)

CAVEAT WARRANT

(General Heading — Use Form 477)

CAVEAT WARRANT

TAKE NOTICE THAT I, (full name and address) apply for a caveat against the issue of any warrant for the arrest of the ship (name) (or description of other property) without notice first being given to me.

AND I UNDERTAKE, within three days after being required to do so, to give bail in this or any other action or counterclaim against that ship (or other property) in this Court in the sum of $(amount), or to pay that sum into Court.

MY ADDRESS FOR SERVICE AND TELEPHONE NUMBER are: (address and telephone number)

(Date)

_____

(Signature)

FORM 493B (Rule 493)

CAVEAT RELEASE

(General Heading — Use Form 477)

CAVEAT RELEASE

TAKE NOTICE THAT I , (full name and address), apply for a caveat against the release of the ship (name) (or description of other property), now under arrest pursuant to a warrant issued (date) without notice first being given to me.

(If person applying for caveat is not a party to the action, add:)
MY ADDRESS FOR SERVICE IS: (address)

(Date)

_____

(Signature)

FORM 493C (Rule 493)

CAVEAT PAYMENT

(General Heading — Use Form 477)

CAVEAT PAYMENT

TAKE NOTICE THAT I, (full name and address), apply for a caveat against the payment of any money out of the proceeds of the sale of the ship (name) (or description of other property), now remaining in Court, without notice first being given to me.

(If person applying for caveat is not a party to the action, add:)
    MY ADDRESS FOR SERVICE is: (address)

(Date)

_____

(Signature)

ACRONYMS AND ABBREVIATIONS

AB	Able Bodied Seaman
ABS	American Bureau of Shipping
AMAC	Association of Maritime Arbitrators of Canada
ASEAN	Association of South East Asian Nations
ASMV	Arrived Sound Market Value
BIMCO	Baltic and International Maritime Council
BLG	Bulk Liquids and Gases
BUNKER	International Convention on Civil Liability for Bunker Oil Pollution Damage
BV	Bureau Veritas (France)
CAPP	Canadian Association of Petroleum Producers
CBMU	Canadian Board of Marine Underwriters
CLC	Convention on Civil Liability for Oil Pollution Damage
CLEE	Convention on Civil Liability for Oil Pollution Damage Resulting from Exploration for and Exploitation of Seabed Mineral Resources
CMI	Comité Maritime International (International Maritime Committee)
CMLA	Canadian Maritime Law Association
CNOPB	Canada–Newfoundland Offshore Petroleum Board
CNSOPB	Canada–Nova Scotia Offshore Petroleum Board
COFRs	Certificates of Financial Responsibility
COLREGS	Convention on the International Regulations for Preventing Collisions at Sea
COMSAR	Radio Communications and Search and Rescue
COS–SAR	International COSPASS–SARSAT Programme Agreement, 1988
CRS	Croatian Register of Shipping
CTA	Canadian Transportation Agency
CTL	Constructive Total Loss
DE	Ship Design and Equipment
DGPS	Differential Global Positioning System
DNV	Det Norske Veritas (Norway)
DR	Dead Reckoning
DSC	Dangerous Goods, Solid Cargoes and Containers
DWT	Deadweight Tonnage

EC	Environment Canada
ECDIS	Electronic Chart Display Information Systems
ECLAC	Economic Commission for Latin America and the Caribbean
ECOWAS	Economic Commission of West African States
ECTOW	Eastern Canada Towing Conditions
EDH	Efficient Deckhand
ERCB	Energy Resources Conservation Board
ESCAP	Economic and Social Commission for Asia and the Pacific
EU	European Union
FAL	*Convention on Facilitation of International Maritime Traffic*
FAO	Food and Agriculture Organisation of the United Nations
FC	Facilitation Committee
FC&S	Free of Capture and Seizure
FD&D	Freight, Demurrage and Defence
FFO	Fixed and Floating Objects
FIATA	International Federation of Freight Forwarders Association
fio	Free In and Out
fios	Free In and Out Stowed
fiost	Free In and Out Stowed and Trimmed
FOB	Free On Board
FOC	Flag of Convenience
FP	Fire Protection
FPSO	Floating Production Storage and Offloading System
FSI	Flag State Implementation
FSU	Floating Storage Units
FUND	*International Convention on the Establishment of an International Fund for Compensation for Oil Pollution Damage*
GA	General Average
GBS	Gravity Based Structure
GL	Germanischer Lloyd (Germany)
GMDSS	Global Maritime Distress and Safety System
GPS	Global Positioning System
GRT	Gross Registered Tonnage
GT	Gross Tonnage
Hague Rules	*International Convention for the Unification of Certain Rules of Law Relating to Bills of Lading, 1924*
Hague-Visby Rules	Hague Rules as amended by the *Visby Protocol 1968* (see Visby Rules below)
IACS	International Association of Classification Societies
IALA	International Association of Lighthouse Authorities
IAPH	International Association of Ports and Harbours
IBA	International Bar Association

ICAO	International Civil Aviation Organization
ICC	International Chamber of Commerce
ICS	International Chamber of Shipping
IFSMA	International Federation of Shipmasters Association
IGA	International Group Agreement
IGO	Inter-Governmental Organization
IHC	International Hull Clauses, 2002
IHO	International Hydrographic Organization
ILO	International Labour Organisation
IMB	International Maritime Bureau
IMDG Code	*International Maritime Dangerous Goods Code*
IMLI	International Maritime Law Institute
IMO	International Maritime Organisation
IMO Convention	*Convention on the Inter-Governmental Maritime Consultative Organization*
IMOSAR	IMO Search and Rescue Manual
IMPA	International Marine Pilots Association
INMARSAT	International Maritime Satellite Organization
INTERTANKO	International Association of Independent Tanker Owners
IOC	Intergovernmental Oceanographic Commission
IOPCF	International Oil Pollution Compensation Fund
IRS	Indian Register of Shipping
ISF	International Shipping Federation
ISM Code	*International Safety Management Code*
ISO	International Organization for Standardization
ISU	International Salvage Union
ITC-Hulls	Institute Time Clauses, Hulls
ITF	International Transport Workers Federation
ITLOS	International Tribunal for the Law of the Sea
ITOPF	International Tanker Owners Pollution Federation
ITU	International Telecommunications Union
IUMI	International Union of Marine Insurers
JMC	Joint Maritime Commission
LC	Legal Committee
LL	*International Convention on Load Lines, 1966*
LLMC	*Convention on Limitation of Liability for Maritime Claims*
LNG	Liquefied Natural Gas
LPG	Liquefied Petroleum Gas
LR	Lloyd's Register of Shipping
LT	Limitation Tonnage
MARPOL	*International Convention for the Prevention of Pollution from Ships, 73/78*

MEPC	Marine Environment Protection Committee
MERSAR	Merchant Ship Search and Rescue Manual
MGA	Managing General Agencies
MODU	Mobile Offshore Drilling Unit
MOU	*Memorandum of Understanding*
MPFC	Marine Pollution Claims Fund
MSC	Maritime Safety Committee
MTO	Multimodal Transport Operator
NAFO	Northwest Atlantic Fisheries Organization
NAV	Safety of Navigation
NEB	National Energy Board
NGO	Non-Governmental Organization
NKK	Nippon Kaiji Kyokai (Japan)
NRT	Net Registered Tonnage
NSUARB	Nova Scotia Utility and Review Board
NT	Net Tonnage
NVOMTO	Non-Vessel/Vehicle Multimodal Transport Operator
NYPE	New York Produce Exchange Time Charter
OAS	Organization of American States
OBO	Ore/Bulk/Oil
OILPOL	*International Convention for the Prevention of Pollution of the Sea by Oil*
OOW	Officer of the Watch
OPRC	*International Convention on Oil Pollution Preparedness, Response and Co-operation*
OS	Ordinary Seamen
P&I	Protection and Indemnity
PAL	*Athens Convention Relating to the Carriage of Passengers and their Luggage by Sea*
pmsi	purchase money security interest
PPSA	Personal Property Security Acts
PRS	Polish Register of Shipping
RADAR	Radio Detection and Ranging
RCMP	Royal Canadian Mounted Police
RDF	Radio Direction Finding
RINA	Registro Italiano Navale (Italy)
Ro-Ro	Roll-on–Roll-off
SAR	*International Convention on Maritime Search and Rescue*
SDR	Special Drawing Right
SFV	*Torremolinos International Convention for the Safety of Fishing Vessels*
SLF	Stability and Load Lines and Fishing Vessel Safety

Acronyms and Abbreviations 831

SMS	Safety Management System
SOLAS	*International Convention on the Safety of Life at Sea*
SOPF	Ship-Source Oil Pollution Fund
STCW	*International Convention on Standards of Training, Certification and Watchkeeping for Seafarers*
STW	Standards of Training and Watchkeeping
SUA	*Convention for the Suppression of Unlawful Acts against the Safety of Maritime Navigation*
TCC	Technical Cooperation Committee
TD	Time Difference
TOC	Technical Co-operation Committee
TOVALOP	Tanker Owners' Voluntary Agreement Concerning Liability for Oil Pollution
TOWCON	International Ocean Towage Agreement
TSB	Transportation Safety Board of Canada
UNCITRAL	United Nations Commission on International Trade Law
UNCLOS	*United Nations Convention on the Law of the Sea*
UNCTAD	United Nations Conference on Trade and Development
UNEP	United Nations Environment Programme
UNFA	*United Nations Fish Stocks Agreement*
UPU	Universal Postal Union
VHF	Very High Frequency
Visby Rules	*Protocol to Amend the International Convention for the Unification of Certain Rules of Law Relating to Bills of Lading, 1968*
VLCC	Very Large Crude Carriers
VMAA	Vancouver Maritime Arbitrators' Association
WHO	World Health Organization
WMO	World Meteorological Organization
WMU	World Maritime University

LEGISLATION

Canada

Admiralty Act, 1891, S.C. 1891, c.29 .... 108, 111, 117, 123, 124
Admiralty Act, 1934, S.C. 1934, c.31 .... 4, 24, 110, 112, 117, 121,
.... 123, 124, 128, 750
An Act Respecting Compensation to the Families of Persons Killed by
    Accident, and in Duels, C.S.C. 1859, c.78 136
Arctic Waters Pollution Prevention Act, R.S.C. 1985, c.A-12 ...... 101, 670, 671,
.... 679, 681
Atomic Energy Control Act, R.S.C. 1985, c.A-16 210
Bank Act, S.C. 1991, c.46 .... 160, 245, 252, 253, 254, 255, 256,
.... 260, 261, 262, 265
Bankruptcy and Insolvency Act, R.S.C. 1985, c.B-3 257
Bills of Lading Act, R.S.C. 1985, c.B-5 .... 420, 421, 422, 425, 426, 432
Canada Evidence Act, R.S.C. 1985, c.C-5 419
Canada Marine Act, S.C. 1998, c.10 .... 4, 67, 175, 294, 563, 671, 679, 682,
.... 728, 729, 781, 798
Canada National Marine Conservation Areas Act, S.C. 2002, c.18 682
Canada Oil and Gas Operations Act, R.S.C. 1985, c.O-7 .... 70, 671, 714
Canada Oil and Gas Operations Act, S.C. 1992, c.35 ....
Canada Shipping Act, 1934, S.C. 1934, c.44 .... 4, 24, 110, 112, 719
Canada Shipping Act, R.S.C. 1985, c.S-9 .... 14, 30, 33, 34, 60, 64, 65, 66,
        67, 68, 69, 74, 122, 142, 143, 144, 157, 161, 162, 169, 170, 171, 172,
        174, 175, 177, 179, 180, 182, 183, 184, 191, 198, 201, 202, 204, 206,
        210, 220, 223, 225, 230, 244, 245, 246, 247, 248, 249, 250, 251, 254,
        255, 257, 259, 260, 261, 284, 285, 286, 293, 372, 373, 378, 442, 469,
        481, 488, 497, 508, 522, 525, 537, 540, 545, 546, 548, 551, 552, 553,
        555, 557, 562, 585, 599, 600, 605, 619, 620, 621, 636, 670, 671, 673,
        674, 676, 677, 679, 680, 681, 682, 686, 696, 714, 721, 722, 733, 735,
        740, 781, 782, 783, 799
Canada Shipping Act, R.S.C. 1985 (3d Supp.), c.6 669
Canada Shipping Act, S.C. 1998, c.6 .... 132, 134, 677, 722

Legislation   833

Canada Shipping Act, 2001, S.C. 2001, c.26 ....4, 14, 15, 30, 33, 34, 41, 60,
    64, 65, 66, 67, 68, 69, 74, 115, 116, 117, 120, 134, 142, 143, 144, 145,
    154, 155, 156, 159, 161, 162, 169, 170, 171, 177, 179, 182, 183, 184,
    198, 201, 202, 204, 206, 207, 210, 220, 223, 224, 225, 228, 230, 235,
    237, 244, 245, 246, 247, 248, 249, 250, 231, 253, 259, 284, 285, 286,
    293, 378, 442, 458, 469, 481, 483, 488, 493, 497, 508, 524, 525, 527,
    538, 540, 546, 551, 585, 599, 600, 605, 607, 619, 620, 621, 636, 659,
    671, 673, 676, 677, 679, 680, 681, 683, 686, 702, 707, 708, 714, 782,
    783
Canada Transportation Act, S.C. 1996, c.10 4
Canada Transportation Accident Investigation and Safety Board Act, S.C.
    1989, c.3 541
Canada Water Act, R.S.C. 1985, c.C-11 ....671, 684, 685
Canada Wildlife Act, R.S.C. 1985, c.W-9 ....671, 684, 685
Canada–Newfoundland Atlantic Accord Implementation Act, S.C. 1987,
    c.3 ....103, 712, 725
Canada–Newfoundland Atlantic Accord Implementation Act, R.S.N.
    1990, c.C-2 ....69, 712
*Canada–Nova Scotia Offshore Petroleum Resources Accord Implementation
    Act*, S.C. 1988, c.28 ....69, 103, 213, 712, 725
*Canada-Nova Scotia Offshore Petroleum Resources Accord Implementation
    (Nova Scotia) Act*, S.N.S. 1987, c.3 214
Canadian Environmental Assessment Act, S.C. 1992, c.37 714
Canadian Environmental Protection Act, 1999, S.C. 1999, c.33 ......4, 373, 671,
    ....674, 680, 684
Canadian Transportation Accident Investigation and Safety Board Act, S.C.
    1989, c.3 ....65, 781
Carriage of Goods by Water Act, R.S.C. 1970, c.15 122
Carriage of Goods by Water Act, R.S.C. 1985, c.C-27 433
Carriage of Goods by Water Act, S.C. 1993, c.21 ....4, 434, 546
Civil Code of Quebec, S.Q. 1991, c.64 ....124, 253, 305, 422
Coastal Fisheries Protection Act, R.S.C. 1985, c.C-33 ....671, 682, 683,
    ....775, 784, 785
Coasting Trade Act, S.C. 1992, c.31 ....24, 179
Commercial Arbitration Act, R.S.C. 1985, c.17 (2d Supp) 473, 805
Constitution Act, 1867 (U.K.), 30 & 31 Vict., c.3, repr. R.S.C. 1985, App. II,
    No. 5 ....24, 99, 100, 101, 102, 103, 104, 108, 110, 111, 117, 118,
    ....121, 125, 127, 129, 131, 132, 134, 137, 151, 254, 758, 759
Contributory Negligence Act, R.S.B.C. 1960, c.74..136
Corporation Securities Registration Act, R.S.O. 1970, c.88 174
Criminal Code, R.S.C. 1985, c.C-46 ..151, 235, 492, 495, 521, 542, 556, 684
Crown Liability Act, R.S.C. 1985, c.C-50 527

834 MARITIME LAW

Customs Act, R.S.C. 1985 c.1 (2d Supp.) 785
Explosives Act, R.S.C. 1985, c.E-17 210
Family Compensation Act, R.S.B.C. 1979, c.120..545
Family Law Act, R.S.O. 1990, c.F-3 136
Federal Court Act, S.C. 1971, c.1 ....110, 112, 118, 119, 121, 123, 124,
  ....125, 127, 129, 130, 132, 536, 750
Federal Court Act, R.S.C. 1985, c.F-7................114, 117, 118, 119, 121, 122,
  143, 144, 145, 149, 152, 163, 173, 251, 273, 278, 279, 280, 284, 285,
  286, 287, 291, 292, 293, 294, 472, 751, 752, 753, 754, 755, 756, 757,
  760, 761, 762, 763, 764, 765, 766, 771, 774, 775, 776, 777, 789
Fisheries Act, R.S.C. 1985, c.F-14 ....101, 671, 682, 683, 784
Fisheries Improvement Loans Act, R.S.C. 1985, c.F-22 245
Harbour Commissions Act, R.S.C. 1985, c.H-1 294
Hazardous Products Act, R.S.C. 1985, c.H-3...210
Immigration Act, R.S.C. 1985 c.I-2..785, 786
Insurance Act, R.S.A. 1980, c.I-5 306
Insurance Act, R.S.N. 1990, c.I-12 306
Insurance Act, R.S.N.S. 1989, c.231 ....125, 306, 354–57
Insurance Act, R.S.N.W.T. 1988, c.I-4 306
Insurance Act, R.S.P.E.I. 1988, c.I-4 306
Insurance Act, R.S.Y. 1986, c.91 306
Insurance (Marine) Act, R.S.B.C. 1996, c.230 ....125, 307, 354–57
Interest Act, R.S.C. 1985, c.I-15 172
Marine Insurance Act, R.S.M. 1987, c.M-40..........................125, 306, 354–57
Marine Insurance Act, R.S.N.B. 1973, c.M-1 ....125, 306, 354–57
Marine Insurance Act, R.S.O. 1990, c.M-2 ....125, 306, 354–57
Marine Insurance Act, S.C. 1993, c.22 ....4, 125, 293, 307, 308, 309, 313,
  314, 319, 320, 321, 322, 324, 325, 326, 327, 328, 329, 331, 332, 338,
  339, 354–57, 628, 629, 631, 632, 642, 644, 647, 650, 652, 733
Marine Liability Act, S.C. 2001, c.6..............4, 13, 68, 115, 116, 117, 120, 133,
  134, 143, 144, 145, 266, 287, 292, 408, 434, 436, 437, 439, 440, 446,
  467, 472, 473, 484, 485, 486, 487, 488, 489, 490, 491, 522, 523, 524,
  526, 530, 536, 537, 546, 547, 549, 551, 552, 553, 557, 558, 559, 629,
  671, 686, 696, 697, 702, 703, 704, 705, 706, 708, 722, 727, 725, 726,
  727, 728, 732, 734, 735, 738, 739, 740, 742, 743, 745, 746, 790, 792,
  805, Appendix 1
Marine Transportation Security Act, S.C. 1994, c.40, as am. by S.C. 2001,
  c.29 ....493, 781
Maritime Conventions Act, 1914, S.C. 1914, c.13..526
Migratory Birds Convention Act, 1994, S.C. 1994, c.22 ....671, 684, 685
Navigable Waters Protection Act, R.S.C. 1985, c.N-22 ....627, 628, 671,
  ....679, 681, 682, 728

Negligence Act, R.S.O. 1990, c.N-1 136
Nuclear Liability Act, R.S.C. 1985, c.N-28..210, 731
Occupational Health and Safety Act, R.S.O. 1990, c.O-1 152
Occupiers' Liability Act, R.S.A. 1980, c.O-4 547
Occupiers' Liability Act, R.S.B.C. 1996, c.337 547
Occupiers' Liability Act, R.S.M. 1987, c.O-8..547
Occupiers' Liability Act, R.S.O. 1990, c.O-2 ....136, 547
Occupiers' Liability Act, S.N.S. 1996, c.27 547
Oceans Act, S.C. 1996, c.31 ....4, 101, 103, 671, 682, 683, 774, 775
Personal Information and Electronic Documents Act, S.C. 2000, c.5 419
Personal Property Security Act, R.S.B.C. 1996, c.359 ....254, 255, 256, 257,
 ....258, 262, 263, 264
Personal Property Security Act, R.S.O. 1990, c.P.10 ....254, 255, 256, 257,
 ....258, 262, 263, 264
Personal Property Security Act, S.N.S. 1995-1996, c.13.... 254, 255, 256, 257,
 ....258, 262, 263, 264
Personal Property Security Act, S.S. 1993, c.P-6.2, ... 255
Pilotage Act, R.S.C. 1985, c.P-14 ....142, 294, 549, 562, 563, 564, 565,
 ....569, 570, 571, 572
Public Service Employment Act, R.S.C. 1985, c.P-33 66
Safe Containers Convention Act, R.S.C. 1985, c.S-1 208
Saskatchewan Insurance Act, R.S.S. 1978, c.S-26 306
Small Claims Courts Act, R.S.O. 1980, c.476..132, 133
Small Vessel Regulations, C.R.C., c.1487....................150, 192, 204, 245, 519,
 ....549, 550, 555, 556, 553
Supreme Court Act, R.S.B.C. 1996, c.443 751
Transportation of Dangerous Goods Act, 1992, S.C. 1992, c.34 ....210, 373
Trustee Act, R.S.O. 1990, c.T-23 136
United Nations Foreign Arbitral Awards Convention Act, R.S.C. 1985,
 c.16 (2d Supp.) 473
Water-Carriage of Goods Act, 1910, S.C. 1910, c.61...................................433
Workmen's Compensation Act, Amended Act, 1954, S.B.C. 1954, c.54..........558

United Kingdom

A Remedy for him who is Wrongfully Pursued in the Court of Admiralty, 1400
 (U.K.), 2 Hen. IV., c.11 105
Administration of Justice Act, 1956 (U.K.), 4 & 5 Eliz. II, c.46..........130, 762,
 ....776, 777
Admiralty Court Act, 1840 (U.K.), 3 & 4 Vict., c.65 ....123, 124, 750
Admiralty Court Act, 1861 (U.K.), 24 Vict., c.10 750

An Act for Compensating the Families of Persons Killed by Accidents, 1846 (U.K.), 9 & 10 Vict., c.93 [Fatal Accidents Act] 302, 303, 551

An Act for Securing Certain Powers and Privileges Intended to be Granted by his Majesty by Two Charters for Assurance of Ships and Merchandises at Sea, for Lending Money Upon Bottomry, and for Restraining Several Extravagant and Unwarrantable Practices Therein Mentioned, 1714 (U.K.), 6 Geo. I., c.18 301

An Act to Amend the Law Relating to Bills of Lading, 1855 (U.K.), 18 & 19 Vict., c.111 420

An Act Touching Policies of Assurances Used Among Merchants, 1601 (U.K.), 43 Eliz., c.12 299

British North America Act, 1867 (U.K.), 30 & 31 Vict., c.3 6

Carriage of Goods by Sea Act, 1992 (U.K.), 1992, c.50 420

Colonial Courts of Admiralty Act, 1890 (U.K.), 53 & 54 Vict., c.27 ..108, 109, ...112, 750

Colonial Laws Validity Act, 1865 (U.K.), 28 & 29 Vict., c.63 110

Harbours, Docks and Piers Clauses Act, 1847 (U.K.), 10 & 11 Vict., c.27 ....536, 539

In What Places the Admiral's Jurisdiction Doth Lie, 1391 (U.K.), 15 Rich II., c.3 749

Law Reform (Contributory Negligence) Act, 1945 (U.K.), 8 & 9 Geo. VI., c.28 536

Marine Insurance Act, 1745 (U.K.), 19 Geo. II., c.37...................................305

Marine Insurance Act, 1906 (U.K.), 6 Edw. VII., c.41........125, 305, 306, 307, ...331, 332, 354–57

Maritime Conventions Act, 1911 (U.K.), 12 Geo. V., c.57...........................526

Merchant Shipping Act, 1854 (U.K.), 17 & 18 Vict., c.104 303

Merchant Shipping Act, 1894 (U.K.), 57 & 58 Vict., c.60 ....189, 718, 719

Merchant Shipping Act, 1995 (U.K.), 1995, c.21 619

Merchant Shipping Act Amendment Act, 1862 (U.K.), 25 & 26 Vict., c.63 496

Pilotage Act, 1983 (U.K.), 1983, c.21..539

Sale of Goods Act, 1893 (U.K.), 56 & 57 Vict., c.71 172

Statute of Westminster, 1931 (U.K.), 22 Geo. V., c.4 ....23, 102, 110, 112, 719

Supreme Court Act, 1981 (U.K.), 29 & 30 Eliz. II, c.54 ....762, 765, 766

Third Parties (Rights Against Insurers) Act, 1930 (U.K.), 20 & 21 Geo. V., c.25 337

Vice-Admiralty Courts Act, 1863 (U.K.), 26 & 27 Vict., c.24 108

Vice-Admiralty Courts Amendment Act, 1867 (U.K.), 30 & 31 Vict., c.45 ..108

What Things the Admiral and his Deputy Shall Meddle, 1389 (U.K.), 13 Rich II., c.5 749

United States

Carriage of Goods by Sea Act, 46 App. U.S.C. §§1300–1315 (1936) 435, 465
Fire Statute, 46 U.S.C. §182 646
Harter Act, 46 U.S.C. §§190–195 (1893) 304, 433
Oil Pollution Act, 33 U.S.C. §§2701–2761 (1990)................28, 312, 666, 708
Wreck Removal Act, 33 U.S.C. §409 724

INTERNATIONAL TREATIES AND AGREEMENTS

1910 *Convention for the Unification of Certain Rules Respecting Collisions between Vessels,* 23 September 1910, 4 B.T.S. 6677, U.K.T.S. 1913 No. 4, see *Ratification of Maritime Conventions,*[1] below note 1, vol.I.3.200 *[Collision Avoidance Rules]* 90, 115, 523, 524, 526, 534, 535, 546

1910 *Convention for the Unification of Certain Rules with Respect to Assistance and Salvage at Sea,* 23 September 1910, 103 U.K.F.S. 441, see *Ratification of Maritime Conventions,* below note 1, vol.I.3.210 *[Assistance and Salvage Convention 1910]* 90, 595–98, 609, 613, 618, 666

1967 *Protocol to amend the Convention for the Unification of Certain Rules of Law Relating to Assistance and Salvage at Sea, 1910,* 27 May 1967, U.K.T.S. 1978 No. 22, see *Ratification of Maritime Conventions,* above note 1, vol. I.3.230 ....92, 596

1914 *Convention on Safety of Life at Sea,* 20 January 1914, 108 F.S.P. 283 *[SOLAS]* 158, 196

1920 *Convention Fixing the Minimum Age for Admission of Children to Employment at Sea,* 9 July 1920, 38 U.N.T.S. 109, see *Ratification of Maritime Conventions,* below note 1, vol I.6.10 *[ILO No. 7]* 218

1920 *Convention Concerning Unemployment Indemnity in Case of Loss or Foundering of the Ship,* 9 July 1920, 38 U.N.T.S. 119, see *Ratification of Maritime Conventions,* below note 1, vol.I.6.30 *[ILO No. 8]* 219

1921 *Convention Fixing the Minimum Age for the Admission of Young Persons to Employment as Trimmers or Stokers,* 11 November 1921, 38 U.N.T.S. 203, see *Ratification of Maritime Conventions,* below note 1, vol.I.6.40 *[ILO No. 15]* 219

1921 *Convention Concerning the Compulsory Medical Examination of Children and Young Persons employed at Sea,* 11 November 1921, 38 U.N.T.S. 217, see *Ratification of Maritime Conventions,* above note 1, vol.I.6.50 *[ILO No. 16]* 219

---

1   Institute of Maritime Law, *Ratification of Maritime Conventions,* 4 vols., Updated looseleaf service (London: Lloyd's Press, 1991–2003) *[Ratification of Maritime Conventions].*

International Treaties and Agreements 839

1924 *International Convention for the Unification of Certain Rules Relating to the Limitation of Liability of Owners of Sea-Going Vessels*, 25 August 1924, 120 L.N.T.S. 123, see *Ratification of Maritime Conventions*, above note 1, vol.I.2.399 ....90, 721

1924 *International Convention for the Unification of Certain Rules of Law Relating to Bills of Lading*, 25 August 1924, 120 L.N.T.S. 155, see *Ratification of Maritime Conventions*, above note 1, vol.I.5.10 [*Hague Rules*] ....90, 116, 122, 305, 319, 345, 351, 359, 393, 408, 409, 413, 430, 432, 434, 435, 436–77, 524, 629, 630, 631, 644, 726, 727, Appendix 1

> **1968** *Protocol to Amend the International Convention for the Unification of Certain Rules of Law Relating to Bills of Lading, 1924,* 23 February 1968, 1412 U.N.T.S. 121 [*Hague-Visby Rules*].........................116, 319, 345, 351, 393, 409, 410, 414, 432, 434, 435, 436–77, 524, 534, 629, 630, 631, 644, 726, 727, Appendix 1

> **1979** *Protocol Amending the International Convention for the Unification of Certain Rules of Law Relating to Bills of Lading, 1924,* 21 December 1979, 1412 U.N.T.S. 121, U.K.T.S. 1984 No. 28 [*SDR Protocol*]............434, 726

1926 *International Convention for the Unification of Certain Rules Concerning the Immunity of State Owned Vessels*, 10 April 1926, 176 L.N.T.S. 199, see *Ratification of Maritime Conventions*, above note 1, vol.I.12.5 90

> **1934** *Protocol Additional to the International Convention for the Unification of Certain Rules Concerning the Immunity of State Owned Vessels of 10 April 1926,* 24 May 1934, 150 L.N.T.S. 269...90

1926 *International Convention for the Unification of certain Rules of Law Relating to Maritime Liens and Mortgages*, 10 April 1926, 120 L.N.T.S. 187, see *Ratification of Maritime Conventions*, above note 1, vol.I.4.10...................90, 244, 266

1926 *Convention Concerning Seamen's Articles of Agreement*, 24 June 1926, 38 U.N.T.S. 295, see *Ratification of Maritime Conventions*, above note 1, vol.I.6.60 [*ILO No. 22*] 219

1936 *Convention Concerning Liability of the Shipowner in Case of Sickness, Injury or Death of Seamen*, 24 October 1936, 40 U.N.T.S. 169, see *Ratification of Maritime Conventions*, above note 1, vol.I.6.110 [*ILO No. 55*] 82

1936 *Convention Concerning Sickness Insurance for Seamen*, 24 October 1936, 40 U.N.T.S. 187, see *Ratification of Maritime Conventions*, above note 1, vol. I.6.120 [*ILO No. 56*]..82

1936 *Convention Fixing the Minimum Age for the Admission of Children to Employment at Sea (Revised)*, 24 October 1936, 40 U.N.T.S. 205, see *Ratification of Maritime Conventions*, above note 1, vol.I.6.100 [*ILO No. 58*] 219

1938 *Convention for the Unification of Certain Rules Relative to the Assistance and Salvaging of Aircraft or by Aircraft at Sea*, 29 September 1938, 8 Hudson 135.... 600

1946 *Convention Concerning Social Security of Seafarers*, 28 June 1946, 148 B.F.S.P. 133, see *Ratification of Maritime Conventions*, above note 1, vol.I.6.180 [*ILO No. 70*] 82

1946 *Convention Concerning Seafarers' Pensions*, 28 June 1946, 442 U.N.T.S. 235, see *Ratification of Maritime Conventions*, above note 1, vol.I.6.190 [*ILO No. 71*] 82

1946 *Convention Concerning Food and Catering for Crews on Board Ship*, 29 June 1946, 264 U.N.T.S. 163, see *Ratification of Maritime Conventions*, above note 1, vol.I.6.210 [*ILO No. 68*] 219

1946 *Convention Concerning the Medical Examination of Seafarers*, 29 June 1946, 214 U.N.T.S. 233, see *Ratification of Maritime Conventions*, above note 1, vol.I.6.220 [*ILO No. 73*]...219

1946 *Convention Concerning the Certification of Able Seamen*, 29 June 1946, 94 U.N.T.S. 11, see *Ratification of Maritime Conventions*, above note 1, vol.I.6.200 [*ILO No. 74*] 219

1948 *Convention on the Intergovernmental Maritime Consultative Organization*, 6 March 1948, 289 U.N.T.S. 48, see *Ratification of Maritime Conventions*, above note 1, vol.I.1.10 [*IMO Convention*] 78

1948 *International Convention on Safety of Life at Sea*, 10 June 1948, 191 U.N.T.S. 3 [*SOLAS 1948*] 196

1952 *International Convention on Certain Rules Concerning Civil Jurisdiction in Matters of Collision*, 10 May 1952, 439 U.N.T.S. 217, see *Ratification of Maritime Conventions*, above note 1, vol.I.2.20 [*1952 Civil Jurisdiction Convention*] 90, 530–32

1952 *International Convention for the Unification of Certain Rules relating to Penal Jurisdiction in Matters of Collision or other Incidents of Navigation*, 10 May 1952, 439 U.N.T.S. 233, see *Ratification of Maritime Conventions*, above note 1, vol.I.2.30 [*1952 Penal Jurisdiction Convention*] 90, 541, 542

1952 *International Convention for the Unification of Certain Rules Relating to the Arrest of Sea-Going Ships*, 10 May 1952, 439 U.N.T.S. 193, see *Ratification of Maritime Conventions*, above note 1, vol.I.2.10 [*Arrest Convention*] 90, 762, 765, 766, 767, 776, 777

1954 *International Convention for the Prevention of Pollution of the Sea by Oil*, 12 May 1954, 327 U.N.T.S. 3 [*OILPOL 1954*] 660, 661, 672–73

1962 *Amendments to the International Convention for the Prevention of Pollution of the Sea by Oil, 1954*, 11 April 1962, 600 U.N.T.S. 332 .... 660, 661, 672

1969 *Amendments to the International Convention for the Prevention of Pollution of the Sea by Oil, of 1954*, 21 October 1969, 1140 U.N.T.S. 340 ....660, 661, 672

1971 *Amendments to the International Convention for the Prevention of Pollution of the Sea by Oil, of 1954, Concerning Tank Arrangements and Size*, 15 October 1971, 11 I.L.M. 267 .... 660, 661, 672

1957 *International Convention Relating to the Limitation of the Liability of Owners of Sea-Going Ships*, 10 October 1957, 1412 U.N.T.S. 73, see *Ratification of Maritime Conventions*, above note 1, vol.I.2.310 .... 91, 686, 721, 722, 724, 732, 734, 735, 738

1979 *Protocol Amending the International Convention Relating to the Limitation of the Liability of Owners of Sea-Going Ships, 1957*, 21 December 1979, 1412 U.N.T.S. 73 .... 721, 722

1957 *International Convention Relating to Stowaways*, 10 October 1957, 1957 A.M.C. No. 2:1980 91

1958 *Convention on the Continental Shelf*, 29 April 1958, 499 U.N.T.S. 311 .. 709, 710

1958 *Convention on the High Seas*, 29 April 1958, 450 U.N.T.S. 82 .... 176, 186, 541, 661

1958 *Convention Concerning Seafarers' National Identity Documents*, 13 May 1958, 389 U.N.T.S. 277, see *Ratification of Maritime Conventions*, above note 1, vol.I.6.260 [*ILO No. 108*] 219

1958 *Convention on the Recognition and Enforcement of Foreign Arbitral Awards*, 10 June 1958, 330 U.N.T.S. 3 .... 477, 478

1960 *International Convention on Safety of Life at Sea*, 17 June 1960, 536 U.N.T.S. 27, see *Ratification of Maritime Conventions*, above note 1, vol.I.3.10 [*SOLAS 1960*] 196, 197

1960 *Convention on Third Party Liability in the Field of Nuclear Energy*, 29 July 1960, 956 U.N.T.S. 251 .... 696, 731

1963 *Convention Supplementary to the Convention on Third Party Liability in the Field of Nuclear Energy, 1960,* 31 January 1963, 1041 U.N.T.S. 358...... 696, 731

1964 *Additional Protocol to the Convention on Third Party Liability in the Field of Nuclear Energy, 1960,* 28 January 1964, 956 U.N.T.S. 335 696

1961 *International Convention for the Unification of Certain Rules Relating to the Carriage of Passengers by Sea and Protocol,* 29 April 1961, 1411 U.N.T.S. 81, see *Ratification of Maritime Conventions,* above note 1, vol.I.5.140 91

1962 *International Convention on the Liability of Operators of Nuclear Ships, with Additional Protocol,* 25 May 1962, 57 A.J.I.L. 268, see *Ratification of Maritime Conventions,* above note 1, vol.I.7.20 ....91, 731

1965 *Convention on Facilitation of International Maritime Traffic,* 9 April 1965, 591 U.N.T.S. 265, see *Ratification of Maritime Conventions,* above note 1, vol. I.5.150 [*FAL 1965*] 237, 238

1966 *International Convention on Load Lines,* 5 April 1966, 640 U.N.T.S. 133, see *Ratification of Maritime Conventions,* above note 1, vol.I.3.50 [*LL 1966*] .. 33, 205, 206, 218, 222

1988 *Protocol of 1988 Relating to the International Convention on Load Lines, 1966,* 11 November 1988, 2 U.S.T. 102, see *Ratification of Maritime Conventions,* above note 1, vol.I.3.60 [*LL Prot 1988*] 205

1967 *Convention on the International Hydrographic Organization,* 3 May 1967, 751 U.N.T.S. 41 2

1967 *International Convention for the Unification of Certain Rules Relating to Maritime Liens and Mortgages,* 27 May 1967, S.D. No. 12 (1967) 3, see *Ratification of Maritime Conventions,* above note 1, vol.I.4.20..............91, 244, 266

1967 *International Convention for the Unification of Certain Rules relating to the Carriage of Passengers' Luggage by Sea,* 27 May 1967, B.P.P. Misc. 7 (1968), see *Ratification of Maritime Conventions,* above note 1, vol.I.5.160 91

1967 *Convention Relating to Registration of Rights in Respect of Vessels under Construction,* 27 May 1967, U.D. 1967–1968 (1):342, see *Ratification of Maritime Conventions,* above note 1, vol.I.4.30 ....91, 161

1969 *International Convention on Tonnage Measurement of Ships,* 23 June 1969, 1291 U.N.T.S. 3 ....181, 734

1969 *International Convention Relating to Intervention on the High Seas in Cases of Oil Pollution Casualties,* 29 November 1969, 970 U.N.T.S. 211 [*Intervention*] 625, 662, 673, 674

International Treaties and Agreements 843

1973 *Protocol Relating to Intervention on the High Seas in Cases of Marine Pollution by Substances Other than Oil, 1973*, 2 November 1973, 1313 U.N.T.S. 3 [*Intervention Protocol*] 673, 674

1969 *International Convention on Civil Liability for Oil Pollution Damage*, 29 November 1969, 973 U.N.T.S. 3 [*CLC 1969*] 116, 310, 311, 661, 662, 665, 667, 686–92, 694, 695, 697, 699, 702, 730, 731

> **1976** *Protocol to the International Convention on Civil Liability for Oil Pollution Damage, 1969*, 19 November 1976, 1225 U.N.T.S. 356 [*CLC Prot 1976*] 665, 667, 685, 687, 689, 693, 698, 699, 730

> **1984** *Protocol of 1984 to Amend the International Convention on Civil Liability for Oil Pollution Damage, 1969*, 25 May 1984, 23 I.L.M. 177 730

> **1992** *Protocol to Amend the International Convention on Civil Liability for Oil Pollution Damage, 1969*, 27 November 1992, U.K.T.S. 1996 No. 87 [*CLC Prot 1992*] 116, 665, 667, 686, 687, 690, 691, 692, 693, 698, 699, 703, 704, 708, 730

1971 *International Convention on the Establishment of an International Fund for Compensation for Oil Pollution Damage*, 18 December 1971, 1110 U.N.T.S. 57 [*FUND 1971*] 87, 116, 662, 663, 665, 667, 692–96, 698, 699, 702, 703, 730, 731

> **1976** *Protocol to Amend the International Convention on the Establishment of an International Fund for Compensation for Oil Pollution Damage of December 18 1971*, 19 November 1976, 16 I.L.M. 621......87, 693, 698, 699, 730

> **1984** *Protocol of 1984 to Amend the International Convention on the Establishment of an International Fund for Compensation for Oil Pollution Damage, 1971*, 25 May 1984, 23 I.L.M. 195 [*FUND Prot 1984*] 665, 667, 693, 698, 699, 730

> **1992** *Protocol to Amend the International Convention on the Establishment of an International Fund for Compensation for Oil Pollution Damage, 1971*, 27 November 1992, 1996 A.T.S. 3 [*FUND Prot 1992*] 87, 117, 667, 692, 693, 694, 698, 699, 703, 704, 705, 708, 730

1971 *Convention Relating to Civil Liability in the Field of Maritime Carriage of Nuclear Material*, 17 December 1971, 974 U.N.T.S. 255 [*NUCLEAR 1971*].... 696, 730

1972 *Convention on the International Regulations for Preventing Collisions at Sea*, 20 October 1972, 1050 U.N.T.S. 16, see *Ratification of Maritime Conventions*, above note 1, vol.I.3.250 [*COLREGS 1972*] 25, 40, 52, 218, 497–535, 561

844   MARITIME LAW

1972 *Convention on the Prevention of Marine Pollution by Dumping of Wastes and Other Matters,* 29 December 1972, 1046 U.N.T.S. 120 [*LC 1972*] 620, 663, 674

   1996 *1996 Protocol to the Convention on the Prevention of Marine Pollution by Dumping of Wastes and Other Matters, 1972,* 7 November 1996, 36 I.L.M. 7 (not yet in force, but accepted by Canada on 15 May 2000); see *Ratification of Maritime Conventions,* above note 1, vols.I.7.150 and 152 674

1972 *International Convention for Safe Containers,* 2 December 1972, 1064 U.N.T.S. 43, see *Ratification of Maritime Conventions,* above note 1, vol.I.3.50 [*CSC 1972*]...207, 208

   1981 *Amendments to Annex I of the International Convention for Safe Containers of 1972,* 2 April 1981, 1263 U.N.T.S. 477 207

   1983 *Amendments to Annex I & II of the International Convention for Safe Containers of 1972,* 13 June 1983, 1348 U.N.T.S. 328 207

   1991 *Amendments to Annex I & II of the International Convention for Safe Containers of 1972,* 17 May 1991, 3138 B.T.S. 6....................................207

   1993 *Amendments to the International Convention for Safe Containers of 1972,* 4 November 1993, 42 S.I.D.A. 1 207

1973 *International Convention for the Prevention of Pollution from Ships,* 2 November 1973, 1340 U.N.T.S. 184 [*MARPOL 1973*] 205, 625, 633, 634, 675, 676, 697

   1978 *Protocol of 1978 Relating to the International Convention for the Prevention of Pollution from Ships of 1973,* 17 February 1978, 1340 U.N.T.S. 61 [*MARPOL 73/78*] 205, 230, 625, 663, 635, 667, 672, 674–75, 679, 697, 710, 715

1974 *Offshore Pollution Liability Agreement,* 4 September 1974 (entered into force 1 May 1975) text of the agreement can be found at <www.opol.org.uk> [*OPOL 1974*] 710, 711

1974 *Convention on a Code of Conduct for Liner Conferences,* 6 April 1974, 1334 U.N.T.S. 15, see *Ratification of Maritime Conventions,* above note 1, vol. I.5.210 84

1974 *International Convention for the Safety of Life at Sea,* 1 November 1974, 1184 U.N.T.S. 2, see *Ratification of Maritime Conventions,* above note 1, vol. I.3.20 [*SOLAS 1974*] 52, 53, 64, 65, 197, 198, 199, 200, 201, 202, 203, 205, 206, 209, 218, 222, 223, 224, 225, 226, 227, 228, 230, 235, 236, 310, 372, 373, 493, 625

International Treaties and Agreements 845

1978 *Protocol relating to the International Convention for the Safety of Life at Sea, 1974*, 17 February 1978, 1276 U.N.T.S. 237, see *Ratification of Maritime Conventions*, above note 1, vol.I.3.30 [*SOLAS Prot 1978*]....197, 198, 201

1988 *Protocol of 1988 Relating to the International Convention for the Safety of Life at Sea, 1974*, 11 November 1988, U.S. Treaty Doc. 102-2, see *Ratification of Maritime Conventions*, above note 1, vol.I.3.40 [*SOLAS Prot 1988*] 197, 201

1974 *Athens Convention Relating to the Carriage of Passengers and their Luggage by Sea*, 13 December 1974, 14 I.L.M. 945 [*PAL 1974*]116, 266, 310, 480, 483–93, 549, 726, 727, 739, 740, 741

1976 *Protocol to the Athens Convention Relating to the Carriage of Passengers and their Luggage by Sea, 1974*, 19 November 1976, 16 I.L.M. 625 727

1990 *Protocol to the Athens Convention Relating to the Carriage of Passengers and their Luggage by Sea, 1974*, 29 March 1990, U.K.T.S. 1989 No. 43 [*PAL Prot 1990*].................................310, 480, 486, 487, 490, 727, 741

2002 *Protocol of 2002 to the Athens Convention Relating to the Carriage of Passengers and their Luggage by Sea, 1974*, 1 November 2002, IMO LEG/CON 13.NF.2 (2003) [*PAL 2002*] 480, 485, 486, 490, 491, 727, 741

1976 *Convention on the International Maritime Satellite Organization*, 3 September 1976, 1143 U.N.T.S. 105, see *Ratification of Maritime Conventions*, above note 1, vol.I.3.260 [*INMARSAT*] 47, 52, 87, 236, 237

1976 *Convention Concerning Annual Leave with Pay for Seafarers*, 29 October 1976, 1138 U.N.T.S. 205, see *Ratification of Maritime Conventions*, above note 1, vol.I.6.320 [*ILO No. 146*]..82

1976 *Convention Concerning Minimum Standards in Merchant Shipping*, 29 October 1976, 1259 U.N.T.S. 335, see *Ratification of Maritime Conventions*, above note 1, vol.I.6.340 [*ILO No. 147*] 217, 218, 548

1976 *Convention on Limitation of Liability for Maritime Claims*, 19 November 1976, 1456 U.N.T.S. 221 [*LLMC 1976*] 116, 134, 266, 446, 484, 485, 491, 492, 695, 696, 700, 705, 721–46, 790

1996 *Protocol of 1996 to Amend the Convention on Limitation of Liability for Maritime Claims, 1976*, 3 May 1996 35 I.L.M. 1406 ....116, 696, 721, 739

1977 *Torremolinos International Convention for the Safety of Fishing Vessels,* 2 April 1977, B.P.P. Misc. 17, see *Ratification of Maritime Conventions,* above note 1, vol.I.3.80 [*SFV 1977*] 202, 203

   1993 *Torremolinos Protocol Relating to the Torremolinos International Convention for the Safety of Fishing Vessels, 1977,* 2 April 1993, B.P.P. Misc. 19, see *Ratification of Maritime Conventions,* above note 1, vol.I.3.85 [*SFV Prot 1993*] 202, 203

1977 *International Convention for the Unification of Certain Rules Concerning Civil Jurisdiction, Choice of Law, and Recognition and Enforcement of Judgments in Matters of Collision,* 16 June 1977, International Maritime Committee Documentation, v. 1 (London Draft) 22, 1977 CMI Doc. 104 532

1977 *Convention on Civil Liability for Oil Pollution Damage Resulting from Exploration for and Exploitation of Seabed Mineral Resources,* 17 December 1976, 16 I.L.M. 1451 [*CLEE 1977*] 711

1978 *United Nations Convention on the Carriage of Goods by Sea,* 31 March 1978, 17 I.L.M. 608 [*Hamburg Rules*] 116, 734, 735, 436, 524, 534, 629, 726, 727

1978 *International Convention on Standards of Training, Certification and Watchkeeping for Seafarers,* 7 July 1978, 1361 U.N.T.S. 2, see *Ratification of Maritime Conventions,* above note 1, vol.I.3.90 [*STCW 1978*] 65, 187, 220, 221, 222, 223, 226, 227, 230, 548, 664, 668

1979 *International Convention on Maritime Search and Rescue,* 27 April 1979, 1405 U.N.T.S. 97, see *Ratification of Maritime Conventions,* above note 1, vol. I.3.280 [*SAR 1979*] 53, 236, 237

1982 *Memorandum of Understanding on Port State Control in Implementing Agreements on Maritime Safety and Protection of the Marine Environment,* 26 January 1982, 21 I.L.M. 1, see *Ratification of Maritime Conventions,* above note 1, vol. I.3.100 [*Paris MOU 1982*] 65, 88, 187, 198, 228, 229, 230, 666, 667, 678

1982 *United Nations Convention on the Law of the Sea,* 10 December 1982, 1833 U.N.T.S. 3, Institute of Maritime Law, see *Ratification of Maritime Conventions,* above note 1, vol.I.1.170 [*UNCLOS*]......7, 21, 41, 76, 87, 100, 101, 176, 177, 178, 186, 189, 228, 229, 234, 498, 540, 542, 618, 621, 622, 625, 659, 664, 665, 670, 672, 683, 710

   1995 *Agreement for the Implementation of the Provisions of the United Nations Convention on the Law of the Sea of 10 December 1982 Relating to the Conservation and Management of Straddling Fish Stocks and Highly Migratory Fish Stocks,* 4 December 1995, 2001 A.T.S. 8 [*UNFA*] 188, 189

International Treaties and Agreements 847

1986 *United Nations Convention on Conditions for Registration of Ships*, 7 February 1986, 26 I.L.M. 1229 186

1988 *Convention for the Suppression of Unlawful Acts against the Safety of Maritime Navigation*, 10 March 1988, 27 I.L.M. 668, see *Ratification of Maritime Conventions*, above note 1, vol.I.3.110 [*SUA 1988*] 234, 235, 492

    1988 *Protocol for the Suppression of Unlawful Acts against the Safety of Fixed Platforms Located on the Continental Shelf*, 10 March 1988, 27 I.L.M. 685, see *Ratification of Maritime Conventions*, above note 1, vol.I.3.120 [*SUA Prot 1988*] 234, 235

1988 *International COSPASS-SARSAT Programme Agreement*, 1 July 1988, 1518 U.N.T.S. 209, see *Ratification of Maritime Conventions*, above note 1, vol. I.3.310 [*COS-SAR 1988*] 237

1989 *Basel Convention on the Control of Transboundary Movements of Hazardous Wastes and their Disposal*, 22 March 1989, Can. T.S. 1992 No. 92 [*Basel Convention*] 373, 665, 676, 684

1989 *International Convention on Salvage*, 28 April 1989, U.K.T.S. 1996 No. 93......116, 596, 597, 598, 599, 600, 603, 609, 610, 611, 612, 613, 614, 618, 619, 622, 636, 637, 655, 666, 729, 730

    1989 *Protocol Concerning Marine Pollution Resulting from Exploration and Exploitation of the Continental Shelf*, 29 March 1989, 19 E.B.L. 32 17

1990 *International Convention on Oil Pollution Preparedness, Response and Co-operation*, 30 November 1990, 30 I.L.M. 733 [*OPRC 1990*] 325, 666, 668, 676, 677, 679, 680, 706

1991 *Convention on the Liability of Operators of Transport Terminals in International Trade 1991*, 19 April 1991, 30 I.L.M. 1503 434

1992 *Latin American Agreement on Port State Control*, 5 November 1992, <http://200.45.69.62/index_i.htm> [*Viña del Mar Agreement*] 87, 667, 678

1993 *FAO Agreement to Promote Compliance with International Conservation and Management Measures by Fishing Vessels on the High Seas* 27th Conf., UN Doc. C/93/26 (1993) 188

1993 *International Convention on Maritime Liens and Mortgages*, 6 May 1993, 33 I.L.M 353, see *Ratification of Maritime Conventions*, above note 1, vol.I.4.2.... 83, 266, 286, 292

848   MARITIME LAW

1993 *Memorandum of Understanding on Port State Control in the Asia-Pacific Region,* 1 December 1993, <www.tokyo-mou.org>, Institute of Maritime Law, see *Ratification of Maritime Conventions,* above note 1, vol.I.3.105 [*Tokyo MOU 1993*] 64, 87, 187, 198, 230, 667, 678

1994 *Protocol for the Protection of the Mediterranean Sea against Pollution Resulting from the Exploration and Exploitation of the Continental Shelf and the Seabed and its Subsoil,* 14 October 1994, online: United Nations Environment Programme <www.unep.ch/seas/main/hconlist.html>...................................17

1995 *International Convention on Standards of Training, Certification and Watchkeeping for Fishing Vessel Personnel,* 7 July 1995, 43 S.I.D.A. 148 [*STCW-F 1995*] 5

1996 *Memorandum of Understanding on Port State Control in the Caribbean Region,* 9 February 1996, 36 I.L.M. 237 [*Caribbean MOU*] 87, 667, 678

1996 *International Convention on Liability and Compensation for Damage in Connection with the Carriage of Hazardous and Noxious Substances by Sea,* 2 May 1996, 35 I.L.M. 1406 [*HNS 1996*] 665, 668, 669, 677, 695, 696, 697–98, 705, 731

1996 *Convention Concerning the Inspection of Seafarer's Working and Living Conditions,* 22 October 1996, online: International Labour Organisation <www.ilo.org>, see *Ratification of Maritime Conventions,* above note 1, vol. I.6.390 [*ILO No 178*] 82

1996 *Convention Concerning Seafarers' Hours of Work and the Manning of Ships,* 22 October 1996, online: International Labour Organisation <www.ilo.org>, see *Ratification of Maritime Conventions,* above note 1, vol.I.6.410 [*ILO No. 180*] 82

1997 *Memorandum of Understanding on Port State Control in the Mediterranean Region,* July 11 1997, online: <www.medmou.org> [*Mediterranean MOU*]......87, 667, 678

1998 *Memorandum of Understanding on Port State Control for the Indian Ocean Region,* June 5 1998, online: <www.iomou.org> [*Indian Ocean MOU*]........87, 667, 678

1999 *International Convention on Arrest of Ships,* 12 March 1999, Doc. A/CONF.188.6. or online: UNCTAD <www.unctad.org/en/docs/imo99d6.pdf>, see *Ratification of Maritime Conventions,* above note 1, vol.I.2.15 91

1999 *Memorandum of Understanding on Port State Control in the West and Central African Region,* October 22 1999, see *Ratification of Maritime Conventions,* above note 1, vol.I.3.135. [*West and Central African MOU*] 667, 678

2000 *Protocol on Preparedness, Response and Co-operation to Pollution Incidents by Hazardous and Noxious Substances,* 15 March 2000, see *Ratification of Maritime Conventions,* above note 1, vol.I.7.232 [*OPRC-HNS Prot 2000*] 668, 677, 707

2001 *International Convention on Civil Liability for Bunker Oil Pollution Damage,* 27 March 2001, IMO LEG/CONF.12/19 [*BUNKER 2001*]..........699, 700, 730

2001 *Convention on the Protection of the Underwater Cultural Heritage,* 2 November 2001, 41 I.L.M. 40 622

2001 *Memorandum of Understanding on Port State Control in the Black Sea Region,* 7 April 2000, see *Ratification of Maritime Conventions,* above note 1, vol.II.3.109................667, 678

TABLE OF CASES

Canada

671122 Ontario Ltd. v. Sagaz Industries Canada Inc., [2001] 2 S.C.R. 983......438
1013799 Ontario Ltd. v Kent Line International (2000), 21 C.C.L.I. (3d) 312 (Ont. S.C.) 323

AG for Canada v. AG for Alberta, [1916] 1 A.C. 588 (P.C.) 125
AG for Canada v. AG for Ontario, [1937] A.C. 355 (P.C.) 125
AG for Ontario v. Reciprocal Insurers, [1924] A.C. 328, 18 Ll. L.R. 53 (P.C.) 125
A.I.M. Steel Ltd. v. Gulf of Georgia Towing Co. (1964), 48 D.L.R. (2d) 549 (B.C.S.C.) 592
A.R. Kitson Trucking Ltd. v. Rivtow Straits Ltd. (1975), 55 D.L.R. (3d) 462 (B.C.S.C.) 441
A/S Ornen v. Duteous (The) (1986), 4 F.T.R. 122, [1987] 1 F.C. 270 528
Aetna Financial Services Ltd. v. Feigelman, [1985] 1 S.C.R. 2..................803, 804
Agricultural Credit Corp. of Saskatchewan v. Pettyjohn (1991), 79 D.L.R. (4th) 22 (Sask. C.A.) 264
Agro Co. of Canada Ltd. v. Regal Scout (The) (1983), 148 D.L.R. (3d) 412 (F.C.T.D.) 472
Albano (The) v. Allan Line Steamship Co., [1907] A.C. 193, (1906), 37 S.C.R. 284 ....511, 513
Alexander v. Gambier Isle (The), [1948] Ex. C.R. 414 606
Alma (The) (1862), 5 N.S.R. 789 611
Amican Navigation Inc. v. Densan Shipping Co. (1997), 137 F.T.R. 132..........788
Amo Containers Ltd. v. Drake Insurance (1984), 51 Nfld. & P.E.I.R. 55 (Nfld. S.C.(T.D.)) 322
Anchor Marine Insurance Co. v. Keith (1884), 9 S.C.R. 483 ....313, 324
Anderson v. Dale & Co., [1994] B.C.J. No. 3347 (B.C.S.C.) (QL) 36

Anderson v. Harrison (1977), 4 B.C.L.R. 320 (S.C.) 481, 482
Anderson v. R. (1919), 59 S.C.R. 379 624
Andrews v. Grand & Toy Alberta Ltd., [1978] 2 S.C.R. 229 530
Anglo-Canadian Timber Products Ltd. v. Gulf of Georgia Towing Co., [1966]
 Ex. C.R. 855 536
Anglo Oriental Rugs Ltd. v. March Shipping Ltd., [1993] O.J. No. 1075 (Gen.
 Div.) (QL) 411
Antares Shipping Corp. v. Capricorn (The), [1977] 2 S.C.R. 422....112, 123, 124,
 268
Anticosti Shipping Co. v. St-Amand, [1959] S.C.R. 372....................411, 441, 465
Aris Steamship Co. v. Associated Metals & Minerals Corp., (The Evie W),
 [1980] 2 S.C.R. 322 ....123, 428
Armada Lines Ltd. v. Chaleur Fertilizers Ltd. (1995), 170 N.R. 372 (F.C.A.),
 rev'd [1997] 2 S.C.R. 617..778, 779
Arnold v. Teno, [1978] 2 S.C.R. 287 530
Asamera Oil Corp. v. Sea Oil & General Corp., [1979] 1 S.C.R. 633 465
Associated Metals and Minerals Corp. v. Evie W (The), [1978] 2 F.C. 710
 (C.A.), aff'd [1980] 2 S.C.R. 322 ....113, 115
Atlantic Consolidated Foods Ltd. v. Doroty (The), [1979] 1 F.C. 283 (T.D.),
 aff'd [1981] 1 F.C. 783 (F.C.A.) 440, 452, 453, 475, 631
Atwood v. R. (1985), 10 C.C.L.I. 62 (F.C.T.D.) 329, 330

B.D.C. Ltd. v. Hofstrand Farms Ltd. (1986) 26 D.L.R. (4th) 1 (S.C.C.) 464
B.W.B. Navigation Co. v. Kiltuish (The) (1922), 21 Ex. C.R. 398 ....516, 588
Balfour Guthrie (Canada) Ltd. v. Far Eastern Steamship Co. (1977),
 82 D.L.R. (3d) 414 (C.A.) 132
Balix Furniture and Appliances Ltd. v. Maritime Insurance Co., [1978] O.J.
 No. 1514 (Co. Ct.) (QL) 324
Balodis v. Prince George (The), [1985] 1 F.C. 890 (T.D.)....................................281
Banco do Brasil S.A. v. Alexandros G. Tsavliris (The) (1987), 12 F.T.R. 278 249
Bank of British North America v. Western Assurance Co. (1884), 7 O.R. 166
 (H.C.) 328
Bank of Montreal v. Hall, [1990] 1 S.C.R. 121 ....252, 254, 261
Bank of Montreal v. Pulsar Ventures Inc. (1987), 42 D.L.R. (4th) 385 (Sask.
 C.A.)..261
Bank of Nova Scotia v. Harvestor Credit Corp. of Canada Ltd. (1990),
 73 D.L.R. (4th) 385 (C.A.)..261
Bank of Scotland v. Nel (The), [2001] 1 F.C. 408, (2000), 189 F.T.R.
 230 (T.D.) 250, 282, 291, 770, 771
Bank of Scotland v. Nel (The), [1998] 4 F.C. 388 (T.D.) 800
Bank of Scotland v. Nel (The) (1997), 140 F.T.R. 271(T.D.) 770, 781, 792, 796,
 797, 800
Barker v. Pacific Pilotage Authority (1982), 42 N.R. 598 (F.C.A.) 572
Bayside Towing v. Canadian Pacific Railway Co., [2001] 2 F.C. 258
 (T.D.) 723, 733, 737
Beaufort Realties (1964) Inc. v. Chomedy Aluminum Co., [1980]
 2 S.C.R. 718 367
Beaulieu v. Reliance Insurance Co. of Philadelphia (1971), 19 D.L.R. (3d) 399,
 aff'd [1972] 1 O.R. 84 (C.A.)..150

Beeco Invest KS v. Canada, [1989] 2 F.C. 110 (C.A.) 742
Behn v. Burness (1863), 3 B. & S. 751, 122 E.R. 281 (Ex. Ct.) 369, 370
Belisle v. Minister of Transport, [1967] Ex. C.R. 141 ....570, 571
Bell Canada v. Quebec, [1988] 1 S.C.R. 749, 51 D.L.R. (4th) 161 138
Bell Telephone Co. of Canada v. Mar-Tirenno (The), [1974] 1 F.C. 294 (T.D.), aff'd (1976), 71 D.L.R. (3d) 608 (C.A.) 523
Benmaple (The) v. Lafayette (The), [1941] S.C.R. 66 514
Benson Brothers Shipbuilding Co. v. Miss Donna (The), [1978] 1 F.C. 379 (T.D.) 277, 290, 774, 800
Bentley v. MacDonald (1977), 27 N.S.R. (2d) 152 (T.D.) 501, 509, 511, 549
Billings v. Zurich Insurance Co. (1987), 27 C.C.L.I. 60 (Ont. Dist. Ct.) 328
Birch Hills Credit Union Ltd. v. CIBC (1988), 52 D.L.R. (4th) 113 (Sask. C.A.) ..261
Bischler v. Stoparyk (1979), 9 Alta. L.R. (2d) 1 (T.D.) 501, 504, 511
Blanc v. Emilien Burke (The) (1919), 19 Ex. C.R. 24, 46 D.L.R. 59 509
Bonabelle (The) v. Hazel (The), [1953] Ex. C.R. 192 603
Bonham v. Sarnor (The) (1918), 21 Ex. C.R. 183 282
Bow Valley Husky (Bermuda) Ltd. v. Saint John Shipbuilding Ltd. (1995), 126 D.L.R. (4th) 1 (Nfld. C.A.), varied [1997] 3 S.C.R. 1210, 153 D.L.R. (4th) 385 ......74, 149, 167, 168, 425, 522, 526, 530,546, 558, 559, 728, 769
Bow Valley Husky (Bermuda) Ltd. v. Saint John Shipbuilding Ltd. (1992), 97 Nfld. & P.E.I.R. 217 (Nfld. C.A.) 131, 135, 136, 137
Braber Equipment Ltd. v. Fraser Surrey Docks Ltd. (1998), 42 B.L.R. (2d) 314 (S.C.), aff'd (1999), 130 B.C.A.C. 307 (B.C.C.A.) 535, 536
Brazeau v. Deroy (1995), 53 A.C.W.S. (3d) 239 (Qc. C.A.) 526
British America Assurance v. William Law & Co. (1892), 21 S.C.R. 325 330
British Columbia (AG) v. Bermuda (The), [1923] Ex. C.R. 107, [1923] 2 D.L.R. 272 ....278, 286
British Columbia Mills, Tug & Barge Co. v. Kelley, [1923] 1 W.W.R. 597, 1 D.L.R. 1015 593
British Columbia Sugar Refining Co. v. Thor I (The), [1965] 2 Ex. C.R. 469 ....450, 457
British Columbia Telephone Co. v. Marpole Towing, [1971] S.C.R. 321 719
Britsky Building Movers v. Dominion Insurance Corp., [1981] I.L.R. 1-1420 (Man. Co. Ct.) 328
Brotchie v. Karey T (The) (1994), 83 F.T.R. 262 788
Brown v. Harvey (1992), 37 A.C.W.S. 5 (B.C.S.C.) 501
Brown v. Marine Atlantic (1998), 163 Nfld. & P.E.I.R. 164 (Nfld. S.C.) 481
Brown & Root Ltd. v. Chimo Shipping Ltd., [1967] S.C.R. 642 431
Bruck Mills Ltd. v. Black Sea Steamship Co., [1973] F.C. 387 (T.D.) 446, 453, 459
Burns v. Cassels (1886), 26 N.B.R. 20, aff'd (1887) 14 S.C.R. 256 364
Burrard Towing v. Reed Stenhouse (1996), 19 B.C.L.R. (3d) 391, 75 B.C.A.C. 254, 35 C.C.L.I. (2d) 145 (C.A.) 324, 334, 591, 592
Burrard Towing v. T.G. McBride & Co., [1968] 1 Ex. C.R. 9 603

C.P. Ships v. Les Industries Lyon Corduroys, [1983] 1 F.C. 736 641
Calvin Austin (The) v. Lovitt (1905), 35 S.C.R. 616 507
Cameron v. Domville (1878), 17 N.B.R. 647 632
Cana Construction Co. v. Canada, [1974] S.C.R. 1159 158
Canada v. Galaxias (The), [1989] 1 F.C. 375 (T.D.) 794

Canada v. Horizons Unbound (1997), 123 F.T.R. 127 792
Canada v. Saint John Shipbuilding and Dry Dock Co. (1981), 43 N.R. 15
 (F.C.A.) 145, 146, 147, 151
Canada v. Saint John Tug Boat Co., [1946] S.C.R. 466.......................................115
Canada v. Saskatchewan Wheat Pool, [1983] 1 S.C.R. 205 481
Canada (AG) v. Brister, [1943] 3 D.L.R. 50(N.S.S.C)...624
Canada (AG) v. Natalie S. (The), [1932] Ex. C.R. 155..115
Canada and Dominion Sugar Co. v. Canadian National (West Indies)
 Steamships, [1947] A.C. 46 (P.C.)..412, 413, 415, 445
Canada Steamship Lines v. John B. Ketchum II, [1925] S.C.R. 81...................516
Canada Steamship Lines v. King (The), [1952] A.C. 192 (P.C.).......................394
Canada Steamship Lines v. Maria Paolina G. (The), [1954] Ex. C.R. 211 514
Canada Steamship Lines v. Montreal Trust Co., [1940] Ex. C.R. 220 578
Canada Steamship Lines v. Paisley (The), [1930] Ex. C.R. 105 583
Canada Steamship Lines v. Rival (The), [1937] 3 D.L.R. 148 (Ex. Ct.).............288
Canada Steamship Lines v. Waldemar Peter (The), [1957] Ex. C.R. 254 501
Canadian Dredging Co. v. Northern Navigation Co, [1923] Ex. C.R. 189,
 [1924] 4 D.L.R. 1195 ....280, 607, 608
Canadian Dredging Company v. Mike Corry (The) (1917), 19 Ex. C.R. 61, 47
 D.L.R. 495 6,15
Canadian General Electric v. Armateurs du St. Laurent Inc., (The Maurice
 Desgagnés), [1977] 1 F.C. 215 (T.D.), revi'd [1977] 2 F.C. 503
 (C.A.) 408, 409
Canadian General Electric v. Pickford & Black Ltd. (The Lake Bosomtwe),
 [1971] S.C.R. 41 442
Canadian Imperial Bank of Commerce v. 281787 Alberta Ltd. (Crockett's
 Western Wear), [1984] 5 W.W.R. 283 (Alta. C.A.) 252
Canadian Imperial Bank of Commerce v. Barkley Sound (The), [1999] B.C.J.
 No. 512 (S.C.) (QL)..289
Canadian Indemnity Co. v. AG of British Columbia, [1977] 2 S.C.R. 504 125
Canadian Klockner Ltd. v. D/SA/S Flint, [1973] 2 Lloyd's L.R. 478 (F.C.T.D.) 430
Canadian National Railway v. Canadian Industries Ltd., [1941] S.C.R. 591,
 [1941] 4 D.L.R. 561 328
Canadian National Railway v. Norsk Pacific Steamship Co. (The Jervis Crown)
 (1989), 26 F.T.R. 81, aff'd [1990] 3 F.C. 114 (C.A.), aff'd [1992] 1 S.C.R.
 1021, 91 D.L.R. (4th) 289 ....425, 430, 727
Canadian National Steamships v. Bayliss, [1937] S.C.R. 261 459
Canadian National Steamships v. Watson, [1939] S.C.R. 11, [1939]
 1 D.L.R. 273 136
Canadian Pacific Ltd. v. Quebec North Shore Paper Co., [1977] 2 S.C.R.
 1054 ....121, 122, 124, 126
Canadian Pacific Navigation Co. v. CF Sargent (The) (1893), 3 B.C.R. 5 606
Canadian Pacific Railway v. Bermuda (The) (1910), 13 Ex. C.R. 389 505
Canadian Pacific Railway v. Camosun (The), [1925] Ex. C.R. 39 506
Canadian Pacific Railway v. Vancouver Tug Boat Co., [1957] Ex. C.R. 95 505
Canadian Salt Co. v. Irving Cedar (The) (2000), 193 F.T.R. 20....536, 580, 581, 582
Canadian Transport Co. v. Hunt, Leuchers, Hepburn (The City Alberni),
 [1947] 2 D.L.R. 647 (Ex. Ct.)...644
Canaport Ltd. v. Beaurivage (The) (1986), 1 F.T.R. 161 529

Table of Cases 855

Canastrand Industries Ltd. v. Lara S. (The), [1993] 2 F.C. 553, aff'd 176
  N.R. 30 (F.C.A.) 425, 430, 431
Captain v. Far Eastern Steamship Co. (1978), 97 D.L.R. (3d) 250
  (B.C.S.C.) 410, 443
Carling O'Keefe Breweries of Canada v. CN Marine (1987), 7 F.T.R. 178 (T.D.),
  varied (1989), 104 N.R. 166 (F.C.A.) 430
Carra v. Lake (1995), 53 A.C.W.S. (3d) 986 (QC.C.A.) 551, 558
Carvill v. Schoffield (1883), 9 S.C.R. 370 370
Cashin v. Canada, [1935] Ex. C.R. 103 115
Catherwood Towing v. Commercial Union Assurance (1996), 26 B.C.L.R.
  (3d) 57 (C.A.) 324, 34, 592
Cavalier (The) v. Liverpool Shipping Co., [1931] Ex. C.R. 205..................... 511
Century 21 Real Estate v. Wenstob (1996), 119 F.T.R. 201 602
Century Insurance Co. of Canada v. Case Existological Laboratories, (The
  Bamcell II), [1983] 2 S.C.R. 47 .... 323, 328, 329, 330
Chaffey v. Schooley (1876), 40 U.C.Q.B. 165 (C.A.) 638, 644
Chamberland v. Fleming (1984), 29 C.C.L.T. 213, 12 D.L.R. (4th) 688 (Alta.
  Q.B.) 550
Champlain (The) v. Canada Steamship Lines Ltd., [1939] Ex. C.R. 89 .... 578, 579
Champoux v. Great Lakes Pilotage Authority, [1976] 2 F.C. 399, 11 N.R. 441,
  67 D.L.R. (3d) 358 (C.A.) 571
Charles Goodfellow Lumber Sales Ltd. v. Verreault, [1971] S.C.R. 522 .... 451, 459
Chastine Maersk (The) v. Trans-Mar Trading Co., [1974] F.C.J. No. 1003 (T.D.)
  (QL) 377
Chernoff v. Chilcott (1988), 27 B.C.L.R. (2d) 283 (C.A.) 720
Chester Sailing Society v. Flinn (1981), 44 N.S.R. (2d) 105
  (S.C.(T.D.)) 501, 509, 512
Chitel v. Rothbart (1982), 29 O.R. (2d) 513 (C.A.) 803
Chubb Insurance Co. of Canada v. Cast Line Ltd., [2001] R.R.A. 765
  (Que. Sup. Ct.) 327
Citizens Insurance Co. of Canada v. Parsons (1881), 7 App. Cas. 96 125
Clackamas (The Ship) v. Schooner Cape d'Or, [1926] S.C.R. 331 504
Clark v. Kona Winds Yacht Charters Ltd. (1990), 34 F.T.R. 211 (T.D.), aff'd
  (1995), 184 N.R. 355 (C.A.) 516, 550
Clark v. Scottish Imperial Insurance (1879), 4 S.C.R. 192 324
Cleeve (The) v. Prince Rupert (The) (1917), 20 Ex. C.R. 441 513
Clift's Marine Sales (1992) Ltd. v. Moorco Inc. (2001), 215 F.T.R. 78 172
Coast Ferries v. Century Insurance Co. of Canada (1975), 48 D.L.R. (3d)
  310 (S.C.C.) 330, 336
Coastal Equipment Agencies Limited v. Comer (The), [1970] 1 Ex.
  C.R. 13 .... 293, 774, 800
Cole v. Canadian Pacific Ltd. (1978), 22 N.B.R. (2d) 328 (Q.B.) 482
Colonial Yacht Harbour Ltd. v. Octavia (The), [1980] 1 F.C. 331 (T.D.) 445
Columbia Transportation Co. v. F.P. Weaver Coal Co., [1950] Ex. C.R. 167 67
Comeau's Sea Foods Ltd. v. Frank and Troy (The), [1971] F.C. 556 (T.D.) 275, 276
Cominco Ltd. v. Bilton (1970), 15 D.L.R. (3d) 60 (S.C.C.) 432, 438
Comorant Bulk Carriers Inc. v. Canficorp Ltd. (1984), 54 N.R. 66
  (F.C.A.) 428, 430, 431
Compagnie des Forges d'Homecourt v. Gibsons & Co., [1920] S.C. 247 513

Coniston (The) v. Walrod (1918), 19 Ex. C.R. 238, 49 D.L.R. 200 527
Connolly v. Dracona (The) (1896), 5 Ex. C.R. 146, aff'd (1896), 5 Ex.
   C.R. 207 ....611, 612
Conohan v. The Cooperators, [2001] 2 F.C. 238 (T.D.) 328
Conrad v. Snair (1995), 131 D.L.R. (4th) 129 (N.S.C.A.) 720
Conrad v. Snair (1994), 135 N.S.R. (2d) 19 (S.C.(T.D.)) 501, 502
Consumers Distributing Co. v. Dart Containerline Co. (1980), 31 N.R. 181
   (F.C.A.) 766
Coutinho, Caro & Co. v. Ermua (The), [1979] 2 F.C. 528 (T.D.), rev'd [1982]
   1 F.C. 252 (C.A.) 413, 465
Cox v. Brown (1996), 4 C.P.C. (4th) 110 (B.C.C.A.) 551
Cox v. Lenneard (The Trade Up), [1998] F.C.J. No. 291 (T.D.) (QL) 6118
Crabbe v. Canada (Minister of Transport), [1972] F.C. 863 (C.A.) 572
Craven v. Strand Holidays (Canada) Ltd. (1982), 40 O.R. (2d) 186 (C.A.)......482
Crawford v. St. Lawrence Insurance Co. (1851), 8 U.C.Q.B. 135 (C.A.) 324
Crelinsten Fruit Co. v. Mormacsaga (The), [1969] 1 Lloyd's L.R. 515
   (Ex. Ct.) 369
Crelinsten Fruit Co. v. Mormacsaga (The), [1968] 2 Lloyd's Rep. 184
   (Ex. Ct.) 430, 465
Croswell v. Daball (1920), 47 O.L.R. 354, aff'd (1921), 49 O.L.R. 85 150
Crown Steamship Co. v. Lady of Gaspe (The) (1914), 17 Ex. C.R. 191 500
Cuba (The) v. McMillan (1896), 26 S.C.R. 651 522
Cull v. Rose (1982), 139 D.L.R. (3d) 559 (Nfld. T.D.).......................107, 109, 131
Curtis v. Jacques (1978), 20 O.R. (2d) 552, 88 D.L.R. (3d) 112
   (H.C.J.) 41, 516, 550
Cyber Sea Technologies Inc. v. Underwater Harvester Remotely Operated
   Vehicle, [2003] 1 F.C. 569 (T.D.)..145, 150, 151

Dagmar Salen (The) v. Puget Sound Navigation Co., [1950] Ex. C.R. 283,
   rev'd in part, [1951] S.C.R. 608...502, 505, 528
Dancey v. Burns (1880), 31 U.C.C.P. 313 ....629, 639
Darnel v. Pacific Pilotage Authority, [1974] 2 F.C. 580 (C.A.) 572
David McNair & Co. \ v. Santa Malta (The), [1967] 2 Lloyd's Rep. 391
   (Ex. Ct.) 458, 561
Davie v. Young Hustler No. 1 (The) (1962), 32 D.L.R. (2d) 470 (Ex. Ct.) 602
Davie Shipping Ltd. v. Canada (1983), 49 N.R. 305 (F.C.A.) 167
Deep Sea Tankers Ltd. v. Tricape (The), [1958] S.C.R. 585, 16 D.L.R. (2d)
   600 ....403, 529
Degroot v. J.T. O'Bryan & Co. (1979), 15 B.C.L.R. 271 (C.A.) 323
Delano Corp. of America v. Saguenay Terminals Ltd., [1965] 2 Ex. C.R. 313..429
Demitri v. General Accident Indemnity (1996), 41 C.C.L.I. (2d) 49 (B.C.S.C.)....328
Desrosiers v. Fishing Vessel Insurance Plan (1994), 87 F.T.R. 101.....................323
Dome Petroleum v. Hunt International Petroleum Co., [1978]
   1 F.C. 11 (T.D.) 74, 148, 149
Dominion Fish Co. v. Isbester (1910), 43 S.C.R. 637..481
Dominion Glass Co. v. Anglo Indian (The), [1944] S.C.R. 409 448
Dominion Shipping Co. v. D'Entremont, [1948] 4 D.L.R. 719........................429
Donnacona Paper Co. v. Desgagne, [1959] Ex. C.R. 215 67
Doris v. Ferdinand (The) (1998), 155 F.T.R. 236 284

Dorland v. Bonter (1849), 5 U.C.Q.B. 583 578
Drew Brown Ltd. v. Orient Trader (The), [1972] 1 Lloyd's Rep. 35 (Ex. Ct.),
    aff'd [1974] S.C.R. 1286 .... 458, 645, 646, 654
Driscoll v. Millville Marine Insurance Co. (1883), 23 N.B.R. 160 (C.A.), rev'd
    (1884), 11 S.C.R. 183.. 324
Duff v. Progress (The), [1928] Ex. C.R. 157... 280
Dumurra (The) v. Maritime Telegraph & Telephone Co., [1977] 2 F.C. 679, 15
    N.R. 382 (C.A.) 569
Dunphy's Ltd. v. Nancy Caines (The), [1950] 2 D.L.R. 64 (Ex. Ct.) 603, 617
Dunsmuir v. Harold (The) (1894), 4 Ex. C.R. 222...................................... 603

Eastaway v. Lavalee (1912), 5 D.L.R. 229 542
Eastern Canada Towing v. Steel & Engine Products (1977), 24 N.S.R. (2d) 452
    (C.A.) 584
Eastern Steamship Co. v. Canada Atlantic Transit Co., [1929] Ex. C.R. 103....514
Eastwest Produce Co. v. Nordnes (The), [1956] Ex. C.R. 328....................... 461
Edmonstone v. Young (1862), 12 U.C.C.P. 437 375
Efford v. Bondy, [1996] B.C.J. No. 171 (S.C.) (QL) 480, 549, 556, 559
Egmont Towing & Sorting Ltd. v. Telendos (The) (1982), 43 N.R. 147
    (F.C.C.A) 501, 505, 507, 509, 512
El Progreso v. Ralph Misener (The) (1986), 6 F.T.R. 46 .... 501, 512, 516
Elders Grain Company v. M/V Ralph Misener (1997), 125 F.T.R. 209 514
Elecnor S.A. v. Soren Toubro (The) (1996), 114 F.T.R. 134 .... 777, 778
Elkhorn Developments v. Sovereign General Insurance (2000), 18 C.C.L.I. (3d)
    203 (B.C.S.C.) 328
Ellerman Lines v. Gibbs, Nathaniel (Canada), [1986] 2 F.C. 463 (C.A.) 639,
    648, 649, 650
Engine & Leasing Co. v. Atlantic Towing Ltd. (1992), 51 F.T.R. 1 (T.D.),
    var'd (1993), 157 N.R. 292 (F.C.A.), aff'd (1993), 164 N.R. 398
    (F.C.A.) 529, 578, 581

Falconbridge Nickel Mines Ltd. v. Chimo Shipping Ltd., [1969] 2 Ex. C.R. 261,
    aff'd [1974] S.C.R. 933, (1973), 37 D.L.R. (3d) 545 .... 147, 441, 446, 452,
    460,, 452, 459, 460, 465
Falconer Fishing Fleet Ltd. v. Island Prince (The), [1948] Ex. C.R. 378.......... 617
Fanad Head (The) v. Adams, [1949] S.C.R. 407... 514
Federal Business Development Bank v. Commonwealth Insurance Co.,
    [1979] B.C.J. No. 578 (S.C.) (QL).. 329
Federal Business Development Bank v. Winder (The), 4135, [1986] 2 F.C.
    154 (T.D.) 290
Federal Commerce and Navigation Co. v. Eisenerz-G.m.b.H. (The Oak Hill),
    [1974] S.C.R. 1225 .... 452, 629, 631, 641, 642, 643, 644, 645, 647, 650
Feoso Oil Ltd. v. Sarla (The) (1995), 184 N.R. 307 (F.C.A.) 761
Ferguson v. Arctic Transportation (1988), 147 F.T.R. 96 549
Field v. Poole (1994), 51 A.C.W.S. (3d) 758 (B.C.S.C.).................... 150, 548, 557
Finansbanken ASA v. GTS Katie (The) (2002), 216 F.T.R. 176 .... 282, 799
Finning Ltd. v. Federal Business Development Bank (1989), 56 D.L.R. (4th)
    379 (B.C.S.C.) 290
Fishery Products Ltd. v. Claudette V (The) (1960), 44 M.P.R. 391 (Ex. Ct.) 617

Fleet Express Lines Ltd. v. Continental Can Co., [1969] 2 O.R. 97 (H.C.J.)....411
Forward v. Birgitte (The) (1904), 9 Ex. C.R. 339 528
Fraser v. Jean & Joyce (The), [1941] Ex. C.R. 43, [1941] 3 D.L.R. 440 287
Fraser River Harbour Commission v. Hiro Maru (The), [1974] 1 F.C. 490
  (T.D.) 67
Fraser River Pile & Dredge v. Can-Dive Services, [1999] 3 S.C.R. 108 327
Fraser River Pile & Dredge v. Empire Tug Boats (1995), 92 F.T.R. 26 688
Fraser Shipyard & Industrial Centre Ltd. v. Expedient Maritime Co.
  (The Atlantis Two) (1999), 170 F.T.R. 1, rev'd (1999),
  170 F.T.R. 57 ....274, 277, 291, 771, 772, 773, 780, 796, 797, 798
Freiya (The) v. RS (The) (1922), 21 Ex. C.R. 232 516
Frisol Bunckering BV v. MV Alexandria (The) (1991), 47 F.T.R. 3 ....781, 763
Fudge v. Charter Marine Insurance (1992), 97 Nfld. & P.E.I.R. 91
  (Nfld. S.C.) 323, 326
Fudge v. Rideau Marine (Kingston) Ltd. (1991), 33 A.C.W.S. (3d) 648 (Ont.
  Gen. Div.) 171
Fugère v. Duchess of York (The), [1924] Ex. C.R. 95 ....281, 282, 283

G.E. Crippen v. Vancouver Tug Boat Co., [1971] 2 Lloyd's Rep. 207
  (Ex. Ct.) 459, 461, 463
Gallagher v. Taylor (1881), 5 S.C.R. 368 ....311, 326
General Accident Indemnity Co. v. Panache IV (The), [1998] 2 F.C. 455,
  (1997) 139 F.T.R. 167..607
General Marine Assurance Co. v. Ocean Marine Insurance Co. (1899), 16
  Qc. S.C. 170 319
General Traders v. Saguenay Shipping, [1983] C.A. 536, [1983] R.D.J. 386
  (Qc. C.A.) 132
Gerow v. British American Assurance Co. (1889), 16 S.C.R. 524 314
Gibb v. McDonell (1850), 7 U.C.Q.B. 356 ....632, 633
Gilling v. Canada, [2001] F.C.T. 1271 775
Giovanni Amendola (The) v. Vae (Le), [1960] Ex. C.R. 492 558
Gleniffer (The) (1892), 3 Ex. C.R. 57..602, 617
Glovertown Shipyards Ltd. v. Hickey, [1999] N.J. No. 169 (Nfld. S.C.
  (T.D.)) (QL) 156, 168, 169
Grace Kennedy & Co. v. Canada Jamaica Line, [1967] 1 Lloyd's Rep. 336 429
Grace Plastics Ltd. v. Bernd Wesch II (The), [1971] F.C. 273 (T.D.) 411, 445
Grain Growers Export Co. v. Canada Steamship Lines Ltd. (1918),
  43 O.L.R. 330 450
Grand Bank Fisheries Ltd. v. Lake & Lake Ltd., [1955] 4 D.L.R. 493, 37
  M.P.R. 97..361, 362
Gravel & Lake Services v. Bay Ocean Management Inc. (2001), 204
  F.T.R. 225 ....583, 586
Great Lakes Paper Co. v. Paterson Steamships Ltd., [1951] 3 D.L.R. 518
  (Ex. Ct.) 427
Greeley v. Tami Joan (The) (1997), 135 F.T.R. 290 290
Green Forest Lumber v. General Security Insurance, [1980] 1 S.C.R. 176 324
Grover v. Bullock (1849), 5 U.C.Q.B. 297 ....629, 635
Guadano v. Hamburg Chicago Line, [1973] F.C. 726 (T.D.) 445, 453, 461

Gulf & Fraser Fishermen's Credit Union v. Calm C Fish Ltd. (The Calm C),
  [1975] 1 Lloyd's L.R. 188 (B.C.C.A.) 250
Gulf & Lake Navigation Co. v. Woodford (The), [1955] 5 S.C.R. 829 607
Gulf Hathi (The) v. R. (1981), 27 B.C.L.R. 92, 58 C.C.C. (2d) 481, 121 D.L.R.
  (3d) 359 (C.A.) 685, 687
Gulf of Georgia Towing Co. v. Sun Diamond (The) (1977), 17 N.R. 356
  (F.C.A.) 605, 606
Gurney v. MacKay (1875), 37 U.C.Q.B. 324 .... 605, 629, 634, 648

H.B. Contracting Ltd. v. Northland Shipping (1962) Co., (1971), 24 D.L.R. (3d)
  209 (B.C.C.A.) 445
H.B. Nickerson & Sons v. Insurance Co. of North America (The J.E. Kenney),
  [1984] 1 F.C. 575 (C.A.) 329
Halcrow v. Lemesurier (1884), 10 Q.L.R. 239, 21 R.L.O.S. 28 (Q.B.) 634
Haley v. Comox (The) (1920), 20 Ex. C.R. 86 153
Hamildoc (The), 1950 A.M.C. 1973 (Qc. C.A.) 450
Hamilton Harbour Commissioners v. AM German (The), [1973] F.C. 1254
  (T.D.) 152
Hamilton Marine & Engineering v. CSL Group (1995), 99 F.T.R. 285 ....586, 587
Harbour Navigation Co. v. Dinteldyk (The), [1925] Ex. C.R. 10...................... 516
Harrison v. Nelson (1991), 28 A.C.W.S. (3d) 6 (F.T.D.) 545
Hartikainen v. Kane (No. 2) (1976), 15 O.R. (2d) 262 (H.C.J.) 526
Hartikainen v. Kane (1975), 10 O.R. (2d) 716 (C.A.) [sub. nom. Heath v.
  Cane] 132
Heath Steele Mines Ltd. v. Erwin Schröder (The), [1969] 1 Lloyd's L.R. 370
  (Ex. Ct.), aff'd [1970] Ex. C.R. 426 .... 373, 374
Heminger v. Porter (The) (1898), 6 Ex. C.R. 208 506
Herbstreit v. Ontario Regional Assessment Commissioner, Region 15 (1982),
  38 O.R. (2d) 642 (Co. Ct.) 152
Herring Un Ltd. v. Nina M. Conrad (The) (1954), 32 M.P.R. 225 (Nfld. S.C.) 618
Hirtle v. Shanalian (The), [1939] Ex. C.R. 50, [1939] 4 D.L.R. 278 514
Hiscock v. Tommie L. Vincent (The) (1964), 49 M.P.R. 302 (Ex. Ct.) 617
Hollandsche Aannaming Maatschappij v. Ryan Leet (The) (1997),
  135 F.T.R. 67 .... 768, 769, 770
Holt Cargo Systems Inc. v. ABC Containerline N.V., [2001] 3 S.C.R. 907 268,
  273, 275, 294
Holt Cargo Systems Inc. v. ABC Containerline N.V. (The Brussel) (2000),
  185 F.T.R. 145 .... 528, 769, 772, 773, 797, 798
Holt Cargo Systems Inc. v. ABC Containerline N.V. (The Brussel), [1997]
  3 F.C. 187, 131 F.T.R. 41, aff'd (1998), 234 N.R. 98 .... 282, 797
Hoover-Owens Rentschler Co. v. Gulf Navigation Co. (1923), 54
  O.L.R. 483 .... 162, 172
Horsley v. MacLaren, [1972] S.C.R. 441, (1971), 22 D.L.R. (3d) 545 ....40, 554
Hovey v. Swan (1978), 19 O.R. (2d) 725, 86 D.L.R. (3d) 478 (H.C.J.) 526
Humphreys v. Florence No. 2 (The), [1948] Ex. C.R. 426 .... 603, 617

IMO (The) v. General Transatlantic Co., [1920] 2 W.W.R. 428, 51 D.L.R. 403
  (P.C.) 500

ITO International Terminal Operators Ltd. v. Miida Electronics Inc. (The Buenos Aires Maru), [1986] 1 S.C.R. 752 ....3, 113, 114, 115, 126, 129, 134, 135, 136, 138, 307, 438, 752, 802
Imperial Oil Ltd. v. Expo Spirit (The) (1986), 6 F.T.R. 156, aff'd (1987), 80 N.R. 259 ....152, 760, 762
Imperial Oil Ltd. v. Petromar Inc, [2001] F.C.A. 391 275
Imperial Oil Ltd. v. Willowbranch (The), [1964] S.C.R. 402....................504, 514
Insurance Co. of North America v. Colonial Steamships Ltd., [1942] S.C.R. 357..421
Insurance Co. of North America v. Thompson (1987), 31 C.C.L.I. 285 (B.C.S.C.) 328
Intermunicipality Realty & Development Corp. v. Gore Mutual Insurance Co., [1978] 2 F.C. 691 (T.D.) 307, 323
International Wrecking & Transportation Co. v. Lobb (1886), 11 O.R. 408 (C.A.) 611, 617
Interocean Shipping Co. v. Atlantic Splendour (The), [1984] 1 F.C. 931 (T.D.)....530
Irish Shipping Ltd. v. R., [1977] 1 F.C. 485 (T.D.), aff'd [1984] 2 F.C. 777......509
Iron Mac Towing v. North Arm Highlander (The) (1979), 28 N.R. 348 (F.C.A.) 605, 611, 617

Jacobsen v. Archer (The) (1894), 3 B.C.R. 374..618
James Yachts v. Thames and Mersey Marine Insurance, [1977] 1 Lloyd's L.R. 206 (B.C.S.C.) 323, 328
Jian Sheng Co. v. Great Tempo, [1998] 3 F.C. 418 (C.A.) 430
Johnson v. Charles S. Neff (The) (1918), 18 Ex. C.R. 159................280, 606, 611
Joint Stock Society Oceangeotechnology v. 1201 (The), [1994] 2 F.C. 265, 72 F.T.R. 211 (T.D.) 585
Jorgensen v. Chasina (The), [1926] 1 W.W.R. 632 281
Joseph A. Likely Ltd. v. AW Duckett & Co. (1916), 53 S.C.R. 471 361
Joys v. Minister of National Revenue (1995), 189 N.R. 175 (F.C.A.) 786

Kaine v. Sorensen (1892), 1 Qc. S.C. 184..577
Kajat v. Arctic Taglu (The) (1997), 135 F.T.R. 161, rev'd (2000), 252 N.S.R. 152..516
Kalamazoo Paper Company v. Canadian Pacific Railway Co., [1950] S.C.R. 356..457
Kaufman v. New York Underwriters Insurance Co., [1955] O.R. 311 (H.C.J.)....330
Kellog Co. v. Kellog, [1941] S.C.R. 242 135
Kelloway v. Engineering Consultants, [1972] F.C. 932 (T.D.) 605
Kennedy v. Surrey (The) (1905), 11 B.C.L.R. 499 278
Kenney v. Cape York (The) (1989), 25 F.T.R. 139 ....501, 522, 727
Keta (The) v. Irene M. (The), [1959] Ex. C.R. 372, [1959] R.L. 280 617
Keystone Transports Ltd. v. Dominion Steel & Coal Co., [1942] S.C.R. 495....459
Keystone Transports Ltd. v. Ottawa Transportation Co., [1927] Ex. C.R. 123 587
Kidd v. Thomson (1899), 26 O.A.R. 220 ....648, 651
King v. Carius, [1975] F.C.J. No. 514 (F.T.D.) (QL) 157
Kingcome Navigation v. Perdia, [1966] Ex. C.R. 656..................................502, 507
Kingdoc (The) v. Canada Steamship Lines, [1931] S.C.R. 288 507
Kirgan Holding S.A. v. Panamax Leader (The) (2002), 225 F.T.R. 273 273

Knox Bros. Ltd. v. Healthfield (The), [1924] Ex. C.R. 73 388
Koskeemo (The) v. Pacific Rover (The), [1974] 1 F.C. 256
  (T.D.) 506, 510, 511, 522
Kuehne & Nagel International Ltd. v. Redirack Ltd. (1991), 47 C.L.R. 241
  (Gen. Div.) 803
Kwok v. British Columbia Ferry Corp. (1987), 20 B.C.L.R. (2d) 318 (S.C.),
  aff'd (1989), 37 B.C.L.R. (2d) 236 (C.A.) 501, 505, 509, 549

Laing v. Boreal Pacific (2000), 264 N.R. 378 (F.C.A.)...329
Larsen v. Gas Boat (The), [1923] Ex. C.R. 704, [1923] 2 D.L.R. 281 603
Leischner v. West Kootenay Power & Light Co. (1986), 24 D.L.R. (4th) 641
  (B.C.C.A.) 549
Letnik v. Metropolitan Toronto (Municipality of), [1988] 2 F.C. 399(C.A.) 525
Leval & Co. v. Colonial Steamships Ltd., [1961] S.C.R. 221 ....457, 458
Lewis v. Canada (1995), 98 F.T.R. 278 328
Lindal v. Lindal, [1981] 2 S.C.R. 629 530
Lionel (The) v. Manchester Merchant (The), [1970] S.C.R. 538 ......500, 508, 516
Lions Gate Lumber Co. v. Francis Salman (The), [1958] Ex. C.R. 259 587
Liznick v. Hamelin, [1994] O.J. No. 624 (Ont. Gen. Div.) (QL) 545, 549
Llido v. The Lowell Thomas Explorer, [1980] 1 F.C. 339 (T.D.) 798
Lorentzen v. Alcoa Rambler (The), [1949] A.C. 236 (P.C.) 511
Lubrolake (The) v. Sarniadoc (The), [1959] Ex. C.R. 131......504, 514, 516, 527
Lutfy Ltd. v. Canadian Pacific Railway Co., [1973] F.C. 1115 (T.D.)................417
Lynch v. Shaw (1859), 17 U.C.Q.B. 241 153

MacDonald v. Atlantic Salvage, [1925] Ex. C.R. 209 509
MacDonald v. Saint John (1885), 25 N.B.R. 318 (C.A.), aff'd (1886),
  14 S.C.R. 1 ....480, 482
Magdalen Islands Steamship Co. v. Diana (The) (1907), 11 Ex. C.R. 40 618
Maggie (The) v. Honovera (The) (1916), 54 S.C.R. 51 507
Magliaro v. Scotia Wholesale Ltd. (1987), 81 N.S.R. (2d) 201 (C.A.) 803
Manchester Liners v. Scotia Trader (The), [1971] F.C. 14 (T.D.)......606, 607, 618
Manning v. Boston Insurance (1962), 34 D.L.R. (2d) 140 (P.E.I.S.C.)......327, 337
Maplehurst (The) v. George Hall Coal Co., [1923] S.C.R. 507 ....516, 522, 587
Margrande Co. Naviera S.A. v. Leacliffe Hall (The), [1970] Ex. C.R. 870 682
Marie Skou (The) v. Nippon Yusen Kaisha Ltd., [1971] S.C.R. 233 ....502, 512,
  514, 522
Marlex Petroleum Inc. v. Har Rai (The), [1982] 2 F.C. 617 (T.D.), rev'd
  [1984] 2 F.C. 345, 4 D.L.R. (4th) 739 (F.C.A.), aff'd, [1987]
  1 S.C.R. 57...5, 272, 273, 285, 291, 727, 761, 762, 798
Marquis v. Astoria (The), [1931] Ex. C.R. 195...269
Martin v. Derrach (1997), 148 Nfld. & P.E.I.R. 127 (P.E.I.S.C.).......................550
Martin v. Ed McWilliams (The) (1919), 18 Ex. C.R. 470..................................292
Marwell Equipment and British Columbia Bridge & Dredging Co. v. Vancouver
  Tug Boat Co. (1960), 26 D.L.R. (2d) 80 (S.C.C.) 328
Mason v. Peters (1982), 139 D.L.R. (3d) 104 (C.A.) 557
Maxine Footwear Co. v. Canadian Government Merchant Marine Ltd., [1959]
  A.C. 589 (P.C.)..446, 451, 453, 458, 475
McAdam v. Ross (1890), 22 N.S.R. 264 481

McBride v. American (The), [1924] Ex. C.R. 227 .... 277, 283, 284
McCain Produce Co. v. Rea (The) (1977), 80 D.L.R. (3d) 105, [1978]
   1 F.C. 686 (T.D.) 279, 291
McCormick v. Sincennes McNaughton Lines (1918), 18 Ex. C.R. 357 577
McCullough v. Samuel Marshall (The), [1924] Ex. C.R. 53 282
McDougall v. Aeromarine of Emsworth Ltd., [1958] 1 W.L.R. 1126 (Q.B.) 162
McElhaney v. Flora (The) (1898), 6 Ex. C.R. 129 281
McFaul v. Montreal Inland Insurance Co. (1845), 2 U.C.Q.B. 59 (C.A.) 323
McKenzie Barge & Derrick Co. v. Rivtow Marine (1968), 70 D.L.R. (2d) 409
   (Ex. Ct.), aff'd (1969), 7 D.L.R. (3d) 96 (S.C.C.) 579
McLeod v. Minnesota Pulp & Paper Co., [1955] Ex. C.R 344 .... 147, 150, 592
McNamara Construction (Western) Ltd. v. R., [1977] 2 S.C.R. 654 .... 3, 121, 122,
   126, 135
Meeker Log and Timber Ltd. v. Sea IMP VIII (The) (1994), 1 B.C.L.R. (3d)
   320 (S.C.) 581
Merchants Marine Insurance v. Barss (1888), 15 S.C.R. 185 324
Merchants Marine Insurance Co. of Canada v. Rumsey (1884), 9 S.C.R. 577 .. 324
Merlo, Merlo & Ray v. Harry R. Jones (The), [1925] Ex. C.R. 183 509
Mesis (The) v. Louis Wolfe & Sons (Vancouver) Ltd., [1977] 1 F.C.
   429 (C.A.) 775
Metaxas v. Galaxias (The), [1990] 2 F.C. 400 (T.D.) 276, 281, 799
Metaxas v. Galaxias (No. 2) (The), [1989] 1 F.C. 386 (T.D.) 282, 483, 548,
   796, 797, 798
Metaxas v. Galaxias (No. 4) (The) (1988), 24 F.T.R. 243 .... 798, 799
Midland Navigation Co. v. Dominion Elevator Co. (1904), 34 S.C.R. 578 389
Monarch Towing & Trading Co. v. British Columbia Cement Co., [1957]
   S.C.R. 816 736
Moncton (City of) v. Aprile Contracting Ltd. (1980), 29 N.B.R. (2d)
   631 (C.A.) 158
Monk Corp. v. Island Fertilizers Ltd., [1991] 1 S.C.R. 779 ...... 128, 129, 136, 307,
   802
Montreal Dry Docks & Ship Repairing Co. v. Halifax Shipyards Ltd. (1920), 60
   S.C.R. 359 .... 276, 277, 289, 290
Montreal Trust Co. v. Canadian Surety Co. (1937), 35 C.S. 278 .... 629, 644
Morguard Investments Ltd. v. De Savoye, [1990] 3 S.C.R. 1077 275
Mormacsaga (The), [1968] 2 Lloyd's L.R. 184 (Ex. Ct.) 394
Morris v. Canada (Min. of Fisheries & Oceans) (1991), 47 F.T.R. 271 330
Mount Royal Walsh Inc. v. Jensen Star (The) (1989), 99 N.R. 42 (F.C.A.) 761,
   763, 770
Mowat v. Boston Marine Insurance (1896), 26 S.C.R. 47 330

N.B. Electric Power Commission v. Maritime Electric Co. (1985), 60 N.R.
   203 (F.C.A.) 472
NHM International Inc. v. F.C. Yachts Ltd. (2003), 227 F.T.R. 42 795
N.M. Paterson & Sons Ltd. v. Mannix Ltd., [1966] S.C.R. 180 .... 387, 459
N.M. Paterson & Sons Ltd. v. Robin Hood Flour Mills Ltd., (The Farrandoc),
   [1968] 1 Ex. C.R. 175 361
N.M. Patterson & Sons Ltd. v. Birchglen (The), [1990] 3 F.C. 301 (T.D.) 285, 286
Nabob Foods Ltd. v. Cape Corso (The), [1954] 2 Lloyd's L.R. 40 (Ex. Ct.) 446

Nanoose Conversion Campaign v. Canada (Minister of Environment) (2000),
    257 N.R. 287(F.C.A.) 674
National Bank of Canada v. Atomic Slipper Co., [1991] 1 S.C.R. 1059 252
Neves v. Kristina Logos (The), 2002 FCA 502, aff'g in part [2001] FCT 1034 282
Neves v. Kristina Logos (The) (1999), 173 F.T.R. 31, varied 2001 FCT 1034
    (T.D.) 784, 792
Neves v. Kristina Logos (The) (1996), 124 F.T.R. 167, aff'd (1998), 225
    N.R. 32 (F.C.A.) 784, 792
Neville Canneries v. Santa Maria (The) (1917), 16 Ex. C.R. 481......................292
New England Fish Co. of Oregon v. Britamerican, [1959] Ex. C.R. 256 507
New Ontario Steamship Co. v. Montreal Transportation Co. (1907),
    11 Ex. C.R. 113, rev'd (1908) 40 S.C.R. 160...506
Newfoundland Processing Ltd. v. South Angela (The), [1997] 1 F.C. 154, (1996)
    121 F.T.R. 178 (T.D.)...685
Nicholson v. Canada, [2000] 3 F.C. 225 (T.D.)...552
Nicholson v. Joyland (The), [1931] Ex. C.R. 70...281
Nickimen Co. v. Executive Venture (The), [1973] F.C. 1108 (T.D.) 645, 651
Nisbet Shipping v. R., [1951] 4 D.L.R. 225 (Ex. Ct.) 115
Nissan Automobile Co. (Canada) v. Continental Shipper (The), [1976]
    2 Lloyd's Rep. 234 (F.C.A.)..461
Noranda Sales Corp. v. Ship British Tay (1994), 77 F.T.R. 8............................771
Nord-Deutsche Versicherungs-Gesellshaft v. R., [1969] 1 Ex. C.R. 117, var'd
    [1971] S.C.R. 849...60, 749
Norlympia Seafoods Ltd. v. Dale & Co., [1983] I.L.R. 1-1688 (B.C.S.C.) 328
Norman v. Canadian National Railway (1980), 27 Nfld. & P.E.I.R. 451
    (Nfld. S.C.)...459
North Star Marine Salvage v. Muren, [1973] F.C. 50, 36 D.L.R. (3d) 136
    (T.D.) 610, 611, 612
Northland Navigation Co. v. Patterson Boiler Works, [1983] 2 F.C. 59 632,
    ....633, 650
Nova Scotia Marine Insurance Co. v. L.P. Churchill & Co. (1896), 26 S.C.R. 65..313

Ocean Towing & Salvage Co. v. Penny Hope (The), [1980] F.C.J. No. 1103
    (T.D.) (QL)...605, 617
Offshore Atlantic v. Marystown Shipyard Ltd. (1988), 31 C.L.R. 12 (Nfld. S.C.
    (T.D.)), rev'd 43 C.L.R. 272 (Nfld. C.A.)..166, 167
O'Keefe & Lynch v. Toronto Insurance and Vessel Agency, [1926] 4 D.L.R. 477
    (Ont. S.C.) 321
Ontario v. Mar-Dive Corp. (1997), 141 D.L.R. (4th) 577 (Ont. Ct. Gen. Div.)....618
Ontario (AG) v. Pembina Exploration Canada, [1989] 1 S.C.R. 206 ......109, 131,
    132, 133
Ontario Central Airlines v. Gustafson (1957), 8 D.L.R. (2d) 584
    (Ont. C.A.) 152, 514
Ontario Gravel Freighting Co. v. Matthews Steamship Co., [1927] S.C.R. 92 516
Orchard v. Aetna Insurance Co. (1856), 5 U.C.C.P. 445 (C.A.) 324
Ordon Estate v. Grail (1996), 30 O.R. (3d) 643 (C.A.), aff'd [1998] 3 S.C.R.
    437 ....3, 8, 13, 99, 115, 116, 125, 131, 133, 134, 135, 136–38, 172, 308,
    ....398, 522, 545, 546, 547, 552, 553, 557, 558

Oregon Stevedoring Co. v. Number Four (The), [1984] F.C.J. No. 121 (T.D.)
(QL) 273, 291
Orr v. Ontario Boaters Brokerage Ltd. (1990), 24 A.C.W.S. (3d) 119 (Ont. Gen.
Div.) 168
Osborn Refrigeration Sales & Service Inc. v. Atlantean I (The), [1979]
2 F.C. 661 (T.D.), aff'd (1982), 7 D.L.R. (4th) 395, 52 N.R. 10
(F.C.A.) 251, 276, 294, 798
Östgöta Enskilda Bank v. Sea Star (The) (1994), 78 F.T.R. 304 294
Outhouse v. Thorshavn (The), [1935] Ex. C.R. 120, [1935] 4 D.L.R. 628 688
Outtrim v. British Columbia, [1948] 3 D.L.R. 273 (B.C.C.A.) 381
Oxley v. Spearwater (1867), 7 N.S.R. 144...285
Oy Nokia Ab v. Martha Russ (The), [1973] F.C. 394 (T.D.), varied [1974]
1 F.C. 410 112
Oyler v. Merriam (1922–24), 56 N.S.R. 64 426

PG du Canada v. Services d'Hôtellerie Maritimes, [1968] C.S. 431 (Qc. S.C.) ..151
PG du Québec v. Vincent, [1984] C.S. 1037 (Qc. S.C.) 150
Pacific Express (The) v. Salvage Princess (The), [1949] Ex. C.R. 230..............736
Pacific Tractor Rentals (V.I.) Ltd. v. Palaquin (The) (1996), 115 F.T.R.
224 ....774, 791
Palleschi v. Romita, [1988] O.J. No. 822 (Ont. Dist. Ct.) (QL) 545
Panagiotis TH. Coumantaros (The) v. Canada (Nat. Harbours Board), [1942]
S.C.R. 450..741
Paramount Enterprises International Inc. v. An Xin Jiang (The) (1997),
146 F.T.R. 161, rev'd in part (1997), 147 F.T.R. 162, aff'd [2001]
2 F.C. 551, 265 N.R. 354 (F.C.A.) 761
Pare v. Rail & Water Terminal (Que), [1978] 1 F.C. 23 (T.D.).........................548
Paterson Steamships Ltd. v. ALCAN, [1951] S.C.R. 852 ....401, 428, 429, 430
Paterson Steamships Ltd. v. Canadian Co-operative Wheat Producers Ltd.,
[1934] A.C. 538 (P.C.) 363, 364, 393
Paterson Timber Co. v. British Columbia (The) (1913), 16 Ex. C.R. 305 592
Pearce v. Leatherby (1905), 6 O.W.R. 606 611
Pembina Resources Ltd. v. ULS International Inc. (1989), [1990] 1 F.C. 666,
28 F.T.R. 180..528, 528, 744
Perrigoue v. British Columbia Ferry Authority, [1966] Ex. C.R. 744........502, 504
Peterborough (The) v. Bell Telephone Co. of Canada, [1952] Ex. C.R. 462 744
Petten v. E.Y.E. Marine Consultants (1998), 180 Nfld. & P.E.I.R. 1 (Nfld.
S.C.(T.D.)) 156, 164, 166
Philip T. Dodge (The) v. Dominion Bridge Co., [1935] 4 D.L.R. 65, [1936] 1
W.W.R. 94 (P.C.)..536
Phoenix Assurance v. Golden Imports (1989), 43 C.C.L.I. 313 (B.C. Co. Ct.)..324
Phoenix Insurance v. McGhee (1890), 18 S.C.R. 61.................................313, 314
Pigeon River Lumber Co. v. Mooring (1909), 13 O.W.R. 190, aff'd
14 O.W.R. 639 147
Pointe Anne Quarries Ltd. v. MF Whalen (The), [1923] 1 D.L.R. 45 (P.C.) 577
Polish Ocean Lines v. Maple Branch (The) (1982), 15 A.C.W.S. (2d) 61 ....505, 512
Porto Seguro Companhia de Seguros Gerais v. Belcan S.A., [1997] 3
S.C.R. 1278...112, 136
Pouliot v. Canada (Minister of Transport), [1965] Que. P.R. 51 (S.C.) 571

Primex Forest Products v. Harken Towing Co., [1997] B.C.J. No. 1644,
(S.C.) (QL) 581
Princess Adelaide (The) v. Fred Olsen & Co., [1931] S.C.R. 254 526
Prins Frederik Willem (The) v. Gayport Shipping, [1960] Ex. C.R. 274 508
Prins Willem III (The), [1972] 2 D.L.R. 124 , [1973] 2 Lloyd's L.R. 124 (Qc.
C.A.) 443
Providence Washington Insurance v. Corbett (1884), 9 S.C.R. 256 314
Providence Washington Insurance v. Gerow (1890), 17 S.C.R. 387 330

Q.N.S. Paper Co. v. Chartwell Ltd, [1989] 2 S.C.R. 683 .... 113, 114, 130, 136
Quebec and Ontario Transportation Co. v. Incan St. Laurent (The), [1979]
2 F.C. 834 (C.A.), aff'd [1980] 2 S.C.R. 242 123
Quebec Marine Ins. Co. v. Commercial Bank of Canada (1870), L.R. 3 P.C. 234 8
Quebec North Shore Paper Co. v. Canadian Pacific Ltd., [1977] 2 S.C.R. 1054 .. 3
Queen Charlotte Fisheries v. Tyee Shell (The), [1966] Ex. C.R. 724 508

R. v. Aqua Clean Ships (1994), 12 C.E.L.R. (N.S.) 241 (B.C. Prov. Ct.) 675
R. v. Aran (The) (1973), 7 C.C.C. (2d) 562 (B.C.S.C.) 685
R. v. Caird (1993), 16 Cr. L.Q. 112 (B.C. Co. Ct.) 685
R. v. Canada Steamship Lines, [1927] S.C.R. 68... 482
R. v. Cole (1976), 31 C.C.C. (2d) 427 (Ont. C.A.)... 541
R. v. Crown Zellerbach Canada Ltd., [1988] 1 S.C.R. 401 579
R. v. Dilkara (The), [1974] 1 W.W.R. 258 (B.C.C.A.).................................685, 687
R. v. Empire Sandy Inc. (1987), 62 O.R. (2d) 641 (C.A.) 201, 481
R. v. Ernst (1979), 50 C.C.C. (2d) 320 (N.S.C.A.) 542
R. v. Esso Resources Canada, [1983] N.W.T.R. 59 (Terr. Ct.)............................ 685
R. v. Fernandez (1980), 29 Nfld. & P.E.I.R. 361 (Nfld. S.C.(T.D.)) 562
R. v. Gatt (1992), 72 C.C.C. (3d) 146 (B.C.S.C.) 150, 151
R. v. General Motors Canada (1984), 48 O.R. (2d) 204 (H.C.J.) 152
R. v. Glenshiel Towing Co. (2001), 154 B.C.A.C. 310....................................... 685
R. v. Guildford (City of) (1975), 27 C.C.C. (2d) 212 (Ont. Co. Ct.)................. 687
R. v. Gulf of Aladdin (1977), 34 C.C.C. (2d) 460 (B.C.C.A) 147
R. v. Harlem (The) (1919), 59 S.C.R. 653.. 511
R. v. Himmerland (1973), 2 C.E.L.R. 17 687
R. v. Hochelaga Shipping and Towing Co., [1940] S.C.R. 153 781
R. v. J.D. Irving Ltd., [1999] 2 F.C. 346 (T.D.) 685
R. v. Levis Ferry, [1962] S.C.R. 629 511
R. v. M.T. Barbro (1992), 121 N.B.R. (2d) 379, 304 A.P.R. 379 (Prov. Ct.) 685
R. v. MV Allunga, [1977] 3 W.W.R. 673 (B.C.C.A.) 685
R. v. M/V Humber Arm (The) (2000), NS Prov. Ct. Case #878518, 19 January
2000 [unreported] 685
R. v. MV Point Vibert (The), [2000] N.S.J. No. 147 (N.S. Prov. Ct.) (QL) 685
R. v. Montreal Shipping Co., [1956] Ex. C.R. 280 443
R. v. Nitrochem (1992), 8 C.E.L.R. (N.S.) 283 (Ont. Prov. Div.) 210
R. v. Nord-Deutsche Versicherungs Gesellschaft, [1971] S.C.R. 849....59, 527, 743
R. v. Petite, [1933] Ex. C.R. 186 509
R. v. S.G. Marshall (The) (1870), 1 P.E.I. 316.. 153
R. v. Saint John Shipbuilding & Drydock Co. (1981), 126 D.L.R. (3d) 353
(F.C.A.) 74

R. v. Salituro, [1991] 3 S.C.R. 654 137
R. v. Sault Ste Marie, [1978] 2 S.C.R. 1299 ....685, 687
R. v. Sauvageau, [1950] S.C.R. 664 624
R. v. Spencer, [1985] 2 S.C.R. 278 275
R. v. Star Luzon (The), [1984] 1 W.W.R. 527 (B.C.S.C.) 146, 685
R. v. Stogdale (1993), 46 M.V.R. (2d) 279 (Ont. Gen. Div.), rev'd (1995), 20
    M.V.R. (3d) 168 (Ont. C.A.) 542
R. v. Sun Diamond (The), [1984] 1 F.C. 3 (T.D.) 681
R. v. Tavares, (27 July 1994), Newfoundland (Prov. Ct.) [Unreported], aff'd
    (1995), 131 Nfld. & P.E.I.R. 271 (Nfld. T.D.), rev'd (1996), 144 Nfld. &
    P.E.I.R. 154 (Nfld. C.A.) 784
R. v. Ulybel Enterprise Ltd. (1997), 150 Nfld. & P.E.I.R. 308 (Nfld. T.D.),
    rev'd in part (1999), 178 Nfld. & P.E.I.R. 321 (Nfld. C.A), rev'd [2001]
    2 S.C.R. 867 784
R. v. Vorgic, [1983] O.J. No. 352 (H.C.J.) (QL) 150
R. v. Wade (1975), 23 C.C.C. (2d) 572 (N.S. Co. Ct.) 542
R. v. Walters (1977), 5 B.C.L.R. 280 (Prov. Ct.) 542
R. v. Westfalia (The), [1975] 2 W.W.R. 134, 54 D.L.R. (3d) 412 (B.C.C.A.) ....685.
R. v. Wholesale Travel Group Inc., [1991] 3 S.C.R. 154..685
R. v. Zingre, [1981] 2 S.C.R. 392 385
Rankin v. Eliza Fisher (The) (1895), 4 Ex. C.R. 461 282
Rast v. Killoran, [1995] B.C.J. No. 1354 (B.C.S.C.) (QL)..........................480, 549
Re Allison (1998), 38 O.R. (3d) 337 (C.A.) 800
Re Bread Man Inc. (1979), 89 D.L.R. (3d) 599 (Ont. H.C.J.) 800
Re Empire Shipping Co. & Hall Bryan Ltd., [1940] 1 D.L.R. 695 (B.S.S.C.)....383
Re The Insurance Act of Canada, [1932] A.C. 41 (P.C.) 125
Re Unus Shipping Co., [1937] 2 D.L.R. 239 (N.S.S.C.) 361
Re Zambesi (The) (1891), 3 Ex. C.R. 67, 2 B.C.R. 91 603
Red Barge Line Ltd. v. Poplarboy (The), [1932] Ex. C.R. 209 514
Rederiet Odfjell A/S v. Vesuvio (The), [1930] Ex. C.R. 207.............................505
Reference Re Mineral and other Natural Resources of the Continental Shelf
    (1983), 145 D.L.R. (3d) 9 (Nfld. C.A.). 102
Reference Re Ownership of Offshore Mineral Rights, [1967] S.C.R. 792 102
Reference Re Ownership of the Bed of the Strait of Georgia, (AG of Canada v.
    AG of British Columbia) (1984), 8 D.L.R. (4th) 161 (S.C.C.) 102
Reference Re s. 92 Motor Vehicle Act, [1982] 2 S.C.R. 486.................................687
Reference Re Special War Revenue Act, Section 16, [1942] S.C.R. 429............125
Reference Re the Seabed and Subsoil of the Continental Shelf Offshore
    Newfoundland (1984), 5 D.L.R. (4th) 385 (S.C.C.) 102
Reide v. Queen of the Isles (The) (1892), 3 Ex. C.R. 258 284
Remorqueurs du Québec v. Keystone Navigation (1990), 45 F.T.R. 64 585
Rhone (The) v. Peter A.B. Widener (The), [1993] 1 S.C.R. 497 ......522, 586, 588,
    720, 732, 735–37
Richardson International Ltd. v. Mys Chikhacheva (The) (2001), 200 F.T.R. 76,
    aff'd [2002] 4 F.C. 80 (C.A.) 285
Richelieu (The) v. Cie de Navigation Saguenay & Lac St. Jean, [1945]
    S.C.R. 659..506, 518
Riverside Landmark v. Northumberland General Insurance (1984), 8 C.C.L.I.
    118 (Ont. S.C.)...328

Robert J. Paisley (The) v. James Richardson & Sons Ltd., [1929] S.C.R. 359, rev'd [1930] 2 D.L.R. 257 (P.C.) 528
Robert Simpson Montreal Limited v. Hamburg America Line Norddeutscher, [1973] F.C. 1356 (C.A.) 118, 121
Robertson v. Maple Prince (The), [1955] Ex. C.R. 225 736
Robertson v. Maple Prince (The), [1955] Ex. C.R. 221 501
Robillard v. St. Roch (The) (1921), 21 Ex. C.R. 132 ....109, 153
Robin Hood Flour Mills v. N.M. Patterson & Sons Ltd., [1967] 1 Ex. C.R. 431 720
Rose v. Borisko Brothers Ltd. (1983), 41 O.R. (2d) 606, 147 D.L.R. (3d) 191 (C.A.) 327
Rose v. Weekes (1984), 7 C.C.L.I. 287 (F.C.T.D.)..314
Ross v. Aragon (The), [1943] Ex. C.R. 41 282
Rover Shipping Co. v. Kaipaki (The), [1948] Ex. C.R. 507 514
Royal Bank of Canada v. Bank of Montreal (1976), 67 D.L.R. (3d) 755 (Sask. C.A.) 260
Royal Bank of Canada v. Nova Scotia (Workers/Workmen's Compensation Board), [1936] S.C.R. 560 252
Royal Bank of Canada v. Queen Charlotte Fisheries Ltd. (1981), 13 B.L.R. 306, aff'd (1983), 50 B.C.L.R. 128 (C.A.) 261
Royal Bank of Scotland v. Kimisis III (The), [1999] F.C.J. No. 300 (T.D.) (QL)..781
Rumely v. Vera M (The), [1923] Ex. C.R. 36 288
Rusden v. Pope (1868), L.R. 3 Ex. 269 249
Russell v. Aetna Insurance Co. (1975), 75 I.L.R. 1-699, [1975] O.J. No. 911 (S.C.C.A.) (QL) 336
Russell v. Canadian General Insurance Co. (1999), 11 C.C.L.I. (3d) 284, (Ont. Ct. Gen. Div.) 336
Russell v. Gloria (The), [1927] Ex. C.R. 162 ....587, 599
Russell v. McColl Brothers (1931), 40 O.W.N. 355 (S.C.) 593

S/S Steamship Co. v. Eastern Caribbean Container Line, [1986] 2 F.C. 27 (C.A.) 376
Sabb Inc. v. Shipping Ltd., [1976] 2 F.C. 175 (T.D.)...763
Sail Labrador Ltd. v. Challenge One (The), [1999] 1 S.C.R. 265 ......174,368, 384
Saint John Shipbuilding and Dry Dock Co. v. Kingsland Maritime Corp. (1981), 126 D.L.R. (3d) 332 (F.C.A.) 413, 412, 440
Schweizerische Metallwerke Selve & Co. v. Atlantic Container Line Ltd (1986), 63 N.R. 104 (F.C.A.) 471
Scindia Steam Navigation Co. v. Canada, [1985] F.C.J. No. 1130 (T.D.) (QL) 787
Scott Steel v. Alarissa (The) (1997), 125 F.T.R. 284, aff'g [1996] 2 F.C. 883 (T.D.) 276, 279, 282, 288, 289, 799
Scottish Metropolitan Assurance Co. v. Canada Steamship Lines Ltd., [1930] S.C.R. 262..336, 579
Sea Lion (The) (1921), 20 Ex. C.R. 137 525
Sea Prince Fishing v. Kalamalka (The) (1967), 61 D.L.R. (2d) 700 (Ex. Ct.) 506, 508, 516
Seafarers' International Union of Canada v. Crosbie Offshore Services Ltd, [1982] 2 F.C. 855, (1982), 135 D.L.R. (3d) 485 (C.A.) 149
Shanalian (The) v. Dr. Brinkley II (The), [1940] S.C.R. 578 ....605, 606, 612

Shaw Savill & Albion Co. v. Electric Reduction Sales Co. (The Mahia),
[1955] 1 Lloyd's Rep. 264 (Qc. S.C.) 372, 374
Shearwater Marine Ltd. v. Guardian Insurance Co. of Canada (1997), 29
B.C.L.R. (3d) 13 (S.C.), aff'd (1998), 60 B.C.L.R. (3d) 37 (C.A.) 328
Sheerwood v. Lake Eyre (The), [1970] Ex. C.R. 672 445
Shelburne Marine v. MacKinnon & Olding (1997), 163 N.S.R. (2d) 257
(S.C.) 727
Sherman v. Good Hope II (The), [1950] Ex. C.R. 430 605
Shibamoto & Co. v. Western Fish Producers (1989), 63 D.L.R. (4th) 549
(F.C.A.), aff'g 29 F.T.R. 311 (T.D.) 74
Shipman v. Morrell (1920), 19 O.W.N. 132 (C.A.) 589
Shipman v. Phinn (1914), 19 D.L.R. 305(H.C.J.), aff'd (1914), 20 D.L.R.
596 (C.A.) 109, 131
Shulman (Guardian ad litem of) v. McCallum, [1991] 6 W.W.R. 470
(B.C.S.C.),aff'd (1993), 105 D.L.R. (4th) 327 (B.C.C.A.) 545
Simpson v. Kruger (The) (1914), 19 Ex. C.R. 64 280
Sincennes-McNaughton v. Steel Chemist (The), [1928] Ex. C.R. 182 511
Skyron and Hel (The), [1994] 2 Lloyd's L.R. 254 .... 504, 517
Smith v. Smith, [1979] 4 W.W.R. 665 (B.C.S.C.) 603
Sociedad Transoceanica Canopus S.A. v. Canada (Nat. Harbours Board),
[1968] 2 Ex. C.R. 330 .... 67, 501, 536
Spellacy v. Marine Management Inc., [1998] N.J. No. 20 (Nfld. S.C. (T.D.))
(QL) 172
Ssangyong Australia Pty. Ltd. v. Looiersgracht (The) (1994), 85
F.T.R 265 .... 767, 768, 770
St. John (City of) v. Donald, [1926] S.C.R. 371 438
St. Lawrence Cement Inc. v. Wakeham & Sons Ltd. (1995), 26 O.R. (3d) 321
(C.A.) 580
St. Lawrence Construction v. Federal Commerce and Navigation Co., [1985]
1 F.C. 767 (C.A.) 454, 644, 647
St. Lawrence Transportation Co. v. Amedee T. (The), [1924] Ex. C.R. 204 280
St. Simeon Navigation Inc v. A. Couturier & Fils Ltée., [1974] S.C.R.
1176 .... 448, 449
Stack v. Leopold (The) (1918), 18 Ex. C.R. 325 292
Stad v. Fireman's Fund Insurance Co., [1979] I.L.R. 1-1070 (B.C.S.C.) ..329, 336
Standard Oil Co. v. Ikala (The), [1929] Ex. C.R. 230 507
Stein v. Kathy K (The), [1972] F.C. 585 (T.D.), aff'd [1976] 2
S.C.R. 802 .... 135, 136, 137, 501, 517, 522, 545, 549, 720, 736
Steves v. Kinnie, [1917] 1 W.W.R. 1250, 33 D.L.R. 776 (B.C.S.C.) 536, 554
Stone v. Rochepoint (The) (1921), 21 Ex. C.R. 143 .... 153, 281, 283
Strandhill (The) v. Walter W. Hodder Co., [1926] S.C.R. 680 .... 269, 270
Sunnyside Greenhouses Ltd. v. Golden West Seeds Ltd. (1972), 27 D.L.R.
(3d) 434 (Alta. C.A.), aff'd [1973] 3 W.W.R. 288 (S.C.C.) 464, 465
Sunrise Co. v. Lake Winnipeg (The) (1987), 12 F.T.R. 57, var'd (1988),
28 F.T.R. 78, aff'd [1991] 1 S.C.R. 3 .... 307, 507, 522, 529
Symes v. City of Windsor (The) (1895), 4 Ex. C.R. 362, aff'd (1895),
4 Ex. C.R. 400 283

Tahsis Co. v. Vancouver Tug Boat Co. (1965), 54 W.W.R. 395 (B.C.S.C.) 444

Table of Cases 869

Thorne Riddell Inc. v. Nicole N. Enterprises Ltd., [1985] 2 F.C. 31 (T.D.) 762
Thornton v. Prince George (Board of Education), [1978] 2 S.C.R. 267............530
Tilley v. Georgian Bay Airways, [1950] O.W.N. 852 (H.C.J.)..............................514
Todd Shipyards Corp. v. Altema Compania Maritima S.A. (The Ioannis
  Daskalelis) (1972), 32 D.L.R. (3d) 571, [1974] S.C.R. 1248....270, 271, 272,
  727, 798
Tolofson v. Jensen, [1994] 3 S.C.R. 1022 275
Toronto Harbour Commissioners. v. Toryoung II (The), [1976] 1 F.C. 191
  (T.D.) 277, 280
Toronto Window Mfg. Co. v. Audrey S (The), [1965] 1 Ex. C.R. 83 574
Translink France Outre Mer S.A. v. Pegasus Lines Ltd. S.A. (1996),
  207 N.R. 293 (C.A.) 761
Transocean Gateway Corp. v. Weser Isle (The), [1974] 2 F.C. 90 (C.A.)..787, 788
Trepanier v. Kloster Cruise Ltd. (1995), 23 O.R. (3d) 398 (Gen. Div.) 482
Trigg v. MI Movers International Transport Services Ltd. (1991), 4 O.R.
  (3d) 562 (C.A.) 482
Triglav v. Terrasses Jewellers Inc., [1983] 1 S.C.R. 283........6, 113, 124, 125, 126,
  127, 128, 307
Tropwood AG v. Sivaco Wire & Nail Co., [1979] 2 S.C.R. 157 ......122, 123, 131
Tucker v. Tecumseh (The) (1905), 10 Ex. C.R. 149 506
Turgel Fur Co. Ltd. v. Northumberland Ferries Ltd. (1966), 59 D.L.R. (2d)
  1 (N.S.S.C.) 459, 482

Ultramar Canada v. Mutual Marine Office (1994), 82 F.T.R. 1 ....653, 654
Ultramar Canada v. Pierson Steamships (1982), 43 C.B.R. (N.S.) 9
  (F.C.T.D.) 294, 798
Union Carbide Corp. v. FednavLtd. (The Hudson Bay) (1997), 131 F.T.R. 241,
  1998 A.M.C. 429 430
United Nations v. Atlantic Seaways Corp., [1979] 2 F.C. 541 (C.A.) 471
Upper Lakes Shipping Ltd. v. Saint John Shipbuilding and Dry Dock Co., [1985]
  F.C.J. No. 526 (T.D.), aff'd (1988), 86 N.R. 40 (F.C.A.) 157, 158, 164, 165
Upson Walton Co. v. Brian Boru (The) (1906), 10 Ex. C.R. 176 281

Vancouver v. Rhodes, [1955] 1 D.L.R. 139 (B.C.S.C.) 719
Vermont Steamship Co. v. Abby Palmer (The) (1904), 9 Ex. C.R. 1 618

Walther Herwig (The) v. Fishery Products Ltd., [1978] 1 F.C. 111, 76 D.L.R.
  (3d) 757 (T.D.)..606, 607
Ward v. Yosemite (The) (1894), 4 Ex. C.R. 241 526
Washington (The), [1976] 2 Lloyd's L.R. 453 (F.C.T.D.) 457, 459
Watkins v. Olafson, [1989] 2 S.C.R. 750, 61 D.L.R. (4th) 577 137
Watts v. John Irwin (The) (1909), 12 Ex. C.R. 374 513
Webb v. Port Bruce Harbour Co. (1861), 19 U.C.Q.B. 623 741
Weir v. Bank of Nova Scotia (1979), 30 Nfld. & P.E.I.R. 223 (Nfld. T.D.)........290
Weir & Lewisporte Shipyards Ltd. v. Bank of Nova Scotia (1979), 30 Nfld. &
  P.E.I.R. 223 (Nfld. S.C.T.D.)..250
Westcan Stevedoring Ltd. v. Armar (The) (1973) F.C. 1232 (T.D.)..........279, 291
Westcoast Food Brokers v. Hoyanger (The) (1979), 31 N.R. 82 (F.C.A.)....448, 461

Western Assurance Co. v. Ontario Coal Co. of Toronto (1892), 21
S.C.R. 383 ....648, 650
Western Canada Steamship Co. v. Canadian Commercial Corp., [1960] S.C.R.
632 ....638, 639, 647
Whitbread v. Walley, [1990] 3 S.C.R. 1273 ....116, 130, 136, 545, 554
William B. Branson Ltd. v. Jadranska Slobodna Plovidba (The Split), [1973] 2
Lloyd's Rep. 535 (F.C.) 461
Williamson v. Loonstra (1973), 34 D.L.R. (3d) 275 (B.C.S.C.) 800
Wire Rope Industries v. British Columbia Marine Shipbuilders, [1981]
1 S.C.R. 363 ....124, 165, 577, 578, 579

Yuri Maru (The) and Woron (The), [1927] A.C. 906 (P.C.).............................109

Z.I. Pompey Industrie v. ECU-Line N.V., [2003] S.C.C. 27 472

United Kingdom

A.E. Reed & Co. v. Page, Son & East Ltd., [1927] 1 K.B. 743 362
AG of Ceylon v. Seindia Steam Navigation Co., [1962] A.C. 60 (P.C.)....413, 448
Accomac (The) (1890), 15 P.D. 208 394
Achille Lauro Fu Gioacchino & Co. v. Total Societa Italiana Per Azioni,
[1968] 2 Lloyd's L.R. 247...364
Achilleus (The), [1985] 2 Lloyd's L.R. 338..508
Acrux (The), [1962] 1 Lloyd's Rep. 405 288
Action S.A. v. Britannic Shipping Corp. (The Aegis Britanic), [1987] 1 Lloyd's
L.R. 119 (C.A.)..398
Adamastos Shipping Co. Ltd. v. Anglo-Saxon Petroleum Co., [1959] A.C. 133....443
Adler v. Dickson (The Himalaya), [1954] 2 Lloyd's Rep. 267 (C.A.).........438, 482
Admiral Shipping Co. v. Weidner, Hopkins & Co., [1916] 1 K.B. 429, aff'd
[1917] 1 K.B. 222..497
Africa (The) (1880), 1 Spinks E.&A. 299, 164 E.R. 173 611
Agapitos v. Agnew (The Ageon), [2002] 2 Lloyd's L.R. 42................................324
Aglaia (The) (1888), L.R. 13 P.D. 160...605
Agra (The) and Elizabeth Jenkins (1867), L.R. 1 P.C. 501 500
Ailsa Craig Fishing Co. Ltd v. Malvern Fishing Co., [1983] 1 W.L.R. 964 165
Akerblom v. Price (1881), 4 Asp. M L.C. 441, (1880), 7 Q.B.D. 127 573
Al Wahab (The), [1983] 2 Lloyd's L.R. 365 334
Alaskan Trader, No. 2 (The), [1983] 2 Lloyd's L.R. 645 (Q.B.) 405
Albacora S.R.L. v. Westcott & Laurance Line Ltd., [1966] 2 Lloyd's Rep. 53
(H.L.)...452, 461, 475
Albazero (The), [1977] A.C. 774 423
Aldora (The), [1975] 1 Lloyd's L.R. 617...590
Aleksandr Marinesko v. Quint Star (The), [1998] 1 Lloyd's L.R. 265 ......505, 517
Alexander Shukoff v. Gothland (1920), 5 Ll. L.R. 237 (H.L.) 566
Alhambra (The) (1881), 6 P.D. 68 (C.A.) 386
Aline (The) (1840), 1 W. Robb. 111, 166 E.R. 514 276
Alletta (The), [1965] 2 Lloyd's Rep. 479 562
Allison v. Bristol Marine Insurance (1876), 1 App. Cas. 209 (H.L.) 376, 378, 397

Alma Shipping Corp. of Monrovia v. Montovani, (The Dione), [1975]
  1 Lloyd's L.R. 115 (C.A.) 404, 405
Amstelmolen (The), [1961] 2 Lloyd's Rep. 1 (C.A.)...390
Andrews v. Little (1887), 3 T.L.R. 544 (C.A.)...483
Angelic Spirit (The) and Y Mariner (The), [1994] 2 Lloyd's L.R. 595 ......511, 512
Anglo-African Merchants v. Bayley, [1970] 1 Q.B. 311; [1969] 2 W.L.R. 686 7
Anglo Saxon Petroleum Co. Ltd. v. Adamastos Shipping Co. Ltd., [1957]
  2 Q.B. 233 (C.A.), aff'd [1959] A.C. 133 455
Anna Salen (The), [1954] 1 Lloyd's Rep. 475..502
Annapolis (The) (1861), Lush. 355, 167 E.R. 151 589
Anns v. Merton London Borough Council, [1978] A.C. 728 452
Antares II (The) and Victory, [1996] 2 Lloyd's L.R. 482 (Q.B. (Adm. Ct.))......566
Antigoni (The), [1991] 1 Lloyd's Rep. 209 (C.A.) 476
Antilope (The) (1873), 1 Asp. M.L.C. 513 605
Ape (The) (1914), 12 Asp. M.L.C. 487 ....566, 567, 568
Apollon (The), [1971] 1 Lloyd's L.R. 476..584
Apollonius (The), [1978] 1 Lloyd's L.R. 53 (Q.B.)..403
Aquila (The) (1798), 1 C. Rob. 36, 165 E.R. 87..620
Aracelio Iglesias (The), [1968] 1 Lloyd's L.R. 131 413
Aramis (The), [1989] 1 Lloyd's L.R. 213 ....421, 423
Ardennes (The), [1951] 1 K.B. 55, [1950] 2 All E.R. 517 ....411, 412
Aries Tanker Corp. v. Total Transport Ltd. (The Aries), [1977] 1 Lloyd's L.R.
  334 (H.L.) 375, 376
Asfar v. Blundell, [1896] 1 Q.B. 123 (C.A.) 375
Athanasia Comminos (The), [1990] 1 Lloyd's L.R. 277 374
Atlantic Duchess (The), [1957] 2 Lloyd's Rep. 55 374
Atlantic Star (The), [1973] 2 All E.R. 175 (H.L.)...268
Attica Sea Carriers Corp. v. Ferrostaal Poseidon Bulk G.m.b.h. (The Puerto
  Buitrago), [1976] 1 Lloyd's L.R. 250 (C.A.) 405
Atwood v. Sellar & Co. (1880), 5 Q.B.D. 286..636, 652
Auriga (The), [1977] 1 Lloyd's L.R. 384...509, 511
Australia Star (The) (1940), 67 Ll. L.R. 110..362
Australian Coastal Shipping Commission v. Green, [1971] 1 Q.B. 456
  (C.A.) 641, 642
Avance (The), [1979] 1 Lloyd's L.R. 143 511

Balli Trading Ltd. v. Afalona Shipping Co. (The Coral), [1993] 1 Lloyd's
  L.R. 1 (C.A.)...387
Bamburi (The) v. Compton, [1982] Com. L.R. 31, [1982] 1 Lloyd's L.R. 312 314
Barbour v. South East Railway (1876), 34 L.T. 67 363
Barclays Bank Ltd. v. Commissioners of Customs and Excise, [1963] 1 Lloyd's
  Rep. 81 .... 411, 415
Basildon (The), [1967] 2 Lloyd's Rep. 134 (Adm. Ct.) 244
Baumwoll v. Furness, [1893] A.C. 8 380
Beechgrove (The), [1916] A.C. 364 569
Benwell Tower (The) (1895), 72 L.T. 664 (Adm. Ct.) 249, 260
Berkshire (The), [1974] 1 Lloyd's L.R. 185 (Q.B.) 428, 429
Berny (The), [1977] 2 Lloyds L.R. 533 (Q.B.) 778
Billings Victory (The) (1949), 82 Ll. L.R. 877 (Adm. Ct.)................506, 512, 522

Birkley v. Presgrave (1801), 1 East 220, 102 E.R. 86 ....629, 631
Black v. Rose (1864), 2 Moore N.S. 277, 15 E.R. 906...375
Blanche (The) (1887), 58 L.T. 592 (Adm. Ct.)...247, 249
Bland v. Ross (The Julia) (1861), 15 E.R. 284 (P.C.) 577
Blenheim (The) (1885), 10 P.D. 167 484
Blower v. Great Western Railway (1872), L.R. 7 C.P. 655...............................363
Blue Anchor Line Ltd. v. Alfred C. Toepfer International G.m.b.H. (The
    Union Amsterdam), [1982] 2 Lloyd's L.R. 432 391
Bold Buccleugh (The) (1851), 7 Moo. P.C. 267 ....173, 277, 278, 286, 287
Boleslaw Chrobry (The), [1974] 2 Lloyd's L.R. 308 527
Boucau (The), [1909] P. 163 538
Bovenkerk (The), [1973] 1 Lloyd's L.R. 63 (Q.B. (Adm. Ct.))..................502, 505
Bowes v. Shand (1877), 2 App. Cas. 455 (H.L.).......................................368, 384
Brabant (The), [1967] 1 Q.B. 588 403
Bradley & Sons v. Federal Steam Navigation Co. (1927), 27 Ll. L.R. 395 362
Bramley Moore (The), [1963] 2 Lloyd's Rep. 429 ....719, 735
Brandt v. Liverpool, Brazil and River Plate Steam Navigation Co., [1924]
    1 K.B. 575 (C.A.) 422, 423
Brass v. Maitland (1856), 6 E. & B. 470, 119 E.R. 940 (Q.B.) 372
Briddon v. Great Northern Railway Co. (1858), 28 L.J. Ex. 51 369
British Aviator (The), [1965] 1 Lloyd's Rep. 271 ....505, 506
British Engineer (The) (1945), 78 Ll. L.R. 31 510
British Patrol (The), [1967] 2 Lloyd's Rep. 16, aff'd [1968] 1 Lloyd's L.R.
    117 (C.A.) 506
British Tenacity (The), [1963] 2 Lloyd's Rep. 1 507
British Trade (The), [1924] P. 104 282
British Westinghouse Electric Co. v. Underground Electric Railways Co.,
    [1912] A.C. 673 (H.L.) 464
Brown v. Tanner (1868), L.R. 3 Ch. App. 597 ....249, 250
Brown, Jenkinson & Co. v. Percy Dalton Ltd., [1957] 2 Lloyd's L.R. 1 (C.A.)....449
Bunge Corp. v. Tradax S.A., [1981] 2 All E.R. 513 (H.L.) 368, 384, 402
Burke Motors Ltd. v. Mersey Docks and Harbours Co., [1986] 1 Lloyd's
    L.R. 155 439
Burns (The), [1907] P. 137 750

C.A. Pisani & Co. v. Brown, Jenkinson & Co. (1939), 64 Ll. L.R. 340 (K.B.)....417
C.M. Palmer (The) and Larnax (The) (1873), 2 Asp. M.C. 94 516
C.V.G. Siderurgicia Del Orinoco S.A. v. London Steamship Owners' Mutual
    Insurance Association Ltd., (The Vainqueur José), [1979] 1 Lloyd's
    L.R. 557 343
Calypso (The) (1828), 2 Hagg. 209, 166 E.R. 221 280
Campania (The), [1901] P. 289..515
Canadian Transport Co. v. Court Line (The Ovington Court), [1940]
    A.C. 934 (H.L.) 387
Cap Palos (The), [1921] P. 458...580, 582
Capitan San Luis (The), [1993] 2 Lloyd's L.R. 573 (Q.B. Adm. Ct.) 725
Captain Gregos (No. 2) (The), [1990] 2 Lloyd's L.R. 395 (C.A.) 422, 423
Cargo Ex Argos (1873), L.R. 5 P.C. 134 377
Cargo Ex Schiller (The) (1877), L.R. 2 P.D. 145 599

Carron Park (The) (1890), 15 P.D. 203 374
Carter v. Boehm (1766), 3 Burr. 1905 322
Castellain v. Preston (1883), 7 A.C. 333 (Q.B.) 327
Castlegate (The), [1893] A.C. 38 281
Cayzer v. Carron Co. (1884), 9 A.C. 873 521
Cella (The) (1888), 13 P.D. 82 ....288, 291
Celtic King (The), [1894] P.175 248
Century Dawn v. Asian Energy (The), [1994] 1 Lloyd's L.R. 138, aff'd
   [1996] 1 Lloyd's L.R. 125 (C.A.) 401
Century Textiles and Industry Ltd. v. Tomoe Shipping Co. (The Aditya
   Vaibhav), [1991] 1 Lloyd's L.R. 573 402
Charles (The) (1872), 1 Asp. M.L.C. 296 605
Charlotte (The) (1848), 3 Wm. Rob. 68, 166 E.R. 888 605
Charlotte Wylie (The) (1846), 2 Wm. Robb. 495, 166 E.R. 842 280
Chartered Bank of India v. Netherlands India Steam Navigation Co. (1883),
   10 Q.B.D. 521 394
Cheikh Boutros Selin El-Khoury v. Ceylon Shipping Lines Ltd. (The Madeleine),
   [1967] 2 Lloyd's Rep. 224 361
Chieftain (The) (1863), Br. & Lush. 212, 8 L.T. 120 282
China National Foreign Trade Transportation Corp. v. Evlogia Shipping Co.
   (The Mihalios Xilas), [1979] 2 Lloyd's L.R. 303 (H.L.) 403
China Pacific S.A. v. Food Corporation of India (The Winson), [1981]
   3 W.L.R. 860 (H.L.) 610
Chippendale v. Holt (1895), 1 Com. Cas. 197 320
Christina (The) (1848), 3 Wm. Rob. 27, 166 E.R. 873 ....567, 568, 586, 587
Circle Freight International v. Medeast Gulf Exports, [1988] 2 Lloyd's L.R.
   427 538
Clan Colquhoun (The), [1936] P. 153 583
Coggs v. Bernard (1703), 2 LD. Raym. 909, 92 E.R. 107 363
Colin & Shields v. W. Weddel & Co., [1952] 1 All E.R. 1021, aff'd [1952]
   2 All E.R. 337 (C.A.) 415
Collins v. Lamport (1864), 11 L.T. 497 (Ch.) 247
Colonial Bank v. European Grain & Shipping Ltd. (The Dominique), [1989]
   1 Lloyd's L.R. 431 (H.L.) 376
Colorado (The), [1923] P. 102 (C.A.) 266, 269, 270, 271
Coltman v. Chamberlain (1890), 25 Q.B.D. 328 244
Compania Maritima San Basilio S.A. v. Oceanus Mutual Underwriting
   Association (Bermuda) Ltd., (The Eurysthenes), [1976] 2 Lloyd's
   L.R. 171 (C.A.) 331
Compania Naviera General v. Kerametal (The Lorna I), [1983] 1 Lloyd's L.R.
   373 (C.A.) 376
Compania Nedelka v. Tradax S.A. (The Tres Flores), [1974] Q.B. 264 389
Concordia (The) (1866), L.R. 1 A. & E. 93 500
Connolly Shaw Ltd. v. A/S Det Nordenfjeldske D/S (1934), 49 Ll. L.R.
   183 (K.B.) 395
Container Transport International Inc. v. Oceanus Mutual U/W Association
   (Bermuda) Ltd., [1984] 1 Lloyd's L.R. 476 323
Corfu Navigation Co. v. Mobil Shipping Co. (The Alpha), [1991] 2 Lloyd's
   L.R. 515 (Q.B.) 643

Coromandel (The) (1857), Swab. 205, 166 E.R. 1097 619
Cranston v. Marshall (1850), 5 Ex. 395, 155 E.R. 172 368
Cremer v. General Carriers S.A. (The Dona Mari), [1973] 2 Lloyd's
  L.R. 366 ....415, 440
Crooks & Co. v. Allan (1879), 5 Q.B.D. 38 654
Crus V (The) (1862), Lush 583, 167 E.R. 266 612
Crusader (The), [1907] P. 15 576
Cunard Carrier (The), Eleranta and Martha, [1977] 2 Lloyd's L.R. 261 398
Cunard Steamship Co. v. Buerger, [1927] A.C. 1 (H.L.)..................................365

Da Ye (The), [1993] 1 Lloyd's L.R. 30 ....502, 511, 513, 515
Dahl v. Nelson (1881), 6 App. Cas. 38 386
Dakin v. Oxley (1864), 15 C.B. (N.S.) 647, 6 E.R. 938 ....375, 376
Darrah (The), [1976] 1 Lloyd's L.R. 285 (C.A.) 390
Davis v. Garrett (1830), 6 Bing. 716, 130 E.R. 1456 ....364, 366, 475
De Silvale v. Kendall (1915), 4 M. & S. 37, 105 E.R. 749 ....376, 397
de Vaux v. Salvador (1836), 111 E.R. 845...303
Decorum Investments Ltd. v. Atkin (The Elena G), [2001] 2 Lloyd's L.R. 378 323
Delfini (The), [1990] 1 Lloyd's L.R. 252..421
Democritos (The), [1976] 2 Lloyd's L.R. 149 (C.A.) 385, 404
Devonshire (S.S.) v. Barge Leslie, [1912] A.C. 634................................582, 586
Diamond (The), [1906] P. 282..458
Dickson & Co. v. Devitt (1916), 21 Com. Cas. 291, 86 L.J. K.B. 315 321
Djerada (The), [1976] 1 Lloyd's L.R. 50 516
Dona Myrto (The), [1959] 1 Lloyd's Rep. 203 ....511, 512
Donoghue v. Stevenson, [1932] A.C. 562...424
Duc d'Aumale (The), [1904] P. 60 490
Dundee (The) (1824), 1 Hag. Adm. 109, 166 E.R. 39 ....286, 521
Dunlop v. Lambert (1839), 6 Cl. & F. 600, 7 E.R. 824 (H.L.) 423

EL Oldendorff & Co. G.m.b.H. v. Tradax Export (The Johanna Oldendorff),
  [1974] A.C. 479 (H.L.) 389
E.R. Wallonia (The), [1987] 2 Lloyd's L.R. 485 ....511, 513, 518
Earle's Shipbuilding Engineering Co. v. Gefion and Fourth Shipbuilding &
  Engineering Co. (1922), 10 Ll. L.R. 305 289
East West Corp. v. DKBS 1912, [2003] 1 Lloyd's Rep. 239 (C.A.)............413, 442
Echo (The), [1917] P. 132...512
Edwards v. Quickenden and Forester, [1939] P. 261 143
Edwin (The) (1864), Br. & Lush. 281, 167 E.R. 365 282
Effort Shipping Co. Ltd. v. Linden Management S.A. (The Giannis NK),
  [1998] A.C. 605 (H.L.) 372, 422, 470
Eglantine, Credo and Inez (The), [1990] 2 Lloyd's L.R. 390 (C.A.) 408, 515
Ek (The), [1966] 1 Lloyd's L.R. 440 513
Elafi (The), [1981] 2 Lloyd's L.R. 679 424
Elder, Dempster & Co. v. Paterson, Zochonis & Co., [1924] A.C. 522....361, 394
Eleftheria (The), [1969] 1 Lloyd's Rep. 237 472
Emblem (The), 8 Cas. 611 (D. Me. 1840) 619
Emily Charlotte v. Newona (1920), 4 Ll. L.R. 156 580
Esso v. Southport Corporation, [1956] A.C. 218 686

Esso Petroleum Co. v. Mardon, [1976] Q.B. 801 612
Estrella (The), [1977] 1 Lloyd's L.R. 525 508
Eugenie (The) (1844), 3 Not. Of Cas. 430 606
Europa (The), [1908] P. 84 363
Europa (The) (1863), 15 E.R. 803 387
Evpo Agnic (The), [1988] 2 Lloyd's L.R. 411 (C.A.) 769

F.J. Wolf (The), [1946] P. 91 513
Faethon (The), [1987] 1 Lloyd's L.R. 538 ....498, 506, 517
Fanchon (The) (1880), 5 P.D. 173 ....247, 250
Federal Commerce & Navigation Ltd. v. Molena Alpha Inc. (The Nanfri), [1978]
  Q.B. 927 (C.A.), aff'd [1979] 1 All E.R. 307 (H.L.) 402
Federal Commerce and Navigation Co. v. Tradax Export S.A. (The Marratha
  Envoy), [1978] A.C. 1 (H.L.) 381, 390
Ferruzzi France S.A. v. Oceania Maritime Inc. (The Palmea), [1988] 2 Lloyd's
  L.R. 261 443
Fibrosa Spolka Akcyjna v. Fairbairn Lawson Combe Barbour Ltd., [1943]
  A.C. 32 397
Fletcher v. Alexander (1868), L.R. 3 C.P. 375..652, 653
Florence (The) (1852), 16 Jur. 572...606
Foreman and Ellams Ltd. v. Federal Steam Navigation Co., [1928] 2 K.B. 424 457
Forfarshire (The), [1908] P. 339 580
Fox v. Nott (1861), 6 H. & N. 630, 158 E.R. 260 422
Fraser & White Ltd. v. Vernan, [1951] 2 Lloyd's Rep. 175 579
Frenkel v. MacAndrews & Co., [1929] A.C. 545 395
Fury Shipping Co. Ltd. v. State Trading Corp. of India Ltd. (The Atlantic Sun),
  [1972] 1 Lloyd's L.R. 509 (Q.B.) 391

G.H. Renton & Co. v. Palmyra Trading Corp. of Panama, [1957] A.C. 149
  (H.L.) 452, 454, 455
G.W. Grace & Co. v. General Steam Navigation Co., [1950] 2 K.B. 383 400
Gannet (The), [1967] 1 Lloyd's Rep. 97 505
Gas Float Whitton No. 2 (The), [1896] P. 42, aff'd [1897] A.C. 337 600
General Accident Fire and Life Assurance Co. v. Tanter (The Zephyr), [1985]
  2 Lloyd's L.R. 529 (C.A.) 320, 321
General Shipping & Forwarding Co. v. British General Ins. Co. (The Borre)
  (1923), 15 Ll. L.R. 175. 325
Generous (The) (1868), L.R. 2 A. & E. 57 612
Genimar (The), [1972] 2 Lloyd's L.R. 17 508
Geogas S.A. v. Trammo Gas Ltd., (The Baleares), [1993] 1 Lloyd's L.R. 215
  (C.A.) 383
Gertor (The) (1894), 7 Asp. 472...576
Glaholm v. Hays (1841), 2 Man. & G. 257, 133 E.R. 743 383
Glastnos (The), [1991] 1 Lloyds L.R. 482 (Q.B.) 770
Global Marine Drilling v. Triton Holdings Ltd., [1999] Scot. J. No. 238
  (QL) 75, 212
Glorious (The) (1933), 44 Ll. L.R. 321 ....503, 515
Glucometer II (The) and St. Michael (The), [1989] 1 Lloyd's L.R. 54.............502

Glyn Mills Currie & Co. v. East and West India Dock Co. (1882), 7 App.
 Cas. 591 411
Glynn v. Margeston & Co., [1893] A.C. 351 ....366, 394
Golden Mistral (The), [1986] 1 Lloyd's L.R. 407 506
Good Friend (The), [1984] 2 Lloyd's L.R. 586..361
Goole and Hull Steamship Towing Co. v. Ocean Marine Insurance Co.
 (1929), 29 Ll. L.R. 242..325
Gosse Millerd Ltd. v. Canadian Government Merchant Marine Ltd., [1929]
 A.C. 223 ....457, 462
Gosse Millerd Ltd. v. Canadian Government Merchant Marine, Ltd. [1928]
 1 K.B. 717 (C.A.) 457, 462
Goulandris (The), [1927] P. 182, (1927) 27 Ll. L.R. 120..................287, 288, 611
Goulandris Bros Ltd. v. B. Goldman & Sons Ltd., [1958] 1 Q.B. 74 645
Grant v. Norway (1851), 10 C.B. 665, 138 E.R. 263 ....431, 432
Great Indian Peninsula Railway v. Turnbull (1885), 53 L.T. 325 (Q.B.) 376
Great Western Railway v. Mostyn (The), [1928] A.C. 57 (H.L.) 536, 539
Grit (The), [1924] P. 246...741
Groves, MacLean & Co. v. Volkart Bros. (1884), 1 T.L.R. 92, aff'd (1885),
 1 T.L.R. 454 (C.A.)..389
Gunnar Knudsen (The), [1961] 2 Lloyd's Rep. 433 515
Guy Mannering (The) (1882), 4 Asp. M.L.C. 553 565

Hadley v. Baxendale (1854), 9 Ex. 341, 156 E.R. 145 ....370, 456, 464
Hain Steamship Co. v. Tate & Lyle Ltd., [1936] 2 All E.R. 597
 (H.L.) 366, 367, 420, 650
Halcrow v. Lemesurier (1884), 10 Q.L.R. 239 (Q.B.)..375
Hales v. London and North Western Railway Co. (1863), 4 B. & S. 66,
 122 E.R. 384 (Q.B.) 369
Hans Hoth (The), [1952] 2 Lloyd's Rep. 341 ....566, 570
Hansen v. Harold Brothers, [1894] 1 Q.B. 612 398
Harman v. Mant (1815), 4 Camp. 161, 171 E.R. 52 388
Harris v. Best, Ryley & Co. (1892), 68 L.T. 76 (C.A.) 387
Hassell (The), [1919] P. 355 516
Heather Bell (The), [1901] P. 143 ....247, 248
Hector (The), [1998] 2 Lloyd's L.R. 287 (Q.B.)...429, 430
Hedley v. Pinkney & Sons Steamship Co., [1894] A.C. 222 362
Heinrich Bjorn (The) (1886), 11 A.C. 270 (H.L.) 764
Hellenic Dolphin (The), [1978] 2 Lloyd's L.R. 336 ....450, 463, 475
Henderson & Co. v. Comptoir d'Escompte de Paris (1873), L.R. 5 P.C. 253....410
Henderson v. H.E. Jenkins & Sons, [1970] A.C. 282 537
Henricksens Rederi A/S v. T.H.Z. Rolimpex (The Brede), [1973] 2 Lloyd's
 L.R. 333 (C.A.)...375
Heranger (S.S) v. S.S. Diamond, [1939] A.C. 94..513
Heyn v. Ocean Steamship Co. (1927), 27 Ll. L.R. 334 463
Hick v. Raymond & Reid, [1893] A.C. 22 (H.L.) 369, 388
Hicks v. Shield (1857), 7 E. & B. 633, 119 E.R. 1380 376
Hill v. Wilson (1879), 4 C.P.D. 329 443
Hjortholm (The) (1935), 52 Ll. L.R. 223 523
Hogarth v. Miller Bros. & Co., [1891] A.C. 48 (H.L.) 401

Hollandia (The), [1983] 1 A.C. 565 689
Homewood (The) (1928), 31 Ll. L.R. 336 14
Hong Kong Fir Shipping Co. v. Kawasaki Kisen Kaisha Ltd., [1962]
 2 Q.B. 26 (C.A.) 361, 362, 370
Hopkinson v. Rolt (1861), 5 L.T. 90 (H.L.) 260
Hopper v. Burness (1876), 1 C.P.D. 137 377
Hughes v. Metropolitan Railway (1877), 2 App. Cas. 439 (H.L.) 166
Hunter v. Prinsep (1808), 10 East 378, 103 E.R. 818 377
Hyundai Merchant Marine Co. Ltd. v. Gesuri Chartering Co. (The Peoina),
 [1991] 1 Lloyd's L.R. 100 (C.A.) 405

Indian Grace (No. 2) (The), [1998] 2 Lloyds L.R. 1 (H.L.) 19
Industrie Chimiche Italia Centrale and Cerealfin S.A. v. Alexander G. Tsalviris &
 Sons Maritime Co. (The Choko Star), [1989] 2 Lloyd's L.R. 42, aff'd
 [1990] 1 Lloyd's L.R. 516 (C.A.). 612
Ingomar (The) (1920), 5 Ll. L.R. 182..588
Ines (The), [1995] 2 Lloyd's L.R. 144 (Q.B.) 429, 430
Integrated Container Service Inc. v. British Traders Insurance Co., [1984] 1
 Lloyd's L.R. 154 (C.A.)...338, 340
Interfoto Library Ltd. v. Stiletto Visual Programmes Ltd., [1989] 1 Q.B. 433
 (C.A.) 482
International Packers London Ltd. v. Ocean Steam Ship Co., [1955] 2 Lloyd's
 Rep. 218 453
Inverkip Steamship Co. v. Bunge & Co., [1917] 2 K.B. 193 (C.A.) 391
Ionian Navigation Co. v. Atlantic Shipping Co., (The Loucas N), [1971]
 1 Lloyd's L.R. 215 (C.A.) 382
Ionna (The), [1985] 2 Lloyd's L.R. 164 402
Iran Torab (The), [1988] 2 Lloyd's L.R. 38...510, 512
Irene's Success (The), [1981] 2 Lloyd's L.R. 635 424
Irvin v. Hine, [1950] 1 K.B. 555, 83 Ll. L.R. 162 314
Isca (The) (1886), 12 P.D. 34 587

J. Thorley Ltd. v. Orchis Steamship Co., [1907] 1 K.B. 660 (C.A.) 366, 475
Jaladhir (The), [1961] 2 Lloyd's Rep. 13 513
Jalamohan (The), [1988] 1 Lloyd's L.R. 443 (Q.B.) 429
James Morrison & Co. v. Shaw, Savill and Albion Co. Ltd., [1916]
 2 K.B. 783 (C.A.) 366, 475
Jan Laurenz (The), [1972] 1 Lloyd's L.R. 404, aff'd [1973] 1 Lloyd's L.R.
 329 (C.A.) 510
Jane Bacon (The) (1878), 27 W.R. 35 587
Jenkyns v. Southampton, etc, Steam Packet Co. (1919), 35 T.L.R. 264 (K.B.) 482
Jones v. European General Express Co. (1920), 90 L.J.K.B. 159 417
Jonge Andries (The), [1857] Swab. 226 572
Julia (The), [1949] A.C. 293 (H.L.) 415
Julia (The) (1861), Lush. 224 577

K/S Merc-Scandia XXXXII v. Certain Lloyd's Underwriters (The Mercadian
 Continent), [2001] 2 Lloyd's L.R. 563..323, 324
Kagu Maru (The) v. Malta (The) (1920), 2 Ll. L.R. 120 (H.L.) 567

Kaituna (The) (1933), 46 Ll. L.R. 200 510
Karin Vatis (The), [1988] 2 Lloyd's L.R. 330 (C.A.)..376
Keith v. Burrows (1877), 2 App. Cas. 636 344
Kenya Railways v. Antares Co. (The Antares), [1987] 1 Lloyd's L.R.
    424 (C.A.) 367, 368, 397
Kingsland (The) (1945), 78 Ll. L.R. 259 516
Kirchner v. Venus (1859), 12 Moo. P.C.C. 361, 14 E.R. 948 ....378, 637
Kish v. Taylor, [1912] A.C. 604..365
Kitano Maru (S.S.) v. S.S. Otranto, [1931] A.C. 194 ....500, 513
Kodros Shipping v. Empreso Cubana, (The Evia) (No. 2), [1983] 1 A.C. 736
    (H.L.) 386
Kong Magnus (The), [1891] P. 223..387
Koningin Juliana (The), [1975], 2 L.R. 111 (H.L.) 506
Koningin Juliana (The), [1974] 2 Lloyd's L.R. 353 (C.A.) 506
Koscierzyna (The) and Hanjin Singapore (The), [1996] 2 Lloyd's L.R. 124,
    130 (C.A.) 505, 512
Koufos v. C. Czarnikow Ltd., (The Heron II), [1969] 1 A.C. 350 (H.L.) 464
Kristiansands Tankredere A/S v. Standard Tankers (Bahamas) Ltd. (The
    Polyglory), [1977] 2 Lloyd's L.R. 353 (Q.B.)...386
Krüger & Co. v. Moel Tryvan Shipping Co., [1907] A.C. 272 432
Kuo International Oil Ltd. v. Daisy Shipping Co., (The Yamatogawa), [1990]
    2 Lloyd's L.R. 39 449
Kuwait Petroleum Corp. v. I & D Oil Carriers Ltd. (The Houda), [1994] 2
    Lloyd's L.R. 541 (C.A.)..414
Kylix (The) and Rustringen (The), [1979] 1 Lloyd's L.R. 133.........................517

Lady Gwendolen (The), [1964] 2 Lloyd's Rep. 99 (Adm. Ct.), aff'd [1965]
    1 Lloyd's Rep. 335 (C.A.)...458, 515, 719, 720
Lamport & Holt Lines v. Coubro & Scrutton (The Raphael), [1982] 2 Lloyd's
    L.R. 42 (C.A.) 394
Law Guarantee & Trust Society v. Russian Bank for Foreign Trade, [1905]
    1 K.B. 815...248
Leduc v. Ward (1888), 20 Q.B.D. 475 (C.A.) 394, 420, 426
Leeds Shipping Co. v. Société Francaise Bunge (The Eastern City), [1958] 2
    Lloyd's Rep. 127 (C.A.)...386
Leesh River Tea Co. v. British India Steam Navigation Co. (The Chyebassa),
    [1967] 2 Q.B. 250, [1966] 2 Lloyd's Rep. 193 (C.A.) 451, 463
Leigh and Sillivan Ltd. v. Aliakmon Shipping Ltd. (The Aliakmon), [1986]
    1 A.C. 785 424
Lennard's Carrying Co. v. Asiatic Petroleum Co., [1915] A.C. 705 (H.L.)........458
Leon Blum (The), [1915] P. 90..458, 589, 590
Leon Corp. v. Atlantic Lines and Navigation Co. (The Leon), [1985] 2 Lloyd's
    L.R. 470 402
Levy v. Costerton (1816), 4 Camp. 389, 171 E.R. 124.......................................361
Lickbarrow v. Mason, [1794] 5 T. R. 367, 101 E.R. 206 ....410, 414, 420
Linde (The), [1969] 2 Lloyd's L.R. 556 505
Litsion Pride (The), [1985] 1 Lloyd's L.R. 437. 323
Liver Alkali Co. v. Johnson (1874), L.R. 9 Ex. 338 363
Liverpool (The), [1893] P. 154 589

Liverpool Marine Credit Co. v. Wilson (1872), L.R. 7 Ch. App. 507..........24, 259
Llanover (The) (1945), 78 Ll. L.R. 461 527
Lochlibo (The) (1850), 166 E.R. 978 568
Lok Vivek (The) and Common Venture (The), [1995] 2 Lloyd's L.R. 230 512
Lomonosoff (The), [1921] P. 97 606
London & Overseas Freighters Ltd. v. Timber Shipping Co. (The London
  Explorer), [1972] A.C. 1 (H.L.)...403
London Dredging Co. v. Greater London Council (The Joseph Rawlinson),
  [1972] 2 Lloyd's L.R. 437..736
Lord Bangor (1896), 8 Asp. 211 587
Louis Dreyfus & Co. v. Lauro (1938), 60 Ll. L.R. 94 (K.B.) 384
Louis Dreyfus & Co. v. Tempus Shipping Co., [1931] A.C. 726 645
Lucile Bloomfield (The), [1966] 2 Lloyd's Rep. 239, aff'd [1967] 1 Lloyd's
  Rep. 341 (C.A.) 517
Luigi Monta of Genoa v. Cechofracht Co., [1956] 2 Q.B. 552 396
Lyon v. Mells (1804), 5 East 428, 102 E.R. 1134 361
Lyrma (No. 2) (The), [1978] 2 Lloyd's L.R. 30 276

Makedonia (The), [1962] 1 Lloyd's Rep. 316..361, 451
Maloja II (The), [1993] 1 Lloyd's L.R. 48.......................502, 511, 512, 515, 517
Manchester Regiment (The) (1938), 60 Ll. L.R. 279 509
Manifest Shipping & Co. Ltd. v. Uni-Polaris Insurance Co. (The Star Sea),
  [2001] 1 Lloyd's L.R. 389 (H.L.), aff'g [1997] 1 Lloyd's L.R. 360 (C.A.)....323
Manor (The), [1907] P. 339 ....247, 248
Manorbier Castle (The) (1922), 16 Asp. M.L.C. 151 538
Marc Rich & Co. AG v. Bishop Rock Marine Co. (The Nicholas H), [1995]
  2 Lloyd's L.R. 299 (H.L.) 157
Marcellino Gonzalez v. James Nourse Ltd., [1936] 1 K.B. 565.......................443
Mardorf Peach & Co. v. Attica Sea Carriers Corp., (The Laconia), [1977]
  A.C. 850 (H.L.) 402
Marechal Suchet (The), [1911] P. 1 ....577, 589
Mareva Corp. Naviera S.A. v. International Bulkcarriers S.A., [1980] 1 All E.R.
  213 (C.A.) 802
Margarine Union G.m.b.H. v. Cambay Prince S.S. Co. (The Wear Breeze),
  [1967] 2 Lloyd's Rep. 315 ....412, 421
Marida Ltd. v. Oswal Steel (The Bijela), [1994] 2 Lloyd's L.R. 1 (H.L.)............635
Maritime Harmony (The), [1982] 2 Lloyd's L.R. 400...............................506, 517
Marston Excelsior Ltd. v. Arbuckle, Smith & Co., [1971] 2 Lloyd's L.R. 306
  (C.A.) 417
Martin Fierro (The), [1974] 2 Lloyd's L.R. 203, aff'd [1975] 2 Lloyd's L.R.
  130 (C.A.) 517
Mary (The) (1880), 5 P.D. 14 586
Mason v. Uxbridge Boat Centre and Wright, [1980] 2 Lloyd's L.R. 592 (Q.B.)....742
Mayhew Foods Ltd. v. Overseas Containers Ltd., [1984] 1 Lloyd's L.R. 317....443
McFadden v. Blue Star Line, [1905] 1 K.B. 697 ....361, 362
McLean and Hope v. Fleming (1871), L.R. 2 Sc. & Div. 128 377
Medina (The) (1877), L.R. 2 P.D. 5..612
Merak (The), [1965] P. 223 (C.A.) 471
Merchant Prince (The) (1892), P. 179 ....537, 538

Merchant's Marine Insurance Co. v. North of England Protection and
 Indemnity Association (1926), 25 Ll. L.R. 446 146
Mersey No. 30 (The), [1952] 2 Lloyd's Rep. 183 506
Micada Compania Naviera S.A. v. Texim, [1968] 2 Lloyd's L.R. 57 (Q.B.) 373, 374
Midland Silicones Ltd. v. Scruttons Ltd., [1962] A.C. 446 (H.L.) 442
Mihalis Angelos (The), [1971] 1 Q.B. 164 ....362, 383
Mills v. Armstrong (The Bernina) (1888), 13 App. Cas. 1 (H.L.) 482
Mineral Dampier (The) v. Hanjin Madras (The), [2001] 2 Lloyd's L.R. 419 502
Minnehaha (The) (1861), Lush. 335, 167 E.R. 151 589
Mitchell, Cotts & Co. v. Steel Brothers & Co., [1916] 2 K.B. 610...................372
Mitsui & Co. v. Novorossiysk Shipping Co. (The Gudermes), [1993]
 1 Lloyd's L.R. 311...423
Moel Tryvan Ship Co. v. Andrew Weir & Co., [1910] 2 K.B. 844 (C.A.) 369, 385
Monarch Steamship Co. v. Karlshamns Oljefabriker (A/B), [1949]
 A.C. 196 ....371, 396
Monroe Brothers Ltd. v. Ryan, [1935] 2 K.B. 28 (C.A.) 384
Monte Ulia v. Banco (The), [1970] 2 Lloyds L.R. 230 (Adm. Ct.), aff'd [1971]
 1 Lloyd's L.R. 49 (C.A.) 776, 777
Montedison v. Icroma (The Caspian Sea), [1980] 1 Lloyd's L.R. 91 (Q.B.) 375
Morviken (The), [1983] 1 Lloyd's L.R. 1 (H.L.)...440
Motor Oil Hellas (Corinth) Refineries v. Shipping Corp. of India (The
 Kanchenjunga), [1990] 1 Lloyd's L.R. 391 (H.L.) 386
Murphy v. Brentwood District Council, [1991] 1 A.C. 398 425
Myrto (The), [1977] 2 Lloyd's L.R. 243 (Q.B.).................................247, 248
Myrto (No. 2) (The), [1984] 2 Lloyd's L.R. 341...781

Navios Enterprise (The) v. Puritan (The), [1998] 2 Lloyd's L.R. 16 ....499, 502
Nelson Line (Liverpool) Ltd. v. James Nelson & Sons Ltd., [1908] A.C. 16....393
Neptune (The) (1824), 1 Hag. 227, 166 E.R. 81 ....276, 287
New Zealand Shipping Co. v. A.M. Satterthwaite & Co. Ltd. (The Eurymedon),
 [1974] 1 Lloyd's L.R. 544 (H.L.) 438
Niobe (The) (1888), 13 P.D. 55..586
Nippon Yusen Kaisha v. International Import and Export Ltd. (The Elbe
 Maru), [1978] 1 Lloyd's L.R. 206..438
Nippon Yusen Kaishu v. Karageorgis, [1975] 3 All E.R. 282 (C.A.)................802
Nippon Yusen Kaisha v. Ramjiban Serowgee, [1938] A.C. 429 4159
Nithsdale (The) (1879), 15 C.L.J. 2681464
Noble Resource Ltd. v. Cavalier Shipping Corp., (The Atlas), [1996] 1 Lloyd's
 L.R. 642 (Q.B.)...413
Nordic Ferry (The), [1991] 2 Lloyd's L.R. 591..............................504, 514, 517
Northampton (The) (1853), 1 Ecc. & Adm. 152 499
Nowy Sacz (The), [1976] 2 Lloyd's L.R. 682 (Adm. Ct.), rev'd [1977]
 2 Lloyd's L.R. 91 (C.A.) 509
Nugent v. Smith (1876), 1 C.P.D. 423 ....363, 459

Olympic (The), [1913] P. 92 623
Optima (The) (1905), 10 Asp. M.L.C. 147, 93 L.T. 638 288
Orchis (The) (1890), 15 P.D. 38 247
Osprey (The), [1967] 1 Lloyd's Rep. 76 506

Ouro Fino (The), [1986] 2 Lloyd's L.R. 466, aff'd [1988] 2 Lloyd's L.R. 325
 (C.A.) 506, 516
Overseas Tankship Ltd. v. Morts Dock & Engineering Co., [1961] A.C. 388 640
Overseas Transportation Co. v. Mineralimportexport (The Sinoe), [1971] 1
 Lloyd's L.R. 514, aff'd 1972] 1 Lloyd's L.R. 201 (C.A.) 398

Pagnan & Fratelli v. Tradax Export S.A., [1969] 2 Lloyd's L.R. 150 (Q.B.) 388
Pan Atlantic Insurance Co. v. Pine Top Insurance Co., [1995] 1 A.C. 501 323
Pan Oak (The), [1992] 2 Lloyd's L.R. 36 (Adm. Ct.) 244
Pantanassa (The), [1970] P. 187 600
Panther (The), [1957] 1 All E.R. 641 687
Patagonier v. Spear & Thorpe (1933), 47 Ll. L.R. 59 413
Pearl (The) (1948), 82 Ll. L.R. 15 523
Pegase (The), [1981] 1 Lloyd's L.R. 175 (Q.B.) 454, 464, 465
Petone (The), [1917] P. 198 282
Petroship B (The), [1986] 2 Lloyd's L.R. 251 513
Photo Production Ltd. v. Securicor Transport Ltd., [1980] A.C. 827 367
Pioneer Container (The), [1994] 2 A.C. 324 (P.C.) 424
Polyduke (The), [1978] 1 Lloyd's L.R. 211..439
Postlethwaite v. Freeland (1880), 5 App. Cas. 599 (H.L.) 388
President of India v. Metcalfe Shipping Co. (The Dunelmia), [1970]
 1 Q.B. 289 ....425, 426
President Van Buren (The) (1924), 16 Asp. M.C. 444 583
Princess Alice (The) (1849), 3 W. Rob. 138 574
Princess Victoria (The), [1953] 2 Lloyd's Rep. 619 719
Pteroti Compania Naviera S.A. v. National Coal Board, [1958] 1 Q.B. 469 390
Pulkovo (The) and Oden (The), [1989] 1 Lloyd's L.R. 280 ....503, 515
Purissima Concepcion (The) (1848), 7 Notes of Cases 150 287
Pyrene Co. v. Scindia Navigation Co., [1954] 2 Q.B. 402 ....441, 452

Queen Mary (The) (1949), 82 Ll. L.R. 303 (H.L.) 59, 510, 513

R. v. Keyn (The Franconia), [1876] 2 Ex. D. 63..103, 109
R.G. Mayer (T/A Granville Coaches) v. P & O Ferries Ltd. (The Lion), [1990]
 2 Lloyd's L.R. 144 (Q.B.) 488
Rainbow (The) (1885), 53 L.T. 91, 5 Asp. 479..285
Raisby (The) (1885), 10 P.D. 114 635
Ramsden (The), [1943] P. 46 585
Rankin v. De Coster, [1975] 2 Lloyd's L.R. 84 488
Rasu Maritime S.A. v. Perusahaan, [1977] 3 All E.R. 324 (C.A.) 802
Re Eddystone Marine Insurance Co., [1892] 2 Ch. 423...................................320
Re Westlake (1881), 16 Ch.D. 604 288
Reardon Smith Line Ltd. v. Black Sea and Baltic General Insurance Co.,
 [1939] A.C. 562 ....364, 386
Rederij v. England (The), [1973] 1 Lloyd's L.R. 373 720
Renton (G.H.) & Co. v. Palmyra Trading Corp. of Panama, [1957] A.C. 149 396
Reward (The) (1841), 1 W. Rob. 177 588
Rewia (The), [1991] 2 Lloyd's L.R. 325 (C.A.)...173, 279, 283
Ripon City (The), [1897] P. 226 ....4, 375

Ritchie v. Atkinson (1808), 10 East. 294, 103 E.R. 787 8
Riverstone Meat Co v. Lancashire Shipping Co. (The Muncaster Castle),
   [1961] A.C. 807 .... 450, 451
Roanoke (The), [1908] P. 231 512
Robertson v. Amazon Tug and Lighterage Co. (1881), 7 Q.B.D. 598 (C.A.) 579
Robinson v. Knights (1873), L.R. 8 C.P. 465 377
Rodocanachi v. Elliott (1874), L.R. 9 C.P. 518, 43 L.J.C.P. 255 314
Rodocanachi, Sons & Co. v. Milburn Bros. (1886), 18 Q.B.D. 67 425
Ropner Shipping Co. v. Cleeves Western Valleys Anthracite Collieries Ltd.,
   [1927] 1 K.B. 879 (C.A.) 371
Roseline (The), [1981] 2 Lloyd's L.R. 410 .... 505, 515
Royalgate (The), [1967] 1 Lloyd's Rep. 352 512

S.A. Sucre Export v. Northern River Shipping Ltd. (The Sormovskiy 3068),
   [1994] 2 Lloyd's L.R. 266 (Q.B.) 413, 414
S.S. Devonshire (The) v. Barge Leslie, [1912] A.C. 634 582
Sabine (The), [1974] 1 Lloyd's L.R. 465 517
Safadi v. Western Assurance (1933), 46 Ll. L.R. 140 (K.B.) 332
Salamis Shipping v. Edm. Van Meerbeek & Co., (The Onisilos), [1971] 2 Q.B.
   500 393
Salomon v. A. Salomon & Co., [1897] A.C. 22 .... 182, 325
Salsi v. Jetspeed Air Services Ltd., [1977] 2 Lloyd's L.R. 57 (Q.B.) 417
Salt Union (The) v. Wood, [1893] 1 Q.B. 370 498
Saltaro (The), [1958] 2 Lloyd's Rep. 232 571
Sametiet M/T Johs Stove v. Istanbul Petrol Rafinerisi A/S (The Johs Stove),
   [1984] 1 Lloyd's L.R. 38 (Q.B.) 390
San Demetrio (The) (1941), 69 Ll. L.R. 5 606
San Nicholas (The), [1976] 1 Lloyd's L.R. 8 (C.A.) 426
San Onofre (The), [1925] A.C. 246 608
Sanday v. Keighley, Maxted & Co. (1922), 10 Ll. L.R. 738 (C.A.) 383
Sandefjord (The), [1953] 2 Lloyd's Rep. 557 573
Sandeman & Sons v. Tyzack & Branfoot Steamship Co., [1913] A.C. 680 463
Sanshin Victory (The), [1980] 2 Lloyd's L.R. 359 .... 515, 516
Santa Anna (The) (1863), 32 L.J.M.P.M. & A. 198. 542
Santiren Shipping Ltd. v. Unimarine (The Chrysovalandou Dyo), [1981]
   1 Lloyd's L.R. 159 (Q.B.) 402
Sanwa (The) and Chayangstar (The), [1998] 1 Lloyd's L.R. 283 .... 502, 505
Saragossa (The) (1892), 7 Asp. M.C. 289 513
Sarpen (The), [1916] P. 306 592
Satef-Huttenes Albertus v. Paloma Tercera Shipping Co. (The Pegase), [1981]
   1 Lloyd's L.R. 175 (Q.B.) 370
Savina (The), [1974] 2 Lloyd's L.R. 317 (Q.B. (Adm. Ct.)), rev'd [1975]
   2 Lloyd's L.R. 141 (C.A.), aff'd [1976] 2 Lloyd's L.R. 123 (H.L.) 511
Saxonia and Eclipse (The) (1862), Lush. 410 516
Scandinavian Trading Tanker Co. A.B. v. Flota Petrolera Ecuatoriana (The
   Scaptrade), [1983] 2 A.C. 694 (H.L.) 402
Scaramanga v. Stamp (1880), 5 C.P.D. 295, 42 L.T. 840 .... 364, 397, 576, 577
Scindia S.S. Co. v. London Assurance Co. (1936), 56 Ll. L.R. 136 336

Table of Cases 883

Semco Salvage & Marine v. Lancer Navigation, (The Nagasaki Spirit), [1997] 1 Lloyd's L.R. 323 (H.L.) 615
Sestriere (The), [1976] 1 Lloyd's L.R. 125 511
Sewell v. Burdick (1884), 10 App. Cas. 74 ....413, 521
Shell International Petroleum Co. v. Gibbs (The Salem) (1983), 2 A.C. 375 (H.L.) 330
Shield v. Wilkins (1850), 5 Ex. 304, 155 E.R. 130 386
Silver v. Ocean Steamship Co., [1930] 1 K.B. 416 ....448, 449, 462
Silver Bullion (The) (1854), 2 Spinks E.A. 70, 164 E.R. 312 288
Simla (The) (1851), 15 Jr. 865 285
Simpson v. Young (1859), 1 F. & F. 708, 175 E.R. 917 368
Siordet v. Hall (1828), 130 E.R. 902 364
Sisters (The) (1876), 1 P.D. 117 522
Skibs. Snefonn v. Kawasaki Kisen Kaisha Ltd. (The Berge Tasta), [1975] 1 Lloyd's L.R. 422 (Q.B.) 379
Skiplander (The) (1877), 3 Asp. M.L.C. 556 604
Slaney (The), [1951] 2 Lloyd's Rep. 538 589
Smith v. Baker, [1891] A.C. 325 548
Smith v. St. Lawrence Tow-Boat Co. (1873), 2 Asp. 41, 28 L.T. 885 ....568, 587
Smith, Hogg & Co. v. Black Sea and Baltic General Insurance Co., [1940] A.C. 997 (H.L.) 371, 377
Smitton v. Orient Steam Navigation Co. (1907), 23 T.L.R. 359 (K.B.) 480, 482
Smjeli (The), [1982] 2 Lloyd's L.R. 74 736
Somes v. British Empire Shipping Co., [1843–60] All E.R. Rep. 844 (H.L.) 289
Spaight v. Tedcastle, [1881] Asp. 406 586
St. Enoch Shipping Co. v. Phosphate Mining Co. (1914), [1916] 2 K.B. 624 ..377
St. George (The) (1926), 25 Ll. L.R. 97 (Adm. Ct.) 243
St. Paul (The), [1909] P. 43 514
Stag Line Ltd. v. Board of Trade, [1950] 2 K.B. 194 389
Stag Line Ltd. v. Foscolo, Mango & Co., [1932] A.C. 328 (H.L.)....446, 454, 455, 467
Standard Oil Co. of New York v. Clan Line Steamers, [1924] A.C. 100 361
Stanton v. Austin (1872), L.R. 7 C.P. 651 388
Stanton v. Richardson (1874), L.R. 9 C.P. 390 ....361, 363
Starsin (The), [2001] 1 Lloyd's L.R. 437 (C.A.) 429, 430, 439
State of Himachal Pradesh (The), [1985] 2 Lloyd's L.R. 573 (Q.B. Adm. Ct.), aff'd [1987] 2 Lloyd's L.R. 97 (C.A.) 513
Statue of Liberty (The), [1970] 2 Lloyd's L.R. 151 (C.A.), aff'd [1971] 2 Lloyd's L.R. 277 (H.L.) 517
Steel v. State Line Steamship Co. (1877), 3 App. Cas. 72 362
Stettin (The) (1889), 14 P.D. 142 411
Strang, Steel & Co. v. A. Scott & Co. (1889), 14 App. Cas. 601 654
Stream Fisher (The), [1927] P. 73 6
Strive Shipping Corp. v. Hellenic Mutual War Risks Association (The Grecia Express), [2002] 2 Lloyd's L.R. 88 323
Svenska Traktor v. Maritime Agencies Ltd., [1953] 2 Q.B. 295 ....444, 445, 460
Swan, Hunter & Wigham Richardson Ltd. v. France Fenwik Tyne & Wear Co. (The Albion), [1953] 2 Lloyd's Rep. 82 580
Sylvan Arrow (The), [1923] P. 220 280

Symington & Co. v. Union Insurance Society of Canton (1928), 30 Ll. L.R. 280 (C.A.) 332

Talabot (The) (1890), 15 P.D. 194 500
Tempus Shipping Co. v. Louis Dreyfus, [1930] 1 K.B. 699 458
Tenes (The), [1989] 2 Lloyd's L.R. 367..505
Tergeste (The), [1903] P. 26 ....289, 290
Terraete (The), [1922] P. 259 (C.A.)..750
Tetroc Ltd. v. Cross-Con (International) Ltd., [1981] 1 Lloyd's L.R. 192 417
Teutonia (The) (1872), L.R. 4 P.C. 171..385
Thames and Mersey Marine Insurance Co. v. Hamilton, Fraser & Co. (The Inchmaree) (1887), 12 App. Cas. 484 335
Thetis (The), [1869] L.R. 2 A. & E. 365 576
Third Chandris v. Unimarine, [1979] 2 All E.R. 972 (C.A.) 802
Thom v. Hutchison Ltd. (1925), 21 Ll. L.R. 169 569
Thomas v. Harrowing Steamship Co., [1915] A.C. 58 (H.L.)............................377
Thomas Powell and Cuba (The) (1866), 14 L.T. 603....................................522
Thompson v. Dominy (1845), 14 M. & W. 403, 153 E.R. 532.............................419
Thorn v. Mayor & Commonality of London (1876), 1 App. Cas 120 158
Toepfer G.m.b.h. v. Tossa Marine Co., (The Derby), [1985] 2 Lloyd's L.R. 25 (C.A.) 361
Tojo Maru (The), [1972] A.C. 242 ....618, 619
Tojo Maru (The), [1971] 1 Lloyd's L.R. 341 (H.L.) 727
Tojo Maru (The), [1968] 1 Lloyd's L.R. 365 513
Tolmidis (The), [1983] 1 Lloyd's L.R. 530 (C.A.).....................................462
Toluca (The), [1981] 2 Lloyd's L.R. 548, aff'd [1984] 1 Lloyd's L.R. 131 (C.A.) 500
Tor Line v. Alltrans Group of Canada Ltd. (The TFL Prosperity), [1984] 1 Lloyd's L.R. 123 (H.L.) 403
Torenia (The), [1983] 2 Lloyd's Rep. 210 476
Torvald Klaveness A/S v. Arni Maritime Corp. (The Gregor), [1995] 1 Lloyd's L.R. 1 (H.L.) 405
Tower Field v. Workington Harbour and Dock Board (1950), 84 Ll. L.R. 233 ....565, 568
Transgrain Shipping BV v. Global Transporte Oceanico S.A. (The Mexico 1), [1990] 1 Lloyd's L.R. 507...388
Transworld Oil (USA) Inc. v. Minos Compania Naveria S.A, (The Leni), [1992] 2 Lloyd's L.R. 48 471
Trask v. Maddox (1863), 15 E.R. 893 606
Treglia v. Smith's Timber Co. (1896), 1 Com. Cas. 360................................386
Troilus (The), [1951] 1 Lloyd's Rep. 467 606
Troy v. Eastern Company of Warehouses (The) (1921), 8 Ll. L.R. 17 (C.A.) 417
Truculent (HMS), [1951] 2 Lloyd's Rep. 308 516

Undaunted (The) (1860), Lush. 90 608
Union Bank of London v. Lenanton (1878), 3 C.P.D. 243, 38 L.T. 698 4
Union of India v. NV Reederj Amsterdam, (The Amstelslot), [1963] 2 Lloyd's Rep. 223 (H.L.) 450
Unique Mariner (The), [1978] 1 Lloyd's L.R. 438 612

Unitia (The), [1953] 1 Lloyd's Rep. 481 517
Universal Cargo Carriers Corp. v. Citati, [1957] 2 Q.B. 401 ....370, 391
Upperton v. Union-Castle Mail Steamship Co. (1902), 19 T.L.R. 123, aff'd
    (1903), 19 T.L.R. 687 (C.A.) 481
Uranienborg (The), [1936] P. 21 584

Venezuela (The), [1980] 1 Lloyd's L.R. 393 (Q.B.) 460
Venizelos A.N.E. of Athens v. Société Commerciale de Cereales of Zurich (The
    Prometheus), [1974] 1 Lloyd's L.R. 350 (Q.B.) 389
Vesta v. Butcher, [1989] 1 All E.R. 402, [1989] 1 Lloyd's L.R. 331 ....321, 322
Vlassopoulos v. British and Foreign Marine Insurance Co. (The Makis), [1929]
    1 K.B. 187 648
Vortigern (The), [1899] P. 140 632

W. Angliss Co. v. P. & O. Steam Navigation Co., [1927] 2 K.B. 456....................450
W. Angliss Co. v. P. & O. Steam Navigation Co. (1927), 28 Ll. L.R. 202 ....450, 459
W.T. Lamb and Sons v. Goring Brick Co., [1932] 1 K.B. 710............................417
Waddle v. Wallsend Shipping Co., [1952] 2 Lloyd's Rep. 105 451
Watson Steamship Co. v. Merryweather & Co., [1913] 18 Com. Cas. 294 404
West Cock (The), [1911] P. 23 ....579, 582
Westbourne (The) (1889), 14 P.D. 132..580
Westenhope (The) (1870), [Unreported] 304
Westminster (The) (1841), 1 W. Rob. 229, 166 E.R. 558....................................612
Whistler International Ltd. v. Kawasaki Kisen Kaisha (The Hill Harmony),
    [2001] 1 A.C. 638 (H.L.) 379
Wibau Maschinenfabric Hartman S.A. v. Mackinnon & Mackenzie (The
    Chanda), [1989] 2 Lloyd's L.R. 494 (Q.B.) 365
Wild Ranger (The) (1863), Br. & Lush. 84 285
Wilhelm (The) (1866), 14 L.T. 636 (Adm. Ct.) 369, 371
Wilson, Sons & Co. v. Xantho (The) (1887), 12 App. Cas. 503 364
Woods v. Russell (1822), 5 B. & Ald. 942, 106 E.R. 1436 (K.B.) 289
Workington Harbour and Dock Board v. Tower Field, [1951] A.C. 112
    (H.L.) 536, 539

Yolanda Barbara (The), [1961] 2 Lloyd's Rep. 337 (Adm. Ct.) 249
Yorkshire Insurance Co. v. Nisbet Shipping Co., [1961] 2 All E.R. 487 327
Young v. Fewson (1837), 8 C. & P. 55, 173 E.R. 396 481

Zim Israel Navigation Co. v. Effy Shipping Corp. (The Effy), [1972] 1 Lloyd's
    L.R. 18 402
Zim Israel Navigation Co. Ltd. v. Tradax Export S.A. (The Timna), [1970]
    2 Lloyd's L.R. 409 (Q.B.), aff'd [1971] 2 Lloyd's L.R. 91 (C.A.) 389

United States

Afran Transport Co. v. Bergechief (The), 274 F.2d 469 (2d Cir. 1960) 502
Alexandre v. Macahan, (City of New York), 147 U.S. 72, 13 S.Ct. 211 (1893)....535
Amerada Hess Corp. v. Mobil Apex (The), 1979 A.M.C. 2406 (2d Cir. 1979) 635

American Steel Co. of Cuba v. Transmarine Corp., 1929 A.M.C. 1516
(D.C.N.Y.) 369
Associated Metals & Minerals Corp. v. Alexander's Unity (The), 41 F.3d 1007
(5th Cir. 1995) 781
Associated Metals & Minerals Corp. v. M/V Arktis Sky, 978 F.2d 47 (2d Cir.
1992) 452
Atlantic Mutual Ins. Co. v. Poseidon Schiffahrt, 313 F.2d 872 (7th Cir. 1963)....435

Bache v. Silver Line Ltd. (The Silver Sandal), 110 F.2d 60 (2d Cir. 1940) 452
Bisso v. Inland Waterways Corp., 349 U.S. 85, 1955 A.M.C. 899 580
Boston (City of) v. Texaco Texas (The), 773 F.2d 1396, 1986 A.M.C. 676
(1st Cir. 1985) 536
Bowman v. Teall, 23 Wend. 307 (N.Y. Sup. Ct. 1840) 369

C. Itoh & Co. (America) Inc. v. Hellenic Lines Ltd., 1979 A.M.C. 1923
(S.D.N.Y.) 470
Chester O. Swain (The), 76 F.2d 890, 1935 A.M.C. 613 (2d Cir. 1935) 516
Citta di Messina (The), 169 F. 472 (D.C.N.Y. 1909)...365
Colby v. Todd Packing Co., 77 F. Supp. 956 (1948) 600

Danner v. United States (The Royal Oak), 99 F. Supp. 880 (D.C.N.Y. 1951)....609

Eagle Terminal Tankers v. Insurance Co. of U.S.S.R. (The Eagle Courier),
637 F.2d 890 (2d Cir. 1981)..631, 648, 649
Edinburgh Assurance v. R.L Burns, 1980 A.M.C. 1261 (D.C. Cal. 1979) 308
Empacadora del Norte S.A. v. M.V. Finnco Victoria, 1983 A.M.C. 1235
(S.D. Tex.) 609

Federal Commerce & Navigation Co. v. Tradox Export S.A., [1978] A.C. 1 381
Fort Myers Shell and Dredging Co. v. Barge NBC 512, 404 F.2d 137, 1969
A.M.C. 186 (5th Cir. 1968) 605
Fruitex Corp. v. GTS Eurofreighter, 1980 A.M.C. 2710 (S.D.N.Y. 1980)..........371

Georgia Ports Authority v. Atlantic Towing Co., 1985 A.M.C. 332
(S.D. Ga. 1983) 537
Giulia (The), 218 F. 744 (2d Cir. 1914) 459
Gray v. Seaboard Air Line Railway Co., 102 S.E. 512 (S.C. 1918) 369
Gulf Stream (The), 43 F. 895 (D.C.N.Y. 1890) 510

Hellenic Army Command v. MV Livorno, 1981 A.M.C. 1288 (D.C.N.Y. 1981)....365
Hellenic Lines v. Louis Dreyfus Corp., 249 F.Supp. 526 at 528 (S.D.N.Y.
1966) 412
Hendry Corporation v. Aircraft Rescue Vessels, 1953 A.M.C. 2115, 113
F. Supp. 198 570
Hoskyn v. Silver Line Ltd. (The Silvercypress), 63 F. Supp. 452
(D.C.N.Y. 1943) 365

Iligan International Steel Mills Inc. v. S.S. John Weyerhaeuser, 507 F.2d 68,
1975 A.M.C. 33 (2d Cir. 1974) 365

Table of Cases 887

Insurance Co. of North America v. S/S American Argosy, 1984 A.M.C. 186
(S.D.N.Y. 1983) 365
Iristo, 1941 A.M.C. 1744 (S.D.N.Y.) 429
Irrawaddy (The), 171 U.S. 187 (1898) 645

J. Gerber & Co. v. S.S. Sabine Howaldt, 1971 A.M.C. 539 329
J.M. Rodriguez & Co. v. Moore – McCormack Lines Inc., 1973 A.M.C. 1463
(N.Y. 1973) 369
Jason (The), 225 U.S. 32 (1908) 645
Jones v. Flying Clipper (The), 116 F. Supp. 386 (D.C.N.Y. 1953) 365
Jones v. Texaco Panama Inc. (The Texaco Ohio), 428 F. Supp. 1333, 1977
A.M.C. 1249 (D.C. La. 1977) 509

Liberty Shipping Lim. Procs., 1973 A.M.C. 2241 (W.D. Wash.) 458
Louis Dreyfus & Co. v. Paterson Steamships Ltd., 1930 A.M.C. 1555 (2d Cir.
1930) 416

Malcolm Baxter, Jr. (The), 277 U.S. 323 (D.N.Y. 1928) 371
Mauch Chunk (The), 154 F. 182 (2d Cir. 1907) 500
Mills v. Renaissance Cruises Inc., 1993 A.M.C. 131 (N.D. Cal. 1992) 496
Morrisey v. S.S.A. & J. Faith, 252 F. Supp. 54 (N.D. Ohio 1965) 460

Navigazione Generale Italiana v. Spencer Kellogg & Sons, 92 F.2d 41 (1937) 648
New Orleans (City of) v. Southern Scrap Material Co., 491 F. Supp. 46 (E.D.
La. 1980) 369

Oliver J. Olson & Co. v. S.S. Marine Leopard, 356 F.2d 728, 1966 A.M.C.
1064 (9th Cir. 1966) 506
Orient Mid-East Lines v. Shipment of Rice on Board S.S. Orient Transporter,
496 F.2d 1032 (5th Cir. 1974) 631

Page Communications Engineers Inc. v. Hellemic Lines Ltd., 356 F. Supp. 456
(D.D.C. 1973) 369
Panola (The), 1925 A.M.C. 1173 (2d Cir. 1925) 369
Pendragon Castle (The), 5 F.2d 56 (1924) 606
Persian (The), 181 F. 439 (2d Cir. 1910) 499
Peter Paul v. Christer Salen (The), 152 F. Supp 410 (S.D.N.Y. 1957) 362
Pioneer Land, 1957 A.M.C. 50 (S.D.N.Y. 1956) 416
Plow City (The), 23 F. Supp. 548 (D. Pa. 1937) 369
Poznam (The), 1927 A.M.C. 723 781
Puerto Rico Ports Authority v. M/V Manhattan Prince, 1990 A.M.C. 1475
(1st Cir. 1990) 566

Re Oil Spill by Amoco Cadiz, 1984 A.M.C. 2123 (7th Cir. 1983) 610
Re Oil Spill by Amoco Cadiz, 954 F.2d 1279 (7th Cir. 1982) 589
Reed & Rice Co. v. Wood, 120 S.E. 874 (Va. C.A. 1924) 369
Reynolds Leasing Co. v. Tug Patrice McAllister, 572 F. Supp. 1131, 1984
A.M.C. 1903 (D.C.N.Y. 1983) 605

Rodi Yachts Inc. v. National Marine, 984 F.2d 880, 1993 A.M.C. 913 (7th Cir. 1993) 525
Rogers v. Saeger, 247 F.2d 758, 1958 A.M.C. 71 (10th Cir. 1957) 537

Sedco Inc. v. S.S. Strathewe, 1986 A.M.C. 2801, 800 F.2d 27 (2d Cir. 1986) 365, 460
Shipping Corp. of India v. Pan American Seafood Inc., 583 F .Supp. 1555 (S.D.N.Y. 1984) 376
Southern Cross, 1940 A.M.C. 59 (S.D.N.Y. 1939) 470
Standard Oil Co. v. Southern Pacific Railroad Co. (The Proteus and The Cushing), 268 U.S. 146, 45 S.Ct. 465, 1925 A.M.C. 779 (1925) 529
Star of Hope (The), 76 U.S. 203 (1869) 629

Tuladi (The), 1927 A.M.C. 894 (E.D. La. 1927)...371

Union Steamship Co. v. New York and Virginia Steamship Co. (The Pennsylvania), 65 U.S. 307 (1860) 506, 533
United States v. Atlantic Mutual Ins. Co., 343 U.S. 236, 72 S.Ct. 666, 96 L.Ed. 907 (U.S. 1952) 535
United States v. Canada, 35 A.J.I.L. 684 (1941) 709
United States v. Lykes Bros. Steamship Co., 511 F.2d 218 (5th Cir. 1975) 460
United States v. Reliable Transfer Co., 421 U.S. 397, 95 S.Ct. 1708, 44 L. Ed. 2d 251, 1975 A.M.C. 541 (1952)..534

Wilburn Boat Co. v. Fireman's Fund Ins. Co., 75 S.Ct. 368, 348 U.S. 310 (1955)..9
Willis v. Tugs Tramp and Mars, 216 F. Supp. 901, 1965 A.M.C. 411 (E.D. Va. 1962) 537

Zim Israel Nav. Co. v. American Press (The), 222 F. Supp. 947, 1964 A.M.C. 1008 (D.C.N.Y. 1963), aff'd 336 F.2d 150, 1964 A.M.C. 2537 (2d Cir. 1964) 500

International

Anders Maersk (The), [1986] 1 Lloyd;s L.R. 483 (H.K. H.C. Adm.) 443

Bankers Trust v. Todd Shipyard (The Halcyon Isle), [1981] A.C. 221 (P.C.) 271, 272, 274, 727, 798
Banque Worms v. Maule (The), [1997] 1 Lloyd's L.R. 419 (P.C.).......................249
Broken Hill Pty. Co. Ltd. v. Hapag-Lloyd Aktiengesellschaft, [1980] 2 N.S.W.L.R. 572 438

Caltex Oil (Australia) Pty. Ltd. v. The Dredge Willemstad (1976), 136 C.L.R. 529 425
Castle Insurance Co. v. Hong Kong Islands Shipping Co., [1984] 1 A.C. 226 (P.C.)..654
Carrington Shipways Pty. Ltd. v. Patrick Operations Pty. Ltd. (The Cape Comorin) (1991), 24 N.S.W.L.R. 745 (C.A.)..417

Table of Cases 889

Dillon v. Baltic Shipping Co. (The Mikhail Lemontov), [1990] 1 Lloyd's L.R. 579 (N.S.W.S.C.) 482

Esmeralda (The), [1988] 1 Lloyd's L.R. 206 (N.S.W.S.C.) 413

Gamlen Chemical Co. v. Shipping Corp of India, [1978] 2 N.S.W.L.R. 12....453, 475

Lotus (The) (France v. Turkey) (1927), P.C.I.J. (Ser. A.) No. 10 541

Kum v. Wah Tat Bank Ltd., [1971] 1 Lloyd's L.R. 439 (P.C.) 415

Maheno (The), [1977] 1 Lloyd's L.R. 81 (N.Z.S.C.) 418
Marbig Rexel Pty. Ltd. v. ABC Container Line N.V., [1992] 2 Lloyd's L.R. 636 (N.S.W.S.C.) 412, 413
Mingren Development (The), [1979] H.K.L.R. 159 781

Namchow Chemical v. Botany Bay Shipping Co. (Aust.) Pty. Ltd., [1982] 2 N.S.W.L.R. 523 (C.A.) 428
Netherlands Insurance Co. v. Karl Ljungberg & Co., [1986] 2 Kkitd;s K,R, 19 (P.C.) 339
Nukila (The), [1997] 2 Lloyd's L.R. 146..334, 336

Octavia (The), [1974] 1 Lloyd's L.R. 344 540

Port Jackson Stevedoring Pty. Ltd. v. Slamon and Spraggon (Australia) Pty. Ltd., (The New York Star), [1980] 2 Lloyd's L.R. 317 (P.C.) 438
Port Jackson Stevedoring Pty. Ltd. v. Slamon and Spraggon (Australia) Pty. Ltd., (The New York Star), [1979] 1 Lloyd's L.R. 298 (H.C.A.) 439

Quadro Shipping NV v. Vizley & Co. (The Protea Trader) (1992) 113 F.L.R. 280 (NS.W.C.A.) 422

Reardon Smith Line v. Australian Wheat Board (The Houston City), [1956] A,C, 266 (P.C.) 385

Sze Hai Tong Bank Ltd. v. Rambler Cycle Co., [1959] A.C. 576 (P.C.) 410, 414

Tasman Express Ltd. v. JJ Case (Australia) Pty. Ltd. (The Canterbuty Express) (1992), 111 F.L.R. 108 (N.S.W.C.A.) 365, 367
Texaco Southampton (The), [1983] 1 Lloyd's L.R. 94 (N.S.W.C.A.)....590, 591, 606

Walumba (The) v. Australian Coatal Shipping Commission, [1964] 2 Lloyd's Rep. 387 (Vic. S.C.) 585

INDEX

Acts of God (see *Hague–Visby Rules*)
Admiralty jurisdiction, 1, 100, 104, 117–20, 133–34, 279
  See also, Canadian maritime law; Federal Court of Canada
Admiralty procedure, 13, 112, 748
  actions, 754–55
  and provincial courts, 748, 751–52, 758–60, 803–4
  arrest proceedings, 5, 9, 145, 295, 531, 760–62, 773–88, 790, 802
  caveats, 788–89
  collision cases, 789–90
  custodia legis expenses, 780–81
  distribution of sale proceeds, 276, 295, 795–1
  in personam actions, 9, 132, 175, 268, 287, 291, 293, 748, 752, 755–56, 758, 759, 761–63, 765, 775, 795
  in rem actions, 9, 132–33, 142, 145, 152, 163, 175, 242, 250, 268, 275, 287, 291, 349, 585, 748, 750–51, 754–81, 787, 791, 795, 797
  intervention rule, 791
  judicial sale of the *res*, 9, 142, 242, 249, 250–51, 267, 278, 288, 295, 791–95
  limitation of liability proceedings, 790–91
  Mareva injunctions, 802–8
  marshal's expenses of arrest, 780–81, 796–97
  priorities proceedings and procedures, 795–801
  sister-ship actions, 277, 531, 751, 764–73, 776–78, 802
  statutory seizures and detentions, 781–86
  See also, Arbitration; Canadian maritime law; Federal Court of Canada; Statutory rights *in rem*; Supreme Court of Canada
Agency doctrine, 172, 321, 423
Allision (*see* Collisions)
Arbitration, 94, 287, 382, 394, 427, 439, 471, 473–74, 490, 588, 595, 596, 611, 613, 617, 694, 791, 804–5
  award enforcement, 473–74
  See also, UNCITRAL

Baltic and International Maritime Council (BIMCO), 93, 381, 435, 579
  BALTIME Charter, 400, 403, 404
  GENCON charter, 382, 383, 384, 392, 393, 394, 396
Bank Act security, 244, 245, 251–56, 259, 260–62, 265
Bareboat charters (*see* Charterparties)
Boating (*see* Pleasure craft)

891

Bottomry, 126, 242–43, 267, 277, 279
See also, Marine insurance

Cabotage, 179, 190
Canada Port Authority, 682, 729
  harbour master, 67, 773
  Canadian Coast Guard, 14–16, 178, 556, 606, 680, 783
  Canadian Criminal Code, 542, 684
  Canadian Marine Pilots' Association (CMPA), 562
  Canadian maritime law, 1, 4, 11, 14–16, 99–100, 201–4, 206–10, 213–15, 218–20, 223, 225–26, 228, 230, 233, 235, 237, 244–45, 251–53, 266, 279, 290, 291–92, 306–8, 360, 408, 433, 436, 439–40, 469, 480, 493, 542, 599, 607, 623, 629, 707–8, 731, 755, 757
  and American maritime law, 5–6, 123, 189, 272–75, 533, 631, 771–73, 781
  and English maritime law, 1, 5, 24, 100, 104–8, 111–12, 122, 123, 130–31, 146, 172, 189, 270–72, 305–6, 429, 536–37, 631, 635, 645, 748–50, 765–66, 776–86, 795, 802–3
  and maritime zones, 100–3, 683, 704, 714, 729, 736
  case law, 99, 113, 117, 126, 145–46
  civil law principles, 113–15, 117, 123–24, 126, 306
  constitutional issues, 99, 101–4, 108, 111–12, 678–79
  enforcement jurisdiction, 678–85
  history, 2–6, 24, 107–17
  integral connection, 128, 129, 136
  international character, 4–8, 24, 114, 115–17, 137, 473–74, 497, 669–72, 701, 741, 744–45
  joint federal–provincial boards, 712–13
  provincial considerations, 3, 4, 10, 100, 102–4, 109–10, 115, 117–18, 124, 126, 131–39, 151, 172, 213–15, 288, 290, 306–7, 545–47, 557, 745
  ratione materiae jurisdiction, 10, 100, 102, 103, 111, 120, 124, 546
  reciprocity, 8
  survival actions, 552
  uniformity, 6, 99, 130–31, 137

  See also, Admiralty procedure; Federal Court of Canada; International maritime law; Supreme Court of Canada
Canadian Register of Ships, 142, 160, 161, 179–80, 245
Canadian Transportation Safety Board (*see* Transportation and Safety Board of Canada)
Cargo insurance, 11, 304–5, 311, 312, 313, 317, 318–19, 325, 591–93, 656
  floating cargo policies, 319
  Institute Standard Conditions for Cargo Contracts, 319
  See also, Institute of London Underwriters; Marine insurance
Cargo ships, 22, 28, 35–39, 58, 185, 197, 199–200, 313
Carriage documents, 11, 415
  as document of title, 408–9, 413–14, 418, 440–41
  bills of lading, 85, 359–60, 380, 407–15, 418–27, 433, 442, 471
  combined transport, 407, 416–18, 435, 440
  delivery orders, 415
  demise clause, 410, 429–30
  electronic transactions, 408, 418–19
  identity of carrier clause, 410, 425, 427–32, 437
  liberty clauses, 382, 394–95, 443–46, 454
  right of action, 420
  sea waybills, 407, 414–15, 418–19, 420, 421, 423, 441
  standard form, 409–10, 412
  transfer of rights and duties, 398, 419–25, 437
  See also, Charterparties; Contracts; General average; *Hague-Visby Rules*
Carriage of goods, 7, 11
  both-to-blame clause, 410
  common law principles, 359–78, 433, 449, 452
  delay, 360, 365, 368–71, 397
  deviation, 360, 364–68, 410, 646–47
  duty of care for cargo, 360, 363–64, 365, 368, 393–94, 424, 449, 644–45
  exclusion clause, 367
  inherent vice, 363, 393
  jurisdiction clause, 471–72

legal effect, 415
quasi-deviation, 365, 367–68, 397
stowage, 361, 365, 372, 387, 425
unreasonable delay, 369–71, 397
war risks clause, 371, 410
See also, Carriage documents; Charterparties; Commercial frustration principle; Contracts; Dangerous goods; General average; *Hague-Visby Rules*; Jettison; Towage; Seaworthiness

Carriage of passengers, 11–12, 549
definitions, 481, 484
at common law, 480–83, 486
burden of proof of fault, 484–86, 490
claims and actions, 489–90
international conventions, 223–26, 310, 480, 483–90, 726–27, 739–41
limitation of liability, 480–93, 554–59, 739–41
luggage, 482, 484–88, 490–91
See also, Maritime safety, passengers; Maritime security

Charterparties, 11, 250, 343, 390
and bills of lading, 382, 398, 425–32, 441
and bulk goods, 358–60, 381, 407, 425
and loss of hire insurance, 315
anti-technicality clause, 402
arbitration clause, 427, 473
arrived ship, 383–84, 388–90
bareboat charters, 379, 380–81
berth charters, 385, 389–90
cancellation rights, 382, 384–85, 399, 400
care of cargo, 372, 387, 392, 393–94
cesser clause, 382, 398
charters by demise, 154, 360, 379, 380–81, 425, 592–93, 762–63, 765–67
delay, 384, 385, 390, 392, 396, 397–98, 401, 403
detention, 390, 391, 398
deviation, 394–95, 397
dispatch money, 391
efficient state, 399, 400–1
exception clause, 366, 390, 393–94, 399, 403
expected ready to load, 384
final voyage, 404–5

free in and out to store and trim (FIOST), 387, 452
gross terms, 387
hire, 402–3, 405
ice clause, 382, 399
incorporation clause, 426–27
laytime, 382, 388–92, 401
notice of readiness, 362, 388–89
off-hire clause, 399, 403
permitted cargoes, 400
port charters, 385, 389
preliminary voyage, 382, 383–86, 390, 400
range of ports, 385, 400, 404
redelivery, 381, 399, 403–5
safe port, 385–86, 400
slot charters, 379–80
standard clauses, 381–83, 399–400, 432
standard forms, 381–82, 400
strike clause, 382, 390, 391–92, 395
time charters, 315, 379, 380, 399–405, 425, 593
time lost waiting, 392
voyage charters, 315, 379, 380, 381–99, 425
war risks clause, 382, 396, 399
WIBON clause, 390
See also, Carriage documents; Carriage of goods; Contracts, carriage; Dangerous goods; Freight; General average; *Hague-Visby Rules*; Seaworthiness

Classification societies, 11, 34, 63–64, 156–57, 158–59, 206, 226, 230–33
Code for Construction and Equipment of Mobile Offshore Drilling Units (MODU Code), 211–12, 711
Collisions, 12, 195, 286, 314, 380, 382, 495–96, 549, 756–57
and *Hague-Visby Rules*, 524
and seamanship, 12, 138, 386, 499, 503, 506, 513, 521–22, 527–28, 550, 554
agony of collision, 512–13, 522
allisions, 11, 195, 496n, 564
Canadian regulations, 498, 504, 507, 510, 511, 516–20, 523, 524, 531, 533
collision avoidance rules, 12, 499–520, 523–24, 526, 554, 568, 587–88
compulsory investigations, 540–41

894 MARITIME LAW

criminal liability and jurisdiction, 521, 527–28, 549, 540–42
fixed and floating objects, 526, 536–40, 554
half-range visibility rule, 503
liability and compensation, 521–35
Lisbon Rules, 532–33
novus actus interveniens, 522, 525
standard of care, 499, 527–28, 554–56, 559
See also, Inevitable accident; Liability; Maritime claims; Navigation, international rules; Towage; United States
Comité Maritime International (CMI), 8, 89–92, 433, 477, 530, 532, 541, 597, 622, 630, 661
Draft Convention on Offshore Mobile Craft, 711
Commercial frustration principle, 370, 391, 397–98
Conflict of laws, 7, 120, 123, 269, 271–72, 530
Container ships, 20, 22, 29, 35–36, 58, 185, 315, 359, 414
Containers (freight), 7, 28, 380, 371, 407–8, 409, 418, 434, 443, 444–45, 465–66, 761
safety, 207–8, 235
Safety Approval Plate, 208
Contracts
and collision damage claims, 538–39
affreightment, 379, 524, 534–35, 591–93
carriage, 7, 304, 362, 364–70, 375–79, 391, 395–97, 398, 408, 410–11, 413, 414, 418–27, 437–44, 447, 449, 455, 456, 462, 465, 466–69, 472, 474, 475, 481, 482–84, 490, 531, 549, 628, 629–30, 640, 644–45, 647
common law of contracts, 105–6, 371, 367–68, 630
fundamental breach, 162, 366–67, 368, 421, 437
privity of contract, 417, 420, 424, 438
ship construction, 161–65, 289, 764
ship purchase, 170–76
warranty clause, 165–69, 362
See also, Carriage documents; Carriage of goods; General average; Hague-Visby Rules; Marine insurance; Salvage; Towage

Craft, 141, 150–51, 253, 507, 549, 562, 692, 738
legal definition, 144–45
See also, Pleasure craft; Ships
Cruise ships, 11, 22, 39–40, 58, 62, 224, 281, 315, 479, 485, 490–93, 548, 549, 741
and marine insurance, 319, 350, 351
See also, Carriage of passengers

Dangerous goods and cargoes, 198, 209–10, 229, 360, 372–74, 422, 469–70, 518, 583
International Maritime Dangerous Goods Code (IMDG Code), 209–10, 373, 583, 698, 699
See also, Marine pollution prevention
Decommissioned ships, 151–52
Demurrage, 390–92, 401, 641
Department of Fisheries and Oceans (DFO), 14–16, 671, 679–83, 703, 706–7, 783–85
See also, Canadian Coast Guard
Department of Transport (see Transport Canada)
Due diligence standard, 287, 304–5, 330, 335–36, 337, 449–51, 457–58, 459, 462–63, 474–75, 534, 548–51, 556, 578, 644, 685

Environment Canada, 671, 683–85
Environmental Damages Fund, 704

Federal Court of Canada
and limitation funds, 725, 745–46
as Admiralty Court, 1, 10, 100, 104, 110, 112–13, 115, 117–21, 126–27, 133–34, 144–45, 175, 278–79, 285, 287, 291–94, 748, 751–61, 795, 805
as court of equity, 276
registry practice, 169, 753–54
territorial scope, 774–75
See also, Admiralty procedure; Canadian maritime law; Statutory rights in rem; Supreme Court of Canada
Ferries, 11, 40, 224, 310, 479, 484, 490, 491, 492, 549, 562
See also, Carriage of passengers; Maritime safety, passengers
Fishing vessels, 40, 159, 160, 163, 184, 188–89, 244, 315, 773, 784–85, 786

International Fishing Vessel Safety
  Certificate, 203
safety, 197, 202–3, 206, 221, 498,
  507, 508–9, 514, 516, 518,
  520
  See also, Bank Act security; Ship
  mortgages
Flags of convenience (*see* Ship
  registration)
Flotilla principle, 586, 723, 735–37
  See also, Towage
Foundering, 195
Freedom of the seas, 21, 194
Freight, 9, 20, 83, 249, 255, 276, 324,
  360, 366, 375–78, 382, 402, 410,
  468, 524, 600, 761
  advance freight, 376–77, 378, 397,
    600
  back freight, 377
  dead freight, 377, 378
  lien, 276, 281, 378
  lump sum freight, 377
  payable on delivery, 375–76
  prepaid freight, 376–77, 422, 600
  recoupment, 376
  set off, 375–76
  See also, General average

General average, 12–13, 312, 360, 382,
  399, 403, 410, 467, 533
  and environmental costs, 634,
    636–37, 655–56
  and freight, 634, 638–40, 652, 653
  and insurance, 656
  and salvage, 634–37, 655
  adjustment process, 632, 647,
    651–54
  at common law, 628, 629, 640, 648,
    650, 654
  artificial general average, 649, 655
  common safety of voyage, 632–34,
    636, 637, 648, 650
  contribution values, 651, 653–54
  definition, 628–29, 632
  expenditures, 634–42, 647, 652,
    655–56
  general average bond, 639, 647, 651,
    654
  indirect loss, 641
  intentional loss, 629, 632, 633,
    642–44, 650
  interest, 654
  New Jason clause, 382, 410, 645–47
  particular average, 642–43

particular loss, 629
peril, 629, 631, 632, 634, 636, 643,
  645, 647–50, 655
port of refuge, 633, 634, 635–39,
  648–49
requirements, 631–50
Rule Paramount, 630, 643–44
sacrifice, 339, 364, 629, 632–34,
  635, 642–43, 647, 652, 653
safe prosecution clause, 649, 655
ship repairs, 634, 635–39, 648–49,
  652, 653
shipowner's lien, 654
substitute expenses, 634, 637–42
termination, 634, 650, 653
valuation of loss, 651–54
York-Antwerp Rules, 628–56
See also, Jettison

Hague-Visby Rules, 305, 319, 345, 351,
  408, 433–36, 476, 534, 629
  and bills of lading, 432, 437–49,
    468–69
  and charterparties, 359, 393–94,
    441–43
  and general average, 629, 630–31,
    644
  and other rules, 445–46
  acts of God, 393, 433, 459
  application, 436–46
  arbitration clause, 471
  arrest, 460
  burden of proof, 449, 453, 463, 470,
    474–76
  care of cargo, 437, 442–43, 449,
    452–53, 455–56, 457, 458,
    460, 461, 474–75
  cargo defects, 460–61
  claims and actions, 470–477
  contracting state, 440
  deck cargo, 409, 444–45
  delay in delivery, 455–56, 466–67,
    474–76
  description of cargo, 448–449, 462,
    468–69
  deviation, 410, 444, 454–455, 467,
    474–75
  discharge and delivery, 442–43,
    448–49, 452–453, 464–65,
    471
  errors in navigation, 456–57, 524,
    534
  exceptions (exclusions), 393,
    456–63, 474, 476

fire, 457–58, 476
freinte de route, 461
Himalaya clause, 126, 410, 438–39
inadequate marks, 460–61
inherent vice, 460–62
insufficient packing, 460–62
latent defects, 462–63
liability, 437–39, 456–67, 726–27
live animals, 409, 444
other causes of loss without fault, 463, 469
paramount clause, 409
particular goods, 445, 453
per kilo limitation, 463–64, 726
per package limitation, 463–64, 726
perils of the sea, 393, 459–60
quarantine, 460
saving life at sea, 460
servants and agents, 436, 437, 457
shippers' faults, 460–61
stevedores, 436, 438–39, 463
stowage, 444–45, 449, 450, 465
strikes and lockouts, 460
tackle-to-tackle rule, 442
theft, 463
time limits, 470–71
war, 460
See also, Carriage documents; Charterparties; Contracts; Dangerous Goods; Seaworthiness
Hamburg Rules, 434–36, 476–77, 524, 629, 726, 727
High seas, 106, 497, 498, 519, 673–74
Hull and machinery insurance, 6, 11, 148, 312–15, 317–25, 341, 577, 621, 656
constructive total loss, 313–14
damage, 314
total loss, 313
See also, Institute of London Underwriters; Marine insurance
Hypothec, 242, 266, 270, 278 *See also*, Maritime liens

Inevitable accident, 522, 525, 554, 590
Inland waters, 109, 130, 132, 134, 150, 197, 206, 207, 531, 533
navigation rules, 497, 498, 507, 510, 519–20, 554
Inland waterways, 59, 116, 197, 207, 497, 519–20, 724
Innocent passage, 21

Inspections and surveys, 148, 183, 198–200, 201, 206, 222, 227, 233, 463, 604 *See also*, Classification societies; Port state control; Ship registration, flag state; Transport Canada
Institute of London Underwriters, 332–40
ABS condition, 334
breach of warranty clause, 335
continuation clause, 335
disbursements clause, 338
duty of assured clause, 338, 339
free capture and seizure clause, 338
general average sacrifice, 339
held covered clause, 335
Inchmaree clause, 335
Institute Cargo Clauses, A, B &C, 318, 334, 340,
Institute Time Clauses, Hulls' (ITC), 333, 339
Institute War and Strike Clauses, Hulls, 317, 334
International Hull Clauses (IHC), 2002, 333–35
London Institute Clauses, 311, 333
navigation (tow and assist) clause, 334–35
notice of assignment clause, 335
perils clause, 335–36
pollution hazard, 336–37
risks clause, 338–39
sale of vessel clause, 335
seaworthiness admitted, 339
sister-ship clause, 337
special Canadian clauses, 333
three-quarters collision liability, 337
transit clause, 339
unrepaired damage clause, 338
valuation clause, 338
Inter-Governmental Maritime Consultative Organization (IMCO) (*see* International Maritime Organisation)
Inter-jurisdictional immunity doctrine, 137–38
Intergovernmental Oceanographic Commission (IOC), 88
International Association of Classification Societies (IACS), 64, 95–96, 232, 233
International Association of Independent Tanker Owners (INTERTANKO), 95

International Association of Lighthouse Authorities (IALA), 92
International Association of Ports and Harbours (IAPH), 92
International Bar Association (IBA), 93
International Chamber of Commerce (ICC), 94, 435
  International Maritime Bureau, 95
International Chamber of Shipping (ICS), 92
International Civil Aviation Organization (ICAO), 86
International Federation of Shipmasters' Associations (IFSMA), 95
International Hazardous and Noxious Substances Fund, 698–99
International Hydrographic Organization (IHO), 86–87
International Labour Organization (ILO), 81–82, 92, 94, 216–20, 229
  International Seafarers' Code, 216
  See also, Maritime labour
International Load Line Certificate, 206
International Marine Pilots' Association (IMPA), 95, 562
International maritime law, 4–8, 89, 540
  and civil law principles, 531
  and common law principles, 531
International Maritime Law Institute, 81
International Maritime Organisation (IMO), 4, 8, 39, 77–81, 87, 89, 92, 93, 116, 155, 186, 199, 205, 207, 220, 222–34, 236, 237, 344, 489, 492, 497–99, 532, 597, 603, 622, 623, 625, 664–65, 667–69, 677, 691, 695, 697, 699, 700, 711, 716
  Maritime Safety Committee, 79–80, 203, 222, 234
  Marine Environment Protection Committee, 80
  See also, MODU Code
International Maritime Satellite Organization (INMARSAT), 87, 236–37
International Oil Pollution Compensation Fund (IOPCF), 87, 692–95, 698, 702–4
International Organization for Standardization (ISO), 93, 207
International Safety Management Code (ISM Code), 156, 174, 187, 223, 226–28, 233, 238, 668, 678

International Salvage Union (ISU), 94, 579, 614, 616
International Ship and Port Facility Security Code (ISPS Code), 235, 493
International Ship Security Certificate, 235
International Shipping Federation (ISF), 95
International Tanker Owners Pollution Federation (ITOPF), 93–94
International Telecommunications Union (ITU), 85, 222
International Transport Workers' Federation (ITF), 94, 185
International Tribunal for the Law of the Sea (ITLOS), 87, 667
International Union of Marine Insurers (IUMI), 93, 656

Jettison (cargo), 339, 599, 604, 632–33
  See also, General average

Latent defect defence, 579
  See also, Hague-Visby Rules
Liability,
  and charterparties, 381, 382, 387, 394, 401, 403, 429–32
  and classification societies, 233
  and combined vessels (towage), 149–50, 578–88, 735–37
  and dangerous goods, 373–74, 422
  and deviation and delay, 454–56, 466–67, 474–76
  and dock, canal and port owners, 722, 734, 741–43
  and freight, 376, 398, 422
  and inland waters, 724
  and marine pollution damage, 142, 145, 351, 528–29, 637, 686–708, 729–31
  and personal injury or death, 316, 480–92, 526, 549, 554–59, 726–27, 734, 738–41
  and pilotage, 549, 563–64, 569–70, 661–62
  and salvage operations, 597–98, 609–10, 614, 722–724, 726, 729–31, 734, 741
  and ship definition, 144–45, 691–92, 724–75
  and strikes, 392, 395
  and towage, 578–83
  apportionment, 558–59

burden of proof, 370, 453, 463, 470, 474–76, 485–86, 490, 500, 528, 535, 538, 579, 651, 721, 732
collision liability, 304, 313, 314–15, 316, 337, 521–42, 719, 726
compensation limits, 310, 370–71, 405, 486–92, 521, 523–24, 525, 527, 529–35, 538, 545–46, 551–53, 557–58, 570, 686–87, 689, 693–94, 696, 698, 706, 721, 725, 734–44, 779
compulsory insurance, 489, 492, 689, 690–91, 699–700, 741
conduct barring limitation, 732–33, 742
contributory negligence, 525–27, 536, 546, 558–59
criminal liability, 542, 556
domestic liability limits, 731
exclusion of liability, 453, 456–63, 474, 476
fault, 457, 459, 463, 476, 481, 484–86, 491, 523–29, 534–37, 538, 540, 554, 558–59, 569–70, 586, 645–47, 686, 689, 719, 720, 725, 732, 735
fixed and floating objects, 526–27, 536–40, 724–25
general average liability, 654, 729–30
indeterminate liability, 728
inscrutable fault, 525
international conventions, 436, 480, 483–84, 488, 522–24, 549, 661–65, 668, 686–701, 720–46
liability for wrecks, 625, 728–29
limitation funds, 134, 690, 692–95, 697–99, 725, 728, 729, 734, 737, 740, 744–46, 790–91
limitation of liability, 13, 145, 302–3, 437–39, 444–45, 463–67, 480–93, 522, 527, 537, 549, 570, 700, 705, 718–22
limitation periods, 135, 175, 470–71, 490, 526, 545, 552, 581–82, 690

negligence, 322, 330, 336, 348, 364, 394, 480–81, 483, 485, 499–501, 513, 517, 521–22, 527–28, 538, 540, 546–47, 551, 554, 570, 586, 599, 609–10, 645, 685, 687, 689, 720, 725, 732, 735–36
nuclear damage liability, 696, 699, 729, 731
privity, 457, 459, 463, 476, 689, 719, 720, 732
right to limitation, 268, 347, 410, 524, 689, 690, 720, 721, 725–34, 742
shipowner liability, 480–81, 537–38, 569–70, 689–91, 718–23, 730–31, 761–63
standard of fault liability, 369
statutory presumption of fault doctrine, 523
strict liability, 368, 369, 370, 372, 393, 528, 539, 582, 685, 686, 696, 703, 725, 730–31
surveyor's liability, 171
tonnage limitation, 13, 32, 150, 446, 467, 483, 488, 491, 588, 686, 687, 690, 719, 734–39, 743
See also Due diligence standard; P&I Insurance; Maritime claims; *Hague-Visby Rules*; *Hamburg Rules*
Lloyd's Register of Shipping, 34, 63, 231, 232
Load limits, 194, 202, 205–7
See also, International Load Line Certificate

Marine insurance, 5–6, 7, 11, 27, 122, 124–26, 159, 171, 255, 529, 696, 733
and case law, 308
and international maritime law, 310–11, 330
and principles of contract law, 304, 330
abandonment notice, 327–28
barratry, 194, 309, 329, 332, 336
brokers, 320–22
Canadian provincial statutes, 306–7
codification of law, 305–6
decisive influence, 323
definitions and terminology, 308–20
deviation, 304, 332, 366–67

disclosure and utmost good faith, 11, 322–24
history, 297–308
hull clubs, 302, 340
inducement, 323
insurable interest, 324–35
loss of hire policies, 315–16, 317, 334
Managing General Agencies, 322, 346
maritime perils, 303, 309, 317, 329–30
markets, 311, 317–18
measure of indemnity, 325–327
mutual protection clubs, 340
proportionality, 326
reinsurance, 317, 320, 329, 343
running-down clause, 303, 337
S.G. form, 300, 305, 319, 329, 330–31
subrogation doctrine, 327
time and voyage policies, 331–32
title insurance, 175–176
underwriters, 300, 308
unvalued policies, 325–27
valued policies, 325–26
warranties, 10, 334–35, 328–29, 332
See also, Cargo insurance; Collisions; Hull and machinery insurance; Institute of London Underwriters; P&I insurance; War risk insurance
Marine liens (*see* Maritime liens; Possessory liens)
Marine pollution prevention, 13, 78, 201, 233, 237, 238, 594, 623–24, 715–16
and salvage operations, 597, 602, 604, 609–10, 613–14, 666
anti-fouling systems, 669, 700–1, 705
ballast water, 669, 673, 677
Canadian regulatory system, 669–72, 673, 678–85, 701–7, 712–14, 782–84
CLC certificate, 690–91, 699
definition, 658–60
dumping, 620, 663, 674
emergency response mechanisms, 666, 676–77, 680, 706–7
floating storage units, 691–92
hazardous and noxious substances, 5, 205, 668, 677, 688–89, 697–99, 707
hazardous wastes, 665, 676, 684

human aspects, 664
international regulation, 7–8, 87–88, 227, 660–69, 672–78, 709–11
liability and compensation, 145, 528–29, 582–83, 661–65, 667, 668, 685–708, 711–12, 730–31
polluter pays principle, 704
radioactive materials, 661, 696, 731
ship source, 28, 658–69, 672–76
ship's bunkers, 624, 687, 699–700, 705
See also, Dangerous goods and cargo; Environment Canada; General average; IMO; *ISM Code*; Liability; Offshore installations and structures; Port state control; Transport Canada; Wreck
Marine Pollution Claims Fund (see Ship–Source Oil Pollution Fund)
Maritime adventure, 12, 195, 267, 268, 308–9, 324, 632, 718, 733
Maritime claims,
and bills of lading, 448–49
and cargo, 10, 126, 304, 340, 345, 351, 363, 368–71, 412, 413–14, 429–32, 433, 436, 468–70, 591–92, 729
and personal injury or death, 29, 134, 424–25, 486–87, 530, 547–53, 739–41, 726
basis of claim, 725–26
cargo claims, 370–71, 422–25, 470–77
collision damage claims, 499, 521, 529–33, 536, 538–39, 798
consequential loss, 726
dependant's claim, 552–53, 557–58
international conventions, 530–33
luggage claims, 487–88, 490
maritime protest, 54
necessaries claims, 11, 106, 124, 242, 270–72, 274, 276, 283–84, 291–93, 761–63, 764, 771–72, 787, 798
pilots' claims, 798
pollution damage claims, 695–98
preventive measures claims, 688–90, 700, 704, 729
relational economic loss, 727–28
restitutio in integrum principle, 532
right to damage claims, 688, 695, 699–700, 703–4
seafarers' claims, 798

900 MARITIME LAW

statutory right of action, 551–552
survival action, 552
See also, Flotilla principle
Maritime communications, 51–53, 85, 87, 196
   Global Marine Distress and Safety System (GMDSS), 52–53, 236
   See also, Maritime search and rescue
Maritime fraud, 194, 323, 325–26
   See also, ICC, International Maritime Bureau
Maritime labour, 5, 10, 61–62, 235, 798–99
   examination and certification, 81, 220–23
   safe working environment, 59–61, 94, 190, 193–94, 215–20, 548, 668
   See also, International Labour Organisation; Maritime claims; Ship registration, flags of convenience
Maritime liens, 5, 11, 241–42, 246, 256, 260, 265–75, 410, 589, 598, 723, 796–99, 800
   and mortgages, 269, 278, 290
   and salvage, 277, 280, 286–88, 598, 611, 798
   and transfer of title, 163, 173–76, 250, 253, 278, 279
   collision liens, 279–80, 286
   definition, 275–79
   enforcement, 268, 269–71, 277–79, 286–87, 291
   extinguishment, 285–88
   foreign liens, 269–75
   forum shopping, 268
   international comity, 271–72, 275
   types, 279–85, 798
   See also, Admiralty procedure; Bottomry; Freight; Possessory liens; Respondentia; Ship mortgages, ranking of; Statutory rights in rem
Maritime organizations, 7–8, 23, 75–96
Maritime property, 9, 141, 193, 266–68, 276, 288, 324, 595, 599–600, 611, 620, 802
Maritime safety, 4, 7–8, 78, 193–94, 238
   international conventions, 5, 195–227, 230, 234–38
   management, 227, 238
   maritime trade facilitation, 202, 226, 237–38

   passengers, 223–26, 233
   risks, 194–95, 223–24
   safety certificates, 156, 197, 200, 203, 206, 225, 229, 596
   See also, Classification societies; Containers; Dangerous goods and cargoes; Inspections and surveys; ISM Code; Load limits; Maritime labour; Maritime security; Offshore installations and structures; Pilotage
Maritime search and rescue, 53, 226, 236–37
   See also, Maritime communications; Maritime safety
Maritime securities (see Ship mortgages; Maritime liens; Statutory rights in rem; Possessory liens)
Maritime security, 95, 194, 226, 233–35, 237, 492–93
   See also, ISPS Code; Piracy; Terrorism
Maritime torts, 4, 9, 130, 424–25, 521, 527, 537, 544–47, 726
   See also, Liability; Maritime claims; Statutory rights in rem
Marshalling doctrine, 800–1

Natural Resources Canada, 671
Naval vessels (see Warships)
Navigation, 7, 42–50, 549
   international rules, 86–87, 230, 496–521, 561
   See also, Maritime communications; Pilotage; Towage

Offshore installations and structures, 4, 343, 548, 600, 775
   Canadian regulatory system, 712–14
   drilling operations and systems, 69–73, 149
   legal definition, 73–74, 147–49, 212–13, 691
   limits of liability, 711–12, 724–25
   marine pollution prevention, 691–92, 708–14
   safety issues, 211–13, 234
   See also, Collisions, fixed and floating objects; MODU Code

Open registries (see Ship registration)

Paramountcy doctrine, 244, 254, 261
Particular average (see General average)

Passenger ships, 28, 39–40, 235, 491–92, 781
  See also, Carriage of passengers; Cruise ships; Ferries; Maritime safety, passengers; Terrorism
Perils of the sea (see Charterparties, exceptions clause; Marine insurance, maritime perils)
Personal watercraft (see Pleasure craft)
Pilotage, 12, 539, 561–62, 773
  and definition of ship, 563
  and salvage operations, 572–73, 606
  and towage, 563–64, 587
  disciplinary proceedings, 570–72
  legal status of pilot, 564
  liability, 563, 569–70
  pilot and master relationship, 564–68
  pilotage authorities, 562–64, 570–72
Piracy, 194, 233, 336, 351
  See also, Maritime security
Pleasure craft, 4, 41, 150–51, 183, 191–92, 206, 221, 245, 258, 315, 380, 479, 507, 514, 516, 562, 680, 715, 773
  and personal injury or death, 550, 551, 554–57
  International Yacht Racing Rules, 509
  proof of competency, 555
  small vessel safety, 203–4
Plimsoll line, 33–34
Port state control, 11, 13, 65, 88, 187, 198–99, 218, 222–23, 226, 227–30, 238, 666–67, 678, 716
Possessory liens, 241–42, 267, 288–90, 378, 398, 654, 796–98

Protection and Indemnity (P&I) insurance, 11, 304–5, 309, 311, 314, 331, 492, 654, 656, 668
  and reinsurance, 320, 343–44, 347, 350
  and war risk cover, 313–18, 351
  certificate of entry, 341
  definition, 340–41, 343
  freight, demurrage & defence cover, 316, 342, 351
  International Group, 94, 320, 344–46, 614, 616
  membership, 343
  mutual risk, 342–43, 492
  non-club P&I cover, 346–47
  offshore energy operations cover, 148, 343, 351, 712
  oil pollution liability, 343, 350, 351, 614–15, 662, 692
  omnibus provision, 342, 350
  overspill claim, 347
  P&I clubs, 6–7, 32, 94, 304, 341–46, 694, 782, 787
  P&I coverage, 312, 316, 347–50, 690
  Pooling Agreement, 311, 344–45, 350
  See also, Marine insurance; Salvage, special compensation clauses

Receiver of Wreck, 66, 620–21
Recreational boating (see Pleasure craft)
Respondentia, 242–43, 267, 277, 279

Safety at sea (see Maritime safety)
Safety management system (see ISM Code)
Sailing vessels (see Pleasure craft)
Salvage, 7, 12, 133, 145, 152, 312, 364, 399, 524, 533, 539
  and definition of ship, 512
  and deviation, 454
  and offshore drilling units, 612
  abandonment, 606–7
  awards, 603–4, 606–9, 617–18, 637
  civil salvage, 595
  claim elements, 605–9
  danger, 605–6
  definition, 594–95
  environmental salvage, 595, 597–98, 609, 613–14, 636–37
  equity principle, 594, 612
  international law, 594–98, 603, 609–11, 613–14, 616, 619, 622, 666
  liability salvage, 595, 614
  life salvage, 595, 596, 618–19
  Lloyd's Open Form, 94, 588, 594, 598, 605, 609–17
  military salvage, 595
  no-cure–no-pay principle, 594–95, 598, 607, 609, 612–13, 615–16, 619, 636
  renumeration, 596, 613, 615–17, 729–30
  salvage contracts, 594, 607, 611–17
  salvage operations, 600–3
  salvage services, 596, 597–98, 603–5, 608, 611, 617
  salvor obligations, 609–10
  shipowner obligations, 610–11

special compensation clauses, 598,
614–17, 729–30
success, 607–9
voluntariness, 606–7
See also, Arbitration; General average;
Maritime liens; Maritime property; Pilotage; Towage; Wreck
Salvage Association, 67
Saving life at sea, 364, 454, 460, 619
See also, Salvage, life salvage
SCOPIC clause (see Salvage, special
compensation clauses)
Seafarers (see Maritime labour)
Seaworthiness, 10, 200, 361–63, 365,
369, 371, 382, 393, 396, 397,
548, 549, 556, 577
and cargo, 362–63, 368, 387, 453
and *Hague-Visby Rules*, 449–51, 457,
474–75
duty at common law, 360, 362, 364,
392–93, 400, 449, 579
warranty of, 329, 593
Ship mortgages, 11, 241
and federal legislation, 244–53
and mortgagee's security, 244, 247
and provincial legislation, 253–58
and sale of ship, 247–50
and transfer of title, 173–76, 182,
246
builder's mortgage, 10, 160–61
collateral loan agreement, 243–44,
246–48
enforcement rights, 243, 257–58,
293
mortgagee rights, 155, 246, 249–51,
290
mortgagor rights and obligations,
153, 155, 243–44, 246–49
personal property security acts
(PPSAs), 253–58, 262–65
pleasure craft, 191, 258, 264
purchase money, 263
ranking of mortgages, 258–66, 269,
290, 294–95, 796, 798, 799
redemption, 246
registration, 174, 179, 241, 243,
245–46
secured party rights, 257–58, 263–65
security interest rule, 263
transfer of, 249, 251
See also, *Bank Act* security; Bottomry; Respondentia
Ship registration, 4, 10, 153–55, 159
and construction contracts, 162

bareboat charters, 154, 177
beneficial ownership, 6, 22, 142,
169, 182, 185, 293, 756,
763–71, 776–78, 779
Certificate of Registry, 179, 182–83,
200, 206
flag state, 6, 22–23, 176–79,
198–200, 217–18, 222, 226,
228, 541–42, 673, 678, 688,
794–95
flags of convenience, 21, 142,
176–82, 184–91
flags of environmental convenience,
188–89
foreign-built ships, 183–84
genuine link, 176–77, 185–86, 188
licencing, 179, 180, 191–92
open registry, 21–22, 185, 226
procedures, 180–84
secondary register, 185
See also, Cabotage; Canadian Register of Ships; Ships,
ownership
Ship-Source Oil Pollution Fund (SOPF),
702–4, 706, 708
Shipping industry
and national maritime zones, 7
globalization, 7–8, 21–23, 75
history, 19–21, 23–24
Ships
basic terminology, 24–34, 53–62
construction issues, 155–69, 245,
715–16
conversion, 157–58, 159
legal definition, 9–10, 73–74,
141–53, 287, 343, 563,
760–61
liner service, 35, 359–60, 380,
407–8, 425
logbooks, 60–61
ownership, 142, 153–55, 164–76,
182, 245
purchase issues, 169–76
tramp vessels, 36–37, 358, 360, 407
types of ships, 20, 22, 28–29, 35–41
See also, Contracts; Fishing vessels;
Ship registration; Pleasure
craft; Vessel; Warships
Small vessels (see Fishing vessels; Pleasure craft)
Statutory rights *in rem*, 242, 267, 270,
796, 799, 800

and maritime liens, 273–74, 277–79, 290–91, 761–62, 764, 765, 771–73, 798
and transfer of title, 292–94, 756–57, 763–64, 771
range of rights, 279, 284, 291–92, 756–57, 760–64
See also, Admiralty procedure, *in rem* actions
Submersibles, 147, 151
See also, Ships, legal definition
Supreme Court of Canada, 108, 110, 111, 215, 271, 557, 559
four-step test, 136–37, 308, 545, 547
maritime law rulings, 3, 8, 102–3, 113–16, 121–30, 132, 134–39, 149, 172–73, 268–70, 307–8, 389, 425, 428–31, 472, 526, 553, 577, 578, 638–39, 641–47, 679, 720, 728, 736–37, 742–43, 779, 784, 803
three-step test, 126–29
See also, Canadian maritime law

Terrorism, 194, 233–34, 492–93 S
See also, War risk insurance
Tonnage, 13, 30–32, 150, 156, 179, 181, 182, 183, 187, 191, 196, 383, 400, 734
International Tonnage Certificate, 159, 181
See also, Liability, tonnage limitation
Towage, 12, 574–77
and carriage of goods, 591–93
and collisions, 504, 516, 582, 586–88
and salvage, 575–76, 588–91, 602–3, 606, 614
and seaworthiness, 577, 578, 579, 582
British Columbia Tugowners' Association Standard Towing Conditions, 578
contract terms and performance, 577–87, 589–93
Eastern Canada Towing Conditions (ECTOW), 578, 584
indemnity clauses, 579–80, 582–583, 614
liability exemption clauses, 579–82
recreational, 550
Towcon, 579, 580
United Kingdom Standard Towing Conditions, 578, 584, 585

Transport Canada, 14–16, 572, 706–7, 783–84
and ship safety and marine pollution prevention, 671, 679–82
Marine Safety Division, 178, 678
Marine Safety Inspectors, 66, 201–2
port wardens, 33, 68
shipping master, 67–68
Steamship Inspection Service, 64–66, 68, 155–157, 158, 180, 781–782
See also, Canada Port Authority; Canadian Register of Ships
Transportation and Safety Board of Canada (TSBC) (Canadian Transportation Accident Investigation and Safety Board), 540–41, 564–65, 568

Underwater cultural heritage (*see* Wreck)
United Nations Commission on International Trade Law (UNCITRAL), 83–85, 92, 435–36, 477
Commercial Arbitration Code, 804–5
United Nations Conference on Trade and Development (UNCTAD), 82–84, 92, 330
Rules for Multimodal Transport Documents, 435
United Nations Conference on Environment and Development (UNCED), 667
United Nations Environment Programme (UNEP), 87, 667
Regional Seas Programme, 666
United States, 22, 268, 274–75, 306, 312, 433, 435, 520, 580, 604, 635, 645
and collisions, 533–35, 537
and marine pollution prevention, 343, 665–67, 672, 707–8
Pennsylvania Rule, 535, 538
See also, General average, New Jason clause
Universal Postal Union (UPU), 86, 238

Vessel, 141
legal definition, 143–53, 600
See also Ships
Vessel traffic separation schemes, 499, 508–9, 514

War risk insurance, 317–18, 351

insurer's rights, 318
mutual war risk associations, 317
terrorism risk coverage, 318
war risk perils, 317–18
See also, Institute of London Underwriters; Marine insurance; P&I insurance
Warships, 31, 41, 177, 197, 205, 221, 234, 498, 529, 531, 562, 596, 756
Windsurfers (see Pleasure craft)
World Health Organization (WHO), 86
World Maritime University, 81
World Meteorological Organization (WMO), 53, 86
Wreck, 12, 133, 145, 152, 276, 287, 504, 620
   and underwater cultural heritage, 620–22
   aircraft definition, 620
   derelict maritime property, 620
   dumped items, 620
   international conventions, 621–22, 623, 625–26
   removal, 582, 622–26, 669, 673
   UNESCO draft convention, 622
   See also Receiver of Wreck; Salvage

Yachts (see Pleasure craft)

ABOUT THE AUTHORS

Professor Edgar Gold, C.M., Q.C., B.A., LL.B. (Dalhousie), Ph.D. (Wales), Dipl. Naut. (CCGC h.c.), MCI Arb. F.N.I., commenced his career in the merchant marine, serving on most types of vessels in worldwide trade for sixteen years. He holds British and Canadian foreign-going Master Mariner's certificates and was in command for several years. He joined the Faculty of Law, Dalhousie University, in 1975 and served as Professor of Law from 1979 to 1994. During this period he was the inaugural director of the faculty's prestigious Marine and Environmental Law Program. He was also cross-appointed as professor in the School for Resource and Environmental Studies, Faculty of Management Studies, Dalhousie University (1987–94). He retains a position as adjunct professor in the Faculty of Law as well as in the Dalhousie Marine Affairs Program. He was the founding executive director of the Oceans Institute of Canada (now the International Oceans Institute of Canada), recognized as Canada's principal centre of excellence in the marine affairs area, until the mid-1990s, and had been directly involved with this institute's predecessors, the Dalhousie Ocean Studies Program, the Canadian Marine Transportation Centre, and the International Institute for Transportation and Ocean Policy Studies since 1978; he was a member of the board of directors of the institute until 1996. He is also an adjunct professor of law at the University of Queensland, Centre for Maritime Law, Brisbane, Australia, as well as at the World Maritime University, Malmö, Sweden.

Dr. Gold was admitted to the Nova Scotia Bar in 1973 and has been a practising lawyer since then. He was appointed Queen's Counsel in 1995. Until 1999 he was a senior partner with the Halifax law firm Huestis Ritch when he became a consultant to the firm. He was a member of the Canada–Nova Scotia Offshore Petroleum Board, 1997–2003. He has been involved in the marine field for more than forty years, has participated in many international ocean-related conferences, including the Third United Nations Conference on the Law of the Sea, has written more than 250 books, monographs, articles, and papers in his field, and is recognized as one of the leading specialists in the world in the international ocean law and marine and environmental policy development areas. He is a past-president of the Canadian Maritime Law Association, a titulary member of the Comité Maritime International, a fellow of the World Academy of Arts and Science, a member of the Chartered Institute of Transport, a fellow of the Nautical Institute, and numerous other professional and academic associations. Dr. Gold has received a number of honours and decorations in Canada and elsewhere, including an honourary degree from the Canadian Coast Guard College in 1992. In 1997 he became a member of the Order of Canada, and was awarded the Commander's Cross of the Order of Merit by the government of the Federal Republic of Germany in the same year.

Professor Gold was the Canadian member of the board of governors (1991–2003) and Visiting Professor at the World Maritime University, Malmö, Sweden, as well as at the IMO–International Maritime Law Institute, Malta. For many years, Dr. Gold has provided advisory services to various sectors of the Canadian government, as well as to a number of other governments and international organizations. He is a member of the Roster of Experts of the Asian Development Bank of the World Bank. He specializes in all areas of maritime law and policy but has particular expertise in marine environmental law and policy; offshore energy; fisheries law and development; maritime transport; and international commercial law and legislation. He also has expertise in alternative dispute resolution methods and is a member of ADR Chambers International, Toronto, as well as an arbitrating Member of the Chartered Institute of Arbitrators (U.K.), the National Transportation Agency (Canada), the Canadian Maritime Arbitration Association, the Vancouver Maritime Arbitrators Association, and the British Columbia International Commercial Arbitration Centre.

Professor Aldo Chircop, N.P., LL.D. (Malta), LL.M., J.S.D. (Dalhousie), is a faculty member in the Marine and Environmental Law Program (Dalhousie Law School), Marine Affairs Program (Faculty of Graduate Studies), and International Development Studies Program (Faculty of Arts and Social Sciences) at Dalhousie University. Since 1992 he has taught maritime law, law of the sea, environmental law, international environmental law, administrative law, and integrated coastal and ocean management. He was director of the Marine Affairs Program between 1992 and 2001, and of the Marine and Environmental Law Program from 2001–2003. His previous responsibilities included directorships of the Mediterranean Institute (University of Malta, 1988–89) and the International Ocean Institute (a global non-governmental organization, 1988–91). He also spent a short period with the Marine Industrial Technology Programme of the United Nations Industrial Development Organization in Vienna (1991). He was also a member of Malta's delegation to the Preparatory Commission, which was given the task of implementing the institutional framework of the *United Nations Convention on the Law of the Sea, 1982.*

Professor Chircop has published widely in the fields of marine and environmental law and policy, law of the sea, and integrated ocean management. He is co-editor of the University of Chicago Press' *Ocean Yearbook*. He is a member of the Nova Scotia Barristers Society, the Canadian Bar Association, and the Canadian Maritime Law Association. He is also counsel to Patterson Palmer Law (Halifax Office). Professor Chircop is on leave of absence from Dalhousie University from 2003–2005, during which time he holds the Canadian Chair in Marine Environmental Protection at the IMO's World Maritime University in Malmö, Sweden.

Professor Hugh M. Kindred, LL.B. (Bristol), LL.M. (London), LL.M. (Illinois), and member of the Bars of England and Nova Scotia, is Professor of Law at Dalhousie University, where he has taught since 1971 in the areas of international law and trade, marine transportation, commercial law, and consumer protection. He is also counsel to the Halifax, Nova Scotia, office of Patterson Palmer Law. From 1985 to 1986 he worked as a senior legal officer in the Shipping Division of the United Nations Conference on Trade and Development. During 1996–97 and again in 2001 he was the director of the Marine and Environmental Law Program at Dalhousie University, and in 1998 he was a visiting professor in Maritime Law at the University of Sydney, Australia.

Among his published work in international, maritime, and commercial law is a book he co-authored with Max Ganado, *Marine Cargo Delays* (1990), and another he co-authored with Dr. Mary Brooks, *Multimodal Transport Rules* (1997). In addition he was the project co-ordinator and co-author of a study in 1982 for Transport Canada on *The Future of the Canadian Carriage of Goods by Water Law* and subsequently assisted the department in the preparation of the Canadian *Carriage of Goods by Water Act, 1993*. He is also the general editor of the widely-used volume *International Law Chiefly as Interpreted and Applied in Canada*, now in its 6th edition (2000).

Professor Kindred has advised governments and other public bodies, including Transport Canada, regarding shipping legislation, and the Nova Scotia Department of Natural Resources concerning maritime boundaries. He is a member of the Canadian Maritime Law Association and past-chair of its Carriage Documentation Committee, and he serves on the board of the Canadian Council on International Law. In 2003 the Canadian Association of Law Teachers presented Professor Kindred with its Award for Academic Excellence.